1

Financial Accounting and Reporting

Business Enterprises

by Vincent W. Lambers, MBA, CPA
Donald T. Hanson, MBA, CPA
William A. Grubbs, MBA, CPA

Published by

2002

Chapter Subjects of Volume 1—FINANCIAL ACCOUNTING AND REPORTING

Chapter One
PARTNERSHIPS

Chapter Two
CORPORATIONS—STOCKHOLDERS' EQUITY
INVESTMENTS IN STOCK

Chapter Three
INVENTORIES

Chapter Four
CONSOLIDATED FINANCIAL STATEMENTS

Chapter Five
EARNINGS PER SHARE, SEGMENT REPORTING

Chapter Six
PRICE LEVEL—FOREIGN EXCHANGE

Chapter Seven
ACCOUNTING THEORY

Chapter Eight
STATEMENT OF CASH FLOWS (FASB STATEMENT #95)

Chapter Nine
BONDS, ACCOUNTING FOR DEBT

Chapter Ten
REVENUE AND EXPENSE RECOGNITION, MISCELLANEOUS ITEMS

Chapter Eleven
OTHER ASSETS, LIABILITIES, AND DISCLOSURES

Chapter Twelve
REPORTING THE RESULTS OF OPERATIONS

Chapter Thirteen
ACCOUNTING FOR INCOME TAXES

Chapter Fourteen
ACCOUNTING FOR LEASES, PENSION AND POSTRETIREMENT PLANS

Introduction and CPA Exam Orientation

The CPA Exam

Accounting is the only profession that has been able to reach an agreement and offer a uniform examination in every state and territory. The Uniform CPA Exam is given in November and May of each year to candidates in the 50 states and territories. The examination is uniform in that all exam questions for all states are prepared by the AICPA Board of Examiners. Candidates are advised by mail of their examination grades about three months after the examination. A uniform release date is established by the State Boards of Accountancy. November exam results are usually released in early February and May results in early August.

Welcome to the CPA Exam!

The CPA Exam has undergone some major format, content and grading changes. The Board of Examiners (BOE) has recently made additional changes in the way the CPA exam is conducted and graded. To sum up, the following changes have occurred in the past five years.

a. Reduced the exam from a 19½ hour three-day exam to a 15½ hour two-day exam.
b. Closed the exam. This means that exam questions are not published or available to outsiders.
c. Substantially reduced the essay and problem content and increased the objective question content, and at the same time, introduced new objective question formats (OOAF). This, we believe, was done to reduce costs and also because of the realization that it is nearly impossible to grade thousands of papers by different graders fairly and objectively over a period of days.
d. Adopted a score of 75 as passing and adopted a new procedure to determine how that score is attained. Under the old procedure, scores between 70 and 74 were not given. This has been changed.
e. Insured that on a nationwide basis at least 30% of all candidates that take a section of the exam will pass. Further, passing levels above 30% will not be restricted.
f. Considerably changed the Content Specifications Guide. For example, Federal Income Tax is now 60% of Accounting and Reporting (ARE), Governmental and Not-for-Profit is 30%, and Managerial Accounting has been reduced to 10%.

The new grading procedure is a modified Angoff standard setting method. Generally, the Angoff method involves convening a panel of judges familiar with the work of entry level professionals, who evaluate each question on each section of the examination. Each panelist's task is to estimate the probability that a "borderline" or "minimally qualified" professional would answer each question correctly.

The modified Angoff procedure resulted in the establishment of Minimum Passing Levels (MPL) beginning with the May 1997 exam. Each exam will be evaluated by the panel and will be given a separate raw score which will be converted to a passing grade of 75.

The initial conversion process resulted in the following scores (MPL) being converted to a passing score of 75.

Exam Section	MPL	Exam Grade
Auditing	65.4	75
Business Law	65.4	75
FARE	61.5	75
ARE	54.8	75

Two things are important for you as a candidate to note:

1. The new method hasn't really changed things very much because the BOE has stated that passing rates under the new procedures are comparable to the prior method with one exception. Under the current procedure, if 40% of the candidates scored 65.4% in Auditing, for example, then all of those candidates would pass. If, on the other hand, only 28% achieved that score, adjustment would be made to equal a 30% passing rate.

2. It should not be lost on the candidate that a raw score of 75% is not needed to pass and as a matter of fact, it is less than 66⅔% (two out of three) and in the case of ARE is less than 55% (11 out of 20). This does not make the exam easy, but more realistic. The prepared candidate will pass and that is what Lambers will do for you.

THE CPA EXAM

What The CPA Exam Will Look Like

The exam changed in 1994 from a 19½ hour, 2½ day test, to a **15½ hour, 2-day test.** In addition, the four old sections of Accounting Practice, Accounting Theory, Auditing and Business Law were reorganized into four new sections. The CPA exam is now a two-day 15½ hour test comprising four sections, all separately graded. Here's what your exam looks like:

THE CPA EXAM

				FORMAT		
SECTION	HOURS	DAY	TIME	4-Option Multiple-choice	Other Objective Answer Formats	Free Response
Business Law and Professional Responsibilities (LPR)	3	Wed.	9:00 am -12 n	50-60%	20-30%	20-30%
Auditing (AUDIT)	4 ½	Wed.	1:30 - 6:00 pm	50-60%	20-30%	20-30%
Accounting and Reporting: Taxation, Managerial, Governmental & Not-for-Profit Organizations (ARE)	3 ½	Thur.	8:30 am - 12 n	50-60%	40-50%	----
Financial Accounting & Reporting (FARE)	4 ½	Thur.	1:30 - 6:00 pm	50-60%	20-30%	20-30%

Multiple-Choice Questions

Multiple-choice questions are usually 60% of the total grade for the Business Law, ARE, and FARE sections of the CPA Exam while Auditing may vary between 50% and 60%. Ten percent of the multiple-choice questions are normally AICPA "test" questions and will not be included in the grade for that section.

Candidates will not be aware of which questions are being tested and should attempt to answer all of the questions.

Candidates should expect 66 questions (60 + 6) on Business Law and FARE. ARE usually consists of 83 questions (75 + 8) and Auditing should be 83 questions if multiple choice is 50% of the total grade or 99 questions (90 + 9) if multiple choice is 60% of the total grade.

Other Objective Answer Format (OOAF)

The OOAF questions are 20-30% of the total grade, except for ARE where the questions are 40-50% of the grade. They are generally multi-part questions worth 5-10 points in total. Examples of OOAF questions are shown on the following pages.

Free Response Questions

Free Response questions are essay questions for Business Law and Auditing and a combination of essays and problems for FARE. Notice that ARE does not have any free response questions and is the only section of the CPA Exam that is completely computer graded.

Writing Skills To Be Graded

With the exception of the Accounting and Reporting section, which is all objective questions, each section contains about 20-30% "free response" questions (essays and problems). The writing skills assessment accounts for 5% of the total points in each area. *Candidates should not underestimate the impact of this 5 point allocation.* It could very well mean the difference between passing and failing. In fact, because many candidates' scores are clustered around the passing point, the difference between success and failure is often 1 point. These 5 points will be allocated to essay responses in each of the three sections. You will not know which essays will be graded for writing skills or how many points will be allocated to any given question. This means you will have to demonstrate good writing skills on all essay responses.

Calculators Will Be Provided

On the plus side for candidates, for both the *Accounting and Reporting* and *Financial Accounting and Reporting* sections, hand-held calculators will be provided as part of the examination materials. This underscores the fact that it is not the math the examiners are concerned with; it is your knowledge of the principles and concepts and your approach to the problems. It will also cut down on the amount of time spent crunching numbers, and allow more material to be tested.

Time Constraints

Since time constraints are no longer listed on the CPA exam, the following time constraints are suggested for the FARE section:

66 Multiple-Choice Questions	160 minutes	60%
2 OOAF Questions	55 minutes	20%
2 Essay or Problem Questions	55 minutes	20%
Total	270 minutes	100%

The above numbers are the "norm" but be prepared to deal with the unexpected. The AICPA will continue to experiment with different configurations for each section of the exam.

CPA Exam Objective Question Formats

The Other Objective Answer Format Questions (OOAFs) that appear on the CPA Exam consist of four new types:

(1) Computational free-response questions (you fill in the answer)
(2) Matching type questions (answer choices are given)
(3) Yes/No; True/False; Increase/Decrease style questions
(4) Graphic questions

Following is an explanation and brief sample of each of these types of questions.

Computational free-response questions:
For the numerical response questions, candidates are required to calculate their own numerical answers—there are no alternatives from which to choose. This type of question eliminates students being able to "guess" correctly at the solution. With traditional multiple-choice, you at least have a 1 in 4 chance of being right. With these questions, however, if you can't compute the answer, you're out of luck.

Example
Following is an example of the manner in which the Objective Answer Sheet should be marked for these numerical response questions. Zeros have already been marked on the Objective Answer Sheet for the ones, tens, and hundreds columns.

Item

99. Proceeds from sale of common stock.
(Answer is $9,000)

Answer Sheet

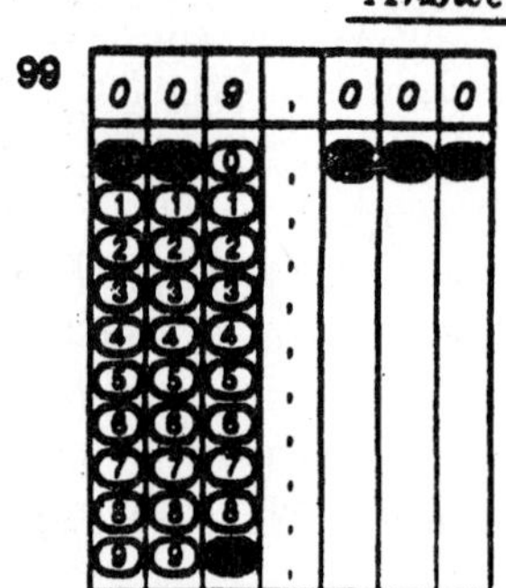

Matching Questions
The Matching questions require candidates to match a list of questions with an equal or unequal number of answers or solutions. With this format, you will have to match one or more answers to each question—they will not necessarily match up evenly. Here's an example from the Auditing section.

Example
Following is an example of the manner in which the answer sheet should be marked for this type of question:

Item

<u>Audit Objective for cash</u>
99. Recorded cash represents cash on hand at the balance sheet date

<u>Audit Procedures for cash</u>
C. Count Cash on hand

Answer Sheet

Item	Audit Procedures (select one per item)
99	Ⓐ Ⓑ ● Ⓓ Ⓔ Ⓕ Ⓖ

Keep in mind that with this type of question, you'd be dealing with multiple situations for which you would have to match one of many items on the left side with one of many items on the right side. Each item may be selected once, more than once, or not at all.

Yes/No; True/False; Increase/Decrease Questions:
Another format is the YES-NO question.

Example
Following is an example of this type of question and the manner in which the answer sheet is to be marked:

Item
99. Does the SEC regulate the securities industry?

Answer Sheet

Item	Yes	No
99	●	Ⓝ

This type of question is basically a derivative of the True/False question. Unlike the numerical questions, this type of question will actually *raise* the probability of guessing right to 50/50 for each item.

Graphic Questions
Graphic questions test candidates' skill in working with auditing and accounting information in symbolic ways. Graphic questions may require candidates to recognize parts of a system or show they are able to extract important information and make correct judgments.

Writing Skills

According to the examiners, what they are looking for in terms of writing skills are the following:

1. *Coherent Organization.* Candidates should organize responses so ideas are arranged logically and the flow of thought is easy to follow. Generally, short paragraphs composed of short sentences, with each paragraph limited to the development of one principal idea, can best emphasize the main points in the answer. Each principal idea should be placed in the first sentence of the paragraph, followed by supporting concepts and examples.

2. *Conciseness.* Candidates should present complete thoughts in the fewest possible words while ensuring important points are covered adequately. Short sentences and simple wording also contribute to concise writing.

3. *Clarity.* A clearly written response prevents uncertainty about the candidate's meaning or reasoning. Clarity involves using words with specific and precise meanings, including proper technical terminology. Well-constructed sentences also contribute to clarity.

4. *Use of Standard English.* Responses should be written using Standard English. Standard English is used to carry on the daily business of the nation. It is the language of business, industry, government, education, and the professions. Standard English is characterized by exacting standards of punctuation and capitalization, by accurate spelling, by exact diction, by an expressive vocabulary, and by knowledgeable choices.

5. *Responsiveness to the Requirements of the Question.* Answers should *address the requirements of the question directly* and demonstrate the candidate's awareness of the purpose of the writing task. Responses should not be broad expositions on the general subject matter.

6. *Appropriateness for the Reader.* Writing appropriate for the reader takes into account the reader's background, knowledge of the subject, interests and concerns. Some questions may ask candidates to prepare a document for a certain reader, such as an engagement memorandum for a CPA's client. When the intended reader is not specified, the candidate should assume the reader is a knowledgeable CPA.

CPA EXAM CONTENT SPECIFICATIONS

Financial Accounting and Reporting

I. Concepts and standards for financial statements (20%)
II. Recognition, measurement, valuation, and presentation of typical items in financial statements in conformity with generally accepted accounting principles (40%)
III. Recognition, measurement, valuation, and presentation of specific types of transactions and events in financial statements in conformity with generally accepted accounting principles (40%)

Accounting and Reporting--taxation, managerial, and governmental and not-for-profit organizations

I. Federal taxation -- individuals (20%)
II. Federal taxation -- corporations (20%)
III. Federal taxation -- partnerships (10%)
IV. Federal taxation -- estates and trusts, exempt organizations, and preparers' responsibilities (10%)
V. Accounting for governmental and not-for-profit organizations (30%)
VI. Managerial accounting (10%)

Auditing

I. Evaluate the prospective client and engagement, decide whether to accept or continue the client and the engagement, enter into an agreement with the client, and plan the engagement (40%)
II. Obtain and document information to form a basis for conclusions (35%)
III. Review the engagement to provide reasonable assurance that objectives are achieved and evaluate information obtained to reach and to document engagement conclusions (5%)
IV. Prepare communications to satisfy engagement objectives (20%)

Business Law and Professional Responsibilities

I. Professional and legal responsibilities (15%)
II. Business organizations (20%)
III. Contracts (10%)
IV. Debtor-creditor relationships (10%)
V. Government regulation of business (15%)
VI. Uniform commercial code (20%)
VII. Property (10%)

Financial Accounting & Reporting	Multiple-Choice				OOAFs				Essays			
	N98	M98	N97	M97	N98	M98	N97	M97	N98	M98	N97	M97
	60 (60%)	60 (60%)	60 (60%)	60 (60%)	20%	20%	20%	20%	20%	20%	20%	20%
I. Concepts and Standards for Financial Statements	7	11	14	0	3%	2%	1%	5%	10%	7%	5%	15%
A. Financial Accounting Concepts	2	0	0	0		2%	1%				2%	5%
B. Financial Accounting Standards for Presentation and Disclosure in General Purpose Financial Statements	3	8	12	0	3%			5%	10%	7%	3%	10%
C. Other Presentations of Financial Data	2	3	2	0								
D. Financial Statement Analysis	0	0	0	0								
II. Recognition, Measurement, Valuation, and Presentation of Typical Items in Financial Statements in Conformity with Generally Accepted Accounting Principles	17	19	24	28	12%	18%	0%	0%	10%	3%	12%	5%
A. Cash, Cash Equivalents, and Marketable Securities	1	2	0	3	1%						7%	
B. Receivables	1	2	1	2								
C. Inventories	2	2	2	2								
D. Property, Plant, and Equipment	2	0	3	3		5%						
E. Investments	0	1	0	2					10%		2%	
F. Intangibles and Other Assets	1	1	1	1								
G. Payables and Accruals	1	2	2	2								
H. Deferred Revenues	1	0	1	1		4%						
I. Notes and Bonds Payable	0	0	3	2	6%					3%		
J. Other Liabilities	1	0	1	2								
K. Equity Accounts	2	3	2	3	5%						3%	3%
L. Revenue, Cost, and Expense Accounts	5	6	8	5		9%						2%

OVERALL POINT DISTRIBUTION

Section I	20 points
Section II	40 points
Section III	40 points
Total	100 points

Financial Accounting & Reporting	Multiple-Choice				OOAFs				Essays			
	N98	**M98**	**N97**	**M97**	**N98**	**M98**	**N97**	**M97**	**N98**	**M98**	**N97**	**M97**
	60 (60%)	**60 (60%)**	**60 (60%)**	**60 (60%)**	**20%**	**20%**	**20%**	**20%**	**20%**	**20%**	**20%**	**20%**
III. Recognition, Measurement, Valuation, and Presentation of Typical Items in Financial Statements in Conformity with Generally Accepted Accounting Principles	36	30	22	32	5%	0%	19%	15%	0%	10%	3%	0%
A. Accounting Changes and Corrections of Errors	0	2	0	2	1%		4%					
B. Business Combinations	2	2	1	3								
C. Cash Flow Components—Financing, Investing, and Operating	2	2	3	0				5%				
D. Contingent Liabilities and Commitments	1	0	1	2						3%		
E. Discontinued Operations	2	2	2	2								
F. Earnings Per Share	2	2	0	2			2%					
G. Employee Benefits	5	3	1	4				5%			3%	
H. Extraordinary Items	3	2	3	3								
I. Financial Instruments	2	1	1	0						3%		
J. Foreign Currency Transactions and Translation	2	1	1	2								
K. Income Taxes	3	2	2	0				5%				
L. Interest Costs	0	2	0	2	4%							
M. Interim Financial Reporting	2	2	0	2			3%					
N. Leases	3	0	0	2			10%			4%		
O. Nonmonetary Transactions	1	1	2	2								
P. Quasi-reorganizations, Reorganizations, and Changes in Entity	1	1	1	0								
Q. Related Parties	2	2	2	2								
R. Research and Development Costs	2	2	2	1								
S. Segment Reporting	1	1	0	1								

OVERVIEW OF THE LAMBERS COURSE BOOKS

Lambers Books Were "Born" in the Classroom

The current edition of the Lambers course books has evolved from the teaching materials originally used by Mr. Lambers when he started the course in 1966. From the beginning, these materials were designed for classroom instruction and were tailored based on the needs of our students. A group of experienced instructors monitor the various segments of the exam on an ongoing basis. These instructors are responsible for the up-to-date quality of the materials in the subjects they teach. The books are kept current for each examination.

We are proud to announce the complete 2002 edition of our 4-volume set.

The 2002 Lambers Textbooks

Vol. 1	***Financial Accounting and Reporting—Business Enterprises***
Vol. 2	***Accounting and Reporting (Taxation, Managerial, Governmental and Not-for-Profit Organizations)***
Vol. 3	***Auditing***
Vol. 4	***Business Law and Professional Responsibilities***

As you can see, the books correspond exactly with the sections of the CPA Exam. Volume I comprises 14 chapters covering the *Financial Accounting and Reporting* section. Volume II consists of 16 chapters covering the *Accounting and Reporting* section. Volume III contains seven chapters covering the scope of *Auditing*. Volume IV, *Business Law*, contains 17 chapters including the new "Professional Responsibilities" chapter. The entire set has over 1,900 pages and 2,400 questions and corresponding solutions from prior exams.

Organized for Efficient Usage

Each chapter in our textbooks is organized into three sections for ease of use. You will notice that the questions and problems are fully integrated with the text. Unlike other CPA Review materials, you do not have to read the material in one book and then refer to a separate book to work the questions. Each chapter contains three sections as follows:

(1) Text. This section provides complete textual coverage of the material. It is written in an informal, easy-to-understand manner to enable you to immediately grasp the concept or principle involved—and remember it. Case examples and illustrations are used extensively throughout. These unique examples and illustrations help give dimension to the abstract concepts and bring the material to life. (*Text* pages are numbered 1-1, 1-2, etc.)

(2) Questions. Questions are included in each chapter in proportion to the frequency each area is tested on the exam. All questions are taken from prior exams. In all, there are over 2,400 questions in the 4-volume set. (The *question* pages are numbered 1Q-1, 1Q-2 etc.)

(3) Solutions. In the third section of each chapter, we provide solutions to all questions, problems and essays. The solutions include full explanations to the multiple-choice questions, so you can understand why the correct answer is correct and also why the incorrect answers are wrong. Analyzing the questions in this manner helps you to understand how the examiners test the concepts you learned. By knowing this, you can avoid the common pitfalls, tricks and traps. (The *solution* pages are numbered 1S-1, 1S-2 etc.)

Coverage Policy

In preparing our books, the authors give as much attention to *omission* as to inclusion of the subject matter. A busy candidate has no time for all possible exam topics, since the range of material questions may be drawn from is virtually unlimited. *Our text focuses on the key areas you need to pass.* Coverage is based on the AICPA's "Content Outlines" as well as our own ongoing analysis of exam frequency and trends.

PassWare ™ Computerized Study Aid

As a supplement to the course books, we offer our own exclusive Computerized Study Aid—*PassWare™*. *PassWare™, on CD-ROM,* works in two modes: "Study" or "Test." You can study a particular topic or take simulated CPA exams. The software provides automatic statistical analysis so you can pinpoint your strengths and weaknesses and chart your progress. *PassWare* was designed to be extremely easy to use. This "accountant-friendly" program is so easy to install, you can be up and studying in minutes. PassWare is cross-referenced to the appropriate chapters in our textbooks. For more information about PassWare™, contact your local Director or call 1-800-CPA-0707.

THE CPA EXAM GRADING PROCESS

Understanding the grading process is essential for success on the CPA Exam because it is graded very differently from how your tests were graded in college. All examination papers are graded by the AICPA's Advisory Grading Service in New York. The graders consist of professors and practitioners (usually from the area). Attorneys grade the Law portion.

The primary objective of the grading process is to ensure that all papers are graded fairly and uniformly. It should be noted that the AICPA is retained by the Board of Examiners in each state to perform this grading service, and it is the State Board and not the AICPA that has the primary responsibility for the grading and issuance of CPA certificates. Some State Boards require candidates to take tests in such subjects as ethics, municipal accounting, economics and finance. These tests are not a part of the Uniform CPA Exam and are not graded by the AICPA. Some State Boards also review the AICPA's grading before issuing results.

Positive Grading and "Grading Guides"

Because it is an enormous task to grade over 70,000 papers for each exam (in 4-5 weeks), the examiners use a system of "Positive Grading." Positive grading is the awarding of points for the demonstration of Grading Concepts. Unlike college, you are **not** penalized for incorrect responses. You must win points by the demonstration of knowledge. Grading concepts are defined as, "an idea, thought or opinion that can be clearly identified or defined."

Grading Guides direct the examiners in awarding *concept value points* for each answer. Initial development of the Grading Guides is done by the Board of Examiners based on their own analysis of all acceptable answers. When the papers are received for grading, a sampling of papers is graded to determine whether the Grading Guides should be amended. When the Grading Guides are finally certified, the grading of all papers begins.

In the initial grading process, each individual grader sees only one answer. This first stage of grading is "assembly line" grading. A candidate's entire paper is not available to the grader, only the one question he or she is grading. In this initial phase of grading, the examiners are trying to determine how the *mainstream* of candidates fared. They are looking for *average* performance.

After the initial grading, the papers for each candidate are assembled and categorized as follows:

(1) Obvious passes
(2) Obvious failures
(3) Marginal

Usually, this grading is done by a section head or more experienced examiner who participated in the development of the Grading Guides. A borderline paper at this point may be graded in total to review it for consistency among subjects. For example, if you pass two subjects, but receive a 70 or greater in a third, that paper would receive a third grading.

At this point, the examiners are looking to give you the few points you need to pass. Format, presentation, and writing skills become very important at this point. If there are still inconsistencies after a third grading, a fourth grading may be called for. However, very few people are passed this way.

Grading Credit for Objective Questions

Since all objective questions are graded by optical scanner, what you fill in is your final answer. Scratch papers are not considered. Since the "Positive Grading" system is used, this means you should *never leave an answer blank.* If you don't know the answer, try to eliminate any possible alternatives and make your best guess.

Grading Credit for Subjective Questions

To grade the Problem and Essay questions, the examiners use the "grading concepts" developed in the Grading Guides. These grading concepts consist of a "check list" of the key words and phrases, a brief description of the applicable concept, and the value of the concept. It allows the examiners to quickly scan your paper and award points if you hit those items in the check list. A key point to remember about the grading of subjective questions is this: **there are always more points available than awarded.** You can never receive all the concept value points that could potentially be earned in any given question.

For example, a typical Grading Guide for computational problems was structured as follows:

Question	*Total concept value points*	*Grading points maximum allowed*	*Concept values needed for 10 points*	*Concept values needed for 7½ points*
4.	19	10	16	11
5.	19	10	16	11

As you can see, there were 19 total concept value points, but the maximum you could get credit for was 16. And all you needed to score 7½ points (passing) was 11 out of the 19—or 58%! This means that you should resist the urge to write a perfect answer to a question you know well. It's a waste of time. Once you hit 16 grading concepts in this example, that's all you can get. Getting concepts 17-19 will earn you *nothing*. You should win the points needed for a passing score and then allocate your time to other questions.

Use your time wisely on these problems and never try to write a perfect answer at the expense of answering the other questions. Also, grading concepts are applied to individual **subparts** of any given question.

For example, if a question has requirements *a-d*, each will have a limited number of points. Make sure you answer every part of every question. You can't answer a and b perfectly to make up for not answering d. If you lacked the time to complete a problem, an explanation of the approach would receive some point credit. It could give you the extra points you need to pass.

STRATEGIES FOR ANSWERING EXAM QUESTIONS

To assist you in answering exam questions, we have developed strategies for answering the various types of questions that will boost your scores significantly. The following are general guidelines for each type of question. During the course, each instructor will use modifications of these general guidelines and have specific suggestions tailored to the individual topic areas.

These question-answering techniques are commonly referred to as the "Solutions Approach." There is no one "solutions approach." It is simply a systematic way of answering questions in the most efficient and effective manner possible. Your job is to experiment with these techniques and modify them if you'd like, as you begin practicing with prior exam questions. Your goal is to have your approach *automatic* by the time you go into the exam.

ANSWERING OBJECTIVE QUESTIONS

The objective questions on the exam will be comprised of the following:

(1) Traditional multiple-choice (50-60% of all 4 sections)
(2) OOAF: Other Objective Answer Formats (40-50% of Accounting and Reporting; 20-30% for the other three sections). These OOAFs should be primarily of three types:

a) Yes/No; Yes/No/Not enough information; Increase/Decrease; Increase/Decrease/No change type questions
b) Matching type questions with four, five or more answers
c) Numerical response questions also include computational matching questions

Be on the lookout for other OOAFs, such as fill-in-the-blank questions. So be ready for anything. Read instructions carefully.

SOLUTIONS APPROACH FOR ANSWERING MULTIPLE-CHOICE QUESTIONS:

1) **Cover the answers.** They are sometimes misleading and may confuse you before you have worked the question. Covering the answers keeps you from turning one simple question into four true or false questions. Also, in many cases, two or more choices may look plausible (and in fact, both may be technically correct), but you are asked to pick the best answer. For these reasons, it is critical that you cover the answers so you can think and formulate your own response first.

2) **Read the last sentence first.** Generally, this will tell you the requirements. Highlight key words and phrases you wish to remember.

3) **Jot down pertinent information.** Write down any formulas or relationships that may help you answer the question. Put down anything that is triggered in your mind by the requirements.

4) **Read the text in light of the requirements.** Highlight key words, phrases and numbers, link appropriate relationships.

5) **Reread the highlighted areas of the requirements.** Make certain you are fully aware of what the question is asking.

6) **Decide on your answer or perform the appropriate calculations** if a numerical response is required, still keeping the answers covered!

7) **Read the alternatives.** If one agrees with yours, select it and move on. If your answer is close, see if it is due to a procedural error. If your answer is totally out of line, reread the requirements and body to see what was missed. If all else fails, try to eliminate any answer choices and make your best guess.

8) **Mark the answer and transfer it onto the gradeable answer sheet.**

SOLUTIONS APPROACH FOR MATCHING TYPE QUESTIONS:

1) **Read the requirements**. Highlight key words and phrases you wish to remember.

2) **Cover the list of possible matching items.** Like the answers to the multiple-choice questions, this will keep you from being misled before you start.

3) **Read the question**. Highlight, circle and underline important items.

4) **Review the items to be matched and jot down notes**. Go through each item to be matched and write down notes indicating your best response in light of the requirements. Don't go and look for the matches before you have finished reviewing your knowledge for all items.

5) **Uncover the list and select the answer that is the best match** based on what you wrote for the item. If your response is not found for a particular item, select the best answer you can find. Remember, for most matching questions, answers on the list of responses may be selected more than once, and others may not be selected at all.

6) **Mark the answer on the gradeable answer sheet.**

SOLUTIONS APPROACH FOR NUMERICAL RESPONSE QUESTIONS:

1) **Read the requirements.** Make sure you read the directions carefully and understand clearly what they are asking you for.

2) **Review the items to be answered and review your knowledge for each one.** Jot down key things you wish to remember.

3) **Read the question in light of the requirements.** Jot down any formulas, relationships, etc., that you will need to perform the appropriate calculations.

4) **Reread the requirements.** Make sure you haven't missed anything. For example, a typical question of this type may have you calculate a labor efficiency variance and have you indicate whether the variance is favorable or unfavorable.

5) **Perform the appropriate calculations.**

6) **Record your answer on the answer sheet and blacken the corresponding ovals.** Make sure you blacken the ovals as well as write in the numerical answer. These questions are machine graded by optical scanner—if you haven't filled in the ovals, you won't get any credit—even if your numerical response was correct!

Important note:
With this type of question, you don't need to employ the technique of covering the answers ... because there aren't any! The good news is that you can't be misled. But the bad news is that you don't have their selections to fall back on. This makes it critical that you really think about how to perform the calculation and make certain that you have not made any math errors. Check and double-check all calculations.

General Comments and Pitfalls to Avoid Regarding Objective Questions

a) Work individual questions in order. Make sure that you flag the ones you skip, so you can go back and answer them later. Remember, there is no penalty for guessing. Make sure you answer everything.

b) Solve group questions as a group. Some objective questions involve a series of questions relating to a specific set of facts. Make sure you account for all key facts.

c) Note layout of answer sheet and don't fall out of sequence. Sometimes the answers may be set up differently. One day they may be going horizontal and the next, vertical. Make sure you check this beforehand to avoid transcription errors.

d) Enter answers directly on your answer sheet. Do not enter them in your test booklet and later transcribe them onto your answer sheet. This will help you avoid errors in copying them over in a hurry.

e) Be decisive. Your first choice was probably correct. Don't second-guess.

f) Watch for wrong-choice indicators. These are words like, "always," "never," "only," "under no circumstances," "identical," etc. These words are usually there for a reason ... and that's to indicate the *incorrect* answer.

g) Watch for negatively stated questions. For example, "Which of the following is not a characteristic of effective internal control?"

h) You must pick up time on objective questions. We have found that the examiners generally allocate too much time to the objective questions and too little time to the problems and essays. Try to pick up time on the multiple-choice and use it for the more demanding problems and essays.

ANSWERING FREE RESPONSE QUESTIONS (PROBLEMS AND ESSAYS)

SOLUTIONS APPROACH TO COMPUTATIONAL PROBLEMS:

1) **Check the estimated time.** Make sure you record the time you start and put down the time you should be finished. And keep checking your time!

2) **Scan or speed-read the problem.** This will give you an indication of the area covered and the main issues involved.

3) **Study the requirements of the problem.** Study (not read) each requirement carefully and obtain a clear understanding of their nature. Underline key words and phrases.

4) **Think about the requirements.** Review your knowledge regarding the solution. Jot down notes about anything that will help you.

5) **Visualize your solution approach.** Think about the problem first in terms of your overall solution. For example, you should be able to visualize a Shareholder's Equity Section, a Corporate Tax Worksheet, or a Statement of Support, Revenue and Expenses and Changes in Fund Balance for a Health and Welfare Organization. If you can picture the correct format, then filling in the numbers becomes simple.

6) **Read the facts and make notations regarding significant items.** Be sure to sort out relevant information from the irrelevant data in light of the requirements. Most problems contain a lot of superfluous information. Underline, circle, or highlight the important data. Make it jump out at you.

7) **Re-Think.** Read the requirements and review the applicable body of knowledge given the background of facts. It may be useful to leave the exam table at this point as this will focus your attention on the solution requirements rather than specific computations or pieces of information.

8) **Study the text and prepare intermediate solutions.** Demonstrate your knowledge of the solutions approach—check data off as you use it. Focus on requirements and ignore irrelevant data. Set up your headings (which may mean just paraphrasing the requirements), prepare journal entries, time diagrams, etc.

9) **Prepare your solution.** Write up your final solution. Label computational sheets and cross-reference statements with schedules and computations. Key your solution to supporting schedules and scratch sheets that are turned in with your paper. Be sure your schedules are properly headed.

10) **Proofread and edit.** If time permits, re-read your solution and make necessary corrections and complete oversights.

General Comments and Pitfalls to Avoid Regarding Problems

a) Do not anticipate the requirements. Furnish the required solution and no more. In general, you don't need to do anything unnecessary. Don't copy too much of the question into the answer. Remember, you are fighting the clock.

b) Present journal entries in good form. When presenting journal entries for computational questions, a brief explanation should be given with each entry unless the requirements state otherwise.

c) Keep within the time budget established for the question. Never steal time from the next question in order to write a "perfect" solution to the current question. An incomplete answer on a ten-point question will not cause you to fail; however, an omitted answer usually will. Make sure you bring a watch and time yourself.

d) Keep moving ahead. Don't get bogged down on something you are not prepared for or possibly an "offbeat" question or problem. Such questions are probably difficult for all candidates and won't be a significant factor in your grade.

e) Work the problems you know first. This will build your confidence and allow you to pick up time for ones that you find more difficult.

f) Flow-through errors. The graders are most interested in the format, organization, and technique in answering the problem. A numerical error that flows through parts of your answer probably won't hurt you. Exam grading guides use the term "Cand Amt," which means the candidate's amount is acceptable if used in the proper order or context in the problem.

g) Outline if you can't finish. This should only be a last resort. If you budget your time and use your solutions approach, you won't run out of time.

h) Don't rewrite the test. Always assume the problem is straightforward. It is rare that assumptions need be made. However, if you feel it is necessary, state the assumption you are making on the notes you turn in.

i) Don't be hasty. Don't be too anxious to rush into answering the questions before you fully understand the requirements and narrative. Take the time to think first. Leave the table and walk around if that helps. The majority of your time in working a problem should be spent thinking and formulating your approach.

j) State the obvious. The grader is looking for a key format or key words in your solution (problem or essay). You cannot be given credit for something you fail to state even if it is obvious.

SOLUTIONS APPROACH TO ESSAY QUESTIONS:

1) **Scan or speed-read the narrative.** Get a feel for the type, general topic addressed, and difficulty of the question.

2) **Study the requirements.** Make certain you are clear about what they're asking you to do. Evaluate? Discuss? Compare? Contrast? Identify?

3) **Construct key word outline.** This step is similar to preparing the intermediate solutions approach to Computational Problems. Think of this in terms of a "macro," or general outline, with only the key words and phrases.

4) **Form your answer in your mind.** Think about how you can verbalize the answer. Each thought must be grouped into ideas that come in sequential steps with one logically following the other. Think in terms of developing and amplifying the broad outline you constructed above.

5) **Reread the requirements and questions in detail.** Highlight, underline, circle important areas. Pay careful attention to any instructions about the type of writing sample required and its *intended reader or purpose.*

6) **Complete key word outline.** This is your "micro" outline, where you fill in all sub-headings to the macro outline in terms of key words, phrases, rules, etc. Be sure to put in any examples you plan to use. This will give you the complete outline. At this point all the hard work is done . . . all that's left is writing your answer out.

7) **Go on to the next essay and complete steps 1-6.** We suggest this to allow your subconscious time to work on the first essay.

8) **Now write your answer to essay 1.** You will find that your ideas will flow more smoothly if you have given them a chance to assimilate in your mind. Your writing cannot be disorganized or disconnected. Try it both ways and see what works for you.

9) **Write answer to question 2.**

10) **Perform steps 1-8 on next essay if applicable** (you may see two or more essays in each area except Accounting and Reporting which is all objective.)

11) **Proofread and edit.** Good writing means good editing. Write on every other line leaving room for these revisions. The edited essay can have inserts, erasures and strike-outs as long as it is legible.

General Comments and Pitfalls to Avoid Regarding Essay Questions

a) Macro-to-micro outline. Once you've finished creating your general (macro) outline, you should know if your answer will be complete and coherent. You'll know if you have left anything out that is relevant to the requirements. (If you aren't sure, you can be certain you have.) You should also know if you have arranged your thoughts in logical, sequential steps. Have you addressed, in a concise way, all the issues required? Make sure you have! Remember the guidelines discussed earlier for good essay writing. The examiners want to see you be direct and answer the question in the most time-effective way possible. They won't forgive you if you lead them on a wild goose chase. The macro-to-micro outline process allows you to start general and build your case with supporting facts and arguments. The macro outline ensures you cover all the bases and the micro outline allows you to get specific and fill in each logical section of your essay. If this is done properly, the actual writing of it will be a piece of cake.

b) Always use full sentences. Phrases and key words that are not in full sentences will not be given credit.

c) Double space your essays. This will make it easier for both you and the grader. It will be easier for the grader to read and you will be able to edit by making notations in between the lines.

d) Make your paragraphs brief. Use no more than 3 or 4 concise sentences in each paragraph. Limit each paragraph to one simple idea.

e) Tell it all. Remember, you are winning points by the demonstration of knowledge. Never omit the obvious. For example, a particular grading guide awarded credit for stating that, "goodwill is an asset." If it's relevant, put it in.

f) The grader will only look at your essay for 25-30 seconds! Believe it or not, although you slave over every word, your essay is graded in under half a minute. This points out how critical it is to be concise, direct and logical. Hit the main points only. The graders will not wade through fluff.

g) Submit your outline for any part you can't finish. If you run out of time, submit your outline for the remainder. A well-developed outline will get some credit.

h) Proofread and edit carefully. Again, this is vitally important in essay writing. Is your answer complete or has relevant information been omitted? A well-thought-out macro/micro outline will eliminate this problem.

Shown below is a Financial Accounting and Reporting (FARE) essay problem and solution showing comments relating to the solution.

FARE

Hudson Company, which is both a wholesaler and a retailer, purchases its inventories from various suppliers.

Additional facts for Hudson's wholesale operations are as follows:

- Hudson incurs substantial warehousing costs.
- Hudson uses the lower of cost or market method.
- The replacement cost of the inventories is below the net realizable value and above the net realizable value less the normal profit margin. The original cost of the inventories is above the replacement cost and below the net realizable value.

Additional facts for Hudson's retail operations are as follows:

- Hudson determines the estimated cost of its ending inventories held for sale at retail using the conventional retail inventory method, which approximates lower of average cost or market.
- Hudson incurs substantial freight-in costs.
- Hudson has net markups and net markdowns.

(3 pts)
a. Theoretically, how should Hudson account for warehousing costs related to its wholesale inventories?

Vince's Comments

a. As a candidate you need to know simply that "all reasonable and necessary *costs of preparing inventory for sale* should be *recorded as inventory cost.*" State in full sentences without elaboration that "*warehousing costs* related to wholesale inventories should be *part of inventory.*" Further state the rule given above in a full sentence underlining "costs of preparing inventory for sale" - "recorded as inventory cost." Finally, the key word "matching" should be included in a simple sentence such as, "This results in proper matching of warehousing costs with revenue when inventories are sold."

(4 pts)
b. 1. In general, why is the lower of cost or market method used to report inventory?

b. 1. Lower of cost or market is consistent with the conservatism principle. LCM produces a more realistic estimate of cash flows from sales. LCM matches anticipated loss in a period of price decline.

b. 2. At which amount should Hudson's wholesale inventories be reported on the balance sheet? Explain the application of the lower of cost or market method in this situation.

b. 2. Hudson's wholesale inventories should be reported at replacement cost. The candidate must know the inventory rules relating to Upper limit and Lower limit as follows:

SP	XX
Minus cost of completion, etc.	XX
NRV—Upper limit	XX
Normal profit margin	XX
Lower limit	XX

Market means *current replacement cost* as used in the terms LCM, except that market cannot be higher than the upper limit or lower than the lower limit. In this case replacement cost (market) is between the upper and lower limits and is less than cost.

Note to the candidate: The answer to **b.**2. requires specific and detailed knowledge. Candidates would be advised that in either case they should not waste time—either you know it or you don't. **b.**1. is not fatal to your overall score in that typically it would contain only 15% of the points that can be earned on the entire problem.

(3 pts)
c. In the calculation of the cost to retail percentage used to determine the estimated cost of its ending retail inventories, how should you treat

1. Freight-in costs?	**c.** 1. Freight-in costs should be included as cost amounts to determine cost to retail percentage.
2. Net Markups?	**c.** 2. Net markups should be included only in the retail amounts to determine cost to retail percent.
3. Net Markdowns?	**c.** 3. Net markdowns should not be deducted from retail to arrive at the cost to retail percentage.

(*Note to candidate*: Freight-in does not have a retail counterpart, similarly a markup or a markdown does not have a cost counterpart).

(2 pts)

d. Why does Hudson's retail inventory method approximate lower of average cost or market?	**d.** Where markdowns are not deducted from retail amounts to determine cost to retail percentage, Hudson produces a lower cost to retail percent than would otherwise result. Application of this lower percentage to ending inventory at retail results in inventory below cost, which approximates LCM.

Maximum points available	*12*
Maximum point credit given	*10*

SOLUTION:

a. Hudson should account for the warehousing costs related to its wholesale inventories as part of inventory. All reasonable and necessary costs of preparing inventory for sale should be recorded as inventory cost. This approach results in proper matching of the warehousing costs with revenue when the wholesale inventories are sold.

b. 1. The lower of cost or market method produces a more realistic estimate of future cash flows to be realized from assets, which is consistent with the principle of conservatism, and recognizes (matches) the anticipated loss in the income statement in the period in which the price decline occurs.

2. Hudson's wholesale inventories should be reported on the balance sheet at replacement cost. According to the lower of cost or market method, replacement cost is defined as market. However, market cannot exceed net realizable value and cannot be less than net realizable value less the normal profit margin. In this instance, replacement cost is below original cost, below net realizable value, and above net realizable value less the normal profit margin. Therefore, Hudson's wholesale inventories should be reported at replacement cost.

c. 1. Hudson's freight-in costs should be included only in the cost amounts to determine the cost to retail percentage.

2. Hudson's net markups should be included only in the retail amounts to determine the cost to retail percentage.

3. Hudson's net markdowns should not be deducted from the retail amounts to determine the cost to retail percentage.

d. By not deducting net markdowns from the retail amounts to determine the cost to retail percentage, Hudson produces a lower cost to retail percentage than would result if net markdowns were deducted. By applying this lower percentage to ending inventory at retail, the inventory is reported at an amount below cost, which approximates lower of average cost or market.

MENTAL AND TECHNICAL PREREQUISITES FOR SUCCESS ON THE CPA EXAM

Technical Prerequisites for Success.

The examination is a test of your overall technical competency. It is a test to measure judgment and intelligence in the application of accounting principles, auditing standards, and procedures to practical problems and to evaluate professional ethics. Keep in mind that you are being tested on a basic level of knowledge in a broad spectrum of areas.

The CPA Exam itself is no more difficult than similar ones given to entrants in law and medicine. However, it is true that the passing rates are proportionately lower on the CPA Exam than on the other two exams. This is primarily due to the fact that accounting students do not study Accounting *exclusively, at a post-graduate level*, as the other two professions do study only Law and only Medicine in Law and Medical school. You have to understand this and look at your preparation now to serve two purposes:

(1) To review the areas you did learn in college that are directly relevant to the CPA Exam.
(2) To gain the knowledge in those areas that will be tested heavily on the exam, but you may have had only light exposure (or no exposure) to in college. These will be areas like Bonds, Consolidations, Auditing, Taxes, Governmental and Not-for-Profit Accounting, Statement of Cash Flows, etc.

Your preparation for the CPA Exam should be geared to obtaining three things:

- **A Basic Technical Knowledge In All Areas**. The emphasis here is on basic. You don't need to know all the intricacies involved in any particular subject. What you do need to know are the major issues involved and you need to have a solid understanding of the underlying principles and concepts so you can respond to different types of questions and unfamiliar fact patterns.

- **Exam-Taking Skills**. You also need weapons. You need exam-taking skills and techniques for each subject area. These will allow you to win the maximum amount of points in the shortest amount of time. We have covered some of the general approaches you will need to learn. The only way you can develop your skill is to PRACTICE by working hundreds of exam questions in each topic area so that answering them correctly becomes second nature.

- **Confidence**. When you walk into that exam, you must be confident. This confidence will come as a by-product of the above two elements. If you've gone to class faithfully, paid close attention, and done your homework, you can be confident that you will be among the best-prepared candidates in the examination room.

Aside from the technical competency, there are other attributes you will need to succeed on the CPA Exam. Remember, this will be unlike any other exam you've taken in your life. It can be a very long and arduous process. But like most things in life, the rewards you receive from your short-term sacrifice will pay off many times over. Preparing for the exam is demanding, both mentally and physically. Following are some tips on helping you through this process effectively.

Goal Setting

Taking the CPA Exam is not an end in itself; it's a means to an end. That end is your goal of becoming a CPA, a professional. That will mean financial security, the opportunity for more fulfilling positions, possibly the opportunity to start your own firm. Keep your ultimate goals in mind as you begin. To a considerable extent, the failure of many people to pass the exam is their failure to be goal-oriented and stay focused through their preparation period. You must stay focused and work every day to make that goal a reality.

Written Plan of Action

We all know the power of goal setting, but have you ever sat down and actually written a goals statement? The importance of a written goals statement has been demonstrated time and again, yet few people actually use one. If you have never previously written a goals statement, you may wonder where to begin. Begin by writing down all the things that becoming a CPA will mean for you. This may be:

- money
- utilization of your skills and talents
- possessions
- recognition by your peers
- influence
- independence
- security

Don't be judgmental; write down all the benefits you will receive by becoming a CPA. If you do not understand why you have set a goal, you cannot really commit yourself to it! And if you can't commit yourself to it and internalize it and feel energized by it, you will never reach it.

Visualizing Your Goal

When you have to go to class on a gorgeous summer day, or you find yourself scraping the car windows to go to class on a cold winter night, it may be easy to lose sight of your goals. In the flux of daily life, it's easy for this to happen. As the saying goes, "When you're knee high in alligators, it's easy to forget your objective was to drain the swamp." That's why you need to visualize your goals on a daily basis. Surround yourself with tokens of the things you want to achieve.

Post the letters **C-P-A** prominently next to your desk at work or on your computer terminal. Picture yourself sitting in a plush office as the CFO of a major company. Think about how it would feel to become a partner in your firm or start your own firm someday. You get the idea. Keep your goals prominently in your mind and around you. You must focus on and experience achieving your goal long before you have actually done it. This will help keep you motivated and focused, and you will be less likely to get off the track.

Expect to Achieve Your Goal

One of the most common differences we see between successful candidates and failing candidates is this:

> ***The successful candidates fully expected to pass the exam and were very confident in their ability to do just that. The failing candidates had more of a "vague hope" and were uncertain about passing.***

By doubting your ability to achieve the goal you have set, you will be sabotaging your chances for success even before you have begun. Many students seem to take the attitude that "if I don't take it too seriously, I can't be too disappointed if I don't pass." This stems from a fear of failure. Whether this has been caused by horror stories about passing rates and years of hearing how hard the exam is during undergraduate days is hard to say. But we guarantee that it is an attitude that will ensure you will never achieve what you set out to. Make no mistake—this is a difficult exam, but it is also a very PASSABLE exam with the proper preparation.

You will be much further ahead with a written goals statement and a commitment to passing than you will if you give it a half-hearted attempt and let matters take their own course. To keep your confidence growing, make sure you do the following:

(1) **Make use of notecards**. You should make two types of notecards. One will be an affirmation of your goal and the benefits you listed in your written goals statement. The other type will be notecards the instructors suggest you make for different topics. When you're stuck in traffic, waiting in line, or sitting at a doctor's office, pull the cards out and review them. This will help instill both the goals and the knowledge you need to achieve them.

(2) **Stick to your program**. Nothing will cause you to fail more surely than falling behind in your study program whether it is attending class or home study. Most passing grades on the exam are just by a few points. Missing just one or two sessions could mean the difference between failure and success.

(3) **Daily Action Plan**. Map out a plan of action that involves what you will do when not watching tapes or attending class. This should consist of a specific time slot set aside to review the materials and work CPA Exam questions.

Organization and Focus

Focus on your objective—don't let minor things distract you. You must organize your life to accommodate the time you will have to devote to preparation. One of our instructors tells his students to look at this as a part-time job you are *required* to do for 4 or 5 months. That's a good way to look at it. Once you are committed to your goal, you must resolutely see it through. You can't let minor interruptions distract you from your task. Beware of all the reasons not to study that will undoubtedly creep in, like:

- I have a cold.
- My favorite show is on tonight.
- My mother-in-law is visiting.
- I had a fight with my boyfriend last night.

These and countless other trivial things will come up, and seem important at the time, but in the long run they will just distract you from achieving your goal. Being focused on your objective is essential for the successful candidate. The minute you allow yourself to be diverted, you are becoming disorganized.

Discipline

This means studying when you feel like it *and when you don't*. Failing candidates study only when they feel like it. Successful candidates study when they do not. The CPA Exam is not like a final exam in college. You can't skip classes and neglect studying for 3 months and then cram for the final. Passing the CPA Exam is earned day in and day out. To stay disciplined, keep visualizing your ultimate goal and thinking about all of the positive benefits once you achieve it. It also helps to think about it from the negative side: do you really want to go through the whole process over again if you don't stick with it and do it right the first time?

NOW MAKE THE COMMITMENT!

At Lambers, we are proud of our past record of achievements. Our success is truly measured by YOUR success. But remember, we can't do it all for you. We have a proven course that has worked for thousands of students and all our experience and resources will be at your disposal. However, your ultimate success or failure will be determined by the commitment you make to preparing, and how assiduously you apply what you learn. Now is the time to make that commitment ... follow that commitment with *action* and you *will* become a CPA.

ACKNOWLEDGMENTS

It would be impossible to write a CPA examination preparation book of any kind without the assistance of the American Institute of Certified Public Accountants, and their various operating divisions, in granting permission to use various materials. We respectfully acknowledge and thank those persons in the American Institute who promptly answered our inquiries.

Those areas of the set for which we received permission to use copyrighted material from the American Institute are:

- *CPA Examination Questions, Problems and Solutions*
- *Opinions of the Accounting Principles Board and The Financial Accounting Standards Board*
- *Statements on Auditing Standards*
- *The Code of Professional Ethics and Interpretations Thereof*

We also wish to thank our editorial advisor, William A. Grubbs, CPA, of Greensboro, North Carolina.

Vincent W. Lambers, CPA
Donald T. Hanson, CPA
Richard DelGaudio, CPA
North Andover, Massachusetts
October 2001

Benefits of Becoming a CPA

First, a little background on the Certified Public Accountant (CPA) designation. The first CPA examination was offered in the state of New York in 1896 and shortly thereafter other states offered an examination for candidates aspiring to be CPA's. Now all states and territories offer examinations for those wishing to become CPA's. Unlike many other professional designations, CPA's are licensed by the state(s) to practice public accounting. The most important aspect of the licensing of CPA's is the "attest to" function. This allows the CPA to attest, in the form of an opinion, as to the condition of the financial statements provided by management. The CPA's opinion may vary from outright refusal to be associated with the statements to acceptance of the statements as fairly representing the financial condition of the enterprise. In carrying out the attest function and other work, the CPA must adhere to certain auditing standards of performance including, but not limited to, independence and designated audit procedures.

The attest function carries with it a heavy responsibility because the CPA's opinion is heavily relied upon by leaders, investors and others who have an interest in the condition of a particular enterprise. Besides the attest function, the CPA's association with other work, such as tax work, carries with it a presumption of excellence because of the standards that are required of CPA's.

Individuals who are CPA's are looked up to in the world of finance and industry especially where accountability is a factor, which is almost always the case. Whether the CPA is in public practice or in an executive position, the designation is recognized as a standard of excellence. Naturally, enterprises in general are willing to pay for the presumption of excellence that the CPA demonstrates, which for the individual results in increased income.

Using the world-famous cliché, the "bottom line" is that the CPA enjoys prestige, higher income, financial security and independence to a much greater extent than the same person without it.

Vincent W. Lambers
President, Lambers CPA Review

Chapter One
Partnerships

Chapter One
Partnerships

DEFINED

"Association of two or more persons to carry on, as co-owners, a business for profit."

AGREEMENTS

Can be expressed (oral or written contract) or implied (actions).
Should be in writing for protection of partners. The agreement governs the formation, operation, distribution of income or loss, and dissolution of the partnership.

DIVISION OF PROFITS

- Profits can be shared in any way agreeable to the partners.
- If the agreement is silent, the law assumes that profits and losses will be shared equally.
- Amount of capital contributed has no effect on profit division unless specified in the agreement.

ADMISSION OF PARTNER

- Admission or withdrawal of a partner generally dissolves the partnership and brings into being a new partnership.
- New articles of partnership should be drawn up.
- A new partner can purchase an interest or invest in the partnership.

Care should be taken to distinguish between a purchase of an interest and the investment in a partnership. The difference is critical to the proper procedure to follow in partnership problems.

1. **Purchase of interest. Example**: A purchases interest of X in XYZ partnership or part of interest of XYZ in XYZ partnership. The amount A paid for his interest is outside the partnership and not recorded in the books.
2. **Investment. Example**: A invests $10,000 in XYZ partnership, thereby increasing the capital of the partnership.

PURCHASE OF AN INTEREST

1. **Payment to an existing partner**
No cash transaction is to be entered on the books in the purchase of an interest. X, Y, and Z have capitals of $10,000, $15,000 and $20,000 respectively. Z sells half of his capital interest to P for the sum of $12,000.

Entry:	Z, Capital	$10,000	
	P, Capital		$10,000

Transaction is between Z and P as to amount and Z has merely transferred one-half of his interest to P.

2. **Payment to more than one partner**
Purchase at book value: P purchases a one-fourth interest for $11,250.

Entry:	X, Capital	$2,500		(25% × $10,000)
	Y, Capital	$3,750		(25% × $15,000)
	Z, Capital	$5,000		(25% × $20,000)
	P, Capital		$11,250	

Purchase at more than book value: Where purchase is at more than book value, goodwill **may** or **may not** be recognized.

Example: P pays $15,000 for a one-fourth interest and XYZ share profits on a 4:3:3 basis.

a. **Goodwill not recognized**. Transfer of capital same as above. The existing partners will divide the $15,000 cash on some agreed basis or as follows:

	X(40)	*Y(30)*	*Z(30)*	*Total*
For Capital	$2,500	$3,750	$5,000	$11,250
Amount in Excess of Capital in P&L Ratio	1,500	1,125	1,125	3,750
	$4,000	$4,875	$6,125	$15,000

b. **Goodwill recognized**. If P is willing to pay $15,000 for a one-fourth interest, the implied value of the partnership is $60,000 ($15,000 × 4). Goodwill must be placed on the books prior to the admission of P to bring total capital to $60,000.

	Debit	Credit	
Goodwill	$15,000		($60,000 – $45,000 XYZ total capital)
X, Capital		$6,000	($15,000 × 40%)
Y, Capital		4,500	($15,000 × 30%)
Z, Capital		4,500	($15,000 × 30%)

To recognize goodwill and increase total capital to $60,000.

	Debit	Credit
(1) X, Capital	$4,000	
(2) Y, Capital	4,875	
(3) Z, Capital	6,125	
P, Capital		$15,000

(1) $16,000 × 1/4 (2) $19,500 × 1/4 (3) $24,500 × 1/4
To record transfer of capital to P.

Purchase at less than book value: P pays $10,000 for a one-fourth interest.

a. **No adjustment of the old partner's capital account.** The same journal entry as in #2 above will be recorded since P will receive $11,250 in capital for $10,000. The existing partners will divide the $10,000 cash on some agreed basis or as follows:

	X(40)	*Y(30)*	*Z(30)*	*Total*
Capital	$2,500	$3,750	$5,000	$11,250
Loss: $11,250 – 10,000 in P&L ratio	(500)	(375)	(375)	(1,250)
Division of Cash	$2,000	$3,375	$4,625	$10,000

b. **Adjustment of old partner's capital account**: In this situation the partners are giving recognition to the loss in value of their interest. Total capital is reduced to $40,000 implied value ($10,000 × 4), with the resulting asset write-down of $5,000.

	X(40)	*Y(30)*	*Z(30)*	*P*	*Total*
Original Capitals	$10,000	$15,000	$20,000		$45,000
Asset write-down					
$45,000 – $40,000 in P&L ratio	(2,000)	(1,500)	(1,500)		(5,000)
	8,000	13,500	18,500		40,000
Capital transfers	(2,000)	(3,375)	(4,625)	10,000	--
	$ 6,000	$10,125	$13,875	$10,000	$40,000

INVESTMENT IN A PARTNERSHIP BY CONTRIBUTION TO THE FIRM'S CAPITAL

Asset values may be adjusted before admission of any new partner(s). An investment may result in the following:

- Recognition of either goodwill or bonus to the old partners.
  Goodwill is placed on the books before admission of a new partner.
  Bonus--part of the capital contributed is credited to the account of the old partners.
- Recognition to the incoming partner in the form of either goodwill or bonus.

1. **No goodwill or bonus.**
A and B have capitals of $10,000 and $20,000 respectively, share profits and losses equally, and C is to be admitted to the firm by making a contribution to the firm's capital. C is to invest $10,000.

Entry:	Cash		$10,000	
		C, Capital		$10,000

Note that C's profit sharing ratio is not determined by the amount of capital contributed, but must result from agreement with the original partners.

2. **Goodwill recognized to old partners**
C is to invest $12,000 for a one-fourth interest. Analysis: Implied value is $48,000 (4 × $12,000). C's contribution plus A and B's capital equals $42,000; therefore, $6,000 in goodwill must be added to total capital.

Entries:	Goodwill		$6,000	
		A, Capital		$3,000
		B, Capital		3,000
	Cash		12,000	
		C, Capital		$12,000

3. **Bonus allowed to old partners**
C is to invest $18,000; capital of A and B plus C's contribution equals $48,000. Since C is contributing $18,000 but is to receive only a one-fourth interest of $12,000 (1/4 × $48,000), a bonus of $6,000 is given to A and B.

Entry:	Cash		$18,000	
		A, Capital		$ 3,000
		B, Capital		3,000
		C, Capital		12,000

Note that in bonus situations total capital equals the old capital plus the partner's contribution.

4. **Goodwill allowed to new partner**
C is to invest $9,000 of miscellaneous business assets and agreed total capital is to be $40,000.

Entry:	Goodwill		$1,000 ($40,000 – $30,000 – $9,000)	
	Misc. Assets		9,000	
		C, Capital		$10,000 (1/4 × 40,000)

5. **Bonus allowed to new partner**
C is to invest $9,000; a bonus is allowed to C.

Entry:	Cash		$9,000	
	A, Capital		375	
	B, Capital		375	
		C, Capital		$9,750 (1/4 × 39,000)

DIVISION OF PROFITS

Division of profits is governed by the partnership agreement. Profits may be divided:

1. Equally
2. On some other fractional basis
3. In capital ratio
4. On average capital ratio
5. By allowing interest on capitals and dividing remainder, and
6. By allowing salaries to the partners and dividing remaining profit.

If the agreement makes no provision for the division of profit and losses, the law assumes they will be shared equally.

1. **Interest on Capital**

- Partner cannot claim interest on capital unless provided for in the partnership agreement.
- Interest on capital should not be included in income statement as an expense.
- Interest paid on partners' loans may be treated as a financial expense.

2. **Partners' Salaries**: Treated as a division of profits. Allocation of partners' "salaries" may exceed partnership income and create a loss to be allocated to all partners according to the partnership agreement.

Method of Distribution

- Allocate salaries, interest first
- Distribute remaining profit (loss) per agreement

Example: A, B, and C agreed to the following distribution of profit:

	A	*B*	*C*
Annual salary	$10,000	$ 8,000	0
Interest on average capital	0	4%	10%
Remainder	40%	40%	20%
Average capital	$50,000	$50,000	$200,000

Profit distribution under three different assumptions:

	A	*B*	*C*	*Total*
Interest allocation	--0--	$ 2,000	$20,000	$22,000
Salary allowance	$10,000	8,000	-0--	18,000
	$10,000	$10,000	$20,000	$40,000
1. Assume $50,000 profit				
Remainder ($50,000 – $40,000)	4,000	4,000	2,000	10,000
2. Assume $20,000 profit				
Remainder ($20,000 – $40,000)	(8,000)	(8,000)	(4,000)	(20,000)
3. Assume $10,000 loss				
Remainder (– $10,000 – $40,000)	(20,000)	(20,000)	(10,000)	(50,000)

RETIREMENT OF A PARTNER

Adjustment of asset values may be required to determine the fair equity of a retiring partner. This may be necessary to:

a. Correct improper operating charges of prior periods (bad debts, accruals, depreciation and recognition of inventories).
b. Give recognition to the existence of goodwill.
c. Give recognition to changes in market values.

Problem: C is to retire from A, B, C partnership. A goodwill value of $6,000 has been agreed upon.

1. **Goodwill recorded on the books for (1) all partners or (2) only the retiring partner.**

		Debit	Credit
(1) Goodwill		$6,000	
	A, Capital		$2,000
	B, Capital		2,000
	C, Capital		2,000
(2) Goodwill		$2,000	
	C, Capital		$2,000

2. **Implied bonus or goodwill**
Assume that A, B and C have capitals of $10,000 each and share profits equally. C is to retire and is to be paid $12,000 from partnership assets. The $2,000 excess of the payment to C over his capital may be recorded as a bonus or as goodwill.

		Debit	Credit
Bonus	A, Capital	$ 1,000	
	B, Capital	1,000	
	C, Capital	10,000	
	Cash		$12,000
Goodwill:	Goodwill	$ 2,000	
	C, Capital		$ 2,000
	C, Capital	12,000	
	Cash		12,000

DISSOLUTION AND LIQUIDATION

1. **Causes of Dissolution**
Dissolution occurs when the existing partnership arrangement is altered for some reason. Liquidation may follow dissolution but often outsiders would be unaware of the end of one partnership and the start of another.

2. **Liquidation—Terminating the Affairs of a Business**
A. **Procedure:**
- (1) Realization of assets—convert assets into cash
- (2) Division of loss or gain on realization, by charges or credits to partner's capital
- (3) Payment of the liabilities
- (4) Payment of the partner's interest

B. **Order of distribution in liquidation**
- (1) Outside creditors
  - (a) Priority claims such as artisans, government, liquidation expenses.
  - (b) Secured creditors to the extent covered by proceeds from sale of pledged assets. Excess claim treated as unsecured credit.
  - (c) Unsecured credit to the extent covered by proceeds from sale of unpledged (or free) assets.
- (2) Partners for loan accounts (right of "offset" reserved, however)
- (3) Partners' capital

As a practical matter partners' loans and capital are considered as one. Any known gain or loss should be distributed before any payments are made to partners.

Problem: A and B have non-cash assets of $40,000, liabilities of $5,000 and capital of $20,000 and $15,000 respectively. Assets are sold for $32,000. Determine amount distributable to A and B in liquidation.

A and B
Statement of Partnership Liquidation

	Assets			*Partners' Capitals*	
	Cash	*Non-Cash*	*Liabilities*	*A 50%*	*B 50%*
		$40,000	$(5,000)	$(20,000)	$(15,000)
Realization and Loss	$32,000	(40,000)		4,000	4,000
	$32,000	--0--	$(5,000)	$(16,000)	$(11,000)
Payment of Liabilities	(5,000)		5,000		
Payment to Partners	(27,000)			16,000	11,000

Problem: Debit balance in partner's capital account. Assets were sold for $50,000.

	Assets			*Partners' Loans*		*Partners' Capitals*	
	Cash	*Non-Cash*	*Liabilities*	*X*	*Y*	*X 80%*	*Y 20%*
	--0--	$80,000	$(15,000)	$(10,000)	$(17,000)	$(20,000)	$(18,000)
Real. and Loss	$50,000	(80,000)				24,000	6,000
	50,000	--0--	(15,000)	(10,000)	(17,000)	4,000	(12,000)
Combine Loan and Capital Acct.				10,000	17,000	(10,000)	(17,000)
	50,000		(15,000)	--0--	--0--	(6,000)	(29,000)
Pay Liabilities	(15,000)		15,000				
Pay Partners	(35,000)					6,000	29,000

NOTE: Right of offset exercised. Neither partner would be paid any cash until there is no danger that possible loss could exceed his capital account and loan account combined.

LIQUIDATION IN INSTALLMENTS -- MAXIMUM POSSIBLE LOSS (MPL)

Where a partnership is liquidated and the full amount to be paid to a partner is determined before any distributions are made, losses have already been distributed to the partners. In these situations it is assured that no partner will receive more than he will be entitled to receive. However, **where a liquidation** occurs in stages and **disbursements are made periodically**, there must be assurance that no partner will receive more than he could possibly be entitled to receive. This can be done by distributing the maximum possible loss to the partners and the remaining capital balance(s) can safely be paid. **The maximum possible loss is the total of the non-cash assets.** The procedure to determine the safe distribution is:

A. Determine the maximum possible loss that the partnership could suffer.
   MPL = Total Assets - Cash (or Non-Cash assets)
B. Distribute the MPL to the partners in P and L ratio.
C. The remaining balance is the amount that can be distributed to each partner.
D. Distribute the amount determined in C.
E. The same calculation must be made each time a distribution is made.

NOTE: Remember, MPL's are not actual losses, only theoretical losses; therefore, the determination of MPL should be done on a separate schedule.

ABC Partnership has the following balance sheet as of December 31st:

Assets		*Liabilities and Capital*	
Cash	$ 35,000	Liabilities	$ 21,000
Receivables	14,000	Partners' Loans	
Other Assets	85,000	A	5,000
		C	8,000
		Partners' Capital	
		A	50,000
		B	35,000
		C	15,000
	$134,000		$134,000

A, B and C share profits and losses on a 5:3:2 basis. Determine the amount the partner(s) will receive by distributing the maximum possible loss.

Solution: The maximum possible loss is $99,000 ($14,000 receivables + $85,000 other assets).

	A (50%)	*B (30%)*	*C (20%)*
Capital balance	$50,000	$35,000	$15,000
Additional loans	5,000	--	8,000
	55,000	35,000	23,000
MPL—$99,000	49,500	29,700	19,800
Amount distributed	$ 5,500	$ 5,300	$ 3,200

NOTE: The cash to be distributed—$14,000—is equal to the cash available—$35,000—less the liabilities of $21,000.

CASH DISTRIBUTION PLANS

Another method of determining the amount(s) that can be distributed to a partner is by preparation of a cash distribution plan. An accountant may be asked by a partnership to devise such a plan, if the partnership should subsequently choose to liquidate, showing how any cash generated by the sale of assets should be distributed. This is similar to the ordinary procedures in liquidation where, as cash is accumulated, the accountant calculates the payments which can safely be made to partners in installments. Once the plan is prepared it may be used to determine all subsequent distributions unless the mix of partners' capital is changed by investment or withdrawal. The use of MPL and the cash distribution plan is necessary because the partners' capital account ratios differ from their P and L ratios. The plan will eventually equalize the partners' capital accounts.

The procedure for a plan for distribution of cash is as follows:

1. Add the loan accounts to the partners' capital accounts.
2. Determine the amount of loss which will extinguish the weakest partner's capital balance.
3. Distribute the loss in (2) to all partners. After one partner is eliminated, repeat the same process with the remaining partners.
4. After all but one of the partners' capital accounts are eliminated, cash distributions are determined by starting with the remaining partner's final balance (which becomes the first cash distribution) and working backwards.

ILLUSTRATION 1:

The ABCD Partnership is being dissolved. All liabilities have been liquidated. The balance of assets on hand is being realized gradually. Following are details of partners' accounts:

	Capital Account (Original Investment)	*P and L Ratio*
A	$30,000	4
B	36,000	3
C	16,000	2
D	22,000	1

PREPARE a schedule showing how cash payments should be made to the partners as assets are realized.

	A (40%)	*B (30%)*		*C (20%)*		*D (10%)*	
Capital balance	$30,000	$36,000		$16,000		$22,000	
Loss (1) $75,000	30,000	22,500		15,000		7,500	
	--0--	13,500		1,000		14,500	
Loss to eliminate C							
$1,000 ÷ 2/6 = $3,000		1,500	(3/6)	1,000	(2/6)	500	(1/6)
		12,000		--0--		14,000	
Loss to eliminate B							
$12,000 ÷3/4 = $16,000		12,000	(3/4)			4,000	(1/4)
First cash payment		--0--				10,000	

Cash distribution plan-- (Liabilities must be paid or cash reserved before payments are made to partners)

1st $10,000 to D
Next $16,000—3/4 to B; 1/4 to D
Next $3,000—3/6 to B; 2/6 to C; 1/6 to D
All remaining cash in P and L ratio

(1) To determine the weakest partner, compare the capital account balance with the P and L ratio. A is weaker than B because A would be charged with 40% of any loss. A is also weaker than C and D even though A has greater total capital. Another method of determining the weakest partner is to divide the capital account by the loss ratio.

$$A = \frac{30{,}000}{.4} = 75{,}000 \text{ loss will eliminate A}$$

$$B = \frac{36{,}000}{.3} = 120{,}000 \text{ loss will eliminate B}$$

$$C = \frac{16{,}000}{.2} = 80{,}000 \text{ loss will eliminate C}$$

$$D = \frac{22{,}000}{.1} = 220{,}000 \text{ loss will eliminate D}$$

We can see from this that D will receive the first cash distribution made to the partners, followed by B, C, and then A.

(2) After each partner is eliminated, the loss which eliminates the next weakest partner is determined by using the loss ratio of the remaining partners, or after A is eliminated 3:2:1. Assume that $20,000 in cash is available for distribution but $5,000 is reserved for payment of liabilities. Following the plan the cash would be distributed as follows:

		A	B	C	D
To D	$10,000				$10,000
To B and D	5,000		$3,750 (3/4)		1,250 (1/4)
	$15,000		$3,750		$11,250

Assume that next month $20,000 is to be distributed. The plan would continue at the point reached last month.

		A	B	C	D
$16,000 – $5,000 =	$11,000		$ 8,250 (3/4)		$2,750 (1/4)
Next	3,000		1,500 (3/6)	$1,000 (2/6)	500 (1/6)
Next	6,000	$2,400	1,800	1,200	600
	$20,000	$2,400	$11,550	$2,200	$3,850

Observe that when all partners have received some cash, the capital accounts are in the same percentage as the P and L ratio and that future distributions can be made in the P and L ratio.

INCORPORATION OF A PARTNERSHIP

Procedures

A. Adjust asset values to bring balances into conformity with values agreed upon for the purpose of transfer to the corporation. The net effect of these adjustments will be carried to the partners' capital accounts in their respective P and L ratios.

B. Change from a partnership to corporation is made by debiting the partners' capital accounts and crediting capital stock account for the shares issued to the partners.

BONUS COMPUTATIONS

Frequently accountants are asked to compute the amount of bonus to be paid a corporate executive, a partner or employee under a profit sharing plan. The factors which may affect the bonus are:

- Net income before tax and/or bonus
- Tax rate—The bonus itself affects the tax since the bonus is deductible. The bonus may be computed before or after the tax depending on the profit sharing arrangement. Partnerships as entities do not pay taxes; however, an imputed tax rate may be used to compute the bonus.
- Bonus percentage—May be before or after bonus and may be applicable to income above a certain amount.

In solving such problems, a good approach is to write the particular problem in equation form with no attempt to quantify the elements of the equation. Then substitute known quantities in the equation and solve for B (Bonus).

Example: A company's bonus plan provides that the company will pay a bonus of one-third of its net income after taxes each year. Income before taxes and before deducting the bonus for the year is $600,000. The tax rate is 40%. What amount is the bonus?

Start with a simple expression of the situation

1. Bonus = Bonus Percent × Net Income

Now begin to substitute quantities

2. B = 33 1/3% (NI – Tax – Bonus)
3. B = 33 1/3% (600,000 – .40 [600,000 – B] – B)

Multiply the factors using the rules of algebra

4. B = 33 1/3% (600,000 – 240,000 + .4B – B)
5. B = 200,000 – 80,000 + 13 1/3% B – 33 1/3% B

Combine like terms when possible

6. **B = $120,000 – 20% B**

Add .2B to both sides of the equation

7. **1.2B = 120,000**

Divide both sides by 1.2

8. **B = 100,000**

Example:

The Wiley Company provides an incentive compensation plan under which its president is to receive a bonus equal to 20% of the company's income in excess of $200,000 before deducting income tax but after deducting the bonus. If income before income tax and bonus is $320,000 and the effective tax rate is 40%, the amount of bonus should be:

Bonus	= 20% (NI – Exclusion – Bonus)
B	= 20% (320,000 – 200,000 – B)
B	= 20% (120,000 – B)
B	= 24,000 – .2B
1.2 B	= 24,000
B	= 24,000 / 1.2
B	= 20,000

Chapter One
Partnerships Questions

FORMATION, ADMISSION OF PARTNERS

1. William desires to purchase a one-fourth capital and profit and loss interest in the partnership of Eli, George, and Dick. The three partners agree to sell William one-fourth of their respective capital and profit and loss interests in exchange for a total payment of $40,000. The capital accounts and the respective percentage interests in profits and losses immediately before the sale to William follow:

	Capital Accounts	*Percentage Interests in Profits and Losses*
Eli	$80,000	60%
George	40,000	30%
Dick	20,000	10%
Total	$140,000	100%

All other assets and liabilities are fairly valued and implied goodwill is to be recorded prior to the acquisition by William. Immediately after William's acquisition, what should be the capital balances of Eli, George, and Dick, respectively?

a. $60,000; $30,000; $15,000.
b. $69,000; $34,500; $16,500.
c. $77,000; $38,500; $19,500.
d. $92,000; $46,000; $22,000.

2. Pat, Helma, and Diane are partners with capital balances of $50,000, $30,000, and $20,000, respectively. The partners share profits and losses equally. For an investment of $50,000 cash, MaryAnn is to be admitted as a partner with a one-fourth interest in capital and profits. Based on this information, the amount of MaryAnn's investment can best be justified by which of the following?

a. MaryAnn will receive a bonus from the other partners upon her admission to the partnership.
b. Assets of the partnership were overvalued immediately prior to MaryAnn's investment.
c. The book value of the partnership's net assets was less than their fair value immediately prior to MaryAnn's investment.
d. MaryAnn is apparently bringing goodwill into the partnership and her capital account will be credited for the appropriate amount.

M91

3. Abel and Carr formed a partnership and agreed to divide initial capital equally, even though Abel contributed $100,000 and Carr contributed $84,000 in identifiable assets. Under the bonus approach to adjust the capital accounts, Carr's unidentifiable asset should be debited for

a. $46,000
b. $16,000
c. $8,000
d. $0

4. The following balance sheet is presented for the partnership of Davis, Wright, and Dover who share profits and losses in the ratio of 5:3:2 respectively:

Cash	$ 60,000
Other assets	540,000
	$600,000
Liabilities	$140,000
Davis, Capital	280,000
Wright, Capital	160,000
Dover, Capital	20,000
	$600,000

Assume that the assets and liabilities are fairly valued on the balance sheet and the partnership decided to admit Hank as a new partner with a one-fifth interest. No goodwill or bonus is to be recorded. How much should Hank contribute in cash or other assets?

a. $120,000.
b. $115,000.
c. $ 92,000.
d. $ 73,600.

M93

5. Kern and Pate are partners with capital balances of $60,000 and $20,000, respectively. Profits and losses are divided in the ratio of 60:40. Kern and Pate decided to form a new partnership with Grant, who invested land valued at $15,000 for a 20% capital interest in the new partnership. Grant's cost of the land was $12,000. The partnership elected to use the bonus method to record the admission of Grant into the partnership. Grant's capital account should be credited for

a. $12,000
b. $15,000
c. $16,000
d. $19,000

N92

6. Cor-Eng Partnership was formed on January 2, 1991. Under the partnership agreement, each partner has an equal initial capital balance accounted for under the goodwill method. Partnership net income or loss is allocated 60% to Cor and 40% to Eng. To form the partnership, Cor originally contributed assets costing $30,000 with a fair value of $60,000 on January 2, 1991, while Eng contributed $20,000 in cash. Drawings by the partners during 1991 totaled $3,000 by Cor and $9,000 by Eng. Cor-Eng's 1991 net income was $25,000. Eng's initial capital balance in Cor-Eng is

a. $20,000
b. $25,000
c. $40,000
d. $60,000

M91

7. Dunn and Grey are partners with capital account balances of $60,000 and $90,000, respectively. They agree to admit Zorn as a partner with a one-third interest in capital and profits, for an investment of $100,000, after revaluing the assets of Dunn and Grey. Goodwill to the original partners should be

a. $0
b. $33,333
c. $50,000
d. $66,667

N86

8. At December 31, 1985, Reed and Quinn are partners with capital balances of $40,000 and $20,000, and they share profit and loss in the ratio of 2:1, respectively. On this date Poe invests $17,000 cash for a one-fifth interest in the capital and profit of the new partnership. Assuming that goodwill is not recorded, how much should be credited to Poe's capital account on December 31, 1985?

a. $12,000
b. $15,000
c. $15,400
d. $17,000

9. Ames and Buell are partners who share profits and losses in the ratio of 3:2, respectively. On August 31, 1990, their capital accounts were as follows:

Ames	$70,000
Buell	60,000
	$130,000

On date they agreed to admit Carter as a partner with a one-third interest in the capital and profits and losses, for an investment of $50,000. The new partnership will begin with a total capital of $180,000. Immediately after Carter's admission, what are the capital balances of the partners?

	Ames	*Buell*	*Carter*
a.	$60,000	$60,000	$60,000
b.	$63,333	$56,667	$60,000
c.	$64,000	$56,000	$60,000
d.	$70,000	$60,000	$50,000

M93

10. Roberts and Smith drafted a partnership agreement that lists the following assets contributed at the partnership's formation:

	Contributed by	
	Roberts	*Smith*
Cash	$20,000	$30,000
Inventory	—	15,000
Building	—	40,000
Furniture & Equipment	15,000	—

The building is subject to a mortgage of $10,000, which the partnership has assumed. The partnership agreement also specifies that profits and losses are to be distributed evenly. What amounts should be recorded as capital for Roberts and Smith at the formation of the partnership?

	Roberts	*Smith*
a.	$35,000	$85,000
b.	$35,000	$75,000
c.	$55,000	$55,000
d.	$60,000	$60,000

N89

11. On July 1, 1988, a partnership was formed by Johnson and Smith. Johnson contributed cash. Smith, previously a sole proprietor, contributed property other than cash including realty subject to a mortgage, which was assumed by the partnership. Smith's capital account at July 1, 1988, should be recorded at

a. Smith's book value of the property at July 1, 1988.
b. Smith's book value of the property less the mortgage payable at July 1, 1988.
c. The fair value of the property less the mortgage payable at July 1, 1988.
d. The fair value of the property at July 1, 1988.

RETIREMENT, LIQUIDATION

M90

12. Allen retired from the partnership of Allen, Beck and Chale. Allen's cash settlement from the partnership was based on new goodwill determined at the date of retirement plus the carrying amount of the other net assets. As a consequence of the settlement, the capital accounts of Beck and Chale were decreased. In accounting for Allen's withdrawal, the partnership could have used the

	Bonus method	*Goodwill method*
a.	No	Yes
b.	No	No
c.	Yes	Yes
d.	Yes	No

13. The following balance sheet is for the partnership of Able, Bayer, and Cain which shares profits and losses in the ratio of 4:4:2, respectively.

Assets	
Cash	$ 20,000
Other assets	180,000 (90,000)
	$200,000

Liabilities and Capital	
Liabilities	$ 50,000
Able, Capital	37,000
Bayer, Capital	65,000
Cain, Capital	48,000
	$200,000

The original partnership was dissolved when its assets, liabilities, and capital were as shown on the above balance sheet and liquidated by selling assets in installments. The first sale of noncash assets having a book value of $90,000 realized $50,000, and all cash available after settlement with creditors was distributed. How much cash should the respective partners receive (to the nearest dollar)?

a. Able $8,000; Bayer $8,000; Cain $4,000.
b. Able $6,667; Bayer $6,667; Cain $6,666.
c. Able $0; Bayer $13,333; Cain $6,667.
d. Able $0; Bayer $3,000; Cain $17,000.

14. The partnership of Jenson, Smith, and Hart share profits and losses in the ratio of 5:3:2, respectively. The partners voted to dissolve the partnership when its assets, liabilities, and capital were as follows:

Assets	
Cash	$ 40,000
Other assets	210,000
	$250,000

Liabilities and Capital	
Liabilities	$ 60,000
Jenson, Capital	48,000
Smith, Capital	72,000
Hart, Capital	70,000
	$250,000

The partnership will be liquidated over a prolonged period of time. As cash is available it will be distributed to the partners. The first sale of noncash assets having a book value of $120,000 realized $90,000. How much cash should be distributed to each partner after this sale?

a. Jenson $0; Smith $28,800; Hart $41,200.
b. Jenson $0; Smith $30,000; Hart $40,000.
c. Jenson $35,000; Smith $21,000; Hart $14,000.
d. Jenson $45,000; Smith $27,000; Hart $18,000.

N90

15. Kent Co. filed a voluntary bankruptcy petition on August 15, 1989, and the statement of affairs reflects the following amounts:

	Book value	*Estimated current value*
Assets:		
Assets pledged with fully secured creditors	$ 300,000	$370,000
Assets pledged with partially secured creditors	180,000	120,000
Free assets	420,000	320,000
	$ 900,000	$810,000

Liabilities:	
Liabilities with priority	$ 70,000
Fully secured creditors	260,000
Partially secured creditors	200,000
Unsecured creditors	540,000
	$1,070,000

Assume that the assets are converted to cash at the estimated current values and the business is liquidated. What amount of cash will be available to pay unsecured nonpriority claims?

a. $240,000
b. $280,000
c. $320,000
d. $360,000

16. On June 30, the balance sheet for the partnership of Williams, Brown and Lowe together with their respective profit and loss ratios was as follows:

Assets, at cost	$300,000
Williams, loan	$ 15,000
Williams, capital (20%)	70,000
Brown, capital (20%)	65,000
Lowe, capital (60%)	150,000
Total	$300,000

Williams has decided to retire from the partnership and by mutual agreement the assets are to be adjusted to their fair value of $360,000 at June 30. It was agreed that the partnership would pay Williams $102,000 cash for his partnership interest exclusive of his loan which is to be repaid in full. No goodwill is to be recorded in this transaction. After William's retirement what are the capital account balances of Brown and Lowe, respectively?

a. $65,000 and $150,000.
b. $72,000 and $171,000.
c. $73,000 and $174,000.
d. $77,000 and $186,000.

17. James Dixon, a partner in an accounting firm, decided to withdraw from the partnership. Dixon's share of the partnership profits and losses was 20%. Upon withdrawing from the partnership he was paid $74,000 in final settlement for his interest. The total of the partners' capital accounts **before** recognition of partnership goodwill prior to Dixon's withdrawal was $210,000. After his withdrawal the remaining partners' capital accounts, excluding their share of goodwill, totaled $160,000. The total agreed upon goodwill of the firm was

a. $120,000
b. $140,000
c. $160,000
d. $250,000

18. The following condensed balance sheet is presented for the partnership of Fisher, Taylor and Simon who share profits and losses in the ratio of 6:2:2, respectively:

Cash	$ 40,000
Other assets	140,000
	$180,000
Liabilities	$ 70,000
Fisher, capital	50,000
Taylor, capital	50,000
Simon, capital	10,000
	$180,000

The assets and liabilities are fairly valued on the above balance sheet, and it was agreed to by all the partners that the partnership would be liquidated after selling the other assets. What would each of the partners receive at this time if the other assets are sold for $80,000?

	Fisher	*Taylor*	*Simon*
a.	$12,500	$37,500	$0
b.	$13,000	$37,000	$0
c.	$14,000	$38,000	$2,000
d.	$50,000	$50,000	$10,000

M92

19. Kamy Corp. is in liquidation under Chapter 7 of the Federal Bankruptcy Code. The bankruptcy trustee has established a new set of books for the bankruptcy estate. After assuming custody of the estate, the trustee discovered an unrecorded invoice of $1,000 for machinery repairs performed before the bankruptcy filing. In addition, a truck with a carrying amount of $20,000 was sold for $12,000 cash. This truck was bought and paid for in the year before the bankruptcy. What amount should be debited to estate equity as a result of these transactions?

a. $0
b. $1,000
c. $8,000
d. $9,000

M91

20. Seco Corp. was forced into bankruptcy and is in the process of liquidating assets and paying claims. Unsecured claims will be paid at the rate of forty cents on the dollar. Hale holds a $30,000 noninterest-bearing note receivable from Seco collateralized by an asset with a book value of $35,000 and a liquidation value of $5,000. The amount to be realized by Hale on this note is

a. $5,000
b. $12,000
c. $15,000
d. $17,000

21. The following condensed balance sheet is presented for the partnership of Cooke, Dorry, and Evans who share profits and losses in the ratio of 4:3:3, respectively:

Cash	$ 90,000
Other assets	820,000
Cooke, loan	30,000
	$940,000
Accounts payable	$210,000
Evans, loan	40,000
Cooke, capital	300,000
Dorry, capital	200,000
Evans, capital	190,000
	$940,000

Assume that the partners decide to liquidate the partnership. If the other assets are sold for $600,000, how much of the available cash should be distributed to Cooke?

a. $170,000.
b. $182,000.
c. $212,000.
d. $300,000.

DISTRIBUTION OF INCOME, BONUS

22. Partners C and K share profits and losses equally after each has been credited in all circumstances with annual salary allowances of $15,000 and $12,000, respectively. Under this arrangement, C will benefit by $3,000 more than K in which of the following circumstances?

a. Only if the partnership has earnings of $27,000 or more for the year.
b. Only if the partnership does not incur a loss for the year.
c. In all earnings or loss situations.
d. Only if the partnership has earnings of at least $3,000 for the year.

23. The Wisper Company provides an incentive compensation plan under which its president is to receive a bonus equal to 10% of the company's income in excess of $100,000 before deducting income tax but after deducting the bonus. If income before income tax and bonus is $320,000 and the effective tax rate is 40%, the amount of the bonus should be

a. $20,000.
b. $22,000.
c. $32,000.
d. $44,000.

24. Malcolm Corporation has an incentive compensation plan under which the sales manager receives a bonus equal to 10% of the company's income after deducting income taxes, but before deducting the bonus. Income before income tax and the bonus is $100,000. The effective income tax rate is 40%. How much is the bonus:

a. $5,400.
b. $6,000.
c. $6,250.
d. $10,000.

N91

25. The Flat and Iron partnership agreement provides for Flat to receive a 20% bonus on profits before the bonus. Remaining profits and losses are divided between Flat and Iron in the ratio of 2 to 3, respectively. Which partner has a greater advantage when the partnership has a profit or when it has a loss?

	Profit	*Loss*
a.	Flat	Iron
b.	Flat	Flat
c.	Iron	Flat
d.	Iron	Iron

N89

26. Beck, the active partner in Beck & Cris, receives an annual bonus of 25% of partnership net income after deducting the bonus. For the year ended December 31, 1988, partnership net income before the bonus amounted to $300,000. Beck's 1988 bonus should be

a. $56,250
b. $60,000
c. $62,500
d. $75,000

M89

27. Ral Corp. has an incentive compensation plan under which a branch manager receives 10% of the branch's income after deduction of the bonus but before deduction of income tax. Branch income for 1988 before the bonus and income tax was $165,000. The tax rate was 30%. The 1988 bonus amounted to

a. $12,600
b. $15,000
c. $16,500
d. $18,000

M89

28. The partnership agreement of Donn, Eddy, and Farr provides for annual distribution of profit or loss in the following sequence:

- Donn, the managing partner, receives a bonus of 10% of profit.
- Each partner receives 6% interest on average capital investment.
- Residual profit or loss is divided equally.

Average capital investments for 1988 were:

Donn	$80,000
Eddy	50,000
Farr	30,000

What portion of the $100,000 partnership profit for 1988 should be allocated to Farr?

a. $28,600
b. $29,800
c. $35,133
d. $41,600

M89

29. The Low and Rhu partnership agreement provides special compensation to Low for managing the business. Low receives a bonus of 15 percent of partnership net income before salary and bonus, and also receives a salary of $45,000. Any remaining profit or loss is to be allocated equally. During 1988, the partnership had net income of $50,000 before the bonus and salary allowance. As a result of these distributions, Rhu's equity in the partnership would

a. Increase.
b. Not change.
c. Decrease the same as Low's.
d. Decrease.

M87

30. Fox, Greg, and Howe are partners with average capital balances during 1986 of $120,000, $60,000, and $40,0000, respectively. Partners receive 10% interest on their average capital balances. After deducting salaries of $30,000 to Fox and $20,000 to Howe, the residual profit or loss is divided equally. In 1986 the partnership sustained a $33,000 loss before interest and salaries to partners. By what amount should Fox's capital account change?

a. $7,000 increase.
b. $11,000 decrease.
c. $35,000 decrease.
d. $42,000 increase.

M91

31. The partnership agreement of Reid and Simm provides that interest at 10% per year is to be credited to each partner on the basis of weighted-average capital balances. A summary of Simm's capital account for the year ended December 31, 1990, is as follows:

Balance, January 1	$140,000
Additional investment, July 1	40,000
Withdrawal, August 1	(15,000)
Balance, December 31	165,000

What amount of interest should be credited to Simm's capital account for 1990?

a. $15,250
b. $15,375
c. $16,500
d. $17,250

ADDITIONAL QUESTIONS

M95

Items 32 and 33 are based on the following:
The following condensed balance sheet is presented for the partnership of Alfa and Beda, who share profits and losses in the ratio of 60:40, respectively.

Cash	$ 45,000
Other assets	625,000
Beda, loan	30,000
	$700,000
Accounts payable	$120,000
Alfa, capital	348,000
Beda, capital	232,000
	$700,000

32. The assets and liabilities are fairly valued on the balance sheet. Alfa and Beda decide to admit Capp as a new partner with a 20% interest. No goodwill or bonus is to be recorded. What amount should Capp contribute in cash or other assets?

a. $110,000
b. $116,000
c. $140,000
d. $145,000

33. Instead of admitting a new partner, Alfa and Beda decide to liquidate the partnership. If other assets are sold for $500,000, what amount of the available cash should be distributed to Alfa?

a. $225,000
b. $273,000
c. $327,000
d. $348,000

N94

34. When Mill retired from the partnership of Mill, Yale, and Lear, the final settlement of Mill's interest exceeded Mill's capital balance. Under the bonus method, the excess

a. Was recorded as goodwill.
b. Was recorded as an expense.
c. Reduced the capital balances of Yale and Lear.
d. Had no effect on the capital balances of Yale and Lear.

N94

35. Able Co. provides an incentive compensation plan under which its president receives a bonus equal to 10% of the corporation's income before income tax but after deduction of the bonus. If the tax rate is 40% and net income after bonus and income tax was $360,000, what was the amount of the bonus?

a. $36,000
b. $60,000
c. $66,000
d. $90,000

M98

36. Eagle and Falk are partners with capital balances of $45,000 and $25,000, respectively. They agree to admit Robb as a partner. After the assets of the partnership are revalued, Robb will have a 25% interest in capital and profits, for an investment of $30,000. What amount should be recorded as goodwill to the original partners?

a. $0
b. $5,000
c. $7,500
d. $20,000

N98

37. Ayers and Smith formed a partnership on July 1, 1998. Ayers contributed cash of $50,000. Smith contributed property with a $36,000 carrying amount, a $40,000 original cost, and a fair value of $80,000. The partnership assumed the $35,000 mortgage attached to the property. What should Smith's capital account be on July 1, 1998?

a. $36,000
b. $40,000
c. $45,000
d. $80,000

Chapter One
Partnerships Problems

NUMBER 1

The partnership of Gary, Jerome, and Paul was formed on January 1, 19X6. The original investments were as follows:

Gary	$ 80,000
Jerome	$120,000
Paul	$180,000

According to the partnership agreement, net income or loss will be divided among the respective partners as follows:

- Salaries of $12,000 for Gary, $10,000 for Jerome, and $8,000 for Paul. Garunteed Pmts
- Interest of 8% on the average capital balances during the year of Gary, Jerome, and Paul.
- Remainder divided equally.

Additional information is as follows:

- Net income of the partnership for the year ended December 31, 19X6, was $70,000.
- Gary invested an additional $20,000 in the partnership on July 1, 19X6.
- Paul withdrew $30,000 from the partnership on October 1, 19X6.
- Gary, Jerome, and Paul made regular drawings against their shares of net income during 19X6 of $10,000 each.

Required:

1. Prepare a schedule showing the division of net income among the three partners. Show supporting computations in good form.
2. Prepare a schedule showing each partner's capital balance at December 31, 19X6. Show supporting computations in good form.

NUMBER 2

On January 1, 1992, the partners of Allen, Brown, and Cox, who share profits and losses in the ratio of 5:3:2, respectively, decide to liquidate their partnership. The partnership trial balance at this date is as follows:

	Debit	*Credit*
Cash	$ 18,000	
Accounts receivable	66,000	
Inventory	52,000	
Machinery and equipment, net	189,000	
Allen, loan	30,000	
Accounts payable		$ 53,000
Brown, loan		20,000
Allen, capital		118,000
Brown, capital		90,000
Cox, capital		74,000
	$355,000	$355,000

The partners plan a program of piecemeal conversion of assets in order to minimize liquidation losses. All available cash, less an amount retained to provide for future expenses, is to be distributed to the partners at the end of each month. A summary of the liquidation transactions is as follows:

January 1992:

a. $51,000 was collected on accounts receivable; the balance is uncollectible.
b. $38,000 was received for the entire inventory.
c. $2,000 liquidation expenses were paid.
d. $50,000 was paid to outside creditors, after offset of a $3,000 credit memorandum received on January 11, 1992.
e. $10,000 cash was retained in the business at the end of the month for potential unrecorded liabilities and anticipated expenses.

February 1992:

f. $4,000 liquidation expenses were paid.
g. $6,000 cash was retained in the business at the end of the month for potential unrecorded liabilities and anticipated expenses.

March 1992:

h. $146,000 was received on sale of all items of machinery and equipment.
i. $5,000 liquidation expenses were paid.
j. No cash was retained in the business.

Required:

Prepare a schedule to compute safe installment payments to the partners as of January 31, 1992. Show supporting computations in good form.

Chapter One
Solutions to Partnerships Questions

1. (b) Purchase of an Interest

X = Total Capital of new partnership
1/4X = $40,000 (William's payment)
X = $160,000

Total capital of new partnership	$160,000		
Less: Total capital of old partnership	140,000		
Implied Goodwill	$ 20,000		

	Eli	*George*	*Dick*	
Capital Balances	$80,000	$40,000	$20,000	
Implied Goodwill ($20,000 in P/L Ratio)	12,000	6,000	2,000	(1)
Total	$92,000	$46,000	$22,000	
Sale—1/4 Interest to Williams	(23,000)	(11,500)	(5,500)	(2)
Capital Balances after Sale	$69,000	$34,500	$16,500	

Journal Entries for #2:

(1) Goodwill	$20,000	
Eli, Capital		$12,000
George, Capital		6,000
Dick, Capital		2,000
To record implied goodwill in P/L Ratio.		
(2) Eli, Capital	$23,000	
George, Capital	11,500	
Dick, Capital	5,500	
Williams, Capital		$40,000
To record acquisition of 1/4 interest by Williams.		

2. (c) Total capital after admittance of new partner $150,000

$150,000 × 1/4 = $37,500
Investment for 1/4 interest = $50,000

MaryAnn paid $50,000 for assets with a net book value of $37,500. Therefore, the book value of the partnership's net assets must have been less than their fair value at the time of her admittance.

3. (d) $0. Under the bonus method an unidentifiable asset (goodwill) is not recorded, rather partners' capital balances are adjusted (bonus) to reflect their proper interest in capital.

4. (b) $115,000. The investment by Hank must be an amount that, when added to the present capital, represents one-fifth of the new total capital. This can be expressed as follows (NC = new capital):

1/5 NC + $460,000 = NC
$460,000 = 4/5 NC
NC = $575,000

New capital $575,000 - old capital $460,000 = $115,000.

5. (d) Under the bonus method, the new partner's capital account is credited for 20% of the new balance of total capital. The new total capital is $95,000 ($60,000 + $20,000 + $15,000). Grant's capital balance will be 20% × $95,000 or $19,000. The bonus to Grant of $4,000 ($19,000 capital balance – $15,000 contribution) will be charged against the old partners capital accounts according to their profit and loss ratio.

6. (d) Under the partnership agreement, each partner has an equal initial capital balance, and goodwill is to be recognized. Cor's original capital balance will be $60,000, the fair market value of the net assets contributed as of the date of contribution. Therefore, Eng's original capital balance will be $60,000, an equal amount, and goodwill of $40,000 will be attributed to Eng ($60,000 capital – $20,000 cash contribution).

7. (c) $50,000

Implied value of new partnership:		
New partner's investment		$100,000
Multiple of interest acquired (1/3)		× 3
		$300,000
Less capital balance before recognition of goodwill:		
Dunn	$ 60,000	
Grey	90,000	
Zorn (new partner)	100,000	250,000
Goodwill to original partners		$ 50,000

8. (c)

Reed capital	$40,000
Quinn capital	20,000
Poe's contribution	17,000
Total capital (New)	$77,000
Poe's interest in capital	× 1/5
Poe's capital balance	$15,400

NOTE: Bonus to old partners of $1,600 would result as Poe contributed $17,000; however only received a capital balance of $15,400.

9. (c)

Carter's capital ($180,000 × 1/3)	$60,000
Carter's investment	50,000
Bonus to Carter	$10,000

Bonus to Carter is shared by the old partners in their P/L ratio (Ames, 3/5; Buell, 2/5).

	Ames	*Buell*	*Carter*
Original capital balances	$70,000	$60,000	—
Carter's investment			$50,000
Bonus to Carter	(6,000)	(4,000)	10,000
New capital balances	$64,000	$56,000	$60,000

NOTE: Only Ames new capital balance needs to be computed as it is different for each of the possible answers.

10. (b) For financial accounting purposes, non-cash contributions are recorded at the fair market value of the net assets contributed, as of the date of contribution. The mortgage balance attributable to the building reduces Smith's capital by the amount of the mortgage assumed by the partnership. Even though profits and losses will be split evenly, the capital balances do not need to be in that ratio.

11. (c) For financial accounting purposes, non-cash contributions are recorded at the fair market value of the net assets contributed as of the date of contribution.

12. (d) Under the bonus method the capital accounts of the non-retiring partners are charged (in proportion to their P & L ratios) for the distribution to the retiring partner in excess of the retiring partner's capital balance (the bonus).

Under the goodwill method, the inherent goodwill (or at least the portion attributable to the retiring partner) is recorded, increasing the retiring partner's capital balance to an amount equal to the retirement distribution. The capital balances of the non-retiring partners would not be decreased by the retirement of a partner, but would be increased if all inherent goodwill were recorded.

13. (d)

	Cash	*Other Assets*	*Liabilities*
Balances	$20,000	$180,000	$(50,000)
Sale of Assets ($40,000 Loss in P/L Ratio)	50,000	(90,000)	—
Balances	$70,000	$ 90,000	$(50,000)
Allow for worst possible loss on remaining assets		(90,000)	
Payment to creditors	(50,000)		50,000
Balances	$20,000	—	—
Distribution of Cash	(20,000)	—	—
Balances	-0-		

	Capital Accounts *Able*	*Bayer*	*Cain*	
Balances	$(37,000)	$(65,000)	$(48,000)	
Sale of Assets ($40,000 Loss in P/L Ratio)	16,000	16,000	8,000	= 40,000
Balances	$(21,000)	$(49,000)	$(40,000)	
Allow for worst possible loss on remaining assets	36,000	36,000	18,000	= 90,000
Payment to creditors	—	—	—	
Balances	$ 15,000	$(13,000)	$(22,000)	
Distribution of Able's deficit - 4:2 ratio	(15,000)	10,000	5,000	Bring Back to zero.
Balances	—	(3,000)	(17,000)	
Distribution of cash	—	3,000	17,000	
Balances	-0-	-0-	-0-	

14. (a) Prepare cash distribution plan as follows:

	Jenson (5)	*Smith (3)*	*Hart (2)*	
Capital balances	48,000	72,000	70,000	
Loss to eliminate weakest partner	(48,000)	28,800	19,200	96,000
	—0—	43,200	50,800	
Loss to eliminate next weakest partner 43,200 ÷ .6		43,200	28,800	72,000
			22,000	

Cash available:

Balance	$ 40,000
Proceeds	90,000
	$130,000
Less: Liabilities	60,000
	$ 70,000 to be distributed as follows:

1st $22,000 to H
Next $48,000—3/5 to S; 2/5 to H or $28,800 to S; $19,200 to H.
Total: S—$28,800; H—$19,200 + 22,000 = $41,200

15. (d) $360,000

Total cash from sale of assets		$810,000
Less distributions to:		
Liabilities with priority	$ 70,000	
Fully secured creditors	260,000	
Partially secured creditors (limited to proceeds from security-pledged assets)	120,000 *	– 450,000
Cash available for unsecured, non-priority claims		$360,000

*Claim of partially secured creditors in excess of security, $80,000 ($200,000 claim – $120,000 assets pledged), would be an unsecured liability (claim).

16. (b)

	Williams	*Brown*	*Lowe*
Original capital balances	$ 70,000	$65,000	$150,000
$60,000 Asset write-up in P/L ratio.	12,000	12,000	36,000
	$ 82,000	$77,000	$186,000
Bonus to Williams ($102,000 – $82,000) distributed in P/L ratio of remaining partners (2/8, 6/8)	20,000	(5,000)	(15,000)
	$102,000	$72,000	$171,000
Cash payment	(102,000)		
Ending capital balances	—0—	$72,000	$171,000

17. (a)

Total capital before goodwill and withdrawal	$210,000
Total capital before goodwill after withdrawal	(160,000)
Capital attributable to Dixon	$ 50,000
Payment to Dixon	(74,000)
Goodwill attributed to Dixon	$ 24,000
Dixon P/L ratio	÷ .20
Total goodwill	$120,000

18. (a)

	Fisher	*Taylor*	*Simon*
Original capital balances	$50,000	$50,000	$10,000
Loss on sale of assets distributed in P/L ratio	(36,000)	(12,000)	(12,000)
	$14,000	$38,000	($2,000)
Distribution of Simon's deficit (6/8, 2/8)	(1,500)	(500)	2,000
Ending capital balances	$12,500	$37,500	—0—

19. (d) Both an unrecorded invoice for repairs (an expense) and the sale of an asset below its carrying value would result in a reduction of "estate equity" for a business liquidating under Chapter 7 of the Federal Bankruptcy Code.

Voluntary or involuntary bankruptcy proceedings under Chapter 7 of the Federal Bankruptcy Code (liquidation), creates an "estate" for the liquidating entity which consists of the entity's assets and is administered by a trustee.

20. (c) $15,000.

Realized on secured credit		
Liquidation value of collateral		$ 5,000
Realized on unsecured credit		
Total claim	$30,000	
Less amount secured	– 5,000	
Unsecured claim	$25,000	
Percent payment on unsecured credit	× 40%	
Payment on unsecured claim		10,000
Total amount realized		$15,000

21. (b)

	Cooke	*Dorry*	*Evans*
Capital balances	$300,000	$200,000	$190,000
Offset Cooke Loan	(30,000)		
	270,000	200,000	190,000
Distribution of loss on sale of assets in P/L ratio	(88,000)	(66,000)	(66,000)
Cash distribution	$182,000	$134,000	$124,000

NOTE: Evans' loan account would be offset to capital if his balance were negative; otherwise it would maintain its priority as a liability.

22. (c) Partners C and K are always credited or charged with the **same amount** of profit and loss, and C's salary is **always** $3,000 greater than K's. Therefore, C will benefit $3,000 more than K in all earnings or loss situations.

23. (a)

X = Net income applicable to 10% bonus
X = $320,000 – $100,000 – 10%X
X = $220,000 – 10%X
110% X = $220,000
X = $200,000
Bonus = 10%X
= $20,000 (10% of net income in excess of $100,000 before tax, after bonus)

or

B = .10 (Net income before taxes – $100,000)
B = .10 ($320,000 – Bonus – $100,000)
B = $32,000 – .1B – $10,000
1.1 B = $22,000
B = $20,000

24. (c)
Bonus = .10 (100,000 – T)
Taxes = .40 (100,000 – B)
B = .10 (100,000 – .4 (100,000 – B))
B = .10 (100,000 – 40,000 + .4B)
B = 10,000 – 4,000 + .04B
.96B = 6,000
B = 6,250

25. (b) Flat has the greater advantage when the partnership has a profit or a loss. When the partnership has a profit, Flat would be allocated 52% of the profits [a 20% bonus plus 32% (40% of the remaining 80% of profits)]. When the partnership has a loss, Flat would be allocated only 40% of the loss (2/5ths).

26. (b)
Bonus = 25% (Net income – Bonus)
B = .25 ($300,000 – Bonus)
B = $75,000 – .25 Bonus
1.25B = $75,000
B = $60,000

27. (b)
Bonus = 10% (NIBT – B)
B = .1 ($165,000 – B)
B = $16,500 – .1B
1.1B = $16,500
B = $16,500 + 1.1
B = $15,000

28.(a)

	Donn	*Eddy*	*Farr*	*Total*
Bonus (10% × $100,000)	$10,000	$ —	$ —	$ 10,000
Interest (6% Avg. Cap.)	4,800	3,000	1,800	9,600
	$14,800	$ 3,000	$ 1,800	$ 19,600
Excess in P/L ratio	26,800	26,800	26,800	80,400
Profit distribution	$41,600	$29,800	$28,600	$100,000

29. (d) Low's 15% bonus and salary exceed the partnership net income, resulting in a $2,500 "loss" to be distributed equally to Low and Rhu.

Distribution of partnership income:

	Low	*Rhu*	*Total*
Bonus (15% × $50,000)	$ 7,500	$ —	$ 7,500
Salary	45,000	—	45,000
			$52,500
Excess in P&L ratio	(1,250)	(1,250)	(2,500)
Profit distribution	$51,250	$(1,250)	$50,000

30. (a)

Partnership loss before interest and salaries to partners	$ 33,000
Partners' interest on average capital balances 10% ($120,000 + $60,000 + $40,000)	22,000
Partners' salaries ($30,000 + 20,000)	50,000
"Residual" partnership loss	$105,000

Change in Fox's Capital Account:

Interest—10% x $120,000	$12,000
Salary	30,000
Share of "residual" partnership loss 1/3 x $105,000	(35,000)
Increase in Fox's capital	$ $7,000

31. (b) $15,375.

Computation of weighted-average capital balance:

Balance 1/1	$140,000
+ additional investment 7/1 ($40,000 × ½ year)	20,000
– withdrawal 8/1 ($15,000 × 5/12 year)	– 6,250
Average capital balance	$153,750

"Interest" credited to Simm's capital:

Average capital balance	$153,750
Rate	× 10%
	$ 15,375

32. (d) $145,000. The investment by Capp must be an amount that, when added to the present capital ($580,000), represents one-fifth of the new total capital. This can be expressed as follows (NC = New Capital):

NC = $580,000 + 1/5 NC
4/5 NC = $580,000
NC = $725,000

New Capital	$725,000
Old Capital	580,000
Investment by Capp	$145,000

33. (b) $273,000.

	Alfa	Beda
Original Capital balances	$348,000	$232,000
Loss on sale of Assets distributed in P/L ratio	(75,000)	(50,000)
Ending Capital balances	$273,000	$182,000

Beda's loan would be offset against Beda's Capital balance.

34. (c) Under the "Bonus Method", Distributions to retiring partners in excess of their capital balance are charged against the other partners capital accounts in proportion to their profit and loss ratios.

35. (b) $60,000. As the tax rate is 40%, net income after bonus and taxes ($360,000) is 60% of net income after bonus **before** taxes.

60% (NIBT - B) = $360,000
NIBT - B = $360,000 ÷ 60%
NIBT - B = $600,000

Bonus = 10% Net income after bonus before tax
= 10% × $600,000
= $60,000

36. (d) Robb's investment of $30,000 for a 25% partnership interest represents an objective basis for the determination of the fair value of the partnership and for the calculation of goodwill. If $30,000 is 25% of the fair value of the partnership, then the total fair value is $120,000 ($30,000 / 25%). The difference between the fair value of the partnership ($120,000) and the total book value of the three partner's capital of $100,000 ($45,000 + $25,000 + $30,000) is goodwill of $20,000.

37. (c) The solution approach would be to prepare the journal entry to form the partnership.

		Debit	Credit
JE	Cash	50,000	
	Property	80,000	
	Mortgage Payable		35,000
	Ayers, capital		50,000
	Smith, capital		45,000

Chapter One
Solutions to Partnerships Problems

NUMBER 1

Partnership of Gary, Jerome, and Paul
DIVISION OF NET INCOME
For the Year Ended December 31, 19X6

	Gary	*Jerome*	*Paul*	*Total*
Salaries	$12,000	$10,000	$ 8,000	$30,000
Interest on average capital balances *(Schedule 1)*	7,200	9,600	13,800	30,600
	19,200	19,600	21,800	60,600
Remainder divided equally	3,133	3,133	3,134	9,400
Division of net income	$22,333	$22,733	$24,934	$70,000

Partnership of Gary, Jerome and Paul
CAPITAL BALANCES
December 31, 19X6

	Gary	*Jerome*	*Paul*	*Total*
Balance at January 1, 19X6	$ 80,000	$120,000	$180,000	$380,000
Additional investment	20,000	—	—	20,000
Withdrawal	—	—	(30,000)	(30,000)
Net income	22,333	22,733	24,934	70,000
Regular drawings	(10,000)	(10,000)	(10,000)	(30,000)
Balance at December 31, 19X6	$112,333	$132,733	$164,934	$410,000

Schedule 1 — Computation of Interest on Average Capital Balances

Gary:		
$ 80,000 × 8% for 6 months	$ 3,200	
$100,000 × 8% for 6 months	4,000	$ 7,200
Jerome:		
$120,000 × 8%		9,600
Paul:		
$180,000 × 8% for 9 months	10,800	
$150,000 × 8% for 3 months	3,000	13,800
		$30,600

NUMBER 2

Allen, Brown, and Cox Partnership
COMPUTATION OF SAFE INSTALLMENT PAYMENTS TO PARTNERS
January 31, 1992

		Residual Equities		
	Total	Allen	Brown	Cox
Profit and loss ratio	100%	50%	30%	20%
Computation of January installment				
Preliquidation balances				
Capital	$282,000	$118,000	$ 90,000	$74,000
Add (deduct) loans	(10,000)	(30,000)	20,000	—
	272,000	88,000	110,000	74,000
Deduct January losses *(Schedule 1)*	(28,000)	(14,000)	(8,400)	(5,600)
Predistribution balances	244,000	74,000	101,600	68,400
Deduct potential losses *(Schedule 1)*	(199,000)	(99,500)	(59,700)	(39,800)
	45,000	(25,500)	41,900	28,600
Deduct potential loss — Allen's debit balance (Brown 3/5; Cox 2/5)	—	25,500	(15,300)	(10,200)
Safe payments to partners	$ 45,000	$ 0	$ 26,600	$18,400

Schedule 1

Computation of Actual and Potential Liquidation Losses
January 1992

	Actual losses	Potential losses
Collection of accounts receivable ($66,000 – $51,000)	$15,000	
Sale of inventory ($52,000 – $38,000)	14,000	
Liquidation expenses	2,000	
Gain resulting from January credit memorandum offset against payments to creditors	(3,000)	
Machinery and equipment, net		$189,000
Potential unrecorded liabilities and anticipated expenses		10,000
Totals	$28,000	$199,000

Chapter Two
Stockholders' Equity and Investments in Stock

STOCKHOLDERS' EQUITY:

Chapter Two

Stockholders' Equity and Investments in Stock

ELEMENTS OF STOCKHOLDERS' EQUITY

Contributed Capital:
  Capital Stock (Legal Capital)
  Capital Contributed in Excess of Par or Stated Value
Retained Earnings
Treasury Stock
Accumulated Other Comprehensive Income

Capital Stock

Capital stock can be common or preferred. Preferred stock has one or more preferences over common stock, usual preference is in dividend payment and/or in liquidation. Capital stock is recorded at:

1. *Par Value:* Par value is established in the articles of incorporation and constitutes legal capital. Legal capital is that portion of corporate capital required by state statute to be retained in the business to afford creditors a minimum degree of protection.
2. *No-Par Value (Stated Value):* Stated value can be set by the board of directors when no-par value is established in the articles of incorporation and functions the same as the par value.
3. *No-Par Value (No Stated Value):* Entire proceeds from the issuance of capital stock is credited to the capital stock account and becomes legal capital.

Capital Contributed in Excess of Par Value of Stock (C.C. in Excess)

In published statements this element of stockholders' equity is normally shown under one title; however, separate accounts must be maintained in the accounting records **by source**. Frequently this account is titled "Additional Paid-In Capital."

This title is used to describe numerous accounts kept for record and statement purposes, such as:

1. Contributions paid in by stockholders and subscribers:
   a. Premiums on par value or stated value stock.
   b. Conversion of convertible bonds or preferred stock.
   c. Forfeited part payments on stock subscriptions.
   d. Assessments on stockholders.
   e. Donations by stockholders, including gifts of assets and forgiveness of indebtedness.
   f. Increments arising from capital stock transactions and changes.
      (1) Donations of stock.
      (2) Purchase and resale of treasury stock at a profit.
      (3) Retirement of stock at a cost less than the amount set up as stated capital.
      (4) Conversion of stock of one class into a smaller amount of stock of another class.
      (5) Reduction of stated or legal capital.
      (6) Issuance of stock dividend recognized at market value which exceeds par.
2. Contributed capital by others, including forgiveness of indebtedness and gifts of assets, such as a plant site given to induce a company to locate in the donor city.

Examples of journal entries for issuance of common stock follow:

Stock Issued at More Than Par or Stated Value

1. 100 shares of $50 par value common issued at $55.

	Dr.	Cr.	
Cash	$5,500		
Common Stock		5,000	(Legal Capital)
C.C. in Excess		500	

2. 100 shares of no-par common, stated value $10, issued at $12.

Cash	$1,200		
Common Stock		1,000	(Legal Capital)
C.C. in Excess		200	

3. 200 shares no-par common (no stated value) issued at $12.

Cash	$2,400		
Common Stock		2,400	(Legal Capital)

Stock Issued for Less Than Par Value

Illegal in some states. Subscribers face contingent liability if corporation becomes insolvent. Contingent liability generally does not pass to subsequent holder unless he had notice or should have known of it. Discount should never be written off against income or retained earnings. It remains open on books. Show on balance sheet as reduction of capital contributed in excess or can be netted against premium received on other shares to arrive at total capital contributed. Because of these factors, stock is rarely issued at a discount.

Subscription of Capital Stock

A subscription of capital stock occurs when an investor contracts to purchase stock, making payment(s) in the future. Usually, a partial payment is made at the time of the contract and the stock is **not** issued until final payment has been made. When a subscription contract is made:

1. **Subscriptions Receivable** is debited for the amount of the future payments. Subscriptions receivable is reported as a current asset or as the SEC requires, a contra stockholders' equity account.
2. **Common or Preferred Stock Subscribed** is credited for the portion of the proceeds representing legal capital. Common or Preferred Stock Subscribed represents a claim against the unissued stock and is reported in stockholders' equity after the issued common or preferred stock.
3. **Additional Paid-in Capital** (in excess of par) is credited for the proceeds in excess of legal capital. Note that the A.P.I.C. is **not** identified as subscribed.

Example: A company accepts subscriptions for 100 shares of common stock ($10 par value) at $25 per share. The agreement calls for an initial payment of 20% with the remainder to be paid in 60 days.

Entry to record subscription:

Cash (20% × $2,500)	$ 500	
Subscriptions receivable: Common stock	2,000	
Common stock **subscribed** (100 × $10 par)		$1,000
A.P.I.C. in excess of par		1,500

When final payment is received, the following entries would be made:

Cash	$2,000	
Subscriptions receivable: Common stock		$2,000
Common stock subscribed	$1,000	
Common stock		$1,000

Default on Subscription

If a subscriber defaults on the subscription contract the accounting treatment depends upon the state law and/or the agreement. The default could result in:

1. Forfeiture of all amounts paid.
2. Refund of amount paid.
3. Partial refund.
4. Issuance of shares in proportion to amount paid for.

Regardless of which alternative is applied, the subscription receivable, common stock subscribed and A.P.I.C. applicable to the shares which will not be issued must be removed from the accounts. The remaining credit will depend upon the alternative applied. Using the prior example and assuming the subscriber forfeits any amounts paid, the default would be recorded as follows:

Common stock subscribed	$1,000	
A.P.I.C. in excess of par	1,500	
Subscription receivable: Common stock		$2,000
A.P.I.C. defaulted subscriptions		500

If the subscriber defaulted and was to receive the proportion of shares paid for, the entry would be as follows:

Common stock subscribed	$1,000	
A.P.I.C. in excess of par ($1,500 × 80%)	1,200	
Common stock ($1,000 × 20%)		$ 200
Subscription receivable: Common stock		2,000

Shares issued = $500 paid ÷ $25 subscription price = 20 shares. Note that A.P.I.C. in excess of par is charged for the subscribed shares which were not issued (80 shares or 80% of the 100 shares subscribed).

Retained Earnings

Retained earnings balance is cumulative net income of a corporation from date of incorporation or reorganization, after deducting losses, distributions to stockholders, transfers to capital accounts, and after accounting for prior period adjustments. Retained earnings include operating profits and other items of net income as included therein by GAAP. Examples of items which are part of net income under GAAP but shown separately on the income statement from operating net income are:

1. Income or loss from discontinued operations
2. Gain or loss on a disposal of a segment of a business
3. Extraordinary items
4. Cumulative effect of a change in method of accounting

Sometimes, portions of the retained earnings of a corporation may have been appropriated for special purposes. This would restrict the payment of dividends from such earnings. Generally, to earmark such appropriations, details would be shown as follows:

Retained Earnings

1. Free (or unappropriated)
2. Appropriated
    a. Reserve for contingencies
    b. Reserve for plant extensions, retirement of preferred stock, etc.

The use of the term **reserve** in this manner is the only proper use of term per AICPA Terminology Bulletin No. 1, Par. 59(3).

Reserves for self-insurance may be set up by appropriating retained earnings. As with other appropriations of retained earnings, losses may not be charged thereto. Losses arising from the self-insurance position of the company would be charged to expense with no effect on the reserve for self-insurance.

To set up appropriated retained earnings:

Retained Earnings	$100,000	
Reserve for Self-Insurance		$100,000

When the reserve is no longer needed, the entry should be reversed. Losses should never be charged against reserve accounts.

TREASURY STOCK

Definition

Treasury stock is a corporation's own stock, once issued and fully paid, and later reacquired but not canceled in accordance with a formal procedure specified by law. Treasury stock may be either common or preferred stock, reacquired by donation, purchase or in settlement of a debt. Stock held in treasury has no cash dividend, liquidation, preemptive or voting rights; however, it does participate in stock splits.

Purchased

1. The **cost** of treasury stock, regardless of par, should be carried as the value of treasury stock as a reduction of stockholders' equity.
2. The total cost of treasury stock carried should also be shown as a restriction of retained earnings in the balance sheet.

STOCKHOLDERS' EQUITY ILLUSTRATION WITH TREASURY STOCK:

Capital Stock:	
Authorized and issued, 10,000 shares of $100 par value of which 500 shares are in the treasury	$1,000,000
Contributed Capital in Excess of Par Value	150,000
Retained Earnings:	
(of which $62,000, representing the cost of treasury stock, is restricted)	784,000
Total	$1,934,000
Less: Cost of Treasury Stock	62,000
Total Stockholders' Equity	$1,872,000

If cost of treasury stock exceeds the Retained Earnings Account, restrict excess against Contributed Capital in Excess of Par Value.

Acquisition for Purposes Other Than Retirement

- "Gains" on sales of treasury stock not previously accounted for as constructively retired should be credited to capital in excess.
- "Losses" should be charged to capital in excess to the extent that previous net "gains" from sales or retirements of the same class of stock are included therein, otherwise to retained earnings.

Note that the terms "gains" and "losses" are used in connection with describing the transaction; however, **treasury stock transactions do not result in net income for financial reporting purposes**. Also, treasury stock transactions are not taxable.

- When state law is at variance with GAAP treatment of treasury stock, the accounting should conform to the applicable law. When state laws relating to acquisition of stock restrict retained earnings for payment of dividends or have other effects of a significant nature, these facts should be **disclosed**.

Accounting Methods

1. Cost (preferable)
2. Par-value or retirement method

Where the "cost" method is used, acquisitions are recorded at cost and the total cost is shown in the balance sheet as a reduction of stockholders' equity. The par-value method, which has theoretical support, results in the shares being recorded at par with the treasury shares shown in the balance sheet as a reduction of capital stock outstanding.

ILLUSTRATIONS: Assume 10,000 shares were originally issued at $15 (par value $10).

	Debit	Credit
Cash	$150,000	
C/S		100,000
C.C. in Excess		50,000

Application of Cost Method Where 200 Shares Were Reacquired at $18:

Treasury Stock	$3,600	
Cash		3,600

If resold at the same price, the entry would be reversed.

If 100 shares were resold at $20, the entry would be:

Cash	$2,000	
Treasury Stock		1,800
C.C. in excess from treasury stock transaction		200

If the remaining 100 shares were resold at $13:

Cash	$1,300	
*C.C. in Excess	200	
Retained Earnings	300	
Treasury Stock		1,800

*Can be used to the extent that "previous net 'gains' from sales or retirements of the same class are included therein, otherwise to retained earnings."

Application of Par Value Method Using the Same Facts

Under the Par Method the excess of cost of treasury stock over par or stated value:

(1) **May be** allocated between A.P.I.C. and retained earnings. The portion allocated to A.P.I.C. is limited to the sum of: a) the pro rata portion of A.P.I.C. on the same issue; and b) all A.P.I.C. from retirements and net "gains" on the sale of treasury stock of the same issue.

(2) **May be** charged entirely to retained earnings.

An excess of par or stated value over cost shall be credited to additional paid in capital (C.C. in excess).

200 shares reacquired at $18:

Treasury Stock (par)	$2,000	
*C.C. in Excess	1,000	
Retained Earnings	600	
Cash		$3,600

*Based on original issue premium of $5 per share.

200 shares reacquired at $15:

Treasury Stock	$2,000	
C.C. in Excess	1,000	
Cash		$3,000

200 shares reacquired at $12:

Treasury Stock	$2,000	
C.C. in Excess	400	
Cash		$2,400

OR

Treasury Stock	$2,000	
C.C. in Excess	1,000	
C.C. in excess from Treasury Stock Transaction		600
Cash		$2,400

(preferable entry)

100 shares are reissued at $11:

Cash	$1,100	
C.C. in Excess		$ 100
Treasury Stock		1,000

Reissuance of treasury shares is given the same treatment as any original issue of stock.

PROBLEM: Hillside Corporation has 80,000 shares of $50 par value common stock authorized, issued, and outstanding. All 80,000 shares were issued at $55 each. Retained earnings of the company are $160,000. If 1,000 shares of Hillside common were reacquired at $62 and the retirement (par value) method of accounting for treasury stock were used, capital stock would decrease by:

a. $62,000 b. $55,000 c. $50,000 d. $0.

Answer: (d) The retirement or par value method does not decrease the number of shares.

Retirement of Treasury Stock

When a corporation's stock is retired, or purchased for constructive retirement (with or without an intention to retire the stock formally in accordance with applicable laws):

1. **An excess of purchase price over par or stated value** may be allocated between C.C in excess and retained earnings. The portion of the excess allocated to C.C. in excess should be limited to the sum of:
   a. All C.C. in excess arising from previous retirements and net "gains" on sales of treasury stock of the same issue, and
   b. The pro rata portion of C.C. in excess paid in, voluntary transfers of retained earnings, capitalization of stock dividends, etc., on the same issue. For this purpose, any remaining C.C. in excess applicable to issues fully retired (formal or constructive) is deemed to be applicable pro rata to shares of common stock.

Alternatively, the excess may be **charged entirely to retained earnings** in recognition of the fact that a corporation can always capitalize or allocate retained earnings for such purposes.

2. **An excess of par or stated value over purchase price** should be credited to C.C. in Excess.

ILLUSTRATIONS

Facts:

10,000 shares, no-par, $10 stated value issued	$100,000
Capital Contributed in Excess, Common	20,000
Capital Contributed in Excess, Common from T/S transactions	1,000
Retained Earnings	40,000
Treasury Stock, 100 shares at cost	2,500
Treasury Stock is retired	

Retirement of Treasury Stock

Method #1:

Capital Stock, stated value $10	1,000	
C.C. in Excess—T.S. transactions	1,000	
C.C. in Excess—Common	200	
Retained Earnings	300	
Treasury Stock		2,500

$$\frac{\text{Shares Retired} \quad 100}{\text{Total Shares} \quad 10{,}000} \times \frac{\$20{,}000}{\text{C.C. in Excess, Common}} = \$200$$

Method #2: (Simplest Method)

Capital Stock, stated value $10	1,000	
Retained Earnings	1,500	
Treasury Stock		2,500

Same facts except that Treasury Stock was acquired at $8 per share or $800.

Capital Stock	1,000	
C.C. in Excess		200
Treasury Stock		800

Donated Stock

General Purpose: Donations may be made to provide stock that may be resold to furnish working capital, to eliminate the water from the stock, to wipe out a deficit, to provide common stock to be given as a bonus to purchasers of a preferred stock, or for other reasons. It may be purchased to buy out a stockholder, or to create a market demand for the stock and thus retard a downward trend in the market value.

If the donated stock is not to be resold, the company should effect a formal reduction of its stated capital.

If the donated stock is to be resold, since the company will part with nothing of value, there is no cost to record in the Treasury Stock account. There would be only a memo entry.

If stock is donated to provide stock that can be sold to raise working capital, no entry other than a memorandum in the Treasury Stock account should be made for the donation. The proceeds of the sale should be credited to C.C. in Excess, Donated Capital.

Retained earnings should never be increased as a result of treasury stock transactions. Cash dividends would not be paid on treasury shares. Stock dividends and stock splits apply to all issued shares, however.

PREFERRED STOCK

Characteristics

a. Fixed dividend rate
b. Preference in liquidation of assets
c. Participating or non-participating. Participation must be stated in problem.
d. Cumulative or non-cumulative.
e. Absence of voting rights

Redemption

What are preferred shares entitled to receive?

Par value
+ Dividends (in arrears if cumulative and any participating dividends)
+ Redemption premium

Conditions of redemption are important. Most preferred shares are entitled to a premium if called (call price, e.g. 105), but may provide no premium in event of liquidation.

Participation in Dividends

Rule #1: When the common stock has a par or stated value, participation is allocated on the aggregate dollar amount of preferred and common stock outstanding. Current dividends should be the same percentage of total par value of each class of stock outstanding.

Problem:	Common—$10 par, 20,000 shares	$200,000
	Preferred—6% cumulative and participating $100 par, 1,000 shares, 2 years' dividends in arrears plus the current year	100,000
	A $51,000 dividend is to be paid	

	Preferred	*Common*	*Total*
Preferred in arrears 2 × $ 6,000	12,000		12,000
Current dividend	6,000		6,000
Common, 1 year at preferred rate 6% × 200,000		12,000	12,000
Remainder divided based on Rule #1			
Preferred 1/3 × 21,000	7,000		7,000
Common 2/3 × 21,000		14,000	14,000
Total Dividend	$25,000	$26,000	$51,000

Rule #2: When the common stock is no-par with no stated value, retained earnings available for participation is based on the number of shares of preferred and common stock outstanding.

Problem: Preferred—6% cumulative and participating, 4,000 shares, $25 par—$100,000
Common—8,000 shares no-par, sold for $250,000
One year's dividends in arrears on the preferred (plus current year)
Common stock gets $1.50 per share dividend (fixed by the Board of Directors)
Retained earnings $51,000

Retained earnings	$51,000
2 years' dividends at $6,000	12,000
	39,000
Amount to common 8,000 × $1.50	12,000
Remainder for distribution	$27,000

Must be based on number of shares:

Preferred	*Common*
4,000 shares	8,000 shares
$9,000	$18,000

COMPUTATION OF BOOK VALUE

Stockholders' Equity must be allocated to the various classes of shareholders. If there is only one class of stock, book value is based on the number of shares issued and outstanding. Exclude treasury shares. If preferred shares have redemption premium, allocate to preferred shareholders.

Common and Preferred Book Value Computation

Problem: Preferred—5% cumulative, $100 par, 5,000 shares sold for $800,000
Common—$2 par, 500,000 shares sold for $1,000,000
Retained earnings $200,000
Preferred dividends, 4 years in arrears including current year.
Compute book value.

	Preferred	*Common*
Balance	$500,000	$1,000,000
4 years dividend @ 5%	100,000	
C.C. in Excess--Preferred		300,000
Balance of Retained Earnings		100,000
Book Value	$600,000	$1,400,000
Book Value Per Share	$120.00	$2.80

Same problem except that preferred stock is participating.

			R.E.	*Preferred*	*Common*
Balance			$200,000	$500,000	$1,000,000
4 years dividends			(100,000)	100,000	
Common at 5%			(50,000)		50,000
Remainder of R.E.					
Preferred	$\frac{\$500{,}000}{1{,}500{,}000}$	× 50,000		16,667	
Common	$\frac{\$1{,}000{,}000}{1{,}500{,}000}$	× 50,000			33,333
C.C. in Excess—Preferred					300,000
Book Value				$616,667	$1,383,333
Book Value Per Share				$123.33	$2.77

ILLUSTRATIVE PROBLEM: The balance sheet of Able Company on December 31st contains the following items:

Provision for Warranty Obligations	$103,732
Bonds Payable	500,000
Reserve for Contingencies	220,000
6% cumulative preferred stock, $50 par (entitled to $55 and accumulated dividends per share liquidation)	
Authorized 6,000 shares, 3,000 shares issued, of which 300 shares are in the treasury	135,000
Common stock, $50 par, authorized 20,000 shares—issued and outstanding, 8,000 shares	400,000
Premium on preferred stock	10,000
Premium on common stock	78,500
Retained earnings	265,000

NOTE: Preferred dividends have been paid or set up as payable through December 31st.

Required: Book value per share—common.
Book value per share—preferred.

SOLUTION TO ILLUSTRATIVE PROBLEM:

	Preferred	*Common*
Par	$135,000	$400,000
Premium	13,500	(13,500)
R.E. and Reserve for Contingencies		485,000
Premium on Preferred		10,000
Premium on Common		78,500
Book Value	$148,500	$960,000
Book Value Per Share	$55	$120

STOCK DIVIDENDS AND STOCK SPLITS

Neither a stock dividend nor a stock split changes stockholders' equity. Distinction centers mainly on the representations of management as to whether the additional stock being distributed to shareholders is a distribution of earnings (stock dividend) or is an effort to improve the marketability of the stock (stock split).

In ARB #43, a guideline was established that where additional shares were issued, less than 20% or 25% of the total shares outstanding indicated a stock dividend; whereas a distribution in excess of that indicated a stock split. The rationale behind the 20-25% guideline was a study of market action when stock distributions were made, in that "where the number of additional shares issued as a stock dividend is so great that it has . . . the effect of materially reducing the share market value . . . the transaction clearly partakes of the nature of a stock split-up." Under such circumstances, there is no need to capitalize retained earnings, other than to satisfy legal requirements.

Stock Dividend
If the transaction is a stock dividend, capitalize retained earnings based on **fair value** of additional shares issued. **Example:** Common, no-par, $10 stated value; $15 market value, 10,000 shares outstanding. A 2% stock dividend is declared.

Retained Earnings	3,000 (FV $15)	
Capital Stock		2,000 ($10 par)
C.C. in Excess		1,000

Stock Split
A stock split, that is, a distribution of additional shares effected to reduce the market price per share, may be recorded in several ways:

1. Stock split with no change in total capital. Requires only a memorandum entry. Example: 100,000 shares of Blue Corp. stock $20 par or stated value split two for one.

Old Capital	100,000 shares @ $20	$2,000,000
New Capital	200,000 shares @ $10	$2,000,000

2. A stock split in which retained earnings are capitalized to the extent of the par or stated value of the shares. Example: Same as above except that the par value remains the same. FV is $40 per share.

Old Capital	100,000 shares @ $20	$2,000,000
New Capital	200,000 shares @ $20	$4,000,000

Retained Earnings	$2,000,000	
C/S		$2,000,000

The Committee on Accounting Procedure of the AICPA recommends that distributions such as the above should not be called a stock dividend, but could be stated as "**a split-up effected in the form of a dividend**," the main difference being that retained earnings are not capitalized based on fair value.

3. Capital stock must be increased to satisfy legal requirements. **Example**: Same facts except a 12 for 1 stock split and state law requires a minimum $2 par or stated value.

Retained Earnings	$400,000	
Capital Stock		$400,000

To increase the Capital Stock account to $2,400,000. Shares outstanding increased to 1,200,000 at $2 stated value.

General Rule: If the distribution is 25% or more, retained earnings will not generally be capitalized based on FV. Capitalize retained earnings based on par or stated value. Closely held corporations may capitalize retained earnings in stock dividend situations based on par value instead of fair value.

Exercise: On December 31, 1985, the stockholders' equity section of the balance sheet of Mason Co. was as follows:

Common stock (par value $1, 1000 shares authorized, 300 shares issued and outstanding)	$ 300
Additional paid-in capital (C.C. in Excess)	1,800
Retained earnings	2,000
	$4,100

On January 2, 1986, the board of directors declared a stock dividend of one share for each three shares owned. Accordingly, 100 additional shares of stock were issued. On January 2, the fair market value of Mason's stock was $10 per share.

The most appropriate presentation of Mason's stockholders' equity on January 2, 1986, following the issuance of the 100 additional shares is:

a. Common stock (par value $1, 1000 shares authorized, 400 shares issued and outstanding)	$ 400
Additional paid-in capital	1,700
Retained earnings	2,000
	$4,100
b. Common stock (par value $1, 1000 shares authorized, 400 shares issued and outstanding)	$ 400
Additional paid-in capital	1,800
Retained earnings	1,900
	$4,100
c. Common stock (par value $1, 1000 shares authorized, 400 shares issued and outstanding)	$ 400
Additional paid-in capital	2,700
Retained earnings	1,000
	$4,100
d. Common stock (par value $1, 1000 shares authorized, 400 shares issued and outstanding)	$ 400
Additional paid-in capital	2,400
Retained earnings	1,300
	$4,100

Solution: (b), since the distribution exceeds 25%. Answer (c) would be correct **if** the distribution is considered a stock dividend.

EXAMPLE: STOCKHOLDERS' EQUITY

GRUBBS CORPORATION
STOCKHOLDERS' EQUITY
DECEMBER 31, 20XX

Preferred Stock 8%--par $100, authorized	1,000 shares	$ 20,000	
Issued and outstanding	200 shares		
Common Stock --par $10, authorized	5,000 shares		
issued	3,000 shares		
outstanding	2,600 shares	30,000	
Total Capital Stock			$ 50,000
Paid-in Capital in excess of par -- Common Stock		40,000	
Paid-in Capital – Treasury Stock Transactions		5,000	
Paid-in Capital – Donations		15,000	
Total Additional Paid-in Capital			$ 60,000
Total Contributed Capital			$110,000
RETAINED EARNINGS			
Restricted for Treasury Stock		$ 10,000	
Not Restricted		150,000	
Total Retained Earnings			$160,000
	Total		$270,000
Less: Treasury Stock - Cost of $25 per share (400 shares)			(10,000)
	Total		$260,000
Accumulated Other Comprehensive Income			75,000
Total Stockholders' Equity			$335,000

QUASI-REORGANIZATION OR CORPORATE READJUSTMENT

Quasi-reorganization: A fresh start in an accounting sense.

1. The corporate entity remains intact.
2. Recorded asset values should be readjusted to the fair value.
3. A deficit is eliminated (usually).
4. Facts must be disclosed.

Why Quasi-Reorganization?
Assets may be overvalued and/or the corporation may have a deficit in its retained earnings account. These factors may hinder the corporation's ability to attract investors because dividends are unlikely.

Procedure: Asset write-downs are charged against retained earnings and capital stock adjustments (reductions in legal capital) are transferred to Additional Paid in Capital in Excess of Par Value, then to Retained Earnings, to eliminate any deficit.

The new retained earnings account is dated to show that it runs from the date of the readjustment and should be disclosed in the financial statements until the date no longer has any special significance. Dating would rarely be needed after 10 years and in only exceptional cases should be discontinued in less than 10 years.

ILLUSTRATIVE PROBLEM:

Current conditions warrant that the Austin Company have a quasi-reorganization (corporate readjustment) at December 31, 20X3. Selected balance sheet items prior to the quasi-reorganization (corporate readjustment) are as follows:

- Inventory was recorded in the accounting records at December 31, 20X3, at its market value of $3,000,000.
- Property, plant, and equipment was recorded in the accounting records at December 31, 20X3, at $6,000,000 net of accumulated depreciation.
- Stockholders' equity consisted of:

Common stock, par value $10 per share; authorized, issued, and outstanding 350,000 shares	$3,500,000
Additional paid-in capital	800,000
Retained earnings (deficit)	(450,000)
Total stockholders' equity	$3,850,000

Additional information is as follows:

- Inventory cost at December 31, 20X3, was $3,250,000.
- Property, plant, and equipment had a fair value of $4,000,000.
- The par value of the common stock is to be reduced from $10 per share to $5 per share.

Required: Prepare the stockholders' equity section of the Austin Company's balance sheet at December 31, 20X3, as it should appear after the quasi-reorganization (corporate readjustment) has been accomplished. Show supporting computations in good form. Ignore income tax and deferred tax considerations.

SOLUTION:

Austin Company
STOCKHOLDERS' EQUITY SECTION OF BALANCE SHEET
AFTER QUASI-REORGANIZATION (CORPORATE READJUSTMENT)
December 31, 20X3

Common stock; par value $5 per share; authorized issued, and outstanding 350,000 shares	$1,750,000
Additional paid-in capital from reduction in par value of common stock (Schedule 1)	100,000
Retained earnings from December 31, 20X3 (Schedule 2)	-0-
Total stockholders' equity	$1,850,000

Schedule 1 -- Computation of Additional Paid-In Capital

Balance at December 31, 20X3	$800,000
Reduction in par value of common stock (350,000 shares x $5 per share)	$1,750,000
Elimination of deficit in retained earnings ($450,000 + $2,000,000)	(2,450,000)
Balance at December 31, 20X3, after quasi-reorganization (corporate readjustment)	$100,000

Schedule 2 -- Computation of Retained Earnings

Balance (deficit) at December 31, 20X3	$ (450,000)
Writedown of property, plant, and equipment	(2,000,000)
Elimination of deficit in retained earnings	2,450,000
Balance at December 31, 20X3, after quasi-reorganization (corporate readjustment)	$ --0--

FASB STATEMENT #115: ACCOUNTING FOR CERTAIN INVESTMENTS IN DEBT AND EQUITY SECURITIES

This statement addresses the accounting and reporting for investments in equity securities that have readily determinable fair values and all investments in debt securities. The fair value of an equity security is readily determinable if sales prices are currently available on a registered securities exchange, publicly reported over-the-counter market, or comparable foreign market.

SFAS #115 does **not** apply to 1) investments accounted for under the equity method nor investments in consolidated subsidiaries; 2) enterprises whose specialized accounting practices include accounting for substantially all investments at market or fair value, such as brokers and dealers in securities, defined benefit pension plans and investment companies; 3) not-for-profit organizations.

Requirements:
At acquisition, investments in equity securities with readily determined fair values, and all investments debt securities must be classified into one of the following three categories and accounted for as follows:

1. Held to Maturity: Debt securities that the entity has the **positive intent** and **ability** to hold to maturity are classified as *held-to-maturity securities* and are reported at **amortized cost.**

On a classified balance sheet, individual held-to-maturity securities should be classified as current assets or noncurrent assets (investments), as appropriate for the individual security.

2. Trading: Debt and equity securities that are bought and held principally for the purpose of selling them in the near term are classified as *trading securities* and are reported at **fair value**, with **unrealized holding gains and losses included in earnings**.

All trading securities should be classified as current asssets on a classified balance sheet.

3. Available for Sale: Debt and equity securities not classified either as held-to-maturity securities or trading securities are classified as *available for sale securities* and are reported at **fair value.**

On a classified balance sheet, individual available-for-sale securities should be classified as current assets or noncurrent assets (investments), as appropriate for the individual security.

SFAS #130, "Reporting Comprehensive Income," amends SFAS #115 to require that **unrealized holding gains and losses** on securities classified as **available-for-sale** (previously reported as a separate component of stockholders' equity) be reported in comprehensive income as a component of **other comprehensive income.**

Reporting changes re: Securities classified as Available-for-Sale:

1. The change in the unrealized holding gain/loss for the period is reported as a component of other comprehensive income in reporting comprehensive income. This includes:
   a. The unrealized holding gain/loss for the period;
   b. Reversal of previously recorded unrealized holding gain/loss for securities sold, (referred to as a reclassification adjustment in the computation of other comprehensive income).

2. The total other comprehensive income for the period is transferred to **accumulated other comprehensive income** which is reported as a separate element of equity. The balance of the unrealized holding gain/loss must be disclosed.

Refer to Chapter 12 for alternative formats for reporting comprehensive income and disclosure of accumulated other comprehensive income.

Transfers Between Categories:
The transfer of a security between categories must be accounted for **at fair value**. At the date of transfer, a security's unrealized holding gain or loss is accounted for as follows:

Transfer	Required accounting
From Trading	Unrealized holding gain or loss at the date of transfer has already been recognized in earnings and shall **not** be reversed.
To Trading	Unrealized holding gain or loss at the date of transfer must be recognized in earnings immediately.
To Available for Sale From Held to Maturity	Unrealized holding gain or loss at the date of transfer must be recognized as a separate component of other comprehensive income.
To Held to Maturity From Available for Sale	Unrealized holding gain or loss at the date of transfer will continue to be reported as a separate component in stockholders' equity, but will be amortized over the remaining life of the security as an adjustment of yield (in a manner consistent with the amortization of any premium or discount). The use of fair value to record the transfer of debt securities (to HTM) may create a premium or discount on the investment (fair value vs. face value) that would be amortized as an adjustment of yield (interest income) over the life of the investment. The amortization of the unrealized holding gain or loss will offset or mitigate the effect on interest income of the amortization of any such premium or discount.

Impairment of Securities (other than Temporary Declines):
For individual securities classified as Available-for-Sale and Held-to-Maturity, a determination must be made as to whether a decline in fair value below amortized cost basis is other than temporary. If the decline is judged to be other than temporary (permanent), the cost basis of the individual security shall be written down to fair value as a new cost basis and the amount of the write-down will be accounted for as a realized loss (included in earnings for the period). The new cost basis will not be changed for subsequent recoveries in fair value. For securities classified as available-for-sale, subsequent increases and decreases (other than permanent decreases) in fair value will be included in unrealized holding gains and losses reported in the separate component of equity.

Income Recognition

Unrealized holding gains and losses:

- *Trading securities*—included in earnings.
- *Available-for-sale securities* (including those classified as current assets) - excluded from earnings and the current change reported as other comprehensive income and the cumulative changes reported as accumulated other comprehensive income in the stockholders' equity.

Dividend and Interest Income: SFAS #115 does not affect the methods used for recognizing and measuring dividend and interest income. Dividends and interest income, including amortization of any premium or discount arising at acquisition, for all three classifications of investments continue to be included in earnings.

Gains and Losses: Realized gains and losses for securities classified as available-for-sale and held-to-maturity continue to be reported in earnings.

Disclosures:

a) As of the date of each balance sheet presented, the following segregated for securities classified as available-for-sale and held-to-maturity:
   1. Aggregate fair value.
   2. Gross unrealized holding gains and losses; and
   3. Amortized cost basis by major security type.
b) As of the date of the most recent balance sheet presented, information about the contractual maturities of debt securities, segregated for securities classified as available-for-sale and held-to-maturity.
c) For each period for which an income statement is presented:
   1. Proceeds from sales of available-for-sale securities and the gross realized gains and losses on those sales.
   2. Basis on which cost was determined for gain or loss computation (specific identification, average, or other).
   3. Gross gains and losses included in earnings from transfers from available-for-sale trading securities.
   4. Change in net unrealized holding gain or loss on available-for-sale securities included as a separate component in other comprehensive income.
   5. Change in net unrealized holding gain or loss on trading securities that has been included in earnings during the period.
   6. For sale or transfer of held-to-maturity securities, the amortized cost, realized or unrealized gain or loss and the circumstances leading to the decision to sell or transfer the securities.

The individual amounts for the three categories of securities do not have to be presented in the balance sheet, if the information is included in the notes to the financial statements.

Overview FASB #115

Marketable Equity and Debt Securities

↓

Includes:

- All Investments in Debt Securities
- Investments in Equity Securities that have a readily determinable fair value (listed on a publicly reported stock exchange)

↓

CLASSIFICATIONS

↓

TRADING SECURITIES

↓

A. Current Assets

↓

B. Report at Fair Value

↓

C. Unrealized Gains/Losses Are Reported on Income Statement

AVAILABLE FOR SALE SECURITIES

↓

A. Current or Noncurrent Assets

↓

B. Report at Fair Value

↓

C. Unrealized Gains/Losses Are Reported as Other Comprehensive Income and Transferred to Accumulated Other Comprehensive Income, a Stockholders' Equity Account

HELD TO MATURITY SECURITIES

↓

A. Positive Intent and Ability to Hold to Maturity

↓

B. Current or Noncurrent Assets

↓

C. Report at Carrying Value

↓

D. Amortize Premium or Discount

↓

E. Do Not Record Unrealized Gains or Losses

Example: Marketable Securities

On December 31, 20x3, Tiger Company provided you with the following information regarding its securities:

Investment	Cost	Fair Value	Unrealized Gain Unrealized (Losses)
Clemson Corp. Stock	$20,000	$19,000	$(1,000)
Wake Corp. Stock	10,000	9,000	(1,000)
Tar Heel Stock	20,000	20,500	500
Total Portfolio	$50,000	$48,500	$(1,500)

Additional Information: During 20x4 the Wake Corp. Stock was sold for $9,600. The fair value of the stocks on December 31, 20x4 were Clemson Stock, $19,200 and Tar Heel Stock, $20,300.

Required:

a. Prepare the adjusting journal entry on December 31, 20x3 assuming the securities are trading securities.
b. Prepare the adjusting journal entry on December 31, 20x3 assuming the securities are available-for- sale securities.
c. Prepare the journal entry to record the sale of the Wake Corp. stock in 20x4.
d. Prepare the adjusting entry needed on December 31, 20x4 assuming
   (1) the securities are trading securities
   (2) the securities are available-for-sale securities
e. Calculate the December 31, 20x4 balance in accumulated other comprehensive income and the securities fair value adjustment accounts for the available-for-sale securities.

Solution:

Trading Securities

20x3

	Debit	Credit
a. Unrealized holding loss	1,500	
Securities fair value adjustment		1,500

Note: Unrealized holding losses on the income statement

	Debit	Credit
Retained earnings	1,500	
Unrealized holding loss		1,500

To close loss to retained earnings.

20x4

	Debit	Credit
c. Cash	9,600	
Loss on trading securities	400	
Trading securities (cost)		10,000

20x4

	Debit	Credit
d. Securities fair value adjustment	1,000	
Unrealized holding gain		1,000
Unrealized holding gain	1,000	
Retained earnings		1,000

Available-For-Sale Securities

20x3

	Debit	Credit
b. Unrealized holding loss	1,500	
Securities fair value adjustment		1,500

Note: Unrealized holding loss is shown as other comprehensive income.

	Debit	Credit
Accumulated other comprehensive income	1,500	
Unrealized holding loss		1,500

To transfer loss to other comprehensive income.

20x4

	Debit	Credit
c. Cash	9,600	
Loss on trading securities	400	
Trading securities (cost)		10,000

20x4

	Debit	Credit
d. Securities fair value adjustment	1,000	
Unrealized holding gain		1,000
Unrealized holding gain	1,000	
Acc.Other Comp. Income		1,000

Details for 20x4 Journal Entries:

Investments	**Cost**	**Fair Value**	**Unrealized Gain Unrealized (Loss)**
Clemson Corp. Stock	$20,000	$19,200	$ (800)
Tar Heel Corp. Stock	20,000	20,300	300
Total portfolio	$40,000	$39,500	$ (500)

Since the required 20x4 balance in the securities fair value adjustment account is a $500 credit, the beginning balance of $1,500 credit must be reduced by a $1,000 debit and an unrealized holding gain recognized.

e. The balance in securities fair value adjustment account would be a $500 credit balance and the accumulated other comprehensive income account would be a $500 debit balance ($1,500 loss in 20x3 less $1,000 gain in 20x4 = $500 balance).

Example: Available-For-Sale Securities with a Reclassification Adjustment

On December 31, 20x1 the Tar Heel company purchased 2,000 shares of available-for-sale securities at a price of $10 per share. These securities had a fair value of $24,000 on December 31, 20x2 and $30,000 on 20x3. All the securities were sold on January 2, 20x4 when the fair value was still $30,000.

Required: Prepare the journal entries for all the transactions of the Tar Heel Company. (For simplicity ignore the tax effect.)

20x1

		Debit	Credit
Dec. 31	Investment in available-for-sale securities	$20,000	
	Cash		$20,000

20x2

		Debit	Credit
Dec. 31	Securities fair value adjustment	4,000	
	Unrealized holding gain on available-for-sale securities		4,000

Note: The unrealized holding gain ($24,000 - $20,000 = $4,000) would appear on the other comprehensive income statement.

		Debit	Credit
Dec. 31	Unrealized holding gain on available-for-sale securities	4,000	
	Accumulated other comprehensive income		4,000

To transfer the unrealized holding gain to accumulated other comprehensive income, which is a stockholders' equity account.

20x3

		Debit	Credit
Dec. 31	Securities fair value adjustment	6,000	
	Unrealized holding gain on available-for-sale securities		6,000
Dec. 31	Unrealized holding gain on available-for-sale securities	6,000	
	Accumulated other comprehensive income		6,000

20x4

		Debit	Credit
Jan. 2	Cash	30,000	
	Investment in available-for-sale securities (cost)		20,000
	Realized gain on sale of available-for-sale securities		10,000

To record the gain on the sale of the securities and report it as a part of current earnings.

		Debit	Credit
Jan. 2	Reclassification adjustment for unrealized holding gain on Available-for-sale securities	10,000	
	Securities fair value adjustment		10,000

To reclassify the cumulative unrealized gain recorded in other comprehensive income in previous periods to prevent the double counting of the realized gain in the current period. The reclassification adjustment account is a part of other comprehensive income.

		Debit	Credit
Jan. 31	Accumulated other comprehensive income	10,000	
	Reclassification adjustment for unrealized holding gain on Available-for-sale securities		10,000

To transfer the reclassification adjustment from the comprehensive income to accumulated other comprehensive income.

To summarize the 20x4 journal entries:

a. The realized gain on the sale of securities would appear as a part of current earnings as a credit of $10,000.
b. The reclassification adjustment would be shown on the other comprehensive income statement as a debit of $10,000.
c. The investment in available-for-sale securities account, the securities fair value adjustment account and the accumulated other comprehensive income account would all have zero balances.

DIVIDENDS

Represent income only to the extent paid from earnings subsequent to the date the investment was acquired. Dividends usually are **not** accrued as the mere passage of time gives no legal right to the receipt of dividends. Dividends may be recorded on the date of (a) declaration, (b) record, or (c) payment (most common—taxed on receipt), and are classified as nonoperating income on the income statement.

Types of Dividends: Assume that an investor owns 100 shares of K Corporation, $100 par value, common stock, which cost $88 per share.

1. **Cash Dividends**: K Corporation paid a cash dividend of $4 per share.

	Debit	Credit
Cash (100 shares × $4)	$400	
Dividend Income		$400

(If recorded before date of payment, debit would be to Dividends Receivable.)

2. **Property Dividends**: K Corporation distributes a property dividend of one share of N Corporation stock for every 10 shares of K Corporation stock held when N Corporation stock is selling at $40 per share.

	Debit	Credit
Investments: N Corp. Stock	$400	
Dividend Income		$400

$$\frac{100 \text{ shares}}{10} = 10 \times 1 \text{ share} \times \$40 \text{ FMV} = \$400$$

3. **Stock Dividends**: Usually **not** income.

a. **Like Kind**: K Corp. distributes a stock dividend of one common share for every ten shares held.

Memorandum entry and recomputation of basic per share

$$\frac{\text{Total Cost}}{\text{Total Shares}} = \frac{\$8,800}{110} = \$80 \text{ per share}$$

There are now more shares representing the same ownership interests. Individual shareholders' relative positions of ownership interests are unchanged.

b. **Unlike Kind**: K Corp. then declares a stock dividend of one preferred share for every ten common shares held when the preferred sold at $150 per share and the common sold at $85 per share.

An allocation of cost is necessary based on the relative fair market values of the different classes of stock.

Computation and resulting entry:

$$\frac{110 \text{ shares}}{10} = 11 \text{ preferred shares}$$

P/S	11 shs. × $150 =	$1,650	$\frac{1,650}{11,000}$	× $8,800 = $1,320
C/S	110 shs. × $ 85 =	9,350	$\frac{9,350}{11,000}$	× 8,800 = $7,480
Total Value		$11,000		$8,800

	Dr.	Cr.
Investments: K Corp. P/S	$1,320	
Investments: K Corp. C/S		$1,320

4. **Liquidating Dividends**: K Corp. paid a cash dividend of $5 per share when retained earnings accumulated subsequent to the investment acquisition would only support a $3 dividend per share.

	Dr.	Cr.
Cash (110 shs. × $5)	$550	
Dividend Income (110 shs. × $3)		$330
Investment: K Corp. C/S (110 shs. × $2)		220

(The $2 per share is a liquidating dividend representing a return of investment.)

STOCK RIGHTS

When an investor purchases stock, he acquires certain legal rights granted by the corporate charter and the laws of the state in which the corporation is organized. A legal right **usually** granted to stockholders is the **pre-emptive right** which allows the individual stockholders to subscribe to any additional issues of the same class of stock on a pro rata basis. This privilege allows the existing stockholders to maintain their relative interests in the corporation's earnings, assets, and management. One right is offered for each share held; however, usually more than one right is required to subscribe to a new share. A warrant is issued with which the shareholder may:

1. exercise the rights and acquire stock,
2. sell the rights, or
3. do nothing allowing the rights to lapse.

After the announcement of the rights offering but before the rights are issued, the stock will sell **Rights-On**—the "right" is a part of the share. When the rights or warrants are issued (usually three days before), the stock will sell **Ex-Rights**—without the "right" as the right is traded separately.

No matter what a stockholder does with the rights, a cost should be assigned to the rights based on the relative fair market values of the stock and the rights at the date of issue.

Example: An investor purchased 100 shares of Co. A common stock for $120 per share, and later received 100 rights to subscribe to 50 additional shares at $100 per share. The market value, after the issuance of the stock rights, of a share of common stock (ex-rights) is $200 and of a right is $40.

Investments: Co. A C/S Rights	$2,000	
Investments: Co. A C/S		$2,000

Stock	100 shs. × $200	= $20,000
Rights	100 shs. × $ 40	= 4,000
Total Value		$24,000

Value of Stock	20,000 / 24,000	× $12,000 (TC)	= $10,000
Value of Rights	4,000 / 24,000	× $12,000	= 2,000
Total Cost (100 shares @ $120)			$12,000

Cost of shares if rights are exercised:

Lot #1: Original Stock		
100 Shares @ 100 per Share		$10,000
Lot #2: New Stock		
Amount Paid (50 shs. × $100)	$5,000	
Value of Rights (100 × $20)	2,000	
50 Shares @ $140 per Share		7,000
		$17,000

(Note: $140 per share = $100 paid + 2 rights @ $20 each.)

STOCK SPLITS

From the investors' viewpoint, there is little or no difference between a stock split and a stock dividend of the same class of stock (refer above). The investors' relative position of ownership interests is unchanged; there are merely more shares representing the ownership rights. As the investor has received nothing which he did not own before the stock split, **no** accounting entry is required—memorandum entry may be made. However, **the basis of a share of stock must be recomputed.**

Example: An investor owns 200 shares of Z Corporation, $50 par value, common stock, which cost $60 per share. Z Corporation announces a 2-for-1 stock split, reducing the par value to $25 per share.

Recomputation of cost per share:

$$\frac{\text{Total Cost}}{\text{Total Shares}} = \frac{\$60 \times 200 \text{ shs.}}{200 \text{ shs.} \times 2} = \frac{\$12{,}000}{400 \text{ shs.}} = \$30 \text{ per share}$$

Later, Z Corporation announces a 3-for-2 stock split. The cost per share would now be $20.

$$\frac{\text{Total Cost}}{\text{Total Shares}} = \frac{\$30 \times 400 \text{ shs.}}{400 \text{ shs.} \times 1\ 1/2} = \frac{\$12{,}000}{600} = \$20 \text{ per share}$$

(Note that the total value of the investment, $12,000, does not change.)

Chapter Two
Stockholders' Equity Questions

ISSUE STOCK

1. On April 1, 1999, Hyde Corp., a newly formed company, had the following stock issued and outstanding:

- Common stock, no par, $1 stated value, 20,000 shares originally issued for $30 per share.
- Preferred stock, $10 par value, 6,000 shares originally issued for $50 per share.

Hyde's April 1, 1999, statement of stockholders' equity should report

	Common stock	*Preferred stock*	*Additional paid-in capital*
a.	$20,000	$60,000	$820,000
b.	$20,000	$300,000	$580,000
c.	$600,000	$300,000	$0
d.	$600,000	$60,000	$240,000

2. Jay & Kay partnership's balance sheet at December 31, 1998, reported the following:

Total assets	$100,000
Total liabilities	20,000
Jay, capital	40,000
Kay, capital	40,000

On January 2, 1999, Jay and Kay dissolved their partnership and transferred all assets and liabilities to a newly-formed corporation. At the date of incorporation, the fair value of the net assets was $12,000 more than the carrying amount on the partnership's books, of which $7,000 was assigned to tangible assets and $5,000 was assigned to goodwill. Jay and Kay were each issued 5,000 shares of the corporation's $1 par value common stock. Immediately following incorporation, additional paid-in capital in excess of par should be credited for

a. $68,000
b. $70,000
c. $77,000
d. $82,000

LUMP SUM ISSUANCE OF STOCK

3. On March 1, 1999, Rya Corp. issued 1,000 shares of its $20 par value common stock and 2,000 shares of its $20 par value convertible preferred stock for a total of $80,000. At this date, Rya's common stock was selling for $36 per share, and the convertible preferred stock was selling for $27 per share. What amount of the proceeds should be allocated to Rya's convertible preferred stock?

a. $60,000
b. $54,000
c. $48,000
d. $44,000

STOCK SUBSCRIPTIONS

4. How should the excess of the subscription price over the par value of common stock subscribed be recorded?

a. As additional paid-in capital when the subscription is received.
b. As additional paid-in capital when the subscription is collected.
c. As retained earnings when the subscription is received.
d. As additional paid-in capital when the capital stock is issued.

DONATED ASSETS

5. Pine City owned a vacant plot of land zoned for industrial use. Pine gave this land to Medi Corp. solely as an incentive for Medi to build a factory on the site. The land had a fair value of $300,000 at the date of the gift. This nonmonetary transaction should be reported by Medi as

a. Extraordinary income.
b. Additional paid-in capital.
c. A credit to retained earnings.
d. A memorandum entry.

RETIRE STOCK

6. In 1999, Fogg, Inc., issued $10 par value common stock for $25 per share. No other common stock transactions occurred until March 31, 2001, when Fogg acquired some of the issued shares for $20 per share and retired them. Which of the following statements correctly states an effect of this acquisition and retirement?

a. 2001 net income is decreased.
b. 2001 net income is increased.
c. Additional paid-in capital is decreased.
d. Retained earnings is increased.

7. The stockholders' equity section of Peter Corporation's balance sheet at December 31, 19X2, was as follows:

Common stock ($10 par value, authorized 1,000,000 shares, issued and outstanding 900,000 shares)	$ 9,000,000
Additional paid-in capital	2,700,000
Retained earnings	1,300,000
Total stockholders' equity	$13,000,000

On January 2, 19X3, Peter purchased and retired 100,000 shares of its stock for $1,800,000. Immediately after retirement of these 100,000 shares, the balances in the additional paid-in capital and retained earnings accounts should be

	Additional paid-in capital	*Retained earnings*
a.	$900,000	$1,300,000
b.	$1,400,000	$800,000
c.	$1,900,000	$1,300,000
d.	$2,400,000	$800,000

TREASURY STOCK – PAR METHOD

8. Ten thousand (10,000) shares of common stock with a par value of $20 per share were initially issued at $25 per share. Subsequently, two thousand (2,000) of these shares were purchased as treasury stock at $30 per share. Assuming that the par value method of accounting for treasury stock transactions is used, what is the effect of the purchase of the treasury stock on each of the following?

	Additional paid-in capital	*Retained earnings*
a.	Decrease	Increase
b.	Decrease	Decrease
c.	Increase	Decrease
d.	Increase	No effect

9. Asp Co. was organized on January 2, 1999, with 30,000 authorized shares of $10 par common stock. During 1999 the corporation had the following capital transactions:

January 5	- issued 20,000 shares at $15 per share.
July 14	- purchased 5,000 shares at $17 per share.
December 27	- reissued the 5,000 shares held in treasury at $20 per share.

Asp used the par value method to record the purchase and reissuance of the treasury shares. In its December 31, 1999, balance sheet, what amount should Asp report as additional paid-in capital in excess of par?

a. $100,000
b. $125,000
c. $140,000
d. $150,000

10. Treasury stock was acquired for cash at a price in excess of its original issue price. The treasury stock was subsequently reissued for cash at a price in excess of its acquisition price. Assuming that the par value method of accounting for treasury stock transactions is used, what is the effect on total stockholders' equity of each of the following events?

	Acquisition of treasury stock	*Reissuance of treasury stock*
a.	No effect	No effect
b.	Increase	Decrease
c.	Decrease	No effect
d.	Decrease	Increase

TREASURY STOCK – COST METHOD

11. If a corporation sells some of its treasury stock at a price that exceeds its cost, this excess should be

a. Reported as a gain in the income statement.
b. Treated as a reduction in the carrying amount of remaining treasury stock.
c. Credited to additional paid-in capital.
d. Credited to retained earnings.

12. Ten thousand shares of $20 par value common stock were initially issued at $25 per share. Subsequently, two thousand of these shares were purchased as treasury stock at $30 per share. Assuming that the cost method of accounting for treasury stock transactions is used, what is the effect of the purchase of the treasury stock on the amount reported in the balance sheet for each of the following?

	Additional paid-in-capital	*Retained earnings*
a.	No effect	No effect
b.	No effect	Decrease
c.	Decrease	No effect
d.	Decrease	Decrease

13. At its date of incorporation, Glean, Inc., issued 100,000 shares of its $10 par common stock at $11 per share. During the current year, Glean acquired 30,000 shares of its common stock at a price of $16 per share and accounted for them by the cost method. Subsequently, these shares were reissued at a price of $12 per share. There have been no other issuances or acquisitions of its own common stock. What effect does the reissuance of the stock have on the following accounts?

	Retained earnings	*Additional paid-in capital*
a.	Decrease	Decrease
b.	No effect	Decrease
c.	Decrease	No effect
d.	No effect	No effect

14. In 1999, Newt Corp. acquired 6,000 shares of its own $1 par value common stock at $18 per share. In 2000, Newt issued 3,000 of these shares at $25 per share. Newt uses the cost method to account for its treasury stock transactions. What accounts and amounts should Newt credit in 2000 to record the issuance of the 3,000 shares?

	Treasury stock	*Additional paid-in capital*	*Retained earnings*	*Common stock*
a.	$54,000		$21,000	
b.	$54,000	$21,000		
c.		$72,000		$3,000
d.		$51,000	$21,000	$3,000

DONATED TREASURY STOCK

15. On December 1, 1999, Line Corp. received a donation of 2,000 shares of its $5 par value common stock from a stockholder. On that date, the stock's market value was $35 per share. The stock was originally issued for $25 per share. By what amount would this donation cause total stockholders' equity to decrease?

a. $70,000
b. $50,000
c. $20,000
d. $0

CASH DIVIDENDS

16. A company declared a cash dividend on its common stock on December 15, 1998, payable on January 12, 1999. How would this dividend affect stockholders' equity on the following dates?

	December 15, 1998	*December 31, 1998*	*January 12, 1999*
a.	Decrease	No effect	Decrease
b.	Decrease	No effect	No effect
c.	No effect	Decrease	No effect
d.	No effect	No effect	Decrease

17. When a company declares a cash dividend, retained earnings is decreased by the amount of the dividend on the date of

a. Declaration
b. Record.
c. Payment.
d. Declaration or record, whichever is earlier.

18. At December 31, 1999 and 2000, Carr Corp. had outstanding 4,000 shares of $100 par value 6% cumulative preferred stock and 20,000 shares of $10 par value common stock. At December 31, 1999, dividends in arrears on the preferred stock were $12,000. Cash dividends declared in 2000 totaled $44,000. Of the $44,000, what amounts were payable on each class of stock?

	Preferred stock	Common stock
a.	$44,000	$0
b.	$36,000	$ 8,000
c.	$32,000	$12,000
d.	$24,000	$20,000

19. Arp Corp.'s outstanding capital stock at December 15, 1990, consisted of the following:

- 30,000 shares of 5% cumulative preferred stock, par value $10 per share, fully participating as to dividends. No dividends were in arrears.
- 200,000 shares of common stock, par value $1 per share.

On December 15, 1990, Arp declared dividends of $100,000. What was the amount of dividends payable to Arp's common stockholders?

a. $10,000
b. $34,000
c. $40,000
d. $47,500

STOCK DIVIDENDS

20. How would the declaration of a 15% stock dividend by a corporation affect each of the following?

	Retained earnings	*Total stockholders' equity*
a.	No effect	No effect
b.	No effect	Decrease
c.	Decrease	No effect
d.	Decrease	Decrease

21. Sprint Company has 1,000,000 shares of common stock authorized with a par value of $3 per share, of which 600,000 shares are outstanding. When the market value was $8 per share, Sprint issued a stock dividend whereby for each six shares held one share was issued as a stock dividend. The par value of the stock was not changed. What entry should Sprint make to record this transaction?

a.	Retained earnings	$300,000	
	Common stock		$300,000
b.	Additional paid-in capital	300,000	
	Common stock		300,000
c.	Retained earnings	800,000	
	Common stock		300,000
	Additional paid-in capital		500,000
d.	Additional paid-in capital	800,000	
	Common stock		300,000
	Retained earnings		500,000

22. Smith Company has 1,000,000 shares of common stock authorized with a par value of $3 per share of which 300,000 shares are outstanding. Smith authorized a stock dividend when the market value was $8 per share, entitling its stockholders to one additional share for each share held. The par value of the stock was **not** changed. What entry, if any, should Smith make to record this transaction?

a.	No entry.		
b.	Retained earnings	$900,000	
	Common stock		$ 900,000
c.	Retained earnings	2,400,000	
	Common stock		900,000
	Capital in excess of par		1,500,000
d.	Stock dividend payable	900,000	
	Retained earnings	900,000	
	Common stock		1,800,000

23. Ray Corp. declared a 5% stock dividend on its 10,000 issued and outstanding shares of $2 par value common stock, which had a fair value of $5 per share before the stock dividend was declared. This stock dividend was distributed 60 days after the declaration date. By what amount did Ray's current liabilities increase as a result of the stock dividend declaration?

a. $0
b. $500
c. $1,000
d. $2,500

24. The following stock dividends were declared and distributed by Sol Corp.:

Percentage of common shares outstanding at declaration date	*Fair value*	*Par value*
10	$15,000	$10,000
28	40,000	30,800

What aggregate amount should be debited to retained earnings for these stock dividends?

a. $40,800
b. $45,800
c. $50,000
d. $55,000

PROPERTY DIVIDENDS

25. A property dividend should be recorded in retained earnings at the property's

a. Market value at date of declaration.
b. Market value at date of issuance (payment).
c. Book value at date of declaration.
d. Book value at date of issuance (payment).

26. On June 27, 1999, Brite Co. distributed to its common stockholders 100,000 outstanding common shares of its investment in Quik, Inc., an unrelated party. The carrying amount on Brite's books of Quik's $1 par common stock was $2 per share. Immediately after the distribution, the market price of Quik's stock was $2.50 per share. In its income statement for the year ended June 30, 1999, what amount should Brite report as gain before income taxes on disposal of the stock?

a. $250,000
b. $200,000
c. $50,000
d. $0

27. On December 1, 1999, Nilo Corp. declared a property dividend of marketable securities to be distributed on December 31, 1999, to stockholders of record on December 15, 1999. On December 1, 1999, the marketable securities had a carrying amount of $60,000 and a fair value of $78,000. What is the effect of this property dividend on Nilo's 1999 retained earnings, after all nominal accounts are closed?

a. $0.
b. $18,000 increase.
c. $60,000 decrease.
d. $78,000 decrease.

LIQUIDATING DIVIDEND

28. On January 2, 1999, the board of directors of Blake Mining Corporation declared a cash dividend of $800,000 to stockholders of record on January 18, 1999, and payable on February 10, 1999. The dividend is permissible under state law in Blake's state of incorporation. Selected data from Blake's December 31, 1999, balance sheet are as follows:

Accumulated depletion	$200,000
Capital stock	1,000,000
Additional paid-in capital	300,000
Retained earnings	600,000

The $800,000 dividend includes a liquidating dividend of

a. $600,000
b. $300,000
c. $200,000
d. $0

STOCK SPLIT

29. What is the most likely effect of a stock split on the par value per share and the number of shares outstanding?

	Par value per share	*Number of shares outstanding*
a.	Decrease	Increase
b.	Decrease	No effect
c.	Increase	Increase
d.	No effect	No effect

30. Effective April 27, 1999, the stockholders of Bennett Corporation approved a two-for-one split of the company's common stock, and an increase in authorized common shares from 100,000 shares (par value $20 per share) to 200,000 shares (par value $10 per share). Bennett's stockholders' equity accounts immediately before issuance of the stock split shares were as follows:

Common stock, par value $20; 100,000 shares authorized; 50,000 shares outstanding	$1,000,000
Additional paid-in capital (premium of $3 per share on issuance of common stock)	150,000
Retained earnings	1,350,000

What should be the balances in Bennett's additional paid-in capital and retained earnings accounts immediately after the stock split is effected?

	Additional paid-in capital	*Retained earnings*
a.	$0	$500,000
b.	$150,000	$350,000
c.	$150,000	$1,350,000
d.	$1,150,000	$350,000

31. On July 1, 1999, Bart Corporation has 200,000 shares of $10 par common stock outstanding and the market price of the stock is $12 per share. On the same date, Bart declared a 1-for-2 reverse stock split. The par of the stock was increased from $10 to $20 and one new $20 par share was issued for each two $10 par shares outstanding. Immediately before the 1-for-2 reverse stock split, Bart's additional paid-in capital was $450,000. What should be the balance in Bart's additional paid-in capital account immediately after the reverse stock split is effected?

a. $0
b. $450,000
c. $650,000
d. $850,000

SHARES OUTSTANDING

32. Nest Co. issued 100,000 shares of common stock. Of these, 5,000 were held as treasury stock at December 31, 1999. During 2000, transactions involving Nest's common stock were as follows:

May 3	- 1,000 shares of treasury stock were sold.
August 6	- 10,000 shares of previously unissued stock were sold.
November 18	- A 2-for-1 stock split took effect.

Laws in Nest's state of incorporation protect treasury stock from dilution. At December 31, 2000, how many shares of Nest's common stock were issued and outstanding?

	Shares	
	Issued	*Outstanding*
a.	220,000	212,000
b.	220,000	216,000
c.	222,000	214,000
d.	222,000	218,000

33. Rudd Corp. had 700,000 shares of common stock authorized and 300,000 shares outstanding at December 31, 1999. The following events occurred during 2000:

January 31	Declared 10% stock dividend
June 30	Purchased 100,000 shares
August 1	Reissued 50,000 shares
November 30	Declared 2-for-1 stock split

At December 31, 2000, how many shares of common stock did Rudd have outstanding?

a. 560,000
b. 600,000
c. 630,000
d. 660,000

RETAINED EARNINGS

34. A retained earnings appropriation can be used to

a. Absorb a fire loss when a company is self-insured.
b. Provide for a contingent loss that is probable and reasonable.
c. Smooth periodic income.
d. Restrict earnings available for dividends.

35. Selected information from the accounts of Row Co. at December 31, 1999, follows:

Total income since incorporation	$420,000
Total cash dividends paid	130,000
Total value of property dividends distributed	30,000
Excess of proceeds over cost of treasury stock sold, accounted for using the cost method	110,000

In its December 31, 1999, financial statements, what amount should Row report as retained earnings?

a. $260,000
b. $290,000
c. $370,000
d. $400,000

STOCK RGHTS

36. A company issued rights to its existing shareholders without consideration. The rights allowed the recipients to purchase unissued common stock for an amount in excess of par value. When the rights are issued, which of the following will be increased?

	Common stock	*Additional paid-in capital*
a.	Yes	Yes
b.	Yes	No
c.	No	No
d.	No	Yes

37. On July 1, 1999, Vail Corp. issued rights to stockholders to subscribe to additional share of its common stock. One right was issued for each share owned. A stockholder could purchase one additional share for 10 rights plus $15 cash. The rights expired on September 30, 1999. On July 1, 1999, the market price of a share with the right attached was $40, while the market price of one right alone was $2. Vail's stockholders' equity on June 30, 1999, comprised the following:

Common stock, $25 par value, 4,000 shares issued and outstanding	$100,000
Additional paid-in capital	60,000
Retained earnings	80,000

By what amount should Vail's retained earnings decrease as a result of issuance of the stock rights on July 1, 1999?

a. $0
b. $5,000
c. $8,000
d. $10,000

BOOK VALUE PER SHARE

38. Hoyt Corp.'s current balance sheet reports the following stockholders' equity:

5% cumulative preferred stock, par value $100 per share; 2,500 shares issued and outstanding	$250,000
Common stock, par value $3.50 per share; 100,000 shares issued and outstanding	350,000
Additional paid-in capital in excess of par value of common stock	125,000
Retained earnings	300,000

Dividends in arrears on the preferred stock amount to $25,000. If Hoyt were to be liquidated, the preferred stockholders would receive par value plus a premium of $50,000. The book value per share of common stock is

a. $7.75
b. $7.50
c. $7.25
d. $7.00

39. Maga Corp.'s stockholders' equity at December 31, 1999, comprised the following:

6% cumulative preferred stock, $100 par; liquidating value $110 per share; authorized, issued, and outstanding 50,000 shares	$5,000,000
Common stock, $5 par; 1,000,000 shares authorized; issued and outstanding 400,000 shares	2,000,000
Retained earnings	1,000,000

Dividends on preferred stock have been paid through 1998 but have **not** been declared for 1999. At December 31, 1999, Maga's book value per common share was

a. $5.50
b. $6.25
c. $6.75
d. $7.50

QUASI-REORGANIZATION

40. The stockholders' equity section of Brown Co.'s December 31, 1999, balance sheet consisted of the following:

Common stock, $30 par, 10,000 shares authorized and outstanding	$300,000
Additional paid-in capital	150,000
Retained earnings (deficit)	(210,000)

On January 2, 2000, Brown put into effect a stockholder-approved quasi-reorganization by reducing the par value of the stock to $5 and eliminating the deficit against additional paid-in capital. Immediately after the quasi-reorganization, what amount should Brown report as additional paid-in capital?

a. $(60,000)
b. $150,000
c. $190,000
d. $400,000

41. The primary purpose of a quasi-reorganizaton is to give a corporation the opportunity to

a. Obtain relief from its creditors.
b. Revalue understated assets to their fair values.
c. Eliminate a deficit in retained earnings.
d. Distribute the stock of a newly created subsidiary to its stockholders in exchange for part of their stock in the corporation.

REVIEW QUESTIONS

STOCKHOLDERS' EQUITY

42. Posy Corp. acquired treasury shares at an amount greater than their par value, but less than their original issue price. Compared to the cost method of accounting for treasury stock, does the par value method report a greater amount for additional paid-in capital and a greater amount for retained earnings?

	Additional paid-in capital	*Retained earnings*
a.	Yes	Yes
b.	Yes	No
c.	No	No
d.	No	Yes

43. In 1999, Elm Corp. bought 10,000 shares of Oil Corp. at a cost of $20,000. On January 15, 2000, Elm declared a property dividend of the Oil stock to shareholders of record on February 1, 2000, payable on February 15, 2000. During 2000, the Oil stock had the following market values:

January 15	$25,000
February 1	26,000
February 15	24,000

The net effect of the foregoing transactions on retained earnings during 2000 should be a reduction of

a. $20,000
b. $24,000
c. $25,000
d. $26,000

44. The condensed balance sheet of Adams & Gray, a partnership, at December 31, 1999, follows:

Current assets	$250,000
Equipment (net)	30,000
Total assets	$280,000
Liabilities	$ 20,000
Adams, capital	160,000
Gray, capital	100,000
Total liabilities and capital	$280,000

On December 31, 1999, the fair values of the assets and liabilities were appraised at $240,000 and $20,000, respectively, by an independent appraiser. On January 2, 2000, the partnership was incorporated and 1,000 shares of $5 par value common stock were issued. Immediately after the incorporation, what amount should the new corporation report as additional paid-in capital?

a. $275,000
b. $260,000
c. $215,000
d. $0.

45. Which of the following **best** describes a possible result of treasury stock transactions by a corporation?

a. May directly decrease but **not** increase retained earnings.
b. May affect total stockholders' equity if the cost method is used instead of the par value method.
c. May increase but **not** decrease reported net earnings.
d. May decrease but **not** increase reported net earnings.

46. Gilbert Corporation issued a 40% stock splitup of its common stock which had a par value of $10 before and after the split-up. At what amount should retained earnings be capitalized for the additional shares issued?

a. There should be **no** capitalization of retained earnings.
b. Par value.
c. Market value on the declaration date.
d. Market value on the payment date.

47. On incorporation, Dee Inc., issued common stock at a price in excess of its par value. No other stock transactions occurred except treasury stock was acquired for an amount exceeding this issue price. If Dee uses the par value method of accounting for treasury stock appropriate for retired stock, what is the effect of the acquisition on the following?

	Net common stock	*Additional paid-in capital*	*Retained earnings*
a.	No effect	Decrease	No effect
b.	Decrease	Decrease	Decrease
c.	Decrease	No effect	Decrease
d.	No effect	Decrease	Decrease

48. The acquisition of treasury stock will cause the number of shares outstanding to decrease if the treasury stock is accounted for by the

	Cost method	*Par value method*
a.	Yes	No
b.	No	No
c.	Yes	Yes
d.	No	Yes

49. Cricket Corp. issued, without consideration, rights allowing stockholders to subscribe for additional shares at an amount greater than par value but less than both market and book values. When the rights are exercised, how are the following accounts affected?

	Retained earnings	*Additional paid-in capital*
a.	Decreased	Not affected
b.	Not affected	Not affected
c.	Decreased	Increased
d.	Not affected	Increased

50. East Co. issued 1,000 shares of its $5 par common stock to Howe as compensation for 1,000 hours of legal services performed. Howe usually bills $160 per hour for legal services. On the date of issuance, the stock was trading on a public exchange at $140 per share. By what amount should the additional paid-in capital account increase as a result of this transaction?

a. $135,000
b. $140,000
c. $155,000
d. $160,000

51. On September 1999, West Corp. made a dividend distribution of one right for each of its 120,000 shares of outstanding common stock. Each right was exercisable for the purchase of 1/100 of a share of West's $50 variable rate preferred stock at an exercise price of $80 per share. On March 20, 2003, none of the rights had been exercised, and West redeemed them by paying each stockholder $0.10 per right. As a result of this redemption, West's stockholders' equity was reduced by

a. $120
b. $2,400
c. $12,000
d. $36,000

52. A clearly identified appropriation of retained earnings for reasonably possible loss contingencies should be

a. Charged with all losses related to that contingency.
b. Transferred to income as losses are realized.
c. Classified in the liability section of the balance sheet.
d. Shown within the stockholders' equity section of the balance sheet.

53. Grid Corp. acquired some of its own common shares at a price greater than both their par value and original issue price but less than their book value. Grid uses the cost method of accounting for treasury stock. What is the impact of this acquisition on total stockholders' equity and the book value per common share?

	Total stockholders' equity	*Book value per share*
a.	Increase	Increase
b.	Increase	Decrease
c.	Decrease	Increase
d.	Decrease	Decrease

54. Long Co. had 100,000 shares of common stock issued and outstanding at January 1, 1999. During 1999, Long took the following actions:

March 15	Declared a 2-for-1 stock split, when the fair value of the stock was $80 per share.
December 15	Declared a $.50 per share cash dividend.

In Long's statement of stockholders' equity for 1999, what amount should Long report as dividends?

a. $ 50,000
b. $100,000
c. $850,000
d. $950,000

55. Cyan Corp. issued 20,000 shares of $5 par common stock at $10 per share. On December 31, 1999, Cyan's retained earnings were $300,000. In March 2000, Cyan reacquired 5,000 shares of its common stock at $20 per share. In June 2000, Cyan sold 1,000 of these shares to its corporate officers for $25 per share. Cyan uses the cost method to record treasury stock. Net income for the year ended December 31, 2000, was $60,000. At December 31, 2000, what amount should Cyan report as retained earnings?

a. $360,000
b. $365,000
c. $375,000
d. $380,000

Items 56 and 57 are based on the following:

The following format was used by Gee, Inc., for its 1999 statement of owners' equity:

	Common stock, $1 par	*Additional paid-in capital*	*Retained earnings*
Balance at 1/1/99	$90,000	$800,000	$175,000
Additions and deductions:			
100% stock dividend			
5% stock dividend	____	____	____
Balance at 12/31/99	____	____	____

When both the 100% and the 5% stock dividends were declared, Gee's common stock was selling for more than its $1 par value.

56. How would the 100% stock dividend affect the additional paid-in capital and retained earnings amounts reported in Gee's 1999 statement of owners' equity?

	Additional paid-in capital	*Retained earnings*
a.	Increase	Increase
b.	Increase	Decrease
c.	No change	Increase
d.	No change	Decrease

57. How would the 5% stock dividend affect the additional paid-in capital and retained earnings amounts reported in Gee's 1999 statement of owners' equity?

	Additional paid-in capital	*Retained earnings*
a.	Increase	Decrease
b.	Increase	Increase
c.	No change	Decrease
d.	No change	Increase

---

58. Georgia, Inc. has an authorized capital of 1,000 shares of $100 par, 8% cumulative preferred stock and 100,000 shares of $10 par common stock. The equity account balances at December 31, 1981, are as follows:

Cumulative preferred stock	$ 50,000
Common stock	90,000
Additional paid-in capital	9,000
Retained earnings	13,000
Treasury stock, common – 100 shares at cost	(2,000)
	$160,000

Dividends on preferred stock are in arrears for the year 1981. The book value of a share of common stock, at December 31, 1981, should be

a. $11.78
b. $11.91
c. $12.22
d. $12.36

INVESTMENT IN STOCK

GENERAL

59. An investor uses the cost method to account for an investment in common stock. Dividends received this year exceeded the investor's share of investee's undistributed earnings since the date of investment. The amount of dividend revenue that should be reported in the investor's income statement for this year would be

a. The portion of the dividends received this year that were in excess of the investor's share of investee's undistributed earnings since the date of investment.
b. The portion of the dividends received this year that were **not** in excess of the investor's share of investee's undistributed earnings since the date of investment.
c. The total amount of dividends received this year.
d. Zero.

DIVIDENDS

60. Bort Co. purchased 2,000 shares of Crel Co. common stock on March 5, 1999, for $72,000. Bort received a $1,000 cash dividend on the Crel stock on July 15, 1999. Crel declared a 10% stock dividend on December 15, 1999, to stockholders of record as of December 31, 1999. The dividend was distributed on January 15, 2000. The market price of the stock was $38 on December 15, 1999, $40 on December 31, 1999, and $42 on January 15, 2000. What amount should Bort record as dividend revenue for the year ended December 31, 1999?

a. $1,000
b. $8,600
c. $9,000
d. $9,400

61. Wood Co. owns 2,000 shares of Arlo, Inc.'s 20,000 shares of $100 par, 6% cumulative, nonparticipating preferred stock and 1,000 shares (2%) of Arlo's common stock. During 1999, Arlo declared and paid dividends of $240,000 on preferred stock. No dividends had been declared or paid during 1998. In addition, Wood received a 5% common stock dividend from Arlo when the quoted market price of Arlo's common stock was $10 per share. What amount should Wood report as dividend income in its 1999 income statement?

a. $12,000
b. $12,500
c. $24,000
d. $24,500

62. Simpson Co. received dividends from its common stock investments during the year ended December 31, 1999, as follows:

- A cash dividend of $8,000 from Wren Corp., in which Simpson owns a 2% interest.
- A cash dividend of $45,000 from Brill Corp., in which Simpson owns a 30% interest. This investment is appropriately accounted for using the equity method.
- A stock dividend of 500 shares from Paul Corp. was received on December 15, 1999, when the quoted market value of Paul's shares was $10 per share. Simpson owns less than 1% of Paul's common stock.

In Simpson's 1999 income statement, dividend revenue should be

a. $58,000
b. $53,000
c. $13,000
d. $8,000

SFAS 115 ACCOUNTING FOR CERTAIN INVESTMENTS IN DEBT AND EQUITY SECURITIES

63. Kale Co. has adopted Statement of Financial Accounting Standards No. 115, Accounting for Certain Investments in Debt and Equity Securities. Kale purchased bonds at a discount on the open market as an investment and intends to hold these bonds to maturity. Kale should account for these bonds at

a. Cost.
b. Amortized cost.
c. Fair value.
d. Lower of cost or market.

64. A company has adopted Statement of Financial Accounting Standards No. 115, *Accounting for Certain Investments in Debt and Equity Securities.* It should report the marketable equity securities that it has classified as trading at

a. Lower of cost or market, with holding gains and losses included in earnings.
b. Lower of cost or market, with holding gains included in earnings only to the extent of previously recognized holding losses.
c. Fair value, with holding gains included **in** earnings only to the extent of previously recognized holding losses.
d. Fair value, with holding gains and losses included in earnings.

65. Data regarding Ball Corp.'s long-term marketable equity securities follow:

	Cost	*Fair value*
December 31, 1999	$150,000	$130,000
December 31, 2000	150,000	160,000

Differences between cost and market values are considered temporary. The decline in market value was considered temporary and was properly accounted for at December 31, 2000. Ball's 2000 statement of changes in stockholders' equity would report an increase of

a. $30,000
b. $20,000
c. $10,000
d. $0

66. At December 31, 1999, Hull Corp. had the following marketable equity securities that were purchased during 1999, its first year of operations:

	Cost	*Fair Value*	*Unrealized gain (loss)*
Trading Securities:			
Security A	$ 90,000	$60,000	$(30,000)
B	15,000	20,000	5,000
Totals	$105,000	$80,000	$(25,000)
Available-for-Sale Securities:			
Security Y	$ 70,000	$ 80,000	$ 10,000
Z	90,000	45,000	(45,000)
Totals	$160,000	$125,000	$(35,000)

All market declines are considered temporary.

Valuation allowances at December 31, 1999, should be established with a corresponding net charge against

	Income	*Stockholders' equity*
a.	$60,000	$0
b.	$30,000	$45,000
c.	$25,000	$35,000
d.	$25,000	$0

67. For a marketable equity securities portfolio included in noncurrent assets, which of the following amounts should be included in the period's net income?

I. Unrealized temporary losses during the period.
II. Realized gains during the period.
III. Changes in the valuation allowance during the period.

a. III only.
b. II only.
c. I and II.
d. I, II, and III.

68. When the fair value of an investment in debt securities exceeds its amortized cost, how should each of the following debt securities be reported at the end of the year?

	Debt securities classified as	
	Held-to-maturity	*Available-for-sale*
a.	Amortized cost	Amortized cost
b.	Amortized cost	Fair value
c.	Fair value	Fair value
d.	Fair value	Amortized cost

69. The following information was extracted from Gil Co.'s December 31, 1994, balance sheet:

Noncurrent assets:	
Long-term investments in marketable equity securities (at fair value)	$96,450
Stockholders' equity:	
Accumulated other comprehensive income**	(25,000)

(** Includes a net unrealized holding loss on long-term investments in marketable equity securities of $19,800.)

Historical cost of the long-term investments in marketable equity securities was

a. $63,595
b. $76,650
c. $96,450
d. $116,250

70. During 1999, Wall Co. purchased 2,000 shares of Hemp Corp. common stock for $31,500 as a short-term investment. The investment was appropriately classified as a Trading Security. The market value of this investment was $29,500 at December 31, 1999. Wall sold all of the Hemp common stock for $14 per share on January 15, 2000, incurring $1,400 in brokerage commissions and taxes. On the sale, Wall should report a realized loss of

a. $4,900
b. $3,500
c. $2,900
d. $1,500

REVIEW QUESTIONS

INVESTMENT IN STOCK

71. The following information pertains to Lark Corp.'s long-term marketable equity securities portfolio:

	December 31,	
	2000	*1999*
Cost	$200,000	$200,000
Fair value	240,000	180,000

Differences between cost and market values are considered to be temporary. The decline in market value was properly accounted for at December 31, 1999. At December 31, 2000, what is the net unrealized holding gain or loss to be reported as

	Other Comprehensive Income	*Accumulated Other Comprehensive Income*
a.	$40,000 Gain	$60,000 Gain
b.	$60,000 Gain	$40,000 Gain
c.	$20,000 Loss	$20,000 Loss
d.	-0-	-0-

72. Reed, Inc., began operations on January 1, 1999. The following information pertains to Reed's December 31, 1999, portfolio of marketable equity securities:

	Current	*Noncurrent*
Aggregate cost	$360,000	$550,000
Aggregate fair value	320,000	450,000
Aggregate lower of cost or market value applied to each security in the portfolio	304,000	420,000

If the market declines are judged to be temporary, what amounts should Reed report as valuation allowances for its current and noncurrent marketable equity securities at December 31, 1999?

	Current	*Noncurrent*
a.	$40,000	$0
b.	$0	$100,000
c.	$40,000	$100,000
d.	$56,000	$130,000

73. In 1997, Cromwell Corporation bought and categorized as available-for-sale 30,000 shares of Fleming Corporation's listed stock for $300,000. This stock was not accounted for by the equity method. In 1999, when the market value had declined to $200,000, Cromwell changed its classification of this investment from current to noncurrent. In January 2000, before Cromwell's 1999 year-end statements were issued, the market value of the Fleming stock had risen to $230,000. How much should Cromwell record as a realized loss in its determination of net income for 1999?

a. $0.
b. $30,000.
c. $70,000.
d. $100,000.

74. On January 2, 1999, Adam Co. purchased as a long-term investment 10,000 shares of Mill Corp.'s common stock for $40 a share. The investment was appropriately classified as an available-for-sale security. On December 31, 1999, the market price of Mill's stock was $35 a share, reflecting a temporary decline in market price. On December 28, 2000, Adam sold 8,000 shares of Mill stock for $30 a share. For the year ended December 31, 2000, Adam should report a loss on disposal of long-term investment of

a. $100,000
b. $90,000
c. $80,000
d. $40,000

75. Stock dividends on common stock should be recorded at their fair market value by the investor when the related investment is accounted for under which of the following methods?

	Cost	Equity
a.	Yes	Yes
b.	Yes	No
c.	No	Yes
d.	No	No

76. On both December 31, 1999, and December 31, 2000, Kopp Co.'s only marketable equity security had the same market value, which was below cost. Kopp considered the decline in value to be temporary in 1999 but other than temporary in 2000. At the end of both years the security was classified as a noncurrent asset. Kopp could not exercise significant influence over the investee. What should be the effects of the determination that the decline was other than temporary on Kopp's 2000 net noncurrent assets and net income?

a. No effect on both net noncurrent assets and net income.
b. No effect on net noncurrent assets and decrease in net income.
c. Decrease in net noncurrent assets and **no** effect on net income.
d. Decrease in both net noncurrent assets and net income.

77. Dey Corp. began operations in 1999. An analysis of Dey's marketable equity securities portfolio acquired in 1999, shows the following totals at December 31, 1999, for securities categorized as trading and available-for-sale:

	Trading assets	*Available-for-sale assets*
Aggregate cost	$45,000	$65,000
Aggregate fair value	39,000	57,000
Aggregate lower of cost or market value applied to each security in the portfolio	38,000	56,000

What valuation allowance should Dey report at December 31, 1999, for the unrealized holding loss included in its 1999 income statement?

a. $14,000
b. $9,000
c. $7,000
d. $6,000

78. During 1999, Scott Corp. purchased marketable equity securities as long-term investments. Pertinent data follow:

Security	Cost	Fair value at 12/31/99
D	$ 36,000	$ 40,000
E	80,000	60,000
F	180,000	186,000
	$296,000	$286,000

Scott appropriately carries these securities at fair value. The amount of unrealized holding loss on these securities in Scott's 1999 income statement should be

a. $20,000
b. $14,000
c. $10,000
d. $0

79. Zinc Co.'s adjusted trial balance at December 31, 1999, includes the following account balances:

Common stock, $3 par	$600,000
Additional paid-in capital	800,000
Treasury stock, at cost	50,000
Accumulated other comprehensive income (Debit)	20,000
Retained earnings appropriated for uninsured earthquake losses	150,000
Retained earnings unappropriated	200,000

What amount should Zinc report as total stockholders' equity in its December 31, 1999, balance sheet?

a. $1,680,000
b. $1,720,000
c. $1,780,000
d. $1,820,000

Recently Released Questions

80. On January 15, 2000 Rice Co. declared its annual cash dividend on common stock for the year ended January 31, 2000. The dividend was paid on February 9, 2000, to stockholders of record as of January 28, 2000. On what date should Rice decrease retained earnings by the amount of the dividend?

a. January 15, 2000
b. January 31, 2000
c. January 28, 2000
d. February 9, 2000

Chapter Two
Stockholders' Equity and Investment in Stock
Problems

NUMBER 1

Part a. Capital stock is an important area of a corporation's equity section. Generally the term "capital stock" embraces common and preferred stock issued by a corporation.

Required:

1. What are the basic rights inherent in ownership of common stock, and how are they exercised?
2. What is preferred stock? Discuss the various preferences afforded preferred stock.

Part b. In dealing with the various equity securities of a corporate entity it is important to understand certain terminology related thereto.

Required: Define the following terms.

1. Treasury stock.
2. Legal capital.
3. Stock right.
4. Stock warrant.

NUMBER 2

For numerous reasons a corporation may reacquire shares of its own capital stock. When a company purchases treasury stock, it has two options as to how to account for the shares: (1) cost method, and (2) par value method.

Required:

Compare and contrast the cost method with the par value method for each of the following:

1. Purchase of shares at a price less than par value.
2. Purchase of shares at a price greater than par value.
3. Subsequent resale of treasury shares at a price less than purchase price, but more than par value.
4. Subsequent resale of treasury shares at a price greater than both purchase price and par value.
5. Effect on net income.

NUMBER 3

Faye, Inc., finances its capital needs approximately one-third from long-term debt and two-thirds from equity. At December 31, 1996, Fay had the following liability and equity account balances:

11% Debenture bonds payable, face amount	$5,000,000
Premium on bonds payable	352,400
Common stock	8,000,000
Additional paid-in capital	2,295,000
Retained earnings	2,465,000
Treasury stock, at cost	325,000

Transactions during 1997 and other information relating to Fay's liabilities and equity accounts were as follows:

- The debenture bonds were issued on December 31, 1994, for $5,378,000 to yield 10%. The bonds mature on December 31, 2009. Interest is payable annually on December 31. Fay uses the interest method to amortize bond premium.
- Fay's common stock shares are traded on the over-the-counter market. At December 31, 1996, Fay had 2,000,000 authorized shares of $10 par common stock.
- On January 15, 1997, Fay reissued 15,000 of its 25,000 shares of treasury stock for $225,000. The treasury stock had been acquired on February 28, 1996.
- On March 2, 1997, Fay issued a 5% stock dividend on all issued shares. The market price of Fay's common stock at time of issuance was $14 per share.
- On November 1, 1997, Fay borrowed $4,000,000 at 9%, evidenced by an unsecured note payable to United Bank. The note is payable in five equal annual principal installments of $800,000. The first principal and interest payment is due on November 1, 1998.
- On December 31, 1997, Fay owned 10,000 shares of Ryan Corp.'s common stock, which represented a 1% ownership interest. Fay accounts for this marketable equity investment as a long-term investment. The stock was purchased on May 1, 1996, at $20 per share. The market price was $21 per share on December 31, 1996, and $18 per share on December 31, 1997.
- Fay's net income for 1997 was $2,860,000.

Required (Include formal schedules of supporting computations with each item referenced to correspond with the items in the solution):
Prepare the stockholders' equity section of Fay's December 31, 1997, balance sheet.

NUMBER 4

Problems may be encountered in accounting for transactions involving the stockholders' equity section of the balance sheet.

Required:

a. Describe the accounting for the subscription of common stock at a price in excess of the par value of the common stock.

b. Describe the accounting for the issuance for cash of no par value common stock at a price in excess of the stated value of the common stock.

c. Explain the significance of the three dates that are important in accounting for cash dividends to stockholders. State the journal entry, if any, needed at each date.

d. Assume retained earnings can be used for stock dividends distributable in shares. What is the effect of an ordinary 10 percent common stock dividend on retained earnings and total stockholders' equity?

NUMBER 5

Mart, Inc., is a public company whose shares are traded in the over-the-counter market. At December 31, 1998, Mart had 6,000,000 authorized shares of $5 par value common stock, of which 2,000,000 shares were issued and outstanding. The stockholders' equity accounts at December 31, 1998, had the following balances:

Common stock	$10,000,000
Additional paid-in capital	7,500,000
Retained earnings	3,250,000

Transactions during 1999 and other information relating to the stockholders' equity accounts were as follows:

- On January 5, 1999, Mart issued at $54 per share, 100,000 shares of $50 par value, 9% cumulative, convertible preferred stock. Each share of preferred stock is convertible, at the option of the holder, into two shares of common stock. Mart had 250,000 authorized shares of preferred stock. The preferred stock has a liquidation value of $55 per share.
- On February 1, 1999, Mart reacquired 20,000 shares of its common stock for $16 per share. Mart uses the cost method to account for treasury stock.
- On March 15, 1999, Mart paid $200,000 for 10,000 shares of common stock of Lew, Inc., a public company whose stock is traded on a national stock exchange. This stock was acquired for long-term investment purposes and had a fair market value of $15 per share on December 31, 1999. This decline in market value was not considered permanent.
- On April 30, 1999, Mart had completed an additional public offering of 500,000 shares of its $5 par value common stock. The stock was sold to the public at $12 per share, net of offering costs.
- On June 17, 1999, Mart declared a cash dividend of $1 per share of common stock, payable on July 10, 1999, to stockholders of record on July 1, 1999.
- On November 6, 1999, Mart sold 10,000 shares of treasury stock for $21 per share.
- On December 7, 1999, Mart declared the yearly cash dividend on preferred stock, payable on January 7, 2000, to stockholders of record on December 31, 1999.
- On January 17, 2000, before the books were closed for 1999, Mart became aware that the ending inventories at December 31, 1998, were overstated by $200,000. The after-tax effect on 1998 net income was $140,000. The appropriate correction entry was recorded the same day.
- After correction of the beginning inventories, net income for 1999 was $2,250,000.

Required:

a. Prepare a statement of retained earnings for the year ended December 31, 1999. Assume that only single period financial statements for 1999 are presented.

b. Prepare the stockholders' equity section of Mart's balance sheet at December 31, 1999.

c. Compute the book value per share of common stock at December 31, 1999.

NUMBER 6

Number 6 consists of 8 items. Select the **best** answer for each item. **Answer all items.**

Min Co. is a publicly-held company whose share are traded in the over-the-counter market. The stockholders' equity accounts at December 31, 1999, had the following balances:

Preferred stock, \$100 par value, 6% cumulative; 5,000 shares authorized; 2,000 issued and outstanding	\$ 200,000
Common stock, \$1 par value, 150,000 shares authorized; 100,000 issued and outstanding	100,000
Additional paid-in capital	800,000
Retained earnings	1,586,000
Total stockholders' equity	\$2,686,000

Transactions during 2000 and other information relating to the stockholders' equity accounts were as follows:

- February 1, 2000-Issued 13,000 shares common stock to Ram Co. in exchange for land. On the date issued, the stock had a market price of \$11 per share. The land had a carrying value on Ram's books of \$135,000, and an assessed value for property taxes of \$90,000.

- March 1, 2000-Purchased 5,000 shares of its own common stock to be held as treasury stock for \$14 per share. Min uses the cost method to account for treasury stock. Transactions in treasury stock are legal in Min's state of incorporation.

- May 10, 2000-Declared a property dividend of marketable securities held by Min to common shareholders. The securities had a carrying value of \$600,000; fair value on relevant dates were:

Date of declaration (May 10, 2000)	\$720,000
Date of record (May 25, 2000)	758,000
Date of distribution (June 1, 2000)	736,000

- October 1, 2000-Reissued 2,000 shares of treasury stock for \$16 per share.

- November 4, 2000-Declared a cash dividend of \$1.50 per share to all common shareholders of record November 15, 2000. The dividend was paid on November 25, 2000.

- December 20, 2000-Declared the required annual cash dividend on preferred stock for 2000. The dividend was paid on January 5, 2001.

- January 16, 2001-Before closing the accounting records for 2000, Min became aware that no amortization had been recorded for 1999 for a patent purchased on July 1, 1999. The patent was properly capitalized at \$320,000 and had an estimated useful life of eight years when purchased. Min's income tax rate is 30%. The appropriate correcting entry was recorded on the same day.

- Adjusted net income for 2000 was \$838,000.

Required:

Items 62 through 68 represent amounts to be reported in Min's financial statements. **Item 69** represents other financial information. For all items, calculate the amounts requested.

Items 62 through 64 represent amounts to be reported on Min's 2000 statement of retained earnings.

62. Preferred dividends.

63. Common dividends-cash.

64. Common dividends-property.

Items 65 through 68 represent amounts to be reported on Min's statement of stockholders' equity at December 31, 2000.

65. Number of common shares issued at December 31, 2000.

66. Amount of common stock issued.

67. Additional paid-in capital, including treasury stock transactions.

68. Treasury stock.

Item 69 represents other financial information for 1999.

69. Book value per share at December 31, 1999, before prior period adjustment.

NUMBER 7

Brady Company has 30,000 shares of $10 par value common stock authorized and 20,000 shares issued and outstanding. On August 15, 2000, Brady purchased 1,000 shares of treasury stock for $12 per share. Brady uses the cost method to account for treasury stock. On September 14, 2000, Brady sold 500 shares of the treasury stock for $14 per share.

In October 2000, Brady declared and distributed 2,000 shares as a stock dividend from unissued shares when the market value of the common stock was $16 per share.

On December 20, 2000, Brady declared a $1 per share cash dividend, payable on January 10, 2001, to shareholders of record on December 31, 2000.

Required:

a. How should Brady account for the purchase and sale of the treasury stock, and how should the treasury stock be presented in Brady's balance sheet at December 31, 2000?

b. How should Brady account for the stock dividend, and how would it affect Brady's stockholders' equity at December 31, 2000? Why?

c. How should Brady account for the cash dividend, and how would it affect Brady's balance sheet at December 31, 2000? Why?

NUMBER 8

Presented below is information pertaining to Cox Stationery Supply, a calendar-year sole proprietorship owned by John Cox. The business maintains its books on the cash basis except that, at year end, the closing inventory and depreciation are recorded. On December 31, 1999, after recording inventory and depreciation, and closing the nominal accounts, Cox had the following general ledger trial balance:

Cox Stationery Supply
TRIAL BALANCE
December 31, 1999

	Dr.	*Cr.*
Cash	$ 16,500	
Merchandise inventory	39,000	
Equipment	52,500	
Accumulated depreciation		$ 20,500
Note payable, bank		10,000
Payroll taxes withheld		1,300
Cox, capital		76,200
	$108,000	$108,000

During the last quarter of 1999, John Cox and Mary Rice, an outside investor, agreed to incorporate the business under the name of Cox Stationers, Inc. Cox will receive 1,000 shares for his business, and Rice will pay $86,000 cash for her 1,000 shares. On January 1, 2000, they received the certificate of incorporation for Cox Stationers, Inc., and the corporation issued 1,000 shares of common stock each to Cox and Rice for the above consideration. The agreement between Cox and Rice requires that the December 31, 1999, balance sheet of the proprietorship should be converted to the accrual basis, with all assets and liabilities stated at current fair values, including Cox's goodwill implicit in the terms of the common stock issuance.

Additional information:

1. Amounts due from customers totaled $23,500 at December 31, 1999. A review of collectibility disclosed that an allowance for doubtful accounts of $3,300 is required.
2. The $39,000 merchandise inventory is based on a physical count of goods priced at cost. Unsalable damaged goods costing $2,500 are included in the count. The current fair value of the total merchandise inventory is $45,000.
3. On July 1, 1999, Cox paid $3,800 to renew the comprehensive insurance coverage for one year.
4. The $10,000 note payable is dated July 1, 1999, bears interest at 12%, and is due July 1, 2000.
5. Unpaid vendors' invoices totaled $30,500 at December 31, 1999.
6. During January 2000, final payroll tax returns filed for Cox Stationery Supply required remittances totaling $2,100.
7. Not included in the trial balance is the $3,500 principal balance at December 31, 1999, of the three-year loan to purchase a delivery van on December 31, 1997. The debt was assumed by the corporation on January 1, 2000. The current fair value of the used equipment is $40,000, including the delivery van.
8. Cox Stationers, Inc., has 7,500 authorized shares of $50 par common stock.

Required:

a. Prepare a schedule to compute Cox's goodwill implicit in the issuance to him of 1,000 shares of common stock for his business.

b. Prepare a formal balance sheet of Cox Stationers, Inc., at January 1, 2000, immediately after the issuance of common stock to Cox and Rice. Journal entries and trial balance worksheet are **not** required.

NUMBER 9

Number 9 consists of 10 items. Select the best answer for each item. Answer all items. Your grade will be based on the total number of correct answers.

Items 1 through 4 are based on the following:

Camp Co. purchased various securities during 1999 to be classified as held-to-maturity securities, trading securities, or available-for-sale securities.

Required:
Items 1 through 4 describe various securities purchased by Camp. For each item, select from the following list the appropriate category for each security. A category may be used once, more than once, or not at all.

Categories:

(H) Held-to-maturity.

(T) Trading.

(A) Available-for-sale.

1. Debt securities bought and held for the purpose of selling in the near term.

2. U.S. Treasury bonds that Camp has both the positive intent and the ability to hold to maturity.

3. $3 million debt security bought and held for the purpose of selling in three years to finance payment of Camp's $2 million long-term note payable when it matures.

4. Convertible preferred stock that Camp does not intend to sell in the near term.

Items 5 through 10 are based on the following:

The following information pertains to Dayle, Inc.'s portfolio of marketable investments for the year ended December 31, 1999:

	Cost	Fair value 12/31/98	1999 activity Purchases	1999 activity Sales	Fair value 12/31/99
Held-to-maturity securities					
Security ABC			$100,000		$95,000
Trading securities					
Security DEF	$150,000	$160,000			155,000
Available-for-sale securities					
Security GHI	190,000	165,000		$175,000	
Security JKL	170,000	175,000			160,000

Security ABC was purchased at par. All declines in fair value are considered to be temporary.

Required:
Items 5 through 10 describe amounts to be reported in Dayle's 1999 financial statements. For each item, select from the following list the correct numerical response. An amount may be selected once, more than once, or not at all.

5. Carrying amount of security ABC at December 31, 1999.

6. Carrying amount of security DEF at December 31, 1999.

7. Carrying amount of security JKL at December 31, 1999.

Items 8 through 10 require a second response. For each item, indicate whether a gain (G) or a loss (L) is to be reported.

8. Recognized gain or loss on sale of security GHI.

9. Unrealized gain or loss to be reported in 1999 income statement.

10. Unrealized gain or loss to be included in Accumulated other comprehensive income, reported in equity at December 31, 1999.

Answer List:

(A) $0

(B) $5,000

(C) $10,000

(D) $15,000

(E) $25,000

(F) $95,000

(G) $100,000

(H) $150,000

(I) $155,000

(J) $160,000

(K) $170,000

Chapter Two
Solutions to Stockholders' Equity Questions

1. (a) Capital stock (common or preferred) is recorded at the:
   a) par value established at incorporation; or
   b) stated value established by the board of directors when no par value is established at incorporation; or
   c) issue price when no par value or stated value has been established.

Amounts in excess of par or stated value constitute APIC.

Common stock: $1 stated value × 20,000 shares			$20,000
Preferred stock: $10 par value × 6,000 shares			$60,000
APIC			
Common	20,000 shares × ($30 – $1) =	$580,000	
Preferred	6,000 shares × ($50 – $10) =	240,000	$820,000

2. (d) $82,000.

Book value of net assets		
(Jay capital + Kay capital)		$80,000
Increase in fair value		
Tangible assets	$7,000	
Goodwill	5,000	12,000
Fair value of net assets (equity)		92,000
Less: Par value of stock issued		
10,000 shares × $1 par		(10,000)
Additional paid-in capital		$82,000

3. (c) $48,000.

	# shares	*Ratio*	*Value*	*Wt.Value*	*% Value*
Common stock	1000	1	$36	$36.00	36/90 = 40%
Preferred stock	2000	2	27	54.00	54/90 = 60%
				$90.00	100%

Proceeds allocated to preferred stock = 60% × $80,000 = $48,000

4. (a) Additional paid-in capital resulting from stock subscriptions is recorded when the stock is subscribed. Only the stock is identified or segregated as subscribed in the capital accounts until the subscription is paid and the stock issued.

5. (b) Donated assets are recorded at fair market value as a credit to Additional paid-in capital—Donated assets.

6. (c) The entries to record the stock issuance and subsequent acquisition and retirement (per share) are as follows:

		Debit	Credit
Issuance:	Cash	25	
	Common stock		10
	APIC in excess of par common		15
Retirement:	Common stock	10	
	APIC in excess of par common	15	
	Cash		20
	APIC: Stock Retirement		5

The net result is a decrease in APIC of $10 per share retired.

Answers (a) and (b) are incorrect as capital stock transactions do not affect net income. Answer (d) is incorrect as capital stock (treasury stock) transactions never increase retained earnings.

7. (d) Entry to record retirement:

Common Stock (100,000 at $10 Par)	$1,000,000	
APIC (100,000 at $3 prorata portion)	300,000	
Retained Earnings	500,000	
Cash		$1,800,000

Prorata portion of APIC = $\frac{\$2,700,000 \text{ APIC}}{900,000 \text{ shares}}$ = $3 per share

8. (b) Under the Par Method the excess of cost of treasury stock over par or stated value:

(1) **May be** allocated between A.P.I.C. and retained earnings. The portion allocated to A.P.I.C. is limited to the sum of: a) the pro rata portion of A.P.I.C. on the same issue; and b) all A.P.I.C. from retirements and net "gains" on the sale of treasury stock of the same issue.
(2) **May be** charged entirely to retained earnings.

Only Answer (b) satisfies the above alternatives—application of alternative #1.

9. (b) $125,000.

APIC in excess of par:

1/5	issue of stock: 20,000 sh @ $5 ($15 price - $10 par)	100,000
7/14	acquisition of Treasury stock: 5,000 sh @ $5 (excess over original issue price is charged to Retained earnings)	(25,000)
12/27	reissue of Treasury shares: 5,000 sh @ $10 ($20 price - $10 par)	50,000
		$125,000

The Par Value method accounts for Treasury stock as a quasi-retirement: 1) T/S is charged for the par of the shares; 2) APIC is charged for the pro-rata portion of APIC attributable to the shares acquired; 3) Retained earnings is charged for the excess of cost over #1 and #2 above or APIC Treasury stock is credited for the excess of #1 and #2 above over cost of the shares acquired.

10. (d) Acquisition of treasury stock (a contra stockholders equity element) will result in a decrease in stockholders' equity whether recorded at cost or par. The subsequent reissuance will increase stockholders' equity as the contra equity is removed. If it is sold at a price in excess of its cost, stockholders' equity will be greater than it was prior to its purchase and sale.

11. (c) Under the cost method, when treasury stock is sold at a price in excess of its cost, the "gain" is credited to APIC - treasury stock transactions.

12. (a) Under the Cost Method of accounting for treasury stock, the purchase of stock is recorded by debiting treasury stock for the full cost. There is no effect on the balance of APIC or Retained Earnings; however, the retained earnings are restricted for dividend purposes in an amount equal to the cost of the stock. When sold, any "gain" (selling price in excess of cost) is credited to APIC (from treasury stock transactions) and any loss (cost in excess of selling price) is charged to APIC and/or retained earnings.

13. (c) The sale of the treasury stock resulted in a "loss" of $4 per share ($12 selling price – $16 cost) or $120,000 (30,000 shares × $4 per share). Under the cost method of accounting for treasury stock transactions, a "loss" on the sale of treasury stock is charged (debited) to APIC from treasury stock transactions to the extent of prior "gains" from the sale of treasury stock, any excess "loss" is charged to retained earnings. As there were no prior treasury stock transactions, the entire "loss" on the sale of the treasury stock ($120,000) would be charged to retained earnings.

14. (b) Entry to record sale of treasury stock:

Cash (3,000 shares × $25)	$75,000	
Treasury stock (3,000 shares × $18 cost)		$54,000
APIC—Treasury stock transactions		21,000

Under the cost method, when treasury stock is sold at a price in excess of its cost, the "gain" is credited to APIC—treasury stock transactions.

Answers (a) and (d) are incorrect, as retained earnings may not be increased by treasury stock transactions. Answers (c) and (d) are incorrect, as treasury stock transactions do not affect the capital stock (common or preferred) accounts.

15. (d) A donation of stock to the corporation causes no reduction of assets and therefore does not affect total stockholders' equity. Under the cost method, there would be only a memorandum entry in the treasury stock account. When reissued, the proceeds would be credited to APIC: Donated Capital. Under the par value method, Treasury Stock would be debited and APIC: Donated Capital would be credited for the par value. When reissued, proceeds in excess of par would be credited to APIC: Donated Capital.

16. (b) Dividends are recorded and reduce stockholders' equity (retained earnings) at the date of declaration.

17. (a) Dividends are recorded as a liability and reduction of retained earnings at the date of declaration.

18. (b)

Total dividend declared		$44,000
Less: Dividend to preferred stock:		
1999 dividends in arrears	$12,000	
2000 dividend		
$400,000 total par × 6%	24,000	36,000
Dividend to common stock		$ 8,000

19. (c) $40,000—Dividends payable to common shareholders.

	Preferred	*Common*	*Total*
Preferred: regular dividend			
5% × $10 par × 30,000 sh.	15,000		15,000
Common at preferred rate			
5% × $1 par × 200,000 sh.		10,000	10,000
			25,000
Participating dividend based on total par values*			
Preferred			
(300,000/500,000) × $75,000	45,000		
Common			75,000
(200,000/500,000) × $75,000		30,000	
Total dividends	$60,000	$40,000	$100,000

*When common stock has a par or stated value, participation is allocated on the aggregate dollar amount of common and preferred stock outstanding. If common stock does not have a par or stated value, participation is based on the number of shares of each class outstanding.

NOTE: If the total dividend is sufficient to provide for a common stock dividend based upon the preferred dividend rate, current dividends will be the same percentage of total par value for each class of stock.

20. (c) Stock dividends do not affect total stockholders' equity as the reduction in retained earnings is offset by an equal increase in the paid-in capital accounts. This is a small stock dividend, less than 20-25 percent of the total outstanding shares, and would be recorded by charging retained earnings for the fair market value of the stock on the date of declaration, and crediting common stock for the par value of the shares issued and APIC for the excess of market value over par value.

21. (c) The number of shares issued is less than the 20-25% guideline established in ARB 43 to determine the treatment of a stock dividend. Therefore, the transaction is considered a dividend and retained earnings should be charged for the FMV at date of declaration.

22. (b) This type of transaction (where the additional shares issued are greater than 20-25% of the total outstanding shares) is a split-up effected in the form of a dividend. Retained earnings should be capitalized in an amount equal to the par value of the shares in the distribution.

$300,000 x 3 = $900,000

23. (a) $0 current liability.
Declaration of a stock dividend does not affect current liabilities as the dividend will not be satisfied with the current assets of the corporation. Rather, shares of stock will be issued to satisfy the dividend. A stock dividend results in a transfer between equity accounts only, the decrease in retained earnings being offset by an equal increase in the paid-in capital accounts.

24. (b) $45,800.

10% stock dividend: *Small stock dividends,* less than 20-25% of the outstanding shares, are recorded at the fair market value of the shares issued as of the date of declaration	$15,000
28% stock dividend: *Large stock dividends,* greater than 20-25% of the outstanding shares, are recorded at the par value of the shares issued as of the date of declaration	30,800
Total charge to retained earnings for stock dividends declared	$45,800

25. (a) A property dividend is a non-monetary transaction and, as such, is appropriately recorded at the fair market value of the asset to be distributed, as of the date of declaration. Any difference between the property's fair market value and its carrying value would be recognized as a gain or loss in the current period.

26. (c)

Fair market value of property dividend	
$2.50 × 100,000 shares	$250,000
Carrying value	
$2.00 × 100,000 shares	200,000
Gain on disposal of investment	$ 50,000

Property dividends are recorded at the fair market value of the property distributed as of the date of declaration, with any gain or loss being recognized in the current period.

27. (c) $60,000 decrease in retained earnings.

Deduction for property dividend		
Fair market value, date of declaration		$78,000
Increase for gain on disposal of investment		
Fair market value, date of declaration	$78,000	
Less: Cost of investment	60,000	
Gain on disposal of investment		18,000
Net decrease in retained earnings		$60,000

Property dividends are nonmonetary transactions and are appropriately recorded at the fair market value of the asset to be distributed, as of the date of declaration, with any gain or loss in disposal of the property recognized in the current period.

28. (c)		
	Dividend declared	$800,000
	Retained earnings at declaration	600,000
	Liquidating dividend	$200,000

A liquidating dividend is a "return **of** capital", a distribution of paid-in capital, as opposed to a "return **on** capital", a distribution of retained earnings.

29. (a) A stock split **increases** the number of shares outstanding. Because a stock split **most likely** does not increase total par value, the par value per share will **decrease.**

30. (c) As the par value was reduced and the number of shares increased proportionately, there is no effect from the stock split on legal capital (total par value of issued stock), A.P.I.C., or retained earnings.

31. (b) As the par value was increased ($10 to $20) and the number of shares decreased proportionately (200,000 to 100,000), there is no effect from the reverse stock split on legal capital (total par value of issued shares), A.P.I.C., or retained earnings.

32. (a) 220,000 shares issued; 212,000 shares outstanding.
Treasury stock is stock which has been issued by a corporation and subsequently reacquired by that corporation, but not formally retired. As the issuing corporation holds the stock it is **not** outstanding stock; however, as the stock has not been formally retired, it is issued stock. Treasury stock participates in stock splits and stock dividends.

			Shares		
	Issued	-	Treasury	=	Outstanding
Shares 1/1/00	100,000		5,000		95,000
5/3 Sale of Treasury stock	--		(1,000)		1,000
8/6 Issuance of stock	10,000		--		10,000
	110,000		4,000		106,000
11/18 2-for-1 stock split	110,000		4,000		106,000
Shares 12/31/00	220,000		8,000		212,000

33. (a)		
1/1	shares outstanding	300,000
1/31	10% stock dividend issued	30,000
6/30	treasury stock purchased	(100,000)
8/1	treasury stock reissued	50,000
	Shares outstanding	280,000
11/30	2-for-1 stock split	280,000
12/31	shares outstanding	560,000

34. (d) An appropriation of retained earnings (a reserve) is used to inform financial statement users of a restriction on the availability of retained earnings for dividends. The entry to record an appropriation charges Retained Earnings and credits Appropriated Retained Earnings. When the appropriation is no longer needed, the only proper entry is to reverse the entry that established the appropriation.

35. (a) $260,000

Total income since incorporation		$420,000
Less:	Cash dividends	(130,000)
	Property dividends (at F.M.V.)	(30,000)
Retained earnings		$260,000

The excess proceeds over the cost of treasury stock sold ("Gain on sale of treasury stock") is accounted for as Additional Paid in Capital.

36. (c) The issuance of stock rights to existing stockholders does not result in a formal journal entry on the books of the issuing corporation. Only a memorandum journal entry is made. These rights merely evidence the stockholders' preemptive right. Furthermore, no formal journal entry is required to record the lapse of stock rights issued to existing stockholders as no formal journal entry was made to record their issuance.

Common stock and additional paid-in capital would be recorded (increase) when the stock rights were exercised and the stock issued.

37. (a) $0 decrease in retained earnings.
The issuance of stock rights to existing stockholders does not result in a formal journal entry on the books of the issuing corporation. Only a memorandum journal entry is made. These rights merely evidence the stockholders' preemptive right. Furthermore, no formal journal entry is required to record the lapse of stock rights issued to existing stockholders as no formal journal entry was made to record their issuance.

38. (d) $7.00 book value per share of common stock.

Total stockholders' equity	$1,025,000
Less: Preferred stock liquidating value	
($250,000 par + $50,000 premium)	(300,000)
Preferred dividends in arrears	(25,000)
Book value of common stock	$ 700,000
Common shares outstanding	÷ 100,000
Book value per common share	$ 7.00

39. (a)

Total stockholders' equity	$8,000,000
Less: Preferred stock liquidating value	
(50,000 shares × $110)	(5,500,000)
Preferred stock dividends in arrears	
($5,000,000 par × 6% × 1 year)	(300,000)
Book value of common stock	$2,200,000
Common shares outstanding	÷ 400,000
Book value per common share	$ 5.50

40. (c) $190,000 APIC

	Common Stock	APIC	Retained Earnings
Beginning balances	$300,000	$150,000	$(210,000)
Reduce Par to $5			
$30 - $5 = $25 to APIC	(250,000)	250,000	
$25 x 10,000 sh.			
Eliminate deficit	———	(210,000)	210,000
Ending balances	$ 50,000	$190,000	-0-

41. (c) A quasi-reorganization is undertaken to reduce a deficit in retained earnings to zero.

Answer (a) is incorrect because a quasi-reorganization is an accounting adjustment. It offers no relief from creditors. Answer (b) is incorrect because assets are usually written down to fair value. Answer (d) is incorrect because a quasi-reorganization does not entail an exchange of stock.

42. (c) Under the par value method, acquisition of treasury stock at an amount greater than par value, but less than original issue price would result in a net decrease in additional paid-in capital equal to the excess of cost over the par value. Retained earnings would not be affected as the cost was not greater than the original issue price.

Under the cost method, treasury stock is recorded at cost and neither additional paid-in capital nor retained earnings are affected.

43. (a) $20,000. Net reduction in retained earnings:

Deduction for property dividend		
Fair market value, date of declaration		$25,000
Increase for gain on disposal of investment		
Fair market value, date of declaration	$25,000	
Less cost of investment	20,000	
Gain on disposal of investment		5,000
Net reduction in retained earnings		$20,000

Property dividends are nonmonetary transactions and are appropriately recorded at the fair market value of the asset to be distributed, as of the date of declaration, with any gain or loss on disposal of the property recognized in the current period.

The net effect of a property dividend is a decrease in retained earnings (and assets) equal to the cost of the asset distributed as a property dividend.

44. (c) Fair value of equity:

Fair value of assets	$240,000
– Fair value of liabilities	(20,000)
	220,000
Less par value of shares issued (1000 × $5)	(5,000)
Additional paid-in capital	$215,000

For financial accounting purposes, non-cash contributions are recorded at the fair market value as of the date of contribution.

45. (a) Per APB #6 par 12a, when a corporation retires its stock the excess paid over par should be allocated between APIC and retained earnings or alternatively charged to retained earnings.

46. (b) The general rule per ARB 43 is if the shares issued are less than 20-25% of the total outstanding shares, retained earnings should be capitalized based on the fair value of the additional shares issued (stock dividend). If the shares issued are 25% or more, the transaction is considered a "split-up effected in the form of a dividend" and requires the capitalization of retained earnings at par value. The distinction is drawn because large distributions have the effect of materially reducing per share market value.

47. (b) Under the par value method, the preferable entry is to charge:

- Treasury stock for the par value of the shares acquired
- APIC for the pro rata portion of APIC attributable to the stock acquired
- Retained earnings for any excess paid over the above amounts.

The treasury stock is reported in the balance sheet as a reduction of the outstanding stock of the same class.

48. (c) Treasury stock is stock which has been issued by a corporation and subsequently reacquired by that corporation, but not formally retired. As the issuing corporation holds the stock it is not outstanding stock (stock held by an investor); however, because the stock has not been formally retired it is issued stock. The cost and par value methods are different techniques of recording treasury stock transactions, but have no effect on the characteristics of the stock.

49. (d) The issuance of stock rights to existing stockholders does not result in a formal journal entry on the books of the issuing corporation. Only a memorandum journal entry is made. These rights merely evidence the stockholders' preemptive right. When the rights are exercised, the issuance of stock is recorded like any other stock issuance, the stock is credited for its par value and additional paid-in capital (in excess of par) is credited for proceeds greater than par value. Retained earnings are not affected by the sale of stock.

50. (a) $135,000. Nonmonetary transactions should be recorded at the fair market value of the assets given or received (whichever is more clearly evident). As the stock is publicly traded, its value at issuance, should be used as the fair value of the transaction.

Fair value of stock (1000 shares @ $140 per share)	$140,000
- Par value of stock (1000 shares @ $5 per share)	5,000
Credit to Additional Paid-in Capital	$135,000

51. (c) $12,000.
When stock rights are issued to shareholders without consideration, only a memo entry is made. Stockholders' equity would be effected when the rights are exercised (increase equity accounts) or redeemed (reduce stockholders' equity). The redemption reduces stockholders' equity $12,000 (120,000 rights @ $.10).

52. (d) An appropriation of R.E. cannot be charged with losses, transferred to income or classified as a liability.

53. (c) Treasury stock results in a decrease in total stockholders' equity equal to the cost of the treasury stock under both the cost method and par value method of recording treasury stock. Under the cost method, treasury stock is recorded at cost, and reported as a contra-account in stockholders' equity.

Treasury stock is issued stock; however, it is not outstanding stock. Book value per common share is based upon the number of shares outstanding (treasury stock is excluded). Therefore, the acquisition of treasury stock at a price (cost) less than its book value would result in an increase in the book value per common share, as the book value of the treasury stock in excess of cost would be attributed to the remaining outstanding shares.

54. (b) $100,000.

Jan. 1	Shares issued and outstanding	100,000
Mar. 15	2 for 1 stock split	x 2
Mar. 15	Shares issued and outstanding	200,000
Dec. 15	Cash Dividend declared (per share)	x $.50
	Dividends for year	$100,000

55. (a) $360,000. Retained earnings at 12/31/00.
Under the cost method of recording Treasury stock transactions:

- The acquisition of T/S does not effect retained earnings.
  T/S is recorded at cost.
- The sale of T/S above cost (at a "gain") does not effect retained earnings.
  "Gain" is credited to APIC Treasury stock.
- The sale of T/S below cost (at a "loss") would reduce retained earnings for the "loss" in excess of APIC from prior Treasury stock transactions.
- Retained earnings is **never** increased by treasury stock transactions.

Therefore, the retained earnings would equal to beginning balance, $300,000 plus net income for the period, $60,000.

56. (d) Additional paid-in capital, no change; Retained earnings, decrease.
Large stock dividends, greater than 20-25% of the total outstanding shares, are considered a split-up effected in the form of a dividend and are recorded at the *par value* of the shares issued. The entry to record the dividend would charge retained earnings and credit common stock for the total par value of the shares issued. Additional paid-in capital would not be affected.

57. (a) Additional paid-in capital, increase; Retained earnings, decrease.
Small stock dividends, less than 20-25% of the total outstanding shares, are recorded at the fair market value of the shares issued as of the date of declaration. The entry to record the dividend would charge retained earnings for the fair market value of the shares issued, and credit common stock for the par value of the shares issued and APIC for the excess of market value over par value.

58. (b)

Total stockholders' equity	$160,000
Less: Preferred stock par	(50,000)
Preferred dividends in arrears	
(50,000 x 8% x 1)	(4,000)
Book value common stock	106,000
Common shares outstanding	÷ 8,900
Book value per share	$ 11.91

Common shares outstanding:	
Total issued (90,000 ÷ $10 par)	9,000
Less: Treasury stock	(100)
Shares outstanding	$8,900

59. (b) Dividends received in excess of an investor's share of the investee's earnings subsequent to the date of the investment are liquidating dividends and represent a return *of* investment. A liquidating dividend is recorded as a reduction of the investment.

60. (a) $1,000 dividend revenue (cash dividends received.)
Stock dividends usually do *not* constitute income to the recipient. Stock dividends reduce the investor's cost per share, as the investment cost ($72,000) is allocated to more shares (2,200 = 2,000 original plus 10% of 2,000).

61. (c) $24,000.

1998	Dividend in arrears ($6 per share x 2000 shares)	$12,000
1999	Current dividend	12,000
Total dividend income		$24,000

The 5% common stock dividend does not constitute income. Stock dividends merely reduce the cost per share (basis) of the investment in common stock.

62. (d) Dividend revenue would consist of the $8,000 dividend from Wren Corporation. This investment would be accounted for using the cost method as Simpson's percentage of ownership is less than 20% (assumption of no significant influence). Under the cost method dividends received are recorded as income.

Under the equity method of accounting for investments, dividends received are treated as a reduction of the investment carrying value (basis). Therefore, the $45,000 dividend from Brill Corp. would not be included in dividend revenue.

Stock dividends do not usually constitute income under either the cost or equity method of accounting for investments. Therefore, the 500 shares received as a stock dividend from Paul Corp. would not be included in dividend revenue.

63. (b) Debt securities that the entity has the **positive intent** and **ability** to hold to maturity are classified as "held-to maturity " and are reported at amortized cost.

64. (d) Debt and equity securities that are bought and held principally for the purpose of selling them in the near term are classified as trading securities and are reported at **fair value** with **unrealized holding gains and losses included in earnings.**

65. (a) $30,000. Marketable equity securities (equity securities with readily determinable fair values) are categorized as either trading securities (which are classified as current assets) or available-for-sale securities (which are classified as current or noncurrent assets), as appropriate. Because Ball's investments are long-term they are categorized as available-for-sale securities.

Available for sale securities are reported at fair value with unrealized holding gains and losses reported as a component of other comprehensive income. The $30,000 unrealized holding gain for 2000 would be included in the other comprehensive income which would be reported as a change in the balance of Accumulated Other Comprehensive Income, a separate element of equity and, therefore, included in a statement of changes in stockholders' equity.

Net unrealized holding gain at 12/31/00	
(Cost $150,000 vs. F.V. $160,000)	$10,000
Net unrealized holding loss @ 12/31/99	
(Cost $150,000 vs. F.V. $130,000)	20,000
Unrealized holding gain for 2000	$30,000

Alternative calculation:

F.V. @ 12/31/00	$160,000
F.V. @ 12/31/99	130,000
Unrealized holding gain for 2000	$ 30,000

66. (c) The unrealized holding loss for the trading securities ($25,000) is recognized in net income and reported on the income statement for the current period. However, the unrealized holding loss (that is temporary in nature) for the available for sale securities ($35,000) is reported as an element of other comprehensive income. This unrealized loss would **not** be included in the determination of net income or included on an "Income Statement". However, they could be included on a "**Statement of Income and Comprehensive Income**" if that alternative reporting format were used. The unrealized holding gains and losses reported in other comprehensive income are included in the balance of accumulated other comprehensive income reported in stockholders' equity.

67. (b) The noncurrent portfolio of marketable equity securities would be categorized as available-for-sale securities. Available-for-sale securities are reported at fair value with unrealized holding gains and losses reported as an element of other comprehensive income and are included in accumulated other comprehensive income in stockholders' equity until realized.

Realized gains and losses for securities classified as available for sale are reported in earnings of the period in which they occur.

68. (b) Held-to-maturity -- Amortized cost; Available-for-sale -- Fair value.

Under FAS #115, debt securities that the entity has the positive intent and ability to hold to maturity are classified as held-to-maturity securities and are reported as amortized cost.

Debt and equity securities not classified either as held-to-maturity or trading securities are classified as available-for sale securities and are reported at fair value, with unrealized holding gains and losses reported as an element of other comprehensive income and included in the balance of accumulated other comprehensive income reported in stockholders' equity.

69. (d) $116,250.

Long-term investments in marketable equity securities at fair value	$ 96,450
Plus: Net unrealized holding loss on long-term marketable equity securities	19,800
Cost of long-term investments in marketable equity securities	$116,250

Unrealized holding gains and losses on the non-current portfolio of investments in marketable equity securities (categorized as available for sale securities) are reported in other comprehensive income and included in the balance of accumulated other comprehensive income reported in stockholders' equity.

70. (a)

Sales price (2,000 shares × $14)	$28,000
Less: Brokerage commission	(1,400)
Net proceeds	$26,600
Less: Cost of investment	(31,500)
Realized loss on trading security	$(4,900)

If these securities had been categorized as available for sale, the total loss of $4,900 would have been recognized (in net income) as the prior year's unrealized holding loss would not have been included (recognized) in earnings (net income), but rather would have been reported as an element of other comprehensive income. A reclassification adjustment for the unrealized holding loss ($2,000) would also be included in other comprehensive income.

71. (b) $60,000 and $40,000.
Marketable equity securities (equity securities with readily determinable fair values) are categorized as either trading securities (which are classified as current assets) or available-for-sale securities (which are classified as current or noncurrent assets), as appropriate.

Because Lark's investments are long-term, they are categorized as available-for-sale securities.

Available for sale securities are reported at fair value with unrealized holding gains and losses reported in other comprehensive income and included in the balance of accumulated other comprehensive income reported in equity. The unrealized holding gain included in other comprehensive income for 2000 would be $60,000 ($240,000 current fair value vs. $180,000 prior period fair value). The net unrealized holding gain, included in the accumulated other comprehensive income as of December 31, 2000 is $40,000 ($60,000 current period unrealized holding gain less $20,000 prior period unrealized holding loss). Alternative calculation shown below.

Net unrealized holding gains at 12/31/00:

Fair value at 12/31/00	$240,000
Cost	200,000
Net unrealized holding gain	$ 40,000

72. (c) $40,000 current; $100,000 noncurrent.
Marketable equity securities (equity securities with readily determinable fair values) are categorized as either trading securities (which are classified as current assets) or available-for-sale securities (which are classified as current or noncurrent assets), as appropriate. Both trading and available-for-sale securities are reported at fair value. Therefore, the carrying value of both the current and noncurrent portfolios of marketable equity securities is the fair value of the portfolio, determined at the balance sheet date, and the valuation allowance, for both portfolios, is equal to the difference between the portfolio's aggregate cost and its aggregate fair value, at the balance sheet date.

The "aggregate lower of cost or market value, *applied to each security in the portfolio*" is irrelevant information.

73. (a) $0. Marketable equity securities categorized as available for sale may be classified as current or non-current as appropriate, and are reported at fair value with unrealized holding gains and losses reported in other comprehensive income and included in the balance of accumulated other comprehensive income reported in stockholders' equity. Therefore, transfer from the current to the noncurrent portfolio (or vice versa) of an available-for-sale security does not affect the reporting or accounting for the security.

Transfers of securities between categories (trading, available-for-sale, held-to-maturity) is accounted for at fair value, with the treatment of unrealized holding gains and losses dependent upon the categories transferred to and from.

74. (c) $80,000.

Proceeds from sale (8,000 shares × $30)	$240,000
Less cost (8,000 shares × $40)	– 320,000
Loss on sale of investment	$(80,000)

Marketable equity securities (equity securities with readily determinable fair values) categorized as available for sale are reported at fair value with unrealized holding gains and losses reported in other comprehensive income and included in the balance of accumulated other comprehensive income reported in stockholders' equity (excluded from earnings). As previously unrealized gains and losses have not been included (recognized) in earnings (net income), the gain or loss on the sale is the difference between the proceeds received and the original cost of the investment. A "reclassification adjustment" for the prior unrealized holding loss ($40,000 = 8,000 shares x $5 per share) would also be included in other comprehensive income for the year.

75. (d) Receipt of stock dividends does not constitute income nor a return of investment and therefore is not recorded under either the cost or equity method of accounting for investments in common stock. The cost of the shares previously held should be allocated to the total shares held after the receipt of a stock dividend or split.

76. (b) Since the decline in value occurred in 1999, the available-for-sale security was reduced to fair value with a related unrealized holding loss reported in other comprehensive income in 1999. In 2000, the asset continues to be carried at the same net value but the unrealized holding loss in accumulated other comprehensive income is removed and recognized as a loss in the determination of net income since the decline is considered to be permanent. The recognition of the loss (write-down to fair value) establishes a new cost basis which will **not** be changed for subsequent recoveries in fair value. However, subsequent unrealized holding gains and losses will be reported in other comprehensive income.

77. (d) $6,000. The valuation allowance related to the unrealized holding loss included in the income statement would be the valuation allowance for the portfolio of marketable equity securities categorized as trading securities. Unrealized holding gains and losses from a non-current portfolio of marketable equity securities (available for sale securities) are reported as an element of other comprehensive income in the reporting of comprehensive income. They would **not** be included in the determination of net income or included on an "Income Statement." However, they could be included on a "**Statement of Income and Comprehensive Income**" if that alternative reporting format were used.

The amount of the valuation allowance for the marketable equity securities categorized as trading securities would be $6,000 ($45,000 aggregate cost – $39,000 aggregate fair value). The reporting value of both the trading and available-for-sale marketable equity securities is their fair value determined at the balance sheet date.

The "aggregate lower of cost or market value *applied to each security* in the portfolio" is irrelevant information.

78. (d) Unrealized holding gains and losses from a non-current portfolio of marketable equity securities (available for sale securities) are reported as an element of other comprehensive income in the reporting of comprehensive income. They would **not** be included in the determination of net income or included on an "Income Statement." However, they could be included on a "**Statement of Income and Comprehensive Income**" if that alternative reporting format were used.

79. (a) $1,680,000 total stockholders' equity.

Common stock		$ 600,000
Additional paid-in capital		800,000
Total paid-in capital		$1,400,000
Retained earnings:		
Appropriated	$150,000	
Unappropriated	200,000	350,000
		$1,750,000
Less: Treasury stock at cost	$ 50,000	
Accumulated other comprehensive income	20,000	(70,000)
Total stockholders' equity		$1,680,000

80. (a) Retained earnings is decreased and a current liability for the cash dividend is recorded on the declaration date, January 15, 2000.

Chapter Two
Solutions to Stockholders' Equity Problems

NUMBER 1

Part a.

1. There are four basic rights inherent in ownership of common stock. The first right is that common shareholders may participate in the actual management of the corporation through participation and voting at the corporate stockholders meeting. Second, a common shareholder has the right to share in the profits of the corporation through dividends declared by the board of directors (elected by the common shareholders) of the corporation. Third, a common shareholder has a pro rata right to the residual assets of the corporation if it liquidates. Finally, common shareholders have the right to maintain their interest (percent of ownership) in the corporation if additional common shares are issued by the corporation, by being given the opportunity to purchase a proportionate number of shares of the new offering. This last is most commonly referred to as a "preemptive right".

2. Preferred stock is a form of capital stock that is afforded special privileges not normally afforded common shareholders in return for giving up one or more rights normally conveyed to common shareholders. The most common right given up by preferred shareholders is the right to participate in management (voting rights), and, in return, the corporation grants one or more preferences to the preferred shareholder. The most common preferences granted to preferred shareholders are these:

a. Dividends may be paid to common shareholders only after dividends have been paid to preferred shareholders.
b. Claim ahead of common shareholders to residual assets (after creditors have been paid) in the case of corporate liquidation.
c. Although the board of directors is under no obligation to declare dividends in any particular year, preferred shareholders may be granted a cumulative provision stating that any dividends not paid in a particular year must be paid in subsequent years before common shareholders may be paid any dividend.
d. Preferred shareholders may be granted a participation clause that allows them to receive additional dividends beyond their normal dividend if common shareholders receive dividends of greater percentage than preferred shareholders. This participation may be on a one-to-one basis (fully participating); common shareholders may be allowed to exceed the rate paid to preferred shareholders by a defined amount before preferred shareholders begin to participate; or, the participation clause may have a maximum rate of participation to which preferred shareholders are entitled.
e. Preferred shareholders may have the right to convert their preferred shares to common shares at a set future price no matter what the current market price of the common stock is.
f. Preferred shareholders may also agree to have their stock callable by the corporation at a higher price than when the stock was originally issued. This item is generally coupled with another preference item to make the issue appear attractive to the market.

Part b.

1. Treasury stock is stock previously issued by the corporation but subsequently repurchased by the corporation and not retired but available for use at a subsequent date by the corporation.

2. Legal capital is that portion of corporate capital required by statute to be retained in the business to afford creditors a minimum degree of protection.

3. A stock right represents a privilege extended by the corporation to acquire additional shares (or fractional shares) of its capital stock.

4. A stock warrant is physical evidence of stock rights. The warrant specifies the number of rights conveyed, the number of shares to which the rightholder is entitled, the price at which the rightholder may purchase the additional shares, and the life of the rights (time period over which the rights may be exercised).

NUMBER 2

1. Under the cost method, treasury stock is debited for the purchase price of the shares even though the purchase price is less than the par value.
Under the par value method, treasury stock is debited for the par value of the shares, and a separate paid-in capital account is credited for the excess of par value over the purchase price.

2. Under the cost method, treasury stock is debited for the purchase price of the shares.
Under the par value method, treasury stock is debited for the par value of the shares, and the debit for the excess of the purchase price over the par value is assigned to additional paid-in capital arising from past transactions in the same class of stock and/or retained earnings.

3. Under the cost method, treasury stock is credited for the original cost (purchase price) of the shares, and the excess of the original cost (purchase price) over the sales price first is debited to additional paid-in capital from earlier sales or retirements of treasury stock, and any remainder then is debited to retained earnings.

Under the par value method, treasury stock is credited for the par value of the shares, and the excess of the sales price over the par value is credited to additional paid-in capital from sale of treasury stock.

4. Under the cost method, treasury stock is credited for the original cost (purchase price) of the shares, and the excess of the sales price over the original cost (purchase price) is credited to additional paid-in capital from sale of treasury stock.

Under the par value method, treasury stock is credited for the par value of the shares, and the excess of the sales price over the par value is credited to additional paid-in capital from sale of treasury stock.

5. There is no effect on net income as a result of treasury stock transactions.

NUMBER 3

Fay, Inc.
STOCKHOLDERS' EQUITY SECTION OF BALANCE SHEET
December 31, 1997

Common stock, $10 par; 2,000,000 shares authorized; 840,000 shares issued; 829,500 shares outstanding		$ 8,400,000 [1]
Additional paid-in capital		2,485,000 [2]
Retained earnings		4,765,000 [3]
		15,650,000
Less: Accumulated other comprehensive income	$ 20,000 [4]	
Treasury stock, at cost, 10,500 shares	130,000 [5]	(150,000)
Total stockholders' equity		$15,500,000

Explanations of Amounts

		Date	Shares	Amount
[1]	Common stock issued			
	Balance	12/31/96	800,000	$8,000,000
	5% stock dividend issued	3/2/97	40,000	400,000
	Balance	12/31/97	840,000	$8,400,000

[2]	Additional paid-in capital	
	Balance, 12/31/96	$2,295,000
	Treasury stock reissued, 1/15/97 [$225,000 – $195,000 ($325,000 × 60%)]	30,000
	Stock dividend issued, 3/2/97 [($14 – $10) × 40,000 shares]	160,000
	Balance, 12/31/97	$2,485,000
[3]	Retained earnings	
	Balance, 12/31/96	$2,465,000
	Stock dividend issued, 3/2/97 ($14 × 40,000 shares)	(560,000)
	Net income for 1997	2,860,000
	Balance, 12/31/97	$4,765,000
[4]	Net unrealized loss on noncurrent marketable equity securities	
	Balance, 12/31/97 [($20 – $18) × 10,000 shares]	$ 20,000
[5]	Treasury stock at cost (10,000 ÷ 25,000 × $325,000)	$130,000

NUMBER 4

a. The subscription of common stock at a price in excess of the par value of the common stock is accounted for at the date of subscription as follows:

- Stock subscriptions receivable is debited for the subscription price of the common stock.
- Common stock subscribed is credited for an amount representing the par value of the common stock that will be issued when the stock subscription is collected.
- Additional paid-in capital is credited for the excess of the subscription price of the common stock over its par value.

b. The issuance for cash of no par value common stock at a price in excess of the stated value of the common stock is accounted for as follows:

- Cash is debited for the proceeds from the issuance of the common stock.
- Common stock is credited for the stated value of the common stock.
- Additional paid-in capital is credited for the excess of the proceeds from the issuance of the common stock over its stated value.

c. The date of declaration is the date when the liability for dividends payable is recorded by a debit to retained earnings and a credit to dividends payable.

The date of stockholders of record is the date that determines which stockholders will receive dividends on the payment date. No journal entry is made at this date.

The date of payment is the date when the dividends are paid and is recorded by a debit to dividends payable and a credit to cash.

d. The effect of an ordinary 10 percent common stock dividend is that an amount equal to the fair value of the additional common stock issued is transferred from retained earnings to common stock and additional paid-in capital. There is no effect on total stockholders' equity.

NUMBER 5

a.

Mart, Inc.
STATEMENT OF RETAINED EARNINGS
For the Year Ended December 31, 1999

Balance, December 31, 1998			
As originally reported			$3,250,000
Less prior period adjustment from error overstating inventories at December 31, 1998	$ 200,000		
Less income tax effect	60,000		140,000
As restated			3,110,000
Net income			2,250,000
			5,360,000
Deduct cash dividends on			
Preferred stock	450,000	[1]	
Common stock	2,480,000	[2]	2,930,000
Balance, December 31, 1999			$2,430,000

b.

Mart, Inc.
STOCKHOLDERS' EQUITY
December 31, 1999

Preferred stock, $50 par value, 9% cumulative, convertible; 250,000 shares authorized; 100,000 shares issued and outstanding			$ 5,000,000	
Common stock, $5 par value; 6,000,000 authorized; 2,500,000 shares issued, of which 10,000 shares are held in treasury			12,500,000	[3]
Additional paid-in capital			11,450,000	[4]
Retained earnings			2,430,000	
			31,380,000	
Less contra accounts:				
Common stock in treasury, 10,000 shares at cost	$160,000	[5]		
Accumulated other comprehensive income	50,000	[6]	210,000	
			$31,170,000	

c.

Mart, Inc.
COMPUTATION OF BOOK VALUE PER SHARE OF COMMON STOCK
December 31, 1999

Total stockholders' equity	$31,170,000
Deduct allocation to preferred stock, at liquidation value [100,000 shares × $55]	5,500,000
Allocation to common stock [Shares outstanding 2,490,000 (2,500,000 – 10,000)]	$25,670,000
Book value per share of common stock [$25,670,000 ÷ 2,490,000]	$10.31

Explanation of Amounts

[1] Preferred stock dividend

Par value of all outstanding preferred stock shares	$ 5,000,000
Dividend rate	9%
Dividends paid on preferred stock	$450,000

[2] Common stock dividend

Number of common stock shares outstanding, 12/31/98	2,000,000
Number of common stock shares issued, 4/30/99	500,000
Total common stock shares issued	2,500,000
Less: Treasury stock shares acquired 2/1/99	20,000
Shares outstanding, 7/1/99	2,480,000
Dividends paid (2,480,000 × $1)	$2,480,000

[3]

Common stock shares issued (see [2] above)	2,500,000
Par value per share	$5
Common stock at par value ($5 × 2,500,000)	$12,500,000

[4] Additional paid-in capital

Balance, December 31, 1998	$ 7,500,000
From issuance of stock:	
100,000 shares of preferred stock on 1/5/99 [100,000 × $4 ($54 – $50)]	400,000
500,000 shares of common stock on 4/30/99 [500,000 × $7 ($12 – $5)]	3,500,000
From sale of 10,000 shares of treasury stock on 11/6/99 [10,000 × $5 ($21 – $16)]	50,000
Balance, December 31, 1999	$11,450,000

[5] Common stock in treasury

	Shares	*Amount of cost*
Stock reacquired, 2/1/99	20,000	$320,000
Stock sold, 11/6/99	10,000	160,000
	10,000	$160,000

[6] Excess of cost of long-term marketable equity security

Cost of marketable equity security	$200,000
Fair market value of marketable equity security, 12/31/99 [$15 × 10,000 shares]	150,000
	$ 50,000

NUMBER 6

62.	$12,000.	Dividend Per share ($100 par x 6%)	$ 6
		x Number of shares outstanding	2,000
		Preferred stock dividends	12,000

63.	$165,000.	Number of common shares outstanding	
		Jan. 1 Beginning balance	100,000
		Feb. 1 Issued for Land	13,000
		Mar. 1 Treasury shares acquired	(5,000)
		Oct. 1 Treasury shares sold	2,000
		Shares outstanding	110,000
		Nov. 4 Declared cash dividend per share	x $1.50
		Cash dividend to common stockholders	$165,000

64. $720,000. Property dividends are recorded at their fair market value at the date of declaration (May 10).

65.	113,000.	Number of common shares issued:	
		Jan. 1 Beginning balance	100,000
		Feb. 1 Issued for land	13,000
		Total shares issued	113,000

Treasury stock is issued stock; however, it is not outstanding stock.

66.	$113,000.	Number of common shares issued	113,000
		Par value per share	x $1
		Amount of common stock issued	$113,000

67.	$934,000.	Additional paid-in capital:	
		Jan. 1. Beginning balance	$800,000
		Feb. 1 Shares issued for land	
		13,000 shares x ($11 - 1 par)	130,000
		Oct. 1 Reissued treasury shares	
		2,000 shares x ($16 - $14 cost)	4,000
		Dec. 31 Ending balance	$934,000

68.	$42,000.	Number of treasury shares	
		Mar. 1 Shares acquired	5,000
		Oct. 1 Shares reissued	(2,000)
		Dec. 31 Treasury shares	3,000
		Cost per share on Mar. 1	x $14
		Total cost of treasury stock @ December 31	$42,000

69.	$24.86.	Total stockholders' equity	12/31/99	$2,686,000
		Less: Preferred stock equity	12/31/99	(200,000)
		Common stock equity	12/31/99	$2,486,000
		# Common shares outstanding		÷ 100,000
		Book value per common share		$ 24.86

NUMBER 7

a. Brady should account for the purchase of the treasury stock on August 15, 2000, by debiting treasury stock and crediting cash for the cost of the purchase (1,000 shares × $12 per share). Brady should account for the sale of the treasury stock on September 14, 2000, by debiting cash for the selling price (500 shares × $14 per share), crediting treasury stock for cost (500 shares × $12 per share), and crediting additional paid-in capital from treasury stock transactions for the excess of the selling price over the cost (500 shares × $2 per share). The remaining treasury stock (500 shares × $12 per share) should be presented separately in the stockholders' equity section of Brady's December 31, 2000, balance sheet as an unallocated reduction of stockholders' equity. These shares are considered issued but not part of common stock outstanding.

b. Brady should account for the stock dividend by debiting retained earnings for $16 per share (the market value of the stock in October 2000, the date of the stock dividend) multiplied by the 2,000 shares distributed. Brady should then credit common stock for the par value of the common stock ($10 per share) multiplied by the 2,000 shares distributed, and credit additional paid-in capital for the excess of the market value ($16 per share) over the par value ($10 per share) multiplied by the 2,000 shares distributed. Total stockholders' equity does not change, but, because this is considered a small stock dividend, recognition has been made of a capitalization of retained earnings equivalent to the market value of the additional shares resulting from the stock dividend.

c. Brady should account for the cash dividend on December 20, 2000, the declaration date, by debiting retained earnings and crediting cash dividends payable for $1 per share multiplied by the number of shares outstanding. A cash dividend is a distribution to the corporation's stockholders. The liability for this distribution is incurred on the declaration date, and it is a current liability because it is payable within one year (January 10, 2001). The effect of the cash dividend on Brady's balance sheet at December 31, 2000, is an increase in current liabilities and a decrease in retained earnings.

NUMBER 8

a.

Computation of Cox's Goodwill
Implicit in the Terms of the Common Stock Issuance

Cash paid by Rice for 1,000 shares			$ 86,000
Contribution by Cox			
Current fair value of assets			
Cash	$ 16,500		
Accounts receivable	20,200		
Merchandise inventory	45,000		
Prepaid insurance	1,900		
Equipment	40,000		
		123,600	
Current fair value of liabilities assumed			
Accounts payable	30,500		
Note payable	10,000		
Loan payable, delivery van	3,500		
Interest payable	600		
Payroll taxes withheld and accrued	2,100		
		46,700	
Net contribution by Cox for 1,000 shares			76,900
Cox's goodwill			$ 9,100

b.

Cox Stationers, Inc.
BALANCE SHEET
January 1, 2000

Assets

Current Assets:			
Cash		$102,500	[1]
Accounts receivable	$23,500		
Less allowance for doubtful accounts	3,300	20,200	
Merchandise inventory		45,000	
Prepaid insurance		1,900	[2]
Total current assets		169,600	
Equipment		40,000	
Goodwill		9,100	
Total assets		$218,700	

Liabilities and Stockholders' Equity

Current Liabilities:		
Note payable, bank	$10,000	
Loan payable, delivery van	3,500	
Accounts payable	30,500	
Accrued interest	600	[3]
Payroll taxes withheld and accrued	2,100	
Total current liabilities	46,700	
Stockholders' Equity:		
Common stock, $50 par; authorized 7,500 shares; issued and outstanding 2,000 shares	100,000	
Additional paid-in capital	72,000	[4]
Total stockholders' equity	172,000	
Total liabilities and stockholders' equity	$218,700	

Explanations of Amounts:

[1] Cash

Balance, 12/31/99	$ 16,500
1/1/00, sale of common stock to Rice	86,000
Balance, 1/1/00	$102,500

[2] Prepaid insurance

Paid, 7/1/99	$ 3,800
Prepaid, 12/31/99 (× 1/2)	$ 1,900

[3] Accrued interest on note payable

Annual interest ($10,000 × 12%)	$ 1,200
July 1-December 31, 1999 (× 1/2)	$ 600

[4] Additional paid-in capital

Total assets	$218,700
Deduct liabilities	46,700
Total stockholders' equity	172,000
Deduct common stock (2,000 shares × $50)	100,000
Additional paid-in capital	$ 72,000

NUMBER 9

1. **T** Investments (debt or equity) bought and held principally for the purpose of selling them in the near term should be classified as trading securities.

2. **H** Investments in debt securities are classified as "held-to maturity " **only** if the entity has the **positive intent and ability** to hold the investment to maturity.

3. **A** Investments in debt or (marketable) equity securities not classified as trading securities or held-to-maturity securities are classified as available-for-sale. As the debt security is to be sold in 3 years it is not a trading security (near term sale) nor a held-to-maturity security.

4. **A** Equity securities (marketable) not classified as trading securities are classified as available-for-sale. As the stock is not intended to be sold in the near term, it is not a trading security. Equity securities can not be classified as held-to-maturity (no maturity date).

5. (G) $100,000. Held-to-maturity securities are reported at amortized cost. As the security was purchased at par or face value, its cost is amortized cost (no premium or discount to amortize).

6. (I) $155,000. Trading securities are reported at their fair market value as of the balance sheet date.

7. (J) $160,000. Available-for-sale securities are reported at their fair market value as of the balance sheet date.

8. (D) $15,000. **Loss** The gain or loss on available-for-sale securities is the difference between the cost of the security and its selling price.

Cost of GHI	$190,000
Selling price	175,000
Loss on sale	15,000

Previous unrealized holding gains and losses have not been recognized in income; the valuation allowance and unrealized holding gain/loss in accumulated other comprehensive income are equal and offset each other.

9. (B) $5,000. **Loss** The unrealized holding gain/loss recognized on the income statement relates to trading securities. As previous unrealized holding gains/loss have been recognized in income, the current unrealized holding gain or loss is the difference between its current fair value and its carrying value (prior fair value).

Fair value 12/31/99		$155,000
Carrying value		
Cost	$150,000	
Valuation allowance	10,000	
Fair value 12/31/98		160,000
Unrealized holding loss, 1999		$ (5,000)

10. (C) $10,000. **Loss** The (net) unrealized holding gain/loss related to available-for-sale securities is included in accumulated other comprehensive income reported in equity.

Fair market value, 12/31/99	$160,000
Cost	170,000
Unrealized holding loss	$ (10,000)

NOTES

(work practice questions here or jot down key concepts!)

Chapter Three
Inventories

Chapter Three
Inventories

DEFINITION

The term "inventory" designates tangible personal property, which is:
1. Held for sale in the ordinary course of business,
2. In process of production for such sale, or
3. To be currently consumed in production of goods and services to be available for sale.

MAJOR CATEGORIES

1. Merchandise—items purchased for resale
2. Raw Materials—materials on hand not yet placed into production
3. Supplies—manufacturing supplies only, others are prepaid expenses
4. Work in process—direct material, labor and overhead cost of unfinished units
5. Finished goods

The major objective of inventory accounting is proper income measurement through the process of matching costs against revenues. The inventory method used should be consistently applied. The primary basis of accounting for inventories is cost which is the price paid plus the direct or indirect cost of bringing the article to its existing condition or location.

METHODS OF INVENTORY MEASUREMENT

1. **Periodic Method.** The asset costs are accumulated in inventory and in related purchases accounts. The cost expiration is determined through use of a cost of goods sold account and is affected by the period change in the asset inventories. A physical inventory is necessary to prepare statements.

2. **Perpetual or Book Inventories.** The cost of goods sold can be determined with each sale or issuance of raw material to production. The physical inventory can be taken on a cycle basis with the objective of verifying the inventory records. A perpetual inventory system is costly to install and maintain.

3. **Gross Profit Method.** The gross profit method is used to estimate the inventory in situations in which it is not desirable or possible to take a physical inventory. It is used mostly for interim financial statements or in determining inventory in the event of a fire or other casualty. The gross profit method is **not** appropriate for year end financial reporting purposes as it does not provide for a "proper determination of the realized income"; an estimate of cost of goods sold and ending inventory is not adequate. The gross profit method does not provide for the taking or pricing (costing) of physical inventory on hand under any cost flow assumption.

Example:

Beginning inventory	$ 12,000
Sales	100,000
Gross profit percentage	25%
Purchases	80,000

Compute the ending inventory.

Sales	$100,000
Gross profit 25%	25,000
Cost of goods sold	$ 75,000

Beginning inventory	$ 12,000
Purchases	80,000
Cost of goods available for sale	$ 92,000
Less: Cost of goods sold	75,000
Ending inventory	$ 17,000

Problem: The Washington Company estimates the cost of its physical inventory at 3/31/X6 for use in an interim financial statement. The rate of markup **on cost** is 25%. The following account balances are available:

Inventory 3/1/X6	$160,000
Purchases during March	86,000
Purchase returns	4,000
Sales during March	140,000

The estimate of the cost of inventory at March 31 would be:

a. $137,000 b. $130,000 c. $112,000 d. $102,000

Answer: (b)

Cost of sales = $140,000 ÷ 1.25 = $112,000
Inventory at 3/31/X6 = $160,000 + $82,000 – $112,000 = $130,000

ADJUSTMENTS TO INVENTORY COST

1. **Cash Discounts.** Should be treated as a reduction of the cost of purchases. Because of the difficulty of associating a discount with a particular purchase, discounts are frequently treated as other income or as a reduction of purchases in the income statement. Theoretically, discounts are cost reductions since income cannot be generated by purchasing goods.

Discounts are usually handled in one of two ways in the accounts:

Use of "Discounts Lost" Account. (Net Price Method) In the use of a "discounts lost" account, it is assumed the discount will be taken and the amount originally recorded in purchases and accounts payable is net of the discount.

Example: Merchandise is purchased for $100 with terms of 2/10 net 30.

Journal Entry:

	Debit	Credit
Purchases	98	
A/P		98

Inventory recorded at cost less discount.

	Debit	Credit
A/P	98	
Cash		98

Payment for inventory within the discount period.

Assume in the above example that the payment is **not** made within the discount period and $100 must be remitted.

	Debit	Credit
A/P	98	
Discounts lost	2	
Cash		100

Inventory A/P paid—no discount taken.

The use of a discounts lost account has two advantages:

a. The inventory can be priced at cost less the discount. In most situations it is impossible to associate the discount with the inventory at a later date.

b. Management can evaluate the effectiveness of the company's handling of discounts. The "discounts lost" account discloses what has been **lost** in discounts not taken. The other method only shows the amount taken (not providing any indication or control of the discounts not taken).

Use of "Discounts" Account. (Gross Price Method) Same example as above.

Journal Entry:

	Dr.	Cr.
Purchases	100	
A/P		100

Inventory recorded at cost.

	Dr.	Cr.
A/P	100	
Discount		2
Cash		98

Payment made taking 2% discount.

If this method is used, discounts are deducted from purchases.

Problem: The use of a Discounts Lost account **implies** that the recorded cost of a purchased inventory item is its:

a. Invoice price
b. Invoice price plus the purchase discount lost.
c. Invoice price less the purchase discount taken.
d. Invoice price less the purchase discount allowable whether or not taken.

Answer: (d).

2. **Transportation Costs.** Should be added to inventory cost.

3. **Purchasing, Handling and Storage Costs.** These costs should also be added to inventory cost, but because of the difficulty of association, are usually expensed as period costs.

4. **Trade Discounts.** Trade discounts (also referred to as volume or quantity discounts) are discounts from a catalog or list price, used to establish a pricing policy and, therefore, do **not** enter into the accounting system. These discounts are usually stated as a percentage of the list price and are deducted from the list or catalog price to determine the recorded invoice price. Each discount applies to the net price computed after deducting the previous discount.

Example: Merchandise is purchased with a list price of $10,000 subject to trade discounts of 20%, 10% and 5%. The invoice price is calculated as follows:

List price	$10,000
Less 20% discount (20% × $10,000)	(2,000)
	$ 8,000
Less 10% discount (10% × $8,000)	(800)
	$ 7,200
Less 5% discount (5% × $7,200)	(360)
Invoice price before cash discount	$ 6,840

INVENTORY VALUATION METHODS

1. **Specific Identification**. Individual inventory lots purchased or manufactured are separately identified. When items are sold or otherwise disposed of, the actual cost of the specific item is assigned to the transaction and the ending inventory consists of the actual costs of the specific items on hand. Usually used for high cost items which are individually identifiable (autos, appliances, jewelry, etc.).

2. **Average Cost**. The average cost flow assumption assumes that all costs and units are merged (commingled) so that no specific item or cost can be separately identified. Both the cost of goods sold and ending inventory are valued at the average unit cost. The average cost method may be used with either the periodic or perpetual inventory system.

a) **Weighted Average—Periodic**: The cost of units is calculated at the end of the period based upon the average price paid (including freight, etc.), weighted by the number of units purchased at each price (the cost of goods available for sale divided by the number of units available for sale).

Illustration of Weighted Average

		Units	*Unit Cost*	*Total Cost*
1/1	Balance	200	$1.50	$ 300
1/5	Purchase	300	$1.60	480
1/15	Sold 400 units			
1/18	Purchase	200	$1.65	330
1/27	Purchase	300	$1.78	534
		1,000		$1,644

Weighted Average Unit Cost = $1,644 ÷ 1,000 units = $1.644 per unit
Ending inventory (600 units @ $1.644) $986.40

b) **Moving Average -- Perpetual**: The cost of units is calculated in the same manner as was used for weighted average except a new weighted average cost is calculated after each purchase. This average cost is used to determine the cost of each unit sold prior to the next purchase.

Illustration of Moving Average

	Total Cost	*Total Units*	*Average Cost*
1/1 Balance	$ 300	200	$1.50
1/5 Purchase			
(300 units @ $1.60 = $480)	$ 780	500	1.56
1/15 Sale			
(400 units @ $1.56 Av. = $624)	$ 156	100	1.56
1/18 Purchase			
(200 units @ $1.65 = $330)	$ 486	300	1.62
1/27 Purchase			
(300 units @ $1.78 = $534)	$1,020	600	1.70

Ending Inventory (600 units @ $1.70) $1,020.

3. **FIFO (First In, First Out)**: An assumption that goods are sold in the chronological order purchased. The ending inventory will consist of the last purchases made during the accounting period.

4. **LIFO (Last In, First Out)**: The last goods purchased are assumed to be sold. The ending inventory consists of the goods first purchased.

The use of LIFO and the techniques for its application stem from federal tax law and regulations. If it is used for either tax or financial statement purposes, it must be used for the other. Historically, LIFO was considered a "cost" method and, therefore, could not be used in conjunction with the lower of cost or market method of inventory valuation. In the early 1980's, federal tax rules re. conformity were relaxed **allowing** the application of LCM with LIFO for financial statement purposes (however, not for tax purposes). The use of LIFO for one type of inventory does not preclude the use of other methods for other inventory categories for either tax or financial statement purposes. You must obtain permission from the Internal Revenue Service to use the LIFO method and/or to change inventory methods.

(1) **Unit Based LIFO**. In the year of changeover to LIFO, the **beginning** inventory in the year of change must be restated. If permission is granted to change to LIFO in 19X2, the January 1, 19X2, inventory must be converted to weighted average and will become the BASE. Conversion to weighted average will mean that all units in the BASE will have the same cost.

For example:
Ending 19X1 inventory on a FIFO basis consisted of:

9/2	1,000 units @ $6.00	$ 6,000
10/15	2,000 units @ $7.00	14,000
11/20	1,000 units @ $8.00	8,000
12/15	1,000 units @ $7.00	7,000
	5,000 units	$35,000

Weighted average $7.00 per unit.

Normally, a LIFO inventory will consist of a base and **layers**, which we call LIFO layers, brought about by subsequent increases in inventory. We must concern ourselves with the valuation of these increases or, as they are sometimes called, increments. In our example, we revalued the beginning inventory of 19X2, the base, to weighted average. Assume that at the end of 19X2 the inventory has **increased** from 5,000 to 7,000 units with purchases during the year as follows:

	Units	*Unit Cost*	*Total*	
1/17	2,400	$7.25	$ 17,400	
2/22	4,600	$7.00	32,200	
6/30	2,000	$8.00	16,000	
7/27	2,500	$9.00	22,500	
10/28	1,500	$8.00	12,000	
	13,000		$100,000	Average $7.70

At this point, an election must be made to value increases in inventory by one of three methods:

1. **FIFO**		2. **LIFO**		3. **Weighted Average**
Purchases		Purchases		
10/28 1,500 @ $8 =	$12,000	1/17 2,000 @ $7.25 = $14,500		2,000 @ $7.70 = $15,400
7/27 500 @ $9 =	4,500			
LIFO LAYER	16,500		14,500	15,400
BASE	35,000		35,000	35,000
INV. VALUE	$51,500		$49,500	$50,400

Subsequent layers must be valued the same way once an election is made to value LIFO layers by any of the three methods. The question may reasonably be asked that--if this is a LIFO inventory method, why is it that increases can be valued by FIFO or weighted average? It is the layers that are valued on a LIFO basis rather than the value of the content of a particular layer or inventory increment. When there is a decrease in inventory, the last layer to be formed is the first to be costed out. Assume an inventory as follows:

1/1/X2	BASE	5,000 units @ $7.00	$35,000
12/31/X2	LAYER	2,000 units @ $7.70	15,400
12/31/X3	LAYER	3,000 units @ $8.00	24,000
12/31/X4	LAYER	1,000 units @ $9.00	9,000
		11,000	$83,400

On 12/31/X5, the inventory dropped to 8,500 units. The ending inventory would be valued at:

1/1/X2	BASE	5,000 units @ $7.00	$35,000
12/31/X2	LAYER	2,000 units @ $7.70	15,400
12/31/X3	LAYER	1,500 units @ $8.00	12,000
		8,500	$62,400

Once the base or a layer has been costed, i.e., charged to cost of goods sold, it is **permanently removed** from the inventory; however, see Chapter 12, Interim Financial Statements, for the treatment of the liquidation of base period inventories during an interim period.

Further, there are some who advocate maintaining the basic LIFO inventory intact even though a temporary liquidation has occurred at year-end. This is done by charging cost of goods sold with current costs and crediting the account, "Excess of Replacement Cost Over LIFO Cost of Basic Inventory Temporarily Liquidated," for that part of replacement cost in excess of LIFO cost. When the inventory is replenished, the "Excess ... " account is removed and the goods acquired replaced in inventory at their LIFO cost. The "Excess ... " account is a current liability.

(2) **Dollar Value LIFO**. As is characteristic of all LIFO methods, the dollar value LIFO inventory consists of a base, and layers when the inventory has increased during the period. In dollar value, however, the inventory is expressed in terms of dollars instead of units. This is necessary if LIFO is to be used in businesses in which units change from year to year and cannot be reduced to a common unit of measurement such as tons, bushels, barrels or cubic yards.

The first year inventory is the base and a price index is constructed from a sampling of inventory items to determine the price change in subsequent years in relation to the base. The price index is used to convert the subsequent year inventory to base year prices so that it can be determined if the inventory has increased. For example:

Assume that the Royster Appliance Company converted to dollar value LIFO on January 1, 19X2, and the inventory in subsequent years was as follows:

	Cost	*Index*
12/31/X1	$15,000	100
12/31/X2	16,800	105
12/31/X3	21,280	112
12/31/X4	22,680	126
12/31/X5	23,970	141
12/31/X6	30,000	150

To determine whether an increment has occurred, express the inventory in all years in terms of base year prices.

			Increase (Decrease)
19X1		$15,000	
19X2	$16,800 + 1.05 =	16,000	$ 1,000
19X3	21,280 + 1.12 =	19,000	3,000
19X4	22,680 + 1.26 =	18,000	(1,000)
19X5	23,970 + 1.41 =	17,000	(1,000)
19X6	30,000 + 1.50 =	20,000	3,000

The inventory by year would be computed as:

19X2	Base year	$15,000
	19X2 Increment $1,000 × 1.05	1,050
		$16,050
19X3	Base year	$15,000
	19X2 Increment	1,050
	19X3 Increment $3,000 × 1.12	3,360
		$19,410
19X4	Base year	$15,000
	19X2 Increment	1,050
	19X3 Increment after $1,000 of 19X3 layer is costed out $2,000 × 1.12	2,240
		$18,290
19X5	Base year	$15,000
	19X2 Increment	1,050
	19X3 Remaining $1,000 of 19X3 layer $1,000 × 1.12	1,120
		$17,170
19X6	Base year	$15,000
	19X2 Increment	1,050
	19X3 Increment	1,120
	19X6 Increment $3,000 × 1.50	4,500
		$21,670

What if you were given the inventory for 19X3, for example $21,280 and the 19X3 inventory in base year prices, but not the price index. You can construct your own index by dividing the base year inventory into the current year inventory.

$$\frac{\text{19X3 Inventory at X3 Prices \$21,280}}{\text{19X3 Inventory at Base Prices \$19,000}} = 1.12$$

5. **Retail Method**—An inventory method in which records are maintained at cost and retail. The method is used to maintain accountability and control of inventory assigned to retail units. Retail units are responsible for the retail price of goods on hand and goods shipped during the period, adjusted for price increases and decreases (markups and markdowns). The relationship of cost to retail is assumed to be the applicable ratio to apply to the ending inventory at retail to determine its cost. This is a valid assumption only if the relationship between cost and retail is relatively constant and that the mix of goods in the ending inventory is similar to that of goods included in the computation of the ratio. We can analyze the retail unit's responsibility in this way.

	Cost	*Retail*
Beginning inventory	X	X
+ Period shipments	X	X
+ Markups (price increases)		X
- Markdowns (price decreases)		(X)
Total responsibility for period	X	X
- Sales (deposited to the credit of company)		(X)
- Employee discounts, sales discounts		(X)
Book inventory at retail		X
Physical inventory at retail		X
Shrink		X

The retail units' book inventory under ideal conditions with no shrinkage, theft, spoilage or recording errors would be exactly the same as the physical at retail. The difference between the book inventory and the physical is called shrink or spoilage.

The retail inventory method may be applied on the basis of the Average, FIFO, and LIFO cost flow assumptions. The lower of cost or market method may also be used in conjunction with the retail method under these flow assumptions by excluding markdowns from the cost to retail ratio (refer to LIFO Method section regarding LIFO and L.C.M.)

Terminology:

Original Retail—Price at which goods first offered for sale.
Additional Markups—Additions that raise selling price above original retail.
Markdowns—Deductions that lower price below original retail.
Markup Cancellations—Deductions that do not decrease price below original retail.
Markdown Cancellations—Additions that do not increase price above original retail.
Net Markups—Additional markups minus markup cancellations.
Net Markdowns—Markdowns minus markdown cancellations.

Net markdowns are not used to determine the cost ratio if the retail method is used to approximate cost or market, whichever is lower.

The following information will be used to illustrate the various retail methods.

The Grand Department Store, Inc., uses the retail-inventory method to estimate ending inventory for its monthly financial statements. The following data pertain to a single department for the month of October:

Inventory, October 1:	
At cost	$17,000
At retail	30,000
Purchases (exclusive of freight and returns):	
At cost	100,151
At retail	146,495
Freight-in	5,100
Purchase returns:	
At cost	2,100
At retail	2,800
Additional markups	2,500
Markup cancellations	265
Markdowns (net)	5,000
Normal spoilage and breakage	3,000
Sales	132,930

- **Conventional Retail Method (Lower of Average Cost or Market)**

In conventional retail, markups are included as part of the cost ratio computation, but markdowns are excluded. This does not affect the computation of the ending inventory at retail, but does affect the cost ratio by reducing the percentage of cost to retail. The exclusion of markdowns in computing the ratio is a feature of conventional retail, its purpose being to approximate lower of cost or market. A more conservative inventory results.

Example:
Grand Department Stores, Inc.—Conventional Retail
(Lower of Average Cost or Market)

	At Cost	*At Retail*
Inventory, October 1	$ 17,000	$ 30,000
Purchases	100,151	146,495
Freight-In	5,100	—
Purchase Returns	(2,100)	(2,800)
Additional Markups	—	2,500
Markup Cancellations		(265)
Available for sale	120,151	175,930
Cost Ratio: $120,151 ÷ $175,930 = 68%		
Markdowns (Net)		(5,000)
Normal spoilage and breakage		(3,000)
Sales (Net)		(132,930)
Inventory, October 31, at retail		$ 35,000
Inventory, October 31, at lower of average cost or market (estimated) $35,000 × 68%	$ 23,800	

- **Average Cost Retail Method:** For a retail cost method both net markups and net markdowns are included in the cost to retail ratio. This has the effect of reducing the retail value (denominator) and increasing the cost percentage.

Example:
Grand Department Stores, Inc.—Average Cost Retail

	At Cost	*At Retail*
Inventory, October 1	$17,000	$ 30,000
Purchases	100,151	146,495
Freight-In	5,100	—
Purchase Returns	(2,100)	(2,800)
Additional Markups		2,500
Mark-up Cancellations		(265)
Net Markdowns		(5,000)
	$120,151	$170,930
Cost Ratio: $120,151 ÷ $170,930 = 70%		
Normal Spoilage and Breakage		(3,000)
Sales (Net)		(132,930)
Inventory, October 31 at Retail		$ 35,000
Inventory, October 31 at Average Cost $35,000 × 70%	$ 24,500	

Note that ending inventory at retail ($35,000) is the same as under conventional retail. The retail method selected does **not** affect the retail value of the ending inventory.

- **FIFO Cost Retail Method**: To compute FIFO Cost Retail, the beginning inventory is excluded from the cost to retail ratio calculation. The cost ratio is then applied to the ending inventory at retail to obtain the cost of the ending inventory.

Example:

Grand Department Stores, Inc.—FIFO Cost Retail

	At Cost	*At Retail*
Inventory, October 1	$ 17,000	$ 30,000
Purchases	$100,151	$146,495
Freight-In	5,100	—
Purchase Returns	(2,100)	(2,800)
Additional Markups	—	2,500
Markup Cancellations		(265)
Net Markdowns		(5,000)
Current Period Inventory	$103,151	$140,930
Cost Ratio: $103,151 ÷ $140,930 = 73%		
Total Available		170,930
Normal Spoilage and Breakage		(3,000)
Sales (Net)		(132,930)
Inventory, October 31 at retail		$ 35,000
Inventory, October 31, at FIFO Cost $35,000 × 73%	$ 25,550	

Note the following:

1. Net Markdowns and Markups are assumed to apply only to the current period's inventory.
2. The Ending Inventory at retail is the same as it was for the Average Cost Methods ($35,000).
3. The Ending Inventory at cost has been valued at the current period's cost ratio (FIFO flow).
4. Although beginning inventory is excluded from the ratio, it must be used to compute the ending inventory at retail.

- **Lower of FIFO Cost or Market Retail Method.** The lower of FIFO cost or market is computed the same way as FIFO cost except net markdowns would be excluded from the cost rates.

Example:

Grand Department Stores, Inc.—Lower of FIFO Cost or Market Retail

Referring to the Retail FIFO Cost Computation, the cost ratio would be computed as follows:

$$\text{Cost ratio} = \frac{\text{Current period cost}}{\text{Current period retail before net markdowns}} = \frac{103{,}151}{140{,}930 + 5{,}000} = 71\%$$

Inventory at October 31, Lower of FIFO Cost or Market
$35,000 × 71% — $24,850

- **LIFO Cost Retail Method:** As in other LIFO methods, retail LIFO consists of a base and layers. To compute LIFO cost retail, the beginning inventory is excluded from the cost to retail ratio calculation (as it was for FIFO). Remember, however, that the beginning inventory must be used to compute the ending inventory at retail. In LIFO retail the ending inventory at retail is compared with the beginning inventory at retail to determine if a layer has been added. If there is an increase, a LIFO layer is established and the current period cost ratio is applied only to that layer to determine its cost. The cost of the layer is then added to the cost of the beginning inventory to determine the cost of the ending inventory. If there is a decrease in ending inventory, the current period ratio is not applicable since there is no LIFO layer. The decrease is included in cost of goods sold on a LIFO basis, in that the latest layer formed is eliminated first.

Example:

Grand Department Stores, Inc.—LIFO Cost Retail

	At Cost	*At Retail*
Inventory, October 1	$ 17,000	$ 30,000
Purchases	$100,151	$146,495
Freight-In	5,100	—
Purchase Returns	(2,100)	(2,800)
Additional markups	—	2,500
Markup cancellations		(265)
Net Markdowns		(5,000)
Current period inventories	$103,151	$140,930
Cost ratio: $103,151 ÷ $140,930 = 73%		
Total available		170,930
Normal spoilage and breakage		(3,000)
Sales (net)		(132,930)
Inventory October 31 at retail		$35,000
Inventory October 31 at LIFO Cost		
Beginning inventory	$17,000	
Layer $5,000 × 73%	3,650	
	$20,650	

Note the following:
1) The ending inventory at retail is the same as it was under the other retail methods.
2) The current year cost to retail ratio is applied only to the increase in inventory at retail.
3) Similarity of set up with FIFO Cost Retail

- **Lower of LIFO Cost or Market Retail:** The lower of LIFO cost or market retail is computed the same as LIFO cost **except** net markdowns would be excluded from the cost ratio computation. (Refer to the section on LIFO method regarding application of L.C.M. with LIFO Cost).

Example:

Grand Department Stores, Inc.—Lower of LIFO Cost or Market Retail

Referring to the Retail LIFO cost computation, the cost ratio would be computed as follows:

$$\text{Cost ratio} = \frac{\text{Current period cost}}{\text{Current period retail before net markdowns}} = \frac{103{,}151}{140{,}930 + 5{,}000} = 71\%$$

Inventory @ October 31, Lower of LIFO Cost or Market

Base	$17,000
Layer $5,000 × 71%	3,550
	$20,550

Dollar Value LIFO Retail. Dollar Value is similar to LIFO retail except that the inventory layers contain an additional dimension; that is, the effect of changes in price levels. Inventory increase at retail can only be determined by converting current year inventory to base year prices. Inventory layers are then computed similar to LIFO retail except that price of the current year is used, such as: (Inventory at retail) × (cost/retail) × (price index).

Determination of Price Level Index in Dollar Value LIFO Retail—The price level index specifically relates to the inventory and is not a measure of general price levels as in price level accounting (sometimes called "replacement cost" accounting). The price index may be one internally generated or if a government index is available for the particular inventory, it may be used. The index must be suitable to convert the ending inventory to base year or at least previous year prices to determine if inventory quantities have increased.

Illustration of Dollar Value LIFO Retail

Procedure to be followed:

1. Compute the ending inventory at retail.
2. Restate the current year inventory in terms of base year prices. Divide the inventory into the base and layers to determine whether there is an increase in quantities.
3. Convert the base and layers into inventory price levels by use of the index and the cost to retail ratio.

Facts:

The James Company switched to dollar value LIFO retail on December 31, 19X1, at which time the inventory, using the dollar value LIFO retail inventory method, at retail was $166,000 and the cost/retail ratio was 76%. Inventory data for subsequent years are as follows:

Year	*Inventory at Respective Year-end Retail Prices*	*Price Index (Base Year 19X1)*	*Cost/Retail Ratio*
19X2	$186,560	106	72%
19X3	198,000	110	75%
19X4	218,500	115	78%
19X5	231,250	125	74%
19X6	264,000	132	73%

Computation of Inventories by Years

		Retail	*Ratio*	*Index*	*Total*
Base		$166,000	76%	100	$126,160
19X2 Layer	(1)	10,000	72%	106	7,632
19X3 Layer	(2)	4,000	75%	110	3,300
19X4 Layer	(3)	10,000	78%	115	8,970
19X5 Layer	(4)	(5,000)	78%	115	(4,485)
19X6 Layer	(5)	15,000	73%	132	14,454
Inventory at 12/31/X6 at cost					$156,031

(1) $186,560 ÷ 1.06 = $176,000 – $166,000 = $10,000

(2) $198,000 ÷ 1.10 = $180,000 – $176,000 = $ 4,000

(3) $218,500 ÷ 1.15 = $190,000 – $180,000 = $10,000

(4) $231,250 ÷ 1.25 = $185,000 – $190,000 = (5,000) decrease
Results in reduction of 19X4 layer—19X5 cost/retail ratio not applicable

(5) $264,000 ÷ 1.32 = $200,000 – $185,000 = $15,000

Illustrative Problem: Under your guidance as of January 1, 19X5, the Penny Wise Discount Store installed the retail method of accounting for its merchandise inventory. When you undertook the preparation of the store's financial statements at June 30, 19X5, the following data were available:

	Cost	*Selling Price*
Inventory, January 1	$26,900	$ 40,000
Markdowns		10,500
Markups		19,500
Markdown cancellations		6,500
Markup cancellations		4,500
Purchases	86,200	111,800
Sales		122,000
Purchase returns and allowances	1,500	1,800
Sales returns and allowances		6,000

Required:

a. Prepare a schedule to compute the Penny Wise Discount Store's June 30, 19X5, inventory under the retail method of accounting for inventories. The inventory is to be valued at cost under the LIFO method.

b. Without prejudice to your solution to part (a), assume that you computed the June 30, 19X5, inventory to be $44,100 at retail and the ratio of cost to retail to be 80%. The general price level has increased from 100 at January 1, 19X5, to 105 at June 30, 19X5.

Prepare a schedule to compute the June 30, 19X5, inventory at the June 30 price level under the dollar-value LIFO method.

Solution—Penny Wise Discount Store

a.

COMPUTATION OF INVENTORY AT LIFO COST UNDER THE RETAIL INVENTORY METHOD
June 30, 19X5

				Cost	*Selling Price*
Inventory, January 1				$ 26,900	$ 40,000
Add:	Purchases			86,200	111,800
	Less purchase returns and allowances			(1,500)	(1,800)
	Markups				19,500
	Less markup cancellations				(4,500)
Goods available for sale				$111,600	$165,000
Less:	Sales at retail		$122,000		
	Sales returns and allowances		6,000		
	Net sales		116,000		
	Markdowns	$10,500			
	Less markdown cancellations	6,500	4,000		120,000
Ending inventory at retail					$ 45,000
Inventory, January 1				$ 26,900	
Add LIFO Layer: [70% of ($45,000 – $40,000)]				3,500	
Inventory, June 30, at LIFO				$ 30,400	

Cost to Retail Ratio

$$\frac{\text{Net purchases at cost}}{\text{Net purchases at retail + net markups – net markdowns}} = \text{Cost to Retail Ratio}$$

$$\frac{\$86,200 - \$1,500}{\$111,800 - \$1,800 + \$19,500 - \$4,500 - \$10,500 + \$6,500} = 70\%$$

b.

COMPUTATION OF INVENTORY UNDER THE DOLLAR-VALUE LIFO COST METHOD
June 30, 19X5

Ending inventory at retail at January 1 price level (44,100 ÷ 1.05)	$42,000
Less beginning inventory at retail	40,000
Inventory increment at retail, January 1 price level	$ 2,000
Inventory increment at retail, June 30 price level ($2,000 × 1.05)	$ 2,100
Beginning inventory at cost	26,900
Inventory increment at cost at June 30 price level ($2,100 × .80)	1,680
Ending inventory at dollar-value LIFO cost	$28,580

LOWER OF COST OR MARKET

ARB 43 states that, "A departure from the cost basis of pricing the inventory is required when the utility of the goods is no longer as great as its cost. Where there is evidence that the utility of goods, in their disposal in the ordinary course of business, will be less than cost . . . the difference should be recognized as a loss of the current period. This is generally accomplished by stating such goods at a lower level commonly designated as market."

As used in the phrase "lower of cost or market", the term market means **current replacement cost** except that:

1. Market should not exceed the net realizable value (NRV) which is the selling price in the ordinary course of business less reasonably predictable costs of completion and disposal, and
2. Market should not be less than NRV reduced by an allowance for an approximately normal profit margin.

For example, assume a selling price of $1.

Selling price	$1.00
Cost of completion and disposal	.15
NRV—Upper limit	.85
Normal profit margin 20%	.20
Lower limit	$.65

This means that market cannot be greater than $.85, the upper limit, nor lower than $.65, the lower limit. Therefore, in determining LC/M compare replacement cost with the upper and lower limit, and

a. If the replacement cost falls between the upper and lower limit, use replacement cost as market.
b. If the replacement cost exceeds the upper limit, use upper limit as market.
c. If lower than the lower limit, use the lower limit.

Then compare market as determined above with cost to determine the inventory value. The lower of cost or market rules resulted from balance sheet conservatism and were modified by the upper and lower limit rules to assure that inventory losses will be taken in the current period and that excessive inventory writedowns cannot be taken which could result in increasing income in the next period. Consider as follows:

a. The upper limit will not allow the inventory item or group to be carried at more than selling price less the cost of completion and disposal. This forces losses into the current period.
b. The lower limit provides a floor that prevents the inventory item from generating a greater than normal profit margin in the next period.

The LC/M rules can be applied to inventory

a. item by item, or
b. components of each major category, or
c. the total inventory.

The basis of stating inventories should be consistently applied and since there are acceptable alternative methods, should be disclosed. An example of the application of the LC/M rules is as follows:

	Cost		*Selling*	*Cost to*	*Normal Profit*
Item	*Original*	*Replacement*	*Price*	*Complete and Sell*	*Margin*
1	$1.18	$1.27	$1.40	.13	.20
2	.69	.72	.98	.14	.30
3	1.90	1.62	2.40	.30	.40
4	.27	.25	.40	.06	.12
5	.90	.96	1.10	.22	.25

Determine the LC/M for the above items.

Solution:	*Item*	*Upper Limit*	*Lower Limit*	*Market*	*Cost*	*LC/M*
	1	$1.27	$1.07	$1.27	$1.18	$1.18
	2	.84	.54	.72	.69	.69
	3	2.10	1.70	1.70	1.90	1.70
	4	.36	.24	.25	.27	.25
	5	.88	.63	.88	.90	.88

STATEMENT OF INVENTORIES ABOVE COST

Only in exceptional cases may inventories be stated above cost. Items, such as precious metals, agricultural, mineral and other products, which are interchangeable and have an immediate marketability may justifiably be stated above cost. Where inventories are stated at sales prices, they should be reduced by expenses to be incurred in disposal.

TREATMENT OF INVENTORY LOSSES

Accrued net losses on firm purchase commitments for goods for inventory are measured in the same way as are inventory losses, and should, if material, be recognized in the accounts and the amounts thereof separately disclosed in the income statement (Statement 10, Inventory Pricing).

1. Illustration of Statement #10—Accrued net losses on firm purchase commitments for goods. On September 1, a purchase commitment is entered into for $40,000. On December 31 of the same year the current market price of such commitment is $25,000. The shipment arrives during January of the following year:

Entry 12/31	Loss on purchase commitments	15,000	
(current liability)	Est. liability on purchase commitments		15,000
Entry 1/21	Purchases	25,000	
	Est. liability on purchase commitments	15,000	
	Accounts payable		40,000

2. Assume that title to goods passed on September 1, 19X7, and delivery will not be made until February 1, 19X8.

9/1/X7	Purchases	40,000	(CGS)
	Accounts payable		40,000
12/31/X7	Loss on purchase commitment	15,000	
	Inventory		15,000

or no entry is necessary if the item is valued at lower of cost or market in the ending inventory.

General Rule: Statement 10 (consistent with FASB #5 re. contingencies) permits taking inventory losses on firm purchase commitments in the period of loss. However, inventory losses should not be anticipated, whereby one accounting period is charged with inventory losses anticipated in a subsequent accounting period. If a reserve for inventory losses is set up, it represents only an appropriation of retained earnings, and in no way should be used to absorb actual losses.

CONSIGNMENTS

As part of their marketing activities, some companies consign goods to others. In such cases, the consignor ships goods to the consignee who acts as an agent of the consignor and receives a commission when the goods are sold. It is, of course, the consignee's responsibility to remit payment for the goods sold on a periodic basis.

The consigned goods, therefore, are a part of the consignor's inventory until sold. Conversely, goods on consignment are not included in the consignee's inventory even though in the consignee's possession.

Goods should be included in inventory at purchase price or cost of production plus cost of shipping to the consignee. Usually, the shipping costs must be allocated to goods sold and unsold.

DEPLETION

Unit of Production Method (Accounting Method)

$$\frac{\text{Cost or value assigned to asset}}{\text{Number of recoverable units}}$$

Example: Assume that $150,000 is paid for mining property estimated to contain 500,000 tons of ore. The unit depletion charge would be $.30.

Depletion, as well as amortization of drilling and development, applicable to units not sold should be included in inventory. Consequently, depletion expense will apply only to units sold. Depletion cost, however, applies to all units extracted.

Percentage Depletion (Income Tax Method, not acceptable for accounting purposes)
Gross income × depletion percentage

Limitation: Depletion expense cannot exceed 50% of the taxable income from the property without the allowance for depletion.

Percentage depletion can be deducted without regard to cost of the property.

Cost Depletion Accounting
For accounting purposes (unit production method) depletion rates are adjusted as it becomes apparent that the recoverable deposit or growth is more or less than previously estimated.

The periodic depletion charge is credited to the Allowance for Depletion account. Assume that depletion cost for ore mined is $50,000, beginning inventory is $10,000 and ending inventory is $15,000.

Depletion Cost (cost of goods produced)	50,000	
Allowance for Depletion		50,000
To record depletion based on ore mined.		

At year end when the ending inventory has been determined:

Ending Inventory	15,000	
Beginning Inventory		10,000
Depletion Cost		5,000

To compute cost of goods sold: $50,000 – $5,000 = $45,000

Illustrative Problem:

Cost of land	$ 200,000
Development cost	150,000
Estimated tonnage	1,750,000

In the first year of operation 100,000 tons were sold for $3.00 a ton. Mining costs were $150,000 and administrative expenses were $75,000, and 125,000 tons were extracted. Prepare an income statement and compute the value of the ending inventory.

Solution:

Sales	100,000 × $3.00		$300,000
Cost of Goods Sold:			
Depletion	100,000 × $ .20	$ 20,000	
Extraction	100,000 × $1.20	120,000	140,000
Gross Profit			$160,000
Expenses			75,000
Net Income			$ 85,000

$$\frac{350{,}000}{1{,}750{,}000} = \$ .20 \text{ depletion cost}$$

$$\frac{150{,}000}{125{,}000} = \$1.20 \text{ extraction cost}$$

1.40 × 25,000 = $35,000

Chapter Three
Inventories Questions

1. When using the periodic-inventory method, which of the following generally would **not** be separately accounted for in the computation of cost of goods sold?

a. Trade discounts applicable to purchases during the period.
b. Cash (purchase) discounts taken during the period.
c. Purchase returns and allowances of merchandise during the period.
d. Cost of transportation-in for merchandise purchased during the period.

N90

2. The following information was derived from the 1989 accounting records of Clem Co.:

	Clem's central warehouse	*Clem's goods held by consignees*
Beginning inventory	$110,000	$12,000
Purchases	480,000	60,000
Freight in	10,000	
Transportation to consignees		5,000
Freight out	30,000	8,000
Ending inventory	145,000	20,000

Clem's 1989 cost of sales was

a. $455,000
b. $485,000
c. $507,000
d. $512,000

M93

3. The following items were included in Opal Co.'s inventory account at December 31, 1992:

Merchandise out on consignment, at sales price, including 40% markup on selling price	$40,000
Goods purchased, in transit, shipped f.o.b. shipping point	36,000
Goods held on consignment by Opal	27,000

By what amount should Opal's inventory account at December 31, 1992, be reduced?

a. $103,000
b. $67,000
c, $51,000
d. $43,000

Items 4 and 5 are based on the following:

During January 1993, Metro Co., which maintains a perpetual inventory system, recorded the following information pertaining to its inventory:

	Units	*Unit cost*	*Total cost*	*Units on hand*
Balance on 1/1/93	1,000	$1	$1,000	1,000
Purchased on 1/7/93	600	3	1,800	1,600
Sold on 1/20/93	900			700
Purchased on 1/25/93	400	5	2,000	1,100

4. Under the moving-average method, what amount should Metro report as inventory at January 31, 1993?

a. $2,640
b. $3,225
c. $3,300
d. $3,900

5. Under the LIFO method, what amount should Metro report as inventory at January 31, 1993?

a. $1,300
b. $2,700
c. $3,900
d. $4,100

M92

6. During periods of rising prices, when the FIFO inventory method is used, a perpetual inventory system results in an ending inventory cost that is

a. The same as in a periodic inventory system.
b. Higher than in a periodic inventory system.
c. Lower than in a periodic inventory system.
d. Higher or lower than in a periodic inventory system, depending on whether physical quantities have increased or decreased.

M90

7. On June 1, 1989, Pitt Corp. sold merchandise with a list price of $5,000 to Burr on account. Pitt allowed trade discounts of 30% and 20%. Credit terms were 2/15, n/40 and the sale was made FOB shipping point. Pitt prepaid $200 of delivery costs for Burr as an accommodation. On June 12, 1989, Pitt received from Burr a remittance in full payment amounting to

a. $2,744
b. $2,940
c. $2,944
d. $3,140

N95

8. A company decided to change its inventory valuation method from FIFO to LIFO in a period of rising prices. What was the result of the change on ending inventory and net income in the year of the change?

	Ending inventory	Net income
a.	Increase	Increase
b.	Increase	Decrease
c.	Decrease	Decrease
d.	Decrease	Increase

N87

9. A company records inventory at the gross invoice price. Theoretically, how should the following affect the costs in inventory?

	Warehousing costs	*Cash discounts available*
a.	Increase	Decrease
b.	No effect	Decrease
c.	No effect	No effect
d.	Increase	No effect

10. The acquisition cost of a heavily used raw material changes frequently. The book value of the inventory of this material at year-end will be the same if perpetual records are kept as it would be under a periodic inventory method only if the book value is computed under the

a. Weighted-average method.
b. First-in, first-out method.
c. Last-in, first-out method.
d. Base-stock method.

M92

11. Kahn Co., in applying the lower of cost or market method, reports its inventory at replacement cost. Which of the following statements are correct?

	The original cost is greater than replacement cost	*The net realizable value, less a normal profit margin, is greater than replacement cost*
a.	Yes	Yes
b.	Yes	No
c.	No	Yes
d.	No	No

12. On May 2, a fire destroyed the entire merchandise inventory on hand of Sanchez Wholesale Corporation. The following information is available:

Sales, Jan. 1 through May 2	$360,000
Inventory, January 1	80,000
Merchandise purchases, January 1 through May 2 (including $40,000 of goods in transit on May 2, shipped F.O.B. shipping point)	330,000
Markup percentage on cost	20%

What is the estimated inventory on May 2 immediately prior to the fire?

a. $70,000.
b. $82,000.
c. $110,000.
d. $122,000.

13. A company using a periodic inventory system neglected to record a purchase of merchandise on account at year end. This merchandise was omitted from the year-end physical count. How will these errors affect assets, liabilities, and stockholders' equity at year end and net earnings for the year?

	Assets	*Liabilities*	*Stock-holders' Equity*	*Net Earnings*
a.	No effect	understate	overstate	overstate
b.	No effect	overstate	understate	understate
c.	Understate	understate	no effect	no effect
d.	Understate	no effect	understate	understate

14. Jamison Corporation's inventory cost on its statement of financial position was **lower** using first-in, first-out than last-in, first-out. Assuming **no** beginning inventory, what direction did the cost of purchases move during the period?

a. Up.
b. Down.
c. Steady.
d. **Cannot** be determined.

15. Moore Corporation has two products in its ending inventory, each accounted for at the lower of cost or market. A profit margin of 30% on selling price is considered normal for each product. Specific data with respect to each product follows:

	Product #1	*Product #2*
Historical cost	$17.00	$ 45.00
Replacement cost	15.00	46.00
Estimated cost to dispose	5.00	26.00
Estimated selling price	30.00	100.00

In pricing its ending inventory using the lower of cost or market, what unit values should Moore use for products #1 and #2 respectively?

a. $15.00 and $44.00.
b. $16.00 and $44.00.
c. $16.00 and $45.00.
d. $17.00 and $46.00.

N94

16. Bren Co.'s beginning inventory at January 1, 1993, was understated by $26,000, and its ending inventory was overstated by $52,000. As a result, Bren's cost of goods sold for 1993 was

a. Understated by $26,000.
b. Overstated by $26,000.
c. Understated by $78,000.
d. Overstated by $78,000.

N90

17. Ashe Co. recorded the following data pertaining to raw material X during January 1990:

Date	Received	Cost	Issued	On hand
1/1/90				
Inventory		$8.00		3,200
1/11/90				
Issue			1,600	1,600
1/22/90				
Purchase	4,800	$9.60		6,400

(Units: Received, Issued, On hand)

The moving-average unit cost of X inventory at January 31, 1990, is

a. $8.80
b. $8.96
c. $9.20
d. $9.60

N90

18. The retail inventory method includes which of the following in the calculation of both cost and retail amounts of goods available for sale?

a. Purchase returns.
b. Sales returns.
c. Net markups.
d. Freight in.

19. The Gunther Company acquired a tract of land containing an extractable natural resource. Gunther is required by its purchase contract to restore the land to a condition suitable for recreational use after it has extracted the natural resource. Geological surveys estimate that the recoverable reserves will be 4,000,000 tons, and that the land will have a value of $1,000,000 after restoration. Relevant cost information follows:

Land	$9,000,000
Estimated restoration costs	1,200,000

If Gunther maintains no inventories of extracted material, what should be the charge to depletion expense per ton of extracted material?

a. $2.00.
b. $2.25.
c. $2.30.
d. $2.55.

N91

20. Thread Co. is selecting its inventory system in preparation for its first year of operations. Thread intends to use either the periodic weighted average method or the perpetual moving average method, and to apply the lower of cost or market rule either to individual items or to the total inventory. Inventory prices are expected to generally increase throughout 1991, although a few individual prices will decrease. What inventory system should Thread select if it wants to maximize the inventory carrying amount at December 31, 1991?

	Inventory method	*Cost or market application*
a.	Perpetual	Total inventory
b.	Perpetual	Individual item
c.	Periodic	Total inventory
d.	Periodic	Individual item

21. Assuming **no** beginning inventory, what can be said about the trend of inventory prices if cost of goods sold computed when inventory is valued using the FIFO method exceeds cost of goods sold when inventory is valued using the LIFO method?

a. Prices decreased.
b. Prices remained unchanged.
c. Prices increased.
d. Price trend **cannot** be determined from information given.

M93

22. On December 1, 1992, Alt Department Store received 505 sweaters on consignment from Todd. Todd's cost for the sweaters was $80 each, and they were priced to sell at $100. Alt's commission on consigned goods is 10%. At December 31, 1992, 5 sweaters remained. In its December 31, 1992, balance sheet, what amount should Alt report as payable for consigned goods?

a. $49,000
b. $45,400
c. $45,000
d. $40,400

M92

23. Anders Co. uses the moving-average method to determine the cost of its inventory. During January 1992, Anders recorded the following information pertaining to its inventory:

	Units	Unit cost	Total cost
Balance on 1/1/92	40,000	$5	$200,000
Sold on 1/17/92	35,000		
Purchased on 1/28/92	20,000	8	160,000

What amount of inventory should Anders report in its January 31, 1992, balance sheet?

a. $200,000
b. $185,000
c. $162,500
d. $150,000

M92

24. Hutch, Inc., uses the conventional retail inventory method to account for inventory. The following information relates to 1991 operations:

	Average Cost	Retail
Beginning inventory and purchases	$600,000	$920,000
Net markups		40,000
Net markdowns		60,000
Sales		780,000

What amount should be reported as cost of sales for 1991?

a. $480,000
b. $487,500
c. $520,000
d. $525,000

25. The Good Trader Company values its inventory by using the retail method (FIFO basis, lower of cost or market). The following information is available for the year 19X8.

	Cost	Retail
Beginning inventory	$ 80,000	$140,000
Purchases	297,000	420,000
Freight-in	4,000	
Shortages	—	8,000
Markups (net)	—	10,000
Markdowns (net)	—	2,000
Sales	—	400,000

At what amount would The Good Trader Company report its ending inventory?

a. $112,000.
b. $113,400.
c. $117,600.
d. $119,000.

26. The double extension method and the linkchain method are two variations of which of the following inventory cost flow methods?

a. Moving average.
b. FIFO.
c. Dollar value LIFO.
d. Conventional (lower of cost or market) retail.

M95

27. During 1994, Kam Co. began offering its goods to selected retailers on a consignment basis. The following information was derived from Kam's 1994 accounting records:

Beginning inventory		$122,000
Purchases		540,000
Freight in		10,000
Transportation to consignees		5,000
Freight out		35,000
Ending inventory	- held by Kam	145,000
	- held by consignees	20,000

In its 1994 income statement, what amount should Kam report as cost of goods sold?

a. $507,000
b. $512,000
c. $527,000
d. $547,000

M90

28. On October 20, 1989, Grimm Co. consigned 40 freezers to Holden Co. for sale at $1,000 each and paid $800 in transportation costs. On December 30, 1989, Holden reported the sale of 10 freezers and remitted $8,500. The remittance was net of the agreed 15% commission. What amount should Grimm recognize as consignment sales revenue for 1989?

a. $7,700
b. $8,500
c. $9,800
d. $10,000

N91

29. On December 28, 1990, Kerr Manufacturing Co. purchased goods costing $50,000. The terms were F.O.B. destination. Some of the costs incurred in connection with the sale and delivery of the goods were as follows:

Packaging for shipment	$1,000
Shipping	1,500
Special handling charges	2,000

These goods were received on December 31, 1990. In Kerr's December 31, 1990, balance sheet, what amount of cost for these goods should be included in inventory?

a. $54,500
b. $53,500
c. $52,000
d. $50,000

M91

30. Kew Co.'s accounts payable balance at December 31, 1990, was $2,200,000 before considering the following data:

- Goods shipped to Kew F.O.B. shipping point on December 22, 1990, were lost in transit. The invoice cost of $40,000 was not recorded by Kew. On January 7, 1991, Kew filed a $40,000 claim against the common carrier.

- On December 27, 1990, a vendor authorized Kew to return, for full credit, goods shipped and billed at $70,000 on December 3, 1990. The returned goods were shipped by Kew on December 28, 1990. A $70,000 credit memo was received and recorded by Kew on January 5, 1991.

- Goods shipped to Kew F.O.B. destination on December 20, 1990, were received on January 6, 1991. The invoice cost was $50,000.

What amount should Kew report as accounts payable in its December 31, 1990, balance sheet?

a. $2,170,000
b. $2,180,000
c. $2,230,000
d. $2,280,000

M93

31. The following information pertains to Deal Corp.'s 1992 cost of goods sold:

Inventory, 12/31/91	$ 90,000
1992 purchases	124,000
1992 write-off of obsolete inventory	34,000
Inventory, 12/31/92	30,000

The inventory written off became obsolete due to an unexpected and unusual technological advance by a competitor. In its 1992 income statement, what amount should Deal report as cost of goods sold?

a. $218,000
b. $184,000
c. $150,000
d. $124,000

32. Dixon Menswear Shop regularly buys shirts from Colt Company and is allowed trade discounts of 20% and 10% from the list price. Dixon purchased shirts from Colt on May 27, and received an invoice with a list price amount of $5,000, and payment terms of 2/10, n/30. Dixon uses the net method to record purchases. Dixon should record the purchase at

a. $3,600
b. $3,528
c. $3,500
d. $3,430

M95

33. Walt Co. adopted the dollar-value LIFO inventory method as of January 1, 1994, when its inventory was valued at $500,000. Walt's entire inventory constitutes a single pool. Using a relevant price index of 1.10, Walt determined that its December 31, 1994, inventory was $577,500 at current year cost, and $525,000 at base year cost. What was Walt's dollar-value LIFO inventory at December 31, 1994?

a. $525,000
b. $527,500
c. $552,500
d. $577,500

N90

34. The replacement cost of an inventory item is below the net realizable value and above the net realizable value less the normal profit margin. The original cost of the inventory item is below the net realizable value less the normal profit margin. Under the lower of cost or market method, the inventory item should be valued at

a. Net realizable value.
b. Net realizable value less the normal profit margin.
c. Original cost.
d. Replacement cost.

35. For external reporting purposes, it is appropriate to use estimated gross profit rates to determine the cost of goods sold for

	Interim financial reporting	*Year-end financial reporting*
a.	Yes	Yes
b.	Yes	No
c.	No	Yes
d.	No	No

M93

36. Moss Co. has determined its December 31, 1992, inventory on a FIFO basis to be $400,000. Information pertaining to that inventory follows:

Estimated selling price	$408,000
Estimated cost of disposal	20,000
Normal profit margin	60,000
Current replacement cost	360,000

Moss records losses that result from applying the lower of cost or market rule. At December 31, 1992, what should be the net carrying value of Moss' inventory?

a. $400,000
b. $388,000
c. $360,000
d. $238,000

N94

37. Mare Co.'s December 31, 1993, balance sheet reported the following current assets:

Cash	$ 70,000
Accounts receivable	120,000
Inventories	60,000
Total	$250,000

An analysis of the accounts disclosed that accounts receivable consisted of the following:

Trade accounts	$ 96,000
Allowance for uncollectible accounts	(2,000)
Selling price of Mare's unsold goods out on consignment, at 130% of cost, **not** included in Mare's ending inventory	26,000
Total	$120,000

At December 31, 1993, the total of Mare's current assets is

a. $224,000
b. $230,000
c. $244,000
d. $270,000

M93

38. On January 1, 1992, Card Corp. signed a three-year, noncancelable purchase contract, which allows Card to purchase up to 500,000 units of a computer part annually from Hart Supply Co. at $.10 per unit and guarantees a minimum annual purchase of 100,000 units. During 1992, the part unexpectedly became obsolete. Card had 250,000 units of this inventory at December 31, 1992, and believes these parts can be sold as scrap for $.02 per unit. What amount of probable loss from the purchase commitment should Card report in its 1992 income statement?

a. $24,000
b. $20,000
c. $16,000
d. $8,000

M90

39. Union Corp. uses the first-in, first-out retail method of inventory valuation. The following information is available:

	Cost	*Retail*
Beginning inventory	$12,000	$ 30,000
Purchases	60,000	110,000
Net additional markups		10,000
Net markdowns		20,000
Sales revenue		90,000

If the lower of cost or market rule is disregarded, what would be the estimated cost of the ending inventory?

a. $24,000
b. $20,800
c. $20,000
d. $19,200

N94

40. Which of the following statements are correct when a company applying the lower of cost or market method reports its inventory at replacement cost?

I. The original cost is less than replacement cost.
II. The net realizable value is greater than replacement cost.

a. I only
b. II only.
c. Both I and II.
d. Neither I nor II.

N94

41. Herc Co.'s inventory at December 31, 1993, was $1,500,000 based on a physical count priced at cost, and before any necessary adjustment for the following:

- Merchandise costing $90,000, shipped FOB shipping point from a vendor on December 30, 1993, was received and recorded on January 5, 1994.

- Goods in the shipping area were excluded from inventory although shipment was not made until January 4, 1994. The goods, billed to the customer FOB shipping point on December 30, 1993, had a cost of $120,000.

What amount should Herc report as inventory in its December 31, 1993, balance sheet?

a. $1,500,000
b. $1,590,000
c. $1,620,000
d. $1,710,000

N90

42. How should the following costs affect a retailer's inventory?

	Freight in	*Interest on inventory loan*
a.	Increase	No effect
b.	Increase	Increase
c.	No effect	Increase
d.	No effect	No effect

43. Which of the following inventory cost flow methods involves computations based on broad inventory pools of similar items?

a. Regular quantity of goods LIFO.
b. Dollar-value LIFO.
c. Weighted average.
d. Moving average.

M90

44. The balance in Kemp Corp.'s accounts payable account at December 31, 1989, was $900,000 before any necessary year-end adjustment relating to the following:

- Goods were in transit to Kemp from a vendor on December 31, 1989. The invoice cost was $50,000. The goods were shipped F.O.B. shipping point on December 29, 1989, and were received on January 4, 1990.
- Goods shipped F.O.B. destination on December 21, 1989, from a vendor to Kemp were received on January 6, 1990. The invoice cost was $25,000.
- On December 27, 1989, Kemp wrote and recorded checks to creditors totaling $40,000 that were mailed on January 10, 1990.

In Kemp's December 31, 1989, balance sheet, the accounts payable should be

a. $940,000
b. $950,000
c. $975,000
d. $990,000

45. Dalton Company adopted the dollar value LIFO inventory method on January 1, 1990. In applying the LIFO method Dalton uses internal price indexes and the multiple-pools approach. The following data were available for Inventory Pool No. 1 for the two years following the adoption of LIFO:

	Current inventory		*Internal*
	At current year cost	*At base year cost*	*price index*
1/1/90	$100,000	$100,000	1.00
12/31/90	126,000	120,000	1.05
12/31/91	140,800	128,000	1.10

Under the dollar value LIFO method the inventory at December 31, 1991, should be

a. $128,000
b. $129,800
c. $130,800
d. $140,800

46. The following balances were reported by Mall Co. at December 31, 1991 and 1990:

	12/31/91	*12/31/90*
Inventory	$260,000	$290,000
Accounts payable	75,000	50,000

Mall paid suppliers $490,000 during the year ended December 31, 1991. What amount should Mall report for cost of goods sold in 1991?

a. $545,000
b. $495,000
c. $485,000
d. $435,000

47. When the double extension approach to the dollar value LIFO inventory cost flow method is used, the inventory layer added in the current year is multiplied by an index number. How would the following be used in the calculation of this index number?

	Ending inventory at current year cost	*Ending inventory at base year cost*
a.	Numerator	Denominator
b.	Numerator	Not Used
c.	Denominator	Numerator
d.	Not Used	Denominator

48. The original cost of an inventory item is below the net realizable value and above the net realizable value less a normal profit margin. The inventory item's replacement cost is below the net realizable value less a normal profit margin. Under the lower of cost or market method, the inventory item should be valued at

a. Original cost.
b. Replacement cost.
c. Net realizable value.
d. Net realizable value less normal profit margin.

49. Dart Company's accounting records indicated the following information:

Inventory, 1/1/86	$ 500,000
Purchases during 1986	2,500,000
Sales during 1986	3,200,000

A physical inventory taken on December 31, 1986, resulted in an ending inventory of $575,000. Dart's gross profit on sales has remained constant at 25% in recent years. Dart suspects some inventory may have been taken by a new employee. At December 31, 1986, what is the estimated cost of missing inventory?

a. $25,000
b. $100,000
c. $175,000
d. $225,000

50. At December 31, 1988, the following information was available from Huff Co.'s accounting records:

	Cost	*Retail*
Inventory, 1/1/88	$147,000	$ 203,000
Purchases	833,000	1,155,000
Additional markups	—	42,000
Available for sale	$980,000	$1,400,000

Sales for the year totaled $1,106,000. Markdowns amounted to $14,000. Under the approximate lower of average cost or market retail method, Huff's inventory at December 31, 1988, was

a. $308,000
b. $280,000
c. $215,600
d. $196,000

51. In January 1991 Huff Mining Corporation purchased a mineral mine for $3,600,000 with removable ore estimated by geological surveys at 2,160,000 tons. The property has an estimated value of $360,000 after the ore has been extracted. Huff incurred $1,080,000 of development costs preparing the property for the extraction of ore. During 1991, 270,000 tons were removed and 240,000 tons were sold. For the year ended December 31, 1991, Huff should include what amount of depletion in its cost of goods sold?

a. $360,000
b. $405,000
c. $480,000
d. $540,000

Recently Released Questions

52. The following information pertained to Azur Co. for the year:

Purchases	$102,800
Purchase discounts	10,280
Freight-in	15,420
Freight-out	5,140
Beginning inventory	30,840
Ending inventory	20,560

What amount should Azur report as a cost of goods sold for the year?

a. $102,800
b. $118,220
c. $123,360
d. $128,500

Chapter Three
Inventories Problems

NUMBER 1

The Jericho Variety Store uses the LIFO retail inventory method. Information relating to the computation of the inventory at December 31, 19X5 follows:

	Cost	*Retail*
Inventory, January 1, 19X5	$ 29,000	$ 45,000
Purchases	120,000	172,000
Freight-in	20,000	
Sales		190,000
Net markups		40,000
Net markdowns		12,000

Required:
Assuming that there was no change in the price index during the year, compute the inventory at December 31, 19X5 using the LIFO cost retail inventory method.

NUMBER 2 consists of three unrelated parts.

Part a. The Frate Company was formed on December 1, 19X8. The following information is available from Frate's inventory records for Product Ply:

	Units	*Unit Cost*
January 1, 19X9 (beginning inventory)	800	$ 9.00
Purchases:		
January 5, 19X9	1,500	$10.00
January 25, 19X9	1,200	$10.50
February 16, 19X9	600	$11.00
March 26, 19X9	900	$11.50

A physical inventory on March 31, 19X9, shows 1,600 units on hand.

Required:
Prepare schedules to compute the ending inventory at March 31, 19X9, under each of the following inventory methods:

1. FIFO.
2. LIFO.
3. Weighted average.

Show supporting computations in good form.

Part b. The Red Department Store uses the retail inventory method. Information relating to the computation of the inventory at December 31, 19X8, is as follows:

	Cost	*Retail*
Inventory at January 1, 19X8	$ 32,000	$ 80,000
Sales		600,000
Purchases	270,000	590,000
Freight in	7,600	
Markups		60,000
Markup cancellations		10,000
Markdowns		25,000
Markdown cancellations		5,000

Estimated normal shrinkage is 2% of sales.

Required:
Prepare a schedule to calculate the estimated ending inventory at the lower of average cost or market at December 31, 19X8, using the retail inventory method. Show supporting computations in good form.

Part c. On November 21, 19X8, a fire at Hodge Company's warehouse caused severe damage to its entire inventory of Product Tex. Hodge estimates that all usable damaged goods can be sold for $10,000. The following information was available from Hodge's accounting records for Product Tex:

Inventory at November 1, 19X8	$100,000
Purchases from November 1, 19X8, to date of fire	140,000
Net sales from November 1, 19X8, to date of fire	220,000

Based on recent history, Hodge had a gross margin (profit) on Product Tex of 30% of net sales.

Required:
Prepare a schedule to calculate the estimated loss on the inventory in the fire, using the gross margin (profit) method. Show supporting computations in good form.

NUMBER 3

In order to effect an approximate matching of current costs with related sales revenue, the last-in, first-out (LIFO) method of pricing inventories has been developed.

Required:

a. Describe the establishment of and subsequent pricing procedures for each of the following LIFO inventory methods:
   1. LIFO applied to units of product when the periodic inventory system is used.
   2. Application of the dollar-value method to a retail LIFO inventory or to LIFO units of product (these applications are similar).

b. Discuss the specific advantages and disadvantages of using the dollar-value-LIFO applications. **Ignore income tax considerations.**

c. Discuss the general advantages and disadvantages claimed for LIFO methods. **Ignore income tax considerations.**

NUMBER 4

M90

Huddell Company, which is both a wholesaler and retailer, purchases merchandise from various suppliers FOB destination, and incurs substantial warehousing costs.

The dollar value LIFO method is used for the wholesale inventories.

Huddell determines the estimated cost of its retail ending inventories using the conventional retail inventory method, which approximates lower of average cost or market.

Required:

a. When should the purchases from various suppliers generally be included in Huddell's inventory? Why?

b. How should Huddell account for the warehousing costs? Why?

c. 1. What are the advantages of using the dollar value LIFO method as opposed to the traditional LIFO method?
   2. How does the application of the dollar value LIFO method differ from the application of the traditional LIFO method?

d. 1. In the calculation of the cost to retail percentage used to determine the estimated cost of its ending retail inventories, how should Huddell use
      - Net markups?
      - Net markdowns?
   2. Why does Huddell's retail inventory method approximate lower of average cost or market?

NUMBER 5

The Acute Company manufactures a single product. On December 31, 19X5, Acute adopted the dollar-value LIFO inventory method. The inventory on that date using the dollar-value LIFO inventory method was determined to be $300,000.

Inventory data for succeeding years are as follows:

Year Ended December 31,	*Inventory at Respective Year-End Prices*	*Relevant Price Index (base year 19X5)*
19X6	$363,000	1.10
19X7	420,000	1.20
19X8	430,000	1.25

Required:
Compute the inventory amounts at December 31, 19X6, 19X7 and 19X8, using the dollar-value LIFO inventory method for each year.

NUMBER 6

Retail, Inc., sells normal brand name household products both from its own store and on consignment through The Mall Space Company.

Required:

a. Should Retail, Inc., include in its inventory normal brand name goods purchased from its suppliers but not yet received if the terms of purchase of FOB shipping point (manufacturer's plant)? Why?

b. Should Retail, Inc., include freight-in expenditures as an inventoriable cost? Why?

c. Retail, Inc., purchased cooking utensils for sale in the ordinary course of business three times during the current year, each time at a higher price than the previous purchase. What would have been the effect on ending inventory and cost of goods sold had Retail, Inc., used the weighted-average cost method instead of the FIFO method?.

d. How and why will Retail, Inc., treat net markdowns when it calculates the estimated cost of ending inventory using the conventional (lower of cost or market) retail inventory method?

e. What are products on consignment and how should they be presented on the balance sheets of Retail, Inc., and The Mall Space Company?

NUMBER 7

M91

Happlia Co. imports expensive household appliances. Each model has many variations and each unit has an identification number. Happlia pays all costs for getting the goods from the port to its central warehouse in Des Moines. After repackaging, the goods are consigned to retailers. A retailer makes a sale, simultaneously buys the appliance from Happlia, and pays the balance due within one week.

To alleviate the overstocking of refrigerators at a Minneapolis retailer, some were reshipped to a Kansas City retailer where they were still held in inventory at December 31, 1990. Happlia paid the costs of this reshipment.

Happlia uses the specific identification inventory costing method.

Required:

a. In regard to the specific identification inventory costing method
   1. Describe its key elements.
   2. Discuss why it is appropriate for Happlia to use this method.

b. 1. What general criteria should Happlia use to determine inventory carrying amounts at December 31, 1990? Ignore lower of cost or market considerations.
   2. Give four examples of costs included in these inventory carrying amounts.

c. What costs should be reported in Happlia's 1990 income statement? Ignore lower of cost or market considerations.

NUMBER 8 *M93*

Blaedon Co. makes ongoing design refinements to lawnmowers that are produced for it by contractors. Blaedon stores the lawnmowers in its own warehouse and sells them at list price, directly to retailers. Blaedon uses the FIFO inventory method. Approximately two-thirds of new lawnmower sales involve trade-ins. For each used lawnmower traded in and returned to Blaedon, retailers receive a $40 allowance regardless of whether the trade-in was associated with a sale of a 1992 or 1993 model. Blaedon's net realizable value on a used lawnmower averages $25.

At December 31, 1992, Blaedon's inventory of new lawnmowers includes both 1992 and 1993 models. When the 1993 model was introduced in September 1992, the list price of the remaining 1992 model lawnmowers was reduced below cost. Blaedon is experiencing rising costs.

Required:

a. At December 31, 1992, how should Blaedon determine the carrying amounts assigned to its lawnmower inventory of
   1. 1993 models?
   2. 1992 models?

b. Considering only the 1993 model lawnmower, explain the impact of the FIFO cost flow assumptions on Blaedon's 1992
   1. Income statement amounts.
   2. Balance sheet amounts.

NUMBER 9

Taylor Company, a household appliance dealer, purchases its inventories from various suppliers. Taylor has consistently stated its inventories at the lower of cost (FIFO) or market.

Required:

a. Taylor is considering alternate methods of accounting for the cash discounts it takes when paying its suppliers promptly. From a theoretical standpoint, discuss the acceptability of each of the following methods:
   1. Financial income when payments are made.
   2. Reduction of cost of goods sold for period when payments are made.
   3. Direct reduction of purchase cost.

b. Identify the effects on both the balance sheet and the income statement of using the LIFO inventory method instead of the FIFO method over a substantial time period when purchase prices of household appliances are rising. State why these effects take place.

c. Why is the lower of cost-or-market rule used for valuing inventories when the FIFO method is used?

NUMBER 10 *M89*

Steel Company, a wholesaler that has been in business for two years, purchases its inventories from various suppliers. During the two years, each purchase has been at a lower price than the previous purchase.

Steel uses the lower of FIFO cost or market method to value inventories. The original cost of the inventories is above replacement cost and below the net realizable value. The net realizable value less the normal profit margin is below the replacement cost.

Required:

a. In general, what criteria should be used to determine which costs should be included in inventory?

b. In general, why is the lower of cost or market rule used to report inventory?

c. At what amount should Steel's inventories be reported on the balance sheet? Explain the application of the lower of cost or market rule in this situation.

d. What would have been the effect on ending inventories and net income for the second year had Steel used the lower of average cost or market inventory method instead of the lower of FIFO cost or market inventory method? Why?

NUMBER 11

M94

York Co. sells one product, which it purchases from various suppliers. York's trial balance at December 31, 1993, included the following accounts:

Sales (33,000 units @ $16)	$528,000
Sales discounts	7,500
Purchases	368,900
Purchase discounts	18,000
Freight-in	5,000
Freight-out	11,000

York Co.'s inventory purchases during 1993 were as follows:

	Units	*Cost per unit*	*Total cost*
Beginning inventory, January 1	8,000	$8.20	$65,600
Purchases, quarter ended March 31	12,000	8.25	99,000
Purchases, quarter ended June 30	15,000	7.90	118,500
Purchases, quarter ended September 30	13,000	7.50	97,500
Purchases, quarter ended December 31	7,000	7.70	53,900
	55,000		$434,500

Additional information:

York's accounting policy is to report inventory in its financial statements at the lower of cost or market, applied to total inventory. Cost is determined under the last-in, first-out (LIFO) method.

York has determined that, at December 31, 1993, the replacement cost of its inventory was $8 per unit and the net realizable value was $8.80 per unit. York's normal profit margin is $1.05 per unit.

Required:

a. Prepare York's schedule of cost of goods sold, with a supporting schedule of ending inventory. York uses the direct method of reporting losses from market decline of inventory.

b. Explain the rule of lower of cost or market and its application in this situation.

Chapter Three
Solutions to Inventories Questions

1. (a) Answers (b)-(d), cash discounts, purchase returns and allowances, and cost of transportation-in all occur after the actual purchase and would be accounted for separately in cost of goods sold. Trade discounts are deducted from a list price in arriving at the price charged the buyer and recorded on the purchase invoice and would not be recorded separately.

2. (d) $512,000

	Warehouse	*Consignees*	*Total*
Beginning inventory	$110,000	$12,000	$122,000
Purchases	480,000	60,000	540,000
Freight-in	10,000	—	10,000
Transportation to consignees	—	5,000	5,000
Cost of goods available for sale			$677,000
Less: Ending inventory	145,000	20,000	(165,000)
Cost of goods sold			$512,000

Consigned goods are a part of the consignor's inventory until sold. Inventory out on consignment is valued at cost plus the cost of shipping to the consignee. Freight-out is a selling expense.

3. (d) Opal's inventory must be reduced by the following:

• The 40% markup on selling price included in merchandise out on consignment (40% × $40,000)	$16,000
• Goods held on consignment which are not part of Opal's inventory	27,000
Total reduction to inventory	$43,000

4. (b) Using the moving average method, a recalculated average cost is computed with each purchase as follows:

	Units	*Cost*	*Total Units*	*Total Cost*	*Average per Unit*
1/1/93	1,000	$1,000	1,000	$1,000	$1.00
1/7/93	600	1,800	1,600	2,800	1.75
1/20/93	(900)	(1,575)*	700	1,225	1.75
1/25/93	400	2,000	1,100	3,225	2.93

*900 units @ $1.75 average cost = $1,575.

Sale of units on January 20 does not affect the moving-average cost, therefore, the moving-average unit cost after the sale is the same as before the sale, $1.75.

5. (b) Using LIFO, the inventory account appears as follows:

	Units	*Cost per Unit*	*Cost*	*Total Units*	*Balance*
1/1/93	1,000	$1.00	$1,000	1,000	$1,000
1/7/93	600	3.00	1,800	1,600	2,800
1/20/93	(600)	3.00	(1,800)		
	(300)	1.00	(300)	700	700
1/25/93	400	5.00	2,000	1,100	2,700

The units sold on 1/20 would be 600 units from the 1/7 purchase and 300 units from the 1/1/ balance.
The ending inventory consists of:

700	units @ $1 =	$ 700	from the 1/1 balance
400	units @ $5 =	2000	from the 1/25 purchase
1100	units	$2700	

6. (a) Under the FIFO method, the cost of the oldest purchases are charged to cost of goods sold and the costs of the most current purchases are assigned to ending inventory. Therefore, the costs assigned to ending inventory and cost of goods sold are the same when a periodic or perpetual inventory system is used with the FIFO cost flow assumption.

7. (c)

List price	$5,000
Less 30% trade discount (30% × $5,000)	– 1,500
	$3,500
Less 20% trade discounts (20% × $3,500)	– 700
Gross sales revenue	$2,800
Less 2% cash discount (2% × $2,800)	– 56
Net sales revenue	$2,744
Add: Burr's delivery costs paid by Pitt	+ 200
Total payment due within discount period	$2,944

Trade discounts are discounts from catalog or list prices used to establish a pricing policy and, therefore, do not enter into the accounting system. (They are deducted prior to arriving at the invoice price.) Each discount applies to the net price computed **after** deducting the previous discount. The delivery costs are appropriately the responsibility of Burr as the merchandise was shipped F.O.B. shipping point.

8. (c) The LIFO inventory method assumes the last unit acquired is the first unit sold. Therefore, during periods of rising prices, LIFO would result in lower ending inventory valuations (earlier purchases constitute inventory), higher cost of goods sold and lower net income than the FIFO inventory method.

9. (a) Theoretically, warehousing costs increase inventory cost and cash discounts (whether taken or not taken) decrease inventory cost. Frequently, these items are difficult to associate with inventory and are therefore expensed or ignored in costing ending inventory.

10. (b) Under the FIFO method, the cost of the oldest purchases is matched with current revenue and the cost of the most current purchases remains in ending inventory. This would result in a book value for inventory under a perpetual system which would be the same as that of the physical inventory taken under a periodic inventory method.

11. (b) In applying the lower of cost or market method, market is defined as current replacement cost, except that:

Upper limit: Market is not to exceed net realizable value (estimated selling price less costs of completion and disposal).
Lower limit: Market should not be less than net realizable value less a normal profit margin.

If, under the *lower* of cost or market method, inventory is reported at replacement cost, it is the market value, and must be less than the original cost and greater than the net realizable value less a normal profit margin (the lower limit on market).

12. (c)

Inventory, 1/1	$ 80,000
Plus: Purchases	330,000
Good available for sale	$410,000
Less: Cost of goods sold ($360,000 ÷ 120%)	300,000
Estimated inventory, 5/2	$110,000

Note: Although the estimated inventory is $110,000, the estimated fire loss would be $70,000 because of the $40,000 of goods in transit included in inventory.

13. (c) If the purchase was omitted from both inventory and accounts payable, both the assets and liabilities will be understated. Because the two errors offset each other, there will be no effect on stockholders' equity and net earnings.

14. (b) If the inventory balance was lower using FIFO than LIFO, then prices during the period were moving downward. By using FIFO during such a period, the higher-priced items are costed out first with lower-priced goods remaining in the ending inventory.

15. (c) Market is defined as current replacement cost, except that:

Upper Limit: Market is not to exceed net realizable value (estimated selling price less costs of completion and disposal).

Lower Limit: Market should not be less than net realizable value reduced by a normal profit margin.

	Product #1	*Product #2*
Selling price	$30.00	$100.00
Less: Cost to dispose	5.00	26.00
Net realizable value (upper limit)	25.00	74.00
Profit margin	9.00	30.00
Lower limit	$16.00	$44.00
Market value	$16.00	$46.00
Cost	17.00	45.00
Lower cost/market	16.00	45.00

16. (c) When beginning inventory is understated, cost of goods sold will be understated by the same amount. When ending is overstated, cost of goods sold will be understated in an equal amount. Therefore, the effect of both of these errors is to understate cost of goods sold by $78,000 ($26,000 + $52,000).

17. (c) $9.20

Inventory 1/11	1,600 units @ $8.00* =	$12,800
Purchase 1/22	4,800 units @ $9.60 =	46,080
	6,400 units	$58,880

Moving average unit cost @ 1/31 = $58,880/6,400 units
= $9.20 per unit

* Sale of unit on January 11 does not affect the moving-average cost; therefore, the moving-average unit cost after the sale is the same as before the sale, $8.00 per unit.

18. (a) Beginning inventory, purchases, and purchase returns are included in the calculation of both cost and retail amounts of goods available for sale in the retail inventory method.

Answer (b) is incorrect, as sales returns is an adjustment of sales, and neither are used in the computation of goods available for sale.

Answer (c) is incorrect as net markups affect only the retail value, and answer (d) is incorrect as freight-in affects only the cost value of goods available for sale.

19. (c) $2.30

Costs:	Land	$ 9,000,000
	Restoration	1,200,000
		10,200,000
Less:	Salvage	1,000,000
		$ 9,200,000
Divided by recoverable reserves		4,000,000 tons
Depletion per ton		$2.30

20. (a) As inventory prices are expected to generally increase during the year, the perpetual inventory system would maximize the inventory carrying value at the end of the period. Under a perpetual inventory system cost of goods sold (used in production) is determined at the time of each sale (issuance of materials to production). Therefore, it would provide for the earlier, lower costs to be transferred out of inventory and the ending inventory to be costed with the later, higher costs.

Application of the lower of cost or market rule to the total inventory would maximize the inventory carrying value at the end of the year, as total inventory cost would be compared with total inventory market value and price increases would offset price decreases. Lower of cost or market applied to individual items given the most conservative (lowest) inventory carrying amount as price increases for some items are not allowed to offset price declines for other items.

21. (a) FIFO-based cost of goods sold contains earlier unit costs and LIFO-based cost of goods sold contains more recent unit costs. Higher cost of goods sold under FIFO indicates that the earlier unit costs were larger than the more recent unit costs, and this is attributable to the fact that prices have decreased.

22. (c) The liability for consigned merchandise is recorded when the merchandise is sold. Since 500 sweaters have been sold, the amount due is the selling price less the 10% commission, or $100 – $10 = $90 × 500 sweaters = $45,000.

23. (b) $185,000 cost of inventory.

Inventory 1/17 (40,000 – 35,000)	5,000 units @ $5 =	$ 25,000 *
Purchase 1/28	20,000 units @ $8 =	160,000
	25,000 units	$185,000

* Sale of units on January 17 does not affect the moving-average cost, therefore, the moving-average unit cost after the sale is the same as before the sale, $5 per unit.

Moving average unit cost at January 31 would be:
$185,000 total cost/25,000 units = $7.40 per unit

24. (d) $525,000 cost of goods sold.

	Cost	*Retail*
Beginning inventories and purchases	$600,000	$920,000
Net markups		40,000
Available for sale	$600,000	$960,000
Cost/retail ratio $600,000/960,000 = .625		
Less: Net markdowns		(60,000)
Sales		(780,000)
Ending inventory at retail		$120,000
Ending inventory at cost ($120,000 × .625)	75,000	
Cost of goods sold	$525,000	

Conventional retail is the lower of *average* cost or market. For a lower of cost or market retail method, net markdowns are excluded from the cost to retail ratio.

25. (a)

	Cost	Retail
Purchases	$297,000	$420,000
Freight-in	4,000	—
Mark-ups	—	10,000
Current period values	$301,000	$430,000
Beginning inventory		140,000
Shortages		(8,000)
Mark-downs		(2,000)
Sales		(400,000)
Ending inventory at retail		$160,000

Current period cost ratio = $301,000 ÷ 430,000 = 70%
Ending inventory, FIFO cost 70% × $160,000 = $112,000

As method is the lower of FIFO cost or market, markdowns are excluded from the cost ratio computation, and the cost ratio computation is made for the current period purchases as it constitutes the ending inventory under FIFO.

Note that if the ending inventory at retail were greater than $430,000, a portion of the beginning inventory would be used, and its cost ratio would be used for its costing.

26. (c) Dollar value LIFO uses price indexes, by year, to compute the increase or decrease in LIFO layers during the period. "Double-extension" and "Chain-link" methods are techniques of computing price indexes for the valuation of inventory. Under "Chain-link", the current price index is computed in relation to the prior period index; under "Double-extension" the current price index is computed in relation to a base year.

27. (b) $512,000. Consigned goods are part of the consignor's inventory until sold. Inventory out on consignment is valued at cost, including the cost of shipping the goods to the consignee. Freight-out is a selling expense.

Beginning inventory		$122,000
Add: Purchases		540,000
Freight-in		10,000
Transportation to consignee		5,000
Cost of goods available for sale		$677,000
Less: Ending inventory:		
on Hand	145,000	
at Consignees	20,000	(165,000)
		$512,000

28. (d) $10,000 = 10 units sold × $1,000 sales price per unit.
Consigned goods are a part of the consignor's inventory until sold, and are valued at cost plus the cost of shipping to the consignee. The consignee acts only as an agent of the consignor and receives a commission when the goods are sold. As the goods were reported sold in December, the consignor (Grimm Co.) would recognize sales revenue of $10,000 and related commission expense of $1,500 ($10,000 × 15%) in December. The cost of goods sold for these units would include $200 ($800 ÷ 40 units = $20 per unit × 10 units sold) of the transportation costs.

29. (d) Title to goods shipped "FOB Destination" transfers to the purchaser when the goods are delivered to the buyer's destination. Costs of transportation and costs while in transit are expenses of the seller, and would not affect the "cost" to the buyer.

30. (a) $2,170,000.

Accounts payable before adjustment	$2,200,000
Add: Goods in transit—FOB shipping point	40,000
Less: Purchase returns in transit	(70,000)
Accounts payable—December 31, 1990	$2,170,000

Title to goods shipped "FOB Shipping Point" transfers to the purchaser at the shipping point when the seller delivers them to a common carrier, which is acting as an agent for the buyer. Such goods, in transit, would be included in the purchaser's inventory and the associated liability included in its accounts payable. Title to goods shipped "FOB Destination" transfers to the purchaser when the goods are delivered to the buyer's destination. Such goods in transit would not be recorded by the purchaser. They are properly included in the seller's inventory.

31. (c)

Beginning balance	$ 90,000
Add: Purchases	124,000
Less: Loss on obsolete inventory	(34,000)
Available for sale	$180,000
Less: Ending inventory	(30,000)
Cost of goods sold	$150,000

32. (b)

List Price	$5,000
Less: Trade discounts	
20% × $5,000	(1,000)
	$4,000
10% × $4,000	(400)
Gross Purchase (Invoice) price	$3,600
Less: Cash discount	
2% × 3,600	72
Net Purchase (Invoice) price	$3,528

Trade discounts are discounts from catalog or list prices used to establish a pricing policy and, therefore, do not enter into the accounting system. (They are deducted prior to arriving at the invoice price.) Each discount applies to the net price computed **after** deducting the previous discount. Under the net price method, purchases are recorded net of any cash discount.

33. (b) $527,500.

Dec 1994 Inventory @ Base Year Cost	$525,000
Jan 1994 Inventory @ Base Year Cost	500,000
1994 Layer	25,000
1994 Price index	× 1.10
1994 Layer @ current (1994) cost	$ 27,500
Jan 1994 Base Layer	500,000
Total inventory Dec 1994	$527,500

34. (c) Original cost. Replacement cost is "market" as it does not exceed the upper limit (net realizable value) and is not less than the lower limit (net realizable value less a normal profit margin). Because original cost is less than "market" (replacement cost), it would be used to value the inventory item.

35. (b) The use of estimated gross profit rates (gross profit method) to determine cost of goods sold for interim reports is appropriate per APB 28 paragraph .14a. However, the method used and any significant adjustments that result from reconciliation with the **annual physical inventory** should be disclosed. The gross profit method is **not** appropriate for year end reporting (Per ARB 43 paragraph 4 and statement 4) as it does not provide for a "proper determination of the realized income;" an estimate of cost of goods sold and ending inventory is not adequate. "The inventory at any given date is the balance of cost applicable to goods in hand remaining after the matching of absorbed costs with current revenues—cost for inventory purposes may be determined under any one of several (flow) assumptions—the major objective in selecting a method should be to choose the one which—most clearly

reflects periodic income." The gross profit method is inappropriate as it does not provide for the taking or pricing of physical inventory on hand under any flow assumption.

36. (c) The inventory would be valued at $360,000, the "market" (replacement cost) as it is lower than the $400,000 FIFO cost.

Replacement cost, $360,000, is "market" as it is:

a) not greater than the upper limit, $388,000 net realizable value ($408,000 selling price – $20,000 cost of disposal); and
b) not less than the lower limit, $328,000 ($388,000 net realizable value – $60,000 normal profit).

37. (c) $244,000. Goods (inventory) out on consignment remain the property of the consignor and must be included in their inventory at cost (including freight charges to transport to the consignee).

Current assets as reported		$250,000
Less unrealized profit on consigned goods		
Selling price of consigned goods	26,000	
Cost of consigned goods (26,000 ÷ 1.3)	20,000	(6,000)
		$244,000

38. (c)

Minimum purchase commitment per year	100,000	units
Years remaining on contract (3–1 for 1992)	× 2	
Minimum total commitment under contract	200,000	units
Probable loss per unit ($.10 cost per unit – $.02 scrap value per unit)	× $.08	
Loss on purchase commitment	$16,000	

39. (a)

	Cost	*Retail*
Purchases	$60,000	$110,000
Net additional markup	—	10,000
Net markdowns	—	(20,000)
Current period value	$60,000	$100,000
Beginning inventory		30,000
Sales		(90,000)
Ending inventory at retail		$ 40,000

Current period cost ratio—$60,000 ÷ $100,000 = 60%
Ending inventory at FIFO cost—$40,000 × 60% = $24,000

As the method is FIFO cost (not L.C.M.) net markdowns are included in the cost ratio computation, and the cost ratio computation is made for the current period purchases as it constitutes the ending inventory under the FIFO method.

Note that if the ending inventory at retail were greater than $100,000, a portion of the beginning inventory would be used, and its cost ratio would be used for its costing.

40. (b) When inventory is reported at replacement cost using the lower of cost or market method, replacement cost is "market" and it is less than the original cost. Therefore, statement I is incorrect.

Under the lower of cost of market method, replacement cost is market provided it is less than the net realizable value (upper limit) and greater than net realizable value less a normal profit (lower limit). Therefore, statement II is correct.

41. (d) $1,710,000

Inventory before adjustments	$1,500,000
Add: Purchase in-transit FOB shipping point	90,000
Add: Goods not shipped to customers	120,000
	$1,710,000

42. (a) Inventory or inventoriable cost should include all reasonable and necessary costs of preparing inventory for sale. These costs include the purchase price of the inventories, and other costs associated with readying inventories for sale, for example, freight-in.

Interest, on an inventory loan or otherwise, is a period cost and expensed in the period incurred. Interest is not an inventoriable cost.

43. (b) Under the dollar value LIFO method, inventory items are grouped into "pools" of similar types of material or use for the computation and use of a price index. The other methods listed are all based upon units.

44. (d)

Accounts payable before adjustment	$900,000
Add: Goods in transit, FOB shipping point	50,000
Add: Payments not disbursed	40,000
	$990,000

Title to goods shipped "FOB Shipping Point" transfers to the purchaser at the shipping point when the seller delivers them to a common carrier, which is acting as an agent for the buyer. Such goods, in transit, would be included in the purchaser's inventory and the associated liability included in its accounts payable. Title to goods shipped "FOB Destination" transfers to the purchaser when the goods are delivered to the buyer's destination. Such goods in transit would not be recorded by the purchaser. They are properly included in the seller's inventory.

Recorded checks which are not disbursed (held back) at the end of an accounting period should be included in the cash balance as of that date.

45. (b)

Date	*Inventory @ base yr. cost*	*Layer @ base yr. cost*	*Price index*	*Layer @ current yr. cost*	*Ending inventory*
1/1/90	$100,000		1.00		100,000
12/31/90	120,000	20,000	1.05	21,000	121,000
12/31/91	128,000	8,000	1.10	8,800	129,800

NOTE: Ending inventory at 1/1/90 is the "base" and two layers have been added.

46. (a) $545,000 cost of goods sold

Payment to suppliers	$490,000
Add: increase in accounts payable ($75,000 – $50,000)	25,000
Purchases	$515,000
Add: decrease in inventory ($290,000 – $260,000)	30,000
Cost of goods sold	$545,000

47. (a) Price index = $\frac{\text{Current ending inventory at current yr. cost}}{\text{Current ending inventory at base yr. cost}}$

48. (d) Net realizable value less a normal profit margin (the lower limit) is "market" as the replacement cost is below this amount. Because "market" (NRV -- normal profit margin) is below the original cost, it would be used to value inventory under the lower of cost or market method.

49. (a)

	Beginning inventory	$ 500,000
+	Purchases	2,500,000
	Cost of goods available for sale	$3,000,000
-	Cost of goods sold ($3,200,000 × 75%*)	2,400,000
	Ending inventory required for 25% gross profit	$ 600,000
	Ending inventory—actual	575,000
	Estimated cost of missing inventory	$ 25,000

*If gross profit (margin) is 25%, then the cost of goods sold is 75% (100% – 25%).

50. (d)

	At cost	*At retail*
Beginning inventory	$147,000	$ 203,000
Purchases	833,000	1,155,000
Additional markups		42,000
	$980,000	$1,400,000
Cost/retail ratio $980,000 ÷ $1,400,000 = 70%		
Less: Markdowns		(14,000)
Sales		(1,106,000)
Ending inventory at retail		$ 280,000
Ending inventory at cost ($280,000 × 70%)	$196,000	

51. (c)

Mineral mine	$3,600,000
Development cost	1,080,000
Total cost	$4,680,000
Less: Estimated residual value	(360,000)
Total cost subject to depletion	$4,320,000

Depletion per ton = $4,320,000 ÷ 2,160,000 tons = $2 per ton
Depletion expense (included in cost of goods sold) = $2 per ton × 240,000 tons sold = $480,000

NOTE: Depletion included in ending inventory equals $60,000 ($2 per ton × 30,000 tons not sold).

52. (b) Answer: B

Cost of Goods sold is calculated as follows:

Beginning Inventory		$ 30,840
+Purchases	102,800	
-Purchase Discounts	(10,280)	
Net Purchases		92,520
+Freight-In		15,420
Available for Sale	$ 138,780	
-Ending Inventory		(20,560)
Cost of Goods Sold		$118,220

Note: Freight out is a selling cost and is not a part of cost of goods sold.

Chapter Three
Solutions to Inventories Problems

NUMBER 1

The Jericho Variety Store
LIFO RETAIL COMPUTATION
December 31, 19X5

	Cost	Retail
Purchases	$120,000	$172,000
Freight-in	20,000	
Net markups		40,000
Net markdowns		(12,000)
	$140,000	200,000
Cost ratio ($140,000 ÷ $200,000)	70%	
Sales		190,000
19X5 layer:		
At retail		10,000
At cost ($10,000 × 70%)	$ 7,000	
Inventory, January 1, 19X5 (base)	$ 29,000	$ 45,000
Inventory, December 31, 19X5	$ 36,000	$ 55,000

NUMBER 2

Part a.

1.

Frate Company
COMPUTATION OF INVENTORY FOR PRODUCT PLY UNDER FIFO INVENTORY METHOD
March 31, 19X9

	Units	Unit cost	Total cost
March 26, 19X9	900	$11.50	$10,350
February 16, 19X9	600	11.00	6,600
January 25, 19X9 (portion)	100	10.50	1,050
March 31, 19X9 (inventory)	1,600		$18,000

2.

Frate Company
COMPUTATION OF INVENTORY FOR PRODUCT PLY UNDER LIFO INVENTORY METHOD
March 31, 19X9

	Units	Unit cost	Total cost
Beginning inventory	800	$ 9.00	$ 7,200
January 5, 19X9 (portion)	800	10.00	8,000
March 31, 19X9, inventory	1,600		$15,200

3.

Frate Company

COMPUTATION OF INVENTORY FOR PRODUCT PLY UNDER WEIGHTED AVERAGE INVENTORY METHOD

March 31, 19X9

	Units	Unit cost	Total cost
Beginning inventory	800	$ 9.00	$ 7,200
January 5, 19X9	1,500	10.00	15,000
January 25, 19X9	1,200	10.50	12,600
February 16, 19X9	600	11.00	6,600
March 26, 19X9	900	11.50	10,350
	5,000		$51,750
Weighted average cost ($51,750 ÷5,000)		$10.35	
March 31, 19X9, inventory	1,600	$10.35	$16,560

Part b.

Red Department Store

COMPUTATION OF ESTIMATED INVENTORY USING RETAIL INVENTORY METHOD

December 31, 19X8

	Cost	Retail
Inventory at January 1, 19X8	$ 32,000	$ 80,000
Purchases	270,000	590,000
Freight in	7,600	
Net markups (60,000 – 10,000)		50,000
Goods available for sale	$309,600	720,000
Cost ratio ($309,600 ÷ $720,000)	43%	
Sales		600,000
Net markdowns (25,000 – 5,000)		20,000
Estimated normal shrinkage (2% × 600,000)		12,000
		632,000
Estimated inventory at retail at December 31, 19X8		$ 88,000
Estimated inventory at December 31, 19X8, lower of cost or market (88,000 × 43%)	$ 37,840	

Part c.

Hodge Company

CALCULATION OF ESTIMATED LOSS ON INVENTORY IN THE FIRE USING GROSS MARGIN (PROFIT) METHOD

November 21, 19X8

Inventory at November 1, 19X8		$100,000
Purchases from November 1, 19X8 to date of fire		140,000
Cost of goods available for sale		240,000
Estimated cost of goods sold		
Net sales from Nov. 1, 19X8 to date of fire	$220,000	
Less estimated gross margin (profit) ($220,000 × 30%)	66,000	154,000
Estimated cost of inventory at date of fire		86,000
Less salvage goods		10,000
Estimated loss on inventory in the fire		$ 76,000

NUMBER 3

a. 1. When LIFO is applied to units of product, the total inventory value is determined by pricing individual items within the inventory. This forms the base layer of the LIFO inventory. When there is an increase in the number of any given unit in the inventory at the end of a period, it is theoretically consistent to value the increase as if it occurred as early in the period as possible. In other words, if the volume of the first purchase of the period exceeds the amount of increase in units, the increase is added to the beginning inventory priced at the unit cost of the first purchase. If the size of the increase exceeds the volume of the first purchase, then the entire cost of the first purchase plus sufficient units priced at the unit cost from the next purchase would be used, etc. In practice, however, the increase is sometimes priced at either the most recent purchase cost or at the average cost for the year. However priced, the increased units represent a new layer of the inventory. Decreases in inventory quantities are removed from the inventory layers in the reverse order of additions.

2. The dollar-value method is applied to a retail LIFO inventory and to LIFO units of product utilizes a number of procedures in common. At the time of adoption of either application, inventory consists of a base pool (or group of pools) to which is assigned a dollar value that is an inherent element of all subsequent inventory amounts, unless a reduction below the original inventory level is sustained. An important element of establishing the pool is segmentation of the inventory into appropriate classes or homogeneous groupings (i.e., similar markups or goods sold to the same type of customer for the same general purpose). It is also essential to compute or ascertain an index value of relevant prices at the time these applications are adopted. Subsequent increments or increases above the basic inventory level are valued through the use of related price-index values. The base-year price index is used in comparison with the current price index prevailing when the inventory increase occurs to determine how much of an apparent change is solely due to price changes and how much represents an actual change in the volume of the inventory. Volume increases (new layers) are then added to the basic inventory at price levels actually prevailing when the physical increases took place. If a decrease should occur in a later period after there has been a succession of increases above the basic inventory, the most recent layers added are the first layers presumed to have been sold or consumed.

b. The pool concept of the dollar-value LIFO applications discussed above makes it unnecessary to match opening and closing quantities of individual items, thereby simplifying recordkeeping. This advantage is limited by the necessity to maintain appropriate classes of inventory within the particular pool, but this is less cumbersome than accounting for individual items of inventory. Under these applications, changes in the specific types of goods making up a particular inventory classification do not affect total inventory pricing unless such changes result in an increase in ending inventory priced at base-year prices. Thus, continuous substitution of new elements of inventory may have little or no effect on the total inventory amount. This is in some contrast with what would occur under a LIFO system maintained strictly on a unit basis where the new units would come into inventory at substantially higher values when prices were rising.

c. The advantage usually cited for the LIFO method and its applications is that it does match current costs against current revenues. Stated another way, its usage, when prices are rising, results in the highest costs being matched against current revenue; conversely, when prices are falling, the lowest costs are matched against current revenue. This minimizes recognition of profits or losses from mere fluctuations in the value of inventories which an entity must continue to hold if it is to remain a going concern. A second advantage of the method is that it provides a better measure of disposable income. Under other methods which, given parallel conditions, would show higher amounts of ending inventory and hence correspondingly higher amounts of income, the income is not as good an indication of the amount that is disposable. Additional investment (perhaps from retained earnings) in inventory must be made if the same quantity is to be maintained on hand. A third advantage of the method is that in conditions of rising prices it tends to give lower inventory valuations. In the event these valuations are accepted for property-tax-valuation purposes there would be an attendant tax saving.

The principal disadvantage concerns the valuation of the inventory for balance-sheet purposes. As more time elapses from the date of adoption of the method, the value reflected on the balance sheet grows more out-of-date. This would mean that if prices changed much over the interval from the date of adoption to the date of the current balance sheet, the balance-sheet value would be somewhat meaningless. Further, LIFO permits a deferral in recognition of gains or losses from the holding of inventories when prices of specific goods are changing at rates different than the rate of prices generally. This has also been criticized as a secret reserve.

Some object to LIFO because it seldom accords with the physical flow of goods. This can be countered by noting that it is said to represent a flow of costs, not a physical flow, but the inconsistency is still there and does not rest easily with some theorists.

The company to company differences in pricing of various layers, because of differences in the timing of adding those layers, may cause significant distortions of comparability even among LIFO companies.

It is possible to manipulate net income to some degree under LIFO simply by refraining from buying or by resorting to heavy buying near the end of an accounting period. Under other flow methods this is not possible and such actions would be reflected simply as inventory variations rather than as variations in cost of goods sold.

In the event inventories are reduced below the level when LIFO was adopted, assuming substantial intervening price rises, the long-term cumulative benefit of having been under such a method can be wiped out in a single period. Ancient costs would be matched against current revenues and highly distorted results would ensue.

While some see the matching of current costs against current revenues as a major advantage of LIFO, others contend that this is a means of achieving an artificial smoothing of income.

NUMBER 4

M90

a. Purchases from various suppliers generally should be included in Huddell's inventory when Huddell receives the goods. Title to goods purchased FOB destination is assumed to pass when the goods are received.

b. Huddell should account for the warehousing costs as additional cost of inventory. All necessary and reasonable costs of readying goods for sale should be included in inventory.

c. 1. The advantages of using the dollar value LIFO method are to reduce the cost of accounting for inventory and to minimize the probability of reporting the liquidation of LIFO inventory layers.

2. The application of dollar value LIFO is based on dollars of inventory, an inventory cost index for each year, and broad inventory pools. The inventory layers are identified with the inventory cost index for the year in which the layer was added. In contrast, traditional LIFO is applied to individual units at their cost.

d. 1. Huddell's net markups should be included only in the retail amounts (denominator) to determine the cost to retail percentage.

Huddell's net markdowns should be ignored in the calculation of the cost to retail percentage.

2. By not deducting net markdowns from the retail amounts to determine the cost to retail percentage, Huddell produces a lower cost to retail percentage than would result if net markdowns were deducted. Applying this lower percentage to ending inventory at retail, the inventory is reported at an amount below cost. This amount is intended to approximate lower of average cost or market.

NUMBER 5

Acute Company
COMPUTATION OF INVENTORIES UNDER THE DOLLAR-VALUE LIFO INVENTORY METHOD

Year ended December 31,	*Inventory at respective year-end prices*	*External price index (base year 19X5)*	*Inventory at base year (19X5) price*
19X6	$363,000	1.10	$330,000
19X7	$420,000	1.20	$350,000
19X8	$430,000	1.25	$344,000

December 31, 19X6

Base	$300,000
19X6 layer at 19X6 cost: ($330,000 – $300,000 = $30,000 × 1.10)	33,000
	$333,000

December 31, 19X7

Base	$300,000
19X6 layer at 19X6 cost	33,000
19X7 layer at 19X7 cost: ($350,000 – $330,000 = $20,000 × 1.20)	24,000
	$357,000

December 31, 19X8

Base	$300,000
19X6 layer at 19X6 cost	33,000
19X7 layer at 19X7 cost: ($344,000 – $350,000 = ($6,000) + $20,000 = $14,000 × 1.20)	16,800
	$349,800

NUMBER 6

a. If the terms of the purchase are FOB shipping point (manufacturer's plant), Retail, Inc., should include in its inventory goods purchased from its suppliers when the goods are shipped. For accounting purposes, title is presumed to pass at that time.

b. Freight-in expenditures should be considered an inventoriable cost because they are part of the price paid or the consideration given to acquire an asset.

c. Because the cooking utensils were purchased three times during the current year, each time at a higher price than previously, Retail, Inc.'s ending inventory would be lower and the cost of goods sold would be higher using the weighted-average cost method instead of the FIFO method.

d. Because Retail, Inc., calculates the estimated cost of its ending inventory using the conventional (lower-of-cost-or-market) retail inventory method, net markdowns are excluded from the computation of the cost ratio and included in the computation of the ending inventory at retail. Net markdowns are excluded in order to approximate a lower-of-cost-or-market valuation. Excluding net markdowns from the computation of the cost ratio reduces the cost ratio, which in turn reduces the estimated cost of the ending inventory.

e. Products on consignment represent inventories owned by Retail, Inc., which are physically transferred to The Mall Space Company. Retail, Inc., retains title to the goods until their sale by The Mall Space Company.
The goods consigned are still included by Retail, Inc., in the inventory section of its balance sheet. Retail, Inc., reclassifies the inventory from regular inventory to consigned inventory. The Mall Space Company, on the other hand, reports neither inventory nor a liability in its balance sheet.

NUMBER 7

a. 1. The specific identification method requires each unit to be clearly distinguished from similar units either by description, identification number, location, or other characteristic. Costs are accumulated for specific units and expensed as the units are sold. Thus, the specific identification method results in recognized cost flows being identical to actual physical flows. Ideally, each unit is relatively expensive and the number of such units relatively few so that recording of costs is not burdensome. Under the specific identification method, if similar items have different costs, cost of goods sold is influenced by the specific units sold.

2. It is appropriate for Happlia to use the specific identification method because each appliance is expensive, and easily identified by number and description. The specific identification method is feasible because Happlia already maintains records of its units held by individual retailers. Management's ability to manipulate cost of goods sold is minimized because once the inventory is in retailer's hands Happlia's management cannot influence the units selected for sales.

b. 1. Happlia should include in inventory carrying amounts all necessary and reasonable costs to get an appliance into a useful condition and place for sale. Common (or joint) costs should be allocated to individual units. Such costs exclude the excess costs incurred in transporting refrigerators to Minneapolis and their reshipment to Kansas City. These unit costs should only include normal freight costs from Des Moines to Kansas City. In addition, costs incurred to provide time utility to the goods, i.e., ensuring that they are available when required, will also be included in inventory carrying amounts.

2. Examples of inventoriable costs include the unit invoice price, plus an allocated proportion of the port handling fees, import duties, freight costs to Des Moines and to retailers, insurance costs, repackaging, and warehousing costs.

c. The 1990 income statement should report in cost of goods sold all inventory costs related to units sold in 1990, regardless of when cash is received from retailers. Excess freight costs incurred for shipping the refrigerators from Minneapolis to Kansas City should be included in determining operating income.

NUMBER 8

a. 1. For its 1993 models, Blaedon should include in inventory carrying amounts all necessary and reasonable costs. These costs may include design costs, purchase price from contractors, freight-in, and warehousing costs.

2. Blaedon's 1992 model inventory should be assigned a carrying amount equal to its net realizable value, which is its current list price reduced by both its disposition costs and two-thirds of the difference between the $40 allowance given and the carrying amount assigned to trade-ins. The trade-ins' carrying amount should equal the $25 average net realizable value less the profit margin, if any, assigned.

b. 1. Using FIFO, Blaedon would assign the earliest lawnmower costs to cost of goods sold. With rising costs, this would result in matching old, relatively low inventory costs against current revenues. Net income would be higher than that reported using certain other inventory methods.

2. Blaedon would assign the latest costs to ending inventory. Normally, the carrying amount of Blaedon's FIFO ending inventory would approximate replacement cost at December 31, 1992. Retained earnings would be higher than that reported using certain other inventory methods.

NUMBER 9

a. 1. Cash discounts should not be accounted for as financial income when payments are made. Income should be recognized when the earning process is complete (when Taylor sells the inventory). Furthermore, cash discounts should not be recorded when the payments are made because in order to properly match a cash discount with the related purchase, the cash discount should be recorded when the related purchase is recorded.

2. Cash discounts should not be accounted for as a reduction of cost of goods sold for period when payments are made. Cost of goods sold should be reduced when the earning process is complete (when Taylor sells the inventory which has been reduced by the cash discounts). Furthermore, cash discounts should not be recorded when the payments are made because in order to properly match a cash discount with the related purchase, the cash discount should be recorded when the related purchase is recorded.

3. Cash discounts should be accounted for as a direct reduction of purchase cost because they reduce the cost of the inventories. Purchases should be recorded net of cash discount to reflect the net cash to be paid. The primary basis of accounting for inventories is cost, which represents the price paid or consideration given to acquire an asset.

b. Inventories would be lower using the LIFO inventory method instead of the FIFO method over a substantial time period when purchase prices of household appliances are rising because the inventories are at the oldest (lower) purchase prices instead of the most recent (higher) purchase prices. Correspondingly, cost of goods sold would be higher because the cost of goods sold is at more recent (higher) purchase prices instead of older (lower) purchase prices. Consequently, net income and retained earnings would be lower.

More cash flow would generally be available using the LIFO inventory method instead of the FIFO method because taxable income is decreased, resulting generally in accrual and payment of lower income taxes. Correspondingly, income tax expense would generally be lower.

c. The lower of cost-or-market rule is used for valuing inventories when the FIFO method is used because of (a) the matching principle, that is, the decline in the utility of the household appliances inventories below its cost should be recognized as a loss in the current period, and (b) the concept of balance sheet conservatism.

NUMBER 10

a. Inventory cost should include all reasonable and necessary costs of preparing inventory for sale. These costs include not only the purchase price of the inventories, but also other costs associated with readying inventories for sale.

b. The lower of cost or market rule produces a realistic estimate of future cash flows to be realized from the sale of inventories. This is consistent with the principle of conservatism, and recognizes (matches) the anticipated loss in the income statement in the period in which the price decline occurs.

c. Steel's inventories should be reported on the balance sheet at market. According to the lower of cost or market rule, market is defined as replacement cost. Market cannot exceed net realizable value and cannot be less than net realizable value less the normal profit margin. In this instance, replacement cost is between net realizable value and net realizable value less the normal profit margin. Therefore, market is established as replacement cost. Since market is less than original cost, inventory should be reported at market.

d. Ending inventories and net income would have been the same under either lower of average cost or market or lower of FIFO cost or market. In periods of declining prices, the lower of cost or market rule results in a write-down of inventory cost to market under both methods, resulting in the same inventory cost. Therefore, net income using either inventory method is the same.

NUMBER 11

a.

York Co.
Schedule of Cost of Goods Sold
For the Year Ended December 31, 1993

Beginning inventory	$ 65,600
Add: Purchases	368,900
Less: Purchase discounts	(18,000)
Add: Freight-in	5,000
Goods available for sale	421,500
Less: Ending inventory	(176,000) [1]
Cost of Goods Sold	$245,500

York Co.
Supporting Schedule of Ending Inventory
December 31, 1993

Inventory at cost (LIFO):

	Units	*Cost per unit*	*Total cost*
Beginning inventory, January 1	8,000	$8.20	$65,600
Purchases, quarter ended March 31	12,000	8.25	99,000
Purchases, quarter ended June 30	2,000	7.90	15,800
	22,000		$180,400

[1] Inventory at market:
22,000 units @ $8 = $176,000

b. Inventory should be valued at the lower of cost or market. Market means current replacement cost, except that:

(1) Market should not exceed the net realizable value; and
(2) Market should not be less than net realizable value reduced by an allowance for an approximately normal profit margin.

In this situation, because replacement cost ($8 per unit) is less than net realizable value, but greater than net realizable value reduced by a normal profit margin, replacement cost is used as market. Because inventory valued at market ($176,000) is lower than inventory valued at cost ($180,400), inventory should be reported in the financial statements at market.

Chapter Four
Consolidated Financial Statements

Chapter Four
Consolidated Financial Statements

BUSINESS COMBINATIONS AND SUBSTANCE OVER FORM

"A business combination occurs when a corporation and one or more incorporated or unincorporated businesses are brought together into one accounting entity. The **single** (accounting/economic) entity carries on the activities of the previously separate, independent enterprises" (APB #16). The accounting concept of a business combination emphasizes the single entity and the independence of the combining companies prior to the combination. In a business combination one or more of the combining companies may lose their separate legal identities; however, dissolution of the legal entities is **not** necessary within the accounting concept of a business combination. Although financial accounting is concerned with both the legal and economic effects of transactions and events, and many of its conventions are based upon legal rules, the economic substance of transactions and events is usually emphasized when the legal form differs from the economic substance and suggests different treatment. Therefore, financial accounting emphasizes the single entity in business combinations even if more than one legal entity continues to exist (substance over form).

TYPES OF BUSINESS COMBINATIONS

Merger: One corporation acquires the assets, liabilities, and operations of another business entity and that entity ceases to exist and is dissolved. All assets and liabilities are recorded on the books of the acquiring corporation.

Consolidation: A new corporation is formed to acquire the assets, liabilities, and operations of two or more separate business entities, and those entities cease to exist and are dissolved. All assets and liabilities are recorded on the books of the new corporation. Note the distinction between Consolidation and Accounting Consolidation shown below.

Acquisition: One corporation (the investor/parent) acquires controlling interest (greater than 50% of the outstanding common stock) in another corporation (the investee/subsidiary). Both corporations continue their separate legal existence. The assets and liabilities, although under the control of a single business entity (the parent), are recorded on two separate sets of books.

ACCOUNTING CONSOLIDATIONS

Preparation of financial statements for the single entity resulting from business combinations classified as mergers and consolidations is accomplished through the normal accounting process, as all assets, liabilities and operations are recorded on a single set of books. However, preparation of single entity financial statements for business combinations classified as acquisitions generally requires the bringing together (**accounting consolidation**) of assets, liabilities, and operations from two sets of books (the parent and subsidiary) as the combining companies continue their separate legal existence, and maintain their own accounting records. This accounting consolidation is based on the financial **accounting concept of substance over form.**

FASB Statement #94 requires that **all** majority-owned subsidiaries (companies in which a parent has a controlling financial interest through direct or indirect ownership of a majority voting interest) be consolidated **except** those in which control is likely to be temporary or if control does not rest with the majority owner (subsidiary is in legal reorganization or in bankruptcy or operates under foreign exchange restrictions, controls, or other governmentally imposed uncertainties so severe that they cast significant doubt on the parent's ability to control the subsidiary).

METHODS OF ACCOUNTING FOR BUSINESS COMBINATIONS

Historically, there were two generally accepted methods of accounting for business combinations – the **Pooling of Interests** Method and the **Purchase** Method. With the release of SFAS 141 in 2001, the purchase method is now required for all business combinations, thus effectively prohibiting future use of the pooling of interests method. Importantly, though, previous combinations that qualified for pooling of interests treatment will continue to be accounted for as poolings in their future consolidated financial reports.

Purchase Method

The purchase method accounts for a business combination as the acquisition of one enterprise by another, and accordingly follows principles normally applicable under historical-cost accounting. The acquiring corporation records the net assets (assets less liabilities assumed) at its cost, not to exceed their fair market value as of the date of acquisition. The total cost is allocated to the individual, identifiable assets and liabilities acquired based upon their fair market values as of the date of acquisition. Any excess of cost over the fair market value of the net assets acquired is attributed to *"goodwill"* (an unidentifiable, intangible asset). The reported income of the acquiring corporation includes the operations of the acquired enterprise **only after the date of acquisition**, and is based upon the cost to the acquiring corporation.

Goodwill

SFAS 142 provides that goodwill will be subject to an annual test for impairment. When the carrying amount of goodwill exceeds its implied fair value, an impairment loss is recognized equal to that excess. This nonamortization approach will be applied to both previously recognized goodwill and newly acquired goodwill.

Negative Goodwill

SFAS 141 states that in some cases, the sum of the amounts assigned to assets acquired and liabilities assumed will exceed the cost of the acquired entity (excess over cost or excess). That excess shall be allocated as a pro rata reduction of the amounts that otherwise would have been assigned to all of the acquired assets except (a) financial assets other than investments accounted for by the equity method, (b) assets to be disposed of by sale, (c) deferred tax assets, (d) prepaid assets relating to pension or other postretirement benefit plans, and (e) any other current assets.

If any excess remains after reducing to zero the amounts that otherwise would have been assigned to those assets, that remaining excess shall be recognized as an **extraordinary item**.

METHODS OF ACCOUNTING FOR INVESTMENTS IN COMMON STOCK

Percent of Common Stock Owned	*Level of Influence (assumed)*	*Valuation of Investment*	*Balance sheet Presentation*	*Income*
<20	Normal	Cost/Fair Value*	Investment	Dividends
20 - 50	Significant	Equity	Investment	% share
>50	Control	*	Consolidate	Consolidate

* If consolidated statements are prepared, the cost and equity methods will produce the same results. If consolidated statements are not prepared because of the restrictions on consolidation (refer above to "Accounting Consolidations"), the **cost method** of accounting for investment must be used. (Refer below to "Restrictions on use of the equity method".)

** Refer to Chapter 2 on use of fair value for equity securities with readily determinable fair values, and use of the Cost/LCM method.

Note: The level of the investor's influence over the operating and financial policies of an investee *controls* the method of accounting used for valuation of the investment, balance sheet presentation and the reporting of income. The percentage of ownership is merely an indication of the degree of influence.

A. **Cost**: Initial investment is recorded at cost. Income is recognized as dividends are distributed from the net accumulated earnings of the investee since the date of acquisition by the investor. Dividends received in excess of earnings subsequent to the date of investment are considered a return of investment (capital) and are recorded as reductions of the cost of the investment. A series of operating losses of an investee or other factors may indicate that a decrease in the value of the investment has occurred which is other than temporary and should accordingly be recognized. Refer to Chapter Two (Corporations—Stockholders' Equity and Investments in Stock) concerning valuation of investments in common stock and examples of the cost method.

Since only dividends paid are reflected on the books of an investor, the investor's statements may not reflect substantial changes in the affairs of an investee. For example, dividends may not be paid for several periods when earnings are high, or dividends could be paid substantially in excess of earnings for a period. Dividends from earnings of prior periods could be paid even though the investee suffered a loss in the current period. Because of these characteristics, the cost method may prevent an investor from reflecting adequately the earnings related to an investment in common stock.

B. **Equity**: Initial investment is recorded at cost. (At date of acquisition the cost and equity methods are the same.) The investor adjusts the carrying value of the investment to recognize its share of earnings or losses after date of acquisition, reflecting such adjustment in income as follows:

DR	Investment
CR	Net Income

Losses would receive similar treatment such as:

DR	Net Income
CR	Investment

The investor also adjusts the carrying value of the investment for changes in the investee's capital. Dividends received reduce the carrying amount of the investment as follows:

DR	Cash
CR	Investment

A series of operating losses or other factors may indicate a decrease in the value of the investment which is other than temporary. If so, such decrease in value should be recognized even though in excess of that recognized by use of the equity method (LCM).

Restrictions on use of the equity method: The equity method may not be used to account for a majority-owned subsidiary if control is likely to be temporary or if it does not rest with the majority owner (if the subsidiary is in legal reorganization or in bankruptcy or operates under foreign exchange restrictions, controls, or other governmentally-imposed uncertainties so severe that they cast significant doubt on the parent's ability to control the subsidiary) per FASB Statement #94. Note that the above restrictions on the use of the equity method are the same as the restrictions on consolidation of subsidiaries. Therefore, **an unconsolidated subsidiary must be accounted for using the cost method**, and the equity method may **not** be used to account for an unconsolidated subsidiary. The equity method is **not** a valid substitute for consolidation.

C. **Consolidation**: The combining of the assets, liabilities, revenues and expenses of subsidiaries (a corporation controlled, directly or indirectly, by another corporation) with the corresponding items of the parent after all intercompany items are eliminated to prevent double accounting. The usual condition for consolidation is ownership of more than 50% of the outstanding voting stock. The purpose of preparing consolidated statements is to present the statements of two or more entities as the statements of a single entity (substance over form). There is a presumption that consolidated statements are more meaningful than separate statements. However, a subsidiary should not be consolidated where control is likely to be temporary or the majority owners do not have control (legal reorganization, bankruptcy, or operates under foreign exchange restrictions, controls, or other governmentally-imposed uncertainties so severe that they cast significant doubt on the parent's ability to control the subsidiary).

The single most important elimination entry is that of the parent's investment account vs. the net assets or stockholders' equity of the subsidiary. At the date of acquisition, the investment represents the cost of the net assets purchased and these two accounts are reciprocal and must be eliminated in the preparation of consolidated statements.

EXAMPLE: On January 1, 20X2 , A Company purchased 80% of the outstanding common stock of B Company for $650,000. At the date of purchase, the book and fair values of Company B's assets and liabilities were the same. The balance sheets of A and B on this date were as follows:

	Co. A	*Co. B*
Current assets	$ 400,000	$ 300,000
Equipment (net)	1,000,000	700,000
Investment in B	650,000	—
Total	$2,050,000	$1,000,000
Liabilities	$ 750,000	$ 200,000
Common stock	500,000	300,000
APIC	200,000	100,000
R/E	600,000	400,000
Total	$2,050,000	$1,000,000

Under the purchase method the cost of the investment is allocated to the individual, identifiable assets and liabilities acquired based upon their fair market values as of the date of acquisition. Any excess of cost over the fair market value of the net assets acquired is attributed to *"goodwill"* (an unidentifiable, intangible asset).

Computation of Goodwill:

Investment cost		$650,000
Fair value of net assets acquired:		
Common stock	$300,000	
APIC	100,000	
R/E	400,000	
Net assets	$800,000	
% acquired	× .80	640,000
Goodwill		$ 10,000

Because Company A did not acquire 100% of the outstanding common stock of Company B, there is a minority interest in the subsidiary equity of $160,000 (20% × $800,000).

Eliminating entry:

Common stock (B)	$300,000	
APIC (B)	100,000	
R/E (B)	400,000	
Goodwill	10,000	
Investment in B		$650,000
Minority interest		160,000

Alternatively, two entries can be made:

#1 To establish minority interest in Company B.

Common stock (20% × $300,000)	$60,000	
APIC (20% × $100,000)	20,000	
R/E (20% × $400,000)	80,000	
Minority interest		$160,000

#2 To eliminate the 80% investment in Company B.

	Dr.	Cr.
Common stock (80% × $300,000)	$240,000	
APIC (80% × $100,000)	80,000	
R/E (80% × $400,000)	320,000	
Goodwill	10,000	
Investment in B		$650,000

The consolidation worksheet would appear as follows:

	Co.A	*Co.B*	*Eliminations* *Dr.(Cr.)*	*Consolidated*
Current assets	$ 400,000	$ 300,000		$ 700,000
Equipment (net)	1,000,000	700,000		1,700,000
Goodwill			10,000	10,000
Investment in B	650,000	—	(650,000)	—
Total	$2,050,000	$1,000,000		$2,410,000
Liabilities	$ 750,000	$ 200,000		$ 950,000
Minority Int.			(160,000)	160,000
Common stock	500,000	300,000	300,000	500,000
APIC	200,000	100,000	100,000	200,000
R/E	600,000	400,000	400,000	600,000
Total	$2,050,000	$1,000,000		$2,410,000

Note the following:

1. The assets of Company B have been combined with the assets of Company A at their fair market value as of the date of acquisition.
2. The equity accounts are those of the single economic entity, Company A.
3. The investment in B and the equity accounts of Company B have been eliminated—they are reciprocal.
4. There is a minority interest established to represent their claim against the assets of the subsidiary.
5. An intangible asset, goodwill, has been established representing the excess of the cost of the investment over the fair market value of the net assets acquired. ~~This new asset would have to be amortized over a maximum period of 40 years, starting January 1, 1989.~~

Negative goodwill: If Company A acquired its investment in B for $620,000 this would result in negative goodwill of $20,000, which would be applied as a reduction in the fair market value of the non-current assets (equipment). The computations and elimination would be as follows:

Computation of negative goodwill

Investment cost	$620,000
Fair value of net assets acquired ($800,000 × 80%)	640,000
Negative goodwill	$ 20,000

Elimination entry

	Dr.	Cr.
Common stock	$300,000	
APIC	100,000	
R/E	400,000	
Equipment		$ 20,000
Minority interest		160,000
Investment		620,000

The consolidation worksheet would appear as follows:

	Co.A	*Co.B*	*Eliminations Dr.(Cr.)*	*Consolidated*
Current assets	$ 400,000	$ 300,000		$ 700,000
Equipment (net)	1,000,000	700,000	(20,000)	1,680,000
Goodwill				
Investment in B	620,000	—	(620,000)	—
Total	$2,020,000	$1,000,000		$2,380,000
Liabilities	$ 720,000	$ 200,000		$ 920,000
Minority Int.			(160,000)	160,000
Common stock	500,000	300,000	300,000	500,000
APIC	200,000	100,000	100,000	200,000
R/E	600,000	400,000	400,000	600,000
Total	$2,020,000	$1,000,000		$2,380,000

Using the facts of the original investment of $650,000 for 80% of the outstanding common stock of B, assume B reported net income of $100,000 for 20X2 and paid dividends of $40,000 during the year.

Equity method: If Company A used the equity method to account for consolidated subsidiaries, it would make the following entries for 1989:

1. To record its share of B's income:

Investment in B (80% × $100,000)	$80,000	
Investment income		$80,000

2. To record dividends received

Cash (80% × $40,000)	$32,000	
Investment in B		$32,000

Computation of goodwill

Investment in B ($650,000 + $80,000 – $32,000)		$698,000
Fair value of net assets acquired @ 12/31/89		
Original amount	$800,000	
Add net income	100,000	
Less dividends	(40,000)	
	$860,000	
% share	× .80	688,000
Goodwill		$ 10,000

Note that the goodwill is the same as that calculated at the date of acquisition. Under the equity method the investment is adjusted for the investor share of the change in net assets subsequent to acquisition (net income and dividends), and the stockholders equity of the subsidiary is also adjusted for this change. Therefore, the difference between the investment and the investors share of the net assets will remain the same.

Computation of minority interest:

20% × $860,000 net assets = $172,000

Eliminating entry:

Common stock	$300,000	
APIC	100,000	
R/E (400,000 + 100,000 – 40,000)	460,000	
Goodwill	10,000	
Minority interest		$172,000
Investment in B		698,000

Cost method: If Company A used the cost method to account for consolidated subsidiaries, it would make the following entry for 1989:

To record dividends received:

Cash (80% × 40,000)	$32,000	
Dividend income		$32,000

Computation of goodwill: The computation of goodwill at 12/31/02 would be the **same as the original computation**. Because the investment is carried at cost as of 1/1/89, it would be compared to the fair value of the net assets acquired on 1/1/89, and the resulting goodwill would be $10,000, the original amount.

Computation of minority interest:

20% × $860,000 net assets at 12/31/02 = $172,000

Note that the computation of the minority interest is the same as under the equity method above. The minority interest has a claim to 20% of the subsidiary equity as of 12/31/02.

Eliminating entry: When the cost method is used to account for the investment in a consolidated subsidiary, the parent's share of the subsidiary's undistributed income, subsequent to acquisition, is **not** eliminated. It is carried forward and combined with the parent's retained earnings. If a single eliminating entry is used it would be as follows:

Common stock	$300,000	
APIC	100,000	
R/E*	412,000	
Goodwill	10,000	
Minority interest		$172,000
Investment in B		650,000

*Retained earnings eliminated

Original retained earnings	$400,000
Undistributed income subsequent to acquisition ($100,000 NI – $40,000 dividend)	60,000
R/E at 12/31/89	$460,000
Less parent's share of undistributed income subsequent to acquisition (80% × $60,000)	(48,000)
R/E to be eliminated	$412,000

If two eliminating entries are used, they are:

#1 To establish minority interest in Company B

Common stock (20% × $300,000)	$60,000	
APIC (20% × $100,000)	20,000	
R/E (20% × $460,000)	92,000	
Minority interest		$172,000

#2	To eliminate the 80% investment in Company B		
	Common stock (80% × $300,000)	$240,000	
	APIC (80% × $100,000)	80,000	
	R/E (80% × $400,000 original amount)	320,000	
	Goodwill	10,000	
	Investment in B		$650,000

Note that when two eliminating entries are used, the entry to eliminate (only) the 80% investment in B at 12/31/02 is the same as the entry to eliminate (only) the investment in B as of 1/1/02. The parent's share of the undistributed subsidiary income, subsequent to acquisition, is not eliminated. It is carried forward and combined with the parent's retained earnings.

The final consolidated balances are the same under the equity and cost methods of accounting for investments in consolidated subsidiaries. Referring to the examples above, under both methods the minority interest was $172,000 and the common stock and APIC of the subsidiary were eliminated. Under the equity method, the parent picked up, in its retained earnings, $80,000 of subsidiary income when it recorded its investment income (equity method, entry #1) and eliminated the subsidiary retained earnings on the consolidation worksheet (equity method, eliminating entry). Under the cost method, the parent picked up, in its retained earnings, $32,000 of subsidiary income when it recorded dividend income and did not eliminate $48,000 of subsidiary retained earnings on the consolidation worksheet. The $48,000 of subsidiary income not eliminated was combined with the parent's retained earnings resulting in $80,000 of subsidiary income ($32,000 + $48,000) being included in the parent's consolidated retained earnings.

Using the facts of the original investment of $650,000 for 80% of the outstanding common stock B, however, assuming the equipment was worth $705,000 with a book value of $700,000, the computation and worksheet would be as follows:

Computation of goodwill:		
Investment		$650,000
Fair value of net assets acquired:		
Book value	$800,000	
Add increase in value of equipment	5,000	
	805,000	
% acquired	× .80	644,000
Goodwill		$ 6,000

Computation of minority interest:
20% × $805,000 F.V. net assets = $161,000

Eliminating entry:		
Common stock (B)	$300,000	
APIC (B)	100,000	
R/E (B)	400,000	
Equipment	5,000 *	
Goodwill	6,000	
Minority interest		$161,000 *
Investment		650,000

* Alternative is to write up equipment only $4,000 (80% × $5,000), the amount attributable to the parent, and compute minority interest based upon the book value of the subsidiary equity ($800,000). All increased depreciation would then be attributed to the parent.

Consolidation worksheet:

	Co. A	*Co. B*	*Eliminations Dr.(Cr.)*	*Consolidated*
Current assets	$ 400,000	$ 300,000		$ 700,000
Equipment (net)	1,000,000	700,000	5,000	$1,705,000
Goodwill			6,000	6,000
Investment	650,000		(650,000)	—
Total	$2,050,000	$1,000,000		$2,411,000
Liabilities	750,000	200,000		950,000
Minority interest			(161,000)	161,000
Common stock	500,000	300,000	300,000	500,000
APIC	200,000	100,000	100,000	200,000
R/E	600,000	400,000	400,000	600,000
Total	$2,050,000	$1,000,000		$2,411,000

Note the following:

1. The assets of B have been combined with the assets of A at their fair market value as of the date of acquisition.
2. The equity accounts are those of the single economic entity, Company A.
3. The minority interest reflects their share of the increase in the value of the equipment.
4. As the recorded value of the equipment has been changed, an adjustment to depreciation expense will be required at the end of the period to reflect the depreciation of this amount over its remaining useful economic life.
5. Goodwill should be tested for impairment.

OTHER POINTS—PURCHASE METHOD

1. An acquiring corporation should not record the previously recorded goodwill of an acquired company.
2. Deferred income taxes recorded previously by an acquired company should not be recorded.
3. Deferred income taxes should not be recorded at date of acquisition.
4. No part of the excess of acquired net assets over cost should be added directly to stockholder's equity at the date of acquisition.
5. **Expenses** incident to consummating a purchase (finders fees, commissions) are considered part of the cost of the acquired company. However, indirect and general expenses related to acquisitions should be charged to expenses when incurred.
6. **Registration fees** incurred in connection with the issuance of securities reduce the fair value of the securities issued and should be charged to APIC.
7. Parent and subsidiaries may have different fiscal periods, but this condition does not preclude consolidation. The subsidiary may prepare statements that closely correspond to the parent's fiscal period, or if the difference is not more than about three months (A.R.B. #51), it is acceptable to use the subsidiary's statements for its fiscal period. Recognition should be given to material intervening events by disclosure.

OTHER INTERCOMPANY ELIMINATIONS AND ADJUSTMENTS

In general, elimination of intercompany receivables and debt; income and expense; sales and purchases; profits and loss on sales of assets is related to the single entity concept of business combinations. While the effect of intercompany transactions is ignored as to the separate entities involved, elimination is necessary when the separate entities purport to show their financial results as one. An entity cannot owe itself, cannot make a profit or suffer a loss from itself nor sell to itself. The adjustments and eliminations necessary to reflect transactions as though a single entity were involved are **not** book entries, but rather worksheet entries. A review of these areas and the special considerations relevant to each follow:

1. **Receivables and payables**

This is the simplest of elimination entries; however, be careful to screen the statements to pick up all such items whether referred to in the problem or not. These take different form such as:

(a) Accounts receivable and accounts payable
(b) Dividends receivable and payable
(c) Advances to subsidiary
(d) Interest receivable and payable
(e) Notes receivable and payable

If the receivable and payable are related to an income, expense or dividend item, eliminate.

DR	LIABILITY	
CR		ASSET

2. **Expense and income**

Eliminate:

(a) Dividend income and dividend paid.
(b) Interest income and interest expense on notes, advances, bonds, etc.

This entry is not necessary if the closing entries have been made and a consolidated balance sheet only is being prepared.

DR	INCOME	
CR		EXPENSE OR DIVIDEND

3. **Sales and purchases**

Eliminate by a debit to sales and a credit to purchases. If a consolidated balance sheet only is being prepared no entry is necessary. If the inventory and purchase accounts have been closed to Cost of Sales, the entry will be

DR	SALES	
CR		COST OF SALES

4. **Profit in Ending Inventory**

Eliminate 100% of gross profit where more than 50% ownership exists. Allocate to the minority interest if the profit resulted from sale by the subsidiary to the parent and that profit is in subsidiary's retained earnings.

Illustration:	*P*	*S*
Intercompany Sales	$70,000	$125,000
Markup on cost	20%	25%
Year-end inventory of intercompany purchases at cost	30,000	24,000
Percentage ownership in S	80%	

Elimination computations:

Sales by S to P of $30,000 remains in ending inventory of P.

Cost 100% + Markup 25% = Selling Price 125%
25/125 × 30,000 = 1/5 × 30,000 = $6,000 profit in S's R/E
Minority interest allocation 20% × $6,000 = $1,200

Sales by P to S—$24,000 remains in ending inventory of S.

Cost 100% + Markup 20% = Selling Price 120%
20/120 × 24,000 = 1/6 × 24,000 = $4,000 profit in P's R/E

Eliminating entry when income accounts **have been closed** (balance sheet only):

(1) R/E — P	$8,800	
Minority Interest	1,200	
Inventory		$10,000

(1) Eliminate against parent's retained earnings even though some profit was earned by the subsidiary, since the parents' R/E will be consolidated R/E.

Alternatively, it is not necessary according to GAAP to allocate to the minority interest; however, exam solutions usually show the allocation method and in some cases allocation is stated as the company's policy.

Journal entry where income and expense **have not been closed**:

To eliminate intercompany sales:		
Sales	$195,000	
Cost of Sales		$195,000

To eliminate intercompany profit in ending inventory:		
Cost of Sales	8,800	
Minority Interest	1,200	
Inventory		10,000

5. **Profit in beginning inventory**

Whereas profit in the ending inventory decreases net income, profit in the beginning inventory has the opposite effect; however, the entry made is as follows:

For profit in beginning inventory		
Retained earnings	$2,000	
Cost of Sales		$2,000
To eliminate profit in the beginning inventory.		

The credit to cost of sales will have the effect of increasing the current year's net income. The debit to retained earnings has the effect of adjusting the beginning retained earnings for the effect of the profit in the prior years' **ending** inventory. This entry coincides with the elimination entry of the prior year which would have been:

R/E or Cost of Sales
    Inventory

If the consolidation policy is to allocate to the minority interest, the entry would be changed accordingly.

6. **Intercompany transactions involving other assets**

From a consolidation standpoint the effects of all intercompany transactions must be eliminated. In the sale of non-depreciable or non-amortizable assets the adjusting entry is relatively simple. For example, land costing P $7,000 was sold to S for $10,000. The adjusting entry would be:

Gain on sale of land or retained earnings	$3,000	
Land		$3,000
To restore land account to cost		

If the asset is depreciable, an adjustment is required involving the present and prior depreciation expense and the allowance for depreciation, in that depreciation taken on a **gain** or depreciation **not taken** on a **loss** must be adjusted. Assume that P acquired S on January 1 and sold two assets to S on April 1.

Asset No.	*Book Value Parent*	*Price Paid Sub.*	*Depreciation Method*	*Life*
1	$16,000	$22,000	SYD	5
2	10,000	8,000	SL	10

The adjusting entry need only involve the depreciation on the profit or loss portion of the assets since the depreciation on the cost portion would have occurred no matter which company owned the assets. The adjustment for Asset #1 would be:

Allowance for depreciation	$1,500	
Depreciation expense or retained earnings		$1,500

$22,000 – $16,000 = 6,000 × 5/15 = 2,000 × 3/4 = $1,500

Adjustment for Asset #2 would be:

Depreciation expense	$150	
Allowance for depreciation		$150

$10,000 – 8,000 = 2,000 ÷ 10 = $200 × 3/4 = $150

The preceding section is a good illustration of the point made earlier that elimination entries are **not book entries** and therefore not recorded on the books of the related entities. Consequently, the same or similar entries must be made year after year because the consolidation starting point is, of course, a trial balance taken from the books of the related entities, which have not been adjusted. For example, use the previous illustration where land costing $7,000 was sold to S for $10,000. The same elimination entry must be made each period (DR R/E $3,000, CR Land $3,000). For depreciable assets, the entire accumulated depreciation related to the gain must be eliminated with the prior year depreciation affecting retained earnings and the current year affecting depreciation expense (except when the closing entries have already been made).

7. **Effect of Purchase of Asset on Minority Interest**

What is the difference between a purchase by a subsidiary from the parent or vice versa? The distinction is very important and frequently misunderstood. The importance of the question centers around allocation of intercompany profit or loss to the minority interest. Obviously, if the subsidiary is 100% owned, there is no difference in the treatment of the sale for consolidation purposes because there is no minority interest.

If the sale is **downstream**, from the parent to the subsidiary, the profit or loss is in the retained earnings of the parent. Since the profit rests in a retained earnings account which does **not** have a minority interest, no allocation is necessary.

If the sale is **upstream**, from the subsidiary to the parent, however, the minority interest is affected by the profit or loss when the sale takes place. Therefore, the minority interest should be affected by the elimination entry, the purpose of which is to **restate the sold asset to cost.**

8. **Intercompany Notes Receivable Discounted**

If intercompany notes receivable are discounted with outsiders (for example, a bank), eliminate the note receivable discounted against notes receivable. Assume the following book entries by P and S:

P	Intercompany N/R	$10,000	
	Cash		$10,000
S	Cash	$10,000	
	Intercompany N/P		$10,000

To record 60 day 9% intercompany note

Thirty days later P discounted S's note at 12% and recorded the following:

Cash	$10,048.50	
Interest Expense	101.50 [1]	
Intercompany Interest Income		$ 150 [2]
Intercompany N/R discounted		10,000

Note: If this entry did not involve affiliated companies, the interest expense and interest income amounts would be netted.

[1] $10,150 × 12% × 1/12 = $101.50
[2] $10,000 × 9% × 2/12 = $150

In consolidation the following elimination entry will be made:

Intercompany N/R discounted	10,000	
Intercompany N/R		10,000
Intercompany Interest Income	150	
Intercompany Interest Expense		150 [3]

[3] Assuming that S recorded interest expense for the note.

Note that the result of the above entries, relating to the notes only, is that a $10,000 N/P remains.

9. **Intercompany Bondholdings**

From a consolidation standpoint, intercompany bondholdings are just like any other debt which along with the related receivable must be eliminated. A complication may arise, however, if bonds are issued at a discount or premium or when purchased as an investment are purchased above or below par. For elimination purposes, the intercompany bonds should be regarded as repurchased by the issuing company and retired, with the resulting gain or loss affecting consolidated retained earnings or net income. Further, the interest expense and interest income for the period must be eliminated. For example:

L acquired 100% of the stock of C on January 1, 20X2. At year end L acquired $500,000 of C's outstanding bonds for $500,000 which includes $10,000 of accrued interest. These bonds were part of $1,000,000 of 8% 20-year bonds which were issued on April 1, 1991, for $960,000. Account balances are as follows:

	L	*C*
Investment in Bonds of C	$490,000	
Bonds Payable		($1,000,000)
Bond Discount		16,500
Interest Receivable	10,000	
Interest Payable (Bonds)		(20,000)
Interest Expense (Bonds)		[1] 82,000

[1] 80,000 cash plus 2,000 bond discount amortization

Objective: Adjust the accounts to eliminate all balances which relate to intercompany transactions. The remaining balances will relate to outsiders only. Elimination entry:

Bonds Payable	$500,000	
Interest Payable	10,000	
Interest Receivable		$ 10,000
Investment in Bonds of C		490,000
Bond Discount		8,250
Gain on purchase of bonds (extraordinary item)		1,750

Supporting Computations

Gain on purchase of bonds:

Par value of intercompany bonds	$500,000
Less: Unamortized discount 16,500 ÷ 2	8,250
Carrying value 12/31/02	491,750
Cost to L	490,000
Gain	$ 1,750

10. **Preferred and Common Stock Investment**
To make proper intercompany elimination where an investment is held in both preferred and common stock, the retained earnings account must be divided between the preferred and common, and intercompany elimination made based on the respective increases in R.E. (common) and R.E. (preferred) since date of acquisition. To break up the R.E. account, remember that preferred are entitled to par, redemption premium (if applicable), and dividends including any that may be in arrears if the stock is cumulative. (Refer to Chapter 2.)

Example: P owns 25% of the $100,000 par value, 8% cumulative preferred shares of S purchased on June 30, 2000, for $30,000. At date of purchase, the preferred dividends were 2 years in arrears. P also owns 90% of the common, and at June 30, 2000, the retained earnings of S was $80,000 and has increased to $190,000 at December 31, 2004, at which date the preferred dividends were 5 years in arrears.

Allocate the retained earnings at date of acquisition of the preferred and determine the change up to 12/31/2004.

R.E.	*Total*	*Preferred*	*Common*
6/30/00	$ 80,000	$ 16,000	$ 64,000
12/31/04	190,000	40,000	150,000
Change—Increase	$110,000	$24,000	$ 86,000

Preferred elimination entry—Cost method

Preferred Stock	$100,000		
R.E.—S	40,000		
Excess of Cost over FV	1,000		
R.E.—P		$ 6,000	($24,000 × 25%)
Investment		30,000	
MI—Preferred Stock		75,000	($100,000 × 75%)
MI—Preferred R.E.		30,000	($40,000 × 75%)

Supporting Computations

Cost of Preferred Stock		$30,000
Elimination:		
Preferred 25% × 100,000 =	25,000	
R/E date of acquisition		
25% × 16,000	4,000	29,000
Excess of cost over FV		$ 1,000
Minority Interest:		
75% × 100,000 (C/S)		$75,000
75% × 40,000 (R/E)		30,000

Addition to R/E — P
P's share of increase from date of acquisition to 12/31/04 — 25% × 24,000 = $6,000.
Elimination entries as to common would be made in the normal manner, using the retained earnings applicable to common instead of total retained earnings.

SFAS 141 Business Combinations

SFAS 141 provides three major changes in financial reporting:

- Eliminates the use of pooling of interest and requires that all business combinations use the purchase method.
- Provides greater guidance in recognizing intangible assets.
- Requires disclosures of the primary reasons for business combinations and expanded purchase price allocation information.

Intangible Assets

Intangible assets include both current assets and non-current assets that lack physical substance. SFAS 141 describes two attributes for recognition of an intangible asset.

- Does the intangible asset arise from contractual or other legal rights?
- Is the intangible asset capable of being separated or divided from the acquired entity and sold, transferred, licensed, rented or exchanged?

Appendix A of SFAS 141 includes a list of intangible assets that meet the recognition criteria.

Illustrative Examples of Intangible Assets That Meet the Criteria for Recognition Separately from Goodwill (SFAS 141)

The following are illustrative examples of intangible assets that, if acquired in a business combination, generally would meet the criteria for recognition as an asset separately from goodwill. Assets designated by the symbol © are those that would generally be recognized separately from goodwill because they meet the contractual-legal criterion. Assets designated by the symbol (s) do not arise from contractual or other legal rights, but should nonetheless be recognized separately from goodwill because they meet the separability criterion. The determination of whether a specific identifiable intangible asset acquired meets the criteria in this Statement for recognition separately from goodwill should be based on the facts and circumstances of each individual business combination.*

Marketing-related intangible assets

1. Trademarks, tradenames c
2. Service marks, collective marks, certification marks c
3. Trade dress (unique color, shape or package design) c
4. Newspaper mastheads c
5. Internet domain names c
6. Noncompetition agreements c

Customer-related intangible assets

1. Customer lists s
2. Order or production backlog c
3. Customer contracts and the related customer relationships c

Artistic-related intangible assets

1. Plays, operas and ballets c
2. Books, magazines, newspapers and other literary works c
3. Musical works such as compositions, song lyrics, advertising jingles c
4. Pictures and photographs c
5. Video and audiovisual material, including motion pictures, music videos, and television programs c

Contract-based intangible assets

1. Licensing, royalty, standstill agreements c
2. Advertising, construction, management, service or supply contracts c
3. Lease agreements c
4. Construction permits c
5. Franchise agreements c
6. Operating and broadcast rights c
7. Use rights such as landing, drilling, water, air, mineral, timber cutting, and so forth c
8. Servicing contracts such as mortgage servicing contracts c
9. Employment contracts c

Technology-based intangible assets

1. Patented technology c
2. Mask works c
3. Internet domain names c
4. Unpatented technology s
5. Databases, including title plants s
6. Trade secrets including secret formulas, processes, recipes c

---

*The intangible assets designated by the symbol © also might meet the separability criterion. However, separability is not a necessary condition for an asset to meet the contractual-legal criterion.

Note: The FASB specifically states that an assembly workforce shall not be recognized as an intangible asset apart from goodwill. Assembled

Purchased In Process Research and Development

SFAS 141 does not change the accounting for purchased in process research and development. The criterion usually used is technological feasibility. If the R & D has not reached technological feasibility, it should be expensed.

Furthermore, any tangible assets or intangible assets associated with the R & D project that have no alternative use should be expensed at the acquisition date.

Disclosures in Financial Statements

I. The notes to the financial statements of a combined entity shall disclose the following information in the period in which a material business combination is completed:
   a. The name and a brief description of the acquired entity and the percentage of voting equity interests acquired.
   b. The primary reason for the acquisition, including a description of the factors that contributed to a purchase price that results in recognition of goodwill.
   c. The period for which the results of operations of the acquired entity are included in the income statement of the combined entity.
   d. The cost of the acquired entity and, if applicable, the number of shares of equity interests (such as common shares, preferred shares, or partnership interests) issued or issuable, the value assigned to those interests, and the basis for determining that value.
   e. A condensed balance sheet disclosing the amount assigned to each major asset and liability caption of the acquired entity at the acquisition date.
   f. Contingent payments, options, or commitments specified in the acquisition agreement and the accounting treatment that will be followed should any such contingency occur.
   g. The amount of purchased research and development assets acquired and written off in the period and the line item in the income statement in which the amounts written off are aggregated.
   h. For any purchase price allocation that has not been finalized, that fact and the reasons therefor. In subsequent periods, the nature and amount of any material adjustments made to the initial allocation of the purchase price shall be disclosed.

II. The notes to the financial statements also shall disclose the following information in the period in which a material business combination is completed if the amounts assigned to goodwill or to other intangible assets acquired are significant in relation to the total cost of the acquired entity:
   a. For intangible assets subject to amortization:
      1. The total amount assigned and the amount assigned to any major **intangible asset class**
      2. The amount of any significant **residual value**, in total and by major intangible asset class

   3. The weighted-average amortization period, in total and by major intangible asset class
b. For intangible assets *not* subject to amortization, the total amount assigned and the amount assigned to any major intangible class
c. For goodwill:
   1. The total amount of goodwill and the amount that is expected to be deductible for tax purposes
   2. The amount of goodwill by reportable segment (if the combined entity is required to disclose segment information in accordance with FASB Statement No. 131, *Disclosures about Segments of an Enterprise and Related Information),* unless not practicable.

SFAS 142 Goodwill and Other Intangible Assets

SFAS 142 provides two major changes in financial reporting related to business combinations. The first major change goodwill will no longer be amortized systematically over time. This nonamortization approach will be applied to both previously recognized and newly acquired goodwill. In the second major change, goodwill will be subject to an annual test for impairment. When the carrying amount of goodwill exceeds its implied fair value, an impairment loss is recognized equal to that excess.

Testing Goodwill for Impairment

SFAS 142 describes the following two-step approach for testing goodwill for impairment:

- The first step of the goodwill impairment test, used to identify potential impairment, compares the fair value of a reporting unit with its carrying amount, including goodwill. If the fair value of a reporting unit exceeds its carrying amount, goodwill of the reporting unit is considered not impaired, thus the second step of the impairment test is unnecessary. If the carrying amount of a reporting unit exceeds its fair value, the second step of the goodwill impairment test shall be performed to measure the amount of impairment loss, if any.
- The second step of the goodwill impairment test, used to measure the amount of impairment loss, compares the implied fair value of reporting unit goodwill with the carrying amount of that goodwill. If the carrying amount of reporting unit goodwill exceeds the implied fair value of that goodwill, an impairment loss shall be recognized in an amount equal to that excess. The loss recognized cannot exceed the carrying amount of goodwill. After a goodwill impairment loss is recognized, the adjusted carrying amount of goodwill shall be its new accounting basis. Subsequent reversal of a previously recognized goodwill impairment loss is prohibited once the measurement of that loss is completed.

Calculation of Implied Fair Value of Goodwill

The implied fair value of goodwill shall be determined in the same manner as the amount of goodwill recognized in a business combination is determined. That is, an entity shall allocate the fair value of a reporting unit to all of the assets and liabilities of that unit (including any unrecognized intangible assets) as if the reporting unit had been acquired in a business combination and the fair value of the reporting unit was the price paid to acquire the reporting unity. The excess of the fair value of a reporting unit over the amounts assigned to its assets and liabilities is the implied fair value of goodwill. That allocation process shall be performed only for purposes of testing goodwill for impairment; an entity shall not write up or write down a recognized asset or liability, nor should it recognize a previously unrecognized intangible asset as a result of that allocation process.

Simple Example

On January 2, 20x2, ABC Company purchased all the outstanding stock of XYZ Corporation for $2,000. The fair value of identifiable assets is $1,600 and $400 of goodwill is recorded.

XYZ recorded a loss for 20x2 and forecast continuing losses. An analysis of the company (reporting unit) indicates that the reporting units fair value is now only $150 above the fair value of the identifiable net assets. Therefore, the implied value of goodwill has fallen to $150. As a result the consolidated unit will report a $250 ($400 - $150) goodwill impairment loss on a separate line on the income statement and report goodwill on a separate line on the balance sheet at $150.

What are Reporting Units?

The FASB noted that goodwill is primarily associated with individual *reporting units* within the consolidated entity. Such goodwill is often considered "synergistic" because it arises from the interaction of the assets of the acquired company with those of the acquirer in specific ways. To better assess potential declines in value for goodwill (in place of amortization), the most specific business level at which goodwill is evident was chosen as the appropriate level for impairment testing. This specific business level is referred to as the reporting unit. The FASB also noted that, in practice, goodwill is often assigned to reporting units either at the level of a reporting segment – as described in SFAS 131 *Disclosures about Segments of an Enterprise and Related Information* – or at a lower level within a segment of a combined enterprise. Consequently, the reporting unit became the designated enterprise component for tests of goodwill impairment. Reporting units may thus include the following:

- A component of an operating segment at a level below the operating segment. Segment management should review and assess performance at this level. Also, the component should be a business in which discrete financial information is available and differ economically from other components of the operating segment.
- The segments of an enterprise
- The entire enterprise

For example, ABC consolidated company includes four operating segments resulting from the parent company and three acquisitions of companies X, Y, and Z. ABC tested each separate reporting unit for goodwill impairment. ABC compared the fair market of each of its reporting units to its carrying value. The comparison revealed that the fair value of each of the reporting units exceeded its carrying value except segment Z.

According to SFAS 142, Segment Z must apply the second step of impairment testing, a comparison of the implied value of its goodwill to its carrying value. The carrying value of its goodwill was $150,000. The following data was used for the test:

Segment Z: December 31, 20x2 fair market value		$3,000,000
Fair values of Segment Z net assets at Dec. 31, 20x2		
Current Assets	$1,000,000	
Property	1,500,000	
Equipment	500,000	
Subscriber list	300,000	
Patented technology	400,000	
Current liabilities	(250,000)	
Long-term debt	(550,000)	
Value assigned to identifiable net assets		(2,900,000)
Value assigned to goodwill		$ 100,000
Carrying value before impairment		(150,000)
Impairment loss		$ 50,000

The necessary comparisons to determine if goodwill is impaired depend first on the fair value computation of the reporting unit and then, if necessary, the fair value computation for goodwill. But how are such values computed? How can fair values be known if the subsidiary is wholly-owned and thus not traded publicly?

Several alternative methods exist for determining the fair values of the reporting units that comprise a consolidated entity.

- First, any quoted market prices that exist can provide a basis for assessing fair value – particularly for subsidiaries with actively traded non-controlling interests.
- Second, a comparable businesses may exist that can help indicate market values.
- Third, there are a variety of present value techniques for assessing the fair value of an identifiable set of future cash flow streams, or profit projections discounted for the riskiness of the future flows.

SFAS 142 Disclosures:

The changes in the carrying amount of goodwill during the period including:

1. The aggregate amount of goodwill acquired
2. The aggregate amount of impairment losses recognized
3. The amount of goodwill included in the gain or loss on disposal of all or a portion of a reporting unit.

For each impairment loss recognized related to an intangible asset, the following information shall be disclosed in the notes to the financial statements that include the period in which the impairment loss is recognized:

a. A description of the impaired intangible asset and the facts and circumstances leading to the impairment
b. The amount of the impairment loss and the method for determining fair value
c. The caption in the income statement or the statement of activities in which the impairment loss is aggregated
d. If applicable, the segment in which the impaired intangible asset is reported under Statement 131.

For each goodwill impairment loss recognized, the following information shall be disclosed in the notes to the financial statements that include the period in which the impairment loss is recognized:

a. A description of the facts and circumstances leading to the impairment
b. The amount of the impairment loss and the method of determining the fair value of the associated reporting unit (whether based on quoted market prices, prices of comparable businesses, a present value or other valuation technique, or a combination thereof)
c. If a recognized impairment loss is an estimate that has not yet been finalized that fact and the reasons therefor and, in subsequent periods, the nature and amount of any significant adjustments made to the initial estimate of the impairment loss.

PARENT COMPANY THEORY vs. ENTITY THEORY—A COMPARISON

The Parent Company theory emphasizes the presentation of the financial statements of the parent company and its share of the subsidiary's assets, liabilities and operating results. The minority interest is shown on the equity side of the consolidated balance sheet between the liabilities and stockholder's equity sections, the minority therefore being regarded as neither a liability nor a part of stockholder's equity under the parent company theory. On the consolidated income statement minority interest is shown as a deduction in arriving at consolidated net income.

The Entity theory of minority interest regards the ownership of the entity to be comprised of two groups of owners—the majority and minority groups. The minority interest is, therefore, classified in the stockholder's equity section of the consolidated balance sheet and the minority portion of the subsidiary's net income is considered to be a segment of the consolidated net income.

A further difference is that in the Entity theory, the excess of cost over fair value (goodwill) is attributed to the enterprise as a whole and recognizes the implied value of the goodwill. This is sometimes referred to as the "grossing up" of goodwill. For example, if goodwill was $20,000 based on 80% ownership, it would follow that goodwill for the enterprise as a whole could be stated as $25,000.

While the question of which of these two concepts is acceptable has not been answered by APB's or FASB's, it would appear that the parent company theory is currently in favor.

Equity Method (20% to 50% Ownership)

Investments in common stock of **all unconsolidated** domestic and foreign **subsidiaries** should be accounted for by the **cost method** in consolidated statements. Further, parent-company financial statements prepared for issuance to stockholders as the financial statements of the primary reporting entity are **not** a valid substitute for consolidated financial statements and not in accordance with GAAP (FASB Statement #94).

The equity method should be followed where an investor's interest in voting stock enables it to exercise **significant influence** over operating and financial policies of an investee even though the investor holds 50% or less of the voting stock. Significant influence may be indicated in several ways such as representation on the board of directors, participation in policy making processes, material intercompany transactions, interchange of managerial personnel or technical dependency. **An investment of 20% or more** (direct or indirect) in the voting stock, **in the absence of evidence to the contrary, is a presumption that an investor has the ability to exercise significant influence over an investee.** Conversely, an investment of less than 20% should lead to a presumption that an investor does not exercise significant influence (unless such ability can be demonstrated) and the cost method should be used.

ADJUSTMENTS TO NET INCOME UNDER THE EQUITY METHOD

Elimination of unrealized intercompany profits and losses: RULE—Eliminate based on the investor's percentage of ownership.

Problem: At the investee's balance sheet date, the investee holds inventory for which the investor recorded a $100,000 gross profit. The investor owns 30% of the common stock of the investee, the investment is accounted for under the equity method. Ignoring income taxes, what adjustments are required?

Solution: The net income of the investee to be included in the investor's income statement should be adjusted for only 30% of the gross profit resulting from intercompany sales and included in the investee's inventory—not 100% where control is exercised in consolidation (over 50% control).

Assume further that investee had net income of $450,000 for the period:

Investee's net income	$450,000
Investor's % share	× .30
Investor's share of net income	$135,000
Less: Intercompany profit	
30% × 100,000	(30,000)
Equity method investment income	$105,000

Journal Entry

Investment	$105,000	
Investment Income		$105,000

GOODWILL AND THE EQUITY METHOD

The calculation of goodwill is the difference between the cost of the investment and the underlying value in the net assets which is the same calculation used in the purchase of a subsidiary.

For example, assume a 40% investment and the net income of the investee is $65,000.

Cost of Investment		$150,000
FV of Net Assets	$350,000	
	X 40%	(140,000)
Excess of Cost Over FV (Goodwill)		10,000

Historically, goodwill implicit in equity method investments was amortized over periods less than or equal to 40 years. However, with the release of SFAS 142, the FASB stated that in applying the equity method, goodwill amortization would not be allowed in future periods. The change will be accounted for prospectively and retroactive adjustments would not be allowed. Instead, the goodwill amount reported for each equity method investment will be tested for **permanent** declines in value as any other asset on the balance sheet is tested for declines in value.

Book value different than fair value: Assume further that the book value of the net assets (S.E.) was $300,000 and that the difference between the FV of the net assets and the carrying value (BV) was attributable to a fixed asset with a remaining useful life of 5 years. We can then make the following computation:

Cost	$150,000
Less: Goodwill	10,000
FV of Identifiable Assets	140,000
BV 40% × $300,000	120,000
Attributable to Fixed Assets	20,000
Annual Additional Depreciation	
20,000 ÷ 5	$ 4,000

This will result in additional depreciation ($4,000) per year for 5 years.

To show the investment account in three parts:

Cost of Assets at BV	$120,000
[1] Cost of Fixed Asset in Excess of BV	20,000
Goodwill (ECOFV)	10,000
	$150,000

[1] Will be written off over the useful life of the asset

If in year 1 the investee had net income of $65,000, the entries to reflect investor's share of investee income ($26,000) and the adjustment to investment income would be:

Investment	$26,000	
Investment Income		$26,000
Investment Income	4,000	
Investment		4,000

A simpler entry would probably be made as follows:

Investment	$22,000	
Investment Income		$22,000

OTHER POINTS

- Sales of stock by an investor should be accounted for as gains or losses for the difference between selling price and carrying amount of stock sold.
- The investor should record its share of the earnings or losses of an investee from the most recent financial statements. A lag in reporting should be consistent from year to year.
- A loss in value that is other than temporary should be recognized.
- In the event that an investor's share of losses exceeds the carrying amount of an investment accounted for by the equity method plus advances, the equity method should be discontinued when the investment is reduced to zero. If the investee subsequently reports net income, the investor should resume applying the equity method only after its share of net income equals the net losses not previously recognized.

CHANGES IN STOCK OWNERSHIP—RETROACTIVE ADJUSTMENTS

When a company buys less than a 20% interest in another company, the investment will ordinarily be recorded at cost unless significant influence can be shown. An increase in the investment by the investor to 20% or above (significant influence is presumed) requires **retroactive application of the equity method** to the period during which the cost method was used. Assume the following:

Year	*Percentage Stock Owned*	*Investee's Net Income*	*Investee's Dividends*	*Undistributed Income*
X1	5%	$150,000	$ 50,000	$100,000
X2	10%	200,000	75,000	125,000
X3	15%	300,000	100,000	200,000
X4	25%	360,000	160,000	200,000

In 19X4 the investor is presumed to have significant influence and should use the equity method with retroactive application. The change from the cost method of accounting to the equity method is required by A.P.B. #18 and necessitates the retroactive adjustment of the investment, results of operations and retained earnings. Prior year statements are therefore restated to reflect the investor's share of net income. Since the investor already included the dividends in net income, only the difference between net income and dividends (the increase in investee's retained earnings) will be included in the adjustment.

Journal Entry to show retroactive application:

	Debit	Credit
Investment	$47,500	
19X1 Investment Income		$ 5,000
19X2 Investment Income		12,500
19X3 Investment Income		30,000

To include in income 5% × $100,000 for X1; 10% × $125,000 for X2; 15% × $200,000 for X3

The actual credits would be to Retained Earnings; however, if comparative statements are prepared, the investment income would be adjusted as shown.

Journal Entries for 19X4:

	Debit	Credit
Investment	$90,000	
Investment Income		$90,000

25% × $360,000 earnings for the year

	Debit	Credit
Cash	$40,000	
Investment		$40,000

25% × 160,000 dividends paid by investee

A comprehensive example of the retroactive adjustment of Investment Income follows:

10,000 shares of S outstanding at $100,000
Capital contributed in excess 48,000

Year	*Shares Purchased by Parent at Beginning of Year*	*Cost*	*Undistributed Income*	*Retained Earnings—S*	*Included in P's R.E.*
X1	None	—0—	1,000	1,000	None
X2	1,000	$ 20,000	10,000	11,000	[1] None
X3	1,000	22,000	14,000	25,000	[2] 3,800
X4	2,000	50,000	50,000	75,000	[3] 23,800
X5	4,000	106,000	75,000	150,000	[4] 83,800

[1] X1, X2—Equity method cannot be used unless significant influence can be shown. Investment should be carried at cost.

[2]	X3	10% × 10,000 =	1,000
		20% × 14,000 =	2,800
			3,800
		Equity Method	
		Intercompany profit eliminated—20%	

[3]	X4	40% × 50,000 =	20,000
		Plus X3 amt. =	3,800
			23,800
		Equity Method	
		Intercompany profit eliminated—40%	

[4]	X5	80% × $75,000	60,000
		Plus X4 amount	23,800
			83,800

Consolidated statements should be prepared. If so, investment may be carried at cost. If consolidated statements cannot be prepared, the cost method must be used. Intercompany profit eliminated—100%.

We can also show how S's stockholder's equity will be handled in making elimination entries in year X5.

STOCKHOLDER'S	MINORITY INTEREST 20% x 298,000 = $59,600
EQUITY	ELIMINATION VS. INVESTMENT ACCOUNT (A) $154,600
$298,000	INCLUDED IN CONSOLIDATED R.E. $83,800

(Stockholder's equity = $148,000 paid-in capital + $150,000 R.E.)

(A) 80% × 100,000 =	$ 80,000
80% × 48,000 =	38,400
Total C/S and C.C.	$118,400
Add: Purchased R.E.	
10% × 1,000 (X2)	100
10% × 11,000 (X3)	1,100
20% × 25,000 (X4)	5,000
40% × 75,000 (X5)	30,000
	$154,600

Remember to apply the rules for purchase accounting to each acquisition to determine if there is an excess of cost over fair value or an excess of fair value over cost. Also a difference in fair value may result in a change in depreciation thereby affecting investment income.

Combined Financial Statements

To justify the preparation of consolidated statements, the controlling financial interest should rest directly or indirectly in one of the companies included in the consolidation. There are circumstances, however, where combined financial statements (as distinguished from consolidated statements) of commonly controlled companies are likely to be more meaningful than their separate statements. For example, combined financial statements would be useful where one individual owns a controlling interest in several corporations which are related in their operations. Combined statements would also be used to present the financial position and the results of operations of a group of unconsolidated subsidiaries. They might also be used to combine the financial statements of companies under common management.

Where combined statements are prepared for a group of related companies, such as a group of unconsolidated subsidiaries or a group of commonly controlled companies, intercompany transactions and profits or losses should be eliminated, and if there are problems in connection with such matters as minority interests, foreign operations, different fiscal periods, or income taxes, they should be treated in the same manner as in consolidated statements. To the extent there is any intercompany investment, it is **offset** against the related equity. If there is no intercompany investment, the individual companies' equities are combined.

Chapter Four
Consolidated Financial Statements Questions

COST METHOD

1. Day Co. received dividends from its common stock investments during the year ended December 31, 2001, as follows:

- A stock dividend of 400 shares from Parr Corp. on July 25, 2001, when the market price of Parr's shares was $20 per share. Day owns less than 1% of Parr's common stock.
- A cash dividend of $15,000 from Lark Corp. in which Day owns a 25% interest. A majority of Lark's directors are also directors of Day.

What amount of dividend revenue should Day report in its 2001 income statement?

a. $23,000
b. $15,000
c. $8,000
d. $0

EQUITY METHOD

2. On July 1, 2000, Denver Corp. purchased 3,000 shares of Eagle Co.'s 10,000 outstanding shares of common stock for $20 per share. On December 15, 2000, Eagle paid $40,000 in dividends to its common stockholders. Eagle's net income for the year ended December 31, 2000, was $120,000, earned evenly throughout the year. In its 2000 income statement, what amount of income from this investment should Denver report?

a. $36,000
b. $18,000
c. $12,000
d. $6,000

3. On January 2, 2000, Well Co. purchased 10% of Rea, Inc.'s outstanding common shares for $400,000. Well is the largest single shareholder in Rea, and Well's officers are a majority on Rea's board of directors. Rea reported net income of $500,000 for 2000, and paid dividends of $150,000. In its December 31, 2000, balance sheet, what amount should Well report as investment in Rea?

a. $450,000
b. $435,000
c. $400,000
d. $385,000

4. On January 1, 2000, Barton Corporation acquired as a long-term investment for $500,000, a 30% common stock interest in Buffer Company. On that date, Buffer had net assets with a book value and current market value of $1,600,000. During 2000 Buffer reported net income of $180,000 and declared and paid cash dividends of $40,000. An impairment test at the end of the year indicated that goodwill had lost 2.5% of its value. What is the amount of income that Barton should report from this investment for 2000?

a. $12,000.
b. $42,000.
c. $53,500.
d. $54,000.

5. Sage, Inc., bought 40% of Adams Corp.'s outstanding common stock on January 2, 2000, for $400,000. The carrying amount of Adams' net assets at the purchase date totaled $900,000. Fair values and carrying amounts were the same for all items except for plant and inventory, for which fair values exceeded their carrying amounts by $90,000 and $10,000, respectively. The plant has an 18-year life. All inventory was sold during 2000. During 2000, Adams reported net income of $120,000 and paid a $20,000 cash dividend. What amount should Sage report in its income statement from its investment in Adams for the year ended December 31, 2000?

a. $48,000
b. $42,000
c. $36,000
d. $32,000

6. Park Co. uses the equity method to account for its January 1, 2000, purchase of Tun Inc.'s common stock. On January 1, 2000, the fair values of Tun's FIFO inventory and land exceeded their carrying amounts. How do these excesses of fair values over carrying amounts affect Park's reported equity in Tun's 2000 earnings?

	Inventory excess	*Land excess*
a.	Decrease	Decrease
b.	Decrease	No effect
c.	Increase	Increase
d.	Increase	No effect

Items 7 through 9 are based on the following:

Grant, Inc. acquired 30% of South Co.'s voting stock for $200,000 on January 2, 2000. Grant's 30% interest in South gave Grant the ability to exercise significant influence over South's operating and financial policies. During 2000, South earned $80,000 and paid dividends of $50,000. South reported earnings of $100,000 for the six months ended June 30, 2001, and $200,000 for the year ended December 31, 2001. On July 1, 2001, Grant sold half of its stock in South for $150,000 cash. South paid dividends of $60,000 on October 1, 2001.

7. Before income taxes, what amount should Grant include in its 2000 income statement as a result of the investment?

a. $15,000
b. $24,000
c. $50,000
d. $80,000

8. In Grant's December 31, 2000, balance sheet, what should be the carrying amount of this investment?

a. $200,000
b. $209,000
c. $224,000
d. $230,000

9. In its 2001 income statement, what amount should Grant report as gain from the sale of half of its investment?

a. $24,500
b. $30,500
c. $35,000
d. $45,500

---

10. Moss Corp. owns 20% of Dubro Corp.'s preferred stock and 80% of its common stock. Dubro's stock outstanding at December 31, 2000, is as follows:

10% cumulative preferred stock	$100,000
Common stock	700,000

Dubro reported net income of $60,000 for the year ended December 31, 2000. What amount should Moss record as equity in earnings of Dubro for the year ended December 31, 2000?

a. $42,000
b. $48,000
c. $48,400
d. $50,000

11. On January 1, 2000, Mega Corp. acquired 10% of the outstanding voting stock of Penny, Inc. On January 2, 2001, Mega gained the ability to exercise significant influence over financial and operating control of Penny by acquiring an additional 20% of Penny's outstanding stock. The two purchases were made at prices proportionate to the value assigned to Penny's net assets, which equaled their carrying amounts. For the years ended December 31, 2000 and 2001, Penny reported the following:

	2000	*2001*
Dividends paid	$200,000	$300,000
Net income	600,000	650,000

In 2001, what amounts should Mega report as current year investment income and as an adjustment, before income taxes, to 2000 investment income?

	2001 investment income	*Adjustment to 2000 investment income*
a.	$195,000	$160,000
b.	$195,000	$100,000
c.	$195,000	$40,000
d.	$105,000	$40,000

12. When the equity method is used to account for investments in common stock, which of the following affect(s) the investor's reported investment income?

	A change in market value of investee's common stock	*Cash dividends from investee*
a.	Yes	Yes
b.	Yes	No
c.	No	Yes
d.	No	No

CONSOLIDATION - GOODWILL

13. Penn Corp. paid $300,000 for the outstanding common stock of Star Co. At that time, Star had the following condensed balance sheet:

	Carrying amounts
Current assets	$ 40,000
Plant and equipment, net	380,000
Liabilities	200,000
Stockholders' equity	220,000

The fair value of the plant and equipment was $60,000 more than its recorded carrying amount. The fair values and carrying amounts were equal for all other assets and liabilities. What amount of goodwill, related to Star's acquisition, should Penn report in its consolidated balance sheet?

a. $20,000
b. $40,000
c. $60,000
d. $80,000

14. On April 1, 2001, Dart Co. paid $620,000 for all the issued and outstanding common stock of Wall Corp. in a transaction properly accounted for as a purchase. The recorded assets and liabilities of Wall Corp. on April 1, 2001, follow:

Cash	$ 60,000
Inventory	180,000
Property and equipment (net of accumulated depreciation of $220,000)	320,000
Goodwill (net of accumulated amortization of $50,000)	100,000
Liabilities	(120,000)
Net assets	$540,000

On April 1, 2001, Wall's inventory had a fair value of $150,000, and the property and equipment (net) had a fair value of $380,000. What is the amount of goodwill resulting from the business combination?

a. $150,000
b. $120,000
c. $50,000
d. $20,000

15. On June 30, 2001, Needle Corporation purchased for cash at $10 per share all 100,000 shares of the outstanding common stock of Thread Company. The total appraised value of identifiable assets less liabilities of Thread was $1,400,000 at June 30, 2001, including the appraised value of Thread's property, plant, and equipment (its only noncurrent asset) of $250,000. The consolidated balance sheet of Needle Corporation and its wholly owned subsidiary at June 30, 2001, should reflect

a. An extraordinary gain of $150,000.
b. Goodwill of $150,000.
c. An extraordinary gain of $400,000.
d. Goodwill of $400,000.

16. In a business combination accounted for as a purchase, the appraisal values of the identifiable assets acquired exceeds the acquisition price. The excess appraisal value should be reported as a

a. Deferred credit.
b. Reduction of the values assigned to current assets and a deferred credit for any unallocated portion.
c. Reduction of the values assigned to noncurrent assets and an extraordinary gain.
d. Pro rata reduction of the values assigned to current and noncurrent assets.

CONSOLIDATION THEORY

17. Which of the following is the **best theoretical** justification for consolidated financial statements?

a. In form the companies are one entity; in substance they are separate.
b. In form the companies are separate; in substance they are one entity.
c. In form and substance the companies are one entity.
d. In form and substance the companies are separate.

18. When a parent-subsidiary relationship exists, consolidated financial statements are prepared in recognition of the accounting concept of

a. Reliability.
b. Materiality.
c. Legal entity.
d. Economic entity.

19. Company X acquired for cash all of the outstanding common stock of Company Y. How should Company X determine in general the amounts to be reported for the inventories and long-term debt acquired from Company Y?

	Inventories	*Long-term debt*
a.	Fair value	Fair value
b.	Fair value	Recorded value
c.	Recorded value	Fair value
d.	Recorded value	Recorded value

20. Company J acquired all of the outstanding common stock of Company K in exchange for cash. The acquisition price exceeds the fair value of net assets acquired. How should Company J determine the amounts to be reported for the plant and equipment and long-term debt acquired from Company K?

	Plant and equipment	*Long-term debt*
a.	K's carrying amount	K's carrying amount
b.	K's carrying amount	Fair value
c.	Fair value	K's carrying amount
d.	Fair value	Fair value

INTERCOMPANY RECEIVABLES

21. Shep Co. has a receivable from its parent, Pep Co. Should this receivable be separately reported in Shep's balance sheet and in Pep's consolidated balance sheet?

	Shep's balance sheet	*Pep's consolidated balance sheet*
a.	Yes	No
b.	Yes	Yes
c.	No	No
d.	No	Yes

22. Wright Corp. has several subsidiaries that are included in its consolidated financial statements. In its December 31, 2000, trial balance, Wright had the following intercompany balances before eliminations:

	Debit	*Credit*
Current receivable due from Main Co.	$ 32,000	
Noncurrent receivable from Main	114,000	
Cash advance to Corn Corp.	6,000	
Cash advance to King Co.		$ 15,000
Intercompany payable to King		101,000

In its December 31, 2000, consolidated balance sheet, what amount should Wright report as intercompany receivables?

a. $152,000
b. $146,000
c. $36,000
d. $0

INTERCOMPANY INVENTORY

23. Parker Corp. owns 80% of Smith Inc.'s common stock. During 2001, Parker sold Smith $250,000 of inventory on the same terms as sales made to third parties. Smith sold all of the inventory purchased from Parker in 2001. The following information pertains to Smith and Parker's sales for 2001:

	Parker	*Smith*
Sales	$1,000,000	$700,000
Cost of sales	400,000	350,000
	$ 600,000	$350,000

What amount should Parker report as cost of sales in its 2001 consolidated income statement?

a. $750,000
b. $680,000
c. $500,000
d. $430,000

24. Clark Co. had the following transactions with affiliated parties during 2000:

- Sales of $60,000 to Dean, Inc., with $20,000 gross profit. Dean had $15,000 of this inventory on hand at year end. Clark owns a 15% interest in Dean and does not exert significant influence.
- Purchases of raw materials totaling $240,000 from Kent Corp., a wholly-owned subsidiary. Kent's gross profit on the sale was $48,000. Clark had $60,000 of this inventory remaining on December 31, 2000.

Before eliminating entries, Clark had consolidated current assets of $320,000. What amount should Clark report in its December 31, 2000, consolidated balance sheet for current assets?

a. $320,000
b. $317,000
c. $308,000
d. $303,000

Items 25 through 27 are based on the following:

Selected information from the separate and consolidated balance sheets and income statements of Pare, Inc. and its subsidiary, Shel Co., as of December 31, 2000, and for the year then ended is as follows:

	Pare	*Shel*	*Consolidated*
Balance sheet accounts			
Accounts receivable	$ 52,000	$38,000	$ 78,000
Inventory	60,000	50,000	104,000
Income statement accounts			
Revenues	$400,000	$280,000	$616,000
Cost of goods sold	300,000	220,000	462,000
Gross profit	100,000	60,000	154,000

Additional information:
During 2000, Pare sold goods to Shel at the same markup on cost that Pare uses for all sales.

25. What was the amount of intercompany sales from Pare to Shel during 2000?

a. $6,000
b. $12,000
c. $58,000
d. $64,000

26. At December 31, 2000, what was the amount of Shel's payable to Pare for intercompany sales?

a. $6,000
b. $12,000
c. $58,000
d. $64,000

27. In Pare's consolidating worksheet, what amount of unrealized intercompany profit was eliminated?

a. $6,000
b. $12,000
c. $58,000
d. $64,000

INTERCOMPANY EQUIPMENT

28. On January 1, 2000, Poe Corp. sold a machine for $900,000 to Saxe Corp., its wholly-owned subsidiary. Poe paid $1,100,000 for this machine, which had accumulated depreciation of $250,000. Poe estimated a $100,000 salvage value and depreciated the machine on the straight-line method over 20 years, a policy which Saxe continued. In Poe's December 31, 2000, consolidated balance sheet, this machine should be included in cost and accumulated depreciation as

	Cost	*Accumulated depreciation*
a.	$1,100,000	$300,000
b.	$1,100,000	$290,000
c.	$900,000	$40,000
d.	$850,000	$42,500

29. Port Inc., owns 100% of Salem Inc. On January 1, 2001, Port sold Salem delivery equipment at a gain. Port had owned the equipment for two years and used a five-year straight-line depreciation rate with no residual value. Salem is using a three-year straight-line depreciation rate with no residual value for the equipment. In the consolidated income statement, Salem's recorded depreciation expense on the equipment for 2001 will be decreased by

a. 20% of the gain on sale.
b. $33^1/_3$% of the gain on the sale.
c. 50% of the gain on the sale.
d. 100% of the gain on the sale.

Items 30 and 31 are based on the following:

Scroll, Inc., a wholly owned subsidiary of Pirn, Inc., began operations on January 1, 2000. The following information is from the condensed 2000 income statements of Pirn and Scroll:

	Pirn	*Scroll*
Sales to Scroll	$100,000	$ —
Sales to others	400,000	300,000
	500,000	300,000
Cost of goods sold:		
Acquired from Pirn	—	80,000
Acquired from others	350,000	190,000
Gross profit	150,000	30,000
Depreciation	40,000	10,000
Other expenses	60,000	15,000
Income from operations	50,000	5,000
Gain on sale of equipment to Scroll	12,000	—
Income before income taxes	$ 38,000	$ 5,000

Additional information:

- Sales by Pirn to Scroll are made on the same terms as those made to third parties.
- Equipment purchased by Scroll from Pirn for $36,000 on January 1, 2000, is depreciated using the straight-line method over four years.

30. In Pirn's December 31, 2000, consolidating worksheet, how much intercompany profit should be eliminated from Scroll's inventory?

a. $30,000
b. $20,000
c. $10,000
d. $6,000

31. What amount should be reported as depreciation expenses in Pirn's 2000 consolidated income statement?

a. $50,000
b. $47,000
c. $44,000
d. $41,000

INTERCOMPANY BONDS

32. P Co. purchased term bonds at a premium on the open market. These bonds represented 20 percent of the outstanding class of bonds issued at a discount by S Co., P's wholly owned subsidiary. P intends to hold the bonds until maturity. In a consolidated balance sheet, the difference between the bond carrying amounts in the two companies would be

a. Included as a decrease to retained earnings/
b. Included as an increase to retained earnings.
c. Reported as a deferred debit to be amortized over the remaining life of the bonds.
d. Reported as a deferred credit to be amortized over the remaining life of the bonds.

33. Wagner, a holder of a $1,000,000 Palmer, Inc., bond, collected the interest due on March 31, 2001, and then sold the bond to Seal, Inc., for $975,000. On that date, Palmer, a 75% owner of Seal, had a $1,075,000 carrying amount for this bond. What was the effect of Seal's purchase of Palmer's bond on the retained earnings and minority interest amounts reported in Palmer's March 31, 2001, consolidated balance sheet?

	Retained earnings	*Minority interest*
a.	$100,000 increase	$0
b.	$75,000 increase	$25,000 increase
c.	$0	$25,000 increase
d.	$0	$100,000 increase

INTERCOMPANY STOCK

34. Sun, Inc. is a wholly-owned subsidiary of Patton, Inc. On June 1, 2000, Patton declared and paid a $1 per share cash dividend to stockholders of record on May 15, 2000. On May 1, 2000, Sun bought 10,000 shares of Patton's common stock for $700,000 on the open market, when the book value per share was $30. What amount of gain should Patton report from this transaction in its consolidated income statement for the year ended December 31, 2000?

a. $0
b. $390,000
c. $400,000
d. $410,000

MINORITY INTEREST

Items 35 through 37 are based on the following:
On January 2, 2000, Pare Co. purchased 75% of Kidd Co.'s outstanding common stock. Selected balance sheet data at December 31, 2000, is as follows:

	Pare	*Kidd*
Total assets	$420,000	$180,000
Liabilities	$120,000	$ 60,000
Common stock	100,000	50,000
Retained earnings	200,000	70,000
	$420,000	$180,000

During 2000, Pare and Kidd paid cash dividends of $25,000 and $5,000, respectively, to their shareholders. There were no other intercompany transactions.

35. In its December 31, 2000, consolidated statement of retained earnings, what amount should Pare report as dividends paid?

a. $5,000
b. $25,000
c. $26,250
d. $30,000

36. In Pare's December 31, 2000, consolidated balance sheet, what amount should be reported as minority interest in net assets?

a. $0
b. $30,000
c. $45,000
d. $105,000

37. In its Dec. 31, 2000, consolidated balance sheet, what amount should Pare report as common stock?

a. $50,000
b. $100,000
c. $137,500
d. $150,000

38. A 70%-owned subsidiary company declares and pays a cash dividend. What effect does the dividend have on the retained earnings and minority interest balances in the parent company's consolidated balance sheet?

a. No effect on either retained earnings or minority interest.
b. No effect on retained earnings and a decrease in minority interest.
c. Decreases in both retained earnings and minority interest.
d. A decrease in retained earnings and no effect on minority interest.

CONSOLIDATED INCOME

39. On September 1, 1999, Phillips, Inc., issued common stock in exchange for 20% of Sago, Inc.'s outstanding common stock. On July 1, 2001, Phillips issued common stock for an additional 75% of Sago's outstanding common stock. Sago continues in existence as Phillips' subsidiary. How much of Sago's 2001 net income should be reported as accruing to Phillips?

a. 20% of Sago's net income to June 30 and all of Sago's net income from July 1 to December 31.
b. 20% of Sago's net income to June 30 and 95% of Sago's net income from July 1 to December 31.
c. 95% of Sago's net income.
d. All of Sago's net income.

CONSOLIDATED RETAINED EARNINGS

40. On June 30, 2001, Pane Corp. exchanged 150,000 shares of its $20 par value common stock for all of Sky Corp.'s common stock. At that date, the fair value of Pane's common stock issued was equal to the book value of Sky's net assets. Both corporations continued to operate as separate businesses, maintaining accounting records with years ending December 31. Information from separate company operations follows:

	Pane	Sky
Retained earnings—12/31/00	$3,200,000	$925,000
Net income—six months ended 6/30/01	800,000	275,000
Dividends paid—3/25/01	750,000	—

If the business combination is accounted for as a purchase, what amount of retained earnings would Pane report in its June 30, 2001, consolidated balance sheet?

a. $5,200,000
b. $4,450,000
c. $3,525,000
d. $3,250,000

41. Poe, Inc. acquired 100% of Shaw Co. in a business combination on September 30, 2000. During 2000, Poe declared quarterly dividends of $25,000 and Shaw declared quarterly dividends of $10,000. What amount should be reported as dividends declared in the December 31, 2000, consolidated statement of retained earnings?

a. $100,000
b. $120,000
c. $130,000
d. $135,000

SUMMARY PROBLEM

Items 42 through 46 are based on the following:

The separate condensed balance sheets and income statements of Purl Corp. and its wholly-owned subsidiary, Scott Corp., are as follows:

BALANCE SHEETS

December 31, 2000

	Purl	Scott
Assets		
Current assets		
Cash	$ 80,000	$ 60,000
Accounts receivable (net)	140,000	25,000
Inventories	90,000	50,000
Total current assets	310,000	135,000
Property, plant, and equipment (net)	625,000	280,000
Investment in Scott (equity method)	390,000	—
Total assets	$1,325,000	$415,000
Liabilities and Stockholders' Equity		
Current liabilities		
Accounts payable	$ 160,000	$ 95,000
Accrued liabilities	110,000	30,000
Total current liabilities	270,000	125,000
Stockholders' equity		
Common stock ($10 par)	300,000	50,000
Additional paid-in capital	—	10,000
Retained earnings	755,000	230,000
Total stockholders' equity	1,055,000	290,000
Total liabilities and stockholders' equity	$1,325,000	$415,000

INCOME STATEMENTS

For the Year Ended December 31, 2000

	Purl	Scott
Sales	$2,000,000	$750,000
Cost of goods sold	1,540,000	500,000
Gross margin	460,000	250,000
Operating expenses	260,000	150,000
Operating income	200,000	100,000
Equity in earnings of Scott	60,000	—
Income before income taxes	260,000	100,000
Provision for income taxes	60,000	30,000
Net income	$ 200,000	$ 70,000

Additional information:

- On January 1, 2000, Purl purchased for $360,000 all of Scott's $10 par, voting common stock. On January 1, 2000, the fair value of Scott's assets and liabilities equaled their carrying amount of $410,000 and $160,000, respectively, except that the fair values of certain items identifiable in Scott's inventory were $10,000 more than their carrying amounts. These items were still on hand at December 31, 2000. An impairment test at the end of the year indicated that goodwill had lost 1/10 of its value.
- During 2000, Purl and Scott paid cash dividends of $100,000 and $30,000, respectively. For tax purposes, Purl receives the 100% exclusion for dividends received from Scott.
- There were no intercompany transactions, except for Purl's receipt of dividends from Scott and Purl's recording of its share of Scott's earnings.
- Both Purl and Scott paid income taxes at the rate of 30%.

In the December 31, 2000, consolidated financial statements of Purl and its subsidiary:

42. Total current assets should be
a. $455,000
b. $445,000
c. $310,000
d. $135,000

43. Total assets should be
a. $1,740,000
b. $1,450,000
c. $1,350,000
d. $1,325,000

44. Total retained earnings should be
a. $985,000
b. $825,000
c. $795,000
d. $755,000

45. Net income should be
a. $270,000
b. $200,000
c. $190,000
d. $170,000

46. Impairment loss-goodwill should be
a. $20,000
b. $10,000
c. $6,000
d. $0

ACQUISITION COST

47. Ecol Corporation issued voting preferred stock with a fair value of $1,000,000 in exchange for all of the outstanding common stock of Ogee Service Company. Ogee has tangible net assets with a book value of $500,000 and a fair value of $600,000. In addition, Ecol Corporation issued stock valued at $100,000 to an investment banker as a "finder's fee" for arranging the combination. As a result of this combination Ecol Corporation should record an increase in net assets of
a. $500,000.
b. $700,000.
c. $600,000.
d. $1,100,000.

48. On August 31, 2001, Wood Corp. issued 100,000 shares of its $20 par value common stock for the net assets of Pine, Inc., in a business combination accounted for by the purchase method. The market value of Wood's common stock on August 31 was $36 per share. Wood paid a fee of $160,000 to the consultant who arranged this acquisition. Costs of registering and issuing the equity securities amounted to $80,000. No goodwill was involved in the purchase. What amount should Wood capitalize as the cost of acquiring Pine's net assets?
a. $3,600,000
b. $3,680,000
c. $3,760,000
d. $3,840,000

49. A business combination is accounted for properly as a purchase. Direct costs of combination, other than registration and issuance costs of equity securities, should be

a. Capitalized as a deferred charge and amortized.
b. Deducted directly from the retained earnings of the combined corporation.
c. Deducted in determining the net income of the combined corporation for the period in which the costs were incurred.
d. Included in the acquisition cost to be allocated to identifiable assets according to their fair values.

COMBINED STATEMENTS

50. For which of the following reporting units is the preparation of combined financial statements most appropriate?
a. A corporation and a majority-owned subsidiary with nonhomogeneous operations.
b. A corporation and a foreign subsidiary with nonintegrated homogeneous operations.
c. Several corporations with related operations with some common individual owners.
d. Several corporations with related operations owned by one individual.

51. Combined statements may be used to present the results of operations of

	Companies under common management	*Commonly controlled companies*
a.	No	Yes
b.	Yes	No
c.	No	No
d.	Yes	Yes

52. Mr. & Mrs. Dart own a majority of the outstanding capital stock of Wall Corp., Black Co., and West, Inc. During 2000, Wall advanced cash to Black and West in the amount of $50,000 and $80,000, respectively. West advanced $70,000 in cash to Black. At December 31, 2000, none of the advances was repaid. In the combined December 31, 2000, balance sheet of these companies,

what amount would be reported as receivables from affiliates?

a. $200,000
b. $130,000
c. $60,000
d. $0

53. Which of the following items should be treated in the same manner in both combined financial statements and consolidated statements?

	Income taxes	*Minority interest*
a.	No	No
b.	No	Yes
c.	Yes	Yes
d.	Yes	No

54. Ahm Corp. owns 90% of Bee Corp.'s common stock and 80% of Cee Corp.'s common stock. The remaining common shares of Bee and Cee are owned by their respective employees. Bee sells exclusively to Cee, Cee buys exclusively from Bee, and Cee sells exclusively to unrelated companies. Selected 2001 information for Bee and Cee follows:

	Bee Corp.	*Cee Corp.*
Sales	$130,000	$91,000
Cost of sales	100,000	65,000
Beginning inventory	None	None
Ending inventory	None	65,000

What amount should be reported as gross profit in Bee and Cee's combined income statement for the year ended December 31, 2001?

a. $26,000
b. $41,000
c. $47,800
d. $56,000

REVIEW QUESTIONS

55. Polk Corp. purchased a 30% interest in Irwin Corp. for an amount which reflects the fact that Irwin's depreciable assets have a market value in excess of their book value. In the separate statements of Polk, this difference should be

a. Charged against investment revenue over the remaining useful life of the assets.
b. Included in the carrying value of the investment until disposition of the stock.
c. Charged against investment revenue in the year of acquisition.
d. Charged to depreciation expense over the remaining useful life of the assets.

56. An investor uses the equity method to account for its 30% investment in common stock of an investee. Amortization of the investor's share of the excess of fair market value over book value of depreciable assets at the date of the purchase should be reported in the investor's income statement as part of

a. Other expense.
b. Depreciation expense.
c. Equity in earnings of investee.
d. Amortization of goodwill.

57. A parent corporation which uses the equity method of accounting for its investment in a 40% owned subsidiary, which earned $20,000 and paid $5,000 in dividends, made the following entries:

Investment in subsidiary	$8,000	
Equity in earnings of subsidiary		$8,000
Cash	2,000	
Dividend revenue		2,000

What effect will these entries have on the parent's statement of financial position?

a. Financial position will be fairly stated.
b. Investment in subsidiary overstated, retained earnings understated.
c. Investment in subsidiary understated, retained earnings understated.
d. Investment in subsidiary overstated, retained earnings overstated.

58. On November 30, 2000, Parlor, Inc., purchased for cash at $15 per share all 250,000 shares of the outstanding common stock of Shaw Co. At November 30, 2000, Shaw's balance sheet showed a carrying amount of net assets of $3,000,000. At that date, the fair value of Shaw's property, plant and equipment exceeded its carrying amount by $400,000. In its November 30, 2000, consolidated balance sheet, what amount should Parlor report as goodwill?

a. $750,000
b. $400,000
c. $350,000
d. $0

59. In a business combination accounted for as a purchase, the appraised values of the identifiable assets acquired exceeded the acquisition price. How should the excess appraised value be reported?

a. As a negative goodwill.
b. As additional paid-in capital.
c. As a reduction of the values assigned to noncurrent assets and an extraordinary gain unallocated portion.
d. As positive goodwill.

60. On June 30, 2000, Purl Corp. issued 150,000 shares of its $20 par common stock for which it received all of Scott Corp.'s common stock. The fair value of the common stock issued is equal to the book value of Scott Corp.'s net assets. Both corporations continued to operate as separate businesses, maintaining accounting records with years ending Dec. 31. Net income from separate company operations and dividends paid were:

	Purl	*Scott*
Net income		
Six months ended 6/30/00	$750,000	$225,000
Six months ended 12/31/00	825,000	375,000
Dividends paid		
March 25, 2000	950,000	—
November 15, 2000	—	300,000

On December 31, 2000, Scott held in its inventory merchandise acquired from Purl on December 1, 2000, for $150,000, which included a $45,000 markup.

Assume that the business combination qualifies for treatment as a purchase. In the 2000 consolidated income statement, net income should be reported at

a. $1,650,000
b. $1,905,000
c. $1,950,000
d. $2,130,000

Items 61 through 64 are based on the following:

Selected information from the separate and consolidated balance sheets and income statements of Pard, Inc. and its subsidiary, Spin Co. as of December 31, 2001, and for the year then ended is as follows:

	Pard	*Spin*	*Consolidated*
Balance sheet accounts			
Accounts receivable	$ 26,000	$ 19,000	$ 39,000
Inventory	30,000	25,000	52,000
Investment in Spin	67,000	—	—
Goodwill	—	—	30,000
Minority interest	—	—	10,000
Stockholders' equity	154,000	50,000	154,000
Income statement accounts			
Revenues	$200,000	$140,000	$308,000
Cost of goods sold	150,000	110,000	231,000
Gross profit	50,000	30,000	77,000
Equity in earnings of Spin	11,000	—	—
Amortization of goodwill	—	—	2,000
Net income	36,000	20,000	40,000

Additional information:

- During 2001, Pard sold goods to Spin at the same markup on cost that Pard uses for all sales. At December 31, 2001, Spin had not paid for all of these goods and still held 37.5% of them in inventory.
- Pard acquired its interest in Spin on January 2, 1998.

61. What was the amount of intercompany sales from Pard to Spin during 2001?

a. $3,000
b. $6,000
c. $29,000
d. $32,000

62. At December 31, 2001, what was the amount of Spin's payable to Pard for intercompany sales?

a. $3,000
b. $6,000
c. $29,000
d. $32,000

63. In Pard's consolidated balance sheet, what was the carrying amount of the inventory that Spin purchased from Pard?

a. $3,000
b. $6,000
c. $9,000
d. $12,000

64. What is the percent of minority interest ownership in Spin?

a. 10%
b. 20%
c. 25%
d. 45%

Items 65 and 66 are based on the following:

Nolan owns 100% of the capital stock of both Twill Corp. and Webb Corp. Twill purchases merchandise inventory from Webb at 140% of Webb's cost. During 2000, merchandise that cost Webb $40,000 was sold to Twill. Twill sold all of this merchandise to unrelated customers for $81,200 during 2000. In preparing combined financial statements for 2000, Nolan's bookkeeper disregarded the common ownership of Twill and Webb.

65. By what amount was unadjusted revenue overstated in the combined income statement for 2000?

a. $16,000
b. $40,000
c. $56,000
d. $81,200

66. What amount should be eliminated from cost of goods sold in the combined income statement for 2000?

a. $56,000
b. $40,000
c. $24,000
d. $16,000

Recently Released Questions

67. Band Co. uses the equity method to account for its investment in Guard, Inc. common stock. How should Band record a 2% stock dividend received from Guard?

a. As dividend revenue at Guard's carrying value of the stock.
b. As dividend revenue at the market value of the stock.
c. As a reduction in the total cost of Guard stock
d. As a memorandum entry reducing the unit cost of all Guard stock owned.

68. Birk co. purchased 30% of Sled Co.'s outstanding common stock on December 31, 2000, for $200,000. On that date, Sled's stockholders' equity was $500,000, and its fair value of its identifiable net assets was $600,000. On December 31, 2000 what amount of good will should Birk attribute to his acquisition?

a. $0
b. $20,000
c. $30,000
d. $50,000

69. On September 29, 1995, Wall Co. paid $860,000 for all the issued and outstanding common stock of Hart Corp. On that date, the carrying amounts of Hart's recorded assets and liabilities had fair values of $840,000 and $140,000, respectively. In Wall's September 30, 1995 balance sheet, what amount should be reported as goodwill?

a. $20,000
b. $160,000
c. $180,000
d. $240,000

NOTES
(work practice questions here or jot down key concepts!)

NOTES

(work practice questions here or jot down key concepts!)

Eliminate Investment -

Chapter Four
Consolidated Financial Statements Problems

NUMBER 1

Brighton Corporation acquired 80 percent of the 1,250 shares of $100 par value common stock outstanding of Solvo Corporation on July 1, 1999 for $158,600. Brighton uses the equity method of accounting for its investment in Solvo.

Enclosed are the balance sheets for both companies for the year ended December 31, 1999. The following information is also available:

1. Solvo Corporation reported net income and dividends for 1999 as follows:

Net income for six months ending:	
June 30	$10,000
December 31	20,000
Dividends declared:	
March 31	4,000
June 30	4,000
September 30	1,000
December 31	8,000

2. Data pertaining to 1999 intercompany sales and ending inventories were as follows:

	Brighton Corporation	*Solvo Corporation*
Intercompany sales:		
January 1 to June 30	$40,000	$95,000
July 1 to December 31	$60,000	$105,000
Markup on cost	20%	25%
Intercompany payable at year end	$13,000	$5,500
Year-end inventory of intercompany purchases at FIFO cost	$25,000	$18,000

3. Sales of equipment by Brighton Corporation to Solvo Corporation during 1999 were as follows:

Date	*Book Value on Brighton's Records*	*Price Paid by Solvo*	*Depreciation Method*	*Estimated Life*
February 1	$11,000	$13,500	Double-Declining Balance	10 years
October 1	14,000	12,000	Straight-line	5 years

For depreciation purposes Solvo Corporation estimates salvage at 10 percent of the equipment's cost.

4. Brighton Corporation acquired $40,000 of the 6 percent Solvo Corporation bonds at par value on July 1, 1999. Interest is paid each July 1 and January 1 by Solvo Corporation.

5. On December 1, 1999, Brighton Corporation discounted $4,000 of noninterest bearing notes payable of Solvo Corporation.

6. An impairment test at December 31, 1999 indicated that goodwill had not lost any of its value.

Required: Prepare a worksheet for the preparation of a consolidated balance sheet for Brighton Corporation and its subsidiary, Solvo, Inc., as of December 31, 1999. Formal statements and journal entries are not required. You may assume that both companies made all of the adjusting entries required for separate financial statements unless an obvious discrepancy exists. Income taxes should not be considered in your solution.

(Use Worksheet #1 on page 4Q-19)

NUMBER 2

Amboy Corporation acquired all of the outstanding $10 par voting common stock of Taft, Inc., on January 1, 2001, in exchange for 50,000 shares of its $10 par voting common stock. On December 31, 2000, Amboy's common stock had a closing market price of $15 per share on a national stock exchange. The acquisition was appropriately accounted for as a purchase. Both companies continued to operate as separate business entities maintaining separate accounting records with years ending December 31.

On December 31, 2001, after year-end adjustments but before the nominal accounts were closed, the companies had condensed general ledger trial balances as follows:

	Amboy	*Taft*
	Dr. (Cr.)	*Dr. (Cr.)*
Net sales	$(1,900,000)	$(1,500,000)
Dividend income from Taft, Inc.	(40,000)	
Gain on sale of warehouse	(30,000)	
Cost of goods sold	1,180,000	870,000
Operating expenses (includes depreciation)	550,000	440,000
Cash	285,000	150,000
Accounts receivable (net)	430,000	350,000
Inventories	530,000	410,000
Land, plant & equipment	660,000	680,000
Accumulated depreciation	(185,000)	(210,000)
Investment in Taft, Inc. (at cost)	750,000	
Accounts payable & accrued expenses	(670,000)	(594,000)
Common stock ($10 par)	(1,200,000)	(400,000)
Additional paid-in capital	(140,000)	(80,000)
Retained earnings (1/1/01)	(220,000)	(156,000)
Dividends paid		40,000
Total	$ -0-	$ -0-

Additional information is as follows:

- There were no changes in the common stock and additional paid-in capital accounts during 2001 except the one necessitated by Amboy's acquisition of Taft.
- At the acquisition date the current value of Taft's machinery exceeded its book value by $54,000. The excess will be amortized over the estimated average remaining life of six years. The fair values of all of Taft's other assets and liabilities were equal to their book values. An impairment test at the end of the year indicated that goodwill had lost $3,000 of its value.
- On July 1, 2001, Amboy sold a warehouse facility to Taft for $129,000 cash. At the date of sale Amboy's book values were $33,000 for the land and $66,000 for the undepreciated cost of the building. Taft allocated the $129,000 purchase price to the land for $43,000 and to the building for $86,000. Taft is depreciating the building over its estimated five-year remaining useful life by the straight-line method with no salvage value.
- During 2001 Amboy purchased merchandise from Taft at an aggregate invoice price of $180,000, which included a 100% markup on Taft's cost. The December 31, 2001, Amboy owed Taft $75,000 on these purchases, and $36,000 of the merchandise purchased remained in Amboy's inventory.

Required:

Complete the worksheet to prepare a consolidated income statement and retaining earnings statement for the year ended December 31, 2001, and a consolidated balance sheet as at December 31, 2001, for Amboy Corporation and its subsidiary, Taft, Inc. Formal consolidated statements and journal entries are not required. Ignore income tax considerations. Supporting computations should be in good form.

(use worksheet #2 on page 4Q-27)

NUMBER 3

The December 31, 2000 condensed balance sheets of Pym Corp. and its 90%-owned subsidiary, Sy Corp., are presented in the worksheet. Additional information follows:

- Pym's investment in Sy was purchased for $1,200,000 cash on January 1, 2000, and is accounted for by the equity method.
- At January 1, 2000, Sy's retained earnings amounted to $600,000, and its common stock amounted to $200,000.
- Sy declared a $1,000 cash dividend in December 2000, payable in January 2001.
- As of December 31, 2000, Pym had not recorded any portion of Sy's 2000 net income or dividend declaration.
- Sy borrowed $100,000 from Pym on June 30, 2000, with the note maturing on June 30, 2001, at 10% interest. Correct accruals have been recorded by both companies.
- During 2000, Pym sold merchandise to Sy at an aggregate invoice price of $300,000, which included a profit of $60,000. At December 31, 2000, Sy had not paid Pym for $90,000 of these purchases, and 5% of the total merchandise purchased from Pym still remained in Sy's inventory.
- Pym's excess cost over book value of Pym's investment in Sy has appropriately been identified as goodwill and an impairment test at the end of the year indicated that goodwill had lost $48,000 of its value.

Required:
Complete the worksheet for Pym Corp. and its subsidiary, Sy Corp., at December 31, 2000. A formal consolidated balance sheet and journal entries are not required.

(use worksheet #3 on page 4Q-28)

NUMBER 4

("Other Objective Answer Format")

Presented below are selected amounts from the separate unconsolidated financial statements of Poe Corp. and its 90%-owned subsidiary, Shaw Co., at December 31, 2001. Additional information follows:

	Poe	*Shaw*
Selected income statement amounts		
Sales	$710,000	$530,000
Cost of goods sold	490,000	370,000
Gain on sale of equipment	----	21,000
Earnings from investment in subsidiary	61,000	----
Interest expense	----	16,000
Depreciation	25,000	20,000
Selected balance sheet amounts		
Cash	$ 50,000	$ 15,000
Inventories	229,000	150,000
Equipment	440,000	360,000
Accumulated depreciation	(200,000)	(120,000)
Investment in Shaw	189,000	----
Investment in bonds	100,000	----
Discount on bonds	(9,000)	----
Bonds payable	----	(200,000)
Common stock	(100,000)	(10,000)
Additional paid-in capital	(250,000)	(40,000)
Retained earnings	(402,000)	(140,000)
Selected statement of retained earnings amounts		
Beginning balance, December 31, 2000	$272,000	$100,000
Net income	210,000	70,000
Dividends paid	80,000	30,000

Additional information:

- On January 2, 2001, Poe, Inc. purchased 90% of Shaw Co.'s 100,000 outstanding common stock for cash of $155,000. On that date, Shaw's stockholders' equity equaled $150,000 and the fair values of Shaw's assets and liabilities equaled their carrying amount. An impairment test at the end of the year indicated that goodwill had lost $2,000 of its value.
- On September 4, 2001, Shaw paid cash dividends of $30,000.
- On December 31, 2001, Poe recorded its equity in Shaw's earnings.

Required:

a. **Items 1 through 3.** Items 1 through 3 below represent transactions between Poe and Shaw during 2001. Determine the dollar amount effect of the consolidating adjustment on 2001 consolidated income before considering minority interest. Ignore income tax considerations.

1. On January 3, 2001, Shaw sold equipment with an original cost of $30,000 and a carrying value of $15,000 to Poe for $36,000. The equipment had a remaining life of three years and was depreciated using the straight-line method by both companies.

2. During 2001, Shaw sold merchandise to Poe for $60,000, which included a profit of $20,000. At December 31, 2001, half of this merchandise remained in Poe's inventory.

3. On December 31, 2001, Poe paid $91,000 to purchase 50% of the outstanding bonds issued by Shaw. The bonds mature on December 31, 2007, and were originally issued at par. The bonds pay interest annually on December 31 of each year, and the interest was paid to the prior investor immediately before Poe's purchase of the bonds.

b. **Item 4.** Determine the amount recorded for impairment loss – Goodwill for 2001.

c. **Items 5 through 16.** Items 5 through 16 below refer to accounts that may or may not be included in Poe and Shaw's consolidated financial statements. The list below refers to the various possibilities of those amounts to be reported in Poe's consolidated financial statements for the year ended December 31, 2001. Consider all transactions stated in items 1 through 4 in determining your answer. Ignore income tax considerations.

Items to be Answered:

5. Cash
6. Equipment
7. Investment in subsidiary
8. Bonds payable
9. Minority interest
10. Common stock
11. Beginning retained earnings
12. Dividends paid
13. Gain on retirement of bonds
14. Cost of goods sold
15. Interest expense
16. Depreciation expense

Responses to be Selected:

A. Sum of amounts on Poe and Shaw's separate unconsolidated financial statements.
B. Less than the sum of amounts on Poe and Shaw's separate unconsolidated financial statements but not the same as the amount on either.
C. Same as amount for Poe only.
D. Same as amount for Shaw only.
E. Eliminated entirely in consolidation.
F. Shown in consolidated financial statements but not in separate unconsolidated financial statements.
G. Neither in consolidated nor in separate unconsolidated financial statements.

CONSOLIDATED FINANCIAL STATEMENTS
WORKSHEET #1

Brighton Corporation & Subsidiary	Brighton Corp.	Salvo Corp.	Adjustments and Eliminations Debit	Adjustments and Eliminations Credit	Consolidated Balances Debit	Consolidated Balances Credit
Assets						
Cash	$ 200000	$ 20 000				
Accounts receivable	205000	55 000				
Notes receivable	180000	11 000		4000		
Notes receivable discounted	(4000)		4000			
Accrued interest receivable	1600	400				
Dividends receivable	6400					
Inventories	300000	75 000				
Plant and equipment	794000	280 600				
Allowance for depreciation	(260000)	(30 000)				
Investment in Solvo Corp. stock	167400			167 400		
Investment in Solvo Corp. bonds	40000					
Advance to Solvo Corp.	35000			35000		
Goodwill			9000			
Totals	$1665400	$ 412 000				
Liabilities and Stockholders' Equity						
Minority Interest				39600		
Accounts payable	220400	54 800				
Notes payable	142000	24 200				
Dividends Payable		8 000	-8000			
Accrued interest payable	22100	3 900				
Other accrued liabilities	7900	3 100				
Advance from Brighton Corp.		35 000	35000			
Bonds payable	600000	85 000				
Capital stock	360000	125 000	125000			
Capital in excess of par value	49000	12 000	12000			
Retained earnings	264000	61 000	61000			
Totals	$1665400	$ 412 000				

NUMBER 5 ("Other Objective Answer Format")

On January 2, 2000, Purl Co. purchased 90% of Strand Co.'s outstanding common stock at a purchase price that was in excess of Strand's stockholders' equity. On that date, the fair values of Strand's assets and liabilities equaled their carrying amounts. Purl has accounted for the acquisition as a purchase. Transactions during 2000 were as follows:

- On February 15, 2000, Strand sold equipment to Purl at a price higher than the equipment's carrying amount. The equipment had a remaining life of three years and was depreciated using the straight-line method by both companies.
- During 2000, Purl sold merchandise to Strand under the same terms it offered to third parties. At December 31, 2000, one-third of this merchandise remained in Strand's inventory.
- On November 15, 2000, both Purl and Strand paid cash dividends to their respective stockholders.
- On December 31, 2000, Purl recorded its equity in Strand's earnings.

Required:
Items 1 through 10 relate to accounts that may or may not be included in Purl and Strand's consolidated financial statements. This list below refers to the possible ways those accounts may be reported in Purl's consolidated financial statements for the year ended December 31, 2000. For each item, select one corresponding letter. An answer may be selected once, more than once, or not at all.

Responses to be Selected:

A. Sum of the amounts on Purl and Strand's separate unconsolidated financial statements.

B. Less than the sum of the amounts on Purl and Strand's separate unconsolidated financial statements, but not the same as the amount on either separate unconsolidated financial statement.

C. Same as the amount for Purl only.

D. Same as the amount for Strand only.

E. Eliminated entirely in consolidation.

F. Shown in the consolidated financial statements but not in the separate unconsolidated financial statements.

Items to be Answered:

1. Cash.
2. Equipment.
3. Investment in subsidiary.
4. Minority interest.
5. Common stock.
6. Beginning retained earnings.
7. Dividends paid.
8. Cost of goods sold.
9. Interest expense.
10. Depreciation expense.

NUMBER 6

Johnson, an investor in Acme Co., asked Smith, CPA for advice on the propriety of Acme's financial reporting for two of its investments. Smith obtained the following information related to the investments from Acme's December 31, 2001, financial statements:

- 20% ownership interest in Kern Co., represented by 200,000 shares of outstanding common stock purchased on January 2, 2001, for $600,000.
- 20% ownership interest in Wand Co., represented by 20,000 shares of outstanding common stock purchased on January 2, 2001, for $300,000.
- On January 2, 2001, the carrying values of the acquired shares of both investments equaled their purchase price.
- Kern reported earnings of $400,000 for the year ended December 31, 2001, and declared and paid dividends of $100,000 during 2001.
- Wand reported earnings of $350,000 for the year ended December 31, 2001, and declared and paid dividends of $60,000 during 2001.
- On December 31, 2001, Kern's and Wand's common stock were trading over-the-counter at $18 and $20 per share, respectively.
- The investment in Kern is accounted for using the equity method.
- The investment in Wand is accounted for as available-for-sale securities.

Smith recalculated the amounts reported in Acme's December 31, 2001, financial statements, and determined that they were correct. Stressing that the information available in the financial statements was limited, Smith advised Johnson that, assuming Acme properly applied generally accepted accounting principles, Acme may have appropriately used two different methods to account for its investments in Kern and Wand, even though the investments represent equal ownership interests.

Smith also informed Johnson that Acme had elected early application of Statement of Financial Accounting Standards No. 130, *Reporting Comprehensive Income,* beginning with the fiscal year ending December 31, 2001.

Required:

a. Prepare a detailed memorandum from Smith to Johnson supporting Smith's conclusion that, under generally accepted accounting principles, correctly applied, Acme may have appropriately used two different methods to account for its investments representing equal ownership interests.

b. Prepare a schedule indicating the amount Acme should report for the two investments in its December 31, 2001, balance sheet and statement of income and comprehensive income. Show all calculations. Ignore income taxes

Do not discuss SFAS No. 115, *Accounting for Investments in Certain Debt and Equity Securities.*

NUMBER 7

Since Grumer Co.'s inception, Monroe Co. has owned 18% of Grumer's outstanding common stock. Monroe provides three key management personnel to Grumer and purchased 25% of Grumer's output during 1999. Grumer is profitable. On January 2, 2000, Monroe purchased additional common stock to finance Grumer's expansion, thereby becoming a 30% owner. Grumer's common stock does not have a quoted market price. The stock has always been issued at its book value, which is assumed to approximate its fair value.

Required:

a. In general, distinguish between investor income reporting under the cost method and under the equity method. Which method is more consistent with accrual accounting? Why?

b. Prior to January 2, 2000, what specific factors should Monroe have considered in determining the appropriate method of accounting for its investment in Grumer?

c. For purposes of your answer to (c) only, assume Monroe used the cost method in accounting for its investment in Grumer prior to January 2, 2000. Describe the book adjustments required on January 2, 2000, when Monroe became owner of 30% of the outstanding common stock of Grumer.

NUMBER 8

Cain Corp. acquired all of the outstanding $10 par value voting common stock of Frey, Inc., on January 1, 2000, in exchange for 25,000 shares of its $10 par value voting common stock. On December 31, 1999, Cain's common stock had a closing market price of $30 per share on a national stock exchange. The acquisition was appropriately accounted for as a purchase. Both companies continued to operate as separate business entities maintaining separate accounting records with years ending December 31.

On December 31, 2000, the companies had condensed financial statements as follows:

	Cain Corp. *Dr. (Cr.)*	*Frey, Inc.* *Dr. (Cr.)*
Income Statement		
Net sales	$(3,800,000)	$(1,500,000)
Dividends from Rey	(40,000)	
Gain on sale of warehouse	(30,000)	
Cost of goods sold	2,360,000	870,000
Operating expenses (including depreciation)	1,100,000	440,000
Net income	$ (410,000)	$ (190,000)
Retained Earnings Statement		
Balance, 1/1/00	$ (440,000)	$ (156,000)
Net income	(410,000)	(190,000)
Dividends paid		40,000
Balance, 12/31/00	$ (850,000)	$ (306,000)
Balance Sheet		
Assets:		
Cash	$ 570,000	$ 150,000
Accounts receivable (net)	860,000	350,000
Inventories	1,060,000	410,000
Land, plant and equipment	1,320,000	680,000
Accumulated depreciation	(370,000)	(210,000)
Investment in Frey (at cost)	750,000	
Total assets	$ 4,190,000	$ 1,380,000
Liabilities and Stockholders' Equity:		
Accounts payable and accrued expenses	$(1,340,000)	$ (594,000)
Common stock ($10 par)	(1,700,000)	(400,000)
Additional paid-in capital	(300,000)	(80,000)
Retained earnings	(850,000)	(306,000)
Total liabilities and stockholders' equity	$(4,190,000)	$(1,380,000)

Additional information follows:

- There were no changes in the common stock and additional paid-in capital accounts during 2000 except the one necessitated by Cain's acquisition of Frey.
- At the acquisition date, the fair value of Frey's machinery exceeded its book value by $54,000. The excess cost will be amortized over the estimated average remaining life of six years. The fair values of all of Frey's other assets and liabilities were equal to their book values. An impairment test at the end of the year indicated that goodwill had lost $3,000 of its value.
- On July 1, 2000, Cain sold a warehouse facility to Frey for $129,000 cash. At the date of sale, Cain's book values were $33,000 for the land and $66,000 for the undepreciated cost of the building. Based on a real estate appraisal, Frey allocated $43,000 of the purchase price to land and $86,000 to building. Frey is depreciating the building over its estimated five-year remaining useful life by the straight-line method with no salvage value.
- During 2000, Cain purchased merchandise from Frey at an aggregate invoice price of $180,000, which included a 100% markup on Frey's cost. At December 31, 2000, Cain owed Frey $86,000 on these purchases, and $36,000 of this merchandise remained in Cain's inventory.

Required:

Complete the worksheet on the following page that would be used to prepare a consolidated income statement and a consolidated retained earnings statement for the year ended December 31, 2000, and a consolidated balance sheet as of December 31, 2000. Formal consolidated statements and adjusting entries are **not** required. Ignore income tax considerations. Supporting computations should be in good form.

NUMBER 8 (cont.)

Cain Corp. and Subsidiary
CONSOLIDATING STATEMENT WORKSHEET
December 31, 2000

Income Statement	*Cain Corp. Dr. (Cr.)*	*Frey, Inc. Dr. (Cr.)*	*Adjustments & Eliminations Dr.*	*Adjustments & Eliminations Cr.*	*Adjusted Balance*
Net sales	(3,800,000)	(1,500,000)			
Dividends from Frey	(40,000)				
Gain on sale of warehouse	(30,000)				
Cost of goods sold	2,360,000	870,000			
Operating expenses (including depreciation)	1,100,000	440,000			
Net income	(410,000)	(190,000)			
Retained Earnings Statement					
Balance, 1/1/00	(440,000)	(156,000)			
Net income	(410,000)	(190,000)			
Dividends paid		40,000			
Balance, 12/31/00	(850,000)	(306,000)			
Balance Sheet					
Assets:					
Cash	570,000	150,000			
Accounts receivable (net)	860,000	350,000			
Inventories	1,060,000	410,000			
Land, plant and equipment	1,320,000	680,000			
Accumulated depreciation	(370,000)	(210,000)			
Investment in Frey (at cost)	750,000				
Total Assets	4,190,000	1,380,000			
Liabilities & Stockholders' Equity: Accounts payable & accrued expenses	(1,340,000)	(594,000)			
Common stock ($10 par)	(1,700,000)	(400,000)			
Additional paid-in capital	(300,000)	(80,000)			
Retained earnings	(850,000)	(306,000)			
Total Liabilities & Stockholders' Equity	(4,190,000)	(1,380,000)			

NUMBER 9

On April 1, 1999, Jared, Inc., purchased 100% of the common stock of Munson Manufacturing Company for $5,850,000 and 20% of its preferred stock for $150,000. At the date of purchase the book and fair values of Munson's assets and liabilities were as follows:

	Book Value	*Fair Value*
Cash	$ 200,000	$ 200,000
Notes receivable	85,000	85,000
Accounts receivable, net	980,000	980,000
Inventories	828,000	700,000
Land	1,560,000	2,100,000
Machinery and equipment	7,850,000	10,600,000
Accumulated depreciation	(3,250,000)	(4,000,000)
Other assets	140,000	50,000
	$8,393,000	$10,715,000
Notes payable	$ 115,000	$ 115,000
Accounts payable	400,000	400,000
Subordinated debentures—7%	5,000,000	5,000,000
Preferred stock; noncumulative, nonparticipating, par value $5 per share, authorized, issued and outstanding 150,000 shares	750,000	—
Common stock; par value $10 per share; authorized, issued, and outstanding 100,000 shares	1,000,000	—
Additional paid-in capital (common stock)	122,000	
Retained earnings	1,006,000	
	$8,393,000	

Additional information:

By the year end, December 31, 1999, the following transactions had occurred:

- The balance of Munson's net accounts receivable at April 1, 1999, had been collected.
- The inventory on hand at April 1, 1999, had been charged to cost of sales. Munson used a perpetual inventory system in accounting for inventories.
- Prior to 1999, Jared had purchased at face value $1,500,000 of Munson's 7% subordinated debentures. These debentures mature on October 31, 2004, with interest payable annually on October 31.
- As of April 1, 1999, the machinery and equipment had an estimated remaining life of six years. Munson uses the straight-line method of depreciation. Munson's depreciation expense calculation for the nine months ended December 31, 1999, was based upon the old depreciation rates.
- The other assets consist entirely of long-term investments made by Munson and do **not** include any investment in Jared.
- During the last nine months of 1999, the following intercompany transactions occurred between Jared and Munson.

Intercompany sales:

	Jared to Munson	*Munson to Jared*
Net sales	$158,000	$230,000
Included in purchaser's inventory at December 31, 1999	36,000	12,000
Balance unpaid at December 31, 1999	16,800	22,000

Jared sells merchandise to Munson at cost. Munson sells merchandise to Jared at regular selling price including a normal gross profit margin of 35 percent. There were **no** intercompany sales between the two companies prior to April 1, 1999.

Accrued interest on intercompany debt is recorded by both companies in their respective accounts receivable and accounts payable accounts.

- The account, "Investment in Munson Manufacturing Company," includes Jared's investment in Munson's debentures and its investment in the common and preferred stock of Munson.

Am impairment test at December 31, 1999 indicated that goodwill had declined in value by $52,500.

Required:
Complete the worksheet to prepare the consolidated trial balance for Jared, Inc., and its subsidiary, Munson Manufacturing Company, at December 31, 1999. Show computations in good form where appropriate to support worksheet entries.

Jared's revenue and expense figures are for the twelve-month period while Munson's are for the last nine months of 1999. You may assume that both companies made all the adjusting entries required for separate financial statements unless stated to the contrary. Round all computations to the nearest dollar. **Ignore income taxes.**

(Use Worksheet #4 on page 4Q-29)

WORKSHEET #2

Amboy Corporation and Subsidiary
CONSOLIDATING STATEMENT WORKSHEET
December 31, 2001

Income Statement	*Amboy Corp.*	*Taft Inc.*	*Adjustments & Eliminations* Debit	Credit	*Adjusted Balance*
Net sales	$(1,900,000)	$(1,500,000)			
Dividends from Taft	(40,000)				
Gain on sale of warehouse	(30,000)				
Cost of goods sold	1,180,000	870,000			
Operating expenses (incl. deprec.)	550,000	440,000			
Net income	$ (240,000)	$ (190,000)			
Retained Earnings Statement					
Balance, 1/1/01	$ (220,000)	$ (156,000)			
Net income	(240,000)	(190,000)			
Dividends paid		40,000			
Balance, 12/31/01	$ (460,000)	$ (306,000)			
Balance Sheet					
Assets:					
Cash	$ 285,000	$ 150,000			
Accounts receivable (net)	430,000	350,000			
Inventories	530,000	410,000			
Land, plant & equipment	660,000	680,000			
Accumulated depreciation	(185,000)	(210,000)			
Investment in Taft (at cost)	750,000				
	$ 2,470,000	$ 1,380,000			
Liabilities & Stockholders' Equity:					
Accounts pay. & accrued exp.	$ (670,000)	$ (594,000)			
Common stock ($10 par)	(1,200,000)	(400,000)			
Additional paid-in capital	(140,000)	(80,000)			
Retained Earnings	(460,000)	(306,000)			
	$(2,470,000)	$(1,380,000)			

WORKSHEET #3
Pym Corp. and Subsidiary
Consolidated Balance Sheet Worksheet
December 31, 2000

	Pym Corp.	Sy Corp.	Adjustments & Eliminations		Consolidated
			Debit	Credit	
Assets					
Cash	75,000	15,000			
Accounts and other current receivables	410,000	120,000	B. 900.	C 100,000 (C) 500 90000	
Merchandise inventory	920,000	670,000		(D) 3000	
Plant and equipment (net)	1,000,000	400,000			
Investment in Sy Corp.	1,200,000		a. 90,900	(B) 900 (A) 1,200,000	
Goodwill			480,000	48,000	
Totals	3,605,000	1,205,000			
Liabilities and Stockholders' Equity					
Accounts payable and other current liabilities	140,000	305,000	(C) 100,000 (C) 500 90,000		
Common stock ($10 par)	500,000	200,000	200,000		
Retained earnings	2,965,000	700,000	600,000 D 3000	(A) 90,900	
Totals	3,605,000	1,205,000			

CONSOLIDATED FINANCIAL STATEMENTS
WORKSHEET #4

CGS - net Inventory

National 45-603 Eye-Ease 45-703 20/20 Buff Made in USA

Jared, Inc. and Subsidiary	Jared, Inc. Dr. (Cr.)	Munson Mfg. Co. Dr. (Cr.)	Adjustments and Eliminations Debit	Adjustments and Eliminations Credit	Consolidated Balances Debit	Consolidated Balances Credit
Cash	$ 822000	$ 580 000				
Notes receivable	--	85 000				
Accounts receivable, net	2758000	1368 400				
Inventories	3204000	1182 000		128000-		
Land	4000000	1560 000	540000			
Machinery and equipment	15875000	7850 000	2750000			
Accumulated depreciation				750000		
machinery and equipment	(6301000)	(3838 750)				
Buildings	1286000	--				
Accumulated depreciation-buildings	(372000)	--				
Investment in Munson Mfg. Co.	7500000	--		5850000-		
Other Assets	263000	140 000		90000		
Goodwill			1400000			
Notes payable	--	(115 000)				
Accounts payable	(1364000)	(204 000)				
Long-term debt	(10000000)	--				
Subordinated debentures - 7%	--	(5000 000)				
Preferred stock	--	(750 000)				
Common stock	(2400000)	(1000 000)	1000000			
Additional paid-in capital	(240000)	(122 000)	122000			
Retained earnings	(12683500)	--				
Retained earnings	--	(1006 000)	1006000			
Sales	(18200000)	(5760 000)				
Cost of sales	10600000	3160 000				
Selling, general, & admin. expense	3448500	1063 900				
Depreciation exp.-machinery & equip.	976000	588 750				
Depreciation exp.-buildings	127000	--				
Interest revenue	(105000)	(1 700)				
Interest expense	806000	269 400				
	$ -0-	$ -0-				

C/S 5850,000
P/S 150,000
SD 1500,000
7,500,000

Chapter Four
Solutions to Consolidated Financial Statements Questions

1. (d) $0 dividend revenue. Receipt of a stock dividend (usually) does not constitute dividend income to the investor, rather it reduces the cost basis per share of the investment. Therefore, the 400 shares received as a stock dividend from Parr Corp. would not be included in dividend income.

2. (b) Denver Corp. acquired 30% of Eagle Company's outstanding common stock. With no evidence to the contrary, an investment of 20% or more is assumed to give significant influence, and would be accounted for using the equity method. Under the equity method the investor recognizes in income its share of the investee's net income or loss subsequent to the date of acquisition.
Investment income = $120,000 × 30% × 1/2 year = $18,000

3. (b) $435,000. The equity method of accounting for investments in common stock should be used if the investor has significant influence over the operating and financial policies of the investee. Well Company's significant influence is demonstrated in its officers being a majority of the investees' board of directors.

Original cost of investment	$400,000
Add: Share of income subsequent to acquisition	
10% x $500,000	50,000
Less: Dividend of investee	
10% x $150,000	(15,000)
	$435,000

4. (c) $53,500.

Cost of investment	$500,000	
FV of net assets purchased—30% × $1,600,000	480,000	
Goodwill	$ 20,000	
The impairment loss from goodwill should be x 2.5%	500	
Buffer's net income	$180,000	
Barton's share (30% × $180,000)		$54,000
Less impairment loss from goodwill		(500)
Income from investment		$53,500

5. (b) $42,000 income from investment in Adams. Under the equity method the investor recognizes in income its share of the investee's net income or loss subsequent to the date of acquisition. Furthermore, the investor should reflect adjustments which would be made in consolidation, based on the investor's percentage ownership, if such adjustments (eliminations) can be recorded between investment income and the investment account.

Sage's share of Adams' net income (40% × $120,000)	$48,000
Less: Amortization of depreciable assets fair value in excess of book value	
$90,000 ÷ 18 yrs. × 40%	(2,000)
Fair value of inventory in excess of book value charged to cost of goods sold	
$10,000 × 40%	(4,000)
Income from investment in Adams	$42,000

There was no goodwill resulting from the investment.

Cost of investment		$400,000
Fair value of net assets acquired		
Book value	$ 900,000	
Fair value in excess of book value		
Plant	90,000	
Inventory	10,000	
Fair value of net assets	1,000,000	
% acquired	× 40%	400,000
Goodwill		—0—

6. (b) Under the equity method, the investor should reflect adjustments which would be made in consolidation, based on the investor's percentage ownership, if such adjustment (eliminations) can be recorded between investment income and the investment account. The fair value of the FIFO inventory in excess of the carrying value would reduce net income of the investee, therefore, the investor would charge investment income and credit the investment account to reflect the decrease in income. The fair value of the land in excess of its carrying value would not affect income as it is not a depreciable asset. No adjustment would be made relative to the land.

7. (b) $24,000 Investment income. As Grant's investment gives it the ability to exercise significant influence over South's operating and financial policies, the equity method would be used to account for the investment. Grant's equity in South's income is $24,000 (30% x $80,000 income).

8. (b) $209,000 Investment carrying value at 12/31/00

Original cost	$200,000
Add: Equity in South's income (#7)	24,000
Less: Dividends received (30% x $50,000)	(15,000)
Carrying value 12/31/00	$209,000

9. (b) $30,500 Gain on sale of investment.

Carrying value 12/31/00 (#8)	$209,000
Add: Equity in South's income 1/1 to 7/1/01	
30% x $100,000	30,000
Carrying value 7/1/01	$239,000
1/2 investment carrying value	$119,500
Sales proceeds on 1/2 of investment	150,000
Gain on sale of investment	$ 30,500

Note: As investment is now reduced to 15%, it will be accounted for by the cost method (assuming no significant influence).

10. (a) $42,000. When an investee has cumulative preferred stock outstanding, an investor should compute its share of investee's earnings after deducting the preferred dividends, whether or not such dividends are declared.

Equity in earnings applicable to common stock		
Net income		$60,000
Less: Preferred dividends ($100,000 par x 10%)		10,000
Net income applicable to common stock		$50,000
Moss' percentage ownership (common)		x 80%
Moss' equity in earning applicable to common stock		$40,000
Equity on earnings applicable to Preferred Stock		
Preferred dividend	$10,000	
Moss' percentage ownership (preferred)	x 20%	2,000
Moss' equity in Dubro's earnings		$42,000

11. (c) $195,000 and $40,000.

2001 investment income:

Penny's 2001 net income	$650,000
Mega's percentage ownership (10% + 20%)	× 30%
Mega's 2001 investment income	$195,000

Because Mega Corp. can exercise "significant influence" over the financial and operating activities of Penny, Inc., it should report its investment and investment income (re: Penny) using the equity method.

Adjustments to 2000 investment income:

Penny's 2000 net income	$600,000
Dividend paid by Penny—2000	(200,000)
Penny's 2000 undistributed net income	$400,000
Mega's percentage ownership 2000	10%
Mega's equity in 2000 undistributed income	$ 40,000

The change from the cost method to the equity method should be made retroactively, restating all prior periods in which the investment was held as if the equity method were used from inception.

There is no goodwill to amortize in 2000 or 2001 as both investments were at "prices proportionate to the value assigned to Penny's net assets." Furthermore, there are no changes in depreciation or amortization to adjust for, as values assigned equaled their carrying amounts.

12. (d) Neither a change in market value of investee's common stock nor cash dividends from investee affect the investor's reported investment income (equity in earnings of investee) under the equity method. Under the equity method, cash dividends would be charged against (reduce) the investment account and have no effect on income. A change in the market value of the investee's common stock would not be recorded under the equity method unless the change were judged a permanent and substantial decline, and then the decline would be charged to a loss account rather than investment income. FAS #115 (chapter 2) does not apply to investments accounted for under the equity method.

13. (a)

Cost		$300,000
Fair value of net assets acquired		
Book value of equity	220,000	
Fair value in excess of book value, plant and equipment	60,000	280,000
Goodwill		$ 20,000

14. (a) $150,000. Goodwill:

Cost of investment		$620,000
Fair value of net assets acquired:		
Cash	$ 60,000	
Inventory	150,000	
Property and equipment (net)	380,000	
Goodwill*	—0—	
	$590,000	
Less liabilities	−120,000	470,000
Goodwill (excess cost over F.V. net assets acquired)		$150,000

**Previously recorded goodwill is valued at -0- (not recorded) by an acquiring company. The acquiring company will determine any goodwill to be recorded based upon its acquisition cost and the fair value of identifiable assets and liabilities acquired.*

15. (a) An extraordinary gain of $150,000.

FV of net assets at 6/30	$1,400,000
Cost (100,000 shs. @ $10)	1,000,000
Excess FV over cost	$ 400,000
Reduce noncurrent assets to zero	250,000
Remaining excess—an extraordinary gain	$ 150,000

According to APB #16 noncurrent assets except marketable securities must be reduced pro-rata by the excess of fair value over cost. If these assets are reduced to zero and a credit balance remains, this balance should be taken into income in the periods benefited.

16. (c) The excess of fair value of net assets acquired over cost (negative goodwill) should be allocated to reduce proportionately the values assigned to noncurrent assets. If the allocation reduces the noncurrent assets to zero value, the remainder of the excess over cost should be classified as an extraordinary gain.

17. (b) Legally, the companies are separate, but due to the parent company's control, they are one entity in substance.

18. (d) Consolidated statements are based on the assumption that they represent the financial position and operating results of a single business (economic) enterprise.

19. (a) In a combination accounted for as a purchase, assets and liabilities acquired are recorded at fair market value.

20. (d) Generally, in a combination accounted for as a purchase, assets and liabilities acquired are recorded at their fair market value, on the date of acquisition (values assigned can **not** exceed cost). As cost exceeds the fair value of the net assets acquired, assets and liabilities would be reported at their fair values, and the excess cost would be recognized as goodwill.

21. (a) Intercompany receivables are eliminated in consolidation; however, in separate (or unconsolidated) statements they are included and would be separately reported.

22. (d) Intercompany receivables (payables) are eliminated in consolidation.

23. (c) $500,000 consolidated cost of goods sold. In consolidation, intercompany sales of $250,000 would be eliminated from the sales and cost of goods sold of the consolidating entities. There would be no further adjustment for intercompany profits in ending inventory as all intercompany purchases were sold to unrelated entities.

Cost of goods sold	
Parker Corp.	$400,000
Smith, Inc.	350,000
	$750,000
Less intercompany sales	(250,000)
Consolidated cost of goods sold	$500,000

24. (c)

Consolidated current assets before adjustment		$320,000
Adjustment to eliminate intercompany profit in ending inventory		
Intercompany inventory from Kent	$60,000	
Kent's gross profit percentage		
$48,000 ÷ $240,000	× 20%	
Intercompany profit in inventory		12,000
Consolidated current assets		$308,000

Dean, Inc., is not included in consolidation (15% ownership by Clark); therefore, intercompany profit with Dean would not be eliminated nor effect consolidated current assets.

25. (d) $64,000.

Consolidated revenues		$616,000
Separate company revenues:		
Pare	$400,000	
Shel	280,000	680,000
Intercompany sales eliminated in consolidation		$ 64,000

26. (b) $12,000.

Consolidated accounts receivable		$ 78,000
Separate company receivables		
Pare	$ 52,000	
Shel	38,000	90,000
Intercompany receivables eliminated in consolidation		$ 12,000

27. (a) $6,000.

Consolidated inventory		$104,000
Separate company inventory		
Pare	$ 60,000	
Shel	50,000	110,000
Unrealized intercompany profit eliminated in consolidation		$ 6,000

28. (a) $1,100,000 cost and $300,000 accumulated depreciation. For consolidation purposes the intercompany sale of an asset is treated as though it had never taken place. Consolidated statements are based on the assumption they represent the financial position and operating results of a single business enterprise and should not include gains or losses on intercompany transactions. An intercompany sale does not provide a new basis for stating cost or related depreciation for consolidation purposes. The depreciation for 2000 should be the parent's cost of $1,100,000 less the salvage value of $100,000 divided by 20 years for a total of $50,000. The 2000 depreciation of $50,000 is added to the accumulated depreciation at January 1 of $250,000 for a December 31, 2000 total of $300,000.

29. (b) For consolidation purposes, the intercompany sale of an asset is treated as though it had never taken place. An intercompany sale does *not* provide a new basis for stating cost or related depreciation for consolidation purposes. Therefore, gains or losses on intercompany transactions and their related effect on depreciation are eliminated. The equipment is being depreciated by the straight-line method, over a 3-year remaining life, with no allowance for residual value. Therefore, the depreciation applicable to the gain on the intercompany sale would be 1/3 (33-1/3%) of the gain and would be eliminated from depreciation expense and accumulated depreciation in consolidation.

30. (d) $6,000 intercompany profit in inventory.

Intercompany purchases in Scroll's inventory:	
Pirn's intercompany sales to Scroll	$100,000
Less: Cost of goods sold from intercompany purchases from Pirn	80,000
Scroll's ending inventory from intercompany purchases	20,000
Pirn's gross profit percentage ($150,000/$500,000)	× 30% *
Intercompany profit in Scroll's inventory	$ 6,000

*Pirn's sales to Scroll are made on the same terms as those made to third parties.

31. (b) $47,000 consolidated depreciation expense.

Depreciation expense:	Pirn	$40,000	
	Scroll	10,000	$50,000
Less depreciation applicable to gain on intercompany sale of equipment $12,000 ÷ 4 yrs.			(3,000)
Consolidated depreciation expense			$47,000

For consolidation purposes the intercompany sale of an asset is treated as though it had never taken place. Therefore, gains or losses on intercompany transactions are eliminated. An intercompany sale does not provide a new basis for stating cost or related depreciation for consolidation purposes.

32. (a) In consolidation, the acquisition of the bonds payable of one of the consolidating companies by another of the consolidating companies is treated (basically) as a retirement of debt. The investment in bonds is eliminated against the bonds payable and its related accounts and any difference is treated as a gain or loss.

The carrying value of the bonds is less than the amount paid to acquire the bonds as they were issued at a discount (below face value) and acquired at a premium (above face value). Therefore, there would be a loss on the elimination of intercompany bonds in consolidation, resulting in a decrease in consolidated retained earnings.

33. (a) In consolidation, the acquisition of the bonds payable of one of the consolidating companies by another of the consolidating companies is treated (basically) as a retirement of debt. The investment in bonds is eliminated against the bonds payable and its related accounts and any difference is treated as a gain or loss.

The carrying value of the bonds ($1,075,000) is greater than the amount paid to acquire the bonds ($975,000); therefore, there would be a gain on the elimination of intercompany bonds in consolidation, resulting in an increase in consolidated retained earnings. Since the bonds are the parent company bonds, the minority interest is not affected.

34. (a) $0. Parent company stock acquired by a subsidiary is usually treated as treasury stock, according "gains" and "losses" from such transactions are not recognized in income. Any intercompany dividends from such stock holdings are eliminated in consolidation.

35. (b) $25,000 Dividends. Under the purchase method, consolidated dividends are the parent's dividends. Dividends paid by the subsidiary are eliminated in consolidation as intercompany/investment or minority interest.

36. (b) $30,000 Minority interest.

Subsidiary (Kidd) net assets	12/31/00	
Common stock		50,000
Retained earnings		70,000
Net assets		120,000
% minority interest		x 25%
Minority interest		30,000

37. (b) $100,000 Consolidated common stock. Under the purchase method, consolidated common stock is the common stock of the parent. Subsidiary common stock is eliminated in consolidation (to investment and/or minority interest).

38. (b) The parent's investment in subsidiary account and its proportionate share of the subsidiary's equity accounts, which include retained earnings, are eliminated in a consolidation. The remainder of the subsidiary's equity is reported separately as the minority interest. Thus, consolidated retained earnings is essentially the parent's retained earnings at year-end. The subsidiary's cash dividend reduces its retained earnings balance and therefore the minority interest but not the parent's retained earnings.

39. (b) Under the purchase method, the parent/investor (Phillips, Inc.) recognizes in income its share of the subsidiary's/investee's (Sago, Inc.) net income or loss subsequent to the date of acquisition. Therefore, for the first six months of 2001, 20% of Sago's net income accrues to Phillips and for the last six months of 2001, 95% (20% + 75%) accrues to Phillips.

40. (d) In a "purchase," acquired retained earnings are eliminated against the investment. Therefore, consolidated retained earnings at acquisition would be the retained earnings of the parent corporation, Pane Corp., of $3,250,000. ($3,200,000 + $800,000 - $750,000)

41. (a) Purchase: $100,000

	Purchase
Poe's dividends ($25,000/QTR x 4)	100,000
Shaw's dividends:	
First 3 QTRS ($10,000/QTR x 3)	NA
4th QTR	Eliminated
Consolidated dividends	$100,000

Poe's (parent's) dividends of $100,000 would be included in consolidated financial statements and Shaw's (subsidiary's) 4th quarter dividend would be eliminated in consolidation as an intercompany transaction (there are no minority interests).

Shaw's first 3 quarterly dividends would be excluded under the Purchase method as pre-acquisition transactions.

42. (a) $455,000. Total current assets:

Scott Company current assets at book value	$135,000
Increase in fair value of Scott's inventory*	10,000
Scott Company current assets at fair value	$145,000
Purl Company current assets at book value	310,000
Consolidated current assets	$455,000

*Inventory was still on hand at December 31.

43. (b) $1,450,000. Total assets:

Scott Company assets at book value		$ 415,000
Increase in fair value of Scott's inventory		10,000
Scott Company assets at fair value		$ 425,000
Purl Company assets at book value		1,325,000
		$1,750,000
Less: Investment in Scott (equity method)		– 390,000
		$1,360,000
Add: Goodwill	$100,000	
The impairment loss from goodwill	– 10,000	90,000
Consolidated total assets		$1,450,000

*Refer to question #46.

Alternative calculation:

Purl Company liabilities and stockholders equity (assets) at book value	$1,325,000
Scott Company liabilities at fair value	125,000
	$1,450,000

44. (d) $755,000 total retained earnings. The consolidated retained earnings will be the same as the parent company's (Purl Company) retained earnings because the equity method used by the parent company adjusts for the parent's share of the subsidiary's net income and the amortization of goodwill.

45. (b) The consolidated net income will be the same as the parent company's (Purl Company) net income because the equity method used by the parent adjusts for the parent's share of the subsidiary's net income and the amortization of goodwill.

Alternative calculation:

Purl Company net income	$200,000
Less: Equity in earnings of Scott	– 60,000
	$140,000
Add: Scott Company net income	70,000
	$210,000
Less: impairment loss-goodwill	– 10,000
Consolidated net income	$200,000

*Refer to answer #46.

46. (b) $10,000. Impairment loss-goodwill

Cost of investment, Jan. 1, 2000		$360,000
Fair value of net assets acquired Jan. 1, 2000:		
Book value assets	$410,000	
Book value liabilities	160,000	
Book value net assets	250,000	
Increase in fair value of inventory	10,000	
Fair value of net asset		260,000
Goodwill, Jan. 1, 2000		100,000
Life		x 10 %
Impairment Loss-goodwill		$ 10,000

47. (d) Increase in Net Assets = Increase in Stockholders' Equity:

Stock issued in business combination	$1,000,000 (FV)
Stock issued as "finder's fee"	100,000 (FV)
Total	$1,100,000

48. (c) $3,760,000. Cost of investment:

Stock issued at fair market value	
100,000 shares × $36 per share	$3,600,000
Consultant's fee	160,000
	$3,760,000

Under the purchase method, direct costs of acquisition are included as part of the cost of the investment, while indirect and general expenses related to the acquisition should be charged to expense when incurred. Cost of registering and issuing equity securities are charged (debited) to A.P.I.C.

49. (d) Under the purchase method, direct costs of acquisition are included as part of the cost of the investment, while indirect and general expenses related to the acquisition should be charged to expense when incurred. Costs of registering and issuing equity securities are charged (debited) to additional paid-in capital.

50. (d) Combined financial statements (as distinguished from consolidated statements) may be used to present the financial position and the results of operations; where one individual owns a controlling interest in several corporations, which are related in their operations; for companies under common management; for a group of unconsolidated subsidiaries.

Answers (a) and (b) are incorrect, as consolidated financial statements should be prepared when controlling financial interest rests directly or indirectly in one of the companies included in the consolidation.

Answer (c) is incorrect as "*some* common individual owners" is not justification for either combined or consolidated financial statements.

51. (d) Combined financial statements (as distinguished from consolidated statements) may be used to present the financial position and results of operations; where one individual owns a controlling interest in several corporations, which are related in their operations; for companies under common management; for a group of unconsolidated subsidiaries.

52. (d) $0 receivables from affiliates. When combined statements are prepared for a group of related companies, intercompany transactions and profits or losses should be eliminated.

53. (c) Per ARB #51, where combined statements are prepared for a group of related companies, intercompany transactions and profit or losses should be eliminated, and if there are problems in connection with such matters as **minority interest**, foreign operations, different fiscal periods, or **income taxes**, they should be **treated in the same manner as in consolidated statements**. To the extent there is any intercompany investment, it is **offset** against the related equity. If there is no intercompany investment, the individual company equities are combined.

54. (b) $41,000 combined gross profit. Where combined statements are prepared for a group of related companies, intercompany transactions and profits or losses should be eliminated. Intercompany sales of $130,000 (Bee to Cee) would be eliminated from combined sales and cost of goods sold (purchases). As Cee sold only half ($65,000) of the intercompany purchases, half of the intercompany profits, $15,000 (1/2 × $30,000 Bee gross profit) would be eliminated from ending inventory and charged back against cost of goods sold.

Sales Bee & Cee ($130,000 + $91,000)		$221,000
Less intercompany sales		(130,000)
Combined sales		$ 91,000
Less combined cost of goods sold		
CGS Bee & Cee ($100,000 + $65,000)	$165,000	
Less intercompany sales	(130,000)	
	$ 35,000	
Add: intercompany profit in ending inventory (1/2 x $30,000)	15,000	50,000
Combined gross profit		$ 41,000

55. (a) The additional depreciation which will result from the excess of market over book value should be charged to investment income over the remaining useful life of the assets per APB #18.

56. (c) Under the equity method, the investor's share of the excess of fair market value over book value of depreciable assets is amortized over the assets' useful economic life as a charge against investment income (equity in earnings of investee) and a credit (reduction) to the investment carrying value.

57. (d) The entries should have been:

	Dr.	*Cr.*
Investment in subsidiary (40% of $20,000)	8000	
Equity in earnings of subsidiary		8000
Cash	2000	
Investment in subsidiary (40% of $5,000)		2000

By erroneously recognizing the $2000 dividend as revenue, retained earnings are overstated. The dividends should have been booked as a reduction of the investment; thus the investment is overstated.

58. (c)

Cost—$15 × 250,000 shares		$3,750,000
Fair value of net assets acquired		
Book value	$3,000,000	
Fair value in excess of book value, P.P.E.	400,000	3,400,000
Goodwill		$ 350,000

59. (c) The excess of fair value over cost (negative goodwill) should be used as a reduction of noncurrent assets . If negative goodwill remains (after reducing noncurrent assets to zero), it should be recorded as an extraordinary gain.

60. (b)

	Purl Corp. net income (parent)	
	Six months ended 6/30/00	$ 750,000
	Six months ended 12/31/00	825,000
	Parent corp. net income for year ended 12/31/00	$1,575,000
Add:	Scott Corp. net income (subsidiary)	
	Six months ended 12/31/00	375,000
		$1,950,000
Less:	Intercompany profit in ending inventory	(45,000)
	Consolidated net income for year ended 12/31/00	$1,905,000

Under the purchase method of accounting for business combinations, the results of operations are combined only **after** the date of acquisition, and are based upon the cost to the acquiring corporation. The effects of intercompany transactions are eliminated as consolidated statements are based on the assumption that they represent the financial position and operating results of a single business enterprise.

61. (d)

Pard's revenue	$200,000
Spin's revenue	140,000
Total individual revenues	$340,000
Consolidated revenues	308,000
Intercompany sales eliminated in consolidation	$ 32,000

62. (b)

Pard's accounts receivable	$26,000
Spin's accounts receivable	19,000
Total individual accounts receivable	$45,000
Consolidated accounts receivable	39,000
Intercompany accounts receivable eliminated in consolidation	$ 6,000

63. (c)

Intercompany sales (refer to answer #61)		$32,000
% in ending inventory		× 37.5%
Intercompany inventory at sales price		$12,000
Less intercompany profit		
Total individual inventory ($30,000 + $25,000)	$55,000	
Consolidated inventory	52,000	
Intercompany profit in inventory eliminated in consolidation		3,000
Consolidated intercompany inventory		$ 9,000

64. (b) % minority interest = $\frac{\text{Minority interest}}{\text{Total subsidiary equity}}$

$$= \frac{10{,}000}{50{,}000}$$

$$= \underline{\underline{20\%}}$$

65. (c) \$56,000 overstatement of revenue. When combined financial statements are prepared, intercompany transactions and profits or losses should be eliminated. Therefore, combined revenues are overstated by the amount of intercompany sales. \$56,000 (140% × \$40,000 cost).

66. (a) \$56,000 elimination of cost of goods sold. When combined financial statements are prepared, intercompany transactions and profits or losses should be eliminated. The amount of intercompany sales of merchandise, \$56,000 (140% × \$40,000 cost) should be eliminated from combined sales and cost of goods sold.

67. (d) Since Band Co. receives additional shares at no cost from the stock dividend, the cost per share would decrease and the transaction would be recorded as a memo entry. This is true regardless of whether the cost or equity basis is used. Since the stock dividend does not include a transfer of assets, it is never considered revenue.

68. (b) The goodwill is the price paid minus 30% of the fair value of net assets:
\$200,000-(30% x 600,000) =\$20,000

69. (b) Goodwill is the price paid less the fair value of net assets: \$860,000 – (\$840,000 - \$140,000) = \$160,000.

NOTES

(work practice questions here or jot down key concepts!)

NOTES

(work practice questions here or jot down key concepts!)

Chapter Four
Solutions to Consolidated Financial Statements Problems

NUMBER 1

Brighton Corporation and Subsidiary
WORKSHEET FOR PREPARATION OF CONSOLIDATED BALANCE SHEET
December 31, 1999

	Brighton	Solvo	Adjustments & Eliminations		Consolidated Balance Sheet	
Assets	*Corporation*	*Corporation*	*Debit*	*Credit*	*Debit*	*Credit*
Cash	$ 200,000	$ 20,000			$ 220,000	
Accounts receivable	205,000	55,000		(3) $18,500	241,500	
Notes receivable	180,000	11,000		(7) 4,000	187,000	
Notes receivable discounted	(4,000)		(7) $4,000			
Accrued interest receivable	1,600	400		(6) 1,200	800	
Dividends receivable	6,400			(2) 6,400		
Inventories	300,000	75,000		(4) 8,000	367,000	
Plant and equipment	794,000	280,600	(5) 2,000		1,076,600	
Allowance for depreciation	(260,000)	(30,000)		(5) 90		$ 290,090
Investment in Solvo Corporation stock	167,400			(1) 167,400		
Investment in Solvo Corporation bonds	40,000			(6) 40,000		
Advance to Solvo Corporation	35,000			(8) 35,000		
	$1,665,400	$412,000				
Liabilities and Stockholders' Equity						
Accounts payable	$ 220,400	$ 54,800	(3) 18,500			256,700
Notes payable	142,000	24,200				166,200
Dividends payable		8,000	(2) 6,400			1,600
Accrued interest payable	22,100	3,900	(6) 1,200			24,800
Other accrued liabilities	7,900	3,100				11,000
Advance from Brighton Corporation		35,000	(8) 35,000			
Bonds payable	600,000	85,000	(6) 40,000			645,000
Capital stock	360,000	125,000	(1) 125,000			360,000
Capital in excess of par value	49,000	12,000	(1) 12,000			49,000
Retained earnings	264,000	61,000	(1) 61,000	(5) 1,910		258,910
			(4) 7,000			
	$1,665,400	$412,000				
Excess of cost over book value of subsidiary interest*			(1) 9,000		9,000	
Minority interest in subsidiary			(4) 1,000	(1) 39,600		38,600
			$322,100	$322,100	$2,101,900	$2,101,900

*~~Goodwill should be amortized. Six months amortization is $112.50 ($9,000 ÷ 40 × 1/2 yr).~~
Debit to retained earnings (income accounts have been closed) and credit to Goodwill.

NUMBER 2

Amboy Corporation and Subsidiary
CONSOLIDATING STATEMENT WORKSHEET
December 31, 2001

Income Statement	*Amboy Corp.*	*Taft Inc.*	*Adjustments & Eliminations Debit*	*Adjustments & Eliminations Credit*	*Adjusted Balance*
Net sales	$(1,900,000)	$(1,500,000)	[6] 180,000		$(3,220,000)
Dividends from Taft	(40,000)		[3] 40,000		---
Gain on sale of warehouse	(30,000)		[4] 30,000		---
Cost of goods sold	1,180,000	870,000		[6] 162,000	1,888,000
Operating expenses (incl. deprec.)	550,000	440,000	[2] 12,000	[5] 2,000	1,000,000
Net income	$ (240,000)	$ (190,000)	[a] 262,000	[a] 164,000	$ (332,000)
Retained Earnings Statement					
Balance, 1/1/01	$ (220,000)	$ (156,000)	[1] 156,000		$ (220,000)
Net income	(240,000)	(190,000)	[a] 262,000	[a] 164,000	(332,000)
Dividends paid		40,000		[3] 40,000	
Balance, 12/31/01	$ (460,000)	$ (306,000)	[b] 418,000	[b] 204,000	$ (552,000)
Balance Sheet					
Assets					
Cash	$ 285,000	$ 150,000			$ 435,000
Accounts receivable (net)	430,000	350,000		[7] 75,000	705,000
Inventories	530,000	410,000		[6] 18,000	922,000
Land, plant & equipment	660,000	680,000	[1] 54,000	[4] 30,000	1,364,000
Accumulated depreciation	(185,000)	(210,000)	[5] 2,000	[2] 9,000	(402,000)
Investment in Taft (at cost)	750,000			[1}750,000	---
Goodwill			[1] 60,000	[2] 3,000	57,000
	$ 2,470,000	$ 1,380,000			$ 3,081,000
Liabilities & Stockholders' Equity					
Accounts Pay. & accrued exp.	$ (670,000)	$ (594,000)	[7] 75,000		$(1,189,000)
Common stock ($10 par)	(1,200,000)	(400,000)	[1] 400,000		(1,200,000)
Additional paid-in capital	(140,000)	(80,000)	[1] 80,000		(140,000)
Retained Earnings	(460,000)	(306,000)	[b] 418,000	[b] 204,000	(552,000)
	$(2,470,000)	$ (1,380,000)	1,089,000	1,089,000	$ (3,081,000)

*Explanations of Adjustments & Eliminations

[1] To eliminate the reciprocal elements in investment, equity, and property accounts. Amboy's investment is carried at cost at December 31, 2001.

[2] To record amortization of current value in excess of book value of Taft's machinery at date of acquisition ($54,000 / 6) and amortization of goodwill ($60,000 / 20) for the year ended December 31, 2001.

[3] To eliminate Amboy 's dividend income from Taft.

[4] To eliminate the intercompany profit on the sale of the warehouse by Amboy to Taft.

[5] To eliminate the excess depreciation on the warehouse building sold by Amboy to Taft [$86,000 - $66,000) / 5] x ½.

[6] To eliminate intercompany sales from Taft to Amboy and the intercompany profit in Amboy's ending inventory as follows:

	Total	*On Hand*
Sales	*$180,000*	*$36,000*
Gross profit	*90,000*	*18,000*

[7] To eliminate Amboy's intercompany balance for merchandise owed to Taft.

NUMBER 3

Pym Corp. and Subsidiary
CONSOLIDATED BALANCE SHEET WORKSHEET
December 31, 2000

	Pym Corp.	Sy Corp.	Adjustments & Eliminations Debit	Adjustments & Eliminations Credit	Consolidated
Assets					
Cash	75,000	15,000			90,000
Accounts and other current receivables	410,000	120,000	[b] 900	[f] 900 [g] 5,000	335,000
				[h] 100,000 [j] 90,000	
Merchandise inventory	920,000	670,000		[i] 3,000	1,587,000
Plant and equipment (net)	1,000,000	400,000			1,400,000
Investment in Sy Corp.	1,200,000		[a] 90,900	[b] 900 [c] 480,000	
				[e] 810,000	
Goodwill			[c] 480,000	[d] 48,000	432,000
Totals	3,605,000	1,205,000			3,844,000
Liabilities and Stockholders' Equity					
Accounts payable and other current liabilities	140,000	305,000	[f] 900 [g] 5,000		249,100
			[h] 100,000 [j] 90,000		
Common stock ($10 par)	500,000	200,000	[e] 200,000		500,000
Retained earnings	2,965,000	700,000	[d] 48,000 [e] 700,000	[a] 90,900	3,004,900
			[i] 3,000		
Minority interest, 10%				[e] 90,000	90,000
Totals	3,605,000	1,205,000	1,718,700	1,718,700	3,844,000

NUMBER 3 cont.

Explanations of Worksheet Adjustments and Eliminations

[a] To record net income of Sy Corp. accruing to Pym Corp.

Sy Corp.'s retained earnings at 12/31/00		$700,000
Sy Corp.'s retained earnings at 1/1/00		600,000
Increase in retained earnings after dividend declaration		100,000
Add dividend declaration		1,000
Sy Corp.'s net income for the year ended 12/31/00		101,000
Pym Corp.'s share, 90%		$ 90,900

[b] To record Pym Corp.'s share of dividend declared by Sy Corp.

90% of $1,000		$ 900

[c] To record goodwill

Purchase price of 90% of Sy Corp.'s common stock		$1,200,000
Sy Corp.'s book value at 1/1/00		
Common stock	$200,000	
Retained earnings	600,000	
Total	$800,000	
Pym Corp.'s share, 90%		720,000
Goodwill		$480,000

[d] To record amortization of goodwill

10% of $480,000		$ 48,000

[e] To eliminate 90% of Sy Corp.'s book value and record minority interest

Common stock		$200,000
Retained earnings at 12/31/00		700,000
Total		$ 900,000
Pym Corp.'s share, 90%		810,000
Minority interest, 10%		90,000
Total		$ 900,000

[f] To eliminate intercompany dividend receivable and payable

90% of $1,000		$ 900

[g] To eliminate intercompany accrued interest

$100,000 @ 10% x ½ year		$ 5,000

[h] To eliminate intercompany loan $ 100,000

[I] To eliminate intercompany profit in Sy Corp.'s 12/31 inventory

Sales from Pym Corp. to Sy Corp.		$ 300,000
5% remaining in Sy Corp.'s 12/31 inventory		15,000
Multiply by 20% (60,000/300,000)		$ 3,000

[j] To eliminate intercompany trade accounts receivable and payable $ 90,000

NUMBER 4

1. $14,000 (decrease in consolidated net income)

Elimination of gain on sale of equipment:		
Sales price to Poe	$36,000	
Shaw's carrying value	15,000	
Intercompany gain eliminated		$21,000
Depreciation adjustment re. gain:		
Straight line depreciation on gain eliminated from cost of equipment $21,000 / 3 yrs.		(7,000)
Net decrease in consolidated net income		$14,000

2. $10,000 (decrease in consolidated net income)
Intercompany profit eliminated from ending inventory is $10,000 ($20,000 intercompany profit x 50% ending inventory from intercompany sales).
The elimination of the intercompany sale of $60,000 (Debit - Sales; Credit - Cost of goods sold) has no effect on consolidated net income.

3. $9,000 (increase in consolidated net income)

Carrying value of Shaw's bonds payable (50% x $200,000)	$100,000
Amount paid for intercompany bonds	91,000
Gain on retirement of bonds	$ 9,000

The elimination of intercompany investment in bonds is treated as a retirement of debt.

4. $2,000 Amortization of goodwill

Cost of investment in Shaw's C/S		$155,000
Fair value of net assets acquired		
Shaw's stockholders' equity	$150,000	
Percent acquired	x 90%	135,000
Goodwill		20,000
Impairment loss - Goodwill		$ 2,000

5. (A) Consolidated cash would be the sum of the individual cash balances on the separate company's books. Consolidation eliminations do not affect cash.

6. (B) Consolidated equipment would be the sum of the individual equipment balances <u>less</u> the gain on the intercompany sale of equipment eliminated in consolidation (see #1 above).

7. (E) Intercompany investments are eliminated in consolidation.

8. (B) Consolidated bonds payable would be the sum of the individual bonds payable <u>less</u> the bonds payable eliminated as a result of the intercompany investment in bonds ($100,000) (refer #3 above).

9. (F) Minority interest represents the non-controlling interest in a subsidiary's net assets which are included in the consolidated financial statements. Minority interest is recorded/set up in consolidation when the subsidiary equity is eliminated against the investment in subsidiary and minority interest. It would not appear in the separate statements or trial balance of either company.

10. (C) Consolidated common stock is the parents' common stock (Poe). The subsidiary equity accounts are eliminated in consolidation.

11. (C) Consolidated beginning retained earnings are the retained earnings of the parent (Poe). The subsidiary retained earnings are eliminated in consolidation.

12. (C) Only the parent company's (Poe) dividends are reported as consolidated dividend distributions. The subsidiary's dividends paid to the parent are eliminated in consolidation and subsidiary distributions to minority interest are charged against the balance of minority interest.

13. (F) "Gain on retirement of bonds" results from the consolidation elimination of the intercompany investment in bonds. No such amount would be reported on the separate financial statements of either company (refer #3 above).

14. (B) Consolidated cost of goods sold would be the sum of the individual C.G.S. <u>less</u> the elimination of the intercompany sales <u>plus</u> the elimination of the intercompany profit in ending inventory (refer #2 above).

15. (D) Interest expense would be the same as the amount shown on Shaw's trial balance. Poe's purchase of Shaw's bonds (intercompany investment) was made on December 31. Therefore, no interest expense would have been eliminated in consolidation as intercompany interest.

16. (B) Consolidated depreciation expense would be the sum of the individual depreciation expenses <u>less</u> the elimination of depreciation attributable to the gain from the intercompany sale of equipment (refer #1 above).

NUMBER 5

1. (A) Consolidated cash would be the sum of the individual cash balances on the combining company's separate financial statements. Consolidation eliminations do not affect cash.

2. (B) Consolidated equipment would be the sum of the individual equipment balances on the combining company's separate financial statements **less** the gain from the intercompany sale of equipment at a price greater than its carrying value. Intercompany gains and loss are eliminated in consolidation.

3. (E) Intercompany investments are eliminated in consolidation.

4. (F) Minority interest represents the non-controlling interest in a subsidiary's net assets which are included in the consolidated financial statements. It is set up/recorded in consolidation when the subsidiary equity is eliminated against the investment in subsidiary and minority interest. It would not appear in the separate statements or trial balances of either company.

5. (C) Consolidated common stock is the parents' common stock (Purl). The subsidiary's equity accounts are eliminated in consolidation (against the investment in subsidiary and minority interest).

6. (C) Consolidated beginning retained earnings are the parents' retained earnings (Purl). The subsidiary's equity accounts are eliminated in consolidation.

7. (C) Only the parents' dividends are reported as consolidated dividends. The subsidiary's dividends paid to the parent are eliminated in consolidation and subsidiary distributions to minority interest are charged against the balance of minority interest.

8. (B) Consolidated cost of goods sold would be the sum of the individual cost of goods sold on the separate financial statements **less** the elimination of the intercompany sales **plus** the elimination of the intercompany profit in ending inventory from the intercompany sales.

9. (A) Consolidated interest expense would be the sum of the individual amounts on the separate financial statements. There is no indication of any intercompany interest bearing debt, which would require elimination of the debt and its related interest amounts.

10. (B) Consolidated depreciation expense would be the sum of the individual depreciation expense balances on the separate financial statements **less** the elimination of depreciation applicable to the amount of the gain from the intercompany sale of equipment.

NUMBER 6

a.

To: Johnson
From: Smith, CPA
Re: Acme Co. Investments in Kern Co. and Wand Co.

The purpose of this memorandum is to explain to you that although Acme's investment in Wand and Kern represent equal ownership interests of 20%, the use of different accounting methods may be appropriate under generally accepted accounting principles.

Under those principles, Acme must use the equity method to account for an investment if Acme's ownership interest allows it to exercise significant influence over the investee company.

Generally, an investor is presumed to be able to exercise significant influence when it has an ownership interest of 20% or more, and is presumed to be unable to exercise significant influence when it has an ownership interest of less than 20%. However, either presumption may be overcome by predominant evidence to the contrary. The determination of whether an investor can exercise significant influence is not always clear and often requires judgment in light of such factors as an investor's representation on the investee's board of directors, participation in policymaking activities, and/or the extent of ownership as compared to that investee's other shareholders.

Acme used the entity method to account for its investment in Kern which indicates that its 20% ownership interest allowed it to exercise significant influence over Kern's operating and financial policies.

Acme accounted for its investment in Wand as available-for-sale securities. Apparently, despite its 20% ownership interest, there was evidence that Acme could not exercise significant influence over Wand's operating and financial policies; hence, Acme did not use the equity method to account for its investment in Ward.

b.

Kern

Balance sheet – Acme reported its investment in Kern at a carrying amount of $660,000.

Calculations:
Equity in earnings = $80,000 ($400,000 x 20%)

Dividend rec'd = $20,000 ($100,000 x 20%)

Carrying amount = $600,000 + $80,000 - $20,000

Statement of Income and Comprehensive Income

Acme's equity in Kern's earnings $80,000

Calculation:
$400,000 x 20%

Wand

Balance sheet – Acme reported its investment in Wand at a fair value of $400,000.

Calculation:
20,000 shares x $20 per share

Statement of Income and Comprehensive Income

Dividend income $12,000

Calculation:
$60,000 x 20%
Unrealized gain $100,000

Calculation: $400,000 -- $300,000

NUMBER 7

a. Under the cost method, the investor recognizes dividends as income when received. Under the equity method, an investor recognizes as income its share of an investee's earnings or losses in the periods in which they are reported by the investee. The amount recognized as income is adjusted for any change in the difference between investment cost and underlying equity in net assets at the investment date. The equity method is more consistent with accrual accounting than is the cost method, because the equity method recognizes income when earned rather than when dividends are received.

b. Monroe should have assessed whether it could have exerted significant influence over Grumer's operating and financial policies. Monroe did not own 20% or more of Grumer's voting stock (which would have given the refutable presumption that it could exercise significant influence); however, the ability to exercise significant influence may be indicated by other factors such as Monroe's provision of three key management personnel and purchase of 25% of Grumer's output.

c. On becoming a 30% owner of Grumer, Monroe should use the equity method to account for its investment. As of January 2, 1990, Monroe's investment and retained earnings accounts must be adjusted retroactively to show balances as if the equity method had been used from the initial purchase date. Both accounts should be increased by 18% of Grumer's undistributed income since formation. (In this case, no adjustment to the undistributed income is necessary since the stock was issued at its book value which was assumed to approximate its fair value.)

NUMBER 8

Cain Corp. and Subsidiary
CONSOLIDATING STATEMENT WORKSHEET
December 31, 2000

Income Statement	Cain Corp. Dr. (Cr.)	Frey, Inc. Dr. (Cr.)	Adjustments & Eliminations Dr.	Adjustments & Eliminations Cr.	Adjusted Balance
Net sales	(3,800,000)	(1,500,000)	[6] 180,000		(5,120,000)
Dividends from Frey	(40,000)		[3] 40,000		
Gain on sale of warehouse	(30,000)		[4] 30,000		
Cost of goods sold	2,360,000	870,000		[6] 162,000	3,068,000
Operating expenses (including depreciation)	1,100,000	440,000	[2] 9,000	[5] 2,000	1,550,000
Impairment loss - Goodwill			[2] 3,000		
Net income	(410,000)	(190,000)	[a] 262,000	[a] 164,000	(502,000)
Retained Earnings Statement					
Balance, 1/1/00	(440,000)	(156,000)	[1] 156,000		(440,000)
Net income	(410,000)	(190,000)	[a] 262,000	[a] 164,000	(502,000)
Dividends paid		40,000		[3] 40,000	
Balance, 12/31/00	(850,000)	(306,000)	[b] 418,000	[b] 204,000	(942,000)
Balance Sheet					
Assets:					
Cash	570,000	150,000			720,000
Accounts receivable (net)	860,000	350,000		[7] 86,000	1,124,000
Inventories	1,060,000	410,000		[6] 18,000	1,452,000
Land, plant and equipment	1,320,000	680,000	[1] 54,000	[4] 30,000	2,024,000
Accumulated depreciation	(370,000)	(210,000)	[5] 2,000	[2] 9,000	(587,000)
Investment in Frey (at cost)	750,000			[1] 750,000	
Goodwill			[1] 60,000	[2] 3,000	57,000
Total Assets	4,190,000	1,380,000			4,790,000
Liabilities & Stockholders' Equity:					
Accounts payable & accrued expenses	(1,340,000)	(594,000)	[7] 86,000		(1,848,000)
Common stock ($10 par)	(1,700,000)	(400,000)	[1] 400,000		(1,700,000)
Additional paid-in capital	(300,000)	(80,000)	[1] 80,000		(300,000)
Retained earnings	(850,000)	(306,000)	[b] 418,000	[b] 204,000	(942,000)
Total Liabilities & Stockholders' Equity	(4,190,000)	(1,380,000)	1,100,000	1,100,000	(4,790,000)

NUMBER 8 (cont.)

Explanations of Adjustments and Eliminations

[1] To eliminate the reciprocal elements in investment, goodwill, equity and property accounts. Cain's investment is carried at cost at December 31, 2000.

[2] To record amortization of the fair value in excess of book value of Frey's machinery at date of acquisition ($54,000 % 6) and impairment loss – Goodwill $3,000 for the year ended December 31, 2000.

[3] To eliminate Cain's dividend revenue from Frey.

[4] To eliminate intercompany profit on the sale of the warehouse by Cain to Frey.

[5] To eliminate the excess depreciation on the warehouse building sold by Cain to Frey [½ × $4,000 ($86,000 – $66,000 × 1/5)].

[6] To eliminate intercompany sales from Cain to Frey and the intercompany profit in Cain's ending inventory as follows:

	Total	*On hand*
Sales	$180,000	$36,000
Gross profit	90,000	18,000

[7] To eliminate Cain's intercompany balance to Frey for the merchandise it purchased.

NUMBER 9

Jared, Inc. and Subsidiary
CONSOLIDATING ENTRIES
December 31, 1999
Not Required

	Debit	Credit
(1)		
Land	$ 540,000	
Machinery and equipment	2,750,000	
Other assets		$90,000
Accumulated depreciation—machinery and equipment		750,000
Investment in Munson Manufacturing Company		2,322,000
Cost of sales		128,000
To adjust Munson's assets to fair value at date of purchase.		
(2)		
Common stock	1,000,000	
Additional paid-in capital (common)	122,000	
Retained earnings	1,006,000	
Investment in Munson Manufacturing Company		2,128,000
To eliminate Jared's investment in Munson's equity at date of purchase.		
(3)		
Excess of cost over fair value of net assets acquired	1,400,000	
Investment in Munson Manufacturing Company		1,400,000
To record excess of cost over fair value of Munson's net assets at date of purchase as follows:		

Purchase price (common stock)		$5,850,000
Less: Adjustment of Munson's assets to fair value (J/E No. 1)	$2,322,000	
Elimination of investment in Munson's equity (J/E No. 2)	2,128,000	4,450,000
Excess		$1,400,000

	Debit	Credit
(4)		
Preferred stock	$150,000	
Investment in Munson Manufacturing Co.		$150,000
To eliminate Jared's investment in Munson's preferred stock at date of purchase.		
(5)		
Depreciation expense—machinery and equipment	236,250	
Accumulated depreciation—machinery and equipment		236,250
To adjust to fair value at date of purchase.		

Machinery and equipment — $10,600,000 – 4,000,000 = 6,600,000 ÷ 6 years =	$1,100,000
Depreciation expense for nine months (1,100,000 × 9/12)	$825,000
Depreciation expense per books	588,750
Adjustment	$236,250

NUMBER 9 (cont.)

(6)

Subordinated debentures—7%	1,500,000	
Accounts payable	17,500	
Investment in Munson Manufacturing Company		1,500,000
Accounts receivable, net		17,500

To eliminate intercompany bonds and related accrued interest for two months.

(7)

Accounts payable	38,800	
Sales	388,000	
Accounts receivable, net		38,800
Cost of sales		388,000

To eliminate intercompany sales and unpaid balances at December 31.

(8)

Cost of sales	4,200	
Inventories		4,200

To eliminate intercompany profit (35%) in Jared's inventory at December 31 ($12,000 × 35% = $4,200).

(9)

Interest revenue	$78,750	
Interest expense		$78,750

To eliminate intercompany interest expense and revenue on debentures for nine months. ($105,000 × 9/12 = $78,750)

(10)

Amortization of excess of cost over fair value of net assets acquired	52,500	
Excess of cost over fair value of net assets acquired		52,500

To record nine months amortization as follows:
Excess of $1,400,000 amortized over twenty years ($1,400,000 ÷ 20 = $70,000 × 9/12 = $52,500)

NUMBER 9 (cont.)

Jared, Inc., and Subsidiary
WORKSHEET TO PREPARE CONSOLIDATED TRIAL BALANCE
December 31, 1999

	Jared, Inc. Dr.(Cr.)	Munson Mfg. Co. Dr.(Cr.)	Adjustments and Eliminations Debit	Adjustments and Eliminations Credit	Consolidated Balances Debit	Consolidated Balances Credit
Cash	$ 822,000	$ 530,000			$ 1,352,000	
Notes receivable	—	85,000			85,000	
Accounts receivable, net	2,758,000	1,368,400		(6) $ 17,500	4,070,100	
				(7) 38,800		
Inventories	3,204,000	1,182,000		(8) 4,200	4,381,800	
Land	4,000,000	1,560,000	(1) $ 540,000		6,100,000	
Machinery and equipment	15,875,000	7,850,000	(1) 2,750,000		26,475,000	
Accumulated depreciation—machinery and equipment	(6,301,000)	(3,838,750)		(1) 750,000		$11,126,000
				(5) 236,250		
Buildings	1,286,000				1,286,000	
Accumulated depreciation—buildings	(372,000)					372,000
Investment in Munson Mfg. Company	7,500,000			(1) 2,322,000		
				(3) 1,400,000		
				(2) 2,128,000		
				(6) 1,500,000		
				(4) 150,000		
Other assets	263,000	140,000		(1) 90,000	313,000	
Excess of cost over fair value of net assets acquired			(3) 1,400,000	(10) 52,500	1,347,500	
Notes payable		(115,000)				115,000
Accounts payable	(1,364,000)	(204,000)	(6) 17,500			1,511,700
			(7) 38,800			
Long-term debt	(10,000,000)					10,000,000
Subordinated debentures - 7%		(5,000,000)	(6) 1,500,000			3,500,000
Preferred stock		(750,000)	(4) 150,000			600,000
Common stock	(2,400,000)	(1,000,000)	(2) 1,000,000			2,400,000
Additional paid-in capital	(240,000)	(122,000)	(2) 122,000			240,000
Retained earnings	(12,683,500)					12,683,500
Retained earnings		(1,006,000)	(2) 1,006,000			
Sales	(18,200,000)	(5,760,000)	(7) 388,000			23,572,000
Cost of sales	10,600,000	3,160,000	(8) 4,200	(7) 388,000	13,248,200	
				(1) 128,000		
Selling, general, and administrative expenses	3,448,500	1,063,900			4,512,400	
Depreciation expense - machinery and equipment	976,000	588,750	(5) 236,250		1,801,000	
Depreciation expense - buildings	127,000				127,000	
Interest revenue	(105,000)	(1,700)	(9) 78,750			27,950
Interest expense	806,000	269,400		(9) 78,750	996,650	
Impairment Loss – Goodwill			(10) 52,500		52,500	
	$ -0-	$ -0-	$9,284,000	$9,284,000	$66,148,150	$66,148,150

NOTES

(work practice questions here or jot down key concepts!)

NOTES

(work practice questions here or jot down key concepts!)

NOTES

(work practice questions here or jot down key concepts!)

NOTES

(work practice questions here or jot down key concepts!)

Chapter Five
Earnings Per Share, Segment Reporting

Chapter Five
Earnings Per Share, Segment Reporting

IN GENERAL

In 1997 the FASB issued SFAS 128 on computing earnings per share. Its purpose is to simplify the calculation of EPS and make it more comparable with international accounting standards.

The objective of FASB 128 is to measure the performance of an entity over the reporting period. The statement requires the reporting of a Basic EPS for companies with a simple capital structure and a Basic EPS plus a Diluted EPS for companies with a complex capital structure.

BASIC EARNINGS PER SHARE

SFAS 128 requires all public companies to disclose Basic EPS if they have a simple capital structure with no **potential common shares** from convertible securities, stock options, warrants, or contingent shares.

Basic EPS must be reported on the face of the income statement for income from continuing operations and net income. The Basic EPS amounts for discontinuing operations, extraordinary items and the cumulative effect of the changes in accounting principles must be disclosed in the face of the income statement **or** in the notes to the financial statements.

Computation of Basic Earnings Per Share

$$\text{Basic EPS} = \frac{\text{Net Income Available to Common Shareholders}}{\text{Weighted Average Number of Common Shares Outstanding}}$$

Net Income Available to Common Shareholders

Income available to common shareholders is net income less preferred dividends for **declared** non cumulative preferred stock. For cumulative preferred stock the current year preferred dividend is deducted **whether it is declared or not.** If the company has preferred stock whose dividend is cumulative only if earned, it must deduct the dividend **earned** in calculating Basic EPS.

$$\text{Basic EPS} = \frac{\text{Net Income - Preferred Dividends}}{\text{Weighted Average Number of Common Shares Outstanding}}$$

Weighted Average Number of Common Shares Outstanding

Takes into account the number of shares outstanding during the period, weighted to reflect the portion of the period outstanding.

Example: T Corporation has 100,000 common shares outstanding on January 1 of the current year and issued 6,000 shares on March 1.

Weighted average shares outstanding for the quarter ended March 31:

100,000 + 1/3 (6,000) = 102,000 (3/1 to 3/31 = 1/3 of period 1/1 to 3/31)

For the 6 months ended June 30:

100,000 + 4/6 (6,000) = 104,000 (3/1 to 6/30 = 4/6 of period 1/1 to 6/30)

For the year ended December 31:

100,000 + 10/12 (6,000) = 105,000 (3/1 to 12/31 = 10/12 of period 1/1 to 6/30)

If T Corporation had reacquired 6,000 shares on March 1 of the current year, the weighted average shares outstanding for the same periods would be:

Quarter ended March 31 — 94,000 + 2/3 (6,000) = 98,000 (1/1 to 3/1 = 2/3 of period)
6 months ended June 30 — 94,000 + 2/6 (6,000) = 96,000 (1/1 to 3/1 = 2/6 of period)
Year ended December 31 — 94,000 + 2/12 (6,000) = 95,000 (1/1 to 3/1 = 2/12 of period)

* Stock dividends and stock splits require **retroactive adjustment to current equivalent shares** as of the beginning of the period(s) being presented for the determination of weighted average shares outstanding. If such changes occur after the close of the period, but before the financial statements are completed, the computation of earnings per share should be based on the new number of shares because the reader's primary interest is presumed to be related to the current capitalization.

Example: The X Corporation completed the following common stock transactions during the period January 1, 1995, through July 1, 1999:

Date	*Transaction*	*No. of Shares*
1/1/95	Issued (original issue)	1,000
1/1/96	Stock dividend to preferred stockholders	50
5/1/97	Shares exchanged for stock of another corporation	600
4/1/98	3 for 2 stock split	
2/1/99	100% stock dividend to common stockholders	
7/1/99	Shares issued to preferred stockholders in exchange for preferred on a 2 for 1 basis	442

Compute the number of shares outstanding, weighted average shares outstanding, and current equivalent shares outstanding for each year.

Solution:

- Shares outstanding:

	1995	1996	1997	1998	1999
Outstanding beginning of year	—0—	1,000	1,050	1,650	2,475
1/1/95 issued	1,000				
1/1/96 dividend to P/S		50			
5/1/97 exchanged			600		
4/1/98 3:2 split (1/2)				825	
2/1/99 dividend to C/S					2,475
7/1/99 exchanged					442
	1,000	1,050	1,650	2,475	5,392

- Weighted average shares outstanding:

	1995	1996	1997	1998	1999
Outstanding beginning of year (100%)	—0—	1,000	1,050	1,650	2,475
'95 1,000 from 1/1 = 100%	1,000				
'96 50 from 1/1 = 100%		50			
'97 600 from 5/1 = 8/12			400		
'98 825 split retroactive to 1/1				825	
'99 2,475 dividend retroactive to 1/1					2,475
442 from 7/1 = 6/12					221
Weighted Average outstanding	1,000	1,050	1,450	2,475	5,171

- Current equivalent shares outstanding:

	1995	1996	1997	1998	1999
Weighted average shares outstanding	1,000	1,050	1,450	2,475	5,171
Adjustment for 3:2 split in 1998 (1/2)	500	525	725	—	—
Current equivalent shares for 1998	1,500	1,575	2,175	2,475	—
Adjustment for 100% stock dividend in 1999	1,500	1,575	2,175	2,475	—
Current equivalent shares for 1999	3,000	3,150	4,350	4,950	5,171

DILUTED EARNINGS PER SHARE

IN GENERAL

Diluted EPS is required for companies with a complex capital structure. A complex structure is one that includes potential common shares as convertible securities, stock options, stock warrants, and contingent shares. The **purpose** of Diluted EPS is to measure the performance of an entity over the reporting period while taking into account the effect of all dilutive potential common shares that were outstanding during the period. All antidilutive potential common shares, securities that if converted or exercised would individually **increase** EPS, are disregarded.

LOSS FROM CONTINUING OPERATIONS

For a company with a loss from continuing operations, the exercise of options or conversions of securities would normally increase the number of potential common shares outstanding and reduce the loss per share. Since this would be antidilutive, SFAS 128 states that if there is a loss from continuing operations, **Diluted EPS would be the same as Basic EPS.**

EXAMPLE OF DILUTIVE EPS WITH CONVERTIBLE PREFERRED STOCK – IF CONVERTED METHOD

In 1999 the Stevens Corp. had 90,000 shares of common stock and 10,000 shares of preferred stock outstanding for the full year. During 1999 Stevens paid preferred dividends of $2.50 per share and the preferred stock is convertible into 20,000 shares of common stock. The net income for the year is $485,000 and the tax rate is 30%.

The capital structure is complex because of the presence of the convertible preferred stock. The first step is to calculate the Basic EPS and then compare it to the Dilutive EPS to determine if the convertible stock is dilutive.

$$\text{Basic EPS} = \frac{\text{Net Income - Preferred Dividends}}{\text{Weighted Average Number of Common Shares Outstanding}}$$

$$= \frac{485{,}000 - (2.50 \text{ per share} \times 10{,}000 \text{ shares})}{90{,}000 \text{ common shares}}$$

$$= \$5.11 \text{ per share}$$

To determine the dilutive effect, assume the convertible preferred stock was converted (if converted method) into 20,000 shares of common stock at January 1, 1999 and the $2.50 per share preferred dividend was not distributed. Therefore, the Diluted EPS would be calculated as follows:

$$\text{Dilutive EPS} = \frac{\text{Net Income}}{\text{Weighted Average Number Of Common Shares Outstanding} + \text{Dilutive Potential Common Shares}}$$

$$= \frac{\$485{,}000}{90{,}000 \text{ shares} + 20{,}000 \text{ shares}}$$

$$= \$4.41 \text{ per share}$$

The convertible preferred stock is dilutive because it reduced the EPS from $5.11 to $4.41. Stevens Corp. would disclose on the face of the income statement a Basic EPS of $5.11 and a Diluted EPS of $4.41.

NOTE: The if converted method assumes the conversion of the preferred stock at the earliest possible date. Since in our example the preferred stock was outstanding for the full year, the earliest date was January 1, 1999. However, if the preferred stock was issued on April 1, 1999, the earliest date for conversion would be April 1, 1999. The if converted method would then assume that the preferred stock was converted into 20,000 on April 1 and weight the shares as having been outstanding for 9 months (20,000 shares x 9/12 = 15,000 shares). The Diluted EPS would use the 15,000 shares as the potential common shares in the denominator of the formula.

EXAMPLE OF DILUTED EPS WITH CONVERTIBLE BONDS – IF CONVERTED METHOD

In 1999 Johnson Company had 100,000 shares of common stock and $1,000,000 of 9% convertible bonds outstanding for the full year. The bonds are convertible into 30,000 shares of common stock, the tax rate is 30% and the net income for the year is $485,000.

$$\text{Basic EPS} = \frac{\text{Net Income}}{\text{Weighted Average Number of Common Shares Outstanding}}$$

$$= \frac{\$485{,}000}{100{,}000 \text{ common shares}}$$

$$= \$4.85 \text{ per share}$$

The Diluted EPS assumes that the bonds were converted into 30,000 shares of common stock on January 1, 1999 and that Johnson Co. did not have bond interest of $90,000 (9% x $1,000,000 of bonds) for the year. Since the bond interest has already been deducted from the $485,000 in net income, the diluted EPS calculation would add back the $90,000 of bond interest and increase the income before tax by $90,000. The tax effect of the increase at 30% would be $27,000 and the net effect of the increase after taxes would be $63,000 ($90,000 - $27,000).

$$\text{Dilutive EPS} = \frac{\text{Net Income} + \text{Interest Expense (Net of Tax)}}{\text{Weighted Average Number of Common Shares Outstanding} + \text{Dilutive Potential Common Shares}}$$

$$= \frac{\$485{,}000 + (\$90{,}000 - \$27{,}000)}{100{,}000 \text{ shares} + 30{,}000 \text{ shares}}$$

$$= \$4.22 \text{ per share}$$

Since the Diluted EPS of $4.22 is lower that the Basic EPS of $4.85, the convertible bonds are dilutive.

TREASURY STOCK METHOD

Earnings per share is computed **as if** the funds obtained from the exercising of options and warrants at the beginning of the period (or at time of issuance, if later) were used to purchase common stock (treasury stock), **at the average market price during the period**. The excess of shares assumed issued, from the exercise of options and warrants, over the shares assumed purchased as treasury stock is considered dilutive and included in the denominator of the Diluted EPS as potential common shares. If the shares assumed purchased exceeds the shares assumed issued, the options and warrants are antidilutive and the options and warrants are excluded from the earnings per share computation. This antidilutive situation occurs when the exercise price exceeds the average market price of the options or warrants.

Example: A corporation has 10,000 warrants outstanding, exercisable at $54 with the average market price per common share during the reporting period being $60. The potential common shares included in the Diluted earnings per share computation is determined as follows:

Number of shares issued from exercise of warrants	10,000
Less: Number of shares purchased with proceeds	
10,000 × $540,000 ÷ $60	9,000
Potential Common Shares	1,000

The $540,000 realized from exercise of the warrants and issuance of 10,000 shares would be sufficient to acquire 9,000 shares of treasury stock. Therefore, 1,000 shares would be added to the weighted average common shares outstanding in computing Diluted earnings per share for the period.

The potential common shares also be determined with the following formula:

$$\text{Potential Common Shares} = \frac{\text{Market price} - \text{Option price}}{\text{Market price}} \times \text{Option Shares}$$

For the example:

$$\frac{\$60 - \$54}{60} \times 10{,}000 = \underline{1{,}000} \text{ C.S.E. shares}$$

ADDITIONAL POINTS

In situations in which an entity has different conversion rates for convertible securities or different stock option or warrant prices over a period of time, the Diluted EPS is based on the most advantageous conversion rate or exercise price from the **point of view of the security holder**. The most advantageous option price is the lowest one and the most advantageous conversion rate is the one that results in the most shares.

CONTINGENT SHARES

In a business combination the purchaser may promise to issue additional shares in the future if a contingency is met. If the contingency is **passage of time**, the contingent shares should be considered potential common shares and included in the denominator for the calculation of Diluted EPS. If the contingency is the **attainment of a certain income or market price level** and this level is met at the end of the year, the contingent shares are considered potential common shares and included in the calculation of the Diluted EPS.

DISCLOSURE REQUIREMENTS

For each period for which a company presents an income statement, it must disclose:

- A reconciliation of the numerators and denominators of basic and diluted EPS from continuing operations, including the individual income and per share effects of all securities used in the computations.
- The effect of preferred dividends in arriving at income available to common stockholders in basic EPS.
- The securities not included in the Diluted EPS computation (because they were antidilutive in the current period) that could potentially dilute Basic EPS in the future.

- A description of any transaction that occurs after the end of the period but before the financial statements are issued that would materially change the number of common shares or potential shares.

Examples of these transactions include the issuance or acquisition of common shares, the issuance of warrants, options, convertible securities and the conversion or exercise of potential common shares outstanding at the end of the period into common shares.

Note: See Appendix B for a Summary of EPS Formulas.

SFAS 131 -- DISCLOSURES ABOUT SEGMENTS OF AN ENTERPRISE AND RELATED INFORMATION

OVERVIEW

SFAS 131 determines the reporting standards for segment reporting, the disclosure of information about different components of an enterprise operation as well as information related to the enterprise's products and services, its geographic areas and its major customers.

OBJECTIVES

The objectives of SFAS 131 are to help users of financial statements:

- Better understand enterprise performance.
- Better assess its prospects for future net cash flows.
- Make more informed judgments about the enterprise as a whole.

IDENTIFYING REPORTABLE OPERATING SEGMENTS (SEE APPENDIX A)

A. MANAGEMENT APPROACH

SFAS 131 adopts a management approach to identifying segments in which segments are based on the way that management organizes segments **internally** for making operating decisions and assessing performance.

Segments can be organized by product or services by geography, by legal entity, or by the type of customer. These are referred to as operating segments.

Operating segments are components of an enterprise which meet three criteria:

1. Engage in business activities and earn revenues and incur expenses.
2. Operating results are regularly reviewed by the chief operating decision-maker to assess performance and make resource allocation decisions.
3. Discrete financial information is available from the internal reporting system.

B. AGGREGATION OF OPERATING SEGMENTS IF APPROPRIATE

After identifying the segments based on internal reporting, management must decide which of the segments should be reported separately. If two or more of the segments have essentially the same business activities in essentially the same economic environment, information for these individual segments may be combined (aggregated). For example, a retail chain may have 20 stores that individually meet the definition of an operating segment but each store is essentially the same. In this case management may desire to combine the 20 stores into one operating segment.

To aggregate similar operating segments the following criteria must be considered:

1. The nature of the products and services provided by each operating segment.
2. The nature of the production process.
3. The type of class of customer.
4. The distribution methods.

5. If applicable, the nature of the regulatory environment.

Segments must be similar in each and every one of these areas to be combined. However, **aggregation** of similar segments **is not required.**

C. **10 PERCENT QUANTITATIVE THRESHOLD TESTS**
Once operating segments have been identified, three quantitative threshold tests are then applied to identify segments of sufficient size to warrant separate disclosure. Any segment meeting even **one** of these tests is separately reportable.

1. ***Revenue test*** – segment revenues, both external and intersegment, are 10 percent or more of the combined revenue, external and intersegment, of all reported operating segments.
2. ***Profit or loss test*** – segment profit or loss is 10 percent or more of the greater (in absolute terms) of the combined reported profit of all profitable segments or the combined reported loss of all segments incurring a loss.
3. ***Asset test*** – segment assets are 10 percent or more of the combined assets of all operating segments.

D. **MANAGEMENT'S JUDGMENT**
Operating segments that were reported in previous periods that do not meet the 10 percent test in the current period may continue to be reported if judged to be of continuing significance to management.

E. **SUFFICIENCY TEST**
If the total external revenue of the operating segments is less than 75% of consolidated revenue, additional operating segments are identified as reportable until the 75% level is reached.

F. **ALL OTHERS**
All other segments that are not reportable should be combined with other business activities such as corporate headquarters and disclosed in an **all other category**.

INFORMATION TO BE DISCLOSED BY OPERATING SEGMENT

A. **GENERAL INFORMATION** about the operating segment including factors used to identify operating segments and the types of products and services from which each segment derives its revenues.

B. **SEGMENT PROFIT OR LOSS AND THE FOLLOWING COMPONENTS OF PROFIT OR LOSS**
1. Revenues from external customers.
2. Revenues from transactions with other operating segments.
3. Interest revenue.
4. Interest expense.
5. Depreciation, depletion, and amortization expense.
6. Other significant noncash items included in segment profit or loss.
7. Unusual items (discontinued operations and extraordinary items).
8. Income tax expense or benefit.
9. Equity in net income of investee accounted for on the equity method.

C. **TOTAL SEGMENT ASSETS AND THE FOLLOWING RELATED ITEMS**
1. Investment in equity method affiliates.
2. Expenditures for additions to long-lived assets.

D. **ADDITIONAL DISCLOSURES**
1. Basis of accounting.
2. Differences in measurement practices between a segment and the complete entity.
3. Reconciliations – the enterprise will need to reconcile the segment amounts disclosed to the corresponding enterprise amounts.

E. INTERIM PERIOD DISCLOSURES

Four items of information must also be disclosed by operating segment in interim financial statements:

1. Revenues from external customers.
2. Intersegment revenues.
3. Segment profit or loss.
4. Total assets for which there has been a material change from the amount disclosed in the last annual report.

ENTERPRISE-WIDE DISCLOSURES

A. INFORMATION ABOUT PRODUCTS AND SERVICES

1. Additional information must be provided if operating segments have not been determined based on differences in products and services, or if the enterprise has only one operating segment.
2. In those situations, revenues derived from transactions with external customers must be disclosed by product or service.

B. INFORMATION ABOUT GEOGRAPHIC AREAS

1. Revenues from external customers and long-lived assets must be reported for:
   - the domestic country.
   - all foreign countries in which the enterprise has assets or derives revenues.
   - each individual foreign country in which the enterprise has material revenues or material long-lived assets.

2. The FASB does not provide any specific guidance with regard to determining materiality of revenues or long-lived assets; this is left to management's judgment.

C. INFORMATION ABOUT MAJOR CUSTOMERS

If revenues from a single customer are 10 percent or more of consolidated revenues, the following disclosures should be made:

1. Amount of revenue to each customer that has 10 percent or more of consolidated revenues.
2. Amount of revenue to domestic government agencies or foreign governments if 10 percent or more of **consolidated** revenues.
3. Identify the industry segment making the sale.
4. Disclosures of the customer's name **is not required.**

Case Example: Assume that an enterprise has seven industry segments some of which incurred operating losses, as follows:

Industry Segment	*Operating Profit or (Operating Loss)*	
A	$100	
B	500	$1,000
C	400	
D	(295)	
E	(600)	
F	(100)	(1,100)
G	(105)	
	$(100)	

The combined operating profit of all industry segments that did not incur a loss (A, B, and C) is $1,000. The absolute amount of the combined operating loss of those segments that did incur a loss (D, E, F, and G) is $1,100. Therefore, Industry Segments B, C, D, and E are significant because the absolute amount of their individual operating profit or operating loss equals or exceeds $110 (10 percent of $1,100). Additional industry segments might also be significant under the revenue and identifiable asset tests.

ILLUSTRATIVE PROBLEM FOR SEGMENT REPORTING

X Corporation operates in various diversified industries within the U.S. as well as in several foreign locations. The company has designated certain operating units as segments in an attempt to comply with the tests in SFAS #131.

Listed below are the designated reporting units along with the revenues, operating profit and assets of each (000's).

	— U.S. —			*— Foreign —*				
	Toys	*Appli-ances*	*Furni-ture*	*Toys*	*Bottles*	*Total*	*Elimina-tions*	*Consol-idated*
Gross revenues	$1,000	$18,000	$4,000	$600	$400	$24,000	$(500)	$23,500
Operating profit (loss)	100	2,000	(800)	(50)	10	1,260	(20)	1,240
Assets	800	6,000	1,000	300	100	8,200	—	8,200

The company combines its foreign and U.S. toy operations as one segment for testing purposes.

Application of tests:

1. Revenues — 10% × gross revenues = $24,000 × .10 = $2,400
   Therefore, appliances and furniture are reportable segments.

2. Operating profit (loss)/profits = 10% × $2,060[1] = $206
   or losses = 10% × 800 = $80

Use 206. Therefore, appliances and furniture are reportable segments.

[1]U.S. toys	$100		
Foreign toys	(50)		
Toys net		$ 50	
Appliances		2,000	
Bottles		10	
		$2,060	Operating profits for test purposes

3. Assets — 10% × $8,200 = $820. Therefore, appliances, furniture and toys are reportable segments.

4. Segments sufficiency test (75% test): .75 × $23,500 (revenues to unaffiliated customers) = $17,625—required. Revenues included in reportable segments exceed the requirement. Therefore, the three segments determined to be reportable are sufficient.

Appendix A – FLOWCHART FOR IDENTIFYING REPORTABLE OPERATING SEGMENTS*

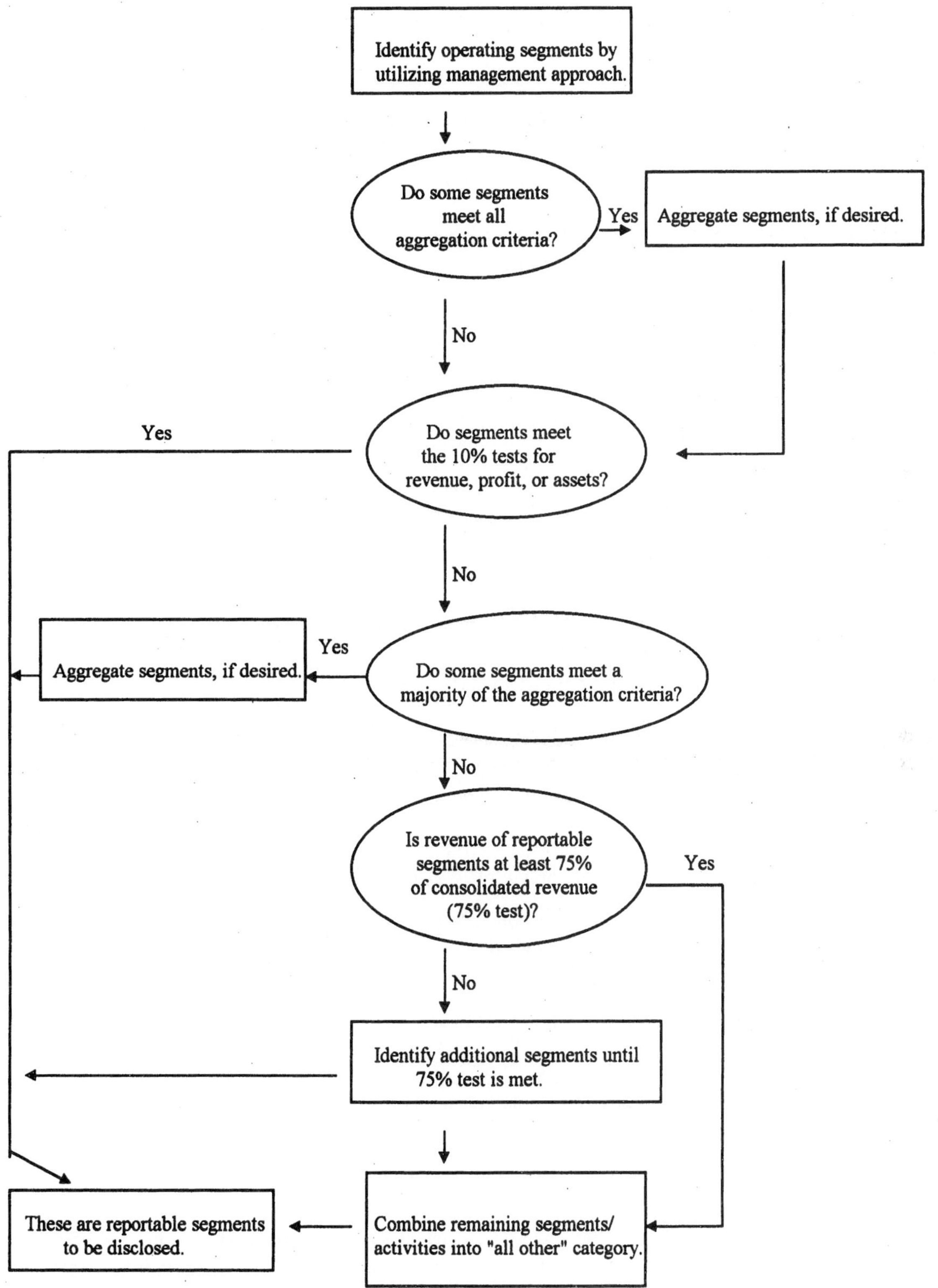

**Adopted from SFAS 131, Appendix B, p. 47.*

APPENDIX B

SUMMARY OF EPS FORMULAS and DISCLOSURE REQUIREMENTS

$$\text{Basic EPS} = \frac{\text{Net Income} - \text{Current years preferred dividends*}}{\text{Weighted average common shares}}$$

$$\text{Diluted EPS with Convertible preferred stock} = \frac{\text{Net Income}}{\text{Weighted average Common Shares} + \text{Weighted average Potential Shares}}$$

$$\text{Diluted EPS with Convertible Bonds} = \frac{\text{Net Income} + (\text{Bond Interest} - \text{Tax Effect})}{\text{Weighted average Common Shares} + \text{Weighted average Potential Shares}}$$

$$\text{Diluted EPS with Stock Options or Warrants} = \frac{\text{Net Income}}{\text{Weighted average Common Shares} + \text{Weighted average Potential Shares (Treasury stock method)}}$$

* Current cumulative preferred dividends are always deducted.
Non-cumulative current dividends are deducted if declared.

DISCLOSURE REQUIREMENTS

For each period for which a company presents an income statement, it must disclose:

- A reconciliation of the numerators and denominators of basic and diluted EPS from continuing operations, including the individual income and per share effects of all securities used in the computations.
- The effect of preferred dividends in arriving at income available to common stockholders in basic EPS.
- The securities not included in the Diluted EPS computation (because they were antidilutive in the current period) that could potentially dilute Basic EPS in the future.
- A description of any transaction that occurs after the end of the period but before the financial statements are issued that would materially change the number of common shares or potential shares.

Examples of these transactions include the issuance or acquisition of common shares, the issuance of warrants, options, convertible securities and the conversion or exercise of potential common shares outstanding at the end of the period into common shares.

Chapter Five
Earnings Per Share, Segment Reporting Questions

EARNINGS PER SHARE

BASIC EARNINGS PER SHARE

1. Rand, Inc., had 20,000 shares of common stock outstanding at January 1, 1993. On May 1, 1993, it issued 10,500 shares of common stock. Outstanding all year were 10,000 shares of nonconvertible preferred stock on which a dividend of $4 per share was paid in December 1993. Net income for 1993 was $96,700. Rand's basic earnings per share for 1993 are

a. $1.86
b. $2.10
c. $2.84
d. $3.58

2. At December 31, 1992 and 1991, Gow Corp. had 100,000 shares of common stock and 10,000 shares of 5%, $100 par value cumulative preferred stock outstanding. No dividends were declared on either the preferred or common stock in 1992 or 1991. Net income for 1992 was $1,000,000. For 1992, basic earnings per common share amounted to

a. $10.00
b. $9.50
c. $9.00
d. $5.00

3. Fay Corporation's capital structure at December 31, 1996, was as follows:

	Shares issued and outstanding
Common stock	200,000
Nonconvertible preferred stock	50,000

On October 1, 1997, Fay issued a 10% stock dividend on its common stock, and paid $100,000 cash dividends on the preferred stock. Net income for the year ended December 31, 1997, was $960,000. Fay's 1997 basic earnings per common share should be

a. $3.91.
b. $4.10.
c. $4.36.
d. $4.68.

4. The following information pertains to Jet Corp.'s outstanding stock for 1999:

Common stock, $5 par value	
Shares outstanding, 1/1/99	20,000
2-for-1 stock split, 4/1/99	20,000
Shares issued, 7/1/99	10,000
Preferred stock, $10 par value, 5% cumulative	
Shares outstanding, 1/1/99	4,000

What are the number of shares Jet should use to calculate 1999 basic earnings per share?

a. 40,000
b. 45,000
c. 50,000
d. 54,000

5. On January 31, 1999, Pack, Inc., split its common stock 2 for 1, and Young, Inc., issued a 5% stock dividend. Both companies issued their December 31, 1998, financial statements on March 1, 1999. Should Pack's 1998 basic earnings per share (EPS) take into consideration the stock split, and should Young's 1998 EPS take into consideration the stock dividend?

	Pack's 1998 EPS	*Young's 1998 EPS*
a.	Yes	No
b.	No	No
c.	Yes	Yes
d.	No	Yes

DILUTED EPS - CONVERTIBLE PREFERRED STOCK

6. During 1994, Moore Corp. had the following two classes of stock issued and outstanding for the entire year.

- 100,000 shares of common stock, $1 par.
- 1,000 shares of 4% preferred stock, $100 par, convertible share for share into common stock.

Moore's 1994 net income was $900,000, and its income tax rate for the year was 30%. In the computation of diluted earnings per share for 1994, the amount to be used in the numerator is

a. $896,000
b. $898,800
c. $900,000
d. $901,200

7. Dunn, Inc., had 200,000 shares of $20 par common stock and 20,000 shares of $100 par, 6%, cumulative, convertible preferred stock outstanding for the entire year ended December 31, 1993. Each share is convertible into five shares of common stock. Dunn's net income for 1993 was $840,000. For the year ended December 31, 1993, the diluted earnings per share is

a. $2.40
b. $2.80
c. $3.60
d. $4.20

DILUTED EPS - CONVERTIBLE BONDS

8. On January 2, 1997, Lang Co. issued at par $10,000 of 4% bonds convertible in total into 1,000 shares of Lang's common stock. No bonds were converted during 1997.
Throughout 1997, Lang had 1,000 shares of common stock outstanding. Lang's 1997 net income was $1,000. Lang's income tax rate is 50%.

No potentially dilutive securities other than the convertible bonds were outstanding during 1997.

Lang's diluted earnings per share for 1997 would be

a. $1.00.
b. $.50.
c. $.70.
d. $.60.

9. On June 30, 1997, Lomond, Inc., issued twenty, $10,000, 7% bonds at par. Each bond was convertible into 200 shares of common stock. On January 1, 1998, 10,000 shares of common stock were outstanding. The bondholders converted all the bonds on July 1, 1998. On the bonds' issuance date, the average Aa corporate bond yield was 12%. During 1998, the average Aa corporate bond yield was 9%. The following amounts were reported in Lomond's income statement for the year ended December 31, 1998:

Revenues	$977,000
Operating expenses	920,000
Interest on bonds	7,000
Income before income tax	50,000
Income tax at 30%	15,000
Net income	$ 35,000

What amount should Lomond report as its 1998 diluted earnings per share?

a. $2.50
b. $2.85
c. $2.92
d. $3.50

DILUTED EPS - CONVERTIBLE BONDS & PREFERRED STOCK

10. Jones Corp.'s capital structure was as follows:

	December 31 1995	1994
Outstanding shares of stock:		
Common	110,000	110,000
Convertible preferred	10,000	10,000
8% convertible bonds	$1,000,000	$1,000,000

During 1995, Jones paid dividends of $3.00 per share on its preferred stock. The preferred shares are convertible into 20,000 shares of common. The 8% bonds are convertible into 30,000 shares of common stock. Net income for 1995 is $850,000. Assume that the income tax rate is 30%.

The diluted earnings per share for 1995 is

a. $5.48
b. $5.66
c. $5.81
d. $6.26

TREASURY STOCK METHOD FOR OPTIONS AND WARRANTS

11. On January 1, 1996, Hage Corporation granted options to purchase 9,000 of its common shares at $7 each. The market price of common was $10.50 per share on March 31, 1996, and averaged $9 per share during the quarter then ended. There was no change in the 50,000 shares of outstanding common stock during the quarter ended March 31, 1996. Net income for the quarter was $8,268. The number of shares to be used in computing diluted earnings per share for the quarter is

a. 59,000.
b. 50,000.
c. 53,000.
d. 52,000.

12. The 1997 net income of Mack Co. was $100,000, and 100,000 shares of its common stock were outstanding during the entire year. In addition, there were outstanding options to purchase 10,000 shares of common stock at $10 per share. These options were granted in 1995 and none had been exercised by December 31, 1997. Market prices of Mack's common stock during 1997 were:

January 1	$20 per share
December 31	$40 per share
Average price	$25 per share

The amount which should be shown as Mack's diluted earnings per share for 1997 is (rounded to the nearest cent)

a. $\frac{\$100,000}{110,000 \text{ shares}} = \$.91.$

b. $\frac{\$100,000}{105,000 \text{ shares}} = \$.95.$

c. $\frac{\$100,000}{106,000 \text{ shares}} = \$.94.$

d. $\frac{\$100,000}{107,500 \text{ shares}} = \$.93.$

13. Dilutive stock options would generally be used in the calculation of

	Basic earnings per share	*Diluted earnings per share*
a.	No	No
b.	No	Yes
c.	Yes	Yes
d.	Yes	No

14. In a diluted earnings per share computation, the treasury stock method is used for options and warrants to reflect assumed reacquisition of common stock at the average market price during the period. If the exercise price of the options or warrants exceeds the average market price, the computation would

a. Fairly present diluted earnings per share on a prospective basis.
b. Fairly present the maximum potential dilution of diluted earnings per share on a prospective basis.
c. Reflect the excess of the number of shares assumed issued over the number of shares assumed reacquired as the potential dilution of earnings per share.
d. Be anti-dilutive.

15. An antidilutive common stock option is

	A potential common share	*Included in computing diluted earnings per share*
a.	No	No
b.	No	Yes
c.	Yes	No
d.	Yes	Yes

CONTINGENT EPS

16. Throughout 1998, J Co. had 10,000 shares of common stock outstanding. There was no potential dilution of earnings per share except as follows:

In 1997, J Co. agreed to issue 2,000 additional shares of its stock to the former stockholders of an acquired company if the acquired company's earnings for any of the five years 1998 through 2002 exceeded $5,000.

Results of operations for 1998 were:

Net income of J Co.	$10,000
Net income of acquired company	4,000
Consolidated net income	$14,000

Diluted earnings per share for 1998 on a consolidated basis would be

a. $\frac{\$14,000}{10,000} = \$1.40.$

b. $\frac{\$14,000}{12,000} = \$1.17.$

c. $\frac{\$15,000}{10,000} = \$1.50.$

d. $\frac{\$15,000}{12,000} = \$1.25.$

EPS REVIEW

17. Timp, Inc., had the following common stock balances and transactions during 1998:

1/1/98	Common stock outstanding	30,000
2/1/98	Issued a 10% common stock dividend	3,000
3/1/98	Issued common stock in a pooling of interests	9,000
7/1/98	Issued common stock for cash	8,000
12/31/98	Common stock outstanding	50,000

What was Timp's 1998 weighted average shares outstanding?

a. 40,000
b. 44,250
c. 44,500
d. 46,000

18. Information relating to the capital structure of the Galaxy Company is as follows:

	December 31	
	1995	1996
Outstanding shares of:		
Common stock	90,000	90,000
Convertible preferred stock	10,000	10,000
9% convertible bonds	$1,000,000	$1,000,000

During 1996 Galaxy paid dividends of $2.50 per share on its preferred stock. The preferred stock is convertible into 20,000 shares of common stock. The 9% convertible bonds are convertible into 30,000 shares of common stock. The net income for the year ended December 31, 1996, is $485,000. Assume that the income tax rate is 50%.

What should be the diluted earnings per share, rounded to the nearest penny, for the year ended December 31, 1996?

a. $3.79.
b. $3.96.
c. $4.11.
d. $4.51.

19. Peters Corp.'s capital structure was as follows:

	December 31	
	1995	1996
Outstanding shares of stock:		
Common	110,000	110,000
Convertible preferred	10,000	10,000
8% convertible bonds	$1,000,000	$1,000,000

During 1996, Peters paid dividends of $3.00 per share on its preferred stock. The preferred shares are convertible into 20,000 shares of common. The 8% bonds are convertible into 30,000 shares of common stock. Net income for 1996 was $850,000. Assume that the income tax rate is 30%. The diluted earnings per share for 1996 is

a. $6.31
b. $5.66
c. $7.08
d. $7.45

20. At December 31, 1992, Lex, Inc. had 600,000 shares of common stock outstanding. On April 1, 1993, an additional 180,000 shares of common stock were issued for cash. Lex also had $5,000,000 of 8% convertible bonds outstanding at December 31, 1993, which are convertible into 150,000 shares of common stock. No bonds were issued or converted into common stock during 1993. What is the number of shares that should be used in computing diluted earnings per share for 1993?

a. 735,000
b. 780,000
c. 885,000
d. 930,000

21. On December 1, 2000, Clay Co. declared and issued a 6% stock dividend on its 100,000 shares of outstanding common stock. There was no other common stock activity during 2000. What number of shares should Clay use in determining basic earnings per share for 2000?

a. 100,000.
b. 100,500.
c. 103,000.
d. 106,000.

22. Mann, Inc., had 300,000 shares of common stock issued and outstanding at December 31, 1997. On July 1, 1998, an additional 50,000 shares of common stock were issued for cash. Mann also had unexercised stock options to purchase 40,000 shares of common stock at $15 per share outstanding at the beginning and end of 1998. The average market price of Mann's common stock was $20 during 1998. What is the number of shares that should be used in computing diluted earnings per share for the year ended December 31, 1998?

a. 325,000.
b. 335,000.
c. 360,000.
d. 365,000.

SEGMENT REPORTING

10% TEST FOR ASSETS

23. In financial reporting for segments of a business enterprise, which of the following should be taken into account in computing the amount of an industry segment's identifiable assets?

	Accumulated depreciation	Marketable securities valuation allowance
a.	No	No
b.	No	Yes
c.	Yes	Yes
d.	Yes	No

10% REVENUE TEST

24. The following information pertains to revenue earned by Timm Co.'s industry segments for the year ended December 31, 1997:

Segment	*Sales to unaffiliated customers*	*Intersegment sales*	*Total revenue*
Alo	$ 5,000	$ 3,000	$ 8,000
Bix	8,000	4,000	12,000
Cee	4,000	--	4,000
Dil	43,000	16,000	59,000
Combined	60,000	23,000	83,000
Elimination	—	(23,000)	(23,000)
Consolidated	$60,000	—	$60,000

In conformity with the revenue test, Timm's reportable segments were

a. Only Dil.
b. Only Bix and Dil.
c. Only Alo, Bix, and Dil.
d. Alo, Bix, Cee, and Dil.

25. The following information pertains to Aria Corp. and its divisions for the year ended December 31, 1995:

Sales to unaffiliated customers	$2,000,000
Intersegment sales of products similar to those sold to unaffiliated customers	600,000
Interest earned on loans to other industry segments	40,000

Aria and all of its divisions are engaged solely in manufacturing operations. Aria has a reportable segment if that segment's revenue exceeds

a. $264,000
b. $260,000
c. $204,000
d. $200,000

COMBINATION OF 10% TEST

26. Correy Corp. and its divisions are engaged solely in manufacturing operations. The following data (consistent with prior years' data) pertain to the industries in which operations were conducted for the year ended December 31, 1996:

Industry	*Total revenue*	*Operating profit*	*Identifiable assets at 12/31/96*
A	$10,000,000	$1,750,000	$20,000,000
B	8,000,000	1,400,000	17,500,000
C	6,000,000	1,200,000	12,500,000
D	3,000,000	550,000	7,500,000
E	4,250,000	675,000	7,000,000
F	1,500,000	225,000	3,000,000
	$32,750,000	$5,800,000	$67,500,000

In its segment information for 1996, how many reportable segments does Correy have?

a. Three
b. Four
c. Five
d. Six

27. Cott Co.'s four business segments have revenues and identifiable assets expressed as percentages of Cott's total revenues and total assets as follows:

	Revenues	*Assets*
Ebon	64%	66%
Fair	14%	18%
Gel	14%	4%
Hak	8%	12%
	100%	100%

Which of these business segments are deemed to be reportable segments?

a. Ebon only.
b. Ebon and Fair only.
c. Ebon, Fair, and Gel only.
d. Ebon, Fair, Gel, and Hak.

MAJOR CUSTOMERS

28. Grum Corp., a publicly-owned corporation, is subject to the requirements for segment reporting. In its income statement for the year ended December 31, 1998, Grum reported consolidated revenues of $50,000,000, operating expenses of $47,000,000, and net income of $3,000,000. Operating expenses include payroll costs of $15,000,000. Grum's combined identifiable assets of all industry segments at December 31, 1998, were $40,000,000.

In its 1998 financial statements, Grum should disclose major customer data if sales to any single customer amount to at least

a. $300,000
b. $1,500,000
c. $4,000,000
d. $5,000,000

RECENTLY DISCLOSED QUESTIONS

M98

29. In computing the weighted-average number of shares outstanding during the year, which of the following midyear events must be treated as if it had occurred at the beginning of the year?

a. Declaration and distribution of a stock dividend.
b. Purchase of treasury stock.
c. Sale of additional common stock.
d. Sale of preferred convertible stock.

30. Deck Co. had 120,000 shares of common stock outstanding at January 1, 1998. On July 1, 1998, it issued 40,000 additional shares of common stock. Outstanding all year were 10,000 shares of nonconvertible cumulative preferred stock. What is the number of shares that Deck should use to calculate 1998 earnings per share?

a. 140,000
b. 150,000
c. 160,000
d. 170,000

Chapter Five
Solutions to Earnings Per Share, Segment Reporting Questions

1. (b)

Common shares outstanding 1/1/93	20,000
Weighted average number of shares issued in 1993 (8/12 × 10,500)	7,000
Denominator of EPS calculation	27,000
Net income	$96,700
Preferred dividends ($4 × 10,000)	– 40,000
Numerator of calculation	$56,700

EPS = $56,700 ÷ 27,000 = $2.10

2. (b)

$$\frac{\$1{,}000{,}000 - \$50{,}000 = \$950{,}000}{100{,}000} = \$9.50 \text{ EPS}$$

Even though no dividends were declared, the preferred dividends are subtracted from the numerator since the preferred shares are cumulative.

3. (a) $960,000 – 100,000 = $860,000—numerator
200,000 + 20,000 = 220,000—denominator
EPS = $3.91

4. (b) The key point is that the stock split is retroactive to the beginning of the year.

Dates Outstanding	*Shares Outstanding*	×	*Fraction of Year*	=	*Weighted Average*
Jan. 1 balance	20,000				
Stock split	× 2				
Jan. 1-June 30	40,000	×	6/12	=	20,000
Shares issued 7/1	10,000				
July 1-Dec. 31	50,000	×	6/12	=	25,000
Weighted average number of shares outstanding					45,000

5. (c) "If changes in common stock resulting from stock dividends or stock splits or reverse splits have been consummated after the close of the period but before the completion of the financial report, the per share computations shall be based on the new number of shares because the readers' primary interest is presumed to be related to the current capitalization. If per share computations reflect those changes in the number of shares after the close of the period, the fact shall be disclosed."

6. (c) The if converted method assumes that the preferred stock was converted to common stock and that preferred dividends were not distributed. Therefore, the numerator in the computation of Diluted EPS would be the net income of $900,000.

7. (b) Diluted EPS is the lesser of $840,000 ÷ 300,000 = $2.80 (assumes conversion) or $840,000 – $120,000 = $720,000 ÷ 200,000 = $3.60 (basic earnings per share); therefore, assuming conversion is dilutive.

8. (d) Diluted EPS = $\dfrac{\$1,000 \text{ NI} + \$200 \text{ after-tax interest}}{1,000 \text{ shs. common} + 1,000 \text{ Potential common shares}}$

$= \dfrac{\$1,200}{2,000}$

$= \$.60$

9. (b) The bonds are potential common shares for the first six months and outstanding shares for the second six months. The interest rates are no longer relevant to the calculation of EPS.

Net income	$35,000
Interest adjustment	
$7,000 – taxes $2,100 = $4,900	4,900
Numerator for calculation of Diluted EPS	$39,900
Denominator =	
Weighted average 10,000 + (200 × 20 × ½) =	12,000
Potential common shares (200 × 20 × ½) =	2,000
	14,000

Diluted EPS = $39,900 ÷ 14,000 = $2.85.

10. (b) $\dfrac{\$850,000 + (\$80,000 - \$24,000)}{\$110,000 + \$20,000 + \$30,000}$ = $906,000 ÷ 160,000 = $5.66

11. (d) Proceeds from exercise of options = 9,000 shs. × $7 = $63,000
Used to repurchase common stock at average market price = $63,000 ÷ $9 = 7,000 shs.

Number of shares if options exercised	9,000
Less: Shares assumed repurchased	7,000
Dilution (Potential Common Shares)	2,000

Shares for Diluted EPS = 50,000 + 2,000 = 52,000

12. (c)

Treasury stock method: $\dfrac{\$25 - \$10}{\$25} \times 10,000 = 6,000$

Diluted EPS = $\dfrac{\$100,000}{100,000 + 6,000}$

13. (b) Dilutive stock options are never used in calculating Basic EPS but are always used in Dilutive EPS.

14. (d) If the exercise price of the options exceeds the average market price, the computation would have the effect of increasing earnings per share (anti-dilution). The anti-dilutive effect should not be recognized in computing the earnings per share.

e.g., number of options = 1,000
exercise price = $60
average market price = $50

Proceeds from exercise of options (1,000 additional shares issued) = 1,000 × $60 = $60,000. Above proceeds used to purchase stock at average market price: $60,000 ÷ $50 = 1,200 shares.

The net effect of the above is to decrease outstanding common shares by 200, which would increase earnings per share.

15. (c) A common stock option is always considered a potential common share but is only included in the calculation of EPS if the result is dilutive.

16. (a) Contingent shares are **not** considered outstanding for computation of Diluted EPS if the condition for their issuance is related to earnings or market value.

$$\text{Diluted EPS} = \frac{\$14{,}000}{10{,}000 \text{ shs.}} = \$1.40$$

17. (d) The issuance of stock for the stock dividend is not weighted but is considered retroactively to the beginning of the year.

Shares outstanding 1/1/98	30,000
10% stock dividend	3,000
Pooling of interests	9,000
Issuance, 7/1/98—8,000 × 6/12	4,000
Weighted average	46,000

18. (a) $485,000 + ($90,000 – 45,000) ÷ 90,000 + 20,000 + 30,000 = $3.79, assuming conversion for the bonds is dilutive.

19. (b) $$\frac{\$850{,}000 + (\$80{,}000 - \$24{,}000)}{\$110{,}000 + \$20{,}000 + \$30{,}000} = \$906{,}000 \div 160{,}000 = \$5.66$$

20. (c)

Shares outstanding 1/1/93	600,000
Weighted average additional shares issued (9/12 × 180,000)	135,000
Potential common shares	150,000
Number of shares to be used in EPS calculation	885,000

21. (d) A stock dividend or stock split that occurs during the year is retroactive to the beginning of the year, or if more than one year is presented, retroactive to the beginning of the earliest accounting period reported. In this case, the 6,000 shares issued (100,000 × 6%) for the stock dividend are retroactive to January 1, 2001 and the number of shares used as a denominator in the calculation of earnings per share would be 106,000 (100,000 + 6,000).

22. (b)

Shares outstanding 1/1/91 =	300,000
Shares issued 7/1/91—50,000 × 6/12 =	25,000
Potential common shares (options) =	10,000
	335,000

Calculation for options: $\frac{20-15}{20} \times 40{,}000 = 10{,}000$

23. (c) All asset (and related contra-asset) accounts which are directly identified with a company's segment are taken into account when testing to determine whether the segment is to be separately reported.

24. (b) Reportable segments are those for which segment revenue including intersegment sales comprise 10% or more of total revenues. Therefore, Bix and Dil are reportable segments—$12,000 and $59,000 are greater than $8,300.

25. (b) The test is 10% of all sales including intersegment sales. Therefore, any segment with revenues of $260,000 or more qualifies as a reporting segment.

26. (c) Those segments qualify which have 10% or more than the related totals of revenues, operating profit and assets. Therefore, segments A, B, C (all three tests), D (asset test), and E (asset and profit tests) qualify as reportable segments.

27. (d) Ebon, Fair and Gel would qualify as reportable segments under the 10% of combined revenue rule of FASB #131. Ebon, Fair and Hak would qualify as reportable segments using the 10% of identifiable assets rule. Since segments have to qualify under only one of the 10% rules, all segments qualify as reportable segments.

28. (d) FASB #131 requires disclosure of major customer data if sales to any major customer is 10% or more of consolidated revenues. Since consolidated revenues amount to $50,000,000, disclosure of major customer data would be required if sales to any single customer amount to $5,000,000. In addition the amount of revenue from each major customer must be disclosed plus the name of the segment making the sale.

29. (a) The calculation of weighted average number of common shares requires the retroactive recognition to the beginning of the year for stock dividends, stock splits, and pooling of interest for all periods presented. Non retroactive treatment would cause a false dilution of earnings per share in the current period as compared to previous periods.

30. (a)
Since the preferred shares are nonconvertible, the requirement is to calculate the weighted average number of common shares for Basic Earnings per share.

Date	shares outstanding	X	fraction of year	=	weighted average
January 1 Balance	120,000	x	6/12	=	60,000
July 1 Issue	40,000				
July 1 Balance	160,000	x	6/12	=	80,000
	Weighted average common shares				140,000

Chapter Six
Price Level—Foreign Exchange

Chapter Six
Price Level—Foreign Exchange

FINANCIAL REPORTING AND CHANGING PRICES

In General

Attributes of assets that accountants might measure are

- Historical cost or
- Current cost

The measuring units that can be used to measure either attribute are

- Nominal dollars or
- Constant dollars

As a result, there are four possibilities:

Historical Cost		*Current Cost*	
Nominal dollars	*Constant dollars*	*Nominal dollars*	*Constant dollars*
—1—	—2—	—3—	—4—

This four-column characterization presents the framework of "Financial Reporting and Changing Prices," and it will be referred to in the discussion that follows.

Working definitions of these four terms follow:

- **Historical cost**—the historical exchange price experienced in an actual transaction.
- **Current cost**—the cost that would be incurred at the present time (its specific measurement is discussed later).
- **Nominal dollars**—dollars that are not adjusted to reflect changes in purchasing power.
- **Constant dollars**—dollars that are restated to reflect changes in purchasing power.

Historical Cost/Constant Dollars

To use the constant dollar measuring unit, price index numbers are the means with which to measure the effects of inflation. The Consumer Price Index-Urban (CPI-U) is the index that is used, and its amount is published monthly. Two index numbers are needed to restate nominal dollars into constant dollars. The period whose nominal dollars are being restated is called the base period, the period into whose dollars' purchasing power the nominal dollars are being restated is the current period.

$$\frac{\text{Current period CPI-U}}{\text{Base period CPI-U}} = \text{conversion factor}$$

Example:

To restate land purchased in January 19X2 for $10,000 into December 19X8 constant dollars, use the appropriate CPI-U numbers.

$$\frac{\text{(December 19X8 =) 180}}{\text{(January 19X2 =) 120}} = 1.5$$

The result is that $10,000 is restated into ($10,000 × 1.5 =) $15,000 in the December 31, 19X8, constant dollar balance sheet. FASB Statement No. 33 allows as an acceptable alternative to have the numerator contain the weighted average CPI-U for the current year, thus

$$\frac{\text{(19X8 average =) 168}}{\text{(January 19X2 =) 120}} = 1.4$$

In average 19X8 constant dollars, the restated cost basis of the land would be ($10,000 × 1.4 =) $14,000.

In the CPA Exam, you will be told whether the constant dollar is based on the year-end CPI-U or the year-average CPI-U.

Monetary items are sums of money whose amount is fixed or determinable without reference to future prices of specific goods or services. They include cash, and those receivables and payables which will be discharged in cash. Such receivables and payables qualify irrespective of their being current or noncurrent. All other financial statement amounts are nonmonetary, e.g., investments (except an investment in debt securities which will be held until maturity—which would be a monetary asset), inventory, plant assets, intangibles, owners' equity balances, revenues and expenses. The monetary-nonmonetary distinction applies when accounting measurements use constant dollars as the measuring unit:

- Only nonmonetary items **are restated** from nominal dollars into constant dollars.
- Gains or losses are **not recognized** as a result of restating nonmonetary items.
- Monetary items are **not restated**—because their sums are fixed.
- Gains or losses **are recorded** to reflect the increase or decrease in purchasing power that results from holding monetary items during inflation.

Example: Assuming that the year-end dollar is the constant dollar, if a company holds $3,000 cash and $7,000 land bought in January 19X7 and during 19X7 the CPI-U moves from 100 to 120, the constant dollar balance sheet as of December 31, 19X7, would disclose $3,000 cash and [$7,000 × (120/100 =) 1.2 =] $8,400 land. The constant dollar income statement would contain a ($3,000 × .2 =) $600 purchasing power loss.

Restatement of a depreciable asset entails restating the related accumulated depreciation and depreciation expense amounts with the same conversion factor used to restate the asset proper. Thus, if the $7,000 land in the last example had instead been a machine being depreciated at a rate of $1,400 per year for 5 years, the constant dollar financial statements would contain the following amounts:

	19X7	*19X8*
Current index	120	156
Machinery:		
(7,000 × 1.2)	$8,400	
(7,000 × 1.56)		$10,920
Depreciation expense:		
(1,400 × 1.2)	$1,680	
(1,400 × 1.56)		$2,184
Accumulated depreciation:		
(1,400 × 1.2)	$1,680	
(2,800 × 1.56)		$4,368

If the $7,000 machinery account had consisted of 3 machines that had been bought at different dates, the cost of each machine is restated individually and the 3 restated amounts are then added together.

	Machine A	*Machine B*	*Machine C*	*Total*
Date acquired	March 19X5	August 19X6	January 19X7	
Base index number	80	90	100	
Cost	$4,000	$2,000	$1,000	$7,000
Conversion factor:				
Dec. 31, 19X7	$\frac{120}{80}$ = 1.50	$\frac{120}{90}$ = 1.33	$\frac{120}{100}$ = 1.20	
Dec. 31, 19X8	$\frac{156}{80}$ = 1.95	$\frac{156}{90}$ = 1.73	$\frac{156}{100}$ = 1.56	

Constant dollars:				
Dec. 31, 19X7	$6,000	$2,666	$1,200	$ 9,866
Dec. 31, 19X8	7,800	$3,460	$1,560	$12,820

If the nonmonetary asset had been Inventory (instead of Land or Machinery), it would be necessary to restate both the asset and the cost of goods sold by using the appropriate conversion factor.

The **purchasing power gain/loss** is the gain/loss from holding monetary items. The calculation of the gain or loss is now illustrated in an example for which the following index numbers apply:

December 19X1	110
December 19X2	132
Average for 19X2	120

Reference to the beginning and ending balance sheets yields the following information. Assuming the average-for-the-year dollar is the constant dollar (i.e., the year-average CPI-U), the purchasing power gain is $454, as follows:

	January 1	*December 31*
Monetary assets	$10,000	$ 12,000
Monetary liabilities	$ 7,000	$ 20,000
Net monetary assets (liabilities)	$ 3,000	$ (8,000)

	Nominal dollars	*Conversion factor*	*Constant dollars*
Net monetary assets (liabilities):			
January 1: $10,000 – $7,000:	$ 3,000	120/110	$ 3,273
Monetary flows:			
In 19X2: ($8,000) – $3,000:	(11,000)		(11,000)
			(7,727)
Net monetary assets (liabilities):			
December 31: $12,000 – ($20,000):	$(8,000)	120/132	$(7,273)
Purchasing power gain			$ 454

The discussion to this point has dealt with the historical cost/constant dollar approach. Certain amounts that would appear in historical cost/constant dollar financial statements may be presented by corporations in schedular form as a supplement to their basic historical cost/nominal dollar financial statements, to be discussed later.

Current Cost Accounting

A second aspect of the expanded financial reporting disclosures set forth in FASB Statement No. 89 entails disclosing certain amounts which would appear in **current cost/constant dollar** financial statements. These are the data that result in the approach depicted in Column 4 of the framework (which appeared in the first paragraph of the discussion). To understand the nature of that approach, we will deal initially with current cost data using the nominal dollar measuring unit, Column 3 in the framework.

The current cost of an asset is the current replacement cost of the asset owned, adjusted for the value of any operating advantages or disadvantages of the asset owned. However, it may not exceed the recoverable amount. which is the higher of the net realizable value or the net present value of the future cash flows.

Use of current cost as the attribute of assets to be measured is implemented either by indexation or by direct pricing. The "indexation" approach should not be confused with general price index numbers (CPI-U) that are used to restate nominal dollars into constant dollars. Instead, it refers to specific indices that are generated either internally or externally for particular classes of goods and services. Direct pricing can be effected by reference to current invoice prices, vendors' price lists or standard manufacturing costs that reflect current costs.

When revaluing an asset to reflect its current cost, the resulting increase (or decrease) from its previous valuation is a holding gain (or a holding loss) and in theory would be recognized as such in a current-cost income statement. For example, if the value of land that had been purchased for $10,000 were to increase subsequently to $16,000, the land asset account would be increased to $16,000, and a $6,000 holding gain would appear in the current-cost income statement. An SFAS #89 current-cost income statement differs from a historical cost income statement in another important respect as well; namely, it reflects depreciation expense and cost of goods sold at their current cost. The holding gain (or loss) would not be a component of Income from Continuing Operations, however.

Proceeding now to the current cost/constant dollar approach (Column 4 in the framework), we observe its dominant characteristics:

- Monetary assets and monetary liabilities are not restated in the balance sheet.
- The effect of inflation on monetary assets and monetary liabilities is calculated and disclosed in the income statement as the purchasing power gain or loss in the manner described earlier.
- Nonmonetary assets (plant assets and inventory) appear in the balance sheet at their current cost, and related expenses appear in the income statement at their current cost (depreciation expense and cost of goods sold).
- The change in the current cost of nonmonetary assets (the holding gain or loss) reflects the change only to the extent not caused by general inflation; an example follows.

Assume that land had been purchased in March for $12,000 when the CPI-U was 130. On December 31, the current cost of the land is $15,000 and the CPI-U is 156. The asset would be valued as $15,000, and assuming the constant dollar is based on the year-end CPI-U, the holding gain that appears in the income statement would be $600. The $600 is based on the following calculation:

$$\$15{,}000 - [\$12{,}000 \times (156/130 =)\ 1.2 =]\ \$14{,}400 = \$600$$

FASB Statement No. 89

The primary disclosure rules set forth by FASB Statement No. 89 are as follows:

1. Disclosures are optional for all companies.
2. The disclosures, if applied, are a supplement to, not a substitute for, financial statements prepared in the traditional (historical cost/nominal dollar) manner.
3. The specific items suggested for disclosure are:
   - Purchasing power gain or loss from holding monetary assets and owing monetary liabilities.
   - Income from continuing operations—with cost of goods sold and depreciation expense on a current cost/constant dollar basis.
   - Inventory and plant assets on a current-cost basis.
   - Changes in the current cost/constant dollar amounts of inventory and plant assets (the holding gain or loss).
   - Five-year comparison of selected historical cost and current cost data—expressed in constant dollars (e.g., sales, dividends per share, market price per share, and some of the already computed amounts).
4. Constant dollars can reflect either end-of-year or average-for-the-year purchasing power. In the five-year summary, however, constant dollars could also reflect the purchasing power of the base year used by the Bureau of Labor Statistics (which is currently 1967).

ACCOUNTING FOR FOREIGN CURRENCY—SFAS #52

In General

This statement encompasses both expressing in dollars **transactions** denominated in a foreign currency, and expressing in dollars the foreign-currency-based **financial statements** of a subsidiary.

To incorporate foreign currency transactions and foreign currency financial statements in its financial statements, include all assets, liabilities, revenue and expenses that are **measured** in foreign currency or **denominated** in foreign currency.

Measure—To quantify an attribute of an item in a unit of measure other than the reporting currency.

Denominate—When asset and liability amounts are fixed in terms of a foreign currency regardless of exchange rate changes.

Illustration: Two foreign branches of a U.S. company, one Swiss and one German, purchase on credit identical assets from a Swiss vendor at identical prices stated in Swiss francs. The German branch measures the cost (an attribute) of that asset in German marks. Although the corresponding liability is also **measured** in marks, it remains **denominated** in Swiss francs since the liability must be settled in a specified number of Swiss francs. The Swiss branch measures the asset and liability in Swiss francs. Its liability is both measured and denominated in Swiss francs. Assets and liabilities can be measured in various currencies. However, currency and rights to receive or obligations to pay fixed amounts of a currency are denominated only in that currency.

Foreign Currency Transactions

These are transactions which are denominated in a foreign currency. A change in the exchange rate between the foreign currency and the dollar results in a gain or loss that is recognized in determining the dollar net income for the period in which the rate changes. (No gain or loss is recognized on hedges of net investments in foreign currency commitments.)

Example—On December 20, a U.S. company purchases inventory from a foreign company for an invoice price of LCU 300,000 when the exchange rate is LCU 6 = $1. The invoice is due in 30 days. On December 31, the exchange rate is LCU 8 = $1 and on the payment date, the exchange rate is LCU 7.5 = $1.

The company would make the following journal entries (in U.S. dollars)

		Debit	Credit	
12/20	Purchase	$50,000		(LCU 300,000 ÷ 6)
	Accounts Payable		$50,000	
12/31	Accounts Payable	$12,500		(LCU 300,000 ÷ 6)
	Exchange Gain		$12,500	(LCU 300,000 ÷ 8)
1/19	Accounts Payable	$37,500		
	Exchange loss	2,500		
	Cash		$40,000	(LCU 300,000 ÷ 7.5)

FOREIGN CURRENCY AND SFAS #133 – ACCOUNTING FOR DERIVATIVES AND HEDGING ACTIVITIES

SFAS #133 looks at foreign currency in the following areas:

Fundamental Decisions

a. Derivative instruments that meet the definition of assets and liabilities should be reported in the financial statements.
b. **Fair value** is the only relevant measure for derivative instruments.

Foreign Currency Hedges

- Fair Value Hedge of an exposed asset or liability.
  Gains and losses are recognized **currently**.

- Fair Value Hedge of a firm commitment.
  Gains and losses are recognized **currently**.

- Cash Flow Hedge of a forecasted transaction denominated in foreign currency.
  Gains and losses are recognized in **comprehensive income**

- Hedge of a Net Investment in a foreign entity.
  Gains or losses are reported in **comprehensive income** as part of the translation adjustment.

Speculation of Foreign Currency

Gain and losses are recognized **currently** based on foreign exchange rates.

A FAIR VALUE HEDGE OF AN ASSET WITH A FORWARD CONTRACT

The Beal Company sells goods to a German Company for 1,000,000 marks on December 15, 1999 and allows the customer 30 days to pay the invoice. The spot rate at that time is $.58 and the company appropriately records a sale of $580,000.

Beal Company is concerned about the fluctuation in the German mark and on December 31, 1999 enters into a 30-day forward contract hedge to sell 1,000,000 marks for $570,000 to AMEX at the forward rate of $.57. At this point, Beal has "locked-in" the amount of cash it will receive from the 1,000,000 marks and eliminated any further risk from foreign currency changes.

Listed below is a table of the changes in exchange rates:

DATE	SPOT RATE	30 DAY FORWARD RATE
December 15, 1999	$.58	$.57
December 31, 1999	.59	.585
January 15, 2000	.56	.56

Journal Entries:

December 15, 1999	Accounts Receivable (DM)	580,000	
	Sales		580,000

To record the sale at the current spot rate.

Note: No entry is made to record the forward contract because its value is zero.

December 31, 1999	Accounts Receivable (DM)	10,000	
	Foreign Currency Transaction Gain		10,000

To adjust the accounts receivable to the Dec. 31 spot rate of $.59 which is $.01 above the December 15 rate (1,000,000 marks x .01 = 10,000).

December 31, 1999	Loss on Forward Contract	15,000	
	Forward Contract (Liability)		15,000

SFAS #133 requires Beal Company to record the forward contract at fair value and to recognize the loss in current earnings. The calculation is the change in the forward rate from $.57 to $.585 or $.015 x 1,000,000 marks = $15,000. Since the current rate is $.585, a forward contract for marks at $.57 is less valuable and a loss should be recognized.

January 15, 2000	Foreign Currency transaction loss	30,000	
	Accounts Receivable (DM)		30,000

To adjust the accounts receivable for the decrease in the spot rate since December 31, 1999 ($.59 - $.56 = $.03 x 1,000,000 marks = $30,000).

January 15, 2000	Forward Contract (Asset)	25,000	
	Gain on Forward Contract		25,000

The change in the value of the forward rate from December 31, 1999 to January 15, 2000 is $.025 ($.585 - $.56) x 1,000,000 marks = $25,000.

January 15, 2000	Foreign Currency (DM)	560,000	
	Accounts Receivable (DM)		560,000

To record the receipt of 1,000,000 marks at the current spot rate of $.56 for a total of $560,000.

January 15, 2000	Cash	570,000	
	Foreign Currency (DM)		560,000
	Forward Contracts		10,000

To record the sale of 1,000,000 marks to AMEX on the forward contract for $570,000 and to remove the forward contract from the books.

A FAIR VALUE HEDGE OF AN ASSET USING A FOREIGN CURRENCY PUT OPTION

As an alternative to the forward contract, Beal Company could hedge its accounts receivable exposure to fluctuations in the value of the mark by purchasing a foreign currency put option. A put option gives Beal the right to sell 1,000,000 marks on January 15, 2000 at a pre-determined price. If the spot rate on January 15 is less than the option price, Beal will exercise the option and sell the 1,000,000 marks. If the spot rate is greater than the option price, Beal will allow the option to expire and sell the 1,000,000 marks at the spot rate. The advantage to Beal is that it does not have to exercise the option.

Using the same basic information as the first example, assume that Beal buys a put option on December 15, 1999 for $9,000 to sell 1,000,000 marks at $.57 on January 15, 2000.

		FOREIGN CURRENCY OPTION	
DATE	SPOT RATE	FAIR VALUE	CHANGE IN FAIR VALUE
December 15, 1999	$.58	$9,000	-0-
December 31, 1999	$.59	$6,000	- $3,000
January 15, 2000	$.56	$10,000	+ $4,000

The journal entries for the transactions will be the same as the first example, so concentrate on the entries affecting the put option.

Date	Account	Debit	Credit
December 15, 1999	Accounts Receivable (DM)	580,000	
	Sales		580,000
	Foreign Currency Option (asset)	9,000	
	Cash		9,000
	To record the purchase of the put option.		
December 31, 1999	Accounts Receivable (DM)	10,000	
	Foreign Currency Transaction Gain		10,000
	Loss on Foreign Currency Option	3,000	
	Foreign Currency Option		3,000
	To record the loss on the foreign currency option.		
January 15, 2000	Foreign Currency transaction loss	30,000	
	Accounts Receivable (DM)		30,000
	Foreign Currency Option	4,000	
	Gain on Foreign Currency Option		4,000
January 15, 2000	Foreign Currency (DM)	560,000	
	Accounts Receivable (DM)		560,000
January 15, 2000	Cash	570,000	
	Foreign Currency (DM)		560,000
	Foreign Currency Option		10,000

To record the exercise of the put option at the option price of $.57 and remove the foreign currency option from the books.

Note: The option was exercised because the option price of $.57 was greater than the spot rate of $.56.

FAIR VALUE HEDGE OF FUTURE FIRM COMMITMENT USING A FORWARD CONTRACT AS A HEDGE

In our previous examples, Beal did not hedge its transactions until the sale was made and the concern was for the exposure of its accounts receivable. Another approach would be for Beal to hedge its transaction when an order is received (a firm commitment).

Assume that Beal received an order on November 15, 1999 in the amount of 1,000,000 German marks for delivery within 60 days. Assume further that payment will be due on the delivery date of January 14, 1999 (60 days). On November 15, 1999, Beal enters into a 60-day forward contract to sell 1,000,000 German marks at the forward rate of $.54.

	FORWARD RATE to 1/14/2000
11/15/99	.54
12/31/99	.55
1/14/00	.535

Journal Entries:

Date	Account	Debit	Credit
November 15, 1999	No Entry The fair value of the forward contract is zero.		
December 31, 1999	Loss on Forward Contract	10,000	
	Forward Contract (liability)		10,000
	The loss on the forward contract is the change in the forward rate of \$.01 x 1,000,000 marks = \$10,000 (.54 - .55 = -.01)		
December 31, 1999	Firm Commitment (asset)	10,000	
	Gain on Firm Commitment		10,000
	To record an offsetting gain on the firm commitment.		
January 15, 2000	Forward Contract (asset)	15,000	
	Gain on Forward Contract		15,000
	To record gain in the change of the rates from December 31. (.55 - .535) = .015 x 1,000,000 = \$15,000		
January 15, 2000	Loss on Firm Commitment	15,000	
	Firm Commitment		15,000
	To record offsetting loss on firm commitment.		
January 15, 2000	Foreign Currency (DM)	535,000	
	Sales		535,000
	To record the sale and receipt of 1,000,000 DM at the current spot rate of \$.535.		
January 15, 2000	Cash	540,000	
	Foreign Currency (DM)		535,000
	Forward Contract		5,000
	To record the sale of the 1,000,000 marks at the forward contract rate of \$.54 and to remove the forward contract from the books.		
January 15, 2000	Firm commitment	5,000	
	Sales		5,000
	The firm commitment and the foreign currency offset and the sales are exactly equal to the cash received (535,000 + 5,000) = \$540,000.		

HEDGE OF A NET INVESTMENT IN A FOREIGN OPERATION

SFAS #52 requires U.S. companies with foreign subsidiaries whose functional currency is the local currency to translate the subsidiary's financial statements into U.S. dollars using the current-rate method. This method produces a translation adjustment for the period that is reported as other comprehensive income.

Companies wanting to hedge its fluctuation from the translated adjustment may use a forward contract or may borrow funds in the local currency.

To hedge the foreign currency exposure, the translation adjustment from the hedging activity must move in the opposite direction from the translation adjustments of the net assets of the subsidiary.

Since our previous examples have all used forward contract, this illustration will use a loss as a hedge.

Assume that the Beal Corp. has an investment in a foreign German subsidiary equal to 10,000,000 marks which at the current spot rate of $.54 would translate into $5,400,000. To hedge its equity investments, Beal borrows 10,000,000 marks for a year on January 1, 2000. Assume that the spot rate for marks on December 31, 2000 is $.51.

Journal Entries:

January 1, 2000	Cash	5,400,000	
	Loan Payable		5,400,000
December 31, 2000	Loan Payable	300,000	
	Gain on Loan – Other Comprehensive Income		300,000

The gain on the loan would be the change in the spot rate from $.54 to $.51 at the end of the year for a net change of $.03 x 10,000,000 = $300,000.

Note: SFAS #133 allows the gain on the loan – other comprehensive income to offset the translated adjustment associated with translating the foreign financial statement into U.S. dollars.

SPECULATION IN FOREIGN CURRENCY

A foreign contract does not have to be used as a hedge; it may be used for speculation. As with any derivative financial instrument, SFAS #133 requires the forward contract to be recorded at fair value and any gains or losses reported in current earnings.

For example, Beal Company expects the value of the German mark to increase in the next 90 days. Accordingly, on December 1, 1999, Beal enters into a 90-day forward contract to buy 1,000,000 marks at the forward rate of $.52.

On December 31, 1999 the forward rate was $.53 and by March 1, 2000 the spot rate had moved to $.55.

Journal Entries:

December 1, 1999	No Entry – the forward contract is at fair value.		
December 31, 1999	Forward Contract	10,000	
	Gain on Forward Contract		10,000
	Increase in forward rate from \$.52 to \$.53 = \$.01 x 1,000,000 marks = \$10,000.		
March 1, 2000	Forward contract	20,000	
	Gain on Forward contract		20,000
	Increase in forward rates from December 31 to March 1 (\$.53 to \$.55) = \$.02 x 1,000,000 marks.		
March 1, 2000	Investment in German Marks	520,000	
	Cash		520,000
	To record the purchase at the forward contract rate of \$.52 x 1,000,000 marks = \$520,000.		
March 1, 2000	Cash	550,000	
	Investment in German Marks		520,000
	Forward Contract		30,000
	To record the sale of 1,000,000 marks at the current spot rate of \$.55.		

RESTATEMENT OF FOREIGN CURRENCY FINANCIAL STATEMENTS

Functional Currency

The rules for expressing foreign currency in dollars depend upon the functional currency involved. An entity's functional currency is the currency of the primary economic environment in which the entity operates; normally, that is the currency of the environment in which an entity primarily generates and expends cash.

Once the functional currency of an entity is determined, such determination remains in effect unless significant changes in the economic facts and circumstances warrant a change in the functional currency.

Functional Currency is the Local Currency

If an entity's operations are relatively self-contained within a particular foreign country, then that country's currency (local currency) would be the functional currency. An example would be an entity whose operations are not integrated with those of the parent, whose buying and selling activities are primarily local, and whose cash flows are primarily in the foreign currency. Since the local currency is the functional currency, the company's financial statements would be **translated** to U.S. dollars using the **current-rate method.**

Current-rate method procedures:

- The assets and liabilities of an entity are translated using the current rate which means the exchange rate at the balance sheet date.
- Equity accounts are translated using historical exchange rates.
- Revenues, expenses, gains, and losses use the weighted average exchange rate for the period.
- The resulting translation adjustment for the current period is reported as other comprehensive income net of tax.

- The cumulative translation adjustment is reported as a part of the accumulated other comprehensive income in the equity section of the statement of financial position.
- Reclassification of Translation Adjustments:
  1. SFAS interpretation #37 states that if an enterprise sales part of its ownership interest in a foreign entity, a **pro rata** portion of the accumulated translation adjustment attributable to that investment shall be recognized in measuring the gain or loss on the sale in the current period.
  2. Since this portion of the translation adjustment would have been recognized in previous periods as other comprehensive income, the translation adjustment would have to be reclassified ("reversed out") in other comprehensive income of the current period to avoid a **double counting** of the translation adjustment gain or loss.

Functional Currency is the Reporting Currency

If the foreign entity is a branch or extension of its U.S. parent, its functional currency would likely be the U.S. dollar (reporting currency). An example would be an entity whose operations are integrated with those of the parent, whose buying and selling activities are primarily in the parent's country and/or the parent's currency, and whose cash flows are available for remittance to the parent. Since the reporting currency is the functional currency, the financial statements would be expressed in dollars using the **remeasurement method.**

Remeasurement method procedures:

Balance sheet accounts are placed in two categories -- monetary and nonmonetary. Monetary items include cash, and those receivables and payables which represent a fixed amount of cash, as opposed, for instance, to an unearned revenue liability which will be satisfied with goods or services. The fact that a receivable or payable is classified as current or noncurrent has no effect on its being monetary in nature. All other balance sheet items are nonmonetary (except an investment in debt securities which will be held until maturity -- which would be a monetary asset).

- Monetary assets and liabilities are remeasured at the current exchange rate.
- Non-monetary accounts are remeasured using the historical exchange rates.
- Revenues, expenses, gains and losses use the weighted average exchange rate for the period except for cost allocations such as depreciation expense which uses the historical rate.
- Foreign exchange gains and losses are reported on the consolidated income statement.

Functional Currency is Neither Local Currency nor Reporting Currency

If the functional currency is a foreign currency other than the local currency, then the foreign currency statements are first remeasured in the functional currency before they are translated to U.S. dollars using the current rate method.

Example: Park Company, a U.S. parent, has a wholly-owned subsidiary, Schnell Corp., which maintains its accounting records in German marks. Because all of Schnell's branch offices are in Switzerland, its functional currency is the Swiss franc. Since the functional currency is the Swiss franc, the financial statements of the subsidiary must first be **remeasured** from German marks into Swiss francs and a foreign exchange remeasurement gain or loss must be recognized.

The remeasured financial statements are then **translated** into U.S. Dollars and a foreign exchange translation gain or loss is calculated. The consolidated financial statements would then report a foreign exchange remeasurement gain or loss on the Income Statement and a translation gain or loss would be reported as other comprehensive income.

Functional Currency in a Highly Inflationary Economy

If a foreign entity is located in a country that is experiencing high inflation (if the cumulative inflation rate is ≥ than 100% over a 3-year period), the foreign currency is considered unstable. In this case, the foreign currency statements are **remeasured** into the reporting currency (the U.S. dollar).

Disclosure

An analysis of the changes during the period in the separate component of other comprehensive income and for the "cumulative translation adjustment" portion of accumulated other comprehensive income is provided in a separate financial statement, in notes to the financial statements, or as part of a statement of changes in equity. At a minimum, the analysis discloses:

a. Beginning and ending amount of cumulative translation adjustments.
b. The aggregate adjustment for the period resulting from translation adjustments and gains and losses from certain hedges and intercompany balances.
c. The amount of income taxes for the period allocated to translation adjustments.
d. The amounts transferred from cumulative translation adjustments and included in determining net income for the period as a result of the sale or complete or substantially complete liquidation of an investment in a foreign entity.

An enterprise's financial statements are not adjusted for a rate change that occurs after the date of the enterprise's financial statements or after the date of the foreign currency statements of a foreign entity if they are consolidated, combined, or accounted for by the equity method in the financial statements of the enterprise. However, disclosure of the rate change and its effects on unsettled balances pertaining to foreign currency transactions, if significant, may be necessary.

Example: Financial statements of the Peso Corporation, a foreign subsidiary of the Dollar Corporation (a U.S. company) are shown below at and for the year ended December 31, 199X. The statements are first translated using the LCU (local currency unit) as the functional currency (translation method), then the dollar as the functional currency (remeasurement).

Assumptions:

1. The parent company organized the subsidiary on December 31, 199W.
2. Exchange rates for the LCU were as follows:

December 31, 199W to March 31, 199X	\$.18
April 1, 199X to June 30, 199X	.13
July 1, 199X to December 31, 199X	.10

3. Inventory was acquired evenly throughout the year and sales were made evenly throughout the year.
4. Fixed assets were acquired by the subsidiary on December 31, 199W.

Peso Corporation
Foreign Currency Financial Statements, Expressed in Dollars
at and for the year ended December 31, 199X

			Current Rate Method		Remeasurement Method	
			Exchange Rate	Dollars	Exchange Rate	Dollars
Income Statement						
Sales	LCU	525,000	[1]$.1275	$66,938	$.1275	$66,938
Costs and expenses:						
Cost of goods sold	LCU	400,000	.1275	$51,000	.1275	$51,000
Depreciation expense		22,000	.1275	2,805	.18	3,960
Selling expenses		31,000	.1275	3,953	.1275	3,953
Other operating expenses		11,000	.1275	1,403	.1275	1,403
Income taxes expense		19,000	.1275	2,423	.1275	2,423
Total costs and expenses	LCU	483,000		$61,584		$62,739
Currency exchange (gain)						(6,854)
Net income	LCU	42,000		$ 5,354		$11,053
Other Comprehensive Income						
Foreign Currency Translation Adjustments				(17,154)		
Comprehensive Loss				($11,800)		
Statement of Retained Earnings						
Retained earnings, beg. of year	LCU	—0—		—0—		—0—
Net income		42,000		5,354		11,053
Retained earnings, end of year	LCU	42,000		$ 5,354		$11,053
Balance Sheet—Assets						
Cash	LCU	10,000	.10	$ 1,000	.10	$ 1,000
Accounts receivable (net)		50,000	.10	5,000	.10	5,000
Inventories (at cost)		95,000	.10	9,500	.1275	12,113
Fixed assets		275,000	.10	27,500	.18	49,500
Accumulated depreciation		(22,000)	.10	(2,200)		[3](3,960)
Total assets	LCU	408,000		$40,800		$63,653
Liabilities & Stockholders' Equity						
Accounts payable	LCU	34,000	.10	$3,400	.10	$3,400
Long-term debt		132,000	.10	13,200	.10	13,200
Common stock 10,000 shares		200,000	.18	36,000	.18	36,000
Retained earnings		42,000		5,354		11,053
Accumulated other comprehensive income		———		[2](17,154)		———
Total liabilities & stockholders' equity	LCU	408,000		$40,800		$63,653

1 $\frac{(\$.18 \times 3) + (\$.13 \times 3) + (\$.10 \times 6)}{12} = .1275$

2 Residual amount (to balance).

3 $\frac{22{,}000}{275{,}000} = \frac{x}{49{,}500}$; x = \$3,960 (or \$.18 in this case)

Chapter Six
Price Level—Foreign Exchange Questions

FINANCIAL REPORTING AND CHANGING PRICES

Items 1 and 2 are based on the following information:

The following schedule lists the general price-level index at the end of each of the five indicated years (assume that the year-end dollar is the constant dollar):

1995	100
1996	110
1997	115
1998	120
1999	140

1. In December 1998, the Meetu Corporation purchased land for $300,000. The land was held until December 1999, when it was sold for $400,000. The historical cost/constant dollar statement of income for the year ended December 31, 1999, should include how much gain or loss on this sale assuming that the year-end dollar is the constant dollar?

a. $20,000 loss.
b. $20,000 general price-level loss.
c. $50,000 gain.
d. $100,000 gain.

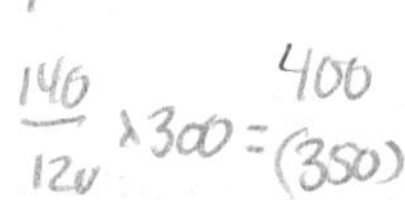

2. On January 1, 1996, the Silver Company purchased equipment for $300,000. The equipment was being depreciated over an estimated life of 10 years on the straight-line method, with **no** estimated salvage value. On December 31, 1999, the equipment was sold for $200,000. The historical cost/constant dollar statement of income prepared for the year ended December 31, 1999, should include how much gain or loss from this sale?

a. $10,600 loss.
b. $16,000 gain.
c. $20,000 gain.
d. $52,000 loss.

---

3. In its financial statements, Hila Co. discloses supplemental information on the effects of changing prices in accordance with Statement of Financial Accounting Standards No. 89, *Financial Reporting and Changing Prices.* Hila computed the increase in current cost of inventory as follows:

Increase in current cost (nominal dollars)	$15,000
Increase in current cost (constant dollars)	$12,000

What amount should Hila disclose as the inflation component of the increase in current cost of inventories?

a. $3,000.
b. $12,000.
c. $15,000.
d. $27,000.

4. The Chalk Company reported sales of $2,000,000 in 1996 and $3,000,000 in 1997 made evenly throughout each year. The consumer price index during 1995 remained constant at 100, and at the end of 1996 and 1997 it was 102 and 104, respectively. What should Chalk report as sales for 1997, restated for general price-level changes assuming that the year-end dollar is the constant dollar?

a. $3,000,000.
b. $3,029,126.
c. $3,058,821.
d. $3,120,000.

Items 5 and 6 are based on the following data:
Rice Wholesaling Corp. accounts for inventory on a FIFO basis. There were 8,000 units in inventory on January 1, 1993. Costs were incurred and goods purchased as follows during 1993:

1993	Historical costs	Units purchased	Units sold
1st quarter	$ 410,000	7,000	7,500
2nd quarter	550,000	8,500	7,300
3rd quarter	425,000	6,500	8,200
4th quarter	630,000	9,000	7,000
	$2,015,000	31,000	30,000

Rice estimates that the current cost per unit of inventory was $57 at January 1, 1993, and $71 at December 31, 1993.

5. In Rice's voluntary supplementary information restated into current cost, the December 31, 1993, inventory should be reported at

a. $576,000
b. $585,000
c. $630,000
d. $639,000

6. In Rice's voluntary supplementary information restated into current cost, the cost of goods sold for 1993 would be

a. $1,920,000
b. $1,944,000
c. $2,100,000
d. $2,130,000

---

7. When does a general purchasing power loss occur, and when is it recognized?

a. It occurs when holding net monetary assets during inflation and is recognized in constant dollar financial statements.
b. It occurs when holding net monetary liabilities during inflation and is recognized in constant dollar financial statements.
c. It occurs when holding net monetary assets during inflation and is recognized in nominal dollar financial statements and in constant dollar financial statements.
d. It occurs when holding net monetary liabilities during inflation and is recognized in nominal dollar financial statements and in constant dollar financial statements.

8. Lewis Company was formed on January 1, 1996. Selected balances from the historical cost balance sheet at December 31, 1997, were as follows:

Land (purchased in 1996)	$120,000
Investment in nonconvertible bonds (purchased in 1996, and expected to be held to maturity)	60,000
Long-term debt	80,000

The average Consumer Price Index was 100 for 1996, and 110 for 1997. In a supplementary constant dollar balance sheet (adjusted for changing prices) at December 31, 1997, these selected account balances should be shown at

	Land	Investment	Long-term debt
a.	$120,000	$60,000	$88,000
b	$120,000	$66,000	$88,000
c	$132,000	$60,000	$80,000
d.	$132,000	$66,000	$80,000

9. When computing purchasing power gain or loss on net monetary items, which of the following accounts is classified as nonmonetary?

a. Unamortized premium on bonds payable.
b. Accumulated depreciation of equipment.
c. Advances to unconsolidated subsidiaries.
d. Allowance for uncollectible accounts.

10. The following information pertains to each unit of merchandise purchased for resale by Vend Co.:

March 1, 1998	
Purchase price	$ 8
Selling price	$12
Price level index	110
December 31, 1998	
Replacement cost	$10
Selling price	$15
Price level index	121

Under current cost accounting, what is the amount of Vend's holding gain on each unit of this merchandise?

a. $0
b. $0.80
c. $1.20
d. $2.00

11. Information with respect to Bruno Co.'s cost of goods sold for 1995 is as follows:

	Historical Cost	Units
Inventory, 1/1/95	$1,060,000	20,000
Production during 1995	5,580,000	90,000
	6,640,000	110,000
Inventory, 12/31/95	2,520,000	40,000
Cost of goods sold	$4,120,000	70,000

Bruno estimates that the current cost per unit of inventory was $58 at January 1, 1995, and $72 at December 31, 1995. In Bruno's supplementary information restated into average current cost, the cost of goods sold for 1995 should be

a. $5,040,000
b. $4,550,000
c. $4,410,000
d. $4,060,000

Items 12 and 13 are based on the following:

In a period of rising general price levels, Pollard Corp. discloses income on a current cost basis in accordance with FASB Statement No. 89, *Financial Reporting and Changing Prices.*

12. Compared to historical cost income from continuing operations, which of the following conditions increases Pollard's current cost income from continuing operations?

a. Current cost of equipment is greater than historical cost.
b. Current cost of land is greater than historical cost.
c. Current cost of cost of goods sold is less than historical cost.
d. Ending net monetary assets are less than beginning net monetary assets.

13. Which of the following contributes to Pollard's purchasing power loss on net monetary items?

a. Refundable deposits with suppliers.
b. Equity investment in unconsolidated subsidiaries.
c. Warranty obligations.
d. Wages payable.

---

14. On January 1, 1998, Nutley Corporation had monetary assets of $2,000,000 and monetary liabilities of $1,000,000. During 1998, Nutley's monetary inflows and outflows were relatively constant and equal so that it ended the year with net monetary assets of $1,000,000. Assume that the Consumer Price Index was 200 on January 1, 1998, and 220 on December 31, 1998. In end of year constant dollars, what is Nutley's purchasing power gain or loss on net monetary items for 1998?

a. $0
b. $50,000 gain
c. $100,000 gain
d. $100,000 loss

15. Details of Poe Corp.'s plant assets at December 31, 1993, are as follows:

Year acquired	*Percent depreciated*	*Historical cost*	*Estimated current cost*
1991	30	$200,000	$280,000
1992	20	60,000	76,000
1993	10	80,000	88,000

Poe calculates depreciation at 10% per annum, using the straight-line method. A full year's depreciation is charged in the year of acquisition. There were no disposals of plant assets. In Poe's voluntary supplementary information restated into current cost, the net current cost (after accumulated depreciation) of the plant assets at December 31, 1993, should be stated as

a. $364,000
b. $336,000
c. $260,000
d. $232,000

16. At both the beginning and end of the year, Lang Co.'s monetary assets exceeded monetary liabilities by $3,000,000. On January 1, the general price level was 125. On December 31, the general price level was 150. How much was Lang's purchasing power loss on net monetary items during the year?

a. $0
b. $600,000
c. $750,000
d. $1,125,000

17. Fair Value, Inc., paid $1,200,000 in December 1997 for certain of its inventory. In December 1998, one half of the inventory was sold for $1,000,000 when the replacement cost of the original inventory was $1,400,000. **Ignoring income taxes,** what amount should be shown as the total gain resulting from the above facts in a current value accounting income statement for 1998?

a. $200,000.
b. $300,000.
c. $400,000.
d. $500,000.

18. The following assets were among those that appeared on Baird Co.'s books at the end of the year:

Demand bank deposits	$650,000
Net long-term receivables	400,000
Patents and trademarks	150,000

In preparing constant dollar financial statements, how much should Baird classify as monetary assets?

a. $1,200,000
b. $1,050,000
c. $800,000
d. $650,000

19. When purchasing power gains or losses are computed, how is each of the following classified?

	Patents	*Unamortized premium on bonds payable*
a.	Nonmonetary	Monetary
b.	Nonmonetary	Nonmonetary
c.	Monetary	Nonmonetary
d.	Monetary	Monetary

20. During a period of inflation, the specific price of a parcel of land increased at a lower rate than the consumer price index. The accounting method that would measure the land at the highest amount is

a. Historical cost/nominal dollar.
b. Current cost/nominal dollar.
c. Current cost/constant dollar.
d. Historical cost/constant dollar.

21. Details of Weaver Corporation's fixed assets at December 31, 2000, are as follows:

Year acquired	*Percent depreciated*	*Historical cost*	*Estimated current cost*
1998	30	$100,000	$140,000
1999	20	30,000	38,000
2000	10	40,000	44,000

Weaver calculates depreciation at 10% per annum, using the straight-line method. A full year's depreciation is charged in the year of acquisition. There were no disposals of fixed assets. In Weaver's supplementary information restated into current cost, the net current cost (after accumulated depreciation) of the fixed assets should be stated as

a. $116,000.
b. $130,000.
c. $168,000.
d. $182,000.

22. Cartwright Corporation prepared the following data needed to compute the purchasing power gain or loss on net monetary items for inclusion in its supplementary information for the year ended December 31, 2000:

	Amount in nominal dollars	
	December 31, 1999	*December 31, 2000*
Monetary assets	$600,000	$1,000,000
Monetary liabilities	$1,566,000	$2,449,000
Net monetary liabilities	$966,000	$1,449,000

Assumed Consumer Price Index numbers:

At December 31, 1999	210
At December 31, 2000	230
Average for 2000	220

Cartwright's purchasing power gain or loss (expressed in average 2000 constant dollars) on net monetary items for the year ended December 31, 2000, should be

a. $109,000 gain.
b. $109,000 loss.
c. $111,000 gain.
d. $111,000 loss.

23. Kerr Company purchased a machine for $115,000 on January 1, 1992, the company's first day of operations. At the end of the year, the current cost of the machine was $125,000. The machine has no salvage value, a five-year life, and is depreciated by the straight line method. For the year ended December 31, 1992, the amount of the current cost depreciation expense which would appear in supplementary current cost financial statements is:

a. $14,000
b. $23,000
c. $24,000
d. $25,000

24. On December 30, 1996, Future, Incorporated, paid $2,000,000 for land. At December 31, 1997, the fair value of the land was $2,200,000. In January 1998, the land was sold for $2,250,000. **Ignoring income taxes,** by what amount should stockholders' equity be increased for 1997 and 1998 as a result of the above facts in current fair value financial statements?

	1997	*1998*
a.	$0	$ 50,000
b.	$0	$250,000
c.	$200,000	$0
d.	$200,000	$ 50,000

25. Manhof Co. prepares supplementary reports on income from continuing operations on a current cost basis in accordance with FASB Statement No. 89, *Financial Reporting and Changing Prices.* How should Manhof compute cost of goods sold on a current cost basis?

a. Number of units sold times average current cost of units during the year.
b. Number of units sold times current cost of units at year end.
c. Number of units sold times current cost of units at the beginning of the year.
d. Beginning inventory at current cost plus cost of goods purchased less ending inventory at current cost.

26. The following items were among those that appeared on Rubi Co.'s books at the end of 1995:

Merchandise inventory	$600,000
Loans to employees	20,000

What amount should Rubi classify as monetary assets in preparing constant dollar financial statements?

a. $0
b. $20,000
c. $600,000
d. $620,000

27. Could current cost financial statements report holding gains for goods sold during the period and holding gains on inventory at the end of the period?

	Goods sold	*Inventory*
a.	Yes	Yes
b.	Yes	No
c.	No	Yes
d.	No	No

28. During a period of inflation in which a liability account balance remains constant, which of the following occurs?
a. A purchasing power loss if the item is a non-monetary liability.
b. A purchasing power gain if the item is a non-monetary liability.
c. A purchasing power loss if the item is a monetary liability.
d. A purchasing power gain if the item is a monetary liability.

29. Deecee Co. adjusted its historical cost income statement by applying specific price indexes to its depreciation expense and cost of goods sold. Deecee's adjusted income statement is prepared according to
a. Fair value accounting.
b. General purchasing power accounting.
c. Current cost accounting.
d. Current cost/general purchasing power accounting.

30. During a period of inflation in which an asset account remains constant, which of the following occurs?
a. A purchasing power gain, if the item is a monetary asset.
b. A purchasing power gain, if the item is a nonmonetary asset.
c. A purchasing power loss, if the item is a monetary asset.
d. A purchasing power loss, if the item is a nonmonetary asset.

FOREIGN EXCHANGE TRANSACTIONS

31. A sale of goods was denominated in a currency other than the entity's functional currency. The sale resulted in a receivable that was fixed in terms of the amount of foreign currency that would be received. The exchange rate between the functional currency and the currency in which the transaction was denominated changed. The effect of the change should be included as a
a. Separate component of stockholders' equity whether the change results in a gain or a loss.
b. Separate component of stockholders' equity if the change results in a gain, and as a component of income if the change results in a loss.
c. Component of income if the change results in a gain, and as a separate component of stockholders' equity if the change results in a loss.
d. Component of income whether the change results in a gain or a loss.

32. On November 15, 1996, Celt, Inc., a U.S. company, ordered merchandise FOB shipping point from a German company for 200,000 marks. The merchandise was shipped and invoiced to Celt on December 10, 1996. Celt paid the invoice on January 10, 1997. The spot rates for marks on the respective dates are as follows:

November 15, 1996	$.4955
December 10, 1996	.4875
December 31, 1996	.4675
January 10, 1997	.4475

In Celt's December 31, 1996, income statement, the foreign exchange gain is
a. $9,600
b. $8,000
c. $4,000
d. $1,600

33. Fogg Co., a U.S. company, contracted to purchase foreign goods. Payment in foreign currency was due one month after the goods were received at Fogg's warehouse. Between the receipt of goods and the time of payment, the exchange rates changed in Fogg's favor. The resulting gain should be included in Fogg's financial statements as a(n)
a. Component of income from continuing operations.
b. Extraordinary item.
c. Deferred credit.
d. Separate component of stockholders' equity.

34. On October 1, 1999, Mild Co., a U.S. company, purchased machinery from Grund, a German company, with payment due on April 1, 2000. If Mild's 1999 operating income included no foreign exchange transaction gain or loss, then the transaction could have

a. Resulted in an extraordinary gain.
b. Been denominated in U.S. dollars.
c. Caused a foreign currency gain to be reported as a contra account against machinery.
d. Caused a foreign currency translation gain to be reported as a separate component of stockholders' equity.

FORWARD CONTRACTS

Items 35 through 37 are based on the following:
On December 12, 1998, Imp Co. entered into three forward exchange contracts, each to purchase 100,000 francs in 90 days. The relevant exchange rates are as follows:

	Spot rate	Forward rate (for March 12, 1999)
December 12, 1998	$.88	$.90
December 31, 1998	.98	.93

35. Imp entered into the first forward contract to hedge a purchase of inventory in November 1998, payable in March 1999. At December 31, 1998, what amount of gain should Imp include in income from this forward contract?

a. $0
b. $3,000
c. $5,000
d. $10,000

36. Imp entered into the second forward contract to hedge a commitment to purchase equipment being manufactured to Imp's specifications. At December 31, 1998, what amount of gain should Imp include in income from this forward contract?

a. $0
b. $3,000
c. $5,000
d. $10,000

37. Imp entered into the third forward contract for speculation. At December 31, 1998, what amount of gain should Imp include in income from this forward contract?

a. $0
b. $3,000
c. $5,000
d. $10,000

LOCAL CURRENCY = FUNCTIONAL CURRENCY

CURRENT RATE METHOD

38. Certain balance sheet accounts of a foreign subsidiary of Rowan, Inc., at December 31, 1996, have been translated into U.S. dollars as follows:

	Translated at Current rates	Translated at Historical rates
Note receivable, long-term	$240,000	$200,000
Prepaid rent	85,000	80,000
Patent	150,000	170,000
	$475,000	$450,000

The subsidiary's functional currency is the currency of the country in which it is located. What total amount should be included in Rowan's December 31, 1996, consolidated balance sheet for the above accounts?

a. $450,000
b. $455,000
c. $475,000
d. $495,000

39. A subsidiary's functional currency is the local currency which has not experienced significant inflation. The appropriate exchange rate for translating the depreciation on plant assets in the income statement of the foreign subsidiary is the

a. Exit exchange rate.
b. Historical exchange rate.
c. Weighted average exchange rate over the economic life of each plant asset.
d. Weighted average exchange rate for the current year.

40. Certain balance sheet accounts of a foreign subsidiary of Post, Inc., at December 31, 1993, have been translated into U.S. dollars as follows:

	Translated at Current rates	Translated at Historical rates
Accounts receivable, long-term	$120,000	$100,000
Prepaid Insurance	55,000	50,000
Copyright	75,000	85,000
	$250,000	$235,000

The subsidiary's functional currency is the currency of the country in which it is located. What total amount should be included in Post's December 31, 1993, consolidated balance sheet for the above accounts?

a. $225,000
b. $235,000
c. $240,000
d. $250,000

FUNCTIONAL CURRENCY = REPORTING CURRENCY

REMEASUREMENT METHOD

41. Gains from remeasuring a foreign subsidiary's financial statements from the local currency, which is not the functional currency, into the parent company's currency should be reported as a(an)

a. Deferred foreign exchange gain.
b. Separate component of stockholders' equity.
c. Extraordinary item, net of income taxes.
d. Part of continuing operations.

42. When remeasuring foreign currency financial statements into the functional currency, which of the following items would be remeasured using historical exchange rates?

a. Inventories carried at cost.
b. Marketable equity securities reported at market values.
c. Bonds payable.
d. Accrued liabilities.

FUNCTIONAL CURRENCY = NEITHER LOCAL NOR REPORTING CURRENCY

43. Park Co.'s wholly-owned subsidiary, Schnell Corp., maintains its accounting records in German marks. Because all of Schnell's branch offices are in Switzerland, its functional currency is the Swiss franc. Remeasurement of Schnell's 2001 financial statements resulted in a $7,600 gain, and translation of its financial statements resulted in an $8,100 gain. What amount should Park report as a foreign exchange gain in its income statement for the year ended December 31, 2001?

a. $0
b. $7,600
c. $8,100
d. $15,700

COMBINATION OF TRANSACTION AND TRANSLATION

44. Fay Corp. had a realized foreign exchange loss of $15,000 for the year ended December 31, 1996, and must also determine whether the following items will require year-end adjustment:

- Fay had an $8,000 loss resulting from the translation of the accounts of its wholly owned foreign subsidiary for the year ended December 31, 1996.
- Fay had an account payable to an unrelated foreign supplier payable in the supplier's local currency. The U.S. dollar equivalent of the payable was $64,000 on the October 31, 1996, invoice date, and it was $60,000 on December 31, 1996. The invoice is payable on January 30, 1997.

In Fay's 1996 consolidated income statement, what amount should be included as foreign exchange loss?

a. $11,000
b. $15,000
c. $19,000
d. $23,000

REVIEW QUESTIONS

45. On September 22, 2001, Yumi Corp. purchased merchandise from an unaffiliated foreign company for 10,000 units of the foreign company's local currency. On that date, the spot rate was $.55. Yumi paid the bill in full on March 20, 2002, when the spot rate was $.65. The spot rate was $.70 on December 31, 2001. What amount should Yumi report as a foreign currency transaction loss in its income statement for the year ended December 31, 2001?

a. $0
b. $500
c. $1,000
d. $1,500

46. On September 1, 1994, Bain Corp. received an order for equipment from a foreign customer for 300,000 local currency units (LCU) when the U.S. dollar equivalent was $96,000. Bain shipped the equipment on October 15, 1994, and billed the customer for 300,000 LCU when the U.S. dollar equivalent was $100,000. Bain received the customer's remittance in full on November 16, 1994, and sold the 300,000 LCU for $105,000. In its income statement for the year ended December 31, 1994, Bain should report a foreign exchange gain of

a. $0
b. $4,000
c. $5,000
d. $9,000

47. On July 1, 1991, Clark Company borrowed 1,680,000 local currency units (LCU) from a foreign lender, evidenced by an interest bearing note due on July 1, 1992, which is denominated in the currency of the lender. The U.S. dollar equivalent of the note principal was as follows:

Date	*Amount*
7/1/91 (date borrowed)	$210,000
12/31/91 (Clark's year end)	240,000
7/1/92 (date repaid)	280,000

In its income statement for 1992, what amount should Clark include as a foreign exchange gain or loss?

a. $70,000 gain.
b. $70,000 loss.
c. $40,000 gain.
d. $40,000 loss.

48. Hunt Co. purchased merchandise for £300,000 from a vendor in London on November 30, 1999. Payment in British pounds was due on January 30, 2000. The exchange rates to purchase one pound were as follows:

	November 30, 1999	*December 31, 1999*
Spot-rate	$1.65	$1.62
30-day rate	1.64	1.59
60-day rate	1.63	1.56

In its December 31, 1999, income statement, what amount should Hunt report as foreign exchange gain?

a. $12,000.
b. $9,000.
c. $6,000.
d. $0.

49. On September 1, 1999, Brady Corp. entered into a foreign exchange contract for speculative purposes by purchasing 50,000 deutsche marks for delivery in 60 days. The rates to exchange $1 for 1 deutsche mark follow:

	9/1/99	*9/30/99*
Spot rate	.75	.70
30-day forward rate	.73	.72
60-day forward rate	.74	.73

In its September 30, 1999, income statement, what amount should Brady report as foreign exchange loss?

a. $2,500
b. $1,500
c. $1,000
d. $500

50. Shore Co. records its transactions in U.S. dollars. A sale of goods resulted in a receivable denominated in Japanese yen, and a purchase of goods resulted in a payable denominated in French francs. Shore recorded a foreign exchange gain on collection of the receivable and an exchange loss on settlement of the payable. The exchange rates are expressed as so many units of foreign currency to one dollar. Did the number of foreign currency units exchangeable for a dollar increase or decrease between the contract and settlement dates?

	Yen exchangeable for $1	*Francs exchangeable for $1*
a.	Increase	Increase
b.	Decrease	Decrease
c.	Decrease	Increase
d.	Increase	Decrease

51. A foreign subsidiary's functional currency is its local currency, which has not experienced significant inflation. The weighted average exchange rate for the current year would be the appropriate exchange rate for translating

	Sales to customers	*Wages expense*
a.	No	No
b.	Yes	Yes
c.	No	Yes
d.	Yes	No

52. Ball Corp. had the following foreign currency transactions during 1996:

- Merchandise was purchased from a foreign supplier on January 20, 1996, for the U.S. dollar equivalent of $90,000. The invoice was paid on March 20, 1996, at the U.S. dollar equivalent of $96,000.
- On July 1, 1996, Ball borrowed the U.S. dollar equivalent of $500,000 evidenced by a note that was payable in the lender's local currency on July 1, 1998. On December 31, 1996, the U.S. dollar equivalents of the principal amount and accrued interest were $520,000 and $26,000, respectively. Interest on the note is 10% per annum.

In Ball's 1996 income statement, what amount should be included as foreign exchange loss?

a. $0
b. $6,000
c. $21,000
d. $27,000

53. The functional currency of Nash, Inc.'s subsidiary is the French franc. Nash borrowed French francs as a partial hedge of its investment in the subsidiary. In preparing consolidated financial statements, Nash's translation loss on its investment in the subsidiary exceeded its exchange gain on the borrowing. How should the effects of the loss and gain be reported in Nash's consolidated financial statements?

a. The translation loss less the exchange gain is reported separately as other comprehensive income.
b. The translation loss less the exchange gain is reported in the income statement.
c. The translation loss is reported separately in the stockholders' equity section of the balance sheet and the exchange gain is reported in the income statement.
d. The translation loss is reported in the income statement and the exchange gain is reported separately in the stockholders' equity section of the balance sheet.

AUTHOR CONSTRUCTED QUESTION

AC

54. A gain in the fair value of a derivative may be included in comprehensive income if the derivative is appropriately designated as a

a. Speculation in Foreign Currency.
b. Hedge of a Foreign Currency exposure of an available-for-sale security.
c. Hedge of a Foreign Currency exposure of a forecasted foreign currency denominated transaction.
d. Hedge of a foreign currency firm commitment.

55. In preparing consolidated financial statements of a U.S. parent company with a foreign subsidiary, the foreign subsidiary's functional currency is the currency

a. In which the subsidiary maintains its accounting records.
b. Of the country in which the subsidiary is located.
c. Of the country in which the parent is located.
d. Of the environment in which the subsidiary primarily generates and expends cash.

Chapter Six
Price Level—Foreign Exchange Problems

NUMBER 1

Skadden, Inc., a retailer, was organized during 1997. Skadden's management has decided to supplement its December 31, 2000 historical dollar financial statements with constant dollar financial statements using average-for-the-year dollars as the constant dollar. The following general ledger trial balance (historical dollar) and additional information have been furnished:

Skadden, Inc.
TRIAL BALANCE
December 31, 2000

	Debit	*Credit*
Cash and receivables (net)	$ 540,000	$ —
Marketable securities (common stock)	400,000	
Inventory	440,000	
Equipment	650,000	
Equipment—Accumulated depreciation		164,000
Accounts payable		300,000
6% First mortgage bonds, due 2000		500,000
Common stock, $10 par		1,000,000
Retained earnings, December 31, 1999	46,000	
Sales		1,900,000
Cost of sales	1,508,000	
Depreciation	65,000	
Other operating expenses and interest	215,000	
	$3,864,000	$3,864,000

1. Monetary assets (cash and receivables) exceeded monetary liabilities (accounts payable and bonds payable) by $445,000 at December 31, 1999. The amounts of monetary items are fixed in terms of numbers of dollars regardless of changes in specific prices or in the general price level.

2. Purchases ($1,840,000 in 2000) and sales are made uniformly throughout the year.

3. Depreciation is computed on a straight-line basis, with a full year's depreciation being taken in the year of acquisition and none in the year of retirement. The depreciation rate is 10 percent and no salvage value is anticipated. Acquisitions and retirements have been made fairly evenly over each year and the retirements in 2000 consisted of assets purchased during 1998 which were scrapped. An analysis of the equipment account reveals the following:

Year	*Beginning Balance*	*Additions*	*Retirements*	*Ending Balance*
1998	—	$550,000	—	$550,000
1999	$550,000	10,000	—	560,000
2000	560,000	150,000	60,000	650,000

4. The bonds were issued in 1998 and the marketable securities were purchased fairly evenly over 2000. Other operating expenses and interest are assumed to be incurred evenly throughout the year.

5. Assume that Consumer Price Index was as follows:

Annual Averages	*Index*
1997	113.9
1998	116.8
1999	121.8
1999 year-end	123.5
2000	126.7
2000 year-end	128.5

Required:

a. Prepare a schedule to convert the Equipment account balance at December 31, 2000 from historical cost to constant dollars assuming the constant dollar is the average-for-the-year dollar.
b. Prepare a schedule to analyze in historical dollars the Equipment—Accumulated Depreciation account for the year 2000.
c. Prepare a schedule to analyze in constant dollars the Equipment—Accumulated Depreciation account for the year 2000.
d. Prepare a schedule to compute Skadden, Inc.'s purchasing power gain or loss on its net holdings of monetary assets for 2000 (ignore income tax implications). The schedule should give consideration to appropriate items on or related to the balance sheet and the income statement.

NUMBER 2

Barden Corp., a manufacturer with large investments in plant and equipment, began operations in 1965. The company's history has been one of expansion in sales, production, and physical facilities. Recently, some concern has been expressed that the conventional financial statements do not provide sufficient information for decisions by investors. After consideration of proposals for various types of supplementary financial statements to be included in the 1999 annual report, management has decided to present a balance sheet as of December 31, 1999, and a statement of income and retained earnings for 1999, both restated for changes in the general price level.

Required:

a. On what basis can it be contended that Barden's conventional statements should be restated for changes in the general price level?
b. Distinguish between financial statements restated for general price-level changes and current-value financial statements.
c. Distinguish between monetary and nonmonetary assets and liabilities, as the terms are used in general price-level accounting. Give examples of each.
d. Outline the procedures Barden should follow in preparing the proposed supplementary statements.
e. Indicate the major similarities and differences between the proposed supplementary statements and the corresponding conventional statements.
f. Assuming that in the future Barden will want to present comparative supplementary statements, can the 1999 supplementary statements be presented in 2000 without adjustments? Explain.

NUMBER 3

Dhia Products Company was incorporated in the State of Florida in 1967 to do business as a manufacturer of medical supplies and equipment. Since incorporating, Dhia has doubled the size about every three years and is now considered one of the leading medical supply companies in the country.

During January 1996, Dhia established a subsidiary, Ban, Ltd., in the emerging nation of Shatha. Dhia owns 90% of the outstanding capital stock of Ban; the remaining 10% of Ban's outstanding capital stock is held by Shatha citizens, as required by Shatha constitutional law. The investment in Ban, accounted for by Dhia by the equity method, represents about 18% of the total assets of Dhia at December 31, 1999, the close of the accounting period for both companies.

Required:
Assume it has been appropriate for Dhia and Ban to prepare consolidated financial statements for each year 1996 through 1999 with the U.S. dollar being the functional currency. But before consolidated financial statements can be prepared, the individual account balances in Ban's December 31, 1999, adjusted trial balance must be translated into the appropriate number of United States dollars. For each of the ten (10) accounts listed below, taken from Ban's adjusted trial balance, specify what exchange rate (for example, average exchange rate for 1999, current exchange rate at December 31, 1999, etc.) should be used to translate the account balances into dollars and explain why that rate is appropriate. Number your answers to correspond with each account listed below.

1. Cash in Shatha National Bank.
2. Trade accounts receivable (all from 1999 revenues).
3. Supplies inventory (all purchased during the last quarter of 1999).
4. Land (purchased in 1996).
5. Short-term note payable to Shatha National Bank.
6. Capital stock (no par or stated value and all issued in January 1996).
7. Retained earnings, January 1, 1999.
8. Sales revenue.
9. Depreciation expense (on buildings).
10. Salaries expense.

NUMBER 4

On January 1, 1998, the Franklin Company formed a foreign subsidiary which issued all of its currently outstanding common stock on that date. Selected captions from the balance sheets, all of which are shown in local currency units (LCU), are as follows:

December 31	*1999*	*1998*
Accounts receivable (net of allowance for uncollectible accounts of 2,200 LCU at December 31, 1999 and 2,000 LCU at December 31, 1998)	40,000 LCU	35,000 LCU
Inventories, at cost	80,000	75,000
Property, plant and equipment (net of allowance for accumulated depreciation of 31,000 LCU at December 31, 1999 and 14,000 LCU at December 31, 1998)	163,000	150,000
Long-term debt	100,000	120,000
Common stock, authorized 10,000 shares, par value 10 LCU per share, issued and outstanding 5,000 shares at December 31, 1999 and December 31, 1998	50,000	50,000

Additional information is as follows:

- Exchange rates are as follows:

January 1, 1998 - July 31, 1998	2 LCU to $1
August 1, 1998 - October 31, 1998	1.8 LCU to $1
November 1, 1998 - June 30, 1999	1.7 LCU to $1
July 1, 1999 - December 31, 1999	1.5 LCU to $1
Average monthly rate for 1998	1.9 LCU to $1
Average monthly rate for 1999	1.6 LCU to $1

- An analysis of the accounts receivable balance is as follows:

Accounts receivable:	*1999*	*1998*
Balance at beginning of year	37,000 LCU	— LCU
Sales (36,000 LCU per month in 1999 and 31,000 LCU per month in 1998)	432,000	372,000
Collections	423,600	334,000
Write-offs (May 1999 and December 1998)	3,200	1,000
Balance at end of year	42,200 LCU	37,000 LCU

Allowance for uncollectible accounts:	*1999*	*1998*
Balance at beginning of year	2,000 LCU	— LCU
Provision for uncollectible accounts	3,400	3,000
Write-offs (May 1999 and December 1998)	3,200	1,000
Balance at end of year	2,200 LCU	2,000 LCU

- An analysis of inventories, for which the first-in, first-out (FIFO) inventory method is used, is as follows:

	1999	*1998*
Inventory at beginning of year	75,000 LCU	— LCU
Purchases (June 1999 and June 1998)	335,000	375,000
Goods available for sale	410,000	375,000
Inventory at end of year	80,000	75,000
Cost of goods sold	330,000 LCU	300,000 LCU

- On January 1, 1998, Franklin's foreign subsidiary purchased land for 24,000 LCU and plant and equipment for 140,000 LCU. On July 4, 1999, additional equipment was purchased for 30,000 LCU. Plant and equipment is being depreciated on a straight-line basis over a ten-year period with no salvage value. A full year's depreciation is taken in the year of purchase.

- On January 15, 1998, 7% bonds with a face value of 120,000 LCU were sold. These bonds mature on January 15, 2004, and interest is paid semiannually on July 15 and January 15. The first payment was made on January 15, 1999.

Required:
Prepare a schedule translating the selected captions above into United States dollars at December 31, 1999, and December 31, 1998, respectively. Show supporting computations in good form and assume that the U.S. dollar is the functional currency.

NUMBER 5

Jay Co.'s 1999 consolidated financial statements include two wholly owned subsidiaries, Jay Co. of Australia (Jay A) and Jay Co. of France (Jay F). Functional currencies are the US dollar for Jay A and the franc for Jay F.

Required:

a. What are the objectives of translating a foreign subsidiary's financial statements?

b. How are gains and losses arising from translating or remeasuring of each subsidiary's financial statements measured and reported in Jay's consolidated financial statements?

c. FASB Statement No. 52 identifies several economic indicators that are to be considered both individually and collectively in determining the functional currency for a consolidated subsidiary. List three of those indicators.

d. What exchange rate is used to incorporate each subsidiary's equipment cost, accumulated depreciation, and depreciation expense in Jay's consolidated financial statements?

Comprehensive Income

Chapter Six
Solutions to Price Level—Foreign Exchange Questions

1. (c)

Selling price of land	$400,000
Less: Cost of land adjusted for price level changes to Dec. 1999 $300,000 × 140 ÷ 120	350,000
Gain on sale	$ 50,000

2. (d)

Cost of equipment	$300,000
Less: Accumulated depreciation ($300,000 ÷ 10 × 4 yrs.)	120,000
Book value	$180,000
Selling price of equipment	$200,000
Less: Book value of equipment adjusted for price level changes from 1/1/96 to 12/31/99 $180,000 × 140 ÷ 100	252,000
Loss on sale of equipment	$(52,000)

3. (a) FASB #89 suggests that inventory and property, plant and equipment be reported at both current cost (current cost — nominal dollars) and current cost adjusted for the change in price level (current cost — constant dollars). The difference between current cost — nominal dollars ($15,000) and current cost — constant dollars ($12,000) is attributable to inflation ($3,000).

4. (b) Sales are evenly distributed throughout the year and are restated to year-end dollars. Indices of prior year do not affect the computation.

$$\frac{\text{Year end index 104}}{\text{Avg. index for year 103}} \times 3{,}000{,}000 = \$3{,}029{,}126$$

5. (d) Current cost per unit—$71 × 9,000 = $639,000

6. (a)

Average current cost of units ($57 + $71 = $128 ÷ 2) =	$ 64
Number of units sold	× 30,000
Cost of goods sold (current cost)	$1,920,000

7. (a) General purchasing power losses occur when net monetary assets are held during a period of inflation. This is because the monetary assets are fixed in terms of dollars and the value of the dollar is decreasing. Conversely, a gain occurs if net monetary liabilities are held during inflation. General purchasing power gains and losses are recognized only in constant dollar (units-of-general-purchasing-power) financial statements.

8. (c) Since the investment and the liability are monetary items, they are reported at their unadjusted balance. The land is adjusted as follows: $120,000 × 110 ÷ 100 = $132,000.

9. (b) The only answer which is not fixed in terms of dollars (or related to an account which is fixed) is the accumulated depreciation of equipment.

10. (d) Holding gains for inventory are measured by comparing current value (replacement cost) at year-end to book value (purchase price). Therefore, the holding gain is $2.00 ($10.00 – $8.00).

11. (b)

Average current unit cost of merchandise	$ 65
Number of units sold	× 70,000
Cost of goods sold (average current cost)	$4,550,000

12. (c) Holding gains for equipment (a) and land (b) are not part of income from continuing operations. The reduction in cost of goods sold is reflected in income from continuing operations (c) and (d) is not applicable for current cost measurement.

13. (a) The purchasing power loss is recognized from holding monetary assets during a period of rising prices. The only monetary asset listed is the refundable deposits. Items (c) and (d) are liabilities, and (b) is a non monetary asset.

14. (d)

Net monetary assets 1/1/98	$1,000,000
Converted to 12/31/98 $	
$1,000,000 × 220/200	$1,100,000
Net monetary assets at 12/31/98	- 1,000,000
Purchasing power loss	$ 100,000

15. (b)

Current cost of plant assets		$444,000
Accumulated depreciation:		
1991 asset	$280,000 × 30% = $84,000	
1992 asset	76,000 × 20% = 15,200	
1993 asset	88,000 × 10% = 8,800	
Total		108,000
Net current cost		$336,000

16. (b) Purchasing power loss = 150 ÷ 125 × $3,000,000 = $600,000

17. (d) $500,000.

Gain from sale of one-half of inventory:		
1,000,000 – (1/2 × 1,200,000) =		400,000
Holding gain from one-half not sold:		
Cost	600,000	
Replacement value	700,000	
Holding gain		100,000
Total gain		500,000

18. (b) Only the deposit and receivables are cash or fixed amounts to be received or paid in the future.

19. (a) A patent is not a fixed or determinable sum of money and is therefore nonmonetary. Premium on bonds payable is directly related to a liability account which is fixed in terms of dollars and is therefore monetary.

20. (d) Since the inflation rate was higher than the rate of increase in the specific value of the land, current cost should not be used, only constant dollar (at historical cost) which would generate the highest amount.

21. (c)

Current Cost	*% depreciated*
$140,000	30% = $ 42,000
38,000	20% = 7,600
44,000	10% = 4,400
Accumulated depreciation	$ 54,000
Current value of assets	222,000
Net current cost	$168,000

22. (a)

Net liabilities, December 31, 2000	$1,449,000		
Net liabilities, December 31, 1999	966,000	× 220 ÷ 210 =	$1,012,000
	483,000	× 220 ÷ 220 =	483,000
Net monetary liabilities restated to 2000 average			$1,495,000
Compared to 2000 actual restated	$1,449,000	× 220 ÷ 230 =	1,386,000
			$ 109,000

23. (c) Assuming that average current cost was used, the average current cost of the machine is $120,000 for 1992, which would generate depreciation expense of $24,000 (5 year life).

24. (d) Stockholders' equity in current value statements would increase by $200,000 in 1997, being the difference between the cost at 12/30/96 and the fair value at 12/31/97. The additional $50,000 would be part of the profit realized in 1998 on the sale. Answer choice (b) is correct for conventional statements under GAAP, but not for current value statements.

25. (a) According to FASB #89, cost of goods sold should be measured by using the current cost at the date of sale. Since Manhof incurs sales throughout the year, cost of goods sold should be calculated by using the number of units sold multiplied by the average current cost per unit during the year.

26. (b) Monetary assets are those which are fixed in terms of settlement amounts, i.e., normally cash, receivables and payables. Therefore, only the loans to employees would be a monetary asset.

27. (a) Cost of goods sold is recorded at the current cost of the merchandise at the time of sale. Therefore, a holding gain would be recorded for merchandise sold during the year as well as for merchandise in inventory at the end of the year.

28. (d) If a monetary liability is held constant during a period of inflation, a purchasing power gain would result. If accounts payable were held constant at $10,000 when the index increased from 110 to 120, a purchasing power gain of $872 would result as follows:

Beginning of year $10,000 × $\frac{115 \text{ (average)}}{110 \text{ (beginning)}}$ = $10,455

End of year $10,000 × $\frac{115}{120 \text{ (end)}}$ = 9,583

Purchasing power gain $ 872 (decrease in liability)

29. (c) FASB # 89 suggest that income from operations be reported on a current cost basis. The adjustment of depreciation expense and cost of goods sold to a current cost basis may be made by using current cost, exit value, capitalization of net cash flows, or by applying specific indexes to the historical cost. Specific price indexes are indexes compiled specifically for inventory or for plant and equipment. Specific indexes should not be confused with a general index such as the CPI-Urban which is normally used to adjust historical cost for the change in price level. Answer (a) is incorrect because current cost of goods would not be the same as fair value (selling price). Answers (b) and (d) are incorrect because both deal with the calculation of purchasing power.

30. (c) A monetary asset held during a period of inflation will lose its purchasing power. For example, a company holding cash during 2001 when the inflation rate was 3% would be able to purchase 3% less at the end of the year compared to the purchasing power of the cash at the beginning of the year.

31. (d) A recognized gain or loss results from settling a receivable or payable which is denominated in other than the company's primary (functional) currency. If the receivable or payable has not been settled, a gain or loss is recognized if the exchange rate changes from the prior date of measurement.

32. (c) Amount recorded in accounts payable by Celt, Inc.

Dec. 10, 1996 (.4875); recorded on date of invoice	$97,500
Balance due Dec. 31, 1996 (.4675)	93,500
Gain reported 12/31/96	$ 4,000

33. (a) Gains or losses on foreign exchange **transactions** are always shown as a component of income from continuing operations.

34. (b) Denominated means that the liability is fixed in terms of the amount of currency in which it will be paid. If the liability is fixed in the amount of U.S. dollars to be paid, fluctuations in the German currency would not affect the amount to be paid and a foreign currency transaction gain or loss would not occur. Answer (a) is incorrect because transaction gains or losses are not extraordinary. Answers (c) and (d) are incorrect because transaction gains or losses are a part of income from continuing operations.

35. (b) SFAS #133 states that the change in the forward rate should be the basis for the calculation of the gain on the forward contract. The change in the forward rate is from $.90 to $.93 or $.03 x 100,000 francs = $3,000.

36. (b) SFAS #133 states that the change in the forward rate should be the basis for the calculation of the gain on the forward contract. The change in the forward rate is from $.90 to $.93 or .$.03 x 100,000 francs = $3,000.

37. (b) SFAS #133 states that the change in the forward rate should be the basis for the calculation of the gain on the forward contract. The change in the forward rate is from $.90 to $.93 or .$.03 x 100,000 francs = $3,000.

38. (c) Since the functional currency is the foreign currency, the accounts are not remeasured and the current rate is used for translation.

39. (d) Income and expense items are generally translated using the weighted average exchange rate for the year when the functional currency is the foreign currency.

40. (d) Since the functional currency of the foreign subsidiary is the foreign currency, all assets are translated into U.S. dollars using the current rate method.

41. (d) Since the subsidiary's functional currency is the parent's currency, the gains are reported as income similar to transaction gains.

42. (a) Under the remeasurement method, nonmonetary items such as inventories or property, plant and equipment would be remeasured using historical exchange rates. Monetary items such as marketable equity securities reported at market value, bonds payable or accrued liabilities would be remeasured using the current exchange rates.

43. (b) This is the exception to the general rules for consolidating foreign subsidiaries. In this case, neither the local currency (German marks) nor the reporting currency (US dollars) is the functional currency. Since the functional currency is the Swiss franc, the financial statements of the subsidiary must first be **remeasured** from German marks into Swiss francs and a foreign exchange remeasurement gain of $7,600 must be recognized.

The remeasured financial statements are then **translated** into US dollars and a foreign exchange translation gain of $8,100 is calculated. The consolidated financial statements would then report a foreign exchange remeasurement gain of $7,600 on the Income Statement and the $8,100 translation gain would be reported as a part of other comprehensive income.

44. (a)

1996 foreign exchange loss	$15,000
Less exchange gain from accounts payable transaction	– 4,000
Reported foreign exchange loss	$11,000

45. (d)

Amount recorded in Accounts Payable on the date of purchase -		
September 22, 2001	10,000 units × $.55 =	$5,500
Amount Due on Accounts Payable at December 31, 2001		
	10,000 units × $.70 =	7,000
Foreign exchange translation loss - 2001		$1,500

46. (c) The sale was recorded when the dollar equivalent for the LCU's was $100,000 and the receivable was settled for $105,000 within the year. Therefore, there is a resulting $5,000 gain recognized.

47. (d) The note would have been adjusted at 12/31/91 to the equivalent of $240,000. Therefore, in 1992, the difference between the repayment equivalent of $280,000 and $40,000 would be recognized as a loss.

48. (b) An adjustment is required at December 31 to properly state Hunt Co.'s liability for the fluctuations in the spot rate. The original purchase was recorded on November 30 at the spot rate of $495,000 (300,000 pounds × $1.65). Since the exchange rate decreased by $.03 on December 31, the following adjusting journal entry should be made:

Accounts Payable	9,000	
Gain on Foreign Currency Transaction		9,000
Calculation: 300,000 pounds × $.03 =	$9,000	

Note: The 30-day and 60-day rates would be used for fluctuations in forward exchange contracts.

49. (c) The key points are to use forward rates for a speculative contract and to use the forward rate at September 30 for the remaining maturity (30 days) of the forward contract. The loss is 50,000 × ($.72 – .74) = $1,000.

50. (b) A gain on settlement of the receivable and a loss on the settlement of payable means that the amount of dollars received and paid at settlement were greater than the amount at the contract date.

Example: LCU 10,000 at exchange rate of 5 LCU for $1 = $20,000.

In order for the settlement amount to be greater than $20,000, the LCU's per $1 must decrease; i.e., LCU 100,000 ÷ 4 LCU = $25,000.

51. (b) Since sales and wages expense are incurred throughout the year, the weighted average current rate is used as the exchange rate.

52. (d)

Transaction loss, $96,000 - $90,000		$ 6,000
Loan balance as recorded 7/1/96	$500,000	
Accrued interest (half year at 10%)	25,000	
Recorded balance of loan and interest at 12/31/96	$525,000	
Translated balance	546,000	
Exchange loss		21,000
Total foreign exchange loss		$27,000

53. (a) Gains and losses on foreign currency transactions that are designated as economic hedges of a net investment in a foreign entity should be reported in the same manner as a translation adjustment. Current changes in translation adjustments are reported as other comprehensive income.

54. (c) SFAS #133 requires that gains or losses on a derivative used as a hedge of a forecasted foreign-currency-denominated transaction should be included in comprehensive income because the transaction is not complete. When the transaction is complete, the gain will be reclassified from comprehensive income to current earnings.

55. (d) SFAS 52 states that an entity's functional currency is the currency of the primary economic environment in which the entity operates; normally, that is the currency of the environment in which an entity primarily generates and expends cash.

Chapter Six
Solutions to Price Level—Foreign Exchange Problems

NUMBER 1

a.

Skadden, Inc.
SCHEDULE TO ANALYZE EQUIPMENT FOR CONSTANT DOLLAR RESTATEMENT
December 31, 2000

Year Acquired	*Amount (Historical)*	*Conversion Factor*		*Amount (Year-average Constant Dollar)*
1998	$490,000	1.085	(126.7/116.8)	$531,650
1999	10,000	1.040	(126.7/121.8)	10,400
2000	150,000	1.000		150,000
	$650,000			$692,050

b.

Skadden, Inc.
SCHEDULE TO ANALYZE EQUIPMENT--ACCUMULATED DEPRECIATION
(Historical Dollars) For the Year 2000

Year Assets Acquired	*Amount (Historical)*		*% Depreciated*	*Balance 12/31/00*
1998	$490,000	*	3/10	$147,000
1999	10,000	*	2/10	2,000
2000	150,000	*	1/10	15,000
	$650,000			$164,000

c.

Skadden, Inc.
SCHEDULE TO ANALYZE EQUIPMENT--ACCUMULATED DEPRECIATION
(Constant Dollars) For the Year 2000

	Accumulated Depreciation Balance 12/31/93	*Conversion Factor*	*Balance Year-Average Constant Dollars*
1998	$147,000	1.085	$159,495
1999	2,000	1.040	2,080
2000	15,000	1.000	15,000
	$164,000		$176,575

d.

Skadden, Inc.
SCHEDULE TO COMPUTE PURCHASING POWER GAIN OR LOSS FOR 2000

	Historical	*Conversion Factor*	*12/31/99 Restated to Average 1993 $'s*	*12/31/00 Historical (restated in Average 1993 $'s)*
Net monetary items:				
Cash & receivables				$540,000
Accounts payable				(300,000)
Bonds payable				(500,000)
Net	$ 445,000	1.040	$462,800	$(260,000)

			Restated to Average 2000 $'s
Purchasing power gain or loss			
Net monetary items--12/31/99	$ 445,000	1.026 (126.7 ÷ 123.5)	$ 456,570
Add: Sales	1,900,000		1,900,000
	2,345,000		$2,356,570
Deduct:			
Purchases	1,840,000		
Operating expenses and interest	215,000		
Purchase of marketable securities	400,000		
Acquisitions of equipment	150,000		
	2,605,000		2,605,000
Net monetary items--historical	$(260,000)		
Net monetary items--historical--restated--12/31/00			(248,430)
Net monetary items--12/31/00 (as above)	$260,000	.986 (126.7 ÷ 128.5)	256,360
Purchasing power loss			$(7,930)

NUMBER 2

a. In general, conventional financial statements reflect transactions in terms of the number of dollars originally involved in those transactions. If prices did not change (i.e., if the dollar were a stable unit of measure), such statements would automatically reflect all transactions in terms of dollars of equal purchasing power. Prices, however, do change, and the effects of the changes are not isolated in conventional statements.

Barden has operated through a period of substantial price changes. Its conventional statements, therefore, simply present combinations of numbers of dollars of varying purchasing power. Such combinations are meaningless if an investor wishes to evaluate the performance of Barden's management over a long period of time to compare Barden to other companies (which present other meaningless combinations). After restatement for general price-level changes, Barden's statements will reflect its transactions in terms of a single unit of measure—the general purchasing power of the dollar at a specified date.

b. Financial statements restated for general price-level changes are based on conventional statements. The historical amounts are restated in terms of the general purchasing power of the dollar at the date of the latest balance sheet presented, as measured by an index based on the price changes of a broad group of goods and services. (Such an index for the United States is the Gross National Product Implicit Price Deflator.) Such statements indicate a company's gain or loss of general purchasing power (general price-level gain or loss). Since the prices of specific items do not necessarily change at the same rate as the general price level, such statements do not purport to show the current values of balance-sheet items or the prices at which transactions would take place currently.

Current-value statements purport to show the current values of individual balance-sheet items and the effects of changes in such values on the results of operations. Many different means of determining current values have been proposed, including replacement costs, resale price, appraisal value, and use of specific (rather than general) price indices. It is sometimes proposed that the portion of the change in value relating to inflation or deflation (change in the general price level) be shown separately from the remaining portion of the change.

c. Monetary assets and liabilities are those for which the amounts in terms of numbers of dollars are fixed (by contract or otherwise) regardless of general price-level changes. Other assets and liabilities are classified as nonmonetary. Examples of monetary items include cash and the usual types of accounts and notes receivable and accounts and notes payable. Examples of nonmonetary items include most inventories, plant and equipment, and liabilities for advances received on sales contracts.

The classification of some items may depend on the purpose for which the company holds them. For example, bonds held for the fixed principal and interest are monetary; bonds held for price speculation are nonmonetary.

d. To prepare the proposed supplementary statements, Barden should:

1. Classify assets and liabilities (at both December 31, 1998, and December 31, 1999) as monetary or nonmonetary.
2. Analyze the nonmonetary balance-sheet items to determine the time of origin.
3. Analyze all 1999 income-statement items and other 1999 items (including dividends) affecting retained earnings to determine the time of origin.
4. Restate the items analyzed in steps 2 and 3 above in terms of December 31, 1999, general purchasing power. This is accomplished by multiplying each historical amount by a "conversion factor" (the ratio of the current index number to the index number at time of origin).
5. Restate the monetary items in the December 31, 1998, balance sheet in terms of December 31, 1999, general purchasing power. Again, conversion factors are used.
6. Apply the "cost or market" rule to the restated amounts of those items to which it applies in the conventional financial statements.
7. Compute the 1999 general price-level gain or loss. This can be accomplished by:
   (a) Analyzing the 1999 changes in net monetary items.
   (b) Restating the changes in terms of December 31, 1999, general purchasing power (most or all of these restated amounts being available from previous computations) to determine what the amount of December 31, 1999, net monetary items would have been had there been no general price-level gain or loss.
   (c) Comparing the amount determined in step (b) above to the actual net monetary items at December 31, 1999, the difference being the general price-level gain or loss.

e. Since monetary assets and liabilities are automatically stated in terms of current general purchasing power, they appear at the same amounts in both conventional statements restated for general price-level changes. Nonmonetary assets and liabilities will usually appear at differing amounts in the two types of statements, as will items appearing on the statement of income and retained earnings. The restated statement of income will include an item not appearing on the conventional statement—the general price-level gain or loss for the year.

f. In presenting comparative supplementary statements at the end of 2000, Barden will have to restate ("roll forward") the 1999 supplementary statements in terms of December 31, 2000, general purchasing power. If this restatement is not made, the supplementary statements will not be presented in comparable terms (units of general purchasing power at a given date).

NUMBER 3

1. The current exchange rate at December 31, 1999, should be used to translate Ban's cash into dollars. The current exchange rate is the appropriate rate to use when it is desired to translate the account balance to reflect the current monetary equivalent number of dollars. With cash, it is desirable to know how many equivalent dollars Ban had at December 31, 1999, so that this amount can be combined with Dhia's cash on the consolidated statement of financial position.

2. The trade accounts receivable amount should be translated into dollars by using the current exchange rate at December 31, 1999. The current exchange rate should be used for accounts receivable because they are claims to cash, and it is desirable to know the current dollar equivalent of these claims.

3. The amount of supplies inventory should be translated into dollars at the average exchange rate for the last quarter of 1999 (or the actual rate(s) of exchange at the date(s) of purchase, if known). Inventories are conventionally stated at historical cost, and cost in this situation is the equivalent dollar amount invested in the inventory at the date(s) the purchase(s) actually took place.
If the inventory is valued at market in accordance with lower of cost or market, current exchange rates would be used.

4. The cost of the land should be translated into dollars at the exchange rate in effect when the land was purchased in 1996. Land should be reported in the statement of financial position at cost; therefore, the cost in dollars should be determined by translating the foreign currency cost into dollars at the rate of exchange on the date the land was purchased.

5. The amount of the short-term note payable to Shatha National Bank should be translated into dollars at the current exchange rate on December 31, 1999. The note payable represents a claim on cash and, like cash, should be restated in current equivalent dollars at the date of the statement of financial position.

6. The capital stock account must be translated into dollars in two parts; the 10% minority interest and the 90% held by Dhia will be treated separately. The amount for capital stock should be translated into dollars at the rate of exchange at the time the stock was issued in January 1996 for the 10% minority interest, and the actual dollars invested by Dhia should be used for the 90% held by Dhia. Legally, capital stock should be stated at the cost of the investment in the company, which should be determined at the date the stock issuance took place.

7. The amount of retained earnings in the adjusted trial balance is not translated by using any exchange rate because the dollar amount shown in the December 31, 1998, financial statements is used. The amount of the beginning retained earnings is the net result of 1996, 1997, and 1998 earnings and dividends; thus, it is a mixture of many different exchange rates and cannot be translated directly. Therefore, the beginning retained earnings is the dollar amount shown at the end of the preceding accounting period in the financial statements.

8. If sales revenue was earned consistently throughout the year, an average exchange rate for 1999 should be used to translate the amount into dollars. An average rate for the year should be used because it best reflects the equivalent dollars of sales, at the time the sales took place, assuming the earning of revenue took place consistently throughout the year.

9. The amount of depreciation expense can be translated into dollars at the historical rates at the time the buildings were purchased, but an accurate and simpler method would be to translate the amount by applying a ratio to the dollar amount of buildings already determined in the working papers. The ratio is based on the relationship of depreciation expense to building cost, both stated in the foreign currency. Therefore, the expense in the foreign currency and in dollars would be the same ratio of building cost, as stated in their respective currencies. Historical exchange rates are generally used when accounting principles require that the account balance in question be stated in terms of unexpired historical cost. Depreciation expense should be based on historical cost. Use of this historical rate accomplishes a conversion of an historical cost in a foreign currency to historical cost in dollars.

10. The amount of salaries expense should be translated into dollars at an average rate of exchange for 1999. An average rate of exchange should be used because salaries probably were incurred consistently throughout the year; thus, when restated by the average exchange rate the salaries expense would be restated in equivalent dollars.

NUMBER 4

Franklin Company's Foreign Subsidiary
TRANSLATION OF SELECTED CAPTIONS INTO UNITED STATES DOLLARS
December 31, 1999 and December 31, 1998

	LCU	Translation Rate	United States Dollars
December 31, 1999			
Accounts receivable (net)	40,000 LCU	1.5 LCU to $1	$26,667
Inventories, at cost	80,000	1.7 LCU to $1	47,059
Property, plant, and equipment (net)	163,000	*Schedule 1*	86,000
Long-term debt	100,000	1.5 LCU to $1	66,667
Common stock	50,000	2 LCU to $1	25,000
December 31, 1998			
Accounts receivable (net)	35,000	1.7 LCU to $1	20,588
Inventories, at cost	75,000	2 LCU to $1	37,500
Property, plant, and equipment (net)	150,000	2 LCU to $1	75,000
Long-term debt	120,000	1.7 LCU to $1	70,588
Common stock	50,000	2 LCU to $1	25,000

Schedule 1

Computation of Translation of Property, Plant, and Equipment (Net) into United States Dollars at December 31, 1999

	LCU	Translation Rate	United States Dollars
Land purchased on January 1, 1998	24,000 LCU	2 LCU to $1	$12,000
Plant and equipment purchased on January 1, 1998:			
Original cost	140,000	2 LCU to $1	70,000
Depreciation for 1998	(14,000)	2 LCU to $1	(7,000)
Depreciation for 1999	(14,000)	2 LCU to $1	(7,000)
	112,000	2 LCU to $1	56,000
Plant and equipment purchased on July 4, 1999:			
Original cost	30,000	1.5 LCU to $1	20,000
Depreciation for 1999	(3,000)	1.5 LCU to $1	(2,000)
	27,000	1.5 LCU to $1	18,000
	163,000 LCU		$86,000

NUMBER 5

a. The objectives of translating a foreign subsidiary's financial statements are to:

- Provide information that is generally compatible with the expected economic effects of a rate change on a subsidiary's cash flows and equity.
- Reflect the subsidiary's financial results and relationships in single currency consolidated financial statements, as measured in its functional currency and in conformity with GAAP.

b. Applying different exchange rates to the various financial statement accounts causes the restated statements to be unbalanced. The amount required to bring the restated statements into balance is termed the gain or loss from the translation or remeasurement. The gain or loss arising from remeasuring Jay A's financial statements is reported in the consolidated income statement. The gain or loss arising from translating Jay F's financial statements is reported separately under stockholders' equity in the balance sheet.

c. The functional currency is the foreign currency or parent's currency that most closely correlates with the following economic indicators:

- Cash flow indicators
- Sales price indicators
- Sales market indicators
- Expense indicators
- Financing indicators
- Intercompany transactions and arrangement indicators

d. All accounts relating to Jay A's equipment are remeasured by the exchange rate prevailing between the US and Australian dollars at the time equipment was purchased.

All accounts relating to Jay F's equipment are translated by the current exchange rates prevailing between the US dollar and French franc. For the equipment cost and accumulated depreciation this is the current exchange rate at December 31, 1999. Depreciation expense is translated at the rate prevailing on the date the depreciation expense was recognized or an appropriate weighted average exchange rate for 1999.

Chapter Seven
Accounting Theory

Read + Re-read closer to exam

Chapter Seven
Accounting Theory

FASB CONCEPTUAL FRAMEWORK

The Financial Accounting Standard Board's conceptual framework consists of five statements identified as Statements of Financial Accounting Concepts "SFAC" 1, 2, 4, 5, and 6. SFAC 3 was superseded by SFAC 6. SFAC 4 deals with non-business organizations. The ideas contained in the conceptual framework for the most part are normative in nature, that is they suggest what financial reporting should be rather than what it currently is, and as a result there is some discrepancy with current accounting practice. Statements of Financial Accounting Concepts are issued by the FASB as guidance in setting accounting principles but are not equivalent to Statements of Financial Accounting Standards. A conceptual statement does not set generally accepted accounting principles but rather address certain issues. Among the major ones:

Objectives of Financial Reporting by Business Enterprises
Qualitative Characteristics of Accounting Information
Elements of Financial Statements of Business Enterprises
Recognition and Measurement in Financial Statements of Business Enterprises

OBJECTIVES OF FINANCIAL REPORTING

Statement of Financial Accounting Concepts No. 1 establishes and identifies three major objectives of general purpose external financial reporting. The objectives are stated in terms of financial reporting:

> Financial reporting should provide information that is **useful** to present and potential investors and creditors and other users **in making rational investment, credit, and similar decisions.** The information should be comprehensible to those who have a reasonable understanding of business and economic activities and are willing to study the information with reasonable diligence.

Investors and creditors include those users who deal directly with an enterprise as well as those who deal through intermediaries.

> The information should help in **assessing the amounts, timing, and uncertainty of prospective cash receipts** from dividends or interest and the proceeds from the sale, redemption, or maturity of securities or loans.

The prospects for those cash receipts are affected by an enterprise's ability to generate enough cash to meet its obligations when due and its other cash operating needs, to reinvest in operations, and to pay cash dividends and may also be affected by perceptions of investors and creditors generally about that ability, which affect market prices of the enterprise's securities. Thus, financial reporting should provide information to help investors, creditors, and others assess the amounts, timing, and uncertainty of prospective net cash inflows to the related enterprise.

> Financial reporting should provide information about the **economic resources** of an enterprise, **the claims to those resources** (obligations of the enterprise to transfer resources to other entities and owners' equity), and the effects of transactions, events, and circumstances **that change resources and claims to those resources.**

In other words, investors, creditors, and others should be able to identify the enterprise's financial strengths and weaknesses and assess its liquidity and solvency. They should be able to measure the enterprise's performance whose primary focus is information about earnings and its components. Information is based on accrual accounting. Information is provided about management's stewardship function. Information is not designed to measure the value of a business. Users make their own decisions, the information is to aid them. Management should identify events and circumstances not directly reported in the financial statements and should explain the financial effects of these on the enterprise.

QUALITATIVE CHARACTERISTICS OF ACCOUNTING INFORMATION

Statement of Financial Accounting Concepts No. 2 defines the characteristics which make accounting information useful. These characteristics guide the selection of accounting policies from available alternatives. The qualitative characteristics of accounting information are those that make the information useful to users in the decision-making process. These characteristics are the basis for evaluating the information against the cost of providing and using it and help distinguish more useful information from that which is less useful. The qualitative characteristics of accounting information should be used when faced with different alternatives.

There is a hierarchy of desirable qualitative characteristics of accounting information.

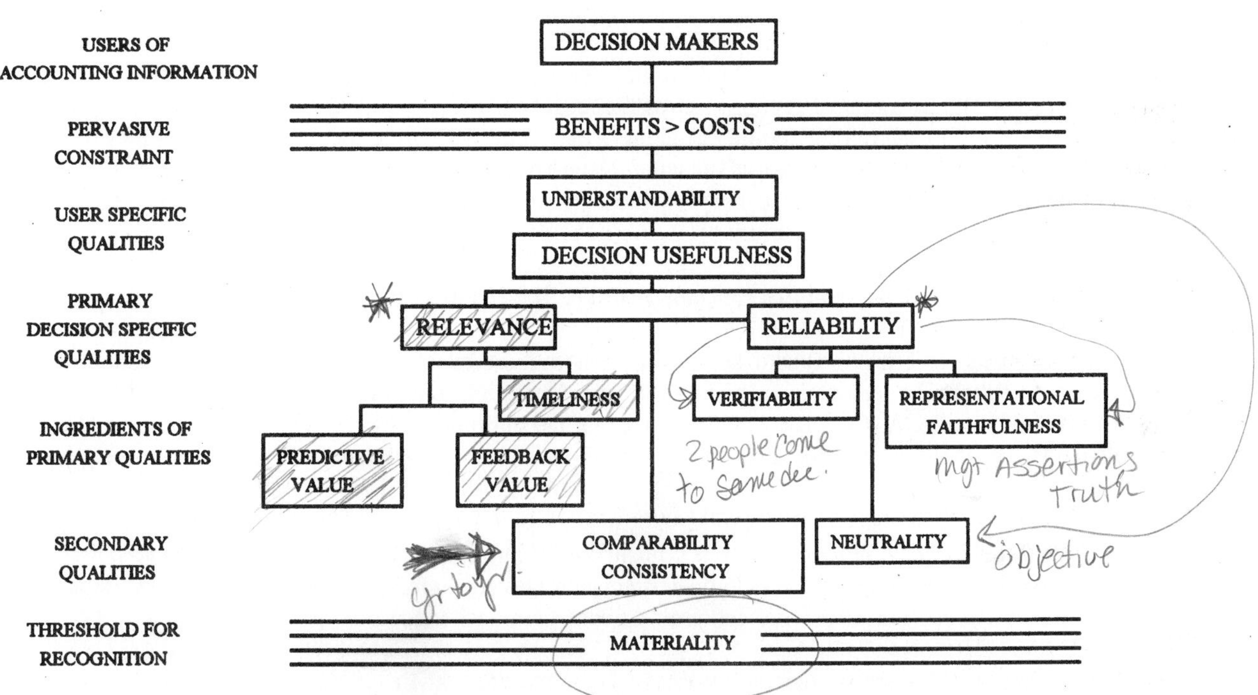

The **primary** qualitative characteristics are **relevance** and **reliability.**

> **Relevance:** To be relevant to investors, creditors, and other users, accounting information must be capable of making a difference in a decision by helping users to form predictions about the outcomes of past, present, and future events or to confirm or correct expectations reducing uncertainty about future events. Unless information is useful in making decisions, there is no reason to report it. While accuracy of information is important, totally accurate information would not be useful if it did not pertain to the decision being made.
>
> **Reliability:** To be reliable, investors, creditors and other users must be able to depend on accounting information to accurately represent the economic conditions or events that it purports to describe.

Relevance has three ingredients:

Predictive value: information can make a difference in decisions by improving the decision makers' capacity to predict.

Feedback value: confirming or correcting previous expectations.

Timeliness: To be useful, information must be timely otherwise the information is irrelevant for the decision process.

Reliability has three ingredients:

Verifiability: Accounting information must be verifiable, that is, several people, making independent evaluations, are likely to obtain the same measures. In other words, there would be a high degree of consensus among independent measurers.

Representational faithfulness: What it is described faithfully discloses the information it represents.

Neutrality: This means rule makers should be concerned with the relevance and reliability of the resulting information, not the effect a new rule may have on a particular interest. Since there are many users of financial accounting information, a general purpose approach is more relevant. The financial statements and footnotes present a complete picture of the current financial position and changes over time, under the assumption that each user will select the elements most relevant to that users purposes.

Information must be trusted to be useful. Trust results from belief that the information is representationally faithful, that is, it is what it claims to be. Financial accounting data is usually based on source documents which can be examined again. This verifiability enhances the reliability of the information. To be relevant, information must have either predictive value or feedback value. To be reliable, information must be neutral. However, sometime the most relevant information may not be the most reliable. For example, future values of assets might be the most relevant information for certain decisions if they could be determined objectively, but they cannot be. Therefore, more objective information based on actual historical transactions is presented under generally accepted accounting principles. Several of the concepts which are included in the hierarchy are closely related to the primary concepts of relevance and reliability.

The **secondary** qualitative characteristics are **comparability and consistency.**

Comparability: Users evaluate accounting information by comparison. Similar companies should account for similar transactions in similar ways. Operating trends should not be disguised by changing accounting methods. Comparability indicates that the information can be compared to other data in order to identify similarities and differences and allow users to make meaningful comparisons between enterprises

Consistency: A goal of this concept is comparison of one company's information from one period to the next. The application of methods over time increases the informational value of comparisons and it indicates that accounting policies and procedures remain unchanged from period to period.

There are two constraints related to the usefulness of accounting information.

Cost/Benefit: The usefulness and benefit to be derived from having certain information must exceed the cost of providing it. The cost/benefit pervasive constraint states that unless the benefits to be derived exceed the costs of providing that information, it should not be provided.

Materiality: Is a consideration if it is probable that a person relying on certain information will be influenced in making investment or credit decisions by an error or omission. The materiality of an item must be considered. A small amount, considered immaterial in normal transactions, might influence users of the information when it pertains to an unusual item.

In order to be useful to a particular individual, the information must be understandable. **Understandability** indicates that a user is able to comprehend the information. If a user does not comprehend the information, it creates a necessity for the user to find help in interpreting the information. Financial information is a tool and is useful only if understood by users of it. The FASB has attempted to develop standards that relate to general purpose of decision makers and their abilities to understand financial information. In other words, the most relevant, reliable, and timely information would be useless if it were presented in a manner that isn't understandable. There must be agreement on accounting methods followed and sufficient explanations to allow a user to comprehend the message.

ELEMENTS OF THE FINANCIAL STATEMENTS

Statement of Financial Accounting Concepts No. 6 deals with the elements of financial statements, which are the building blocks with which financial statements are constructed. SFAC 6 defines ten elements that are directly related to measuring the performance and status of an enterprise. The Balance-sheet elements include assets, liabilities, and equity, which describe amounts of resources or claims to resources at a moment in time. The Income Statement elements include income, revenue, expenses, gains. and losses and describe the effects of transactions and other events and circumstances that affect an enterprise during intervals of time. These two classes of elements are related because assets, liabilities, and equity are changed by elements of the other class and at any time. All elements are defined in relation to a particular entity such as a business enterprise, an educational or charitable organization, or a governmental unit.

> **Assets** are probable future economic benefits obtained or controlled by a particular enterprise as a result of past transactions or events. An asset has the capacity to contribute to future net cash inflows. A particular enterprise can obtain the benefit and control others' access to it. The transaction or other event giving rise to the enterprise's right to the benefit has already occurred.

The common characteristic possessed by all assets and economic resources is "service potential" or "future economic benefit," the capacity to provide services or benefits to the entities that use them. In a business enterprise, that service potential or future economic benefit eventually results in net cash inflows to the enterprise. That characteristic is the primary basis of the definition of assets in this statement. A separate item that reduces or increases the carrying amount of an asset is sometimes found in financial statements. For example, an estimate of uncollectible amounts reduces receivables to the amount expected to be collected, or a premium on a bond receivable increases the receivable to its cost or present value. Those "valuation accounts" are part of the related assets and are neither assets in their own right nor liabilities.

> **Liabilities** are probable future sacrifices of economic benefits arising from present obligations of a particular enterprise to transfer assets or provide services to other enterprises in the future as a result of past transactions or events. A liability is a present duty to other entities that entails settlement by probable future transfer or use of assets at a specified or determinable date, on occurrence of a specified event, or on demand. The duty obligates a particular enterprise, leaving it little or no discretion to avoid the future sacrifice. The transaction or other event obligating the enterprise has already happened.

Uncertainty about economic and business activities and results is pervasive, and it often clouds whether a particular item qualifies as an asset or a liability of a particular enterprise at the time the definitions are applied. The presence or absence of future economic benefit that can be obtained and controlled by the enterprise or of the enterprise's legal, equitable, or constructive obligation to sacrifice assets in the future can often be discerned reliably only with hindsight. As a result, some items that with hindsight actually qualified as assets or liabilities of the enterprise under the definitions may, as a practical matter, have been recognized as expenses, losses, revenues, or gains or remained unrecognized in its financial statements because of uncertainty about whether they qualified as assets or liabilities of the enterprise or because of recognition and measurement considerations stemming from uncertainty at the time of assessment. Conversely, some items that with hindsight did not qualify under the definitions may have been included as assets or liabilities because of judgments made in the face of uncertainty at the time of assessment. A highly significant practical consequence of the features described above is that the existence or amount (or both) of most assets and many liabilities can be probable but not certain. Estimates and approximations will often be required unless financial statements are to be restricted to reporting only cash transactions.

> **Equity** is the residual interest in the assets of an enterprise that remains after deducting its liabilities. In a business enterprise, the equity is the ownership interest. It involves a relationship between an enterprise and its owners in their ownership capacity rather than as employees, suppliers, customers, lenders, or

some other non-owner role. Since it ranks after liabilities as a claim to, or interest in, the assets of the enterprise, it is a residual interest.

Equity is the same as net assets, the difference between the enterprise's assets and its liabilities. Equity is enhanced or impeded by changes in net assets. Events that affect a business enterprise can be placed into three classes:

1. changes in assets and liabilities not associated with changes in equity
2. changes in assets and liabilities that are accompanied by changes in equity
3. changes in equity that do not affect assets or liabilities.

For example, exchanges of assets for other assets. An enterprise may have several classes of equity (for example, one or more classes each of common stock or preferred stock) with different degrees of risk stemming from different rights to participate in distributions of enterprise assets or different priorities of claims on enterprise assets in the event of liquidation. In contrast, a not-for-profit organization has no ownership interest or profit purpose in the same sense as a business enterprise and thus receives no investments of assets by owners and distributes no assets to owners. Rather, its net assets often are increased by receipts of assets from resource providers (contributors, donors, grantors, and the like) who do not expect to receive either repayment or economic benefits proportionate to the assets provided, but who are nonetheless interested in how the organization makes use of those assets and often impose temporary or permanent restrictions on their use.

Although the line between equity and liabilities is clear in concept, it may be obscured in practice. Applying the definitions to particular situations may involve practical problems because several kinds of securities issued by business enterprises seem to have characteristics of both liabilities and equity in varying degrees or because the names given some securities may not accurately describe their essential characteristics. For example, convertible debt instruments have both liability and residual interest characteristics, which may create problems in accounting for them.

Similarly, the line between net assets and liabilities of not-for-profit organizations may be obscured in practice because donors' restrictions that specify the use of contributed assets may seem to result in liabilities, although most do not. The essence of a not-for-profit organization is that it obtains and uses resources to provide specific types of goods or services, and the nature of those goods or services is often critical in donors' decisions to contribute cash or other assets to a particular organization. Most donors contribute assets (restricted as well as unrestricted) to an organization to increase its capacity to provide those goods or services and receipt of donated assets not only increases the assets of the organization but also imposes a fiduciary responsibility on its management to use those assets effectively and efficiently in pursuit of those service objectives. That responsibility pertains to all of the organization's assets and does not constitute an equitable or constructive obligation. In other words, a not-for-profit organization's fiduciary responsibility to use assets to provide services to beneficiaries does not itself create a duty of the organization to pay cash, transfer other assets, or provide services to one or more creditors. Rather, an obligation to a creditor results when the organization buys supplies for a project, its employees work on it, and the like, and the organization therefore owes suppliers, employees, and others for goods and services they have provided to it. A donor's restriction focuses that fiduciary responsibility on a stipulated use for specified contributed assets but does not change the basic nature of the organization's fiduciary responsibility to use its assets to provide services to beneficiaries. A donor's gift of cash to be spent for a stipulated purpose or of another asset to be used for a stipulated purpose—for example, a mansion to be used as a museum, a house to be used as a dormitory, or a sculpture to be displayed in a cemetery—imposes a responsibility to spend the cash or use the asset in accordance with the donor's instructions. In its effect on the liabilities of the organization, a donor's restriction is essentially the same as management's designating a specified use for certain assets. That is, the responsibility imposed by earmarking assets for specified uses is fundamentally different, both economically and legally, from the responsibility imposed by incurring a liability, which involves a creditor's claim. Consequently, most donor-imposed restrictions on an organization's use of contributed assets do not create obligations that qualify as liabilities of the organization.

Investments by owners are increases in net assets of a particular enterprise resulting from transfers to it from other enterprises of something of value to obtain or increase ownership interests (or equity) in it. Assets are most commonly received as investments by owners, but that which is received may also include services or satisfaction or conversion of liabilities of the enterprise.

Distributions to owners are decreases in net assets of a particular enterprise resulting from transferring assets, rendering services, or incurring liabilities by the enterprise to owners. Distributions to owners decrease ownership interests or equity in the enterprise.

Comprehensive income is the change in equity (net assets) of an enterprise, during a period, from transactions and other events and circumstances from nonowner sources. It includes all changes in equity during a period except those resulting from investments by owners and distributions to owners.

Over the life of a business enterprise, its comprehensive income equals the net of its cash receipts and cash outlays, excluding cash investments by owners and cash distributions to owners. That characteristic holds whether the amounts of cash and comprehensive income are measured in nominal dollars or constant dollars. Timing of recognition of revenues, expenses, gains, and losses is also a major difference between accounting based on cash receipts and outlays and accrual accounting. Accrual accounting may encompass various timing possibilities—for example, when goods or services are provided or when cash is received.

Revenues are inflows or other enhancements of assets of an enterprise or settlements of its liabilities or a combination of both, during a period, from delivering or producing goods, rendering services, or other activities that constitute the enterprise's ongoing major or central operations. Revenues represent cash inflows that have occurred or will eventuate as a result of the enterprise's major operations during the period.

Expenses are outflows or other uses of assets or incurrences of liabilities (or a combination of both), during a period, from delivering or producing goods, rendering services, or carrying out other activities that constitute the enterprise's ongoing major or central operations. Expenses represent cash outflows that have occurred or will occur because of the enterprise's major operations during the period.

Gains are increases in equity, or net assets, from peripheral or incidental transactions of an enterprise and from all other transactions and other events and circumstances affecting the enterprise, during a period, except those that result from revenues or investments by owners.

Losses are decreases in equity (net assets) from peripheral or incidental transactions of an enterprise and from all other transactions and other events and circumstances affecting the enterprise, during a period, except those that result from expenses or distributions to owners.

Articulation is a term used to describe the interrelationship of the elements of the financial statements. Some elements reflect aspects of the enterprise at a point in time, at December 31, 19xx, such as assets, liabilities, and equity. The remaining elements of the financial statements describe effects of transactions and other events and circumstances that occur over periods of time. These two types of elements are related in such a way that assets, liabilities and equity are changed by elements of the other type and at any time are their cumulative result, and an increase or decrease in an asset cannot occur without a corresponding increase or decrease in another asset, liability, or equity. The resulting financial statements are, therefore interrelated, even though they include different elements which reflect different characteristics of the enterprise and its activities.

RECOGNITION AND MEASUREMENT IN FINANCIAL STATEMENTS OF BUSINESS ENTERPRISES

Statement of Financial Accounting Concepts No. 5 sets forth recognition criteria and guidance on what information should be incorporated into financial statements and when. The statement makes the following major conclusions:

> Financial statements are a central feature of financial reporting as a principal means of communicating financial information to those outside an entity. Some useful information is better provided by financial statements and some is better provided, or can only be provided, by notes to financial statements, supplementary information, or other means of financial reporting. For items that meet criteria for recognition, disclosure by other means is not a substitute for recognition in financial statements.
>
> Recognition is the process of formally incorporating an item into the financial statements of an entity as an asset, liability, revenue, expense, or the like. A recognized item is depicted in both words and numbers, with the amount included in the statement totals.

A full set of financial statements for a period should show:

- Financial position at the end of the period
- Earnings for the period
- Comprehensive income for the period*
- Cash flows during the period
- Investments by and distributions to owners during the period.

* In June 1997 the FASB adopted SFAS #130 which requires the disclosure of comprehensive income. (See Chapter 12 for complete disclosure requirements.)

Following are some characteristics of financial statements identified in SFAC 5:

General purpose financial statements are directed toward the common interests of various users and are feasible only because groups of users of financial information have similar needs.

Financial statements, individually and collectively, contribute to meeting the objectives of financial reporting. No one financial statement is likely to provide all the financial statement information that is useful for a particular kind of decision.

The parts of a financial statement also contribute to meeting the objectives of financial reporting and may be more useful to those who make investment, credit, and similar decisions than the whole.

Financial statements result from simplifying, condensing, and aggregating masses of data. As a result, they convey information that would be obscured if great detail were provided. Although those simplifications, condensations, and aggregations are both necessary and useful, the Board believes that it is important to avoid focusing attention almost exclusively on "the bottom line," earnings per share, or other highly simplified condensations.

A statement of financial position provides information about an entity's assets, liabilities, and equity and their relationships to each other at a moment in time. The statement delineates the entity's resource structure—major classes and amounts of assets—and its financing structure—major classes and amounts of liabilities and equity.

A statement of financial position does not purport to show the value of a business enterprise but, together with other financial statements and other information, should provide information that is useful to those who desire to make their own estimates of the enterprise's value. Those estimates are part of financial analysis, not of financial reporting, but financial accounting aids financial analysis.

Statements of earnings and of comprehensive income together reflect the extent to which and the ways in which the equity of an entity increased or decreased from all sources other than transactions with owners during a period.

The concept of earnings set forth in this Statement is similar to net income for a period in present practice; however, it excludes certain accounting adjustments of earlier periods that are recognized in the current period—cumulative effect of a change in accounting principle is the principal example from present practice. The Board expects the concept of earnings to be subject to the process of gradual change or evolution that has characterized the development of net income.

Earnings is a measure of entity performance during a period. It measures the extent to which asset inflows revenues and gains associated with cash-to-cash cycles substantially completed during the period exceed asset outflows expenses and losses associated, directly or indirectly, with the same cycles.

Further guidance in applying the criteria for recognizing components of earnings is necessary because of the widely acknowledged importance of earnings as a primary measure of entity performance. Guidance for recognizing components of earnings is concerned with identifying which cycles are substantially complete and with associating particular revenues, gains, expenses, and losses with those cycles.

The monetary unit or measurement scale in current practice in financial statements is nominal units of money, that is, unadjusted for changes in purchasing power of money over time. The Board expects that nominal units of money will continue to be used to measure items recognized in financial statements.

Earnings and comprehensive income are not the same because certain gains and losses are included in comprehensive income but are excluded from earnings. Those items fall into three classes that are illustrated by certain present practices:

- Foreign currency translation adjustments
- Minimum pension liability adjustments
- Unrealized gains and losses on certain investments in debt and equity securities (example: available-for-sale marketable securities)

THREE OTHER EXAMPLES OF OTHER COMPREHENSIVE INCOME

SFAS #133 – Accounting for derivatives and hedging activities added the following additional items to be included in comprehensive income:

- Gains or losses on cash flow hedges.
- Gains or losses on hedges of forecasted foreign-currency-denominated transactions.
- Gains or losses on hedging of a net investment in a foreign operation are reported in ***comprehensive income*** as part of the translation adjustment.

A variety of terms are used for net income in present practice. The Board anticipates that a variety of terms will be used in future financial statements as names for earnings for example, net income, profit, or net loss and for comprehensive income for example, total nonowner changes in equity or comprehensive loss.

Comprehensive income is a broad measure of the effects of transactions and other events on an entity, comprising all recognized changes in equity net assets of the entity during a period from transactions and other events and circumstances except those resulting from investments by owners and distributions to owners. Comprehensive income is closely related to the concept of capital maintenance. The full set of financial statements discussed in this Statement is based on the concept of **financial** capital maintenance. The concept of capital maintenance applied to a particular enterprise will have a direct effect on what is included in comprehensive income. Under the financial capital approach, the effects of changing prices will be included in comprehensive income. Under the physical capital approach, the effects of changing prices will not be included. In other words, physical and financial can be used to separate return **on** capital (earnings) from return **of** capital (capital recovery). Assume the company has $ 1,000 in inventory and at the end of the year the company sells it for $1,500. Also consider that at the end of the year the company needs to spend $1,200 to replace the inventory.

Under the financial capital approach, $1,000 is considered return of investment and $500 is considered return on capital or income. In other words, the effects of changing prices on assets and liabilities are holding gains and losses and part of the return on capital being earned by the enterprise. The objective is to maintain purchasing power.

Under the physical capital approach, $1,200 is considered the sum that must be reinvested to replenish the inventory, and $300 is considered return on capital or income. In other words, the operating capability of the enterprise must be maintained. As a result, changing prices would be part of capital maintenance rather than return on capital. The effects of those changes, referred to as capital maintenance adjustments, are included directly in equity. The objective is to maintain operating capacity.

Future standards may change what is recognized as components of earnings. Future standards may also recognize certain changes in net assets as components of comprehensive income but not of earnings.

A statement of cash flows directly or indirectly reflects an entity's cash receipts classified by major sources and its cash payments classified by major uses during a period, including cash flow information about its operating, financing, and investing activities.

A statement of investments by and distributions to owners reflects an entity's capital transactions during a period—the extent to which and in what ways the equity increased or decreased from transactions with owners as owners.

An item and information about it should meet four fundamental recognition criteria to be recognized and should be recognized when the criteria are met, subject to a cost-benefit constraint and a materiality threshold. Those criteria are:

- *Definitions* -- The item meets the definition of an element of financial statements.
- *Measurability* -- It has a relevant attribute measurable with sufficient reliability.
- *Relevance* -- The information about it is capable of making a difference in user decisions.
- *Reliability* -- The information is representationally faithful, verifiable, and neutral.

Items currently reported in the financial statements are measured by different attributes (for example, historical cost, current [replacement] cost, current market value, net realizable value, and present value of future cash flows), depending on the nature of the item and the relevance and reliability of the attribute measured. The Board expects use of different attributes to continue.

Guidance for recognizing revenues and gains is based on their being:

- *Realized or realizable* -- Revenues and gains are generally not recognized as components of earnings until realized or realizable and
- *Earned* -- Revenues are not recognized until earned. Revenues are considered to have been earned when the entity has substantially accomplished what it must do to be entitled to the benefits represented by the revenues. For gains, being earned is generally less significant than being realized or realizable.

Guidance for expenses and losses is intended to recognize:

- *Consumption of benefit* -- Expenses are generally recognized when an entity's economic benefits are consumed in revenue-earning activities or otherwise or
- *Loss or lack of benefit* -- Expenses or losses are recognized if it becomes evident that previously recognized future economic benefits of assets have been reduced or eliminated, or that liabilities have been incurred or increased, without associated economic benefits.

In a limited number of situations, the Board may determine that the most useful information results from recognizing the effects of certain events in comprehensive income but not in earnings, and set standards accordingly. Certain changes in net assets that meet the fundamental recognition criteria may qualify for recognition in comprehensive income even though they do not qualify for recognition as components of earnings.

Information based on current prices should be recognized if it is sufficiently relevant and reliable to justify the costs involved and more relevant than alternative information.

Most aspects of current practice are consistent with the recognition criteria and guidance in this Statement, but the criteria and guidance do not foreclose the possibility of future changes in practice. When evidence indicates that information that is more useful (relevant and reliable) than information currently reported is available at a justifiable cost, it should be included in financial statements.

The statement included the following diagram illustrating the umbrella of financial reporting and GAAP.

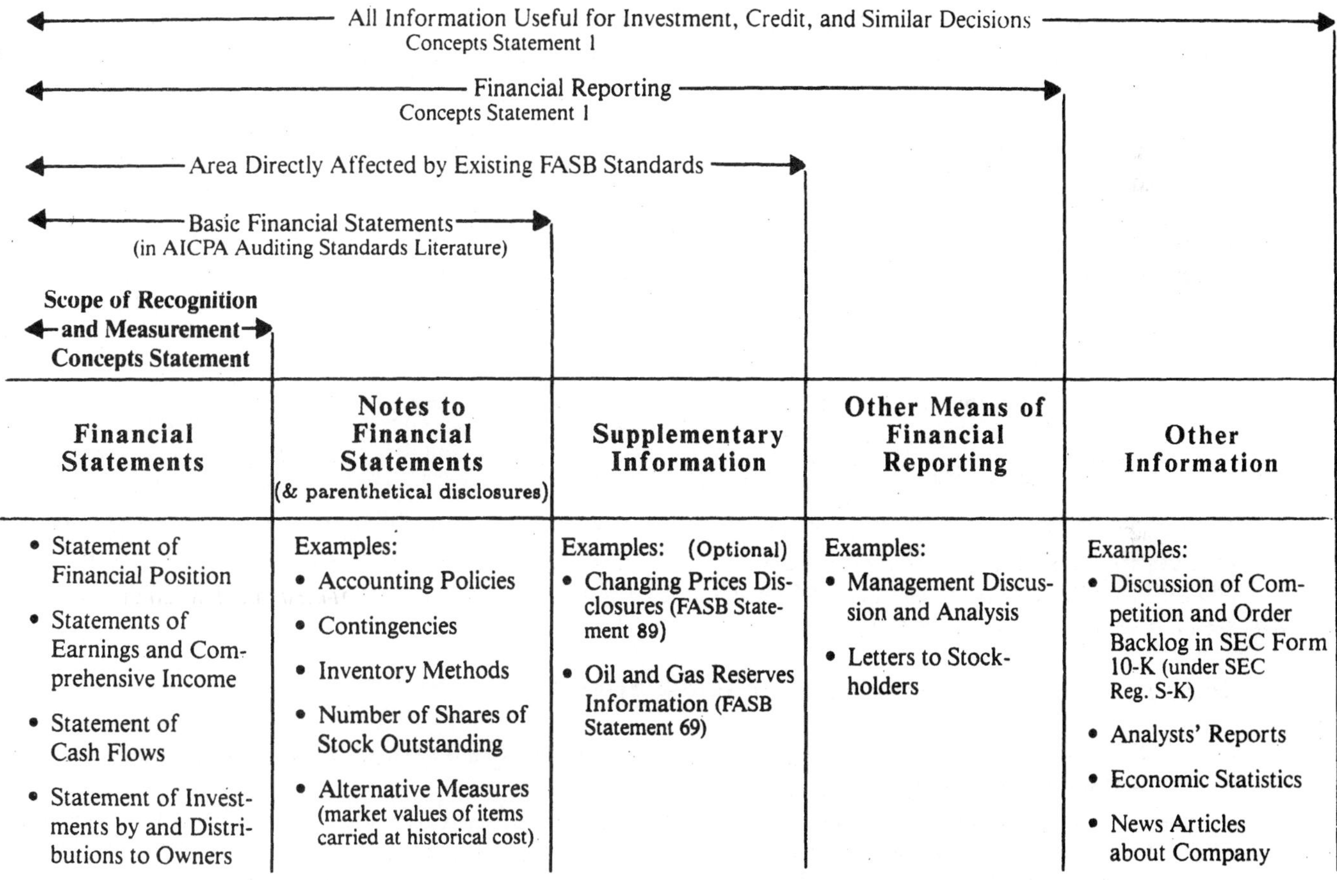

GENERALLY ACCEPTED ACCOUNTING PRINCIPLES

An accounting principle is "generally accepted" if it is an official pronouncement or has other substantial authoritative support. GAAP is a technical term in financial accounting, encompassing the conventions, rules, and procedures necessary to define accepted accounting practice at a particular time. The standard of "generally accepted accounting principles" includes not only broad guidelines of general application, but also detailed practices and procedures. GAAP is conventional—that is, principles become generally accepted by tacit agreement. The principles have developed on the basis of experience, reason, custom, usage, and practical necessity. In recent years, Opinions of the Accounting Principles Board and standards of the Financial Accounting Standards Board have received considerable emphasis as a major determinant of the composition of generally accepted accounting principles.

GAAP is the result of an evolutionary process and can be expected to change over time. Principles change in response to changes in economic and social conditions, to new knowledge and technology, and to demands by users for more useful information. GAAP as defined by rule 203 of the Code of Professional Conduct of the American Institute of Certified Public Accountants, includes:

Accounting Research Bulletins
Accounting Principles Board Opinions
Financial Accounting Standards Board Statements
Financial Accounting Standards Board Interpretations

The AICPA issued ARBs at the beginning and created the APB later. Some of these bulletins and opinions have been superseded by the Financial Accounting Standards Board, issuing the Statements Financial Accounting Standards. In addition to statements, the FASB issues interpretations that cover various clarifications of previous official pronouncements. Statements of Financial Accounting Concepts are also issued by the FASB. A conceptual statement does not have the same authority under Code of Conduct rule 203 as statements and interpretations. Instead, they are viewed as general frameworks on which specific rules will be built.

If an area is not covered by an official pronouncement, then GAAP consists of other support, such as pronouncements of the SEC or other regulatory bodies, textbooks, or industry practice. Generally accepted accounting principles are divided into three sections: pervasive principles, which relate to financial accounting as a whole and provide a basis for the other principles; broad operating principles, which guide the recording, measuring, and communicating processes of financial accounting; and detailed principles, which indicate the practical application of the pervasive and broad operating principles. Depicted below is the GAAP Hierarchy.

GAAP HIERARCHY SUMMARY* (SAS 69)

Note: If a specified accounting procedure cannot be found in category 10a, the auditor/accountant would proceed to the next lowest category.

Established Accounting Principles:

10a. FASB Statements and Interpretations, APB Opinions, and AICPA Accounting Research Bulletins.

10b. FASB Technical Bulletins, AICPA Industry Audit and Accounting Guides, and AICPA Statements of Position.

10c. Consensus positions of the FASB Emerging Issues Task Force and AICPA Practice Bulletins.

10d. AICPA accounting interpretations, "Qs and As" published by the FASB staff, as well as industry practices widely recognized and prevalent.

Other Accounting Literature:**

11. Other accounting literature, including FASB Concepts Statements; APB Statements; AICPA Issues Papers; International Accounting Standards Committee Statements; GASB Statements, Interpretations, and Technical Bulletins; pronouncements of other professional associations or regulatory agencies; AICPA *Technical Practice Aids*; and accounting textbooks, handbooks, and articles.

* Paragraph references correspond to the paragraphs of this Statement that describe the categories of the GAAP hierarchy.

** In the absence of established accounting principles, the auditor may consider other accounting literature, depending on its relevance in the circumstances.

The pervasive principles are few in number and fundamental in nature. The broad operating principles derived from the pervasive principles are more numerous and more specific, and guide the application of a series of detailed principles. The detailed principles are numerous and specific. When more than one pronouncement relates to a given issue or type of transaction, an individual can determine which pronouncement is the most authoritative based upon this hierarchy.

Financial statements can be prepared using principles other than those defined in official pronouncements if, due to very unusual conditions, following the official pronouncement would seriously mislead the statement's reader. The independent CPA is required to follow GAAP via Rule 203 of the AICPA Code of Professional Conduct. This rule indicates that an opinion shall not be issued if statements contain a departure from accounting principles unless the CPA can demonstrate that due to unusual circumstances the financial statements would otherwise be misleading. If such a departure exists, the report should describe the departure, the approximate effect on the financial statements, and the reasons why compliance with the principle would result in a misleading statement. Justification for departure from the official pronouncements would not include reasons such as materiality of the amount or industry practice that is contrary to the pronouncements. Circumstances that permit departure from an official pronouncement are extremely rare, and, in fact, very few audit opinions have indicated a departure from the official pronouncement concept of GAAP.

UNDERLYING PRINCIPLES

Revenue Recognition: Revenue is recognized when it is earned, measurable and collectible, that is when the income earning process is complete and an exchange has taken place.

Matching: Dictates that efforts and expenses be matched with the revenue of the period. Some costs are recognized as expenses on the basis of a presumed direct association with specific revenue. Examples of expenses that are recognized by associating cause and effect are sales commissions and costs of products sold or services provided. In the absence of a direct match, some costs are associated with specific accounting periods as expenses in a systematic and rational manner among the periods in which benefits are provided. Examples of items that are recognized in a systematic and rational manner are depreciation of fixed assets, amortization of intangible assets, and allocation of rent and insurance. Some costs associated with the current accounting period are expensed immediately because costs incurred during the period provide no future benefits, costs recorded as assets in prior periods no longer provide discernible benefits, or allocating costs serve no useful purpose. Examples include officers' salaries, selling costs, amounts paid to settle lawsuits.

Unit of Measure: While adequate disclosure requires information about nonmonetary events, comparability and understandability of financial information are enhanced if it is presented in terms of a common denominator. Measurement in terms of money is not completely accurate since the value of money changes over time, but it is the most understandable basis available. The US. dollar is the unit of measure in financial accounting in the United States. Changes in its general purchasing power are not recognized in the basic financial statements.

Historical Cost: As a measurement basis, historical cost is the most objectively determinable and it is the proper basis for recording assets, equity, costs, and expenses. However, five measurement attributes are used in current practice.

Historical cost - historical proceeds
Current replacement cost
Current market value
Net realizable value
Present - discounted value of future cash flows

Separate Entity: Accounting information is reported as if the business were separate from its owners, customers, employees, and creditors. When consolidated statements are prepared for a group of related businesses, the group is the assumed entity; separate statements for each business assume a different definition of the entity to enhance the usefulness of information.

Disclosure: For information to be relevant, there must be adequate disclosure. This implies knowledge of the use to which the information will be put to differentiate between relevant and irrelevant disclosures.

Going Concern: Unless there is other evidence, accounting information assumes the company will continue in operation long enough to realize its objectives and fulfill its legal obligations.

Objectivity/Verifiability: Information should be free from bias on the part of the individual who prepared the information. If several independent individuals examined the same transactions and used the same reporting principles, the accounting information prepared by each should be the same.

Periodicity: Because of the need for timely information, accounting information is reported for set time intervals. While different time periods might be appropriate for different types of companies, it is generally accepted that information related to annual periods is reported annually.

Consistency: To achieve comparability of accounting information over time, the same accounting methods must be followed. If accounting methods are changed from period to period the effects of the change are disclosed.

MODIFYING CONVENTIONS

Conservatism: Historically, managers, investors, and accountants have generally preferred that possible errors in measurement be in the direction of understatement rather than overstatement of net income and net assets. This has led to the convention of conservatism, which is expressed in rules adopted by the profession as a whole, such as the rule that inventory should be measured at the lower of cost or market. These rules may result in stated net income and net assets at amounts lower than would otherwise result from applying the pervasive measurement principles. Therefore, when confronted with alternative accounting procedures, the accountant follows that which has the least favorable impact on current income. If there are no reasons that make one accounting treatment preferable to another, the least favorable effect on current operations is selected. Losses may be anticipated while gains are normally not recognized in the accounts until they are realized. There is a relationship between the relevance and reliability of accounting information with the convention of conservatism. Conservatism ensures that the uncertainty and risks inherent in business situations are adequately considered. Conservatism should not imply the deliberate understatement of assets and profits and should lead toward fairness of presentation. An attempt to understate results on a consistent basis will lead accounting information to be unreliable.

Emphasis on Income: Over the years, financial statement users, and accountants have increasingly tended to emphasize the importance of net income and that trend has affected the emphasis in financial accounting. Accounting principles that are deemed to increase the usefulness of the income statement are, therefore, sometimes adopted by the profession as a whole regardless of their effect on the balance sheet or other financial statements. For example, the last-in, first-out method of inventory pricing may result in balance sheet amounts for inventories that become further removed from current prices with the passage of time. LIFO, however, is often supported on the grounds that it usually produces an amount for cost of goods sold in determining net income that more closely reflects current prices.

Application of Judgment: Sometimes, strict adherence to the pervasive measurement principles produces results that are considered by the accounting profession to be unreasonable in the circumstances or misleading. The exception to the usual revenue realization rule for long-term, construction-type contracts, for example, is justified in part because adherence to realization at the time of sale would produce results that are considered to be unreasonable. The judgment of the profession is that revenue should be recognized in this situation as construction progresses.

Materiality: If information is insignificant, it has no effect on the decisions of an accounting information user, therefore, there is no need to report that information. Materiality cannot be precisely defined, but is related to absolute values and relationships of an amount to other accounting information.

Industry Practices: Departure from strict compliance with GAAP may exist in some cases due to the peculiar nature of the industry in which an enterprise operates.

Substance over Form: The economic substance of a transaction determines the accounting treatment, even though the legal form of the transaction may indicate a different treatment. In some cases, strict adherence to GAAP produces results that are unreasonable. because the legal form of a transaction does not fully represent the underlying intentions of that transaction. For example, some leases are actually purchases of assets, although the legal form of the transaction is a lease, the true intent of a transaction differs from its legal form, the profession supports reporting substance rather than legal form.

Summary of Conceptual Framework

Objectives

Provide Information

1. Useful in rational investment and credit decisions
2. Useful in assessing future cash flows
3. About enterprise resources, claims to resources and changes in them

Qualitative Characteristics

1. **Pervasive Constraint**
   Benefits exceed costs
2. **User Specific Qualities**
   A. Understandability
   B. Decision usefulness
3. **Primary Qualities**
   A. Relevance
      1. Predictive Value
      2. Feedback Value
      3. Timeliness
   B. Reliability
      1. Verifiability
      2. Representational faithfulness
      3. Neutrality
4. **Secondary Qualities**
   A. Comparability
   B. Consistency

Elements

1. Assets
2. Liabilities
3. Equity
4. Investment by owners
5. Distribution to owners
6. Comprehensive income
7. Revenues
8. Expenses
9. Gains
10. Losses

Recognition and Measurement Concepts

ASSUMPTIONS

1. Economic entity
2. Going concern
3. Monetary unit
4. Periodicity

UNDERLYING PRINCIPLES

1. Historical cost
2. Revenue recognition
3. Matching
4. Full disclosure
5. Consistency

MODIFYING CONVENTIONS

1. Cost-benefit
2. Materiality
3. Industry practice
4. Conservatism
5. Substance over form
6. Judgment

Chapter Seven
Accounting Theory Questions

OFFICIAL PRONOUNCEMENTS

1. FASB Interpretations of Statements of Financial Accounting Standards have the same authority as the FASB
a. Statements of Financial Accounting Concepts.
b. Emerging Issues Task Force Consensus.
c. Technical Bulletins.
d. Statements of Financial Accounting Standards.

2. Which of the following accounting pronouncements is the most authoritative?
a. FASB Statement of Financial Accounting Concepts.
b. FASB Technical Bulletin.
c. AICPA Accounting Principles Board Opinion.
d. AICPA Statement of Position.

DEFINITIONS

3. According to the FASB's conceptual framework, the process of reporting an item in the financial statements of an entity is
a. Recognition.
b. Realization.
c. Allocation.
d. Matching.

4. Determining periodic earnings and financial position depends on measuring economic resources and obligations and changes in them as these changes occur. This explanation pertains to
a. Disclosure.
b. Accrual accounting.
c. Materiality.
d. The matching concept.

SFAC #2 -- A HIERARCHY OF ACCOUNTING QUALITIES

5. Which of the following is considered a pervasive constraint by Statement of Financial Accounting Concepts No. 2?
a. Benefits/costs.
b. Conservatism.
c. Timeliness.
d. Verifiability.

6. Under Statement of Financial Accounting Concepts No. 2, which of the following relates to both relevance and reliability?
a. Timeliness.
b. Materiality.
c. Verifiability.
d. Neutrality.

7. According to the FASB conceptual framework, predictive value is an ingredient of

	Reliability	*Relevance*
a.	Yes	Yes
b.	No	Yes
c.	No	No
d.	Yes	No

8. According to the FASB conceptual framework, which of the following relates to both relevance and reliability?
a. Comparability.
b. Feedback value.
c. Verifiability.
d. Timeliness.

9. According to the FASB conceptual framework, predictive value is an ingredient of

	Relevance	*Reliability*
a.	No	No
b.	Yes	Yes
c.	No	Yes
d.	Yes	No

10. According to the FASB Conceptual Framework, which of the following relates to both relevance and reliability?

	Consistency	*Verifiability*
a.	Yes	Yes
b.	Yes	No
c.	No	Yes
d.	No	No

SFAC #5 -- COMPREHENSIVE INCOME

11. According to the FASB Conceptual Framework, earnings
a. Are the same as comprehensive income.
b. Exclude certain gains and losses that are included in comprehensive income.
c. Include certain gains and losses that are excluded from comprehensive income.
d. Include certain losses that are excluded from comprehensive income.

12. According to the FASB's conceptual framework, comprehensive income includes which of the following?

	Operating income	*Investments by owners*
a.	Yes	No
b.	Yes	Yes
c.	No	Yes
d.	No	No

13. Under FASB Statement of Financial Accounting Concepts No. 5, which of the following items would cause earnings to differ from comprehensive income for an enterprise in an industry **not** having specialized accounting principles?
a. Unrealized loss on investments in available-for-sale marketable equity securities.
b. Unrealized loss on investments in trading marketable equity securities.
c. Loss on exchange of similar assets.
d. Loss on exchange of dissimilar assets.

14. According to the FASB's conceptual framework, comprehensive income includes which of the following?

	Gross margin	*Operating income*
a.	No	Yes
b.	No	No
c.	Yes	No
d.	Yes	Yes

15. Under Statements of Financial Accounting Concepts, comprehensive income includes which of the following?

	Gains	*Gross Margin*
a.	No	No
b.	No	Yes
c.	Yes	No
d.	Yes	Yes

BASIC THEORY

16. The principle of objectivity includes the concept of
a. Summarization.
b. Classification.
c. Conservatism.
d. Verifiability.

17. What is the underlying concept that supports the immediate recognition of a contingent loss?
a. Substance over form.
b. Consistency.
c. Matching.
d. Conservatism.

18. Revenue is generally recognized when the earning process is virtually complete and an exchange has taken place. What principle is described herein?
a. Consistency.
b. Matching.
c. Realization.
d. Conservatism.

19. Periodic net earnings are conventionally measured by a

a. Transactions approach.
b. Transactions approach including recognition of unrealized gains and losses.
c. Capital maintenance approach.
d. Market value approach including recognition of all realized gains and some unrealized losses.

20. Under what condition is it proper to recognize revenues prior to the sale of the merchandise?

a. When the ultimate sale of the goods is at an assured sales price.
b. When the revenue is to be reported as an installment sale.
c. When the concept of internal consistency (of amounts of revenue) must be complied with.
d. When management has a long-established policy to do so.

REVIEW QUESTIONS

21. Under Statement of Financial Accounting Concepts No. 2, feedback value is an ingredient of the primary quality of

	Relevance	*Reliability*
a.	No	No
b.	No	Yes
c.	Yes	Yes
d.	Yes	No

22. According to the FASB's conceptual framework, asset valuation accounts are

a. Assets.
b. Neither assets nor liabilities.
c. Part of stockholders' equity.
d. Liabilities.

23. According to the FASB conceptual framework, which of the following is an essential characteristic of an asset?

a. The claims to an asset's benefits are legally enforceable.
b. An asset is tangible.
c. An asset is obtained at a cost.
d. An asset provides future benefits.

24. According to the FASB conceptual framework, which of the following situations violates the concept of reliability?

a. Financial statements were issued nine months late.
b. Report data on segments having the same expected risks and growth rates to analysts estimating future profits.
c. Financial statements included property with a carrying amount increased to management's estimates of market value.
d. Management reports to stockholders regularly refer to new projects undertaken, but the financial statements never report project results.

25. Under Statement of Financial Accounting Concepts No. 2, timeliness is an ingredient of the primary quality of

a. Reliability.
b. Relevance.
c. Verifiability.
d. Representational faithfulness.

26. According to the FASB conceptual framework, an entity's revenue may result from

a. A decrease in an asset from primary operations.
b. An increase in an asset from incidental transactions.
c. An increase in a liability from incidental transactions.
d. A decrease in a liability from primary operations.

27. The FASB's conceptual framework classifies gains and losses based on whether they are related to an entity's major ongoing or central operations. These gains or losses may be classified as

	Nonoperating	*Operating*
a.	Yes	No
b.	Yes	Yes
c.	No	Yes
d.	No	No

28. Under Statement of Financial Accounting Concepts No. 2, which of the following interacts with both relevance and reliability to contribute to the usefulness of information?

a. Comparability.
b. Timeliness.
c. Neutrality.
d. Predictive value.

29. According to Statements of Financial Accounting Concepts, neutrality is an ingredient of

	Reliability	*Relevance*
a.	Yes	Yes
b.	Yes	No
c.	No	Yes
d.	No	No

30. The basis for classifying assets as current or noncurrent is the period of time normally elapsed from the time the accounting entity expends cash to the time it converts

a. Inventory back into cash, or 12 months, whichever is shorter.
b. Receivables back into cash, or 12 months, whichever is longer.
c. Tangible fixed assets back into cash, or 12 months, whichever is longer.
d. Inventory back into cash, or 12 months, whichever is longer.

31. Which of the following is an application of the principle of systematic and rational allocation?

a. Amortization of intangible assets.
b. Sales commissions.
c. Research and development costs.
d. Officers' salaries.

32. In analyzing a company's financial statements, which financial statement would a potential investor primarily use to assess the company's liquidity and financial flexibility?

a. Balance sheet.
b. Income statement.
c. Statement of retained earnings.
d. Statement of cash flows.

33. FASB's conceptual framework explains both financial and physical capital maintenance concepts. Which capital maintenance concept is applied to currently reported net income, and which is applied to comprehensive income?

	Currently reported net income	*Comprehensive income*
a.	Financial capital	Physical capital
b.	Physical capital	Physical capital
c.	Financial capital	Financial capital
d.	Physical capital	Financial capital

34. According to the FASB conceptual framework, the objectives of financial reporting for business enterprises are based on

a. The need for conservatism.
b. Reporting on management's stewardship.
c. Generally accepted accounting principles.
d. The needs of the users of the information.

35. According to the FASB conceptual framework, which of the following statements conforms to the realization concept?

a. Equipment depreciation was assigned to a production department and then to product unit costs.
b. Depreciated equipment was sold in exchange for a note receivable.
c. Cash was collected on accounts receivable.
d. Product unit costs were assigned to cost of goods sold when the units were sold.

36. In the hierarchy of generally accepted accounting principles, APB Opinions have the same authority as AICPA.

a. Statements of Position.
b. Industry Audit and Accounting Guides.
c. Issues Papers.
d. Accounting Research Bulletins.

37. What are the Statements of Financial Accounting Concepts intended to establish?

a. Generally accepted accounting principles in financial reporting by business enterprises.
b. The meaning of "Present fairly in accordance with generally accepted accounting principles."
c. The objectives and concepts for use in developing standards of financial accounting and reporting.
d. The hierarchy of sources of generally accepted accounting principles.

38. Reporting inventory at the lower of cost or market is a departure from the accounting principle of

a. Historical cost.
b. Consistency.
c. Conservatism.
d. Full disclosure.

39. During a period when an enterprise is under the direction of a particular management, its financial statements will directly provide information about

a. Both enterprise performance and management performance.
b. Management performance but **not** directly provide information about enterprise performance.
c. Enterprise performance but **not** directly provide information about management performance.
d. Neither enterprise performance nor management performance.

40. What is the purpose of information presented in notes to the financial statements?

a. To provide disclosures required by generally accepted accounting principles.
b. To correct improper presentation in the financial statements.
c. To provide recognition of amounts **not** included in the totals of the financial statements.
d. To present management's responses to auditor comments.

41. According to the FASB conceptual framework, which of the following situations violates the concept of reliability?

a. Data on segments having the same expected risks and growth rates are reported to analysts estimating future profits.
b. Financial statements are issued nine months late.
c. Management reports to stockholders regularly refer to new projects undertaken, but the financial statements never report project results.
d. Financial statements include property with a carrying amount increased to management's estimate of market value.

42. One of the elements of a financial statement is comprehensive income. Comprehensive income excludes changes in equity resulting from which of the following?

a. Loss from discontinued operations.
b. Prior period error correction.
c. Dividends paid to stockholders.
d. Unrealized loss on investments in noncurrent marketable equity securities.

43. According to the FASB conceptual framework, the objectives of financial reporting for business enterprises are based on

a. Generally accepted accounting principles.
b. Reporting on management's stewardship.
c. The need for conservatism.
d. The needs of the users of the information.

44. According to the FASB conceptual framework, the usefulness of providing information in financial statements is subject to the constraint of

a. Consistency.
b. Cost-benefit.
c. Reliability.
d. Representational faithfulness.

RECENTLY DISCLOSED QUESTIONS

M98

45. According to the FASB conceptual framework, comprehensive income includes which of the following?

	Loss on Discontinued Operations	Investment by Owners
a.	Yes	Yes
b.	Yes	No
c.	No	Yes
d.	No	No

Chapter Seven
Accounting Theory Problems

NUMBER 1

The concept of the accounting entity often is considered to be the most fundamental of accounting concepts, one that pervades all of accounting.

Required:

a. 1. What is an accounting entity? Explain.

2. Explain why the accounting entity concept is so fundamental that it pervades all of accounting.

b. For each of the following indicate whether the accounting concept of entity is applicable; discuss and give illustrations.

1. A unit created by or under law.
2. The product-line segment of an enterprise.
3. A combination of legal units and/or product-line segments.
4. All of the activities of an owner or a group of owners.
5. An industry.
6. The economy of the United States.

NUMBER 2

Valuation of assets is an important topic in accounting theory. Suggested valuation methods include the following:

Historical cost (past purchase prices)
Historical cost adjusted to reflect general price-level changes
Discounted cash flow (future exchange prices)
Market price (current selling prices)
Replacement cost (current purchase prices)

Required:

1. Why is the valuation of assets a significant issue?
2. Explain the basic theory underlying **each** of the valuation methods cited above. **Do not discuss advantages and disadvantages of each method.**

NUMBER 3

N93

Mono Tech Co. began operations in 1989 and confined its activities to one project. It purchased equipment to be used exclusively for research and development on the project, and other equipment that is to be used initially for research and development and subsequently for production. In 1990, Mono constructed and paid for a pilot plant that was used until December 1991 to determine the best manufacturing process for the project's product. In December 1991, Mono obtained a patent and received cash from the sale of the pilot plant. In 1992, a factory was constructed and commercial manufacture of the product began.

Required:

a. 1. According to the FASB conceptual framework, what are the three essential characteristics of an asset?

2. How do Mono's project expenditures through 1991 meet the FASB conceptual framework's three essential characteristics of an asset? Do **not** discuss why the expenditures may **not** meet the characteristics of an asset.

3. Why is it difficult to justify the classification of research and development expenditures as assets?

Chapter Seven
Solutions to Accounting Theory Questions

1. (d) FASB Statements of Financial Accounting Standards and Interpretations of those Standards are generally accepted accounting principles as designated by rule 203 of the AICPA's Code of Conduct. All of the other choices may be considered in determining GAAP, but are at a lower level of authority.

2. (c) The most authoritative accounting pronouncements are Accounting Research Bulletins, APB Opinions and FASB Statements of Financial Accounting Standards. FASB Statements of Financial Accounting Concepts, FASB Technical Bulletins and AICPA Statements of Position carry less authority.

3. (a) SFAC #5 defines "recognition" as the process of formally incorporating an item into the financial statements of an entity as an asset, liability, revenue, or expense.

4. (b) Accrual accounting requires measurement based upon changes in economic conditions rather than changes in cash. The other responses do not concur at all with the information given.

5. (a) SFAC #2 identified benefits/costs as pervasive constraints of accounting information.

6. (b) Timeliness relates only to relevance and verifiability and neutrality relates only to reliability. Materiality relates to both relevance and reliability.

7. (b) As indicated in the hierarchy of accounting qualities, predictive value is an ingredient of relevance but not reliability.

8. (a) In the Hierarchy of Accounting Qualities (SFAC #2), comparability relates to both relevance and reliability.

9. (d) As indicated in the hierarchy of accounting qualities in SFAC #2, predictive value is an ingredient of relevance but not reliability.

10. (b) SFAC #2 points out that consistency (comparability) relates to both relevance and reliability. However, verifiability relates only to reliability.

11. (b) Comprehensive income is broader than earnings and includes certain gains and losses not included in earnings. Examples are holding losses or gains on available-for-sale marketable equity securities, foreign currency translation adjustments and minimum pension liability adjustments.

12. (a) Comprehensive income includes any type of inflow which culminates an earnings process. There is no earnings process involved in investment by owners.

13. (a) The losses described in (b), (c) and (d) are recognized in earnings as well as in comprehensive income. An unrealized loss on investments in available-for-sale marketable equity securities is not recognized in current earnings but is a factor in measuring comprehensive income.

14. (d) Comprehensive income is a broad measure of the changes in equity over a period except for contributions from, or distributions to, owners.

15. (d) Comprehensive income includes all income items which ultimately increase equity from transactions related to nonowner sources.

16. (d) Objectivity implies the independent verifiability of financial information.

17. (d) The immediate recognition of a contingent loss is an example of **conservatism.** Concepts Statement #2 defines conservatism as "a prudent reaction to uncertainty to try to ensure that uncertainty and risks inherent in business situations are adequately considered."

18. (c) Realization occurs when the earnings process is complete, e.g., an exchange has taken place and the company received cash or has a claim against another company.

19. (a) Periodic net earnings are normally measured by matching expense transactions and revenue transactions.

20. (a) Only when the ultimate sales price of the product is assured may revenue be recognized prior to sale.

21. (d) Feedback value is an ingredient of the primary quality of relevance.

22. (b) Financial Accounting Concepts #6 states that valuation accounts are part of the related assets or liabilities and neither assets nor liabilities in their own right.

23. (d) By definition, the key element of an asset is its future use or potential.

24. (c) For information to be reliable it must be neutral, verifiable and must represent what it purports to represent (representational faithfulness). To present property at market value instead of carrying is a misrepresentation which causes the financial statements to be unreliable.

25. (b) Timeliness is an ingredient of relevance.

26. (d) SFAC #6 states that gains and losses but not revenues and expenses result from incidental or peripheral transactions. Revenues result from decreases in liabilities or increases in assets from primary operations.

27. (b) Gains or losses are part of comprehensive income but may or may not be from operations or operations-related activities.

28. (a) Comparability interacts with both relevance and reliability.

29. (b) Neutrality is the absence of bias. Concepts Statement #2 lists neutrality, verifiability, and representational faithfulness as elements of **reliability.**

30. (d) Current assets are those assets which are expected to be used or realized in cash during the next operating cycle, which can be defined as the time elapsed from the time the company spends cash until it turns inventory back into cash, or 12 months, whichever is longer.

31. (a) The other responses are not subject to allocation on a systematic and rational basis.

32. (a) Concepts Statement #5 states that the balance sheet includes "information that is often used in assessing an entity's liquidity and financial flexibility." The current assets are listed in order of liquidity which should allow an assessment of their nearness to cash. An overall analysis of the balance sheet should indicate the financial flexibility to respond to unexpected events.

33. (c) The financial capital maintenance concept defines income as the change in net resources other than owner transactions. Therefore, the dollar investment is subtracted to determine income. This concept is used in the definitions of GAAP net income and comprehensive income. The physical capital maintenance concept defines income as the change in physical production capabilities other than owner transactions. Thus, the current values of assets and liabilities invested in the firm must be deducted to determine net income. Increases or decreases due to price changes for the same capability are not included in net income. This concept is not currently used for GAAP for either net or comprehensive income.

34. (d) The function of reporting is to provide information that is useful to those who make economic decisions. Conservatism, management's stewardship, and generally accepted accounting principles are used in providing the information, not the objective per se.

35. (b) Revenues and gains are **realized** when products or other assets are exchanged for cash or claims to cash. The depreciated equipment was sold in exchange for a note receivable, meaning that the resulting gain had been realized. Choice (a) deals with allocation, (c) deals with conversion of accounts receivable into cash, and (d) deals with matching.

36. (d) In the GAAP hierarchy the highest level of authority is given to FASB Statements and Interpretations, APB Opinions, and the AICPA Accounting Research Bulletins which all have the same weight. The Statements of Position, Industry Audit and Accounting Guides, and the Issues Papers all have a lower weight.

37. (c) FASB C-1 intends to establish objectives and concepts for use in developing the standards of financial accounting and reporting to be used as a guideline that will lead to consistent standards. **GAAP** is a technical term that encompasses the conventions, rules, and procedures not only in broad guidelines but also detailed procedures developed on the basis of experience, reason, custom and practical need. **ASB** (Auditing Standards Board) is responsible for developing choice (b). The AICPA's Code of Conduct establishes the hierarchy of sources.

38. (a) ARB 43 states that "a departure from the cost basis of pricing the inventory is required when the utility of the goods is no longer as great as its costs...and the difference should be recognized as a loss of the current period." This utility is considered to be their market value, therefore the term **Lower of Cost or Market. Consistency** is the application of the same accounting principle from one period to the next. **Conservatism** is the practice of avoiding an overly optimistic presentation of assets, income and owner's equity in the financial statements.

39. (c) Financial statements provide information about the financial position or operations of an organization for a stated period, but they do not directly provide information about management performance.

40. (a) Notes to the financial statements provide disclosures required by GAAP necessary to better explain essential additional information to complement the information recognized in the financial statements. The notes are considered an **"integral part of the financial statements."**

41. (d) For information to be reliable, it must be verifiable, free from bias (neutral) and faithfully represent what is described. Financial statements which include property whose carrying amount has been increased to **management's estimate of fair value** can not be considered reliable. The write up to fair value can not be verified and is certainly not free from bias.

42. (c) Comprehensive income is the change in equity (net assets) of an enterprise during a period from transactions and other events and circumstances from nonowner sources. It includes all changes in equity during a period except those resulting from investments by owners or distributions to owners. In this case, **dividends paid to stockholders** would be distributions to owners and not a part of comprehensive income.

43. (d) FASB #1 Concepts Statement states that one objective of financial reporting is to provide information that is **useful to present and potential investors and creditors and other users** in making rational investment, credit and other similar decisions.

44. (b) FASB Concepts Statement #2 in its hierarchy of accounting qualities lists cost/benefits as a pervasive constraint. This means that financial information will not be required unless its benefits (usefulness) exceed its cost to product the information.

45. (b) SFAC 6 defines comprehensive income as a broad measure of the effects of transactions and the events on an entity, comprising all recognized changes in net assets of an entity during a period from transactions and other events and circumstances except those resulting from investments by owners and distributions to owners. Therefore, investments by owners in this example would not be a part of comprehensive income.

Chapter Seven
Solutions to Accounting Theory Problems

NUMBER 1

a. 1. The conventional or traditional approach has been to define the accounting entity in terms of a specific firm or enterprise unit that is separate and apart from the owner or owners and from other enterprises having separate legal and accounting frames of reference. For example, partnerships and sole proprietorships were accounted for separately from the owners although such a distinction might not exist legally. Thus it was recognized that the transactions of the enterprise should be accounted for and reported upon separately from those of the owners.

An extension of this approach is to define the accounting entity in terms of an economic unit that controls resources, makes and carries out commitments and conducts economic activity. In the broadest sense an accounting entity could embrace any object, event or attribute of an object or event for which there is an input-output relationship. Such an accounting entity may be an individual, a profit-seeking or not-for-profit enterprise or any subdivision or attribute thereof for which a system of accounts is maintained. Thus this approach is oriented toward the unit for which financial reports are prepared.

An alternative approach is to define the accounting entity in terms of an area of economic interest to a particular individual, group or institution. The boundaries of such an economic entity would be identified by determining (1) the interested individual, group or institution and (2) the nature of that individual's, group's or institution's interest. Thus this approach is oriented to the users of financial reports.

2. The accounting entity concept defines the area of interest and thus narrows the range and establishes the boundaries of the possible objects, activities or attributes of objects or activities that may be selected for inclusion in accounting records and reports. Further, postulates as to the nature of the entity also may aid in determining (1) what information to include in reports of the entity and (2) how to best present information of the entity so that relevant features are disclosed and irrelevant features do not cloud the presentation.

The applicability of all the other generally accepted concepts (or principles or postulates) of accounting (e.g., continuity, money measurement and time periods) depends upon the established boundaries and nature of the accounting entity. The other accounting concepts lack significance without reference to an entity. The entity must be defined before the balance of the accounting model can be applied and the accounting can begin. Thus the accounting entity concept is so fundamental that is pervades all of accounting.

b. 1. Yes, units created by or under law would include corporations, partnerships and, occasionally, sole proprietorships. Thus legal units probably are the most common types of accounting entities.

2. Yes, a product line or other segment of an enterprise, such as a division, department, profit center, branch or cost center, could be an accounting entity. The stimuli for financial reporting by segment include investors, the Securities and Exchange Commission, financial executives and the accounting profession (SFAS #14).

3. Yes, most large corporations issue consolidated financial reports for two or more legal entities that constitute a controlled economic entity. Accounting for investments in subsidiary companies by the equity method also is an example of an accounting unit that extends beyond the legal entity. The financial reports for a business enterprise that includes two or more product-line segments would also be a form of a consolidated report that most commonly would be considered to be the report of a single legal entity.

4. Yes, although the accounting entity often is defined in terms of a business enterprise that is separate and distinct from other activities of the owner or owners, it also is possible for an accounting entity to embrace all of the activities of an owner or a group of owners. Examples include financial statements for an individual (personal financial statements) and the financial report of a person's estate.

5. Yes, the accounting entity could embrace an industry. Examples include financial data compiled for an industry by a trade association (industry averages) or by the federal government. Probably the best examples of an industry being the accounting entity are in the accounting systems prescribed by the Federal Power Commission and the Federal Communications Commission which define the original cost of an asset in terms of the cost to the person first devoting it to public service.

6. Yes, the accounting entity concept can embrace the economy of the United States. An example is the national income accounts compiled by the U.S. Department of Commerce. Another area where the entity concept is applicable is in the yet to be developed area of socio-economic accounting.

NUMBER 2

1. Valuation of assets is a significant issue because of its effect on the statement of financial position and earnings statement. The valuation method used affects the measurement of total assets and the timing and amount of periodic net earnings. This relationship between asset valuation and measurement of net earnings is referred to as articulation between these two financial statements.

2. **Historical-cost** valuation reports assets at their acquisition cost (net of depreciation, depletion, or amortization, if applicable) and is the total of exchange prices to obtain an asset and render it suitable to use. Such valuation is measured by cash or cash equivalent sacrificed in exchange for the asset. There is an inherent assumption that a stable monetary unit exists.

Because acquisition cost is the vital measurement, that amount for limited life assets is allocated on a reasonable basis to future periods as expense or as a factor in the cost of goods sold (if inventory). It is, therefore, the actual past purchase price that affects future period's measurement of net earnings under the matching concept. Because of this emphasis on matching each period's revenue and expense, the earnings emerges as the primary financial statement based on a transactions approach and the statement of financial position becomes partly a statement of unallocated past costs for nonmonetary assets.

Concerning allocation to the earnings statement under historical-cost valuation, gains are normally recognized in the period they are realized through sale or usage. Unrealized gains are not considered. Unrealized losses, theoretically, should be treated the same as unrealized gains; nonetheless, conventional accounting practice permits recognition of some unrealized losses. This inconsistent treatment is justified under the doctrine of conservatism.

Historical cost adjusted to reflect general price-level changes is a valuation method which uses the historical cost (discussed above) of nonmonetary assets and applies a general price-level index (CPI) to reflect changes in the standard unit of purchasing power, the dollar, so that the information reported is not biased by changes in the ability of the dollar to command goods and services. In this way, information reported in successive periods (time series data) would be expressed in terms of a constant dollar. Nonmonetary assets are, therefore, stated in terms of the units of general purchasing power as of the date of the statement. These adjusted amounts do not measure any form of "current value" except by coincidence.

Monetary assets (cash, accounts receivable, etc.) are fixed claims to units of purchasing power which are the same as the units of dollars. Nonetheless, holding net monetary assets (monetary assets in excess of monetary liabilities) during a period of rising prices causes a purchasing power loss because these assets represent a fixed claim to reduced purchasing power. A purchasing power gain occurs by holding net monetary assets during periods of falling prices (or by being a net debtor in periods of rising prices). These purchasing power losses and gains would be shown on a company's earnings statement. They reflect, in part, the stewardship of management during a period of changing price levels.

Discounted-cash-flow valuation is one method which yields a "current-value" measurement. Under this approach, assets are reported at the present value of their expected future net cash inflows. Thus, it is considered a future exchange price. It reflects the notion that assets represent future service potential (economic benefits) and an attempt should be made to measure this potential (benefit) for reporting.

When using the discounted-cash-flow approach, net earnings would be equal to the discounted amount of stockholders' equity at the beginning of the period multiplied by the rate used to discount the future net cash flow. This reflects the amount that could be paid out to stockholders and still leave the business as "well off" at the end of the period as it was at the beginning.

Market-price valuation yields a different "current-value" measurement. Under this approach, assets are reported at their present realizable sales prices at the date of the statement of financial position. These selling prices should be market selling prices of similar assets under conditions of orderly sales, rather than liquidating selling prices under conditions of forced sales. Use of current market selling prices is an indicator of present cash equivalents of the assets and reflects existing market alternatives; such usage does not assume that these assets will necessarily be sold at those prices.

When using the market-price approach, net earnings would equal net assets (assets minus liabilities) at the end of the period plus capital withdrawals and dividends, less capital additions, less net assets at the beginning of the period. Net earnings are, therefore, based on the valuation of the firm's assets (and liabilities) because these assets generate such earnings. Net earnings are not based on a transactions approach and, therefore, do not include arbitrary cost allocations to an accounting period.

Replacement-cost valuation yields another, and different "current-value" measurement. Under this approach, assets are reported at their quoted market price to acquire them (replacement in kind). Current replacement cost, which may be approximated by use of a specific price index or by appraisals, reflects supply and demand for the specific asset(s) in question. Replacement cost valuation can be based upon replacement in kind or replacement of equivalent services or benefits.

When using the replacement-cost approach, net earnings include earnings computed by the transactions approach and gains or losses from holding assets (and liabilities) whose purchase prices rise or fall. The earnings statement thus contains some unrealized items (from a conventional viewpoint). Part of the traditionally determined net earnings would, under replacement-cost accounting, be reclassified as holding gains or losses. The earnings statement would show earnings from operations by deducting from current revenue the cost to replace the goods and services consumed in generating that revenue, plus holding gains or less holding losses resulting from changes in the replacement cost of the resources (and obligations) held.

NUMBER 3

a. 1. The essential characteristics of an asset are:
   1. The asset has future economic benefits.
   2. The asset is obtained or controlled by the entity as a result of past transactions or events.

2. The expenditures for the project provided no immediate revenue or income. Any benefits are probable future economic gains due to the successful completion of the project, the patent and the construction of the manufacturing facility.

   Any assets coming from project expenditures were specifically from past transactions controlled by Mono. The patent has probable future economic benefit.

3. The issue of the probable economic benefit is not clear since any future value following from research and development has not yet been identified or measured. Furthermore, R & D expenditures do not have three essential characteristics of an asset. It is due to this uncertainty that R & D expenditures are expensed as incurred.

Chapter Eight
Statement of Cash Flows (FASB Statement #95) and Financial Statement Analysis

Chapter Eight
Statement of Cash Flows (FASB Statement #95) and Financial Statement Analysis

A Statement of Cash Flows is a financial statement which shows the cash receipts, cash payments and net change in cash from the operating, investing, and financing activities of an enterprise during a period, in a manner that reconciles beginning and ending cash balances. FASB Statement #95 requires that **all** business enterprises include a statement of cash flows in a complete set of financial statements. When both the balance sheet (financial position) and income statement (results of operations) are provided, a statement of cash flows must be provided for **each** period for which an income statement is provided. A statement of cash flows is generally not required for defined benefit pension plans and other employee benefit plans; investment companies subject to the Investment Company Act of 1940; and trusts or similar funds (SFAS #95 and #102).

The theoretical foundation for the statement of cash flows and its classifications of cash flows is established in FASB Concepts #1 and #5. Concept #1 states that, "financial reporting should provide information to help ... (external users) ... in assessing the amount, timing, and uncertainty of prospective cash receipts..." and that, "expected cash flows to investors and creditors are related to expected cash flows to the enterprise." Concept #5 of the FASB states, "Classification in financial statements facilitates analysis by grouping items with essentially similar characteristics and separating items with essentially different characteristics. Analysis aimed at objectives such as predicting amounts, timing, and uncertainty of future cash flows **requires** financial information segregated into reasonably homogeneous groups."

Previous accounting practice has been to segregate cash (or funds) flow by sources and uses. The major disadvantages of this grouping are that it does not focus on categories of related cash flows, and has resulted in a lack of comparability among enterprises due to differing definitions of funds, reporting formats and/or classification of transaction. It is also contended that this classification of cash flows frequently explains little concerning an enterprise's ability to meet obligations, pay dividends, or needs for external financing.

To implement the guidelines established in the FASB concepts and to promote consistent, comparable reporting by enterprises, the FASB decided that cash flows must be grouped according to operating, investing and financing activities, thereby enabling significant relationships within and among the three types of enterprise activities to be evaluated.

PURPOSE OF STATEMENT

The primary purpose of the Statement of Cash Flows is to provide **external** users with relevant information concerning an enterprise's gross cash receipts and payments during a period. This information, if used with related disclosures and information in the other financial statements, should help external users to assess:

1. The enterprise's ability to generate positive net cash flows in the future
2. The enterprise's ability to meet its obligations and pay dividends
3. The enterprise's need for external financing
4. The reasons for differences between net income and associated cash receipts and payments
5. The effects on financial position of both cash and non-cash investing and financing transactions during the period.

Focus on Cash and Cash Equivalents

The primary focus of the statement is on gross cash receipts and payments. However, enterprises commonly invest temporarily idle cash as part of their cash management activities, purchasing and selling short-term, highly liquid investments such as treasury bills, commercial paper and money market funds. These investments are referred to as cash equivalents and are usually reported with cash on the balance sheet. Whether cash is on hand, on deposit or invested in short-term financial instruments that are readily convertible to known amounts of cash is largely irrelevant to users' assessment of liquidity and future cash flows. Because these transactions relate to cash management activities rather than the operating, investing and financing activities of the enterprise and because the distinction between cash and cash equivalents is largely irrelevant to external users, the details of these transactions are **not** reported in a statement of cash flows and the focus of the statement is changed to explain the change in **cash and cash equivalents.**

Requirements for cash equivalents: Cash equivalents are short-term, highly liquid investments that are both:
a) Readily converted to **known** amounts of cash
b) So near maturity that they present **insignificant risk** of change in value because of changes in interest rates.

Generally, only investments with original maturities (to the enterprise holding the investment) of three (3) months or less qualify under this definition. Furthermore, the investment should relate to the cash management activities of the enterprise (investment of temporarily idle cash balances) rather than its investing activities (such as bank's or investment company's trading as part of their investment portfolio). Enterprises must develop a clear and consistent policy for determining which short-term highly liquid investments, that satisfy the above criteria for cash equivalents are, and are not treated as cash equivalents for statement purposes. This policy must be disclosed in the footnotes to the financial statements. Any change in the policy should be treated as a change in accounting principle that will require a company to restate financial statements presented for comparative purposes.

REQUIREMENTS: STRUCTURE AND DISCLOSURES

1. The statement shall use descriptive terms such as **cash** or **cash and cash equivalents** rather than ambiguous terms such as funds.

2. The statement shall group and classify cash receipts and cash payments as resulting from **operating, investing** or **financing** activities of the enterprise.

3. Generally, cash receipts and payments must be presented as **gross amounts** rather than as net changes in related balance sheet amounts. **Exception:** Net amounts of related cash receipts and payments may be used for:
   a. When the enterprise is substantively holding or disbursing cash on behalf of its customers (demand deposits of banks, customer accounts payable of a broker-dealer).
   b. Investments (other than cash equivalents), loans receivable (including credit card receivables), and debt, providing that the original maturity of the asset or liability is three (3) months or less. (Because the turnover is quick, the amounts are large, and the maturities are short, information on gross receipts and payments is deemed no more relevant than information about only the net changes.)

4. The statement shall report **net cash provided or used** by operating, investing and financing activities and the **net effect** of those flows on cash and cash equivalents during the period in a manner that reconciles beginning and ending cash and cash equivalents.

5. The total amounts of cash and cash equivalents at the beginning and end of the period shown in the statement of cash flows shall be the **same amounts** as similarly titled line items or subtotals shown on the balance sheet as of those dates.

6. A reconciliation of net income to net cash flow from operating activities shall be provided regardless of whether the direct or indirect method of reporting net cash flow from operating activities is used. The reconciliation shall separately report all major classes of reconciling items.
* If the **direct method** is used, the reconciliation shall be provided in a separate schedule.
* If the **indirect method** is used, the reconciliation may be either reported within the statement of cash flows or provided in a separate schedule, with the statement of cash flows reporting only the net cash flow from operating activities.
  In addition, if the indirect method is used, cash payments for interest (net of amounts capitalized) and income taxes during the period shall be provided in related disclosures.

7. Noncash investing and financing activities that affect recognized assets or liabilities shall be reported in related disclosures (either narrative or summarized in a schedule). For transactions that are part cash and part noncash, only the cash portion shall be reported in the statement of cash flows. The related disclosures shall clearly describe the cash and noncash aspects of such transaction.

8. Cash flow per share shall **not** be reported in financial statements. Neither cash flow per share, nor any component thereof, is an acceptable alternative to net income or earnings per share as a measure of performance.

9. An enterprise shall disclose its policy for determining which investments are treated as cash equivalents.

CLASSIFICATIONS OF CASH FLOWS

OPERATING ACTIVITIES: Include all transactions and other events that are not defined as investing or financing activities. Operating activities generally involve producing and delivering goods and/or providing services to customers. Cash flows from operating activities are generally the cash effects of transactions and other events that enter into the determination of net income.

Cash inflows from operating activities include cash receipts from:

1. Sale of goods or services.
2. Collection or sale (discounting) of accounts and both short- and long-term notes receivable from customers arising from sales (trade).
3. Interest on loans and investments in debt securities of other enterprises (return **on** investment).
4. Dividends on investments in equity securities of other enterprises (return **on** investment).
5. Settlement of lawsuits.
6. Refunds from suppliers.
7. Insurance settlements except those that are directly related to investing or financing activities, such as from destruction of a building.

Cash outflows from operating activities include cash payment for:

1. Acquisition of materials for manufacture or goods for resale.
2. Principal payments on accounts and both short- and long-term notes payable to suppliers for materials or goods.
3. Suppliers and employees for other goods or services.
4. Taxes (FASB Statement #95 concluded that allocating income taxes to operating, investing and financing activities would be complex and arbitrary and that the benefits would not justify the cost).
5. Other government imposed duties, fines, fees and penalties.
6. Interest paid to creditors (net of amounts capitalized).
7. Settlement of lawsuits.
8. Contribution to charity.
9. Refunds to customers.

INVESTING ACTIVITIES: Include transactions relating to making and collecting loans, acquiring and disposing of: debt or equity investments (other than cash equivalents); property, plant and equipment; and other productive assets. Generally, investing activities relate to the acquisition and disposal of assets other than those directly related to the enterprise's operations (such as trade accounts and notes receivable, inventory, prepaid expenses).

Cash inflows from investing activities include cash receipts from:

1. Collection of non-trade loan/note principal (not interest on the loan which relates to operating activities).
2. Sale of non-trade loans/notes receivable (discounting).
3. Sale of debt or equity investments in other enterprises.
4. Returns of equity investments in other enterprises (liquidating dividends, but **not** regular dividends which are a return **on** investment).
5. Sale of productive assets (land, buildings, equipment, natural resources, intangibles).
6. Sale of a business unit (discontinued operations).

Cash outflows from investing activities include cash payments for:
1. Loans made to other entities.
2. Purchase of loans from another entity.
3. To acquire debt or equity investments in other entities.
4. Acquisition of productive assets including interest capitalized as part of the cost of those assets. (Includes payments soon before, at, or soon after the time of purchase. Incurring directly related debt to the seller is a financing transaction and subsequent payments of principal are, therefore, financing cash flow.)
5. Acquisition of a business.

Cash flows from securities, loans and other assets acquired specifically for resale (SFAS #102 and SFAS #115)
1. Banks, brokers and dealers in securities, and other enterprises may carry securities and other assets in a trading account. Cash receipts and cash payments resulting from purchases and sales of securities and other assets shall be classified as operating cash flows if those assets are acquired specifically for resale and are carried at market value in a trading account.
2. Some loans are similar to securities in a trading account in that they are originated or purchased specifically for resale and are held for short periods of time. Cash receipts and cash payments resulting from acquisitions and sales of loans also shall be classified as operating cash flows if those loans are acquired specifically for resale and are carried at market value or at the lower of cost or market value. Cash receipts resulting from sales of loans that were not specifically acquired for resale shall be classified as investing cash inflows. That is, if loans were acquired as investments, cash receipts from sales of those loans shall be classified as investing cash inflows regardless of a change in the purpose for holding those loans.

FINANCING ACTIVITIES: Include transactions related to obtaining resources from owners and providing them with a return on, and return of their investment; borrowing money and repaying or otherwise settling the obligation; and obtaining and paying for other resources obtained from creditors on long-term credit.

Cash inflows from financing activities include cash receipts from:
1. Issuing equity securities (stocks, detachable warrants).
2. Issuing bonds, notes and other short-term or long-term debt.

Cash outflows from financing activities include cash payments for:
1. Dividends or other distributions to owners.
2. Repurchase of the enterprise's equity securities (treasury stock).
3. Repayment of amounts borrowed.
4. Other principal payments to creditors who have extended long-term credit (includes principal payments on seller-financed debt directly related to the acquisition of productive assets, and principal payments on capitalized leases).

NONCASH INVESTING AND FINANCING ACTIVITIES: Includes transactions which result in no cash inflow or outflow during the period; however, they affect the assets, liabilities and/or equity of the enterprise. Although these items do not affect the current cash flows of the enterprise, they frequently have a significant effect on the current financial position and on prospective cash flows of the enterprise. For example, a capitalized lease affects both the assets and liabilities of the current period and requires future lease payments in cash; conversion of debt to equity affects the capital structure of the current period and generally eliminate future, nondiscretionary payments of interest.

Noncash investing and financing activities (to be disclosed in a related schedule or narrative) include:
1. Conversion of debt to equity.
2. Acquisition of assets by issuance of debt or equity securities or the assumption of debt.
3. Acquisition of assets by entering into a capital lease.
4. Exchanges of noncash assets or liabilities for other noncash assets or liabilities.

Items With Possible Alternative Classification (Marginal Items)

The FASB recognized that the most appropriate classification of items will not always be clear. Certain cash receipts and payments may have aspects of more than one class of cash flow as the three classifications are not clearly mutually exclusive. In those circumstances, the appropriate classification should depend on the nature of the activity that is **likely** to be the **predominant** source of cash flows. For example, the acquisition and sale of equipment to be used by the enterprise or rented to others generally are investing activities. However, equipment may be acquired or produced to be used by the enterprise or rented to others for a short period and then sold. In those circumstances, the acquisition or production and subsequent sale of the equipment should be considered operating activities.

DIRECT METHOD OF REPORTING OPERATING CASH FLOW

FASB Statement #95 **encourages** enterprises to use the direct method in reporting cash flows from operating activities; however, it does not require its use. The direct method reports major classes of gross cash receipts and gross cash payments and the resulting net cash flow from operating activities. Basically, the direct method results in the reporting of a cash basis income statement in the operating activities section of the statement of cash flows.

If the direct method is used, the following classes of operating cash receipts and payments should, **at a minimum, be separately reported**:

a. Cash collected from customers, including lessees, licensees, and the like
b. Interest and dividends received
c. Other operating cash receipts, if any
d. Cash paid to employees and other suppliers of goods or services, including suppliers of insurance, advertising, and the like.
e. Interest paid (exclusive of amounts capitalized)
f. Income taxes paid
g. Other operating cash payments, if any.

Enterprises are encouraged to provide further breakdowns of operating cash receipts and payments that they consider meaningful and feasible. For example, a retailer or manufacturer might decide to further divide cash paid to employees and suppliers [category (d) above] into payments for costs of inventory and payments for selling, general, and administrative expenses.

Advantages of Direct Method

- The principal advantage of the direct method is that it shows gross operating cash receipts and payments. Knowledge of specific sources of operating cash flows is useful in estimating future cash flows. Commercial lenders generally maintain that amounts of operating cash receipts and payments are particularly important in assessing an enterprise's external borrowing needs and its ability to repay borrowings.
- The direct method is more consistent with the objectives of a statement of cash flows—to provide information concerning gross cash receipts and payments during a period.

Disadvantages of Direct Method

- The direct method does not link the net income reported on the income statement to the cash flow from operating activities.
- The direct method does not provide information about intervals of lead and lags between cash flows and income by showing how the changes in current assets and current liabilities, relating to operations, affect operating cash flows.

Additional Required Disclosures

To avoid the disadvantages associated with the direct method and gain the benefits associated with the indirect method (refer below), FASB Statement #95 requires that if the direct method is used, a reconciliation of net income to net cash flow from operating activities must be provided in a separate disclosure. The reconciliation must meet the same requirements as those for the indirect method (refer below).

Example: The Hiram Supply Company had the following income statement for the year ended December 31, 19X1:

Sales		$70,000
Cost of goods sold		30,000
Gross profit		$40,000
Operating expenses		
Salaries	$10,000	
Depreciation	5,000	
Interest	3,000	18,000
Income before income taxes		$22,000
Income taxes		3,300
Net income		$18,700

Hiram Supply Company also reported the following changes in current assets and liabilities related to operations:

Accounts receivable	$8,000 increase
Inventory	2,500 increase
Accounts payable	1,300 decrease
Salaries payable	1,000 increase

Under the direct method, the cash flows from the operating activities section of the statement of cash flows would appear as follows:

Cash flows from operating activities:		
Cash received from customers	$62,000	
Cash paid to suppliers	*(33,800)	
Cash paid to employees	*(9,000)	
Interest paid	(3,000)	
Income taxes paid	(3,300)	
Net cash provided by operating activities		$12,900

*Amount may be combined as cash paid to suppliers and employees.

Supporting computations:

Cash received from customers:	
Sales	$70,000
Less increase in accounts receivable	(8,000)
Cash collected	$62,000

Cash paid to suppliers:	
Cost of goods sold	$30,000
Add increase in inventory	2,500
Purchases	$32,500
Add decrease in accounts payable	1,300
Cash paid to suppliers	$33,800

Cash paid to employees:	
Salaries expense	$10,000
Less increase in salaries payable	(1,000)
Cash paid to employees	$ 9,000

INDIRECT METHOD OF REPORTING OPERATING CASH FLOWS

The indirect method reports the **same** amount for **net cash flow** from operating activities; however, it does not report major classes of gross cash receipts and payments from operating activities. Rather, the indirect method starts with net income and adjusts it for revenue and expense items that were not the result of operating cash transactions in the current period, to reconcile it to net cash flow from operating activities. The reconciliation must **separately** report all major classes of reconciling items, including **at a minimum, separately reporting changes during the period in receivables, inventory, and payables**, pertaining to operating activities **and clearly identify all adjustments to net income as reconciling items.** The reconciliation may be either within the statement of cash flows or in a separate schedule with the statement reporting only the net cash flow from operating activities.

Common reconciling items to adjust net income to net cash flow from operating activities are:

Additions to net income

- decreases in receivables and inventory related to operations
- decrease in prepaid expenses
- increase in payables related to operations
- increases in accrued expenses and deferred income taxes
- depreciation, depletion and amortization expenses
- amortization of discount on notes or bonds payable
- amortization of premium on investments in notes or bonds
- loss on the sale or disposal of productive assets
- loss recognized under the equity method
- loss on discontinued operations
- loss on retirement of debt

Deductions from net income

- increases in receivables and inventory related to operations
- increase in prepaid expenses
- decrease in payables related to operations
- decreases in accrued expenses and deferred income taxes
- amortization of premium on notes or bonds payable
- amortization of discount on investments in notes or bonds
- gain on sale or disposal of productive assets
- undistributed income recognized under the equity method
- gain on discontinued operations
- gain on retirement of debt

Advantages of Indirect Method

- The principal advantage of the indirect method is that it focuses on the differences between net income and net cash flow from operating activities, linking the income statement to the statement of cash flows. Identifying differences between income items and related cash flows can assist external users to identify differences between enterprises in the measurement and recognition of noncash items that affect income.
- The indirect method provides information about intervals of leads and lags between cash flows and income by showing how the changes in current assets and current liabilities, relating to operations, affect operating cash flows. External users frequently assess future cash flows by first estimating future income (based in part on reports of past income) and then converting those estimates to estimates of future cash flows by allowing for leads and lags between income and cash flows.

Disadvantages of Indirect Method

- The indirect method does not show gross operating cash receipts and payments.
- The indirect method is inconsistent with the statement objective of providing information concerning gross cash receipts and payments during a period.

Additional Required Disclosures

If the indirect method is used, related disclosures must include the amounts paid for **interest** (exclusive of amounts capitalized) and **income taxes**. This information, together with the information included in the reconciliation of net income to net cash flow from operating activities, should enable external users to indirectly approximate the cash receipts and payments related to operations, and thereby partially avoid the inherent disadvantages of this method.

Example: Using the facts of the example for the direct method (Hiram Supply Company), the cash flows from the operating activities section of the statement of cash flows, under the indirect method, would appear as follows:

Cash flows from operating activities:		
Net income	$18,700	
Adjustments to reconcile net income to net cash provided by operating activities:		
Depreciation expense	5,000	
Increase in accounts receivable	(8,000)	
Increase in inventory	(2,500)	
Decrease in accounts payable	(1,300)	
Increase in salaries payable	1,000	
Net cash provided by operating activities		$12,900

STEPS FOR PREPARATION OF THE STATEMENT AND REQUIRED DISCLOSURES

1. Prepare the **heading** and format for the statement of cash flows and for supplemental schedules (such as noncash investing and financing activities), if required. Amounts can be filled in as determined.
2. Determine the balance of cash and cash equivalents as of the beginning and end of the period, and the net change in cash and cash equivalents during the period.
3. Determine the changes in all other balance sheet amounts if this information is not provided.
4. Determine the cash flow from operating activities. Analysis and use of amounts related to operations will depend on whether the direct or indirect method of reporting cash flow from operating activities is used.
   Direct method: Convert income statement amounts to major classes of operating cash receipts and payments by adjusting for:
   a. noncash revenue and expenses (such as gains and depreciation)
   b. changes in balance sheet amounts related to operations (primarily changes in current assets, other than cash, and current liabilities which relate to an enterprise's operating cycle, such as receivables, inventory and payables).

   Indirect method: Convert net income to cash flow from operations by adjusting for:
   a. noncash revenue and expenses
   b. changes in balance sheet amounts related to operations including, at a minimum, separately reported changes in receivables, inventory and payables related to operating activities
   c. items which are not operating activities.
5. Analyze all other changes in balance sheet amounts to determine and classify:
   a. gross cash receipts and payments relating to investing and financing activities
   b. noncash investing and financing activities for required supplemental disclosure.
6. Proof of totals: The total of the net cash flows from operating (step 4), investing, and financing (step 5) activities should equal the net change in cash and cash equivalents (step 2). The net increase (decrease) in cash and cash equivalents, per the statement, plus the beginning balance of cash and cash equivalents (step 2) should equal the ending balance of cash and cash equivalents (step 2).

Illustrative Problem

Following are the balance sheets of the Trowel Company as of December 31, 19X2, and 19X1, and its income statement for the year ended December 31, 19X2.

Trowel Company
BALANCE SHEET
December 31, 19X2 and 19X1

	19X2	19X1	Increase (Decrease)
Assets:			
Cash and cash equivalents	$ 2,530	$ 600	$1,930
Accounts receivable (net of allowance for doubtful accounts of $450 and $600)	1,785	1,770	15
Notes receivable	150	400	(250)
Inventory	1,025	1,230	(205)
Prepaid expenses	135	110	25
Property, plant and equipment	7,560	6,460	1,100
Accumulated depreciation	(2,300)	(2,100)	(200)
Investments	275	250	25
Intangibles (net)	25	40	(15)
Total assets	$11,185	$8,760	$2,425
Liabilities:			
Accounts payable and accrued expenses	$ 835	$1,085	$(250)
Interest payable	45	30	15
Income taxes payable	25	50	(25)
Short-term debt	750	450	300
Capital lease obligation	725	—	725
Long-term debt	2,050	2,150	(100)
Deferred taxes	525	375	150
Other liabilities	275	225	50
Total liabilities	5,230	4,365	
Stockholders' equity:			
Common stock	3,000	2,000	1,000
Retained earnings	2,955	2,395	560
Total stockholders' equity	5,955	4,395	
Total liabilities and stockholders' equity	$11,185	$8,760	$2,425

Trowel Company
INCOME STATEMENT
For the Year Ended December 31, 19X2

Sales		$13,965
Operating expenses:		
Cost of goods sold	$10,290	
Selling, general and administrative expenses	1,890	
Depreciation and amortization	445	12,625
Operating income		$ 1,340
Other revenues and expenses:		
Equity in income of affiliate	$ 45	
Gain on sale of equipment	80	
Interest income	55	
Insurance proceeds	15	
Interest expense	(235)	
Loss from patent infringement lawsuit	(30)	(70)
Income before taxes		$ 1,270
Provision for income taxes		510
Net income		$ 760

Additional information:

a. During 19X2, Trowel Company wrote off $350 of accounts receivable as uncollectible and included in its selling, general and administrative expenses a provision for bad debts expense of $200 for the year.
b. During 19X2, Trowel collected $100 on a note receivable from the sale of inventory and $150 on a note resulting from the sale of property. Interest on these notes amounted to $55 during 19X2 and was collected during the year.
c. Selling, general and administrative expenses include an accrual of $50 for deferred compensation. The obligation for the deferred compensation was included in other liabilities.
d. Trowel Company received dividends of $20 from an affiliate accounted for using the equity method.
e. Trowel Company collected insurance proceeds of $15 from a business interruption claim.
f. Trowel Company paid $30 to settle a lawsuit relating to patent infringement.
g. For 19X2, Trowel Company's depreciation totaled $430, and amortization of intangible assets totaled $15.
h. Trowel Company constructed and placed in services a new plant facility at a cost of $1,000, including capitalized interest of $10.
i. During 19X2, Trowel Company sold equipment with a book value of $520 and an original cost of $750 for $600 cash. It also entered into a capital lease for new equipment with a fair value of $850. Principal payments under the lease obligation totaled $125 during 19X2.
j. Trowel Company borrowed and repaid various amounts during the year under a line-of-credit agreement, which provides for repayments within 60 days of the date borrowed. The result of these activities was a net increase of $300 in short-term debt.
k. Trowel Company issued $400 of long-term debt securities during 19X2.
l. Trowel Company issued $1,000 of additional common stock of which $500 was issued for cash, and $500 was issued upon conversion of long-term debt.
m. Trowel Company paid dividends of $200 during 19X2.

STATEMENT OF CASH FLOWS
For the Year Ended December 31, 19X2
(Direct Method)

Cash flows from operating activities:		
Cash received from customers	$13,850	
Cash paid to suppliers and employees	(12,000)	
Dividends received from affiliate	20	
Interest received	55	
Insurance proceeds received	15	
Interest paid (net of amount capitalized)	(220)	
Cash paid to settle lawsuit for patent infringement	(30)	
Income taxes paid	(385)	
Net cash provided by operating activities		$1,305
Cash flows from investing activities:		
Collection on note from sale of property	$ 150	
Payments to construct new plant facility	(1,000)	
Proceeds from sale of equipment	600	
Net cash used in investing activities		(250)
Cash flows from financing activities:		
Net borrowings under line of credit	$ 300	
Principal payment on capital lease obligations	(125)	
Proceeds from issuance of long-term debt	400	
Proceeds from issuance of common stock	500	
Dividends paid	(200)	
Net cash provided by financing activities		875
Net increase in cash and cash equivalents		$1,930
Cash and cash equivalents, January 1, 19X2		600
Cash and cash equivalents, December 31, 19X2		$2,530

Note: For explanation of statement amounts refer below to Analysis and Supporting Computations (Direct Method), which follows the same sequence as the amounts in the statement.

Schedule of Noncash Investing and Financing Activities

- A capital lease obligation of $850 was incurred when the company entered into a lease for new equipment.
- Additional common stock was issued upon the conversion of $500 of long-term debt.

If the direct method is used, a separate schedule, "Reconciliation of Net Income to Net Cash Provided by Operating Activities" is required. The schedule would be the same as the "Cash flow from operating activities" section of the statement of cash flows, using the indirect method, except that the title of the schedule would be as shown above. Refer below to the statement of cash flows using the indirect method.

Analysis and Supporting Computations (Direct Method):

- Sequence of analysis and computations follows the sequence of amounts in the statement of cash flows.
- Letters in parentheses refer to additional information provided in the illustrative problem.

Computation of Cash Flows from Operating Activities

1. Cash received from customers:

Sales		$13,965
Less increase in accounts receivable:		
Increase in A/R—net	$ 15	
Increase in allowance from bad debts expense	200 (a)	
Increase in A/R from uncollected sales		(215) *
Add: Collection on trade notes receivable		100 (b)
Cash received from customers		$13,850

*Alternative computation:

Beginning balance ($1,770 A/R net + $600 allowance)	$2,370
Less accounts written off as uncollectible	(350) (a)
Adjusted beginning balance	$2,020
Ending balance ($1,785 A/R net + $450 allowance)	2,235
Increase in A/R from uncollected sales	$ 215

2. Cash paid to suppliers and employees*

Cost of goods sold		$10,290
Selling, general and administrative expenses	$1,890	
Less bad debts expense	(200) (a)	
S.G. & A. expenses requiring cash payments		1,690
Adjustments for changes in related balance sheet amounts:		
Less decrease in inventory [1]		(205)
Add increase in prepaid expenses [2]		25
Add decrease in accounts payable and accrued expenses [3]		250
Less increase in other liabilities [4]		(50) (c)
Total cash paid to suppliers and employees		$12,000

*Cash paid to suppliers and employees cannot be broken down to amounts paid suppliers and amounts paid employees as prepaid expenses, and accounts payable and accrued expenses are not broken down in that manner.

1 The decrease in inventory has been charged to cost of goods sold; however, it does not require the payment of cash in the current period, therefore it is deducted from expenses to determine cash flow.

2 The increase in prepaid expenses resulted from a payment of cash that was not charged to expenses, therefore it is added to expenses to determine cash flow.

3 The decrease in accounts payable and accrued expenses required cash payment, however, did not affect expenses; therefore, it is added to expenses to determine cash flow.

4 The increase in other liabilities resulted from the accrual of an expense that did not require cash payment; therefore, it is deducted from expenses to determine cash flow.

3. Depreciation and amortization are not cash flow items and, therefore, are excluded from the computation of cash flow from operating activities.

4. Dividends received from affiliate:

Equity in income of affiliate	$ 45
Less dividends received	(20) (d)
Increase in investment account	$ 25

Under the equity method of accounting for investments, the investor debits investment and credits equity in income of affiliate for its share of the investee's income. When dividends are received, the investor debits cash and credits the investment account. (Refer to Chapter 4, Equity Method.) Equity in income of affiliate is not a cash flow item and is excluded from cash flow from operating activities.

5. Gain on sale of equipment is excluded from the computation of cash flows from operating activities because: 1) it is not the gross cash flow from the sale of the equipment, and 2) sale of equipment is an investing activity, not an operating activity.

6. Interest received is the same amount as interest income reported on the income statement ($55). Additional information (b) states that interest of $55 was collected on the notes receivable. This amount agrees to the interest income; therefore, there are no accruals to adjust for.

7. Insurance proceeds received is the same amount as reported on the income statement ($15). Refer to additional information (e).

8. Interest paid:

Interest expense	$235
Less increase in interest payable	(15)
	$220

Interest paid is qualified as "net of amount capitalized" as interest was capitalized as part of the cost of constructed assets. Refer to additional information (h).

9. Payment for settlement of patent infringement lawsuit is the same amount as the related loss in the income statement. Refer to additional information (f).

10. Income taxes paid:

Provision for income taxes	$510
Add decrease in income taxes payable	25
	$535
Less increase in deferred taxes payable	(150)
	$385

Computation and classification of cash flows from investing and financing activities and identification of noncash investing and financing activities.

11. Change in notes receivable (b):

Collection of trade note receivable	$100	(operating)
Collection of note receivable from sale of property	150	(investing)
Decrease in notes receivable	$250	

12. Changes in P.P. & E. and Accumulated Depreciation:

	P.P.&E.	*Accumulated depreciation*	
Depreciation expense (g)		$430	(operating)
Construction of new facility (h)	$1,000		(investing)
Sale of equipment for $600 (i)	(750)		(investing)
($750 cost – $520 book value)		(230)	
Asset under capital lease (i)	850		(noncash)*
Net change	$1,100	$200	

*The capital lease for new equipment is a noncash investing (asset acquisition) and financing (capital lease obligation) activity.

13. Change in investments:

Equity in income of affiliate	$45 (operating/noncash)
Less dividends received (d)	(20) (operating)
Increase in investments from undistributed affiliate income	$25

Refer to #4 above regarding the equity method.

14. Change in intangibles: The $15 decrease in intangibles results from amortization expense of $15. Refer to additional information (g).

15. Change in short-term debt: The $300 increase resulted from net borrowings under a line-of-credit agreement. These activities may be shown net as the original maturity of the debt(s) was three (3) months or less. Refer to additional information (j) and requirements section #3.

16. Change in capital lease obligation:

Original amount of capital lease (i)	$850 (noncash)*
Less: Principal payments (i)	(125) (financing)
Increase in capital lease obligation	$725

*The capital lease obligation for the acquisition of new equipment is a noncash investing (asset acquisition) and financing (capital lease obligation) activity.

17. Change in long-term debt:

Issuance of debt securities for cash (k)	$ 400 (financing)
Retirement of debt securities by conversion to common stock (l)	(500) (noncash)*
Decrease in long-term debt	$(100)

*The conversion of bonds to common stock is a noncash financing activity.

18. Change in common stock:

Issuance of stock for cash	$ 500 (financing)
Issuance of stock on conversion of long-term debt	500 (noncash)*
Increase in common stock	$1,000

*The issuance of common stock upon the conversion of long-term debt is a noncash financing activity.

19. Increase in retained earnings:

Net income	$ 760 (operating)
Less dividends paid	(200) (financing)
Increase in retained earnings	$ 560

Trowel Company
STATEMENT OF CASH FLOWS
For the Year Ended December 31, 19X2
(Indirect Method)

Cash flow from operating activities:		
Net income	$760	
Adjustments to reconcile net income to net cash provided by operating activities:		
Depreciation and amortization expense	445	
Bad debts expense	200	
Undistributed income of affiliate	(25)	
Gain on sale of equipment	(80)	
Increase in accounts receivable	(215)	
Collection of trade notes receivable	100	
Decrease in inventory	205	
Increase in prepaid expenses	(25)	
Decrease in accounts payable and accrued expenses	(250)	
Increase in interest payable	15	
Decrease in income taxes payable	(25)	
Increase in deferred taxes	150	
Increase in other liabilities	50	
Net cash flow from operating activities		$1,305
Cash flows from investing activities:		
Collection on note from sale of property	$ 150	
Payments to construct new plant facility	(1,000)	
Proceeds from sale of equipment	600	
Net cash used in investing activities		(250)
Cash flows from financing activities:		
Net borrowings under line of credit	$ 300	
Principal payment on capital lease obligations	(125)	
Proceeds from issuance of long-term debt	400	
Proceeds from issuance of common stock	500	
Dividends paid	(200)	
Net cash provided by financing activities		875
Net increase in cash and cash equivalents		$1,930
Cash and cash equivalents, January 1, 19X2		600
Cash and cash equivalents, December 31, 19X2		$2,530

Note: For explanation of statement amounts, refer below to Analysis and Supporting Computations (Indirect Method) which follows the same sequence as the amounts in the statement.

If the indirect method is used, supplemental disclosures must be made for:

1. Interest paid (net of amounts capitalized)
2. Income taxes paid
3. Noncash investing and financing activities

These amounts would be the same as in the prior example of the statement of cash flows using the direct method.

Analysis and Supporting Computations (Indirect Method)

- Only analysis and computations relating to cash flow from operating activities are shown in this section. Amounts relating to investing and financing activities are the same as when the direct method is used. Refer to "Analysis and Supporting Computation (Direct Method)" for explanation of amounts related to investing and financing activities.
- Sequence of analysis and computations follow the sequence of amounts shown in the statement.
- Letters in parentheses refer to additional information provided in the illustrative problem.

Computation of cash flow from operating activities:

1. Depreciation and amortization expense are not cash flow items; therefore, the expense for these items would be added back to net income to determine cash flow from operating activities.

2. Bad debts is a noncash expense and would be added to net income to determine cash flow (a).

3.

Equity in income of affiliate	$45
Less dividends received (d)	(20)
Undistributed affiliate income and increase in investments	$25

4. Gain on sale of equipment relates to investing activities rather than operating activities. Therefore, the gain is deducted from net income to remove its effect.

5.

Increase in accounts receivable—net	$ 15
Increase in allowance from bad debts expense (a)	200
Increase in accounts receivable	$215

Alternative computation of increase in accounts receivable:

Beginning balance ($1,770 A/R net + $600 allowance)	$2,370
Less accounts written off (a)	(350)
Adjusted beginning balance	2,020
Ending balance ($1,785 A/R net + $450 allowance)	2,235
Increase in A/R from uncollected sales	$ 215

6. Collection of trade note receivable (b) in the amount of $100 resulted in cash flow from operation; however, it would not have been included in revenues (and net income) of the current period.

7. The decrease in inventory would have increased cost of goods sold and decreased net income in the current period. Because the decrease is not a cash flow item, it is added to net income to determine cash from operating activities.

8. An increase in prepaid expenses results from cash payments which are not charged to expenses in the current period. The increase is therefore deducted from net income to determine cash flows from operating activities.

9. The decrease in accounts payable and accrued expenses resulted from cash payments which were not charged to expense. The decrease is deducted from net income to determine cash flow related to operating activities.

10. The increase in interest payable results from accrual of unpaid interest expense. The increase is added to net income to remove the effect of unpaid interest expense.

11. A decrease in income taxes payable results from cash payments which are not charged to income taxes in the current period. Therefore, the decrease is deducted from net income to determine cash flow from operating activities.

12. The increase in deferred taxes results from accrual of current period taxes for income determination which are not paid in the current period. The increase is therefore added to net income to determine cash flow from operating activities.

13. The increase in other liabilities results from accrual of deferred compensation (c). Because compensation relates to operating activities, the increase is added to net income to determine cash flow from operating activities.

FINANCIAL STATEMENT ANALYSIS

A candidate for the CPA Examination must be able to demonstrate a working knowledge of the **basic** techniques of financial statement analysis. Financial analysis is the process of interpreting the financial statements of an enterprise to identify and evaluate its strengths and weaknesses as reflected in those statements. Accountants rely upon techniques of financial analysis in the performance of the audit function to assist in designing the audit program with respect to scope and specific items to be evaluated. Because of their familiarity with the development of financial statements, accountants are also frequently called upon to analyze and interpret the results of operations as reflected in the statements for management.

Basic techniques of financial statement analysis include:

1. Comparative financial statements and horizontal analysis,
2. Common size statements (vertical analysis),
3. Ratio analysis.

Comparative Financial Statements and Horizontal Analysis

Financial statements for two or more years and statements of percentages indicating the relative change in items on the statements over time facilitate the identification, comparison and evaluation of trends. They also provide perspective in evaluating the reasonableness of current performance.

Common Size Statements

Statements which express each item on a particular financial statement as a percentage of a base amount emphasize the relationship among the items included, the relative importance of amounts included, and the significance of changes in items from one period to the next.

Ratio Analysis

Ratio analysis develops comparisons and measures relationships between two amounts from a single statement or from two different statements. A ratio may be expressed as a percentage (25%), a fraction (1/4) or a comparison of numbers (4 to 1). The essence of ratio analysis is to point out areas where further investigation is warranted.

a. **Basic ratio computations:**

RATIO	COMPUTATION	SIGNIFICANCE
1. Current ratio	$\frac{\text{Current Assets}}{\text{Current Liabilities}}$	Primary measure liquidity–able to meet current obligations
2. Quick ratio (acid test)	$\frac{\text{C+M/S+Rec}}{\text{CL}}$ or $\frac{\text{CA – Inv.}}{\text{CL}}$	Degree of immediate liquidity
3. Receivables turnover	$\frac{\text{Net Credit Sales}}{\text{Av. Rec. (net)}}$	Liquidity of receivables–efficiency and collection period
4. No. of days sales in receivables or Av. collection period	(a) $\frac{\text{Av. Rec. (net)}}{\text{Daily Cr. Sales}}$ OR	No. of days to collect receivables–efficiency of collections

Ratio	Formula	Measures
	(b) $\dfrac{365}{\text{Rec. Turnover}}$	
5. Inventory turnover	$\dfrac{\text{Cost of Goods Sold}}{\text{Av. Inv.}}$	Liquidity of inventory and inventory efficiency
6. Days supply in inventory	$\dfrac{365}{\text{Inv. Turnover}}$	Efficiency inv. mgmt. over- under-stocking
7. Asset turnover	$\dfrac{\text{Net Sales}}{\text{Total Assets}}$	Efficiency of resource utilization
8. Profit margin (return on sales)	$\dfrac{\text{Net Income}}{\text{Net Sales}}$	Profit margin per dollar of sales
9. Return on investment (ROI)	$\dfrac{\text{Net Income}}{\text{Total Assets}}$	Earning power of business—profitability—measure of management performance
10. Return on stockholders' equity	$\dfrac{\text{Net Income}}{\text{Stockholders' Equity}}$	Earning power per dollar of owner's investment
11. Debt-equity	$\dfrac{\text{Debt}}{\text{Equity}}$	Relative debt funds—financial structure
12. Equity to total assets (equity ratio)	$\dfrac{\text{Owner's Equity}}{\text{Total Assets}}$	% equity financing—protection of creditors
13. Book value per share	$\dfrac{\text{Common stock equity}}{\text{No. shares C/S}}$	CSE=TSE–Liquidating value P/S–cumulative dividends P/S
14. Times interest earned	$\dfrac{\text{Net Income Before Interest and Taxes}}{\text{Interest Expense}}$	Protection of creditors
15. Times fixed charges earned	$\dfrac{\text{Net Income Before Interest and Taxes}}{\text{Interest + Preferred Dividends}}$	Operating risk
16. E.P.S.	$\dfrac{\text{Net Income Available for C/S}}{\text{Av. No. Shares C/S}}$	Earnings per unit of ownership—dividend potential
17. Dividend Payout	$\dfrac{\text{Dividends per share}}{\text{EPS}}$	% profit paid out to owners—% retained for internal finance of growth
18. Price-earning ratio	$\dfrac{\text{Market value per sh. C/S}}{\text{EPS}}$	Indication of relative value of stock risk
19. Dividend yield	$\dfrac{\text{Dividend per share}}{\text{Market value per share}}$	Investment profitability

b. The DuPont System

The rate of return on investment is generally considered the most important ratio for providing information concerning the general profitability of the firm and the overall effectiveness of management. The DuPont system of analysis highlights and examines in detail the elements comprising the rate of return on investment, emphasizing the effect that various elements of the financial statements have on this ratio. The two major elements which interact to determine R.O.I. are asset turnover and profit margin. The relationship is as follows:

$$\text{R.O.I.} = \text{Asset Turnover} \times \text{Profit Margin}$$

or

$$\frac{\text{Net Income}}{\text{Total Assets}} = \frac{\text{Sales}}{\text{Total Assets}} \times \frac{\text{Net Income}}{\text{Sales}}$$

The component elements of asset turnover and profit margin are further subdivided to their component elements as illustrated in the following chart:

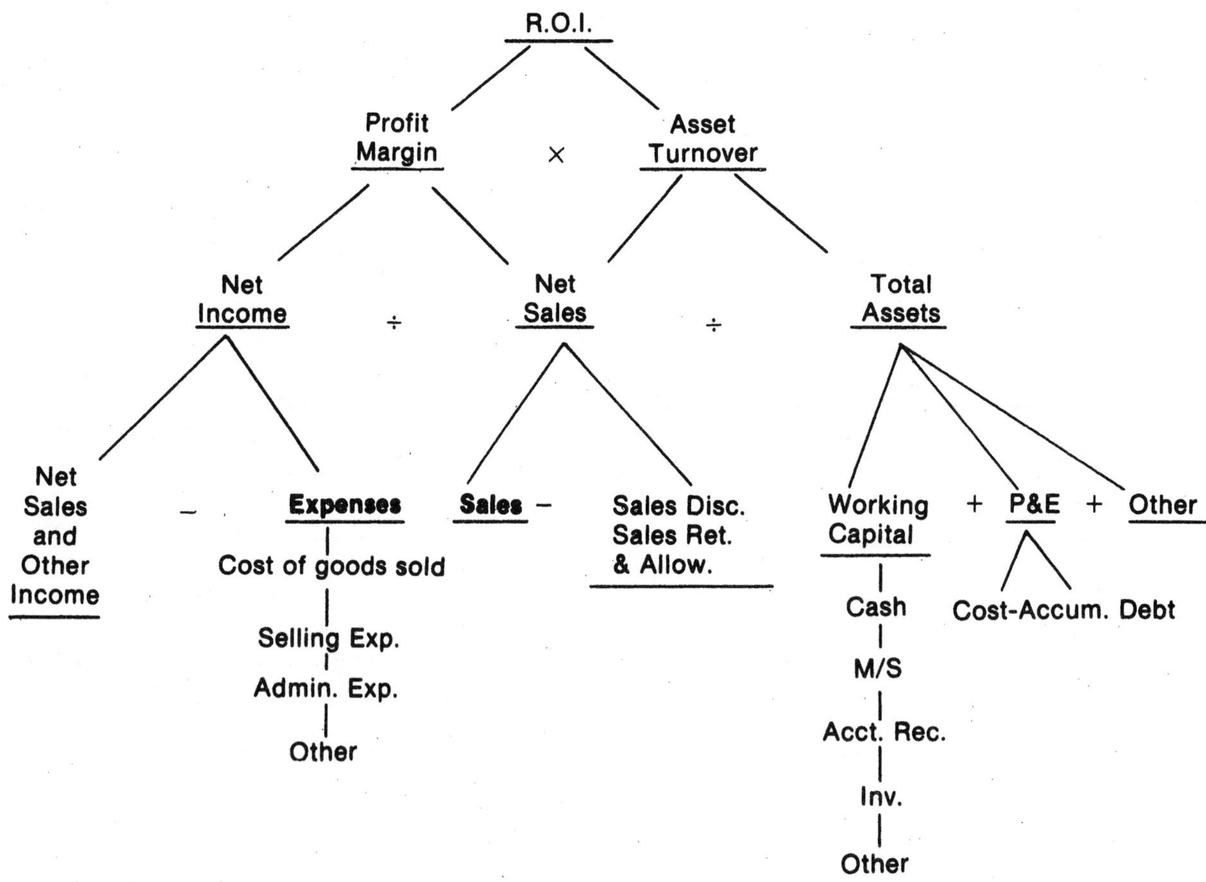

- A long-term investment was sold in 1988 for $135,000. There were no other transactions affecting long-term investments in 1988.
- 10,000 shares of common stock were issued in 1988 for $22 a share.
- Short-term investments consist of treasury bills maturing on 6/30/89.

14. Net cash provided by Dice's 1988 operating activities was
a. $690,000
b. $915,000
c. $940,000
d. $950,000

15. Net cash used in Dice's 1988 investing activities was:
a. $1,115,000
b. $895,000
c. $865,000
d. $815,000

16. Net cash provided by Dice's 1988 financing activities was
a. $305,000
b. $440,000
c. $455,000
d. $545,000

Items 17 and 18 are based on the following:
In preparing its cash flow statement for the year ended December 31, 1994, Reve Co. collected the following data:

Gain on sale of equipment	$(6,000)
Proceeds from sale of equipment	10,000
Purchase of A.S., Inc. bonds (par value $200,000)	(180,000)
Amortization of bond discount	2,000
Dividends declared	(45,000)
Dividends paid	(38,000)
Proceeds from sale of treasury stock (carrying amount $65,000)	75,000

In its December 31, 1994, statement of cash flows,

17. What amount should Reve report as net cash used in investing activities?
a. $170,000
b. $176,000
c. $188,000
d. $194,000

18. What amount should Reve report as net cash provided by financing activities?
a. $20,000
b. $27,000
c. $30,000
d. $37,000

Items 19 and 20 are based on the following:
Kollar Corp.'s transactions for the year ended December 31, 1988, included the following:

- Purchased real estate for $550,000 cash which was borrowed from a bank.
- Sold investment securities for $500,000.
- Paid dividends of $600,000.
- Issued 500 shares of common stock for $250,000.
- Purchased machinery and equipment for $125,000 cash.
- Paid $450,000 toward a bank loan.
- Reduced accounts receivable by $100,000.
- Increased accounts payable by $200,000.

19. Kollar's net cash used in investing activities for 1988 was
a. $675,000
b. $375,000
c. $175,000
d. $50,000

20. Kollar's net cash used in financing activities for 1988 was
a. $50,000
b. $250,000
c. $450,000
d. $500,000

M91

21. Bee Co. uses the direct write-off method to account for uncollectible accounts receivable. During an accounting period, Bee's cash collections from customers equal sales adjusted for the addition or deduction of the following amounts:

	Accounts written-off	*Increase in accounts receivable balance*
a.	Deduction	Deduction
b.	Addition	Deduction
c.	Deduction	Addition
d.	Addition	Addition

M91

22. In 1990, a tornado completely destroyed a building belonging to Holland Corp. The building cost $100,000 and had accumulated depreciation of $48,000 at the time

of the loss. Holland received a cash settlement from the insurance company and reported an extraordinary loss of $21,000. In Holland's 1990 cash flow statement, the net change reported in the cash flows from investing activities section should be a

a. $10,000 increase.
b. $21,000 decrease.
c. $31,000 increase.
d. $52,000 decrease.

M91

23. During 1990, Teb, Inc., had the following activities related to its financial operations:

Payment for the early retirement of long-term bonds payable (carrying value $740,000)	$750,000
Distribution in 1990 of cash dividend declared in 1989 to preferred shareholders	62,000
Carrying value of convertible preferred stock in Teb, converted into common shares	120,000
Proceeds from sale of treasury stock (carrying value at cost, $86,000)	95,000

In Teb's 1990 statement of cash flows, net cash used in financing activities should be

a. $717,000
b. $716,000
c. $597,000
d. $535,000

24. Alp, Inc., had the following activities during 1990:

- Acquired 2,000 shares of stock in Maybel, Inc., for $26,000.
- Sold an investment in Rate Motors for $35,000 when the carrying value was $33,000.
- Acquired a $50,000, 4-year certificate of deposit from a bank. (During the year, interest of $3,750 was paid to Alp.)
- Collected dividends of $1,200 on stock investments.

In Alp's 1990 statement of cash flows, net cash used in investing activities should be

a. $37,250
b. $38,050
c. $39,800
d. $41,000

25. On September 1, 1992, Canary Co. sold used equipment for a cash amount equaling its carrying amount for both book and tax purposes. On September 15, 1992, Canary replaced the equipment by paying cash and signing a note payable for new equipment. The cash paid for the new equipment exceeded the cash received for the old equipment. How should these equipment transactions be reported in Canary's 1992 statement of cash flows?

a. Cash outflow equal to the cash paid less the cash received.
b. Cash outflow equal to the cash paid and note payable less the cash received.
c. Cash inflow equal to the cash received and a cash outflow equal to the cash paid and note payable.
d. Cash inflow equal to the cash received and a cash outflow equal to the cash paid.

26. Mend Co. purchased a three-month U.S. Treasury bill. Mend's policy is to treat as cash equivalents all highly liquid investments with an original maturity of three months or less when purchased. How should this purchase be reported in Mend's statement of cash flows?

a. As an outflow from operating activities.
b. As an outflow from investing activities.
c. As an outflow from financing activities.
d. Not reported.

N95

27. Which of the following is **not** disclosed on the statement of cash flows when prepared under the direct method, either on the face of the statement or in a separate schedule?

a. The major classes of gross cash receipts and gross cash payments.
b. The amount of income taxes paid.
c. A reconciliation of net income to net cash flow from operations.
d. A reconciliation of ending retained earnings to net cash flow from operations.

R97

28. In its 1996 income statement, Kilm Co. reported cost of goods sold of $450,000. Changes occurred in several balance sheet accounts as follows:

Inventory	$160,000 decrease
Accounts payable - suppliers	40,000 decrease

What amount should Kilm report as cash paid to suppliers in its 1996 cash flow statement, prepared under the direct method?

a. $250,000
b. $330,000
c. $570,000
d. $650,000

FINANCIAL STATEMENT ANALYSIS

29. What effect would the sale of a company's trading securities at their carrying amounts for cash have on each of the following ratios?

	Current ratio	*Quick ratio*
a.	No effect	No effect
b.	Increase	Increase
c.	No effect	Increase
d.	Increase	No effect

30. At December 30, 1993, Vida Co. had cash of $200,000, a current ratio of 1.5:1 and a quick ratio of .5:1. On December 31, 1993, all cash was used to reduce accounts payable. How did these cash payments affect the ratios?

	Current ratio	*Quick ratio*
a.	Increased	Decreased
b.	Increased	No effect
c.	Decreased	Increased
d.	Decreased	No effect

31. The following information pertains to Bala Co. for the year ended December 31, 1991:

Sales	$600,000
Net income	100,000
Capital investment	400,000

Which of the following equations should be used to compute Bala's return on investment?

a. (4/6) x (6/1) = ROI
b. (6/4) x (1/6) = ROI
c. (4/6) x (1/6) = ROI
d. (6/4) x (6/1) = ROI

32. In analyzing a company's financial statements, which financial statement would a potential investor primarily use to assess the company's liquidity and financial flexibility?

a. Balance sheet.
b. Income statement.
c. Statement of retained earnings.
d. Statement of cash flows.

Items 33 and 34 are based on the following:
At December 31, 1992, Curry Co. had the following balances in selected asset accounts:

	1992	*Increase over 1991*
Cash	$ 300	$100
Accounts receivable, net	1,200	400
Inventory	500	200
Prepaid expenses	100	40
Other assets	400	150
Total assets	$2,500	$890

Curry also had current liabilities of $1,000 at December 31, 1992, and net credit sales of $7,200 for the year then ended.

33. What is Curry's acid-test ratio at December 31, 1992?

a. 1.5
b. 1.6
c. 2.0
d. 2.1

34. What was the average number of days to collect Curry's accounts receivable during 1992?

a. 30.4
b. 40.6
c. 50.7
d. 60.8

Items 35 through 37 are based on the following:
Selected data pertaining to Lore Co. for the calendar year 1994 is as follows:

Net cash sales	$3,000
Cost of goods sold	18,000
Inventory at beginning of year	6,000
Purchases	24,000
Accounts receivable at beginning of year	20,000
Accounts receivable at end of year	22,000

35. The accounts receivable turnover for 1994 was 5.0 times. What were Lore's 1994 net credit sales?

a. $105,000
b. $107,000
c. $110,000
d. $210,000

36. What was the inventory turnover for 1994?

a. 1.2 times.
b. 1.5 times.
c. 2.0 times.
d. 3.0 times.

37. Lore would use which of the following to determine the average days sales in inventory?

	Numerator	*Denominator*
a.	365	Average inventory
b.	365	Inventory turnover
c.	Average inventory	Sales divided by 3
d.	Sales divided by 365	Inventory turnover

---

38. Selected information for 1999 for the Prince Company is as follows:

Cost of goods sold	$5,400,000
Average inventory	1,800,000
Net sales	7,200,000
Average receivables	960,000
Net income	720,000

Assuming a business year consisting of 360 days, what was the average number of days in the operating cycle for 1999?

a. 72.
b. 84.
c. 144.
d. 168.

39. A company's return on investment is the

a. Profit margin percentage divided by the capital turnover.
b. Profit margin percentage multiplied by the capital turnover.
c. Capital turnover divided by invested capital.
d. Capital turnover multiplied by invested capital.

40. How is the average inventory used in the calculation of each of the following?

	Acid test (quick ratio)	*Inventory turnover rate*
a.	Numerator	Numerator
b.	Numerator	Denominator
c.	Not used	Denominator
d.	Not used	Numerator

41. Zenk Co. wrote off obsolete inventory of $100,000 during 1991. What was the effect of this write-off on Zenk's ratio analysis?

a. Decrease in current ratio but **not** in quick ratio.
b. Decrease in quick ratio but **not** in current ratio.
c. Increase in current ratio but **not** in quick ratio.
d. Increase in quick ratio but **not** in current ratio.

42. Gil Corp. has current assets of $90,000 and current liabilities of $180,000. Which of the following transactions would improve Gil's current ratio?

a. Refinancing a $30,000 long-term mortgage with a short-term note.
b. Purchasing $50,000 of merchandise inventory with a short-term account payable.
c. Paying $20,000 of short-term accounts payable.
d. Collecting $10,000 of short-term accounts receivable.

43. During 1989, Rand Co. purchased $960,000 of inventory. The cost of goods sold for 1989 was $900,000, and the ending inventory at December 31, 1989, was $180,000. What was the inventory turnover for 1989?

a. 6.4
b. 6.0
c. 5.3
d. 5.0

44. The following computations were made from Clay Co.'s 1991 books:

Number of days' sales in inventory	61
Number of days' sales in trade accounts receivable	33

What was the number of days in Clay's 1991 operating cycle?

a. 33
b. 47
c. 61
d. 94

45. Which combination of changes in asset turnover and income as a percentage of sales will maximize the return on investment?

	Asset turnover	*Income as a % of sales*
a.	Increase	Decrease
b.	Increase	Increase
c.	Decrease	Increase
d.	Decrease	Decrease

46. Are the following ratios useful in assessing the liquidity position of a company?

	Defensive-interval ratio	*Return on stockholders' equity*
a.	Yes	Yes
b.	Yes	No
c.	No	Yes
d.	No	No

47. On December 31, 1991, Northpark Co. collected a receivable due from a major customer. Which of the following ratios would be increased by this transaction?

a. Inventory turnover ratio.
b. Receivable turnover ratio.
c. Current ratio.
d. Quick ratio.

48. Successful use of leverage is evidenced by a

a. Rate of return on investment greater than the rate of return on stockholders' equity.
b. Rate of return on investment greater than the cost of debt.
c. Rate of return on sales greater than the rate of return on stockholders' equity.
d. Rate of return on sales greater than the cost of debt.

49. Barr Co. has total debt of $420,000 and stockholders' equity of $700,000. Barr is seeking capital to fund an expansion. Barr is planning to issue an additional $300,000 in common stock, and is negotiating with a bank to borrow additional funds. The bank is requiring a debt-to-equity ratio of .75. What is the maximum additional amount Barr will be able to borrow?

a. $225,000
b. $330,000
c. $525,000
d. $750,000

50. The following data pertain to Ruhl Corp.'s operations for the year ended December 31, 1989:

Operating income	$800,000
Interest expense	100,000
Income before income tax	700,000
Income tax expense	210,000
Net income	$490,000

The times interest earned ratio is

a. 8.0 to 1.
b. 7.0 to 1.
c. 5.6 to 1.
d. 4.9 to 1.

Recently Released Questions

1999

51. North Bank is analyzing Belle Corp's financial statements for a possible extension of credit. Belle's quick ratio is significantly better than the industry average. Which of the following factors should North consider as a possible limitation of using this ratio when evaluating Belle's credit worthiness?

a. Fluctuating market prices of short-term investments may adversely affect the ratio.
b. Increasing market prices for Belle's inventory may adversely affect the ratio.
c. Belle may need to sell its available-for-sale investments to meet its current obligations.
d. Belle may need to liquidate its inventory to meet its long-term obligations.

1999

52. Trans Co. had the following balances at December 31, 1999:

Cash in checking account	$35,000
Cash in money market account	$75,000
U.S. Treasury bill, purchased 11/1/1999 maturing 1/31/2000	$350,000
U.S. Treasury bill, purchased 12/1/1999 maturing 3/31/2000	$400,000

Trans' policy is to treat as cash equivalents all highly liquid investments with a maturity of three months or less when purchased. What amount should Trans report as cash and cash equivalents in its December 31, 1999 balance sheet?

a. $110,000
b. $385,000
c. $460,000
d. $860,000

2000

53. Inch Co. had the following balances at December 31, 1999:

Cash in checking account	$35,000
Cash in money market account	$75,000
U.S. Treasury bill, purchased 12/1/99, maturing 2/28/00	$200,000
U.S. Treasury bill, purchased 12/1/98, maturing 5/31/00	$150,000

Inch's policy is to treat as cash equivalents all highly-liquid investments with a maturity of 3 months or less when purchased. What amount should Inch report as cash and cash equivalents in its December 31, 1999 balance sheet?

a. $110,000
b. $235,000
c. $310,000
d. $460,000

Chapter Eight
Statement of Cash Flows and Financial Statement Analysis Problems

NUMBER 1

Presented below are the balance sheets of Farrell Corporation as of December 31, 19X1, and 19X0, and the statement of income and retained earnings for the year ended December 31, 19X1.

Farrell Corporation
BALANCE SHEETS
December 31, 19X1 and 19X0

Assets	*19X1*	*19X0*	*Increase (Decrease)*
Cash	$ 275,000	$ 180,000	$ 95,000
Accounts receivable, net	295,000	305,000	(10,000)
Inventories	549,000	431,000	118,000
Investment in Hall, Inc., at equity	73,000	60,000	13,000
Land	350,000	200,000	150,000
Plant and equipment	624,000	606,000	18,000
Less accumulated depreciation	(139,000)	(107,000)	(32,000)
Goodwill	16,000	20,000	(4,000)
Total assets	$2,043,000	$1,695,000	$348,000

Liabilities and Stockholders' Equity			
Accounts payable and accrued expenses	$ 604,000	$ 563,000	$ 41,000
Note payable, long-term	150,000	—	150,000
Bonds payable	160,000	210,000	(50,000)
Deferred income taxes	41,000	30,000	11,000
Common stock, par value $10	430,000	400,000	30,000
Additional paid-in capital	226,000	175,000	51,000
Retained earnings	432,000	334,000	98,000
Treasury stock, at cost	—	(17,000)	17,000
Total liabilities and stockholders' equity	$2,043,000	$1,695,000	$348,000

Farrell Corporation
STATEMENT OF INCOME AND RETAINED EARNINGS
For the Year Ended December 31, 19X1

Net sales	$1,950,000
Operating expenses:	
Cost of sales	1,150,000
Selling and administrative expenses	505,000
Depreciation	53,000
	1,708,000
Operating income	242,000
Other (income) expense:	
Interest expense	15,000
Equity in net income of Hall, Inc.	(13,000)
Loss on sale of equipment	5,000
Amortization of goodwill	4,000
	11,000
Income before income taxes	231,000
Income taxes:	
Current	79,000
Deferred	11,000
Provision for income taxes	90,000
Net income	141,000
Retained earnings, January 1, 19X1	334,000
	475,000
Cash dividends, paid August 14, 19X1	43,000
Retained earnings, December 31, 19X1	$ 432,000

Additional information:

- On January 2, 19X1, Farrell sold equipment costing $45,000, with a book value of $24,000, for $19,000 cash.
- On April 1, 19X1, Farrell issued 1,000 shares of common stock for $23,000 cash.
- On May 15, 19X1, Farrell sold all of its treasury stock for $25,000 cash.
- On June 1, 19X1, individuals holding $50,000 face value of Farrell's bonds exercised their conversion privilege. Each of the 50 bonds was converted into 40 shares of Farrell's common stock.
- On July 1, 19X1, Farrell purchased equipment for $63,000 cash.
- On December 31, 19X1, land with a fair market value of $150,000 was purchased through the issuance of a long-term note in the amount of $150,000. The note bears interest at the rate of 15% and is due on December 31, 19X6.
- Deferred income taxes represent timing differences relating to the use of accelerated depreciation methods for income tax reporting and the straight-line method for financial statement reporting.

Required:
Using the indirect method, prepare the statement of cash flows of Farrell Corporation for the year ended December 31, 19X1. Supplementary disclosures and schedules are not required.

NUMBER 2

The following is Omega Corp.'s comparative balance sheet accounts worksheet at December 31, 1992, and 1991, with a column showing the increase (decrease) from 1991 to 1992.

Comparative balance sheet worksheet	1992	1991	Increase (Decrease)
Cash	$ 800,000	$ 700,000	$100,000
Accounts receivable	1,128,000	1,168,000	(40,000)
Inventories	1,850,000	1,715,000	135,000
Property, plant and equipment	3,307,000	2,967,000	340,000
Accumulated depreciation	(1,165,000)	(1,040,000)	(125,000)
Investment in Belle Co.	305,000	275,000	30,000
Loan receivable	270,000	—	270,000
Total assets	$6,495,000	$5,785,000	$710,000
Accounts payable	$1,015,000	$ 955,000	$ 60,000
Income taxes payable	30,000	50,000	(20,000)
Dividends payable	80,000	90,000	(10,000)
Capital lease obligation	400,000	—	400,000
Capital stock, common, $1 par	500,000	500,000	—
Additional paid-in capital	1,500,000	1,500,000	—
Retained earnings	2,970,000	2,690,000	280,000
Total liabilities and stockholders' equity	$6,495,000	$5,785,000	$710,000

Additional information:

- On December 31, 1991, Omega acquired 25% of Belle Co.'s common stock for $275,000. On that date, the carrying value of Belle's assets and liabilities, which approximated their fair values, was $1,100,000. Belle reported income of $120,000 for the year ended December 31, 1992. No dividend was paid on Belle's common stock during the year.
- During 1992, Omega loaned $300,000 to Chase Co., an unrelated company. Chase made the first semi-annual principal repayment of $30,000, plus interest at 10%, on October 1, 1992.
- On January 2, 1992, Omega sold equipment costing $60,000, with a carrying amount of $35,000, for $40,000 cash.
- On December 31, 1992, Omega entered into a capital lease for an office building. The present value of the annual rental payments is $400,000, which equals the fair value of the building. Omega made the first rental payment of $60,000 when due on January 2, 1993.
- Net income for 1992 was $360,000.
- Omega declared and paid cash dividends for 1992 and 1991 as follows:

	1992	1991
Declared	December 15, 1992	December 15, 1991
Paid	February 28, 1993	February 28, 1992
Amount	$80,000	$90,000

Required:
Prepare a statement of cash flows for Omega, Inc., for the year ended December 31, 1992, using the indirect method. Supplemental schedules and disclosures are **not required**. A worksheet is **not required**.

NUMBER 3

N90

Presented below are the condensed statements of financial position of Linden Consulting Associates as of December 31, 1989 and 1988, and the condensed statement of income for the year ended December 31, 1989.

Linden Consulting Associates
CONDENSED STATEMENTS OF FINANCIAL POSITION
December 31, 1989 and 1988

Assets	*1989*	*1988*	*Net change increase (decrease)*
Cash	$ 652,000	$ 280,000	$372,000
Accounts receivable, net	446,000	368,000	78,000
Investment in Zach, Inc., at equity	550,000	466,000	84,000
Property and equipment	1,270,000	1,100,000	170,000
Accumulated depreciation	(190,000)	(130,000)	(60,000)
Excess of cost over book value of investment in Zach, Inc. (net)	152,000	156,000	(4,000)
Total assets	$2,880,000	$2,240,000	$640,000
Liabilities and Partners' Equity			
Accounts payable and accrued expenses	$ 320,000	$ 270,000	$ 50,000
Mortgage payable	250,000	270,000	(20,000)
Partners' equity	2,310,000	1,700,000	610,000
Total liabilities and partners' equity	$2,880,000	$2,240,000	$640,000

Linden Consulting Associates
CONDENSED STATEMENT OF INCOME
For the Year Ended December 31, 1989

Fee revenue	$2,664,000
Operating expenses	1,940,000
Operating income	724,000
Equity in earnings of Zach, Inc. (net of $4,000 amortization of excess of cost over book value)	176,000
Net income	$ 900,000

NUMBER 3 (cont.)

Additional information:

- On December 31, 1988, partners' capital and profit sharing percentages were as follows:

	Capital	*Profit sharing %*
Garr	$1,020,000	60%
Pat	680,000	40%
	$1,700,000	

- On January 1, 1989, Garr and Pat admitted Scott to the partnership for a cash payment of $340,000 to Linden Consulting Associates as the agreed amount of Scott's beginning capital account. In addition, Scott paid a $50,000 cash bonus directly to Garr and Pat. This amount was divided $30,000 to Garr and $20,000 to Pat. The new profit sharing arrangement is as follows:

Garr	50%
Pat	30%
Scott	20%

- On October 1, 1989, Linden purchased and paid for an office computer costing $170,000, including $15,000 for sales tax, delivery, and installation. There were no dispositions of property and equipment during 1989.

- Throughout 1989, Linden owned 25% of Zach, Inc.'s common stock. As a result of this ownership interest, Linden can exercise significant influence over Zach's operating and financial policies. During 1989, Zach paid dividends totaling $384,000 and reported net income of $720,000. Linden's 1989 amortization of excess of cost over book value in Zach was $4,000.

- Partners' drawings for 1989 were as follows:

Garr	$280,000
Pat	200,000
Scott	150,000
	$630,000

Required:

a. Using the direct method, prepare Linden's statement of cash flows for the year ended December 31, 1989.
b. Prepare a reconciliation of net income to net cash provided by operating activities.
c. Prepare an analysis of changes in partners' capital accounts for the year ended December 31, 1989.

NUMBER 4 ("Other Objective Answer Format")

Question Number 4(a) consists of 5 items. These items require numerical answers and selection of the proper cash flow category. **Answer all items.** Your grade will be based on the total number of correct answers.

Following are selected balance sheet accounts of Zach Corp. at December 31, 1991 and 1990, and the increases or decreases in each account from 1990 to 1991. Also presented is selected income statement information for the year ended December 31, 1991, and additional information.

Selected balance sheet accounts	*1991*	*1990*	*Increase (Decrease)*
Assets:			
Accounts receivable	$ 34,000	$ 24,000	$10,000
Property, plant, and equipment	277,000	247,000	30,000
Accumulated depreciation	(178,000)	(167,000)	(11,000)
Liabilities and stockholders' equity:			
Bonds payable	49,000	46,000	3,000
Dividends payable	8,000	5,000	3,000
Common stock, $1 par	22,000	19,000	3,000
Additional paid-in capital	9,000	3,000	6,000
Retained earnings	104,000	91,000	13,000

Selected income statement information for the year ended December 31, 1991

Sales revenue	$155,000
Depreciation	33,000
Gain on sale of equipment	13,000
Net income	28,000

Additional information

- Accounts receivable relate to sales of merchandise.
- During 1991, equipment costing $40,000 was sold for cash.
- During 1991, $20,000 of bonds payable were issued in exchange for property, plant, and equipment. There was no amortization of bond discount or premium.

Required:
Items A through E represent activities that will be reported in Zach's statement of cash flows for the year ended December 31, 1991. The following two responses are required for each item:

- Determine the amount that should be reported in Zach's 1991 statement of cash flows.
- Using the list below, determine the category in which the amount should be reported in the statement of cash flows.

O. Operating activity
I. Investing activity
F. Financing activity

Items to be answered:

A. Cash collections from customers (direct method).
B. Payments for purchase of property, plant, and equipment.
C. Proceeds from sale of equipment.
D. Cash dividends paid.
E. Redemption of bonds payable.

NUMBER 5

Number 5 is based on the following information. It consists of items 1 through 6.

The following condensed trial balance of Probe Co., a publicly-held company, has been adjusted except for income tax expense.

Probe Co.
CONDENSED TRIAL BALANCE

	12/31/93 Balances Dr. (Cr.)	*12/31/92 Balances Dr. (Cr.)*	*Net change Dr. (Cr.)*
Cash	$ 473,000	$ 817,000	$ (344,000)
Accounts receivable, net	670,000	610,000	60,000
Property, plant, and equipment	1,070,000	995,000	75,000
Accumulated depreciation	(345,000)	(280,000)	(65,000)
Dividends payable	(25,000)	(10,000)	(15,000)
Income taxes payable	35,000	(150,000)	185,000
Deferred income tax liability	(42,000)	(42,000)	--
Bonds payable	(500,000)	(1,000,000)	500,000
Unamortized premium on bonds	(71,000)	(150,000)	79,000
Common stock	(350,000)	(150,000)	(200,000)
Additional paid-in capital	(430,000)	(375,000)	(55,000)
Retained earnings	(185,000)	(265,000)	80,000
Sales	(2,420,000)		
Cost of sales	1,863,000		
Selling and administrative expenses	220,000		
Interest income	(14,000)		
Interest expense	46,000		
Depreciation	88,000		
Loss on sale of equipment	7,000		
Gain on extinguishment of bonds	(90,000)		
	$ 0	$ 0	$300,000

Additional information:

- During 1993 equipment with an original cost of $50,000 was sold for cash, and equipment costing $125,000 was purchased.
- On January 1, 1993, bonds with a par value of $500,000 and related premium of $75,000 were redeemed. The $1,000 face value, 10% par bonds had been issued on January 1, 1984, to yield 8%. Interest is payable annually every December 31 through 2003.
- Probe's tax payments during 1993 were debited to Income Taxes Payable. Probe elected early adoption of Statement of Financial Accounting Standards No. 109, *Accounting for Income Taxes*, for the year ended December 31, 1992, and recorded a deferred income tax liability of $42,000 based on temporary differences of $120,000 and an enacted tax rate of 35%. Probe's 1993 financial statement income before income taxes was greater than its 1993 taxable income, due entirely to temporary differences, by $60,000. Probe's cumulative net taxable temporary differences at December 31, 1993, were $180,000. Probe's enacted tax rate for the current and future years is 30%.
- 60,000 shares of common stock, $2.50 par, were outstanding on December 31, 1992. Probe issued an additional 80,000 shares on April 1, 1993.
- There were no changes to retained earnings other than dividends declared.

Required:
For each transaction in **items 1 through 6,** the following two responses are required:

- Determine the amount to be reported in Probe's 1993 statement of cash flows prepared using the indirect method.

- Select from the list below where the specific item should be separately reported on the statement of cash flows prepared using the indirect method.

  O. Operating.
  I. Investing.
  F Financing.
  S. Supplementary information.
  N. Not reported on Probe's statement of cash flows.

1. Cash paid for income taxes.
2. Cash paid for interest.
3. Redemption of bonds payable.
4. Issuance of common stock.
5. Cash dividends paid.
6. Proceeds from sale of equipment.

NUMBER 6 ("Other Objective Answer Format")

M93

Question Number 6 consists of 6 items. Select the **best** answer for each item. **Answer all items.** Your grade will be based on the total number of correct answers.

Items 1 through 6 are based on the following:

Daley, Inc., is consistently profitable. Daley's normal financial statement relationships are as follows:

I.	Current ratio	3 to 1
II.	Inventory turnover	4 times
III.	Total debt/total assets ratio	0.5 to 1

Required:
For items 1 through 6, determine whether each 1992 transaction or event increased, decreased, or had no effect on each of the 1992 ratios. For each ratio select only one of the three alternatives.

Items to be answered:
1. Daley issued a stock dividend.
2. Daley declared, but did not pay, a cash dividend.
3. Customers returned invoiced goods for which they had not paid.
4. Accounts payable were paid on December 31, 1992.
5. Daley recorded both as receivable from an insurance company and a loss from fire damage to a factory building.
6. Early in 1992, Daley increased the selling price of one of its products that had a demand in excess of capacity. The number of units sold in 1991 and 1992 was the same.

Chapter Eight
Solutions to Statement of Cash Flows and Financial Statement Analysis Questions

1. (c)	Cash in checking account	$ 350,000
	Cash in money market account	250,000
	U.S. Treasury bill purchased 12/1/92, maturing 2/28/93 (3 months)	800,000
	Cash and cash equivalents 12/31/92	$1,400,000

Generally, only investments with *original* maturities (to the enterprise holding the investment) of three (3) months or less qualify as cash equivalents. Therefore, the treasury bills purchased 3/1/92, maturing 2/28/93, would **not** be included as cash equivalents at 12/31/92.

2. (d)	Revenue	$1,980,000	
	Less increase in accounts receivable		
	Balance 12/31/86	$415,000	
	Balance	550,000	(135,000)
	Cash receipts from customers		$1,845,000

If accounts receivable had been written off during the year, the beginning balance would have to be adjusted for the write-off before the change in accounts receivable was determined.

The increase in the allowance account results from the current provision for bad debts expense and does not relate to the increase in receivables from unpaid revenues.

3. (c) Per FAS #95, cash flow per share shall not be reported in financial statements. Neither cash flow per share, nor any component thereof, is an acceptable alternative to net income or earnings per share as a measure of performance.

Per FAS #95, noncash investing and financing activities that affect recognized assets or liabilities shall be reported in related disclosures (either narrative or summarized in a schedule).

4. (a) All choices will be adjustments to net earnings when converting to cash provided because they do not involve the use of cash. The amortization of premium on bonds payable was originally a credit (increase to net earnings); therefore it must be subtracted from net earnings to arrive at cash provided by operations. Answers (b)-(d) are all items that should be added to convert net earnings to cash provided.

5. (d) All interest paid to creditors, except amounts capitalized, are classified as cash flows from operating activities.

6. (c) A gain on the sale of equipment is a noncash credit to income, therefore, it is deducted from net income to determine net cash flow from operating activities. Furthermore, the sale of equipment is an investing activity, and the cash receipts from the sale would be classified as investing activities on the statement of cash flows.

7. (a) For transactions that are part cash and part noncash, only the cash portion is reported in the statement of cash flows. The related disclosures (of noncash investing and financing activities) should clearly describe the cash and noncash aspects of such transactions.

8. (c) The financing portion of this transaction is a noncash transaction and would only be reported in related disclosures (narrative or schedule). In subsequent periods, payments of the mortgage note payable would be classified as cash outflows for financing activities.

9. (c) Generally, investing activities relate to the acquisition and disposal of assets other than those directly related to the enterprise's operations (such as trade receivables, inventory and prepaid expenses). Answer (a) is incorrect, as operating activities generally involve producing and delivering goods and/or providing services to customers. Sale of productive assets would not constitute sales to customers. Answer (b) is incorrect, as financing activities relate to obtaining and settling equity and debt financing other than that directly related to the enterprise's operations (such as trade payables and accrued expenses) and providing a return on investment to owners (dividends). Interest paid to creditors (net of amounts capitalized) is classified as an operating activities cash flow. Answer (d) is incorrect, as it is not a classification of cash flow for the statement of cash flows.

10. (a) Dividends received from investments.

Dividends received from investments are classified as a cash flow from operating activities. Under the direct method of reporting cash flows from operating activities, major classes of operating cash receipts and payments are shown in the operating activities section of the statement of cash flows.

Answer (b) is incorrect because: 1) gains are not cash flows, and 2) proceeds from the sale of equipment would be classified as investing activities, not operating activities.

Answer (c) is incorrect because: 1) gains are not cash flows, and 2) the cash payment to retire debt would be classified as financing activities, not operating activities.

Answer (d) is incorrect, as a change in accounting method is not a cash flow item.

11. (d) Cash flow per share should *not* be reported in financial statements. Neither cash flow per share, nor any component thereof, is an acceptable alternative to net income or earnings per share as a measure of performance.

12. (c) $429,200. Collections from customers:

Sales		$438,000
Less increase in accounts receivable:		
Accounts receivable Jan. 1	$21,600	
Accounts receivable Dec. 31	30,400	– 8,800
Cash collected from customers		$429,200

As no accounts receivable were written off or recovered during the year, the increase in accounts receivable represents uncollected sales and the beginning balance of accounts receivable does not require adjustment for such events.

13. (d) $75,700. Net cash provided by operating activities:

Net income	$75,000
Adjustments to reconcile net income to net cash provided by operating activities:	
Increase in accounts receivable ($11,500 – $14,500)	– 3,000
Bad debt expense (increase in the allowance for uncollectible accounts, $400 – $500)	+ 100
Decrease in prepaid rent ($6,200 – $4,100)	+ 2,100
Increase in accounts payable ($9,700 – $11,200)	+ 1,500
Net cash provided by operating activities	$75,700

The increase in accounts receivable attributed to uncollected sales.
The decrease in prepaid rent attributed to expense not requiring cash payment in the current period.
The increase in accounts payable attributed to purchases not requiring cash payment in the current period.

14. (c) Cash flow from operating activities:

Net income	$690,000
Adjustments to reconcile net income to net cash provided by operating activities:	
Depreciation	* 250,000
Amortization of goodwill	10,000
Gain on sale of long-term investment	(35,000)
Increase in inventory	(80,000)
Increase in accounts payable and accrued liabilities	105,000
Net cash provided by operating activities	$940,000

*There was no net change in accumulated depreciation; therefore, depreciation expense equaled the accumulated depreciation on the equipment sold of $250,000 ($400,000 cost - $150,000 carrying value).

15. (a) Cash flow from investing activities:

Purchase of short-term investments	$(300,000)
Proceeds from sale of long-term investments	135,000
Purchase of plant assets	(1,100,000)
Proceeds from sale of equipment	150,000
Net cash used in investing activities	$(1,115,000)

Purchase of plant assets:

Net increase in plant assets	$ 700,000
Add cost of equipment sold	400,000
Purchases of plant assets	$1,100,000

16. (a) Cash flows from financing activities:

Proceeds from short-term debt	$325,000
Proceeds from issuance of common stock	220,000
Dividends paid	(240,000)
Net cash provided by financing activities	$305,000

*Note that the total of the net cash provided by (used in) operating activities (#6), investing activities (#7) and financing activities (above) equals the net change in cash during the period.

Cash provided by (used in):

Operating activities	$940,000
Investing activities	(1,115,000)
Financing activities	305,000
Net increase in cash	$130,000

17. (a) $170,000.

Proceeds from sale of equipment	$10,000
Payment to acquire A.S. Inc. bonds	(180,000)
Net cash used in investing activities	$(170,000)

Gain on sale of equipment and amortization of bond discount are noncash items and would only be used to reconcile net income to net cash from operating activities.

18. (d) $37,000.

Payment at Dividends	$(38,000)
Proceeds from sale of treasury stock	75,000
Net cash provided by Financing Activities	37,000

Declaration of dividends is not a cash flow item.

19. (c) Cash flows from investment activities

Payment for purchase of real estate	$(550,000)
Proceeds from sale of investments	500,000
Payment to acquire machinery and equipment	(125,000)
Net cash used in investing activities	$ (175,000)

20. (b) Cash flows from financing activities

Proceeds from bank loan	$ 550,000
Payment of dividends	(600,000)
Proceeds from issuance of common stock	250,000
Payment of bank loan	(450,000)
Net cash used in financing activities	$(250,000)

Note: The reduction in accounts receivable and increase in accounts payable relate to operating activities.

21. (a) The write-off of accounts receivable is a non-cash decrease in accounts receivable. Therefore, the increase (decrease) in accounts receivable for the period does not represent the true uncollected sales (additional collections). The write-off, as a non-cash decrease in accounts receivable, would be deducted from sales to determine cash collections from customers.

The increase in accounts receivable represents (results from) uncollected sales, and would be deducted from sales to determine cash collections from customers.

22. (c) $31,000 increase.

Building cost	$100,000
Less accumulated depreciation	- 48,000
Book value	$ 52,000
Reported loss	- 21,000
Proceeds from insurance	$31,000

23. (a) $717,000. Net cash used in financing activities:

Payment for retirement of debt	-	$750,000
Payment of cash dividend	-	62,000
Proceeds from sale of treasury stock	+	95,000
Net cash used in financing activities	-	$717,000

The conversion of preferred stock to common stock is a non-cash financing activity and would be disclosed in a related schedule or footnote.

24. (d) $41,000. Net cash used in investing activities:

Payment for acquisition of investment in Maybel, Inc.	- $26,000
Proceeds from sale of investment in Rate Motors	+ 35,000
Payment for acquisition of certificate of deposit	- 50,000
Net cash used in investing activities	- $41,000

Collection of dividends on investments in stock ($12,000) is classified as a cash flow from operating activities (dividend income).

25. (d) On the statement of cash flows, the amounts reported as investing activities reflect the actual inflows and outflows of cash. The amount of the note issued is reflected as a non-cash significant investing and financing activity in a separate notation or schedule.

26. (d) The U.S. Treasury bills qualify as cash equivalents. As such, they are part of the change (cash and cash equivalents) being explained by the statement and are not operating, investing or financing cash flows which explain the change.

27. (d) The cash flow statement prepared under the direct method would include the major classes of gross cash receipts and payments, and the cash payments would include the amount of income taxes paid. A unique feature of the direct method is that it requires a supplemental schedule showing a reconciliation of net income to net cash from operating activities (the indirect method).

Neither the direct nor indirect method requires a reconciliation of ending retained earnings to net cash flow from operations.

28. (b) $330,000.

Cost of goods sold	$ 450,000
Less decrease in inventory	- 160,000
Purchases	$ 290,000
Add decrease in A/P - suppliers	40,000
Payments to suppliers	$ 330,000

The decrease in inventory is included in cost of goods sold; however, was not purchased during the current period. The decrease in accounts payable - suppliers results from payments to suppliers in excess of current period purchases.

29. (a) The sale of trading securities at their carrying amounts for cash would not effect either the current ratio or the quick ratio. Neither current assets nor quick assets (cash + marketable securities + S.T. receivables) would be affected by the sale as both trading securities and cash are current and quick assets, and the sale was at carrying value (no gain or loss).

30. (a) Current ratio -- increased; Quick ratio -- decreased.

Current ratio = Current assets ÷ Current liabilities.
When the current ratio is greater than 1 to 1, an equal decrease in current assets and current liabilities will result in an increase in the current ratio. The decrease in current liabilities (the smaller number) is proportionately greater than the decrease in current assets, resulting in an increase in the ratio.

Quick ratio = Cash + Mkt. Sec. + Rec. / Current liabilities.
When the quick ratio is less than 1:1, an equal decrease in quick assets and current liabilities will result in a decrease in the ratio. The decrease in current liabilities (the larger number) is proportionately smaller than the decrease in quick assets, resulting in a decrease in the ratio.

31. (b) (6/4) x (1/6) = ROI.
Rate of return in investment = Turnover x margin
Turnover = Sales/Investment (assets) = 600,000/400,000 = 6/4
Margin = Net income/Sales = 100,000/600,000 = 1/6
ROI = (6/4) x (1/6)

32. (a) Per FASB Concept #5, the balance sheet is intended to help external users to assess a company's liquidity, financial flexibility, and operating capability. Liquidity is used to describe the amount of time until an asset is converted into cash or a liability is paid. Financial flexibility refers to a company's ability to use its financial resources to adapt to change.

33. (a) Acid-test (quick) ratio

$$= \frac{\text{Cash + marketable securities + accounts receivable}}{\text{Current liabilities}}$$

$$= \frac{300 + 1200}{1000}$$

$$= \underline{1.5}$$

34. (c) Daily credit sales = Credit sales/365 = $7200/365 = $19.72

Average accounts receivable = $\frac{\text{Beginning balance + ending balance}}{2}$

$= \frac{800 + 1200}{2}$

= $1000

Days sales in accounts receivable = $\frac{\text{Average accounts receivable}}{\text{Daily credit sales}}$

$= \frac{\$1000}{\$19.72} = \underline{50.7}$

Alternative computation:

Accounts receivable turnover = Credit sales/Average accounts receivable

= $7200/$1000

= 7.2 times

Days sales in accounts receivable = $\frac{365}{\text{Accounts receivable turnover}}$

$= \frac{365}{7.2}$

= <u>50.7</u>

35. (a) $105,000.

Accounts Receivable Turnover = $\frac{\text{Credit sales}}{\text{Average Accts Receivable}}$

5.0 = $\frac{\text{Credit sales}}{\$21,000}$

5.0 x $21,000 = Credit sales

$<u>105,000</u> = Credit sales

Average Accounts Receivable = $\frac{\text{Beginning balance + Ending balance}}{2}$

$= \frac{\$20,000 + 22,000}{2}$

<u>$21,000</u>

36. (c) 2.0 times.

$$\text{Inventory Turnover} = \frac{\text{Cost of Goods Sold}}{\text{Aver. Inventory}} = \frac{18{,}000}{9{,}000} = \underline{2.0} \text{ times}$$

$$\text{Average inventory} = \frac{\text{Beginning Balance + Ending Balance}}{2} = \frac{\$6{,}000 + \$12{,}000}{2} = \underline{\$9{,}000}$$

Ending inventory:

Beginning inventory	$ 6,000
+ Purchases	24,000
Cost of goods available for sale	30,000
- Cost of goods sold	(18,000)
Ending inventory	12,000

37. (b) Average days sales in inventory =

$$\frac{\text{365 Days (in year)}}{\text{Times Inventory Turnover (in year)}}$$

or

$$\frac{\text{Average Inventory}}{\text{Average daily cost of goods sold}}$$

38. (d) The average number of days in the operating cycle is equal to the average number of days in the inventory -- cost of goods sold cycle plus the average number of days in the accounts receivable-sales cycle.

Average daily CGS = CGS / 360 = 5,400,000 / 360 =	15,000/day
Average daily sales = sales / 360 = 7,200,000 / 360 =	20,000/day
Day's sales in inventory = av. inv. / CGS/day = 1,800,000 / 15,000 =	120 days
+ day's sales in accts. rec. = av. A.R. / sales/day = 960,000 / 20,000 =	48 days
	168 days

39. (b) Rate of return on investment (or asset) can be broken down to its component margin and turnover. An increase (decrease) in either will result in an increase (decrease) in the R.O.I. The relationship of R.O.I. , margin and turnover is as follows:

$$\text{R.O.I.} = \frac{\textit{Net income}}{\text{Investment}} = \underset{\textit{(Margin)}}{\frac{\textit{Net income}}{\text{Sales}}} \times \underset{\textit{(Turnover)}}{\frac{\textit{Sales}}{\text{Investment}}}$$

40. (c) The acid test or quick ratio is equal to cash + marketable securities + receivables divided by current liabilities, or current assets minus inventory divided by current liabilities. Neither average inventory nor inventory is used in the computation of this ratio.

The inventory is equal to cost of goods sold divided by average inventory.

41. (a)

$$\text{Current ratio} = \frac{\text{Current assets}}{\text{Current liabilities}}$$

$$\text{Quick (acid test) ratio} = \frac{\text{Cash + Marketable securities + Receivables}}{\text{Current liabilities}}$$

or

$$= \frac{\text{Current assets - Inventory}}{\text{Current liabilities}}$$

As inventory is excluded in the quick ratio, the write-off of obsoleted inventory would have no effect on the quick ratio; however, it would decrease the current ratio as the write-off would reduce current assets.

42. b) The current ratio is equal to current assets divided by current liabilities. Any transaction which will increase current assets proportionately more than current liabilities or decrease current liabilities proportionately more than current assets will increase the current ratio.

Purchasing $50,000 of inventory with a short-term account payable will increase both current assets and current liabilities by $50,000. However, because the current ratio is less than 1 to 1, the purchase will increase current assets proportionately more than current liabilities, and increase the current ratio.

Answer (a) is incorrect as it will increase only current liabilities, decreasing the current ratio. Answer (c) is incorrect as it will decrease current assets proportionately more than current liabilities, decreasing the current ratio. Answer (d) is incorrect as it will not affect either current assets or current liabilities. Therefore, the current ratio will be unchanged.

43. (b) 6.0 (times).

Inventory turnover	=	Cost of goods sold / Average inventory
	=	$900,000 / $150,000
	=	6.0 times
Average inventory	=	Beginning + ending balance / 2
	=	($120,000 + $180,000) / 2
	=	$150,000

Computation of beginning inventory:

Cost of goods sold	$ 900,000
+ Ending inventory	180,000
Cost of goods available for sale	$1,080,000
- Purchases	- 960,000
Beginning inventory	$ 120,000

Alternative: If purchases were $960,000 and cost of goods sold were $900,000, inventory increased $60,000. Beginning inventory would equal the ending inventory of $180,000 less the increase of $60,000, or $120,000.

44. (d) 94 days.
The operating cycle is the average time for a company to expend cash for inventory, process and sell the inventory, and collect the resulting receivables, converting them back into cash. The number of days in the operating cycle (94) is equal to the number of days' sales in inventory (61), plus the number of days' sales in accounts receivable (33).

45. (b) The rate of return on investment (assets) can be broken down to its components margin (income as a percentage of sales) and asset turnover. An increase (decrease) in either will result in an increase (decrease) in rate of return on investment (ROI). The relationship of ROI, margin and turnover is as follows:

				(Margin)		(Turnover)
ROI	=	Net Income / Investment (Assets)	=	Net income / Sales	x	Sales / Investment (Assets)

46. (b) The defensive - interval ratio is a measure of liquidity, the entities' ability to meet operating cash needs without external cash flows.

$$\text{Defensive-interval Ratio} = \frac{\text{Cash + S.T. Mk. Sec. + S.T. Rec.}}{\text{Aver. daily expenditures for operations}}$$

The rate of return on stockholders' equity is a measure of profitability (to the owners).

47. (b) Receivable turnover ratio.
Accounts receivable turnover = Sales/Average accounts receivable.
Collection of accounts receivable would reduce the accounts receivable balance and, thereby, the average accounts receivable which would result in an increase in the accounts receivable turnover.

48. (b) Leverage (financial) results from the use of fixed cost debt securities in the capital structure of an entity. Successful use of leverage (favorable leverage) results when invested funds earn more than the cost of borrowing the funds.

49. (b) $330,000.

Current stockholders' equity	$ 700,000
Planned issuance of stock	300,000
Planned stockholders' equity	$1,000,000

Debt-equity ratio = Debt/Equity
.75 = Debt/$1,000,000
Debt = $750,000

Maximum allowable debt	$750,000
Current debt	- 420,000
Maximum additional debt	$330,000

50. (a)

$$\text{Times interest earned} = \frac{\text{Net income before interest and taxes}}{\text{Interest expense}}$$

$$= \frac{\$800,000}{\$100,000}$$

= 8 or 8 to 1

51. (a) The quick ratio includes the current assets that can be "quickly" converted to cash such as cash, marketable securities and receivables. Therefore, fluctuating market prices for short-term investments (marketable securities) may adversely affect the ratio. Answers (b) and (d) are incorrect because inventory is not included in the Quick Ratio. Answer (c) is incorrect because Available-For-Sale securities may be either current or non-current assets.

52. (c) Cash and Cash Equivalents should include cash in the checking account, the money market account, and the U.S. Treasury bill purchased 1/1/99. ($35,000 + $75,000 + $350,000 = $460,000). The 1st Treasury bill has a maturity from the purchase date of three months which meets the Trans Co. definition of a cash equivalent. The second Treasury bill has a maturity of four months and would not be considered a cash equivalent.

53. (c) Cash equivalents are the cash in the checking account ($35,000), the cash in the money market account ($75,000) and the Treasury bill that has a maturity of three months from the purchase date ($200,000) for a total of $310,000. The $150,000 Treasury bill is not a cash equivalent because the maturity date is six months from the purchase date.

Chapter Eight
Solutions to Statement of Cash Flows Problems

NUMBER 1

Farrell Corporation
STATEMENT OF CASH FLOWS WORKSHEET
For the Year Ended December 31, 19X1
(Not Required)

Assets	*19X0*	*Dr.*	*Cr.*	*19X1*
Cash	$180,000	(x) $ 95,000		$ 275,000
Accounts receivable	305,000		(7) 10,000	295,000
Inventories	431,000	(8) 118,000		549,000
Investment in Hall, Inc.	60,000	(5) 13,000		73,000
Land	200,000	(10) 150,000		350,000
Plant and equipment	606,000	(15) 63,000	(4) 45,000	624,000
Less accumulated depreciation	(107,000)	(4) 21,000	(2) 53,000	(139,000)
Goodwill	20,000		(3) 4,000	16,000
Total assets	$1,695,000			$2,043,000
Liabilities and stockholders' equity				
Accounts payable and accrued expenses	$563,000		(9) 41,000	$604,000
Note payable, long-term	—		(10) 150,000	150,000
Bonds payable	210,000	(12) 50,000		160,000
Deferred income taxes	30,000		(6) 11,000	41,000
Common stock	400,000		(11) 10,000 (12) 20,000	430,000
Additional paid-in capital	175,000		(11) 13,000 (12) 30,000 (13) 8,000	226,000
Retained earnings	334,000	(14) 43,000	(1) 141,000	432,000
Treasury stock	(17,000)		(13) 17,000	—
Total liabilities and equity	$1,695,000	$553,000	$553,000	$2,043,000
Cash flows from operating activities:				
Net Income		(1) $141,000		
Depreciation		(2) 53,000		
Amortization of goodwill		(3) 4,000		
Loss on sale of equipment		(4) 5,000		
Equity in net income of Hall, Inc.			(5) 13,000	
Deferred income taxes		(6) 11,000		
Decrease in accounts receivable		(7) 10,000		
Increase in inventories			(8) 118,000	
Increase in accounts payable and accrued expenses		(9) 41,000		
Cash flows from investing activities:				
Sale of equipment		(4) 19,000		
Purchase of equipment			(15) 63,000	
Cash flows from financing activities:				
Sale of common stock		(11) 23,000		
Sale of treasury stock		(13) 25,000		
Cash dividends			(14) 43,000	
Noncash investing and financing activities:				
Issuance of note payable to purchase land		(10) 150,000		
Purchase of land by issuance of note payable			(10) 150,000	
Issuance of common stock to convert bonds		(12) 50,000		
Conversion of bonds to common stock			(12) 50,000	
Net increase in cash			(X) 95,000	
		$532,000	$532,000	

Farrell Corporation
STATEMENT OF CASH FLOWS
For the Year Ended December 31, 19X1

Cash flow from operating activities:		
Net income	$141,000	
Adjustments to reconcile net income to net cash provided by operating activities:		
Depreciation	53,000	
Amortization of goodwill	4,000	
Loss on sale of equipment	5,000	
Undistributed earnings of Hall, Inc.	(13,000)	
Increase in deferred income taxes	11,000	
Decrease in accounts receivable	10,000	
Increase in inventories	(118,000)	
Increase in accounts payable and accrued expenses	41,000	
Net cash provided by operating activities		$134,000
Cash flows from investing activities:		
Proceeds from sale of equipment	$ 19,000	
Payments to acquire equipment	(63,000)	
Net cash used in investing activities		(44,000)
Cash flows from financing activities:		
Proceeds from issuance of common stock	$ 23,000	
Proceeds from sale of treasury stock	25,000	
Dividends paid	(43,000)	
Net cash provided by financing activities		5,000
Net increase in cash		$ 95,000
Cash, January 1, 19X1		180,000
Cash, December 31, 19X1		$275,000

NUMBER 2

Omega Corp.
STATEMENT OF CASH FLOWS
For the Year Ended December 31, 1992

Cash flows from operating activities:		
Net income		$360,000
Adjustments to reconcile net income to net cash provided by operating activities:		
Depreciation	$150,000 [1]	
Gain on sale of equipment	(5,000) [2]	
Undistributed earnings of Belle Co.	(30,000) [3]	
Changes in assets and liabilities:		
Decrease in accounts receivable	40,000	
Increase in inventories	(135,000)	
Increase in accounts payable	60,000	
Decrease in income taxes payable	(20,000)	
		60,000
Net cash provided by operating activities		420,000
Cash flows from investing activities:		
Proceeds from sale of equipment	40,000	
Loan to Chase Co.	(300,000)	
Principal payment of loan receivable	30,000	
Net cash used in investing activities		(230,000)
Cash flows from financing activities:		
Dividends paid	(90,000)	
Net cash used in financing activities		(90,000)
Net increase in cash		100,000
Cash at beginning of year		700,000
Cash at end of year		$800,000

Explanation of Amounts:

[1]	Depreciation		
	Net increase in accumulated depreciation for the year ended December 31, 1992		$125,000
	Accumulated depreciation on equipment sold:		
	Cost	$60,000	
	Carrying value	35,000	25,000
	Depreciation for 1992		$150,000
[2]	Gain on sale of equipment		
	Proceeds		$ 40,000
	Carrying value		35,000
	Gain		$ 5,000
[3]	Undistributed earnings of Belle Co.		
	Belle's net income for 1992		$120,000
	Omega's ownership		25%
	Undistributed earnings of Belle Co.		$ 30,000

NUMBER 3

a.

Linden Consulting Associates
STATEMENT OF CASH FLOWS
For the Year Ended December 31, 1989
Increase (Decrease) in Cash

Cash flows from operating activities:		
Cash received from customers	$2,586,000 [1]	
Cash paid to suppliers and employees	(1,830,000) [2]	
Dividends received from affiliate	96,000	
Net cash provided by operating activities		$ 852,000
Cash flows from investing activities:		
Purchased property and equipment		(170,000)
Cash flows from financing activities:		
Principal payment of mortgage payable	(20,000)	
Proceeds for admission of new partner	340,000	
Drawings against partners' capital accounts	(630,000)	
Net cash used in financing activities		(310,000)
Net increase in cash		372,000
Cash at beginning of year		280,000
Cash at end of year		$ 652,000

Explanation of amounts:

[1] Fee revenue		$2,664,000
Less ending accounts receivable balance		(446,000)
Add beginning accounts receivable balance		368,000
		$2,586,000
[2] Operating expenses		$1,940,000
Less: Depreciation	$ 60,000	
Ending accounts payable balance	320,000	(380,000)
Add beginning accounts payable balance		270,000
		$1,830,000

b.

Reconciliation of net income to net cash provided by operating activities:

Net income		$900,000
Adjustments to reconcile net income to net cash provided by operating activities:		
Depreciation and amortization	$64,000	
Undistributed earnings of affiliate	(84,000) [1]	
Change in assets and liabilities:		
Increase in accounts receivable	(78,000)	
Increase in accounts payable and accrued expenses	50,000	
Total adjustments		(48,000)
Net cash provided by operating activities		$852,000

[1] Linden's share of Zach, Inc.'s:	
Reported net income for 1989 (25% × $720,000)	$180,000
Cash dividends paid for 1989 (25% × $384,000)	96,000
Undistributed earnings for 1989	$ 84,000

c.

Linden Consulting Associates

ANALYSIS OF CHANGES IN PARTNERS' CAPITAL ACCOUNTS

For the Year Ended December 31, 1989

	Total	*Garr*	*Pat*	*Scott*
Balance, December 31, 1988	$1,700,000	$1,020,000	$680,000	$ —
Capital investment	340,000	—	—	340,000
Allocation of net income	900,000	450,000	270,000	180,000
Balance before drawings	2,940,000	1,470,000	950,000	520,000
Drawings	630,000	280,000	200,000	150,000
Balance, December 31, 1989	$2,310,000	$1,190,000	$750,000	$370,000

NUMBER 4

A. Cash collections from customers — $145,000 (O)

Revenue from sales	$155,000
Less increase in accounts receivable	(10,000)
	$145,000

B. Payment for purchases of property, plant and equipment — $50,000 (I)

Cost of equipment sold	$40,000
Add: increase in property, plant and equipment	30,000
Total acquisitions of P.P.&E.	$70,000
Less: P.P.&E. acquired through issuance of bonds payable (non-cash acquisition)	(20,000)
Payments to acquire P.P.&E.	$50,000

C. Proceeds from sale of equipment — $31,000 (I)

Cost of equipment sold		$40,000
Less: Accumulated depreciation		
Depreciation expense	$33,000	
Less increase in accumulated depreciation	(11,000)	
Accumulated depreciation applicable to equipment sold		(22,000)
Book value of equipment sold		$18,000
Add: Gain on sale of equipment		13,000
Proceeds from sale of equipment		$31,000

D. Cash dividends paid — $12,000 (F)

Net income	$28,000
Less increase in retained earnings	13,000
Dividends declared	$15,000
Less increase in dividends payable	(3,000)
Dividends paid	$12,000

E. Redemption of bonds payable — $17,000 (F)

Bonds payable issued to acquire P.P.&E.	$20,000
Less increase in bonds payable	(3,000)
Payments to redeem bonds payable	$17,000

NUMBER 5

1. $185,000. Supplementary Information.
   The "additional information" states that Probe's tax payments during 1993 were debited to income taxes payable; therefore, the change in the account ($185,000 debit) represents the cash paid for income taxes.

   When the indirect method is used to represent cash flows from operating activities, FAS #95 requires supplementary disclosure of cash paid for interest and taxes.

2. $50,000. Supplementary Information.
   Cash paid for interest:

Interest expense	$46,000
+ Bond premium amortization	4,000
Cash paid	$50,000

Bond Premium Amortization:

Beginning balance	$150,000
- Premium retired	(75,000)
	75,000
- Ending balance	(71,000)
Amortization of bond premium	4,000

When the indirect method is used to report cash flows from operating activities, FAS # 95 requires supplementary disclosure of cash paid for interest and taxes.

3. $485,000. Financing.
   Cash paid to retire bonds:

Bond payable (Face value)	$500,000
+ Premium on bond payable	75,000
Carrying value of bond payable	$575,000
- Gain on retirement of bond payable	(90,000)
Cash payment to retire bond	$485,000

Issuance and retirement of debt are financing activities.

4. $255,000. Financing.
   Cash received from issuance of common stock:

Increase in common stock (par)	$200,000
Increase in A.P.I.C.	55,000
	$255,000

Issuance and retirement of stock and acquisition and sale of treasury stock are financing activities.

5. $65,000. Financing.
   Cash dividends paid:

Decrease in retained earnings	$80,000
- Increase in dividend payable	(15,000)
Cash payment	$65,000

The "additional information" states there were no changes to retained earnings other than dividends declared. Payment of dividends is a financing activity.

6. $20,000. Investing.

Cash received from sale of equipment:

Cost of equipment sold	$50,000
- Accumulated depreciation	(23,000)
Book value of equipment sold	$27,000
- Loss on sale	(7,000)
Cash received	$20,000

Accumulated depreciation on equipment sold

Depreciation expense	$88,000
- Increase in accumulated depreciation	(65,000)
Accumulated depreciation on equipment sold	$23,000

Acquisition and disposal of fixed assets are Investing Activities.

NUMBER 6

I. Current ratio = Current assets ÷ current liabilities

II. Inventory turnover = Cost of goods sold ÷ Average inventory
Average inventory = (beginning inventory + ending inventory) ÷ 2

III. Total debt ÷ total asset ratio (debt ratio)

1. I, II, and III—no effect.
A stock dividend reduces retained earnings and increases paid-in capital by an equal amount; therefore, it has no effect in total stockholders' equity, or any of the elements in the above ratios.

2. I—decrease; II—no effect; III—increase.
Declaration of a cash dividend increases current liabilities and decreases retained earnings (thus stockholders' equity). The increase in current liabilities would decrease the current ratio (I) and increase the debt ratio (II).

3. I and II—decrease; III—increase.
The return of merchandise would decrease current assets (accounts receivable decreases by the sales value; inventory increases by the cost of the items) resulting in a decrease of the current ratio (I).
The return of merchandise would reduce cost of goods sold and increase inventory resulting in a decrease in inventory turnover (II).
The return of merchandise does not effect total debt; however, the decrease in assets (current) will cause the debt ratio (III) to increase.

4. I—increase; II—no effect; III—decrease.
The payment of accounts payable reduces current assets and current liabilities by an equal dollar amount.
As the current ratio is greater than 1 to 1, the decrease in current assets is proportionately smaller than the decrease in current liabilities, resulting in an increase in the current ratio (I).
As the debt ratio is less than 1 to 1, the decrease in debt is proportionately greater than the decrease in assets, resulting in a decrease in the debt ratio (III).
The inventory turnover (II) is not effected as the payment of accounts payable does not effect any of its elements.

5. I—increase; II—no effect; III—increase.
The increase in receivables would increase current assets and the current ratio (I).
The inventory turnover (II) is not effected as this transaction does not effect any of its elements. As the fire damage resulted in a loss, the insurance receivable is less than the book value of the building and total assets have decreased. The decrease in assets results in an increase in the debt ratio (III).

6. I—increase; II—no effect; III—decrease.
An increase in selling price with no decrease in units sold would result in an increase in proceeds from sale (cash or accounts receivable) increasing current assets and the current ratio (I). The inventory turnover (II) would not be effected as none of its elements are effected.
The increase in assets would result in a decrease in the debt ratio (III).

Chapter Nine
Bonds, Accounting for Debt

Chapter Nine
Bonds, Accounting for Debt

BONDS ISSUED

Long-term certificates of indebtedness usually issued in denominations of $1,000 with the market price being quoted in 100's. The terms of the debt issue are specified in the **indenture** (contract between issuer and investor) which is policed by a **trustee** (representative of investors). Interest is normally paid semi-annually based on a stated percentage of the face value of the bond issue, referred to as the **coupon or nominal rate**. This fixed dollar interest is adjusted to the prevailing market (yield) rate of interest for securities of equivalent risk by changes in the market price of the bond issue. The market value of the bonds will vary inversely with changes in the market rate of interest.

Issuance:

Bonds are recorded as liabilities at their face value when issued. The issuance of bonds above or below their face value reflects the difference between the market rate of interest and the coupon rate on the date of issuance, as follows:

IF	*Bonds Sell*
Market Rate < Coupon Rate	Above F.V. @ Premium
Market Rate = Coupon Rate	At F.V.
Market Rate > Coupon Rate	Below F.V. @ Discount

(Note: Market price and market rate [yield] are inversely related.)

Any difference between the amount paid and the face value should be recorded separately as a Premium or Discount on bonds payable.

Journal entries to record issuance at Premium and Discount:

Cash	$102,000		
Bonds Payable		$100,000	Premium
Premium on Bonds Payable		2,000	(102)
Cash	$ 98,000		
Discount on Bonds Payable	2,000		Discount
Bonds Payable		$100,000	(98)

The carrying value of the liability will be its face value plus any premium or less any discount, and will be periodically adjusted by the amortization of the premium or discount to interest expense over the life of the issue so as to reflect the face value at maturity. The discount or premium should not be reported separately as a deferred charge or credit, as it does not represent an asset or liability separable from the debt which gave rise to it (APB #21).

Issue costs are treated separately as deferred charges and amortized over the life of the bond issue. They should **not** be combined with a discount or used to reduce a premium. Issue costs include all costs of issuing the bond, such as underwriting, accounting, and legal fees, S.E.C. registration, printing, etc., and represent an asset which is carried on the balance sheet as a deferred charge (APB #21).

In order to establish the proceeds of a bond issue, the present value of the interest payments and the maturity payment of face value are computed using the factors for the yield rate.

Example: On January 2, 19XX, Firm A issued 7% bonds, face value $1,000,000 due at the end of 5 years with interest paid annually.

	Case A-Yield Rate 8%	Case B-Yield Rate 6%
Present value of 1	.68058	.74726
Present value of annuity	3.99271	4.21236

	Case A	Case B
P.V. of interest payments	3.9927 × $70,000 = $279,490	4.21236 × $70,000 = $ 294,865
P.V. of principal payments	.68058 × $1,000,000 = 680,580	.74726 × $1,000,000 = 747,260
	$960,070	$1,042,125

Amortization of Bond Discount and Premium:

The discount or premium on a bond issue should be amortized over the life of the issue to reflect the face value at maturity. There are two methods of bond premium or discount amortization:

1. **The effective interest method (preferable per APB #21).**
2. **The straight-line method (allowed if not materially different than the interest method).**

SFAS #91 requires an enterprise which acquires or originates a loan (lender and purchaser) to defer loan origination fees and costs and recognize such amounts as adjustments of the yield using the interest method. The charges (revenues) may not be offset against the costs of the loan. These adjustments are to be made on a contract by contract basis (unless aggregation of the adjustments causes immaterial differences). The straight-line method may only be used for demand loans or revolving lines of credit under certain circumstances.

Sale at Discount—Case Example A (above)

(1) Effective Interest Method Amortization

Year	*(1) Interest Expense (4) × 8%*	*(2) Interest Paid*	*(3) Discount Amort. (1) – (2)*	*(4) Carrying Value EOY (4) + (3)*	*(5) Interest Rate (1) ÷ (4)*
Issue	—	—	—	$ 960,070	—
1	$ 76,806	$70,000	$ 6,806	966,876	8%
2	77,350	70,000	7,350	974,226	8%
3	77,938	70,000	7,938	982,164	8%
4	78,573	70,000	8,573	990,737	8%
5	79,263	70,000	9,263	1,000,000	8%
	$389,930		$39,930		

(2) Straight-Line Method Amortization

Year	*(1) Interest Paid*	*(2) Discount Amort. 39,930÷5 yr.*	*(3) Interest Expense (1)+(2)*	*(4) Carrying Value EOY (4)+(2)*	*(5) Interest Rate (3)÷(4)*
Issue	—	—	—	960,070	—
1	70,000	7,986	77,986	968,056	8.12%
2	70,000	7,986	77,986	976,042	8.06%
3	70,000	7,986	77,986	984,028	7.99%
4	70,000	7,986	77,986	992,014	7.93%
5	70,000	7,986	77,986	1,000,000	7.86%
		$39,930	$389,930		

Note: (1) Total discount amortizations are the same.
(2) Total interest expenses are the same.
(3) The effective interest method results in:
- constant rate of interest
- increasing interest expense per period
- increasing discount amortization per period

(4) The straight-line method results in:
- varying interest rate
- constant interest expense and discount amortization

Journal entry to record interest expense and amortization for Year 1:

	Effective Interest		*Straight-Line*	
Interest Expense	$76,806		$77,986	
Cash		$70,000		$70,000
Discount on Bonds Payable		6,806		7,986

Sale at Premium—Case Example B (previous)

(1) Effective Interest Method

Year	*(1) Interest Expense (4) × 6%*	*(2) Interest Paid*	*(3) Premium Amort. (1)–(2)*	*(4) Carrying Value (4)–(3)*	*(5) Interest Rate (1)÷(4)*
Issue	—	—	—	$1,042,125	6%
1	$ 62,527	$70,000	$ 7,473	1,034,652	6%
2	62,079	70,000	7,921	1,026,731	6%
3	61,604	70,000	8,396	1,018,335	6%
4	61,100	70,000	8,900	1,009,435	6%
5	60,565	70,000	9,435	1,000,000	6%
	$307,875		$42,125		

(2) Straight-Line Method

Year	*(1) Interest Paid*	*(2) Premium Amort. 42,125÷5 yrs.*	*(3) Interest Expense (1)–(2)*	*(4) Carrying Value (4)–(2)*	*(5) Interest Rate (3)÷(4)*
Issue	—	—	—	$1,042,125	—
1	$70,000	$ 8,425	$ 61,575	1,033,700	5.91%
2	70,000	8,425	61,575	1,025,275	5.96%
3	70,000	8,425	61,575	1,016,850	6.01%
4	70,000	8,425	61,575	1,008,425	6.06%
5	70,000	8,425	61,575	1,000,000	6.11%
		$42,125	$307,875		

Note: (a) Total premium amortizations are the same.
(b) Total interest expenses are the same.
(c) The effective interest method results in:
- constant rate of interest
- decreasing interest expense per period
- increasing premium amortization

(d) The straight-line method results in:
- varying rate of interest per period
- constant interest expense and premium amortization

Journal entry to record interest expense and amortization for Year 1:

	Effective Interest		Straight-Line	
Interest Expense	$62,527		$61,575	
Premium on Bonds Payable	7,473		8,425	
Cash		$70,000		$70,000

Issuance of Bonds Between Interest Dates:

Bonds issued between interest dates are sold for their market value (refer above) plus accrued interest since the last interest payment date. For example, if $1,000,000 F.V., 6% bonds, interest payment dates 1/1 and 7/1, are issued on 3/1 at 102, the price paid for the five-year bonds would be computed as follows:

Market value on 3/1 (102% × $1,000,000)	$1,020,000
Accrued interest 1/1 to 3/1 ($1,000,000 × 6% × 2/12)	10,000
Total to be paid on 3/1	$1,030,000

Journal entry to record issuance on 3/1:

	Debit	Credit
Cash	$1,030,000	
Bonds Payable		$1,000,000
Premium on bonds payable		20,000
Bond interest payable*		10,000

*The credit could also be made to interest expense, in which case, on 7/1 there would be no charge to bond interest payable and the charge to interest expense would be for $28,621 (6 months interest of $30,000 less the premium amortization of $1,379).

The journal entry to record the payment of interest on 7/1 would be (assuming straight-line amortization):

	Debit	Credit
Bond interest payable	$10,000	
Premium on bonds payable (20,000/58 × 4)	1,379	
Interest expense	18,621	
Cash 1,000,000 × 6% × 1/2		$30,000

If the bonds had been sold at a discount, it **would not** have affected the accrued interest as of 3/1; however, it would affect the interest expense recognized on 7/1, as the amortization of the discount for 4 months would increase interest expense. The debit to bond interest payable on 7/1 would also be unaffected.

Gains or Losses From Debt Extinguishment—APB #26, SFAS #4, 64, 125

Determining Gain or Loss on Redemption or Purchase: APB #26 states that: " . . . A difference between the reacquisition price and the net carrying amount of the extinguished debt should be recognized currently in income of the period of extinguishment as losses or gains and identified as a separate item . . . **Gains and losses should not be amortized to future periods.**"

When bonds are redeemed or purchased prior to maturity, the gain or loss is determined by the difference between the carrying value of the bonds and the amount given up to acquire the bonds. If the bonds are redeemed at a time other than a scheduled interest payment date, the accrued interest, including amortization of bond premium or discount, and the amortization of bond issue costs should be determined and recorded up to the date of redemption or purchase.

SFAS #4 states that: "Gains and losses from extinguishment of debt that are included in the determination of net income shall be aggregated and if **material**, classified as an **extraordinary item**, net of related income tax effect . . . the following information . . . shall be disclosed (except when such extinguishments are made to satisfy sinking-fund requirements that a company must meet within one year of the date of the extinguishment—SFAS #64) . . . (a) a description of the extinguishment transaction, including the source of any funds used to extinguish debt if it is practicable to identify the source, (b) the income tax effect in the period of extinguishment, (c) the per share amount of the aggregate gain or loss net of related income tax effect." Note that APB #30 re extraordinary items

does not apply to gains or losses from extinguishment of debt. (See Chapter 12 for coverage of SFAS #15 which relates to financial reporting for troubled debt restructuring.)

According to SFAS 125, a liability is not extinguished by an in-substance defeasance. It is derecognized only if the debtor:

- pays the creditor and is relieved of its obligation or
- is legally released from being the primary obligor.

Balance Sheet Presentation—Long-Term Debt

Bond Discount:

	Current Year	*Previous Year*
Principal Amount	$24,000,000	$24,000,000
Less unamortized discount	2,070,000	2,192,000
Long-term debt less unamortized discount	$21,930,000	$21,808,000

Bond Premium:

Principal Amount	$24,000,000	$24,000,000
Add unamortized premium	600,000	650,000
Long-term debt plus unamortized premium	$24,600,000	$24,650,000

INVESTMENT IN BONDS

Valuation:

The acquisition of bonds as an investment is initially recorded at **cost** which includes the costs of acquisition. Any difference between the cost and face value of the bonds should be amortized over the remaining life of the bond issue, **except for short-term investments**.

After acquisition, the carrying value of the investment in bonds is **not** usually adjusted for subsequent changes in the market rate of interest or resultant changes in the market value of the bonds; however, when a **substantial decline** in market value occurs, and it is evident that it is **not a mere temporary decline**, the loss in value should be recognized currently in income (refer LCM). Investment in bonds is usually reported on the balance sheet at cost with the market value being disclosed parenthetically or in the notes to the financial statements.

Amortization of Bond Discount and Premium:

The discount or premium on a bond investment should be amortized over the life of the bond so as to reflect the face value as the book value at maturity, and to adjust the interest earned over the life of the investment to the effective yield. There are two methods of bond premium or discount amortization:

1. The effective interest method (preferable per APB #21).
2. The straight-line method (allowable if result is not materially different).

Example: Referring to Case Examples A and B, entries to record the investment in the bonds and the first year's interest income on the investor's books by the effective interest and straight-line methods would be:

(a) Purchase at Discount—investment of $960,070

1. Acquisition:

Investment in Bonds	$960,070	
Cash		$960,070

2. First year's interest income:

	Effective Interest		*Straight-Line*	
Cash	$70,000		$70,000	
Investment in Bonds	6,806		7,986	
Interest Income		$76,806		$77,986

(b) Purchase at Premium—investment of $1,042,125

1. Acquisition:

Investment in Bonds	$1,042,125	
Cash		$1,042,125

2. First year's interest income:

	Effective Interest		*Straight-Line*	
Cash	$70,000		$70,000	
Investment in Bonds		$ 7,473		$ 8,425
Interest Income		62,527		61,575

Note that separate accounts for Bond Discount or Premium were not used; the investments were recorded at net cost, and the amortization of the discount or premium was directly to the investment account. Alternatively, separate accounts for premium or discount could be used; however, this method is usually not used.

Purchase of Bond Investments Between Interest Dates:

Bonds purchased between interest dates are purchased at cost (refer above) plus accrued interest since the last interest payment date. The entry to record the purchase of the bonds will include a receivable for the interest "purchased" which will be received when the first interest payment is received.

Example: $100,000 FV, 6% bonds are purchased on April 1 at 96, cost of acquisition $500. Interest payment dates are 1/1 and 7/1, and the bonds mature in 8 3/4 years—35 quarters.

Amount Paid for Bonds

Market value on 4/1 ($100,000 × 96%)	$96,000
Acquisition Costs	500
Cost of Bond Investment	$96,500
Accrued Interest 1/1 to 4/1 ($100,000 × 6% × 3/12)	1,500
Total Paid on 4/1	$98,000

Journal entry to record purchase on 4/1:

Investment in Bonds	$96,500	
Bond interest receivable	1,500	
Cash		$98,000

Journal entry to record first interest payment on 7/1:

Cash ($100,000 × 6% × 1/2)	$3,000	
Investment in bonds (3,500/35 quarters)	100	
Interest receivable		$1,500
Interest income		1,600

Journal entry to record accrual of interest at 12/31:

Bond interest receivable	$3,000	
Investment in bonds (2 quarters)	200	
Interest income		$3,200

CONVERTIBLES AND WARRANTS

Issuance of Convertible Debt and Debt With Stock Purchase Warrants (APB #14)

Rule #1. Convertible debt and debt with *nondetachable* warrants:

No portion of the proceeds from the issuance should be accounted for as attributable to the conversion privilege or the nondetachable stock purchase warrants. The debt securities should be recorded as shown previously, with appropriate recognition of any premium or discount.

Rule #2. Debt with *detachable* warrants:
The portion of the proceeds of the debt securities issued with detachable stock purchase warrants which is allocable to the warrants should be accounted for as paid-in capital. The allocation should be based on the relative fair market values of the two securities at the time of issuance. Any resulting discount or premium on the debt securities should be accounted for as such.

Example: The A Company issued $100,000, 8%, 20-year bonds payable with stock purchase warrants. Each $1,000 bond carried 20 warrants and each warrant was for one share of $10 par value common stock at an option price of $50. At the date of issuance, the debentures sold at 105 including the warrants.

Journal entries to record the issuance:

1. **If warrants are nondetachable** (or if bonds were convertible to 20 shares—conversion price $50):

Cash	$105,000	
Bonds Payable		$100,000
Premium on Bonds Payable		5,000
(recorded as debt only)		

2. **If warrants are detachable** and traded separately for $5 immediately after issue:

Cash	$105,000	
Discount on Bonds Payable	5,000	
Bonds Payable		$100,000
Common Stock Warrants		10,000

Computation of Paid-In Capital Attributable to Warrants

Proceeds $100,000 × 1.05	$105,000
Less FMV Warrants (20 × 100 × $5)	10,000
Proceeds Attributable to Bonds	$ 95,000
Resulting Discount	5,000
Face Value of Bonds	$100,000

$$\frac{\text{FMV of Warrants}}{\text{FMV of Bonds \& Warrants}} = \frac{10{,}000}{105{,}000} \times \$105{,}000 = \underline{\$10{,}000}$$

Conversion of Debt:

At the date of conversion, the carrying value of the bonds must be removed from the accounts and the issuance of the new common stock recorded. There are two methods by which the issuance may be recorded:

1. Record the stock issuance **at the fair market value** of the stock or bonds, whichever is more clearly evident, recognizing a gain or loss on conversion as the difference between the carrying value of the bonds and the fair market value of the stock or bonds.
2. Record the stock issuance **at the carrying value (book value)** of the bonds. Upon conversion, if the par value of the stock issued is greater than the book value of the bonds, the excess is recorded as a debit to retained earnings. If the carrying value of the bonds is greater than the par value of the stock issued, the excess is credited to paid-in capital in excess of par.

The first method is generally viewed as theoretically preferable; however, **the second method is generally used in practice.**

Example: The B Company has outstanding $100,000 of 8% convertible bonds with an unamortized bond premium of $5,000. The conversion privilege provides for a conversion ratio of 20 to 1 (20 shares for each bond) for B Company's $10 par value common stock. A bondholder tenders for conversion a $1,000 bond when the market price of the common stock is $60.

Journal entries to record conversion:

1. Conversion Recorded at Fair Market Value:

Bonds Payable	$1,000	
Premium on Bonds Payable	50	
Loss on Bond Conversion	150	
Common Stock (20 shares of $10 par)		$ 200
Paid-in Capital in Excess of Par		1,000
Computation of Loss:		
FMV Stock: 20 shares × $60		$1,200
BV Bonds: Face Value	$1,000	
Premium 5,000 + 100	50	1,050
Loss on Conversion		$ 150

2. Conversion Recorded at Book Value of Bonds:

Bonds Payable	$1,000	
Premiums on Bonds Payable	50	
Common Stock		$200
Paid-in Capital in Excess of Par		850

Prior to recording the conversion of the debt securities, all account balances related to the bonds must be brought up to date—amortization bond discount or premium and accrued interest from the last interest payment date to the date of conversion must be recorded.

Convertible bonds which are reacquired by the exercise of the call provision, by the issuer, should be accounted for in accordance with APB #26 and SFAS #4. (See section on "Determining Gain or Loss on a Redemption or Purchase.")

Exercise of Warrants:

Warrants give the holder the option to buy a specified number of shares of stock, at a specified price, for a specified period of time. Upon exercise of the warrants, the holder must pay the price stated in the warrants and surrender the warrants to the issuing corporation. The issuance of the stock is recorded at the **amount paid** for the shares **which includes any paid-in capital attributed to the warrants at issuance** (refer above to Rule #2).

Example: Referring to the A Co. example, in which each bond carried 20 warrants each convertible into one share of common stock and assuming that 50 bondholders exercise their warrants:

(a) Number of Warrants Exercised	50 bonds × 20	= 1,000 warrants
(b) Amount Paid for Stock	1,000 shares × $50	= $50,000

Journal entries to record exercise of warrants:

1. **If warrants were nondetachable:****

Cash	50,000	
Common Stock (1,000 shares × $10)		$10,000
Paid-in Capital in Excess of Par		40,000

2. **If warrants were detachable:**

Cash	$50,000	
Common Stock Warrants*	5,000	
Common Stock		$10,000
Paid-in Capital in Excess of Par		45,000

*1,000 warrants exercised 1,000 at $5 of paid-in capital attributable to warrants at issuance.
**This treatment presumes that the bonds remain outstanding after the warrants are exercised.

Convertible Stock and Stock with Stock Purchase Warrants:

Although APB #14 related specifically to the issuance of convertible debt and debt with stock purchase warrants, the reasoning is also applicable to the issuance of stock with stock purchase warrants and convertible stock. Therefore, the issuance of convertible stock and stock with stock purchase warrants is given the **same accounting treatment as convertible debt and debt with stock purchase warrants**. Furthermore, its conversion or the exercise of its warrants is accounted for in the same manner as convertible debt or debt with stock purchase warrants.

Investments in Convertible Securities and Securities with Stock Purchase Warrants

Valuation: The accounting for investments in convertible securities and securities with stock purchase warrants follows the accounting for their issuance.

1. **Convertible securities and securities with nondetachable warrants:**
   The investment is recorded at cost which includes the costs of acquisition. No portion of the cost is attributed to the conversion privilege or the nondetachable stock purchase warrants.
2. **Securities with detachable warrants:**
   The investment in securities with detachable stock purchase warrants constitutes the acquisition of two separate securities and requires that the cost of the investment be allocated to the different securities according to their relative market values.

Example: Referring to the same A Co. example, the acquisition of **one** of the bonds as an investment would be recorded as follows:

1. **If warrants are nondetachable (or if bonds were convertible to 20 shares):**

Investment in Bonds	$1,050	
Cash		$1,050

2. **If warrants are detachable:**

Investment in Bonds	$950	
Investment in Stock Warrants	100	
Cash		$1,050

Computation of Costs Attributable to Warrants

$$\frac{\text{MV of Warrants}}{\text{MV of Bond \& Warrants}} = \frac{5}{1{,}050} \times \$1{,}050 = \$5 \text{ per warrant}$$

20 warrants/bond × $5 = $100

Subsequent to acquisition, the valuation of the investment in bonds or stock account would be accounted for as explained in the earlier sections on investments in stocks and bonds.

Conversion of Investment Securities:

At conversion, the carrying value of the investment being converted must be removed from the accounts and the receipt of the investment in stock recorded. There are two methods by which the investment in stock may be recorded:

1. Record the new investment at its **fair market value**, or the fair market value of the converted security, whichever is more clearly evident, recognizing a gain or loss on the conversion at the difference between the carrying value of the converted security and the fair market value used to record the new investment.
2. Record the new investment at the **carrying value** of the security converted, recognizing no gain or loss on the conversion.

The first method is generally viewed as theoretically preferable; however, the second method is generally used in practice.

Example: Referring to the A Co. example, assuming that the **investor's** books also reflect a carrying value of $1,050 for one of these bonds, the journal entries to record the conversion would be:

1. **Conversion recorded at fair market value:**

Investment in Common Stock	$1,200	
Investment in Bonds		$1,050
Gain on Conversion of Bond Investment		150
Computation of Gain		
FMV on Stock: 20 shares @ $60 =	$1,200	
BV of Bonds Surrendered	1,050	
Gain on Conversion	$ 150	

2. **Conversion recorded at book value of converted security:**

Investment in Common Stock	$1,050	
Investment in Bonds		$1,050

Prior to conversion of the convertible security, all account balances related to the convertible security must be brought up to date so as to reflect the current carrying value at conversion.

Exercise of Warrants:

Investments in stock are initially recorded at cost, including the cost of acquisition. When warrants are exercised to acquire stock investments, the **cost includes the book value of the warrants surrendered** and the amount paid in cash as specified in the warrants.

Example: Referring again to the A Co. example, assuming an investor owns 50 bonds and exercises all of his warrants to purchase stock, the journal entries to record his purchase would be:

1. **If warrants are nondetachable:**

Investment in Common Stock	$102,500	
Cash		$50,000
Investment in Bonds		$52,500

Computation

50 bonds × 20 warrants per bond = 1,000. 1000 shares × $50 = $50,000.

2. **If warrants are detachable:**

Investment in Common Stock	$55,000	
Cash		$50,000
Investment in Stock Warrants		5,000

Computation

Amount Paid:	1,000 shares at $50 = $50,000
Plus:	1,000 warrants at $5 = 5,000 = $55,000 Total Cost

DISCLOSURE OF LONG-TERM OBLIGATIONS—SFAS #47, #129

Long-Term Borrowings and Stock Redemptions

SFAS #47 requires the following information to be disclosed regarding long-term borrowings and capital stock for each of the five years following the latest balance sheet:

(a) The combined aggregate amount of maturities and sinking fund requirements for all long-term borrowings.

(b) The amount of redemption requirements for all issues of capital stock that are redeemable at fixed or determinable prices on fixed or determinable dates, separately by issue or combined.

Example:
D Company has outstanding two long-term borrowings and one issue of preferred stock with mandatory redemption requirements. The first borrowing is a $100 million sinking fund debenture with annual sinking fund payments of $10 million in 19X2, 19X3, and 19X4, $15 million in 19X5 and 19X6, and $20 million in 19X7 and 19X8. The second borrowing is a $50 million note due in 19X5. The $30 million issue of preferred stock requires a 5 percent annual cumulative sinking fund payment of $1.5 million until retired.

D's disclosures might be as follows:

Maturities and sinking fund requirements on long-term debt and sinking fund requirements on preferred stock subject to mandatory redemption are as follows (000's):

	Long-term debt	*Preferred stock*
19X2	$10,000	$1,500
19X3	10,000	1,500
19X4	10,000	1,500
19X5	65,000	1,500
19X6	15,000	1,500

Unconditional Purchase Obligations

An unconditional purchase obligation is the amount which a company is obligated to pay for a contract which calls for the purchase of a minimum quantity of goods at a fixed minimum price. For such obligations which are noncancelable and have a remaining term in excess of one year (and have not been pre-recorded on the balance sheet), the following shall be disclosed.

(a) The nature and term of the obligation(s).
(b) The amount of the fixed and determinable portion of the obligation(s) as of the date of the latest balance sheet presented in the aggregate and, if determinable, for each of the five succeeding fiscal years.
(c) The nature of any variable components of the obligation(s).
(d) The amounts purchased under the obligation(s) for each period for which an income statement is presented.

For those unconditional purchase obligations **which have been recorded on the balance sheet** (asset and related liability), the aggregate amount of payments which have been recognized (on the balance sheet) shall be disclosed.

Case Example of Unrecorded Purchase Obligation

F Company has entered into a take-or-pay contract with an ammonia plant. F is obligated to purchase 50 percent of the planned capacity production of the plant each period while the debt used to finance the plant remains outstanding. The monthly payment equals the sum of 50 percent of raw material costs, operating expenses, depreciation, interest on the debt used to finance the plant, and a return on the owner's equity investment.

F's disclosure might be as follows:

To assure a long-term supply, the company has contracted to purchase half the output of an ammonia plant through the year 2005 and to make minimum annual payments as follows, whether or not it is able to take delivery (in thousands):

19X2 through 19X6 ($6,000 per annum)	$ 30,000
Later years	120,000
Total	150,000
Less: Amount representing interest	*(65,000)
Total at present value	*$ 85,000

In addition F must reimburse the owner of the plant for a proportional share of raw material costs and operating expenses of the plant. F's total purchases under the agreement were (in thousands) $7,000, $7,100, and $7,200 in 19X9, 19X0, and 19X1, respectively.

*not required disclosure

DISCLOSURES ABOUT FAIR VALUE OF FINANCIAL INSTRUMENTS — SFAS #107

SFAS #107 requires all entities to disclose the fair value of many financial instruments. These disclosures are for both assets and liabilities and also include financial instruments not shown on the balance sheet ("off-balance-sheet"). Examples include accounts, notes, loans receivable and payable, investment securities, options, standby letters of credit and financial guarantees and bonds.

If it is not practical to estimate these fair values, descriptive information about the financial instruments such as the terms of the instrument and why it is not possible to estimate the fair value should be provided.

It is important to note that the disclosure of fair values are provided as **supplemental information** and do not normally replace the historical cost basis used on the balance sheet. (An exception to this traditional reliance on historical cost is the valuing of certain investments in debt and equity securities at fair market value. See SFAS #115 in chapter 2).

FASB #107 requires disclosure of information about significant concentrations of **risk for all financial instruments**. Concentrations of credit exist when a company has a business activity, economic characteristic, or location that is common to most of its financial instruments.

SFAS #107 lists a number of items that are covered in other standards and are exempted from coverage by this standard: obligations for pension and other post-retirement benefits, employee stock option and deferred compensation plans, substantially extinguished debt and the related assets in trust, many insurance contracts, lease contracts, obligations and rights resulting from warranties, unconditional purchase obligations, equity method investments, minority interests in consolidated statements, and instruments classified as stockholders' equity on the balance sheet.

SFAS #126, *Exemption from Certain Required Disclosures about Financial Instruments for Certain Nonpublic Entities*, amends SFAS #107, *Disclosures about Fair Value of Financial Instruments*, to make such disclosures optional for entities that are nonpublic, have total assets of less than $100 million, and have not held or issued any derivative financial instruments, other than loan commitments, during the reporting period.

DERIVATIVES – BACKGROUND

Derivatives are financial devices that "derive" their value from other financial instruments.

Examples of derivatives are futures contracts, forward contracts, interest rate swaps and put options.

Derivatives may be freestanding or embedded in a host contract that is itself not a derivative. The combination of a host contract and an embedded derivative is a hybrid instrument.

A common example of an embedded derivative is the conversion feature of convertible debt. It represents a call option on the issuer's stock.

STATEMENT OF FINANCIAL ACCOUNTING STANDARDS NO. 133 – ACCOUNTING FOR DERIVATIVE INSTRUMENTS AND HEDGING ACTIVITIES

The pronouncement addresses the accounting for derivative instruments including certain derivative instruments embedded in other contracts, and hedging activities.

Fundamental Decisions

a. Derivative instruments that meet the definition of assets and liabilities should be reported in the financial statements.
b. Fair value is the only relevant measure for derivative instruments.

Types of Derivative Instruments

a. Fair value hedges of assets, liabilities & commitments.
b. Cash flow hedges.
c. Foreign currency hedges.

Gains or Losses on Derivative Instruments

a. Fair Value Hedges: Gains or losses on fair value hedges are recognized in *current earnings.*
b. Cash Flow Hedges: Gains or losses on cash flow hedges are reported as a component of *comprehensive income* because the gain or loss on the hedged item will not occur until a future period. The other comprehensive income will be reclassified to income when the gain or loss on the transaction is recognized in earnings.
c. Foreign Currency Hedges:
   1. Gains or losses on hedged firm commitments are recognized *currently.*
   2. Gains or losses on hedged assets and liabilities are recognized *currently.*
   3. Gains or losses on hedges of available-for-sale securities are recognized *currently.*
   4. Gains or losses on hedges of forecasted foreign-currency-denominated transactions are reported as a component of comprehensive income and reclassified to earnings when the transaction is complete. These hedges are considered cash flow hedges.
   5. Gains or losses on hedging of a net investment in a foreign operation are reported in *comprehensive income* as part of the translation adjustment.

Note: Foreign currency hedges are covered in Chapter Six.

Embedded Derivatives

a. Embedded derivatives must be accounted for separately from the related host contract if the following conditions are met:
   1. The economic characteristics and risks of the embedded derivative instrument are **not clearly and closely related** to the economic characteristics of the host.
   2. The hybrid instrument is not **remeasured at fair value** under otherwise applicable GAAP, with changes in fair value reported in earnings as they occur.
   3. A freestanding instrument with the same terms as the embedded derivative would be subject to the requirements of SFAS 133.
b. If an embedded derivative is accounted for separately, the host contract is accounted for based on the accounting standards that are applicable to instruments of its type. The separated derivative should be accounted for under SFAS #133. If separating the two instruments is impossible, the entire contract must be measured at fair value, with gains and losses recognized in earnings. It may not be designated as a hedging instrument because nonderivatives usually do not qualify as hedging instruments.

Disclosures

a. Disclose the objectives for holding or issuing derivative instruments.
b. Disclose the context needed to understand these objectives.
c. Disclose the strategies for achieving these objectives.
d. Risk management policies.
e. Details about fair value hedges, cash flow hedges, and hedges of a net investment in a foreign operation.

FASB Definition of Derivative Instruments

A derivative instrument is a financial instrument or other contract with all three of the following characteristics:

a. It has: (1) one or more underlyings and (2) one or more notional amounts or payment provisions or both. Those terms determine the amount of the settlement or settlements, and, in some cases, whether or not a settlement is required.
b. It requires no initial net investment or an initial net investment that is smaller than would be required for other types of contracts that would be expected to have a similar response to changes in market factors.
c. Its terms require or permit net settlement. It can readily be settled net by a means outside the contract, or it provides for delivery of an asset that puts the recipient in a position not substantially different from net settlement.

Definitions of *Underlying, Notional Amount,* and *Payment Provisions:*

a. An **underlying** is a specified interest rate, security price, commodity price, foreign exchange rate, index of prices or rates, or other variable. An underlying may be a price or rate of an asset or liability but is not the asset or liability itself.
b. A **notional amount** is a number of currency units, shares, bushels, pounds, or other units specified in the contract. The settlement of a derivative instrument with a notional amount is determined by interaction of that notional amount with the underlying. The interaction may be simple multiplication, or it may involve a formula with leverage factors or other constants.
c. A **payment provision** specifies a fixed or determinable settlement to be made if the underlying behaves in a specified manner.

Example: FAIR VALUE HEDGE

ABC Company has an inventory of 1,000,000 pounds of a commodity called widgets which has a cost of $.48 per pound. The company hedges the fair value of its inventory by selling a futures contract on September 1, 1999 for 1,000,000 pounds at $.63 per pound for delivery on March 1, 2000. The following table lists the market rates and the company's estimates of the changes in the fair value of its inventory.

DATE	SPOT RATE	FUTURE RATE FOR MARCH 1 DELIVERY	CHANGE IN VALUE OF INVENTORY
September 1, 1999	.61	.63	
December 31, 1999	.59	.61	$22,000 loss
March 1, 2000	.62	.62	$31,000 gain

On March 1, 2000, ABC **bought** a futures contract for 1,000,000 pounds of widgets at $.62 per pound which offsets the company's sale of the futures contract on September, 1999 and closes its futures position. ABC sold its inventory on March 1, 2000 at the market rate of $.63 per pound.

Journal Entries:

1999, September 1

No journal entry because the futures rate of $.63 per pound and the fair value are the same and the futures contract is an executory contract.

1999, December 31

		Debit	Credit
JE	Loss on Inventory	20,000	
	Inventory – widgets		20,000

To record the company's estimate of the inventory loss.

1999, December 31

	Debit	Credit
Received from broker	20,000	
Gain on futures contract		20,000

*ABC has a futures sale for a contract price of $.63 per pound but could theoretically buy a contract on December 31 to deliver the widgets for $.61 per pound for a net gain of $.02 per pound x 1,000 pounds or $20,000.

2000, March 1

		Debit	Credit
JE	Inventory – widgets	31,000	
	Gain on Inventory		31,000
JE	Loss on futures contract	10,000	
	Receivable from broker		10,000

ABC has a futures sale for a contract price of $.63 per pound and buys a contract to settle the futures obligation for $.62 per pound for a net gain of $.01 per pound or a total gain of $10,000. Since the company anticipated a $20,000 gain on December 31, 1999, the company must recognize a $10,000 loss on March 1, 2000 in order to recognize a total gain of $10,000.

2000, March 1

		Debit	Credit
JE	Accounts receivable	620,000	
	Cost of goods sold	491,000	
	Sales		620,000
	Inventory – widgets		491,000

To record sale and cost of goods sold.

Sale = 1,000,000 pounds x $.62 = 620,000.

Cost of goods sold = 1,000,000 pounds x the original cost of $.48 per pound for a total cost of $480,000. The cost of $480,000 is reduced by the loss on the inventory in 1999 of $20,000 but increased by the year 2000's gain of $31,000 for a net cost of $491,000 ($480,000 - $20,000 + $31,000).

FAIR VALUE HEDGE – INTEREST RATE SWAP

ABC Inc. borrows $500,000 for 3 years at a fixed interest rate of 7% annually. On the same date, ABC enters into an interest rate swap in which the company receives a 7% fixed rate but pays a variable rate on $500,000 based on an agreed upon standard index for interest rates. ABC designates the interest swap as a fair value hedge of the risks associated with a change in market interest rates. Assuming that the hedge meets the criteria for an effective hedge, changes in fair values of the interest rate swap will be used to measure the changes in the fair value of the debt.

The following table lists the changes in fair value of the debt and the variable interest rates from the agreed-upon index.

DATE	FAIR VALUE OF DEBT	FAIR VALUE OF INTEREST RATE SWAP	INDEX VARIABLE INTEREST RATES
Dec. 31, 2000	500,000	-0-	6.2%
Dec. 31, 2001	480,000	\$20,000 loss	6.8%
Dec. 31, 2002	505,000	\$5,000 gain	6.0%

Journal entries:

Date	Account	Debit	Credit
Dec. 31, 2000	Cash	500,000	
	Notes Payable		500,000
	To record the borrowing		
Dec. 31, 2001	Interest Expense	35,000	
	Cash		35,000
	To record the annual interest of \$500,000 x 7% = \$35,000.		
Dec. 31, 2001	Cash	4,000	
	Interest expense		4,000
	On the interest rate swap, ABC receives 7% of \$500,000 or \$35,000 and pays the variable rate of 6.2% x \$500,000 or \$31,000, for a net decrease in interest expense of \$4,000.		
Dec. 31, 2001	Notes payable	20,000	
	Gain from hedge		20,000
	The year-end increase in interest rates reduced the debt's fair value.		
Dec. 31, 2001	Loss from hedge	20,000	
	Interest rate swap contract		20,000
	To record the decrease in value of the interest rate swap.		
Dec. 31, 2002	Interest Expense	35,000	
	Cash		35,000
	To record annual interest cost.		
Dec. 31, 2002	Cash	1,000	
	Interest Expense		1,000
	ABC receives \$35,000 from the fixed rate and pays 6.8% x \$500,000 or \$34,000 for the variable rate, for a net decrease in interest expense of \$1,000.		

Dec. 31, 2002	Loss from hedge	25,000	
	Notes payable		25,000

The decrease in interest rates to 6% increased the debts fair value from $480,000 to $505,000, for a loss of $25,000.

Dec. 31, 2002	Interest rate swap	25,000	
	Gain from hedge		25,000

To record increase in value of the hedge from a loss of $20,000 to a gain of $5,000, for a total of $25,000.

CASH FLOW HEDGE – Forecasted Transaction

On January 1, 1999, XYZ Company decides that it will purchase 200,000 pounds of commodity A on July 1, 2000 at the spot rate. The company further decides to purchase a futures contract for 200,000 pounds of commodity A at the June 30 futures price of $2.50 per pound to hedge the forecasted transaction. The effectiveness of the hedge will be measured by the changes in the cash flows of forecasted purchase vs. the changes in the fair value of the futures contract. On June 30, 1999, XYZ purchases 200,000 pounds of commodity A at $2.60 per pound.

Journal Entries:

June 1, 1999

No journal entry because the futures contract is at the spot rate which is the fair value. (For simplicity, margin deposits are ignored.)

June 30, 1999	Inventory – Commodity A	520,000	
	Cash		520,000

To record the purchase of 200,000 pounds of commodity A at $2.60 per pound.

June 30, 1999	Futures Contract (Asset)	20,000	
	Gain on hedge – other Comprehensive Income		20,000

The gain is the difference between the current rate of $2.60 per pound and the futures contract price of $2.50 per pound of $.10 x 200,000 pounds or $20,000.

June 30, 1999	Cash	20,000	
	Futures contract (Asset)		20,000

To record the net cash settlement of the futures contract.

Author's Note: For an example using a put option instead of a futures contract, see Chapter 6 on Foreign Currency.

CONTINGENCIES—SFAS #5

Summary

If the contingency is **probable** or **likely** to occur, and both of the following conditions are present, the contingency loss should be recognized.

1. It is **probable** that an asset has been impaired or a liability incurred at the balance sheet date, and
2. The amount of loss can be reasonably estimated.

In such cases, an adjustment should be made and the contingency loss recognized.
If the chance of occurrence is only reasonably possible or less than likely, disclosure should be made.
If the event is probable but the amount of loss cannot be reasonably estimated, disclosure should be made.

Definitions

Contingency. A situation involving uncertainty as to possible loss that will be resolved when one or more future events occur or fail to occur. Examples are: Litigation, threat of expropriation, collectibility of receivables, claims arising from product warranties or product defects, self-insured risks, and possible catastrophe losses of property and casualty insurance companies.

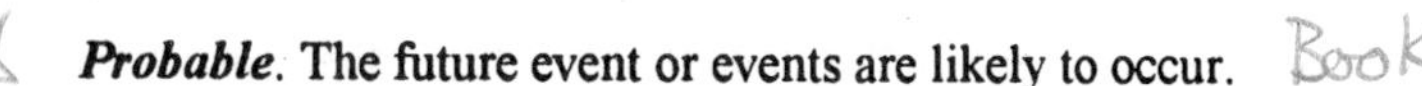

Probable. The future event or events are likely to occur.

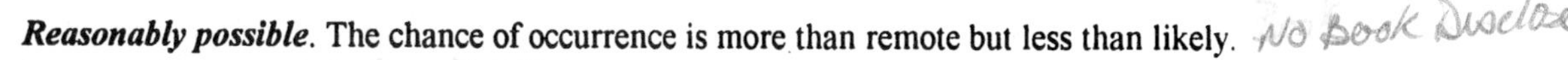

Reasonably possible. The chance of occurrence is more than remote but less than likely.

Remote. The chance of occurrence is slight.

Conditions Required for Recognition of Contingency Loss

1. It must be **probable** that an asset has been impaired or a liability incurred at the date of the financial statements. It must be **probable** that a future event or events confirming the fact of loss will occur.
2. The amount of loss can be reasonably estimated.

Examples of loss contingencies included:

a. Collectibility of receivables.
b. Obligations related to product warranties and product defects.
c. Risk of loss or damage of enterprise property by fire, explosion, or other hazards.
d. Threat of expropriation of assets.
e. Pending or threatened litigation.
f. Actual or possible claims and assessments.
g. Risk of loss from catastrophies assumed by property and casualty insurance companies including reinsurance companies.
h. Guarantees of indebtedness of others.
i. Obligations of commercial banks under "standby letters of credit."
j. Agreements to repurchase receivables (or to repurchase the related property) that have been sold.

Estimation of the Amount of a Loss

Where it is probable that an asset has been impaired or a liability incurred, the amount of loss estimable is within a range of amounts. If so, the provision for loss should be:

a. The amount within the range that appears to be the best estimate of loss, or
b. Where no amount is a better estimate than any other, the **minimum** amount in the range should be accrued.

Example: Hokum, Inc., has been involved in litigation and it is probable that an unfavorable verdict will result in payment of damages between $3 million and $9 million. No amount in the range appears to be a better estimate than any other amount. A loss of $3 million should be accrued for the year, the minimum amount of the range of estimated loss. Disclosure of the nature of the contingency and the exposure to an additional amount of loss of up to $6 million should be made.

Disclosure

If no accrual is made for a loss contingency because one or both of the conditions for accrual are not met, **disclosure should** be made when there is at least a **reasonable possibility** that a loss may have been incurred. The disclosure should include the nature of the contingency, an estimate of the probable loss or range of loss, or state that such an estimate cannot be made.

Examples of **situations that normally meet the conditions for accrual** are losses from **uncollectible receivables and obligations related to product warranties and product defects**. Conversely, accrual for loss or damage of property, loss from injury to others, damage to property of others and business interruption (sometimes called self-insured risks) should not be made until the loss has taken place.

Self-Insured Risks

The mere absence of insurance does not fulfill the requirements for accrual. Casualties are random in their occurrence and there is no diminution in the value of the property until the event has occurred.

Earnings Variability

Some have advocated the recognition of estimated losses from contingencies without regard to whether it is probable that an asset has been impaired or a liability incurred to avoid reporting net income that fluctuates widely from period to period. The FASB concluded that "financial statement users have indicated that information about earnings variability is important to them." If the nature of an enterprise's operations is such that **irregularities in the incurrence of losses cause variations in periodic net income, that fact should not be obscured by accruing for anticipated losses that do not relate to the current period.**

Gain Contingencies

These **should not be recognized**, since to do so might be to recognize revenue prior to its realization. **Disclosure should be made**, but care exercised to avoid misleading implications as to the likelihood of realization.

General or Unspecified Business Risks

So-called "reserves for general contingencies" or similar type reserves do not meet the criteria for accrual. These type reserves or other appropriations of retained earnings should not be shown outside the Stockholders' Equity section of the balance sheet and **losses should not be charged** to appropriations of retained earnings. The only proper disposition of an appropriation (reserve) of retained earnings, contingency or otherwise, is reversal.

Remote Contingencies

Even though the possibility of loss is remote, disclosure of certain types of loss contingencies which are now being disclosed should be continued. These are: guarantees of indebtedness of others, obligations of commercial banks under "standby letters of credit," and guarantees to purchase receivables that have been sold or otherwise assigned. Disclosure of these type contingencies and others that have the same characteristics should be continued.

STATEMENT OF POSITION 94-6: DISCLOSURE OF CERTAIN SIGNIFICANT RISKS AND UNCERTAINTIES

The AICPA in the form statement of position (SOP) 94-6 added to the required disclosures of financial instruments and contingencies (SFAS #5)

The SOP uses two terms that should be defined:

- **Near term** – a period of time not to exceed one year from the date of the financial statements.
- **Severe impact** – the threshold is higher than that of materiality, yet lower than that of catastrophic in nature.

The additional disclosures are in four areas:

- **Nature of operations**
- **Use of estimates in the preparation of financial statements**
- **Certain significant estimates**
- **Current vulnerability due to certain concentrations**

Nature of Operations

The SOP requires that users of financial statements be informed about the following specific areas of operations (these disclosures do not have to be quantified):

- Description of the major products and/or services provided by the Company.
- Principle markets and locations of the markets.
- Relative importance of the operations of each (line of) business and the basis for such a determination (sales, asset commitment, income, etc.)

Use of Estimates in the Preparation of Financial Statements

This is a general disclosure that puts users on notice that preparation of financial statements requires the use of estimates on the part of management.

Certain Significant Estimates

In this area the SOP requires a significant increase in disclosure responsibilities in financial statements. Disclosure may have to be made regarding estimates that are not required under current first-level GAAP.

Two Tests

Estimates used in the preparation of financial statements are subject to the following two tests:

1. Could it be at least reasonably possible that the estimate of the effect on the financial statements of the estimate (at the financial statement date) in question will change in the near-term due to one or more future confirming events?
2. Would that potential change have a material effect on the financial statements?

Disclosures

Such disclosure surrounding estimates meeting the criteria should, at a minimum, include (where applicable):

- The nature of the uncertainty.
- An indication that it is **at least reasonably possible** that one or more of the confirming events may occur.
- If this is a potential loss contingency (SFAS #5), there should be an estimate of the potential loss or a statement that such an estimate is not possible. (It is encouraged, but not required, to include the factors that make the estimation especially subject to change.)
- Disclosure of risk reduction techniques employed by the Company is encouraged, not required.

Examples

The SOP offers numerous examples of assets and/or liabilities that involve estimation, and may need to be disclosed under this requirement. Some of those examples include:

- Inventories
- Specialized equipment
- Certain valuation allowances
- Litigation related obligations

Conditions

The SOP also offers examples of conditions that might indicate those areas that are particularly sensitive:

- A significant decrease in the market value of an asset.
- A change (perhaps brought on by technology) in the usage of a particular asset.
- Changing legal environment.
- Significant cost over-runs.
- A continuing loss trend.

Current Vulnerability Due to Certain Concentrations

The idea of disclosing areas of potential exposure from concentrations was introduced in SFAS #107 and is expanded in SOP 94-6.

The SOP addresses those concentrations (defined below) that meet each of the following **three criteria**:

1. The concentration exists at the balance sheet date.
2. The concentration subjects the Company to potential near-term risk (potentially severe-impact).
3. It is at least reasonably possible that the adverse events could occur that would cause the severe-impact condition.

Concentration

There are four defined concentrations for purposes of this disclosure:

a. Volume of business transacted with any customer, supplier, lender, grantor, or creditor.
b. Product or service revenue generation.
c. Available sources of supply, labor, services, material, licenses and/or other rights used in operations.
d. Market and/or geographic areas in which the Company conducts business.

Concentrations – Labor Supply

Concentrations related to labor supply subject to collective bargaining must disclose the following: Percentage of labor force

- Covered by collective bargaining.
- Under agreements that will expire within a one-year period.

Concentration – Outside of Entity's Home Country

Concentrations related to operations outside of the entity's home country must disclose the carrying amounts of net assets and geographic areas in which the assets are located.

Concentrations related to financial instruments, and concentrations other than described above are not subject to the SOP provisions.

ESTIMATED LIABILITIES

The CPA exam often includes questions regarding liabilities which must be accrued due to obligations incurred in the company's operations. Such liabilities include obligations for gift certificates, coupon and premium offers, deposits, trading stamps, warranties, and similar items. The expense recognition and resulting liability balance is usually based upon estimates of occurrences which are matched with the recognition of revenues.

Example #1: In packages of its products, Curran Co. includes coupons that may be presented at retail stores to obtain discounts on other Curran products. Retailers are reimbursed for the face amount of coupons redeemed plus 10% of that amount for handling costs. Curran honors requests for coupon redemption by retailers up to three months after the consumer expiration date. Curran estimates that 70% of all coupons issued will ultimately be redeemed. Information relating to coupons issued by Curran during the current year is as follows:

Consumer expiration date	12/31/XX
Total face amount of coupons issued	$600,000
Total payments to retailers as of the end of the current year	220,000

The company must recognize $462,000 as the expense of the coupon offer which is matched against the revenues which were recognized from the sale of the product which contain the coupons. Since $220,000 has already been paid, the remaining $242,000 is the remaining liability at year end.

Expense = $600,000 × 70% = $420,000 + (10% × $420,000) = $462,000

Example #2: Marr Co. sells its products in reusable containers. The customer is charged a deposit for each container delivered and receives a refund for each container returned within two years after the year of delivery. Marr accounts for the containers not returned within the time limit as being retired by sale at the deposit amount. Information for 1999 is as follows:

Container deposits at December 31, 1998, from deliveries in:

1997	$150,000	
1998	430,000	$580,000
Deposits for containers delivered in 1999		780,000

Deposits for containers returned in 1999 from deliveries in:

1997	$ 90,000	
1998	250,000	
1999	286,000	$626,000

At December 31, 1999, the liability for deposits on returnable containers would appear as follows:

Deposit Liability Account

	Debit	Credit	
		$580,000	Balance 12/31/98
		780,000	1992 deposits
1999 returns	$626,000		
1997 deposits not returned ($150,000 – 90,000)	60,000		
		$674,000	Balance 12/31/99

CLASSIFICATION OF SHORT-TERM OBLIGATIONS—SFAS #6

SUMMARY

Short-term obligations such as trade accounts payable and normal accrued liabilities should always be classified as current. Other short-term obligations (maturing within one year) must also be classified as current unless the company **intends to** and **has the ability to refinance** such obligations **within one year**. Ability to refinance must be demonstrated by either accomplishing the refinancing or entering into an agreement to do so before the balance sheet is issued.

Criteria For Current Liability Classification

Short-term obligations arising from transactions in the normal course of business that are due in customary terms shall be classified as current liabilities. Examples are obligations for items which have entered into the operating cycle, such as payables incurred in the acquisition of materials and supplies to be used in the production of goods or in providing services to be offered for sale; collections received in advance of the delivery of goods or performance of services; and debts which arise from operations directly related to the operating cycle, such as accruals for wages, salaries, commissions, rentals, royalties, and income and other taxes.

Criteria For Exclusion as a Current Liability

1. The enterprise intends to refinance the obligation on a long-term basis, and
2. The enterprise's intent to refinance on a long-term basis is supported by an ability to consummate the refinancing demonstrated in either of the following ways:
   a. Post-balance-sheet-date issuance of a long-term obligation or equity securities. **After the date of an enterprise's balance sheet but before that balance sheet is issued**, a long-term obligation or equity securities have been issued for the purpose of refinancing the short-term obligation on a long-term basis; or

b. Financing agreement. Before the balance sheet is issued, the **enterprise has entered into a financing agreement that clearly permits the enterprise to refinance** the short-term obligation on a long-term basis on terms that are readily determinable, and all of the following conditions are met:
   (1) The agreement does not expire within one year or within the operating cycle, if greater, from the date of the enterprise's balance sheet. Further, during that period the agreement cannot be cancelable by the lender or the prospective lender or investor except for violation of a provision with which compliance is objectively determinable or measurable. Additionally, obligations incurred under the agreement cannot be callable during that period.
   (2) No violation of any provision in the financing agreement exists at the balance-sheet date and no available information indicates that a violation has occurred thereafter but prior to the issuance of the balance sheet, or, if one exists at the balance-sheet date or has occurred thereafter, a waiver has been obtained.
   (3) The lender or the prospective lender or investor with which the enterprise has entered into the financing agreement is expected to be financially capable of honoring the agreement.

Disclosure

The total of current liabilities shall be presented in classified balance sheets. If a short-term obligation is excluded from current liabilities pursuant to the provisions of this Statement, the notes to the financial statements shall include a general description of the financing agreement and the terms of any new obligation incurred or expected to be incurred or equity securities issued or expected to be issued as a result of a refinancing.

CLASSIFICATION OF CALLABLE OBLIGATIONS—SFAS #78

In determining the classification of debt for balance-sheet and/or disclosure purposes, the following should be classified as current:

1. Demand obligations or those which will become demand within one year from the balance sheet date.
2. Long-term obligations which are callable by the lender because of a violation of the debt agreement.

Exceptions include:

a. When the creditor has waived or lost the right to demand repayment within one year.
b. When the long-term obligation includes a grace period for curing the violation and it is probable that such violation will be cured prior to the end of the grace period.

Appendix
STATEMENT OF POSITION 94-6: DISCLOSURE OF CERTAIN SIGNIFICANT RISKS AND UNCERTAINTIES

Companies are required to disclose information about the nature of their operations, the use of estimates in preparing financial statements, certain significant estimates, and vulnerabilities due to certain concentrations. [17] An example of such a disclosure is provided below.

Chesapeake Corporation

Risks and Uncertainties: Chesapeake operates in three business segments which offer a diversity of products over a broad geographic base. The Company is not dependent on any single customer, group of customers, market, geographic area or supplier of materials, labor or services. Financial statements include, where necessary, amounts based on the judgments and estimates of management. These estimates include allowances for bad debts, accruals for landfill closing costs, environmental remediation costs, loss contingencies for litigation, self-insured medical and workers' compensation insurance and income taxes and determinations of discount and other rate assumptions for pensions and postretirement benefit expenses.

[17] "Disclosure of Certain Significant Risks and Uncertainties," *Statement of Position* 94-6 (New York: AICPA, 1994)

Chapter Nine
Bonds, Accounting for Debt
Questions

ISSUANCE OF BONDS

1. The market price of a bond issued at a discount is the present value of its principal amount at the market (effective) rate of interest
a. Less the present value of all future interest payments at the market (effective) rate of interest.
b. Less the present value of all future interest payments at the rate of interest stated on the bond.
c. Plus the present value of all future interest payments at the market (effective) rate of interest.
d. Plus the present value of all future interest payments at the rate of interest stated on the bond.

2. The following information pertains to Camp Corp.'s issuance of bonds on July 1, 1998:

Face amount	$800,000
Terms	10 years
Stated interest rate	6%
Interest payment dates	Annually on July 1
Yield	9%

	At 6%	*At 9%*
Present value of 1 for 10 periods	0.558	0.422
Future value of 1 for 10 periods	1.791	2.367
Present value of ordinary annuity of 1 for 10 periods	7.360	6.418

What should be the issue price for each $1,000 bond?
a. $1,000
b. $864
c. $807
d. $700

3. The issue price of a bond is equal to the present value of the future cash flows for interest and principal when the bond is issued

	At par	*At a discount*	*At a premium*
a.	Yes	No	Yes
b.	Yes	No	No
c.	No	Yes	Yes
d.	Yes	Yes	Yes

4. On July 1, 2001, Eagle Corp. issued 600 of its 10%, $1,000 bonds at 99 plus accrued interest. The bonds are dated April 1, 2001 and mature on April 1, 2011. Interest is payable semiannually on April 1 and October 1. What amount did Eagle receive from the bond issuance?
a. $579,000
b. $594,000
c. $600,000
d. $609,000

5. On July 1, 1996, Howe Corp. issued 300 of its 10%, $1,000 bonds at 99 plus accrued interest. The bonds are dated April 1, 1996, and mature on April 1, 2006. Interest is payable semiannually on April 1 and October 1. What amount did Howe receive from the bond issuance?
a. $304,500
b. $300,000
c. $297,000
d. $289,500

BOND ISSUE COST

6. During 1999, Lake Co. issued 3,000 of its 9%, $1,000 face value bonds at 101½. In connection with the sale of these bonds, Lake paid the following expenses:

Promotion costs	$ 20,000
Engraving and printing	25,000
Underwriters' commissions	200,000

What amount should Lake record as bond issue costs to be amortized over the term of the bonds?
a. $0
b. $220,000
c. $225,000
d. $245,000

7. Dixon Co. incurred costs of $3,300 when it issued, on August 31, 1998, 5-year debenture bonds dated April 1, 1998. What amount of bond issue expense should Dixon report in its income statement for the year ended December 31, 1998?

a. $220
b. $240
c. $495
d. $3,300

INTEREST EXPENSE AND AMORTIZATION OF BOND DISCOUNT OR BOND PREMIUM

8. On January 2, 2001, West Co. issued 9% bonds in the amount of $500,000, which mature on January 2, 2011. The bonds were issued for $469,500 to yield 10%. Interest is payable annually on December 31. West uses the interest method of amortizing bond discount. In its June 30, 2001, balance sheet, what amount should West report as bonds payable?

a. $469,500
b. $470,475
c. $471,025
d. $500,000

9. On May 1, 1999, Bolt Corp. issued 11% bonds in the face amount of $1,000,000 that mature on May 1, 2009. The bonds were issued to yield 10%, resulting in bond premium of $62,000. Bolt uses the effective interest method of amortizing bond premium. Interest is payable semiannually on November 1 and May 1. In its October 31, 1999, balance sheet, what amount should Bolt report as unamortized bond premium?

a. $62,000
b. $60,100
c. $58,900
d. $58,590

10. Webb Co. has outstanding a 7%, 10-year $100,000 face-value bond. The bond was originally sold to yield 6% annual interest. Webb uses the effective interest rate method to amortize bond premium. On June 30, 1999, the carrying amount of the outstanding bond was $105,000. What amount of unamortized premium on bond should Webb report in its June 30, 2000, balance sheet?

a. $1,050.
b. $3,950.
c. $4,300.
d. $4,500.

11. On July 1, 1997, Day Co. received $103,288 for $100,000 face amount, 12% bonds, a price that yields 10%. Interest expense for the six months ended December 31, 1997, should be

a. $6,197
b. $6,000
c. $5,164
d. $5,000

12. A bond issued on June 1, 2000, has interest payment dates of April 1 and October 1. Bond interest expense for the year ended December 31, 2000, is for a period of

a. Three months.
b. Four months.
c. Six months.
d. Seven months.

13. On November 1, 1998, Mason Corp. issued $800,000 of its 10-year, 8% term bonds dated October 1, 1998. The bonds were sold to yield 10%, with total proceeds of $700,000 plus accrued interest. Interest is paid every April 1 and October 1. What amount should Mason report for interest payable in its December 31, 1998, balance sheet?

a. $17,500
b. $16,000
c. $11,667
d. $10,667

14. On March 1, 1997, Clark Co. issued bonds at a discount. Clark incorrectly used the straight-line method instead of the effective interest method to amortize the discount. How were the following amounts, as of December 31, 1997, affected by the error?

	Bond carrying amount	*Retained earnings*
a.	Overstated	Overstated
b.	Understated	Understated
c.	Overstated	Understated
d.	Understated	Overstated

RETIREMENT OF BONDS

15. On June 30, 1999, King Co. had outstanding 9%, $5,000,000 face value bonds maturing on June 30, 2004. Interest was payable semiannually every June 30 and December 31. On June 30, 1999, after amortization was recorded for the period, the unamortized bond premium and bond issue costs were $30,000 and $50,000, respectively. On that date, King acquired all its outstanding bonds on the open market at 98 and retired them. At June 30, 1999, what amount should King recognize as gain before income taxes on redemption of bonds?

a. $ 20,000
b. $ 80,000
c. $120,000
d. $180,000

16. On July 31, 2000, Dome Co. issued $1,000,000 of 10%, 15-year bonds at par and used a portion of the proceeds to call its 600 outstanding 11%, $1,000 face value bonds, due on July 31, 2010, at 102. On that date, unamortized bond premium relating to the 11% bonds was $65,000. In its 2000 income statement, what amount should Dome report as gain or loss, before income taxes, from retirement of bonds?

a. $ 53,000 gain.
b. $0.
c. $(65,000) loss.
d. $(77,000) loss.

17. In open market transactions, Oak Corp. simultaneously sold its long-term investment in Maple Corp. bonds and purchased its own outstanding bonds. The broker remitted the net cash from the two transactions. Oak's gain on the purchase of its own bonds exceeded its loss on the sale of Maple's bonds. Oak should report the

a. Net effect of the two transactions as an extraordinary gain.
b. Net effect of the two transactions in income before extraordinary items.
c. Effect of its own bond transaction gain in income before extraordinary items, and report the Maple bond transaction as an extraordinary loss.
d. Effect of its own bond transaction as an extraordinary gain, and report the Maple bond transaction loss in income before extraordinary items.

CONVERTIBLE BONDS

18. On June 30, 1996, Hamm Corp. had outstanding $2,000,000 face amount of 8% convertible bonds maturing on June 30, 2001. Interest is payable on June 30 and December 31. Each $1,000 bond is convertible into 40 shares of Hamm's $20 par common stock. After amortization through June 30, 1996, the unamortized balance in the premium on bonds payable account was $50,000. On June 30, 1996, all of the bonds were converted when Hamm's common stock had a market price of $30 per share. Under the book value method, what amount should Hamm credit to additional paid-in capital in recording the conversion?

a. $350,000
b. $400,000
c. $450,000
d. $800,000

19. Clay Corp. had $600,000 convertible 8% bonds outstanding at June 30, 1997. Each $1,000 bond was convertible into 10 shares of Clay's $50 par value common stock. On July 1, 1997, the interest was paid to bondholders, and the bonds were converted into common stock, which had a fair market value of $75 per share. The unamortized premium on these bonds was $12,000 at the date of conversion. Under the book value method, this conversion increased the following elements of the stockholders' equity section by

	Common stock	*Additional paid-in capital*
a.	$300,000	$312,000
b.	$306,000	$306,000
c.	$450,000	$162,000
d.	$600,000	$ 12,000

20. On April 30, 1995, Witt Corp. had outstanding 8%, $1,000,000 face amount, convertible bonds maturing on April 30, 1999. Interest is payable on April 30 and October 31. On April 30, 1995, all these bonds were converted into 40,000 shares of $20 par common stock. On the date of conversion:

- Unamortized bond discount was $30,000.
- Each bond had a market price of $1,080.
- Each share of stock had a market price of $28.

Under the book value method, what amount should Witt record as a loss on conversion of bonds?

a. $150,000
b. $110,000
c. $30,000
d. $0

21. When bonds payable are converted into common stock, any gain or loss would be recognized when using the

	Book value method	*Market value method*
a.	Yes	Yes
b.	No	Yes
c.	No	No
d.	Yes	No

BOND ISSUED WITH STOCK WARRANTS

22. On December 30, 1999, Fort, Inc. issued 1,000 of its 8%, 10-year, $1,000 face value bonds with detachable stock warrants at par. Each bond carried a detachable warrant for one share of Fort's common stock at a specified option price of $25 per share. Immediately after issuance, the market value of the bonds without the warrants was $1,080,000 and the market value of the warrants was $120,000. In its December 31, 1999, balance sheet, what amount should Fort report as bonds payable?

a. $1,000,000.
b. $975,000.
c. $900,000.
d. $880,000.

23. Ray Corp. issued bonds with a face amount of $200,000. Each $1,000 bond contained detachable stock warrants for 100 shares of Ray's common stock. Total proceeds from the issue amounted to $240,000. The market value of each warrant was $2, and the market value of the bonds without the warrants was $196,000. The bonds were issued at a discount of

a. $0.
b. $678.
c. $4,000.
d. $33,898.

24. On March 1, 1999, Evan Corp. issued $500,000 of 10% nonconvertible bonds at 103, due on February 28, 2009. Each $1,000 bond was issued with 30 detachable stock warrants, each of which entitled the holder to purchase, for $50, one share of Evan's $25 par common stock. On March 1, 1999, the market price of each warrant was $4. By what amount should the bond issue proceeds increase stockholders' equity?

a. $0
b. $15,000
c. $45,000
d. $60,000

25. Roaster Company issued bonds with detachable stock warrants. Each warrant granted an option to buy one share of $40 par value common stock for $75 per share. Five hundred warrants were originally issued, and $4,000 was appropriately credited to "warrants." If 90% of these warrants are exercised when the market price of the common stock is $85 per share, how much should be credited to "capital in excess of par" on this transaction?

a. $19,350.
b. $19,750.
c. $23,850.
d. $24,250.

BOND TERMS

26. Blue Corp.'s December 31, 1991, balance sheet contained the following items in the long-term liabilities section:

9¾% registered debentures, callable in 2002, due in 2007	$700,000
9½% collateral trust bonds, convertible into common stock beginning in 2000, due in 2010	600,000
10% subordinated debentures ($30,000 maturing annually beginning in 1997)	300,000

What is the total amount of Blue's term bonds?

a. $600,000
b. $700,000
c. $1,000,000
d. $1,300,000

27. Hancock Co.'s December 31, 1990, balance sheet contained the following items in the long-term liabilities section:

Unsecured	
9.375% registered bonds ($25,000 maturing annually beginning in 1994)	$275,000
11.5% convertible bonds, callable beginning in 1999, due 2010	125,000
Secured	
9.875% guaranty security bonds, due 2010	$250,000
10.0% commodity backed bonds ($50,000 maturing annually beginning in 1995)	200,000

What are the total amounts of serial bonds and debenture bonds?

	Serial bonds	*Debenture bonds*
a.	$475,000	$400,000
b.	$475,000	$125,000
c.	$450,000	$400,000
d.	$200,000	$650,000

DISCLOSURE OF BONDS

28. Witt Corp. has outstanding at December 31, 1996, two long-term borrowings with annual sinking fund requirements and maturities as follows:

	Sinking fund requirements	*Maturities*
1996	$1,000,000	$ —
1997	1,500,000	2,000,000
1998	1,500,000	2,000,000
1999	2,000,000	2,500,000
2000	2,000,000	3,000,000
	$8,000,000	$9,500,000

In the notes to its December 31, 1996, balance sheet, how should Witt report the above data?

a. No disclosure is required.
b. Only sinking fund payments totaling $8,000,000 for the next five years detailed by year need be disclosed.
c. Only maturities totaling $9,500,000 for the next five years detailed by year need be disclosed.
d. The combined aggregate of $17,500,000 of maturities and sinking fund requirements detailed by year should be disclosed.

CLASSIFICATION OF BONDS

29. Included in Witt Corp.'s liability account balances at December 31, 1995, were the following:

14% note payable issued October 1, 1995, maturing September 30, 1996	$500,000
16% note payable issued April 1, 1993, payable in six equal annual installments of $200,000 beginning April 1, 1994	800,000

Witt's December 31, 1995, financial statements were issued on March 31, 1996. On January 15, 1996, the entire $800,000 balance of the 16% note was refinanced by issuance of a long-term obligation payable in a lump sum. In addition, on March 10, 1996, Witt consummated a noncancelable agreement with the lender to refinance the 14%, $500,000 note on a long-term basis, on readily determinable terms that have not yet been implemented. Both parties are financially capable of honoring the agreement, and there have been no violations of the agreement's provisions. On the December 31, 1995 at Witt should classify as short-term obligations is

a. $700,000
b. $500,000
c. $200,000
d. $0

30. On December 31, 1999, Largo, Inc. had a $750,000 note payable outstanding, due July 31, 2000. Largo borrowed the money to finance construction of a new plant. Largo planned to refinance the note by issuing long-term bonds. Because Largo temporarily had excess cash, it prepaid $250,000 of the note on January 12, 2000. In February 2000, Largo completed a $1,500,000 bond offering. Largo will use the bond offering proceeds to repay the note payable at its maturity and to pay construction costs during 2000. On March 3, 2000, Largo issued its 1999 financial statements. What amount of the note payable should Largo include in the current liabilities section of its December 31, 1999, balance sheet?

a. $750,000
b. $500,000
c. $250,000
d. $0

31. Cali, Inc., had a $4,000,000 note payable due on March 15, 2002. On January 28, 2002, before the issuance of its 2001 financial statements, Cali issued long-term bonds in the amount of $4,500,000. Proceeds from the bonds were used to repay the note when it came due. How should Cali classify the note in its December 31, 2001, financial statements?

a. As a current liability, with separate disclosure of the note refinancing.
b. As a current liability, with no separate disclosure required.
c. As a noncurrent liability, with separate disclosure of the note refinancing.
d. As a noncurrent liability, with no separate disclosure required.

32. Mill Co.'s trial balance included the following account balances at December 31, 1999:

Accounts payable	$15,000
Bonds payable, due 2000	25,000
Discount on bonds payable, due 2000	3,000
Dividends payable 1/31/00	8,000
Notes payable, due 2001	20,000

What amount should be included in the current liability section of Mill's December 31, 1999, balance sheet?

a. $45,000.
b. $51,000.
c. $65,000.
d. $78,000.

BOND SINKING FUND

33. On March 1, 1995, a company established a sinking fund in connection with an issue of bonds due in 2007. At December 31, 1999, the independent trustee held cash in the sinking fund account representing the annual deposits to the fund and the interest earned on those deposits. How should the sinking fund be reported in the company's balance sheet at December 31, 1999?

a. The cash in the sinking fund should appear as a current asset.
b. Only the accumulated deposits should appear as a noncurrent asset.
c. The entire balance in the sinking fund account should appear as a current asset.
d. The entire balance in the sinking fund account should appear as a noncurrent asset.

INVESTMENT IN BONDS

34. On July 1, 1993, Fox Company purchased 400 of the $1,000 face amount, 8% bonds of Dey Corporation for $369,200 to yield 10% per annum. The bonds, which mature on July 1, 1998, pay interest semiannually on January 1 and July 1. Fox uses the interest method of amortization and the bonds are appropriately recorded as a long-term investment. The bonds should be reported on Fox's December 31, 1993, balance sheet at

a. $397,540
b. $374,120
c. $371,660
d. $366,740

35. Jent Corp. purchased bonds at a discount of $10,000. Subsequently, Jent sold these bonds at a premium of $14,000. During the period that Jent held this investment, amortization of the discount amounted to $2,000. What amount should Jent report as gain on the sale of the bonds?

a. $12,000.
b. $22,000.
c. $24,000.
d. $26,000.

36. An investor purchased a bond classified as a long-term investment between interest dates at a discount. At the purchase date, the carrying amount of the bond is more than the

	Cash paid to seller	*Face amount of bond*
a.	No	Yes
b.	No	No
c.	Yes	No
d.	Yes	Yes

37. An investor purchased a bond as a long-term investment on January 2. The investor's carrying value at the end of the first year would be highest if the bond was purchased at a

a. Discount and amortized by the straight-line method.
b. Discount and amortized by the effective interest method.
c. Premium and amortized by the straight-line method.
d. Premium and amortized by the effective interest method.

CONTINGENCIES

38. Management can estimate the amount of loss that will occur if a foreign government expropriates some company assets. If expropriation is reasonably possible, a loss contingency should be
a. Disclosed but **not** accrued as a liability.
b. Disclosed and accrued as a liability.
c. Accrued as a liability but **not** disclosed.
d. Neither accrued as a liability **nor** disclosed.

39. Snelling Co. did not record an accrual for a contingent loss, but disclosed the nature of the contingency and the range of the possible loss. How likely is the loss?
a. Remote.
b. Reasonably possible.
c. Probable.
d. Certain.

40. During 1996, Tedd Co. became involved in a tax dispute with the IRS. At December 31, 1996, Tedd's tax advisor believed that an unfavorable outcome was probable. A reasonable estimate of additional taxes was $400,000, but could be as much as $600,000. After the 1996 financial statements were issued, Tedd received and accepted an IRS settlement offer of $450,000. What amount of accrued liability should Tedd have reported in its December 31, 1996, balance sheet?
a. $400,000
b. $450,000
c. $500,000
d. $600,000

41. On February 5, 2000, an employee filed a $2,000,000 lawsuit against Steel Co. for damages suffered when one of Steel's plants exploded on December 29, 1999. Steel's legal counsel expects the company will lose the lawsuit and estimates the loss to be between $500,000 and $1,000,000. The employee has offered to settle the lawsuit out of court for $900,000, but Steel will not agree to the settlement. In its December 31, 1999, balance sheet, what amount should Steel report as liability from lawsuit.
a. $2,000,000
b. $1,000,000
c. $900,000
d. $500,000

42. Brite Corp. had the following liabilities at December 31, 2000:

Accounts payable	$ 55,000
Unsecured notes, 8%, due 7/1/01	400,000
Accrued expenses	35,000
Contingent liability	450,000
Deferred income tax liability	25,000
Senior bonds, 7%, due 3/31/01	1,000,000

The contingent liability is an accrual for possible losses on a $1,000,000 lawsuit filed against Brite. Brite's legal counsel expects the suit to be settled in 2002, and has estimated that Brite will be liable for damages in the range of $450,000 to $750,000.

The deferred income tax liability is not related to an asset for financial reporting and is expected to reverse in 2002.

What amount should Brite report in its December 31, 2000, balance sheet for current liabilities?
a. $515,000.
b. $940,000.
c. $1,490,000.
d. $1,515,000.

43. Eagle Co. has cosigned the mortgage note on the home of its president, guaranteeing the indebtedness in the event that the president should default. Eagle considers the likelihood of default to be remote. How should the guarantee be treated in Eagle's financial statements?
a. Disclosed only.
b. Accrued only.
c. Accrued and disclosed.
d. Neither accrued nor disclosed.

44. During January 1999, Haze Corp. won a litigation award for $15,000 which was tripled to $45,000 to include punitive damages. The defendant, who is financially stable, has appealed only the $30,000 punitive damages. Haze was awarded $50,000 in an unrelated suit it filed, which is being appealed by the defendant. Counsel is unable to estimate the outcome of these appeals. In its 1999 financial statements, Haze should report what amount of pretax gain?
a. $15,000
b. $45,000
c. $50,000
d. $95,000

ESCROW ACCOUNTS LIABILITY

45. Kent Co., a division of National Realty, Inc., maintains escrow accounts and pays real estate taxes for National's mortgage customers. Escrow funds are kept in interest-bearing accounts. Interest, less a 10% service fee, is credited to the mortgagee's account and used to reduce future escrow payments. Additional information follows:

Escrow accounts liability, 1/1/99	$ 700,000
Escrow payments received during 1999	1,580,000
Real estate taxes paid during 1999	1,720,000
Interest on escrow funds during 1999	50,000

What amount should Kent report as escrow accounts liability in its December 31, 1999, balance sheet?

a. $510,000.
b. $515,000.
c. $605,000.
d. $610,000.

CREDIT RISK

46. Disclosure of information about significant concentrations of credit risk is required for

a. All financial instruments.
b. Financial instruments with off-balance-sheet credit risk only.
c. Financial instruments with off-balance-sheet market risk only.
d. Financial instruments with off-balance-sheet risk of accounting loss only.

UNCONDITIONAL PURCHASE OBLIGATIONS

47. Brad Corp. has unconditional purchase obligations associated with product financing arrangements. These obligations are reported as liabilities on Brad's balance sheet, with the related assets also recognized. In the notes to Brad's financial statements, the aggregate amount of payments for these obligations should be disclosed for each of how many years following the date of the latest balance sheet?

a. 0
b. 1
c. 5
d. 10

MISCELLANEOUS TAX LIABILITIES

48. Lime Co.'s payroll for the month ended January 31, 2002, is summarized as follows:

Total wages	$10,000
Federal income tax withheld	1,200

All wages paid were subject to FICA. FICA tax rates were 7% each for employee and employer. Lime remits payroll taxes on the 15th of the following month. In its financial statements for the month ended January 31, 2002, what amounts should Lime report as total payroll tax liability and as payroll tax expense?

	Liability	Expense
a.	$1,200	$1,400
b.	$1,900	$1,400
c.	$1,900	$ 700
d.	$2,600	$ 700

49. Under state law, Acme may pay 3% of eligible gross wages or it may reimburse the state directly for actual unemployment claims. Acme believes that actual unemployment claims will be 2% of eligible gross wages and has chosen to reimburse the state. Eligible gross wages are defined as the first $10,000 of gross wages paid to each employee. Acme had five employees each of whom earned $20,000 during 2000. In its December 31, 2000, balance sheet, what amount should Acme report as accrued liability for unemployment claims?

a. $1,000.
b. $1,500.
c. $2,000.
d. $3,000.

50. Which of the following statements is correct regarding the provision for income taxes in the financial statements of a sole proprietorship?

a. The provision for income taxes should be based on business income using individual tax rates.
b. The provision for income taxes should be based on business income using corporate tax rates.
c. The provision for income taxes should be based on the proprietor's total taxable income, allocated to the proprietorship at the percentage that business income bears to the proprietor's total income.
d. No provision for income taxes is required.

WARRANTIES

51. During 1997, Gum Co. introduced a new product carrying a two-year warranty against defects: The estimated warranty costs related to dollar sales are 2% within 12 months following the sale and 4% in the second 12 months following the sale. Sales and actual warranty expenditures for the years ended December 31, 1997 and 1998, are as follows:

	Sales	Actual warranty expenditures
1997	$150,000	$2,250
1998	250,000	7,500
	$400,000	$9,750

What amount should Gum report as estimated warranty liability in its December 31, 1998, balance sheet?

a. $2,500
b. $4,250
c. $11,250
d. $14,250

52. Vadis Co. sells appliances that include a three-year warranty. Service calls under the warranty are performed by an independent mechanic under a contract with Vadis. Based on experience, warranty costs are estimated at $30 for each machine sold. When should Vadis recognize these warranty costs?

a. Evenly over the life of the warranty
b. When the service calls are performed.
c. When payments are made to the mechanic.
d. When the machines are sold.

COUPONS

53. In packages of its products, the Kent Food Company includes coupons which may be presented to grocers for discounts on certain products of Kent on or before a stated expiration date. The grocers are reimbursed when they send the coupons to Kent. In Kent's experience, 40% of such coupons are redeemed, and one month generally elapses between the date a grocer receives a coupon from a consumer and the date Kent receives it. During 1994, Kent issued two series of coupons as follows:

Issued on	Total value	Consumer expiration date	Amount disbursed as of 12/31/94
1/1/94	$100,000	6/30/94	$34,000
7/1/94	120,000	12/31/94	40,000

Kent's December 31, 1994, balance sheet should include a liability for unredeemed coupons of

a. $0
b. $8,000
c. $14,000
d. $48,000

54. In December 2001, Mill Co. began including one coupon in each package of candy that it sells and offering a toy in exchange for 50 cents and five coupons. The toys cost Mill 80 cents each. Eventually 60% of the coupons will be redeemed. During December, Mill sold 110,000 packages of candy and no coupons were redeemed. In its December 31, 2001, balance sheet, what amount should Mill report as estimated liability for coupons?

a. $ 3,960
b. $10,560
c. $19,800
d. $52,800

GIFT CERTIFICATES

55. A retail store received cash and issued gift certificates that are redeemable in merchandise. The gift certificates lapse one year after they are issued. How would the deferred revenue account be affected by each of the following transactions?

	Redemption of certificates	Lapse of certificates
a.	Decrease	No effect
b.	Decrease	Decrease
c.	No effect	No effect
d.	No effect	Decrease

56. Regal Department Store sells gift certificates, redeemable for store merchandise, that expire one year after their issuance. Regal has the following information pertaining to its gift certificates sales and redemptions:

Unredeemed at 12/31/97	$ 75,000
1998 sales	250,000
1998 redemptions of prior year sales	25,000
1998 redemptions of current year sales	175,000

Regal's experience indicates that 10% of gift certificates sold will not be redeemed. In its December 31, 1998, balance sheet, what amount should Regal report as unearned revenue?

a. $125,000
b. $112,500
c. $100,000
d. $50,000

REVIEW QUESTIONS

57. On April 1, 1999, Hill Corp. issued 200 of its $1,000 face value bonds at 101 plus accrued interest. The bonds were dated November 1, 1998, and bear interest at an annual rate of 9% payable semiannually on November 1 and May 1. What amount did Hill receive from the bond issuance?

a. $194,500
b. $200,000
c. $202,000
d. $209,500

58. During 2000, Smith Co. filed suit against West, Inc. seeking damages for patent infringement. At December 31, 2000, Smith's legal counsel believed that it was probable that Smith would be successful against West for an estimated amount in the range of $75,000 to $150,000, with all amounts in the range considered equally likely. In March 2001, Smith was awarded $100,000 and received full payment thereof. In its 2000 financial statements, issued in February 2001, how should this award by reported?

a. As a receivable and revenue of $100,000.
b. As a receivable and deferred revenue of $100,000.
c. As a disclosure of a contingent gain of $100,000.
d. As a disclosure of a contingent gain of an undetermined amount in the range of $75,000 to $150,000.

59. A bond issued on June 1, 1998, has interest payment dates of April 1 and October 1. Bond interest expense for the year ended December 31, 1998, is for a period of

a. Seven months.
b. Six months.
c. Four months.
d. Three months.

60. At December 31, 1997, Cain, Inc., owed notes payable of $1,750,000, due on May 15, 1998. Cain expects to retire this debt with proceeds from the sale of 100,000 shares of its common stock. The stock was sold for $15 per share on March 10, 1998, prior to the issuance of the year-end financial statements. In Cain's December 31, 1997, balance sheet, what amount of the notes payable should be excluded from current liabilities?

a. $0
b. $250,000
c. $1,500,000
d. $1,750,000

61. On January 2, 1999, Gill Co. issued $2,000,000 of 10-year, 8% bonds at par. The bonds, dated January 1, 1999, pay interest semi-annually on January 1 and July 1. Bond issue costs were $250,000. What amount of bond issue costs are unamortized at June 30, 2000?

a. $237,500.
b. $225,000.
c. $220,800.
d. $212,500.

62. Aneen's Video Mart sells 1- and 2-year mail order subscriptions for its video-of-the-month business. Subscriptions are collected in advance and credited to sales. An analysis of the recorded sales activity revealed the following:

	1996	*1997*
Sales	$420,000	$500,000
Less cancellations	20,000	30,000
Net sales	$400,000	$470,000
Subscriptions expirations:		
1996	$120,000	
1997	155,000	$130,000
1998	125,000	200,000
1999		140,000
	$400,000	$470,000

In Aneen's December 31, 1997, balance sheet, the balance for unearned subscription revenue should be

a. $495,000
b. $470,000
c. $465,000
d. $340,000

63. During 2001, Haft Co. became involved in a tax dispute with the IRS. At December 31, 2001, Haft's tax advisor believed that an unfavorable outcome was probable. A reasonable estimate of additional taxes was $200,000 but could be as much as $300,000. After the 2001 financial statements were issued, Haft received and accepted an IRS settlement offer of $275,000. What amount of accrued liability should Haft have reported in its December 31, 2001 balance sheet?

a. $200,000
b. $250,000
c. $275,000
d. $300,000

Items 64 and 65 are based on the following:
On January 2, 1995, Chard Co. issued 10-year convertible bonds at 105. During 1998, these bonds were converted into common stock having an aggregate par value equal to the total face amount of the bonds. At conversion, the market price of Chard's common stock was 50 percent above its par value.

64. On January 2, 1993, cash proceeds from the issuance of the convertible bonds should be reported as
a. Contributed capital for the entire proceeds.
b. Contributed capital for the portion of the proceeds attributable to the conversion feature and as a liability for the balance.
c. A liability for the face amount of the bonds and contributed capital for the premium over the face amount.
d. A liability for the entire proceeds.

65. Depending on whether the book value method or the market value method was used, Chard would recognize gains or losses on conversion when using the

	Book value method	*Market value method*
a.	Either gain or loss	Gain
b.	Either gain or loss	Loss
c.	Neither gain **nor** loss	Loss
d.	Neither gain **nor** loss	Gain

66. Lyle, Inc. is preparing its financial statements for the year ended December 31, 1999. Accounts payable amounted to $360,000 before any necessary year-end adjustment related to the following:

- At December 31, 1999, Lyle has a $50,000 debit balance in its accounts payable to Ross, a supplier, resulting from a $50,000 advance payment for goods to be manufactured to Lyle's specifications.

- Checks in the amount of $100,000 were written to vendors and recorded on December 29, 1999. The checks were mailed on January 5, 2000.

What amount should Lyle report as accounts payable in its December 31, 1999, balance sheet?
a. $510,000.
b. $410,000.
c. $310,000.
d. $210,000.

67. On July 1, 1999, York Co. purchased as a long-term investment $1,000,000 of Park, Inc.'s 8% bonds for $946,000, including accrued interest of $40,000. The bonds were purchased to yield 10% interest. The bonds mature on January 1, 2006, and pay interest annually on January 1. York uses the effective interest method of amortization. In its December 31, 1999, balance sheet, what amount should York report as investment in bonds?
a. $911,300
b. $916,600
c. $953,300
d. $960,600

68. On January 1, 1995, Purl Corp. purchased as a long-term investment $500,000 face value of Shaw, Inc.'s 8% bonds for $456,200. The bonds were purchased to yield 10% interest. The bonds mature on January 1, 2001, and pay interest annually on January 1. Purl uses the interest method of amortization. What amount (rounded to nearest $100) should Purl report on its December 31, 1996, balance sheet for this long-term investment?
a. $468,000
b. $466,200
c. $461,800
d. $456,200

69. Pam, Inc., has $1,000,000 of notes payable due June 15, 1996. At the financial statement date of December 31, 1995, Pam signed an agreement to borrow up to $1,000,000 to refinance the notes payable on a long-term basis. The financing agreement called for borrowings not to exceed 80% of the value of the collateral Pam was providing. At the date of issue of the December 31, 1995, financial statements, the value of the collateral was $1,200,000 and was not expected to fall below this amount during 1996. In its December 31, 1995, balance sheet, Pam should classify notes payable as

	Short-term obligations	*Long-term obligations*
a.	$0	$1,000,000
b.	$40,000	$960,000
c.	$200,000	$800,000
d.	$1,000,000	$0

70. On March 31, 1999, Ashley, Inc.'s bondholders exchanged their convertible bonds for common stock. The carrying amount of these bonds on Ashley's books was less than the market value but greater than the par value of the common stock issued. If Ashley used the book value method of accounting for the conversion, which of the following statements correctly states an effect of this conversion?

a. Stockholders' equity is increased.
b. Additional paid-in capital is decreased.
c. Retained earnings is increased.
d. An extraordinary loss is recognized.

71. Blue Co. issued preferred stock with detachable common stock warrants at a price which exceeded both the par value and the market value of the preferred stock. At the time the warrants are exercised, Blue's total stockholders' equity is increased by the

	Cash received upon exercise of the warrants	*Carrying amount of warrants*
a.	Yes	No
b.	Yes	Yes
c.	No	No
d.	No	Yes

72. On January 1, 1991, Fox Corp. issued 1,000 of its 10%, $1,000 bonds for $1,040,000. These bonds were to mature on January 1, 2001, but were callable at 101 any time after December 31, 1994. Interest was payable semiannually on July 1 and January 1. On July 1, 1996, Fox called all of the bonds and retired them. Bond premium was amortized on a straight-line basis. Before income taxes, Fox's gain or loss in 1996 on this early extinguishment of debt was

a. $30,000 gain.
b. $12,000 gain.
c. $10,000 loss.
d. $8,000 gain.

73. In May 1996, Caso Co. filed suit against Wayne, Inc. seeking $1,900,000 damages for patent infringement. A court verdict in November 1999 awarded Caso $1,5000,000 in damages, but Wayne's appeal is not expected to be decided before 2001. Caso's counsel believes it is probable that Caso will be successful against Wayne for an estimated amount in the range between $800,000 and $1,100,000, with $1,000,000 considered the most likely amount. What amount should Caso record as income from the lawsuit in the year ended December 31, 1999?

a. $0
b. $800,000
c. $1,000,000
d. $1,500,000

74. On December 31, 1992, Arnold, Inc., issued $200,000, 8% serial bonds, to be repaid in the amount of $40,000 each year. Interest is payable annually on December 31. The bonds were issued to yield 10% a year. The bond proceeds were $190,280 based on the present values at December 31, 1999, of the five annual payments as follows:

Due date	*Amounts due Principal*	*Interest*	*Present value at 12/31/99*
12/31/00	$40,000	$16,000	$ 50,900
12/31/01	40,000	12,800	43,610
12/31/02	40,000	9,600	37,250
12/31/03	40,000	6,400	31,690
12/31/04	40,000	3,200	26,830
			$190,280

Arnold amortizes the bond discount by the interest method. In its December 31, 2000, balance sheet, at what amount should Arnold report the carrying value of the bonds?

a. $139,380
b. $149,100.
c. $150,280.
d. $153,308.

75. On February 24, 1993, Bart Company purchased 2,000 shares of Winn Corp.'s newly issued 6% cumulative $75 par preferred stock for $152,000. Each share carried one detachable stock warrant entitling the holder to acquire at $10, one share of Winn no-par common stock. On February 25, 1993, the market price of the preferred stock ex-warrants was $72 a share and the market price of the stock warrants was $8 a warrant. On December 29, 1993, Bart sold all the stock warrants for $20,500. The gain on the sale of the stock warrants was

a. $0
b. $500
c. $4,500
d. $5,300

76. On January 2, 1994, Nast Co. issued 8% bonds with a face amount of $1,000,000 that mature on January 2, 2000. The bonds were issued to yield 12%, resulting in a discount of $150,000. Nast incorrectly used the straight-line method instead of the effective interest method to amortize the discount. How is the carrying amount of the bonds affected by the error?

	At December 31, 2001	At January 2, 2007
a.	Overstated	Understated
b.	Overstated	No effect
c.	Understated	Overstated
d.	Understated	No effect

77. On January 1, 2001, Oak Co. issued 400 of its 8%, $1,000 bonds at 97 plus accrued interest. The bonds are dated October 1, 2000, and mature on October 1, 2010. Interest is payable semiannually on April 1 and October 1. Accrued interest for the period October 1, 2000, to January 1, 2001, amounted to $8,000. On January 1, 2001, what amount should Oak report as bonds payable, net of discount?

a. $380,300.
b. $388,000.
c. $388,300.
d. $392,000.

78. Dunn Trading Stamp Co. records stamp service revenue and provides for the cost of redemptions in the year stamps are sold to licensees. Dunn's past experience indicates that only 80% of the stamps sold to licensees will be redeemed. Dunn's liability for stamp redemptions was $6,000,000 at December 31, 1995. Additional information for 1996 is as follows:

Stamp service revenue from stamps sold to licensees	$4,000,000
Cost of redemptions (stamps sold prior to 1/1/96)	2,750,000

If all the stamps sold in 1996 were presented for redemption in 1997, the redemption cost would be $2,250,000. What amount should Dunn report as a liability for stamp redemptions at December 31, 1996?

a. $7,250,000
b. $5,500,000
c. $5,050,000
d. $3,250,000

79. On January 31, 1999, Beau Corp. issued $300,000 maturity value, 12% bonds for $300,000 cash. The bonds are dated December 31, 1998, and mature on December 31, 2008. Interest will be paid semiannually on June 30 and December 31. What amount of accrued interest payable should Beau report in its September 30, 1999, balance sheet?

a. $27,000.
b. $24,000.
c. $18,000.
d. $9,000.

80. On July 1, 1999, Cove Corp., a closely-held corporation, issued 6% bonds with a maturity value of $60,000, together with 1,000 shares of its $5 par value common stock, for a combined cash amount of $110,000. The market value of Cove's stock cannot be ascertained. If the bonds were issued separately, they would have sold for $40,000 on an 8% yield to maturity basis. What amount should Cove report for additional paid-in capital on the issuance of the stock?

a. $75,000
b. $65,000
c. $55,000
d. $45,000

81. Hudson Hotel collects 15% in city sales taxes on room rentals, in addition to a $2 per room, per night, occupancy tax. Sales taxes for each month are due at the end of the following month, and occupancy taxes are due 15 days after the end of each calendar quarter. On January 3, 2001, Hudson paid its November 1993 sales taxes and its fourth quarter 2000 occupancy taxes. Additional information pertaining to Hudson's operations is:

1993	Room rentals	Room nights
October	$100,000	1,100
November	110,000	1,200
December	150,000	1,800

What amounts should Hudson report as sales taxes payable and occupancy taxes payable in its December 31, 2000, balance sheet?

	Sales taxes	Occupancy taxes
a.	$39,000	$6,000
b.	$39,000	$8,200
c.	$54,000	$6,000
d.	$54,000	$8,200

82. Grim Corporation operates a plant in a foreign country. It is probable that the plant will be expropriated. However, the foreign government has indicated that Grim will receive a definite amount of compensation for the plant. The amount of compensation is less than the fair market value, but exceeds the carrying amount of the plant. The contingency should be reported

a. As a valuation allowance as a part of stockholders' equity.
b. As a fixed asset valuation allowance account.
c. In the notes to the financial statements.
d. In the income statement.

83. Ivy Co. operates a retail store. All items are sold subject to a 6% state sales tax, which Ivy collects and records as sales revenue. Ivy files quarterly sales tax returns when due, by the 20th day following the end of the sales quarter. However, in accordance with state requirements, Ivy remits sales tax collected by the 20th day of the month following any month such collections exceed $500. Ivy takes these payments as credits on the quarterly sales tax return. The sales taxes paid by Ivy are charged against sales revenue.

Following is a monthly summary appearing in Ivy's first quarter 2002 sales revenue account:

	Debit	*Credit*
January	$ ---	$10,600
February	600	7,420
March	---	8,480
	$600	$26,500

In its March 31, 2002, balance sheet, what amount should Ivy report as sales taxes payable

a. $600
b. $900
c. $1,500
d. $1,590

84. Adams, Inc., owns 50 shares of the outstanding common stock of Bland Corporation, which has several hundred thousand shares publicly traded. These 50 shares were purchased by Adams in 1990 for $100 per share. On August 30, 1992, Bland distributed 50 stock rights to Adams. Adams was entitled to buy one new share of Bland common stock for $90 cash and two of these rights. On August 30, 1992, each share of stock had a market value of $132 ex-rights, and each right had a market value of $18. What cost should be recorded for each new share that Adams acquires by exercising the rights?

a. $90.
b. $114.
c. $126.
d. $132.

Items 85 and 86 are based on the following:

House Publishers offered a contest in which the winner would receive $1,000,000, payable over 20 years. On December 31, 2000, House announced the winner of the contest and signed a note payable to the winner for $1,000,000, payable in $50,000 installments every January 2. Also on December 31, 2000, House purchased an annuity for $418,250 to provide the $950,000 prize monies remaining after the first $50,000 installment, which was paid on January 2, 2001.

85. In its December 31, 2000, balance sheet, what amount should House report as note payable-contest winner, net of current portion?

a. $368,250
b. $418,250
c. $900,000
d. $950,000

86. In its 2000 income statement, what should House report as contest prize expense?

a. $0
b. $418,250
c. $468,250
d. $1,000,000

---

87. On July 1, 1996, Pell Co. purchased Green Corp. ten-year, 8% bonds with a face amount of $500,000 for $420,000. The bonds mature on June 30, 2004, and pay interest semiannually on June 30 and December 31. Using the interest method, Pell recorded bond discount amortization of $1,800 for the six months ended December 31, 1996. From this long-term investment, Pell should report 1996 revenue of

a. $16,800
b. $18,200
c. $20,000
d. $21,800

88. Ames, Inc., has $500,000 of notes payable due June 15, 1998. Ames signed an agreement on December 1, 1997, to borrow up to $500,000 to refinance the notes payable on a long-term basis with no payments due until 1999. The financing agreement stipulated that borrowings may not exceed 80% of the value of the collateral Ames was providing. At the date of issuance of the December 31, 1997, financial statements, the value of the collateral was $600,000 and is not expected to fall below this amount during 1998. In Ames' December 31, 1997, balance sheet, the obligation for these notes payable should be classified as

	Short-term	*Long-term*
a.	$500,000	$0
b.	$100,000	$400,000
c.	$20,000	$480,000
d.	$0	$500,000

RECENTLY DISCLOSED and AUTHOR CONSTRUCTED QUESTIONS

N96

89. Which of the following risks are inherent in an interest rate swap agreement?

I. The risk of exchanging a lower interest rate for a higher interest rate.
II. The risk of nonperformance by the counterparty to the agreement.

a. I only.
b. II only.
c. Both I and II.
d. Neither I nor II.

N96

90. If it is not practicable for an entity to estimate the fair value of a financial instrument, which of the following should be disclosed?

I. Information pertinent to estimating the fair value of the financial instrument.
II. The reasons it is not practicable to estimate fair value.

a. I only.
b. II only.
c. Both I and II.
d. Neither I nor II.

M96

91. On December 1, 1995, Money Co. gave Home Co. a $200,000, 11% loan. Money paid proceeds of $194,000 after the deduction of a $6,000 non refundable loan origination fee. Principal and interest are due in 60 monthly installments of $4,310, beginning January 1, 1996. The repayments yield an effective interest rate of 11% at a present value of $200,000 and 12.4% at a present value of $194,000. What amount of income from this loan should Money report in its 1995 income statement?
a. $0
b. $1,833
c. $2,005
d. $7,833

AC

92. For a bond issue which sells for less than its par value, the market rate of interest is
a. Dependent on rate stated on the bond.
b. Equal to rate stated on the bond.
c. Less than rate stated on the bond.
d. Higher than rate stated on the bond.

AC

93. The loss from a decrease in the fair value of a derivative that is designated as a hedge would be included in current earnings if the derivative is a hedge of
a. Cash flows.
b. A forecasted foreign currency transaction.
c. A net investment in a foreign operation.
d. A foreign currency exposure of an available-for-sale security.

AC

94. In SFAS 133, Accounting for Derivatives and Hedging Activities, the FASB used the term "underlying." Which of the following items is an example of an "underlying?"
a. A specified interest rate.
b. Number of currency units.
c. Number of pounds.
d. An embedded derivative.

AC

95. A gain on a forecasted cash flow hedge should be reported as
a. An extraordinary item.
b. Change in accounting estimate.
c. Other comprehensive income.
d. Income from continuing operations.

AC

96. On October 15, 1999, Gilmore Inc. invested in a derivative designated as a hedge of the fair value of an asset. By December 31, 1999, the fair value of the hedged asset had decreased by $200,000 but the fair value of the derivative had increased by $220,000. The net effect on 1999 earnings would be

a. $200,000
b. $0
c. $20,000
d. $220,000

AC

97. Helgeson Corporation had the following transaction in the last quarter of 1999. Which of the transactions is most likely to result in a derivative subject to SFAS 133 – Accounting for Derivative Instruments and Hedging Activities?

a. Invested in land with the anticipation of an increase in fair value.
b. Purchased available-for-sale securities.
c. Negotiated a two-year loan with a Swiss bank to take advantage of lower European interest rates.
d. Based on a forecasted purchase of cocoa beans, Helgeson bought a futures contract to protect itself from changes in market prices of cocoa beans.

AC

98. On November 1, 1999, Cox Corp. enters into a derivative contract to hedge the forecasted cash flows associated with a future sale of 100,000 bushels (notional amount) of corn. The future sale date is January 11, 2000. The fair value of the derivative contract at December 31, 1999 increased by $15,000 which was the same amount as the decrease in the value of corn. The fair value of the derivative contract increased by an additional $8,000 from January 1 to January 15, which again corresponded to the decrease in the value of the corn. On January 15, 2000, the corn was sold and the derivative was settled. The gains from the derivative should be recognized in 1999 and 2000 as

	1999 *Other Comprehensive Income*	*2000* *Earnings (Income)*
a.	-0-	-0-
b.	$15,000	$23,000
c.	$15,000	$8,000
d.	$23,000	$23,000

AC

99. SFAS 133 defines a derivative as a financial instrument that has the following elements.

a. One or more underlying and one or more notional amounts or payment provisions or both; requires either no initial investment or an immaterial net investment and requires or permits net settlement.
b. One underlying; one notional amount and a net settlement provision.
c. An embedded contract; a conversion clause; and a net settlement amount.
d. An underlying; a notional amount; and an effective hedge.

Author's Note:
See Chapter 6 for questions on Derivatives and Foreign Currency.

100. Perk, Inc. issued $500,000, 10% bonds to yield 8%. Bond issuance costs were $10,000. How should Perk calculate the net proceeds to be received from the issuance?

a. Discount the bonds at the stated rate of interest.
b. Discount the bonds at the market rate of interest.
c. Discount the bonds at the stated rate of interest and deduct bond issuance costs.
d. Discount the bonds at the market rate of interest and deduct bond issuance costs.

101. Whether recognized or unrecognized in an entity's financial statements, disclosure of the fair values of the entity's financial instruments is required when

a. It is practicable to estimate those values.
b. The entity maintains accurate cost records.
c. Aggregated fair values are material to the entity.
d. Individual fair values are material to the entity.

102. For the week ended June 30, 1995, Free Co. paid gross wages of $20,000, from which federal income taxes of $2,500 and FICA were withheld. All wages paid were subject to FICA tax rates of 7% each for employer and employee. Free makes all payroll-related disbursements from a special payroll checking account to cover net payroll and related payroll taxes for the week ended June 30, 1995. What is the amount needed to cover the net payroll and related payroll taxes?

a. $21,400
b. $22,800
c. $23,900
d. $25,300

Chapter Nine
Bonds, Accounting for Debt Problems

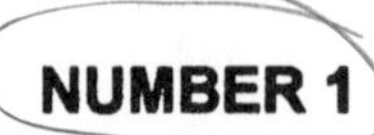

NUMBER 1

Question Number 1 consists of 5 items. Select the **best** answer for each item. **Answer all items.**

Items 1 through 5 are based on the following:
Hamnoff, Inc.'s $50 par value common stock has always traded above par. During 1999, Hamnoff had several transactions that affected the following balance sheet accounts:

I. Bond discount
II. Bond premium
III. Bonds payable
IV. Common stock
V. Additional paid-in capital
VI. Retained earnings

Required:
For items 1 through 5, determine whether the transaction increased, decreased, or had no effect on each of the balances in the above accounts.

1. Hamnoff issued bonds payable with a nominal rate of interest that was less than the market rate of interest.
2. Hamnoff issued convertible bonds, which are common stock equivalents, for an amount in excess of the bonds' face amount.
3. Hamnoff issued common stock when the convertible bonds described in item 2 were submitted for conversion. Each $1,000 bond was converted into 20 common shares. The book value method was used for the early conversion.
4. Hamnoff issued bonds, with detachable stock warrants, for an amount equal to the face amount of the bonds. The stock warrants have a determinable value.
5. Hamnoff declared and issued a 2% stock dividend.

Your answer sheet should be organized as follows:

	Bond/ Discount	Bond/ Premium	Bonds/ Payable	Common Stock	Additional Paid-in Capital	Retained Earnings

NUMBER 2

Lino Corporation's liability account balances at December 31, 1993, included the following:

Note payable to bank	$800,000
Liability under capital lease	280,000
Deferred income taxes	100,000

Additional information:

- The note payable, dated October 1, 1993, bears interest at an annual rate of 10% payable semiannually on April 1 and October 1. Principal payments are due annually on October 1 in four equal installments.
- The capital lease is for a 10-year period beginning December 31, 1988. Equal annual payments of $100,000 are due on December 31 of each year. The 16% interest rate implicit in the lease is known by Lino. At December 31, 1993, the present value of the four remaining lease payments discounted at 16% was $280,000.
- Deferred income taxes are provided in recognition of timing differences between financial statement and income tax reporting of depreciation. For the year ended December 31, 1994, depreciation per tax return exceeded book depreciation by $50,000. Lino's income tax rate for 1994 was 30%.
- On July 1, 1994, Lino issued $1,000,000 face amount of 10-year, 10% bonds for $750,000, to yield 15%. Interest is payable annually on July 1. Bond discount is amortized by the interest method.
- All required principal and interest payments were made on schedule in 1994.

Required:

a. Prepare the long-term liabilities section of Lino's balance sheet at December 31, 1994.

b. Prepare a schedule showing interest expense that should appear in Lino's income statement for the year ended December 31, 1994.

NUMBER 3

Part a.

On January 1, 1992, MyKoo Corporation issued $1,000,000 in five-year, 5% serial bonds to be repaid in the amount of $200,000 on January 1, of 1993, 1994, 1995, 1996, and 1997. Interest is payable at the end of each year. The bonds were sold to yield a rate of 6%. Information on present value and future amount factors is as follows:

Present value of an ordinary annuity of $1 for 5 years		*Future amount of an ordinary annuity of $1 for 5 years*	
5%	6%	5%	6%
4.3295	4.2124	5.5256	5.6371

Number of years	*Present Value of $1*		*Future amount of $1*	
	5%	6%	5%	6%
1	.9524	.9434	1.0500	1.0600
2	.9070	.8900	1.1025	1.1236
3	.8638	.8396	1.1576	1.1910
4	.8227	.7921	1.2155	1.2625
5	.7835	.7473	1.2763	1.3382

Required:

1. Prepare a schedule showing the computation of the total amount received from the issuance of the serial bonds. Show supporting computations in good form.
2. Assume the bonds were originally sold at a discount of $26,247. Prepare a schedule of amortization of the bond discount for the first two years after issuance, using the interest (effective rate) method. Show supporting computations in good form.

Part b.

On January 1, 1998, when its $30 par value common stock was selling for $80 per share, a corporation issued $10,000,000 of 4% convertible debentures due in ten years. The conversion option allowed the holder of each $1,000 bond to convert the bond into five shares of the corporation's $30 par value common stock. The debentures were issued for $11,000,000. The present value of the bond payments at the time of issuance was $8,500,000 and the corporation believes the difference between the present value and the amount paid is attributable to the conversion feature.

On January 1, 1999, the corporation's $30 par value common stock was split 3 for 1. On January 1, 2000, when the corporation's $10 par value common stock was selling for $90 per share, holders of 40% of the convertible debentures exercised their conversion options. The corporation uses the straight-line method for amortizing any bond discounts or premiums.

Required:

1. Prepare in general journal format the entry to record the original issuance of the convertible debentures.
2. Prepare in general journal format the entry to record the exercise of the conversion option, using the book value method. Show supporting computations in good form.

Part c.

On July 1, 1998, Salem Corporation issued $2,000,000 of 7% bonds payable in ten years. The bonds pay interest semiannually. The bonds include detachable warrants giving the bondholder the right to purchase for $30, one share of $1 par value common stock at any time during the next ten years. The bonds were sold for $2,000,000. The value of the warrants at the time of issuance was $100,000.

Required:

Prepare in general journal format the entry to record the issuance of the bonds.

NUMBER 4

On June 30, 1995, Corval Co. issued 15-year 12% bonds at a premium (effective yield 10%). On November 30, 1998, Corval transferred both cash and property to the bondholders to extinguish the entire debt. The fair value of the transferred property equaled its carrying amount. The fair value of the cash and property transferred exceeded the bonds carrying amount. [Ignore income taxes.]

Required:

a. Explain the purpose of the effective interest method and the effect of applying the method in 1995 on Corval's bond premium.

b. What would have been the effect on 1995 interest expense, net income, and the carrying amount of the bonds if Corval had incorrectly adopted the straight-line method instead of the effective interest method?

c. How should Corval calculate and report the effects of the November 30, 1998, transaction in its 1998 income statement? Why is this presentation appropriate?

d. How should Corval report the effects of the November 30, 1998, transaction in its statement of cash flows using the indirect method?

NUMBER 5

Part a.

On January 1, 1999, the Hopewell Company sold its 8% bonds that had a face value of $1,000,000. Interest is payable at December 31, each year. The bonds mature on January 1, 2007. The bonds were sold to yield a rate of 10%. The present value of an ordinary annuity of $1 for 10 periods at 10% is 6.1446. The present value of $1 for 10 periods at 10% is 0.3855.

Required:

Prepare a schedule to compute the total amount received from the sale of the bonds. Show supporting computations in good form.

Part b.

On September 1, 1999, the Junction Company sold at 104, (plus accrued interest) four thousand of its 9%, ten-year, $1,000 face value, nonconvertible bonds with detachable stock warrants. Each bond carried two detachable warrants; each warrant was for one share of common stock, at a specified option price of $15 per share. Shortly after issuance, the warrants were quoted on the market for $3 each. No market value can be determined for the bonds above. Interest is payable on December 1, and June 1. Bond issue costs of $40,000 were incurred.

Required:

Prepare in general journal format the entry to record the issuance of the bonds. Show supporting computations in good form.

Part c.

On December 1, 1996, The Cone Company issued its 7%, $2,000,000 face value bonds for $2,200,000, plus accrued interest. Interest is payable on November 1 and May 1. On December 31, 1998, the book value of the bonds, inclusive of the unamortized premium, was $2,100,000. On July 1, 1999, Cone reacquired the bonds at 98, plus accrued interest. Cone appropriately uses the straight-line method for the amortization of bond premium because the results do not materially differ from using the interest method.

Required:

Prepare a schedule to compute the gain or loss on this early extinguishment of debt. Show supporting computations in good form.

NUMBER 6

On June 1, 1998, Warner, Inc., purchased as a long-term investment 800 of the $1,000 face value, 8% bonds of Universal Corporation for $738,300. The bonds were purchased to yield 10% interest. Interest is payable semiannually on December 1 and June 1. The bonds mature on June 1, 2003. Warner uses the effective interest method of amortization. On November 1, 1999, Warner sold the bonds for $785,000. This amount includes the appropriate accrued interest.

Required:

Prepare a schedule showing the income or loss before income taxes from the bond investment that Warner should record for the years ended December 31, 1998, and 1999. Show supporting computations in good form.

NUMBER 7

On January 2, 1994, Drew Company issued 9% term bonds dated January 2, 1994, at an effective annual interest rate (yield) of 10%. Drew uses the effective interest method of amortization. On July 1, 1996, the bonds were extinguished early when Drew acquired them in the open market for a price greater than their face amount.

On September 1, 1996, Drew issued for cash 7% nonconvertible bonds dated September 1, 1996, with detachable stock purchase warrants. Immediately after issuance, both the bonds and the warrants had separately determined market values.

Required:

a. 1. Were the 9% term bonds issued at face amount, at a discount, or at a premium? Why?
   2. Would the amount of interest expense for the 9% term bonds using the effective interest method of amortization be higher in the first or second year of the life of the bond issue? Why?

b. 1. How should gain or loss on early extinguishment of debt be determined? Does the early extinguishment of the 9% term bonds result in a gain or loss? Why?
   2. How should Drew report the early extinguishment of the 9% term bonds on the 1996 income statement?

c. How should Drew account for the issuance of the 7% nonconvertible bonds with detachable stock purchase warrants?

NUMBER 8

M98

The following information relates to the obligations of Villa Watch Co. as of December 31, 1997:

- Accounts payable for goods and services purchased on open account amount to $35,000 at December 31, 1997.
- On December 15, 1997, Villa declared a cash dividend of $.05 per common share, payable on January 12, 1998 to shareholders of record as of December 31, 1997. Villa had 1 million shares of common stock issued and outstanding throughout 1997.
- On December 30, 1997, Villa entered a 6-year capital lease on a warehouse and made the first annual lease payment of $100,000. Villa's incremental borrowing rate was 12%, and the interest rate implicit in the lease, which was known to Villa, was 10%. The rounded present value factors for an annuity due for 6 years are 4.6 at 12% and 4.8 at 10%.
- On July 1, 1997, Villa issued $500,000, 8% bonds for $440,000 to yield 10%. The bonds mature on June 30, 2003 and pay interest annually every June 30. At December 31, 1997, the bonds were trading on the open market at 86 to yield 12%. Villa uses the effective-interest method.
- Villa's 1997 pretax financial income was $850,000 and its taxable income was $600,000. The difference is due to $100,000 of permanent differences and $150,000 of temporary differences related to noncurrent assets. At December 31, 1997, Villa had cumulative taxable differences of $300,000 related to noncurrent assets. Villa's effective tax rate is 30%. Villa made no estimated tax payments during the year.

- Contingency information:

    - -- Villa has been named a liable party for toxic waste cleanup on its land and must pay an as-yet undetermined amount for environmental remediation activities.

    - -- An adjoining landowner, Clear Toothpaste Co., sold its property because of possible toxic contamination of the water supply and resulting potential adverse public reaction toward its product. Clear sued Villa for damages. There is a reasonable possibility that Clear will prevail and be awarded between $250,000 and $600,000.

    - -- As a result of comprehensive risk assessment, Villa has discontinued rockslide insurance for its warehouse, which is located at the base of a mountain. The warehouse has never sustained rockslide damage, and the probability of sustaining future damage is only slight.

Required:

a. Prepare the liabilities section of Villa's December 31, 1997 balance sheet.

b. Discuss the information Villa is required to disclose, either in the body of the financial statements or the notes thereto, related to bonds payable and capital leases included in the liabilities presented above.

c. Explain how Villa should account for each contingency in its 1997 financial statements. Discuss the theoretical justification for each accounting treatment.

NUMBER 9

Cope Company is a manufacturer of household appliances. During the year, the following information became available:

- Probable warranty costs on its household appliances are estimated to be 1% of sales.
- One of its manufacturing plants is located in a foreign country. There is a threat of expropriation of this plant. The threat of expropriation is deemed to be reasonably possible. Any compensation from the foreign government would be less than the carrying amount of the plant.
- It is probable that damages will be received by Cope next year as a result of a lawsuit filed this year against another household appliances manufacturer.

Required:

In answering the following, do not discuss deferred income tax implications.

a. How should Cope report the probable warranty costs? Why?

b. How should Cope report the threat of expropriation of assets? Why?

c. How should Cope report this year the probable damages that may be received next year? Why?

NUMBER 10

Coyn, CPA, has been approached by Howe, the chief financial officer of Chatham Co. Howe is aware that the Financial Accounting Standards Board is engaged in an ongoing project to improve disclosure of information about financial instruments and has recently issued two related Statements of Financial Accounting Standards: SFAS 107, *Disclosures about Fair Value of Financial Instruments;* and *Financial Instruments with Concentration of Credit Risk; SFAS 133 Derivative Financial Instruments.* In accordance with these pronouncements, Howe has prepared the following footnote for Chatham's financial statements:

Note 12: Financial Instruments
The Company uses various financial instruments, including **derivative financial instruments**, to manage its interest rate and foreign currency exchange rate risks. Other financial instruments that potentially subject the Company to **concentrations of credit risk** consist principally of trade receivables.

Howe will be meeting with Chatham's board of directors to review the financial statements, and has asked Coyn to prepare a handout for the board explaining the terms used in the footnote.

Required: Prepare the requested handout. Including the following:

a. What is a **financial instrument**? Define and give an example of **derivative financial instruments**.

b. Define both **market risk and credit risk**. What is meant by the term **concentration of credit risk**?

c. Define **fair value**. Discuss the methods Chatham's management might use to estimate the fair values of its various financial instruments.

NUMBER 11

N98

Number 11 consists of 11 items. Select the **best** answer for each item.

On July 1, 1997, Ring Co. issued $250,000, 14% bonds payable at a premium. The bonds are due in ten years. Interest is payable semiannually every June 30 and December 31. On December 31, 1997, and June 30, 1998, Ring made the semi-annual interest payments due and recorded interest expense and amortization of bond premium.

With the proceeds of the bond issuance, Ring retired other debt. Ring recorded a gain on the early extinguishment of the other debt.

Required:

Items 1 through 7, contained in the partially-completed amortization table below, represent formulas used to calculate information needed to complete the table. Select your answers from the following list of formulas. Each formula may be selected once, more than once, or not at all. "Stated interest rate" and "effective interest rate" are stated on an annual basis.

	Cash paid	*Interest expense*	*Amortization*	*Carrying amount*	*Unamortized premium*
7/1/97				(1)	
12/31/97	(2)	$14,100	(3)	$349,100	(4)
6/30/98	$17,500	(5)	$3,536	(6)	

Effective Annual Interest Rate: (7)

A	Face amount x stated interest rate.	**J**	(Face amount x stated interest rate) x ½.
B	Face amount x effective interest rate.	**K**	(Face amount x effective interest rate) x ½.
C	Carrying amount x stated interest rate.	**L**	(Carrying amount at the beginning of the period x stated interest rate) x ½.
D	Carrying amount x effective interest rate.	**M**	(Carrying amount at the beginning of the period x effective interest rate) x ½.
E	Present value of face amount + present value of all future interest payments at date of issuance.	**N**	Carrying amount – face amount.
F	Carrying amount of bonds in the previous period – amortization for the current period.	**O**	(Interest expense/carrying amount at the beginning of the period) x 2.
G	Carrying amount of bonds in the previous period + amortization for the current period.	**P**	(Cash paid/carrying amount) x 2.
H	Cash paid – interest expense.	**Q**	Face amount – unamortized premium.
I	Cash paid + interest expense.		

Items 8 through 11 describe amounts that will be reported in Ring's 1997 statement of cash flows prepared using the indirect method or disclosed in the related notes. For each item, select from the following list where the amount should be reported or disclosed. An answer may be selected once, more than once, or not at all.

Statement of Cash Flows Items:

O	Operating activities.
I	Investing activities.
F	Financing activities.
S	Supplemental schedule.

8. Proceeds received from sale of bonds.
9. Interest paid.
10. Amortization of bond premium.
11. Gain on early extinguishment of debt.

Chapter Nine
Solutions to Bonds, Accounting for Debt Questions

1. (c) At issuance, a bond is valued at the present value of the principal and interest payments, discounted at the prevailing market rate of interest at the date of issuance of the bond. Per APB #21, "Interest on Receivables and Payables."

2. (c)

Present value of interest payments per bond: 6.418 × $60	$385
Present value of principal per bond: .422 × $1,000	422
Proceeds per bond	$807

3. (d) The issue price of any bond is equivalent to the present value (at the yield rate) of all cash payments (principal and interest) at the issue date.

4. (d) The requirement is to calculate the cash proceeds from the sale of bonds **between interest dates:**

CASH PROCEEDS FROM:

A. **BONDS** $600,000 X 99% =	$594,000
B. **ACCRUED INTEREST** $600,000 x 10% x 3/12 =	15,000
Total Cash Proceeds	$609,000

5. (a)

Proceeds of the bond issue—$300,000 × .99 =	$297,000
Accrued interest—$300,000 × 10% × 3/12 =	7,500
Total cash received	$304,500

6. (d) All of the costs are directly related to the issuance of the bonds and should be recorded as bond issue costs. Other costs that may be considered bond issue costs are legal, accounting and other professional fees and registration costs.

7. (b)

Issue costs	$3,300
No. of months bonds were outstanding in 1998 =	4
No. of months bonds will be outstanding if held to maturity =	55
1998 amortization = 4/55 × $3,300 =	$240

8. (b) Journal entry to record the first six months interest:

Interest Expense (10% x 469,500 x 6/12)	23,475	
Interest Payable (9% x 500,000 x 6/12)		22,500
Bond Discount		975

The amount that West should report as bonds payable on its June 30, 2001 is $470,475. (January 2 balance $469,500 + $975 Bond Amortization)

9. (b)

Carrying value 5/1/99 ($1,000,000 + $62,000)	$1,062,000
Yield rate for six months (10% × 6/12)	× 5%
Interest expense at 10/31/99	$ 53,100
Interest Paid ($1,000,000 × 11% × 6/12)	55,000
Premium amortization	$ (1,900)
Original premium	62,000
Unamortized Premium at 10/31/99	$ 60,100

10. (c) The journal entry to record the interest and amortization of the bond premium for the year is:

Bond Premium		700	
Interest Expense	(a)	6,300	
Cash	(b)		7,000

a. Effective rate × CV at beginning of year = interest expense
6% × $105,000 = $6,300

b. Face interest × face value of bonds = cash interest
7% × $100,000 = $7,000

The balance in the bond premium account at June 30, 2000 would be the beginning balance less the amortization in the above journal entry ($5,000 – 700 = $4,300).

11. (c) Carrying value 7/1/97	$103,288
Yield rate (10% × ½)	× 5%
Interest expense	$ 5,164

12. (d) Interest expense begins on June 1, 2000 when the bond is issued and continues for the **seven** months ending December 31, 2000.

13. (b) Interest payable is accrued at the stated interest of 8% for the three months since the last payment date of October 1.
$800,000 × .08 × 3/12 = $16,000

14. (c) When bonds are issued at a discount, using the straight-line method of amortization will cause interest expense to be greater in the first year than using the effective interest method (see chart in the chapter). Therefore, amortization under the straight-line method is greater causing the carrying value to be overstated. Since the expense was greater, retained earnings is understated.

15. (b) Carrying value of bonds at 6/30/99 is $4,980,000 ($5,000,000 + $30,000 – $50,000).

Carrying value of the bonds	$4,980,000
Repurchase price (98% × $5,000,000)	4,900,000
Gain before taxes on redemption of bonds	$80,000

16. (a) The journal entry to record the retirement of the bonds:

JE	Bonds Payable	600,000	
	Premium to Bonds	65,000	
	Cash*		612,000
	Extraordinary Gain on Retirement of Bonds		53,000

* Cash Paid = $600,000 x 102% = $612,000

17. (d) Each transaction must be reported separately since the gain on early extinguishment of the company's debt is reported as an extraordinary item and the loss on the sale of the investment is an ordinary loss.

18. (c) The journal entry to record the conversion would be as follows:

		Debit	Credit
6/30/96	Bonds payable	$2,000,000	
	Premium on bonds payable	50,000	
	Common stock (80,000 shares × $20)		$1,600,000
	APIC (residual)		450,000

19. (a) The journal entry to record the conversion would be as follows:

		Debit	Credit
7/1/97	Bonds payable	$600,000	
	Premium	12,000	
	Common stock (par)		*$300,000
	APIC		** 312,000

*10 × $600 × $50 = $300,000 (par value of shares issued)
**$612,000 – $300,000 = $312,000 (book value of bonds converted less par value of shares issued)

20. (d) Using the book value method, no gain or loss is recognized. The journal entry for the conversion would be:

4/30/95

	Debit	Credit
Bonds payable	$1,000,000	
Discount on bonds payable		$ 30,000
Common stock (par)		800,000
APIC		170,000

21. (b) The book value method only transfers the carrying value of the bonds to equity and no differential exists. The market value method normally records the stock issued at its fair value at the date of conversion causing a difference between the book value of the bonds converted and the value of the stock issued. This difference is recognized as gain or loss.

22. (c) Since the stock warrants are detachable, the FMV provides an objective basis for the allocation of a portion of the cash proceeds to the stock warrants. The allocation is calculated as follows:

	FMV	Ratio to Total FMV	×	Cash Proceeds	=	Allocation
Bonds	1,080,000	1080k / 1200k = 90	×	1,000,000	=	$ 900,000
Warrants	120,000	120k / 1200k = 10%	×	1,000,000	=	100,000
Total	1,200,000					$1,000,000

23. (b)

Market value of the bonds	$196,000
Market value of the warrants ($2 × 100 × $200)	40,000
Total market price	$236,000

Ratio attributable to the bonds 196/236 = .83

Amount allocated to bonds:

.83 × 240,000 =	$199,322
Face value	200,000
Discount on bonds	$ 678

24. (d) Since no market value is given for the bonds, the amount attributable to the warrants (stockholders' equity) is $4 each × 30 warrants per bond = $120 × 500 bonds = $60,000.

25. (a) 500 warrants × 90% = 450 exercised for 1 share each.

Option Price	$ 75
Less: par value	40
Premium paid in per share	$ 35
Times number of shares issued	× 450
Total premium paid at exercise	$ 15,750
Add: warrants exercised (4,000 × 90%)	3,600
Total premium on shares issued	$ 19,350

26. (d) Term bonds are bonds that are due on a specific date. The 9¾% registered debentures and the 9½% collateral trust bonds are term bonds ($700,000 + $600,000 = $1,300,000). The 10% subordinated debentures are serial bonds.

27. (a) Serial bonds are those which retire over the life of the bond issue ($275,000 + $200,000). Debenture bonds are unsecured bonds ($275,000 + $125,000).

28. (d) SFAS #47 requires that the aggregate maturities and sinking fund requirements be disclosed for each of five years after the balance sheet.

29. (d) Both of the liabilities would be reported as long-term since, at the time the statements were issued, the company clearly had the intent and the ability to convert the obligations to long-term commitments. The fact that the $500,000 refinancing had not yet been implemented at the date the statements were issued does not preclude the classification as long-term.

30. (c) FASB #6 states that the amount excluded from current liabilities through refinancing cannot exceed the amount actually refinanced. Therefore, Largo should consider the $500,000 paid by the refinancing to be a long-term liability and the $250,000 a current liability on the December 31, 1999 balance sheet. The refinancing was completed before the issuance of the financial statements and meets both criteria (intent & financial ability) for the classification of the $500,000 as a long-term liability.

31. (c) Normally this note would be classified as a current liability. However, FASB # 6 states that if Cali Inc. **intends** to refinance the note and has the **ability** to refinance the obligation within one year, the note should be classified as noncurrent. The ability to refinance must be demonstrated by either accomplishing the refinancing or entering into an agreement to do so before the financial statements are issued. In this case, Cali Inc. refinanced the note (accomplished the refinancing) on January 28, 2002 before the financial statements were issued. Therefore, both the intent and ability criteria were met and the note should be classified on the December 31, 2001 balance sheet as noncurrent with a separate disclosure of the criteria used in making the classification decision.

32. (a) Current liabilities are obligations that are expected to be paid within one year of the operating cycle whichever is longer.

Accounts payable	$15,000
Bonds less discount	22,000
Dividends payable	8,000
Total liabilities 12/31/99	$45,000

The notes payable are not classified as current liabilities because they are not due until 2001.

33. (d) Since the sinking is restricted for the payment of bonds, it is not available for the payment of current liabilities and cannot be considered a current asset. Therefore, it is classified as a non-current asset.

34. (c)

Carrying value 7/1/93	$369,200
Yield rate—10% × 1/2 =	× 5%
Interest revenue for 1993	18,460
Interest receivable at 12/31/93	16,000
Amortization	2,460
Carrying value at beginning of the period	369,200
Carrying value 12/31/93	$371,660

35. (b) Assume for simplicity that the face amount of the bonds is $100,000. The journal entry to record the sale would be:

Cash	114,000	
Investment-Carrying value (a)		92,000
Gain on sale of bonds		22,000

a. CV of Bonds = Cost + Discount Amortization
$92,000 = $90,000 + $2,000

36. (b) Example—A $100,000 bond purchased at a cost of $95,000 plus the additional cash paid for accrued interest of $5,000 = cash paid of $100,000. Therefore, the $95,000 carrying value is less than the cash paid to the seller (a \ b) and less than the face value (b \ c)

37. (d) The carrying value is highest if the bonds were purchased above face value (at a premium). When the interest method of amortization is used, the lowest amount of amortization is recorded in the first year, such amount being less than using the straight-line method (see amortization table in the chapter). Therefore, the carrying value of the investment would be higher using the interest method.

38. (a) The key words are "reasonably possible". FASB #5 states that if a loss contingency is reasonably possible, it should be **disclosed but not accrued.** A loss contingency is accrued only if the loss contingency is probable and the amount of the loss can be reasonably estimated.

39. (b) Since no amount was accrued, the loss was not probable, but since a range of potential loss was disclosed, the loss is reasonably possible.

40. (a) The minimum amount within the range must be accrued since an unfavorable outcome is probable.

41. (d) When a contingent loss is probable but counsel can only estimate a range of losses, Steel Co. should accrue the lower end of the range ($500,000) and disclose the possibility of an additional loss up to $500,000. See FASB Interpretation #14.

42. (c) Current liabilities are obligations that are expected to be paid within one year or the operating cycle whichever is longer. The current liabilities on the December 31, 2000, balance sheet are calculated as:

Accounts payable	$ 55,000
Unsecured notes - due 7/1/01	400,000
Accrued expenses	35,000
Serial Bonds - due 3/31/01	1,000,000
Liabilities 12/31/01	$1,490,000

The contingent liability is not a liability at this point because Brite Corp. considers the loss to be **possible** but not probable. Since the deferred tax liability is not related to an asset for financial reporting, the reversal date is used to classify the liability as either current or noncurrent. In this case the reversal date is 2002 and the deferred tax liability is classified as noncurrent.

43. (a) Loss contingencies are classified as probable, reasonable possible and remote. Remote contingencies are generally not disclosed. FASB #5 makes an exception for guarantees of indebtedness. Guarantees of indebtedness must be disclosed even though the probability of loss is remote. Remote contingencies are never accrued.

44. (a) As a general rule, gain contingencies are not recognized until realized. In the first case the defendant is only appealing $30,000 of the $45,000 award so $15,000 should be recognized as a pretax gain on the 1999 financial statements. In the second case the total award is being appealed so none of the $50,000 should be recognized as a pretax gain.

45. (c)

Escrow liability	1/1/99	$ 700,000
Add payments received in 1999		1,580,000
Int. on escrow funds - 1999 (a)		45,000
Less payment made in 1999		(1,720,000)
Escrow liability 12/31/99		$ 605,000

(a) Interest of $50,000 is reduced by 10% service fee ($50,000 – 5,000 = $45,000).

46. (a) FASB #107 requires disclosure of information about significant concentrations of risk **for all financial instruments.** Concentrations of credit exists when a company has a business activity, economic characteristic, or location that it common to most of its financial instruments.

47. (c) FASB #47 states that the aggregate amount of payments for unconditional purchase obligations that have been recognized on the purchaser's balance sheet shall be disclosed for each of the *five* years following the date of the latest balance sheet.

48. (d) The payroll tax liability consists of the federal tax withheld, $1,200, the FICA tax withheld, $700, and the employer's share of the FICA, $700, for a total of $2,600. The payroll tax expense would be the employer's share of the FICA, which is $700.

49. (a) The December 31, 2000 accrued liability for unemployment claims should be the number of employees times $10,000 times 2% rate (5 × $10,000 × 2%) = $1,000.

50. (d) A sole proprietorship is not a taxable entity and is not required to record a provision for income taxes. Income from a sole proprietorship will be taxed on the owner's individual tax return.

51. (d)

1997 and 1998 sales =	$400,000
Warranty % =	6%
1997 and 1998 allowance	$ 24,000
Actual expenditure	– 9,750
12/31/98 remaining liability	$ 14,250

52. (d) Under the accrual accounting, the warranty costs should be recognized in the same accounting period (matching) as the revenue is recognized. In this case, a proper matching of revenue vs. expense would be to recognize the warranty costs when the **machines are sold.** Answers (a), (b), and (c) all recognize revenue in the current period and the warranty costs in a later period which would not be matching.

53. (b) All redemptions of the first series of coupons are final since the latest date of submission would be 7/30/94. From the second series of coupons the liability at 12/31/94 would be as follows:

Value	$120,000
Probability of redemption	40%
Total expected cost of promotion	$ 48,000
Paid during 1994	40,000
Balance due	$ 8,000

54. (a)

PROJECTED COUPONS RETURNED:	
Packages of candy sold	110,000
Times Expected Redemption Rate	x 60%
Equals Projected Coupons Returned	66,000
Divided by Coupons Required for each toy	5 coupons
EQUALS EXPECTED TOYS TO BE MAILED	= 13,200 Toys
Times cost per toy ($.80 - .50)	x .30
LIABILITY ON BALANCE SHEET AT December 31, 2001	$ 3,960

55. (b) As gift certificates are sold, the deferred revenue account increases. As the gift certificates are redeemed or lapse, revenue is recognized and the liability account is reduced.

56. (d) Two key points: The 1997 certificates that were not redeemed by December 31, 1998 have expired and Regal's total liability for 1998 sales is for the 90% of the certificates that are expected to be returned. The approach is to set up a T-account for the unearned revenue.

UNEARNED REVENUE

Debit		Credit	
		12/31/97 balance	$ 75,000
1997 redeemed	$ 25,000		
1997 expired	50,000		
		1998 sales	
1998 redeemed	$ 175,000	(250,000 × 90%)	225,000
		12/31/98 balance	$ 50,000

57. (d)

Issue price of the bonds ($200,000 × 1.01)	$202,000
Accrued interest ($200,000 × .09 × 5/12)	+ 7,500
Total proceeds from bond issue	$209,500

58. (d) FASB #5 states that gain contingencies should not be recognized until realized. Gain contingencies should be disclosed but the disclosure should be made in a careful and responsible manner in order to avoid misleading implications as to the likelihood of realization.

59. (a) The expense on the bond issue is based upon the number of months that the bonds have been outstanding during the year; in this case, since June 1, 1998. The dates on which interest is paid is not significant in this question.

60. (c) Since the debt was refinanced to the extent of $1,500,000 prior to the issuance of the financial statements, the liability is classified as long-term to the extent of the refinancing.

61. (d)

Bond Issue Cost 1/2/99		$250,000
Less amortization		
1999	$250,000 / 10 years	(25,000)
2000	$250,000 / 10 years × 6/12	(12,500)
Balance	6/30/00	$212,500

62. (c) The liability balance at 12/31/97 should include those subscriptions for periods after that date.

1998 expirations ($125,000 + $200,000)	$325,000
1999 expirations	140,000
Total	$465,000

63. (a) FASB #5 states that a contingent loss should be accrued if the loss is **probable** and the amount of the loss is reasonably estimable. In this case, the loss is probable and a reasonable estimate of the loss is $200,000. This is the amount of the accrued liability that should appear on the December 31, 2001 balance sheet. In addition, Haft Co. should **disclose** the possibility of an additional loss of $100,000 which would bring the total potential loss to $300,000.

64. (d) Convertible bonds are debt securities reported entirely as a liability.

65. (c) The book value method records the stock issued at the book value of the converted bonds. There is no gain or loss recognized. The market value method results in recognized gain or loss usually based upon the difference between the fair market value of the stock issued compared to the carrying value of the converted bonds. The face value of the bonds was equal to the par value of the stock when the bonds were issued. At the time of conversion, the common stock had increased in value. Therefore, using the market value method to record the conversion results in a loss (credits to equity accounts are greater than debits to the bond liability account).

66. (a)

Accounts payable balance before adjustments		$360,000
Add:	Debit balance in A/P to Ross is an asset to Lyle and should be taken out of A/P	50,000
Add:	Checks written by Lyle and recorded as a reduction in A/P on December 29, 1999, should be added back to the A/P because the checks were not mailed until January 5, 2000.	$100,000
Adjusted A/P balance - December 31, 1999		$510,000

67. (a)

Interest revenue is $906,000 × 10% × 6/12 =	$ 45,300
Interest receivable is $1,000,000 × 8% × 6/12 =	40,000
Amortization of bond discount	5,300
Cost of investment in bonds 7/1/99	$906,000
Investment in bonds 12/31/99	$911,300

68. (a) Amortization schedule:

Date	(10%) Interest Revenue	Cash Receipt	Amortization	Carrying Value
1/1/95				$456,200
12/31/95	$45,600*	$40,000	$5,600	461,800
12/31/96	46,200*	40,000	6,200	468,000

*Rounded per instructions

69. (b) SFAS #6 indicates that "if amounts that could be obtained under the financing agreement fluctuate (...in proportion to the value of collateral), the amount to be excluded from current liabilities shall be limited to ... the minimum amount expected to be available ...". Therefore, in this case, only 80% of $1,200,000, or $960,000, could be classified as long-term.

70. (a) Under the book value approach, the book value of the bonds in transferred to stockholders' equity. This amount is allocated between the common stock account at par and the additional paid-in capital account.

71. (a) When the warrants are exercised, the carrying value of the warrants and the cash received are debited and the par value and APIC is credited for the same total amount. The carrying value of the warrants is a transfer from one equity account to another. Therefore, total equity is increased only by the cash received.

72. (d)

Bond premium at issue	$ 40,000	
Amortization of premium 1/1/91 through 7/1/96:		
$40,000 ÷ 20 = $2,000 per period		
$2,000 × 11 periods	22,000	
Unamortized premium 7/1/96	$ 18,000	
Face value	+1,000,000	
Carrying value 7/1/96	$1,018,000	
Call (redemption) price	1,010,000	$1,000,000 × 1.01
Gain on extinguishment	$ 8,000	

73. (a) FASB #5, following the concept of conservatism, states that gain contingencies should not be recognized in the financial statements until realized. Adequate disclosure should be made in the footnotes but care should be taken to avoid misleading implications as to the likelihood of realization of the contingent gain.

74. (d)

Interest expense for 12/31/00 = 10% × $190,280 =	$ 19,028
Cash payment for interest	16,000
Amortization of discount	$ 3,028
Payment for bond dated 12/31/00	40,000
Net decrease in carrying value	$ 36,972
Original carrying value at issuance	190,280
Carrying value at 12/31/00	$153,308

75. (d) Price per share ex-warrants

Price per share ex-warrants	$72
Price per warrant	8
Total	$80

Carrying value assigned to warrants: 8/80 × $152,000 = $15,200

Selling price	$20,500
Carrying value	15,200
Gain	$ 5,300

76. (b) In the early years of the bond's life, the straight-line method of bond amortization will result in a **higher** interest expense and **higher** discount amortization than the effective interest method. Thus, the bond amortization will be overstated in 2001 which will cause an **overstatement** of the bonds at December 31, 2001. However, both the straight-line method and the effective interest method will amortize the bond discount to zero by January 2, 2007 and the carrying amount of the bonds will be $1,000,000 for both amortization methods. Therefore, the effect of the error in amortization methods **will not have any effect** on the carrying value of the bonds at January 2, 2007.

77. (b) The bonds were sold at 97 and their carrying value would be $388,000 ($400,000 × 97% = $388,000). The journal entry is:

Cash	396,000	
Bond Discount	12,000	
Bonds Payable		400,000
Accrued Interest Payable		8,000

78. (c)

Liability for Stamp Redemptions (000's)

	Debit	Credit	
		$6,000	Balance 12/31/95
1996 redemptions of pre-'96 stamps	$2,750		
		1,800	Additional liability for 1996 sales, $2,250 × .8
		$5,050	Balance 12/31/96

79. (d) The interest payable at September 30, 1999 will be for the three month's interest that has accrued since the last interest was paid on June 30, 1999 ($300,000 × 12% × 3/12 = $9000).

80. (b) The fair market value of the bonds is given at $40,000 but the FMV of Cove's stock cannot be determined because it is a closely-held corporation. The bond is recorded at FMV and the remainder of the proceeds ($70,000) is assumed to be the FMV of the stock. Since there are 1,000 shares of common stock at a par value of $5 each, a total of $5,000 would be allocated to the common stock account and the remaining $65,000 would be credited to additional paid-in capital.

81. (b) KEY POINT: At January 3, 2001, Hudson Hotel has a liability for sales taxes for both November and December. Therefore, the sales tax payable would be 15% × ($110,000 + 150,000) = $39,000. The liability for occupancy taxes at December 31, 2000 would be the room nights for October, November, and December times the $2 per night occupancy tax.

(1,110 + 1,200 + 1,800) × $2 per night = $8,200

82. (c) Since the appropriation will result in a gain, the transaction is disclosed in the notes to the financial statements and recognized only when realized.

83. (b) The key point is that Ivy Co. includes its sales taxes in the **sales revenue account:**

Sales including sales tax	$26,500
Divided by	106%
Equals Taxable Sales	$25,000
Times the sales tax rate	x 6%
Equals **Total** Sales Tax Payable	$ 1,500
Less Sales Taxes already paid	(600)
Sales Tax Payable at March 31, 2002	$ 900

84. (b) Original cost of Adams investment in stock to be allocated between the original stock investment and the rights is $5,000 (50 shares × $100 per share).

Allocation of Cost to rights

FMV of stock ex-rights	$132
FMV of rights	18
Total FMV	$150

$\frac{\text{Value of Rights}}{\text{Value of Rights and Stock}} \times \text{Total Cost} = \frac{18}{150} \times \$5{,}000 = \$600$ Cost Assigned to rights.

Cost of each new share purchased with rights	
Cash payment	$ 90
Add: cost of rights ($600 ÷ 50 = $12 × 2 rights)	24
	$114

85. (b) The note payable-contest winner should be reported on the December 31, 2000 balance sheet at the present value of future payments or $418,250.

86. (c) The amount reported on the 2000 income statement for contest prize expense should be the $468,250 which is the first installment plus the present value of the future payments ($50,000 + $418,250 = $468,250).

87. (d) Six months interest revenue at stated rate.

8% × 1/2 × $500,000 =	$20,000
Amortization recorded	1,800
Revenue for 1993	$21,800

Since no yield rate was given, the $1,800 amortization must be accepted. Note that the amortization is added to the stated revenue amount since the bonds **were acquired** at a discount.

88. (c) Since the minimum coverage for collateral during 1998 was $480,000 (80% × $600,000), only that amount can be reported as long-term. The other $20,000 must be reported as a current liability.

89. (c) An interest rate swap agreement involves the exchange of cash flows determined by various interest rates. Fluctuations in interest rates after the agreement is entered into may result in the risk of exchanging a lower interest rate for a higher interest rate. Financial instruments, including swaps, also bear credit risk or the risk that a counterparty to the agreement will not perform as expected.

91. (c) Interest Income = Effective Interest Rate x December 1 carrying value x 1 month
= 12.4% x $194,000 x 1/12
= $2004.66 or $2005.00 rounded

92. (d) A bond issued at a discount reflects that the market rate is greater than the contract rate.

93. (d) SFAS #133 requires that gains or losses on hedges of foreign currency exposure of an available-for-sale security must be recognized currently. Choices (a), (b) and (c) are examples of losses that would be included in comprehensive income.

94. (a) Examples of an underlying include a **specified interest rate,** security price, commodity price, foreign exchange rate, index of prices or rates on other variables. An underlying may be a price or rate of an asset or liability, but is not the asset or liability itself.

Choices (b) and (c) are examples of notional amounts and an embedded derivative is not related to the question.

95. (c) SFAS #133 requires that gain or losses from forecasted cash flow hedges be reported as other comprehensive income.

96. (c) The net effect on 1999 earnings of the gain from the derivative and the loss in the fair value of the asset is $20,000 ($220,000 - $200,000 = $20,000).

97. (d) Helgeson's purchase of a futures contract to hedge against future market fluctuations would include the three elements in the SFAS #133 – Definition of a Derivative.

The future's contract would have an underlying (price per pound of cocoa beans) and a notional amount (number of pounds of cocoa beans); no initial investment; and the net settlement amount of the futures contract.

98. (b) The $15,000 gain on the derivative in 1999 is recognized in comprehensive income until the transaction is completed. When the transaction is completed in 2000 (the corn is sold), the $15,000 gain is reclassified in 2000 from other comprehensive income to current earnings. This reclassification plus the $8,000 gain in January would total at $23,000 gain in 2000 ($15,000 + $8,000 = $23,000).

99. (a) Answer (a) is the SFAS #133 definition of a derivative.

100. (d) The issue price of a bond is always the present value of future cash flows (discounted amount) at the market rate of interest. The issue price of the bonds less the bond issue cost is the net proceeds. Answers (a) & (c) are incorrect because they use the stated rate of interest. Answer (b) is wrong because it does not deduct the bond issues cost.

101. (a)If it is practicable to estimate the values. SFAS 107 requires entities to disclose the fair value of its financial instruments regardless of whether they are recognized or not on the entity's financial statements.
If it is not practical to estimate these fair values, descriptive information about the financial instruments such as the terms of the instrument and why it is not possible to estimate the fair value should be provided.
It is important to note that the disclosure of fair values is provided as supplemental information and does not normally replace the historical cost basis used on the balance sheet. (An exception to this traditional reliance on historical cost is the valuing of certain investments in debt and equity securities at fair market value. See SFAS #115 in Chapter 2.)

102. (a) The amount needed to cover the net payroll and related payroll taxes should be the $20,000 gross wages plus the employer's share of the FICA taxes (7% x $20,000 = $1400) for a total of $21,400.

Chapter Nine
Solutions to Bonds, Accounting for Debt Problems

NUMBER 1

	Bond/ Discount	Bond/ Premium	Bonds/ Payable	Common Stock	Additional Paid-in Capital	Retained Earnings
1	Increased	No Effect	Increased	No Effect	No Effect	No Effect
2	No Effect	Increased	Increased	No Effect	No Effect	No Effect
3	No Effect	Decrease	Decrease	Increased	Increased	No Effect
4	Increased	No Effect	Increased	No Effect	Increased	No Effect
5	No Effect	No Effect	No Effect	Increased	Increased	Decrease

1. If bonds are issued with a nominal (face) rate of interest that is less than the market rate of interest, the bonds will be issued at a discount. The journal entry is:

Cash	xxx	
Bond discount	xxx	
Bonds payable		xxx

Therefore, both the bond discount and the bonds payable are **increased.**

2. If convertible bonds are issued at an amount in excess of the bonds' face value, the bonds are issued at a premium.

Cash	xxx	
Bond premium		xxx
Bonds payable		xxx

Therefore, both the bond premium and the bonds payable accounts are **increased.**

3. If convertible bonds are converted to common stock using the book value method, a gain or loss on conversion is not recognized.

Bonds payable	xxx	
Bond premium	xxx	
Common stock-par		xxx
PIC - Excess of par		xxx

Therefore, the bonds payable and bond premium are **decreased** and the common stock and PIC - excess of par are **increased.**

4. If bonds are issued at **FACE VALUE** with detachable stock warrants that have a determinable value, a portion of the cash proceeds will be allocated to the stock warrants and the bonds will be a sold at a discount.

Cash	xxx	
Bond discount	xxx	
Bonds payable		xxx
PIC - Stock warrants		xxx

Therefore, the bond discount, bonds payable and PIC - stock warrant accounts **increased.**

5. If a 2% stock dividend is declared and issued, the dividend is considered a **small** stock dividend and the amount of retained earnings capitalized is the FMV of the stock. In this case the FMV is in excess of par.

Retained earnings	xxx	
Common stock - par		xxx
PIC - excess of par		xxx

Therefore, retained earnings would **decrease** while common stock and paid-in-capital would **increase.**

NUMBER 2

N88

a.

Lino Corporation
LONG-TERM LIABILITIES SECTION OF BALANCE SHEET
December 31, 1994

10% note payable to bank, due in annual installments of $200,000, less current installment	$ 400,000	(1)
Liability under capital lease, net present value of lease payments, less current installment	160,768	(2)
10% bonds payable due July 1, 2004, less unamortized discount of $243,750	756,250	(3)
Deferred income taxes	115,000	(4)
Total long-term liabilities	$1,432,018	

b.

Lino Corporation
INTEREST EXPENSE
For the Year Ended December 31, 1994

Note payable to bank	$ 75,000	(5)
Liability under capital lease	44,800	(2)
Bonds payable	56,250	(3)
Total	$176,050	

Explanations of Amounts

(1) 10% Note Payable to bank

Note payable, 12/31/93	$800,000
Less installment paid 10/1/94	200,000
Balance, 12/31/94	600,000
Less current installment due 10/1/95	200,000
Long-term portion, 12/31/94	$400,000

(2) Liability under capital lease

Liability under capital lease, 12/31/93		$280,000
Less principal portion of 12/31/94 payment		
Lease payment	$100,000	
Less imputed interest ($280,000 × 16%)	44,800	55,200
		224,800
Balance, 12/31/94		
Less current principal payment due 12/31/95		
Lease payment	100,000	
Less imputed interest ($224,800 × 16%)	35,968	64,032
Long-term portion, 12/31/94		$160,768

(3)	Bonds payable		
	Bonds payable issued 7/1/94		$750,000
	Add amortization of bond discount		
	Effective interest ($750,000 × 15% × 6/12)	56,250	
	Less accrued interest payable 12/31/94		
	($1,000,000 × 10% × 6/12)	50,000	6,250
	Balance, 12/31/94		$756,250
(4)	Deferred income taxes		
	Deferred income taxes, 12/31/93		$100,000
	Add timing difference—excess of tax depreciation		
	over book depreciation of $50,000 × 30%		15,000
	Balance, 12/31/94		$115,000
(5)	Interest expense on note payable to bank		
	1/1/94 to 9/30/94 ($800,000 × 10% × 9/12)		$ 60,000
	10/1/94 to 12/31/94 ($600,000 × 10% × 3/12)		15,000
	Interest, year ended 12/31/94		$ 75,000

NUMBER 3

Part a.

1.

MyKoo Corporation

SCHEDULE OF TOTAL AMOUNT RECEIVED FOR SERIAL BOND

Present value of interest to be paid at the end of each year for 5 years at an annual yield of 6% computed as follows:

Interest Payment Date	*Bonds outstanding*	*Interest at 5%*	*Present value factor at 6%*	*Present value of interest payments*
12/31/92	$1,000,000	$50,000	.9434	$47,170
12/31/93	800,000	40,000	.8900	35,600
12/31/94	600,000	30,000	.8396	25,188
12/31/95	400,000	20,000	.7921	15,842
12/31/96	200,000	10,000	.7473	7,473

Total present value of interest payments	$131,273
Present value of amount to be paid on January 1 each year for 5 years at an annual yield of 6% ($200,000 × 4.2124)	842,480
Present value (amount received) of all payments	$973,753

2.

MyKoo Corporation
AMORTIZATION OF BOND DISCOUNT
Interest (Effective Rate) Method

Year	(A) Carrying value of bonds \$1,000,000 —E—F	(B) Effective interest expense (6% × A)	(C) Interest payments	(D) Amortization of bond discount (B—C)	(E) Bond discount balance (E—D)	(F) Cumulative principal payments
Issue	$973,753				$26,247	
1	782,178	$ 58,425	$ 50,000	$ 8,425	17,822	$ 200,000
2	589,108	46,930	40,000	6,930	10,892	400,000
3	394,454	35,346	30,000	5,346	5,546	600,000
4	198,121	23,667	20,000	3,667	1,879	800,000
5	0	* 11,879	10,000	1,879	0	$1,000,000
		$176,247*	$150,000	$26,247		

*Rounding differences ignored.

Note: Computations for years 3, 4, and 5 are not part of requirement but are included in answer so that complete schedule can be presented.

Part b.

1.

Entry	Debit	Credit
Cash	$11,000,000	
Bonds payable		$10,000,000
Premium on bonds payable		1,000,000

To record issuance of $10,000,000 of 4% convertible debentures for $11,000,000. The bonds mature in ten years, and each $1,000 bond is convertible into five shares of $30 par value common stock.

2.

Entry	Debit	Credit
Bonds payable	$4,000,000	
Premium on bonds payable *(Schedule 1)*	320,000	
Common stock, $10 par *(Schedule 2)*		$ 600,000
Additional paid-in capital		3,720,000

To record conversion of 40% of the outstanding 4% convertible debentures after giving effect to the 3-for-1 stock split.

Schedule 1
Computation of Unamortized Premium on Bonds Converted

Premium on bonds payable on Jan. 1, 1991		$1,000,000
Amortization for 1991 ($1,000,000 ÷ 10)	$100,000	
Amortization for 1992 ($1,000,000 ÷ 10)	100,000	200,000
Premium on bonds payable on Jan. 1, 1993		$ 800,000
Bonds converted		40%
		$ 320,000

Schedule 2
Computation of Common Stock Resulting from Conversion

Number of shares convertible on January 1, 1993:		
Number of bonds ($10,000,000 ÷ $1,000)	10,000	
Number of shares for each bond	5	
		50,000
Stock split on January 1, 1992		3
		150,000
Bonds converted		40%
Number of shares converted		60,000
Par value		$ 10
		$600,000

Part c.

Entry 7/1/91	*Debit*	*Credit*
Cash	$2,000,000	
Discount on bonds payable	100,000	
Bonds payable		$2,000,000
Additional paid in capital (stock purchase warrants)		100,000

To record issuance of $2,000,000 of 7% bonds with detachable warrants. The bonds mature in ten years, and each detachable warrant gives the bondholder the right to purchase for $30, one share of $1 par value common stock.

NUMBER 4

a. The purpose of the effective interest method is to provide periodic interest expense based on a constant rate over the life of the bonds. The impact of applying the effective interest method on Corval's bond premium is to decrease the premium by a lesser amount in 1995 compared to using the straight-line method of amortization.

b. Under the straight-line interest method, the premium is amortized at a constant periodic amount, and in 1995 the premium amortization would have been greater than amortization under the effective interest method. Consequently, for 1995, interest expense would have been understated, net income would have been overstated, and the carrying amount of the bonds would have been understated.

c. The November 30, 1998, transaction is reported as an extraordinary loss after income from continuing operations. This loss equals the excess of the fair value of the cash and property transferred over the bonds' carrying amount on November 30, 1998. This presentation is appropriate because this is an early extinguishment of debt.

d. The gross amount of the extraordinary loss is added to net income under cash flows from operating activities. The cash payment is reported as a cash outflow from financing activities. Corval should disclose details of the noncash elements of the transaction either on the same page as the statement of cash flows or in the notes to the financial statements.

NUMBER 5

Part a.

Hopewell Company
COMPUTATION OF TOTAL AMOUNT RECEIVED FROM SALE OF BONDS
January 1, 1999

Present value of the future principal ($1,000,000 × 0.3855)	$385,500
Present value of future annual interest payments	
($80,000 [$1,000,000 × 8%] × 6.1446)	491,568
Amount received from sale of bonds	$877,068

Part b.

Junction Company
JOURNAL ENTRY
September 1, 1999

	Debit	*Credit*
Cash	$4,210,000	
Bond issue costs deferred	40,000	
Bonds payable (4,000 × $1,000)		$4,000,000
Premium on bonds payable *(Schedule 1)*		136,000
Detachable stock warrants *(Schedule 1)*		24,000
Bond interest expense *(Schedule 2)*		90,000
To record the issuance of the bonds.		

Schedule 1

Premium on Bonds Payable and Value of Stock Warrants

Sales price (4,000 × $1,040)	$4,160,000
Face value of bonds	4,000,000
	$ 160,000
Deduct value assigned to stock warrants	
(4,000 × 2 = 8,000 warrants × $3)	24,000
Premium on bonds payable	$ 136,000

Schedule 2

Accrued Bond Interest to Date of Sale

Face value of bonds	$4,000,000
Interest rate	9%
Annual interest	$ 360,000
Accrued interest (3 months)—(360,000 × 3/12)	$ 90,000

Part c.

Cone Company
COMPUTATION OF GAIN ON EARLY EXTINGUISHMENT OF DEBT
July 1, 1999

Book value of bonds on December 1, 1996	$2,200,000
Book value of bonds on December 31, 1998	2,100,000
Amortization for 25 months	$ 100,000
Monthly amortization ($100,000 ÷ 25)	$ 4,000
Book value of bonds on December 31, 1998	$2,100,000
Amortization for 1996 to July 1, 1999 ($4,000 × 6 months)	24,000
Book value of bonds on July 1, 1999	2,076,000
Cost of reacquisition (2,000 × $980)	1,960,000
Gain on early extinguishment of debt	$ 116,000

NUMBER 6

Warner, Inc.
INCOME BEFORE INCOME TAXES FROM BOND INVESTMENT
For the Years Ended December 31, 1998 and 1999

	1998	*1999*
Interest income before amortization (Schedules 1 and 2)	$37,333	$53,334
Amortization of bond discount (Schedule 3)	5,775	8,817
Gain on sale of bonds (Schedule 4)	—	5,441
Income before income taxes	$43,108	$67,592

Schedule 1
Interest Income Before Amortization for 1998

Face value of bonds (800 × $1,000)	$800,000
Interest rate	× 8%
Interest for year	$ 64,000

Interest received December 1, 1998 ($64,000 × 1/2)	$32,000
Interest accrued at December 31, 1998 ($64,000 × 1/12)	5,333
Interest income before amortization for 1998	$37,333

Schedule 2
Interest Income Before Amortization for 1999

Interest accrued at December 31, 1998, reversed	$(5,333)
Interest received June 1, 1998 (6 months)	32,000
Accrued interest paid by buyer (June 1 to November 1, 5/12 × $64,000)	26,667
Interest income before amortization for 1999	$53,334

Schedule 3

Amortization of Bond Discount—Effective Interest Method for 1998 and 1999

Face value of bonds (800 × $1,000)		$800,000
Purchase price of bonds		738,300
Bond discount		61,700
Amortization of bond discount for 1998		
6 months ended December 1, 1998		
($738,300 × 5% = $36,915 effective		
interest – $32,000 cash interest)	$4,915	
Month of December 1998		
($743,215 ($738,300 + $4,915) × 5% = $37,161 effective		
interest = $32,000 cash interest = $5,161 × 1/6)	860	5,775
Balance of unamortized bond discount, December 31, 1998		55,925
Amortization of bond discount for 1999		
5 months ended June 1, 1992 ($5,161 – $860)	4,301	
5 months ended November 1, 1999		
($748,376 [$743,215 + $5,161] × 5% = $37,419		
effective interest - $32,000 cash		
interest = $5,419 × 5/6)	4,516	8,817
Balance of unamortized bond discount, November 1, 1999		$47,108

Schedule 4

Gain on Sale of Bonds for 1999

Selling price of bonds		
Selling price of bonds, including accrued interest paid by buyer		$785,000
Accrued interest paid by buyer (Schedule 2)		(26,667)
Selling price of bonds		$758,333
Book value of bonds		
Purchase price of bonds	738,300	
Amortization of bond discount for 1998 (Schedule 3)	5,775	
Amortization of bond discount for 1999 (Schedule 3)	8,817	
Book value of bonds at date of sale		752,892
Gain on sale of bonds		$ 5,441

Warner, Inc.
SCHEDULE OF INTEREST INCOME AND BOND DISCOUNT AMORTIZATION — EFFECTIVE INTEREST METHOD (8% Bonds Purchased to Yield 10%)
(Not Required)

Date	*Cash interest (4% semiannual)*	*Effective interest (5% semiannual)*	*Discount amortization*	*Balance unamortized discount*	*Carrying value of bonds*
6-1-98	—	—	—	$61,700[b]	$738,300[a]
12-1-98	$ 32,000	$ 36,915	$ 4,915	56,785	743,215
6-1-99	32,000	37,161	5,161	51,624	748,376
12-1-99	32,000	37,419	5,419	46,205	753,795
6-1-00	32,000	37,690	5,690	40,515	759,485
12-1-00	32,000	37,974	5,974	34,541	765,459
6-1-01	32,000	38,273	6,273	28,268	771,732
12-1-01	32,000	38,587	6,587	21,681	778,319
6-1-02	32,000	38,916	6,916	14,765	785,235
12-1-02	32,000	39,262	7,262	7,503	792,497
6-1-03	32,000	39,625	7,625	(122)	800,122
6-1-03	—	(122)[c]	(122)[c]	122[c]	800,000
	$320,000	$381,700	$61,700	—0—	$800,000

[a] Price paid for $800,000 bonds equals present value of principal plus present value of interest payments:

Principal – $800,000 × .614 (present value of $1 at 5% for 10 periods)	$491,200
Interest payments - $32,000 (4% × $800,000) × 7.722 (present value of an annuity of $1 at 5% for 10 periods)	247,100
	$738,300

[b] $800,000 – $738,300 = $61,700.

[c] Adjustment for fractional differences.

NUMBER 7

a. 1. The 9% bonds were issued at a discount (less than face amount). Although the bonds provide for payment of interest of 9% of face amount, this rate was less than the prevailing or market rate for bonds of similar quality at the time the bonds were issued. Thus, the issue price of the bonds, which is the present value of the principal and interest payments discounted at 10%, is less than the face amount.

2. The amount of interest expense would be higher in the second year of the life of the bond issue than in the first year of the life of the bond issue. According to the effective interest method of amortization, the 10% effective interest rate is applied to the bond carrying amount. In a discount situation, the bond carrying amount increases each year, and this results in a greater interest expense in each successive year.

b. 1. Gain or loss on early extinguishment of debt should be determined by comparing the carrying amount of the bonds at the date of extinguishment with the acquisition price. If the carrying amount exceeds the acquisition price, a gain results. If the carrying amount is less than the acquisition price, a loss results.

In this case, a loss results. The term bonds were issued at a discount. Therefore, the carrying amount of the bonds at the date of extinguishment must be less than the face amount, which is less than the acquisition price.

2. Drew should report the loss from early extinguishment of debt in its 1996 income statement as an extraordinary item, net of income taxes.

c. The proceeds from the issuance of the 7% nonconvertible bonds with detachable stock purchase warrants should be recorded as an increase in cash. These proceeds should be allocated between the bonds and the warrants on the basis of their relative market values. The portion of the proceeds allocable to the bonds should be accounted for as long-term debt, while the portion allocable to the warrants should be accounted for as paid-in capital.

NUMBER 8

a.

Villa Co.
BALANCE SHEET – LIABILITIES SECTION
December 31, 1997

Accounts payable	$ 35,000	
Accrued interest payable	20,000	[2]
Income taxes payable	180,000	[3]
Dividends payable	50,000	
Current portion, long-term debt	62,000	[1]
Total current liabilities	347,000	
Capital lease payable, minus $62,000 current portion	318,000	[1]
Bonds payable	442,000	[2]
Deferred tax liability	90,000	[3]
Total liabilities	$1,197,000	

[1] $100,000 x 4.8 = $480,000
$480,000 - $100,000 = $380,000
$380,000 x 10% = $38,000
$100,000 - $38,000 = $62,000
$380,000 - $62,000 = $318,000

[2] 500K x 8% x ½ = 20K
440K x 10% x ½ = 22K
440K + (22K - 20K) = 442,000

[3] 600K x 30% = 180K
300K x 30% = 90K

b. Villa should disclose the following information about the capital leases, either in the body of the financial statements or in the notes thereto:

- The gross amount of assets recorded under the capital leases, presented by major classes. This information may be combined with owned assets.
- Future minimum lease payments as of the balance sheet date, in the aggregate and for each of the 5 succeeding years.
- A general description of the leasing arrangement, including the existence and terms of renewal, escalation clauses, and restrictions imposed by the lease agreements.

Villa should disclose the following information about the bonds payable, either in the body of the financial statements or in the notes thereto:

- The face amount.
- The nature and terms of the bonds and a discussion of their credit and market risk, cash requirements, and related accounting policies.
- The fair value of the bonds and the method used to estimate their fair value. The price at which the bonds are trading is the most reasonable estimate of their fair value at December 31, 1997.

c. Villa should account for each contingency in a slightly different way because the likelihood of Villa's incurring a loss differs in each situation.

For the toxic waste cleanup, a loss has been incurred. In the notes to its financial statements, Villa should disclose the nature of the loss on cleanup and indicate that an estimate of the loss, or range of the loss, cannot be made. No accrual should be made because the loss cannot be reasonably estimated and accrual of an uncertain amount would impair the integrity of the financial statements.

With regard to Clear's claim, it is only reasonably possible, and not probable, that Villa will have to pay. Accordingly, Villa should not accrue the loss. Villa should disclose the existence and nature of Clear's claim in the notes to its financial statements. Disclosure should include an estimate of the potential range of loss.

Regarding the lack of rockslide insurance, no asset has been impaired and no liability has been incurred. Accordingly, Villa should not accrue a loss. Given that the likelihood of a rockslide is remote, disclosure of the uninsured risk, while permitted, is not required.

NUMBER 9

a. Cope should report the probable warranty costs as an expense in the income statement and a liability in the balance sheet because both of the following required conditions for accrual were met:

- It is considered probable that liabilities have been incurred.
- The amount of loss can be reasonably estimated.

In addition, it may be necessary for Cope to disclose the nature of the probable warranty costs in the notes to the financial statements.

b. Cope should disclose the nature of the threat of expropriation of assets in the notes to the financial statements. In addition, an estimate of the possible loss or range of loss should be disclosed in the notes to the financial statements.

Cope should not report the threat of expropriation of assets as an expense in the income statement nor as a liability in the balance sheet because it does not meet both required conditions for accrual. The actual expropriation of assets is only reasonably possible instead of probable.

c. Adequate disclosure should be made of contingencies that result in gains, but care should be exercised to avoid misleading implications as to the likelihood of realization.

Cope should not report this year the probable damages that may be received next year as a gain in the income statement nor as an asset in the balance sheet. Gain contingencies usually are not recorded in the accounts until the gains are realized.

NUMBER 10

a. A financial instrument is cash, evidence of an ownership interest in an entity, or a contractual right to receive or deliver cash or another financial instrument. A derivative financial instrument is a product whose value is derived, at least in part, from the value and characteristics of one or more underlying assets. Examples of derivative financial instruments include: futures; forward, swap, or options contracts; interest-rate caps; and fixed-rate loan commitments.

b. Market risk is the possibility that future changes in market prices may make a financial instrument less valuable or more burdensome. Credit risk is the possibility that a loss may occur from the failure of the other party to perform according to the terms of a contract. Concentrations of credit risk exist when receivables have common characteristics that may affect their collection. One common characteristic might be that the receivables are due from companies in the same industry or in the same region of the country.

c. The fair value of a financial instrument is the amount at which the instrument could be exchanged in a current transaction between willing parties, other than in a forced or liquidation sale. Quoted market price, if available, is the best evidence of the fair value of a financial instrument. If quoted prices are not available, Chatham's management's best estimate of fair value might be based on valuation techniques or on the quoted market price of a financial instrument with similar characteristics.

NUMBER 11

1. **E**
2. **J**
3. **H**
4. **N**
5. **M**
6. **F**
7. **O**
8. **F**
9. **S**
10. **O**
11. **O**

Solution:

Author's Note: This problem is similar to a problem on the November 1995 exam. The difference is that the November exam required the calculation of the **dollar amounts** for the solution. To assist the candidates in preparation for future exams, our approach will first calculate the amounts as required by the November 1995 exam and then answer the procedural questions from the November 1998 exam.

SOLUTIONS APPROACH:

The key to the problem is to change the format for the amortization table to make the calculations easier. The suggested format and the numbers given are listed below:

DATE	FACE AMOUNT	+	BOND PREMIUM	=	CARRYING VALUE	FACE INTEREST PAID	EFFECTIVE INTEREST EXPENSE	=	AMORTZ.
7/1/97					(1)				
Interest & Amtz.						(2)	$14,100		(3)
12/31/97			(4)		$349,100				
Interest & Amtz.						$17,500	(5)		$3,536
6/30/98					(6)				

1. The problem states that the face amount of the bonds issued is $250,000. Place $250,000 in the face amount column for July 1.

2. The interest paid is the same each 6 months so $17,500 should be added to the face interest paid column for 1997 (answer 2). The interest paid divided by the face amount of the bonds ($17,500 / $250,000) equals a semi-annual interest rate of 7% or an annual rate of 14%. This calculation was required for the November 1995 exam problem.

3. For 1997 the $17,500 paid for interest minus the $14,100 interest expense (given) should equal the amortization of the bond premium of $3,400. (Answer 3). Also place the $3,400 amortization under the bond premium column and the carrying value column.

4. The December 31, 1997 carrying value of $349,100 (given) plus the $3,400 amortization would equal the July 1 carrying value of $352,500 (Answer 1).

5. The July 1 carrying value of $352,500 minus the face value of the bonds ($250,000) is the balance in the bond premium at July 1 of $102,500.

6. The July total of the bond premium, $102,500 minus the $3,400 amortization equals the balance in the bond premium column at 12/31/97 of $99,100 (Answer 4).

7. The July 1 carrying value times the effective interest rate is the interest expense for the first 6 months. So the $14,100 interest expense divided by the July 1 carrying value of $352,500 is an effective rate of 4% each six months and an annual rate of 8%. This calculation was required for the November 1995 exam problem (Answer 7).

8. The interest paid and the bond amortization for the second 6 months is given. The difference is the bond interest expense. ($17,500 - $3,536 = $13,964 interest expense) (Answer 5).

9. Place the amortization for the second 6 months ($3,536) as a subtraction in the bond premium column and the carrying value column and foot the columns. The balance in the face amount column is $250,000 and the bond premium is $95,564 for a total carrying value of $345,564 (Answer 6).

DATE	FACE AMOUNT	+	BOND PREMIUM	=	CARRYING VALUE	FACE INTEREST PAID	-	EFFECTIVE INTEREST EXPENSE	=	AMORTZ.
7/1/97	$250,000	+	$102,500	=	$352,500					
Interest & Amtz.			($3,400)		($3,400)	$17,500	-	$14,100	=	$3,400
12/31/97	$250,000	+	$99,100	=	$349,100					
Interest & Amtz.			($3,536)		($3,536)	$17,500	-	$13,964	=	$3,536
6/30/98	$250,000	+	$95,564	=	$345,564					

PROCEDURAL ANSWERS FOR NOVEMBER 1998 EXAM:

1. Answer **E**
   Carrying amount 7/1/97 (just theory).

2. Answer **J**
   Cash paid for interest each 6 months is ($250,000 x 14% x ½ = $17,500).

3. Answer **H**
   Bond premium amortization for the first 6 months is the cash paid for interest minus the interest expense. ($17,500 - $14,100 = $3,400).

4. Answer **N**
   Unamortized bond premium is the carrying amount of the bonds minus the face amount of the bonds ($349,100 - $250,000) = $99,100)

5. Answer **M**
   Interest expense for the second 6 months is the carrying value times the effective interest rate times ½ year ($349,100 x 8% x ½ = $13,964).

6. Answer **F**
   The carrying amount at 6/30/98 is the 12/31/97 carrying value minus the amortization for the second 6 months ($349,100 - $3,536 = $345,564).

7. Answer **O**
   The effective annual interest rate is the interest expense divided by the carrying amount at the beginning of the period times two ($14,100 / $352,500 is an effective rate of 4% times 2 equals an annual rate of 8%).

8. Answer **F**
   Proceeds received from the sale of bonds is a financing activity.

9. Answer **S**
   Interest paid is not a part of the cash flow statement using the indirect method. However, the interest is disclosed in a supplemental schedule.

10. Answer **O**
    Amortization of bond premium does not affect cash and is shown as a deduction from net income in calculating cash generated from operations (operating activities).

11. **Answer O**
Gain on early extinguishment of debt does not affect cash and is shown as a deduction from net income in calculating cash generated from operations (operating activities).

Chapter Ten
Revenue and Expense Recognition, Miscellaneous Items

Chapter Ten
Revenue and Expense Recognition, Miscellaneous Items

CONTRACT ACCOUNTING

Methods of Income Measurement

1. **Percentage of Completion**: Income is recognized as work on a contract progresses based on a percentage of **estimated** total income, either as:
   a. a percentage of incurred costs to date to estimated total costs, or
   b. any other measure of progress toward completion that may be appropriate having due regard for work performed.

2. **Completed Contract**: Profit is measured when contract is complete. Results in deferral of profit until year contract is substantially finished. This method does not measure current performance and may result in erratic reporting of income. When the completed-contract method is used, general and administrative costs are usually treated as period costs; however, it may be appropriate to allocate such costs to contracts in progress. In any case, there should not be excessive deferral of overhead costs, which might occur if total overhead is assigned to abnormally few or small contracts in progress.

Percentage-of-Completion Method

The completed-contract method does not present a significant income measurement problem. Costs are accumulated and deferred until the contract is substantially complete at which time contract costs are matched with the income generated.

The percentage-of-completion method, however, presents some accounting problems which can easily cause confusion. Ordinarily, the act of billing, a debit to accounts receivable, results in a credit to a revenue account. In percentage of completion, revenue does not coincide with the act of billing, since the contract may provide for billings to be made either ahead of or after various stages of completion. Further, revenue earned is determined periodically, not necessarily at the time billings are permitted under the provisions of the contract.

Costs and Estimated Earnings in Excess of Billings

"Billings in excess of costs and estimated earnings" is offset against "Costs and estimated earnings in excess of billings" when the **same** contract is involved in both accounts. Where different contracts are involved, their status with regard to this account should not be netted. ARB 43 states, "...current assets may include costs and recognized income not yet billed with respect to certain contracts; and liabilities (in most cases current liabilities) may include billings in excess of costs and recognized income with respect to other contracts."

Other titles found in current accounting literature were:

Construction in Progress
Unbilled Construction in Progress—At Contract Price
Billings on Construction in Process
Partial Billings on Contract

Contract Accounting problems in past CPA exams have followed ARB #43.

Completed-Contract Method

Contact Costs are recorded:

Contract Costs
    Cash, A/P, etc.

Progress Billings are made:

Accounts Receivable—Contracts
    Progress Billings

Contract is completed and the full contract price has been billed:

Progress billings
    Contract Costs
    Income on Long-Term Contracts

The balance sheet would show as a current asset the following, prior to completion of the contract, assuming costs of $125,000 and billings of $65,000.

Contract Costs to date	$125,000
Less: Progress billings	65,000
Costs on uncompleted contracts in excess of billings	$ 60,000

If progress billings exceed costs, show the balance as a current liability, "Billings on uncompleted contracts in excess of costs." ARB 43 states, "When the completed-contract method is used, an excess of accumulated costs over related billings should be shown in the balance sheet as a current asset, and an excess of accumulated billings over related costs shown among the liabilities, in most cases as a current liability."

"If costs exceed billings on some contracts, and billings exceed costs on others, the contracts should ordinarily be segregated so that the figures on the asset side include only those contracts on which costs exceed billings, those on the liability side include only those on which billings exceed costs."

Treatment of Losses on Contracts in Progress

Losses should be provided for in full when it is apparent that the contract will result in a loss. This applies to both methods.

Journal Entry:

Loss on Contract
    Allowance for Contract Loss

ARB #43 states: "When the current estimate of total contract costs indicates a loss, in most circumstances provision should be made for the loss on the entire contract."

Illustrative Problem #1

Facts: Total contract price $9,000,000
Estimated costs 8,000,000
3-year contract

Year	*Actual Costs*	*Estimated Additional Costs to Complete*	*Billings*	*Collections*
1	$1,944,000	$6,156,000	$1,800,000	$1,620,000
2	5,232,000	2,024,000	4,950,000	4,455,000
3	1,844,000	—	2,250,000	2,925,000

Required:
Prepare journal entries for the above contract assuming:

1. Percentage of completion
2. Completed contract

The contract calls for the customer to retain 10% of contract billings until the last payment is submitted.

Solution:

(1) Percentage of Completion:

	Year #1		*Year #2*		*Year #3*	
Cost of contract work	$1,944,000		$5,232,000		$1,844,000	
Materials, Cash, etc.		$1,944,000		$5,232,000		$1,844,000
Accounts receivable	1,800,000		4,950,000		2,250,000	
Billings in excess of cost and estimated earnings		1,800,000		4,950,000		2,250,000
Cash	1,620,000		4,455,000		2,925,000	
Accounts receivable		1,620,000		4,455,000		2,925,000
Cost and estimated earnings in excess of billings	2,160,000		4,860,000		1,980,000	
Revenue from contracts		2,160,000		4,860,000		1,980,000
Loss on contract			44,000			
Allowance for contract loss				44,000		
Closing Entries:						
Revenue from contracts	2,160,000		4,860,000		1,980,000	
Allowance for contract loss					44,000	
Cost of contract work		1,944,000		5,232,000		1,844,000
Loss on contract				44,000		
Income summary		216,000	416,000			180,000

SCHEDULES

Revenue to be recognized

	Year #1	*Year #2*	*Year #3*
Costs incurred to date	$1,944,000	$1,944,000+5,232,000=7,176,000	
Total costs	1,944,000+6,156,000=8,100,000	7,176,000+2,024,000=9,200,000	
% =	24%	78%	100%
× 9,000,000 =	2,160,000	7,020,000	9,000,000
Less prior years' revenue		2,160,000	7,020,000
		4,860,000	1,980,000

Accumulated Profit (Loss) on contract and allowance for contract loss

	Year #1	Year #2	Year #3
Revenue recognized	$2,160,000	$4,860,000	$1,980,000
Current costs	1,944,000	5,232,000	1,844,000
Profit (loss)	216,000	(372,000)	136,000
Cumulative—Year #2		(156,000)	
Provision for additional loss	______	(44,000)	44,000
[9,000,000 – (1,944,000 + 5,232,000 + 2,024,000)]		(200,000)	180,000
Cumulative—Year #3			(20,000)
[9,000,000 – (1,944,000 + 5,232,000 + 1,844,000)]			

(2) Completed Contract:

	Year #1		Year #2		Year #3	
Construction in progress	$1,944,000		$5,232,000		$1,844,000	
Materials, cash, etc.		$1,944,000		$5,232,000		$1,844,000
Accounts receivable	1,800,000		4,950,000		2,250,000	
Progress billings		1,800,000		4,950,000		2,250,000
Cash	1,620,000		4,455,000		2,925,000	
Accounts receivable		1,620,000		4,455,000		2,925,000
Provision for contract loss			200,000			
Allowance for loss				200,000		
Contract costs					9,020,000	
Progress billings					9,000,000	
Construction in progress						9,020,000
Contract revenues						9,000,000
Closing entries:						
Income summary			200,000			
Provision for contract loss				200,000		
Contract revenues					9,000,000	
Allowance for loss					200,000	
Contract costs						9,020,000
Income summary						180,000

Illustrative Problem #2

Following is data related to the DeWitt Construction Company and the completed-contract method and the percentage-of-completion method of accounting for long-term contracts for reporting in the Company's financial statements. DeWitt commenced doing business on January 1, 19XA.

Construction activities for the year ended December 31, 19XA:

Project	*Total Contract Price*	*Billings Through December 31, 19XA*	*Cash Collections Through December 31, 19XA*	*Contract Costs Incurred Through December 31, 19XA*	*Estimated Additional Costs to Complete Contracts*
A	$ 520,000	$ 350,000	$ 310,000	$ 424,000	$106,000
B	670,000	210,000	210,000	126,000	504,000
C	475,000	475,000	395,000	315,000	—
D	200,000	70,000	50,000	112,750	92,250
E	460,000	400,000	400,000	370,000	30,000
	$2,325,000	$1,505,000	$1,365,000	$1,347,750	$732,250

All contracts are with different customers.
Any work remaining to be done on the contracts is expected to be completed in 19XB.

DeWitt Construction Company
BALANCE SHEET
December 31, 19XA

Assets

	Completed-Contract Method		*Percentage-of Completion Method*	
Cash	XXXX		XXXX	
Accounts receivable:				
Due on contracts	$140,000	(1)	$140,000	(5)
Cost of uncompleted contracts in excess of billings	116,750	(2)	—	
Costs and estimated earnings in excess of billings on uncompleted contracts	—		127,250	(6)
Property, plant, and equipment, net	XXXX		XXXX	
Other assets	XXXX		XXXX	
	$ XXXX		$ XXXX	

Liabilities and Stockholders' Equity

Accounts payable and accrued liabilities	XXXX		XXXX	
Billings on uncompleted contracts in excess of costs	$114,000	(3)	—	
Billings in excess of costs and estimated earnings	—		$76,000	(7)
Estimated losses on uncompleted contracts	15,000	(4)	—	
Notes payable	XXXX		XXXX	
Common stock	XXXX		XXXX	
Retained earnings	XXXX		XXXX	
	$ XXXX		$ XXXX	

Explanations:

(1)(5) Total billings of $1,505,000 less cash collections of $1,365,000.
(2)(3) See Schedule #3 below.
(4) See Schedule #1 below.
(6)(7) See Schedule #4 below.

Schedule #1
DeWitt Construction Company
SCHEDULE OF REVENUE AND INCOME (LOSS)
THAT WOULD BE REPORTED UNDER THE
COMPLETED-CONTRACT METHOD AND THE PERCENTAGE-OF-COMPLETION METHOD
For the Year Ended December 31, 19XA

1.

Completed-Contract Project	*Revenue to be Reported*	*Costs Incurred*	*Provision for Loss*	*Income (Loss) to be Reported*
A			$10,000	$ (10,000)
C	$475,000	$315,000		160,000
D			5,000	(5,000)
Totals	$475,000	$315,000	$15,000	$145,000

Percentage-of-Completion Project	*Revenue to be Reported (Schedule 2)*	*Costs Incurred*	*Provision for Loss*	*Income (Loss) to be Reported*
A	$ 416,000	$ 424,000	$2,000	$(10,000)
B	134,000	126,000		8,000
C	475,000	315,000		160,000
D	110,000	112,750	2,250	(5,000)
E	425,500	370,000		55,500
	$1,560,500	$1,347,750	$4,250	$208,500

Schedule #2
DeWitt Construction Company
COMPUTATION OF REVENUE RECOGNIZED UNDER THE
PERCENTAGE-OF-COMPLETION METHOD
For the Year Ended December 31, 19XA

Projects			
A	$\frac{424{,}000}{530{,}000}$	× 520,000 =	$ 416,000
B	$\frac{126{,}000}{630{,}000}$	× 670,000 =	134,000
C	$\frac{315{,}000}{315{,}000}$	× 475,000 =	475,000
D	$\frac{112{,}750}{205{,}000}$	× 200,000 =	110,000
E	$\frac{370{,}000}{400{,}000}$	× 460,000 =	425,500
			$1,560,500

Schedule #3
DeWitt Construction Company
COMPUTATION OF COSTS IN EXCESS OF BILLINGS AND BILLINGS IN EXCESS OF COSTS INCURRED UNDER THE COMPLETED-CONTRACT METHOD
For the Year Ended December 31, 19XA

Project	Construction in Process	Related Billings	Costs in Excess of Billings	Billings in Excess of Costs
A	$ 424,000	$ 350,000	$ 74,000	
B	126,000	210,000		$ 84,000
D	112,750	70,000	42,750	
E	370,000	400,000	—	30,000
	$1,032,750	$1,030,000	$116,750	$114,000

Schedule #4
DeWitt Construction Company
COMPUTATION OF COSTS AND ESTIMATED EARNINGS IN EXCESS OF BILLINGS AND BILLINGS IN EXCESS OF COSTS AND ESTIMATED EARNINGS UNDER THE PERCENTAGE-OF-COMPLETION METHOD
For the Year Ended December 31, 19XA

Project	Costs and Estimated Earnings or Losses	Related Billings	Costs and Estimated Earnings in Excess of Billings	Billings in Excess of Costs and Estimated Earnings
A	$ 414,000	$ 350,000	$ 64,000	
B	134,000	210,000		$76,000
D	107,750	70,000	37,750	
E	425,500	400,000	25,500	
	$1,081,250	$1,030,000	$127,250	$76,000

INSTALLMENT SALES

Sales are made with payment to be received in the current and future accounting periods. Payments received are partly a return of cost and profit.

Key Points:

1. Each year's accounts receivable are maintained separately.
2. Each year has separate gross profit and cost of sales percentage.
3. Unrealized gross profit is the gross profit percentage times the accounts receivable balance for that year.
4. Realized gross profit is the gross profit percentage times the collections of the A/R for a given year.

Accounting Problems:

a. Defaults on installment contracts—loss on defaults would be the balance on the contract times the cost of sales percentage for that year.

For example: In 19X2, $15,000 in 19X1 contracts was defaulted. The cost of sales percentage in 19X1 was 58%. Entry would be:

Loss on defaulted contracts	$8,700	
Deferred gross profit 19X1	6,300	
Installment Accounts Receivable		$15,000
To record loss and clear deferred gross profit account.		

b. Merchandise may be repossessed—
Assume the same facts as in (a) except that merchandise with a wholesale market value of $3,200 was repossessed. Entry:

Loss on defaulted contracts	$5,500	
Deferred gross profit in 19X1	6,300	
Used merchandise inventory	3,200	
Installment Accounts Receivable		$15,000

c. Trade-Ins—
Trade-ins should be placed on the books at estimated inventory market value. Gross profit is computed based on estimated value of trade-in. Example: Merchandise costing $1,000 was sold for $1,500. A trade-in of $175 was taken having an inventory value of $125. Entry:

Installment A/R	$1,325	
Trade-in inventory	125	
Installment Sales		$1,450

Note: Gross profit on sale is $450 and percentage of gross profit is $450/1,450 or 31%.

Illustrative Problem:

FACTS: Sale Oct. 15 $8,000

Cost	6,000
Gross profit	2,000
Ratio gross profit to selling price	25%
Down Payment	2,000
Monthly Payments	500

Solution:

10/15	Cash	$2,000	
	Installment A/R	6,000	
	Installment Sales		$8,000
	Cost of Installment Sales	6,000	
	Inventory		6,000
11/15 & 12/15	Cash	$500	
	Installment A/R		$500
12/31	Closing Entries:		
	Installment Sales	$8,000	
	Cost of Installment Sales		$6,000
	Deferred G.P. on Inst. Sales		1,250
	Realized G.P. on Inst. Sales		750
	Realized G.P. on Inst. Sales	750	
	Revenue and Exp.		750

Matching Costs and Revenue
Even though procedure of deferring income and not deferring expenses does not result in matching of costs and revenues, it is permissible because of the difficulty of matching costs with revenue.

When Installment Accounting Is Acceptable
AICPA position on Installment Accounting:

> "Profit is deemed to be realized when a sale in the ordinary course of business is effected, unless the circumstances are such that the **collection** of the sale price is **not reasonably assured**." (Emphasis supplied) The Board believes that in the absence of the above circumstances, the installment method of accounting is **not acceptable**. The Board believes that revenues should be ordinarily accounted for at the time a transaction is completed with appropriate provision for uncollectible accounts. Therefore, the installment method would appear to be acceptable, only where receivables are collectible over extended periods, and, because of the terms of the transactions or other conditions, there is no reasonable basis for estimating the degree of collectibility.

Cost-Recovery Method
The Board has also indicated that the **cost-recovery** method may be used where the installment method is also acceptable. Under the cost-recovery method, equal amounts of revenue and expense are recognized as collections are made until all costs have been recovered, postponing any recognition of profit until that time.

Interest
If installment sales contracts call for interest on uncollected balances, the interest should be taken into income during the period in which it accrues.

Balance Sheet Presentation
Installment receivables may be classified as a current asset if they conform to normal trade practices. Balances should be shown by years (parenthetically). Deferred gross profit should be shown as a contra account from installment accounts receivable.

CORRECTION OF ERRORS

SFAS #16 defines accounting errors which qualify as prior period adjustments. Such errors should result in correction of the statements of prior years, if material. These errors usually result from mistake, oversight or misuse of facts.

Types of Errors
Errors which affect the net income of two or more periods and/or the balance sheet of one or more periods can be grouped as counterbalancing and noncounterbalancing errors.

Counterbalancing Errors
This type of error affects the net income of two or more periods, but has no effect on retained earnings for the years for which the statements are being corrected. Assume that the years 1997, 1998, and 1999, are under review and that net income for the three years is to be corrected and a balance sheet is to be prepared for the year ended December 31, 1999. The following are examples of counterbalancing errors.

a. $3,000 of 1996 advertising was paid and recorded as an expense in 1997.
b. The ending inventory for 1997 was understated by $2,500.
c. 1997 real estate taxes of $6,000 payable in 1998 were not accrued as an expense in 1997.
d. The 1999 beginning inventory was overstated by $12,000.
e. A three-year insurance policy totaling $27,000 was paid on January 1, 1997, and charged to expense.

If statements are to be presented only for these years, the specific accounts should be corrected as follows:

	Dr. (Cr.)		
		Net Income for Years	
	1997	1998	1999
a. Advertising Expense	[1]($3,000)		
b. 1997 Ending Inventory	($2,500)	$2,500	
c. Real Estate Taxes	$6,000	($6,000)	
d. 1999 Beginning Inventory		$12,000	($12,000)
e. Insurance Expense	($18,000)	9,000	9,000

[1] Beginning retained earnings requires a counterbalancing debit of $3,000.

Noncounterbalancing Errors

Such errors require an adjustment to a balance sheet account at the end of the period for which corrections are being made. Examples of such errors are failure to properly record depreciation, amortization or to provide for uncollectible accounts receivable.

For example: Equipment purchased in 1997 costing $11,000 was expensed. The equipment has a ten-year useful life and a $1,000 salvage value. The company uses straight-line depreciation but does not take depreciation in the year of purchase. Correct the years 1997, 1998, and 1999.

	Dr. (Cr.)		
		Net Income for Years	
	1997	1998	1999
Equipment Adjustment	($11,000)	$1,000	$1,000

Journal Entry:

	Dr.	Cr.
Equipment	$11,000	
Allowance for Depreciation		$2,000
Retained Earnings (12/31/99)		9,000

ACCOUNTING FOR STOCK OPTIONS AS COMPENSATION

Stock options for compensation are accounted for using either of the following methods:

- Intrinsic Value Method (APB #25)
- Fair Value Method (SFAS #123)

Intrinsic Value Method – Stock Options

When stock options are granted to employees, compensation expenses is measured by the difference between the exercise price and the fair value of the stock at the **measurement date.**

The measurement date is the first date on which **both** the exercise price and the number of shares to be granted are known.

On the measurement date a journal entry is made for the total compensation cost. The entry is a debit to deferred compensation cost and a credit to paid-in capital – stock options. Both of these accounts are reported in the stockholders' equity section of the statement of financial position.

Deferred compensation expense is allocated equally over the periods in which the employee performs the service (service period). The service period is the time between the grant date and the first date the employee can exercise the option (the vesting date).

When the intrinsic value method is used for the calculation of compensation cost, SFAS #123 requires pro-forma disclosure of net income and earnings-per-share as if the fair value method had been used.

Fair Value Method – Stock Options

The fair value method calculates compensation expense based on the fair value of the options expected to vest on the date the options are **granted** to the employees. The computation is done with an option – pricing model (such as the Black-Scholes option pricing method) that considers the following:

a. the stock price at the grant date
b. exercise price
c. expected life of the option
d. volatility of the stock
e. expected dividend from the stock
f. a risk-free interest rate for the expected term of the stock option

Total compensation cost is determined at the grant date and allocated equally to the periods benefited by the employee's service.

Example

To illustrate the two methods of accounting for a stock option plan, assume that on December 1, 1999 the stockholders of Gerlack Corp. approve a plan to grant the corporation's ten executives options to purchase 1,000 shares each of the company's $5 par value common stock. The options are granted on January 1, 2000 and may be exercised at any time between January 1, 2002 and January 1, 2005. The option price is $55, the market price is $65 and the service period is two years.

Total Compensation Cost – Intrinsic Value Method

Market value at grant date of 10,000 shares at $65	$650,000
Option price at grant date of 10,000 shares at $55	(550,000)
Total compensation expense	$100,000

Total Compensation Expense – Fair Value Method

Assume that Gerlack Corp. applies the Black-Scholes pricing model and determines that the total compensation expense is **$250,000.**

Basic Journal Entries

	Intrinsic Value		Fair Value	
January 1, 2000 – grant date				
(To record total compensation)				
Deferred compensation cost	$100,000		No	
Paid-in capital stock options		$100,000	entry	
December 31, 2000				
(To record compensation expense)				
Compensation expense	$50,000		$125,000	
Deferred compensation cost		$50,000		
Paid-in capital stock options				$125,000
($100,000 + 2) and ($250,000 + 2)				
December 31, 2001				
(To record compensation expense)				
Compensation expense	$50,000		$125,000	
Deferred compensation cost		$50,000		
Paid-in capital stock options				$125,000

January 2, 2002
(Assume 90% of the stock options are exercised)

Cash (9,000 shares x $55 per share)	$495,000		$495,000	
Paid-in capital stock options	90,000*		225,000**	
Common Stock (9,000 shares x $5 par)		$ 45,000		$ 45,000
Paid-in capital in excess of par		$540,000		$675,000

* 90% x total paid-in capital stock options of $100,000
** 90% x total paid-in capital stock options of $250,000

January 2, 2005
(Assume the remaining 10% of stock options expire)

Paid-in capital stock options	$10,000*		$25,000**	
Paid-in capital expired stock options		$10,000		$25,000

* 10% x total paid-in capital stock options of $100,000
** 10% x total paid-in capital stock options of $250,000

NOTE:
If the stock option is forfeited because an employee leaves the company and fails to meet the service requirement, the compensation expense associated with the employee is adjusted as a change in accounting estimate in the current period. The journal entry would be a debit to paid-in capital stock options and a credit to either deferred compensation expense or compensation expense (intrinsic value method) or a credit to compensation expense (fair value method).

SUMMARY OF ACCOUNTING FOR STOCK-BASED COMPENSATION – SFAS #123

This pronouncement applies to stock purchase plans, stock options, and stock appreciation rights. It also applies to the issue of equity instruments for goods or services from nonemployees.

I. The measurement of the cost of stock compensation plans under APB #25 is **still** permissible. SFAS #123 **encourages** but does not require the use of the fair value based method.

   A. When APB #25 is used for the calculation of compensation cost, SFAS #123 requires **pro-forma** disclosure of net income and earnings per share as if the fair value based method had been used.

   B. In justifying a change in accounting principle, the fair value method is preferred.

II. The recognition of compensation cost using the fair value based method is based on the value of the award at the **grant date** and is amortized over the service period which is usually equal to the vesting period.

   A. **Stock Options**
   The fair value of stock options is calculated using an option-pricing model. This model considers the stock price at the grant date, the exercise price, the expected life of the option, the volatility of the stock, expected dividends from the stock, and a risk-free interest rate for the expected term of the stock option.

   B. **Restricted Stock**
   The fair value based method measures the value of nonvested stock (restricted stock) at the market price on the grant date unless a restriction applies after the vesting date. In that case the restriction would have to be considered.

   C. **Stock Purchase Plans**
   Entities that offer stock purchase plans do not incur any compensation cost if the plan allows a small discount of 5% or less, offers the plan to substantially all of its full-time employees and the plan does not have any other option feature except the discount.

D. **Stock Appreciation Rights**
Stock appreciation rights allow employees to receive as compensation an amount equal to the excess of the market price of the entities stock over a stated amount. The compensation is allocated over the periods benefited. If the rights are for past services, the cost is charged to the current period.

III. Issuance of equity instruments to nonemployees for goods or services.

The cost of the goods or services is based on the fair value of the equity instruments or the fair value of the goods or services whichever is more objective.

IV. DISCLOSURES

A. Vesting requirements, maximum term of options granted, and number of shares authorized of grants or options or other equity instruments.
B. The number and weighted-average exercise prices of each group of options.
C. The weighted-average grant-date fair value of options granted during the year, classified according to whether the exercise price equals, exceeds, or is less than the fair value of the stock at the date of the grant.
D. A description of methods used and assumptions made in determining fair values of the options.
E. Total compensation cost recognized for the year.
F. The range of exercise prices and weighted-average remaining contractual life for all options still outstanding.
Reminder: If APB #25 is used for the calculation of compensation cost, SFAS #123 requires pro-forma disclosure of net income and earnings per share as if the fair value based method had been used.

ESOPS

Companies with Employee Stock Ownership Plans (ESOPs) recognize expense when cash and/or stocks are contributed to the plan (stocks measured at FMV). When the ESOP borrows funds to purchase company stock, the company reports an equal reduction in shareholders' equity and an increase in debt for the endorsed note payable of the ESOP when the loan is so guaranteed.

Deferred Compensation Contracts

Deferred compensation contracts should be accounted for individually on an accrual basis. If the contract is equivalent to a pension plan, apply SFAS #87, "Accounting for the Cost of Pension Plans." Deferred compensation contracts customarily include requirements such as continued employment for a specified period and availability for consulting services and agreements not to compete after retirement, which, if not complied with, remove the employer's obligations for future payments. The estimated amounts to be paid under each contract should be accrued over the period of active employment from the time the contract is entered into, unless it is evident that future services are commensurate with the payments to be made. If both current and future services are involved, only the portion applicable to the current services should be accrued.

Where contracts provide for periodic payments to employees or their surviving spouses for life, the estimated amount of future payments should be accrued over the period of active employment. Estimates should be based on the life expectancy of each individual concerned or on the estimated cost of an annuity contract.

CASH TO ACCRUAL

At times, incomplete or cash basis statements are presented, and candidates are asked to convert such statements to the accrual basis (or vice versa) based on supplemental information furnished. To convert to the accrual basis:

1. Cash sales must be adjusted to sales recognized under GAAP.
2. Purchases must be converted to the accrual basis.
3. Cost of goods sold must be computed taking into account purchases in (2) above and beginning and ending inventories.
4. Expenses must be converted to the accrual basis recognizing accrued expenses at the beginning and end of the period.

5. Other items of revenue and cost expirations under GAAP must be recognized such as:
   Income tax allocation
   Amortization of intangibles
   Receivables and payables requiring imputed interest computations

TIMING OF REVENUE AND EXPENSES—ACCRUAL BASIS

The timing of revenue and expense recognition has been the subject of exam questions in recent years. These questions generally relate to insurance expense, warranty expense, royalty expense or revenue, service contract revenue, and similar areas. In most cases, the question will describe the company's recognition policy. Income and expense in these areas are recognized on a strict accrual basis and the cash exchanges generally should not impact the recognition of income or expense. It is helpful to understand the function of the related balance sheet account.

Example #1: Under Hart Company's accounting system, all insurance premiums paid are debited to prepaid insurance. For interim financial reports, Hart makes monthly estimated charges to insurance expense with credits to prepaid insurance. Additional information for the year ended December 31, 1999, is as follows:

Prepaid insurance at December 31, 1998	$210,000
Charges to insurance expense during 1999 (including a year-end adjustment of $35,000)	875,000
Unexpired insurance premiums at December 31, 1999	245,000

What was the total amount of insurance premiums paid by Hart during 1999?
   a. $910,000
   b. $875,000
   c. $840,000
   d. $665,000

Solution:

	Prepaid Insurance		
Balance 12/31/98	210,000		
		875,000	1999 expense charges
Premiums paid	?		
Balance 12/31/99	245,000		

In order to generate a balance of $245,000 in the "prepaid insurance" account, the premiums paid in 1999 must have been $910,000.

$$\$210{,}000 - 875{,}000 + X = \$245{,}000$$
$$X = \$910{,}000 \quad \text{Answer (a)}$$

Example #2: Lane Company acquires copyrights from authors, paying advance royalties in some cases, and in others, paying royalties within 30 days of year end. Lane reported royalty expense of $375,000 for the year ended December 31, 1999. The following data are included in Lane's December 31 balance sheets:

	1998	*1999*
Prepaid royalties	$60,000	$50,000
Royalties payable	75,000	90,000

During 1999 Lane made royalty payments totaling
   a. $350,000
   b. $370,000
   c. $380,000
   d. $400,000

Solution: The net effect of the balance sheet accounts is a net credit of $25,000 (asset decreased by $10,000 and liability increased by $15,000). Therefore, if the expense was $375,000 for the year and the impact on the prepaid and accrual accounts was a credit of $25,000, then the cash payment must have been $350,000—answer (a).

PERSONAL FINANCIAL STATEMENTS

- A statement of financial position is **required.**
- A statement of changes in net worth is **optional.**
- Income statements and statements of cash flows are not usually disclosed.
- In presenting Personal Financial Statement, assets and liabilities are reported at estimated current values.

Features of Personal Financial Statements

Title of Statement:	Statement of Financial Position
Categories:	Assets – listed in order of liquidity (not a current/non-current basis) Liabilities – listed in order of maturity (not a current/non-current basis) Estimated income taxes on the excess of the estimated current values of assets over their tax basis. Net Worth
Data Presentation:	Use estimated fair market value Cost may be shown in comparison if desired Use accrual basis of accounting

Other Points:

1. Income taxes should be accrued on unrealized asset appreciation.
2. Deferred income taxes should be included where appropriate to reflect timing differences between financial statement and income tax reporting.

BANK RECONCILIATIONS

Because of the differences in the timing of recording transactions, the cash balance per books and the balance per the bank statement will not agree. Further, it is probable that neither the bank statement nor the balance per books represents the correct balance of cash at the date of reconciliation. The basic form of the standard bank reconciliation is therefore an adjustment of both balances to the balances of cash on hand, as follows:

Balance per bank 12/31/X1		$65,000
Less: Outstanding checks		14,000
		$51,000
Add: Deposits in transit	$7,000	
Check erroneously charged	500	7,500
Correct bank balance 12/31/X1		$58,500
Balance per books 12/31/X1		$53,112
Less: Bank Service Charge	12	
NSF check of Vulcan Co.	600	612
		$52,500
Add: Bank loan of 12/16 unrecorded		6,000
Correct bank balance 12/31/X1		$58,500

Adjusting entries should be made for any items reconciling the book balance:

(1) Bank Service Charge, Expense	12	
Account Receivable, Vulcan Co.	600	
Cash		612
To record bank service charge and reinstate A/R		
(2) Cash	6,000	
Notes Payable		6,000
To record note payable		

RECOGNIZING REVENUE WHEN RIGHT OF RETURN EXISTS—SFAS #48

If an enterprise sells its product but gives the buyer rights to return the product, revenue from the sales transaction shall be recognized at time of sale only if all of the following conditions are met:

(a) The seller's price to the buyer is substantially fixed or determinable at the date of sale.
(b) The buyer has paid the seller, or the buyer is obligated to pay the seller and the obligation is not contingent on resale of the product.
(c) The buyer's obligation to the seller would not be changed in the event of theft or physical destruction or damage of the product.
(d) The buyer acquiring the product for resale has economic substance apart from that provided by the seller.
(e) The seller does not have significant obligations for the future performance to directly bring about resale of the product by the buyer.
(f) The amount of future returns can be reasonably estimated.

Sales revenue and cost of sales that are not recognized at time of sale because the foregoing conditions are not met shall be recognized either when the return privilege has substantially expired or if those conditions subsequently are met, whichever occurs first.

If sales revenue is recognized because the above conditions are met, any costs or losses that may be expected in connection with any returns shall be accrued in accordance with FASB Statement No. 5, Accounting for Contingencies. Sales revenue and cost of sales reported in the income statement shall be reduced to reflect estimated returns.

ACCOUNTING FOR FRANCHISE FEE REVENUE—SFAS #45

Franchise fee revenue from an individual franchise sale is ordinarily recognized when all material services or conditions relating to the sale have been substantially performed or satisfied by the franchisor. Installment or cost recovery accounting methods should be used to account for franchise fee revenue only in those exceptional cases when the franchise revenue is collectible over an extended period **and** no reasonable basis exists for estimating collectibility.

If an initial franchise fee is substantial in comparison to the continuing franchise fee and the services to be performed in the future, a portion of the initial fee should be deferred and amortized over the life of the franchise. The portion deferred should be an amount sufficient to cover the costs of (and reasonable profit on) the continuing services to be provided.

If the franchise agreement contains other options for which there is reasonable expectation for exercise, then that portion of the initial franchise fee attributable to such option should be deferred and, upon exercise, allocated to the asset acquired as a result of such exercise.

Franchisor Disclosures

(a) The nature of all significant franchising commitments and agreements.

(b) Revenue and related costs deferred (and the period due to be collected) for any fees accounted for using the installment or cost recovery method.

(c) Segregation of initial franchise fees from other franchise fee revenue.

(d) Revenue and costs related to franchisor-owned outlets shall be distinguished from revenue and costs related to franchised outlets when practicable. That may be done by segregating revenue and costs related to franchised outlets. If there are significant changes in franchisor-owned outlets or franchised outlets during the period, the number of (a) franchises sold, (b) franchises purchased during the period, (c) franchised outlets in operation and (d) franchisor-owned outlets in operation shall be disclosed.

Illustrative Problem

Southern Fried Shrimp sells franchises to independent operators throughout the Southeastern part of the United States. The contract with the franchisee includes the following provisions:

- The franchisee is charged an initial fee of $25,000. Of this amount $5,000 is payable when the agreement is signed and a $4,000 noninterest bearing note is payable at the end of each of the five subsequent years.
- All of the initial franchise fee collected by Southern Fried Shrimp is to be refunded and the remaining obligation canceled if, for any reason, the franchisee fails to open his franchise.
- In return for the initial franchise fee Southern Fried Shrimp agrees to (1) assist the franchisee in selecting the location for his business, (2) negotiate the lease for the land, (3) obtain financing and assist with building design, (4) supervise construction, (5) establish accounting and tax records and (6) provide expert advice over a five-year period relating to such matters as employee and management training, quality control and promotion.
- In addition to the initial franchise fee the franchisee is required to pay to Southern Fried Shrimp a monthly fee of 2% of sales for menu planning, recipe innovations and the privilege of purchasing ingredients from Southern Fried Shrimp at or below prevailing market prices.

Management of Southern Fried Shrimp estimates that the value of the services rendered to the franchisee at the time the contract is signed amounts to at least $5,000. All franchisees to date have opened their locations at the scheduled time and none has defaulted on any of the notes receivable.

The credit ratings of all franchisees would entitle them to borrow at the current interest rate of 10%. The present value of an ordinary annuity of five annual receipts of $4,000 each discounted at 10% is $15,163.

Required:

Given the nature of Southern Fried Shrimp's agreement with its franchisees, when should revenue be recognized? Discuss the question of revenue recognition for both the initial franchise fee and the additional monthly fee of 2% of sales and give illustrative entries for both types of revenue.

Illustrative Solution

Because the initial cash collection of $5,000 must be refunded if the franchisee fails to open, it is not fully earned until the franchisee begins operations so that Southern Fried Shrimp should record the initial franchise fee as follows:

	Debit	Credit
Cash	$ 5,000	
Notes Receivable	20,000	
Discount on Notes Receivable		$ 4,837
Unearned Initial Franchise Fee		20,163

When the franchisee begins operations, the $5,000 would be earned and the following entry should be made:

	Debit	Credit
Unearned Initial Franchise Fee	$ 5,000	
Earned Initial Franchise Fee		$ 5,000

After Southern Fried Shrimp has experienced the opening of a large number of franchises, it should be possible to develop probability measures so that the expected value of the retained initial franchise fee can be determined and recorded as earned at the time of receipt.

Interest at 10% should be accrued each year by a debit to Discount on Notes Receivable and a credit to Interest Revenue. Each year as the services are rendered an appropriate amount would be transferred from Unearned Initial Franchise Fee to Earned Initial Franchise Fee. Since these annual payments are not refundable, the Earned Initial Franchise Fee revenue might be recognized at the time the $4,000 is collected, but this may result in the mismatching of cost and revenue.

At the time that a franchise opens, only two steps remain before Southern Fried Shrimp will have fully earned the entire franchise fee. First, it must provide expert advice over the five-year period. Second, it must wait until the end of each of the next five years so that it may collect each of the $4,000 notes. Since collection has not been a problem, it could be maintained that a substantial portion of the $15,163, the present value of the notes, should be recognized as revenue when a franchisee begins operations. At some time in the future, after Southern Fried Shrimp has experienced a large number of franchises that have opened and operated for five years or more, it should be possible to develop probability measures so that the earned portion of the present value of the notes may be recognized as revenue at the time the franchisee begins operations.

The monthly fee of 2% of sales should be recorded as revenue at the end of each month. This fee is for current services rendered and should be recognized as the services are performed.

REAL ESTATE SALES—SFAS #66

Sales of Real Estate (other than retail land sales)

Profit is recognized in full when real estate is sold, provided (a) the profit is determinable, (collectibility of the sales price is reasonably assured or the amount that will not be collectible can be estimated), and (b) the seller is not obliged to perform significant activities after the sale to earn the profit. Unless both conditions exist, recognition of all or part of the profit shall be postponed.

Full profit on real estate sales transactions shall not be recognized until **all** of the following criteria are met:

(a) A sale is consummated (usually at closing).
(b) The buyer's initial and continuing investments are adequate to demonstrate a commitment to pay for the property.
(c) The seller's receivable is not subject to future subordination.
(d) The seller has transferred to the buyer the usual risks and rewards of ownership in a transaction that is in substance a sale and the seller does not have a substantial continuing involvement with the property.

ACCOUNTING FOR FUTURES CONTRACTS—SFAS #80

A gain or loss resulting from a change in the market value of a futures contract should be recognized in income except when such a contract is a hedge of specified assets, liabilities or firm commitments. Such an exception must result from a hedge against price or interest rate risk; terms of the transaction must be identified, and it should be probable that such a transaction will occur.

COMPREHENSIVE BASES OF ACCOUNTING OTHER THAN GAAP

The following accounting bases may be used to prepare financial statements in conformity with a comprehensive basis of accounting other than GAAP:

a. Basis of accounting used by an entity to file its income tax return.
b. Cash receipts and disbursements basis of accounting.
c. Cash basis.
d. Modifications of cash basis such as accruing income taxes and recording depreciation.
e. A definite set of criteria having substantial support that is applied to all material items. For example: constant dollar or current cost statements.

Chapter Ten
Revenue and Expense Recognition, Miscellaneous Items Questions

LONG-TERM CONTRACTS

1. The percentage-of-completion method of accounting for long-term construction-type contracts is preferable when
a. Estimates of costs to complete and extent of progress toward completion are reasonably dependable.
b. The collectibility of progress billings from the customer is reasonably assured.
c. A contractor is involved in numerous projects.
d. The contracts are of a relatively short duration.

2. How should the balances of progress billings and construction in progress be shown at reporting dates prior to the completion of a long-term contract?
a. Progress billings as deferred income, construction in progress as a deferred expense.
b. Progress billings as income, construction in progress as inventory.
c. Net, as a current asset if debit balance and current liability if credit balance.
d. Net, as income from construction if credit balance, and loss from construction if debit balance.

Items 3 and 4 are based on the following data relating to a construction job started by Syl Co. during 1993:

Total contract price	$100,000
Actual costs during 1993	20,000
Estimated remaining costs	40,000
Billed to customer during 1993	30,000
Received from customer during 1993	10,000

3. Under the completed contract method, how much should Syl recognize as gross profit for 1993?
a. $0
b. $4,000
c. $10,000
d. $12,000

4. Under the percentage-of-completion method, how much should Syl recognize as gross profit for 1993?
a. $0
b. $13,333
c. $26,667
d. $33,333

---

5. Hansen Construction, Inc., has consistently used the percentage-of-completion method of recognizing income. During 1997 Hansen started work on a $3,000,000 fixed-price construction contract. The accounting records disclosed the following data for the year ended December 31, 1997:

Costs incurred	$ 930,000
Estimated cost to complete	2,170,000
Progress billings	1,100,000
Collections	700,000

How much loss should Hansen have recognized in 1997?
a. $230,000
b. $100,000
c. $30,000
d. $0

6. During 1995, Mitchell Corp. started a construction job with a total contract price of $600,000. The job was completed on December 15, 1996. Additional data are as follows:

	1995	*1996*
Actual costs incurred	$225,000	$255,000
Estimated remaining costs	225,000	—
Billed to customer	240,000	360,000
Received from customer	200,000	400,000

Under the completed contract method, what amount should Mitchell recognize as gross profit for 1996?
a. $45,000
b. $72,000
c. $80,000
d. $120,000

7. Mill Construction Co. uses the percentage-of-completion method of accounting. During 1996, Mill contracted to build an apartment complex for Drew for $20,000,000. Mill estimated that total costs would amount to $16,000,000 over the period of construction. In connection with this contract, Mill incurred $2,000,000 of construction costs during 1996. Mill billed and collected $3,000,000 from Drew in 1996. What amount should Mill recognize as gross profit for 1996?

a. $250,000
b. $375,000
c. $500,000
d. $600,000

8. Cord Builders, Inc., has consistently used the percentage-of-completion method of accounting for construction-type contracts. During 1991 Cord started work on a $9,000,000 fixed-price construction contract that was completed in 1993. Cord's accounting records disclosed the following:

	December 31, 1991	1992
Cumulative contract costs incurred	$3,900,000	$6,300,000
Estimated total costs at completion	7,800,000	8,100,000

How much income would Cord have recognized on this contract for the year ended December 31, 1992?

a. $100,000
b. $300,000
c. $600,000
d. $700,000

Items 9 and 10 are based on the following data pertaining to Pell Co.'s construction jobs, which commenced during 1999:

	Project 1	*Project 2*
Contract price	$420,000	$300,000
Costs incurred during 1999	240,000	280,000
Estimated costs to complete	120,000	40,000
Billed to customers during 1999	150,000	270,000
Received from customers during 1999	90,000	250,000

9. If Pell used the completed contract method, what amount of gross profit (loss) would Pell report in its 1999 income statement?

a. $(20,000)
b. $0
c. $340,000
d. $420,000

10. If Pell used the percentage-of-completion method, what amount of gross profit (loss) would Pell report in its 1999 income statement?

a. $(20,000)
b. $20,000
c. $22,500
d. $40,000

THEORY REVIEW

11. A company uses the completed-contract method to account for a long-term construction contract. Revenue is recognized when recorded progress billings

	Are collected	*Exceed recorded costs*
a.	Yes	Yes
b.	No	No
c.	Yes	No
d.	No	Yes

12. A company used the percentage-of-completion method of accounting for a 5-year construction contract. Which of the following items will the company use to calculate the income recognized in the third year?

	Progress billings to date	*Income previously recognized*
a.	Yes	No
b.	No	Yes
c.	No	No
d.	Yes	Yes

13. The calculation of the income recognized in the third year of a five-year construction contract accounted for using the percentage-of-completion method includes the ratio of

a. Total costs incurred to date to total estimated costs.
b. Total costs incurred to date to total billings to date.
c. Costs incurred in year 3 to total estimated costs.
d. Costs incurred in year 3 to total billings to date.

14. Which of the following would be used in the calculation of the income recognized in the fourth and final year of a contract accounted for by the percentage-of-completion method?

	Actual total costs	*Income previously recognized*
a.	Yes	Yes
b.	Yes	No
c.	No	Yes
d.	No	No

INSTALLMENT SALES

15. The installment method of recognizing revenue
a. Should be used only in cases where there is no reasonable basis for estimating the collectibility of receivables.
b. Is not a generally accepted accounting principle under any circumstances.
c. Should be used for book purposes only if it is used for tax purposes.
d. Is an acceptable alternative accounting principle for a firm which makes installment sales.

16. Ryan, Inc., began operations on January 1, 1993, and appropriately uses the installment method of accounting. The following data are available for 1993:

Installment accounts receivable, 12/31/93	$ 600,000
Installment sales for 1993	1,050,000
Gross profit on sales	40%

Under the installment method, Ryan's deferred gross profit at December 31, 1993, would be
a. $360,000
b. $270,000
c. $240,000
d. $180,000

17. Karr Co. began operations on January 1, 1995, and appropriately uses the installment method of accounting. The following information pertains to Karr's operations for 1995:

Installment sales	$800,000
Cost of installment sales	480,000
General and administrative expenses	80,000
Collections on installment sales	300,000

The balance in the deferred gross profit account at December 31, 1995, should be
a. $120,000
b. $150,000
c. $200,000
d. $320,000

18. Green Company, which began operations on January 1, 1997, appropriately uses the installment method of accounting. The following information is available for 1997:

Gross profit on sales	40%
Deferred gross profit at 12/31/97	$240,000
Cash collected, including down payments	450,000

What is the total amount of Green's installment sales for 1997?
a. $600,000
b. $690,000
c. $850,000
d. $1,050,000

19. Hill Company began operations on January 1, 1994, and appropriately uses the installment method of accounting. Data available for 1994 are as follows:

Installment accounts receivable, 12/31/94	$500,000
Installment sales	900,000
Cost of goods sold, as percentage of sales	60%

Using the installment method, Hill's realized gross profit for 1994 would be
a. $360,000
b. $240,000
c. $200,000
d. $160,000

20. Dolce Co., which began operations on January 1, 1997, appropriately uses the installment method of accounting to record revenues. The following information is available for the years ended December 31, 1997 and 1998:

	1997	*1998*
Sales	$1,000,000	$2,000,000
Gross profit realized on sales made in:		
1997	150,000	90,000
1998	—	200,000
Gross profit percentages	30%	40%

What amount of installment accounts receivable should Dolce report in its December 31, 1998, balance sheet?

a. $1,225,000
b. $1,300,000
c. $1,700,000
d. $1,775,000

COST-RECOVERY METHOD

21. According to the cost-recovery method of accounting, gross profit on an installment sale is recognized in income

a. After cash collections equal to the cost of sales have been received.
b. In proportion to the cash collections.
c. On the date the final cash collection is received.
d. On the date of sale.

22. Several of Fox, Inc.'s customers are having cash flow problems. Information pertaining to these customers for the years ended March 31, 1998 and 1999, follows:

	3/31/98	*3/31/99*
Sales	$10,000	$15,000
Cost of sales	8,000	9,000
Cash collections		
on 1998 sales	7,000	3,000
on 1999 sales	--	12,000

If the cost-recovery method is used, what amount would Fox report as gross profit from sales to these customers for the year ended March 31, 1999?

a. $2,000
b. $3,000
c. $5,000
d. $15,000

ERRORS

23. Loeb Corp. frequently borrows from the bank in order to maintain sufficient operating cash. The following loans were at a 12% interest rate, with interest payable at maturity. Loeb repaid each loan on its scheduled maturity date.

Date of loan	*Amount*	*Maturity date*	*Term of loan*
11/1/96	$ 5,000	10/31/97	1 Year
2/1/97	15,000	7/31/97	6 Months
5/1/97	8,000	1/31/98	9 Months

Loeb records interest expense when the loans are repaid. As a result, interest expense of $1,500 was recorded in 1997. If no correction is made, by what amount would 1997 interest expense be understated?

a. $540
b. $620
c. $640
d. $720

Items 24, 25, 26 are based on the following information:

Declaration, Inc., is a calendar year corporation. Its financial statements for the years 1999 and 1998 contained errors as follows:

	1999	*1998*
Ending inventory	$1,000 understated	$3,000 overstated
Depreciation expense	$800 understated	$2,500 overstated

24. Assume that the proper correcting entries were made at December 31, 1998. By how much will 1999 income before income taxes be overstated or understated?

a. $200 understated.
b. $500 overstated.
c. $2,700 understated.
d. $3,200 understated.

25. Assume that no correcting entries were made at December 31, 1998. Ignoring income taxes, by how much will retained earnings at December 31, 1999, be overstated or understated?

a. $200 understated.
b. $500 overstated.
c. $2,700 understated.
d. $3,200 understated.

26. Assume that no correcting entries were made at December 31, 1998, or December 31, 1999, and that no additional errors occurred in 2000. Ignoring income taxes, by how much will working capital at December 31, 2000, be overstated or understated?

a. $0.
b. $1,000 overstated.
c. $1,000 understated.
d. $1,700 understated.

EMPLOYEE STOCK OPTIONS

27. On June 1, 1998, Oak Corp. granted stock options to certain key employees as additional compensation. The options were for 1,000 shares of Oak's $2 par value common stock at an option price of $15 per share. Market price of this stock on June 1, 1998, was $20 per share. The options were exercisable beginning January 2, 1999, and expire on December 31, 2000. On April 1, 1999, when Oak's stock was trading at $21 per share, all the options were exercised. What amount of pretax compensation should Oak report in 1998 in connection with the options?

a. $6,000
b. $5,000
c. $2,500
d. $2,000

28. On January 1, 1994, Doro Corp. granted an employee an option to purchase 3,000 shares of Doro's $5 par value common stock at $20 per share. The option became exercisable on December 31, 1995, after the employee completed two years of service. The option was exercised on January 10, 1996. The market prices of Doro's stock were as follows:

January 1, 1994	$30
December 31, 1995	50
January 10, 1996	45

For 1995, Doro should recognize compensation expense of

a. $45,000
b. $37,500
c. $15,000
d. $0

29. On January 2, 2000, Kine Co. granted Morgan, its president, compensatory stock options to buy 1,000 shares of Kine's $10 par common stock. The options call for a price of $20 per share and are exercisable for 3 years following the grant date. Morgan exercised the options on December 31, 2000. The market price of the stock was $50 on January 2, 2000, and $70 on December 31, 2000. By what net amount should stockholders' equity increase as a result of the grant and exercise of the options?

a. $20,000.
b. $30,000.
c. $50,000.
d. $70,000.

30. When a balance-sheet account, which had no previous balance, is debited in connection with a compensatory stock option plan because the services relate to a future period, the balance of the account should be reported as a

a. Deferred charge.
b. Prepaid expense.
c. Reduction of stockholders' equity.
d. Deferred credit.

31. In a compensatory stock option plan for which the grant, measurement, and exercise date are all different, the stock options outstanding account should be reduced at the

a. Date of grant.
b. Measurement date.
c. Beginning of the service period.
d. Exercise date.

STOCK APPRECIATION RIGHTS

32. On January 2, 1996, Morey Corp. granted Dean, its president, 20,000 stock appreciation rights for past services. Those rights are exercisable immediately and expire on January 1, 1999. On exercise, Dean is entitled to receive cash for the excess of the stock's market price on the exercise date over the market price on the grant date. Dean did not exercise any of the rights during 1996. The market price of Morey's stock was $30 on January 2, 1996, and $45 on December 31, 1996. As a result of the stock appreciation rights, Morey should recognize compensation expense for 1996 of

a. $0
b. $100,000
c. $300,000
d. $600,000

33. Wolf Co.'s grant of 30,000 stock appreciation rights enables key employees to receive cash equal to the difference between $20 and the market price of the stock on the date each right is exercised. The service period is 1996 through 1998, and the rights are exercisable in 1999 and 2000. The market price of the stock was $25 and $28 at December 31, 1996 and 1997, respectively. What amount should Wolf report as the liability under the stock appreciation rights plan in its December 31, 1997, balance sheet?

a. $0
b. $130,000
c. $160,000
d. $240,000

EMPLOYEE STOCK PURCHASE PLAN

34. Wall Corp.'s employee stock purchase plan specifies the following:

- For every $1 withheld from employees' wages for the purchase of Wall's common stock, Wall contributes $2.
- The stock is purchased from Wall's treasury stock at market price on the date of purchase.

The following information pertains to the plan's 1997 transactions:

• Employee withholdings for the year	$ 350,000
• Market value of 150,000 shares issued	1,050,000
• Carrying amount of treasury stock issued (cost)	900,000

Before payroll taxes, what amount should Wall recognize as expense in 1997 for the stock purchase plan?

a. $1,050,000
b. $900,000
c. $700,000
d. $550,000

ESOPS

35. On January 1, 1995, Heath Corp. established an employee stock ownership plan (ESOP). Selected transactions relating to the ESOP during 1995 were as follows:

- On April 1, 1995, Heath contributed $45,000 cash and 3,000 shares of its $10 par value common stock to the ESOP. On this date, the market price of the stock was $18 a share.
- On October 1, 1995, the ESOP borrowed $100,000 from Union National Bank and acquired 6,000 shares of Heath's common stock in the open market at $17 a share. The note is for one year, bears interest at 10%, and is guaranteed by Heath.
- On December 15, 1995, the ESOP distributed 8,000 shares of Heath's common stock to employees of Heath in accordance with the plan formula. On this date, the market price of the stock was $20 a share.

In its 1995 income statement, what amount should Heath report as compensation expense relating to the ESOP?

a. $99,000
b. $155,000
c. $199,000
d. $259,000

WHAT IS CASH?

36. On December 31, 1998, West Company had the following cash balances:

Cash in banks	$1,800,000
Petty cash funds (all funds were reimbursed on 12/31/98)	50,000

Cash in banks includes $600,000 of compensating balances against short-term borrowing arrangements at December 31, 1998. The compensating balances are not legally restricted as to withdrawal by West. In the current assets section of West's December 31, 1998, balance sheet, what total amount should be reported as cash?

a. $1,200,000
b. $1,250,000
c. $1,800,000
d. $1,850,000

BANK RECONCILIATIONS

37. Poe, Inc., had the following bank reconciliation at March 31, 1997:

Balance per bank statement, 3/31/97	$46,500
Add deposit in transit	10,300
	56,800
Less outstanding checks	12,600
Balance per books, 3/31/97	$44,200

Data per bank for the month of April 1997 follow:

Deposits	$58,400
Disbursements	49,700

All reconciling items at March 31, 1997, cleared the bank in April. Outstanding checks at April 30, 1997, totaled $7,000. There were no deposits in transit at April 30, 1997. What is the cash balance per books at April 30, 1997?

a. $48,200
b. $52,900
c. $55,200
d. $58,500

FRANCHISES

38. On December 31, 1997, Rice, Inc., authorized Graf to operate as a franchisee for an initial franchise fee of $150,000. Of this amount, $60,000 was received upon signing the agreement and the balance, represented by a note, is due in three annual payments of $30,000 each beginning December 31, 1998. The present value on December 31, 1997, of the three annual payments appropriately discounted is $72,000. According to the agreement, the nonrefundable down payment represents a fair measure of the services already performed by Rice; however, substantial future services are required of Rice. Collectibility of the note is reasonably certain. In Rice's December 31, 1997, balance sheet, unearned franchise fees from Graf's franchise should be reported as

a. $132,000
b. $100,000
c. $90,000
d. $72,000

39. On January 2, 1995, Rex Enterprises, Inc., authorized Adam Company to operate as a franchise over a 20-year period for an initial franchise fee of $60,000 received on signing the agreement. Adam started operations on June 30, 1995, by which date Rex had performed all of the required initial services. In its income statement for the six months ended June 30, 1995, what amount should Rex report as revenue from franchise fees in connection with Adam's franchise?

a. $0
b. $1,500
c. $30,000
d. $60,000

40. On July 1, 1993, Hart signed an agreement to operate as a franchisee of Ace Printers for an initial franchise fee of $120,000. The same date, Hart paid $40,000 and agreed to pay the balance in four equal annual payments of $20,000 beginning July 1, 1994. The down payment is not refundable and no future services are required of the franchiser. Hart can borrow at 14% for a loan of this type. Present and future value factors are as follows:

Present value of 1 at 14% for 4 periods	0.59
Future amount of 1 at 14% for 4 periods	1.69
Present value of an ordinary annuity of 1 at 14% for 4 periods	2.91

Hart should record the acquisition cost of the franchise on July 1, 1993, at

a. $135,200
b. $120,000
c. $98,200
d. $87,200

TIMING OF REVENUE/EXPENSE

41. On October 1, 1998, Acme Fuel Co. sold 100,000 gallons of heating oil to Karn Co. at $3 per gallon. Fifty thousand gallons were delivered on December 15, 1998, and the remaining 50,000 gallons were delivered on January 15, 1999. Payment terms were: 50% due on October 1, 1998, 25% due on first delivery, and the remaining 25% due on second delivery. What amount of revenue should Acme recognize from this sale during 1998?

a. $75,000
b. $150,000
c. $225,000
d. $300,000

42. In 1997, Super Comics Corp. sold a comic strip to Fantasy, Inc. and will receive royalties of 20% of future revenues associated with the comic strip. At December 31, 1998, Super reported royalties receivable of $75,000 from Fantasy. During 1999, Super received royalty payments of $200,000. Fantasy reported revenues of $1,500,000 in 1999 from the comic strip. In its 1999 income statement, what amount should Super report as royalty revenue?

a. $125,000
b. $175,000
c. $200,000
d. $300,000

43. Beal Company sells contracts agreeing to service equipment for a three-year period. Information for the year ended December 31, 1992, is as follows:

Cash receipts from service contracts sold	$960,000
Service contract revenue recognized	780,000
Unearned service contract revenue, 1/1/92	570,000

In its December 31, 1992, balance sheet, what amount should Beal report as unearned service contract revenue?

a. $390,000
b. $510,000
c. $640,000
d. $750,000

44. On February 12, 1999, VIP Publishing, Inc. purchased the copyright to a book for $15,000 and agreed to pay royalties equal to 10% of book sales, with a guaranteed minimum royalty of $60,000. VIP had book sales of $800,000 in 1999. In its 1999 income statement, what amount should VIP report as royalty expense?

a. $60,000
b. $75,000
c. $80,000
d. $95,000

45. A state requires quarterly sales tax returns to be filed with the sales tax bureau by the 20th day following the end of the calendar quarter. However, the state further requires that sales taxes collected be remitted to the sales tax bureau by the 20th day of the month following any month such collections exceed $500. These payments can be taken as credits on the quarterly sales tax return.

Taft Corp. operates a retail hardware store. All items are sold subject to a 6% state sales tax, which Taft collects and records as sales revenue. The sales taxes paid by Taft are charged against sales revenue. Taft pays the sales taxes when they are due.

Following is a monthly summary appearing in Taft's first quarter 1996 sales revenue account:

	Debit	*Credit*
January	$ —	$10,600
February	600	7,420
March	—	9,540
	$600	$27,560

In its financial statements for the quarter ended March 31, 1996, Taft's sales revenue and sales taxes payable would be

	Sales revenue	*Sales taxes payable*
a.	$27,560	$1,560
b.	$26,960	$600
c.	$26,000	$1,560
d.	$26,000	$960

46. At December 31, 1997, Ashe Co. had a $990,000 balance in its advertising expense account before any year-end adjustments relating to the following:

- Radio advertising spots broadcast during December 1997 were billed to Ashe on January 4, 1998. The invoice cost of $50,000 was paid on January 15, 1998.
- Included in the $990,000 is $60,000 for newspaper advertising for a January 1998 sales promotional campaign.

Ashe's advertising expense for the year ended December 31, 1997, should be

a. $930,000
b. $980,000
c. $1,000,000
d. $1,040,000

CASH VS. ACCRUAL

47. On April 1, 2000, Ivy began operating a service proprietorship with an initial cash investment of $1,000. The proprietorship provided $3,200 of services in April and received full payment in May. The proprietorship incurred expenses of $1,500 in April which were paid in June. During May, Ivy drew $500 against her capital account.

What was the proprietorship's income for the two months ended May 31, 2000, under the following methods of accounting?

	Cash-basis	*Accrual-basis*
a.	$1,200	$1,200
b.	$1,700	$1,700
c.	$2,700	$1,200
d.	$3,200	$1,700

48. Reid Partners, Ltd., which began operations on January 1, 1997, has elected to use cash-basis accounting for tax purposes and accrual-basis accounting for its financial statements. Reid reported sales of $175,000 and $80,000 in its tax returns for the years ended December 31, 1998 and 1997, respectively. Reid reported accounts receivable of $30,000 and $50,000 in its balance sheets as of December 31, 1998 and 1997, respectively. What amount should Reid report as sales in its income statement for the year ended December 31, 1998?

a. $145,000
b. $155,000
c. $195,000
d. $205,000

49. Class Corp. maintains its accounting records on the cash basis but restates its financial statements to the accrual method of accounting. Class had $60,000 in cash-basis pretax income for 1999. The following information pertains to Class's operations for the years ended December 31, 1999 and 1998:

	1999	*1998*
Accounts receivable	$40,000	$20,000
Accounts payable	15,000	30,000

Under the accrual method, what amount of income before taxes should Class report in its December 31, 1999 income statement?

a. $25,000
b. $55,000
c. $65,000
d. $95,000

OTHER BASES OF ACCOUNTING

50. Which of the following accounting bases may be used to prepare financial statements in conformity with a comprehensive basis of accounting other than generally accepted accounting principles?

I. Basis of accounting used by an entity to file its income tax return.
II. Cash receipts and disbursements basis of accounting.

a. I only.
b. II only.
c. Both I and II.
d. Neither I nor II.

PERSONAL FINANCIAL STATEMENTS

51. Personal financial statements usually consist of

a. A statement of net worth and a statement of changes in net worth.
b. A statement of net worth, an income statement, and a statement of changes in net worth.
c. A statement of financial condition and a statement of changes in net worth.
d. A statement of financial condition, a statement of changes in net worth, and a statement of cash flows.

52. Personal financial statements should report assets and liabilities at

a. Estimated current values at the date of the financial statements and, as additional information, at historical cost.
b. Estimated current values at the date of the financial statements.
c. Historical cost and, as additional information, at estimated current values at the date of the financial statements.
d. Historical cost.

53. A business interest that constitutes a large part of an individual's total assets should be presented in a personal statement of financial condition as

a. A single amount equal to the proprietorship equity.
b. A single amount equal to the estimated current value of the business interest.
c. A separate listing of the individual assets and liabilities, at cost.
d. Separate line items of both total assets and total liabilities, at cost.

54. The following information pertains to an insurance policy that Barton owns on his life:

Face amount	$100,000
Accumulated premiums paid up to December 31, 1998	8,000
Cash value at December 31, 1998	12,000
Policy loan	3,000

In Barton's personal statement of financial condition at December 31, 1998, what amount should be reported for the investment in life insurance?

a. $97,000
b. $12,000
c. $9,000
d. $8,000

55. In personal financial statements, how should estimated income taxes on the excess of the estimated current values of assets over their tax bases be reported in the statement of financial condition?

a. As liabilities.
b. As deductions from the related assets.
c. Between liabilities and net worth.
d. In a footnote disclosure only.

56. For the purpose of estimating income taxes to be reported in personal financial statements, assets and liabilities measured at their tax bases should be compared to assets and liabilities measured at their

	Assets	*Liabilities*
a.	Estimated current value	Estimated current amount
b.	Historical cost	Historical cost
c.	Estimated current value	Historical cost
d.	Historical cost	Estimated current amount

57. Shea, a calendar-year taxpayer, is preparing a personal statement of financial condition as of April 30, 1999. Shea's 1998 income tax liability was paid in full on April 15, 1999. Shea's tax on income earned from January through April 1999 is estimated at $30,000. In addition, $25,000 is estimated for income tax on the differences between the estimated current values of Shea's assets and the current amounts of liabilities and their tax bases at April 30, 1999. No withholdings or payments have been made towards the 1999 income tax liability. In Shea's statement of financial condition at April 30, 1999, what is the total of the amount or amounts that should be reported for income taxes?

a. $0
b. $25,000
c. $30,000
d. $55,000

58. Dale Hall's holdings at December 31, 1996, included the following:

- 5,000 shares of Arno Corp. common stock purchased in 1991 for $85,000. The market value of the stock was $120,000 at December 31, 1996.
- A life insurance policy with a cash value of $50,000 at December 31, 1996.

120
50

In Hall's December 31, 1996, personal statement of financial condition, the above items should be reported at

a. $170,000
b. $135,000
c. $120,000
d. $85,000

REVIEW QUESTIONS

59. Wren Co. sells equipment on installment contracts. Which of the following statements best justifies Wren's use of the cost recovery method of revenue recognition to account for these installment sales?

a. The sales contract provides that title to the equipment only passes to the purchaser when all payments have been made.
b. No cash payments are due until one year from the date of sale.
c. Sales are subject to a high rate of return.
d. There is **no** reasonable basis for estimating collectibility.

60. Gow Constructors, Inc., has consistently used the percentage-of-completion method of recognizing income. In 1996, Gow started work on an $18,000,000 construction contract that was completed in 1997. The following information was taken from Gow's 1996 accounting records:

Progress billings	$6,600,000
Costs incurred	5,400,000
Collections	4,200,000
Estimated costs to complete	10,800,000

What amount of gross profit should Gow have recognized in 1996 on this contract?

a. $1,400,000
b. $1,200,000
c. $900,000
d. $600,000

61. Cash collection is a critical event for income recognition in the

	Cost-recovery method	*Installment method*
a.	No	No
b.	Yes	Yes
c.	No	Yes
d.	Yes	No

62. Compared to the accrual basis of accounting, the cash basis of accounting understates income by the net decrease during the accounting period of

	Accounts receivable	*Accrued expenses*
a.	Yes	Yes
b.	Yes	No
c.	No	No
d.	No	Yes

63. At the end of 1996, Ritzcar Co. failed to accrue sale commissions earned during 1996 but paid in 1997. The error was not repeated in 1997. What was the effect of this error on 1996 ending working capital and on the 1997 ending retained earnings balance?

	1996 ending working capital	*1997 ending retained earnings*
a.	Overstated	Overstated
b.	No effect	Overstated
c.	No effect	No effect
d.	Overstated	No effect

64. On July 1, 2000, Ran County issued realty tax assessments for its fiscal year ended June 30, 2001. On September 1, 2000, Day Co. purchased a warehouse in Ran County. The purchase price was reduced by a credit for accrued realty taxes. Day did not record the entire year's real estate tax obligation, but instead records tax expenses at the end of each month by adjusting prepaid real estate taxes or real estate taxes payable, as appropriate. On November 1, 2000, Day paid the first of two equal installments of $12,000 for realty taxes. What amount of this payment should Day record as a debit to real estate taxes payable?

a. $ 4,000
b. $ 8,000
c. $10,000
d. $12,000

65. For $50 a month, Rawl Co. visits its customers' premises and performs insect control services. If customers experience problems between regularly scheduled visits, Rawl makes service calls at no additional charge. Instead of paying monthly, customers may pay an annual fee of $540 in advance. For a customer who pays the annual fee in advance, Rawl should recognize the related revenue

a. When the cash is collected.
b. At the end of the fiscal year.
c. At the end of the contract year after all of the services have been performed.
d. Evenly over the contract year as the services are performed.

66. Black Co. requires advance payments with special orders for machinery constructed to customer specifications. These advances are nonrefundable. Information for 2000 is as follows:

Customer advances-balance 12/31/99		$ 118,000
Advances received with orders in 2000		184,000
Advances applied to orders shipped in 2000	164,000	
Advances applicable to orders canceled in 2000		50,000

In Black's December 31, 2000, balance sheet, what amount should be reported as a current liability for advances from customer?

a. $0
b. $ 88,000
c. $138,000
d. $148,000

67. Ward, a consultant, keeps her accounting records on a cash basis. During 2001, Ward collected $200,000 in fees from clients. At December 31, 2000, Ward had accounts receivable of $40,000. At December 31, 2001, Ward had accounts receivable of $60,000, and unearned fees of $5,000. On an accrual basis, what was Ward's service revenue for 2001?

a. $175,000
b. $180,000
c. $215,000
d. $225,000

68. Which of the following is used in calculating the income recognized in the fourth and final year of a contract accounted for by the percentage-of-completion method?

	Actual total costs	*Income previously recognized*
a.	Yes	Yes
b.	Yes	No
c.	No	Yes
d.	No	No

69. According to the installment method of accounting, gross profit on an installment sale is recognized in income

a. On the date of sale.
b. On the date the final cash collection is received.
c. In proportion to the cash collection.
d. After cash collections equal to the cost of sales have been received.

70. Under a royalty agreement with another company, Wand Co. will pay royalties for the assignment of a patent for three years. The royalties paid should be reported as expense

a. In the period paid.
b. In the period incurred.
c. At the date the royalty agreement began.
d. At the date the royalty agreement expired.

71. Leslie Shaw's personal statement of financial condition at December 31, 1993, shows net worth of $400,000 before consideration of employee stock options owned on that date. Information relating to the stock options is as follows:

- Options to purchase 10,000 shares of Korn Corporation stock.
- Option exercise price is $10 a share.
- Options expire on June 30, 1993.
- Market price of the stock is $25 a share on December 31, 1993.
- Assume that exercise of the options in 1994 would result in ordinary income taxable at 35%.

After giving effect to the stock options, Shaw's net worth at December 31, 1993, would be

a. $497,500
b. $550,000
c. $562,500
d. $650,000

72. Each of Potter Pie Co.'s 21 new franchisees contracted to pay an initial franchise fee of $30,000. By December 31, 1998, each franchisee had paid a non-refundable $10,000 fee and signed a note to pay $10,000 principal plus the market rate of interest on December 31, 1999, and December 31, 2000. Experience indicates that one franchisee will default on the additional payments. Services for the initial fee will be performed in 1999. What amount of net unearned franchise fees would Potter report at December 31, 1998?

a. $400,000
b. $600,000
c. $610,000
d. $630,000

73. A company uses the completed-contract method to account for a long-term construction contract. Revenue is recognized when progress billings are

	Recorded	*Collected*
a.	No	Yes
b.	Yes	Yes
c.	Yes	No
d.	No	No

74. On January 1, 1998, Sip Co. signed a 5-year contract enabling it to use a patented manufacturing process beginning in 1998. A royalty is payable for each product produced, subject to a minimum annual fee. Any royalties in excess of the minimum will be paid annually. On the contract date, Sip prepaid a sum equal to two years' minimum annual fees. In 1998, only minimum fees were incurred. The royalty prepayment should be reported in Sip's December 31, 1998, financial statements as

a. An expense only.
b. A current asset and an expense.
c. A current asset and noncurrent asset.
d. A noncurrent asset.

75. Bren Co.'s beginning inventory at January 1, 2000, was understated by $26,000, and its ending inventory was overstated by $52,000. As a result, Bren's cost of goods sold for 2000 was

a. Understated by $26,000.
b. Overstated by $26,000.
c. Understated by $78,000.
d. Overstated by $78,000.

Items 76 and 77 are based on the following:
Baker Co. is a real estate developer that began operations on January 2, 1997. Baker appropriately uses the installment method of revenue recognition. Baker's sales are made on the basis of a 10% downpayment, with the balance payable over 30 years. Baker's gross profit percentage is 40%. Relevant information for Baker's first two years of operations is as follows:

	1998	*1997*
Sales	$16,000,000	$14,000,000
Cash collections	2,020,000	1,400,000

76. At December 31, 1997, Baker's deferred gross profit was
a. $5,040,000
b. $5,600,000
c. $8,400,000
d. $12,600,000

77. Baker's realized gross profit for 1998 was
a. $6,400,000
b. $2,020,000
c. $1,212,000
d. $808,000

---

78. Since there is no reasonable basis for estimating the degree of collectibility, Astor Co. uses the installment method of revenue recognition for the following sales:

	2000	*1999*
Sales	$900,000	$600,000
Collections from:		
1999 sales	100,000	200,000
2000 sales	300,000	----
Accounts written off:		
1999 sales	150,000	50,000
2000 sales	50,000	----
Gross profit percentage	40%	30%

What amount should Astor report as deferred gross profit in its December 31, 2000, balance sheet for the 1999 and 2000 sales?
a. $150,000.
b. $160,000.
c. $225,000.
d. $250,000.

79. Clint owns 50% of Vohl Corp.'s common stock. Clint paid $20,000 for this stock in 1993. At December 31, 1998, Clint's 50% stock ownership in Vohl had a fair value of $180,000. Vohl's cumulative net income and cash dividends declared for the five years ended December 31, 1998, were $300,000 and $40,000, respectively. In Clint's personal statement of financial condition at December 31, 1998, what amount should be shown as the investment in Vohl?
a. $20,000
b. $150,000
c. $170,000
d. $180,000

80. On January 1, 1996, Pall Corp. granted stock options to key employees for the purchase of 40,000 shares of the company's common stock at $25 per share. The options are intended to compensate employees for the next two years. The options are exercisable within a four-year period beginning January 1, 1998, by the grantees still in the employ of the company. The market price of Pall's common stock was $33 per share at the date of grant. No stock options were terminated during the year. What amount should Pall charge to compensation expense for the year ended December 31, 1996?
a. $320,000
b. $160,000
c. $80,000
d. $0

81. In preparing its bank reconciliation at December 31, 1994, Case Company has available the following data:

Balance per bank statement, 12/31/94	$38,075
Deposit in transit, 12/31/94	5,200
Outstanding checks, 12/31/94	6,750
Amount erroneously credited by bank to Case's account, 12/28/94	400
Bank service charges for December	75

Case's adjusted cash in bank balance at December 31, 1994, is
a. $36,525
b. $36,450
c. $36,125
d. $36,050

82. On January 2, 1999, Yardley Co. sold a plant to Ivory, Inc. for $1,500,000. On that date, the plant's carrying cost was $1,000,000. Ivory gave Yardley $300,000 cash and a $1,200,000 note, payable in 4 annual installments of $300,000 plus 12% interest. Ivory made the first principal and interest payment of $444,000 on December 31, 1999. Yardley uses the installment method of revenue recognition. In its 1999 income statement, what amount of realized gross profit should Yardley report?

a. $344,000
b. $200,000
c. $148,000
d. $100,000

83. On April 30, 1997, White sold land with a book value of $600,000 to Smith for its fair value of $800,000. Smith gave White a 12%, $800,000 note secured only by the land. At the date of sale, Smith was in a very poor financial position and its continuation as a going concern was very questionable. White should

a. Use the cost recovery method of accounting.
b. Record the note at its discounted value.
c. Record a $200,000 gain on the sale of the land.
d. Fully reserve the note.

84. Jen has been employed by Komp, Inc. since February 1, 1996. Jen is covered by Komp's Section 401(k) deferred compensation plan. Jen's contributions have been 10% of salaries. Komp has made matching contributions of 5%. Jen's salaries were $21,000 in 1996, $23,000 in 1997, and $26,000 in 1998. Employer contributions vest after an employee completes three years of continuous employment. The balance in Jen's 401(k) account was $11,900 at December 31, 1998, which included earnings of $1,200 on Jen's contributions. What amount should be reported for Jen's vested interest in the 401(k) plan in Jen's December 31, 1998, personal statement of financial condition?

a. $11,900
b. $8,200
c. $7,000
d. $1,200

85. Zach Corp. pays commissions to its sales staff at the rate of 3% of net sales. Sales staff are not paid salaries but are given monthly advances of $15,000. Advances are charged to commission expense, and reconciliations against commissions are prepared quarterly. Net sales for the year ended March 31, 1999, were $15,000,000. The unadjusted balance in the commissions expense account on March 31, 1999, was $400,000. March advances were paid on April 3, 1999. In its income statement for the year ended March 31, 1999, what amount should Zach report as commission expense?

a. $465,000
b. $450,000
c. $415,000
d. $400,000

86. The estimated current values of Lane's personal assets at December 31, 1997, totaled $1,000,000, with tax bases aggregating $600,000. Included in these assets was a vested interest in a deferred profit-sharing plan with a current value of $80,000 and a tax basis of $70,000. The estimated current amounts of Lane's personal liabilities equaled their tax bases at December 31, 1997. Lane's 1997 effective income tax rate was 30%. In Lane's personal statement of financial condition at December 31, 1997, what amount should be provided for estimated income taxes relating to the excess of current values over tax bases?

a. $120,000
b. $117,000
c. $3,000
d. $0

87. Luge Co., which began operations on January 2, 1999, appropriately uses the installment sales method of accounting. The following information is available for 1999:

Installment accounts receivable, December 31, 1999	$800,000
Deferred gross profit, December 31, 1992 (before recognition of realized gross profit for 1999)	560,000
Gross profit on sales	40%

For the year ended December 31, 1999, cash collections and realized gross profit on sales should be

	Cash collections	*Realized gross profit*
a.	$400,000	$320,000
b.	$400,000	$240,000
c.	$600,000	$320,000
d.	$600,000	$240,000

88. A company uses the completed-contract method to account for a four-year construction contract which is presently in its third year. Progress billings were recorded and collected in the third year. Based on events occurring in the third year, there is now an anticipated loss on the contract. When would the effect of each of the following be reported in the company's income statement?

	Third year progress billings	*Anticipated loss*
a.	Not third year	Third year
b.	Not third year	Fourth year
c.	Third year	Third year
d.	Third year	Fourth year

89. Pie Co. uses the installment sales method to recognize revenue. Customers pay the installment notes in 24 equal monthly amounts, which include 12% interest. What is an installment note's receivable balance six months after the sale?

a. 75% of the original sales price.
b. Less than 75% of the original sales price.
c. The present value of the remaining monthly payments discounted at 12%.
d. Less than the present value of the remaining monthly payments discounted at 12%.

90. Moran is preparing a personal statement of financial condition as of April 30, 1998. Included in Moran's assets are the following:

- 50% of the voting stock of Crow Corp. A stockholders' agreement restricts the sale of the stock and, under certain circumstances, requires Crow to repurchase the stock based on carrying amounts of net assets plus an agreed amount for goodwill. At April 30, 1998, the buyout value of this stock is $337,500. Moran's tax basis for the stock is $215,000.
- Jewelry with a fair value aggregating $35,000 based on an independent appraisal on April 30, 1998, for insurance purposes. This jewelry was acquired by purchase and gift over a 10-year period and has a total tax basis of $20,000.

At what total amount should the Crow stock and jewelry be reported in Moran's April 30, 1998, personal statement of financial condition?

a. $372,500
b. $357,500
c. $250,000
d. $235,000

91. Wren Corp.'s trademark was licensed to Mont Co. for royalties of 15% of sales of the trademarked items. Royalties are payable semi-annually on March 15 for sales in July through December of the prior year, and on September 15 for sales in January through June of the same year. Wren received the following royalties from Mont:

	March 15	*September 15*
1999	$10,000	$15,000
2000	12,000	17,000

Mont estimated that sales of the trademarked items would total $60,000 for July through December 1993.

In Wren's 2000 income statement, the royalty revenue should be

a. $26,000
b. $29,000
c. $38,000
d. $41,000

92. Adam Co. reported sales revenue of $2,300,000 in its income statement for the year ended December 31, 1996. Additional information was as follows:

	12/31/95	*12/31/96*
Accounts receivable	$500,000	$650,000
Allowance for uncollectible accounts	(30,000)	(55,000)

Uncollectible accounts totaling $10,000 were written off during 1996. Under the **cash basis of accounting,** Adam would have reported 1996 sales of

a. $2,140,000
b. $2,150,000
c. $2,175,000
d. $2,450,000

93. State Co. recognizes construction revenue and expenses using the percentage-of-completion method. During 1996, a single long-term project was begun, which continued through 1997. Information on the project follows:

	1996	*1997*
Accounts receivable from construction contract	$100,000	$300,000
Construction expenses	105,000	192,000
Construction in progress	122,000	364,000
Partial billings on contract	100,000	420,000

Profit recognized from the long-term construction contract in 1997 should be

a. $50,000
b. $108,000
c. $128,000
d. $228,000

94. The bookkeeper of Latsch Company, which has an accounting year ending December 31, made the following errors:

- A $1,000 collection from a customer was received on December 29, 1999, but not recorded until the date of its deposit in the bank, January 4, 2000.
- A supplier's $1,600 invoice for inventory items received in December 1999 was not recorded until January 1993. (Inventories at December 31, 1999 and 2000, were stated correctly, based on physical count.)
- Depreciation for 1999 was understated by $900.
- In September 1999, a $200 invoice for office supplies was charged to the Utilities Expense account. Office supplies are expensed as purchased.
- December 31, 1999, sales on account of $3,000 were recorded in January 2000.

Assume that no other errors have occurred and that no correcting entries have been made. **Ignore income taxes.**

Net income for 1999 was

a. Understated by $500.
b. Understated by $2,100.
c. Overstated by $2,500.
d. Neither understated nor overstated.

95. Assume the same facts as above. Working capital at December 31, 1999, was

a. Understated by $3,000.
b. Understated by $500.
c. Understated by $1,400.
d. Neither understated or overstated.

96. Assume the same facts as above. Total assets at December 31, 2000, were

a. Overstated by $2,500.
b. Overstated by $2,100.
c. Understated by $2,500.
d. None of the above.

RECENTLY DISCLOSED MULTIPLE CHOICE QUESTIONS

97. Troop Co. frequently borrows from the bank to maintain sufficient operating cash. The following loans were at a 12% interest rate, with interest payable at maturity. Troop repaid each loan on its scheduled maturity date.

Date of Loan	*Amount*	*Maturity Date*	*Term of Loan*
11/1/95	$10,000	10/31/96	1 year
2/1/96	30,000	7/31/96	6 months
5/1/96	16,000	1/31/97	9 months

Troop records interest expense when the loans are repaid. Accordingly, interest expense of $3,000 was recorded in 1996. If **no** correction is made, by what amount would 1996 interest expense be understated?

a. $1,080
b. $1,240
c. $1,280
d. $1,440

M98

98. Which statements are usually included in a set of personal financial statements?

a. A statement of net worth and an income statement.
b. A statement of financial condition and a statement of changes in net worth.
c. A statement of net worth, an income statement, and a statement of cash flows.
d. A statement of financial condition, a statement of changes in net worth, and a statement of cash flows.

M98

99. At May 31, 1997, Quay owned a $10,000 whole-life insurance policy with a cash-surrender value of $4,500, net of loans of $2,500. In Quay's May 31, 1997 personal statement of financial condition, what amount should be reported as investment in life insurance?

a. $4,500
b. $7,000
c. $7,500
d. $10,000

N98

100. Which of the following is **not** a comprehensive basis of accounting other than generally accepted accounting principles?

a. Cash receipts and disbursements basis of accounting.
b. Basis of accounting used by an entity to file its income tax return.
c. Basis of accounting used by an entity to comply with the financial reporting requirements of a government regulatory agency.
d. Basis of accounting used by an entity to comply with the financial reporting requirements of a lending institution.

N98

101. Bear Co., which began operations on January 2, 1997, appropriately uses the installment sales method of accounting. The following information is available for 1997:

Installment sales	$1,400,000
Realized gross profit on installment sales	240,000
Gross profit percentage on sales	40%

For the year ended December 31, 1997, what amounts should Bear report as accounts receivable and deferred gross profit?

	Accounts receivable	*Deferred gross profits*
a.	$600,000	$320,000
b.	$600,000	$360,000
c.	$800,000	$320,000
d.	$800,000	$560,000

1999

102. Income tax-basis financial statements differ from those prepared under GAAP in that income tax-basis financial statements

a. Do **not** include nontaxable revenues and nondeductible expenses in determining income.
b. Include detailed information about current and deferred income tax liabilities.
c. Contain **no** disclosures about capital and operating lease transactions.
d. Recognize certain revenues and expenses in different reporting periods.

Chapter Ten
Revenue and Expense Recognition, Miscellaneous Items Problems

NUMBER 1

London, Inc. began operation of its construction division on October 1, 1998, and entered into contracts for two separate projects. The Beta project contract price was $600,000 and provided for penalties of $10,000 per week for late completion. Although during 1999 the Beta project had been on schedule for timely completion, it was completed four weeks late in August 2000. The Gamma project's original contract price was $800,000. Change orders during 2000 added $40,000 to the original contract price.

The following data pertains to the separate long-term construction projects in progress:

	Beta	*Gamma*
As of September 30, 1999:		
Costs incurred to date	$360,000	$410,000
Estimated costs to complete	40,000	410,000
Billings	315,000	440,000
Cash collections	275,000	365,000
As of September 30, 2000:		
Costs incurred to date	450,000	720,000
Estimated costs to complete	----	180,000
Billings	560,000	710,000
Cash collections	560,000	625,000

Additional Information:

- London accounts for its long-term construction contracts using the percentage-of-completion method for financial reporting purposes and the completed-contract method for income tax purposes.
- London elected early application of FASB 109, *Accounting for Income Taxes,* for the year ended September 30, 1999. Enacted rates are 25% for 1999 and 30% for future years.
- London's income before income taxes from all divisions, before considering revenues from long-term construction projects, was $300,000 for the year ended September 30, 1999. There were no other temporary or permanent differences.

Required:

a. Prepare a schedule showing London's gross profit (loss) recognized for the years ended September 30, 1999, and 2000, under the percentage-of-completion method.

b. Prepare a schedule showing London's balances in the following accounts at September 30, 1999, under the percentage-of-completion method:

- Accounts receivable
- Costs and estimated earnings in excess of billings
- Billings in excess of costs and estimated earnings

c. Prepare a schedule reconciling London's financial statement income and taxable income for the year ended September 30, 1999, and showing all components of taxes payable and current and deferred income tax expense for the year then ended. Do not consider estimated tax requirements.

NUMBER 2

The Deytyme Construction Company began operations January 1, 19X7. During the year, Deytyme entered into a contract with Redbeard Razor Corporation to construct a manufacturing facility. At that time, Deytyme estimated that it would take five years to complete the facility at a total cost of $4,800,000. The total contract price for construction of the facility is $6,000,000. During the year, Deytyme incurred $1,250,000 in construction costs related to the construction project. The estimated cost to complete the contract is $3,750,000. Redbeard was billed and paid 30% of the contract price.

Required:
Prepare schedules to compute the amount of gross profit to be recognized for the year ended December 31, 19X7, and the amount to be shown as "cost of uncompleted contract in excess of related billings" or "billings on uncompleted contract in excess of related costs" at December 31, 19X7, under each of the following methods:

1. Completed-contract method.
2. Percentage-of-completion method.

Show supporting computations in good form.

NUMBER 3

The following information pertains to Baron Flowers, a calendar-year sole proprietorship, which maintained its books on the cash basis during the year.

Baron Flowers
TRIAL BALANCE
December 31, 2001

	Dr.	Cr.
Cash	$ 25,600	
Accounts Receivable, 12/31/00	16,200	
Inventory, 12/31/00	62,000	
Furniture & fixtures	118,200	
Land improvements	45,000	
Accumulated depreciation, 12/31/00		$ 32,400
Accounts payable, 12/31/00		17,000
Baron, Drawings		
Baron, Capital, 12/31/00		124,600
Sales		653,000
Purchases	305,100	
Salaries	174.000	
Payroll taxes	12,400	
Insurance	8,700	
Rent	34,200	
Utilities	12,600	
Living expenses	13,000	
	----------	----------
	$827,000	$827,000

Baron has developed plans to expand into the wholesale flower market and is in the process of negotiating a bank loan to finance the expansion. The bank is requesting 2001 financial statements prepared on the accrual basis of accounting from Baron. During the course of a review engagement, Muir, Baron's accountant, obtained the following additional information.

1. **Amounts due from customers totaled $32,000 at December 31, 2001.**

2. **An analysis of the above receivables revealed that an allowance for uncollectible accounts of $3,800 should be provided.**

3. **Unpaid invoices for flower purchases totaled $30,500 and $17,000, at December 31, 2001, and December 31, 2000, respectively.**

4. **The inventory totaled $72,800 based on a physical count of the goods at December 31, 2001. The inventory was priced at cost, which approximates market value.**

5. **On May 1, 2001, Baron paid $8,700 to renew its comprehensive insurance coverage for one year. The premium on the previous policy, which expired on April 30, 2001, was $7,800.**

6. **On January 2, 2001, Baron entered into a twenty-five-year operating lease for the vacant lot adjacent to Baron's retail store for use as a parking lot. As agreed in the lease, Baron paved and fenced in the lot at a cost of $45,000. The improvements were completed on April 1, 2001, and have an estimated useful life of fifteen years. No provision for depreciation or amortization has been recorded. Depreciation on furniture and fixtures was $12,000 for 2001.**

7. Accrued expenses at December 31, 2000 and 2001, were as follows:

	2000	*2001*
Utilities	$ 900	$1,500
Payroll taxes	1,100	1,600
	$2,000	$3,100

8. Baron is being sued for $400,000. The coverage under the comprehensive insurance policy is limited to $250,000. Baron's attorney believes that an unfavorable outcome is probable and that a reasonable estimate of the settlement is $300,000.

9. The salaries account includes $4,000 per month paid to the proprietor. Baron also receives $250 per week for living expenses.

Required:

a. Using the worksheet on the following page, prepare the adjustments necessary to convert the trial balance of Baron Flowers to the accrual basis of accounting for the year ended December 31, 2001. Formal journal entries are not required to support your adjustments. However, use the numbers given with the additional information to cross-reference the postings in the adjustment columns on the worksheet.

b. Write a brief memo to Baron explaining why the bank would require financial statements prepared on the accrual basis instead of the cash basis.

NUMBER 4

At December 31, 1996, Roko Co. has two fixed price construction contracts in progress. Both contracts have monthly billings supported by certified surveys of work completed. The contracts are:

- The Ski Park contract, begun in 1995, is 80% complete, is progressing according to bid estimates, and is expected to be profitable.
- The Nassu Village contract, a project to construct 100 condominium units, was begun in 1996. Thirty-five units have been completed. Work on the remaining units is delayed by conflicting recommendations on how to overcome unexpected subsoil problems. While the total cost of the project is uncertain, a loss is not anticipated.

Required:

a. Identify the alternatives available to account for long-term construction contracts, and specify the criteria used to determine which method is applicable to a given contract.

b. Identify the appropriate accounting method for each of Roko's two contracts, and describe each contract's effect on net income for 1996.

c. Indicate how the accounts related to the Ski Park contract should be reported on the balance sheet at December 31, 1996.

a.

Baron Flowers

WORKSHEET TO CONVERT TRIAL BALANCE TO ACCRUAL BASIS

December 31, 2001

	Cash basis		Adjustments		Accrual Basis*	
Account title	**Dr.**	**Cr.**	**Dr.**	**Cr.**	**Dr.***	**Cr.***
Cash	**25,600**					
Accounts receivable	**16,200**		(1) 15,800			
Inventory	**62,000**		(4) 10,800			
Furniture & fixtures	**118,200**					
Land improvements	**45,000**					
Accumulated depreciation & amortization		**32,400**		(6) 14,000		
Accounts payable		**17,000**		(3) 13,500		
Baron, Drawings			(9) 48000 (9) 13,000			
Baron, Capital		**124,600**				
Allowance Uncollectable				(2) 3,800		
PRepaid Insurance			(5) 2900			
Accrued Exp.				(7) 1100		
Litigation Contingency				(8) 50,000		
Sales		**653,000**		(1) 15,800		
Purchases	**305,100**		(3) 13,500	(4) 10,800		
Salaries	**174,000**			(9) 48000		
Payroll taxes	**12,400**		(7) 500			
Insurance	**8,700**			(5) 2900		
Rent	**34,200**					
Utilities	**12,600**		(7) 600			
Living expenses	**13,000**			(9) 13,000		
Bad Debt Expense			(2) 3800			
Depreciation Expense			(6) 14,000			
Litigation Expense			(8) 50000			
	827,000	**827,000**				

*** Completion of these columns is not required.**

NUMBER 5

The Maple Corporation sells farm machinery on the installment plan. On July 1, 19X9, Maple entered into an installment sale contract with Agriculture, Inc., for an eight-year period. Equal annual payments under the installment sale are $100,000 and are due on July 1. The first payment was made on July 1, 19X9.

Additional information is as follows:

- The amount that would be realized on an outright sale of similar farm machinery is $556,000.
- The cost of the farm machinery sold to Agriculture is $417,000.
- The finance charges relating to the installment period are $244,000 based on a stated interest rate of 12%, which is appropriate.
- Circumstances are such that the collection of the installments due under the contract is reasonably assured.

Required:
What income or loss before income taxes should Maple record for the year ended December 31, 19X9, as a result of the above transaction? Show supporting computations in good form.

NUMBER 6

On November 5, 1993, Gunpowder Corp.'s board of directors approved a stock option plan for key executives. On January 2, 1994, a specific number of stock options were granted. These options were exercisable between January 2, 1996, and December 31, 1997, at 90% of the quoted market price on January 2, 1994. The service period is for 1994 and 1995. Some options were forfeited when an executive resigned in 1995. All other options were exercised during 1996.

Required:
a. When is Gunpowder's stock option measurement date? Why?
b. How should Gunpowder determine the compensation expense, if any, for the stock option plan in 1994?
c. What is the effect of forfeiture of the stock options on Gunpowder's financial statements for 1995? Why?
d. What is the effect of the stock option plan on the balance sheet at December 31, 1996? Be specific as to the changes in balance sheet accounts between November 5, 1996, and December 31, 1996.

NUMBER 7

On January 1, 1995, Holt, Inc., granted stock options to officers and key employees for the purchase of 20,000 shares of the company's $10 par common stock at $25 per share. The options were exercisable within a four-year period beginning January 1, 1997, by grantees still in the employ of the company, and expiring December 31, 2000. The market price of Holt's common stock was $33 per share at the date of grant. Holt prepares a formal journal entry to record this award.

On April 1, 1996, 2,000 option shares were terminated when the employees resigned from the company. The market value of the common stock was $35 per share on this date.

On March 31, 1997, 12,000 option shares were exercised when the market value of the common stock was $40 per share.

Required:
Prepare journal entries to record issuance of the stock options, termination of the stock options, exercise of the stock options, and charges to compensation expense, for the years ended December 31, 1995, 1996 and 1997. Show supporting computations in good form.

NUMBER 8

After a two-year search for a buyer, Hobson, Inc., sold its idle plant facility to Jackson Company for $700,000 on January 1, 1997. On this date the plant had a depreciated cost on Hobson's books of $500,000. Under the agreement Jackson paid $100,000 cash on January 1, 1997, and signed a $600,000 note bearing interest at 10%. The note was payable in installments of $100,000, $200,000 and $300,000 on January 1, 1998, 1999 and 2000, respectively. The note was secured by a mortgage on the property sold. Hobson appropriately accounted for the sale under the cost recovery method since there was no reasonable basis for estimating the degree of collectibility of the note receivable. Jackson repaid the note with three late installment payments, which were accepted by Hobson, as follows:

Date of payment	*Principal*	*Interest*
July 1, 1998	$100,000	$90,000
December 31, 1999	200,000	75,000
February 1, 2000	300,000	32,500

Required:
Prepare a schedule (using the format shown below) to record the initial transaction for the sale of the idle plant facility, the application of subsequent cash collections on the note, and the necessary journal entry on the date the transaction is complete.

Date	*Cash received Debit*	*Note receivable Dr.(Cr.)*	*Idle plant (net) (Credit)*	*Deferred income Dr.(Cr.)*	*Income rec-ognized (Credit)*
January 1, 1997	$100,000				
July 1, 1998	190,000				
December 31, 1999	275,000				
February 1, 2000	332,500				
February 1, 2000					

NUMBER 9

On July 1, 1998, Bow Construction Co. commenced operations and began constructing a building for Crecy under a fixed price contract. Anticipated completion date was June 15, 2000. Bow projects a large profit because it purchased most of the contract materials at exceptionally low prices in August 1998.

At the end of each month, Crecy is billed for completed work; for which it pays within 30 days. On December 31, 1999, all costs incurred exceed billings on the contract.

For the Crecy contract, Bow uses the percentage-of-completion (cost-to-cost) method for financial statement purposes. For income tax purposes, Bow qualifies for and uses the completed-contract method. Bow has no other contracts and no other differences between financial statement and income tax reporting.

Required:
a. How should Bow determine that the percentage-of-completion method is appropriate for the Crecy contract?
b. How should Bow calculate its 1999 income to be recognized on the Crecy contract? Explain any special treatment of unused material costs and why it is required.
c. Ignoring income tax effects, specify how the accounts related to the Crecy contract should be reported on Bow's December 31, 1999, balance sheet.
d. Assuming Bow has elected early adoption of FASB Statement No. 109, *Accounting for Income Taxes,* what are the income tax effects of the Crecy contract on Bow's 1999 balance sheet and income statement?

Chapter Ten
Solutions to Revenue and Expense Recognition, Miscellaneous Items Questions

1. (a) In order to use the percentage-of-completion method, both the estimated costs of completion and an estimate of the extent of completion must be reasonably dependable.

2. (c) The excess of cost of billings is a current asset, and the excess of billings over cost is a current liability.

3. (a) Since the contract is not yet complete, no gross profit is recognized in 1993.

4. (b)

1993 actual costs	$ 20,000
Total estimated costs	÷ 60,000
Ratio	= 1/3
Contract price	× 100,000
Revenue	33,333
1993 actual costs	– 20,000
Gross profit	$ 13,333

5. (b) Since the total cost of the contract, $3,100,000 ($930,000 + $2,170,000) is projected to exceed the contract price of $3,000,000, the excess cost of $100,000 must be recognized as a loss in 1997.

6. (d) Under the completed-contract method, revenues are not recognized until the year of completion. Therefore, in 1996, the entire contract price of $600,000 would be recognized as revenue and the costs incurred of $480,000 would be deducted in determining the gross profit of $120,000.

7. (c)

Current period's (first year) actual costs =	$ 2,000,000	= 12.5%
Total estimated costs =	$16,000,000	
Revenue for 1996 = 12.5% × $20,000,000 =	$ 2,500,000	
Costs for 1996 =	2,000,000	
Gross profit =	$ 500,000	

8. (a) Year-to-date income through 12/31/92:

Revenues $6,300 ÷ 8,100 × $9,000,000 =	$7,000,000	
Costs	6,300,000	
Income recognized through 12/31/92		$700,000
Income recognized in 1991:		
Revenues $3,900 ÷ 7,800 × $9,000,000 =	$4,500,000	
Costs	– 3,900,000	
		– 600,000
Income recognized in 1992		$100,000

9. (a) Under the completed-contract method all revenue and expenses are deferred on profitable contracts until the contract is complete, but losses are recognized immediately (conservatism) on unprofitable contracts. Project #1 is projecting a profit of $60,000 ($420,000 – $240,000 – $120,000) and is estimating $120,000 in additional cost to complete the contract. Since the contract is profitable and is not complete, Pell should not recognize any gross profit in 1999 under the completed-contract method.

Project #2 is projecting a loss of $20,000 ($300,000 – $280,000 – $40,000) and the loss should be recognized in full for 1999.

10. (b) Using the percentage-of-completion method, Pell should recognize the portion of the estimated gross profit that is associated with the percentage of the contract that is complete for profitable contracts, but with unprofitable contracts, the company should recognize the total estimated loss immediately. Project #1 is 66 2/3% complete. The percentage complete is computed by dividing the cost to date ($240,000) by the estimated total cost of the contract ($360,000). This percentage is then multiplied by the total estimated gross profit on the contract to calculate the gross profit recognized in 1999. In this case 66 2/3% × $60,000 = $40,000 profit recognized.

Project #2 is projecting a loss of $20,000 ($300,000 – $280,000 – $40,000) and the loss should be recognized in full for 1999.

In summary, Project #1 should recognize a profit of $40,000 and Project #2 should recognize a loss of $20,000, for a net of a $20,000 profit.

11. (b) Using the completed-contract method, all revenue is recognized in the year the contract is completed. The period of collection or if progress billings exceed costs have no impact on the period of revenue recognition.

12. (b) Under the percentage-of-completion method for long-term contracts, the income recognized each period is the total income recognized to date less the income recognized in prior periods. Progress billings are not a part of the calculation of income recognized.

13. (a) Income recognized in the third year of a five-year construction contract using percentage-of-completion method would be calculated by multiplying the ratio of the total cost incurred to date divided by the estimated total cost times the estimated total gross profit on the contract less the gross profit recognized in years one and two. Note that billings on the contract do not affect the calculation of income recognized.

14. (a) Actual costs are deducted from revenues in the fourth year and the revenues recognized are determined by the difference between the contract price and revenues previously recognized.

15. (a) According to APB #10 (par. 12), the installment method of accounting is not acceptable unless "collection of the sale price is not reasonably assured."

16. (c)	Uncollected accounts receivable at 12/31/93	$600,000
	Gross profit percentage	× 40%
	Deferred gross profit 12/31/93	$240,000

17. (c)	Accounts receivable at 12/31/95 = $800,000 - 300,000 =	$500,000
	Gross profit rate = 1 – (480,000 ÷ 800,000) =	40%
	Deferred gross profit at 12/31/95 =	$200,000

18. (d)	1997 sales not yet collected = $240,000 ÷ 4 =	$ 600,000
	+ 1997 sales collected	450,000
		$1,050,000

19. (d) Sales of $400,000 have been collected. Therefore, the gross profit of 40% has been realized, or $160,000.

20. (c)

	Year of sale	
	1997	*1998*
a. Gross profit realized	$ 240,000	$ 200,000
b. Percentage	30%	40%
c. Collections on sales (a/b)	$ 800,000	$ 500,000
Total sales	1,000,000	2,000,000
Balance uncollected	$ 200,000	$1,500,000

Total accounts receivable at 12/31/98 = $1,700,000

21. (a) Under the cost-recovery method, gross profit is recognized only after the entire cost of the product(s) sold has been received.

22. (c) Under the cost-recovery method, gross profit is not recognized until the total cost is collected. In 1998 the cost of sales was $8,000 but collections were only $7,000 so Fox did not recognize any gross profit in 1998. By the end of 1999 total collections from 1998 sales were $10,000 ($7,000 in 1998 and $3,000 in 1999). At this point collections exceeded cost of sales by $2,000 and that amount should be recognized as gross profit in 1999 from 1998 sales.

The 1999 collections from 1999 sales were $12,000 and the cost of sales was $9,000. At this point the cost had been recovered and the differences between the collections ($12,000) and the cost of sales ($9,000) equals $3,000.

The $3,000 is the amount that should be reported as gross profit from 1999 sales.
In summary, the total gross profit recognized at March 31, 1999 should be $2,000 from 1998 sales and $3,000 from 1999 sales for a total of $5,000.

23. (a)

Interest expense recorded			$1,500
Correct interest expense:			
$ 5,000 × 12% × 10/12	=	$500	
$15,000 × 12% × 6/12	=	900	
$ 8,000 × 12% × 8/12	=	640	2,040
Understatement of interest expense			$ 540

24. (a) Proper correcting entries were made at 12/31/98, so the errors made in 1998 will have no effect on net income in 1999.

The ending inventory for 1999 is understated by $1,000. This will cause cost of goods to be overstated by $1,000 and net income to be understated by $1,000 (before taxes).

Depreciation understated by $800 will cause income to be overstated by $800. The net effect of these errors is a $200 understatement of income.

25. (c) The $3,000 overstatement of ending inventory in 1998 has no effect on the retained earnings at the end of 1999 because the error was automatically counterbalanced in the next fiscal period. (Income for 1998 was overstated and income for 1999 was understated by this error.).

The overstatement of depreciation expense in 1998 will cause retained earnings to be understated by $2,500. Adding the $200 understatement of income for 1999 as determined in #35, we find the total understatement of retained earnings to be $2,700.

26. (a) There will be no over/understatement of working capital at 12/31/00, because the inventory errors will have been counterbalanced, and the depreciation errors have no effect on working capital, which is defined as current assets less current liabilities.

27. (b) Compensation cost is the difference between the market price of the stock at June 1, 1998, the measurement date, and the option price times the number of options granted. ($20 – $15) × 1,000 options = $5,000. The benefit period is the period from June 1, 1998 to the first date the options may be exercised (January 2, 1999). Therefore, all the cost should be recognized in 1998.

28. (c)

Difference between market price and option price on measurement date, 1/1/94 ($30 – $20) =	$ 10
Number of shares	3,000
Total compensation expense	$30,000

The expense is recognized equally over the years of service—1994 and 1995. Therefore, the 1995 expense is one-half of the total, or $15,000.

29. (a) The compensation from the stock option program is measured by the difference between the market price of the stock and the option price at the measurement date of January 2, 2000.

$50 – $20 = $30 per share × 1,000 options - $30,000

The journal entries are:

a.	Jan. 2	Deferred Compensation - PIC	$30,000	
		PIC Stock options outstanding		30,000
b.	Dec. 31	Compensation Expense	30,000	
		Deferred Compensation - PIC		30,000
c.	Dec. 31	Cash	20,000	
		PIC - Stock options outstanding	30,000	
		Common Stock - Par		10,000
		PIC - Excess of Par		40,000

The net effect on total stockholders' equity is:

STOCKHOLDERS' EQUITY

a.	Def. Comp. - PIC	30,000	a.	PIC - Stock options out.	30,000
b.	Compensation expense	30,000	b.	Def. Comp. - PIC	30,000
c.	PIC - Stock options out.	30,000	c.	Common Stock - Par	10,000
			c.	PIC - Excess of Par	40,000
				NET EFFECT	**20,000**

30. (c) The account, "Deferred Compensation," is reported contra to the related stockholders' equity account.

31. (d) The stock options outstanding account is reduced when the stock options are exercised or when the stock options expire.

32. (c)

Market price, date of grant	$ 30
Market price, December 31, 1996	45
Compensation per right	15
Number of rights	20,000
Total compensation	$300,000

All of the compensation is recognized in the year of the grant since the rights were issued for past services.

33. (c) The expense for the rights are recorded over the service period of 1996, 1997 and 1998. Since the rights are not exercisable until 1999, the expense must be estimated based on the most recent market price.

Market price 12/31/97	$ 28
Base	20
Compensation per share as of 12/31/97	$ 8
No. of shares	30,000
Total compensation	$240,000
Liability accrued in 1996 and 1997 (2/3)	$160,000

34. (c) The matching funds ($350,000 × 2) are recognized as expense for the year. The difference between the market price and the carrying value of the treasury stock would be recorded as follows:

1997 Summary Entry

Liability for stock purchase plan	$1,050,000[1]	
Treasury stock		$900,000
APIC		150,000

[1]$350,000 employee contribution and $700,000 employer contribution.

35. (a) A company records compensation expense based upon cash or stocks (at fair market value) contributed to the plan during the year. Therefore, the $45,000 cash and $54,000 value of the shares contributed to the plan are reported as compensation expense. The second and third transactions noted in the question do not result in any expense recognition.

36. (d) Generally, cash held by a bank as a compensating balance is included as cash on the balance sheet.

37. (a)

Balance per books 3/31/97		$44,200
Deposits, April 1997:		
Per bank	$58,400	
Less D.I.T., 3/31/97	10,300	48,100
Cash available		$92,300
Disbursements, April 1997:		
Per bank	$49,700	
Plus outstanding checks 4/30/97	+ 7,000	
Less outstanding checks 3/31/97	– 12,600	44,100
Cash balance per books 4/30/97		$48,200

38. (d) The present value of the notes receivable represents the value of the services to be provided after 1997. As the services are rendered the amount will be transferred from the unearned revenue account to the revenue account.

39. (d) Since the franchiser has performed all of the required initial services, all of the initial franchise fee is recognized as revenue in 1995.

40. (c) Since the initial fee does not include any service or product obligation on the part of the franchiser, the entire cash payment and present value of the note represents the acquisition cost to the franchisee.

$40,000 + (2.91 × $20,000) = $98,200.

41. (b) The earnings process is completed upon delivery of the product. Therefore, in 1998, revenue for 50,000 gallons at $3 each is recognized. The payment terms do not affect revenue recognition.

42. (d) Royalty revenue is 20% of Fantasy's reported revenues. For 1999 the royalty revenue would be 20% × $1,500,000 or $300,000.

43. (d)

Unearned Service Contract Revenue Account

	Debit	Credit	
		$570,000	Balance 1/1/92
		960,000	1992 Cash receipts
1992 Revenue	$780,000		
		$750,000	Balance 12/31/92

44. (c) Royalty expense is the higher of 10% of sales or a minimum of $60,000. The 10% of sales (10% × $800,000 = $80,000) is higher than the minimum and should be reported as royalty expense.

45. (d) Sales revenue = \$27,560 ÷ 1.06 = \$26,000 (the credit to the revenue account includes the 6% sales taxes).

Sales taxes for the quarter = \$27,560 – \$26,000 =	\$1,560
Sales taxes paid	– 600
Balance of sales taxes payable	\$ 960

46. (b) The \$50,000 for radio ads should be accrued at 12/31/97. The \$60,000 is a prepayment and should not be expensed in 1997. (\$990,000 + 50,000 – 60,000 = \$980,000)

47. (d)

a. Cash Basis income: Revenue collected in May — \$3200

b. Accrual Basis income:	Revenue	\$3200
	Expenses	(1500)
	Income	\$1700

Note: Ivy's cash investment of \$1,000 would have increased her capital account and the withdrawal of \$500. would decrease the capital account.

48. (b) The approach is to set up a T-account and calculate sales.

ACCOUNTS RECEIVABLE			
Beginning balance	\$50,000	Cash collections	\$175,000
Sales (Calculate)	155,000	Write-offs	0
Ending balance	\$30,000		

49. (d)	
Cash basis pretax income - 1999	\$60,000
Less A/R 12/31/98	(20,000)
Plus A/R 12/31/99	40,000
Plus A/P 12/31/98	30,000
Less A/P 12/31/99	(15,000)
Pretax accrual income - 1999	\$95,000

The beginning A/R should be subtracted because it represents revenues that were earned in 1998 but collected in 1999. The ending A/R should be added because it is revenue earned in 1999 that will be collected in 2000. The beginning A/P should be added because it was deducted on the cash basis when paid in 1999 but on the accrual basis is considered as an expense of 1998. The ending A/P should be subtracted because it is an expense on the accrual basis for 1999.

50. (c) The following accounting bases may be used to prepare financial statements in conformity with a comprehensive basis of accounting other than GAAP:

a. Basis of accounting used by an entity to file its income tax return.
b. Cash receipts and disbursements basis of accounting.
c. Cash basis.
d. Modifications of cash basis such as accruing income taxes and recording depreciation.
e. A definite set of criteria having substantial support that is applied to all material items. For example: constant dollar or current cost statements.

51. (c) The key word is **usually.** Personal financial statements **must** present a statement of financial position but **usually** include both a statement of financial position and a statement of changes in net worth.

52. (b) Personal financial statements should report assets and liabilities at estimated current values at the date of the financial statements.

53. (b) Assets are included in personal financial statements at their fair market values. Therefore, the business interest would be included as a single amount (business entity theory) at its FMV.

54. (c) An investment in life insurance should be reported at its cash value less any outstanding loans for personal financial statements (AICPA Position Statement 82-1). The cash value of the policy at December 31, 1998 is $12,000 and the outstanding loan is for $3,000. The net value of $9,000 should be reported.

55. (c) Income taxes which would be due if the assets were liquidated are reported between liabilities and net worth. The amount is not a true liability but reflects the person's position on a current value basis.

56. (a) Estimated income taxes for personal financial statements are based on the differences between the estimated current value of the assets and liabilities and their tax basis at the reporting date. The estimated tax liability should be shown on the statement of financial condition between the liabilities and net worth.

57. (d) In the statement of financial condition at April 30, 1999, the income tax liability is the estimated tax on earnings since January 1, 1999 (the 1998 tax liability was paid) plus the estimated tax on the differences between current values and bases of assets and liabilities.

58. (a) Assets are included at fair market value or $120,000 + $50,000 = $170,000.

59. (d) Either the cost recovery or the installment method may be used when there is no reasonable basis for estimating the collectibility of the sales price. The cost recovery method is the more conservative of the two approaches and is used when the degree of uncertainty is too great to justify the use of the installment method.

60. (d) Percentage of completion:

Costs incurred $5,400,000/Total costs ($5,400,000 + $10,800,000) =	1/3
Contract price =	$18,000,000
Revenue to be recognized in 1996	$ 6,000,000
1996 contract costs	5,400,000
Gross profit	$ 600,000

61. (b) Cash is the critical event for income recognition in both the cost recovery and installment methods. The installment method defers the recognition of the gross profit initially and recognizes the gross profit in the future by multiplying the cash collections × gross profit rate. The cost recovery method defers the recognition of profit of any type until the cumulative cash receipts are greater than the cost of the asset sold.

62. (d) A net decrease in accounts receivable means that cash collections exceeded accrual sales. Therefore the cash basis would **overstate** income when compared to accrual basis. A net decrease in accrued expenses indicates that cash payments for expenses are greater than accrual expenses. Therefore cash basis would **understate** income versus accrual basis.

63. (d) 1996 current liabilities were too low producing a higher working capital amount (overstated). Since an expense was not recorded in 1996 but was recorded in 1997, the retained earnings balance at the end of 1997 was correct.

64. (b)

JE	Accrued Real Estate Taxes Payable	8,000	
	Prepaid Taxes	4,000	
	Cash		12,000

To record the payment of six months taxes at $2,000 per month; four months ($8,000) for the accrued taxes for July 1 through October 31; and prepaid taxes ($4,000) for the two months of November and December. The cost of $2,000 per month is calculated by dividing the semi-annual installment of $12,000 by six months.

65. (d) The question is when should revenues be recognized and the appropriate expenses be "matched" against them. Since Rawl Co. makes monthly service calls to the customers and incurs most of its cost at that point, the revenue should be recognized monthly or **"evenly over the contract year as the services are performed."**

66. (b)
The solutions approach is to use a "T" account.

Current Liability for Advances from Customers

		Beginning Balance	$118,000
Orders Shipped	164,000		
		Orders Received	184,000
Advances Canceled	50,000		
		Ending Balance	$ 88,000

67. (c)

Cash Collected	$200,000
Plus - Increase in Accounts Receivable	20,000
Less - Increase in Unearned Fees	(5,000)
SERVICE REVENUE EARNED	$215,000

68. (a)
The income recognized in the fourth and final year of the contract using the percentage-of-completion method would be calculated as follows:

Contract Price	XXXX
Less - Actual Total Cost	(XXXX)
Total Actual Gross Profit	XXXX
Less - Income Previously Recognized	(XXXX)
Income Recognized in Year Four	XXXX

Therefore, both Actual Total Cost and Income Previously Recognized are used in the calculation.

69. (c) The gross profit recognized on an installment sale in any given year is calculated by multiplying the gross profit percentage by the portion of the sales price collected in that year or by multiplying the percentage of the sales price collected **(in proportion to the cash collection)** times the total gross profit on the sale. Answer (a) is incorrect because it recognizes revenue at the point of sale and answer (d) describes the cost recovery method of revenue recognition. Answer (b) is incorrect because it does not represent any revenue recognition method that is currently used.

70. (b) In accrual accounting, revenues are recognized when earned and expenses when **incurred**. In this question, when the three-year royalty contract is paid, the company should debit the asset, Prepaid Royalties, and credit cash. As the asset is used and the expense **incurred,** the company should increase Royalty Expense and decrease the Prepaid Royalties account.

71. (a) The value of the options, which is the amount reported in the financial statement, is the value of the benefit from the options:

Benefit per share ($25 – 10) =	$ 15
Number of shares	× 10,000
Total benefit before tax	$150,000
Tax rate at 35%	52,500
Benefit after tax	$ 97,500

72. (c) Since none of the services have been rendered in 1998, all fees are unearned. The question asks for "net" unearned fees. Therefore, the allowance for uncollectible fees are taken into account. The journal entry to record the transactions is summarized as follows:

12/31/98

Cash (21 × 10,000)	$210,000	
Notes receivable (21 × 20,000)	420,000	
Allowance for uncollectible notes		$ 20,000
Unearned franchise fees		610,000

73. (d) Under the completed-contract method, revenues are recognized only when the job is complete. Recording or collection of progress billings has no effect on the income statement.

74. (b) Sip paid two years' minimum annual fees on January 1, 1998. One-half of the fees are for royalty fees expense for 1998 and the other one-half represents a prepayment for 1999. The prepayment would be a current asset on the December 31, 1998 balance sheet.

75. (c) The understatement of beginning inventory and the overstatement of ending inventory both cause the cost of goods sold to be understated. The total understatement is $78,000 ($26,000 + $52,000).

76. (a)

	1997
Sales	$14,000,000
Collections	1,400,000
Accounts receivable at 12/31/97	$12,600,000
Gross profit rate	× 40%
Deferred gross profit 12/31/97	$ 5,040,000

77. (d)

1998 collections	$2,020,000
Gross profit rate	× 40%
Realized gross profit	$ 808,000

78. (d) The deferred gross profit on the balance sheet at December 31, 2000 should be the balances in the accounts receivable accounts for 1999 and 2000 multiplied times the appropriate gross profit percentage:

Accounts Receivable	2000	1999
Total Sales	900,000	600,000
Less Collections	(300,000)	(300,000)
Write offs	(50,000)	(200,000)
Accounts Receivable Balance	550,000	100,000
× Gross Profit Rate	× 40%	× 30%
Deferred Gross Profit 12/31/00	220,000	30,000

The Combined Deferred Gross Profit on the Balance Sheet is $250,000 ($220,000 + $30,000).

79. (d) Assets should be reported on personal statements of financial condition at estimated current value. The current value of the investment in stock at December 31, 1998 is $180,000.

80. (b) Employee benefit at the measurement date is $8 per share ($33 – 25). Total compensation is $8 × 40,000 = $320,000 spread over the two years for which services are being compensated, 1996 and 1997. Therefore, the 1996 expense is $160,000.

81. (c)

Balance per bank 12/31/94		$38,075
Deposits in transit		+5,200
		43,275
Outstanding checks	$6,750	
Bank error	400	–7,150
Adjusted bank balance		$36,125

This amount is equal to the reconciled balance per the books.

82. (b) The gross profit percentage on the sale is 33 1/3% (gross profit $500,000 divided by sales $1,500,000). The total cash collected is $600,000, the $300,000 down payment plus the first installment of $300,000. The gross profit recognized in 1999 is the gross profit percentage × the total cash collected in 1999. In this case, the 33 1/3% × $600,000 = $200,000 gross profit recognized.

83. (a) The cost-recovery method should be used. Under this method, equal amounts of revenue and cost are recognized when a payment is received. When all cost are recovered, then profit is recognized.

84. (b) Jen should not include the employer's matching contribution on the personal financial statements because the contribution does not vest until the employee has had three years of continuous employment with Komp. Jen's vesting date will not occur until February 1, 1999.

The personal statement of financial condition should include Jen's contribution, 10% × ($21,000 + $23,000 + $26,000), which totals $7,000 plus the earnings of $1,200 for a grand total of $8,200.

85. (b) Commissions expense is 3% of sales for the year (3% × $15,000,000 = $450,000).

86. (a)

Value of assets in excess of basis	$400,000
Tax rate	× 30%
Provision for estimated taxes	$120,000

87. (d) The sales for 1999 are calculated by dividing the deferred gross profit at December 31, 1999 by the gross profit percentage ($560,000 × 40% = $1,400,000 in sales). Cash collections are total sales less the December 31, 1999 balance in installment accounts receivable ($1,400,000 – $800,000 = $600,000 cash collections). The gross profit realized is the cash collections times the gross profit percentage ($600,000 × 40% = $240,000).

88. (a) Under either the completed-contract or the percentage-of-completion method, progress billings are reflected only on the balance sheet and an anticipated loss must be provided for in the year in which the loss is first projected.

89. (c) Since the installment note at face value includes the 12% interest, the correct balance at the end of six months should be the face amount of the note reduced for the six payments less the unamortized discount on the note. This amount should be equal to the present value of the remaining monthly payments discounted at 12%.

90. (a) The assets are included at fair market value—$337,500 + $35,000 = $372,500.

91. (a)

2000 September 15 Payment	$17,000	for January 1 through June 30, 2000
Accrual - $60,000 × 15%	9,000	for July 1 through December 31, 2000
	$26,000	TOTAL ROYALTY REVENUE

92. (a) Accrual basis revenue	$2,300,000
Less: Increase in accounts receivable	(150,000)
Accounts receivable written off	(10,000)
1996 sales on cash basis	$2,140,000

93. (a) The key point is that the construction in progress account (CIP) under percentage completion represents the cost plus the gross profit recognized. Therefore, the 1997 balance in CIP is the beginning of $122,000 plus the 1997 cost of $192,000=$314,000 plus the profit in 1997. The profit recognized in 1997 would be the ending balance of CIP of $364,000 less $314,000 for a total of $50,000.

94.-96. Entries to correct errors:

1) Cash	$1,000	
Accounts Receivable		$1,000
2) Purchases	1,600	
Accounts Payable		1,600
3) Depreciation	900	
Accumulated Depreciation		900
4) Office supplies expense	200	
Utilities expense		200
5) Accounts Receivable	3,000	
Sales		3,000

94. (a) Adjustments to net income:	*Dr.*	*Cr.*
2) Purchases	$1,600	
3) Depreciation	900	
5) Sales		3,000
Net adjustment		$ 500

Net income understated by $500

95. (c) Effect on Working capital:	*Dr.*	*Cr.*
(1)	—	—
(2)		1,600
(3)	—	—
(4)	—	—
(5)	3,000	
	$1,400	

Working capital understated by $1,400

96. (d) Effect on assets:	*Dr.*	*Cr.*
(1)	—	—
(2)	—	—
(3)		900
(4)	—	—
(5)	—	
		$900

Assets overstated by $900

97. (a) The correct amount of 1996 interest expense is $4,080, as computed below:

11/1/95 note	
Interest from 1/1/96 to 10/31/96	
($10,000 x 12% x 10/12)	$1,000
2/1/96 note	
Interest from 2/1/96 to 7/31/96	
($30,000 x 12% x 6/12)	1,800
5/1/96 note	
Interest from 5/1/96 to 12/31/96	
($16,000 x 12% x 8/12)	1,280
	$4,080

Since interest expense of $3,000 was recorded, 1996 interest expense was understated by $1,080 ($4,080 - $3,000).

98. (b) The key word is "usually." Personal Financial Statements must include a statement of financial position and **"usually"** include an optional statement of changes in net worth.

99. (a) As a general rule in accounting, assets are not offset against related liabilities. An exception to this rule is found in personal financial statements. Cash surrender value is reported as an asset, net of loans, on the statement of financial position for personal financial statements. In this example, cash surrender value of $7,000 less the loans of $2,500 are reported at the net amount of $4,500.

100. (d) The following accounting bases may be used to prepare financial statements in conformity with a comprehensive basis of accounting other than GAAP:

a. Basis of accounting used by an entity to file its income tax return.
b. Cash receipts and disbursements basis of accounting.
c. Cash basis.
d. Modifications of cash basis such as accruing income taxes and recording depreciation.
e. A definite set of criteria having substantial support that is applied to all material items. For example: constant dollar or current cost statements.
f. Basis of accounting used by an entity to comply with the financial reporting requirements of a government regulatory agency.

101. (c)

1).	Total Deferred Gross Profit	=	Total Sales x Gross Profit Rate		
		=	$1,400,000 x 40%		
		=	$560,000		
2).	Ending Balance in Deferred Gross Profit	=	Total Gross Profit (see 1 above)	--	Realized Gross Profit
		=	$560,000	--	$240,000
		=	$320,000		
3).	Realized Gross Profit	=	A/R Collected x Gross Profit Rate		
	$240,000	=	A/R collected x 40%		
	A/R collected	=	$240,000 / 40%		
		=	$600,000		
4).	Ending balance in A/R	=	Total Sales	--	A/R collected (see 3 above)
		=	$1,400,000	--	$600,000
		=	$800,000		

102. (d) Income tax-basis financial statements differ from those prepared under GAAP in that income tax-basis financial statements recognize certain revenues and expenses in different reporting periods. For example, GAAP requires the recognition of warranty expenses on accrual basis but tax-basis reporting requires the use of cash basis. Magazine subscriptions are recognized as revenue under GAAP when earned but recognized on tax-basis when the cash is collected. These temporary differences create deferred assets or deferred liabilities.

Chapter Ten
Solutions to Revenue and Expense Recognition, Miscellaneous Items Problems

NUMBER 1

a.

London Inc.
SCHEDULE OF GROSS PROFIT (LOSS)

	Beta	Gamma
For the Year Ended September 30, 1999:		
Estimated gross profit (loss):		
Contract price	$600,000	$800,000
Less total costs	400,000	820,000
Estimated gross profit (loss)	$200,000	$(20,000)
Percent complete:		
Costs incurred to date divided by	$360,000	$410,000
Total costs	400,000	820,000
Percent complete	90%	50%
Gross profit (loss) recognized	$180,000	$(20,000)
For the Year Ended September 30, 2000:		
Estimated gross profit (loss):		
Contract price	$560,000	$840,000
Less total costs	$450,000	$900,000
Estimated gross profit (loss)	$110,000	$(60,000)
Percent complete:		
Costs incurred to date divided by	$450,000	$720,000
Total costs	450,000	900,000
Percent complete	100%	80%
Gross profit (loss) recognized	110,000	(60,000)
Less gross profit (loss) recognized in prior year	180,000	(20,000)
Gross profit (loss) recognized	$(70,000)	$(40,000)

b.

London Inc.
SCHEDULE OF SELECTED BALANCE SHEET ACCOUNTS
September 30, 1999

Accounts receivable		$115,000
Costs and estimated earnings in excess of billings:		
Construction in progress (Beta)	$540,000	
Less: Billings	315,000	
Costs and estimated earnings in excess of billings		225,000

Billings in excess of costs and estimated earnings	
Billings (Gamma)	$440,000
Less: Construction in Progress	($390,000)
Billings in excess of costs and estimated earnings	$50,000

c.

London Inc.

SCHEDULE OF INCOME TAXES PAYABLE AND INCOME TAX EXPENSE

September 30, 1999

Financial statement income:		
From other divisions		$300,000
From Beta project		180,000
From Gamma project		(20,000)
Total financial statement income		$460,000
Less temporary differences:		
Beta project income		(180,000)
Gamma project loss		20,000
Total taxable income		$300,000
Taxes payable ($300,000 × 25%)		$75,000
Deferred tax liability ($160,000 × 30%)		48,000
Tax expense:		
Current	$75,000	
Deferred	48,000	123,000

NUMBER 2

1.

Computation of Gross Profit to Be Recognized Under Completed-Contract Method

No computation necessary. No gross profit is to be recognized prior to completion of contract.

Computation of Billings on Uncompleted Contract in Excess of Related Costs Under Completed-Contract Method

Construction costs incurred during the year	$1,250,000
Partial billings on contract (30% × $6,000,000)	1,800,000
	$ (550,000)

2.

Computation of Gross Profit to Be Recognized Under Percentage-of-Completion Method

Total contract price	$6,000,000
Total estimated cost ($1,250,000 + $3,750,000)	5,000,000
Estimated total gross profit from contract	$1,000,000
Percentage-of-completion	25%
Gross profit to be recognized during the year ($1,000,000 × 25%)	$ 250,000

Computation of Billings on Uncompleted Contract in Excess of Related Costs Under Percentage-of-Completion Method

Construction costs incurred during the year	$1,250,000
Gross profit to be recognized during the year (above)	250,000
Total charged to construction-in-progress	1,500,000
Partial billings on contract (30% × $6,000,000)	1,800,000
	$ (300,000)

NUMBER 3

a.

Baron Flowers
WORKSHEET TO CONVERT TRIAL BALANCE TO ACCRUAL BASIS
December 31, 2001

	Cash basis		*Adjustments*		*Accrual Basis**	
Account title	*Dr.*	*Cr.*	*Dr.*	*Cr.*	*Dr.**	*Cr.**
Cash	25,600				25,600	
Accounts receivable	16,200		(1) 15,800		32,000	
Inventory	62,000		(4) 10,800		72,800	
Furniture & fixtures	118,200				118,200	
Land improvements	45,000				45,000	
Accumulated depreciation & amortization		32,400		(6) 14,250		46,650
Accounts payable		17,000		(3) 13,500		30,500
Baron, Drawings			(9) 61,000		61,000	
Baron, Capital		124,600	(7) 2,000	(5) 2,600		125,200
Allowance for uncollectible accounts				(2) 3,800		3,800
Prepaid insurance			(5) 2,900		2,900	
Accrued expenses				(7) 3,100		3,100
Estimated liability from lawsuit				(8) 50,000		50,000
Sales		653,000		(1) 15,800		668,800
Purchases	305,100		(3) 13,500		318,600	
Salaries	174,000			(9) 48,000	126,000	
Payroll taxes	12,400		(7) 500		12,900	
Insurance	8,700			(5) 300	8,400	
Rent	34,200				34,200	
Utilities	12,600		(7) 600		13,200	
Living expenses	13,000			(9) 13,000		
Income summary—inventory			(4) 62,000	(4) 72,800		10,800
Uncollectible accounts			(2) 3,800		3,800	
Depreciation & amortization			(6) 14,250		14,250	
Estimated loss from lawsuit			(8) 50,000		50,000	
	827,000	827,000	237,150	237,150	938,850	938,850

* Completion of these columns was not required.

Explanations of Adjustments

[1] To convert 2001 sales to accrual basis.

Accounts receivable balances:	
December 31, 2001	$32,000
December 31, 2000	16,200
Increase in sales	$15,800

[2] To record provision for uncollectible accounts.

[3] To convert 2001 purchases to accrual basis.

Accounts payable balances:	
December 31, 2001	$30,500
December 31, 2000	17,000
Increase in purchases	$13,500

[4] To record increase in inventory from 12/31/00 to 12/31/01.

Inventory balances:	
December 31, 2001	$72,800
December 31, 2000	62,000
Increase in inventory	$10,800

[5] To adjust prepaid insurance.

Prepaid balances:	
December 31, 2001 ($8,700 x 4/12)	$2,900
December 31, 2000 ($7,800 x 4/12)	2,600
Decrease in insurance expense	$300

[6] To record 2001 depreciation and amortization expense.

Cost of leasehold improvement	$45,000
Estimated life	15 years
Amortization ($45,000 x 1/15 x 9/12)	2,250
Depreciation expense on fixtures and equipment	$12,000
	$14,250

[7] To convert expenses to accrual basis.

	Balances December 31,		*Increase in*
	2001	*2000*	*expenses*
Utilities	$1,500	$ 900	$ 600
Payroll taxes	1,600	1,100	500
	$3,100	$2,000	$1,100

[8] To record lawsuit liability at 12/31/01.

Attorney's estimate of probable loss	$300,000
Amount covered by insurance	250,000
Baron's estimated liability	$50,000

[9] To record Baron's drawings for 2001.

Salary ($4,000 x 12)	$48,000
Living expenses	13,000
	$61,000

b.

To: Baron Flowers
From: Muir
Re: Accrual basis financial statements

You have asked me to explain why the bank would require financial statements prepared on the accrual basis instead of the cash basis. The bank is concerned about your ability to repay the loan. To assess that ability, it wants information about your earnings for the period, total assets, and all claims on those assets. This information about your enterprise's performance and financial position is provided more completely by accrual basis financial statements than by cash-basis financial statements.

Under the cash basis, revenues are recognized when received and expenses when paid. Earnings can be manipulated by the timing of cash receipts and disbursements. Accrual basis accounting, while grounded in cash flows, reports transactions and other events with cash consequences at the time the transactions and events occur. Revenues and expenses are reported in the accounting period benefited and reflect receivables and payables, not just what the enterprise was able to collect or chose to pay.

NUMBER 4

a. The two alternative accounting methods to account for long-term construction contracts are the percentage-of-completion method and the completed-contract method. The percentage-of-completion method must be used if both of the following conditions are met at the statement date:

- Reasonable estimates of profitability at completion.
- Reliable measures of progress toward completion.

If one or both of these conditions are not met at the statement date, the completed-contract method must be used.

b. The Ski Park contract must be accounted for by the percentage-of-completion method. Eighty percent of the estimated total income on the contract should be recognized as of December 31, 1996. Therefore, the 1996 income to be recognized will equal 80% of the estimated total income less the income reported under the contract in 1995.

The Nassu Village contract must be accounted for by the completed-contract method. Therefore no income or loss is recognized in 1996 under this contract.

c. The receivable on the Ski Park contract should be reported as a current asset. If costs plus gross profit to date exceed billings, the difference should be reported as a current asset. If billings exceed cost plus gross profit to date, the difference should be reported as a current liability.

NUMBER 5

Maple Corporation
INCOME BEFORE INCOME TAXES ON INSTALLMENT SALE CONTRACT
For the Year Ended December 31, 19X9

Sales	$556,000
Cost of sales	417,000
Gross profit	139,000
Interest income *(Schedule 1)*	27,360
Income before income taxes	$166,360

Schedule 1

Computation of Interest Income on Installment Sale Contract

Cash selling price	$556,000
Deduct payment made July 1, 19X9	100,000
	456,000
Interest rate	× 12%
Annual interest	$ 54,720
Interest July 1, 19X9 to December 31, 19X9 ($54,720 × 1/2)	$ 27,360

NUMBER 6

a. Gunpowder's stock option measurement date is January 2, 1994. The stock option measurement date is the first date on which the employer knows both:
   - The number of shares that an individual is entitled to receive, and
   - The option or purchase price.

b. The compensation expense for 1994 is equal to the market price of Gunpowder's stock on January 2, 1994, less the option price, times the number of options outstanding times one-half.

c. When options are forfeited, compensation expense, contributed capital-stock options, and deferred compensation (if used) are all decreased. This is necessary because the total compensation expense is less than that estimated in 1994.

d. Cash was increased by the stock option price [90% of the quoted market price on January 2, 1994] multiplied by the number of shares issued. Retained earnings was reduced by the compensation expense recorded in 1994 and 1995. Contributed capital was increased by the balancing amount for the above entries.

NUMBER 7

Holt, Inc.
JOURNAL ENTRY (1)
January 1, 1995

		Debit	*Credit*
Deferred compensation cost		$160,000	
Common stock options			$160,000
To record compensatory stock options at grant date:			
Compensation per share ($33 – $25)	$ 8		
Stock option shares	× 20,000		
Common stock options and deferred compensation cost	$160,000		

Holt, Inc.
JOURNAL ENTRY (2)
December 31, 1995

	Debit	*Credit*
Compensation expense	$80,000	
Deferred compensation cost ($160,000 ÷ 2)		$80,000
To record compensation expense for 1995, based on write-off of deferred compensation cost over the stipulated two-year period of service		

Holt, Inc.
JOURNAL ENTRY (3)
April 1, 1996

		Debit	*Credit*
Common stock options		$16,000	
Deferred compensation cost			$8,000
Compensation expense			8,000
To record termination of 2,000 option shares held by employees at date they resigned their positions:			
Option shares terminated	2,000		
Compensation per share	× $8		
Common stock options and deferred compensation	$16,000		
Expensed year ended December 31, 1995 ($16,000 ÷ 2)	8,000		
Deferred compensation cost at April 1, 1996	$ 8,000		

Holt, Inc.
JOURNAL ENTRY (4)
December 31, 1996

	Debit	Credit
Compensation expense	$72,000	
Deferred compensation cost ($160,000 – $80,000 – $8,000)		$72,000
To record compensation expense for 1996 and write-off of remaining deferred compensation cost		

Holt, Inc.
JOURNAL ENTRY (5)
March 31, 1997

	Debit	Credit
Cash (12,000 × $25)	$300,000	
Common stock options (12,000 × $8)	96,000	
Common stock (12,000 × $10)		$120,000
Additional paid-in capital		276,000
To record issuance of 12,000 shares of $10 par common stock in exchange for 12,000 stock options and cash of $25 per share		

Holt, Inc.
December 31, 1997
(Not required)

No entry for compensation expense for the stock options is required for year ended December 31, 1997, because the deferred compensation cost was properly expensed during 1995 and 1996.

NUMBER 8

Hobson, Inc.
APPLICATION OF CASH RECEIPTS FROM SALE OF IDLE PLANT FACILITY TO COST RECOVERY, DEFERRED INCOME, AND INCOME RECOGNIZED UNDER THE COST RECOVERY METHOD OF ACCOUNTING
For the Period January 1, 1997, to February 1, 2000

Date	Cash received Debit	Note receivable Dr. (Cr.)	Idle plant (net) (Credit)	Deferred income Dr. (Cr.)	Income recognized (Credit)
January 1, 1997	$100,000	$600,000	$(500,000)	$(200,000)	
July 1, 1998	190,000	(100,000)		(90,000)	
December 31, 1999	275,000	(200,000)		(10,000)	$ (65,000)*
February 1, 2000	332,500	(300,000)			(32,500)
February 1, 2000				300,000	(300,000)

*Total cash received	$565,000	($100,000 + $190,000 + $275,000)
Idle plant (net)	500,000	
Income recognized	$ 65,000	

NUMBER 9

a. Bow must have a system that is capable of meeting both of the following conditions for the Crecy contract:

- Reasonable estimates of profitability at completion.
- Reliable measures of progress toward completion.

b. At December 31, 1999, Bow should calculate the percentage of completion by comparing the costs incurred to date, less costs of unused materials, to the estimated total cost to complete Crecy. Income to date equals the percentage-of-completion multiplied by the estimated total profit to be earned on the contract. The 1999 income equals the income to be recognized to December 31, 1999, less the income reported under the contract in 1998.

When contract materials are purchased but not used, costs of the unused materials are excluded from income recognition calculations. Otherwise, the early period income reported may be overstated compared with the income earning efforts of that period.

c. Bow should report a current asset for the Crecy accounts receivable, and another for the excess of costs incurred plus total profit recognized over contract billings.

d. Assuming Bow has elected early adoption of FASB Statement No. 109, *Accounting for Income Taxes,* Bow should report a current deferred tax liability equal to its total net income reported in 1998 and 1999 multiplied by its enacted 2000 average tax rate. A deferred income tax expense should be recognized for the increase during 1999 in the deferred tax liability balance.

Chapter Eleven
Other Assets, Liabilities and Disclosures

10-15%.

Chapter Eleven
Other Assets, Liabilities and Disclosures

ACCOUNTS RECEIVABLE

DISCLOSURE

Accounts receivable should be disclosed on the statement of financial position at net realizable value:

Accounts Receivable (gross)	XX
Less Allowance for Uncollectible Accounts	(XX)
Net Realizable Value	XX

ACCOUNTING FOR UNCOLLECTIBLE ACCOUNTS

There are two approaches to accounting for uncollectible accounts:

- Allowance method
- Direct write-off method

A. Allowance Method

The allowance method is preferred by GAAP because it matches uncollectible accounts expense with credit sales in the same accounting period and establishes a valuation account to report the accounts receivable at net realizable value.

The normal journal entries are:

1. **To establish uncollectible accounts:**

JE Bad debt expense	XX	
Allowance from uncollectible accounts		XX

2. **To write off an uncollectible account:**

JE Allowance from uncollectible accounts	XX	
Accounts receivable		XX

3. **To record the recovery of an account previously written off:**

JE Accounts receivable	XX	
Allowance for uncollectible accounts		XX
JE Cash	XX	
Accounts receivable		XX

NOTE: The effect of the two above journal entries is

JE Cash	XX	
Allowance for uncollectible accounts		XX

T-Account Summary of the above journal entries:

Allowance for Doubtful Accounts

Debit	Credit
	Beginning balance
Write-offs	Estimated expense
	Recoveries
	Ending balance

Methods of estimating uncollectible accounts:
The allowance method uses two approaches to estimate the charges to bad debt expense.

- Balance sheet approach
- Income statement approach

Balance Sheet Approach:
The balance sheet approach analyzes accounts receivable and uses either a percentage of accounts receivable or an aging of accounts receivable to determine the **required balance** in the **allowance for uncollectible accounts.**

Income Statement Approach:
The income statement approach analyzes credit sales and uses a percentage of credit sales to determine the **required balance in the bad debt expense account.**

Example:
X Company had credit sales of $100,000 in the current year. The allowance for doubtful accounts had a balance of $1,200 at the beginning of the year. Writeoffs of $1,600 were recorded during the year, recoveries were $300. The Company estimates bad debt expense at 1% of credit sales and an aging of the accounts receivable at year-end indicates that the required balance in the allowance account is $1,100.

To record estimated uncollectible accounts:

	Income Statement Approach		Balance Sheet Approach	
JE Bad debt expense	$1,000*		$1,200**	
Allowance for uncollectible accounts		$1,000		$1,200

* 1% X credit sales of $100,000 = $1,000

** The beginning balance in the allowance account of $1,200 – the write-offs of $1,600 + the recoveries of $300 = a debit balance of $100. The aging of accounts receivable indicates a required balance in the allowance account at the end of the year of $1,100. Therefore, the journal entry should be for $1,200 (the debit balance of $100 + the ending balance of $1,100 in the allowance account).

B. Direct Write-off Method
The direct write-off method may be used if bad debts are immaterial. This method is also used for tax purposes. Using the direct write-off method recognizes bad debt expense only upon the actual write-off of the account receivable. No allowance account is used. Recoveries are normally credited to the current year's expense account.

In the above example, if the direct write-off method had been used, the expense for the year would have been the $1,600 in writeoffs less the $300 in recoveries or $1,300. The net journal entry would be a debit to bad debt expense and a credit to accounts receivable for $1,300. Note that the direct write-off method does not use an allowance for uncollectible accounts.

PLEDGING, ASSIGNING AND FACTORING RECEIVABLES

PLEDGING (SECURED BORROWING)

Pledging is an agreement in which receivables are used as collateral for loans. The customers are usually unaware that the receivables have been pledged and continue to remit their payments to the company.

The only accounting issue associated with pledging is proper disclosure. The accounts receivable continue to be shown as a current asset but must be labeled as having been pledged. This identification can be done by a footnote or parenthetical disclosure. The related liability should also be identified as secured by the accounts receivable.

ASSIGNMENT OF RECEIVABLES (SECURED BORROWING)

The assignment of receivables is a more formalized type of collateral for a loan. The lender will identify specific receivables that will be used for the loan and approve the receivables to be used for collateral. The receivables usually remain on the books of the company seeking the loan and the customers are normally unaware that their accounts have been assigned. The accounting problem is adequate disclosure. The financial statements must disclose either by footnote or parenthetically that the receivables have been assigned and the related liability should disclose that receivables are being used as collateral for the loan.

FACTORING (SALE OF RECEIVABLES)

In order to accelerate the receipt of cash, some companies will sell (factor their receivables). Factoring is common in the furniture, textile and apparel industries. Factoring may be done on a with recourse or without recourse basis.

Factoring (Sale) Without Recourse

If receivables are factored without recourse, the buyer of the receivables assumes the risk of collection and absorbs the loss for any uncollectible accounts. The receivables are removed from the books of the seller and the **title** and **control** of the receivables are transferred to the buyer. SFAS 140 pointed out that a common form of factoring is the **credit card sale,** which is a means of transferring receivables without recourse, or with all of the risks and benefits of ownership.

Example: Burns Furniture Co. factors $250,000 of accounts receivable to commercial factors on a without recourse basis. Commercial factors charges 2% of accounts receivable as a finance charge and retains 4% of the accounts receivable as a contingency to cover possible sales discounts and sales returns and allowance.
The journal entry for Burns is as follows:

JE	Cash	$235,000	
	Due from factor (4% x $250,000)	10,000	
	Loss on sale of receivables (2% x $250,000)	5,000	
	Accounts receivable		$250,000

Factoring (Sale) With Recourse

If accounts receivable are sold with recourse, the seller guarantees payment to the buyer if any of the accounts receivable become uncollectible. In recording this type of transaction, SFAS 125 requires a **financial components** approach because the seller retains a continuing involvement with the receivables. The financial components approach assigns a value to the recourse provision.

Example: Use the same facts as in the previous example but assume that the recourse obligation is valued at $4,000. Burns Furniture Co. recorded the following journal entry:

JE	Cash	$235,000	
	Due from factor	10,000	
	Loss on sale of receivables*	9,000	
	Accounts receivable		$250,000
	Recourse liability		4,000

*The loss on the receivables is the finance charge of $5,000 plus the $4,000 estimated costs of the recourse obligation.

SUMMARY OF SFAS 140 - ACCOUNTING FOR TRANSFERS AND SERVICING OF FINANCIAL ASSETS AND EXTINGUISHMENT OF LIABILITIES

SFAS 140 adopted a financial components approach to the transfer of financial assets based on control. The financial components approach replaces the old approach of viewing transferred financial assets as an inseparable unit that had been entirely sold or entirely retained. Values are now assigned to financial components such as recourse provisions, servicing rights and agreements to reacquire.

BASIC ACCOUNTING ISSUE

The basic accounting issue is whether the transferred assets result in a sale or secured borrowing. A sale results when a transferor gives up control. After a transfer, an entity recognizes the assets and liabilities it controls and derecognizes the assets it no longer controls and derecognizes liabilities that have been extinguished.

CONTROL IS SURRENDERED – SALE IS RECORDED

Control is considered to have been surrendered if the three following conditions have been met:

- The transferred assets are isolated from or beyond the reach of the transferor and its creditors (even a bankruptcy trustee).
- The transferee has a right to freely exchange or pledge the assets transferred without unreasonable constraints or conditions imposed on its contractual right.

  or

  The holders of beneficial interest in a qualifying special-purpose entity can pledge or exchange those interests freely without unreasonable constraints or conditions imposed on their right.
- The transferor does not maintain control through an agreement to repurchase or redeem the transferred assets prior to maturity or an agreement, not obtainable elsewhere, to repurchase or redeem the transferred assets.

If these three conditions are met, the transaction is considered a sale and if the three conditions are not met, the transaction is considered a secured borrowing.

Example: An application of SFAS 140 can be seen in our previous discussion of transfer of receivables either by factoring, pledging, or assignment.

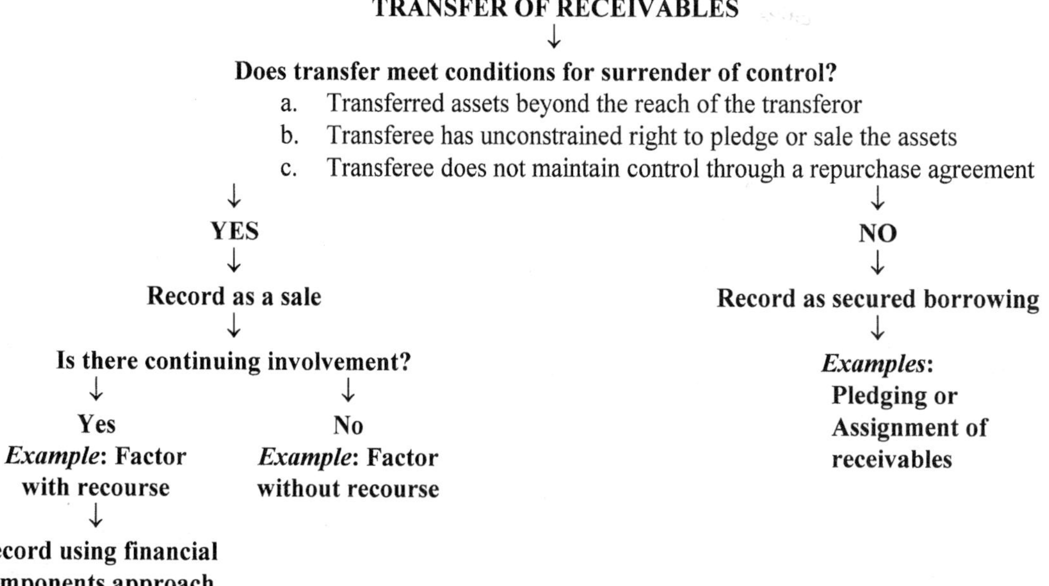

TRANSFER OF RECEIVABLES
Does transfer meet conditions for surrender of control?
a. Transferred assets beyond the reach of the transferor
b. Transferee has unconstrained right to pledge or sale the assets
c. Transferee does not maintain control through a repurchase agreement
YES
Record as a sale
Is there continuing involvement?
Yes
Example: Factor with recourse
Record using financial components approach
No
Example: Factor without recourse
NO
Record as secured borrowing
Examples:
Pledging or Assignment of receivables

SFAS 140 added the following three new terms to our accounting vocabulary:

- **Securitization** is the transfer of a portfolio of financial assets (e.g., trade receivables, mortgage loans, automobile loans, and credit card receivables) to a special-purpose entity, often a trust, and the sale of beneficial interests in the special-purpose entity to investors. The proceeds of the sale of these interests are paid to the transferor. Amounts of interest and principal collected on the securitized assets are paid to the investors in accordance with the legal agreement that established the special-purpose entity.
- A **servicing asset** is a contract under which future revenues from servicing fees, late charges, etc., are expected to more than adequately compensate the servicer. A **servicing liability** arises when such compensation is inadequate.
- An **undivided interest** is partial ownership as a tenant in common, for example, the right to the interest but not the principal of a security. This interest also may be pro rata, for example, a right to a proportion of the interest payments on a security

FIXED ASSETS

In General

Fixed assets should be carried at cost of acquisition or construction in the historical accounts, unless such cost is no longer meaningful. Cost of land should ordinarily be shown separately. Cost of construction includes direct costs and overhead costs incurred, such as engineering, supervision and administration, interest, and taxes. Items treated as fixed assets should have at least one year of expected useful life to the enterprise, and normally the life is considerably longer. Items no longer in service should be written off in order that fixed assets will represent the cost of properties in service.

Classification

Those tangible assets used in operations and not intended for sale in the ordinary course of business are classified on the balance sheet as fixed assets provided they have an expected service life of more than one year. No one designation of this category has been accepted, and captions such as "fixed assets," "property, plant, and equipment," "general property," "properties," and numerous others are found in published financial statements. Depreciable and nondepreciable property ordinarily should be shown separately, and a further classification is often given.

Property Stated on Cost Basis

Cost means cost in cash or its equivalent. Preferably, the words "at cost" are appended to the principal plant caption to avoid any possibility of misunderstanding. Although cost is the accepted basis of reporting property, plant, and equipment, there are situations in which cost is no longer meaningful. By carrying plant at cost, less accumulated depreciation, there is a representation that the remaining balance of the investment is properly chargeable to future operations and has a fair chance to be recovered. If this assumption appears no longer valid with respect to material items, it may be prudent to recognize the loss by reducing the book value to the estimated remaining useful cost to the enterprise.

Components of Cost

The cost of properties acquired by purchase is the net price paid on a cash basis, plus all incidental payments necessary to put the asset in condition and location for use, such as freight and installation costs. When several assets are acquired at a group price, the price paid is allocated between the assets based on their relative value, as determined by such evidence as independent appraisal by professional appraisers or real estate brokers, or assessed valuations for property tax purposes.

If property other than cash is the consideration in a transaction, a fair measure of the actual cash cost is the amount of money which would have been realized if such property had first been directly converted into cash. If the property has no determinable fair market value, the market value of the properties received in the exchange may be used. A gain or loss will occur when fair market value differs from the book value of the property given up. In practice, exchanges of fixed assets often are recorded at the book values of the properties given up.

If the consideration employed in acquiring properties is in the form of the capital stock of the buying enterprise, a fair measure of actual cost is the amount of money which could have been raised through the issue of the securities for cash. If the securities are of uncertain value, however, an alternative measurement would be the estimated fair market price of the property acquired.

The principle of costing of self-constructed property, plant, and equipment is similar to the principle of costing of purchased assets of this type—they are recorded at the price paid to get them in condition and location for use. The practical problems involved in determining their cost are the same problems that are encountered in determining the cost of goods manufactured for resale. The direct costs of materials and labor are readily identified and charged to construction work in process. Indirect or overhead costs may be specifically identifiable items, as well as those allocated to construction in process on supportable cost-incurrence principles. Overhead costs include supervision, engineering and interest during construction. Enterprises which do not normally carry out their own construction usually follow the incremental cost method by limiting the overhead charged to construction to the increase which can be directly attributed to the work done on the plant and equipment. *(See "Capitalization of Interest" later in this chapter.)*

Land and land rights. These asset accounts should include the purchase cost of land owned in fee and of rights, interest, and privileges held in land owned by others. The following incidental costs are also properly included, among others: commissions to agents, attorneys' fees, demolition, clearing and grading, streets, sewer lines, and relocating or reconstructing property of others elsewhere in order to acquire possession.

Buildings. A building is a relatively permanent structure designed to house or safeguard property or persons, and its total cost should include not only the cost of the shell, but also expenditures for service equipment and fixtures made a permanent part of the structure. In addition to direct costs of construction, it is proper to capitalize such items as permits, architects' and engineers' fees, legal fees, and overhead directly applicable to construction.

Machinery and equipment. It is important to include all costs of purchase or manufacture together with all costs of installation. The latter would include such costs as transportation, labor, and testing during an experimental period. If machines are purchased under an agreement providing for royalties to be paid on units of production, these royalty payments are not costs of acquisitions and should be charged to operating expenses.

Accounting for Retirements

The asset accounts for property, plant, and equipment should include the costs of only those units which are used and useful to the enterprise; the allowance for depreciation accounts should relate to those units, and to no others. Although these objectives are theoretically simple, they are in practice difficult to achieve.

Idle plant, reserve, and stand-by equipment. Plant assets on the balance sheet may include property in use and property held with reasonable expectation of its being used in the business. It is not customary to segregate or indicate the existence of temporarily idle plant, reserve, or standby equipment. Property abandoned but not physically retired and facilities still owned but no longer adapted for use in the business, if material in amount, should be removed from plant accounts and recorded separately at an estimated realizable amount, appropriately explained.

Classification of Capital Expenditures

Additions. Additions represent entirely new units or extensions and enlargements of old units. Expenditures for additions are capitalized by charging either old or new asset accounts depending on the nature of the addition.

Betterments. A betterment does not add to existing plant. Expenditures for betterments represent increases in the quality of existing plant by rearrangements in plant layout or the substitution of improved components for old components so that the facilities are better in some way than they were when acquired. Such increases in the quality of improved facilities are measured by their increased productivity, greater capacity, or longer life. The cost of betterments is accounted for by charges to the appropriate property accounts and the elimination of the cost and accumulated depreciation associated with the replaced components, if any.

Extraordinary repairs. Expenditures to replace parts or otherwise to restore assets to their previously efficient operating condition are regarded as repairs. To be classified as an extraordinary repair, an expenditure must benefit future periods by increasing the useful life of an existing asset. Expenditures for extraordinary repairs are capitalized by charges to the appropriate accumulated depreciation account or by eliminating from the accounts the cost and accumulated depreciation on the replaced parts and charging the asset account for the cost of the repairs. The latter treatment is preferred because it maintains the integrity of the accounts in that the actual cost of the asset in use is recorded.

Deferred maintenance. Deferred maintenance is an amount equal to the expenditure necessary to restore a plant or item of equipment to normal operating efficiency. Accounting for deferred maintenance involves the establishment of an allowance account by a charge to operations in the period during which it occurs. Actual repairs and other deferred maintenance expenditures are then charged to the allowance account when they occur.

Replacements. Replacements involve an "in kind" substitution of a new asset for an old asset or part. Accounting for major replacements requires entries to retire the old asset or part and to record the cost of the new asset or part. Minor replacements are treated as period costs.

DEPRECIATION METHODS

Accounting for depreciation is a system of accounting to distribute the cost (or other book value) of tangible capital assets, less salvage, over their useful lives in a systematic and rational manner. Under generally accepted accounting principles as presently understood, depreciation accounting is a process of allocation, not of valuation, through which the productive effort (cost) to be matched with productive accomplishment (revenue) for the period is measured. Depreciation accounting, therefore, is concerned with the timing of the expiration of the cost of tangible fixed assets.

Straight Line

Asset cost is allocated based on time.

$$\frac{\text{Cost} - \text{Salvage Value}}{\text{Useful Life}} = \text{Depreciation}$$

Units-of-Production Method

Cost less salvage value is spread over the service life of the asset such as production hours, miles, etc. For example, if a machine costing $10,000 has a productive life of 14,000 hours and 3,500 hours are used in year 1, depreciation in year 1 will be $2,500.

Decreasing Charge Methods

Called accelerated depreciation because the depreciation charge is greatest initially and decreases during the later years of useful life. Uneven expense is justified by proponents of this method on the basis that when the asset is new, repairs are lower, and in later years of useful life when depreciation is low, repairs would ordinarily be higher. This results in more even annual charges to operations during the asset life. Decreasing charge methods are also justified on the basis of greater expected output when the asset is new. Methods used are:

a. Declining balance (at a percentage of the straight line rate)
b. Sum-of-the-years' digits

Assume that an asset cost $20,000, has a $2,000 salvage value and a 5-year estimated life.

Depreciation computation:

a. **Declining balance** at 200% of the straight-line rate.

Year	*S/L Rate*	*200% Rate*	*Depreciation*
1	20%	40%	$ 8,000
2	20%	40%	4,800
3	20%	40%	2,880
4	20%	40%	1,728
5	20%	40%	592
		Total	$18,000

Computations:

Year (1) $20,000 × 40% = $8,000
Year (2) $20,000 – 8,000 = 12,000 × 40% = $4,800
Year (3) $12,000 – 4,800 = 7,200 × 40% = $2,880
Year (4) $ 7,200 – 2,880 = 4,320 × 40% = $1,728
Year (5) $ 4,320 – 1,728 = 2,592 × 40% = $1,037 (limited to $592)

Salvage value is ignored in the declining-balance method computations. However, depreciation is only recorded until the book value of the asset equals salvage value. In the above example, at the end of the asset's useful life $18,000 has been assigned to depreciation with $2,000 as salvage value. The example shows a rate of 200% of the straight-line rate, whereas the rate can be any amount over 100%, usually 125%, 150%, 175% or 200%.

b. **Sum-of-the-years' digits.**

Year		*Digits*	*Depreciation Fraction*
1		5	5/15
2		4	4/15
3		3	3/15
4		2	2/15
5		1	1/15
	Total	15	15/15

Depreciation amounts are computed as follows:

Year	Cost Less Salvage	Fraction	Depreciation
1	$18,000	5/15	$ 6,000
2	18,000	4/15	4,800
3	18,000	3/15	3,600
4	18,000	2/15	2,400
5	18,000	1/15	1,200
	Total	15/15	$18,000

Illustrative Problem:

Thompson Corporation, a manufacturer of steel products, began operations on October 1, 1995. The accounting department of Thompson has started the fixed-asset and depreciation schedule presented below. You have been asked to assist in completing this schedule. In addition to ascertaining that the data already on the schedule are correct, you have obtained the following information from the company's records and personnel:

- Depreciation is computed from the first of the month of acquisition to the first of the month of disposition.
- Land A and Building A were acquired from a predecessor corporation. Thompson paid $812,500 for the land and building together. At the time of acquisition, the land had an appraised value of $72,000 and the building had an appraised value of $828,000.
- Land B was acquired on October 2, 1995, in exchange for 3,000 newly issued shares of Thompson's common stock. At the date of acquisition, the stock had a par value of $5 per share and a fair value of $25 per share. During October 1995, Thompson paid $10,400 to demolish an existing building on this land so it could construct a new building.
- Construction of Building B on the newly acquired land began on October 1, 1996. By September 30, 1997, Thompson had paid $210,000 of the estimated total construction costs of $300,000. Estimated completion and occupancy are July 1998.
- Certain equipment was donated to the corporation by a local university. An independent appraisal of the equipment when donated placed the fair value at $16,000 and the salvage value at $2,000.
- Machinery A's total cost of $110,000 includes installation expense of $550 and normal repairs and maintenance of $11,000. Salvage value is estimated as $5,500. Machinery A was sold on February 1, 1997.
- On October 1, 1996, Machinery B was acquired with a down payment of $4,000 and the remaining payments to be made in ten annual installments of $4,000 each beginning October 1, 1996. The prevailing interest rate was 8%. The following data were abstracted from present-value tables:

Present value of $1.00 at 8%		*Present value of annuity of $1.00 in arrears at 8%*	
10 years	.463	10 years	6.710
11 years	.429	11 years	7.139
15 years	.315	15 years	8.559

Thompson Corporation
FIXED ASSET AND DEPRECIATION SCHEDULE
For Fiscal Years Ended September 30, 1996, and September 30, 1997

						Depreciation Expense Year Ended Sept. 30,	
Assets	*Acquisition Date*	*Cost*	*Salvage*	*Depreciation Method*	*Estimated Life in Years*	*1996*	*1997*
Land A	October 1, 1995	$ (1)	N/A	N/A	N/A	N/A	N/A
Building A	October 1, 1995	(2)	$47,500	Straight Line	(3)	$14,000	$ (4)
Land B	October 2, 1995	(5)	N/A	N/A	N/A	N/A	N/A
Building B	Under Construction	210,000 to date	—	Straight Line	Thirty	—	(6)
Donated Equipment	October 2, 1995	(7)	2,000	150% Declining Balance	Ten	(8)	(9)
Machinery A	October 2, 1995	(10)	5,500	Sum of Years' Digits	Ten	(11)	(12)
Machinery B	October 1, 1996	(13)	—	Straight Line	Fifteen	—	(14)

N/A—Not applicable

Required: For each numbered item (1) to (14), supply the correct amount. Round each answer to the nearest dollar.

Do not recopy schedule. Show supporting computations in good form.

1. ____________________
2. ____________________
3. ____________________
4. ____________________
5. ____________________
6. ____________________
7. ____________________
8. ____________________
9. ____________________
10. ____________________
11. ____________________
12. ____________________
13. ____________________
14. ____________________

Illustrative Solution:

Computations for Fixed Asset and Depreciation Schedule

(1) \$65,000.	Allocated in proportion to appraised values (72/900 × \$812,500).
(2) \$747,500.	Allocated in proportion to appraised values (828/900 × \$812,500).
(3) Fifty years.	Cost less salvage (\$747,500 – \$47,500) divided by annual depreciation (\$14,000).
(4) \$14,000.	Same as prior year since it is straight-line depreciation.
(5) \$85,400.	(Number of shares [3,000] times fair value [\$25]) plus demolition cost of existing building (\$10,400).
(6) None.	No depreciation before use.
(7) \$16,000.	Fair market value.
(8) \$2,400.	Cost (\$16,000) times percentage (15%).
(9) \$2,040.	Cost (\$16,000) less prior year's depreciation (\$2,400) equals \$13,600. Multiply \$13,600 times 15%.
(10) \$99,000.	Total cost (\$110,000) less repairs and maintenance (\$11,000).
(11) \$17,000.	Cost less salvage (\$99,000 – \$5,500) times 10/55.
(12) \$5,100.	Cost less salvage (\$99,000 – \$5,500) times 9/55 times one-third of a year.
(13) \$30,840.	(Annual payment [\$4,000] times present value of annuity at 8% for 10 years [6.71]) plus down payment (\$4,000). This can be computed from an annuity due table since the payments are at the beginning of each year. To convert from an annuity in arrears to an annuity due factor, proceed as follows: For eleven payments use the present value in arrears for 10 years (6.710) plus 1.00. Multiply this factor (7.710) times \$4,000 annual payment.
(14) \$2,056.	Cost (\$30,840) divided by estimated life (15 years).

Group and Composite Depreciation

Depreciation on homogenous (group) assets or on heterogeneous (composite) assets with similar characteristics may be computed by compiling the assets into a single asset account for depreciation purposes. A rate is established based upon the average life of the assets in the account and the rate is applied to the balance in the asset account each period to compute the depreciation expense. A retirement of an asset is recorded by crediting the asset account for the original cost of the asset and debiting the accumulated depreciation account for the difference between the original cost and the proceeds received. **Gains and losses on retirements are not usually recognized.** A gain or loss is normally recognized only after the last asset within the group is retired.

SFAS #121 -- ACCOUNTING FOR THE IMPAIRMENT OF LONG-LIVED ASSETS AND FOR LONG-LIVED ASSETS TO BE DISPOSED OF (COVERS LONG-LIVED ASSETS AND IDENTIFIABLE INTANGIBLE ASSETS)

I. Impairment of Long-Lived Assets

A. Review for Impairment

When events and circumstances indicate that the carrying amount of the asset is not recoverable, it is assumed to be impaired. Examples of possible events and circumstances are listed below:

1. Drop-off in demand; coupled with the company's inability to keep pace with advancing technology.
2. A current period operating loss.
3. A significant decrease in the fair value of the asset.
4. A negative cash flow.

B. Impairment Test

If the future net cash flows (not present value) expected to be generated by the asset are less than the carrying value, an impairment loss should be recognized.

C. Measurement of the Impairment Loss

The loss is the amount by which the carrying amount exceeds the **fair value.** If the fair value is not available, the **present value** of future cash flows may be used.

Note: After the impairment loss is recognized, the adjusted carrying amount is considered the new "cost" and the restoration of the impairment loss is prohibited.

II. **Assets to be Disposed of**

A. Assets to be disposed of should be reported at the lower of the carrying amount or fair value less the cost to sell.

B. Unlike the impaired long-lived assets, future changes in the estimated fair value including recoveries may be reflected as adjustments to the carrying value of the assets to be disposed of as long as the adjusted carrying value does not exceed the **initial** carrying value.

III. NOTE: SFAS #121 does not apply to disposal of a segment of a business.

Example of Asset Impairment:

AMC Corporation experienced its first loss in 1997. The loss along with a decrease in demand for its products and an inability to keep pace with advancing technology has management concerned about possible impairment of its assets. The three-year old factory is being depreciated over 20 years and the machinery over 10 years, but because of the decrease in demand AMC believes that a more realistic estimate would be five years. The carrying value of the factory and machinery is $2,500,000. The company projects total (not discounted) net cash flows for the next five years to be $2,000,000. Since it is difficult to estimate the fair value of the factory and the machinery, AMC calculates the present value of the net cash flows for the next five years as a substitute for the fair market value ($1,400,000). (The discount rate used is the rate of return used for evaluating capital budgeting projects.)

The calculation of the potential impairment is done in two steps:

A. The Impairment Test

B. Calculation of the Loss

A. **Impairment Test**

Compare the carrying value of the factory and machinery	$2,500,000
vs.	
Nondiscounted expected net cash flows	$2,000,000
Since the net cash flows are **less** than the carrying value, an impairment loss must be recognized.	

B. **Calculation of the Loss**

Carrying value of the factory and machinery	$2,500,000
vs.	
Fair Market Value (Present Value of Future Cash Flows	$1,400,000
IMPAIRMENT LOSS TO BE RECOGNIZED	$1,100,000

RESEARCH AND DEVELOPMENT COSTS—SFAS #2

Under this statement all items defined as research and development (R&D) costs are to be **expensed when incurred**. The statement defines the inclusions and exclusions as to research and development costs as well as elements of cost to be identified as research and development activities.

Definition of R&D Costs

a. **Research** is planned search or critical investigation aimed at discovery of new knowledge with the hope that such knowledge will be useful in developing a new product or service (hereinafter "product") or a new process or technique (hereinafter "process") or in bringing about a significant improvement to an existing product or process.

b. **Development** is the translation of research findings or other knowledge into a plan or design for a new product or process or for a significant improvement to an existing product or process whether intended for sale or use. It includes the conceptual formulation, design, and testing of product alternatives, construction of prototypes, and operation of pilot plants. It does not include routine or periodic alterations to existing products, production lines, manufacturing processes, and other ongoing operations, even though those alterations may represent improvements, and it does not include market research or market testing activities.

Activities Included in R&D Costs

a. Laboratory research aimed at discovery of new knowledge.
b. Searching for applications of new research findings or other knowledge.
c. Conceptual formulation and design of possible product or process alternatives.
d. Testing in search for or evaluation of product or process alternatives.
e. Modification of the formulation or design of a product or process.
f. Design, construction, and testing of pre-production prototypes and models.
g. Design of tools, jigs, molds, and dies involving new technology.
h. Design, construction, and operation of a pilot plant that is not of a scale economically feasible to the enterprise for commercial production.
i. Engineering activity required to advance the design of a product to the point that it meets specific functional and economic requirements and is ready for manufacture.

Exclusions from R&D Costs

a. Engineering follow-through in an early phase of commercial production.
b. Quality control during commercial production, including routine testing of products.
c. Trouble-shooting in connection with breakdowns during commercial production.
d. Routine, ongoing efforts to refine, enrich, or otherwise improve upon the qualities of an existing product.
e. Adaptation of an existing capability to a particular requirement or customer's need as part of a continuing commercial activity.
f. Seasonal or other periodic design changes to existing products.
g. Routine design of tools, jigs, molds, and dies.
h. Activity, including design and construction engineering, related to the construction, relocation, rearrangements, or start-up of facilities or equipment other than (1) pilot plants (see paragraph h. above), and (2) facilities or equipment whose sole use is for a particular research and development project (see below).
i. Legal work in connection with patent applications or litigation, and the sale or licensing of patents. Legal Exp.

Elements of Costs Identified with R&D Activities

a. **Materials, equipment, and facilities.** The costs of materials (whether from the enterprise's normal inventory or acquired specially for research and development activities) and equipment or facilities that are acquired or constructed for R&D activities and that have alternative future uses (in R&D projects or otherwise) shall be capitalized as tangible assets when acquired or constructed. The cost of such materials consumed in R&D activities and the depreciation of such equipment or facilities used in those activities are R&D costs. However, the costs of materials, equipment, or facilities that are acquired or constructed for a particular R&D project that have no alternative future uses (in other R&D projects or otherwise), and, therefore, no separate economic values, are R&D costs at the time the costs are incurred.

b. **Personnel.** Salaries, wages and other related costs of personnel engaged in R&D activities should be included in R&D costs.

c. **Intangibles purchased from others.** The costs of intangibles that are purchased from others for use in R&D activities and that have alternative future uses (in R&D projects or otherwise) shall be capitalized and amortized as intangible assets in accordance with APB Opinion No. 17 (section 5141). The amortization of those intangible assets used in R&D activities is an R&D cost. However, the costs of intangibles that are purchased from others for a particular R&D project and that have no alternative future uses (in other R&D projects or otherwise), and, therefore, no separate economic values, are R&D costs at the time the costs are incurred.

d. **Contract services.** The costs of services performed by others in connection with the R&D activities of an enterprise, including R&D conducted by others in behalf of the enterprise, shall be included in R&D costs.
e. **Indirect costs.** R&D costs shall include a reasonable allocation of indirect costs. However, general and administrative costs that are not clearly related to R&D activities shall not be included as R&D costs.

Outside Funding—SFAS #68

When a research and development arrangement is funded by others and the enterprise is obligated to repay any of the funds provided by the other parties regardless of the outcome of the research and development, the enterprise shall estimate and recognize that liability.

To conclude that a liability does not exist, the transfer of the financial risk involved with research and development from the enterprise to the other parties must be substantive and genuine. To the extent that the enterprise is committed to repay any of the funds provided by the other parties regardless of the outcome of the research and development, all or part of the risk has not been transferred. If conditions suggest that it is probable (see SFAS #5) that the enterprise will repay any of the funds regardless of the outcome of the research and development, there is a presumption that the enterprise has an obligation to repay the other parties. That presumption can be overcome only by substantial evidence to the contrary.

An enterprise that incurs a liability to repay the other parties shall charge the research and development costs to expense as incurred. The amount of funds provided by the other parties might exceed the enterprise's liability. If so, the enterprise shall charge its portion of the research and development costs to expense in the same manner as the liability is incurred. For example, the liability might arise as the initial funds are expended, or the liability might arise on a pro rata basis.

ACCOUNTING FOR NONMONETARY TRANSACTIONS—APB #29

Summary

When nonmonetary transactions occur, the fair values of the items exchanged are compared and the resulting gain or loss is recognized. Exceptions to the general rule:

1. If fair value is not determinable, recorded value should be used.
2. Exchange of similar type assets, e.g., a machine for a machine of the same general type, does not culminate the earning process, and a gain is not recorded. unless Cash is Recieved
3. If monetary consideration is received in an exchange of similar assets, partial gain is recognized. The gain is the percentage of monetary consideration to total consideration X total gain.
4. When similar assets are exchanged, and monetary consideration is paid, **gain** should not be recognized on the transaction, but the "income tax method" should be used in recording the new asset. However, if a loss is indicated by the terms of a transaction, such loss should be recognized.

Definitions

Monetary assets and liabilities. Assets and liabilities whose amounts are fixed in terms of units of currency by contract or otherwise. Examples are cash, short- or long-term accounts and notes receivable in cash, and short- or long-term accounts and notes payable in cash.

Nonmonetary assets and liabilities. Assets and liabilities other than monetary ones. Examples are inventories; investments in common stocks; property, plant and equipment; and liabilities for rent collected in advance.

Exchange (or exchange transaction). A reciprocal transfer between an enterprise and another entity that results in the enterprise's acquiring assets or services or satisfying liabilities by surrendering other assets or services or incurring other obligations.

Nonreciprocal transfer. A transfer of assets or services in one direction, either from an enterprise to its owners (whether or not in exchange for their ownership interests) or another entity, or from owners or another entity to the enterprise. An entity's reacquisition of its outstanding stock is an example of a nonreciprocal transfer.

Similar productive assets. Productive assets that are of the same general type, that perform the same function, or that are employed in the same line of business. Examples include the trade of player contracts by professional sports organizations, exchange of leases on mineral properties, exchange of one form of interest in an oil-producing property for another form of interest, exchange of real estate for real estate.

Monetary assets are as defined in price-level accounting; i.e., assets and liabilities whose amounts are fixed in terms of currency by contract or otherwise, such as cash, accounts and notes receivable, and accounts and notes payable. Nonmonetary assets are everything else, including investments in securities, inventories, fixed assets, etc.

Exchange of Dissimilar Assets

If dissimilar assets are exchanged, the cost of the nonmonetary asset received is the fair value of the asset surrendered to obtain it, and a gain or loss should be recognized; which is measured by the difference between the fair value and the book value of the asset given up. If the fair value of the asset given up is unknown, or the fair value of the asset received is more clearly evident, then the latter should be used to record the cost of the asset received. In such situations the gain or loss is computed as the difference between the fair value received and the book value of the asset given up. This is the case in the following example:

Dissimilar assets are exchanged. The asset received has a fair value of $1,000. The asset given up has a book value of $500.

Asset Received	$1,000	
Asset Given Up		$500
Gain		500
(earnings process is considered culminated)		

If a monetary consideration was involved in the exchange of dissimilar assets, the gain or loss would be the same.

Exchange of Similar Productive Assets

1. **No monetary consideration—gain indicated.** If the assets were similar, the treatment for dissimilar assets would be modified so as to result in no gain. Assume the same facts as above:

Asset Received	$500	
Asset Given Up		$500

2. **No monetary consideration—loss indicated.** Regardless of the circumstances, an indicated loss is recognized. Assume the asset received has a fair value of $2,000, whereas the asset exchanged cost $4,000 with accumulated depreciation of $1,600. The indicated loss of $400 would be recorded as follows:

Loss	$ 400	
Accumulated Depreciation	1,600	
New Asset	2,000	
Old Asset		$4,000

3. **Monetary consideration received.** Assume that similar assets are exchanged. The asset given up has a book value of $800. The asset received has a fair value of $900 and $600 in cash is received.

Asset Received	$480	
Cash	600	
Asset Given Up		$800
Gain		280
(earnings process partially culminated)		

The cash received is considered to be a partial realization of the F.V. of the asset given up and gain is recognized pro-rata. The gain can be computed as:

$$\frac{600 \text{ (Cash)}}{1{,}500 \text{ (Total Proceeds)}} \times \text{Gain } (700) = \$280$$

If a loss is indicated in such an exchange, the entire loss should be recognized.

4. **Monetary consideration paid.** If cash is paid in addition to a similar asset exchanged, no gain should be recognized; the cash paid merely increases the recorded cost. Treatment is the same as the "income tax method." Ex.:

Asset Received	$1,000	
Asset Given Up (BV)		$600
Cash		400

5. **Monetary consideration paid—loss indicated.** If a loss is indicated by a transaction, the entire loss should be recognized. For example, assume the following: An old machine that cost $6,000, with accumulated depreciation of $3,000, was traded in on a new machine, with a $5,500 cash payment. The new machine has a list price of $8,000, but normally sells for $7,500 without a trade-in.

Computation of Indicated Loss:

Book value of old machine ($6,000 – $3,000)		$3,000
Cost of new machine	$7,500	
Less: Cash paid	5,500	
Value received for old machine		2,000
Indicated loss		$1,000

Journal Entry to Record the Loss:

New machine	$7,500	
Accumulated depreciation	3,000	
Loss	1,000	
Old machine		$6,000
Cash		5,500

Nonreciprocal Transfers to Owners

Nonreciprocal transfers are payments to or from an entity, such as dividends, contributions to others or from others, and sales of stock. Gain or loss should be recognized on nonreciprocal transfers to owners and others.

For example, nonmonetary assets worth $10,000, book value $6,000 are distributed to shareholders.

Assets	$ 4,000	
Gain		$ 4,000
Dividends Paid	10,000	
Assets		10,000

Other Points

An exchange of a product or property held for sale in the ordinary course of business for a product or property to be sold in the same line of business to facilitate sales to customers does not culminate the earnings process. No gain or loss should be recorded.

A difference between the amount of gain or loss recognized for tax purposes and that recognized for accounting purposes may constitute a timing difference to be accounted for according to SFAS #109, *Accounting for Income Taxes*.

An enterprise that engages in one or more nonmonetary transactions during a period should **disclose** in financial statements for the period the nature of the transactions, the basis of accounting for the assets transferred, and gains or losses recognized on transfers.

INTANGIBLE ASSETS

SFAS 142 and Goodwill

SFAS 142 provides two major changes in financial reporting related to business combinations. The first major change is that goodwill will no longer be amortized systematically over time. This non-amortization approach will be applied to both previously recognized and newly acquired goodwill. In the second major change, goodwill will be subject to an annual test for impairment. When the carrying amount of goodwill exceeds its implied fair value, an impairment loss is recognized equal to that excess. **(see chapter 4)**

SFAS 142 *and Other Intangible Assets*

SFAS 142 recommends that all identified intangible assets should be amortized over their economic useful life, unless such life is considered *indefinite.* The term *indefinite life* is defined as a life that extends beyond the foreseeable future. A recognized intangible asset with an indefinite life should not be amortized unless and until its life is determined to be finite. Importantly, indefinite does not mean infinite. Also, the useful life on an intangible asset should not be considered indefinite because a precise finite life is not known.

For those intangible assets with finite lives, the method of amortization should reflect the pattern of decline in the economic usefulness of the asset. If no such pattern is apparent, the straight-line method of amortization should be used. The amount to be amortized should be the value assigned to the intangible asset less any residual value. In most cases the residual value is presumed to be zero. However, that presumption may be overcome if the acquiring enterprise has a commitment from a third party to purchase the intangible at the end of its useful life, or an observable market exists for the intangible asset that provides a basis for estimating a terminal value.

The length of the amortization period for identifiable intangibles (i.e., those not included in goodwill), depends primarily on the assumed economic life of the asset. Factors that should be considered in determining the useful life of an intangible asset include

- Legal, regulatory, or contractual provisions
- The effects of obsolescence, demand, competition, industry stability, rate of technological change, and expected changes in distribution channels
- The expected use of the intangible asset by the enterprise
- The level of maintenance expenditure required to obtain the asset's expected future benefits

Note: SFAS 142 eliminated the arbitrary limit of 40 years for amortization of intangibles.

Any recognized intangible assets considered to possess indefinite lives are not amortized but instead are tested for impairment on an annual basis. To test for impairment, the carrying amount of the intangible asset is compared to its fair value. If the fair value is less than the carrying amount, then the intangible asset is considered impaired and an impairment loss is recognized and the asset's carrying value is reduced accordingly.

Internally Generated Cost of Intangibles

The cost of developing, maintaining, or restoring intangible assets which are not specifically identifiable, have indeterminate lives, or are inherent in a continuing business, should be expensed.

ORGANIZATION COST AND COST OF START-UP ACTIVITIES – SOP 98-5

In 1998 the AICPA decided that organizational cost and start-up cost should be **expensed** as incurred. For entities that had capitalized organizational cost in the past, the adoption of the new method should be reported as the cumulative effect of a change in accounting principle, but entities are not required to report the pro forma effects of retroactive application.

CAPITALIZATION OF INTEREST COST—SFAS #34

Material interest costs incurred by a firm for assets constructed or produced for its use or assets which are intended to be leased or sold should be capitalized as part of the cost of the asset. Interest is not to be capitalized for routinely manufactured inventories, inventories produced in large quantities (inventories requiring aging, for example), assets which are ready for use, or assets which are not yet ready for use but are not in the process of completion (a building which is one-half completed but construction is halted due to litigation). In this case, interest would continue to be capitalized when construction continues.

Interest costs are initially capitalized during planning stages and capitalization continues even if such capitalization raises the asset cost above market value. (The reduction of the asset to market is a separate accounting transaction.)

The amount of interest to be capitalized is based upon the Company's actual borrowings. The amount to be capitalized is that portion of interest incurred during the construction or acquisition period which could have been avoided had the assets not been acquired. If there is a specific borrowing related to the qualifying asset, the interest on such borrowing is the amount used. If the borrowing is less than the cost of the asset, then the interest capitalized for the excess is the amount paid for recent borrowings. If the Company has no specific or other recent borrowings, then the rate to be used is the average rate of old borrowings.

When computing the amount of interest to be capitalized, such interest should be compounded; i.e., the amount is based on all costs previously incurred including interest. The amount of interest to be capitalized cannot exceed the total interest cost for the period, both of which must be disclosed.

FORMULA FOR CAPITALIZATION OF INTEREST

Average accumulated expenditures during construction	X	Appropriate Interest Rate	X	Construction Period

Example:
X Company began construction of a new plant on January 1, 1999 and the expenditures incurred evenly throughout the year totaled $4,000,000 on December 31. X Company had the following debt structure at year-end.

Mortgage on plant under construction at an 8% interest rate	$1,500,000
Other borrowings at a weighted average interest rate of 10%	500,000

Calculation of Average Accumulated Expenditures for 1999:

$$= \frac{\text{January 1 total expenditures} + \text{December 31 total expenditures}}{2}$$

$$= \frac{0 + \$4,000,000.}{2}$$

= $2,000,000 Average accumulated expenditures

Formula Amount of Capitalized Interest:

Average accumulated expenditures during construction	X	Appropriate Interest Rate	X	Construction Period		
$1,500,000*	X	8% mortgage rate	X	1 year	=	$120,000
500,000	X	10% other interest rate	X	1 year	=	50,000
formula amount of interest capitalized					=	$170,000

*The steps used in selecting the interest rates for the $2,000,000 of average accumulated expenditures are to first use the 8% interest rate on the $1,500,000 mortgage and then use the 10% interest rate on the other borrowings for the remaining $500,000.

Calculation of Actual Interest Cost:

Mortgage Interest	=	**$1,500,000**	**X**	**8%**	**X**	**1 year**	=	**$120,000**
Other borrowings	=	**$ 800,000**	**X**	**10%**	**X**	**1 year**	=	**$80,000**
Actual interest cost							=	**$200,000**

The amount of interest capitalized is the lower of the formula amount of interest and the actual interest. In this case the formula amount of interest is lower and the amount capitalized would be $170,000.

SFAS 142 Intangible Asset Disclosure

For intangible assets acquired either individually or with a group of assets, the following information shall be disclosed in the notes to the financial statements in the period of acquisition:

a. For intangible assets subject to amortization:
   1. The total amount assigned and the amount assigned to any major **intangible asset class**
   2. The amount of any significant residual value, in total and by major intangible asset class

3. The weighted-average amortization period, in total and by major intangible asset class

b. For intangible assets *not* subject to amortization, the total amount assigned and the amount assigned to any major intangible asset class
c. The amount of research and development assets acquired and written off in the period and the line item in the income statement in which the amounts written off are aggregated.

The following information shall be disclosed in the financial statements or the notes to the financial statements for each period for which a statement of financial position is presented:

a. For intangible assets subject to amortization:
    1. The gross carrying amount and accumulated amortization, in total and by major intangible asset class
    2. The aggregate amortization expense for the period
    3. The estimated aggregate amortization expense for each of the five succeeding fiscal years
b. For intangible assets *not* subject to amortization, the total carrying amount and the carrying amount for each major intangible asset class

INTEREST ON RECEIVABLES AND PAYABLES—APB #21

How should a note **receivable** or note **payable** be recorded when the face amount does not represent the present value of the consideration given or received in the exchange?

Example: A Co. gives B Co. a note for $5,000 as payment for equipment which has a fair or cash value of $3,500. The note is to be paid $1,000 per year with no interest stipulated. In such case the note should be recorded at the fair value of the equipment or the market value of the note. This requires recognition of the interest element which exists in the transaction.

Entry for A. Co.:

	Debit	Credit
Equipment	$3,500	
Discount on N/P	$1,500	
Notes Payable		$5,000

Entry for B Co.:

	Debit	Credit
N/R	$5,000	
Discount on N/R		$1,500
Sales		$3,500

As the periodic payments are made by A to B, A will recognize interest expense and B will recognize interest income. (Note: This example presumes that both parties recognize the interest element involved and record the transaction correctly. There is no requirement that parties to a transaction coordinate the entries.)

Scope of APB #21

The opinion does **not** apply to the following situations:

a. Receivables and payables arising from transactions with customers or suppliers in the normal course of business which are due in customary trade terms not exceeding approximately one year;
b. amounts which do not require repayment in the future, but rather will be applied to the purchase price of the property, goods, or service involved (e.g., deposits or progress payments on construction contracts, advance payments for acquisition of resources and raw materials, advances to encourage exploration in the extractive industries);
c. amounts intended to provide security for one party to an agreement (e.g., security deposits, retainages on contracts);
d. the customary cash lending activities and demand or savings deposit activities of financial institutions whose primary business is lending money;
e. transactions where interest rates are affected by the tax attributes or legal restrictions prescribed by a governmental agency (e.g., industrial revenue bonds, tax exempt obligations, government guaranteed obligations, income tax settlements); and
f. transactions between parent and subsidiaries and between subsidiaries of a common parent.

The opinion **applies** to situations which otherwise qualify where the debt instrument contains no provision for interest or an unrealistic interest rate.

Note Exchanged for Cash

A note issued or received for cash with no other right or privilege exchanged has a value equal to the cash proceeds. **Example**: A loans B $10,000 at 4% interest. The rate for similar loans at the time of the transaction is 9%. No other rights or privileges are included in the exchange. The note would be recorded at the $10,000 amount and the interest at 4%.

Other Rights or Privileges Included

When unstated rights or privileges are exchanged along with a note, such items should be given accounting recognition.

Example: On January 1, Sell Co. received a 5-year $100,000 interest-free loan from Buy, Inc., in exchange for a contract to supply spare parts at a certain price for five years. Sell Co. normally would pay 10% for the use of the funds. The present value of 1 at 10% for five periods is .62092. Sell should record the loan in the following manner:

Cash	$100,000	
Discount on Note Payable	37,908	
Note Payable		$100,000
Unearned Income		37,908

Calculations:	Present Value of Note	- $100,000 × .62092 = $62,092
	Discount on Note	- $100,000 – 62,092 = $37,908
	Unearned Income	- Amortized over the life of the contract

During the year, Sell Co. sold an estimated 10% of the amount to be involved in the 5-year contract and amortized 10% of the unearned income.

Unearned Income	3,791	
Sales		3,791

At year end, Sell Co. recorded interest as follows:

Interest Expense	$6,209	(10% × 62,092)
Discount on Note Payable		$6,209

Sell Co. would show the following for Notes Payable:

Notes Payable	$100,000	
Less Discount	31,699	($37,908 – 6,209)
	$ 68,301	

Note Exchanged for Property, Goods, or Service

There is a general presumption that the stated interest rate represents fair and adequate compensation for the goods or services. This does not apply, however, if (1) interest is not stated, (2) is unreasonable, or (3) the stated face amount of the note is materially different from the current cash sales price for the same or similar items or from the market value of the note at the date of the transaction.

In such cases, the property exchanged for the note should be recorded at the fair value of the **property** or **note**, whichever is more clearly determinable. Any resulting discount or premium should, of course, be accounted for as interest using an imputed rate.

1. **Asset acquired for note—periodic payments**

An asset was acquired in exchange for a $100,000 note, payable $10,000 a year for 10 years. The interest for similar risks is 6%. The present value of an ordinary annuity of 1 at 6% for 10 periods is 7.36.

Face amount	$100,000
P.V. of ten $10,000 payments over a 10-year period at 6%	73,600
Discount—to be amortized as interest expense	$ 26,400

1st year:

Amount of note		$73,600
Payment	$10,000	
Interest @ 6%	4,416	5,584
		$68,016

5th year:

Amount of note		$42,123
Payment	$10,000	
Interest @ 6%	2,528	7,472
		$34,651

Last Payment:

Amount of note	$ 9,433
Interest @ 6%	567
Payment	$10,000

Recording the Asset

Asset	$ 73,600	
Note discount	26,400	
Notes Payable		$100,000

Stacking machine purchased for $100,000 to be paid over 10 years @ $10,000 per year.

Balance Sheet Presentation

	Year 0	*Year 1*
Notes Payable	$100,000	$90,000
Less: Discount on Note Payable	26,400	21,984
	$ 73,600	$68,016

Entry to record first payment

Interest Expense	$ 4,416	
Notes Payable	10,000	
Cash		$10,000
Note discount		4,416

First payment of $10,000 on Note Payable
Interest at 6% × $73,600

2. **Asset acquired for note—lump sum payment**

The same asset was acquired for a $100,000 note to be paid in a lump sum at the end of 10 years. The present value of 1 at 6% for 10 periods is .5584.

Face amount	$100,000
P.V. of one $100,000 payment to be paid in 10 years	55,840
Discount—to be amortized as interest expense	$ 44,160

1st year:

Amount of note	$55,840
Interest payable at 6%	3,350
Total payable	$59,190

2nd year:

Interest payable at 6%	3,551
Total payable	$62,741

Note: The amount payable at the end of any year can be obtained from "present value of 1" interest tables.

10th year:

Amount of note	$ 55,840
Nine years' interest	38,500
	94,340
Interest at 6%	5,660
Total amount payable	$100,000

Recording the Asset

Asset	$55,840	
Note discount	44,160	
Notes Payable		$100,000

Stacking machine purchased for $100,000 to be paid at the end of 10 years.

Balance Sheet Presentation

	Year 0	*Year 1*
Notes Payable	$100,000	$100,000
Less: Discount on Notes Payable	44,160	40,810
	$ 55,840	$ 59,190

Interest Expense	$3,350	
Note discount		$3,350

Amortization of note discount for year 1—6% × 55,840

Statement Presentation of Discount and Premium

The discount or premium resulting from the determination of present value in cash or noncash transactions is not an asset or liability separable from the note which gives rise to it. Therefore, **the discount or premium should be reported in the balance sheet as a direct deduction from or addition to the face amount of the note.** It should not be classified as a deferred charge or deferred credit. The description of the note should include the effective interest rate; the face amount should also be disclosed in the financial statements or in the notes to the statements. Amortization of discount or premium should be reported as interest in the statement of income. Issue costs should be reported in the balance sheet as deferred charges.

Discounting a Note Receivable

When a company discounts a note which it is holding, the proceeds are determined by taking the (bank's) discount rate and applying it against the maturity value of the note for the period the bank will be holding the note. This amount is the bank's discount and is subtracted from the maturity value to arrive at the proceeds.

Example: Terms of note: $10,000, 12% 90-day note
Discounted after 30 days
Maturity value: $10,300 ($10,000 × 12% × 90/360)
Bank's discount rate = 15%
$10,300 × 15% × 60/360 = $257.50
Proceeds = $10,300 – 257.50 = $10,042.50

Q 57+58

RELATED PARTY DISCLOSURES—SFAS #57

SFAS #57 established formal requirements for disclosures which are to be made of material related party transactions (not compensation). Related party transactions include those between the company and its parent, subsidiary, (also between subsidiaries of a common parent), principal owners or management (including their families), affiliates, or a pension trust managed by the company.

Required disclosures do not include transactions which are eliminated in consolidation but include:

a. The nature of the relationship.
b. A description of the transaction (includes transactions to which no or small amounts are ascribed).
c. Other information necessary to understand the effects of the transactions or the financial statements.
d. Amounts of the transactions for each period and the effects of any change in the method of establishing the terms from that used in the preceding period.
e. Balance due from or to related parties at balance sheet date for each balance sheet presented.
f. Nature of control relationships when reporting company and one or more other companies are under common control; (applies even if no transactions between companies) if such common control could result in financial results significantly different than those that would have been obtained if the companies were autonomous.

In addition, companies may not imply that related party transactions were on terms equivalent to those as if they were at arm's length (unless such representations can be substantiated).

ACCOUNTING FOR COMPENSATED ABSENCES—SFAS #43

An employer shall accrue a liability for employees' compensation for future absences if all of the following conditions are met:

(a) The employer's obligation relating to employees' rights to receive compensation for future absences is attributable to employees' services already rendered.
(b) The obligation relates to rights that vest or accumulate.
(c) Payment of the compensation is probable, and
(d) The amount can be reasonably estimated.

If an employer meets conditions (a), (b), and (c) and does not accrue a liability because condition (d) is not met, that fact shall be disclosed.

Notwithstanding the conditions specified above, an employer is not required to accrue a liability for nonvesting accumulating rights to receive sick pay benefits (that is, compensation for an employee's absence due to illness) since the lower degree of reliability of estimates of future sick pay does not justify such an accrual.

Statement of Financial Accounting Standards No. 143 – Accounting for Asset Retirement Obligations

In FASB's words, Statement No. 143's stated objective is to "establish accounting standards for recognition and measurement of a liability for an asset retirement obligation and an associated asset retirement cost."

Statement No. 143 applies to tangible long-lived assets, including individual assets, functional groups of related assets and significant parts of assets. It covers a company's **legal obligations** resulting from the acquisition, construction, development or normal operation of a capital asset.

Basic Approach

- A business must recognize an asset retirement obligation for a long-lived asset at the point an obligating event takes place – provided it can reasonably estimate its fair value (or at the earliest date it can make a reasonable estimate).
- The entity must record the obligation at its fair value, either the amount at which the liability could be settled in a current transaction between willing parties in an active market, or – more likely—at a substitute for market value, such as the present value of the estimated future cash flows required to satisfy the obligation.
- To offset the credit portion of the asset retirement liability entry, businesses must capitalize the asset retirement costs as an increase in the carrying amount of the related long-term asset.
- Businesses must include certain costs in the income statement during the asset's life—namely depreciation on the asset, including additional capitalized retirement costs, and interest for the accretion of the asset retirement liability due to the passage of time.

This statement is particularly applicable to industries such as oil refineries, electric power plants and mines which all have unusually long lives. Therefore, the calculation of the fair value of the retirement obligation will probably be based on projections of the present value of future cash flows using educated guesses about inflation, labor cost, technological advances and profit margins. This discount rate used is what the FASB calls a **credit-adjusted risk-free rate.** Therefore, the effect of the entity's credit standing is reflected in the discount rate rather than in the estimated cash flows.

Example:

- XYZ purchases an asset for $1,000,000
- Company incurs an obligation upon installation to retire the asset
- Straight-line depreciation over a 10-year life
- 10% credit-adjusted risk-free discount rate
- Because of the difficulty in projecting cash flows the company used three different estimates and weights them based on probability.

Estimates	Estimated Cash Outflow Year 10	Probability	Weighting
1	300,000	20%	$ 60,000
2	500,000	60%	300,000
3	550,000	20%	110,000
	Expected cash outflow		$470,000

Present value at 10% =
470,000 x pv of $1 (.38554) = $181,204

XYZ would make the following journal entries to record the purchase of the asset and record the asset retirement liability:

		Debit	Credit
JE	Tangible Asset (cost)	1,000,000	
	Cash		1,000,000
JE	Tangible Asset	181,204	
	Asset Retirement Liability		181,204

At the end of the first year the following entries would be made:

		Debit	Credit
JE	Depreciation Expense	118,120	
	Accumulated Depreciation		118,120
	($1,181,204 / 10 years = $118,120)		
JE	Interest Expense (accretion)	18,120	
	Asset Retirement Liability		18,120
	(10% x $181,204 = $18,120)		

Note: The increase in the asset retirement liability will total $470,000 at the end of 10 years.

This is similar to our recording of a non-interest bearing note payable earlier in the chapter.

Disclosures

An entity shall disclose the following information about its asset retirement obligations:

- A general description of the asset retirement obligations and the associated long-lived assets
- The fair value of assets that are legally restricted for purposes of settling asset retirement obligations
- A reconciliation of the beginning and ending aggregate carrying amount of asset retirement obligations showing separately the changes attributable to
  1. liabilities incurred in the current period
  2. liabilities settled in the current period
  3. accretion expense
  4. revisions in estimated cash flows, whenever there is a significant change in one or more of those four components during the reporting period.

If the fair value of an asset retirement obligation cannot be reasonably estimated, that fact and the reasons therefor shall be disclosed.

Chapter Eleven
Other Assets, Liabilities and Disclosures Questions

ACCOUNTS RECEIVABLE DOUBTFUL ACCOUNTS

1. Which method of recording uncollectible accounts expense is consistent with accrual accounting'?

	Allowance	*Direct write-off*
a.	Yes	Yes
b.	Yes	No
c.	No	Yes
d.	No	No

2. The following information pertains to Oro Corp.:

Credit sales for the year ended December 31, 1995	$450,000
Credit balance in allowance for uncollectible accounts at January 1, 1995	10,800
Bad debts written off during 1995	18,000

According to past experience, 3% of Oro's credit sales have been uncollectible. After provision is made for bad debt expense for the year ended December 31, 1995, the allowance for uncollectible accounts balance would be

a. $6,300
b. $13,500
c. $24,300
d. $31,500

3. The following accounts were abstracted from Roxy Co.'s unadjusted trial balance at December 31, 1996:

	Debit	*Credit*
Accounts receivable	$1,000,000	
Allowance for uncollectible accounts	8,000	
Net credit sales		$3,000,000

Roxy estimates that 3% of the gross accounts receivable will become uncollectible. After adjustment at December 31, 1996, the allowance for uncollectible accounts should have a credit balance of

a. $90,000
b. $82,000
c. $38,000
d. $30,000

4. The following information pertains to Tara Co.'s accounts receivable at December 31, 1999:

Days outstanding	*Amount*	*Estimated % uncollectible*
0 - 60	$120,000	1%
61 - 120	90,000	2%
Over 120	100,000	6%
	$310,000	

During 1999, Tara wrote off $7,000 in receivables and recovered $4,000 that had been written off in prior years. Tara's December 31, 1998, allowance for uncollectible accounts was $22,000. Under the aging method, what amount of allowance for uncollectible accounts should Tara report at December 31, 1999?

a. $9,000
b. $10,000
c. $13,000
d. $19,000

5. Inge Co. determined that the net value of its accounts receivable at December 31, 2000, based on an aging of the receivables, was $325,000. Additional information is as follows:

Allowance for uncollectible accounts - 1/1/00	$ 30,000
Uncollectible accounts written off during 2000	18,000
Uncollectible accounts recovered during 2000	2,000
Accounts receivable at 12/31/00	350,000

For 2000, what would be Inge's uncollectible accounts expense?

a. $ 5,000
b. $11,000
c. $15,000
d. $21,000

6. The following information relates to Jay Co.'s accounts receivable for 1999:

Accounts receivable, 1/1/99	$ 650,000
Credit sales for 1999	2,700,000
Sales returns for 1999	75,000
Accounts written off during 1999	40,000
Collections from customers during 1999	2,150,000
Estimated future sales returns at 12/31/99	50,000
Estimated uncollectible accounts at 12/31/99	110,000

What amount should Jay report for accounts receivable, before allowances for sales returns and uncollectible accounts, at December 31, 1999?

a. $1,200,000
b. $1,125,000
c. $1,085,000
d. $925,000

7. Wren Company had the following account balances at December 31, 1994:

Accounts receivable	$ 900,000
Allowance for doubtful accounts (before any provision for 1994 doubtful accounts expense)	16,000
Credit sales for 1994	1,750,000

Wren is considering the following methods of estimating doubtful accounts expense for 1994:

- Based on credit sales at 2%
- Based on accounts receivable at 5%

What amount should Wren charge to doubtful accounts expense under each method?

	Percentage of credit sales	*Percentage of accounts receivable*
a.	$51,000	$45,000
b.	$51,000	$29,000
c.	$35,000	$45,000
d.	$35,000	$29,000

8. A company uses the allowance method to recognize uncollectible accounts expense. What is the effect at the time of the collection of an account previously written off on each of the following accounts?

	Allowance for uncollectible accounts	*Uncollectible accounts expense*
a.	No effect	Decrease
b.	Increase	Decrease
c.	Increase	No effect
d.	No effect	No effect

9. Gibbs Co. uses the allowance method for recognizing uncollectible accounts. Ignoring deferred taxes, the entry to record the write-off of a specific uncollectible account

a. Affects **neither** net income **nor** working capital.
b. Affects **neither** net income **nor** accounts receivable.
c. Decreases both net income and accounts receivable.
d. Decreases both net income and working capital.

10. Which of the following is a method to generate cash from accounts receivable?

	Assignment	Factoring
a.	Yes	No
b.	Yes	Yes
c.	No	Yes
d.	No	No

11. Gar Co. factored its receivables without recourse with Ross Bank. Gar received cash as a result of this transaction, which is best described as a

a. Loan from Ross collateralized by Gar's accounts receivable.
b. Loan from Ross to be repaid by the proceeds from Gar's accounts receivables.
c. Sale of Gar's accounts receivable to Ross, with the risk of uncollectible accounts retained by Gar.
d. Sale of Gar's accounts receivable to Ross, with the risk of uncollectible accounts transferred to Ross.

FIXED ASSETS

WHAT IS COST?

12. On December 1, 1998, Boyd Co. purchased a $400,000 tract of land for a factory site. Boyd razed an old building on the property and sold the materials it salvaged from the demolition. Boyd incurred additional costs and realized salvage proceeds during December 1998 as follows:

Demolition of old building	$50,000
Legal fees for purchase contract and recording ownership	10,000
Title guarantee insurance	12,000
Proceeds from sale of salvaged materials	8,000

In its December 31, 1998, balance sheet, Boyd should report a balance in the land account of

a. $464,000
b. $460,000
c. $442,000
d. $422,000

13. Merry Co. purchased a machine costing $125,000 for its manufacturing operations and paid shipping costs of $20,000. Merry spent an additional $10,000 testing and preparing the machine for use. What amount should Merry record as the cost of the machine?

a. $155,000.
b. $145,000.
c. $135,000.
d. $125,000.

14. During 1995, Yvo Corp. installed a production assembly line to manufacture furniture. In 1996, Yvo purchased a new machine and rearranged the assembly line to install this machine. The rearrangement did not increase the estimated useful life of the assembly line, but it did result in significantly more efficient production. The following expenditures were incurred in connection with this project:

Machine	$75,000
Labor to install machine	14,000
Parts added in rearranging the assembly line to provide future benefits	40,000
Labor and overhead to rearrange the assembly line	18,000

What amount of the above expenditures should be capitalized in 1996?

a. $147,000
b. $107,000
c. $89,000
d. $75,000

15. Lano Corp.'s forest land was condemned for use as a national park. Compensation for the condemnation exceeded the forest land's carrying amount. Lano purchased similar, but larger, replacement forest land for an amount greater than the condemnation award. As a result of the condemnation and replacement, what is the net effect on the carrying amount of forest land reported in Lano's balance sheet?

a. The amount is increased by the excess of the replacement forest land's cost over the condemned forest land's carrying amount.
b. The amount is increased by the excess of the replacement forest land's cost over the condemnation award.
c. The amount is increased by the excess of the condemnation award over the condemned forest land's carrying amount.
d. No effect, because the condemned forest land's carrying amount is used as the replacement forest land's carrying amount.

DEPRECIATION

16. On January 2, 2000, Lem Corp. bought machinery under a contract that required a down payment of $10,000, plus 24 monthly payments of $5,000 each, for total cash payments of $130,000. The cash equivalent price of the machinery was $110,000. The machinery has an estimated useful life of ten years and estimated salvage value of $5,000. Lem uses straight-line depreciation. In its 2000 income statement, what amount should Lem report as depreciation for this machinery?

a. $10,500.
b. $11,000.
c. $12,500.
d. $13,000.

17. Turtle Co. purchased equipment on January 2, 1998, for $50,000. The equipment had an estimated five-year service life. Turtle's policy for five-year assets is to use the 200% double-declining depreciation method for the first two years of the asset's life, and then switch to the straight-line depreciation method. In its December 31, 2000, balance sheet, what amount should Turtle report as accumulated depreciation for equipment?

a. $30,000.
b. $38,000.
c. $39,200.
d. $42,000.

18. Vore Corp. bought equipment on January 2, 1995 for $200,000. This equipment had an estimated useful life of five years and a salvage value of $20,000. Depreciation was computed by the 150% declining balance method. The accumulated depreciation balance at December 31, 1996, should be

a. $102,000
b. $98,000
c. $91,800
d. $72,000

19. On April 1, 1995, Kew Co. purchased new machinery for $300,000. The machinery has an estimated useful life of five years, and depreciation is computed by the sum-of-the-years'-digits method. The accumulated depreciation on this machinery at March 31, 1997, should be

a. $192,000
b. $180,000
c. $120,000
d. $100,000

20. The graph below depicts three depreciation expense patterns over time.

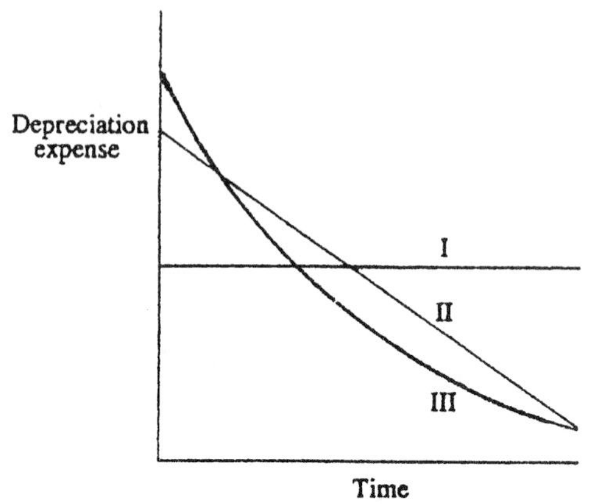

Which depreciation expense pattern corresponds to the sum-of-the-years'-digits method and which corresponds to the double-declining balance method?

	Sum-of-the-years-digits	*Double-declining balance*
a.	III	II
b.	II	I
c.	I	III
d.	II	III

21. On January 2, 1996, Reed Co. purchased a machine for $800,000 and established an annual depreciation charge of $100,000 over an eight-year life. During 1999, after issuing its 1998 financial statements, Reed concluded that: (1) the machine suffered permanent impairment of its operational value, and (2) $200,000 is a reasonable estimate of the amount expected to be recovered through use of the machine for the period January 1, 1999, through December 31, 2003. In Reed's December 31, 1999, balance sheet, the machine should be reported at a carrying amount of

a. $0
b. $100,000
c. $160,000
d. $400,000

22. Depreciation is computed on the original cost less estimated salvage value under which of the following depreciation methods?

	Double-declining balance	*Productive output*
a.	No	No
b.	No	Yes
c.	Yes	Yes
d.	Yes	No

23. In which of the following situations is the units-of-production method of depreciation most appropriate?

a. An asset's service potential declines with use.
b. An asset's service potential declines with the passage of time.
c. An asset is subject to rapid obsolescence.
d. An asset incurs increasing repairs and maintenance with use.

24. Net income is understated if, in the first year, estimated salvage value is excluded from the depreciation computation when using the

	Straight-line method	*Production or use method*
a.	Yes	No
b.	Yes	Yes
c.	No	No
d.	No	Yes

DISPOSAL OF FIXED ASSETS

25. On December 31, 1996, a building owned by Pine Corp. was totally destroyed by fire. The building had fire insurance coverage up to $500,000. Other pertinent information as of December 31, 1996, follows:

Building, carrying amount	$520,000
Building, fair market value	550,000
Removal and clean-up costs	10,000

During January 1997, before the 1996 financial statements were issued, Pine received insurance proceeds of $500,000. On what amount should Pine base the determination of its loss on involuntary conversion?

a. $520,000
b. $530,000
c. $550,000
d. $560,000

26. Weir Co. uses straight-line depreciation for its property, plant, and equipment, which, stated at cost, consisted of the following:

	12/31/99	*12/31/98*
Land	$ 25,000	$ 25,000
Buildings	195,000	195,000
Machinery & Equipment	695,000	650,000
	915,000	870,000
Less accumulated depreciation	400,000	370,000
	$515,000	$500,000

Weir's depreciation expense for 1999 and 1998 was $55,000 and $50,000, respectively. What amount was debited to accumulated depreciation during 1999 because of property, plant, and equipment retirements?

a. $40,000.
b. $25,000.
c. $20,000.
d. $10,000.

COMPOSITE DEPRECIATION

27. A company using the composite depreciation method for its fleet of trucks, cars, and campers retired one of its trucks and received cash from a salvage company. The net carrying amount of these composite asset accounts would be decreased by the

a. Cash proceeds received and original cost of the truck.
b. Cash proceeds received.
c. Original cost of the truck less the cash proceeds.
d. Original cost of the truck.

CAPITALIZED INTEREST

28. Cole Co. began constructing a building for its own use in January 2000. During 2000, Cole incurred interest of $50,000 on specific construction debt, and $20,000 on other borrowings. Interest computed on the weighted-average amount of accumulated expenditures for the building during 2000 was $40,000. What amount of interest cost should Cole capitalize?

a. $20,000.
b. $40,000.
c. $50,000.
d. $70,000.

29. Clay Company started construction of a new office building on January 1, 1991, and moved into the finished building on July 1, 1992. Of the building's $2,500,000 total cost, $2,000,000 was incurred in 1991 evenly throughout the year. Clay's incremental borrowing rate was 12% throughout 1991, and the total amount of interest incurred by Clay during 1991 was $102,000. What amount should Clay report as capitalized interest at December 31, 1991?

a. $102,000
b. $120,000
c. $150,000
d. $240,000

30. During 1987, Belardo Corporation constructed and manufactured certain assets, and incurred the following interest costs in connection with those activities:

	Interest costs incurred
Warehouse constructed for Belardo's own use	$20,000
Special-order machine for sale to unrelated customer, produced according to customer's specifications	9,000
Inventories routinely manufactured, produced on a repetitive basis	7,000

All of these assets required an extended period of time for completion. Assuming the effect of interest capitalization is material, what is the total amount of interest costs to be capitalized?

a. $0.
b. $20,000.
c. $29,000.
d. $36,000.

NON-MONETARY TRANSACTIONS

NON-RECIPROCAL TRANSFERS

31. On June 27, 1999, Brite Co. distributed to its common stockholders 100,000 outstanding common shares of its investment in Quik, Inc., an unrelated party. The carrying amount on Brite's books of Quik's $1 par common stock was $2 per share. Immediately after the distribution, the market price of Quik's stock was $2.50 per share. In its income statement for the year ended June 30, 1999, what amount should Brite report as gain before income taxes on disposal of the stock?

a. $250,000
b. $200,000
c. $50,000
d. $0

TRADE DISSIMILAR ASSETS

32. In October 1996 Allen Company exchanged a used packaging machine, having a book value of $120,000, for a dissimilar new machine and paid a cash difference of $15,000. The market value of the used packaging machine was determined to be $140,000. In its income statement for the year ended December 31, 1996, how much gain should Allen recognize on this exchange?

a. $0
b. $5,000
c. $15,000
d. $20,000

33. Caine Motor Sales exchanged a car from its inventory for a computer to be used as a long-term asset. The following information relates to this exchange that took place on July 31, 1993:

Carrying amount of the car	$30,000
Listed selling price of the car	45,000
Fair value of the computer	43,000
Cash difference paid by Caine	5,000

On July 31, 1993, what amount of profit should Caine recognize on this exchange?

a. $0
b. $8,000
c. $10,000
d. $13,000

TRADE SIMILAR ASSETS - PAY BOOT

34. On December 30, 1990, Diamond Company traded in an old machine with a book value of $10,000 for a similar new machine having a list price of $32,000, and paid a cash difference of $19,000. Diamond should record the new machine at

a. $32,000.
b. $29,000.
c. $22,000.
d. $19,000.

35. Pine Football Company had a player contract with Duff that is recorded in its books at $500,000 on July 1, 1995. Ace Football Company had a player contract with Terry that is recorded in its books at $600,000 on July 1, 1995. On this date, Pine traded Duff to Ace for Terry and paid a cash difference of $50,000. The fair value of the Terry contract was $700,000 on the exchange date. After the exchange, the Terry contract should be recorded in Pine's books at

a. $550,000
b. $600,000
c. $650,000
d. $700,000

36. On March 31, 1995, Winn Company traded in an old machine having a carrying amount of $16,800, and paid a cash difference of $6,000 for a new machine having a total cash price of $20,500. On March 31, 1995, what amount of loss should Winn recognize on this exchange?

a. $0
b. $2,300
c. $3,700
d. $6,000

20,500
16 800 6000
22 800

TRADE SIMILAR ASSETS - RECEIVE BOOT

37. Good Deal Company received $20,000 in cash and a used computer with a fair value of $180,000 from Harvest Corporation for Good Deal's existing computer having a fair value of $200,000 and an undepreciated cost of $160,000 recorded on its books. How much gain should Good Deal recognize on this exchange, and at what amount should the acquired computer be recorded, respectively?

a. Zero and $140,000.
b. $4,000 and $144,000.
c. $20,000 and $160,000.
d. $40,000 and $180,000.

Cash 20
New Asst 144
Gain 4
160

38. Bensol Co. and Sable Co. exchanged similar trucks with fair values in excess of carrying amounts. In addition, Bensol paid Sable to compensate for the difference in truck values. As a consequence of the exchange, Sable recognizes

a. A gain equal to the difference between the fair value and carrying amount of the truck given up.
b. A gain determined by the proportion of cash received to the total consideration.
c. A loss determined by the proportion of cash received to the total consideration.
d. Neither a gain **nor** a loss.

39. May Co. and Sty Co. exchanged nonmonetary assets. The exchange did not culminate an earning process for either May or Sty. May paid cash to Sty in connection with the exchange. To the extent that the amount of cash exceeds a proportionate share of the carrying amount of the asset surrendered, a realized gain on the exchange should be recognized by

	May	*Sty*
a.	Yes	Yes
b.	Yes	No
c.	No	Yes
d.	No	No

INTANGIBLE ASSETS

40. Which of the following costs of goodwill should be capitalized and amortized?

	Maintaining goodwill	*Developing goodwill*
a.	Yes	No
b.	No	No
c.	Yes	Yes
d.	No	Yes

41. Hy Corp. bought Patent A for $40,000 and Patent B for $60,000. Hy also paid acquisition costs of $5,000 for Patent A and $7,000 for Patent B. Both patents were challenged in legal actions. Hy paid $20,000 in legal fees for a successful defense of Patent A and $30,000 in legal fees for an unsuccessful defense of Patent B. What amount should Hy capitalized for patents?

a. $162,000
b. $112,000
c. $65,000
d. $45,000

42. During 2001, Jase Co. incurred research and development costs of $136,000 in its laboratories relating to a patent that was granted on July 1, 2001. Costs of registering the patent equaled $34,000. The patent's legal life is 17 years, and its estimated economic life is 10 years. In its December 31, 2001, balance sheet, what amount should Jase report as patent, net of accumulated amortization?

a. $ 32,300
b. $ 33,000
c. $161,500
d. $165,000

43. On January 2, 1999, Judd Co. bought a trademark from Krug Co. for $500,000. Judd retained an independent consultant, who estimated the trademark's remaining life to be 50 years. Its unamortized cost on Krug's accounting records was $380,000. Judd decided to amortize the trademark over the maximum period allowed. In Judd's December 31, 1999, balance sheet, what amount should be reported as accumulated amortization?

a. $7,600.
b. $9,500.
c. $10,000.
d. $12,500.

44. On January 2, 2000, Rafa Co. purchased a franchise with a useful life of ten years for $50,000. An additional franchise fee of 3% of franchise operation revenues must be paid each year to the franchisor. Revenues from franchise operations amounted to $400,000 during 2000. In its December 31, 2000, balance sheet, what amount should Rafa report as an intangible asset-franchise?

a. $33,000.
b. $43,800.
c. $45,000.
d. $50,000.

ORGANIZATION COST

45. On January 1, 1999, Kew Corp. incurred organization costs of $24,000. For tax purposes, Kew is amortizing these costs over the maximum period allowed by the IRS. For financial reporting purposes, Kew is following GAAP. What portion of organization cost would Kew defer to years subsequent to 1999?

a. $23,400
b. $19,200
c. $4,800
d. $0

COMPUTER SOFTWARE

46. On December 31, 1997, Bit Co. had capitalized costs for a new computer software product with an economic life of five years. Sales for 1998 were 30 percent of expected total sales of the software. At December 31, 1998, the software had a net realizable value equal to 90 percent of the capitalized cost. What percentage of the original capitalized cost should be reported as the net amount on Bit's December 31, 1998, balance sheet?

a. 70%
b. 72%
c. 80%
d. 90%

LEASEHOLD IMPROVEMENTS

47. On January 1, 1995, Nobb Corp. signed a 12-year lease for warehouse space. Nobb has an option to renew the lease for an additional 8-year period on or before January 1, 1999. During January 1997, Nobb made substantial improvements to the warehouse. The cost of these improvements was $540,000, with an estimated useful life of 15 years. At December 31, 1997, Nobb intended to exercise the renewal option. Nobb has taken a full year's amortization on this leasehold. In Nobb's December 31, 1997, balance sheet, the carrying amount of this leasehold improvement should be

a. $486,000
b. $504,000
c. $510,000
d. $513,000

RESEARCH AND DEVELOPMENT

48. Which of the following costs is included in research and development expense?

a. Ongoing efforts to improve existing products.
b. Troubleshooting in connection with breakdowns during commercial production.
c. Periodic design changes to existing products.
d. Design, construction and testing of preproduction prototypes and models.

49. Cody Corp. incurred the following costs during 1996:

Design of tools, jigs, molds and dies involving new technology	$125,000
Modification of the formulation of a process	160,000
Trouble-shooting in connection with breakdowns during commercial production	100,000
Adaptation of an existing capability to a particular customer's need as part of a continuing commercial activity	110,000

In its 1996 income statement, Cody should report research and development expense of

a. $125,000
b. $160,000
c. $235,000
d. $285,000

50. West, Inc., made the following expenditures relating to Product Y:

- Legal costs to file a patent on Product Y—$10,000. Production of the finished product would not have been undertaken without the patent.
- Special equipment to be used solely for development of Product Y—$60,000. The equipment has no other use and has an estimated useful life of four years.
- Labor and material costs incurred in producing a prototype model—$200,000.
- Cost of testing the prototype—$80,000.

What is the total amount of costs that will be expensed when incurred?
a. $280,000
b. $295,000
c. $340,000
d. $350,000

NOTES - APB #21

51. Ogden Corp. lends a supplier cash which is to be repaid five years hence with no stated interest. At the same time a purchase contract is entered into for the supplier's products. Ogden will be required to recognize interest revenue in connection with the loan
a. Under no circumstances.
b. If the contract price is equal to the prevailing market rate.
c. If the contract price is less than the prevailing market rate.
d. If the contract price is more than the prevailing market rate.

52. On December 30, 1996, Bart, Inc., purchased a machine from Fell Corp. in exchange for a noninterest bearing note requiring eight payments of $20,000. The first payment was made on December 30, 1996, and the others are due annually on December 30. At the date of issuance, the prevailing rate of interest for this type of note was 11%. Present value factors are as follows:

Period	*Present value of ordinary annuity of 1 at 11%*	*Present value of annuity in advance of 1 at 11%*
7	4.712	5.231
8	5.146	5.712

On Bart's December 31, 1996, balance sheet, the note payable to Fell was
a. $94,240
b. $102,920
c. $104,620
d. $114,240

53. On January 1, 1995, Ott Company sold goods to Fox Company. Fox signed a noninterest-bearing note requiring payment of $60,000 annually for seven years. The first payment was made on January 1, 1995. The prevailing rate of interest for this type of note at date of issuance was 10%. Information on present value factors is as follows:

Periods	*Present value of 1 at 10%*	*Present value of ordinary annuity of 1 at 10%*
6	.56	4.36
7	.51	4.87

Ott should record the sales revenue in January 1995 of
a. $321,600
b. $292,200
c. $261,600
d. $214,200

Items 54 and 55 are based on the following:
On January 2, 1999, Emme Co. sold equipment with a carrying amount of $480,000 in exchange for a $600,000 noninterest bearing note due January 2, 2002. There was no established exchange price for the equipment. The prevailing rate of interest for a note of this type at January 2, 1999, was 10%. The present value of 1 at 10% for three periods is 0.75.

54. In Emme's 1999 income statement, what amount should be reported as interest income?
a. $9,000.
b. $45,000.
c. $50,000.
d. $60,000.

450,000
x 10%

55. In Emme's 1999 income statement, what amount should be reported as gain (loss) on sale of machinery?
a. ($30,000) loss.
b. $30,000 gain.
c. $120,000 gain.
d. $270,000 gain.

---

56. On December 31, 1998, Jet Co. received two $10,000 notes receivable from customers in exchange for services rendered. On both notes, interest is calculated on the outstanding principal balance at the annual rate of 3% and payable at maturity. The note from Hart Corp., made under customary trade terms, is due in nine months and the note from Maxx, Inc., is due in five years. The market interest rate for similar notes on December 31, 1998, was 8%. The compound interest factors to convert future values into present values at 8% follow:

Present value of $1 due in nine months: .944
Present value of $1 due in five years .680

At what amounts should these two notes receivable be reported in Jet's December 31, 1998, balance sheet?

	Hart	*Maxx*
a.	$9,440	$6,800
b.	$9,652	$7,820
c.	$10,000	$6,800
d.	$10,000	$7,820

DISCOUNTING NOTES

57. After being held for 40 days, a 120-day 12% interest-bearing note receivable was discounted at a bank at 15%. The proceeds received from the bank equal

a. Maturity value less the discount at 12%.
b. Maturity value less the discount at 15%.
c. Face value less the discount at 12%.
d. Face value less the discount at 15%.

58. Roth, Inc. received from a customer a one-year, $500,000 note bearing annual interest of 8%. After holding the note for six months, Roth discounted the note at Regional Bank at an effective interest rate of 10%. What amount of cash did Roth receive from the bank?

a. $540,000.
b. $523,810.
c. $513,000.
d. $495,238.

NOTES - GENERAL

59. Frame Co. has an 8% note receivable dated June 30, 1998, in the original amount of $150,000. Payments of $50,000 in principal plus accrued interest are due annually on July 1, 1999, 2000, and 2001. In its June 30, 2000, balance sheet, what amount should Frame report as a current asset for interest on the note receivable?

a. $0.
b. $4,000.
c. $8,000.
d. $12,000.

60. On August 15, 1998, Benet Co. sold goods for which it received a note bearing the market rate of interest on that date. The four-month note was dated July 15, 1998. Note principal, together with all interest, is due November 15, 1998. When the note was recorded on August 15, which of the following accounts increased?

a. Unearned discount.
b. Interest receivable.
c. Prepaid interest.
d. Interest revenue.

61. On June 1, 1996, Yola Corp. loaned Dale $500,000 on a 12% note, payable in five annual installments of $100,000 beginning January 2, 1997. In connection with this loan, Dale was required to deposit $5,000 in a noninterest-bearing escrow account. The amount held in escrow is to be returned to Dale after all principal and interest payments have been made. Interest on the note is payable on the first day of each month beginning July 1, 1996. Dale made timely payments through November 1, 1996. On January 2, 1997, Yola received payment of the first principal installment plus all interest due. At December 31, 1996, Yola's interest receivable on the loan to Dale should be

a. $0
b. $5,000
c. $10,000
d. $15,000

62. Leaf Co. purchased from Oak Co. a $20,000, 8%, 5-year note that required five equal annual year-end payments of $5,009. The note was discounted to yield a 9% rate to Leaf. At the date of purchase, Leaf recorded the note at its present value of $19,485. What should be the total interest revenue earned by Leaf over the life of this note?

a. $5,045
b. $5,560
c. $8,000
d. $9,000

COMPENSATED ABSENCES

63. On January 1, 1998, Baker Co. decided to grant its employees 10 vacation days and five sick days each year. Sick days may not be carried over to the next year. Each employee took an average of three sick days in 1998. During 1998, each of Baker's six employees earned $100 per day and earned 10 vacation days. These vacation days were taken during 1999. What amount should Baker report for compensated absence expense for the year ended December 31, 1998?

a. $0
b. $6,000
c. $7,200
d. $9,000

64. North Corp. has an employee benefit plan for compensated absences that gives employees 10 paid vacation days and 10 paid sick days. Both vacation and sick days can be carried over indefinitely. Employees can elect to receive payment in lieu of vacation days; however, no payment is given for sick days not taken. At December 31, 1999, North's unadjusted balance of liability for compensated absences was $21,000. North estimated that there were 150 vacation days and 75 sick days available at December 31, 1999. North's employees earn an average of $100 per day. In its December 31, 1999, balance sheet, what amount of liability for compensated absences is North required to report?

a. $36,000
b. $22,500
c. $21,000
d. $15,000

PAYROLL TAXES

65. Bloy Corp.'s payroll for the pay period ended October 31, 1996, is summarized as follows:

Department payroll	*Total wages*	*Federal income tax withheld*	*Amount of wages subject to payroll taxes* — *F.I.C.A.*	*Unemployment*
Factory	$ 60,000	$ 7,000	$56,000	$18,000
Sales	22,000	3,000	16,000	2,000
Office	18,000	2,000	8,000	—
	$100,000	$12,000	$80,000	$20,000

Assume the following payroll tax rates:

F.I.C.A. for employer and employee	7% each
Unemployment	3%

What amount should Bloy accrue as its share of payroll taxes in its October 31, 1996, balance sheet?

a. $18,200
b. $12,600
c. $11,800
d. $6,200

CASH SURRENDER VALUE OF LIFE INSURANCE

66. In 1993, Chain, Inc. purchased a $1,000,000 life insurance policy on its president, of which Chain is the beneficiary. Information regarding the policy for the year ended December 31, 1998, follows:

Cash surrender value, 1/1/98	$ 87,000
Cash surrender value, 12/31/98	108,000
Annual advance premium paid 1/1/98	40,000

During 1998, dividends of $6,000 were applied to increase the cash surrender value of the policy. What amount should Chain report as life insurance expense for 1998?

a. $40,000
b. $25,000
c. $19,000
d. $13,000

RELATED PARTY TRANSACTIONS

67. Dean Co. acquired 100% of Morey Corp. prior to 1996. During 1996, the individual companies included in their financial statements the following:

	Dean	*Morey*
Officers' salaries	$ 75,000	$ 50,000
Officers' expenses	20,000	10,000
Loans to officers	125,000	50,000
Intercompany sales	150,000	—

What amount should be reported as related party disclosures in the notes to Dean's 1996 consolidated financial statements?

a. $150,000
b. $155,000
c. $175,000
d. $330,000

CLASSIFICATION OF ASSETS

68. The following is Gold Corp.'s June 30, 1999, trial balance:

Cash overdraft		$ 10,000
Accounts receivable, net	$ 35,000	
Inventory	58,000	
Prepaid expenses	12,000	
Land held for resale	100,000	
Property, plant, and equipment, net	95,000	
Accounts payable and accrued expenses		32,000
Common stock		25,000
Additional paid-in capital		150,000
Retained earnings		83,000
	$300,000	$300,000

Additional Information:

- Checks amounting to $30,000 were written to vendors and recorded on June 29, 1999, resulting in a cash overdraft of $10,000. The checks were mailed on July 9, 1999.
- Land held for resale was sold for cash on July 15, 1999.
- Gold issued its financial statements on July 31, 1999.

In its June 30, 1999, balance sheet, what amount should Gold report as current assets?

a. $225,000
b. $205,000
c. $195,000
d. $125,000

REVIEW QUESTIONS

Items 69 and 70 are based on the following:

The following trial balance of Trey Co. at December 31, 2000, has been adjusted except for income tax expense.

	Dr.	*Cr.*
Cash	$ 550,000	
Accounts receivable, net	1,650,000	
Prepaid taxes	300,000	
Accounts payable		$ 120,000
Common stock		500,000
Additional paid-in capital		680,000
Retained earnings		630,000
Foreign currency translation adjustment	430,000	
Revenues		3,600,000
Expenses	2,600,000	
	$5,530,000	$5,530,000

Additional information:

- During 2000, estimated tax payments of $300,000 were charged to prepaid taxes. Trey has not yet recorded income tax expense. There were no differences between financial statement and income tax income, and Trey's tax rate is 30%.
- Included in accounts receivable is $500,000 due from a customer. Special terms granted to this customer require payment in equal semi- annual installments of $125,000 every April 1 and October 1.

69. In Trey's December 31, 2000, balance sheet, what amount should be reported as total current assets?

a. $1,950,000
b. $2,200,000
c. $2,250,000
d. $2,500,000

70. In Trey's December 31, 2000, balance sheet, what amount should be reported as total retained earnings?

a. $1,029,000
b. $1,200,000
c. $1,330,000
d. $1,630,000

71. An increase in the cash surrender value of a life insurance policy owned by a company would be recorded by

a. Decreasing annual insurance expense.
b. Increasing investment income.
c. Recording a memorandum entry only.
d. Decreasing a deferred charge.

72. On November 1, 1999, Davis Co. discounted with recourse at 10% a one-year, noninterest bearing, $20,500 note receivable maturing on January 31, 2000. What amount of contingent liability for this note must Davis disclose in its financial statements for the year ended December 31, 1999?

a. $0.
b. $20,000.
c. $20,333.
d. $20,500.

73. Gei Co. determined that, due to obsolescence, equipment with an original cost of $900,000 and accumulated depreciation at January 1, 1999, of $420,000 had suffered permanent impairment, and as a result should have a carrying value of only $300,000 as of the beginning of the year. In addition, the remaining useful life of the equipment was reduced from 8 years to 3. In its December 31, 1999, balance sheet, what amount should Gei report as accumulated depreciation?

a. $100,000.
b. $520,000.
c. $600,000.
d. $700,000.

74. On December 30, 2001, Chang Co. sold a machine to Door Co. in exchange for a noninterest-bearing note requiring ten annual payments of $10,000. Door made the first payment on December 30, 2001. The market interest rate for similar notes at date of issuance was 8%. Information on present value factors is as follows:

Period	*Present value of $1 at 8%*	*Present value of ordinary annuity of $1 at 8%*
9	0.50	6.25
10	0.46	6.71

In its December 31, 2001, balance sheet, what amount should Chang report as note receivable?

a. $45,000
b. $46,000
c. $62,500
d. $67,100

75. At January 1, 2001, Jamin Co. had a credit balance of $260,000 in its allowance for uncollectible accounts. Based on past experience, 2% of Jamin's credit sales have been uncollectible. During 2001, Jamin wrote off $325,000 of uncollectible accounts. Credit sales for 2001 were $9,000,000. In its December 31, 2001, balance sheet, what amount should Jamin report as allowance for uncollectible accounts?

a. $115,000
b. $180,000
c. $245,000
d. $440,000

76. Theoretically, which of the following costs incurred in connection with a machine purchased for use in a company's manufacturing operations would be capitalized?

	Insurance on machine while in transit	*Testing and preparation of machine for use*
a.	Yes	Yes
b.	Yes	No
c.	No	Yes
d.	No	No

77. During 1997, Burr Co. had the following transactions pertaining to its new office building:

Purchase price of land	$ 60,000
Legal fees for contracts to purchase land	2,000
Architects' fees	8,000
Demolition of old building on site	5,000
Sale of scrap from old building	3,000
Construction cost of new building (fully completed)	350,000

In Burr's December 31, 1997, balance sheet, what amounts should be reported as the cost of land and cost of building?

	Land	*Building*
a.	$60,000	$360,000
b.	$62,000	$360,000
c.	$64,000	$358,000
d.	$65,000	$362,000

78. The following information pertains to Eagle Co.'s 2000 sales:

Cash sales	
Gross	$ 80,000
Returns and allowances	4,000
Credit sales	
Gross	120,000
Discounts	6,000

On January 1, 2000, customers owed Eagle $40,000. On December 31, 2000, customers owed Eagle $30,000. Eagle uses the direct writeoff method for bad debts. No bad debts were recorded in 2000. Under the cash basis of accounting, what amount of net revenue should Eagle report for 2000?

a. $76,000
b. $170,000
c. $190,000
d. $200,000

79. Rye Co. purchased a machine with a four-year estimated useful life and an estimated 10% salvage value for $80,000 on January 1, 1999. In its income statement, what would Rye report as the depreciation expense for 2001 using the double-declining-balance method?

a. $ 9,000
b. $10,000
c. $18,000
d. $20,000

80. On March 1, 2000, Fine Co. borrowed $10,000 and signed a two-year note bearing interest at 12% per annum compounded annually. Interest is payable in full at maturity on February 28, 2002. What amount should Fine report as a liability for accrued interest at December 31, 2001?

a. $0
b. $1,000
c. $1,200
d. $2,320

81. Gray Co. was granted a patent on January 2, 1998, and appropriately capitalized $45,000 of related costs. Gray was amortizing the patent over its estimated useful life of fifteen years. During 2001, Gray paid $15,000 in legal costs in successfully defending an attempted infringement of the patent. After the legal action was completed, Gray sold the patent to the plaintiff for $75,000. Gray's policy is to take no amortization in the year of disposal. In its 2001 income statement, what amount should Gray report as gain from sale of patent?

a. $15,000
b. $24,000
c. $27,000
d. $39,000

82. On January 1, 1995, Crater, Inc. purchased equipment having an estimated salvage value equal to 20% of its original cost at the end of a 10-year life. The equipment was sold December 31, 1999, for 50% of its original cost. If the equipment's disposition resulted in a reported loss, which of the following depreciation methods did Crater use?

a. Double-declining balance.
b. Sum-of-the-years'-digits.
c. Straight-line.
d. Composite.

83. On January 1, 1992, Elia Company sold a building, which had a carrying amount of $350,000, receiving a $125,000 down payment and, as additional consideration, a $400,000 noninterest bearing note due on January 1, 1995. There was no established exchange price for the building, and the note had no ready market. The prevailing rate of interest for a note of this type at January 1, 1992, was 10%. The present value of 1 at 10% for three periods is 0.75. What amount of interest income should be included in Elia's 1992 income statement?

a. $0
b. $30,000
c. $35,000
d. $40,000

84. On Merf's April 30, 2000, balance sheet a note receivable was reported as a noncurrent asset and its accrued interest for eight months was reported as a current asset. Which of the following terms would fit Merf's note receivable?

a. Both principal and interest amounts are payable on August 31, 2000, and August 31, 2001.
b. Principal and interest are due December 31, 2000.
c. Both principal and interest amounts are payable on December 31, 2000, and December 31, 2001.
d. Principal is due August 31, 2001, and interest is due August 31, 2000, and August 31, 2001.

85. On October 1, 1997, Shaw Corp. purchased a machine for $126,000 that was placed in service on November 30, 1997. Shaw incurred additional costs for this machine, as follows:

Shipping	$3,000
Installation	4,000
Testing	5,000

In Shaw's December 31, 1997, balance sheet, the machine's cost should be reported as

a. $126,000
b. $129,000
c. $133,000
d. $138,000

86. Brill Co. made the following expenditures during 1999:

Costs to develop computer software for internal use in Brill's general management information system	$100,000
Costs of market research activities	75,000

What amount of these expenditures should Brill report in its 1999 income statement as research and development expenses?

a. $175,000.
b. $100,000.
c. $75,000.
d. $0.

87. On January 2, 1996, Lava, Inc. purchased a patent for a new consumer product for $90,000. At the time of purchase, the patent was valid for 15 years; however, the patent's useful life was estimated to be only 10 years due to the competitive nature of the product. On December 31, 1999, the product was permanently withdrawn from sale under governmental order because of a potential health hazard in the product. What amount should Lava charge against income during 1999, assuming amortization is recorded at the end of each year?

a. $ 9,000.
b. $54,000.
c. $63,000.
d. $72,000.

88. Ace Co. sold to King Co. a $20,000, 8%, 5-year note that required five equal annual year-end payments. This note was discounted to yield a 9% rate to King. The present value factors of an ordinary annuity of $1 for five periods are as follows:

8%	3.992
9%	3.890

What should be the total interest revenue earned by King on this note?

a. $9,000
b. $8,000
c. $5,560
d. $5,050

89. Gavin Co. grants all employees two weeks of paid vacation for each full year of employment. Unused vacation time can be accumulated and carried forward to succeeding years and will be paid at the salaries in effect when vacations are taken or when employment is terminated. There was no employee turnover in 1996. Additional information relating to the year ended December 31, 1996, is as follows:

Liability for accumulated vacations at 12/31/95	$35,000
Pre-1996 accrued vacations taken from 1/1/96 to 9/30/96 (the authorized period for vacations)	20,000
Vacations earned for work in 1996 (adjusted to current rates)	30,000

Gavin granted a 10% salary increase to all employees on October 1, 1996, its annual salary increase date. For the year ended December 31, 1996, Gavin should report vacation pay expense of

a. $45,000
b. $33,500
c. $31,500
d. $30,000

90. Malden, Inc. has two patents that have allegedly been infringed by competitors. After investigation, legal counsel informed Malden that it had a weak case on patent A34 and a strong case in regard to patent B19. Malden incurred additional legal fees to stop infringement on B19. Both patents have a remaining legal life of 8 years. How should Malden account for these legal costs incurred relating to the two patents?

a. Expense costs for A34 and capitalize costs for B19.
b. Expense costs for both A34 and B19.
c. Capitalize costs for both A34 and B19.
d. Capitalize costs for A34 and expense costs for B19.

91. During 2000, Orr Co. incurred the following costs:

Research and development services performed by Key Corp. for Orr	$150,000
Design, construction, and testing of preproduction prototypes and models	200,000
Testing in search for new products or process alternatives	175,000

In its 2000 income statement, what should Orr report as research and development expense?

a. $150,000
b. $200,000
c. $350,000
d. $525,000

92. During 1999, Lyle Co. incurred $400,000 of research and development costs in its laboratory to develop a product for which a patent was granted on July 1, 1999. Legal fees and other costs associated with the patent totaled $82,000. The estimated economic life of the patent is 10 years. What amount should Lyle capitalize for the patent on July 1, 1999?

a. $0
b. $82,000
c. $400,000
d. $482,000

93. Tobin Corp. incurred $160,000 of research and development costs to develop a product for which a patent was granted on January 2, 1990. Legal fees and other costs associated with registration of the patent totaled $30,000. On March 31, 1995, Tobin paid $45,000 for legal fees in a successful defense of the patent. The total amount capitalized for this patent through March 31, 1995, should be

a. $75,000
b. $190,000
c. $205,000
d. $235,000

94. Amble, Inc. exchanged a truck with a carrying amount of $12,000 and a fair value of $20,000 for a truck and $5,000 cash. The fair value of the truck received was $15,000. At what amount should Amble record the truck received in the exchange?

a. $7,000
b. $9,000
c. $12,000
d. $15,000

95. During 1999, Beam Co. paid $1,000 cash and traded inventory, which had a carrying amount of $20,000 and a fair value of $21,000, for other inventory in the same line of business with a fair value of $22,000. What amount of gain (loss) should Beam record related to the inventory exchange?

a. $2,000
b. $1,000
c. $0
d. ($1,000)

96. A fixed asset with a five-year estimated useful life and no residual value is sold at the end of the second year of its useful life. How would using the sum-of-the-years'-digits method of depreciation instead of the double declining balance method of depreciation affect a gain or loss on the sale of the fixed asset?

	Gain	*Loss*
a.	Decrease	Decrease
b.	Decrease	Increase
c.	Increase	Decrease
d.	Increase	Increase

97. Scott Co. exchanged similar nonmonetary assets with Dale Co. No cash was exchanged. The carrying amount of the asset surrendered by Scott exceeded both the fair value of the asset received and Dale's carrying amount of that asset. Scott should recognize the difference between the carrying amount of the asset it surrendered and

a. The fair value of the asset it received as a loss.
b. The fair value of the asset it received as a gain.
c. Dale's carrying amount of the asset it received as a loss.
d. Dale's carrying amount of the asset it received as a gain.

98. The following information pertains to Rik Co.'s two employees:

Name	*Weekly salary*	*Number of weeks worked in 1998*	*Vacation rights vest or accumulate*
Ryan	$800	52	Yes
Todd	600	52	No

Neither Ryan nor Todd took the usual two-week vacation in 1998. In Rik's December 31, 1998, financial statements, what amount of vacation expense and liability should be reported?

a. $2,800
b. $1,600
c. $1,400
d. $0

99. Fay Corp. pays its outside salespersons fixed monthly salaries and commissions on net sales. Sales commissions are computed and paid on a monthly basis (in the month following the month of sale), and the fixed salaries are treated as advances against commissions. However, if the fixed salaries for salespersons exceed their sales commissions earned for a month, such excess is not charged back to them. Pertinent data for the month of March 1995 for the three salespersons are as follows:

Salesperson	*Fixed salary*	*Net sales*	*Commission rate*
A	$10,000	$ 200,000	4%
B	14,000	400,000	6%
C	18,000	600,000	6%
Totals	$42,000	$1,200,000	

What amount should Fay accrue for sales commissions payable at March 31, 1995?

a. $70,000
b. $68,000
c. $28,000
d. $26,000

100. Of the following items, the one which should be classified as a current asset is

a. Trade installment receivables normally collectible in 18 months.
b. Cash designated for the redemption of callable preferred stock.
c. Cash surrender value of a life insurance policy of which the company is beneficiary.
d. A deposit on machinery ordered, delivery of which will be made within six months.

101. On the December 31, 1996, balance sheet of Mann Co., the current receivables consisted of the following:

Trade accounts receivable	$ 93,000
Allowance for uncollectible accounts	(2,000)
Claim against shipper for goods lost in transit (November 1996)	3,000
Selling price of unsold goods sent by Mann on consignment at 130% of cost (**not** included in Mann's ending inventory)	26,000
Security deposit on lease of warehouse used for storing some inventories	30,000
Total	$150,000

At December 31, 1996, the correct total of Mann's current net receivables was

a. $94,000
b. $120,000
c. $124,000
d. $150,000

102. When the allowance method of recognizing uncollectible accounts is used, the entries at the time of collection of a small account previously written off would

a. Increase the allowance for uncollectible accounts.
b. Increase net income.
c. Decrease the allowance for uncollectible accounts.
d. Have **no** effect on the allowance for uncollectible accounts.

103. Delta, Inc. sells to wholesalers on terms of 2/15, net 30. Delta has no cash sales but 50% of Delta's customers take advantage of the discount. Delta uses the gross method of recording sales and trade receivables. An analysis of Delta's trade receivables balances at December 31, 2000, revealed the following:

Age	*Amount*	*Collectible*
0 - 15 days	$100,000	100%
16 - 30 days	60,000	95%
31 - 60 days	5,000	90%
Over 60 days	2,500	$500
	$167,500	

In its December 31, 2000, balance sheet, what amount should Delta report for allowance for discounts?

a. $1,000.
b. $1,620.
c. $1,675.
d. $2,000.

104. On July 1, 1998, Balt Co. exchanged a truck for 25 shares of Ace Corp.'s common stock. On that date, the truck's carrying amount was $2,500, and its fair value was $3,000. Also, the book value of Ace's stock was $60 per share. On December 31, 1998, Ace had 250 shares of common stock outstanding and its book value per share was $50. What amount should Balt report in its December 31, 1998, balance sheet as investment in Ace?

a. $3,000
b. $2,500
c. $1,500
d. $1,250

105. On December 31, 1999, Roth Co. issued a $10,000 face value note payable to Wake Co. in exchange for services rendered to Roth. The note, made at usual trade terms, is due in nine months and bears interest, payable at maturity, at the annual rate of 3%. The market interest rate is 8%. The compound interest factor of $1 due in nine months at 8% is .944. At what amount should the note payable be reported in Roth's December 31, 1999, balance sheet?

a. $10,300.
b. $10,000.
c. $9,652.
d. $9,440.

106. Slad Co. exchanged similar productive assets with Gil Co. and, in addition, paid Gil cash of $100,000. The following information pertains to this exchange:

<u>Assets</u>	*Carrying* *<u>amounts</u>*	*Fair* *<u>values</u>*
Relinquished by Gil	$75,000	$140,000
Relinquished by Slad	40,000	40,000

On Slad's books, the assets acquired should be recorded at what amount?

a. $75,000
b. $100,000
c. $140,000
d. $175,000

107. A building suffered uninsured fire damage. The damaged portion of the building was refurbished with higher quality materials. The cost and related accumulated depreciation of the damaged portion are identifiable. To account for these events, the owner should

a. Reduce accumulated depreciation equal to the cost of refurbishing.
b. Record a loss in the current period equal to the sum of the cost of refurbishing and the carrying amount of the damaged portion of the building.
c. Capitalize the cost of refurbishing and record a loss in the current period equal to the carrying amount of the damaged portion of the building.
d. Capitalize the cost of refurbishing by adding the cost to the carrying amount of the building.

RECENTLY DISCLOSED QUESTIONS

M97

108. On January 2, 1993, Jann Co. purchased a $150,000 whole-life insurance policy on its president. The annual premium is $4,000. The company is both the owner and the beneficiary. Jann charged officers' life insurance expense as follows:

1993	$ 4,000
1994	3,600
1995	3,000
1996	<u>2,200</u>
Total	<u>$12,800</u>

In its December 31, 1996 balance sheet, what amount should Jann report as investment in cash surrender value of officers' life insurance?

a. $0
b. $3,200
c. $12,800
d. $16,000

M97

109. When a loan receivable is impaired but foreclosure is **not** probable, which of the following may the creditor use to measure the impairment?

I. The loan's observable market price.
II. The fair value of the collateral if the loan is collateral dependent.

a. I only.
b. II only.
c. Either I or II.
d. Neither I nor II.

N96

110. Which of the following related-party transactions by a company should be disclosed in the notes to the financial statements?

I. Payment per diem expenses to members of the board of directors.
II. Consulting fees paid to a marketing research firm, one of whose partners is also a director of the company.

a. I only.
b. II only.
c. Both I and II.
d. Neither I nor II.

M98

111. Lemu Co. and Young Co. are under the common management of Ego Co. Ego can significantly influence the operating results of both Lemu and Young. While Lemu had no transactions with Ego during the year, Young sold merchandise to Ego under the same terms given to unrelated parties. In the notes to their respective financial statements, should Lemu and Young disclose their relationship with Ego?

	Lemu	Young
a.	Yes	Yes
b.	Yes	No
c.	No	Yes
d.	No	No

N98

112. Wizard Co. purchased two machines for \$250,000 each on January 2, 1997. The machines were put into use immediately. Machine A has a useful life of five years and can only be used on one research project. Machine B will be used for two years on a research and development project and then used by the production division for an additional eight years. Wizard uses the straightline method of depreciation. What amount should Wizard include in 1997 research and development expense?

a. \$75,000
b. \$275,000
c. \$375,000
d. \$500,000

1999

113. Spiro Corp. uses the sum-of-the-years' digits method to depreciate equipment purchased in January 1996 for \$20,000. The estimated salvage value of the equipment is \$2,000 and the estimated useful life is four years. What should Spiro report as the asset's carrying amount as of December 31, 1998?

a. \$1,800
b. \$2,000
c. \$3,800
d. \$4,500

1999

114. Dex Co. has entered into a joint venture with an affiliate to secure access to additional inventory. Under the joint venture agreement, Dex will purchase the output of the venture at prices negotiated on an arms-length basis. Which of the following is(are) required to be disclosed about the related party transaction?

I. The amount due to the affiliate at the balance sheet date.
II. The dollar amount of the purchases during the year.

a. I only
b. II only
c. Both I and II
d. Neither I nor II.

2000

115. In its December 31, 1999 balance sheet, Fleet Co. reported accounts receivable of \$100,000 before allowance for uncollectible accounts of \$10,000. Credit sales during 2000 were \$611,000, and collections from customers, excluding recoveries, totaled \$591,000. During 2000, accounts receivable of \$45,000 were written off and \$17,000 were recovered. Fleet estimated that \$15,000 of the accounts receivable at December 31, 2000 were uncollectible. In its December 31, 2000 balance sheet, what amount should Fleet report as accounts receivable before allowance for uncollectible accounts?

a. \$58,000
b. \$67,000
c. \$75,000
d. \$82,000

2000

116. Samm Corp. purchased a plot of land for \$100,000. The cost to raze a building on the property amounted to \$50,000 and Samm received \$10,000 from the sale of scrap materials. Samm built a new plant on the site at a total cost of \$800,000 including excavation costs of \$30,000. What amount should Samm capitalize in its land account?

a. \$150,000
b. \$140,000
c. \$130,000
d. \$100,000

1999

117. In its December 31 balance sheet, Butler Co. reported trade accounts receivable of $250,000 and related allowance for uncollectible accounts of $20,000. What is the total amount of risk of accounting loss related to Butler's trade accounts receivable, and what amount of that risk is off-balance sheet risk?

	Risk of Accounting Loss	Off-Balance Sheet Risk
a.	$0	$0
b.	$230,000	$0
c.	$230,000	$20,000
d.	$250,000	$20,000

118. The Maddox Corporation acquired land, buildings, and equipment from a bankrupt company at a lump-sum price of $90,000. At the time of acquisition, Maddox paid $6,000 to have the assets appraised. The appraisal disclosed the following values:

Land	$60,000
Buildings	40,000
Equipment	20,000

What cost should be assigned to the land, buildings, and equipment, respectively?

a. $30,000, $30,000, and $30,000
b. $32,000, $32,000, and $32,000
c. $45,000, $30,000, and $15,000
d. $48,000, $32,000, and $16,000

Chapter Eleven
Other Assets, Liabilities, and Disclosures Problems

NUMBER 1

Gregor Wholesalers Co. sells industrial equipment for a standard three-year note receivable. Revenue is recognized at time of sale. Each note is secured by a lien on the equipment and has a face amount equal to the equipment's list price. Each note's stated interest rate is below the customer's market rate at date of sale. All notes are to be collected in three equal annual installments beginning one year after sale. Some of the notes are subsequently discounted at a bank with recourse, some are subsequently discounted without recourse, and some are retained by Gregor. At year end, Gregor evaluates all outstanding notes receivable and provides for estimated losses arising from defaults.

Required:

a. What is the appropriate valuation basis for Gregor's notes receivable at the date it sells equipment?

b. How should Gregor account for the discounting, without recourse, of a February 1, 1999, note receivable discounted on May 1, 1999? Why is it appropriate to account for it in this way?

c. At December 31, 1999, how should Gregor measure and account for the impact of estimated losses resulting from notes receivable that it

1. Retained and did **not** discount?
2. Discounted at a bank with recourse?

NUMBER 2

Sigma Co. began operations on January 1, 1997. On December 31, 1997, Sigma provided for uncollectible accounts based on 1% of annual credit sales. On January 1, 1998, Sigma changed its method of determining its allowance for uncollectible accounts by applying certain percentages to the accounts receivable aging as follows:

Days past invoice date	*Percent deemed to be uncollectible*
0– 30	1
31– 90	5
91–180	20
Over 180	80

In addition, Sigma wrote off all accounts receivable that were over one year old. The following additional information relates to the years ended December 31, 1998, and 1997:

	1998	*1997*
Credit sales	$3,000,000	$2,800,000
Collections	2,915,000	2,400,000
Accounts written off	27,000	None
Recovery of accounts previously written off	7,000	None
Days past invoice date at 12/31		
0– 30	300,000	250,000
31– 90	80,000	90,000
91–180	60,000	45,000
Over 180	25,000	15,000

Required:

a. Prepare a schedule showing the calculation of the allowance for uncollectible accounts at December 31, 1998.

b. Prepare a schedule showing the computation of the provision for uncollectible accounts for the year ended December 31, 1998.

NUMBER 3

Winter Sports Co. rents winter sports equipment to the public. Snowmobiles are depreciated by the double declining balance method. Before the season began, the estimated lives of several snowmobiles were extended because engines were replaced. Winter was given thirty days to pay for the engines. Winter gave the old engines to a local mechanic who agreed to provide repairs and maintenance service in the next year equal to the fair value of the engines. Rental skis, poles, and boots are capitalized and depreciated according to the inventory (appraisal) method.

Required:

a. How would Winter account for the purchase of the new engines and the transfer of the old engines to the local mechanic if the old engines' costs are
   1. Known?
   2. Unknown?

b. 1. What are two assumptions underlying use of an accelerated depreciation method?
   2. How should Winter calculate the snowmobiles' depreciation?

c. How should Winter calculate and report the costs of the skis, poles, and boots in its balance sheets and income statements?

NUMBER 4

Number 4 consists of 14 items. Select the best answer for each item. Answer all items. Your grade will be based on the total number of correct answers.

Items 61 through 66 represent expenditures for goods held for resale and equipment.

Required:
For items 61 through 66, determine for each item whether the expenditure should be capitalized C or expensed as a period cost E.

61. Freight charges paid for goods held for resale.
62. In-transit insurance on goods held for resale purchased F.O.B. shipping point.
63. Interest on note payable for goods held for resale.
64. Installation of equipment.
65. Testing of newly-purchased equipment.
66. Cost of current year service contract on equipment.

Items 67 through 70 are based on the following 1993 transactions:

- Link Co. purchased an office building and the land on which it is located by paying $800,000 cash and assuming an existing mortgage of $200,000. The property is assessed at $960,000 for realty tax purposes, of which 60% is allocated to the building.

- Link leased construction equipment under a 7-year capital lease requiring annual year-end payments of $100,000. Link's incremental borrowing rate is 9%, while the lessor s implicit rate, which is not known to Link, is 8%. Present value factors for an ordinary annuity for seven periods are 5.21 at 8% and 5.03 at 9%. Fair value of the equipment is $515,000.

- Link paid $50,000 and gave a plot of undeveloped land with a carrying amount of $320,000 and a fair value of $450,000 to Club Co. in exchange for a plot of undeveloped land with a fair value of $500,000. The land was carried on Club's books at $350,000.

Required:

For **items 67 through 70**, calculate the amount to be recorded for each item.

67. Building.
68. Leased equipment.
69. Land received from Club on Link's books.
70. Land received from Link on Club's books.

Items 71 through 74 are based on the following information:

On January 2, 1999, Half, Inc. purchased a manufacturing machine for $864,000. The machine has an 8-year estimated life and a $144,000 estimated salvage value. Half expects to manufacture 1,800,000 units over the life of the machine. During 2000, Half manufactured 300,000 units.

Required:

Items 71 through 74 represent various depreciation methods. For each item, calculate depreciation expense for 1993 (the second year of ownership) for the machine described above under the method listed.

71. Straight-line.
72. Double-declining balance.
73. Sum-of-the-years'-digits.
74. Units of production.

NUMBER 5

Nan Co.'s property, plant, and equipment and accumulated depreciation and amortization balances at December 31, 1994, are:

	Cost	*Accumulated Depreciation*
Land	$ 275,000	—
Buildings	2,800,000	$ 672,900
Machinery and equipment	1,380,000	367,500
Automobiles and trucks	210,000	114,326
Leasehold improvements	432,000	108,000
Totals	$5,097,000	$1,262,726

Additional information follows:

Depreciation and amortization methods and useful lives
Buildings—150% declining balance; 25 years.
Machinery and equipment—straight-line; 10 years.
Automobiles and trucks—150% declining balance; five years, all acquired after 1992.
Leasehold improvements—straight-line.
Depreciation is computed to the nearest month.

Salvage values of depreciable assets are immaterial except for automobiles and trucks which have estimated salvage values equal to 15% of cost.

Other additional information

- Nan entered into a twelve-year operating lease starting January 1, 1992. The leasehold improvements were completed on December 31, 1991, and the facility was occupied on January 1, 1992.
- On January 6, 1995, Nan completed its self-construction of a building on its own land. Direct costs of construction were $1,095,000. Construction of the building required 15,000 direct labor hours. Nan's construction department has an overhead allocation system for outside jobs based on an activity denominator of 100,000 direct labor hours, budgeted fixed costs of $2,500,000, and budgeted variable costs of $27 per direct labor hour.
- On July 1, 1995, machinery and equipment were purchased at a total invoice cost of $325,000. Additional costs of $23,000 to rectify damage on delivery and $18,000 for concrete embedding of machinery were incurred. A wall had to be demolished to enable a large machine to be moved into the plant. The wall demolition cost $7,000, and rebuilding of the wall cost $19,000.
- On August 30, 1995, Nan purchased a new automobile for $25,000.
- On September 30, 1995, a truck with a cost of $48,000 and a carrying amount of $30,000 on December 31, 1994, was sold for $23,500.
- On November 4, 1995, Nan purchased a tract of land for investment purposes for $700,000. Nan thinks it might use the land as a potential future building site.
- On December 20, 1995, a machine with a cost of $17,000, a carrying amount of $2,975 on date of disposition, and a market value of $4,000 was given to a corporate officer in partial liquidation of a debt.

Required: Use the worksheet below and on the next page.

a. Analyze the changes in each of the property, plant, and equipment accounts during 1995 by completing Schedule No.1.

b. 1. For each asset category, prepare a schedule showing calculations for depreciation or amortization expense for the year ended December 31, 1995. Round computations to the nearest whole dollar.
2. Analyze the changes in accumulated depreciation and amortization by completing Schedule No. 2.

c. Prepare a schedule showing gain or loss on disposition of property, plant, and equipment.

a.

Schedule 1

Nan Co.

ANALYSIS OF CHANGES IN PROPERTY, PLANT, AND EQUIPMENT

For the Year Ended December 31, 1995

	Balance 12/31/94	*Increase*	*Decrease*	*Balance 12/31/95*
Land	$ 275,000			
Buildings	2,800,000			
Machinery & equipment	1,380,000			
Automobiles and trucks	210,000			
Leasehold improvements	432,000			
Totals	$5,097,000			

b.2.

Schedule 2

Nan Co.
ANALYSIS OF CHANGES IN ACCUMULATED DEPRECIATION AND AMORTIZATION
For the Year Ended December 31, 1995

	Balance 12/31/94	*Increase*	*Decrease*	*Balance 12/31/95*
Buildings	$ 672,900			
Machinery & equipment	367,500			
Automobiles and trucks	114,326			
Leasehold improvements	108,000			
Totals	$1,262,726			

NUMBER 6

Kern, Inc., had the following long-term receivable account balances at December 31, 1996:

Note receivable from the sale of an idle building	$750,000
Note receivable from an officer	200,000

Transactions during 1997 and other information relating to Kern's long-term receivables follow:

- The $750,000 note receivable is dated May 1, 1996, bears interest at 9%, and represents the balance of the consideration Kern received from the sale of its idle building to Able Co. Principal payments of $250,000 plus interest are due annually beginning May 1, 1997. Able made its first principal and interest payment on May 1, 1997. Collection of the remaining note installments is reasonably assured.
- The $200,000 note receivable is dated December 31, 1994, bears interest at 8%, and is due on December 31, 1999. The note is due from Frank Black, president of Kern, Inc., and is collateralized by 5,000 shares of Kern's common stock. Interest is payable annually on December 31, and all interest payments were made through December 31, 1997. The quoted market price of Kern's common stock was $45 per share on December 31, 1997.
- On April 1, 1997, Kern sold a patent to Frey Corp. in exchange for a $100,000 noninterest-bearing note due on April 1, 1999. There was no established exchange price for the patent, and the note had no ready market. The prevailing interest rate for this type of note was 10% at April 1, 1997. The present value of $1 for two periods at 10% is 0.826. The patent had a carrying amount of $40,000 at January 1, 1997, and the amortization for the year ended December 31, 1997, would have been $8,000. Kern is reasonably assured of collecting the note receivable from Frey.
- On July 1, 1997, Kern sold a parcel of land to Barr Co. for $400,000 under an installment sale contract. Barr made a $120,000 cash down payment on July 1, 1997, and signed a four-year 10% note for the $280,000 balance. The equal annual payments of principal and interest on the note will be $88,332, payable on July 1 of each year from 1998 through 2001. The fair value of the land at the date of sale was $400,000. The cost of the land to Kern was $300,000. Collection of the remaining note installments is reasonably assured.

Required:
Prepare the following and show supporting computations:

a. Long-term receivables section of Kern's December 31, 1997, balance sheet.
b. Schedule showing current portion of long-term receivables and accrued interest receivable to be reported in Kern's December 31, 1997, balance sheet.
c. Schedule showing interest revenue from long-term receivables and gains recognized on sale of assets to be reported in Kern's 1997 income statement.

NUMBER 7

On January 1, 1997, the Pitt Company sold a patent to Chatham, Inc., which had a net carrying value on Pitt's books of $10,000. Chatham gave Pitt an $80,000 noninterest-bearing note payable in five equal annual installments of $16,000, with the first payment due and paid on January 1, 1998. There was no established exchange price for the patent, and the note has no ready market. The prevailing rate of interest for a note of this type at January 1, 1997, was 12%. Information on present value and future amount factors is as follows:

	Period				
	1	*2*	*3*	*4*	*5*
Present value of $1 at 12%	0.89	0.80	0.71	0.64	0.57
Present value of an annuity of $1 at 12%	0.89	1.69	2.40	3.04	3.60
Future amount of $1 at 12%	1.12	1.25	1.40	1.57	1.76
Future amount of an annuity of $1 at 12%	1.00	2.12	3.37	4.78	6.35

Required:
Prepare a schedule showing the income or loss before income taxes (rounded to the nearest dollar) that Pitt should record for the years ended December 31, 1997 and 1998, as a result of the above facts. Show supporting computations in good form.

NUMBER 8

M90

Magrath Company has an operating cycle of less than one year and provides credit terms for all of its customers. On April 1, 1996, the company factored, without recourse, some of its accounts receivable.

On July 1, 1996, Magrath sold special order merchandise and received a noninterest-bearing note due June 30, 1998. The market rate of interest for this note is determinable.

Magrath uses the allowance method to account for uncollectible accounts. During 1996, some accounts were written off as uncollectible and other accounts previously written off as uncollectible were collected.

Required:
a. How should Magrath account for and report the accounts receivable factored on April 1, 1996? Why is this accounting treatment appropriate?
b. How should Magrath report the effects of the noninterest-bearing note on its income statement for the year ended December 31, 1996, and its December 31, 1996, balance sheet?
c. How should Magrath account for the collection of the accounts previously written off as uncollectible?
d. What are the two basic approaches to estimating uncollectible accounts under the allowance method? What is the rationale for each approach?

NUMBER 9

Portland Co. uses the straight-line depreciation method for depreciable assets. All assets are depreciated individually except manufacturing machinery, which is depreciated by the composite method.

During the year, Portland exchanged a delivery truck with Maine Co. for a larger delivery truck. It paid cash equal to 10% of the larger truck's value.

Required:
a. What factors should have influenced Portland's selection of the straight-line depreciation method?
b. How should Portland account for and report the truck exchange transaction?
c. 1. What benefits should Portland derive from using the composite method rather than the individual basis for manufacturing machinery?
2. How should Portland have calculated the manufacturing machinery's annual depreciation expense in its first year of operation?

NUMBER 10

The following problem consists of 8 items. Select the **best** answer for each item. **Answer all items.**

During 1999, Sloan, Inc. began a project to construct new corporate headquarters. Sloan purchased land with an existing building for $750,000. The land was valued at $700,000 and the building at $50,000. Sloan planned to demolish the building and construct a new office building on the site. Items 1 through 8 represent various expenditures by Sloan for this project.

Required:
For each expenditure in Items 1 through 8, select from the list below the appropriate accounting treatment.

L. Classify as land and do not depreciate.
B. Classify as building and depreciate.
E. Expense.

Items to be answered:
1. Purchase of land for $700,000.
2. Interest of $147,000 on construction financing incurred after completion of construction.
3. Interest of $186,000 on construction financing paid during construction.
4. Purchase of building for $50,000.
5. $18,500 payment of delinquent real estate taxes assumed by Sloan on purchase.
6. $12,000 liability insurance premium during the construction period.
7. $65,000 cost of razing existing building.
8. Moving costs of $136,000.

Chapter Eleven
Solutions to Other Assets, Liabilities and Disclosures Questions

1. (b) A primary objective of accrual accounting is the proper matching of revenues and expenses. Since the allowance method accrues uncollectible accounts expense in order to match the cost against the revenues recognized in the period, it **is** consistent with accrual accounting. On the other hand, the direct write-off method usually writes off an account in a period that is different from the period in which the revenue is recognized and would **not** be consistent with the accrual method.

2. (a)

Allowance for Doubtful Accounts

	Debit	Credit	
		$ 10,800	—Balance 1/1/95
		13,500	—1995 expense[1]
1995 writeoffs	$18,000		
		$ 6,300	—Balance 12/31/95

[1]3% × $450,000

3. (d) The allowance account must be adjusted so that the ending balance is equal to the estimated uncollectible accounts receivable estimate—3% × 1,000,000 = $30,000.

4. (a) The aging method is a balance sheet approach that calculates the required ending balance in the allowance for uncollectible accounts. The calculation is as follows:

Estimated % Uncollectible	×	Amount	=	Required Balance
1%	×	$120,000	=	$1200
2%	×	$90,000	=	$1800
6%	×	$100,000	=	$6000
Total required balance				$9000

5. (b)

I. Calculate the ending balance in the allowance for uncollectible accounts.

GIVEN:	ACCOUNTS RECEIVABLE BALANCE 12/31/2000	$350,000
	Allowance for uncollectible accounts (calculate)	(25,000)
GIVEN:	NET VALUE OF A/R AT 12/31/2000	$325,000

II. Using a "T" account for the allowance and the ending balance from "I", calculate the uncollectible accounts expense.

ALLOWANCE FOR UNCOLLECTIBLE ACCOUNTS

Debit		Credit	
Accounts written off	18,000	Beginning Balance	30,000
		Uncollectible recovery	2,000
		EXPENSE (calculate)	11,000
		Ending Balance (See I above)	25,000

6. (c) The approach is to set up the T-account for accounts receivable.

Accounts Receivable			
Beginning balance	$ 650,000	Write offs	$ 40,000
Credit sales	2,700,000	Sales returns	75,000
		Collections	2,150,000
Ending balance	$1,085,000		

Note that the journal entry for the estimated sales returns would be a debit to sales returns and a credit to the allowance for sales returns and would not affect the accounts receivables account.

7. (d) The estimate based upon sales is the expense for the year:

$1,750,000 × 2% = $35,000

The estimate based on accounts receivable is the balance in the allowance account:

Allowance before 1994 expenses =	$16,000
Ending balance ($900,000 × 5%) =	45,000
Computed expense	$29,000

8. (c) The collection of cash has the impact of increasing the allowance account. (The allowance account was decreased when the account was written off.) The write-off of the account as well as the subsequent collection of the account has no effect on the expense.

9. (a) The entry to write off an account is a debit to the allowance account and a credit to the accounts receivable account. Since the allowance account is a contra account to accounts receivable and since both are balance sheet accounts, only (a) above is correct.

10. (b) The assignment of accounts receivable may be required when a company's receivables are collateral for a loan. Factoring normally involves an outright sale of a company's receivables. In either case, they are both used to generate cash from accounts receivable.

11. (d) The key phrase is "without recourse" which means that Gar Co. has transferred the risk for the uncollectible accounts to Ross Bank and Ross does not have any recourse against Gar Co. if the accounts are not collected. Thus, Gar has sold the accounts receivable to Ross Bank along with the risk associated with the uncollectible accounts.

12. (a) All of the items listed are considered in the cost of the land with the proceeds from the salvaged materials a reduction in the cost.

13. (a) The cost of the machine should include all the necessary cost to purchase the machine and get it ready for use. In this case that would include the purchase price of the machine plus the shipping and testing.

$125,000 + 20,000 + $10,000 = $155,000

14. (a) All of the expenditures constitute a betterment and are therefore capitalized.

15. (a) The total realized gain is reported on the income statement. Therefore the new land is recorded at its full cost.

16. (a) The key point is that the cost of the machinery should be cash equivalent price of $110,000. The $130,000 total cash payments include $20,000 in interest. Interest cost should only be capitalized for assets that are being constructed.

Cost	$110,000
Less Salvage Value	(5,000)
Depreciation Base	$105,000 / 10 years =
Depreciation per year	$10,500

17. (b)

	Carrying Value	Accumulated Depreciation
COST	$50,000	
1998 Depreciation		
40% × $50,000	(20,000)	$20,000
1999 Depreciation		
40% × ($50,000 - 20,000)	(12,000)	12,000
Balance 12/31/99	$18,000	$32,000
2000 Depreciation		
$18,000 / 3 years	(6,000)	6,000
Balance 12/31/00	$12,000	$38,000

Note: The percentage used in 200% double declining balance is **double** the straight line percentage (2 × 20% = 40%).

18. (a)

Equipment cost	$200,000
Depreciation rate (1.5/5)	30%
Expense for 1995	$ 60,000
Carrying value 1/1/96—$140,000	
Expense for 1996 (.3 × $140,000)	+ 42,000
Accumulated depreciation at 12/31/96 ($60,000 + $42,000)	$102,000

Salvage is not considered in the calculations.

19. (b) 5/15 + 4/15 = 9/15 × $300,000 = $180,000.

20. (d) The double-declining balance method has the highest depreciation in the first year (III). The sum-of-the-years'-digits method is slightly less in the first year and declines at a constant rate (II). The straight-line method is represented by (I).

21. (c) Since the machine suffered a permanent impairment of value, its carrying value should be adjusted to $200,000 at January 1, 1999. At 12/31/99, one year's depreciation of $40,000 ($200,000 ÷ 5 years) is recorded. The carrying amount of the machine at 12/31/99 is the new cost ($200,000) less the accumulated depreciation ($40,000) for a net of $160,000.

22. (b) Salvage value is normally used in the computation of depreciation except when using declining balance methods.

23. (a) The units-of-production method of depreciation measures depreciation based on use and is therefore a variable cost. Other depreciation methods such as straight line or accelerated methods are fixed costs and measure depreciation in relation to the passage of time.

24. (b) Salvage value is used in computing depreciation expense under both the straight-line and the units-of-production methods. If salvage value were excluded from the calculation in either method, the expense would be greater and as a result, net income would be understated.

25. (b) The loss is based upon the difference between the insurance proceeds and the carrying value (plus direct costs of removal). Therefore, the base used for determining the loss is $530,000.

26. (b) The solutions approach would be to set up a "T" and solve for the debit to Accumulated Depreciation.

Accumulated Depreciation			
		Balance 1/1/99	$370,000
Retirements	$25,000	Depreciation - 1999	55,000
		Balance 12/31/99	$400,000

27. (b) Using the composite depreciation method, when an asset is sold the asset account is credited for the entire sales price. No gain or loss is recognized.

28. (b) Interest is capitalized on a building under construction because the building has not begun to generate revenue. To charge the interest incurred to interest expense during this construction period would be an improper matching of expenses and revenues. The interest cost capitalized is the lesser of the formula amount or the actual interest cost incurred. In this case the formula amount ($40,000) is the smaller amount and should be the amount charged to the building account. The formula for interest capitalization is:

Average Accumulated Expenditures × Appropriate Interest Rate × Time Period.

29. (a) Average costs incurred in 1991 amounted to $1,000,000 which at 12% amounts to $120,000 interest cost. However, since the company's actual interest cost was less than $120,000, the actual interest cost is used.

30. (c) Interest incurred for routinely manufactured inventories is not capitalized. The other interest costs are appropriately capitalized under SFAS #34.

31. (c) This is a non-reciprocal transfer. Non-reciprocal transfers are recorded at FMV (100,000 shares × $2.50 per share = $250,000). The difference between the FMV ($250,000) and the carrying value ($200,000) is recorded as a $50,000 gain.

32. (d) The gain is measured by the difference between the market value and the book value of the machine exchanged or $140,000 – $120,000 = $20,000. Since the assets are dissimilar, the entire gain is recognized. The new machine will be recorded at $140,000 + $15,000 or $155,000.

33. (b) Since the exchange is for a dissimilar asset, the entire gain of $8,000 is recognized.

Fair value of computer given up		$43,000
Book value of auto	$30,000	
Cash paid	5,000	35,000
Gain		$ 8,000

34. (b)

Book value of old asset	$10,000
Cash paid	19,000
Recorded cost of new asset	$29,000

35. (a) The company records the new contract at the book value of the old contract plus the cash paid or $500,000 + $50,000 = $550,000.

36. (b) In order to determine the loss, the trade-in value must be compared to the book value:

Cash price of new machine =	$20,500
Cash payment	6,000
Trade-in	14,500
Book value of old machine	16,800
Loss to be recognized	$ 2,300

Such losses on exchanges of similar productive assets are recognized assuming materiality.

37. (b) Computation (See APB 29, par. 21 and 22):

$$\text{Ratio:}\quad \frac{\text{Monetary Consideration}}{\text{Total Consideration}} = \frac{\$20{,}000}{\$20{,}000 + \$180{,}000} = 10\%$$

Portion of book value applicable to monetary consideration = 10% × $160,000 = $16,000

Monetary consideration	$20,000
Less: Applicable book value	16,000
Gain realized	$ 4,000

Book value of asset given up	$160,000
Less: Book value applicable to monetary consideration	16,000
Recorded amount of acquired asset	$144,000

38. (b) Sable has a theoretical gain because the fair market value of the truck traded exceeds its carrying value. The general rule for a trade of similar nonmonetary assets with a gain is that the gain should not be recognized because the earnings process is not complete (Sable still has a truck generating revenue). However, an exception to the general rule is made if boot is received. In that case a portion of the theoretical gain is recognized based on the following formula:

$$\text{Gain Recognized} = \frac{\text{Boot (Cash)}}{\text{Total Consideration Received (Boot + FMV of Asset Received)}} \times \text{Total Theoretical Gain}$$

39. (c) Only the company which receives cash recognizes a gain to the extent that the cash received is in proportion to total value of assets received.

40. (b) Goodwill is capitalized and amortized when incurred in the purchase of another entity. The cost of maintaining or developing goodwill is not capitalized because there is not an objective basis for measuring its value.

41. (c) Since the legal action for Patent B was unsuccessful, the related costs would be written off. Only the costs for Patent A are carried as an asset including the legal fees.

42. (a) The research development costs should be expensed because of the uncertainty associated with any R & D effort. However, the cost of registering the patent should be capitalized because it benefits future periods and should be amortized over its useful life of 10 years. In this case, the amortization for the last six months of 2001 would be $1700 ($34,000 divided by 10 years x 6/12). The amount presented on the balance sheet would be the cost of $34,000 less the $1700 amortization or $32,300.

43. (c) $500,000 / 50 years = $10,000 per year.
Note: SFAS 142 eliminated the arbitrary limit of 40 years for amortization of intangibles.

44. (c)

Cost	$50,000
Less 2000 Amortization	
$50,000 / 10 years	(5,000)
December 31, 2000 Balance	$45,000

The 3% franchise fee is a current variable expense and should not be capitalized because it does not benefit future periods.

45. (d) SOP 98-5 requires that organization cost be expensed as incurred. Therefore, none of the organization cost may be deferred.

46. (a) Using a service life method, the capitalized costs would be amortized on the basis of percentage of total projected sales. Therefore, 30% of the costs would be amortized in 1998.

47. (b) Since the estimated life of the improvements (15 years) was less than the remaining lease term plus the option period (10 + 8 years), the 15-year amortization period is used:

Cost of improvements	$540,000
1997 amortization ($540,000 ÷ 15)	– 36,000
Carrying value 12/31/97	$504,000

48. (d) Research and development expenses are incurred prior to the production process in researching and developing a new product or process. Answers (a), (b) and (c) are incurred after production was in process. Only (d) is a pre-production R&D expense.

49. (d) Only the pre-production costs are recognized as R&D expenses. The $100,000 and $110,000 expenditures are costs incurred as part of the company's normal production.

50. (c) All costs incurred for producing and testing the prototype are R&D costs. The legal costs are capitalized as part of the cost of the patent. The special equipment, having no alternative use, is considered an R&D cost—it is not depreciated.

51. (c) If the purchase contract allows Ogden to purchase goods from the supplier for less than the prevailing market value, the difference between the contract price and the market rate should be recognized as interest revenue in connection with the loan (Per APB 21, Par. 7).

52. (a) There are seven payments due, the first one year after the initial date of the transaction. Therefore, the correct factor to use is the present value of an ordinary annuity for seven periods (4.712) or the present value of an annuity in advance for eight periods less one (5.712 – 1).

$$4.712 \times \$20,000 = \$94,240$$

53. (a) The sales price is equivalent to the present value of the note payments:

Present value of first payment	$ 60,000
Present value of last six payments:	
$60,000 × 4.36	261,600
Sales price	$321,600

Note that the present value of annuity factors which are given are "ordinary" annuity factors. Therefore, the present value of the first payment must be considered separately.

54. (b) In an exchange of a noninterest bearing note for equipment in which the fair market value of the equipment can not be determined, the present value of the note must be computed using an imputed interest rate. The present value of the note is then assumed to equal the FMV of equipment. The interest income recognized on the note is the present value of the note at the beginning of the period ($600,000 × 0.75 = $450,000) times the imputed interest rate ($450,000 × 10% × 12/12 = $45,000).

55. (a) The journal entry to record the transaction is as follows:

Notes Receivable	600,000	
Loss on Sale of Machinery	30,000	
Discount on Notes Receivable		150,000
Equipment (carrying value)		480,000

56. (d) The note from Hart is reported at face value since it is made under customary terms and is for less than one year.
The carrying value of the Maxx note is reported at its discounted value as follows:

Amount to be paid in five years:	
$10,000 + ($300 × 5) =	$11,500
Present value factor	.680
Carrying value	$ 7,820

57. (b) The proceeds received when a note is discounted at the bank is the maturity value of the note less the bank discount.

58. (c) The key point in calculating the cash received from discounting a note is to remember that the bank calculates its discount on the maturity value of the note times the bank discount rate times the time period that the note is held by the bank.

Face value of the note	$500,000
Interest to maturity	
$500,000 × 8% × 12/12 =	40,000
MATURITY VALUE OF THE NOTE	$540,000
Less Bank Discount	
$540,000 × 10% × 6/12 =	(27,000)
Cash proceeds	$513,000

59. (c) As of June 30, 2000, one payment of $50,000 has been made on the $150,000 original principal of the note. So the balance of the note from July 1, 1999 to June 30, 2000 has been $100,000. Therefore, the accrued interest receivable, the current asset, should be the accrued interest for 12 months ($100,000 × 8% × 12/12 = $8,000).

60. (b) Since the note is dated July 15 and received on August 15, the assumption is that the selling price is equal to the principal of the note plus one month's interest. Therefore, interest receivable is increased on the date of the transaction.

61. (c)

Face value of the note	$500,000
Interest rate	12%
Annual interest	$ 60,000
Two months accrual (2/12)	$10,000

62. (b)

TOTAL CASH PAYMENTS	$5,009 × 5 years	-	$25,045
Less Present Value of the note			19,485
Total Interest Revenue			$ 5,560

63. (None - *credit was given for all answers.*) The vacation days were earned in 1998 and should be accrued in 1998. The cost accrued should be 6 employees × 10 days × $100 per day for a total of $6,000. The question is whether to accrue the sick pay. The key to the question is the word "should". The problem asks what Baker Co. should accrue for sick pay. Since Baker estimates three days of sick pay will be taken, it should accrue three days to properly match expenses and revenues. The cost accrued should be 6 employees × 3 days × $100 for a total of $1800. In summary the total accrued for compensated absences would be the vacation pay of $6,000 plus the sick pay of $1,800 for a total of $7,800.

64. (d) The liability for compensated absences at December 31, 1999, is $15,000 for the 150 vacation days times $100 per day. The key word in dealing with sick pay is the word "required". The problem asks what is the liability required at December 31, 1999. Since the accrual of sick pay is optional, North Corp. would not be required to accrue a liability for sick pay.

65. (d)	Wages subject to FICA = $80,000 × 7% =	$5,600
	Wages subject to unemployment = $20,000 × 3% =	600
	Total payroll taxes accrued	$6,200

66. (c) Insurance expense is the difference between the annual advance premium and the increase in the cash surrender value of the policy. In this case the annual premium was $40,000 and the increase in the cash surrender value ($87,000 to $108,000) was $21,000. The difference of $19,000 would be reported as life insurance expense. The dividends in the problem are not a factor because they are included in the 12/31/98 cash surrender value.

67. (c) The intercompany sales are eliminated in the consolidated statements and the officers' expenses and salaries are not related party transactions. Only the loans to officers need be disclosed.

68. (a) Current assets are assets that are expected to be converted to cash, used, or sold within one year or the operating cycle whichever is **longer**. In this case cash must be adjusted because even though the checks were recorded in June, they were not mailed and legally paid until July. Therefore, the checks ($30,000) must be added to the negative cash balance (-$10,000) to reach the adjusted cash balance of $20,000. In addition, the land held for resale should be reclassified to a current asset because Gold Corp. is selling the land in July of 1999. In summary, the total current assets would be the adjusted cash ($20,000), the accounts receivable net ($35,000), inventory ($58,000), prepaid expenses ($12,000), and the land for resale ($100,000) for a total of $225,000.

69. (a) Two Key Points:

1. One half of the $500,000 accounts receivable with the special terms is current and the other half is noncurrent.

2. The income before tax is $1,000,000 ($3,600,000 Revenues less 2,600,000 in Expenses). Therefore, taxes are $300,000 (1,000,000 x 30%). After recording the tax expense and crediting the prepaid tax, the prepaid tax would have a **zero** balance.

Therefore, the total current assets would include the cash of $550,000 plus the accounts receivable of $1,650,000 reduced by the $250,000 noncurrent portion for a total of $1,950,000.

70. (c)

Beginning Balance in Retained Earnings			$ 630,000
Plus:	Revenue	$3,600,000	
	Expenses	(2,600,000)	
	Income before tax	1,000,000	
	Tax Expense (30%)	(300,000)	
	Net Income		700,000
Ending Balance in Retained Earnings			$1,330,000

*Note: The Foreign Currency **translation** adjustment account is a stockholders' equity account and does not affect the income statement.*

71. (a) The answer can be determined by reviewing the journal entry for insurance costs:

JE	Insurance Expense (Annual)	XX	
	Cash Surrender Value of Life Insurance	XX	
	Cash		XX

72. (d) A note discounted with recourse creates a contingent liability for the face of the note plus any interest due on the note. Since this note is a noninterest bearing note, the contingent liability disclosed in the financial statements would be $20,500.

73. (d)

	Carrying Value	*Accumulated Depreciation*
Cost	$900,000	
Accumulated Depreciation	(420,000)	$420,000
Carrying Value 1/1/99	$480,000	
Writedown (loss) due to obsolescence	(180,000)	180,000
Adjusted Carrying Value 1/1/99	$300,000	
Depreciation for 1999 $300,000 / 3 years	(100,000)	100,000
Balance 12/31/99	$200,000	$700,000

74. (c) Since the first payment was made on December 30, 2001, the note should be reported on the December 31, 2001 balance sheet at $62,500 which is the present value of the remaining nine payments ($10,000 x 6.25).

75. (a) The key point is that Jamin Co. is using the income statement approach for estimating uncollectible accounts. In this case, the estimated uncollectible accrued expense would be $180,000 (2% x $9,000,000 credit sales). Therefore, the ending balance in the allowance account should be calculated as follows:

ALLOWANCE FOR UNCOLLECTIBLE ACCOUNTS	
Beginning Balance	$260,000
Accrual (see above)	180,000
Write offs	(325,000)
Ending Balance	$115,000

76. (a) Theoretically all necessary cost to purchase the machine and get it ready for use should be capitalized. Both of these costs are necessary to purchase the asset and should be capitalized.

77. (c) Costs attributable to land: $60,000 + $2,000 + $5,000 – $3,000 = $64,000
Costs attributable to building: $8,000 + $350,000 = $358,000

78. (d)

I. Collections from CASH sales		
Gross Sales	$80,000	
less Returns & Allowances	(4,000)	
Collections from cash sales		$76,000
II. Collections from CREDIT sales		
Accounts Receivable 1/1/00	$40,000	
Credit Sales (120,000 - 6,000)	114,000	
Less Accounts Receivable 12/31/00	(30,000)	
Collections from credit sales		124,000
TOTAL CASH COLLECTIONS		$200,000

79. (b) Two Key Points:

A. Under DDB the salvage value is ignored in the initial years.

B. The percentage used is double the straight-line percentage. In this case, the percentage is 50% (2 x 25%).

DEPRECIATION SCHEDULE FOR CALCULATION OF DEPRECIATION EXPENSE			
1999	$ 80,000 x 50%	=	$40,000
2000	($80,000 - 40,000) x 50%	=	$20,000
2001	($80,000 - 40,000 - 20,000) x 50%	=	$10,000

80. (d) The accrued interest at end of the first year, February 28, 2001, is $1200 ($10,000 X 12% = 1200). The interest for the remaining 10 months is compounded based on the carrying amount of the total liability at February 28, 2001, $11,200 ($10,000 principal plus the $1200 accrued interest). Therefore, the interest is $11,200 x 12% X 10/12 = $1120 for the last 10 months. The accrued interest liability at December 31, 2001 would be the total interest for the two time periods, $1200 + $1120 = $2320.

81. (b) The $45,000 capitalized cost of the patent was amortized at $3,000 per year ($45,000/15 years) for 1998, 1999, and 2000, which reduced the carrying amount to $36,000. The cost of the successful defense of the patent ($15,000) is added to the carrying amount for a total of $51,000. Therefore, the gain on the sale is $24,000 ($75,000 - $51,000).

82. (c) On theory questions such as Crater, Inc., the solutions approach is to set up a **simple** numerical example:

Cost of equipment	$20,000
Salvage value (20%)	$4,000
Sold equipment	$10,000

Sum-of-the-years-digits approach:

Accumulated depreciation Years 1 - 5 = $16,000 × $\frac{(10+9+8+7+6)}{55}$ = $11,636

Gain/loss	=	Selling price – book value
	=	$10,000 – ($20,000 – $11,636)
	=	$10,000 – $8,364
Gain	=	$1,636

Double-declining balance method will depreciate the asset faster than sum-of-the-years-digits because it ignores salvage value initially. Therefore, DDB would report a higher gain than SYD.

Composite method does not recognize a gain or loss on early retirement.

Straight-line method

- Depreciation = ($20,000 – 4,000) ÷ 10 years = $1,600
- Accumulated Dep. = $1,600 × 5 years = $8,000
- Loss = Selling price – book value = $10,000 – ($20,000 – 8,000)
  = $2,000 loss

83. (b)

Carrying value of note on 1/1/92 = .75 × $400,000 =	$300,000
Interest rate	10%
Interest income	$ 30,000

84. (d) The principal would have to be due in 2001 to be considered as a noncurrent asset at April 30, 2000. The accrued interest for eight months (since August 31, 1999) is a current asset at April 30, 2000. Since the principal is due August 31, 2001, additional interest would have to be recorded for the period September 1, 2000 to August 31, 2001. Therefore, the answer is (d). This is the only answer in which the principal is due in 2001 and includes interest for the two fiscal years.

85. (d) All costs incurred until the machine is ready for use are part of the machine's cost.

86. (d) Research and development is the search for new knowledge in the hope of developing a new product or service. Since Brill Co.'s costs to develop computer software is for **internal** use and not for a new product, these costs would be charged to general and administrative expenses and not research and development. The marketing research costs would be charged to selling expenses.

87. (c)

Cost 1/1/96	$90,000
Less Amortization	
$90,000 / 10 years = $9,000	
per year × 3 years	(27,000)
CARRYING VALUE 1/1/99	$63,000

Since the patent will not benefit Lava Inc. beyond the current year, the total 1/1/99 carrying value should be charged to the income statement in 1999. The $9,000 amortization per year would be charged to expense and the remaining $54,000 would be charged as a loss on the patent.

88. (c) Annual payments on the note:

Payment × 3,992 = $20,000
Payment = $5,010

Present value of the payments @ 9%:

$5,010 × 3.890 = $19,490

This amount represents the purchase price of the note.

Total of all payments—$5,010 × 5 =	$25,050
Carrying value of the note	19,490
Interest to be recognized	$ 5,560

89. (c)

Balance in the liability account at 10/1/96	$15,000
Additional expense due to pay raise @ 10%	$ 1,500
1996 expense at current pay rates	30,000
Total expense for 1996	$31,500

90. (a) Since the case on patent A34 is weak, the legal cost should be charged to expense. The company has a strong case on patent B19 and the legal cost should be capitalized. The theory for capitalization of the legal costs is that the costs will benefit future periods.

91. (d) Research and Development costs incurred from employing outside companies, **preproduction** cost and cost incurred for searching for new products or process alternatives would all be considered R & D costs. Therefore, the total costs of $525,000 ($150,000 + 200,000 + 175,000) would be the answer.

92. (b) The legal fees and other cost associated with the patent should be capitalized because these costs will benefit future periods. The total of these costs are $82,000. The R&D costs should be expensed.

93. (a) The costs capitalized as patent are the direct costs of obtaining the patent other than research and development expenditures which are expensed. The registration costs of $30,000 and the legal fees of $45,000 paid for the successful defense of the patent are charged to the patent account.

94. (b) The theoretical gain on the trade is $8,000 (FMV old truck $20,000 – $12,000 carrying value). Therefore, the transaction is a trade of similar items with a theoretical gain and a receipt of boot. In that case Amble, Inc. should allocate the carrying value of the truck exchanged between the portion of the carrying value sold and the portion traded:

a. Portion of carrying value sold $= \dfrac{\text{Boot}}{\text{Boot + FMV of new truck}} \times$ Carrying value

$= \dfrac{\$5,000}{\$5,000 + \$15,000} \times \$12,000$

Portion of carrying value sold = $3,000

b. Portion of carrying value traded	=	Total carrying value	–	Portion of CV sold
	=	$12,000	–	$3,000
Portion of carrying value traded	=	$9,000		

The portion of the carrying value traded is the cost of the new truck - $9,000. The theory is that the earnings process is not complete on the portion of the asset traded, and since similar assets were traded, none of the theoretical gain should be recognized. The earnings process is assumed to be complete on the portion of the CV sold and the gain should be recognized ($5,000 – $3,000 = $2,000 gain recognized).

95. (c) The theoretical gain on the trade is the FMV of the inventory ($21,000) less the carrying value of the inventory ($20,000) for a total gain of $1,000. In a trade of similar assets in which Beam pays boot and has a theoretical gain, the gain is not recognized ($0) and the inventory received is recorded at the carrying value of the inventory traded ($20,000) plus the boot ($1,000) for a total of $21,000. The theory is that the earnings process is not complete.

96. (b) The method which records the most depreciation in the first two years would cause the higher gain or lower loss upon sale. The percent of cost depreciated in the first two years is:

Sum of years' digits depreciation is 5/15 + 4/15 or 9/15 or 60%.

Double declining balance is 40% + (40% × 60%) or 64%.

Therefore, using sum-of-the-years' digits would reduce the gain and increase the loss upon sale.

97. (a) When similar or dissimilar assets are exchanged and a loss is realized on the disposal of the asset, such loss is recognized for the difference between the carrying value and the fair market value of the asset surrendered.

98. (b) Only Ryan's vacation pay is accrued since Todd's does not vest or accumulate.

99. (c) The amount accrued as commissions for each salesperson will be any commissions due over and above the fixed salary as follows:

	Fixed salary	*Commissions*	*Excess*
A	$10,000	$ 8,000	$— 0 —
B	$14,000	$24,000	$10,000
C	$18,000	$36,000	$18,000

The accrual is $28,000.

100. (a) Trade installment receivables normally collectible in 18 months would be classified as current, since this is industry practice.

101. (a) The goods on consignment have not been sold and the amount is not included in accounts receivable. The security deposit is not a receivable. The claim against the shipper is appropriately included as a receivable.

102. (a) A recovery of an account which was previously written off is usually reinstated into accounts receivable with a debit entry to accounts receivable and a credit to the allowance account.

103. (a) The allowance for sales discounts should be calculated from the group of sales in the 0 - 15 days category that could qualify for the sales discount. Since only 50% of this group is expected to take advantage of the discount, the calculation would be $100,000 × 50% × 2% = $1,000.

104. (a) In a trade of dissimilar items, the earnings process is assumed to be complete and the new asset received is recorded at the FMV of the consideration given up and a gain or loss is recognized. In this case the investment in Ace should be recorded at $3,000; the FMV of the truck traded.

105. (b) Normally when a note is exchanged for services and the stated interest rate is substantially below the imputed interest rate, the note is recorded at the FMV of the services or the present value of the note, whichever is more reliable. However, if the note arose in the normal course of business (customary or usual trade terms) and the term of the note does not exceed one year, APB #21 makes an exception to the normal rule and allows the note to be recorded at face value.

106. (c)		
	Carrying value of Slad's asset	$ 40,000
	Cash paid by Slad	100,000
	Recorded cost on Slad's books	$140,000

107. (c) The key point is that the cost and related accumulated depreciation of the damaged portion are identifiable and can be removed from the accounts with the appropriate loss recognized. The new cost of refurbishing should be capitalized and depreciated over the future periods benefited.

108. (b) The amount of the investment in cash surrender value to be reported on Jann Co.'s December 31, 1996 balance sheet is $3,200. This is calculated by comparing the amount paid for annual premiums, $16,000 (4 years x $4,000), to the amount charged to life insurance expense of $12,800 ($16,000 - $12,800 = $3,200).

109. (c) According to SFAS 114, when a loan receivable is impaired but foreclosure is not probable, a creditor may measure the impairment by using either the loan's observable market price or the fair value of the collateral if the loan is collateral dependent.

110. (b) SFAS 57 established formal requirements for disclosure of material related-party transactions. Consulting fees paid to a marketing research firm, one of whose partners is also a director of the company is an example of a related-party transaction that must be disclosed. Expense allowances incurred in the ordinary course of business such as the payments per diem expenses of the members of the board of directors are specifically excluded from disclosure.

111. (a) SFAS #57 requires the disclosure of related parties in situations in which one party controls or can significantly influence the management or operating policies of the reporting entity. Since Lemu and Young are under common management of Ego Co., the relationship must be disclosed.

112. (b) The key point is that if a machine can only be used on one project, the total cost of that machine should be charged to expense in the year of acquisition because the future life of a research project is uncertain. Therefore, the cost of machine A ($250,000) should be charged to expense in 1997.

Machine B has other uses beyond R&D and should be depreciated over the useful life of 10 years ($250,000 / 10 years) for an annual depreciation of $25,000.

The total cost included in R&D expense should be $250,000 for machine A and $25,000 for machine B, for a total cost of $275,000.

113. (c) Under the sum-of-the-year's digits method, the denominator in the fraction is used to calculate the yearly depreciation as the sum of the year's digits or 1 + 2 + 3 + 4=10. The numerators are the year's digits in declining order or 4,3,2,1. Therefore, the fraction used in 1996 would be 4/10; 1997 3/10; 1996 2/10 for an accumulated total of 9/10.

The accumulated depreciation would then be 9/10 x ($20,000 cost- $2,000 salvage value) for a total of $16,200.

The equipment's carrying value at December 31, 1998 would be the cost of $20,000 less the accumulated depreciation of $16,200 for a total of $3,800.

114. (c) SFAS 57 requires that joint ventures with an affiliate disclose the nature of the relationship, the dollar amount of purchases during the year and the amount due to the affiliate at the balance sheet date.

115. (c) The solutions approach is to use a "T" account.

Accounts Receivable

Beginning Balance	100,000	Collections	591,000
Credit Sales	611,000	Write-offs	45,000
Ending Balance	75, 000		

Note: The $17,000 of recoveries do not affect accounts receivable. A recovery is a debit to cash and a credit to the allowance for uncollectible accounts.

116. (b) The cost of the land should be the necessary cost to purchase the land and get it ready for its intended use. Therefore, the purchase price plus the cost of razing the old building less the sale of scrap materials should be capitalized ($100,000 + $50,000 – $10,000 = $140,000). The excavation cost to build the foundation would be a cost of the building.

117. (b) The risk of loss associated with the trade accounts receivable is the net realizable value of the receivables ($250,000 - $20,000 = $230,000). There is not an off-balance sheet risk associated with trade accounts receivable.

118. (d) Ratio of purchase price of $96,000

Land	$60,000-3/6	$48,000
Bldgs	$40,000-2/6	32,000
Equip.	$20,000-1/6	16,000
	$120,000	$96,000

Chapter Eleven
Solutions to Other Assets, Liabilities and Disclosures Problems

NUMBER 1

a. The appropriate valuation basis of a note receivable at the date of sale is its discounted present value of the future amounts receivable for principal and interest using the customer's market rate of interest, if known or determinable, at the date of the equipment's sale.

b. Gregor should increase the carrying amount of the note receivable by the effective interest revenue earned for the period February 1 to May 1, 2002. Gregor should account for the discounting of the note receivable without recourse by increasing cash for the proceeds received, eliminating the carrying amount of the note receivable, and recognizing a loss (gain) for the resulting difference.

This reporting is appropriate since the note's carrying amount is correctly recorded at the date it was discounted and the discounting of a note receivable without recourse is equivalent to a sale of that note. Thus the difference between the cash received and the carrying amount of the note at the date it is discounted is reported as a loss (gain).

c. **1.** For notes receivable not discounted, Gregor should recognize an uncollectible notes expense. The expense equals the adjustment required to bring the balance of the allowance for uncollectible notes receivable equal to the estimated uncollectible amounts less the fair values of recoverable equipment.

2. For notes receivable discounted with recourse, Gregor should recognize an uncollectible notes expense. The expense equals the estimated amounts payable for customers' defaults less the fair values of recoverable equipment.

NUMBER 2

a.

Sigma Co.
SCHEDULE OF CALCULATION OF
ALLOWANCE FOR UNCOLLECTIBLE ACCOUNTS
December 31, 1998

0 to 30 days	$300,000	×	1%	$ 3,000
31 to 90 days	80,000	×	5%	4,000
91 to 180 days	60,000	×	20%	12,000
Over 180 days	25,000	×	80%	20,000
Accounts receivable	$465,000			
Allowance for uncollectible accounts				$39,000

b. Computation of 1998 provision:

Balance, December 31, 1997	$28,000
Writeoffs during 1998	(27,000)
Recoveries during 1998	7,000
Balance before 1998 provision	8,000
Required allowance at December 31, 1998	39,000
1998 provision	$31,000

NUMBER 3

a. 1. When the old engines' costs are known, the snowmobiles account is decreased by the old engines' costs, and accumulated depreciation is decreased by the accumulated depreciation on the old engines. A current asset would be recorded for the fair value of the future repair and maintenance services. The net difference between the old engines' carrying amounts and their fair values is recorded as an operating gain or loss. To record the new engines' acquisition, both the snowmobiles account and accounts payable are increased by the new engines' costs.

2. If the old engines' costs are unknown then either the snowmobiles account would be increased or accumulated depreciation would be decreased by the difference between the new engines' costs and the old engines' fair values.

b. 1. Assumptions underlying use of an accelerated depreciation method include:

- An asset is more productive in the earlier years of its estimated useful life. Therefore, greater depreciation charges in the earlier years would be matched against the greater revenues generated in the earlier years.
- Repair and maintenance costs are often higher in later periods and an accelerated depreciation method results in a more nearly annual constant total cost over the years of use.
- An asset may become obsolete before the end of its originally estimated useful life. The risk associated with estimated long-term cash flows is greater than the risk associated with near-term cash flows. Accelerated depreciation recognizes this condition.

2. Winter should calculate snowmobile depreciation by applying twice the straight-line rate to their carrying amounts.

c. Under the inventory (appraisal) method, Winter calculates the ending undepreciated cost on the skis, poles, and boots by multiplying the physical quantities of these items on hand by an appraised amount. This ending undepreciated cost is classified as a noncurrent asset. Depreciation included in continuing operations equals the sum of the beginning balance and purchases for the year less the ending undepreciated cost.

NUMBER 4

61. (C) All necessary cost to purchase the inventory and get it ready to sell should be capitalized. Freight cost are cost of purchasing the inventory and should be capitalized.

62. (C) The purchaser has the responsibility for paying the freight and insurance on merchandise shipped F.O.B. shipping point. Since the insurance on goods in transit is a cost of buying the inventory, it should be capitalized.

63. (E) Interest is never capitalized on inventory produced in the normal course of business. Interest may be capitalized on a internally constructed assets or assets produced as discrete products for sale.

64. (C) All necessary cost to purchase equipment and get it ready for use should be capitalized. Installation cost would be a necessary cost to get the machine ready for use and should be capitalized.

65. (C) Testing of newly-purchased equipment should be capitalized because it is a necessary cost of getting the asset ready for use.

66. (E) Routine costs such as the current year service contract on equipment do not benefit the company beyond the current year and should not be capitalized.

67. $600,000. The total cost of the office building and the land is $1,000,000 ($800,000 cash paid plus the $200,000 mortgage assumed). The portion of the cost allocated to the building is <u>$600,000</u> (60% x the total cost of $1,000,000).

68. $503,000. The problem states that this is a **capital** lease. The amount capitalized should be the annual payment times the present value factor for seven periods at 9% ($100,000 x 5.03 = <u>$503,000</u>).

69. $370,000. Link has a theoretical gain of $130,000 on the trade (FMV of $450,000 - $320,000 carrying value). In a trade of similar assets, (Land for Land), the earnings process is not complete and the theoretical gain is not recognized. The cost of the land for Link is the carrying value of the land traded plus the boot ($320,000 + $50,000 = $370,000).

70. $315,000. Club Co. has a theoretical gain of $150,000 on the trade (FMV of $500,000 - $350,000 carrying value). In a trade of similar assets with a theoretical gain, the carrying value ($350,000) of the asset is divided into a portion sold on which a gain may be recognized and the portion traded on which the gain is not recognized because the earnings process is not complete. The division of the carrying value is shown below:

PORTION SOLD $= \dfrac{\text{Boot}}{\text{Boot - FMV of } \textbf{Asset Received}} \times$ Carrying Value Traded

$= \dfrac{50,000}{50,000 + 450,000} = \dfrac{1}{10} \times \$350,000$

$= \$35,000$

PORTION TRADED = 9/10 x $350,000
= $315,000 which becomes the "cost" of the land received.

71. $90,000. The straight-line depreciation per year is the cost - salvage value divided by the useful life:

$\dfrac{\$864,000 - \$144,000}{8 \text{ years}} = \$90,000$ per year

72. $162,000. The double-declining balance depreciation expense is calculated by multiplying a constant rate times the declining book value. The salvage value is ignored initially and the constant rate is twice the straight rate. In this case, the straight line rate is 1/8 per year and the DDB rate would be 2 x 1/8 or 2/8 or 25%. Therefore, depreciation expense would be as follows:

1999	25% x $864,000	=	$216,000
2000	25% x ($864,000 - 216,000)	=	162,000

73. $140,000. SYD depreciation is calculated by taking a declining fraction and multiplying it times a constant depreciation base. The depreciation base is the cost minus the salvage value ($864,000 - 144,000 = $720,000). The denominator for the fraction is the sum of all the numbers in the sequence one through eight or the formula n(n+1) /2 which is 8(8+1) /2 = 36. The numerator for the first year is the highest number in the sequence (8) and for the second year the next highest number (7). Therefore:

1999	8/36	x	$720,000	=	$160,000
2000	7/36	x	$720,000	=	140,000

74. $120,000. The units-of-production calculates a depreciation cost per unit of production:

Depreciation per unit of Production $= \dfrac{\text{Cost - Salvage Value}}{\text{ESTIMATED PRODUCTION}}$

$= \dfrac{\$864,000 - 144,000}{1800,000 \text{ units}}$

= $.40 per unit

2000 Depreciation = Depreciation per unit x units produced in 2000
= $.40 x 300,000 units
= $120,000

NUMBER 5

a.

Schedule 1

Nan Co.
ANALYSIS OF CHANGES IN PROPERTY, PLANT, AND EQUIPMENT
For the Year Ended December 31, 1995

	Balance 12/31/94	*Increase*	*Decrease*	*Balance 12/31/95*
Land	$ 275,000	$ —	$ —	$ 275,000
Buildings	2,800,000	1,875,000 [1]		4,675,000
Machinery & equipment	1,380,000	369,000 [2]	17,000	1,732,000
Automobiles and trucks	210,000	25,000	48,000	187,000
Leasehold improvements	432,000	—	—	432,000
Totals	$5,097,000	$2,269,000	$65,000	$7,301,000

Explanations of amounts:

[1] Construction cost of building

Direct costs		$1,095,000
Overhead costs		
Fixed (15,000 hours × $25)	$375,000	
Variable (15,000 hours × $27)	405,000	780,000
		$1,875,000

[2] Machinery and equipment purchased

Invoice cost	$325,000
Installation cost (concrete embedding)	18,000
Cost of gaining access to factory ($19,000 + $7,000)	26,000
Total acquisition cost	$369,000

b.1.

Nan Co.
SCHEDULE OF DEPRECIATION AND AMORTIZATION EXPENSE
For the Year Ended December 31, 1995

Buildings		
Carrying amount, 1/1/95 ($2,800,000 – $672,900)	$2,127,100	
Building completed 1/6/95	1,875,000	
Total subject to depreciation	4,002,100	
150% declining balance [(100% ÷ 25) × 1.5]	× 6%	
Depreciation for 1995		$240,126
Machinery and equipment		
Balance, 1/1/95	$1,380,000	
Straight-line (100% ÷ 10)	× 10%	$138,000
Purchased 7/1/95	369,000	
Straight-line (10% × 6/12)	× 5%	18,450
Depreciation for 1995		$156,450

Automobiles and trucks		
Carrying amount, 1/1/95 ($210,000 – $114,326)	$95,674	
Deduct carrying amount, 1/1/95 on truck sold 9/30/95	30,000	
Amount subject to depreciation	65,674	
150% declining balance [(100% ÷ 5) × 1.5]	× 30%	$19,702
Automobile purchased 8/30/95	25,000	
150% declining balance (30% × 4/12)	× 10%	2,500
Truck sold 9/30/95—depreciation for 1995 (1/1 to 9/30/95) ($30,000 × 30% × 9/12)		6,750
Depreciation for 1995		$28,952

Leasehold improvements	
Amortization for 1995 ($432,000 ÷ 12 years)	$36,000

b.2.

Schedule 2

Nan Co.
ANALYSIS OF CHANGES IN ACCUMULATED DEPRECIATION AND AMORTIZATION
For the Year Ended December 31, 1995

	Balance 12/31/94	*Increase*	*Decrease*	*Balance 12/31/95*
Buildings	$ 672,900	$240,126	$ —	$ 913,026
Machinery & equipment	367,500	156,450	14,025 [1]	509,925
Automobiles and trucks	114,326	28,952	24,750 [2]	118,528
Leasehold improvements	108,000	36,000	—	144,000
Totals	$1,262,726	$461,528	$38,775	$1,685,479

	[1]	*[2]*
Cost	$17,000	$48,000
Carrying Amount	2,975	23,250 *
Accumulated Depreciation	$14,025	$24,750

*($30,000 - $6,750)

c.

Nan Co.
GAIN ON DISPOSITION OF PROPERTY, PLANT, AND EQUIPMENT
For the Year Ended December 31, 1995

	Selling price	*Carrying amount*	*Gain*
Sale of truck	$23,500	$23,250	$ 250
Machine exchanged for debt	4,000	2,975	1,025
	$27,500	$26,225	$1,275

NUMBER 6

a.

Kern, Inc.
LONG-TERM RECEIVABLES SECTION OF BALANCE SHEET
December 31, 1997

9% note receivable from sale of idle building, due in annual installments of $250,000 to May 1, 1999, less current installment	$250,000	[1]
8% note receivable from officer, due December 31, 1999, collateralized by 5,000 shares of Kern, Inc., common stock with a fair value of $225,000	200,000	
Noninterest bearing note from sale of patent, net of 10% imputed interest, due April 1, 1999	88,795	[2]
Installment contract receivable, due in annual installments of $88,332 to July 1, 2001, less current installment	219,668	[3]
Total long-term receivables	$758,463	

b.

Kern, Inc.
SELECTED BALANCE SHEET ACCOUNTS
December 31, 1997

Current portion of long-term receivables:		
Note receivable from sale of idle building	$250,000	[1]
Installment contract receivable	60,332	[3]
Total	$310,332	
Accrued interest receivable:		
Note receivable from sale of idle building	$30,000	[4]
Installment contract receivable	14,000	[5]
Total	$44,000	

c.

Kern, Inc.
INTEREST REVENUE FROM LONG-TERM RECEIVABLES AND GAINS RECOGNIZED ON SALE OF ASSETS
For the year ended December 31, 1997

Interest revenue:		
Note receivable from sale of idle building	$52,500	[6]
Note receivable from sale of patent	6,195	[2]
Note receivable from officer	16,000	[7]
Installment contract receivable from sale of land	14,000	[5]
Total interest revenue	$88,695	
Gains recognized on sale of assets:		
Patent	$ 44,600	[8]
Land	100,000	[9]
Total gains recognized	$144,600	

Explanation of amounts:

[1] Long-term portion of 9% note receivable at 12/31/97			
Face amount, 5/1/96		$750,000	
Less installment received 5/1/97		250,000	
Balance, 12/31/97		500,000	
Less installment due 5/1/98		250,000	
Long-term portion, 12/31/97		$250,000	
[2] Noninterest bearing note, net of imputed interest at 12/31/97			
Face amount, 4/1/97		$100,000	
Less imputed interest [$100,000 – $82,600 ($100,000 × 0.826)]		17,400	
Balance, 4/1/97		82,600	
Add interest earned to 12/31/97 [$82,600 × 10% × 9/12]		6,195	
Balance, 12/31/97		$ 88,795	
[3] Long-term portion of installment contract receivable at 12/31/97			
Contract selling price, 7/1/97		$400,000	
Less cash down payment		120,000	
Balance, 12/31/97		280,000	
Less installment due 7/1/98 [$88,332 – $28,000 ($280,000 × 10%)]		60,332	
Long-term portion, 12/31/97		$219,668	
[4] Accrued interest—note receivable, sale of idle building at 12/31/97			
Interest accrued from 5/1 to 12/31/97 [$500,000 × 9% × 8/12]		$ 30,000	
[5] Accrued interest—installment contract at 12/31/97			
Interest accrued from 7/1 to 12/31/97 [$280,000 × 10% × ½]		$ 14,000	
[6] Interest revenue—note receivable, sale of idle building, for 1997			
Interest earned from 1/1 to 5/1/97 [$750,000 × 9% × 4/12)		$ 22,500	
Interest earned from 5/1 to 12/31/97 [$500,000 × 9% × 8/12]		30,000	
Interest revenue		$ 52,500	
[7] Interest revenue—note receivable, officer, for 1997			
Interest earned 1/1 to 12/31/97 [$200,000 × 8%]		$ 16,000	
[8] Gain recognized on sale of patent			
Stated selling price		$100,000	
Less imputed interest		17,400	[2]
Actual selling price		82,600	
Less cost of patent (net)			
Carrying value 1/1/97	$40,000		
Less amortization 1/1 to 4/1/97 [$8,000 × ¼]	2,000	38,000	
Gain recognized		$ 44,600	
[9] Gain recognized on sale of land			
Selling price		$400,000	
Less cost		300,000	
Gain recognized		$100,000	

NUMBER 7

Pitt Company
INCOME BEFORE INCOME TAXES ON SALE OF PATENT
For the Years Ended December 31, 1997, and 1998

		1997	*1998*
Profit on Sale			
Sales price ($16,000 × 3.60)	$57,600		
Cost of patent, net of amortization	10,000	$47,600	—
Interest income *(Schedules 1 and 2)*		6,912	$5,821
Income before income taxes		$54,512	$5,821

Schedule 1—Computation of Interest Income for 1997

Sales price	$57,600
Interest rate	× 12%
Interest income	$ 6,912

Schedule 2—Computation of Interest Income for 1998

Balance at December 31, 1997 ($57,600 + $6,912)	$64,512
Deduct payment made on January 1, 1998	16,000
	48,512
Interest rate	× 12%
Interest income	$ 5,821

NUMBER 8

a. To account for the accounts receivable factored on April 1, 1996, Magrath should decrease accounts receivable by the amount of accounts receivable factored, increase cash by the amount received from the factor, and record a loss equal to the difference. The loss should be reported in the income statement. Factoring of accounts receivable on a without recourse basis is equivalent to a sale.

b. The carrying amount of the note at July 1, 1996, is the maturity amount discounted for two years at the market interest rate. For the noninterest-bearing note receivable, the interest revenue for 1996 should be determined by multiplying the carrying amount of the note at July 1, 1996, times the market rate of interest at the date of the note times one-half.

The noninterest-bearing note receivable should be reported in the December 31, 1996, balance sheet, as a noncurrent asset at its face amount less the unamortized discount.

c. Magrath should account for the collection of the accounts previously written off as uncollectible as follows:
* Increase both accounts receivable and the allowance for uncollectible accounts.
* Increase cash and decrease accounts receivable.

d. One approach estimates uncollectible accounts based on credit sales. This approach focuses on income determination by attempting to match uncollectible accounts expense with the revenues generated.

The other allowance approach estimates uncollectible accounts based on the balance in or aging of receivables. The approach focuses on asset valuation by attempting to report receivables at realizable value.

NUMBER 9

a. Portland should have selected the straight-line depreciation method when approximately the same amount of an asset's service potential is used up each period. If the reasons for the decline in service potential are unclear, then the selection of the straight-line method could be influenced by the ease of recordkeeping, its use for similar assets, and its use by others in the industry.

b. Portland should record depreciation expense to the date of the exchange. If the original truck's carrying amount is greater than its fair value, a loss results. The truck's capitalized cost and accumulated depreciation are eliminated, and the loss on trade-in is reported as part of income from continuing operations. The newly acquired truck is recorded at fair value. If the original truck's carrying amount is less than its fair value at trade-in, then there is an unrecognized gain. The newly acquired truck is recorded at fair value less the unrecognized gain. Cash is decreased by the amount paid.

c. 1. By associating depreciation with a group of machines instead of each individual machine, Portland's bookkeeping process is greatly simplified. Also, since actual machine lives vary from the average depreciable life, unrecognized net losses on early dispositions are expected to be offset by continuing depreciation on machines usable beyond the average depreciable life. Periodic income does not fluctuate as a result of recognizing gains and losses on manufacturing machine dispositions.

2. Portland should divide the depreciable cost (capitalized cost less residual value) of each machine by its estimated life to obtain its annual depreciation. The sum of the individual annual depreciation amounts should then be divided by the sum of the individual capitalized costs to obtain the annual composite depreciation rate.

NUMBER 10

1. Land - The purchase price of the land is capitalized as a part of the cost of the land. Land is a permanent asset and is not depreciated.

2. Expense - Interest incurred after completion of the building is charged to interest expense.

3. Building - Interest incurred during construction is capitalized as a part of the cost of the building and depreciated. The theory is that the building is not yet generating revenue and to charge the interest to expense will result in an improper matching of expenses and revenue.

4. Land - All costs associated with the purchase of the land and getting the land ready for its intended use should be capitalized. Since the land was purchased as a building site, the cost of the building which will be razed is considered a part of the land.

5. Land - The real estate taxes paid are a necessary cost associated with the purchase of the land.

6. Building - Liability insurance during construction is a normal cost of the construction and should be capitalized as a part of the cost of the building and depreciated.

7. Land - The cost of tearing down the building is a necessary cost of getting the land ready for its intended use and should be capitalized as a part of the cost of the land.

8. Expense - Moving costs are not acquisition cost or cost of getting the land ready for its intended use or normal cost of construction. Therefore, the costs should be charged to expense of the period.

Chapter Twelve
Reporting the Results of Operations

Chapter Twelve
Reporting the Results of Operations

INCOME STATEMENT- MULTI-STEP FORMAT

This approach is called multi-step because of the number of "steps" or sub-totals between the beginning net sales number and the calculation of income from continuing operations. Examples of the "steps" are the calculation of gross profit, operating profit, and income from continuing operations before income taxes.

Complex Corporation
Statement of Earnings
For the Years Ended December 31,
(in thousands)

	19X3	*19X2*
Net sales	$5,000	$4,000
Cost of sales	2,800	1,900
GROSS PROFIT	2,200	2,100
Operating expenses	1,000	850
Selling expenses	100	100
Administrative expenses	500	450
	1,600	1,400
OPERATING PROFIT	600	700
Other income, principally interest	(80)	(60)
Other expenses, principally interest	20	30
Income from continuing operations before income taxes	660	730
Provision for income taxes	300	350
INCOME FROM CONTINUING OPERATIONS	$ 360	$ 380
Discontinued operations:		
Loss from operations of discontinued widget division net of applicable income taxes of $70		($100)
Loss on disposal of widget division less estimated income taxes of $100		(150)
Adjustment to actual loss net of income taxes of $10	$ (15)	$(250)
NET INCOME BEFORE EXTRAORDINARY GAIN AND CUMULATIVE EFFECT OF CHANGE IN ACCOUNTING PRINCIPLE	345	130
Extraordinary gain from settlement with State for condemnation of property net of income taxes of $30		70
Cumulative effect of change from the declining balance to straight-line method of depreciation on previously owned assets net of income taxes of $60	75	
NET INCOME	$420	$200
Earnings per common share (100,000 shares):		
Income from continuing operations	$3.60	$3.80
*Loss from operations of discontinued widget division		(1.00)
*Loss on disposal of widget division	(.15)	(1.50)
Income before extraordinary gain and cumulative effect of accounting change	3.45	1.30
*Extraordinary gain net of income taxes		.70
Cumulative effect of changing to a different depreciation method net of taxes	.75	
Net income	$4.20	$2.00

Pro forma amounts assuming the new depreciation method is applied retroactively:		
Income from continuing operations	$360	$390
Income per share*	3.60	3.90
Net income before extraordinary gain and cumulative effect of accounting change	345	140
Income per share*	3.45	1.40
Net income	345	210
Net income per share*	3.45	2.10

*specific per share disclosure not required

INCOME STATEMENT- SINGLE STEP FORMAT

A single-step approach lists all revenues together and then lists all expenses together regardless of the source. The approach is called single-step because a single calculation of total revenues less total expenses equals income from continuing operations. A single-step income statement would differ from a multi-step income statement only in the calculation of income from continuing operations as shown below. The calculation of discontinued operations, extraordinary items, changes in accounting principles, earnings per share, etc., would be the same under both the single-step and the multi-step method.

Complex Corporation
Partial Income Statement
For the Years Ended December 31,
(in thousands)

Single-Step Format

REVENUES	*19X3*	*19X2*
Net sales	$5,000	$4,000
Other Income – Principally Interest	80	60
Total Revenues	$5,080	$4,060
EXPENSES		
Cost of Sales	2,800	1,900
Operating Expenses	1,000	850
Selling Expenses	100	100
Administrative Expenses	500	450
Other Expenses – Principally Interest	20	30
Provision for Income Taxes	300	350
Total Expenses	4,720	3,680
Income from Continuing Operations	$360	$380

DISCLOSURE OF ACCOUNTING POLICIES—APB #22

Issuance of financial statements, purporting to present fairly such statements in accordance with GAAP **should include a description of all significant accounting policies**. This applies to profit or not-for-profit entities and situations where one or more of the basic statements are appropriately issued purporting to present financial position, results of operations or changes in financial position. Disclosure is not required for interim unaudited statements issued between annual reporting dates where the entity has not changed accounting policies since the end of the preceding year.

Disclosure should include accounting principles and methods of applying them that involve the following criteria:

a. A selection from existing acceptable alternatives. (Where there is only one acceptable application of GAAP, no disclosure is required.)
b. Principles and methods peculiar to the industry in which the reporting entity operates, even if such principles and methods are predominantly followed in that industry.
c. Unusual or innovative applications of generally accepted accounting principles (and, as applicable, of principles and methods peculiar to the industry in which the reporting entity operates).

Examples of disclosures by a business entity commonly required with respect to accounting policies would include, among others, those relating to **basis of consolidation, depreciation methods, amortization of intangibles, inventory pricing, recognition of profit on long-term construction-type contracts, and recognition of revenue from franchising and leasing operations**. This is not all-inclusive.

Disclosure need not duplicate details furnished elsewhere in the financial statements. In some cases, disclosure may be cross-referenced to other required disclosure; for example, the disclosure of a change in accounting principle as required by Opinion No. 20.

Format for disclosure is flexible, but it is suggested that disclosure be included separately under the heading: **Summary of Significant Accounting Policies.**

ACCOUNTING CHANGES—APB #20

In General

APB #20 defines various types of changes in accounting principles and the manner of reporting each type. The opinion also defines and establishes reporting requirements for special types of accounting changes, change in an accounting estimate, change in entities, and the correction of an error.

Change in Accounting Principle

Changes in accounting principles require **a retroactive computation of the effect of the change on prior periods**. The cumulative effect on net income of prior periods is included in the net income of the current period (except special changes) as a **segregated** item described as, for example, "**cumulative effect on prior years of changing to a different depreciation method**." The "accounting change" income caption is included in the income statement between "extraordinary items and net income."

The after-tax effect of the change in accounting principle on "income before extraordinary items" and on net income is disclosed.

Prior periods are not restated; however, "income before extraordinary items" and net income computed **on a pro forma basis**, along with the related per share amounts, should be shown for prior periods on the face of the income statements.

It is presumed that once an accounting principle is adopted for events and transactions of a similar type, it should not be changed without justification. It is therefore required that the **nature and justification** of a change in accounting principle be disclosed in the financial statements of the year of change.

Examples of a Change in Accounting Principle:

1. A change in inventory accounting methods
2. A change in depreciation accounting methods
3. A change in accounting for long-term construction-type contracts
4. A change in composition of the elements of cost included in inventory.

The initial adoption of an accounting principle in recognition of events or transactions occurring for the first time or items that were previously immaterial is **not** a change in accounting principle; similarly with respect to adoption or modification of an accounting principle because of events or transactions clearly different in substance from those previously occurring.

Changes in Methods of Accounting for Long-Lived Assets

Retroactive recognition is **not** required for the adoption of a new depreciation or amortization method for newly acquired, identifiable, long-lived assets of the same class while continuing to depreciate (amortize) existing assets of the same class using the previous method. A description of the nature of the change in method and its effect on income before extraordinary items and net income should be disclosed, along with the related per share amounts. **If the new method is applied to previously recorded assets of the same class, the cumulative effect of the change should be applied.**

Case Example:

The Wing Company purchased a machine on January 1, 19X5, for $240,000. At the date of acquisition, the machine had an estimated useful life of ten years with an estimated salvage value of $20,000. The machine is being depreciated on a straight-line basis. On January 1, 19X8, Wing appropriately adopted the sum-of-the-years-digits method of depreciation for this machine.

Required:

1. Prepare a schedule computing the cumulative effect on prior years of changing to a different depreciation method for the year ended December 31, 19X8. The income tax rate was 30% in all years.
2. Prepare a schedule computing the book value of this machine, net of accumulated depreciation, that would be included in Wing's balance sheet at December 31, 19X8.

1.

Wing Company

COMPUTATION OF CUMULATIVE EFFECT ON PRIOR YEARS OF CHANGING TO A DIFFERENT DEPRECIATION METHOD

For the year ended December 31, 19X8

	Straight-line method	*Sum-of-the-years digits method*		*Increase*
Depreciation for 19X5	$22,000	$ 40,000	($220,000 × 10/55)	$18,000
19X6	22,000	36,000	($220,000 × 9/55)	14,000
19X7	22,000	32,000	($220,000 × 8/55)	10,000
	$66,000	$108,000		42,000
Income tax effect at 30%				12,600
Cumulative effect of change				$29,400

2.

Wing Company
COMPUTATION OF BOOK VALUE OF MACHINES, NET OF ACCUMULATED DEPRECIATION
December 31, 19X8

Cost of machine at date of purchase		$240,000
Depreciation for 19X5 *(Schedule I)*	$22,000	
19X6 *(Schedule I)*	22,000	
19X7 *(Schedule I)*	22,000	
		66,000
Book value of machine at December 31, 19X7		174,000
Excess of sum-of-the-years digits depreciation method over straight-line depreciation method *(Computation per Requirement 2)*	42,000	
Depreciation for 19X8, using sum-of-the-years digits method ($220,000 × 7/55—*Computation format per Requirement 2)*	28,000	70,000
Book value of machine at December 31, 19X8		$104,000

Schedule I—Computation of Depreciation for 19X5, 19X6, and 19X7

Cost of machine at date of purchase	$240,000
Estimated salvage value	20,000
Amount subject to depreciation	220,000
Depreciation rate	10%
Straight-line annual depreciation expense	$ 22,000

Special Changes in Accounting Principle

The Accounting Principles Board concluded that for some types of accounting changes, restatement of prior years' statements was advantageous because of the ordinarily large credits to income that may result. The special situations are primarily:

1. A change from the LIFO method of inventory pricing to another method.
2. A change in method of accounting for long-term construction-type contracts. For example, from completed contract to percentage of completion or vice versa.

These type changes require the cumulative effect of the accounting change to be reported as an adjustment to retained earnings (net of tax) and require retroactive restatement of prior period financial statements when presented.

This exemption is available only once for changes made at the time a company's financial statements are first used for these purposes and is not available to companies whose securities are widely held.

Pro Forma Amounts Not Determinable

In those rare situations where the pro forma amounts cannot be computed (e.g., breakdown of data for specific periods not available) or reasonably estimated for prior periods but the cumulative effect on retained earnings is determinable, **the cumulative effect should be reported in the year of change** with disclosure of the reason for not showing the pro forma amounts otherwise required.

The cumulative effect on the beginning retained earnings of the current period may also not be determinable (e.g., a change from FIFO to LIFO in accounting for inventories). The required disclosure can then be limited to showing the effect of the change on the results of operations of the change period and the reason for omitting the required disclosures.

Change In Accounting Estimates

Changes in accounting estimates are an essential part of accounting and adjustments of these estimates are necessary as events occur and experience is acquired. Changes in estimates may involve:

- Uncollectible receivables
- Inventory obsolescence
- Service lives and salvage value of assets
- Warranty costs
- Periods benefited by a deferred cost
- Recoverable mineral reserves

Changes in accounting estimates should affect the period of change only or the period of change and future periods if the change affects both. No restatements of prior periods or pro forma computations are required. The effect of a change in estimate should be disclosed.

Change In Estimate Effected By A Change In Accounting Principle

For example, a company may change from deferring and amortizing a cost to recording it as an expense when incurred because future benefits are doubtful. Since the change in accounting principle is inseparable from the effect of the accounting estimate, **this type of change should be treated as a change in accounting estimate**. Therefore, only the year of change and future periods will be affected.

Changes In The Reporting Entity

This type of change requires the restatement of all prior periods to show financial information for the new reporting entity. Examples of such changes are:

1. Consolidated or combined statements instead of individual statements.
2. Changes among the specific subsidiaries for which consolidated statements are presented.
3. Changes the companies included in combined financial statements. Combined statements are different from consolidated statements. Examples:
   a. One individual owns a controlling interest in several corporations.
   b. The financial position and results of operations of a group of unconsolidated subsidiaries.
   c. Combined statements of companies under common management. Intercompany transactions, minority interests, etc., are treated in the same manner as in consolidated statements.

Correction of an Error

A correction of an error is **not an accounting change** and should be **reported as a prior period adjustment**. This requires adjustment of financial statements of the year(s) affected. Correction of errors would include:

* Mathematical mistakes
* Mistakes in the application of an accounting principle
* Oversight or misuse of information available when the financial statements were prepared.

In contrast, a change in accounting estimate results from new information, better insight or improved judgment.

A change of an accounting principle **not** generally accepted to one that is generally accepted is a correction of an error (changing from the direct write-off method for bad debts to the allowance method when bad debts are material).

Accounting Changes Made to Conform to AICPA Recommendations

An enterprise making a change in accounting principle to conform with the recommendations of an AICPA statement of position should report the change as specified in the statement. If not specified, the change should be reported in accordance with APB #20.

PRIOR PERIOD ADJUSTMENTS—SFAS #16

Reporting Criteria

A prior period adjustment is required for the correction of an error in the financial statements of a prior period. Items such as income tax settlements or assessments, litigation claims or settlements, proceeds from renegotiation proceedings, initiated in a prior year should be included in the determination of net income for the applicable current period as stipulated in APB #30. Most such items will not qualify for extraordinary item treatment, but may fulfill the criteria for being either unusual or infrequent, thus requiring disclosure as a separate component of income from continuing operations.

Adjustments of prior year income tax provisions which result from income tax settlements should be reported as part of the income tax provision in the year of settlement. If such treatment causes a material distortion in the income tax provision as compared to the earnings before income taxes, an explanation as to the adjustment should be given in the footnote for income taxes.

Disclosure and Presentation

Items qualifying for prior period adjustment treatment will result in adjustment of the financial statements of the affected period(s) along with the related income tax effect (if appropriate) when such statements are included in the annual report. The adjustment of net income in the affected year will result in a change in retained earnings for such year and subsequent years, including the beginning retained earnings for the current year.

When single period statements only are being presented, disclosure should be made of the effects of such restatement on the beginning retained earnings.

Example: A material error was made in the preparation of the income statement for the year ended 12/31/97 is discovered when preparing the income statement for the year ended 12/31/99:

	Year Ended 12/31	
	1999	*1998*
Net Income	$ 420,000	$ 380,000
Retained earnings at beginning of year:		
As previously reported	1,200,000	950,000
Adjustments (Note 1)	(60,000)	(30,000)
As Restated	1,140,000	920,000
	1,560,000	1,300,000
Dividends	180,000	160,000
Retained earnings at end of period:	$1,380,000	$1,140,000

NOTE 1: The balance of retained earnings at December 31, 1998, has been restated to reflect a retroactive charge of $60,000 for amortization of goodwill not previously recognized. Of this amount, $30,000 ($.02 per share) is applicable to 1998 and has been reflected as an expense for that year; the remaining $30,000 (applicable to 1990) is being charged to retained earnings at January 1, 1998.

DISCONTINUED OPERATIONS—APB #30

In General

APB #30 added a new component of reporting net income; i.e., "Discontinued Operations," which includes results of operations of a "segment of a business" that has been sold, abandoned, spun off or otherwise disposed of, or is the subject of a formal plan for disposal. This type of situation will not be reported as an "extraordinary item."

The new net income captions will appear on the income statement as follows (from APB Opinion #30):

Income from continuing operations before income taxes	$xxxx	
Provision for income taxes	xxx	
Income from continuing operations		$xxxx
Discontinued operations (Note: .....):		
Income (loss) from operations of discontinued Division X (less applicable income taxes of $......)	$xxxx	
Loss on disposal of Division X, including provision of $...... for operating losses during phase-out period (less applicable income taxes of $......)	xxxx	xxxx
Net Income		$xxxx

Segment of a Business Criteria

Activities must represent:

1. A separate major line of business, or
2. A separate class of customer

The segment can be in the form of:

a subsidiary,
a division,
a department,
and in some cases a joint venture,

provided that its assets, results of operations and activities can be clearly distinguished from other activities. Difficulty in segregating assets or results of operations of a "disposed" segment of a business suggests that the transaction should not be classified as such.

Other disposals of assets **not** considered to be "disposal of a segment of a business":

1. Disposal of a part of a line of business
2. Shifting of production or marketing activities for a particular line from one location to another
3. The phasing out of a product line or class of service and other changes because of **technological improvements**.

Case Examples:

The following are illustrative of disposals which should be classified as "disposals of a segment of a business":

(1) A sale by a diversified company of a major division which represents the company's only activities in the electronics industry. The assets and results of operations of the division are clearly segregated for internal financial reporting purposes from the other assets and results of operations of the company.

(2) A sale by a meat packing company of a 25% interest in a professional football team which has been accounted for under the equity method. All other activities of the company are in the meat packing business.

(3) A sale by a communications company of all its radio stations which represent 30% of gross revenues. The company's remaining activities are three television stations and a publishing company. The assets and results of operations of the radio stations are clearly distinguishable physically, operationally and for financial reporting purposes.

(4) A food distributor disposes of one of its two divisions. One division sells food wholesale primarily to supermarket chains and the other division sells food through its chain of fast-food restaurants, some of which are franchised and some of which are company-owned. Both divisions are in the business of distribution of food. However, the nature of selling food through fast-food outlets is vastly different than that of wholesaling food to supermarket chains. Thus by having two major classes of customers, the company has two segments of its business.

The following disposals should **not** be classified as disposals of a segment of a business:

(5) The sale of a major foreign subsidiary engaged in silver mining by a mining company which represents all of the company's activities in that particular country. Even though the subsidiary being sold may account for a significant percentage of gross revenue of the consolidated group and all of its revenues in the particular country, the fact that the company continues to engage in silver mining activities in other countries would indicate that there was a sale of a part of a line of business.

(6) The sale by a petrochemical company of a 25% interest in a petrochemical plant which is accounted for as an investment in a corporate joint venture under the equity method. Since the remaining activities of the company are in the same line of business as the 25% interest which has been sold, there has not been a sale of a major line of business but rather a sale of part of a line of business.

(7) A manufacturer of children's wear discontinues all of its operations in Italy which were composed of designing and selling children's wear for the Italian market. In the context of determining a segment of a business by class of customer, the nationality of customers or slight variations in product lines in order to appeal to particular groups are not determining factors.

(8) A diversified company sells a subsidiary which manufactures furniture. The company has retained its other furniture manufacturing subsidiary. The disposal of the subsidiary, therefore, is not a disposal of a segment of the business but rather a disposal of part of a line of business. Such disposals are incident to the evolution of the entity's business.

(9) The sale of all assets (including the plant) related to the manufacture of men's woolen suits by an apparel manufacturer in order to concentrate activities in the manufacture of men's suits from synthetic products. This would represent a disposal of a product line as distinguished from the disposal of a major line of business.

Measurement and Disposal Dates

Measurement date—the date management having authority to do so commits itself to a **formal** plan to dispose of a segment of the business whether by sale or abandonment. The plan should include as a minimum:

1. Identification of major assets to be disposed of
2. Expected method of disposal
3. Period required for completion
4. An active program to find a buyer, if the assets are to be sold
5. An estimate of the results of operations from the measurement date to the disposal date.

Disposal date—date of closing the sale or the cessation of operations if disposal is by abandonment.

Determining Gain or Loss on Disposal

1. Expected losses should be **provided for** at the measurement date.
2. Expected gains should be recognized when realized.

Estimated net losses from operations should be included in the computation of an estimated gain or loss on disposal. If it is expected that income will be generated from operations during the disposal period, such income should be included in the estimated gain or loss on disposal, limited to the amount of loss otherwise recognizable from the disposal with the remainder recognized as income when realized.

Example 1:

On August 1, 1999, the measurement date, Downturn Corp. decided to dispose of its Housewares division. The Housewares division had operating income from January 1, 1999 to August 1, 1999 of $100,000 but incurred a loss of $50,000 during the phase-out period from August 2, 1999 to December 1, 1999. The division was sold on December 1 at a gain of $200,000.

Downturn's income from continuing operations before tax for 1999 was $1,000,000 and its tax rate was 30%.

The 1999 condensed income statement for Downturn Corp. is as follows:

Income from continuing operations before taxes		$1,000,000
Less income taxes of 30%		300,000
Income from continuing operations		700,000
Discontinued operations		
Income from operations of Housewares Division up to the measurement date less income taxes of $30,000	$ 70,000	
Gain on disposal of Housewares Division less income tax of $45,000	105,000	175,000
Net Income		$875,000

Note: The gain on disposal is a combination of the loss during phase-out of $50,000 and the gain on the sale of $200,000 for a total gain on disposal of $150,000 less taxes of $45,000 for a net gain of $105,000.

Example 2:
Assume the same facts as in *Example 1* but assume that the disposal date was March 1, 2000, the $50,000 loss was for the phase-out period from August 1 to December 31, and that Housewares incurred an additional $20,000 loss for the phase-out period from January 1 to March 1, 2000. Assume the division was sold at a loss of $200,000 on March 1, 2000. A time line may be helpful in viewing the facts:

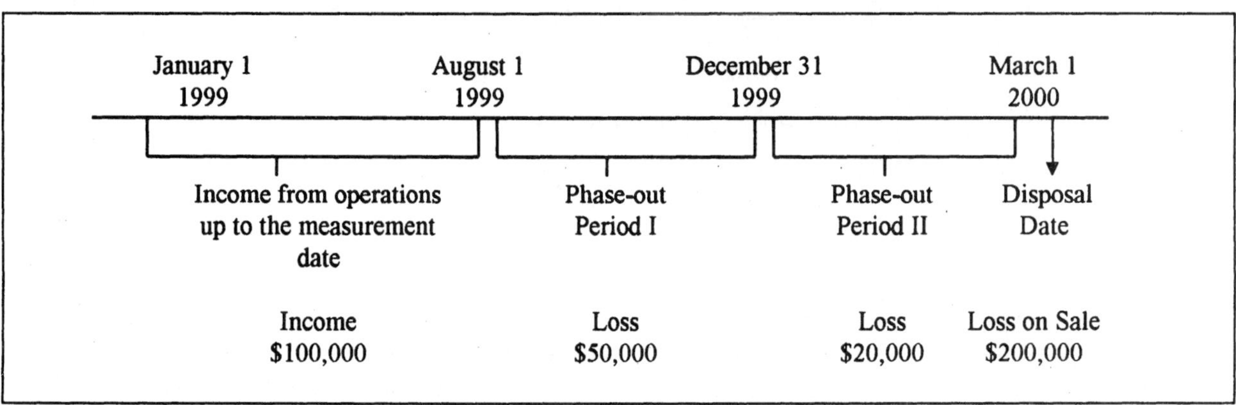

The 1999 condensed income statement for Downturn Corp. is as follows:

Income from continuing operations before taxes		$1,000,000
Less income taxes of 30%		300,000
Income from continuing operations		700,000
Discontinued operations		
Income from operations of Housewares Division up to the measurement date less income taxes of $30,000	$ 70,000	
Loss on disposal of Housewares Division less income tax of $81,000	(189,000)	(119,000)
Net Income		$581,000

Note: The loss on disposal in 1999 is conservatively viewed as one transaction that includes the phase-out losses of $50,000 and $20,000 plus the expected loss on the sale of $200,000 for a total lost of $270,000 less the tax effect of $81,000 for a net loss of $189,000.

Example 3:
Assume the same facts as in *Example 1* except that Downturn Corp. earned $80,000 during the phase-out period from August 2 to December 31, 1999, incurred a $40,000 phase-out loss from January 1 to March 1, 2000, and sold the division for a $200,000 gain on March 1, 2000. Also assume that Downturn Corporation's income from continuing operations was $1,500,000.

The 1999 condensed income statement for Downturn Corp. is as follows:

Income from continuing operations before taxes		$1,000,000
Less income taxes of 30%		300,000
Income from continuing operations		700,000
Discontinued operations		
Income from operations of Housewares Division up to the measurement date less income taxes of $30,000	$ 70,000	
Gain on disposal of Housewares Division less income tax of $24,000	56,000	126,000
Net Income		$826,000

The 2000 condensed income statement for Downturn Corp. is as follows:

Income from continuing operations before taxes		$1,500,000
Less income taxes of 30%		450,000
Income from continuing operations		1,050,000
Discontinued operations		
Income from operations of Housewares Division up to the measurement date less income taxes	$ 0	
Gain on disposal of Housewares Division less income tax of $48,000	112,000	112,000
Net Income		$1,162,000

Note: This is the exception to the one-transaction concept because the combination of the unrealized loss of $40,000 during the phase-out period from January 1 to March 1, 2000 and the unrealized gain on the sale of $200,000 results in an anticipated total unrealized gain of $160,000. Conservatism dictates that anticipated gains should not be recognized until realized in the year 2000. Therefore, the $160,000 gain on disposal less the tax effect of $48,000 for a net gain of $112,000 should be shown on the 2000 income statement.

This means that the income during the phase-out period from August 1 to December 31, 1999 of $80,000 less the tax effect of $24,000 for a net gain on disposal of $56,000 should be shown on the 1999 income statement.

Listed below are some additional cases to help you understand how the gain (loss) on disposal of a segment is reported. The cases use the same measurement and disposal dates as in the previous example. All situations are reported on a pretax basis.

CALCULATION OF GAIN OR LOSS ON DISPOSAL OF A SEGMENT

	Income (Loss) during phase-out Aug. 1 – Dec. 31, 1999	Expected Income (Loss) during phase-out Jan. 1 – March 1, 2000	Expected Gain (Loss) on sale of segment	Gain (Loss) on disposal of segment
Case 1	(50,000)	(80,000)	70,000	1999 (60,000)
Case 2	(50,000)	(80,000)	(70,000)	1999 (200,000)
Case 3	50,000	80,000	(140,000)	1999 (10,000)
Case 4	(50,000)	(80,000)	140,000	1999 0 2000 10,000
Case 5	50,000	80,000	70,000	1999 50,000 2000 150,000
Case 6	50,000	(20,000)	(20,000)	1999 10,000 2000 0
Case 7	50,000	(20,000)	40,000	1999 50,000 2000 20,000
Case 8	50,000	(60,000)	30,000	1999 20,000 2000 0

SOLUTIONS TO ABOVE CASES

Case 1: The expected gain on the sale of $70,000 is used to offset the cumulative phase-out losses of $130,000 for a net loss on disposal of $60,000.

Case 2: The cumulative total losses are $200,000.

Case 3: The expected loss on the sale of $140,000 offsets the cumulative income of $130,000 during the phase-out period for a net loss of $10,000.

Case 4: This is the most difficult case. The anticipated gain on the sale of $140,000 in the year 2000 is used to offset the cumulative phase-out losses for a net gain of $10,000. Since conservatism does not anticipate gains, the gain is recognized in the year 2000 instead of 1999.

Case 5: Since conservatism does not allow the anticipation of income or gains, the $50,000 of realized income would be recognized in 1999 and the phase-out income of $80,000 plus the gain on the sale of $70,000 for a cumulative total of $150,000 would be recognized when realized in the year 2000.

Case 6: The $50,000 realized income for 1999 is offset by the $40,000 cumulative phase-out loss and expected loss on sale in 2000 for a net gain on disposal of $10,000.

Case 7: The $20,000 unrealized phase-out loss in 2000 is combined with the unrealized gain on the sale of $40,000 for an anticipated net gain of $20,000. Since conservatism does not allow the anticipation of gain, the $20,000 net gain is recognized in the year 2000. Therefore, the $50,000 of realized income in 1999 is shown as the 1999 gain on disposal.

Case 8: The unrealized phase-out loss of $60,000 in 2000 less the expected gain on sale of $30,000 is an anticipated net loss of $30,000 in 2000. Conservatism would combine the anticipated net loss of $30,000 with the $50,000 of 1999 phase-out income for a total gain on disposal of $20,000.

Other Points

Projections of operating income or loss should not ordinarily cover more than one year.

Adjustments, costs, and expenses that should have been recognized on a going concern basis up to the measurement date should not be included in the gain or loss on disposal. Examples: Adjustments of accruals on long-term contracts; write-down or write-off of receivables, inventories, property, plant equipment, research and development costs or other intangible assets.

Costs or adjustments directly associated with the decision to dispose include such items as severance pay, additional pension costs, employee relocation expenses, and future rentals on long-term leases. The notes to the financial statements encompassing the measurement date should include pertinent details of the disposal including what, when and how the disposal will be made, the remaining asset and liabilities of the segment at the balance sheet date, the income or loss from operations and the proceeds from disposal from the measurement date to the balance sheet date.

EXTRAORDINARY ITEMS—APB #30

Criteria

Extraordinary items should be both

a. Unusual and
b. Infrequent

Unusual Nature: The underlying event or transaction should possess a high degree of abnormality and be of a type clearly unrelated to, or only incidentally related to, the ordinary and typical activities of the entity, taking into account the environment in which the entity operates.

The environment in which the entity operates is a primary consideration in determining whether an underlying event or transaction is abnormal and significantly different from the ordinary and typical activities of the entity. This includes the characteristics of the industry, the geographical location of operations, and nature and extent of governmental regulation. Unusual nature is not established by the fact that an event or transaction is beyond the control of management.

Infrequency: The underlying event or transaction should be of a type that would not reasonably be expected to recur in the foreseeable future, taking into account the environment in which the entity operates.

Determining the probability of recurrence of a particular event or transaction in the foreseeable future should take into account the entity environment. A transaction of an entity not reasonably expected to recur in the foreseeable future is considered to occur infrequently. By definition, extraordinary items occur infrequently.

Case Examples:
Events or transactions which would meet both criteria in the circumstances described are:

(1) A large portion of a tobacco manufacturer's crops are destroyed by a hailstorm. Severe damage from hail storms in the locality where the manufacturer grows tobacco is rare.
(2) A steel fabricating company sells the only land it owns. The land was acquired ten years ago for future expansion, but shortly thereafter the company abandoned all plans for expansion and held the land for appreciation.

(3) A company sells a block of common stock of a publicly traded company. The block of shares, which represents less than 10% of the publicly held company, is the only security investment the company has ever owned.
(4) An earthquake destroys one of the oil refineries owned by a large multinational oil company.

The following are illustrative of **events or transactions which do not meet both criteria in the circumstances described and thus should not be reported as extraordinary items**:
(5) A citrus grower's Florida crop is damaged by frost. Frost damage is normally experienced every three or four years. The criterion of infrequency of occurrence taking into account the environment in which the company operates would not be met since the history of losses caused by frost damage provides evidence that such damage may reasonably be expected to recur in the foreseeable future.
(6) A company which operates a chain of warehouses sells the excess land surrounding one of its warehouses. When the company buys property to establish a new warehouse, it usually buys more land than it expects to use for the warehouse with the expectation that the land will appreciate in value. In the past five years, there have been two instances in which the company sold such excess land. The criterion of infrequency of occurrence has not been met since past experience indicates that such sales may reasonably be expected to recur in the foreseeable future.
(7) A large diversified company sells a block of shares from its portfolio of securities which it has acquired for investment purposes. This is the first sale from its portfolio of securities. Since the company owns several securities for investment purposes, it should be concluded that sales of such securities are related to its ordinary and typical activities in the environment in which it operates and thus the criterion of unusual nature would not be met.
(8) A textile manufacturer with only one plant moves to another location. It has not relocated a plant in twenty years and has no plans to do so in the foreseeable future. Notwithstanding the infrequency of occurrence of the event as it relates to this particular company, moving from one location to another is an occurrence which is a consequence of customary and continuing business activities, some of which are finding more favorable labor markets, more modern facilities, and proximity to customers or suppliers. Therefore, the criterion of unusual nature has not been met and the moving expenses (and related gains and losses) should not be reported as an extraordinary item. Another example of an event which is a consequence of customary typical business activities (namely financing) is an unsuccessful public registration, the cost of which should not be reported as an extraordinary item.

Items Not Extraordinary (because they are usual and can be expected to recur)
a. Write-down or write-off of receivables, inventories, equipment leased to others, and other intangible assets.
b. Gains or losses from exchange or translation of foreign currencies, including those relating to major devaluations and revaluations.
c. Gains or losses on disposal of segment of a business.
d. Other gains or losses from sale or abandonment of property, plant, or equipment used in the business.
e. Effects of a strike, including those against competitors and major suppliers.
f. Adjustment of accruals on long-term contracts.

Rarely, an event such as the above may also meet the extraordinary criteria of unusualness and infrequency of occurrence. If so, gains and losses such as (a) and (d) above should be included in the extraordinary items if they are the direct result of a major casualty, an expropriation or a prohibition under a newly enacted law or regulation. Any portion of such losses that would have resulted from a valuation of assets on a going concern basis should not be included in extraordinary items.

Materiality

Items that are material in relation to income before extraordinary items, the trend in annual earnings or other appropriate criteria, should be shown separately as extraordinary items. Items should be considered individually and not in the aggregate.

Adjustment of Amounts Reported in Prior Periods

Items reported under the guidelines of the opinion require estimates based on judgment. Adjustment of such estimates in the current period should not be reported as prior period adjustments unless they meet such criteria. Such adjustments should be disclosed in the current period in the same manner as the original item. Correction of an error should be handled according to the provisions of APB #20.

Disclosure of Unusual or Infrequently Occurring Items

A material event or transaction meeting one but not both of the extraordinary item criteria (unusualness and infrequency) should be reported as a separate component of income from continuing operations. The nature and financial effects of each event or transaction should be disclosed on the face of the income statement or in the notes to the financial statements.

Important Income Statement Presentation Differences

Opinion No. 30 contains reporting criteria for three different reporting situations which require different presentation on the income statement. These are:

1. **Disposals of a Segment of a Business** (to be reported separately along with the related tax effect)
2. **Extraordinary Items** (to be reported separately along with the related tax effect).
3. **Exclusions** (events or transactions which are **not** disposals of a segment of a business and **not** extraordinary items). Gains or losses which are **not** disposals of a segment of a business should be reported separately as a component of income from **continuing** operations. However, the related tax effect should **not** be shown separately as to imply the disposal is that of a segment of a business. Similarly with other material items which do **not** qualify as extraordinary items, which should be reported separately as part of continuing operations. The related income tax effect should not be shown separately.

INTERIM FINANCIAL STATEMENTS—APB #28

In General

The results for each interim period should be based on the accounting principles and practices used by an enterprise in the preparation of its latest annual financial statements unless a change in an accounting practice or policy has been adopted in the current year. Certain accounting principles and practices followed for annual reporting purposes may require modification at interim reporting dates so that the reported results for the interim period may better relate to the results of operations for the annual period. Some modifications are necessary at interim dates in accounting principles or practices followed for annual periods.

Interim financial information is essential to provide investors and others with timely information of the progress of the enterprise. Accordingly, **each interim period should be viewed primarily as an integral part of an annual period**.

Seasonal fluctuations in revenue and irregular incurrence of costs and expenses limit the comparability of operating results for interim periods.

Guidelines for Preparing Interim Statements

1. Revenue should be recognized as earned based on criteria used for the full year.
2. Costs and expenses associated directly with or allocated to products sold require the same treatment in interim statements as in fiscal-year financial statements.

Exceptions for Cost of Goods Sold

- If the gross profit method is used for preparing interim statements, such fact should be disclosed including any year-end adjustments resulting therefrom.
- If LIFO is used and the LIFO base is temporarily depleted during an interim period, the inventory reported at the interim date should not reflect the LIFO liquidation and the cost of goods sold should include the estimated cost of replacing the depleted LIFO base. Example: Assume that at the end of the 2nd quarter, the ending inventory was $25,000 below the LIFO base and the condition is temporary. Perpetual system is used.

Journal Entries:
(1) At the end of the 2nd quarter

Cost of Good Sold	$25,000	
Allowance for temporary LIFO liquidation		$25,000

(2) When the inventory is replaced by purchase of $40,000 in merchandise

Inventory	$15,000	
Allowance for temporary LIFO liquidation	25,000	
Accounts Payable		$40,000

- LCM writedowns of inventories should be used in interim periods unless such writedowns are considered temporary.
- Standard cost variances should be reported for interim periods similar to fiscal year reporting; however, planned price or volume variances which are expected to be absorbed should be deferred until year end.

3. Costs other than product costs should be associated with interim periods based on benefits derived, time expired or activity associated with the period.
4. Seasonal variations in revenues, costs, etc., should be disclosed. For example, fixed costs can be allocated to interim periods based on expected sales activity where revenues follow a seasonal pattern.
5. Income tax expense should be based on an estimated effective rate for the year as a whole.
6. Extraordinary items and disposals of a segment of a business should be reflected in the period in which they occurred. Contingencies should be disclosed in interim reports in the same manner required for annual reports.
7. The tax effects of losses that arise in the early portion of a fiscal year (in the event carryback of such losses is not possible) should be recognized only when realization is assured beyond any reasonable doubt. An established seasonal pattern of loss in early interim periods offset by income in later interim periods should constitute evidence that realization is assured beyond reasonable doubt. The tax benefit of interim losses carried forward to a later interim period would reduce each later interim period's tax provision.
8. Each report of interim financial information should indicate any change in accounting principles or practices from those applied in (a) the comparable interim period of the prior annual period, (b) the preceding interim periods in the current annual period, and (c) the prior annual report.
9. When publicly traded companies report summarized financial information to their security holders at interim dates (including reports on 4th quarters), the following data should be reported, as a minimum:
(a) Sales, provision for income taxes, extraordinary items, cumulative effect of a change in accounting principles or practices, and net income; (b) primary and fully diluted earnings per share data; (c) seasonal revenue, costs or expenses; (d) significant changes in estimates or provisions for income taxes; (e) disposal of a segment of a business and extraordinary, unusual or infrequent occurring items; (f) contingent items; (g) changes in accounting principles or estimates; (h) significant changes in financial position.

Treatment of Nonrecurring Adjustments Under SFAS #16

SFAS #16 requires that prior **interim** periods be restated for nonrecurring adjustments due to adjustment or settlement of litigation, income taxes, renegotiation proceedings or rate-making for utilities provided that each such adjustment meets **each** of the following criteria:

1. The adjustment is material.
2. The adjustment is specifically related to business activities of a specific prior interim period of the current year.
3. The amount of the adjustment or settlement could not have been reasonably estimated prior to the current interim period but becomes "reasonably estimable" during the current interim period.

An example of such an adjustment would be a change in the statutory rate of income tax which was enacted in September and applicable to the entire calendar year.

The adjustment should be reported as a restatement of the applicable prior interim periods with any amount applicable to prior fiscal years being reflected in the determination of net income of the first interim period of the current fiscal year.

REPORTING ACCOUNTING CHANGES IN INTERIM FINANCIAL STATEMENTS—SFAS #3

Summary: If an accounting change (APB 20) is made in other than the first interim period of a fiscal year, the cumulative effect of the change on retained earnings at the beginning of that year will be included in the determination of net income of the first interim period of the year of change. This is accomplished by restatement of that period's financial information. In those rare situations where cumulative effect of the change on retained earnings cannot be computed (principally a change to the LIFO method) specific disclosures are required.

Cumulative Effect Type Accounting Changes Other Than Changes to LIFO

1. If a cumulative effect type accounting change is made during the **first** interim period of an enterprise's fiscal year, the cumulative effect of the change on retained earnings at the **beginning of that fiscal year** shall be included in net income of the first interim period.
2. If a cumulative effect type accounting change is made in **other than the first** interim period of an enterprise's fiscal year, **no** cumulative effect of the change shall be included in net income of the period of change. Instead, financial information for the pre-change interim periods of the fiscal year in which the change is made shall be restated by applying the newly adopted accounting principle to those pre-change interim periods. **The cumulative effect of the change on retained earnings at the beginning of that fiscal year shall be included in restated net income of the first interim period of the fiscal year in which the change is made.**

Changes to the LIFO Method of Inventory Pricing and Similar Situations

1. If a change of that type is made in the **first** interim period of an enterprise's fiscal year, the disclosures specified below shall be made.
2. If the change is made in **other than** the first interim period of an enterprise's fiscal year, the disclosure specified below shall be made and in addition, interim periods of that fiscal year shall be re-stated by applying the newly adopted accounting principle to those pre-change interim periods. Whenever financial information that includes those pre-change interim periods is presented, it shall be presented on the restated basis.

Disclosures

The following disclosures will be made in interim financial reports:

a. Nature of and justification of the change.
b. Effect of the change on income from continuing operations, net income, and related per share amounts for the interim period in which the change is made. In addition, in other than the first interim period of a fiscal year, financial reports for the period of change shall also disclose (i) the effect of the change on income from continuing operations, net income, and related per share amounts for each pre-change interim period of that fiscal year, and (ii) income from continuing operations, net income, and related per share amounts for each pre-change interim period as restated.
c. In financial reports for the interim period in which the new accounting principle is adopted, disclosure shall be made of income from continuing operations, net income, and related per share amounts computed on a pro forma basis for (i) the interim period in which the change is made, and (ii) any interim periods of prior fiscal years for which financial information is being presented.

SFAS #130 - REPORTING COMPREHENSIVE INCOME

Definition

Comprehensive income is net income plus other comprehensive income.

Other Comprehensive Income

Other comprehensive income includes the following items and <u>changes</u> in each item:

a. Foreign currency translation adjustments
b. Minimum pension liability adjustments
c. Unrealized gains and losses on certain investments in debt and equity securities (example: available-for-sale marketable securities)

Disclosure of Comprehensive Income

The FASB permits four alternative disclosures of the components of the comprehensive income (see **Formats A, B, C and D** on the following pages) and a disclosure of **accumulated other comprehensive income** in the equity section of The Statement of Financial Position (see the pages following **Formats A, B, C and D**).

a. **Format A** includes other comprehensive income as an integral part of the Statement of Income and Comprehensive Income.

b. **Format B** shows other comprehensive income as a separate Statement of Comprehensive Income following the Income Statement.

c. **Formats C and D** include other comprehensive income as a part of the Statement of Changes in equity.

Although the SFAS-130 does not require a single display presentation for elements of comprehensive income and the total of comprehensive income, it does require that these items be presented in a financial statement that is displayed with the same prominence as other financial statements, which together constitute a full set of financial statements.

The total of other comprehensive income for a period is transferred to a stockholder's equity account called accumulated other comprehensive income. The accumulated balance in this account for each classification must be disclosed in the balance sheet, a statement of changes in equity on the footnotes.

A total for comprehensive income is reported in interim financial statements.

Tax Effect

Other comprehensive items may be shown net of tax effects or before tax effects with one amount shown for the total tax (see **Format A** and the pages following **Formats A, B, C and D**).

Reclassification Adjustments

a. Reclassification of adjustments are made to avoid <u>**double accounting**</u> of items that are part of net income that may be included in the other comprehensive income of the current or earlier periods.

   (*Example*: Realized gains on available-for-sale marketable equity securities recognized as a part of current net income were included in other comprehensive income as unrealized holding gains in a previous period. These unrealized holding gains must be deducted in the current period from other comprehensive income to avoid double accounting of the gains.)

b. Reclassification adjustments must be shown <u>**separately**</u> for foreign currency items and unrealized gains and losses on certain investment in debt and equity securities.

c. Reclassification adjustments are <u>**not**</u> used with minimum pension liability adjustments.

Earnings Per Share Not Required

Earnings per share numbers are <u>**not**</u> calculated for other comprehensive income or comprehensive income.

Other Terms

Although SFAS #130 uses the term "comprehensive income," other equivalent terms such as **total nonowner changes in equity** may be used.

Three Additional Examples of Other Comprehensive Income

SFAS #133 – Accounting for derivatives and hedging activities added the following additional items to be included in comprehensive income:

- Gains or losses on cash flow hedges.
- Gains or losses on hedges of forecasted foreign-currency-denominated transactions.
- Gains or losses on hedging of a net investment in a foreign operation are reported in ***comprehensive income*** as part of the translation adjustment.

Note: See Chapter 9 for coverage of derivatives.

Examples of Disclosures

The following pages include examples of disclosures taken from SFAS #130.

Format A: One-Statement Approach

Enterprise
Statement of Income and Comprehensive Income
Year Ended December 31, 19X9

Revenues		$140,000
Expenses		(25,000)
Other gains and losses		8,000
Gain on sale of securities		2,000
Income from operations before tax		125,000
Income tax expense		(31,250)
Income before extraordinary item and cumulative effect of accounting change		93,750
Extraordinary item, net of tax		(28,000)
Income before cumulative effect of accounting change		65,750
Cumulative effect of accounting change, net of tax		(2,500)
[Net income		63,250]
Other comprehensive income, net of tax:		
Foreign currency translation adjustments[a]		8,000
Unrealized gains on securities:[b]		
Unrealized holding gains arising during period	$13,000	
Less: reclassification adjustment for gains included in net income	(1,500)	11,500
Minimum pension liability adjustment[c]		(2,500)
Other comprehensive income		17,000
[Comprehensive income		$80,250]

Alternatively, components of other comprehensive income could be displayed before tax with one amount shown for the aggregate income tax expense or benefit:

Other comprehensive income, before tax:		
Foreign currency translation adjustments[a]		$10,666
Unrealized gains on securities:[b]		
Unrealized holding gains arising during period	$17,333	
Less: reclassification adjustment for gains included in net income	(2,000)	15,333
Minimum pension liability adjustment[c]		(3,333)
Other comprehensive income, before tax		22,666
[Income tax expense related to items of other comprehensive income		(5,666)]
Other comprehensive income, net of tax		$17,000

---

[a] It is assumed that there was no sale or liquidation of an investment in a foreign entity. Therefore, there is no reclassification adjustment for this period.

[b] This illustrates the gross display. Alternatively, a net display can be used, with disclosure of the gross amounts (current-period gain and reclassification adjustment) in the notes to the financial statements.

[c] This illustrates the required net display for this classification.

Format B: Two-Statement Approach

Enterprise
Statement of Income
Year Ended December 31, 19X9

Revenues	$140,000
Expenses	(25,000)
Other gains and losses	8,000
Gain on sale of securities	2,000
Income from operations before tax	125,000
Income tax expense	(31,250)
Income before extraordinary item and cumulative effect of accounting change	93,750
Extraordinary item, net of tax	(28,000)
Income before cumulative effect of accounting change	65,750
Cumulative effect of accounting change, net of tax	(2,500)
[Net income	$ 63,250]

Enterprise
Statement of Comprehensive Income
Year Ended December 31, 19X9

[Net income		$ 63,250]
Other comprehensive income, net of tax:		
Foreign currency translation adjustments[a]		8,000
Unrealized gains on securities:[b]		
Unrealized holding gains arising during period	$13,000	
Less: reclassification adjustment for gains included in net income	(1,500)	11,500
Minimum pension liability adjustment[c]		(2,500)
Other comprehensive income		17,000
[Comprehensive income		$80,250]

Alternatively, components of other comprehensive income could be displayed before tax with one amount shown for the aggregate income tax expense or benefit as illustrated in Format A.

---

[a] It is assumed that there was no sale or liquidation of an investment in a foreign entity. Therefore, there is no reclassification adjustment for this period.

[b] This illustrates the gross display. Alternatively, a net display can be used, with disclosure of the gross amounts (current-period gain and reclassification adjustment) in the notes to the financial statements.

[c] This illustrates the required net display for this classification.

Format C: Statement-of-Changes-in-Equity Approach (Alternative 1)

Enterprise
Statement of Changes in Equity
Year Ended December 31, 19X9

	Total	Comprehensive Income	Retained Earnings	Accumulated Other Comprehensive Income	Common Stock	Paid-in Capital
Beginning balance	$563,500		$88,500	$25,000	$150,000	$300,000
Comprehensive Income						
Net income	63,250	[$63,250]	63,250			
Other comprehensive income, net of tax						
Unrealized gains on securities, net of reclassification adjustment (see disclosure)	11,500	11,500				
Foreign currency translation adjustments[a]	8,000	8,000				
Minimum pension liability adjustment	(2,500)	(2,500)				
Other comprehensive income		17,000		17,000		
Comprehensive income		[$80,250]				
Common stock issued	150,000				50,000	100,000
Dividends declared on common stock	(10,000)		(10,000)			
Ending balance	$783,750		$141,750	$42,000	$200,000	$400,000

Disclosure of reclassification amount:[b]	
Unrealized holding gains arising during period	$13,000
Less: reclassification adjustment for gains included in net income	(1,500)
Net unrealized gains on securities	$11,500

---

[a] Alternatively, an enterprise can omit the separate column labeled "Comprehensive Income" by displaying an aggregate amount for comprehensive income ($80,250) in the "Total" column.

[b] It is assumed that there was no sale or liquidation of an investment in a foreign entity. Therefore, there is no reclassification adjustment for this period.

Format D: Statement-of-Changes-in-Equity Approach (Alternative 2)

Enterprise
Statement of Changes in Equity
Year Ended December 31, 19X9

Retained earnings		
Balance at January 1	$88,500	
Net income	63,250	[$63,250]
Dividends declared on common stock	(10,000)	
Balance at December 31	141,750	
Accumulated other comprehensive income [a]		
Balance at January 1	25,000	
Unrealized gains on securities, net of reclassification Adjustment (see disclosure)		11,500
Foreign currency translation adjustments		8,000
Minimum pension liability adjustment		(2,500)
Other comprehensive income	17,000	17,000
Comprehensive income		[$80,250]
Balance at December 31	42,000	
Common stock		
Balance at January 1	150,000	
Shares issued	50,000	
Balance at December 31	200,000	
Paid-in capital		
Balance at January 1	300,000	
Common stock issued	100,000	
Balance at December 31	400,000	
Total equity	$783,750	

Disclosure of reclassification amount: [b]	
Unrealized holding gains arising during period	$13,000
Less: reclassification adjustment for gains included in net income	(1,500)
Net unrealized gains on securities	$11,500

---

[a] All items of other comprehensive income are displayed net of tax.

[b] It is assumed that there was no sale or liquidation of an investment in a foreign entity. Therefore, there is no reclassification adjustment for this period.

All Formats: Accompanying Statement of Financial Position

Enterprise
Statement of Financial Position
December 31, 19X9

Assets:	
Cash	$ 150,000
Accounts receivable	175,000
Available-for-sale securities	112,000
Plant and equipment	985,000
Total assets	$1,422,000
Liabilities:	
Accounts payable	$ 112,500
Accrued liabilities	79,250
Pension liability	128,000
Notes payable	318,500
Total liabilities	$ 638,250
Equity:	
Common stock	$ 200,000
Paid-in capital	400,000
Retained earnings	141,750
[Accumulated other comprehensive income	42,000]
Total equity	$ 783,750
Total liabilities and equity	$1,422,000

All Formats: Required Disclosure of Related Tax Effects Allocated to Each Component of Other Comprehensive Income

Enterprise
Notes to Financial Statements
Year Ended December 31, 19X9

	Before-Tax Amount	Tax (Expense) or Benefit	Net-of-Tax Amount
Foreign currency translation adjustment	$10,666	$(2,666)	$ 8,000
Unrealized gains on securities:			
Unrealized holding gains arising during period	17,333	(4,333)	13,000
Less: reclassification adjustment for gains realized In net income	(2,000)	500	(1,500)
Net unrealized gains	15,333	(3,833)	11,500
Minimum pension liability adjustment	(3,333)	833	(2,500)
Other comprehensive income	$22,666	$(5,666)	$17,000

Alternatively, the tax amounts for each component can be displayed parenthetically on the face of the financial statement in which comprehensive income is reported.

All Formats: Disclosure of Accumulated Other Comprehensive Income Balances

Enterprise
Notes to Financial Statements
Year Ended December 31, 19X9

	Foreign Currency Items	Unrealized Gains on Securities	Minimum Pension Liability Adjustment	Accumulated Other Comprehensive Income
Beginning balance	$(500)	$25,500	$ 0	$25,000
Current-period change	8,000	11,500	(2,500)	17,000
Ending balance	$7,500	$37,000	$(2,500)	$42,000

Alternatively, the balances of each classification within accumulated other comprehensive income can be displayed in a statement of changes in equity or in a statement of financial position.

PROSPECTIVE FINANCIAL INFORMATION

The AICPA in its 1998 content specification outline added Prospective Financial Information to its coverage of FARE. This area is discussed in Statement on Standards for Attestation Engagements #200 (AT200) entitled "Financial Forecasts and Projections."

Definitions

Prospective Financial Statements

- **Include:**
  a. Financial forecast
  b. Financial projections
  c. Summaries of significant assumptions
  d. Accounting policies
- **Exclude:**
  a. Pro forma financial statements
  b. Partial presentations
  c. Financial statements for periods that have expired
  d. Statements used solely in support service litigation

Financial Forecast

- Prospective financial statements that present, to the best of the responsible party's knowledge and belief, an entity's <u>expected</u> financial position; results of operations; and changes in financial position.
- A financial forecast is based on assumptions reflecting conditions that are expected to exist and the course of action that is expected to be taken.
- A financial forecast may be expressed in specific monetary amounts or as a range.

Financial Projections

- Prospective financial statements that present, to the best of the responsible party's knowledge and belief, (given one or more hypothetical assumptions) an entity's expected financial position, results of operations, and cash flows.
- A financial projection is sometimes prepared to present one or more hypothetical courses of actions for valuation, as in response to a question such as "what would happen if…?"
- A financial projection is based on assumptions that are expected to exist and the course of action that is expected to be taken, **given** one or more hypothetical assumptions.
- A financial projection my contain a range.

Responsible Party

The responsible party usually is management, but it can be persons outside the entity, such as a party considering acquiring the entity.

AT200 Financial Forecasts and Projections

This standard provides guidance to the accountants concerning performance and reporting for engagements to **examine, compile, or apply agreed-upon procedures** to prospective financial statements if these statements are (or reasonably might be) expected to be used by another (third) party **and**

- if the accountant submits to his client or others prospective financial statements that he **assembled or assisted in assembling**.
- **<u>Or</u>** if the accountant **reports** on prospective financial statements.

Assumptions

Although the accountant may assist in identifying assumptions, gathering information and assembling the statement, the **responsible party** is responsible for the preparation and presentation of the prospective financial statements.

Users of Prospective Financial Statements

Prospective financial statements are for either "**general use**" or "**limited use.**"

- **General Use**

  General use refers to use of statements by persons with whom the responsible party is not negotiating directly; for example, in an offering statement of an entity's debt or equity interest.

  Since the users are unable to ask the responsible party directly about the presentation, the presentation more useful to them is one that portrays the expected results.

  Only financial forecasts are appropriate for general use.

- **Limited Use**

  "Limited use" of prospective financial statements refers to use of prospective financial statements by the responsible party alone or by the responsible party and third parties with whom the responsible party is negotiating directly. Examples include use in negotiations for a bank loan, submission to a regulatory agency, and use solely within the entity.

  Third-party recipients of prospective financial statements intended for limited use can ask questions of the responsible party and negotiate terms directly with it.

  Either financial forecasts or financial projections are appropriate for limited use.

ACCOUNTING AND REPORTING BY DEVELOPMENT STAGE ENTERPRISES—SFAS #7

Summary: Some development stage enterprises have developed specialized accounting and reporting practices. Such enterprises are now required to present financial statements in conformity with generally accepted accounting principles with revenue and expense recognition to be the same as applied to established enterprises. Further, development stage companies are required to disclose additional information.

Development Stage Enterprise Defined

An enterprise is considered in the development stage if it is devoting substantially all of its efforts to establishing a new business and **either** planned **principal operations have not begun**, or if operations have begun, **there has been no significant revenue therefrom**.

Financial Accounting and Reporting

Financial statements should present financial position, changes in financial position and results of operations in conformity with generally accepted accounting principles that apply to established operating enterprises. GAAP should be applied to expense and revenue recognition; deferral of costs and capitalization should be subject to the same assessment of recoverability that would be applicable in an established operating enterprise. For a subsidiary or investee, the recoverability of costs should be assessed within the entity for which separate financial statements are being presented.

Disclosures

The basic financial statement(s) to be presented should include the following information:

(a) A balance sheet showing any accumulated net losses with a descriptive caption such as "deficit accumulated during the development stage" in the stockholders' equity section.

(b) An income statement, showing amounts of revenue and expenses for each period covered by the income statement and cumulative amounts from the enterprise's inception.

(c) A statement of cash flows showing the investing and financing activities for each period and cumulative amounts from the enterprise's inception.

(d) A statement of stockholders' equity showing from the enterprise's inception:
1. For each issuance, the date and number of shares of stock, warrants, rights, or other equity securities issued for cash or other consideration.
2. For each issuance, the dollar amounts assigned to the consideration received for shares of stock, warrants, rights, or other equity securities. Dollar amounts should be assigned to any noncash consideration received.
3. For each issuance involving noncash consideration, the nature of the noncash consideration and the basis for assigning amounts.

The financial statements should be identified as those of a development stage enterprise and include a description of the activities in which the enterprise is engaged.

Transition from Development Stage

The first fiscal year in which an enterprise is no longer considered in the development stage should disclose its prior status as a development stage enterprise.

ACCOUNTING BY DEBTORS AND CREDITORS FOR TROUBLED DEBT RESTRUCTURINGS—SFAS #15 and SFAS #114

A restructuring of a debt constitutes a "Troubled Debt Restructuring" when a creditor, for economic or legal reasons related to the debtor's financial difficulties, grants a **concession** (by agreement or imposition of law or a court) to the debtor that it **would not otherwise consider**. A creditor participates in a troubled debt restructuring because it no longer expects its investment to earn the original rate of return expected and may view loss of all or part of its investment as likely if the debt is not restructured. For the purposes of this statement, debt represents a contractual right to receive, or obligation to pay, money that is already included as an asset or liability in the creditor's or debtor's balance sheet at the time of the restructuring and consists of such items as accounts receivable or payable, notes, debentures, bonds (secured or unsecured, convertible or nonconvertible), and related accrued interest. "Debt" does not include lease agreements or employment-related agreements.

Accounting by Debtors

The accounting treatment for troubled debt restructuring depends on the type of restructuring as follows:

- Transfer of Assets in Full Settlement: The excess of the carrying value of the debt settled over the **fair value of the assets** transferred to the creditor should be recognized as a gain on debt restructuring. A difference between the fair value and carrying value of the **asset transferred** to the creditor should be recognized as a gain or loss on the transfer of assets, included in the determination of net income for the period of transfer. and reported in accordance with APB #30. (Note that a gain on debt restructuring **and** a gain or loss on the transfer of assets may be reported.)
- Grant of an Equity Interest in Full Settlement: The excess of the carrying value of the debt settled over the fair value of the equity interest granted to the creditors should be recognized as a gain on debt restructuring. The equity interest granted is to be recorded at its fair value.
- Modification of Terms:
  a. Total future cash payments of interest and principal equal or exceed the carrying value of the debt. The carrying value of the debt should not change and the effects of changes in the amount or timing (or both) of future interest or principal (or both) payments are reflected in future periods. Interest expense is computed in a way that a constant effective interest rate is applied to the carrying amount of the debt at the beginning of each period between restructuring and maturity (refer to Chapter 9, Amortization of Bond Discount and Premium—Effective Interest Method). The new effective interest rate is the discount rate that equates the present value of the future cash payments specified by the new terms with the carrying value of the debt.
  b. Total future cash payments of interest and principal are less than the carrying value of the debt. The carrying value of the debt is reduced to an amount equal to the total future cash payments specified by the new terms and a gain is recognized on the reduction of the debt equal to the amount of the reduction. Thereafter, all future cash payments are accounted for as reductions of the carrying value of the debt and no interest expense is recognized for any period between restructuring and maturity.

- Combination of Above Types: The **fair value** of assets transferred or equity interest granted in partial settlement shall **first** be applied to the **reduction of the carrying value** of the debt; then, the modification of terms is accounted for as prescribed above. No gain on debt restructuring is recognized unless the remaining carrying value of the debt (after application of fair value of assets transferred and equity interest granted) exceeds the total future cash payments.

Gains recognized on debt restructuring should be aggregated, included in the determination of net income for the period of restructuring, and, if material, classified as an extraordinary item, net of related income tax effect, in accordance with SFAS #4 (refer to Chapter 9).

Accounting by Creditors

The accounting for troubled debt restructuring depends on the type of restructuring as follows:

- Receipt of Assets in Full Settlement (including equity interest in debtor): The assets received are to be recorded at their fair market value when received, and the excess of the carrying value of the investment in the receivable (debt) satisfied over the fair value of the assets received should be recognized as a loss. Subsequently, the creditor should account for the assets received the same as if the assets had been acquired for cash.
- Modification of Terms: SFAS #114 requires the creditor to recognize a new value for the loan receivable. This new value is the present value of the future cash flows from the restructured agreement discounted at the **historical** (original) interest rate (**not** the interest rate in the restructuring agreement). An ordinary loss is recognized as the difference between the carrying value of the loan and the present value of the future cash flows. Interest revenue after the restructuring should be based on the historical (original) interest rate times the new carrying value of the loan receivable.

Losses recognized on debt restructuring, to the extent that they are not offset against allowance for uncollectible amounts or other valuation accounts, should be included in the determination of net income for the period of the restructuring and reported according to APB #30.

Troubled Debt Restructuring

Trouble Company which is experiencing financial difficulty has a note payable of $500,000 and the current year's interest of $50,000 outstanding at December 31 of the current year. The note is a 10% obligation due at the end of the following year.

A. Lender accepts land from Trouble Company in full payment of the note. The land has a fair value of $400,000 and a book value of $220,000. The entry to be made upon execution of the agreement:

Trouble Co. (000)			*Lender (000)*		
Accrued interest payable	$ 50				
Note payable	500		Land	$400	
Land		$220	Loan loss	150	
Gain on disposal of fixed asset		180	Note receivable		$500
			Accrued interest receivable		50
Extraordinary gain from early extinguishment of debt		150			

B. Lender accepts Trouble Company stock with a par value of $100,000 and a fair market value of $400,000 in full payment of the note.

Accrued interest payable	$ 50				
Note payable	500		Investment in Trouble Co.	$400	
Common stock		$100	Loan loss	150	
Capital in excess of par		300	Note receivable		$500
Extraordinary gain from early extinguishment of debt		150	Accrued interest receivable		50

C. Lender agrees to extend the note for two years beyond the original due date, forgive the $50,000 accrued interest, reduce the principal of the note to $400,000, and revise the interest rate to 8%.

DEBTOR - TROUBLE CO.

Future cash payments = $400,000 + ($32,000 × 3) =	$496,000
Carrying value (including interest) =	550,000
Extraordinary gain	$ 54,000

Journal entry when agreement is signed:

Accrued interest payable	$50,000	
Note payable	4,000	
Extraordinary Gain		$54,000

CREDITOR - LENDER

In accordance with SFAS #114 the creditor should record the note receivable at the present value of future cash flows at the **historical** interest rate of 10% based on the restructured receipts of $400,000 for the principal and $32,000 per year for the interest ($400,000 × 8% = $32,000).

Present value of future cash flows at 10%:

	FUTURE RECEIPTS	X	PRESENT VALUE OF 1 FACTOR	=	TOTAL PRESENT VALUE
Year 1	32,000	x	.909091	=	$ 29,091
Year 2	32,000	x	.826446	=	26,446
Year 3	32,000	x	.751315	=	24,042
Year 4	400,000	x	.751315	=	300,526
			Total Present Value		$ 380,105
			Carrying value on books (500,000 + 50,000)		550,000
			Loss on loan restructuring		$ 169,895

Journal entry when agreement is signed:

Loss on loan restructuring	169,895	
Interest receivable		50,000
Notes receivable		119,895

Journal entries to record interest revenue and receipt of the interest and principal are based on the amortization table listed below:

	Year 1		Year 2		Year 3	
a. Cash	32,000		32,000		32,000	
Notes receivable	6,010		6,612		7,273	
Interest revenue		38,010		38,612		39,273

b. Cash		400,000	
Notes receivable			400,000

Amortization of "Discount" on Notes Receivable

	10% Interest	8% Cash Interest	Addition to Carrying Value (Amtz. Discount)	Carrying Value of Notes Receivable
Balance				380,105
Year 1	38,010	32,000	6010	386,115
Year 2	38,612	32,000	6612	392,727
Year 3	39,273	32,000	7273	400,000

D. Lender agrees to extend the note for two years beyond the original due date, forgive the accrued interest, reduce the principal amount of the note to $450,000 and revise the interest rate to 9%.

DEBTOR - TROUBLE CO.

Future cash payments = $450,000 + ($40,500 × 3) =	$571,500
Carrying value (including interest) =	550,000
Future interest to be recognized*	$ 21,500

Journal entry when agreement is signed:

Accrued interest payable	$50,000	
Note payable		$50,000

Journal entry when first cash payment is made:

*Interest expense	$ 7,700	
Note payable	32,800	
Cash		$40,500

*Represents an interest rate of 1.4% on the new carrying value of $550,000.

CREDITOR - LENDER

Journal entry when agreement is signed:

Loss on loan restructuring	111,191	
Interest receivable		50,000
Note receivable		61,191

The present value of future payments of $40,500 interest per year and $450,000 principal are as follows: Year 1 - $40,500 × .909091 = $36,818; Year 2 - $40,500 × .826446 = $33,471; Year 3 - $40,500 × .751315 = $30,428 and Year 3 - $450,000 × .751315 = $338,092 for a total of $438,809. The loss on loan restructuring is the carrying value less the present value of future cash flows ($550,000 - 438,809 = $111,191).

Journal entry when first cash payment is made:

Cash	40,500	
Notes receivable	3,381	
Interest revenue (a)		43,881

(a) Interest revenue is the historical interest rate × the total present value (10% × 438,809 = $43,881).

Loan Impairments - Creditors

A loan impairment should be differentiated from a debt restructuring. An impairment does not involve a formal restructuring but is a conclusion by the creditor, based on its normal review procedures, that there is a problem with the collectibility of the loan receivable. SFAS #114 states that a loan is impaired when **it is probable that a creditor will be unable to collect all amounts due according to the contracted terms.** The calculation of the loss on impairment is similar to the calculation of the loss on debt restructuring in which there is a modification of terms. The creditor calculates the present value of future cash flows using the historical (original) interest rate and the difference between the cash flows and the carrying value of the loan is the loss. The loss should be charged to Bad Debt Expense and credited to the Allowance for Doubtful Loans.

SFAS #114 allows an alternative calculation in which the impaired loan may be measured at the loan's observable market price of the fair value of the collateral.

Example of Loan Impairment:

On January 1, 2002 ABC Corporation received a $50,000, 3-year non-interest bearing note yielding 8% from XYZ Corporation. At December 31, 2002 ABC determines through its normal credit review procedures that it is **probable** that XYZ will not be able to pay but $40,000 of the $50,000 loan. The loss on impairment would be calculated:

Carrying Value - 12/31/02 (a)	$42,867
Less present value of future cash receipts	
($40,000 × PV of 1 for 2 periods at 8% = 40,000 × .857339)	(34,294)
Loss on Impairment at 12/31/02	8,573

The journal entry to record the impairment:

Bad Debt Expense	8,573	
Allowance for Doubtful Loans		8,573

Note: ABC's future interest revenue will be based on the new carrying value of $34,294.

(a). The calculation of the carrying value of the loan at 12/31/02:

Balance 1/1/02 = Present Value of $50,000 for 3 periods at 8% (50,000 × .793832)	$39,692
Plus Amortization of Discount on the note for 2002 = 8% × January 1 carrying value (8% × 39,692)	3,175
Total carrying value 12/31/02	$42,867

Chapter Twelve
Reporting the Results of Operations Questions

INCOME STATEMENT FORMAT

Items 1 and 2 are based on the following:
Vane Co's trial balance of income statement accounts for the year ended December 31, 2000, included the following:

	Debit	*Credit*
Sales		$575,000
Cost of sales	$240,000	
Administrative expenses	70,000	
Loss on sale of equipment	10,000	
Sales commissions	50,000	
Interest revenue		25,000
Freight out	15,000	
Loss on early retirement of long-term debt	20,000	
Uncollectible accounts expense	15,000	
Totals	$420,000	$600,000
Other information:		
Finished goods inventory:		
January 1, 2000		$400,000
December 31, 2000		360,000

Vane's income tax rate is 30%. In Vane's 2000 multiple-step income statement,

1. What amount should Vane report as the cost of goods manufactured?
a. $200,000.
b. $215,000.
c. $280,000.
d. $295,000.

2. What amount should Vane report as income after income taxes from continuing operations?
a. $126,000.
b. $129,500.
c. $140,000.
d. $147,000.

---

3. Brock Corporation reports operating expenses in two categories: (1) selling and (2) general and administrative. The adjusted trial balance at December 31, 1996, included the following expense and loss accounts:

Accounting and legal fees	$120,000
Advertising	150,000
Freight out	80,000
Interest	70,000
Loss on sale of long-term investment	30,000
Officers' salaries	225,000
Rent for office space	220,000
Sales salaries and commissions	140,000

One-half of the rented premises is occupied by the sales department.

Brock's total selling expenses for 1996 are
a. $480,000
b. $400,000
c. $370,000
d. $360,000

4. In Baer Food Co.'s 1997 single-step income statement, the section titled "Revenues" consisted of the following:

Net sales revenue		$187,000
Results from discontinued operations:		
Loss from operations of segment (net of $1,200 tax effect)	$(2,400)	
Gain on disposal of segment (net of $7,200 tax effect)	14,400	12,000
Interest revenue		10,200
Gain on sale of equipment		4,700
Cumulative change in 1995 and 1996 income due to change in depreciation method (net of $750 tax effect)		1,500
Total revenues		$215,400

In the revenues section of the 1997 income statement, Baer Food should have reported total revenues of
a. $216,300
b. $215,400
c. $203,700
d. $201,900

DISCONTINUED OPERATIONS

5. On September 30, 1996, a commitment was made to dispose of a business segment in early 1997. The segment operating loss for the period October 1 to December 31, 1996, should be included in the 1996 income statement as part of

a. Loss on disposal of the discontinued segment.
b. Operating loss of the discontinued segment.
c. Income or loss from continuing operations.
d. Extraordinary gains or losses.

6. On December 1, 1997, Shine Co. agreed to sell a business segment on March 1, 1998. Throughout 1997 the segment had operating losses that were expected to continue until the segment's disposition. However, the gain on disposition was expected to exceed the segment's total operating losses in 1997 and 1998. The amount of estimated net gain from disposal recognized in 1997 equals

a. Zero.
b. The entire estimated net gain.
c. All of the segment's 1997 operating losses.
d. The segment's December 1997 operating losses.

7. On November 1, 1999, Smith Co. contracted to dispose of an industry segment on February 28, 2000. Throughout 1999 the segment had operating losses. These losses were expected to continue until the segment's disposition. If a loss is anticipated on final disposition, how much of the operating losses should be included in the loss on disposal reported in Smith's 1999 income statements?

I. Operating losses for the period January 1 to October 31, 1999.
II. Operating losses for the period November 1 to December 31, 1999.
III. Estimated operating losses for the period January 1 to February 28, 2000.

a. II only.
b. II and III only.
c. I and III only.
d. I and II only.

8. On October 1, 1994, Burns Corp. approved a formal plan to sell Hall division, a business segment. The sale was scheduled to take place on March 31, 1995. Hall had operating income of $100,000 for the quarter ended December 31, 1994, and expected to incur an operating loss of $50,000 for the first quarter of 1995. Burns estimated that it would incur a $375,000 loss on the sale of Hall's assets. Burns' income tax rate for 1994 was 30%. In its 1994 income statement, Burns should report a loss on the disposal of Hall division of

a. $325,000
b. $297,500
c. $262,500
d. $227,500

9. On May 15, 1996, Munn, Inc., approved a plan to dispose of a segment of its business. It is expected that the sale will occur on February 1, 1997, at a selling price of $500,000. During 1996, disposal costs incurred by Munn totaled $75,000. The segment had actual or estimated operating losses as follows:

1/1/96 to 5/14/96	$130,000
5/15/96 to 12/31/96	50,000
1/1/97 to 1/31/97	15,000

The carrying amount of the segment at the date of sale was expected to be $850,000. Before income taxes, what amount should Munn report as a loss on disposal of the segment in its 1996 income statement?

a. $490,000
b. $475,000
c. $440,000
d. $425,000

10. On December 31, 1997, Greer Co. entered into an agreement to sell its Hart segment's assets. On that date, Greer estimated the gain from the disposition of the assets in 1998 would be $700,000 and Hart's 1998 operating losses would be $200,000. Hart's actual operating losses were $300,000 in both 1997 and 1998, and the actual gain on disposition of Hart's assets in 1998 was $650,000. Disregarding income taxes, what net gain (loss) should be reported for discontinued operations in Greer's comparative 1998 and 1997 income statements?

	1998	1997
a.	$50,000	$(300,000)
b.	$0	$50,000
c.	$350,000	$(300,000)
d.	$(150,000)	$200,000

CHANGES IN ACCOUNTING PRINCIPLES-NORMAL CHANGE

11. On August 31, 1999, Harvey Co. decided to change from the FIFO periodic inventory system to the weighted average periodic inventory system. Harvey is on a calendar year basis. The cumulative effect of the change is determined

a. As of January 1, 1999.
b. As of August 31, 1999.
c. During the eight months ending August 31, 1999, by a weighted average of the purchases.
d. During 1999 by a weighted average of the purchases.

12. On December 31, 1995, Kerr, Inc., appropriately changed its inventory valuation method to FIFO cost

from weighted-average cost for financial statement and income tax purposes. The change will result in a \$700,000 increase in the beginning inventory at January 1, 1995. Assume a 30% income tax rate. The cumulative effect of this accounting change reported for the year ended December 31, 1995, is

a. \$0
b. \$210,000
c. \$490,000
d. \$700,000

13. On January 1, 1992, Pell Corp. purchased a machine having an estimated useful life of 10 years and no salvage. The machine was depreciated by the double declining balance method for both financial statement and income tax reporting. On January 1, 1997, Pell changed to the straight-line method for financial statement reporting but not for income tax reporting. Accumulated depreciation at December 31, 1996, was \$560,000. If the straight-line method had been used, the accumulated depreciation at December 31, 1996, would have been \$420,000. Pell's enacted income tax rate for 1997 and thereafter is 30%. The amount shown in the 1997 income statement for the cumulative effect of changing to the straight-line method should be

a. \$98,000 debit.
b. \$98,000 credit.
c. \$140,000 credit.
d. \$140,000 debit.

14. On January 2, 1996, Union Co. purchased a machine for \$264,000 and depreciated it by the straight-line method using an estimated useful life of eight years with no salvage value. On January 2, 1999, Union determined that the machine had a useful life of six years from the date of acquisition and will have a salvage value of \$24,000. An accounting change was made in 1999 to reflect the additional data. The accumulated depreciation for this machine should have a balance at December 31, 1999, of

a. \$176,000.
b. \$160,000.
c. \$154,000.
d. \$146,000.

CHANGES IN ACCOUNTING PRINCIPLES-EXCEPTIONS

15. On January 1, 1992, Poe Construction, Inc., changed to the percentage-of-completion method of income recognition for financial statement reporting but not for income tax reporting. Poe can justify this change in accounting principle. As of December 31, 1991, Poe compiled data showing that income under the completed-contract method aggregated \$700,000. If the percentage-of-completion method had been used, the accumulated income through December 31, 1991, would have been \$880,000. Assuming an income tax rate of 40% for all years, the cumulative effect of this accounting change should be reported by Poe in the 1992

a. Retained earnings statement as a \$180,000 credit adjustment to the beginning balance.
b. Income statement as a \$180,000 credit.
c. Retained earnings statement as a \$108,000 credit adjustment to the beginning balance.
d. Income statement as a \$108,000 credit.

16. Milton Co. began operations on January 1, 1996. On January 1, 1998, Milton changed its inventory method from LIFO to FIFO for both financial and income tax reporting. If FIFO had been used in prior years, Milton's inventories would have been higher by \$60,000 and \$40,000 at December 31, 1998 and 1997, respectively. Milton has a 30% income tax rate. What amount should Milton report as the cumulative effect of this accounting change in its income statement for the year ended December 31, 1998?

a. \$0
b. \$14,000
c. \$28,000
d. \$42,000

REVIEW

17. The cumulative effect of changing to a new accounting principle should be recorded separately as a component of income after continuing operations for a change from the

a. Straight-line method of depreciation for previously recorded assets to the sum-of-the-years'-digits method.
b. LIFO method of inventory pricing to the FIFO method.
c. Percentage-of-completion method of accounting for long-term construction-type contracts to the completed-contract method.
d. Cash basis of accounting for vacation pay to the accrual basis.

18. Is the cumulative effect of an inventory pricing change on prior years earnings reported separately between extraordinary items and net income for a change from

	LIFO to weighted average?	*FIFO to weighted average?*
a.	Yes	Yes
b.	Yes	No
c.	No	No
d.	No	Yes

CHANGES IN ACCOUNTING ESTIMATES

19. When a company changes the expected service life of an asset because additional information has been obtained, which of the following should be reported?

	Pro forma effect of retroactive application	*Cumulative effect of a change in accounting principle*
a.	Yes	Yes
b.	No	Yes
c.	Yes	No
d.	No	No

20. During 1999, Krey Co. increased the estimated quantity of copper recoverable from its mine. Krey uses the units of production depletion method. As a result of the change, which of the following should be reported in Krey's 1999 financial statements?

	Cumulative effect of a change in accounting principle	*Pro forma effects of retroactive application of new depletion base*
a.	Yes	Yes
b.	Yes	No
c.	No	No
d.	No	Yes

21. On January 1, 1993, Lane, Inc., acquired equipment for $100,000 with an estimated 10-year useful life. Lane estimated a $10,000 salvage value and used the straight-line method of depreciation. During 1997, after its 1996 financial statements had been issued, Lane determined that, due to obsolescence, this equipment's remaining useful life was only four more years and its salvage value would be $4,000. In Lane's December 31, 1997, balance sheet, what was the carrying amount of this asset?

a. $51,500
b. $49,000
c. $41,500
d. $39,000

22. For 1998, Pac Co. estimated its two-year equipment warranty costs based on $100 per unit sold in 1998. Experience during 1999 indicated that the estimate should have been based on $110 per unit. The effect of this $10 difference from the estimate is reported

a. In 1999 income from continuing operations.
b. As an accounting change, net of tax, below 1999 income from continuing operations.
c. As an accounting change requiring 1998 financial statements to be restated.
d. As a correction of an error requiring 1998 financial statements to be restated.

CHANGES IN REPORTING ENTITY

23. Presenting consolidated financial statements this year when statements of individual companies were presented last year is

a. A correction of an error.
b. An accounting change that should be reported prospectively.
c. An accounting change that should be reported by restating the financial statements of all prior periods presented.
d. Not an accounting change.

24. Matt Co. included a foreign subsidiary in its 1998 consolidated financial statements. The subsidiary was acquired in 1992 and was excluded from previous consolidations. The change was caused by the elimination of foreign exchange controls. Including the subsidiary in the 1998 consolidated financial statements results in an accounting change that should be reported

a. By footnote disclosure only.
b. Currently and prospectively.
c. Currently with footnote disclosure of pro forma effects of retroactive application.
d. By restating the financial statements of all prior periods presented.

25. A change in accounting entity is actually a change in accounting

a. Principle.
b. Estimate.
c. Method.
d. Concept.

EXTRAORDINARY ITEMS

26. A gain or loss from a transaction that is unusual in nature and infrequent in occurrence should be reported separately as a component of income

a. Before cumulative effect of accounting changes and after discontinued operations of a segment of a business.
b. After cumulative effect of accounting changes and after discontinued operations of a segment of a business.
c. Before cumulative effect of accounting changes and before discontinued operations of a segment of a business.

d. After cumulative effect of accounting changes and before discontinued operations of a segment of a business.

27. An extraordinary item should be reported separately on the income statement as a component of income

	Before discontinued operations of a segment of a business	*Net of income taxes*
a.	No	No
b.	No	Yes
c.	Yes	Yes
d.	Yes	No

28. On July 1, 1992, Dolan Corp. incurred an extraordinary loss of $300,000, net of income tax saving. Dolan's operating income for the full year ending December 31, 1992, was expected to be $500,000. In Dolan's income statement for the quarter ended September 30, 1992, how much of this extraordinary loss should be disclosed separately?

a. $300,000
b. $150,000
c. $75,000
d. $0

29. On March 1, 1994, Somar Co. issued 20-year bonds at a discount. By September 1, 1999, the bonds were quoted at 106 when Somar exercised its right to retire the bonds at 105. How should Somar report the bond retirement on its 1999 income statement?

a. A gain in continuing operations.
b. A loss in continuing operations.
c. An extraordinary gain.
d. An extraordinary loss.

30. Midway Co. had the following transactions during 1999:

- $1,200,000 pretax loss on foreign currency exchange due to a major unexpected devaluation by the foreign government.
- $500,000 pretax loss from discontinued operations of a division.
- $800,000 pretax loss on equipment damaged by a hurricane. This was the first hurricane ever to strike in Midway's area. Midway also received $1,000,000 from its insurance company to replace a building, with a carrying value of $300,000, that had been destroyed by the hurricane.

What amount should Midway report in its 1999 income statement as extraordinary loss before income taxes?

a. $100,000
b. $1,300,000
c. $1,800,000
d. $2,500,000

31. The effect of a transaction that is infrequent in occurrence but **not** unusual in nature should be presented separately as a component of income from continuing operations when the transaction results in

	Loss	*Gain*
a.	Yes	Yes
b.	No	Yes
c.	No	No
d.	Yes	No

PRIOR PERIOD ADJUSTMENTS

32. Conn Co. reported a retained earnings balance of $400,000 at December 31, 1998. In August 1999, Conn determined that insurance premiums of $60,000 for the three-year period beginning January 1, 1998, had been paid and fully expensed in 1998. Conn has a 30% income tax rate. What amount should Conn report as adjusted beginning retained earnings in its 1999 statement of retained earnings?

a. $420,000.
b. $428,000.
c. $440,000.
d. $442,000.

33. Foy Corp. failed to accrue warranty costs of $50,000 in its December 31, 1999, financial statements. In addition, a change from straight-line to accelerated depreciation made at the beginning of 2000 resulted in a cumulative effect of $30,000 on Foy's retained earnings. Both the $50,000 and the $30,000 are net of related income taxes. What amount should Foy report as prior period adjustment in 2000?

a. $0
b. $30,000
c. $50,000
d. $80,000

34. Which of the following should be reported as a prior period adjustment?

	Change in estimated lives of depreciable assets	*Change from unaccepted principle to accepted principle*
a.	Yes	Yes
b.	No	Yes
c.	Yes	No
d.	No	No

DISCLOSURE OF ACCOUNTING POLICIES

35. The stock of Gates, Inc., is widely held, and the company is under the jurisdiction of the Securities and Exchange Commission. In the annual report, information about the significant accounting policies adopted by Gates should be

a. Omitted because it tends to confuse users of the report.
b. Included as an integral part of the financial statements.
c. Presented as supplementary information.
d. Omitted because all policies must comply with the regulations of the Securities and Exchange Commission.

36. Which of the following should be disclosed in the summary of significant accounting policies?

	Composition of inventories	*Maturity dates of long-term debt*
a.	Yes	Yes
b.	Yes	No
c.	No	No
d.	No	Yes

37. Which of the following should be disclosed in the summary of significant accounting policies?

	Composition of plant assets	*Inventory pricing*
a.	Yes	Yes
b.	No	Yes
c.	No	No
d.	Yes	No

INTERIM FINANCIAL REPORTING

38. For interim financial reporting, an extraordinary gain occurring in the second quarter should be

a. Recognized ratably over the last three quarters.
b. Recognized ratably over all four quarters with the first quarter being restated.
c. Recognized in the second quarter.
d. Disclosed by footnote only in the second quarter.

39. Which of the following reporting practices is permissible for interim financial reporting?

a. Use of the gross-profit method for interim inventory pricing.
b. Use of the direct-costing method for determining manufacturing inventories.
c. Deferral of unplanned variances under a standard-cost system until year end.
d. Deferral of inventory market declines until year end.

40. Farr Corp. had the following transactions during the quarter ended March 31, 1997:

Loss on early extinguishment of debt	$ 70,000
Payment of fire insurance premium for calendar year 1997	100,000

What amount should be included in Farr's income statement for the quarter ended March 31, 1997?

	Extraordinary loss	*Insurance expense*
a.	$70,000	$100,000
b.	$70,000	$25,000
c.	$17,500	$25,000
d.	$0	$100,000

41. For interim financial reporting, a company's income tax provision for the second quarter of 1999 should be determined using the

a. Effective tax rate expected to be applicable for the full year of 1999 as estimated at the end of the first quarter of 1999.
b. Effective tax rate expected to be applicable for the full year of 1999 as estimated at the end of the second quarter of 1999.
c. Effective tax rate expected to be applicable for the second quarter of 1999.
d. Statutory tax rate for 1999.

42. During the first quarter of 2000, Tech Co. had income before taxes of $200,000, and its effective income tax rate was 15%. Tech's 1999 effective annual income tax rate was 30%, but Tech expects its 2000 effective annual income tax rate to be 25%. In its first quarter interim income statement, what amount of income tax expense should Tech report?

a. $0
b. $30,000
c. $50,000
d. $60,000

43. An inventory loss from a market price decline occurred in the first quarter, and the decline was not expected to reverse during the fiscal year. However, in the third quarter the inventory's market price recovery exceeded the market decline that occurred in the first quarter. For interim financial reporting, the dollar amount of net inventory should

a. Decrease in the first quarter by the amount of the market price decline and increase in the third quarter by the amount of the decrease in the first quarter.
b. Decrease in the first quarter by the amount of the market price decline and increase in the third

quarter by the amount of the market price recovery.
c. Decrease in the first quarter by the amount of the market price decline and **not** be affected in the third quarter.
d. Not be affected in either the first quarter or the third quarter.

44. Due to a decline in market price in the second quarter, Petal Co. incurred an inventory loss. The market price is expected to return to previous levels by the end of the year. At the end of the year the decline had not reversed. When should the loss be reported in Petal's interim income statements?
a. Ratably over the second, third, and fourth quarters.
b. Ratably over the third and fourth quarters.
c. In the second quarter only.
d. In the fourth quarter only.

TROUBLED-DEBT RESTRUCTURING

45. Colt, Inc., is indebted to Kent under an $800,000, 10%, four-year note dated December 31, 1989. Annual interest of $80,000 was paid on December 31, 1990 and 1991. During 1992 Colt experienced financial difficulties and is likely to default unless concessions are made. On December 31, 1992, Kent agreed to restructure the debt as follows:

- Interest of $80,000 for 1992, due December 31, 1992, was made payable December 31, 1993.
- Interest for 1993 was waived.
- The principal amount was reduced to $700,000.

Assuming an income tax rate of 40%, how much should Colt report as extraordinary gain in its income statement for the year ended December 31, 1992?
a. $0
b. $60,000
c. $100,000
d. $108,000

46. During 1989 Peterson Company experienced financial difficulties and is likely to default on a $500,000, 15%, three-year note dated January 1, 1981, payable to Forest National Bank. On December 31, 1988, the bank agreed to settle the note and unpaid interest of $75,000 for 1989 for $50,000 cash and marketable securities having a current market value of $375,000. Peterson's acquisition cost of the securities is $385,000. Ignoring income taxes, what amount should Peterson report as a gain from the debt restructuring in its 1989 income statement?
a. $65,000.
b. $75,000.
c. $140,000.
d. $150,000.

47. Wood Corp., a debtor-in-possession under Chapter 11 of the Federal Bankruptcy Code, granted an equity interest to a creditor in full settlement of a $28,000 debt owed to the creditor. At the date of this transaction, the equity interest had a fair value of $25,000. What amount should Wood recognize as an extraordinary gain on restructuring of debt?
a. $0
b. $3,000
c. $25,000
d. $28,000

48. On October 15, 1998, Kam Corp. informed Finn Co. that Kam would be unable to repay its $100,000 note due on October 31 to Finn. Finn agreed to accept title to Kam's computer equipment in full settlement of the note. The equipment's carrying value was $80,000 and its fair value was $75,000. Kam's tax rate is 30%. What amounts should Kam report as ordinary gain (loss) and extraordinary gain for the year ended September 30, 1999?

	Ordinary gain (loss)	*Extraordinary gain*
a.	$(5,000)	$17,500
b.	$0	$20,000
c.	$0	$14,000
d.	$20,000	$0

DEVELOPMENT STAGE ENTERPRISES

49. A development stage enterprise
a. Issues an income statement that shows only cumulative amounts from the enterprise's inception.
b. Issues an income statement that is the same as an established operating enterprise, but does **not** show cumulative amounts from the enterprise's inception as additional information.
c. Issues an income statement that is the same as an established operating enterprise, and shows cumulative amounts from the enterprise's inception as additional information.
d. Does **not** issue an income statement.

50. A development stage enterprise should use the same generally accepted accounting principles that apply to established operating enterprises for

	Deferral of costs	*Expensing of costs when incurred*
a.	Yes	Yes
b.	Yes	No
c.	No	No
d.	No	Yes

51. Deficits accumulated during the development stage of a company should be
a. Reported as organization costs.
b. Reported as a part of stockholders' equity.
c. Capitalized and written off in the first year of principal operations.
d. Capitalized and amortized over a five-year period beginning when principal operations commence.

52. Tanker Oil Co., a developmental stage enterprise, incurred the following costs during its first year of operations:

Legal fees for incorporation and other related matters	$55,000
Underwriters' fees for initial stock offering	40,000
Explorations costs and purchases of mineral rights	60,000

Tanker had no revenue during its first year of operation. What amount may Tanker capitalize as organizational costs?
a. $155,000
b. $115,000
c. $95,000
d. $55,000

REVIEW QUESTIONS

53. Pear Co.'s income statement for the year ended December 31, 1999, as prepared by Pear's controller, reported income before taxes of $125,000. The auditor questioned the following amounts that had been included before taxes:

Equity in earnings of Cinn Co.	$40,000
Dividends received from Cinn	8,000
Adjustments to profits of prior years for arithmetical errors in depreciation	(35,000)

Pear owns 40% of Cinn's common stock. Pear's December 31, 1999, income statement should report income before taxes of
a. $85,000
b. $117,000
c. $120,000
d. $152,000

Items 54 and 55 are based on the following:

During 2001, Orca Corp. decided to change from the FIFO method of inventory valuation to the weighted-average method. Inventory balances under each method were as follows:

	FIFO	*Weighted-average*
January 1, 2001	$71,000	$77,000
December 31, 2001	79,000	83,000

Orca's income tax rate is 30%.

54. In its 2001 financial statements, what amount should Orca report as the cumulative effect of this accounting change?
a. $2,800
b. $4,000
c. $4,200
d. $6,000

55. Orca should report the cumulative effect of this accounting change as a(an)
a. Prior period adjustment.
b. Component of income from continuing operations.
c. Extraordinary item.
d. Component of income after extraordinary items.

---

56. During January 2000, Doe Corp. agreed to sell the assets and product line of its Hart division. The sale was completed on January 15, 2001, and resulted in a gain on disposal of $900,000. Hart's operating losses were $600,000 for 2000 and $50,000 for the period January 1 through January 15, 2001. Disregarding income taxes, what amount of net gain (loss) should be reported in Doe's comparative 2001 and 2000 income statements?

	2001	*2000*
a.	$0	$250,000
b.	$250,000	$0
c.	$850,000	$(600,000)
d.	$900,000	$(650,000)

57. Conceptually, interim financial statements can be described as emphasizing
a. Timeliness over reliability.
b. Reliability over relevance.
c. Relevance over comparability.
d. Comparability over neutrality.

58. Which of the following information should be disclosed in the summary of significant accounting policies?

a. Refinancing of debt subsequent to the balance sheet date.
b. Guarantees of indebtedness of others.
c. Criteria for determining which investments are treated as cash equivalents.
d. Adequacy of pension plan assets relative to vested benefits.

59. In Yew Co.'s 1999 annual report, Yew described its social awareness expenditures during the year as follows:

"The Company contributed $250,000 in cash to youth and educational programs. The Company also gave $140,000 to health and human-service organizations, of which $80,000 was contributed by employees through payroll deductions. In addition, consistent with the Company's commitment to the environment, the Company spent $100,000 to redesign product packaging."

What amount of the above should be included in Yew's income statement as charitable contributions expense?
a. $310,000.
b. $390,000.
c. $410,000.
d. $490,000.

60. Which of the following should be included in general and administrative expenses?

	Interest	*Advertising*
a.	Yes	Yes
b.	Yes	No
c.	No	Yes
d.	No	No

61. On October 1, 2001, Host Co. approved a plan to dispose of a segment of its business. Host expected that the sale would occur on April 1, 2002, at an estimated gain of $350,000. The segment had actual and estimated operating losses as follows:

1/1/01 to 9/30/01	$(300,000)
10/1/01 to 12/31/01	(200,000)
1/1/02 to 3/31/02	(400,000)

In its 2001 income statement, what should Host report as a loss on disposal of the segment before income taxes?
a. $200,000
b. $250,000
c. $500,000
d. $600,000

62. In open market transactions, Gold Corp. simultaneously sold its long-term investment in Iron Corp. bonds and purchased its own outstanding bonds. The broker remitted the net cash from the two transactions. Gold's gain on the purchase of its own bonds exceeded its loss on the sale of the Iron bonds. Gold should report the
a. Net effect of the two transactions as an extraordinary gain.
b. Net effect of the two transactions in income before extraordinary items.
c. Effect of its own bond transaction gain in income before extraordinary items, and report the Iron bond transaction as an extraordinary loss.
d Effect of its own bond transaction as an extraordinary gain, and report the Iron bond transaction loss in income before extraordinary items.

63. Lore Co. changed from the cash basis of accounting to the accrual basis of accounting during 2001. The cumulative effect of this change should be reported in Lore's 2001 financial statements as a
a. Prior-period adjustment resulting from the correction of an error.
b. Prior-period adjustment resulting from the change in accounting principle.
c. Component of income before extraordinary item.
d. Component of income after extraordinary item.

64. Grey Company holds an overdue note receivable of $800,000 plus recorded accrued interest of $64,000. As the result of a court imposed settlement on December 31, 1993, Grey agreed to the following restructuring arrangement:

- Reduced the principal obligation to $600,000.
- Forgave the $64,000 accrued interest.
- Extended the maturity date to December 31, 1995.
- Annual interest of $60,000 is to be paid to Grey on December 31, 1994 and 1995.

On December 31, 1993, Grey must recognize a loss from restructuring of
a. $144,000
b. $200,000
c. $204,000
d. $264,000

65. On January 2, 1999, to better reflect the variable use of its only machine, Holly, Inc. elected to change its method of depreciation from the straight-line method to the units-of-production method. The original cost of the machine on January 2, 1997, was $50,000, and its estimated life was 10 years. Holly

estimates that the machine's total life is 50,000 machine hours.

Machine hours usage was 8,500 during 1998 and 3,500 during 1997.

Holly's income tax rate is 30%. Holly should report the accounting change in its 1999 financial statements as a(an)

a. Cumulative effect of a change in accounting principle of $2,000 in its income statement.
b. Adjustment to beginning retained earnings of $2,000.
c. Cumulative effect of a change in accounting principle of $1,400 in its income statement.
d. Adjustment to beginning retained earnings of $1,400.

66. Goddard has used the FIFO method of inventory valuation since it began operations in 1994. Goddard decided to change to the weighted-average method for determining inventory costs at the beginning of 1997. The following schedule shows year-end inventory balances under the FIFO and weighted-average methods:

Year	*FIFO*	*Weighted average*
1994	$45,000	$54,000
1995	78,000	71,000
1996	83,000	78,000

What amount, before income taxes, should be reported in the 1997 income statement as the cumulative effect of the change in accounting principle?

a. $5,000 decrease.
b. $3,000 decrease.
c. $2,000 increase.
d. $0.

67. Which of the following facts concerning fixed assets should be included in the summary of significant accounting policies?

	Depreciation method	*Composition*
a.	No	Yes
b.	Yes	Yes
c.	Yes	No
d.	No	No

68. An Accounting Principles Board Opinion is concerned with disclosure of accounting policies. A singular feature of this particular opinion is that it

a. Calls for disclosure of every accounting policy followed by a reporting entity.
b. Applies to immaterial items whereas most opinions are concerned solely with material items.
c. Applies also to accounting policy disclosures by not-for-profit entities, whereas most opinions are concerned solely with accounting practices of profit-oriented entities.
d. Prescribes a rigid format for the disclosure of policies to be reported upon.

69. The first examination of Rudd Corp.'s financial statements was made for the year ended December 31, 1995. The auditor found that Rudd had purchased another company in January 1993 and had recorded goodwill of $100,000 in connection with this purchase. It was determined that the goodwill had an estimated useful life of only five years because of obsolescence. No amortization of goodwill had ever been recorded. For the December 31, 1995, financial statements, Rudd should debit

	Amortization expense	*Retained earnings*
a.	$0	$100,000
b.	$20,000	$40,000
c.	$33,333	$0
d.	$60,000	$0

70. In 1992, May Corp. acquired land by paying $75,000 down and signing a note with a maturity value of $1,000,000. On the note's due date, December 31, 1997, May owed $40,000 of accrued interest and $1,000,000 principal on the note. May was in financial difficulty and was unable to make any payments. May and the bank agreed to amend the note as follows:

- The $40,000 of interest due on December 31, 1997, was forgiven.
- The principal of the note was reduced from $1,000,000 to $950,000 and the maturity date extended 1 year to December 31, 1998.
- May would be required to make one interest payment totaling $30,000 on December 31, 1998.

As a result of the troubled debt restructuring, May should report a gain, before taxes, in its 1997 income statement of

a. $40,000
b. $50,000
c. $60,000
d. $90,000

71. On October 1, 2000, Wand, Inc. committed itself to a formal plan to sell its Kam division's assets. On

that date, Wand estimated that the loss from the disposal of assets in February 2001 would be $25,000. Wand also estimated that Kam would incur operating losses of $100,000 for the period of October 1, 2000, through December 31, 2000, and $50,000 for the period January 1, 2001 through February 28, 2001. These estimates were materially correct. Disregarding income taxes, what should Wand report as loss from discontinued operations in its comparative 2000 and 2001 income statements?

	2000	*2001*
a.	$175,000	$0
b.	$125,000	$50,000
c.	$100,000	$75,000
d.	$0	$175,000

72. Under East Co.'s accounting system, all insurance premiums paid are debited to prepaid insurance. For interim financial reports, East makes monthly estimated charges to insurance expense with credits to prepaid insurance. Additional information for the year ended December 31, 1997, is as follows:

Prepaid insurance at December 31, 1996	$105,000
Charges to insurance expense during 1997 (including a year-end adjustment of $17,500)	437,500
Prepaid insurance at December 31, 1997	122,500

What was the total amount of insurance premiums paid by East during 1997?

a. $332,500
b. $420,000
c. $437,500
d. $455,000

73. Vilo Corp. has estimated that total depreciation expense for the year ending December 31, 1996, will amount to $60,000, and that 1996 year-end bonuses to employees will total $120,000. In Vilo's interim income statement for the six months ended June 30, 1996, what is the total amount of expense relating to these two items that should be reported?

a. $0
b. $30,000
c. $90,000
d. $180,000

74. On March 15, 1994, Rex Company paid property taxes of $180,000 on its factory building for calendar year 1994. On April 1, 1994, Rex made $300,000 in unanticipated repairs to its plant equipment. The repairs will benefit operations for the remainder of the calendar year. What total amount of these expenses should be included in Rex's quarterly income statement for the three months ended June 30, 1994?

a. $75,000
b. $145,000
c. $195,000
d. $345,000

75. The summary of significant accounting policies should disclose the

a. Pro forma effect of retroactive application of an accounting change.
b. Basis of profit recognition on long-term construction contracts.
c. Adequacy of pension plan assets in relation to vested benefits.
d. Future minimum lease payments in the aggregate and for each of the five succeeding fiscal years.

76. Kent Co. incurred the following infrequent losses during 1998:

- A $300,000 loss was incurred on disposal of one of four dissimilar factories.
- A major currency devaluation caused a $120,000 exchange loss on an amount remitted by a foreign customer.
- Inventory valued at $190,000 was made worthless by a competitor's unexpected production innovation.

In its 1998 income statement, what amount should Kent report as losses that are **not** considered extraordinary?

a. $610,000
b. $490,000
c. $420,000
d. $310,000

77. Bolte Corp. had the following infrequent gains during 1996:

- $210,000 on reacquisition and retirement of bonds.
- $75,000 on repayment at maturity of a long-term note denominated in a foreign currency.
- $240,000 on sale of a plant facility (Bolte continues similar operations at another location.)

In its 1996 income statement, what amount should Bolte report as total infrequent gains which are **not** considered extraordinary?

a. $450,000
b. $315,000
c. $285,000
d. $240,000

78. A change in the periods benefited by a deferred cost because additional information has been obtained is

a. A correction of an error.
b. An accounting change that should be reported by restating the financial statements of all prior periods presented.
c. An accounting change that should be reported in the period of change and future periods if the change affects both.
d. Not an accounting change.

Items 79 and 80 are based on the following:
On January 1, 1997, Warren Co. purchased a $600,000 machine, with a five-year useful life and no salvage value. The machine was depreciated by an accelerated method for book and tax purposes. The machine's carrying amount was $240,000 on December 31, 1998. On January 1, 1999, Warren changed retroactively to the straight-line method for financial statement purposes. Warren can justify the change. Warren's income tax rate is 30%.

79. In its 1999 income statement, what amount should Warren report as the cumulative effect of this change?

a. $120,000
b. $84,000
c. $36,000
d. $0

80. On January 1, 1999, what amount should Warren report as deferred income tax liability as a result of the change?

a. $120,000
b. $72,000
c. $36,000
d. $0

---

81. Lex Corp. was a development stage enterprise from October 10, 1994, (inception) to December 31, 1995. The year ended December 31, 1996, is the first year in which Lex is an established operating enterprise. The following are among the costs incurred by Lex:

	For the period 10/10/94 to 12/31/95	*For the year ended 12/31/96*
Leasehold improvements, equipment, and furniture	$1,000,000	$ 300,000
Security deposits	60,000	30,000
Research and development	750,000	900,000
Laboratory operations	175,000	550,000
General and administrative	225,000	685,000
Depreciation	25,000	115,000
	$2,235,000	$2,580,000

From its inception through the period ended December 31, 1996, what is the total amount of costs incurred by Lex that should be charged to operations?

a. $3,425,000
b. $2,250,000
c. $1,175,000
d. $1,350,000

Items 82 and 83 are based on the following:
On December 31, 1999, the Board of Directors of Maxx Manufacturing, Inc. committed to a plan to discontinue the operations of its Alpha division in 2000. Maxx estimated that Alpha's 2000 operating loss would be $500,000 and that Alpha's facilities would be sold for $300,000 less than their carrying amounts. Alpha's 1999 operating loss was $1,400,000. Maxx's effective tax rate is 30%.

82. In its 1999 income statement, what amount should Maxx report as loss from discontinued operations?

a. $980,000
b. $1,330,000
c. $1,400,000
d. $1,900,000

83. In its 1999 income statement, what amount should Maxx report as loss on disposal of discontinued operations?

a. $210,000
b. $300,000
c. $560,000
d. $800,000

---

84. On January 1, 1995, Dart, Inc., entered into an agreement to sell the assets and product line of its Jay Division, considered a segment of the business. The sale was consummated on December 31, 1995, and resulted in a gain on disposition of $400,000. The division's operations resulted in losses before income tax of $225,000 in 1995 and $125,000 in 1994. Dart's income tax rate is 30% for both years. In a comparative statement of income for 1995 and 1994, as components under the caption Discontinued Operations, Dart should report a gain (loss) amounting to:

	1995	*1994*
a.	$122,500	($87,500)
b.	$122,500	$0
c.	($157,500)	($87,500)
d.	($157,500)	$0

85. Financial reporting by a development stage enterprise differs from financial reporting for an established operating enterprise in regard to footnote disclosures

a. Only.
b. And expense recognition principles only.
c. And revenue recognition principles only.
d. And revenue and expense recognition principles.

86. Which of the following statements is correct regarding accounting changes that result in financial statements that are, in effect, the statements of a different reporting entity?

a. Cumulative-effect adjustments should be reported as separate items on the financial statements pertaining to the year of change.
b. No restatements or adjustments are required if the changes involve consolidated methods of accounting for subsidiaries.
c. No restatements or adjustments are required if the changes involve the cost or equity methods of accounting for investments.
d. The financial statements of all prior periods presented should be restated.

87. On April 30, 1996, Carty Corp. approved a plan to dispose of a segment of its business. The estimated disposal loss is $480,000, including severance pay of $55,000 and employee relocation costs of $25,000, both of which are directly associated with the decision to dispose of the segment. Also included is the segment's estimated operating loss of $100,000 for the period from May 1, 1996, to the disposal date. A $120,000 operating loss from January 1, 1996, to April 30, 1996, is **not** included in the estimated disposal loss of $480,000. Before income taxes, what amount should be reported in Carty's income statement for the year ended December 31, 1996, as the loss from discontinued operations?

a. $600,000
b. $480,000
c. $455,000
d. $425,000

88. The following items were among those that were reported on Lee Co.'s income statement for the year ended December 31, 1996:

Legal and audit fees	$170,000
Rent for office space	240,000
Interest on inventory floor plan	210,000
Loss on abandoned data processing equipment used in operations	35,000

The office space is used equally by Lee's sales and accounting departments. What amount of the above-listed items should be classified as general and administrative expenses in Lee's multiple-step income statement?

a. $290,000
b. $325,000
c. $410,000
d. $500,000

RECENTLY RELEASED QUESTIONS

M97

89. How should the effect of a change in accounting principle that is inseparable from the effect of a change in accounting estimate be reported?

a. As a component of income from continuing operations.
b. By restating the financial statements of all prior periods presented.
c. As a correction of an error.
d. By footnote disclosure only.

M97

90. In September 1996, Koff Co.'s operating plant was destroyed by an earthquake. Earthquakes are rare in the area in which the plant was located. The portion of the resultant loss not covered by insurance was $700,000. Koff's income tax rate for 1996 is 40%. In its 1996 income statement, what amount should Koff report as extraordinary loss?

a. $0
b. $280,000
c. $420,000
d. $700,000

99

91. When a full set of general-purpose financial statements is presented, comprehensive income and its components should

a. Appear as a part of discontinued operations, extraordinary items, and cumulative effect of a change in accounting principle.
b. Be reported net of related income tax effect, in total and individually.
c. Appear in a supplemental schedule in the notes to financial statements.
d. Be displayed in a financial statement that has the same prominence as other financial statements.

92. Which of the following disclosures should prospective financial statements include?

	Summary of significant *accounting policies*	Summary of *significant assumptions*
a.	Yes	Yes
b.	Yes	No
c.	No	Yes
d.	No	No

99

93. At December 31, 1998, Off-Line Co. changed its method of accounting for demo costs from writing off the costs over two years to expensing the costs immediately. Off-Line made the change in recognition of an increasing number of demos placed with customers that did not result in sales. Off-Line had deferred demo costs of $500,000 at December 31, 1997, $300,000 of which were to be written off in 1998 and the remainder in 1999. Off-Line's income tax rate is 30%. In its 1998 income statement, what amount should Off-Line report as cumulative effect of change in accounting principle?

a. $140,000
b. $200,000
c. $350,000
d. $500,000

99

94. Casey Corporation entered into a troubled-debt restructuring agreement with First State Bank. First State agreed to accept land with a carrying amount of $85,000 and a fair value of $120,000 in exchange for a note with a carrying amount of $185,000. Disregarding income taxes, what amount should Casey report as extraordinary gain in its income statement?

a. $0
b. $35,000
c. $65,000
d. $100,000

95. Wilson Corp. experienced a $50,000 decline in the market value of its inventory in the first quarter of its fiscal year. Wilson had expected this decline to reverse in the third quarter, and in fact, the third quarter recovery exceeded the previous decline by $10,000. Wilson's inventory did not experience any other declines in market value during the fiscal year. What amounts of loss and/or gain should Wilson report in its interim financial statements for the first and third quarters?

	First quarter	*Third quarter*
a.	$0	$0
b.	$0	$10,000 gain
c.	$50,000 loss	$50,000 gain
d.	$50,000 loss	$60,000 gain

00

96. On February 2, Flint Corp's board of directors voted to discontinue operations of its frozen food division and to sell the division's assets on the open market as soon as possible. The division reported net operating losses of $20,000 in January and $30,000 in February. On February 26, sale of the division's assets resulted in a gain of $90,000. What amount of gain from disposal of a segment should Flint recognize in its income statement for the 3 months ended March 31?

a. $0
b. $40,000
c. $60,000
d. $90,000

00

97. Ace Corporation entered into a troubled-debt restructuring agreement with National Bank. National agreed to accept land with a carrying amount of $75,000 and a fair value of $100,000 in exchange for a note with a carrying amount of $150,000. Disregarding income taxes, what amount should Ace report as extraordinary gain in its income statement?

a. $0
b. $25,000
c. $50,000
d. $75,000

Chapter Twelve
Reporting the Results of Operations Problems

NUMBER 1

Number 1 consists of 8 items. Select the **best** answer for each item. **Items 1 through 8** are based on the following:

Pucket Corp. is in the process of preparing its financial statements for the year ended December 31, 1998. Items 1 through 8 represent various transactions or situations that occurred during 1998.

Required:
For items 1 through 8, select from the list of financial statement categories below the category in which the item should be presented. A financial statement category may be selected once, more than once, or not at all.

Financial Statement Categories:

a. Income from continuing operations, with **no** separate disclosure.
b. Income from continuing operations, with separate disclosure (either on the face of statement or in the notes).
c. Extraordinary items.
d. Separate component of stockholders' equity.
e. None of the above categories include this item.

Items to be answered:

1. An increase in the unrealized excess of cost over market value of short-term marketable equity securities.
2. An increase in the unrealized excess of cost over market value of long-term marketable equity securities.
3. Income from operations of a discontinued segment in the segment's disposal year, but before the measurement date.
4. A gain on remeasuring a foreign subsidiary's financial statements from the local currency into the functional currency.
5. A loss on translating a foreign subsidiary's financial statements from the functional local currency into the reporting currency.
6. A loss caused by a major earthquake in an area previously considered to be subject to only minor tremors.
7. The probable receipt of $1,000,000 from a pending lawsuit.
8. The purchase of research and development services. There were **no** other research and development activities.

NUMBER 2

The Century Company, a diversified manufacturing company, had four separate operating divisions engaged in the manufacture of products in each of the following areas: food products, health aids, textiles, and office equipment.

Financial data for the two years ended December 31, 1998, and 1997 are presented below:

	Net Sales		*Cost of Sales*		*Operating Expenses*	
	1998	1997	1998	1997	1998	1997
Food products	$3,500,000	$3,000,000	$2,400,000	$1,800,000	$ 550,000	$ 275,000
Health aids	2,000,000	1,270,000	1,100,000	700,000	300,000	125,000
Textiles	1,580,000	1,400,000	500,000	900,000	200,000	150,000
Office equipment	920,000	1,330,000	800,000	1,000,000	650,000	750,000
	$8,000,000	$7,000,000	$4,800,000	$4,400,000	$1,700,000	$1,300,000

On January 1, 1998, Century adopted a plan to sell the assets and product line of the office equipment division and expected to realize a gain on this disposal. On September 1, 1998, the division's assets and product line were sold for $2,100,000 cash resulting in a gain of $640,000 (exclusive of operations during the phase-out period).

The company's textiles division had six manufacturing plants which produced a variety of textile products. In April 1998, the company sold one of these plants and realized a gain of $130,000. After the sale, the operations at the plant that was sold were transferred to the remaining five textile plants which the company continued to operate.

In August 1998, the main warehouse of the food products division, located on the banks of the Bayer River, was flooded when the river overflowed. The resulting damage of $420,000 is not included in the financial data given above. Historical records indicate that the Bayer River normally overflows every four to five years causing flood damage to adjacent property.

For the two years ended December 31, 1998 and 1997, the company had interest revenue earned on investments of $70,000 and $40,000 respectively.

For the two years ended December 31, 1998 and 1997, the company's net income was $1,344,000 and $938,000 respectively.

The provision for income tax expense for each of the two years should be computed at a rate of 30%.

Required:
Prepare in proper form a comparative statement of income of the Century Company for the two years ended December 31, 1998, and December 31, 1997. Footnotes are **not** required.

NUMBER 3

The following condensed trial balance of Powell Corp., a publicly-owned company, has been adjusted except for income tax expense:

Powell Corp.
CONDENSED TRIAL BALANCE
June 30, 1999

	Debit	*Credit*
Total assets	$25,080,000	
Total liabilities		$ 9,900,000
5% cumulative preferred stock		1,970,000
Common stock		10,000,000
Retained earnings		2,900,000
Machine sales		750,000
Service revenues		250,000
Interest revenue		10,000
Gain on sale of factory		250,000
Foreign currency translation adjustments		30,000
Cost of sales - machines	425,000	
Cost of services	100,000	
Administrative expenses	300,000	
Research and development expenses	110,000	
Interest expense	5,000	
Loss from asset disposal	40,000	
	$26,060,000	$26,060,000

Other information and financial data for the year ended June 30, 1999, follows:

- The weighted average number of common shares outstanding during 1999 was 200,000. The potential dilution from the exercise of stock options held by Powell's officers and directors was not material.
- There were no dividends-in-arrears on Powell's preferred stock at July 1, 1998. On May 1, 1999, Powell's directors declared a 5% preferred stock dividend to be paid in August 1999.
- During 1999, one of Powell's foreign factories was expropriated by the foreign government, and Powell received a $900,000 payment from the foreign government in settlement. The carrying value of the plant was $650,000. Powell has never disposed of a factory.
- Administrative expensed includes a $5,000 premium payment for a $1,000,000 life insurance policy on Powell's president, of which the corporation is the beneficiary.
- Powell depreciates its assets using the straight-line method for financial reporting purposes and an accelerated method for tax purposes. The differences between book and tax depreciation are as follows:

June 30	*Financial statements over (under) tax depreciation*
1999	$(15,000)
2000	10,000
2001	5,000

There were no other temporary differences.

- Powell's enacted tax rate for the current and future years is 30%. Powell elected early application of FASB Statement No. 109, *Accounting for Income Taxes.*

Required:

a. Prepare a combined single-step income statement and statement of comprehensive income for the year ended June 30, 1999.

b. Prepare a schedule reconciling Powell's financial statement net income to taxable income for the year ended June 30, 1999.

NUMBER 4

The following pro forma statement of income and changes in equity accounts was prepared by the newly-hired staff accountant of Topaz, Inc., a nonpublic company, for the year ended December 31, 1995.

Topaz, Inc.
STATEMENT OF INCOME AND CHANGES IN RETAINED EARNINGS
December 31, 1995

Revenues and gains
Gross sales
Purchase discounts
Recovery of accounts receivable written off in prior years
Interest revenue
Gain on early extinguishment of debt
Total revenues and gains

Expenses and losses
Cost of goods sold
Sales returns and allowances
Selling expenses
General and Administrative expenses
Cash dividends declared
Total expenses and losses
Income before discontinued operations and extraordinary item

Discontinued operations
Loss on disposal of discontinued styles, net of tax effect

Extraordinary item
Correction of errors in prior years' statements, net of tax effect

Retained earnings at beginning of year
Income taxes
Net income

Additional information
- Topaz uses the allowance method to account for uncollectible accounts.
- The loss on disposal of discontinued styles resulted from the sale of outdated styles within a product line.
- Topaz had no temporary tax differences at the beginning or the end of the year.

Required:
Identify the weaknesses in classification and presentation in the above Statement of Income and Changes in Retained Earnings. Explain the proper classification and presentation. **Do not prepare a corrected statement.**

NUMBER 5

The following condensed trial balance of Probe Co., a publicly-held company, has been adjusted except for income tax expense.

Probe Co.

CONDENSED TRIAL BALANCE

	12/31/00 Balances Dr. (Cr.)	*12/31/99 Balances Dr. (Cr.)*	*Net change Dr. (Cr.)*
Cash	$ 493,000	$ 817,000	$ (344,000)
Accounts receivable, net	670,000	610,000	60,000
Property, plant, and equipment	1,070,000	995,000	75,000
Accumulated depreciation	(345,000)	(280,000)	(65,000)
Dividends payable	(25,000)	(10,000)	(15,000)
Income taxes payable	35,000	(150,000)	185,000
Deferred income tax liability	(42,000)	(42,000)	--
Bonds payable	(500,000)	(1,000,000)	500,000
Unamortized premium on bonds	(71,000)	(150,000)	79,000
Common stock	(350,000)	(150,000)	(200,000)
Additional paid-in capital	(430,000)	(375,000)	(55,000)
Retained earnings	(185,000)	(265,000)	80,000
Sales	(2,420,000)		
Cost of sales	1,863,000		
Selling and administrative expenses	220,000		
Interest income	(14,000)		
Interest expense	46,000		
Depreciation	88,000		
Loss on sale of equipment	7,000		
Gain on extinguishment of bonds	(90,000)		
Unrealized holding gain on Available-For-Sale securities	(20,000)		
	$ 0	$ 0	$300,000

Additional information:

- During 2000 equipment with an original cost of $50,000 was sold for cash, and equipment costing $125,000 was purchased.
- On January 1, 2000, bonds with a par value of $500,000 and related premium of $75,000 were redeemed. The $1,000 face value, 10% par bonds had been issued on January 1, 2001, to yield 8%. Interest is payable annually every December 31 through 2010.
- Probe's tax payments during 2000 were debited to Income Taxes Payable. Probe elected early adoption of Statement of Financial Accounting Standards No. 109, *Accounting for Income Taxes*, for the year ended December 31, 1999, and recorded a deferred income tax liability of $42,000 based on temporary differences of $120,000 and an enacted tax rate of 35%. Probe's 2000 financial statement income before income taxes was greater than its 2000 taxable income, due entirely to temporary differences, by $60,000. Probe's cumulative net taxable temporary differences at December 31, 2000, were $180,000. Probe's enacted tax rate for the current and future years is 30%.
- 60,000 shares of common stock, $2.50 par, were outstanding on December 31, 1999. Probe issued an additional 80,000 shares on April 1, 2000.
- There were no changes to retained earnings other than dividends declared.

Required: Prepare a combined multiple-step income statement and statement of comprehensive income for the year ended December 31, 2000, with earnings per share information and supporting computations for current and deferred income tax expense.

NUMBER 6

Interim financial reporting has become an important topic in accounting. There has been considerable discussion as to the proper method of reflecting results of operations at interim dates. Accordingly, the Accounting Principles Board issued an opinion clarifying some aspects of interim financial reporting.

Required:

a. Discuss generally how revenue should be recognized at interim dates and specifically how revenue should be recognized for industries subject to large seasonal fluctuations in revenue and for long-term contracts using the percentage-of-completion method at annual reporting dates.

b. Discuss generally how product and period costs should be recognized at interim dates. Also discuss how inventory and cost of goods sold may be afforded special accounting treatment at interim dates.

c. Discuss how the provision for income taxes is computed and reflected in interim financial statements.

NUMBER 7

Hillside Company had a loss during the year ended December 31, 1995, that is properly reported as an extraordinary item.

On July 1, 1995, Hillside committed itself to a formal plan for sale of a business segment. A loss is expected from the proposed sale. Segment operating losses were incurred continuously throughout 1995, and were expected to continue until final disposition in 1996. Costs were incurred in 1995 to relocate segment employees.

Required:

a. How should Hillside report the extraordinary item in its income statement? Why?

b. How should Hillside report the effect of the discontinued operations in its 1995 income statement?

c. How should Hillside report the costs that were incurred to relocate employees of the discontinued segment? Why?

Do not discuss earnings per share requirements.

NUMBER 8

Question 8 consists of 10 items. Select the **best** answer for each item. **Answer all items.**
On January 2, 2000, Quo, Inc. hired Reed to be its controller. During the year, Reed, working closely with Quo's president and outside accountants, made changes in accounting policies, corrected several errors dating from 1999 and before, and instituted new accounting policies.

Quo's 2000 financial statements will be presented in comparative form with its 1999 financial statements.

Required:

Items 1 through 10 represent Quo's transactions. List A represents possible classifications of these transactions as: a change in accounting principle, a change in accounting estimate, a correction of an error in previously presented financial statements, or neither an accounting change nor an accounting error.

List B represents the general accounting treatment required for these transactions. These treatments are:

- Cumulative effect approach - Include the cumulative effect of the adjustment resulting from the accounting change or error correction in the 2000 financial statements, and do **not** restate the 1999 financial statements.
- Retroactive restatement approach - Restate the 1999 financial statements and adjust 1999 beginning retained earnings if the error or change affects a period prior to 1999.
- Prospective approach - Report 2000 and future financial statements on the new basis, but **do not** restate 1999 financial statements.

For each item, select one from List A and one from List B.

	List A (*Select one*)		List B (*Select one*)
A.	Change in accounting principle.	X.	Cumulative effect approach.
B.	Change in accounting estimate.	Y.	Retroactive restatement approach.
C.	Correction of an error in previously presented financial statements.	Z.	Prospective approach.
D.	Neither an accounting change not an accounting error.		

Items to be answered:

1. Quo manufactures heavy equipment to customer specifications on a contract basis. On the basis that it is preferable, accounting for these long-term contracts was switched from the completed-contract method to the percentage-of-completion method.
2. As a result of a production breakthrough, Quo determined that manufacturing equipment previously depreciated over 15 years should be depreciated over 20 years.
3. The equipment that Quo manufactures is sold with a five-year warranty. Because of a production breakthrough, Quo reduced its computation of warranty costs from 3% of sales to 1% of sales.
4. Quo changed from LIFO to FIFO to account for its finished goods inventory.
5. Quo changed form FIFO to average cost to account for its raw materials and work in process inventories.
6. Quo sells extended service contracts on its products. Because related services are performed over several years, in 2000 Quo changed from the cash method to the accrual method of recognizing income from these service contracts.
7. During 2000, Quo determined that an insurance premium paid and entirely expensed in 1999 was for the period January 1, 1999, through January 1, 2001.
8. Quo changed its method of depreciating office equipment from an accelerated method to the straight-line method to more closely reflect costs in later years.
9. Quo instituted a pension plan for all employees in 2000 and adopted Statement of Financial Accounting Standards No. 87, *Employers' Accounting for Pensions.* Quo had not previously had a pension plan.
10. During 2000, Quo increased its investment in Worth, Inc. from a 10% interest, purchased in 1999, to 30%, and acquired a seat on Worth's board of directors. As a result of its increased investment, Quo changed its method of accounting for investment in subsidiary from the cost method to the equity method.

Chapter Twelve
Solutions to Reporting the Results of Operations Questions

1. (a) The solutions approach is to use a "T" account and solve for the missing number.

Finish Goods Inventory

Beginning Inventory	400,000	Cost of Goods Sold	240,000
Cost of Goods Mfg.	200,000		
Available for Sale	600,000		
Ending Inventory	360,000		

2. (c) The solutions approach would be to subtract the extraordinary item loss on early retirement of long-term debt ($20,000) from the debit column and adjust the debit balance to $400,000. Then combine the debit and credit balances to calculate income from continuing operations before tax of $200,000 ($600,000 – 400,000). Income from continuing operations after taxes would then be $140,000 ($200,000 – 60,000 tax).

3. (a) Selling expenses include:

Advertising	$150,000
Freight-out	80,000
Rent (½)	110,000
Sales salaries and commissions	140,000
Total	$480,000

4. (d) In a single-step income statement, revenues include sales as well as miscellaneous income:

Sales	$187,000
Interest	10,200
Gain	4,700
Total	$201,900

The discontinued operations and the cumulative effect of the accounting change are reported below income from continuing operations..

5. (a) All activities which take place after the measurement date, September 30, 1996, are reported as part of the disposal under discontinued operations. The operating results from January 1 until September 30, 1996, would be reported as an operating loss of a discontinued segment.

6. (a) The anticipated 1998 gain is recognized only to the extent of the loss on disposal (from operations in December 1997) since the gain is not realized in 1997. Therefore the *net* gain recognized from disposal in 1997 is zero.

7. (b) The discontinued operations portion of the income statement consists of two sections: the income/loss up to the measurement date (January 1 to October 31, 1999) and the gain/loss on disposal. In this case Smith Co. has a loss on disposal. APB #30 requires that the loss on disposal include the anticipated losses during the phase-out period (November 1, 1999 to February 28, 2000) plus the expected loss on final disposition.

8. (d) A gain on the disposal of a segment of the business is generally recognized only when realized. However, such gain can be recognized to the extent of operating losses after the measurement date. Transactions after the measurement are projected as follows:

Results of operations ($100,000 – $50,000)	$ 50,000
Loss on sale of assets	(375,000)
Net loss on disposal	$325,000
Less taxes—30%	97,500
Net loss on disposal	$227,500

9. (a) Loss after the measurement date:

Losses on sale ($500,000 – $850,000)	$350,000
Disposal costs	75,000
Operating losses (after 5/15/96)	65,000
Loss on disposal	$490,000

10. (c) Greer Co. recognizes the operating loss of $300,000 in 1997 under "Discontinued Operations" but does not recognize the net gain on disposal since the gain has not yet been realized. In 1998, the actual gain of $650,000 less the 1998 operating loss of $300,000 is reported as net gain on disposal of the segment under "Discontinued Operations" for the net amount of $350,000.

11. (a) The cumulative effect of a change in accounting principle is calculated at the beginning of the period of the change (APB #20).

12. (c) The cumulative effect is the difference in the asset account after the income tax impact.
$700,000 – ($700,000 × .3) = $490,000.

13. (b) The cumulative effect is reported net of taxes in the income statement:

Difference in accumulated depreciation at 1/1/97	$140,000
Income tax effect at 30%	42,000
Cumulative effect of the change	$ 98,000

Since the change was from an accelerated method to straight-line, the accumulated depreciation account is reduced and income is increased (credit).

14. (d)

	Carrying Value	Accumulated Depreciation
Cost 1/2/96	$264,000	
Depreciation 1996-1998 $264 / 8 yrs. × 3 yrs.	(99,000)	$ 99,000
Carrying value 1/2/99	$165,000	
Depreciation - 1999		
$\frac{\$165,000 - 24,000}{3 \text{ years}}$	(47,000)	47,000
Balance 12/31/99	$118,000	$146,000

15. (c) This is a special change in accounting principle requiring restatement of prior years being reported. The cumulative effect of the change is therefore credited to retained earnings (APB #20) net of the income tax effect.

16. (a) Generally the cumulative effect net of taxes of a change in accounting principle is shown on the income statement after the extraordinary items section. APB #20 provides an exception to this general rule for certain changes in accounting principles. The two most common examples of this exception are a change from LIFO to another inventory method and a change in the accounting for long-term contracts. In this case the change from LIFO to FIFO is an exception and should be accounted for by restating all prior periods' financial statements to reflect the change.

17. (a) The cumulative effect of the change is shown as a component of income, net of tax, after income from continuing operations for changes in accounting principle. Only item (a) is such a change. Items (b) and (c) are special changes in accounting principle requiring the cumulative effect to be reported as an adjustment to "Retained Earnings." Item (d) is the correction of an error.

18. (d) The cumulative effect of changing from LIFO is a special change and is reported in the statement of retained earnings. The change from FIFO is reported after any extraordinary items in the income statement.

19. (d) A change in the expected service life of an asset is a change in accounting estimate which does not require either of the two items as shown. Both of the items in the question are required for a change in accounting principle, not a change in estimate.

20. (c) The change in the estimated quantity of copper recoverable from a mine is a change in accounting **estimate** and should be accounted for in current and future periods. The cumulative effect and pro forma effects are used for changes in accounting principles and would not be appropriate for a change in estimate.

21. (b)

Cost of the asset 1/1/93	$100,000
Depreciation, 1993-1996:	
$90,000/10 × 4 =	36,000
Carrying value 12/31/96	$ 64,000
Depreciation for 1997:	
$64,000 – $4,000 = $60,000 ÷ 4	15,000
Carrying value 12/31/97	$ 49,000

22. (a) The change in the estimate for warranty costs is based on new information obtained from experience and qualifies as a change in accounting estimate. A change in accounting estimate affects current and future periods and is not accounted for by restating prior periods. The accounting change is a part of continuing operations but is not reported net of taxes.

23. (c) This is a change in accounting entity which requires restatement of prior periods being presented.

24. (d) The change is a change in accounting entity which reports the new group of companies as if the same group was the reporting entity in the past. Therefore, prior period statements are restated and retained earnings is adjusted for the differential.

25. (a) A change in accounting entity is "one special type of change in accounting principle" (APB Opinion No. 20, paragraph no. 12).

26. (a) See comprehensive income statement p. 12-1.

27. (b) An extraordinary item is reported net of tax **after** income from discontinued operations.

28. (a) An extraordinary item is reported net of tax in its entirety in the quarterly period in which it occurs.

29. (d) FASB #4 requires that gains and losses from extinguishment of debt be reported as extraordinary items. In this case the extraordinary item will be a loss because Somar issued the bonds at a discount but retired them at a price (105) in excess of the face value of the bonds.

30. (a) Extraordinary items are transactions that are **both** unusual in nature and infrequent in occurrence. Neither the loss on foreign currency or the discontinued operations loss would be considered unusual or infrequent. Since the hurricane is the first ever to strike the Midway's area, it should be an extraordinary item. The pretax loss would be $100,000 (equipment loss $800,000 minus $700,000 building gain).

31. (a) A transaction which is infrequent but does not qualify as extraordinary is reported separately in the income statement whether it is a gain or loss.

32. (b) The insurance premiums of $60,000 were charged in error to insurance expense on the 1998 income statements. The premiums should have been allocated equally at $20,000 per year for 1998, 1999, and 2000. Therefore, the beginning retained earnings at 1999 are understated by $28,000 - the effect of the error ($40,000) less the $12,000 tax effect ($40,000 × 30%). The corrected retained earnings would be the beginning balance plus the correction of the error ($400,000 + 28,000 = $428,000).

33. (c) The failure to accrue warranty costs of $50,000 in 1999 is an accounting error that was discovered in 2000. Since the error affected the income statement of 1999, it is considered a prior period adjustment. The change in depreciation method is a change in accounting principle and is the type of change that should be reported on the 2000 income statement.

34. (b) A prior-period adjustment is the correction of an error made in a prior period by reporting the adjustment net of tax in the statement of retained earnings. A change from an unaccepted accounting principle to an acceptable accounting principle is such a transaction. A change in the estimated lives of depreciable assets is a change in estimate, not a prior period adjustment.

35. (b) Per APB 22, Par. 8, disclosure of significant accounting policies should be included as an integral part of the financial statements.

36. (c) Neither the composition of inventories nor the maturity of debt is a significant accounting policy with existing acceptable alternatives. These disclosures should be provided in later footnotes but not as part of the footnote which discloses the summary of significant accounting policies.

37. (b) Inventory pricing is a significant accounting policy which should be disclosed according to APB Opinion #22 but the composition of plant assets is not a policy disclosure.

38. (c) Gains and losses are generally recognized in the quarter in which they are transacted, not allocated to other interim quarters.

39. (a) The gross-profit method of inventory pricing is acceptable for interim reporting per APB 28, par. 14(a).
(b) Direct costing is never an acceptable method for financial reporting, because it excludes fixed manufacturing overhead in determining inventories.
(c) Planned variances that are expected to be absorbed by the end of the annual period should be deferred, but unplanned variances should be reported at the end of the interim period. APB 28, 14(d).
(d) Inventory market declines should not be deferred unless they are temporary and no loss is expected to be incurred. APB 28, Par. 14(c).

40. (b) The extraordinary loss is reported in the quarter in which it is transacted. The insurance expense is an anticipated expense and is allocated to each quarter of the year.

41. (b) The company should use the effective tax rate expected to be applicable for the full year of 1999 as estimated at the end of the second quarter of 1999 because the interim period is considered an integral part of the accounting year.

42. (c) Tech's first quarter taxes would be calculated using the expected 2000 effective annual rate of 25%. The tax expense would be $50,000 ($200,000 × 25%).

43. (a) The inventory decline in the first quarter should be recognized in that quarter because at that point it was the company's judgment that the decline was not expected to reverse during the fiscal year. However, the decline was recovered in the third quarter. In that case the recovery recognized is limited to the amount of the decrease in the first quarter. To do otherwise would violate the cost principle for inventory.

44. (d) It was Petal's best estimate at the end of the second quarter that the decline in market price was temporary and would be restored by the end of the year. In that case the inventory loss was not recognized in the second quarter. Since the price decline had not been restored by the end of the year, the loss would have to be recognized in the fourth quarter.

45. (b)		
	Liability balance on 12/31/92 =	$800,000
	Accrued interest	80,000
	Total carrying value	$880,000
	Future cash payments	780,000
	Gain	$100,000
	Net of tax =	$ 60,000

46. (d)		
	Carrying value of obligation	$500,000
	Plus accrued interest	75,000
		$575,000
	Fair market value of assets sacrificed	
	($375,000 + $50,000)	425,000
	Gain	$150,000

47. (b) The extinguishment in a troubled situation is classified as an extraordinary gain for the difference between the fair value of the equity interest and the carrying value of the liability.

48. (a) An ordinary loss of $5,000 should be recognized to reduce the equipment from its carrying value of $80,000 to the fair market value of $75,000. Kam Corp. should recognize an extraordinary pre-tax gain of $25,000 because it was able to pay a $100,000 note by giving Finn Co. computer equipment with a fair market value of only $75,000. The extraordinary gain should be reported at $17,500 which is after taxes of 30% ($25,000 × 70%).

49. (c) A development stage enterprise generally presents the same financial statements as an established enterprise with an income statement for the current period as well as from inception.

50. (a) A development stage enterprise generally uses the same GAAP as an established company.

51. (b) As with any company, deficits are reported as a negative component of stockholders' equity.

52. (d) Since developmental stage enterprises follow GAAP, the answer is not affected by the fact that Tanker Oil Co. is in the developmental stage. Legal fees for incorporation and other related matters are normally part of the organizational cost because they are necessary cost of getting the organization started. Underwriters' fees for initial stock offering are usually treated as reductions in paid-in capital and exploration costs and purchase of mineral rights are considered to be costs of the natural resource.

53. (d) Pear's 40% interest in Cinn's common stock implies that Pear has significant influence over Cinn and should account its investment and earnings on the equity basis. Therefore, the equity in earnings of Cinn Co. is properly included on the income statement but the dividends received from Cinn should be a reduction of the investment and excluded from the income statement. The arithmetical errors are prior period adjustments and should be shown as deductions from beginning retained earnings in the statement of retained earnings. The adjusted 1999 income before taxes is computed below:

Controller's income	$125,000
Less dividend received	(8,000)
Plus errors	35,000
Correct income	$152,000

54. (c) The key point to recognize is that all changes in accounting principle are effective as of the beginning of the year. Therefore, the gross effect of the change in the January 1, 2001 balances would be $6,000 ($77,000 - 71,000). The cumulative effect of the change to be reported on income statement is gross change less the tax effect:

$6,000 - ($6,000 × 30%) = $4,200.

55. (d) The requirement is to determine the **placement** of the cumulative effect of a change in accounting principle on the income statement. The abbreviation for December (DEC) is a useful acronym for remembering the order of the lower sections of the income statement: D = Discontinued Operations; E = Extraordinary items; and C = Change in Accounting Principle. Therefore, the answer to the question is that the change in accounting principle would be **after** the extraordinary items.

56. (b) The measurement date is January 2000. Therefore, the gain on disposal is the net of the operating losses during the phase-out period of $650,000 ($600,000 for 2000 and $50,000 for January 2001) vs. the gain on the sale of $900,000 for a net gain of $250,000. Since conservatism dictates that gains not be anticipated, none of the gain is recognized in 2000 and the net gain is recognized in 2001.

57. (a) Interim Statements are affected by estimates, cost allocations, seasonality and other factors which may affect the usefulness of the information. Therefore, the emphasis on timeliness over reliability.

58. (c) FASB #95 on Cash Flows requires the disclosure as a part of significant accounting policies of a firm's policy for determining which investments are considered cash equivalents.

59. (a)

Contributed to youth and education programs	$250,000
Company's share - share of contribution to the Health and Human-service organizations = $140,000 – 80,000	60,000
Total charitable contribution expense	$310,000

60. (d) Since interest expense is not an operating expense, it should be shown on the income statement as a part of **Other Expenses and Losses.** On a multi-step income statement the operating expenses are split between selling expenses and general and administrative expenses. The advertising expense would be considered a selling expense and not a general and administrative expense.

61. (b) The general rule for the calculation of the gain or loss on the disposal of a segment is to take the income or loss during the phase out period and add or subtract the gain or loss on the sale of the segment. The calculation becomes more complicated when the time from the measurement date (October 1) through the phase out period to the disposal date (April 1) covers more than one calendar year. In this case the "single transaction" theory is used and disposal is viewed one transaction occurring in 2001. Under this approach the $600,000 ($200,000 + $400,000) loss during the phase out period is netted against the estimated gain on sale ($350,000) and a $250,000 loss on disposal before taxes is calculated. The gain on the sale may be used to offset anticipated losses but if the gain exceeds losses, conservatism would require that the net gain be recognized in 2002.

62. (d) The key point is that these are two separate transactions and should not be netted as one transaction. FASB #4 requires that the gain on the extinguishment of debt be classified as an extraordinary item. The loss on the investment in bonds does not meet the criteria of unusual and infrequent to be classified as extraordinary and should be considered a part of income before extraordinary items.

63. (a) The change from cash basis which is not GAAP to accrual basis which is GAAP is a correction of an error and should be reported as a prior period adjustment net of taxes.

64. (a)

Carrying value of receivable 12/31/93 =	$864,000
Future cash receipts: $60,000 + 60,000 + 600,000 =	720,000
Loss from restructuring	$144,000

65. (c)

Calculation of Accumulated Depreciation - January 2, 1999

	Straight-line Method	Units-of-Production Method
1997 Depreciation		
a. Straight-line method $50,000 / 10 years	$ 5,000	
b. Units-of-Production 3500 hours × $1 per hour*		$ 3,500
1998 Depreciation		
a. Straight-line method	5,000	
b. Units-of-Production 8500 hours × $1 per hour*	______	8,500
Total accumulated depreciation 1/2/99	$10,000	$12,000

The difference between the accumulated depreciation using the units-of-production method versus the straight-line method times the tax rate should be reported as the change in accounting principle on the 1999 income statement

$12,000 – 10,000 = $2,000 × 40% = $1,400

* The depreciation per machine hour is the cost of the machine divided by the estimated total usage in machine hours ($50,000 / 50,000 machine hours = $1 per machine hour).

66. (a) The cumulative effect reported on the income statement represents the adjustment at the beginning of the year as if the weighted average method had been used in prior periods. For inventory, this amount is the difference in the beginning of the year balances—$5,000.

67. (c) The depreciation method is one of several alternatives and is therefore included in the summary of significant accounting policies. The composition of fixed assets is included in a separate footnote but not in the summary of significant accounting policies.

68. (c) The singular feature of APB 22 is that it applies to not-for-profit entities.

69. (b) The amortization for prior years, $40,000, should be debited to retained earnings as a prior period adjustment and the current year's amortization, $20,000, should be charged to expense.

70. (c) The future cash payment of $980,000 is $60,000 less than the carrying value of the note and the accrued interest. This amount is recognized as a gain.

71. (a)

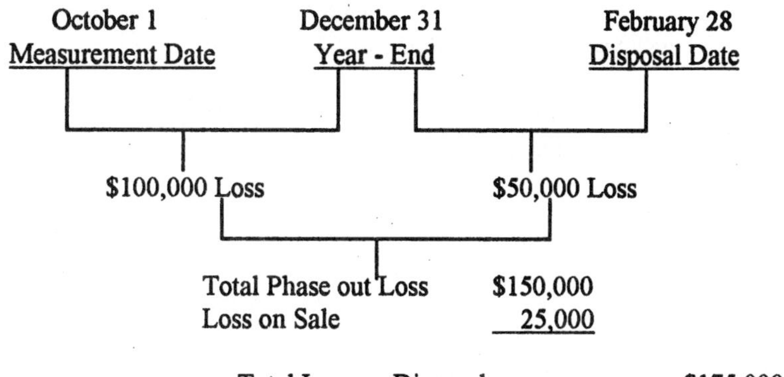

Total Loss on Disposal $175,000

The key point is to view the disposal as a "single transaction" occurring on the October 1, 2000 measurement date. Therefore, in this case all actual and anticipated losses would be recognized in 2000.

72. (d)

Increase in prepaid insurance in 1997 ($122,500 – $105,000)	$ 17,500
Expense recognized in 1997	+ 437,500
Total premiums paid in 1997	$455,000

73. (c) Both depreciation and bonuses are anticipated, recurring expenses which should be allocated to each interim period.

Expense for the year	$180,000
1/2 for six months ended 6/30/96	90,000

74. (b) Property taxes—anticipated recurring expenses—allocated equally to all four quarters—$180,000 ÷ 4 = $45,000 per quarter.
Repairs—unanticipated expense allocated to remaining quarters—$300,000 ÷ 3 = $100,000.
Total expenses allocated to the second quarter = $145,000.

75. (b) The summary of significant accounting policies should include alternative acceptable accounting policies such as either percentage of completion or completed contract for long-term construction contracts. The other alternative answers relate to specific disclosures to be made in separate footnotes.

76. (a) None of the transactions are classified as extraordinary since they all relate to operational activities or assets and cannot be considered to be unusual.

77. (b) The $210,000 gain is extraordinary whether infrequent or not. The $75,000 gain due to translation and the $240,000 gain on disposal of plant are not unusual and do not qualify as extraordinary.

78. (c) The described change is a change in estimate which is prospective in nature affecting the reporting of only current and future periods.

79. (b) The accumulated depreciation at January 2, 1999 using the accelerated method is the cost of the machine ($600,000) less the book value $240,000 which equals $360,000. The accumulated depreciation for 1997 and 1998 under the straight-line method would be the cost of $600,000 × 2/5 = $240,000. Therefore, the total (gross) effect of the change is the difference in the accumulated depreciations ($360,000 – $240,000 = $120,000). The tax effect is $36,000 (30% × $120,000). APB #20 requires that the cumulative effect of the change that is reported on the income statement be net of taxes. So, the amount reported should be $84,000, the total change ($120,000) minus the tax effect ($36,000).

80. (c) Since the change in accounting principle is for book purposes but not for tax purposes, the effect is to create a temporary difference in taxes which is reflected as a deferred tax liability of $36,000. The journal entry is as follows:

Accumulated depreciation	$120,000	
Cumulative effect of a change in accounting principles		$ 84,000
Deferred tax liability		$ 36,000

81. (a) As with any company, the operating expenses include research and development costs, laboratory operations, general and administrative and depreciation expenses.

82. (a) The discontinued operations section of the income statement consists of two parts: income (loss) from operations up to the measurement date of the discontinued segment and gain (loss) on disposal. In this case the question relates to the first part of the discontinued operations section. The measurement date is December 31, 1999, so the amount reported would be the 1999 operating loss net of taxes:

$1,400,000 – (30% × $1,400,000) = $980,000 loss

83. (c) The loss on disposal of a discontinued segment consists of two parts: The income (loss) during the phase-out period plus/minus the gain (loss) on the sale of the discontinued operation. If the disposal does not occur until the following year and the disposal results in a loss, the loss must be recognized in the year in which a formal commitment was made to sell the segment. In this case the formal commitment was made on December 31, 1999 (the measurement date) and the loss on disposal should be recognized in 1999. The loss on disposal should include the loss during phase-out (2000 loss of $500,000) plus the loss on the sale ($300,000) reported net of tax:

$800,000 – (30% × $800,000) = $560,000 loss

84. (a) The results of operations for the prior year, 1994, would be recharacterized when that year is reported in comparison with 1995 as operations from a discontinued segment. Therefore, the 1994 net operating loss of $87,500 ($125,000 – $37,500 tax) is reported under discontinued operations in 1995.

The 1995 operating loss and gain on disposal are all part of discontinued operations and would be reported net of tax as follows:

Gain on sale	$400,000
Operating loss	(225,000)
Net gain	$175,000
Income tax effect at 30%	(52,500)
Net gain from discontinued operations	$122,500

85. (a) GAAP is no different for development stage enterprises than for operating companies. Development stage enterprises do present additional disclosures and reporting periods in the financial statements.

86. (d) A change in reporting entity is accounted for by restating the financial statements of a prior period presented. A change in reporting entity is considered a special type of change in accounting principle.

87. (a) The loss from discontinued operations includes both the $480,000 loss on disposal and the $120,000 loss from operations prior to the measurement date.

88. (a) General and administrative expenses include:

Legal and audit fees	$170,000
Rent for office space (½)	120,000
Total	$290,000

The interest and the loss would be reported as other (non-operating) items in a multiple-step income statement.

89. (a) A change in accounting principle that is inseparable from a change in accounting estimate is accounted for as **change in accounting estimate (APB #30).** A change in accounting estimate affects current and future periods and is reported in the continuing operations sections of the income statement.

90. (c) APB #30 states that a transaction that is both unusual in nature and infrequent in occurrence is an extraordinary item. Since the question indicates that earthquakes are rare in the area in which Koff's plant is located, this would be considered an extraordinary item. The extraordinary item is reported as the gross amount of the loss of $700,000 less the 40% tax effect of $280,000 for a net extraordinary item of $420,000.

91. (d) SFAS 130 does not require a single display presentation for elements of comprehensive income and the total of comprehensive income, but it does require that these items be presented in a financial statement that is displayed with the same prominence as other financial statements, which together constitute a full set of financial statements.

92. (a) Standards for Attestation Engagements #200 requires the following disclosures:

Prospective Financial Statements:

- **Include**
  a. Financial forecast
  b. Financial projections
  c. Summaries of significant assumptions*
  d. Accounting policies*
- **Exclude**
  a. Pro forma financial statements
  b. Partial presentations
  c. Financial statements for periods that have expired
  d. Statements used solely in support service litigation

93. (c) The cumulative effect of a change in accounting principle is always computed at the beginning of the year of the change:

January 1, 1998 Balance	$500,000	
Less the tax effect of 30%	(150,000)	
Net effect of the change on the 1998 Income Statement		$350,000

94. (c) The extraordinary gain on Casey Corp.'s books is the difference between the carrying value of the note ($185,000) and fair value/the land ($120,000) for a gain of $65,000.

Note: Casey would adjust the carrying value of the land from $85,000 to the fair value of $120,000 and recognize an ordinary gain of $35,000.

95. (a) For interim statements (not year-end statements) a company may use its judgment in recording a quarterly decline in the market value of its inventory. In this case, Wilson correctly used its judgment by not recording the loss in the first quarter and then recording a gain in the third quarter for the market recovery.

96. (c) The gain from disposal of a business segment is the gain on the sale of $90,000 less the operating loss during the phase-out period $30,000 for a net gain of $60,000. The phase-out period is the time frame from the measurement date February 2nd until the disposal date of February 26.

97. (c) The extraordinary gain is the carrying value of the note ($150,000) less the fair value of the land ($100,000) for a net gain of $50,000. The journal entry to adjust the land to its fair value would result in an ordinary gain of $25,000.

Chapter Twelve
Solutions to Reporting the Results of Operations Problems

NUMBER 1

1. (b) An increase in the unrealized excess of cost over market value of short-term marketable equity securities (unrealized loss on **current** marketable equity securities) should be included in income from continuing operations. In addition FASB #12 requires separate disclosure (either on the face of the statement or in the notes) of the change in the valuation allowance.

2. (d) An increase in the unrealized excess of cost over market value of long-term marketable equity securities (unrealized loss on **long-term** marketable securities) should be included in the stockholders' equity section of the balance sheet. FASB #12 requires separate disclosure of the change in the valuation allowance.

3. (e) Income from discontinued segment consist of two sections: income from discontinued operations up to the measurement date and gain/loss on disposal. In this case the problem is referring to part one of the discontinued operations portion of the income statement. Discontinued operations are located on the income statement between continuing operations and extraordinary items.

4. (b) The key word is "remeasuring". Remeasuring means that the functional currency is not the local currency. A gain on remeasuring a foreign subsidiary's financial statements from the local currency into the functional currency is reported as a part of continuing operations. Separate disclosure should be made for the aggregate gain or loss for the period.

5.(d) The key word is "translating". In translating a foreign subsidiary's financial statements (the local currency is the functional currency), the translation loss adjustment is reported as a separate component of stockholders' equity.

6. (c) Extraordinary items are transactions that are both unusual and infrequent. Since this earthquake occurred in an area previously considered to be subject to only minor tremors, it would be considered to be unusual and infrequent and it would be reported as an extraordinary item.

7. (e) The probable receipt of $1,000,000 from a pending lawsuit is a contingent gain. Contingent gains are not recognized (accrued) until realized. Disclosure of the contingent gain should be made, but care should be taken to avoid misleading implications as to the likelihood of realization.

8. (b) The outside purchase of R&D services are recognized as a part of the R&D expense of the period and are reported as a part of continuing operations. In addition, separate disclosure of total R&D should be made.

NUMBER 2

The Century Company
COMPARATIVE STATEMENT OF INCOME
For the Two Years Ended December 31, 1998 and December 31, 1997

	1998	*1997*
Net Sales	$7,080,000	$5,670,000
Cost of sales	4,000,000	3,400,000
Gross profit on sales	$3,080,000	$2,270,000
Operating expenses	1,050,000	550,000
Operating income	$2,030,000	$1,720,000
Other revenue and (expenses)		
Interest revenue	70,000	40,000
Gain on sale of plant	130,000	—
Loss due to flood damage	$ (420,000)	—
	$ (220,000)	$ 40,000
Income from continuing operations before income taxes	$1,810,000	$1,760,000
Less provision for income taxes	543,000	528,000
Income from continuing operations	$1,267,000	$1,232,000
Discontinued operations		
(Loss) from operations of discontinued office equipment division (less income taxes of $126,000)	—	(294,000)
Gain on disposal of office equipment division (less applicable income taxes of $33,000)	77,000	—
Net income	$1,344,000	$ 938,000

NUMBER 3

a.

Powell Corp.

INCOME STATEMENT
For the Year Ended June 30, 1999

Revenues:		
Machine sales	$750,000	
Service revenues	250,000	
Interest revenue	10,000	
Total revenues		$1,010,000
Expenses:		
Cost of sales - machines	425,000	
Cost of services	100,000	
Administrative expenses	300,000	
Research and development expenses	110,000	
Interest expense	5,000	
Loss from asset disposal	40,000	
Current income tax expense	6,000	
Deferred income tax expense	4,500	
Total expenses and losses		990,500
Income before extraordinary gain		19,500
Extraordinary gain, net of income taxes of $75,000		175,000
Net income		$ 194,500
Other comprehensive income		
Foreign currency translation adjustments net of income taxes of $9,000		21,000
Comprehensive income		$215,000
Earnings (loss) per share:		
Income before extraordinary gain*		($0.40)
Net income		$0.47

b.

Net income	$194,500
Add:	
Taxes on extraordinary gain	75,000
Provision for income taxes	10,500
Financial statement income before income taxes	280,000
Permanent difference - officer's life insurance	5,000
Temporary difference - excess of tax over financial statement depreciation	(15,000)
Taxable income	$270,000

$$\frac{\text{* Income before extraordinary gain 19,500 – Preferred dividends of \$100,000}}{\text{200,000 shares}} = (\$0.40)$$

NUMBER 4

There are a number of weaknesses noted in the Statement of Income and Changes in Retained Earnings.

The first weakness noted is the heading. An income statement reports the results of an entity's earning activities for an accounting period. Accordingly, the statement should be titled "For the Year Ended December 31, 1995."

The ***Revenues and gains*** section improperly includes several items. "Purchase discounts" should reduce the cost of purchases or cost of goods sold. It is not theoretically sound to consider as revenue savings on purchases. Also, under the allowance method of accounting for uncollectible account, recovery of accounts receivable written off in previous years should be credited to the allowance for uncollectible accounts.

The ***Expenses and losses*** section also contains errors. Sales returns and allowances should be offset against or deducted from gross sales. Cash dividends are not an expense, but should be shown as a reduction of retained earnings.

Discontinued operations includes a loss that does not meet the criteria for discontinued operations. The loss on disposal of discontinued styles should be classified as ordinary and usual and be reported in the ***Expenses and losses*** section of the income statement. An ordinary loss should not be shown net of tax effect.

Income before extraordinary item should be shown before the extraordinary item. The caption for the extraordinary item is properly positioned on the income statement, but contains two errors. First, early extinguishment of debt, incorrectly reported under "Revenues and gains," is always reported as an extraordinary item, net of tax effect.

Second, the error discovered from the previous year is not an extraordinary item, but should be treated as a prior period adjustment. Accordingly, the retained earnings balance at the beginning of the year should be adjusted by the amount of the error correction, net of tax effect, and the income statement should include a subtotal titled "Retained earnings at beginning of year as restated." Cash dividends declared should be deducted from this subtotal.

Income taxes and net income should be shown elsewhere on the Statement. Income taxes should be deducted in arriving at income before extraordinary item, either included as the last item in the expenses section or shown as a separate line item before income before extraordinary item. Net income should be reported immediately before beginning retained earnings.

NUMBER 5

Probe Co.
STATEMENT OF INCOME AND COMPREHENSIVE INCOME
For the Year Ended December 31, 2000

Sales			$2,420,000
Cost of sales			1,863,000
Gross profit			557,000
Selling and administrative expenses	$220,000		
Depreciation	88,000		308,000
Operating income			249,000
Other income (expenses):			
Interest income	14,000		
Interest expense	(46,000)		
Loss on sale of equipment	(7,000)		(39,000)
Income before income tax and extraordinary item			210,000
Income tax:			
Current	45,000	[1]	
Deferred	12,000	[2]	57,000
Income before extraordinary item			153,000
Extraordinary item:			
Gain on extinguishment of debt, net of income taxes of $27,000			63,000
Net income			$216,000
Other comprehensive income, net of tax			
Unrealized holding gain on Available-for-Sale securities net of income taxes of $6,000			$14,000
Comprehensive income			$230,000
Earnings per share			
Earnings before extraordinary item			$1.275 [3]
Extraordinary item			.525 Optional
Net income			$1.800

[1] Current income tax expense:

Income before income tax and extraordinary item	$210,000
Differences between financial statement and taxable income	(60,000)
Income subject to tax	150,000
Income tax rate	× 30%
Income tax excluding extraordinary item	$45,000

[2] Deferred income tax expense:

Cumulative temporary differences - 12/31/00	$180,000
Income tax rate	× 30%
Deferred tax liability -- 12/31/00	54,000
Deferred tax liability -- 12/31/99	42,000
Deferred tax expense for 2000	$12,000

[3] Earnings per share:

Weighted average number of shares outstanding for 2000:

January through March	60,000 × 3	180,000
April through December	140,000 × 9	1,260,000
Total		1,440,000
		÷ 12
		120,000
Income before extraordinary item		153,000
Earnings per share	(153,000 ÷ 120,000)	1,275

NUMBER 6

a. Sales and other revenues should be recognized for interim financial statement purposes in the same manner as revenues are recognized for annual reporting purposes. This means normally at the point of sale or, in the case of services, at completion of the earnings process.

In the case of industries whose sales vary greatly due to the seasonal nature of business, revenues should still be recognized as earned, but a disclosure should be made of the seasonal nature of the business in the notes.

In the case of long-term contracts recognizing earnings on the percentage-of-completion basis, the current state of completion of the contract should be estimated and revenue recognized at interim dates in the same manner as at the normal year end.

b. For interim reporting purposes, product costs (costs directly attributable to the production of goods or services) should be matched with the product and associated revenues in the same manner as for annual reporting purposes.

Period costs (costs not directly associated with the production of a particular good or service) should be charged to earnings as incurred or allocated among interim periods based on an estimate of time expired, benefit received, or other activity associated with the particular interim period(s). Also, if a gain or loss occurs during an interim period and is a type that would not be deferred at year end, the gain or loss should be recognized in full in the interim period in which it occurs. Finally, in allocating period costs among interim periods, the basis for allocation must be supportable and may not be based on merely an arbitrary assignment of costs between interim periods.

The AICPA Accounting Principles Board allowed for some variances from the normal method of determining cost of goods sold and valuation of inventories at interim dates in Opinion no. 28, but these methods are allowable only at interim dates and must be fully disclosed in a footnote to the financial statements. Some companies use the gross profit method of estimating cost of goods sold and ending inventory at interim dates instead of taking a complete physical inventory. This is an allowable procedure at interim dates, but the company must disclose the method used and any significant variances that subsequently result from reconciliation of the results obtained using the gross profit method and the results obtained after taking the annual physical inventory.

At interim dates, companies using the LIFO cost-flow assumption may temporarily have a reduction in inventory level that results in a liquidation of base period tiers of inventory. If this liquidation is considered temporary and is expected to be replaced prior to year end, the company should charge cost of goods sold at current prices. The difference between the carrying value of the inventory and the current replacement cost of the inventory is a current liability for replacement of LIFO base inventory temporarily depleted. When the temporary liquidation is replaced, inventory is debited for the original LIFO value and the liability is removed.

Inventory losses from a decline in market value at interim dates should not be deferred but should be recognized in the period in which they occur. However, if in a subsequent interim period the market price of the written-down inventory increases, a gain should be recognized for the recovery up to the amount of the loss previously recognized. If a temporary decline in market value below cost can reasonably be expected to be recovered prior to year end, no loss should be recognized.

Finally, if a company uses a standard costing system to compute cost of goods sold and to value inventories, variances from standard should be treated at interim dates in the same manner as at year end. However, if variances occur at an interim date that are expected to be absorbed prior to year end, the variances should be deferred instead of being immediately recognized.

c. The AICPA Accounting Principles Board stated that the provision for income taxes shown in interim financial statements must be based upon the effective tax rate expected for the entire annual period for ordinary earnings. The effective tax rate is, in accordance with previous APB opinions, based on earnings for financial statement purposes as opposed to taxable income which may consider timing differences. This effective tax rate is the combined federal and state(s) income tax rate applied to expected annual earnings, taking into consideration all anticipated investment tax credits, foreign tax rates, percentage depletion capital gains rates, and other available tax planning alternatives. Ordinary earnings do not include unusual or extraordinary items, discontinued operations, or cumulative effects of changes in accounting principles, all of which will be separately reported or reported net of their related tax effect in reports for the interim period or for the fiscal year. The amount shown as the provision for income taxes at interim dates should be computed on a year-to-date basis. For example, the provision for income taxes for the second quarter of a company's fiscal year is the result of applying the expected rate to year-to-date earnings and subtracting the provision recorded for the first quarter. There are several variables in this computation (expected earnings may change, tax rates may change), and the year-to-date method of computation provides the only continuous method of approximating the provision for income taxes at interim dates. However, if the effective rate or expected annual earnings change between interim periods, the change is not reflected retroactively but the effect of the change is absorbed in the current interim period.

NUMBER 7

a. Hillside should report the extraordinary item separately, net of applicable income taxes, below the continuing operations section in the income statement. Exclusion of extraordinary items from the results of continuing operations is intended to produce a measure of income from continuing operations that is useful in projecting future operating cash flows.

b. Hillside should report the discontinued operations separately in the 1995 income statement immediately below income from continuing operations. Discontinued operations should be comprised of two categories, with each category reported net of income taxes:

- Loss from operations of the discontinued segment from the beginning of the year to the measurement date.
- Loss on disposal of the discontinued segment, including the provision for operating losses during the phase-out period.

c. Hillside should include the costs incurred to relocate employees in the loss on disposal of the discontinued segment in its 1995 income statement. These costs are a direct result of the commitment to dispose of its segment.

NUMBER 8

1. AY Changing the method of accounting for long-term contracts is a change in accounting principle that must be accounted for retroactively.

2. BZ A change in the useful life of equipment based on new information or additional experience is a change in accounting estimate that should be accounted for in current and future (prospective) years.

3. BZ The change in estimated warranty costs is a change in accounting estimate that should be accounted for in current and future (prospective) years.

4. AY A change from LIFO to another acceptable inventory method is a change in accounting principle that must be accounted for retroactively.

5. AX A change from FIFO to another acceptable inventory method is a change in accounting principle that is accounted for by reporting the cumulative effect of the change net of tax on the income statement. The pro-forma effect of the change should also be disclosed.

6. CY A change from the cash basis (an incorrect method) to the accrual basis is a correction of an error and should be accounted for retroactively.

7. CY Charging the entire insurance premium to expense is an error and should be accounted for retroactively.

8. AX A change in depreciation methods is a change in accounting principle that is accounted for by reporting the cumulative effect of the change net of taxes on the income statement. Since Quo is presenting comparative statements, the pro-forma effect of the change should also be disclosed.

9. DZ Since Quo had not previously had a pension plan, the implementation of the pension plan in 2000 would not be an accounting change. The pension cost would accrue in 2000 and future years (prospectively).

10. DY A change in accounting principle occurs when an accounting principle different from the one used previously for reporting purposes is adopted. For a change to occur, a choice between two or more accounting principles must exist. In this case, the change in Quo's situation dictates that the equity method be used to account for the investment. Consequently, this is not an accounting change. However, APB 18 requires that the investment account be retroactively restated to reflect balances as if the equity method had always been used.

Chapter Thirteen
Accounting for Income Taxes

Chapter Thirteen
Accounting for Income Taxes

INCOME TAX ALLOCATION—SFAS #109

Income tax allocation in accounting is necessary because of the accrual concept that costs incurred in an accounting period should be matched with the income that resulted in such costs, regardless of when such costs are ultimately paid. Income taxes—federal, state, local, and foreign—are significant costs which must be matched with the income that gave rise to the taxes to fulfill the major objective of corporate financial reporting.

Principal Problem Areas

1. Transactions affect book income in one period and taxable income in another, and result in **temporary differences**.
2. Recognition of the tax effects of a net operating loss. Will the effect be recognized in the period of the loss or in the period the taxable income is reduced by means of carrybacks and carryforwards?
3. The treatment of tax effects of extraordinary items, disposal of a segment of a business, and discontinued operations referred to as intraperiod income tax allocation.

The FASB's conclusions regarding these problem areas are as follows:

1. There should be interperiod income tax allocation and the "asset and liability" method should be used.
2. The deferred tax account will be calculated using future enacted tax rates.
3. Carrybacks should affect the loss periods; carryforwards will usually be recognized subject to a valuation allowance.
4. The statements will disclose the income taxes currently payable and the expense related to the period.
5. Deferred taxes should be classified net current and net noncurrent.
6. Tax allocation within a period (intraperiod) is appropriate in that the tax effects of all items which are segregated from income from continuing operations should be shown along with the related tax effect of such items.
7. Tax allocation within a period (intraperiod) is also appropriate for other comprehensive income items included in comprehensive income. (SFAS #130)

Basic Principles and Objectives

One objective of accounting for income taxes is to recognize the amount of taxes payable or refundable for the current year. A second objective is to recognize **deferred tax liabilities and assets** for the future **tax consequences** of events that have been recognized in an enterprise's financial statements or tax returns.

Ideally, the second objective might be stated more specifically to recognize the *expected* future tax consequences of events that have been recognized in the financial statements or tax returns. However, that objective is realistically constrained because (a) the tax payment or refund that results from a particular tax return is a joint result of all the items included in that return, (b) taxes that will be paid or refunded in future years are the joint result of events of the current or prior years and events of future years, and (c) information available about the future is limited. As a result, attribution of taxes to individual items and events is arbitrary and, except in the simplest situations, requires estimates and approximations.

To implement the objectives in light of those constraints, the following basic principles are applied in accounting for income taxes at the date of the financial statements:

a. A current tax liability or asset is recognized for the estimated taxes payable or refundable on tax returns for the current year.
b. A deferred tax liability or asset is recognized for the estimated future tax effects attributable to **temporary differences** and carryforwards.
c. The measurement of current and deferred tax liabilities and assets is based on provisions of the enacted tax law; the effects of future changes in tax laws or rates are not anticipated.
d. The measurement of deferred tax assets is reduced, if necessary, by the amount of any tax benefits that, based on available evidence, are not expected to be realized.

TEMPORARY DIFFERENCES

The tax consequences of most events recognized in the current year's financial statements are included in determining income taxes currently payable. However, because tax laws and financial accounting standards differ in their recognition and measurement of assets, liabilities, equity, revenues, expenses, gains, and losses, differences arise between the following:

a. The amount of taxable income and pretax financial income for a year

b. The tax bases of assets or liabilities and their reported amounts in financial statements.

An assumption inherent in an enterprise's statement of financial position prepared in accordance with generally accepted accounting principles is that the reported amounts of assets and liabilities will be recovered and settled, respectively.

Because of that assumption, a difference between the tax basis of an asset or a liability and its reported amount in the statement of financial position will result in taxable or deductible amounts in some future year without regard to other future events. Examples follow:

a. *Revenues or gains that are taxable after they are recognized in financial income* (installment sale).

b. *Expenses or losses that are deductible after they are recognized in financial income* (a product warranty liability).

c. *Revenues or gains that are taxable before they are recognized in financial income* (subscriptions received in advance).

d. *Expenses or losses that are deductible before they are recognized in financial income* (depreciable property).

These examples pertain to revenues, expenses, gains, or losses that are included in taxable income of an earlier or later year than the year in which they are recognized in financial income. Those differences between taxable income and pretax financial income also create differences between the tax basis of an asset or liability and its reported amount in the financial statements. The differences result in taxable or deductible amounts when the reported amount of an asset or liability in the financial statements is recovered or settled, respectively. SFAS #109 refers collectively to these differences as **temporary differences.**

Example:

In 1999 Noll Corp. reported income before depreciation of $900,000. Noll deducted depreciation for financial reporting of $400,000 and $600,000 on its 1999 tax return. The $200,000 temporary depreciation difference is expected to reverse equally over the next three years. Noll's enacted tax rates are 30% for 1999 and 25% for the following three years.

Required: Prepare the tax journal entry for 1999.

Solution:

	Book	Tax
Income before depreciation	$900,000	$900,000
Depreciation Expense	(400,000)	(600,000)
Income before tax	500,000	300,000
Income taxes (see JE)		
Currently payable	(90,000)	(90,000)
Deferred taxes	(50,000)	(0)
Net Income	$360,000	$210,000

Journal Entry:

Income tax expense – current	90,000	
Income tax expense – deferred	50,000*	
Income tax payable		90,000**
Deferred tax payable		50,000

* The deferred tax of $50,000 is the temporary difference of $200,000 times the future enacted tax rate of 25%.

** The income tax payable is the taxable income of $300,000 times the current tax rate of 30%.

PERMANENT DIFFERENCES

A permanent difference arises when revenues are exempt from taxation or expenses are not allowable as deductions for tax purposes. Permanent differences cause differences in book **net income** and tax **net income**. Permanent differences do **not** cause differences in taxes (only temporary differences can create differences in taxes). Some examples of common permanent differences are listed below:

a. State and municipal bond interest income: included in book income but not included in taxable income.
b. Dividends received exclusion: deducted for taxable income but not for book income.
c. Life insurance premiums on executives when the corporation is the beneficiary: deducted as an expense for book purposes but not deducted for tax purposes. Conversely, proceeds received from life insurance policies are included in book income but excluded from taxable income.
d. Payment of fines and penalties: included in book income but not included in taxable income.

The following problem illustrates the effect of permanent differences:

Example:
Seaboard Corp. has income of $200,000 for books and taxes before considering the permanent differences listed below:
a. Interest income on municipal bonds is $30,000.
b. Life insurance premiums of $20,000 have been paid on Seaboard executives and the Corporation is the beneficiary.

Assuming a 30% tax rate, what would be the journal entry to record the taxes?

Solution:

	Book	Tax
Income before permanent differences	$200,000	$200,000
Interest income on municipal bonds	30,000	0
Life insurance premiums on executives	(20,000)	0
Income before taxes	$210,000	$200,000
Taxes at 30% (see below*)	(60,000)	(60,000)
Net income	$150,000	$140,000

* Entry to record taxes:

Income tax expense - current	60,000	
Tax payable		60,000

*Note from the above problem that the permanent differences cause a difference in net income but do **not** cause a difference in taxes.*

Deferred Tax Assets and Liabilities

An enterprise shall recognize a deferred tax liability or asset for all temporary differences and operating loss and tax credit carryforwards in accordance with the provisions below. **Deferred tax expense or benefit** is the change during the year in an enterprise's deferred tax liabilities and assets.

The statement requires comprehensive allocation using the liability method. This method is balance-sheet oriented. The total tax that will be assessed on temporary differences when they reverse is accrued and reported.

The deferred tax amount that is reported as an asset or liability on the balance sheet represents the effect of all temporary differences, which will reverse in the future using current tax rates and laws and those in existence in the year(s) in which the temporary differences reverse. Therefore, income tax expense is equal to income taxes currently payable plus or minus the change in the deferred tax account.

An Enacted Change in Tax Laws or Rates

A deferred tax liability or asset shall be adjusted for the effect of a change in tax law or rates. The effect shall be included in income from continuing operations for the period that includes the enactment date.

Annual Computation of a Deferred Tax Liability or Asset

Deferred taxes shall be determined separately for each tax-paying component (an individual entity or group of entities that is consolidated for tax purposes) in each tax jurisdiction. That determination includes the following procedures:

a. Identify (1) the types and amounts of existing temporary differences and (2) the nature and amount of each type of operating loss and tax credit carryforward and the remaining length of the carryforward period.
b. Measure the total deferred tax liability for taxable temporary differences using the tax rate in effect when temporary difference reverses.
c. Measure the total deferred tax asset for deductible temporary differences and operating loss carryforwards using the applicable tax rate.
d. Measure deferred tax assets for each type of tax credit carryforward.
e. Reduce deferred tax assets by a **valuation allowance** if, based on the weight of available evidence, it is *more likely than not* (a likelihood of more than 50 percent) that some portion or all of the deferred tax assets will not be realized. The valuation allowance should be sufficient to reduce the deferred tax asset to the amount that is more likely than not to be realized.

The objective is to measure a deferred tax liability or asset using the enacted tax rate(s) expected to apply to taxable income in the periods in which the deferred tax liability or asset is expected to be settled or realized. Under current U.S. federal tax law, if taxable income exceeds a specified amount, all taxable income is taxed, in substance, at a single flat tax rate. That tax rate shall be used for measurement of a deferred tax liability or asset by enterprises for which graduated tax rates are not a significant factor. Enterprises for which graduated tax rates are a significant factor shall measure a deferred tax liability or asset using the average graduated tax rate applicable to the amount of estimated annual taxable income in the periods in which the deferred tax liability or asset is estimated to be settled or realized.

VALUATION ALLOWANCE

All available evidence, both positive and negative, should be considered to determine whether, based on the weight of that evidence, a valuation allowance is needed. Information about an enterprise's current financial position and its results of operations for the current and preceding years ordinarily is readily available. That historical information is supplemented by all currently available information about future years. Sometimes, however, historical information may not be available (for example, start-up operations) or it may not be as relevant (for example, if there has been a significant, recent change in circumstances) and special attention is required.

Future realization of the tax benefit of an existing deductible temporary difference or carryforward ultimately depends on the existence of sufficient taxable income of the appropriate character (for example, ordinary income or capital gain) within the carryback, carryforward period available under the tax law. The following four possible sources of taxable income may be available under the tax law to realize a tax benefit for deductible temporary differences and carryforwards:

a. Future reversals of existing taxable temporary differences.
b. Future taxable income exclusive of reversing temporary differences and carryforwards.
c. Taxable income in prior carryback year(s) if carryback is permitted under the tax law.
d. **Tax-planning strategies** that would, if necessary, be implemented to, for example:
   (1) Accelerate taxable amounts to utilize expiring carryforwards
   (2) Change the character of taxable or deductible amounts from ordinary income or loss to capital gain or loss.
   (3) Switch from tax-exempt to taxable investments.

Forming a conclusion that a valuation allowance is not needed is difficult when there is negative evidence such as cumulative losses in recent years. Other examples of negative evidence include (but are not limited to) the following:

a. A history of operating loss or tax credit carryforwards expiring unused
b. Losses expected in early future years (by a presently profitable entity)
c. Unsettled circumstances that, if unfavorably resolved, would adversely affect future operations and profit levels on a continuing basis in future years
d. A carryback, carryforward period that is so brief that it would limit realization of tax benefits if (1) a significant deductible temporary difference is expected to reverse in a single year or (2) the enterprise operates in a traditionally cyclical business.

Examples (not prerequisites) of positive evidence that might support a conclusion that a valuation allowance is not needed when there is negative evidence include (but are not limited to) the following:

a. Existing contracts or firm sales backlog that will produce more than enough taxable income to realize the deferred tax asset based on existing sales prices and cost structures
b. An excess of appreciated asset value of the tax basis of the entity's net assets in an amount sufficient to realize the deferred tax asset
c. A strong earnings history exclusive of the loss that created the future deductible amount (tax loss carryforward or deductible temporary difference) coupled with evidence indicating that the loss (for example, an unusual, infrequent, or extraordinary item) is an aberration rather than a continuing condition.

An enterprise must use judgment in considering the relative impact of negative and positive evidence. The weight given to the potential effect of negative and positive evidence should be commensurate with the extent to which it can be objectively verified. The more negative evidence that exists (a) the more positive evidence is necessary and (b) the more difficult it is to support a conclusion that a valuation allowance is not needed for some portion or all of the deferred tax asset.

A Change in the Valuation Allowance

The effect of a change in the beginning-of-the-year balance of a valuation allowance that results from a change in circumstances that causes a change in judgment about the realizability of the related deferred tax asset in future years ordinarily shall be included in income from continuing operations. Exceptions include certain temporary differences of an acquired corporation and adjustments to beginning retained earnings for certain accounting changes or prior period adjustments.

FINANCIAL STATEMENT PRESENTATION

In a classified statement of financial position, an enterprise shall separate deferred tax liabilities and assets into a current amount and a noncurrent amount. Deferred tax liabilities and assets shall be classified as current or noncurrent based on the classification of the related asset or liability for financial reporting. A deferred tax liability or asset that is not related to an asset or liability for financial reporting, including deferred tax assets related to carryforwards, shall be classified according to the expected reversal date of the temporary difference. The valuation allowance for a particular tax jurisdiction shall be allocated between current and noncurrent deferred tax assets for that tax jurisdiction on a pro rata basis.

For a particular tax-paying component of an enterprise and within a particular tax jurisdiction, (a) all current deferred tax liabilities and assets shall be offset and presented as a single amount and (b) all noncurrent deferred tax liabilities and assets shall be offset and presented as a single amount.

Financial Statement Disclosure

The components of the net deferred tax liability or asset recognized in an enterprise's statement of financial position shall be disclosed as follows:

a. The total of all deferred tax liabilities.
b. The total of all deferred tax assets.
c. The total valuation allowance recognized for deferred tax assets.

The net change during the year in the total valuation allowance also shall be disclosed. A **public enterprise** shall disclose the approximate tax effect of each type of temporary difference and carryforward that gives rise to a significant portion of deferred tax liabilities and deferred tax assets (before allocation of valuation allowances). A **nonpublic enterprise** shall disclose the types of significant temporary differences and carryforwards but may omit disclosure of the tax effects of each type. A public enterprise that is not subject to income taxes because its income is taxed directly to its owners shall disclose that fact and the net difference between the tax bases and the reported amounts of the enterprise's assets and liabilities.

The significant components of income tax expense attributable to continuing operations for each year presented shall be disclosed in the financial statements or notes thereto. Those components would include, for example:

a. **Current tax expense or benefit**
b. Deferred tax expense or benefit (exclusive of the effects of other components listed below)
c. Investment tax credits
d. Government grants (to the extent recognized as a reduction of income tax expense)
e. The benefits of operating loss carryforwards
f. Tax expense that results from allocating certain tax benefits either directly to contributed capital or to reduce goodwill or other noncurrent intangible assets of an acquired entity
g. Adjustments of a deferred tax liability or asset for enacted changes in tax laws or rates or a change in the tax status of the enterprise
h. Adjustments of the beginning-of-the-year balance of a valuation allowance because of a change in circumstances that causes a change in judgment about the realizability of the related deferred tax asset in future years.

The amount of income tax expense or benefit allocated to continuing operations and the amounts separately allocated to other items shall be disclosed for each year for which those items are presented.

A public enterprise shall disclose a reconciliation using percentages or dollar amounts of (a) the reported amount of income tax expense attributable to continuing operations for the year to (b) the amount of income tax expense that would result from applying domestic federal statutory tax rates to pretax income from continuing operations. The "statutory" tax rates shall be the regular tax rates if there are alternative tax systems. The estimated amount and the nature of each significant reconciling item shall be disclosed. A nonpublic enterprise shall disclose the nature of significant reconciling items but may omit a numerical reconciliation.

An enterprise shall disclose the amounts and expiration dates of operating loss and tax credit carryforwards for tax purposes.

LOSS CARRYBACKS AND LOSS CARRYFORWARDS

The 1997 tax law allows a pretax operating loss to be carried back to the **two** preceding periods resulting in a tax credit. The tax rate in existence at each of prior balance sheet dates is used to calculate the amount of the tax credit. Losses remaining after the carrybacks may be carried forward for **20** years to offset income if income exists in any of the future **20** years.

FASB #109 requires that the tax benefit of a loss carryforward be recognized as a deferred tax asset in the year of the loss. The deferred tax asset may be reduced by a valuation allowance if necessary. Companies at the time of the loss may forgo the loss carryback and elect to use only the carryforward provision.

Example of loss carryback and loss carryforward:

BG Corp. has reported combined income before taxes of $150,000 for the years 1998 and 1999. In 2000 the Corporation has a pretax loss (NOL) of $250,000. The tax rate is 30% for 1998 and 1999 and 25% for the year 2000.

Solution:
In 2000 BG Corp. would take $150,000 of the NOL and carry it back for two years. At a 30% tax rate, the Corporation would receive a $45,000 tax refund (30% × $150,000). The journal entry would be:

Tax refund receivable	$45,000	
Tax benefit of operating loss carryback		$45,000

The remaining $100,000 of the NOL should be recognized as a carryforward in 2000. The tax benefit of the carryforward is $25,000 (25% × $100,000). However, the company feels that based on the weight of evidence available, it is more likely than not that $10,000 of the tax benefit will not be realized. The Company's entries to record the tax benefit and the valuation allowance are as follows:

Deferred tax asset	$ 25,000	
Tax benefit of operating loss carryforward		$25,000
Tax benefit of loss carryforward	$ 10,000	
Allowance to reduce deferred tax assets to expected realizable value		$10,000

Income Statement Presentation
The income statement for the year 2000 would appear as follows:

Loss before income taxes		($250,000)
Less:		
Benefit from operating loss carryback	$45,000	
Benefit from operating loss carryforward	15,000	60,000
Net Loss		($190,000)

Balance Sheet Disclosure

Deferred tax asset	$ 25,000
Less:	
Allowance to reduce deferred tax assets to expected realizable value	(10,000)
Expected realizable value	$ 15,000

Illustrations - Temporary Differences
Example #1—Deferred Tax Liability *(one difference)*
Asset acquired in 1999 for $10,000. For financial reporting, the asset is depreciated over five years using straight-line. For tax purposes, the asset is recovered using MACRS three-year class. Assume a current (and future) tax rate of 30%. The company's taxable income for 1999 is $100,000.

a) Depreciation	*1999*	*2000*	*2001*	*2002*	*2003*
Tax (rounded)	$3,300	$4,400	$1,500	$ 800	- 0 -
Book	2,000	2,000	2,000	2,000	2,000

b) Net taxable or deductible amounts in each year:

	1999	*2000*	*2001*	*2002*	*2003*
Taxable			$500	$1,200	$2,000
Deductible	$1,300	$2,400			

c) Flow of deferred tax liability account:

Year	*Deductible (Taxable) amount*	*Change in account (30%)*	*Balance in account*
1999	$1,300	+ $390	$ (390)
2000	2,400	+ 720	(1,110)
2001	(500)	- 150	(960)
2002	(1,200)	- 360	(600)
2003	(2,000)	- 600	-0-

The journal entry for income tax expense at 12/31/99 would be:

12/31/99	Income tax expense	$30,390	
	Deferred income tax liability		$ 390
	Income tax payable (.30 × $100,000)		30,000

The journal entry for income tax expense for 12/31/00 assuming a taxable income of $100,000 would be:

12/31/00	Income tax expense	$30,720	
	Deferred income tax liability		$ 720
	Income tax payable		30,000

Example #2—Multiple Temporary Differences

Using the same facts as in Example #1, assume that, in addition, the company recognized a warranty expense of $3,000 for financial reporting in 2000 which (the company estimates) will be recognized for tax purposes as follows:

2000—$300; 2001—$400; 2002—$1,000; 2003—$1,300

The deferred tax asset is determined independently from the deferred tax liability.

Flow of deferred tax asset account:

Year	*Taxable (Deductible) amount*	*Change in account (30%)*	*Balance in account*
2000	$2,700[1]	+$810	$810
2001	(400)	- 120	690
2002	(1,000)	- 300	390
2003	(1,300)	- 390	-0-

Since the deferred tax asset is greater than the liability, the need for a valuation allowance must be evaluated. It is assumed that no such allowance is required in this example.

[1]$3,000 –$300

12/31/00	Income tax expense	$29,910	
	Deferred tax asset	810	
	Income tax payable		$30,000
	Deferred tax liability		720

ILLUSTRATIVE PROBLEM

In January 2000, you began the examination of the financial statements for the year ended Dec. 31, 1999, of Sesame Corporation, a new audit client. During your examination the following information was disclosed:

1. The 1999 federal tax return reported taxable income of $175,000 and taxes due of $52,500. Taxable incomes were reported for 1996, 1997 and 1998. The company had a deferred tax asset balance of $20,025 at 12/31/98. Sesame Corp. implements the provisions of SFAS #109 for the year ended 12/31/99 for the first time.
2. On Jan. 2, 1997, equipment was purchased at a cost of $225,000. The equipment had an estimated useful life of five years and no salvage value. The MACRS (5-year) method of recovery was used for income tax reporting and the straight-line method was used on the financial statements.
3. On Jan. 8, 1998, $60,000 was collected in advance rental of a building for a three-year period. The $60,000 was reported as taxable income in 1998, but $40,000 was reported as deferred revenue in 1998 in the financial statements. The building will continue to be rented for the foreseeable future.
4. On Jan. 5, 1999, office equipment was purchased for $10,000. The office equipment has an estimated life of 10 years and no salvage value. Straight-line depreciation was used for both financial and income tax reporting purposes. Management, however, elected to write off $5,000 of the cost of the equipment for income tax purposes in 1999 and use straight-line over 5 years for the remaining $5,000 cost. As a result, the total depreciation for this equipment on the tax return was $5,500. (Half-year convention is used).
5. On Feb. 12, 1999, the Corporation sold land with a book and tax basis of $150,000 for $200,000. The gain, reported in full in 1999 on the financial statements, was reported by the installment method on the income tax return equally over a period of 5 years.
6. On Mar. 15, 1999, a patent developed at a cost of $34,000 was granted. The Corporation is amortizing the patent over a period of 4 years on the financial statements and over 17 years on its income tax return. The Corporation elected to record a full year's amortization in 1999 on both its financial statements and income tax return.
7. The income tax rates for 1997, 1998 and 1999 are assumed to be 30% for each year.

Required:

a. For each item causing a temporary difference, prepare a schedule showing the taxable or deductible amount for each year.
b. Prepare a schedule showing the taxable and deductible amounts for 1999 for each item.
c. Compute the deferred tax asset and liability at 12/31/99.
d. Compute the 1999 income tax expense.

Solution:

a. Net taxable or deductible amounts:

(2) Equipment

Schedule	*1997*	*1998*	*1999*	*2000*	*2001*	*2002*
Tax (MACRS)	$45,000	$72,000	$43,200	$ 25,920	$ 25,920	$12,960
Book (S.L.)	45,000	45,000	45,000	45,000	45,000	- 0 -
Difference	$ - 0 -	$27,000	$(1,800)	$(19,080)	$(19,080)	$12,960
Taxable amounts			$ 1,800	$19,080	$19,080	
Deductible amounts		$27,000				$12,960

(3) Rental receipts

	1998	*1999*	*2000*
Book income	$20,000	$20,000	$20,000
Tax income	60,000		
Difference	$(40,000)	$20,000	$20,000
Deductible amount		$20,000	$20,000
Taxable amount	$40,000		

(4) Office equipment

	1999	*2000*	*2001*	*2002*	*2003*	*2004*	*2005-2008*	
Tax depreciation	$5,500	$1,000	$1,000	$1,000	$1,000	$ 500	$ -0-	
Book depreciation	1,000	1,000	1,000	1,000	1,000	1,000	4,000	($1,000 ea.)
Difference	$4,500	- 0 -	- 0 -	- 0 -	- 0 -	$(500)	$(4,000)	
Taxable amounts						$500	$4,000	
Deductible amount	$4,500							

(5) Installment gain:

	1999	*2000*	*2001*	*2002*	*2003*
Book income	$50,000				
Tax income	10,000	10,000	10,000	10,000	10,000
Difference	$40,000	$(10,000)	$(10,000)	$(10,000)	$(10,000)
Deductible amount	$40,000				
Taxable amounts		$10,000	$10,000	$10,000	$10,000

(6) Patent

	1999	*2000*	*2001*	*2002*	*2003*	*2004*	*2005*	*2006*	*After*
Tax amortization	$2,000	$2,000	$2,000	$2,000	$2,000	$2,000	$2,000	$2,000	$18,000
Book amortization	8,500	8,500	8,500	8,500					
Difference	$6,500	$6,500	$6,500	$6,500	$(2,000)	$(2,000)	$(2,000)	$(2,000)	$(18,000)
Taxable amounts	$6,500	$6,500	$6,500	$6,500					
Deductible amounts					$2,000	$2,000	$2,000	$2,000	$18,000

b. Taxable and deductible amounts for 1999:

		Taxable	*Deductible*
(2)	Equipment $27,000 – $1,800		$25,200
(3)	Rental income $40,000 – $20,000	$20,000	
(4)	Office equipment		4,500
(5)	Installment gain		40,000
(6)	Patent	6,500	

c. Deferred tax balances:

Totals	$26,500	$69,700
Tax rate	30%	30%
Asset	$7,950	
Liability		$20,910
Current portion:		
$20,000 × .3 =	$6,000	

d. Income tax expense for 1999:

Income tax payable		$52,500
Change in deferred tax accounts:		
Liability at 12/31/99	$20,910	
Asset	– 7,950	
		12,960
Income tax expense		$65,460

Note: The $20,025 deferred tax asset balance at 12/31/98 would be shown on the income statement at 12/31/99 as an accounting change due to the implementation of a new accounting standard in accordance with APB 20.

UNDISTRIBUTED EARNINGS — INVESTEE AND SUBSIDIARY

An additional deferred tax problem relates to the temporary difference between the earnings of an investee or subsidiary accounted for by the equity method and a dividend distributed by them. The tax effect of this temporary difference depends upon whether the temporary difference will ultimately be distributed as future dividends or future capital gains. If the assumption is made that the temporary difference (undistributed earnings) is to be distributed as future dividends and the corporation is a domestic corporation, the tax effect of the temporary difference would normally be adjusted for the dividends received deduction.

Example - Deferred tax effects of domestic investee
ABC Corp. owns 30% of the outstanding stock of Investee Corp., a domestic corporation. ABC's net income for the current year is $60,000 and its dividends are $20,000. The Company accounts for its investment on the equity basis and assumes that future distributions of undistributed earnings will be as dividends. The tax rate for all years is assumed to be 40%.

Solution:
ABC's income before taxes would include $18,000 of income from earnings of investee ($60,000 × 30%). The company would also receive $6,000 in dividends from Investee ($20,000 × 30%). This creates a temporary difference between the earnings and dividends of $12,000. Since the Company assumes that the difference will be distributed as future dividends, it is eligible for the 80% dividends received deduction. This means that 80% of the $12,000 temporary difference ($9,600) will never be taxed and is considered a permanent difference. Therefore, only 20% of the $12,000 temporary difference ($2,400) will be taxable. The deferred tax liability on ABC's books from the temporary difference will be $960 ($2,400 × 40%).

Note: The rule for the 80% dividends received deduction is that the investment must be in a domestic corporation and that the ownership percentage must be equal to or greater than 20% but less than 80%. For investments in a domestic corporation in which the ownership is less than 20%, a **70%** dividends received deduction is allowed. This investment would normally be accounted for by using the cost method and the company would recognize dividend income for both financial and tax purposes. In this case, a temporary tax difference would not exist.

Example - Deferred tax effects of a domestic subsidiary
ABC also owns 60% interest in Subsidiary Corp., a domestic corporation. Subsidiary's net income and dividends for the current year are $100,000 and $40,000 respectively. ABC accounts for its investment on the equity basis and assumes that all undistributed earnings will be distributed as dividends. The tax rate for all years is 40%.

Solution:
ABC's income before taxes would include earnings from Subsidiary Corp. of $60,000 ($100,000 × 60%), and dividends of $24,000 ($40,000 × 60%). This creates a temporary difference between earnings and dividends of $36,000. Since ABC is a domestic corporation and the ownership interest is between 20% or more and less than 80%, it is eligible for the 80% dividend received deduction. Therefore, 80% of the temporary difference (undistributed earnings) will never be taxed and is considered a permanent difference. Only 20% of the temporary difference is considered taxable. The deferred tax liability on ABC's books would be $2,880: the temporary difference ($36,000) times 20% times the future enacted tax rate of 40%.

Note: The dividends received deduction is 100% for investments in domestic corporations in which the ownership percentage is 80% or above. This means that 100% of the dividends would never be taxed and would be considered a permanent difference. In this case, the company would **not** have a temporary tax difference.

DIFFERING VIEWPOINTS

(1) Asset and liability method (method to be used)
(2) "Deferred" method
(3) Net of tax method

The asset and liability approach to deferred taxes is most consistent with the definitions established in the Concepts Statements for assets and liabilities. This method recognizes a deferred tax liability (or asset) which represents the amount of taxes payable or recoverable in future years as a result of temporary differences at the end of the current year. This method emphasizes those rates in effect when the tax difference reverses (future rates).

In the deferred method, the tax effects of income tax allocation are deferred currently and current tax rates are used. If the current taxes are reduced below the income tax expense per books, a deferred credit arises. Similarly, where income tax payable exceeds the income tax expense, a deferred charge arises. In this method, the emphasis is on the income statement and matches tax expense with related revenues and expenses for the year in which they are recognized in pretax financial income.

The label "deferred" or "liability" is really the principal difference between the first two methods. One other difference relates to tax rates. In the deferred method, current tax rates are used; whereas, in the liability method, rates expected to prevail when the differences reverse are used. In the "net of tax" method, the tax effects under either the deferred or liability method are recognized in the valuation of assets and liabilities and the related revenues and expenses. The tax effects are applied to reduce specific assets or liabilities on the basis that tax deductibility or taxability are factors in their valuation.

Another viewpoint, partial allocation, is not acceptable. Partial allocation advocates maintain that the tax expense should be the tax payable with the possible exception of non recurring differences that lead to material distortions of tax expense and net income. Holders of this view state that comprehensive tax allocation advocates rely on the "revolving" account approach which suggests a similarity between deferred tax accruals and other balance sheet items, like accounts payable, where the individual items within an account balance remain constant or grow. They argue that deferred tax accruals are not owed to anyone, there is no payable date, and represent at best vague estimates of future amounts due depending on future tax rates and other factors.

INTRAPERIOD TAX ALLOCATION

- **Income Statement**

Income tax expense or benefit for the year shall be allocated among continuing operations, discontinued operations, extraordinary items, and changes in accounting principles. The amount allocated to continuing operations is the tax effect of the pretax income or loss from continuing operations that occurred during the year, plus or minus income tax effects of changes in circumstances that cause a change in judgment about the realization of deferred tax assets in future years, changes in tax laws or rates, and changes in tax status.

If there is only one item other than continuing operations, the portion of income tax expense or benefit for the year that remains after the allocation to continuing operations is allocated to that item. If there are two or more items other than continuing operations, the amount that remains after the allocation to continuing operations shall be allocated among those other items in proportion to their individual effects on income tax expense or benefit for the year.

- **Comprehensive Income**
  a. Other comprehensive items are shown net of tax effects or before tax effects with one amount shown for the total tax. (See Chapter 12)
  b. Accumulated other comprehensive income shown in the equity section of the statement of financial position is shown net of tax. (See Chapter 12)

- **Stockholder's Equity**

  Accounting errors are shown net of tax as adjustments to beginning retained earnings.

CHAPTER OVERVIEW

EXAMPLES OF TEMPORARY DIFFERENCES

TRANSACTIONS	FINANCIAL REPORTING	IRS – TAX REPORTING	FINANCIAL IBT* IS > < TAXABLE IBT	DEFERRED TAX
1. Sales	Accrual	Installment	Greater	Liability
2. Long-term Contracts	Percentage Completion	Completed Contract	Greater	Liability
3. Investments	Equity	Cost	Greater	Liability
4. Depreciation	Straight Line	SYD	Greater	Liability
5. Prepaid Expenses	Accrual	Cash	Greater	Liability
6. Rent Received in Advance	Accrual	Cash	Less	Asset
7. Subscriptions Received in Advance	Accrual	Cash	Less	Asset
8. Warranty Cost	Accrual	Cash	Less	Asset
9. Estimated Litigation Losses	Accrual	Cash	Less	Asset
10. Unrealized Loss on Marketable Securities	Accrual	Cash	Less	Asset

*Income Before Taxes

Generally { Asset - Revenue - Create Liability - (deferred)
Liability - Expenses - Create deferred Assets -

Chapter Thirteen
Accounting for Income Taxes Questions

The following former CPA exam questions and problems were originally intended for application with SFAS #96. The questions have been modified for compliance with SFAS #109 where necessary. In any questions with potential deferred tax assets, it should be assumed that a valuation allowance is not required unless specifically mentioned in the question or problem.

TEMPORARY DIFFERENCES; DEFERRED TAX LIABILITY

1. Tower Corp. began operations on January 1, 1997. For financial reporting, Tower recognizes revenues from all sales under the accrual method. However, in its income tax returns, Tower reports qualifying sales under the installment method. Tower's gross profit on these installment sales under each method was as follows:

Year	*Accrual method*	*Installment method*
1997	$1,600,000	$ 600,000
1998	2,600,000	1,400,000

The income tax rate is 30% for 1997 and future years. There are no other temporary or permanent differences. In its December 31, 1998, balance sheet, what amount should Tower report as a liability for deferred income taxes?

a. $840,000
b. $660,000
c. $600,000
d. $360,000

2. Huff Corp. began operations on January 1, 1998. Huff recognizes revenues from all sales under the accrual method for financial reporting purposes and appropriately uses the installment method for income tax purposes. Huff's gross margin on installment sales under each method was as follows:

Year	*Accrual method*	*Installment method*
1998	$ 800,000	$300,000
1999	1,300,000	700,000

Huff elected early application of FASB Statement No. 109, *Accounting for Income Taxes.* Enacted income tax rates are 30% for 1999 and 25% thereafter. There are no other temporary differences. In Huff's December 31, 1999, balance sheet, the deferred income tax liability should be

a. $150,000
b. $180,000
c. $275,000
d. $330,000

3. Scott Corp. received cash of $20,000 that was included in revenues in its 1999 financial statements, of which $12,000 will not be taxable until 2000. Scott's enacted tax rate is 30% for 1999, and 25% for 2000. Scott elected early application of FASB Statement No. 109, *Accounting for Income Taxes.* What amount should Scott report in its 1999 balance sheet for deferred income tax liability?

a. $2,000
b. $2,400
c. $3,000
d. $3,600

CURRENT TAX LIABILITY OR CURRENT PORTION OF TAX EXPENSE

4. On January 2, 1999, Ross Co. purchased a machine for $70,000. This machine has a 5-year useful life, a residual value of $10,000, and is depreciated using the straight-line method for financial statement purposes. For tax purposes, depreciation expense was $25,000 for 1999 and $20,000 for 2000. Ross elected early application of FASB Statement No. 109, *Accounting for Income Taxes.* Ross' 2000 income, before income taxes and depreciation expense, was $100,000 and its tax rate was 30%. If Ross had made **no** estimated tax payments during 2000, what amount of current income tax liability would Ross report in its December 31, 2000, balance sheet?

a. $26,400
b. $25,800
c. $24,000
d. $22,500

5. For the year ended December 31, 2001, Tyre Co. reported pretax financial statement income of $750,000. Its taxable income was $650,000. The difference is due to accelerated depreciation for income tax purposes. Tyre's effective income tax rate is 30%, and Tyre made estimated tax payments during 2001 of $90,000. What amount should Tyre report as current income tax expense for 2001?

a. $105,000
b. $135,000
c. $195,000
d. $225,000

6. Pine Corp.'s books showed pretax income of $800,000 for the year ended December 31, 1996. In the computation of federal income taxes, the following data were considered:

Gain on an involuntary conversion (Pine has elected to replace the property within the statutory period using total proceeds.)	$350,000
Depreciation deducted for tax purposes in excess of depreciation deducted for book purposes	50,000
Federal estimated tax payments, 1996	70,000
Enacted federal tax rate, 1996	30%

What amount should Pine report as its current federal income tax liability on its December 31, 1996, balance sheet?

a. $50,000
b. $65,000
c. $120,000
d. $135,000

COMBINATION OF PERMANENT AND TEMPORARY DIFFERENCES

7. For the year ended December 31, 1998, Mont Co.'s books showed income of $600,000 before provision for income tax expense. To compute taxable income for federal income tax purposes, the following items should be noted:

Income from exempt municipal bonds	$ 60,000
Depreciation deducted for tax purposes in excess of depreciation recorded on the books	120,000
Proceeds received from life insurance on death of officer	100,000
Estimated tax payments	0
Enacted corporate tax rate	30%

Ignoring the alternative minimum tax provisions, what amount should Mont report at December 31, 1998, as its current federal income tax liability?

a. $96,000
b. $114,000
c. $150,000
d. $162,000

8. Stone Co. began operations in 1999 and reported $225,000 in income before income taxes for the year. Stone's 1999 tax depreciation exceeded its book depreciation by $25,000. Stone also had nondeductible book expenses of $10,000 related to permanent differences. Stone's tax rate for 1999 was 40%, and the enacted rate for years after 1999 is 35%. Stone elected early adoption of FASB Statement No. 109, *Accounting for Income Taxes.* In its December 31, 1999, balance sheet, what amount of deferred income tax liability should Stone report?

a. $8,750
b. $10,000
c. $12,250
d. $14,000

Items 9 and 10 are based on the following:
Kent, Inc.'s reconciliation between financial statement and taxable income for 2000 follows:

Pretax financial income	$150,000
Permanent difference	(12,000)
	138,000
Temporary difference - depreciation	(9,000)
Taxable income	$129,000

Additional information:

	At 12/31/99	12/31/00
Cumulative temporary differences (future taxable amounts)	$11,000	$20,000

The enacted tax rate was 34% for 1999, and 40% for 2000 and years thereafter.

9. In its December 31, 2000, balance sheet, what amount should Kent report as deferred income tax liability?

a. $3,600
b. $6,800
c. $7,340
d. $8,000

10. In its 2000 income statement, what amount should Kent report as current portion of income tax expense?

a. $51,600
b. $55,200
c. $55,800
d. $60,000

Items 11 and 12 are based on the following:
Bee Corp. prepared the following reconciliation between book income and taxable income for the year ended December 31, 1999:

Pretax accounting income	$500,000
Taxable income	300,000
Difference	$200,000
Differences:	
Interest on municipal bonds	$ 50,000
Lower depreciation per financial statements	150,000
Total differences	$200,000

Bee elected early application of FASB Statement No. 109, *Accounting for Income Taxes,* in its financial statements for the year ended December 31, 1999.

Bee's effective income tax rate for 1999 is 30%. The depreciation difference will reverse equally over the next three years at enacted tax rates as follows:

Years	*Tax rates*
2000	30%
2001	25%
2002	25%

11. In Bee's 1999 income statement, the current portion of its provision for income taxes should be

a. $150,000
b. $125,000
c. $90,000
d. $75,000

12. In Bee's 1999 income statement, the deferred portion of its provision for income taxes should be

a. $60,000
b. $50,000
c. $45,000
d. $40,000

DEFERRED TAX ASSET

13. Quinn Co. reported a net deferred tax asset of $9,000 in its December 31, 2000, balance sheet. For 2001, Quinn reported pretax financial statement income of $300,000. Temporary differences of $100,000 resulted in taxable income of $200,000 for 2001. At December 31, 2001, Quinn had cumulative taxable differences of $70,000. Quinn's effective income tax rate is 30%. In its December 31, 2001, income statement, what should Quinn report as deferred income tax expense?

a. $12,000
b. $21,000
c. $30,000
d. $60,000

14. On its December 31, 2001, balance sheet, Shin Co. had income taxes payable of $13,000 and a current deferred tax asset of $20,000 before determining the need for a valuation account. Shin had reported a current deferred tax asset of $15,000 at December 31, 2000. No estimated tax payments were made during 2001. At December 31, 2001, Shin determined that it was more likely than not that 10% of the deferred tax asset would not be realized. In its 2001 income statement, what amount should Shin report as total income tax expense?

a. $8,000
b. $8,500
c. $10,000
d. $13,000

15. West Corp. leased a building and received the $36,000 annual rental payment on June 15, 1999. The beginning of the lease was July 1, 1999. Rental income is taxable when received. West's tax rates are 30% for 1999 and 40% thereafter. West has elected early adoption of FASB Statement No. 109, *Accounting for Income Taxes.* West had no other permanent or temporary differences. West determined that no valuation allowance was needed. What amount of deferred tax asset should West report in its December 31, 1999, balance sheet?

a. $5,400
b. $7,200
c. $10,800
d. $14,400

CLASSIFICATION OF DEFERRED TAX ACCOUNTS

16. At December 31, 2001, Bren Co. had the following deferred income tax items:

- A deferred income tax liability of $15,000 related to a noncurrent asset
- A deferred income tax asset of $3,000 related to a noncurrent liability
- A deferred income tax asset of $8,000 related to a current liability

Which of the following should Bren report in the noncurrent section of its December 31, 2001, balance sheet?

a. A noncurrent asset of $3,000 and a noncurrent liability of $15,000.
b. A noncurrent liability of $12,000.
c. A noncurrent asset of $11,000 and a noncurrent liability of $15,000.
d. A noncurrent liability of $4,000.

17. In 1999, Rand, Inc., reported for financial statement purposes the following items, which were not included in taxable income:

Installment gain to be collected equally in 2000 through 2002	$1,500,000
Estimated future warranty costs to be paid equally in 2000 through 2002	2,100,000

Rand has paid income taxes in the amount of $900,000 for the three year period ended December 31, 1999. There were no temporary differences in prior years. Rand's enacted tax rates are 30% for 1999 and 25% for 2000 through 2002.

Rand elected early application of FASB Statement No. 109, *Accounting for Income Taxes.* In Rand's December 31, 1999, balance sheet, what amounts of the deferred tax asset should be classified as current and noncurrent?

	Current	*Noncurrent*
a.	$60,000	$100,000
b.	$60,000	$120,000
c.	$50,000	$100,000
d.	$50,000	$120,000

18. Thorn Co. applies Statement of Financial Accounting Standards No. 109, *Accounting for Income Taxes.* At the end of 2000, the tax effects of temporary differences were as follows:

	Deferred tax assets liabilities	*Related asset classification*
Accelerated tax depreciation	($75,000)	Noncurrent asset
Additional costs in inventory for tax purposes	25,000	Current asset
	($50,000)	

A valuation allowance was not considered necessary. Thorn anticipates that $10,000 of the deferred tax liability will reverse in 2001. In Thorn's December 31, 2000, balance sheet, what amount should Thorn report as noncurrent deferred tax liability?

a. $40,000
b. $50,000
c. $65,000
d. $75,000

19. Because Jab Co. uses different methods to depreciate equipment for financial statement and income tax purposes, Jab has temporary differences that will reverse during the next year and add to taxable income. Deferred income taxes that are based on these temporary differences should be classified in Jab's balance sheet as a

a. Contra account to current assets.
b. Contra account to noncurrent assets.
c. Current liability.
d. Noncurrent liability.

DEFERRED TAX THEORY

20. Temporary differences arise when expenses are deductible for tax purposes

	After they are recognized in financial income	*Before they are recognized in financial income*
a.	No	No
b.	No	Yes
c.	Yes	Yes
d.	Yes	No

21. Rein Inc. reported deferred tax assets and deferred tax liabilities at the end of 1997 and at the end of 1998. According to FASB Statement No. 109, *Accounting for Income Taxes,* for the year ended 1998 Rein should report deferred income tax expense or benefit equal to the

a. Decrease in the deferred tax assets.
b. Increase in the deferred tax liabilities.
c. Amount of the current tax liability plus the sum of the net changes in deferred tax assets and deferred tax liabilities.
d. Sum of the net changes in deferred tax assets and deferred tax liabilities.

22. The liability method of accounting for deferred income taxes should be used for

	Intraperiod income tax allocation	*Permanent differences*
a.	Yes	Yes
b.	Yes	No
c.	No	No
d.	No	Yes

23. Orleans Co., a cash basis taxpayer, prepares accrual basis financial statements. Since 1999, Orleans has applied FASB Statement No. 109, *Accounting for Income Taxes.* In its 2000 balance sheet, Orleans' deferred income tax liabilities increased compared to 1999. Which of the following changes would cause this increase in deferred income tax liabilities?

I. An increase in prepaid insurance.
II. An increase in rent receivable.
III. An increase in warranty obligations.

a. I only.
b. I and II.
c. II and III.
d. III only.

INVESTEE UNDISTRIBUTED EARNINGS

24. Rico Corp. owns 40% of Dee Corp.'s voting common stock and accounts for its investment using the equity method. During 1999, Dee reported earnings of $225,000 and paid dividends of $75,000. Rico assumes that all of Dee's undistributed earnings will be distributed as dividends in future years. Rico's income tax rate is 30%. Rico elected early application of FASB Statement No. 109, *Accounting for Income Taxes.* Ignoring the dividends received deduction, what amount of deferred income tax liability should Rico report in its 1999 financial statements?

a. $27,000
b. $18,000
c. $9,000
d. $0

25. Taft Corp. uses the equity method to account for its 25% investment in Flame, Inc. During 1999, Taft received dividends of $30,000 from Flame and recorded $180,000 as its equity in the earnings of Flame. Additional information follows:

- All the undistributed earnings of Flame will be distributed as dividends in future periods.
- The dividends received from Flame are eligible for the 80% dividends received deduction.
- There are no other temporary differences.
- Enacted income tax rates are 30% for 1999 and thereafter.

Taft elected early application of FASB Statement No. 109, *Accounting for Income Taxes.* In its December 31, 1999, balance sheet, what amount should Taft report for deferred income tax liability?

a. $9,000
b. $10,800
c. $45,000
d. $54,000

LOSS CARRYBACKS AND CARRYFORWARDS

26. Mobe Co. reported the following operating income (loss) for its first three years of operations:

1999	$ 300,000
2000	(700,000)
2001	$1,200,000

For each year, there were no deferred income taxes, and Mobe's effective income tax rate was 30%. In its 2000 income tax return, Mobe elected to carry back the maximum amount of loss possible. In its 2001 income statement, what amount should Mobe report as total income tax expense?

a. $120,000
b. $150,000
c. $240,000
d. $360,000

27. Bishop Corporation began operations in 1997 and had operating losses of $200,000 in 1997 and $150,000 in 1998. For the year ended December 31, 1999, Bishop had pretax book income of $300,000. For the three-year period 1997 to 1999, assume an income tax rate of 40% and no permanent or temporary differences between book and taxable income. In Bishop's 1999 income statement, how much should be reported as total income tax expense?

a. $0
b. $40,000
c. $60,000
d. $120,000

28. Town, a calendar-year corporation incorporated in January 1996, experienced a $600,000 net operating loss (NOL) in 1999. For the years 1997 - 1998, Town reported a taxable income in each year, and a total of $450,000 for the two years. Assume that: (1) there is no difference between pretax accounting income and taxable income for all years, (2) the income tax rate is 40% for all years, (3) the NOL will be carried back to the profit years 1997 - 1998 to the extent of $450,000, and $150,000 will be carried forward to future periods. Town believes that it is more likely than not that the full tax benefit of the loss carryforward will be realized. In its 1999 income statement, what amount should Town report as the reduction of loss due to NOL carryback and carryforward?

a. $180,000
b. $240,000
c. $270,000
d. $360,000

INTRAPERIOD TAX ALLOCATIONS

29. Which of the following is not affected by tax allocation within a period?

a. Income before extraordinary items.
b. Extraordinary items.
c. Adjustments of prior periods.
d. Operating revenues.

30. Which of the following requires intra-period tax allocation?

a. That portion of dividends reduced by the dividends received deduction by corporations under existing federal income tax law.
b. The excess of accelerated depreciation used for tax purposes over straight-line depreciation used for financial reporting purposes.
c. Extraordinary gains or losses as defined by the Accounting Principles Board.
d. All differences between taxable income and financial statement earnings.

31. The amount of income tax applicable to transactions that must be reported using intraperiod income tax allocation is computed

a. By multiplying the item by the effective income tax rate.
b. As the difference between the tax computed based on taxable income without including the item and the tax computed based on taxable income including the item.
c. As the difference between the tax computed on the item based on the amount used for financial reporting and the amount used in computing taxable income.
d. By multiplying the item by the difference between the effective income tax rate and the statutory income tax rate.

REVIEW QUESTIONS

32. An example of intraperiod income tax allocation is

a. Interest income on municipal obligations.
b. Estimated expenses for major repairs accrued for financial statement purposes in one year, but deducted for income tax purposes when paid in a subsequent year.
c. Rental income included in income for income tax purposes when collected, but deferred for financial statement purposes until earned in a subsequent year.
d. Reporting the cumulative effect on prior years of changing to a different depreciation method in the income statement, net of direct tax effects.

Items 33 and 34 are based on the following:
Venus Corp.'s worksheet for calculating current and deferred income taxes for 1999 follows:

	1999	*2000*	*2001*
Pretax income	$ 1,400		
Temporary differences:			
Depreciation	(800)	(1,200)	$2,000
Warranty costs	400	(100)	(300)
Taxable income	$ 1,000	(1,300)	1,700
Enacted rate	30%	30%	25%

Venus elected early adoption of FASB Statement No. 109, *Accounting for Income Taxes.* Venus had no prior deferred tax balances. In its 1999 income statement, what amount should Venus report as:

33. Current income tax expense?
a. $420
b. $350
c. $300
d. $0

34. Deferred income tax expense?
a. $350
b. $300
c. $120
d. $95

---

35. On December 31, 1999, Oak Co. recognized a receivable for taxes paid in prior years and refundable through the carryback of all of its 1999 operating loss. Also, Oak had a 1999 deferred tax liability derived from the temporary difference between tax and financial statement depreciation, which reverses over the period 2000-2004. The amount of this tax liability is less than the amount of the tax asset. Which of the following 1999 balance sheet sections should report tax-related items in accordance with FASB Statement No. 109, *Accounting for Income Taxes?*

I. Current assets.
II. Current liabilities.
III. Noncurrent liabilities.

a. I only.
b. I and III.
c. I, II, and III.
d. II and III.

36. Leer Corp.'s pretax income in 1997 was $100,000. The temporary differences between amounts reported in the financial statements and the tax return are as follows:

- Depreciation in the financial statements was $8,000 more than tax depreciation.
- The equity method of accounting resulting in financial statement income of $35,000. A $25,000 dividend was received during the year, which is eligible for the 80% dividends received deduction.

Leer's effective income tax rate was 30% in 1997. In its 1997 income statement, Leer should report a current provision for income taxes of
a. $26,400
b. $23,400
c. $21,900
d. $18,600

37. In its 1999 income statement, Noll Corp. reported depreciation of $400,000 and interest revenue on municipal obligations of $60,000. Noll reported depreciation of $550,000 on its 1999 income tax return. The difference in depreciation is the only temporary difference, and it will reverse equally over the next three years. Noll's enacted income tax rates are 35% for 1999, 30% for 1993 and 25% for 2000 and 2002. Noll elected early application of FASB Statement No. 109, *Accounting for Income Taxes.* What amount should be included in the deferred income tax liability in Noll's December 31, 1999, balance sheet?
a. $40,000
b. $52,500
c. $63,000
d. $73,500

38. For the year ended December 31, 2000, Grim Co.'s pretax financial statement income was $200,000 and its taxable income was $150,000. The difference is due to the following:

Interest on municipal bonds	$70,000
Premium expense on keyperson life insurance	(20,000)
Total	$50,000

Grim's enacted income tax rate is 30%. In its 2000 income statement, what amount should Grim report as current provision for income tax expense?
a. $45,000.
b. $51,000.
c. $60,000.
d. $66,000.

39. Dix, Inc., a calendar-year corporation, reported the following operating income (loss) before income tax for its first three years of operations:

1997	$100,000
1998	(200,000)
1999	400,000

There are no permanent or temporary differences between operating income (loss) for financial and income tax reporting purposes. When filing its 1998 tax return, Dix did not elect to forego the carryback of its loss for 1998. Assume a 40% tax rate for all years. What amount should Dix report as its income tax liability at December 31, 1999?

a. $160,000
b. $120,000
c. $80,000
d. $60,000

40. Bart, Inc., a newly organized corporation, uses the equity method of accounting for its 30% investment in Rex Co.'s common stock. During 1999, Rex paid dividends of $300,000 and reported earnings of $900,000. In addition:

- The dividends received from Rex are eligible for the 80% dividends received deduction.
- All the undistributed earnings of Rex will be distributed in future years.
- There are no other temporary differences.
- Bart's 1999 income tax rate is 30%.
- The enacted income tax rate after 1999 is 25%.

Bart elected early application of FASB Statement No. 109, *Accounting for Income Taxes.* In Bart's December 31, 1999, balance sheet, the deferred income tax liability should be

a. $10,800
b. $9,000
c. $5,400
d. $4,500

41. Cahn Co. applies straight-line amortization to its trademark costs for both income taxes and financial statement reporting. However, for tax purposes a 5-year period is used and for financial statement purposes a 10-year period is used. Cahn has no other temporary differences, has an operating cycle of less than 1 year, and has taxable income in all years. Cahn should report both current and noncurrent deferred income tax liabilities at the end of

	Year 1	*Year 8*
a.	No	Yes
b.	No	No
c.	Yes	Yes
d.	Yes	No

42. Rom Corp. began business in 1999 and reported taxable income of $50,000 on its 1999 tax return. Rom elected early application of FASB Statement No. 109, *Accounting for Income Taxes.* Rom's enacted tax rate is 30% for 1999 and future years. The following is a schedule of Rom's December 31, 1999, temporary differences in thousands of dollars:

	12/31/99 Book basis over (under) tax basis	*Future taxable (deductible) amounts*			
		2000	*2001*	*2002*	*2003*
Equipment	10	(5)	5	5	5
Warranty liability	(20)	(10)	(10)		
Deferred compensation liability	(15)		(5)		(10)
Installment receivables	30	10		20	
Totals	5	(5)	(10)	25	(5)

What amount should Rom report as current deferred tax assets in its December 31, 1999, balance sheet?

a. $0
b. $1,500
c. $4,500
d. $6,000

Items 43 through 45 are based on the following:
The following trial balance of Shaw Corp. at December 31, 1999, has been adjusted except for income tax expense.

Shaw Corp.
TRIAL BALANCE
December 31, 1999

	Dr.	*Cr.*
Cash	$ 675,000	
Accounts receivable (net)	2,695,000	
Inventory	2,185,000	
Property, plant and equipment (net)	7,366,000	
Accounts payable and accrued liabilities		$ 1,801,000
Income tax payable		654,000
Deferred income tax liability		85,000
Common stock		2,300,000
Additional paid-in capital		3,680,000
Retained earnings, 1/1/99		3,350,000
Net sales and other revenues		13,360,000
Costs and expenses	11,180,000	
Income tax expense	1,129,000	
	$25,230,000	$25,230,000

Other financial data for the year ended December 31, 1999:

Included in accounts receivable is $1,000,000 due from a customer and payable in quarterly installments of $125,000. The last payment is due December 30, 2001.

The balance in the deferred income tax liability account pertains to a temporary difference not related to a balance sheet account that arose in a prior year, of which $15,000 is expected to be paid in 2000. Shaw elected to apply the provisions of FASB Statement No. 109, *Accounting for Income Taxes,* in its financial statements for the year ended December 31, 1999.

During the year, estimated tax payments of $475,000 were charged to income tax expense. The current and future tax rate on all types of income is 30%.

In Shaw's December 31, 1999, balance sheet,

43. The current assets total is
a. $6,030,000
b. $5,555,000
c. $5,530,000
d. $5,055,000

44. The current liabilities total is
a. $1,995,000
b. $2,065,000
c. $2,470,000
d. $2,540,000

45. The final retained earnings balance is
a. $4,401,000
b. $4,486,000
c. $4,876,000
d. $5,055,000

---

46. As a result of differences between depreciation for financial reporting purposes and tax purposes, the financial reporting basis of Noor Co.'s sole depreciable asset, acquired in 2001, exceeded its tax basis by $250,000 at December 31, 2001. This difference will reverse in future years. The enacted tax rate is 30% for 2001, and 40% for future years. Noor has no other temporary differences. In its December 31, 2001, balance sheet, how should Noor report the deferred tax effect of this difference?
a. As an asset of $75,000.
b. As an asset of $100,000.
c. As a liability of $75,000.
d. As a liability of $100,000.

RECENTLY DISCLOSED QUESTIONS

N98

47. Black Co., organized on January 2, 1997, had pretax financial statement income of $500,000 and taxable income of $800,000 for the year ended December 31, 1997. The only temporary differences are accrued product warranty costs, which Black expects to pay as follows:

1998	$100,000
1999	$50,000
2000	$50,000
2001	$100,000

The enacted income tax rates are 25% for 1997, 30% for 1998 through 2000, and 35% for 2001. Black believes that future years' operations will produce profits. In its December 31, 1997, balance sheet, what amount should Black report as deferred tax asset?

a. $50,000
b. $75,000
c. $90,000
d. $95,000

1999

48. Under current generally accepted accounting principles, which approach is used to determine income tax expense?

a. Asset and liability approach.
b. A with and without approach.
c. Net of tax approach.
d. Periodic expense approach.

Chapter Thirteen
Accounting for Income Taxes Problems

NUMBER 1

M94

Chris Green, CPA, is auditing Rayne Co.'s 2000 financial statements. The controller, Dunn, has provided Green with the following information:

For the year ended December 31, 2000, Rayne has adopted Statement of Financial Accounting Standards No. 109, *Accounting for Income Taxes.* Dunn has prepared a schedule of all differences between financial statement and income tax return income. Dunn believes that as a result of pending legislation, the enacted tax rate at December 31, 2000, will be increased for 2001. Dunn is uncertain which differences to include and which rates to apply in computing deferred taxes under FASB 109. Dunn has requested an overview of FAS 109 from Green.

Required:

a. Prepare a brief memo to Dunn from Green:
- identifying the objectives of accounting for income taxes,
- defining temporary differences,
- explaining how to measure deferred tax assets and liabilities, and
- explaining how to measure deferred income tax expense or benefit.

NUMBER 2

Income tax allocation is an integral part of generally accepted accounting principles. The applications of intraperiod tax allocation (within a period) and interperiod tax allocation (among periods) are both required.

Required:

1. Explain the need for **intraperiod** tax allocation.
2. Accountants who favor **interperiod** tax allocation argue that income taxes are an expense rather than a distribution of earnings. Explain the significance of this argument. **Do not explain the definitions of expense or distribution of earnings.**
3. Indicate and explain whether each of the following **independent** situations should be treated as a temporary difference or a permanent difference.
   a. Estimated warranty costs (covering a three-year warranty) are expensed for accounting purposes at the time of sale but deducted for income tax purposes when incurred.
   b. Depreciation for accounting and income tax purposes differs because of different bases of carrying the related property. The different bases are a result of a business combination treated as a purchase for accounting purposes and as a tax-free exchange for income tax purposes.
   c. A company properly uses the equity method to account for its 30% investment in another company. The investee pays dividends that are about 10% of its annual earnings.

NUMBER 3

Number 3 consists of 2 parts. Each part consists of 4 items. Select the **best** answer for each item.

Required:

a. **Items 1 through 4** describe circumstances resulting in differences between financial statement income and taxable income. For each numbered item, determine whether the difference is:

List

A. A temporary difference resulting in a deferred tax asset.

B. A temporary difference resulting in a deferred tax liability.

C. A permanent difference.

An answer may be selected once, more than once, or not at all.

1. For plant assets, the depreciation expense deducted for tax purposes is in excess of the depreciation expense used for financial reporting purposes.
2. A landlord collects some rents in advance. Rents received are taxable in the period in which they are received.
3. Interest is received on an investment in tax-exempt municipal obligations.
4. Costs of guarantees and warranties are estimated and accrued for financial reporting purposes.

b. The following partially completed worksheet contain Lane Co.'s reconciliation between financial statement income and taxable income for the 3 years ended April 30, 1997, and additional information.

Lane Co.
INCOME TAX WORKSHEET
For the Three Years Ended April 30, 1997

	April 30, 1995	April 30, 1996	April 30, 1997
Pretax financial income	$900,000	$1,000,000	$1,200,000
Permanent differences	100,000	100,000	100,000
Temporary differences	200,000	100,000	150,000
Taxable income	$600,000	$800,000	$950,000
Cumulative temporary differences (future taxable amounts)	$200,000	$ (6)	$450,000
Tax rate	20%	25%	30%
Deferred tax liability	$ 40,000	$ 75,000	$ (8)
Deferred tax expense	$ --	$ (7)	$ --
Current tax expense	$ (5)	$ --	$ --

The tax rate changes were enacted at the beginning of each tax year and were not known to Lane at the end of the prior year.

Required:

Items 5 through 8 represent amounts omitted from the worksheet. For each item, determine the amount omitted from the worksheet. Select the amount from the following list. An answer may be used once, more than once, or not at all.

5. Current tax expense for the year ended April 30, 1995.

6. Cumulative temporary differences at April 30, 1996.

7. Deferred tax expense for the year ended April 30, 1996.

8. Deferred tax liability at April 30, 1997.

Amount

A. $25,000

B. $35,000

C. $45,000

D. $75,000

E. $100,000

F. $112,500

G. $120,000

H. $135,000

I. $140,000

J. $160,000

K. $180,000

L. $200,000

M. $300,000

N. $400,000

Chapter Thirteen
Solutions to Accounting for Income Taxes Questions

1. (b) The gross profit from sales for 1997 and 1998 under the accrual method totals \$4,200,000 and the total under the installment method is \$2,000,000. This creates a temporary difference of \$2,200,000. The deferred tax liability on the December 31, 1998 balance sheet will be the temporary difference times the enacted future tax rate of 30% (\$2,200,000 × 30% = \$660,000 deferred tax liability).

2. (c) The deferred tax liability is the amount of the difference in gross margin \$2,100,000 - \$1,000,000 = \$1,100,000 at the future tax rate of 25% or \$275,000.

3. (c) The deferred tax liability is recognized at the rate anticipated in the period when the temporary difference reverses. Therefore, the deferred tax liability is \$12,000 × 25% or \$3,000.

4. (c) In 2000, the company would increase its deferred tax liability by \$2,400 [30% × (20,000 – 12,000)]. The current tax liability would be for only the amount due to be paid in 2000, taxable income of \$80,000 × 30% = \$24,000.

5. (c) The key point is that the **current portion** of tax expense is equal to the total tax liability **for the year.**
\$650,000 × 30% = \$195,000

6. (a)

Pretax (book) income	\$800,000
Nontaxable gain	(350,000)
Depreciation difference	(50,000)
Taxable income	\$400,000
Tax rate	30%
Current taxes due	\$120,000
Estimated tax payments	(70,000)
Current tax liability	\$ 50,000

7. (a) Taxable Income for Federal tax purposes:

Income per books before tax	\$600,000
Less the following permanent & temporary differences	
Income - municipal bonds	(60,000)
Excess depreciation	(120,000)
Proceeds life insurance	(100,000)
Taxable income - Fed. Tax	\$320,000

Since the federal tax rate is 30%, the federal tax liability at December 31, 1998 would be \$96,000 (\$320,000 × 30%).

8. (a) The nondeductible book expenses are permanent differences and do not affect taxes. The temporary depreciation difference (\$25,000) times the enacted future tax rate (35%) will be the deferred tax liability on the December 31, 1999 balance sheet (\$25,000 × 35% = \$8,750 deferred tax liability).

9. (d) The cumulative temporary difference at December 31, 2000 is \$20,000. This difference will reverse as future taxable amounts after 2000. Therefore, the appropriate tax rate for the future years is 40% and the deferred tax liability should be \$8,000 (\$20,000 × 40%).

10. (a) The **current** portion of income tax expense equals the current tax payable for the year.
\$129,000 × 40% current tax rate = \$51,600

11. (c) $300,000 × 30% = $90,000.

12. (d) Difference in depreciation to be reversed in future years at future tax rates:
($100,000 × 25% = $25,000) + ($50,000 × 30% = $15,000) = $40,000

13. (c) The income statement for 2001 would report the following:

Income Tax Expense		
Current Portion	($200,000 × 30%)	$60,000
Deferred Portion	($100,000 × 30%)	30,000
Total Income Tax Expense		$90,000

14. (c)
A. The journal entry to record the current taxes before the allowance entry is as follows:

	Debit	Credit
JE Income Tax Expense	8,000	
Deferred Tax Asset	5,000	
Income Tax Payable		13,000

B. The entry to record the allowance:

	Debit	Credit
JE Income Tax Expense	2,000	
Allowance to Reduce the Deferred Tax Asset to Realizable Value		2,000

Note: Calculation is 10% X 20,000 = 2,000

Total income tax expense is the total of the two JEs or $10,000.

15. (b) The annual rent of $36,000 is taxable in 1999 but only $18,000 is considered rental income for financial purposes. This creates a temporary difference of $18,000 which will be taxed at the future enacted tax rate of 40%. Therefore, the deferred tax asset at December 31, 1999 is $7,200 ($18,000 × 40%).

16. (b) In determining the deferred tax account that should appear on the balance sheet, the noncurrent deferred tax liability ($15,000) would be netted against the noncurrent deferred tax asset ($3,000). As a result a noncurrent deferred tax liability of $12,000 ($15,000 - 3,000) would be shown on the December 31, 2001 balance sheet.

17. (c) The excess deductible amount which reverses in 2000 is classified as current. The excess deductible amounts which reverse after 2000 are classified as noncurrent. All amounts are deferred at the reversal year rate of 25%.

18. (d) The classification of deferred tax account depends upon the classification of the asset or liability which created the deferred tax. In this case the deferred tax liability is related to a temporary difference in depreciation created by a noncurrent asset account. Since the related asset is noncurrent, the deferred tax liability ($75,000) will also be classified as noncurrent.

19. (d) Jab Co.'s use of different depreciation methods for tax versus financial reporting purposes will result in a deferred tax account. Since the reversal next year will **add** to taxable income, the deferred tax account has to be a liability. The classification of the deferred tax liability is noncurrent because the related asset (equipment) that created the deferred tax is noncurrent.

20. (c) Temporary differences may arise when expenses are deducted on the tax return after they are recognized on the books (warranty costs) or before they are recognized on the books (depreciation).

21. (d) The deferred income tax expense or benefit is the sum of the net changes in the deferred tax assets and deferred tax liabilities.

22. (c) The liability method is used for recognizing temporary tax differences. It is not used for permanent differences since there is no timing difference. Intraperiod allocation does not refer to timing or temporary differences but only to how the income tax expense is spread throughout the income statement.

23. (b) The increases in deferred tax liabilities would take place in those instances where the company's provision for income taxes is greater than its current tax payable. This cash basis taxpayer would generate a tax deduction but not an expense with the payment of an insurance premium in advance. The company would recognize rent income but not for tax purposes with an increase in rent receivable. This event would also lead to an increase in the tax provision but not in the current tax payable. An increase in the warranty obligation generates a non-deductible expense causing a tax provision which is less than the related current liability. Such an event would generate a deferred tax asset.

24. (b) Increase in investment:

Investee earnings	$225,000
Investee dividends	75,000
Excess	$150,000
Ownership percentage	40%
Pre-tax increase in equity	$ 60,000
Tax rate (future)	30%
Increase in deferred tax liability	$ 18,000

25. (a) The temporary difference between book income ($180,000) and the taxable dividends ($30,000) is $150,000. Since all the undistributed earnings will be distributed as dividends in the future, the temporary difference ($150,000) needs to be reduced by the 80% dividend exclusion to determine the taxable amount. The taxable amount would be $30,000 ($150,000 – 80% × $150,000). Therefore, the deferred tax liability will be the taxable portion of the temporary difference ($30,000) times the future enacted tax rate (30%) for a total of $9,000.

26. (c) In this question, it is helpful to look at the tax journal entries for both 2000 and 2001:

2000 JE	Tax Receivable ($300,000 × 30%)	90,000	
	Deferred Tax Asset ($400,000 × 30%)	120,000	
	Tax Benefits of Loss Carryforward & Loss Carryback		210,000

FASB #109 requires the recognition of both the Tax Loss Carryback ($90,000) and the Loss Carryforward ($120,000) in the year of the loss (2000).

2000 JE	Tax Benefit of Loss Carryforward	120,000	
	Allowance to Reduce Deferred Tax Asset to Realizable Value		120,000

FASB #109 also requires that an allowance against the deferred tax asset be established if it is **more likely than not** that none of the asset will be realized. In this case, the company is young and in 2000 does not have a pattern of earnings and the conservative approach would be to record the allowance.

2001 JE	Income Tax Expense ($1,200,000 × 30%)	360,000	
	Deferred Tax Asset		120,000
	Income Tax Payable ($1,200,000 - $400,000 × 30%)		240,000

Since the IRS does not allow the recognition of the loss carryforward in 2000, the loss carryforward is used to reduce the taxable income for 2001.

2001 JE	Allowance to Reduce Deferred Tax Asset to Realizable Value	120,000	
	Tax Benefit of Loss Carryforward		120,000

Since Mobe Co. has a profit in 2001, the allowance account is not needed and the tax benefits of the loss carryforward is recognized for book purposes.

The total tax expense would be the $360,000 less the tax benefits of the loss carryforward ($120,000) for a net tax expense of <u>$240,000</u>.

27. (d) FASB #109 requires that the tax benefit of the loss carryforward be recognized in the year of the loss and a deferred tax asset account be created. This may be adjusted by an allowance if it is more likely than not that the full tax benefit of the loss carryforward may not be realized. This problem does not mention an allowance. Therefore, Bishop should set up a deferred tax asset account and recognize a tax benefit of the loss carryforward of $80,000 in 1997 ($200,000 × 40%) and a $60,000 tax benefit in 1998 ($150,000 × 40%). Since the full benefit of the loss carryforwards was recognized in 1997 and 1998, the loss carryforwards do not affect the calculation of the tax expense for 1999. The tax expense for 1999 to be shown on the income statement is $120,000 ($300,000 × 40%).

Note: The IRS does not allow for early recognition of loss carryforwards, so for tax purposes $300,000 of the loss carryforwards would be recognized in 1999 and used to offset the 1999 pretax income of $300,000 in calculating the tax liability. The tax liability would then be zero.
The journal entry for 1999:

Income tax expense	$120,000	
Deferred tax asset		$120,000

28. (b) FASB #109 requires that the tax benefit of loss carryforwards be recognized in the year of the loss. In this case the tax benefit of the loss carryforward is $60,000 ($150,000 × 40%). The tax benefit of the loss carryback is $180,000 ($450,000 × 40%). Therefore, the combined benefit of the carryback and carryforward is $240,000 ($60,000 + $180,000).

29. (d) Intraperiod tax allocation should be applied to apportion income tax expense in amounts attributable to income before extraordinary items, and prior period adjustments.

30. (c) The income tax effects of extraordinary gains and losses must be included in extraordinary items in an income statement. Answers (a), (b) and (d) relate to inter-period allocation.

31. (b) The purpose of intraperiod tax allocation is to isolate the tax effect of a particular component of income. The calculation entails comparing the total tax obligation with that which would have existed had it not been for the component, the tax effect of which is being measured.

32. (d) Only item (d) requires intraperiod allocation of income tax. Item (a) results in a permanent difference and items (b) and (c) result in temporary differences.

33. (c) Income tax expense should be reported in two components: the amount currently payable (current portion) and the deferred portion. In this case, the current portion is the taxable income ($1,000) times the current tax rate of 30% for a total price of $300.

34. (d) The deferred portion of the income tax expense is calculated by considering the two temporary differences. The $800 depreciation difference will reverse in 2001 when the tax rate is 25%. This will create a deferred tax liability of $200 ($800 × 25%). The warranty cost will reverse partly in 2000 ($100) when the tax rate is 30% and partly ($300) in 2001 when the tax rate is 25%. This will create a deferred tax asset in 1999 of $105 ($100 × 30% + $300 × 25%). The deferred tax rate liability will increase tax expense by $200 and the deferred tax asset will decrease tax expense by $105 for a net increase in deferred tax expense of $95.

Note: The balance sheet will show a current deferred tax asset of $30 and a noncurrent deferred tax liability of $125 ($200 – $75).

35. (b) The receivable is classified as a current asset and the deferred tax liability which arises from the temporary difference (depreciation) is reported as a noncurrent liability due to the nature of the related asset.

36. (b)		
Pretax income		$100,000
Excess book depreciation		+ 8,000
Excess taxable investee income:		
Financial income	$35,000	
Taxable amount		
$25,000 × .2 =	– 5,000	– 30,000
Current taxable amount		$78,000
Tax rate		30%
Current tax provision		$23,400

37. (a) The municipal bond interest is a permanent difference and does not generate deferred income taxes. The depreciation difference of $150,000 generates deferred tax liability as follows:

2000 reversal—$50,000 × 30% =	$15,000
2001 and 2002 reversal—$100,000 × 25% =	25,000
	$40,000

38. (a) The current provision for income tax expense is the taxable income ($150,000) times the current tax rate (30%) for a total provision of $45,000. Since the municipal interest income and the keyperson life insurance expense are permanent differences, the tax expense and the tax liability for the year are both $45,000. Only temporary differences cause differences in taxes.

39. (b) The tax benefit of loss carryback would be $40,000 ($100,000 × 40%) and would result in a tax refund in 1998. The other $100,000 of the loss would be carried forward to offset a portion of the 1999 income. The tax liability would be the 1999 pretax income of $400,000 less the loss carryforward of $100,000 times the 40% tax rate for a total liability of $120,000.

40. (b)	
1997 undistributed earnings	$600,000
Ownership percentage	30%
Bart Inc.'s deferred income	$180,000
Portion taxable in future	20%
Taxable amount	$ 36,000
Tax rate to be applied	25%
Deferred tax liability	$ 9,000

41. (b) Since the related asset is not a current asset, the deferred tax liability will be classified as noncurrent at the end of year 1 as well as at the end of year 8.

42. (a) SFAS #109 requires classification based upon the related asset or liability or if no asset or liability is related, classification is based on the expected date of reversal.

Since the current portion of the warranty liability and the installment receivables are the same, the current deferred tax asset would be offset by the current deferred tax liability.

43. (d) Current assets:

Cash	$ 675,000
Accounts receivable	2,695,000
Inventory	2,185,000
	5,555,000
Less noncurrent portion of installment note	(500,000)
Total current assets	$5,055,000

44. (a) Current liabilities:

Accounts payable and accruals	$1,801,000
Income tax payable (see below)	179,000
	$1,980,000
Plus current portion of deferred tax liability	15,000
Total current liabilities	$1,995,000

Income tax payable:

Revenues	$13,360,000
Expenses	11,180,000
Pre-tax income	$ 2,180,000
Tax rate	30%
Tax provision	$ 654,000
Prepayments	475,000
Tax payable	$ 179,000

45. (c)

Retained earnings 1/1/99	$3,350,000
1999 income ($2,180,000 – $654,000)	1,526,000
Retained earnings 12/31/99	$4,876,000

46. (d) The key point is that the liability will reverse after 2001 when the tax rate is 40%. Therefore, the deferred tax liability that should appear on the December 31, 2001 balance sheet is $100,000 ($250,000 × 40%).

47. (d) Deferred taxes are calculated using future enacted tax rates.

Year	*Temporary Differences*	*x*	*Enacted Tax Rates*	=	*Deferred Tax Asset*
1998	$100,000	x	30%	=	$30,000
1999	$ 50,000	x	30%	=	15,000
2000	$ 50,000	x	30%	=	15,000
2001	$100,000	x	35%	=	35,000
			Total Deferred Tax Asset		$95,000

48. (a) SFAS 109 requires a balance sheet emphasis in the calculation of taxes. A balance sheet approach would stress the asset and liability calculation. For example, the calculation of a deferred tax liability uses the enacted future tax rate whereas an income statement approach would use the current year's tax rate.

Chapter Thirteen
Solutions to Accounting for Income Taxes Problems

NUMBER 1

a.

To: Dunn
From: Green
Re: Accounting for income taxes

Below is a brief overview of accounting for income taxes in accordance with FAS 109.

The objectives of accounting for income taxes are to recognize (a) the amount of taxes payable or refundable for the current year, and (b) deferred tax liabilities and assets for the estimated future tax consequences of temporary differences and carryforwards. Temporary differences are differences between the tax basis of assets or liabilities and their reported amounts in the financial statements that will result in taxable or deductible amounts in future years.

Deferred tax assets and liabilities are measured based on the provisions of enacted tax law; the effects of future changes in the tax laws or rates are not anticipated. The measurement of deferred tax assets is reduced, if necessary, by a valuation allowance to reflect the net asset amount that is more likely than not to be realized. Deferred income tax expense or benefit is measured as the change during the year in an enterprise's deferred tax liabilities and assets.

NUMBER 2

1. Intraperiod tax allocation is necessary to obtain an appropriate relationship between income tax expense and each element of earnings (continuing operations, discontinued operations, extraordinary items, and cumulative effects of accounting changes) or between income tax expense and prior-period adjustments. Income tax expense attributable to earnings before extraordinary items is computed based solely on the earnings before extraordinary items to prevent distortion of the results of continuing operations. The extraordinary items are shown net of the corresponding income tax consequences. Any prior-period adjustment is shown net of the corresponding income tax consequences as an adjustment to beginning retained earnings.

2. Some accountants cite the argument that income taxes are an expense rather than a distribution of earnings. They apply the matching concept of accrual accounting, thus relating the income taxes presented on the earnings statement to the earnings that gave rise to those taxes. Their argument is that income tax expense for financial reporting should be related to the respective pretax accounting earnings. Implicit in this argument is the notion that a distribution of earnings is not allocated to periods.

3. a. Temporary difference. The full estimated three years of warranty expenses reduce the current year's pretax accounting earnings, but will reduce taxable income in varying amounts each respective year, as incurred. Assuming the estimate as to each warranty is valid, the total amounts deducted for accounting for tax purposes will be equal over the three-year period for a given warranty. This is an example of an expense that, in the first period, reduces pretax accounting earnings more than taxable income and, in later years, reverses and reduces taxable income without affecting pretax accounting earnings.

   b. Permanent difference. This difference in depreciation for pretax accounting earnings and taxable income will never reverse because the depreciation is based on different recorded amounts of the assets in question. The income tax expense per books would be reflected based on the amount actually paid (or due) in this situation.

c. Temporary difference. The investor's share of earnings of an investee (other than subsidiaries and corporate joint ventures) accounted for by the equity method is included in pretax accounting earnings, while only dividends received are included in taxable income. This difference between pretax accounting earnings and taxable income is assumed to be related either to probable future dividend distributions or to anticipated realization on disposal of the investment and is a factor in determining income tax expense. Future dividends imply ordinary income, and future disposal of an investment implies capital-gains income. Because dividend income is subject to an 80% dividends-received deduction, the effective rate would, in this case, be lower for the ordinary dividend income than for capital gains.

NUMBER 3

Part a:

1. (b)

In situations in which tax depreciation exceeds financial (book) depreciation, the taxable income will be less than the financial income and will create a temporary difference resulting in a deferred tax liability. Since the depreciation is related to a long-term plant or equipment asset, the deferred tax liability will always be classified as a non-current liability.

The journal entry is:

Deferred Tax Expense	XX	
Deferred Tax Liability		XX

2. (a)

Rent collected in advance will be taxable as rent revenue in the year received, but will be recognized for financial purposes when earned in a later period. Therefore, taxable income in the current year will exceed financial income and a deferred tax asset will be created. The classification of the deferred tax asset will depend upon the classification of the related liability for unearned rent.

The journal entry is:

Deferred Tax Asset	XX	
Deferred Tax Expense		XX

3. (c)

Municipal interest would be included as interest revenues for financial reporting but since it is tax exempt, the interest would be excluded for calculating taxable income. This would create a permanent difference. A permanent difference causes a difference in financial net income vs. net income reported for taxes but will not cause a difference in the provision for taxes.

4. (a)

Estimated guarantees and warranties are accrued as expenses for financial reporting but are not tax deductible expenses until paid (cash basis.) This temporary difference causes financial income to be lower than taxable income which creates a deferred tax asset. Since the liability for accrued guarantees and warranties is normally part current and part long-term, the related deferred tax asset will be part current and part non-current.

Part b:

5. (g)

Current tax expense is $120,000. The current tax expense is the taxable income, $600,000, times the current tax rate of 20% for a total of $120,000.

6. (m) $300,000

The cumulative temporary differences at April 30, 1996 will be the $300,000 (the temporary differences for 1995 of $200,000 plus the $100,000 temporary differences for 1996.) Since the temporary differences are <u>deducted</u> from pretax financial income to arrive at taxable income, the differences represent <u>increases</u> in the cumulative total temporary differences. (See Question #7)

7. (b) $35,000

The solution approach is to prepare the following schedule:

<u>SCHEDULE TO CALCULATE THE APRIL 30, 1996 DEFERRED TAX LIABILITY</u>
<u>BASED ON THE 1996 TAX RATE OF 25%</u>

YEAR	CHANGE	TAX TEMPORARY DIFFERENCE	X	TAX RATE	=	BALANCE
1995	INCREASE	$200,000	X	20%	=	$40,000
1996	INCREASE	$100,000		(PLUG JE)		$35,000
1996	CUMULATIVE TOTAL	$300,000	X	25%		$75,000

The 1996 JE:

Tax Expense	200,000	
Deferred Tax Expense	35,000	
Tax Payable		200,000 *
Deferred Tax Payable		35,000

* Taxable income $800,000 x 25% = $200,000

8. (h) $135,000

The balance in deferred tax liability at April 30, 1997 is the cumulative temporary differences of $450,000 times the 1997 tax of 30% for an ending balance of $135,000.

Chapter Fourteen
Accounting for Leases, Pension and Postretirement Plans

Chapter Fourteen
Accounting for Leases, Pension and Postretirement Plans

ACCOUNTING FOR LEASES—SFAS #13

In General

A lease is in **form** a rental of property, but may be in **substance** the acquisition of an asset and the related obligation. This has financial accounting and reporting implications for both the lessor and the lessee.

The **lessee** should, if certain criteria are met, treat the lease as a **capital lease** and record an asset and related obligation equal to the present value of the minimum lease payments. If the criteria are not met, the lease should be treated as an **operating lease** (lease payments are charged to expense when payable on a straight-line basis).

The **lessor** should treat the lease as a **sales-type lease** if a profit or loss is involved and certain criteria are met. Sales-type leases are usually confined to manufacturers and dealer lessors, but not necessarily. If the lease is not a **sales-type lease**, but the incidence of ownership has been relinquished by the lessor due to the terms of the lease (in effect, a capital lease for the lessee), the lease should be classified as a **direct financing lease**.

Leases that meet the criteria of **leveraged leases** are not to be treated as direct financing leases. Operating leases are those which do not qualify for treatment in the other categories, and lease rentals received are credited to income.

Classification of Leases

Lessees can classify leases as:

1. Capital leases, or
2. Operating leases

Lessors can classify leases as either:

1. Sales-type leases
2. Direct financing leases
3. Leveraged leases
4. Operating leases

Lessee Lease Categories

Capital Leases. The lessee will record an asset and an obligation equal to the present value of the minimum lease payments during the lease term, not to exceed fair value, if at least one of the following criteria are met:

a. The lease transfers ownership of the property at the end of the lease term.
b. The lease contains a bargain purchase option.
c. The lease term is **75%** or more of the economic life of the property.
d. The present value of the minimum lease payments (excluding reimbursements for other costs) is **90%** or more of the fair value of the leased property.

In general, minimum lease payments are those required to be made in connection with the lease, except that **executory costs** such as insurance, maintenance and taxes should be excluded. **Charge executory costs to lease expense.** Minimum lease payments are increased by: any guarantee of the residual value at the expiration of the lease term; any payment required because of failure to renew or extend the lease. Minimum lease payments are increased by escalator provisions in the lease agreement or commitment, where property is being constructed or acquired for later use.

If the lease meets criterion (a) or (b), the asset should be amortized consistent with the lessee's normal depreciation policy for owned assets. If not, and the lease falls under either criterion (c) or (d) as a capital lease, normal depreciation policies should be followed except that the period of amortization should be the lease term. The lease should be amortized to its expected value, if any, at the end of the lease term.

Operating Leases. Rent is charged to expense over the lease term on a straight-line basis. If prepayments are made under the lease terms, such prepayments will be classified as assets and amortized over the life of the lease. Assume a 10-year lease providing for a $10,000 advance payment on 1/1/97 and $4,000 annual payments:

Date	Account	Debit	Credit
1/1/97	Leasehold	$10,000	
	Cash		$10,000
12/31/97	Rent Expense	5,000	
	Leasehold		1,000
	Cash		4,000

Lessor Lease Categories

Sales-Type Leases. Leases which give rise to a profit or loss at the inception of the lease; i.e., the fair value of the leased property is greater or less than the lessor cost or carrying value, if different, and:

a. The lease meets the capital lease criteria for lessees, and
b. Both of the following conditions are met:
    1. Collectibility of the lease payments is reasonably predictable, and
    2. There are no important uncertainties that exist as to unreimbursable costs yet to be incurred by the lessor.

However, a lease of real estate which otherwise would be classified as a sales type lease shall be classified as an operating lease by the lessor unless **at the beginning of the lease term** such lease also complies with SFAS #66 relative to sales of real estate. This provision relates to the adequacy of the buyer's initial and continuing investment in the property acquired and the conditions relating to the seller's continued involvement with the property sold.

Direct Financing Leases. Leases that meet all the above criteria of sales-type leases except that no manufacturer or dealer profit or loss is involved, and the lease is not a leveraged lease. Otherwise, the lease should be classified as an operating lease. In direct financing leases, the cost of the leased property and the fair value are the same at the inception of the lease. SFAS #23 defines "Inception of the Lease" as the date of the lease agreement or commitment, if earlier. A commitment shall be in writing and specifically set forth the principal provisions of the transaction. A preliminary agreement does not qualify.

A renewal or extension of an existing sales-type or direct financing lease which otherwise qualifies as a sales-type lease shall be classified as a direct financing lease unless the renewal or extension occurs within the last few months of the existing lease in which case it shall be classified as a sales-type lease.

Operating Leases. Rent is reported as income as it becomes receivable over the lease term on a straight-line basis. Initial direct costs should be deferred and allocated over the lease term in proportion to the recognition of rental income, but may be expensed as incurred if the effect is not material. The leased property should be included with or near property, plant and equipment in the balance sheet.

Computing the Present Value of Minimum Lease Payments

Lessee—The present value of the minimum lease payments should be computed using the lessee's **incremental borrowing rate** (the rate the lessee would pay if the asset were purchased with borrowed funds). Exception: See Lessor below.

Lessor—The rate **implicit in the lease** must be used. If the lessee knows the lessor's implicit rate and it is less than the lessee borrowing rate, the lessee should also use the implicit rate.

Computation of the Rate Implicit in the Lease

The implicit rate is the interest rate necessary to make the present value of the minimum lease payments plus the unguaranteed residual value of the leased property equal to the fair value of the leased property less any investment tax credit retained by the lessor.

Example: A crane is leased for $750 per month for 84 months. The lessee receives the investment credit of 10%. The leased property reverts to the lessor at the end of the lease. The cost of the property to the lessor is $40,000.

Computation of implicit rate by the lessor:

Fair Value of Lessor's Property (Normal Selling Price)	$42,490
Minimum Lease Payments (84 × $750)	63,000
Present Value of an Annuity of $1 at 1% per period, 84 periods (months) (56.6484 × $750)	42,490

Note: The 1% per month rate is shown in this example without details as to its computation. The computation is complex, particularly when the present value of the residual value is involved, and CPA exam candidates would not have the means to compute the rate, but may be required to solve a problem with the rate given.

Question: Referring to the previous example, assume the lessee's borrowing rate is 13% and the lessee knows the lessor's implicit rate. What rate will the lessee use in determining the amount to be capitalized?
Answer: 12%, because the rate implicit in the lease is less than the lessee's incremental borrowing rate.

Question: Capitalize the lease for the lessee assuming the lessee's incremental borrowing rate is 12%.

Answer:			
	Lease payments (84 × $750)	=	$63,000
	Present value of $63,000 (84 periods at 1% per period, 750 × 56.6484)	=	42,490
	Interest expense over the lease term		$20,510

Initial Direct Costs

1. Sales-type lease—charge to income in the period in which the sale is recorded.
2. Direct financing lease—part of the gross investment in the lease along with the minimum lease payments and the unguaranteed residual value.

Costs To Be Included As Initial Direct Costs, SFAS #91, #98

Costs incurred by lessor to originate a lease and costs directly associated with lessor activities related to the lease. Such activities include evaluating lessee's financial condition or collateral, negotiations and processing activities. Employment costs are included insofar as they relate directly to the initiation of the lease.

Recording Capital Leases by Lessee (See Appendix A)

Journal entries, assuming the date of lease is 1/1/97 and the property has a 7-year useful life and no salvage value. Facts are as previously given.

Date	Account	Debit	Credit
1/1/97	Leased property under capital lease[1]	$42,490	
	Obligations under capital leases[2]		$42,490
	To record capital lease		
1/31/97	Interest expense 1% × 42,490	425	
	Obligations under capital leases	325	
	Cash		750
	To record first payment under capital lease		
	Depreciation expense	506	
	A/D leased property under capital leases		506
	To record 1 month's depreciation		

[1]Classified on B/S separately under Property, Plant and Equipment. May not exceed FV.
[2]Classified separately under Long-Term Liabilities, except that current portion should be classified as such.

Recording Sales-Type Leases by Lessor (See Appendix A)

Assume the same facts as above, and the lessee classified the lease as a capital lease, collection of the lease payments is reasonably predictable, and there are no important uncertainties as to reimbursable costs. The lease is properly classified as a sales-type lease. The leased property reverts to the lessor at the termination of the lease.

1. Gross investment in the lease:

Minimum lease payments 84 × 750	$63,000[1]

[1]The gross investment in the lease would be increased by the unguaranteed residual value reverting to the lessor.

2. Normal selling price (fair value) $42,490

3. Rate implicit in the lease
It is the rate at which the present value of the gross investment is equal to the fair value (less any investment credit if retained by the lessor) or the rate at which $42,490 is the present value of $63,000. That rate is 1% per month.

Note: The computation of the rate would probably be done by computer. CPA candidates in the past have not been required to make such computations.

Application of the rate to the gross investment is:
P.V. of 84 monthly $750 payments:
$750 × 56.6484 (P.V. of annuity of $1 at 1% compounded monthly) $42,490

4. Computation of unearned income
"Unearned income" is the difference between the gross investment and the present value of the components of the gross investment.

Gross investment	$ 63,000
P.V. of minimum lease rentals	(42,490)
Unearned income	$ 20,510

Journal entries recording the lease, assuming that in addition to the above, initial direct costs are $500. Note that this transaction results in a gross profit in the year of sale of $2,490.

Minimum lease receivables	$63,000	
Cost of sales	40,000	
Sales		$42,490
Property or Inventory		40,000
Unearned income		20,510

Journal entries recording initial direct cost:

Selling expense (initial direct cost)	500	
Cash		500

When the first monthly payment is received:

Cash	750	
Unearned income	[1]425	
Minimum lease receivables		750
Lease income		[1]425

[1]1% × $42,490 = 425

Note: This lease would be recorded by the lessee as a capital lease.

Recording Direct Financing Leases by Lessor

Assume the same facts as shown for a sales-type lease above, except that the cost of the leased property is the same as the lessor's fair value ($42,490) at the inception of the lease and that no investment credit is available. Note: Frequently the lessee may acquire the property and be reimbursed by the lessor.

Journal entries recording the lease:

	Dr	Cr
Minimum lease payments receivable (gross investment)	$63,000	
Property		$42,490
Unearned income		20,510
Initial direct cost (gross investment)	* 500	
Cash		500

When the first annual payment is received:

	Dr	Cr
Cash	750	
Unearned income	[1]425	
Minimum lease payments receivable		750
Lease income		[1]425

[1]1% × $42,490 = 425 *adjustment of interest rate due to the initial direct cost omitted

Note: This lease would be recorded by the lessee as a capital lease.

Recording Leveraged Leases

The lessor's investment is recorded net of nonrecourse debt.

DR Rentals Receivable (total rent receivable less principal and interest on nonrecourse debt)
DR Investment Tax Credit Receivable
DR Estimated Residual Value
CR Unearned Deferred Income (investment credit plus pretax income)
CR Cash (investment outlay)

Note to students: We have not included examples of leverage lease computations because of their specialized nature and complexity. We do not expect the **computations** to be CPA exam material.

Comprehensive Example:

Dumont Corporation, a lessor of office machines, purchased a new machine for $500,000 on December 31, 1999, which was delivered the same day (by prior arrangement) to Finley Company, the lessee. The following information relating to the lease transaction is available:

- The leased asset has an estimated useful life of seven years which coincides with the lease term.
- At the end of the lease term, the machine will revert to Dumont, at which time it is expected to have a residual value of $60,000 (none of which is guaranteed by Finley).
- Dumont's implicit interest rate (on its net investment) is 12%, which is known by Finley.
- Finley's incremental borrowing rate is 14% at December 31, 1999.
- Lease rentals consist of seven equal annual payments, the first of which was paid on December 31, 1999.
- The lease is appropriately accounted for as a direct financing lease by Dumont and as a capital lease by Finley. Both lessor and lessee are calendar-year corporations and depreciate all fixed assets on the straight-line basis.

Information on present value factors is as follows:

Present value of $1 for seven periods at 12%	0.452
Present value of $1 for seven periods at 14%	0.400
Present value of an annuity of $1 in advance for seven periods at 12%	5.111
Present value of an annuity of $1 in advance for seven periods at 14%	4.889

Required:
1. Compute the annual rental.
2. Compute the amount to be recorded by the lessee for the leased asset and lease obligation as well as Finley's expenses for the year ended December 31, 2000.
3. Compute the gross lease rentals receivable by Dumont and the unearned interest at December 31, 1999.

Solution:
1.

Dumont Corporation
COMPUTATION OF ANNUAL RENTAL UNDER DIRECT FINANCING LEASE
Dated December 31, 1999

Cost of leased machine	$500,000
Deduct present value of estimated residual value	
$60,000 × 0.452 (present value of $1 at 12% for 7 periods)	27,120
Net investment to be recovered	472,880
Present value of an annuity of $1 in advance	
for 7 periods at 12%	÷ 5.111
Annual rental	$ 92,522

2.

Finley Company
LEASED ASSET AND OBLIGATION, 12/31/99
Expenses Year Ended December 31, 2000

Asset and initial liability under capital lease—$92,522 × 5.111	
(present value of an annuity of $1 in advance for 7 periods at 12%*)	$472,880
Deduct lease payment on December 31, 1999	92,522
Balance December 31, 1999 (after initial payment)	380,358
Interest rate	* × 12%
Interest expense year ended December 31, 2000	$ 45,643
Depreciation ($472,880 ÷ 7)	67,554
Total expense on lease	$113,197

* Finley Company must use Dumont Corporation's (Lessor's) implicit rate of 12% (which is known to it), since it is lower than
Finley's incremental borrowing rate of 14%.

3.

Dumont Corporation
COMPUTATION OF GROSS LEASE RENTALS RECEIVABLE AND UNEARNED INTEREST REVENUE AT INCEPTION OF DIRECT FINANCING LEASE
Dated December 31, 1999

Gross lease rentals receivable ($92,522 × 7)		$647,654
Deduct recovery of net investment in		
machine on capital lease		
Cost of machine	$500,000	
Residual value of machine	(60,000)	440,000
Unearned interest revenue		$207,654

Disclosures—Lessor

When leasing is a significant part of the lessor's business activities, the following information should be disclosed in the financial statements or footnotes along with a general description of the lessor's leasing activities.

For Sales-Type and Direct Financing Leases

1. The components of the net investment as of the date of each balance sheet presented:
   a. Future minimum lease payments to be received, less executory costs and the accumulated allowance for uncollectible minimum lease payments receivable.
   b. The unguaranteed residual values estimated to be recovered.
   c. Unearned income.
   d. For direct financing leases, initial direct costs.
2. Future minimum lease payments to be received for each of the five succeeding fiscal years.
3. Total contingent rentals included in income for each period presented.

For Operating Leases

1. The cost and carrying amount by major classes of property and the amount of accumulated depreciation in total.
2. Minimum future rentals in total and for each of the next five years.
3. Total contingent rentals in income for each period presented.

Disclosures—Lessee

For capital leases:

1. The gross amount of assets recorded under capital leases as of the date of each balance sheet presented by major classes according to nature or function. This information may be combined with the comparable information for owned assets.
2. Future minimum lease payments as of the date of the latest balance sheet presented, in the aggregate and for each of the five succeeding fiscal years, with separate deductions from the total for the amount representing executory costs, including any profit thereon, included in the minimum lease payments and for the amount of the imputed interest necessary to reduce the net minimum lease payments to present value.
3. The total of minimum sublease rentals to be received in the future under noncancelable subleases as of the date of the latest balance sheet presented.
4. Total contingent rentals actually incurred for each period for which an income statement is presented.

For operating leases having initial or remaining noncancelable lease terms in excess of one year:

1. Future minimum rental payments required as of the date of the latest balance sheet presented, in the aggregate and for each of the five succeeding fiscal years.
2. The total of minimum rentals to be received in the future under noncancelable subleases as of the date of the latest balance sheet presented.

For all operating leases, rental expense for each period for which an income statement is presented, with separate amounts for minimum rentals, contingent rentals, and sublease rentals. Rental payments under leases with terms of a month or less that were not renewed need not be included.

A general description of the lessee's leasing arrangements including, but not limited to, the following:

1. The basis on which contingent rental payments are determined.
2. The existence and terms of renewal or purchase options and escalation clauses.
3. Restrictions imposed by lease agreements, such as those concerning dividends, additional debt, and further leasing.

Real Estate Leases

Special provisions apply to the following categories of real estate leases:

1. Land only
2. Land and buildings
3. Equipment and real estate, and
4. Part of a building

If the lease is in category 3, the minimum lease payments should be estimated by whatever means are appropriate and the equipment should be considered separately according to its classification by both lessors and lessees.

Related Party Leases

Classification is the same as other leases except where the terms of the lease have been significantly affected by the relationship. In such cases, the economic substance of the transaction should be recognized in classifying the lease instead of its legal form. The nature and extent of leasing transactions with related parties should be disclosed.

In consolidated statements or statements accounted for on the equity basis, profit or loss on lease transactions should be treated according to generally accepted accounting principles for such statements.

Subsidiaries whose principal business activity is leasing property or facilities to the parent or other affiliates should be consolidated. The equity method is not adequate for fair presentation.

Sale-Leaseback Transactions

A sale-leaseback transaction is essentially a financing arrangement whereby the property is sold and leased back to the seller.

The sale and the leaseback cannot be accounted for as independent transactions. Any gain or loss on the sale should be deferred and amortized as follows:

a. If the transactions meet the criteria for treatment as a capital lease, over the useful life of the asset, or
b. Over the period of time the asset is expected to be used if classified as an operating lease.

If the fair value of the property at the time of the transaction is less than its **undepreciated cost**, a loss should be recognized for the difference immediately.

If the seller retains use of a minor part (if the present value of the rentals is 10% or less of the fair value of the asset sold) of the property, SFAS #28 requires the sale and lease to be accounted for based on their separate terms (unless the rentals called for are unreasonable relative to current market conditions in which case an appropriate amount would be deferred or accrued by adjusting the profit or loss on the sale).

If the seller retains more than a minor part but less than substantially all of the use of the property and the profit on the sale exceeds the present value of the minimum lease payments, the excess would be recognized as profit at the date of the sale.

Criteria for Sale-Leaseback Accounting (SFAS #98)

Sale-leaseback accounting shall be used by a seller-lessee only if a sale-leaseback transaction includes all of the following:

a. A normal leaseback as described below.
b. Payment terms and provisions that adequately demonstrate the buyer-lessor's initial and continuing investment in the property.
c. Payment terms and provisions that transfer **all** of the other risks and rewards of ownership as demonstrated by the absence of **any** other continuing involvement by the seller-lessee.

A **normal leaseback** is a lessee-lessor relationship that involves the active use of the property by the seller-lessee in consideration of payment of rent, and excludes other continuing involvement provisions or conditions.

A sale-leaseback transaction that does not qualify for sale-leaseback accounting because of any form of continuing involvement by the seller-lessee other than a normal leaseback shall be accounted for by the deposit method or as a financing. Continuing involvement includes provisions where:

a. The seller-lessee has an obligation or an option to repurchase the property or the buyer-lessor can compel the seller-lessee to repurchase the property.
b. The seller-lessee guarantees the buyer-lessor's investment or a return on that investment for a limited or extended period of time.

The financial statements of a seller-lessee shall include a description of the terms of the sale-leaseback transaction, including future commitments, obligations, provisions, or circumstances that require or result in the seller-lessee's continuing involvement.

The financial statements of a seller-lessee that has accounted for a sale-leaseback transaction by the deposit method or as a financing according to the provisions of this Statement also shall disclose:

a. The obligation for future minimum lease payments as of the date of the latest balance sheet presented in the aggregate and for each of the five succeeding fiscal years.
b. The total of minimum sublease rentals, if any, to be received in the future under noncancelable subleases in the aggregate and for each of the five succeeding fiscal years.

Example: On January 1, 2000, Marsh Company sold an airplane with an estimated useful life of ten years. At the same time, Marsh leased back the airplane as follows in the three separate situations:

	A	B	C
Sales price (fair value)	$500,000	$500,000	$500,000
Book value	100,000	100,000	100,000
Lease period	1 year	3 years	9 years
Annual rental	$50,000	$60,000	$74,000
Present value of lease rentals in advance at 10%	$50,000	$164,000	$469,000
Criterion met—Use of	minor part	more than minor part, less than substantially all	substantially all

Journal entries (ignoring income taxes):

a) 1/1/00

	Dr	Cr
Cash	500,000	
Aircraft (net)		100,000
Gain		400,000

Since a minor part of the use of the asset is being leased back, the entire gain is recognized.

	Dr	Cr
Rent expense	50,000	
Cash		50,000

Rent expense is recorded for an operating lease.

b) 1/1/00

	Dr	Cr
Cash	500,000	
Aircraft (net)		100,000
Gain		236,000
Deferred gain		164,000

Since more than a minor part but less than substantially all of the asset's use is being leased back, gain is recognized to the extent of the excess of the gain over the present value of the lease payments.

	Dr	Cr
Rent expense	5,333	
Deferred gain	54,667	
Cash		60,000

Rent expense and amortization of the deferred gain under an operating lease is recorded. The amortization is for the 2000 year.

c) 1/1/00

	Dr	Cr
Cash	500,000	
Aircraft (net)		100,000
Gain		- 0 -
Deferred gain		400,000

	Dr	Cr
Leased aircraft	469,000	
Lease liability		469,000

Lease liability	74,000	
Cash		74,000

The entire gain is deferred and a capitalized lease is recorded.

12/31/00

Interest expense	39,500	
Liability		39,500
Depreciation expense	7,667	
Deferred gain	44,444	
Accumulated depreciation		52,111

469,000 ÷ 9 = 52,111
400,000 ÷ 9 = 44,444
Difference 7,667

Interest and depreciation is recorded on a capitalized lease.

APPENDIX A

LEASES

LESSEE'S POINT OF VIEW

↓

CAPITALIZABLE LEASE

↓

CRITERIA: **MEET ONE**

A. Transfer title
B. Bargain purchase option
C. 75% or more of asset's useful life
D. Present Value of Future Lease Payments is 90% or more of the asset's fair market value

THEORY: "Substance over Form"
"Purchase an Asset on Installments"

↓

ACCOUNTING

↓

Annuity Due
Annuity in Advance

20X2			
Jan. 1	Leased Asset	XXX	
	Lease Liability		XXX
Jan. 1	Lease Liability	XXX	
	Cash		XXX
Dec. 31	Dep. Exp. - Lease Asset	XXX	
	Acc. Dep.- Lease Asset		XXX
Dec. 31	Interest Expense	XXX	
	Interest Payable		XXX
20X3			
Jan. 1	Interest Payable	XXX	
	Lease Liability	XXX	
	Cash		XXX

↓

Ordinary Annuity
Annuity in Arrears

20X2			
Jan. 1	Leased Asset	XXX	
	Lease Liability		XXX
Jan. 1	No Entry		
Dec. 31	Dep. Exp.– Lease Asset	XXX	
	Acc. Dep. – Lease Asset		XXX
Dec. 31	Interest Expense	XXX	
	Lease Liability	XXX	
	Cash		XXX
20X3			
Jan. 1	No Entry		

↓

CALCULATION OF PRESENT VALUE OF FUTURE LEASE PAYMENTS

USE LOWER OF TWO INTEREST RATES

A. Present Value of Lease Payments (Exclude Executory Cost)	XXX
PLUS **EITHER**	
B. PV of BARGAIN PURCHASE OPTION	XXX
OR	
PV of GUARANTEED RESIDUAL	-------
TOTAL PRESENT VALUE	XXX

CANNOT EXCEED FMV!

APPENDIX B

LEASES
LESSOR'S POINT OF VIEW
↓
CAPITALIZABLE LEASE
↓

CRITERIA: **MEET ONE**

A. Transfer title
B. Bargain purchase option
C. 75% or more of asset's useful life
D. Present Value of Future Lease Payments is 90% or more of the asset's fair market value

PLUS

CRITERIA: **MEET BOTH**

A. No problem with collectibility of lease receivable
B. No important uncertainties surround the amount of unreimbursable cost yet to be incurred by the lessor under the lease

THEORY: "SUBSTANCE OVER FORM"
↓
TYPES OF LEASES

↓ **DIRECT FINANCING**	↓ **SALES TYPE**
Lessor = "Bank"	Lessor = "Bank and Manufacturer or Dealer"
Interest Revenue	Interest Revenue & Gross Profit

↓
ACCOUNTING

Direct financing ↓

JE Lease Receivable	XXX	
Unearned Interest		XXX
Inventory of Leased Assets		XXX

Sales type ↓

JE Lease Receivable	XXX	
Unearned Interest		XXX
Sales		XXX
JE Cost of Goods Sold	XXX	
Inventory		XXX

↓

JE Cash	XXX	
Lease Receivable		XXX
JE Unearned Interest	XXX	
Interest Revenue		XXX

APPENDIX C

ACCOUNTING FOR PENSIONS SFAS #87
↓

↓ NET PERIODIC PENSION COST		↓ MINIMUM LIABILITY COMPUTATION	
(Pension Expense)			
a. Service cost	X X	Accumulated benefit obligation	X X
		- Plan assets at fair value	X X
		=Minimum liability	X X
b. Interest on project benefit obligation	X X		
c. Actual and expected return on plan assets	X X		
d. Amortization of unrecognized prior service cost	X X		
e. Amortization of unrecognized net gain or loss	X X		
Total – Pension expense	X X		

EMPLOYER'S ACCOUNTING FOR PENSIONS

In reviewing for Pensions, the candidate should focus on the following key points:

1. Terminology (see glossary)
2. Differences between a defined contribution plan and a defined benefit plan.
3. Calculation of pension expense (5 elements-ignore element #6).
4. Journal entry to record a pension expense and employer funding.
5. Calculation, journal entry and reporting of minimum pension liability.
6. Calculation of actual return on plan assets and the balance in the projected benefit obligation (see worksheet).
7. Pension plan disclosures. (SFAS #132)

Types of Pension Plans

- **Defined benefit pension plan**
  A pension plan that defines an amount of pension benefit to be provided, usually as a function of one or more factors such as age, years of service, or compensation. Any pension plan that is not a defined contribution pension plan is, for purposes of this Statement, a defined benefit pension plan.

- **Defined contribution pension plan**
  A plan that provides pension benefits in return for services rendered, provides an individual account for each participant, and specifies how contributions to the individual's account are to be determined instead of specifying the amount of benefits the individual is to receive. Under a defined contribution pension plan, the benefits a participant will receive depend solely on the amount contributed to the participant's account, the returns earned on investments of those contributions, and forfeitures of other participants' benefits that may be allocated to such participant's account.

EMPLOYER'S ACCOUNTING FOR PENSIONS-SFAS #87

In General

Statement #87 applies measurement, recognition and disclosure requirements primarily for a single employer defined benefit pension plan.

NET PERIODIC PENSION COST (PENSION EXPENSE)

The employer's net periodic pension cost includes:

1. **Service cost**—The present value of benefits earned by employees during the period according to the pension benefit formula contained within the pension plan.
2. **Interest cost**—The increase in the projected benefit obligation due to the passage of time. Such interest costs are to be measured based upon rates at which the pension benefits could be effectively settled (PBGC annuity rates and high quality fixed income rates).
3. **Actual return on plan assets**—Based upon the fair value of plan assets at the beginning and end of the period, adjusted for contributions and benefit payments. Although the actual return is disclosed as a component of pension cost, pension expense will include an amount equal to the expected return in plan assets. The difference between expected return and the actual return is included in the gain or loss component (#5) below.
4. **Amortization of unrecognized prior service cost**—The cost of retroactive benefits is amortized by assigning an equal amount to each future period of service of each employee who is active at the date of the initiation of the plan (or amendment). If essentially all of the employees are inactive, such cost shall be amortized based upon the remaining life expectancy of those participants. The amortization can, alternatively, be computed using a straight-line approach based upon the average remaining service life of the employees or any other rational approach which results in a faster write-off than the service-life approach first discussed above (disclosure of method is required).
5. **Amortization of cumulative unrecognized gains or losses using the "corridor" approach.**
   - Gains & Losses consist of the following two items:
     a. Changes in the amount of the projected benefit obligation or plan assets resulting from experience which is different from what was assumed, or from changes In assumptions.

     b. The difference between the actual return on plan assets and the expected return on plan assets.

   - Amortization using the corridor approach:
     a. The corridor was arbitrarily established by the FASB as 10% of the greater of the beginning period balance in the projected benefit obligation or the market related value of the plan assets. This corridor establishes a threshold for amortization.

     b. The excess of the beginning of the period cumulative unrecognized gains or losses over the corridor amount is amortized in the same manner as the prior period costs.

6. **Amortization of net obligation or net assets at date of implementation**—An employer must determine, as of the beginning of the year in which SFAS #87 is initially applied, both the amount of the projected benefit obligation as well as the fair value of plan assets (plus previously recognized unfunded accrued pension cost or minus previously recognized prepaid pension cost). The differential is amortized over the average remaining service period of employees expected to receive benefits under the plan (or the employer may use 15 years if greater).

RECOGNITION OF ASSET AND LIABILITY ON THE BALANCE SHEET

Pension Cost

If the net pension cost (expense) recognized pursuant to SFAS #87 exceeds the employer's contribution to the pension plan, the excess is recognized as an **accrued pension liability.** If the employer contributes more than the net pension cost; an asset, **prepaid pension cost**, is recognized.

Accounting Entries

XYZ Corporation adopts a defined benefit pension plan on January 1, 1999, with no retroactive benefits to employees. The company uses a 10% rate as appropriate for settling any projected benefit obligation and the expected return on assets is also projected at 10%. Using the benefits/years of service approach, the actuary has determined a service cost of $300,000 for 1999 and $330,000 for 2000.

Accounting entries assuming these amounts are funded:

	1999		*2000*	
Pension Expense	$300,000		$330,000	
Cash		$300,000		$330,000

Accounting entries assuming the company funds $275,000 in 1999 and $300,000 in 2000:

1999	Pension expense	$300,000	
	Cash		$275,000
	Accrued pension liability		25,000
2000	Pension expense computation:		
	Service cost		$330,000
	Interest on projected benefit obligation 10% × $300,000		30,000
	Return on assets—$275,000 × 10%		(27,500)
			$332,500
	Pension expense	$332,500	
	Cash		$300,000
	Accrued pension liability		32,500

Accounting entries assuming the company funds $320,000 in 1999 and $340,000 in 2000:

1999:	Pension expense	$300,000	
	Prepaid pension cost	20,000	
	Cash		$320,000
2000:	Pension expense computation:		
	Service cost		$330,000
	Interest on PBO 10% × $300,000		30,000
	Return on assets 10% × $320,000		(32,000)
			$328,000
	Pension expense	$328,000	
	Prepaid pension cost	12,000	
	Cash		$340,000

Minimum Pension Liability

In addition to the journal entry to record pension cost, the FASB was concerned that a company may need to record an **additional pension liability** to report a minimum liability on the balance sheet. After much discussion the FASB decided that the minimum liability should be the excess of the accumulated benefit obligation over the fair value of the plan assets at the end of the accounting period.

The offset to the recording of the additional pension liability is a debit to **deferred pension cost-intangible asset.** This deferred pension cost account is limited to the amount of the unrecognized prior service cost. If the additional pension liability which must be recorded is greater than the unrecognized service cost, the excess is recognized net of tax as an other comprehensive income account called **excess of additional pension liability over unrecognized**

prior service cost. The change in the account is shown in the calculation of comprehensive income and the accumulated balance in the account is reported net of tax as a part of accumulated other comprehensive income in the equity section of the balance sheet.

EXAMPLE OF MINIMUM PENSION LIABILITY

ABC Company provides the following information relative to its defined benefit plan for the years 1999 and 2000.

	December 31	
	1999	2000
Accrued Pension Liability	$20,000	-0-
Prepaid Pension Cost	-0-	$ 10,000
Unrecognized Prior Service Cost	$75,000	$ 60,000
Minimum Pension Liability		
Accumulated Benefit Obligation	$80,000	$160,000
Fair Value of Plan Assets	90,000	120,000
Minimum Pension Liability	-0-	$ 40,000

Instruction: Prepare the journal entry required by the minimum pension liability calculation.

Solution:

1999 A journal entry is not required because the fair value of the plan assets exceed the accumulated benefit obligation. The FASB does not permit the recognition of a net investment in the pension plan when the plan assets exceed the pension obligation.

ABC's balance sheet would report an accrued pension liability of $20,000.

2000 JE

	Debit	Credit
Intangible Asset-Deferred Pension Cost	$50,000	
Additional Pension Liability		$50,000*

*Minimum Liability required	$40,000
Plus balance in prepaid pension cost	10,000
Additional Pension Liability	$50,000

ABC's balance sheet would report the following balances:

Intangible Asset- Deferred Pension Cost	$50,000
Pension Liability	$40,000

Note: The additional pension liability account is netted against the prepaid pension cost account for a balance of $40,000.

PENSION DISCLOSURES

The pension plan and post-retirement benefit plan disclosures were combined in SFAS #132. These disclosures are listed after the section on post-retirement benefits on page 14-25.

Comprehensive Illustration
XYZ Corp. implements a noncontributory defined benefit pension plan on January 1, 1999, and the company anticipates relatively constant employment levels in the future with a turnover rate approximating 5% each year. The independent trustee administering the plan indicates a prior service cost of $1,000,000 at 1/1/99. The settlement rate as well as the rate of return on assets is 8%. The average remaining service life of the employees is 20 years and the company uses a straight-line approach to amortization.

Additional information for the years ended December 31:

	1999	*2000*
Annual service cost	$450,000	$500,000
Accumulated benefit obligation, 12/31	$1,400,000	$2,000,000
Fair value of plan assets	$500,000	*$1,100,000
Company cash contribution (made 12/31)	$500,000	$550,000

*reflects gain of $10,000, immaterial, therefore not amortized

Determination of pension expense:	*1999*	*2000*
1. Service cost	$450,000	$500,000
2. Interest on projected benefit obligation		
8% × 1,000,000 and 8% × $1,530,000	80,000	122,400
3. Earnings on assets		
8% × 500,000		(40,000)
4. Amortization of prior service cost		
5% × 1,000,000	50,000	50,000
5. Gains and losses (not greater than 10% of P.B.O.)	0	0
Expense	$580,000	$632,400

Asset-Liability to be Recognized

	1999	*2000*
Accrued pension at January 1	$ - 0 -	$(80,000)
Pension expense	(580,000)	(632,400)
Cash contribution	500,000	550,000
Accrued pension liability at December 31, 1999	$(80,000)	
Accrued pension liability at December 31, 2000		$(162,400)

Computation of additional liability:		
Plan assets December 31	$ 500,000	$1,100,000
Accumulated benefit obligation	1,400,000	2,000,000
Minimum pension liability	(900,000)	(900,000)
Accrued pension liability (above)	80,000	162,400
Additional liability required	$ 820,000	$737,600
Intangible asset to be recognized (adjustment)	820,000	$(82,400)

Journal entries:

		DR	*CR*
Dec. 31, 1999	Pension expense	$580,000	
	Cash		$500,000
	Accrued pension liability		80,000
	Deferred pension cost-intangible asset	$820,000	
	Additional pension liability		$820,000
	To establish additional liability required		
Dec. 31, 2000	Pension expense	$632,400	
	Accrued pension liability		$ 82,400
	Cash		550,000

Additional pension liability	$82,400	
Deferred pension cost-intangible asset		$82,400
To adjust additional pension liability required		

ILLUSTRATION FOR SFAS #130-COMPREHENSIVE INCOME

Using the same illustration assume that at December 31, 1999, the unrecognized prior service cost is $750,000 instead of $950,000 and that the tax rate is 30%.

In this case the journal entry to establish the additional pension liability becomes more complicated. The original entry was a debit to deferred pension cost for $820,000 and a credit to additional pension liability for $820,000. Under the new assumption, the debit to deferred pension cost - intangible asset cannot exceed the unrecognized prior service cost of $750,000. The additional debit of $70,000 is to an account called excess of additional pension liability over unrecognized prior service cost. The journal entry is as follows:

December 31, 1992			
JE	Deferred pension cost - Intangible asset	$750,000	
	Excess of additional pension liability over unrecognized prior service cost	70,000	
	Additional pension liability		$820,000

The **change** in the excess of additional pension liability over unrecognized prior service cost account is reported as other comprehensive income net of the 30% tax effect in the calculation of comprehensive income (#130). The **accumulated balance** in the account is included net of taxes as a part of the accumulated other comprehensive income shown in the equity section of the statement of financial position (see Chapter 12 for a review of comprehensive income).

AMORTIZATION OF CUMULATIVE UNRECOGNIZED GAINS AND LOSSES (CORRIDOR METHOD)

In our comprehensive example the amortization gains or losses (step 5) was zero because the cumulative unrecognized gains or losses did not exceed the "corridor" (threshold) account. Please use the following example to prepare for the amortization calculation.

Example: Magic Corporation obtained the following information from its actuary. All amounts given are as of **1/1/99** (beginning of the year).

	1/1/99
Projected benefit obligation	$1,500.00
Market-related asset value	$1,600.00
Cumulative unrecognized loss	$200.00
Average remaining service period	5 years

Required: What amount of the cumulative unrecognized net loss should be amortized (step 5) as part of pension expense in 1999?

Solution:

Step 1- Calculate the corridor amount.

10% of the **greater** of the January 1 projected benefit obligation or market related asset value.

10% X $1,600.000 = $160,000 corridor

Step 2- Calculate the **amount** to be amortized by comparing the cumulative unrecognized loss to the corridor.

$200,000 - $160,000= $40,000 amount to be amortized.

Step 3- Calculate the amortization amount to be included in the 1999 pension expense by dividing the amortization by the average remaining service period.

$40,000 ÷ 5 years = $8,000 (the 1999 amortization).

PENSION SUMMARY WITH WORKSHEET

Please study the following problem and worksheet solution. Although the CPA exam does not usually test the worksheet, the worksheet is an excellent way to view the relationships among the various accounts.

- Study the calculation of Pension Expense.
- The calculation of interest is the January 1 projected benefit obligation x 9% (9% x $575,000 = $51,750.)
- Note that when the expected return on plan assets is different from the actual return, the expected return is used in the calculation of the pension expense. This is shown on the worksheet as follows:

Actual return on the plan assets	$52,000
Less unexpected gain	(5,000)
Expected return on plan assets	$47,000

- Review the components of the projected benefit obligation.
- Review the components of the plan assets.
- Notice the two elements included under cumulative unrecognized gain or loss. The beginning balance in this column is zero so there is no amortization for 1999.
- Notice that the pension benefits are paid by the pension trustee and not by the corporation.
- Study the reconciliation schedule which is part of the pension disclosure.

Problem:
Grubbs Corporation sponsors a defined benefit pension plan for its employees. On January 1, **1999** the following balances relate to this plan:

Plan assets	$450,000
Projected benefit obligation	575,000
Prepaid/accrued pension liability	25,000
Unrecognized prior service cost	100,000

As a result of the operation of the plan during **1999** the following additional data are provided by the actuary:

Service cost for 1999	$ 85,000
Interest/Discount/Settlement rate of 9%	
Actual return on plan assets in 1999	52,000
Amortization of prior service cost	19,000
Expected return on plan assets	47,000
Unexpected loss from change in projected benefit obligation, due to change in actuarial predictions	76,000
Contributions in 1999	99,000
Benefits paid retirees in 1999	81,000

Required: Complete the following pension worksheet.

Solution:

GRUBBS CORP.
Pension Work Sheet

Items	General Journal Entries			Memo Record			
	Annual Pension Expense	Cash	Prepaid/ Accrued Cost	Projected Benefit Obligation	Plan Assets	Unrecognized Prior Service Cost	Cumulative Net Gain or Loss
Bal. January 1, 1999			25,000 Cr.	575,000 Cr.	450,000 Dr.	100,000 Dr.	
1. Service Cost	85,000 Dr.			85,000 Cr.			
2. Interest Cost	51,750 Dr.			51,750 Cr.			
3a. Actual Return	52,000 Cr.				52,000 Dr.		
3b. Unexpected Gain	5,000 Dr.						5,000 Cr.
4. Amortization of PSC	19,000 Dr.					19,000 Cr.	
5. Liability increase				76,000 Cr.			76,000 Dr.
6. Contributions		99,000 Cr.			99,000 Dr.		
7. Benefits				81,000 Dr.	81,000 Cr.		
Journal Entry	108,750 Dr.	99,000 Cr.	9,750 Cr.				
Bal. Dec. 31, 1999			34,750 Cr.	706,750 Cr.	520,000 Dr.	81,000 Dr.	71,000 Dr.

Reconciliation Schedule -- 12/31/99	
Projected benefit obligation (Credit)	($706,750)
Plan assets at fair value (Debit)	520,000
Funded status	(186,750)
Unrecognized prior service cost (Debit)	81,000
Unrecognized net loss (Debit)	71,000
Prepaid/Accrued Pension Cost - Liability	($34,750)

ACCOUNTING FOR SETTLEMENTS AND CURTAILMENTS OF DEFINED BENEFIT PENSION PLANS, SFAS #88

A settlement of a pension obligation is an irrevocable elimination of an employer's pension liability usually through an annuity contract or a lump sum cash payment.

A curtailment is an event which significantly reduces the expected future service of employees or eliminates the accrual of benefits for some or all employees. Curtailments generally include plan suspension or termination, plant closings or discontinuation of a business segment.

FASB Statement No. 88 requires that the net gain or loss from a settlement or curtailment be included in the net income of the period. When a plan is *settled,* the net gain or loss is the unrecognized net gain or loss that has not been recognized as part of pension expense plus any remaining unrecognized net asset existing when *FASB Statement No. 87* was initially applied. When a plan is *curtailed,* the portion of the unrecognized prior service cost associated with the estimated reduced future benefits is a loss. This amount is combined with any gain or loss from a change in the projected benefit obligation due to the curtailment in order to determine the net gain or loss.

Termination Benefits Paid to Employees

Such benefits may include lump-sum cash payments, payments over future periods, or similar inducements. *SFAS No. 88* requires that a company record a loss and a liability for these *termination benefits* when the following two conditions are met:

1. The employee accepts the offer.
2. The amount can be reasonably estimated.

The amount of the loss includes the amount of any lump-sum payments and the present value of any expected future benefits.

PENSION TERMS

Accumulated benefit obligation

The actuarial present value of benefits (whether vested or nonvested) attributed by the pension benefit formula to employee service rendered before a specified date and based on employee service and compensation (if applicable) prior to that date. The accumulated benefit obligation differs from the projected benefit obligation in that it includes no assumption about future compensation levels. For plans with flat-benefit or non-pay-related pension benefit formulas, the accumulated benefit obligation and the projected benefit obligation are the same.

Actual return on plan assets component (of net periodic pension cost)

The difference between fair value of plan assets at the end of the period and the fair value at the beginning of the period, adjusted for contributions and payments of benefits during the period.

Benefit/years-of-service approach

One of three benefit approaches. Under this approach, an equal portion of the total estimated benefit is attributed to each year of service. The actuarial present value of the benefits is derived after the benefits are attributed to the periods.

Expected return on plan assets

An amount calculated as a basis for determining the extent of delayed recognition of the effects of changes in the fair value of assets. The expected return on plan assets is determined based on the expected long-term rate of return on plan assets and the market-related value of plan assets.

Flat-benefit formula (Flat-benefit plan)

A benefit formula that bases benefits on a fixed amount per year of service, such as $20 of monthly retirement income for each year of credited service. A flat-benefit plan is a plan with such a formula.

Fund

Used as a verb, to pay over to a funding agency (as to fund future pension benefits or to fund pension cost). Used as a noun, asset accumulated in the hands of a funding agency for the purpose of meeting pension benefits when they become due.

Market-related value of plan assets

A balance used to calculate the expected return on plan assets. Market-related value can be either fair market value or a calculated value that recognizes changes in fair value in a systematic and rational manner over not more than five years. Different ways of calculating market-related value may be used for different classes of assets, but the manner of determining market-related value shall be applied consistently from year to year for each asset class.

Measurement date

The date as of which plan assets and obligations are measured.

Net periodic pension cost

The amount recognized in an employer's financial statements as the cost of a pension plan for a period. Components of net periodic pension cost are service cost, interest cost, actual return on plan assets, gain or loss, amortization of unrecognized prior service cost, and amortization of the unrecognized net obligation or asset existing at the date of initial application of this Statement. This Statement uses the term **net periodic pension cost** instead of **net pension expense** because part of the cost recognized in a period may be capitalized along with other costs as part of an asset such as inventory.

Participant

Any employee or former employee, or any member or former member of a trade or other employee association, or the beneficiaries of those individuals, for whom there are pension plan benefits.

PBGC

The Pension Benefit Guaranty Corporation.

Prepaid pension cost

Cumulative employer contributions in excess of accrued net pension cost.

Prior service cost

The cost of retroactive benefits granted in a plan amendment. See also *Unrecognized prior service cost.*

Projected benefit obligation

The actuarial present value as of a date of all benefits attributed by the pension benefit formula to employee service rendered prior to that date. The projected benefit obligation is measured using assumptions as to future compensation levels if the pension benefit formula is based on those future compensation levels (pay-related, final-pay, final-average-pay, or career-average-pay plans).

Retroactive benefits

Benefits granted in a plan amendment (or initiation) that are attributed by the pension benefit formula to employee services rendered in periods prior to the amendment. The cost of the retroactive benefits is referred to as prior service cost.

Service cost component (of net periodic pension cost)

The actuarial present value of benefits attributed by the pension benefit formula to services rendered by employees during that period. The service cost component is a portion of the projected benefit obligation and is unaffected by the funded status of the plan.

Single-employer plan

A pension plan that is maintained by one employer. The term also may be used to describe a plan that is maintained by related parties such as a parent and its subsidiaries.

Unfunded accrued pension cost

Cumulative net pension cost accrued in excess of the employer's contributions.

Unfunded accumulated benefit obligation

The excess of the accumulated benefit obligation over plan assets.

Unfunded projected benefit obligation

The excess of the projected benefit obligation over plan assets.

Unrecognized net gain or loss

The cumulative net gain or loss that has not been recognized as part of the net periodic pension cost. See *Gain or loss*.

Unrecognized prior service cost

That portion of prior service cost that has not been recognized as a part of net periodic pension cost.

Vested benefits

Benefits for which the employee's right to receive a present or future pension benefit is no longer contingent on remaining in the service of the employer. (Other conditions, such as inadequacy of the pension fund, may prevent the employee from receiving the vested benefit.) Under graded vesting, the initial vested right may be to receive in the future a stated percentage of a pension based on the number of years of accumulated credited service;

thereafter, the percentage may increase with the number of years of service or of age until the right to receive the entire benefit has vested.

ACCOUNTING FOR POSTRETIREMENT BENEFITS—SFAS #106

The Statement applies to *all* postretirement benefits expected to be provided by an employer to current and former employees, their beneficiaries, and dependents. Postretirement benefits include health care, life insurance, and other welfare benefits such as tuition assistance, day care, legal services, and housing subsidies provided after retirement.

A plan is an arrangement to provide current and former employees with benefits after they retire in exchange for the employees' services over a specified period of time, upon attaining a specified age while in service, or both. Benefits may commence immediately upon termination of service or may be deferred until retired employees attain a specified age.

The expected postretirement benefit obligation for an employee is the *actuarial present value* as of a particular date of the postretirement benefits expected to be paid by the employer's plan to or on behalf of the employee. Measurement of the expected postretirement benefit obligation is based on the expected amount and timing of future benefits, taking into consideration the expected future cost of providing the benefits and the extent to which those costs are shared by the employer, the employee, or others.

The accumulated postretirement benefit obligation as of a particular date is the actuarial present value of all future benefits attributed to an employee's service rendered to that date. Prior to the date on which an employee attains *full eligibility* for the benefits that employee is expected to earn under the terms of the postretirement benefit plan (the *full eligibility date*), the accumulated postretirement benefit obligation for an employee is a portion of the expected postretirement benefit obligation.

The service cost component of net periodic postretirement benefit cost is the actuarial present value of benefits attributed to services rendered by employees during the period. The other components of net periodic postretirement benefit cost are **interest cost** (interest on the accumulated postretirement benefit obligation, which is a discounted amount), **actual return on plan assets, amortization of unrecognized prior service cost, amortization of the transition obligation or transition asset, and the gain or loss component.**

Measurement of Cost and Obligations

An employer's cost-sharing policy, as evidenced by past practice or communication, shall constitute the cost-sharing provisions of the substantive plan, even if such practices are in contrast to the written plan. Otherwise, the written plan shall be considered to be the substantive plan.

Contributions expected to be received from active employees toward the cost of their postretirement benefits and from retired plan participants are treated similarly for purposes of measuring an employer's expected postretirement benefit obligation. That obligation is measured as the actuarial present value of the benefits expected to be provided under the plan, reduced by the actuarial present value of contributions expected to be received from the plan participants during their remaining active service and postretirement periods.

Automatic benefit changes specified by the plan that are expected to occur shall be included in measurements of the expected and accumulated postretirement benefit obligations and the service cost component of net periodic postretirement benefit cost. Also, *plan amendments* shall be included in the computation of the expected and accumulated postretirement benefit obligations once they have been contractually agreed to.

The service cost component of postretirement benefit cost, any **prior service cost,** and the accumulated postretirement benefit obligation are measured using actuarial assumptions and present value techniques to calculate the actuarial present value of the expected future benefits attributed to periods of employee service. Each assumption used shall reflect the best estimate solely with respect to that individual assumption. All assumptions shall presume that the plan will continue in effect in the absence of evidence that it will not continue. Principal actuarial assumptions include the time value of money *(discount rates);* participation rates (for *contributory plans*); retirement age; and factors affecting the amount and timing of future benefit payments.

Assumed discount rates shall reflect the time value of money as of the **measurement date** in determining the present value of future cash outflows currently expected to be required to satisfy the postretirement benefit obligation. In making that assumption, employers shall look to rates of return on high-quality fixed-income investments currently available whose cash flows match the timing and amount of expected benefit payments.

The expected long-term rate of return on plan assets shall reflect the average rate of earnings expected on the existing assets that qualify as *plan assets* and contributions to the plan expected to be made during the period.

Recognition of Net Periodic Postretirement Benefit Cost

The following components shall be included in the net postretirement benefit cost recognized for a period by an employer sponsoring a defined benefit postretirement plan:

a. Service cost.
b. Interest cost.
c. Actual return on plan assets, if any.
d. Amortization of unrecognized prior service cost, if any.
e. Gain or loss (including the effects of changes in assumptions) to the extent recognized.
f. Amortization of the unrecognized obligation or asset existing at the date of initial application of the Statement, referred to as the **unrecognized transition obligation** or **unrecognized transition asset.**

Service Cost

The service cost component recognized in a period shall be determined as the portion of the expected postretirement benefit obligation attributed to employee service during that period. The measurement of the service cost component requires identification of the substantive plan and the use of assumptions and an attribution method.

Interest Cost

The interest cost component recognized in a period shall be determined as the increase in the accumulated postretirement benefit obligation to recognize the effects of the passage of time. Measuring the accumulated postretirement benefit obligation as a present value requires accrual of an interest cost at rates equal to the assumed discount rates.

For a funded plan, the actual return on plan assets shall be determined based on the *fair value* of plan assets at the beginning and end of the period, adjusted for contributions and benefit payments.

Prior Service Cost

Plan amendments or the initiation of a plan may include provisions that attribute the increase or reduction in benefits to employee service rendered in prior periods or only to employee service to be rendered in future periods. For purposes of measuring the accumulated postretirement benefit obligation, the effect of a plan amendment on a plan participant's expected postretirement benefit obligation shall be attributed to each year of service in that plan participant's attribution period, including years of service already rendered by that plan participant, in accordance with the attribution of the expected postretirement benefit obligation to years of service.

The cost of benefit improvements is the increase in the accumulated postretirement benefit obligation as a result of the plan amendment, measured at the date of the amendment.

The prior service cost is amortized by assigning an equal amount to each remaining year of service to the full eligibility date of each plan participant active at the date of the amendment who was not yet fully eligible for benefits at that date. If all or almost all of a plan's participants are fully eligible for benefits, the prior service cost shall be amortized based on the remaining life expectancy of those plan participants rather than on the remaining years of service to the full eligibility dates of the active plan participants.

To reduce the complexity and detail of the computations required, consistent use of an alternative amortization approach that more rapidly reduces unrecognized prior service cost is permitted. For example, a straight-line amortization of the cost over the average remaining years of service to full eligibility for benefits of the active plan participants is acceptable.

Gains and Losses

Gains and losses are changes in the amount of either the accumulated postretirement benefit obligation or plan assets resulting from experience different from that assumed or from changes in assumptions. The Statement generally does not distinguish between those sources of gains and losses.

As a minimum, amortization of an **unrecognized net gain or loss** (excluding plan asset gains and losses not yet reflected in market-related value) shall be included as a component of net postretirement benefit cost for a year if, as of the beginning of the year, that unrecognized net gain or loss exceeds 10 percent of the greater of the accumulated postretirement benefit obligation or the market-related value of plan assets. If amortization is required, the minimum amortization shall be that excess divided by the average remaining service period of active plan participants. If all or almost all of a plan's participants are inactive, the average remaining life expectancy of the inactive participants shall be used instead of the average remaining service period.

Case Example:

XYZ Company maintains an unfunded postretirement healthcare plan which provides its employees with full benefits at age 60. Its four employees were hired at age 30 and the company uses a 10% discount rate. The company implements the provisions of SFAS #106 for 1999. Expected retirement age is 65.

Information at 1/1/99:

Employee	*Age*	*Actuarially Expected Postretirement Benefit Obligation*	*Actuarially Accumulated Postretirement Benefit Obligation*
A	40	$ 25,000	$ 15,000
B	50	$ 35,000	$ 25,000
C	60	$ 55,000	$ 55,000
D	70	$ 30,000	$ 30,000
		$145,000	$125,000

The EPBO and the APBO are the same for employees C and D since they have reached the time for full eligibility.

Computation of Net Periodic Postretirement Benefit Cost

(1)	Service cost (actuarially determined)	$ 2,000
(2)	Interest cost—$125,000 × 10%	$12,500
(3)	Return on plan assets (unfunded plan)	$0
(4)	Amortization of prior service cost	$0
(5)	Gain or loss	$0
(6)	Amortization of transition obligation—$125,000 ÷ 20	$ 6,250
	Total	$20,750

The company chooses to amortize the benefits over the 20-year optional period. The transition amount is the same as the APBO since this is an unfunded plan.

STATEMENT OF FINANCIAL ACCOUNTING STANDARDS NO. 132

In SFAS #132, the FASB **combined** the disclosures for pensions and other post-retirement benefits.

Disclosures about Pensions and Other Postretirement Benefits

An employer that sponsors one or more defined benefit pension plans or one or more defined benefit postretirement plans shall provide the following information:

a. A reconciliation of beginning and ending balances of the benefit obligation showing separately, if applicable, the effects during the period attributable to each of the following: service cost, interest cost, contributions by plan participants, actuarial gains and losses, foreign currency exchange rate changes, benefits paid, plan amendments, business combinations, divestitures, curtailments, settlements, and special termination benefits.

b. A reconciliation of beginning and ending balances of the fair value of plan assets showing separately, if applicable, the effects during the period attributable to each of the following: actual return on plan assets, foreign currency exchange rates, contributions by the employer, contributions by plan participants, benefits paid, business combinations, divestitures, and settlements.

c. The funded status of the plans, the amounts not recognized in the statement of financial position, and the amounts recognized in the statement of financial position, including:

1. The amount of any unamortized prior service cost.

2. The amount of any unrecognized net gain or loss (including asset gains and losses not yet reflected in market-related value.)

3. The amount of any remaining unamortized, unrecognized net obligation or net asset existing at the initial date of application of Statement 87 or 106.

4. The net pension or other postretirement benefit prepaid assets or accrued liabilities.

5. Any intangible asset and the amount of accumulated other comprehensive income recognized.

d. The amount of net periodic benefit cost recognized, showing separately the service cost component, the interest cost component, the expected return on plan assets for the period, the amortization of the unrecognized transition obligation or transition asset, the amount of recognized gains and losses, the amount of prior service cost recognized, and the amount of gain or loss recognized due to a settlement or curtailment.

e. The amount included within other comprehensive income for the period arising from a change in the additional minimum pension liability.

f. On a weighted-average basis, the following assumptions used in the accounting for the plans: assumed discount rate, rate of compensation increase (for pay-related plans), and expected long-term rate of return on plan assets.

g. The assumed health care cost trend rate(s) for the next year used to measure the expected cost of benefits covered by the plan (gross eligible charges) and a general description of the direction and pattern of change in the assumed trend rates thereafter, together with the ultimate trend rate(s) and when that rate is expected to be achieved.

h. The effect of a one-percentage-point increase and the effect of a one-percentage-point decrease in the assumed health care cost trend rates on (1) the aggregate of the service and interest cost components of net periodic postretirement health care benefit cost and (2) the accumulated postretirement benefit obligation for health care benefits. (For purposes of this disclosure, all other assumptions shall be held constant, and the effects shall be measured based on the substantive plan that is the basis for the accounting.)

i. If applicable, the amounts and types of securities of the employer and related parties included in plan assets, the approximate amount of future annual benefits of plan participants covered by insurance contracts issued by the employer or related parties, and any significant transactions between the employer or related parties and the plan during the period.

SELECTED GLOSSARY

Accumulated postretirement benefit obligation

The actuarial present value of benefits attributed to employee service rendered to a particular date. Prior to an employee's full eligibility date, the accumulated postretirement benefit obligation as of a particular date for an employee is the portion of the expected postretirement benefit obligation attributed to that employee's service rendered to that date; on and after the full eligibility date, the accumulated and expected postretirement benefit obligations for an employee are the same.

Active plan participant

Any active employee who has rendered service during the credited service period and is expected to receive benefits, including benefits to or for any beneficiaries and covered dependents, under the postretirement benefit plan. Also refer to **Plan participant.**

Actual return on plan assets (component of net periodic postretirement benefit cost)

The change in the fair value of the plan's assets for a period including the decrease due to expenses incurred during the period (such as income tax expense incurred by the fund, if applicable), adjusted for contributions and benefit payments during the period.

Attribution

The process of assigning postretirement benefit cost to periods of employee service.

Attribution period

The period of an employee's service to which the expected postretirement benefit obligation for that employee is assigned. The beginning of the attribution period is the employee's date of hire unless the plan's benefit formula grants credit only for service from a later date, in which case the beginning of the attribution period is generally the beginning of that credited service period. The end of the attribution period is the full eligibility date. Within the attribution period, an equal amount of the expected postretirement benefit formula attributes a disproportionate share of the expected postretirement benefit obligation to employees' early years of service. In that case, benefits are attributed in accordance with the plan's benefit formula.

Benefit formula

The basis for determining benefits to which participants may be entitled under a postretirement benefit plan. A plan's benefit formula specifies the years of service to be rendered, age to be attained while in service, or a combination of both that must be met for an employee to be eligible to receive benefits under the plan.

Curtailment (of a postretirement benefit plan)

An event that significantly reduces the expected years of future service of active plan participants or eliminates the accrual of defined benefits for some or all of the future services of a significant number of active plan participants.

Defined benefit postretirement plan

A plan that defines postretirement benefits in terms of monetary amounts (for example, $100,000 of life insurance) or benefit coverage to be provided (for example, up to $200 per day for hospitalization, 80 percent of the cost of specified surgical procedures, and so forth). Any postretirement benefit plan that is not a defined contribution postretirement plan is, for purposes of this Statement, a defined benefit postretirement plan.

Defined contribution postretirement plan

A plan that provides postretirement benefits in return for services rendered, provides an individual account for each plan participant, and specifies how contributions to the individual's account are to be determined rather than specifies the amount of benefits the individual is to receive.

Expected long-term rate of return on plan assets

An assumption about the rate of return on plan assets reflecting the average rate of earnings expected on existing plan assets and expected contributions to the plan during the period.

Expected postretirement benefit obligation

The actuarial present value as of a particular date of the benefits expected to be paid to or for an employee, the employee's beneficiaries, and any covered dependents pursuant to the terms of the postretirement benefit plan.

Expected return on plan assets

An amount calculated as a basis for determining the extent of delayed recognition of the effects of changes in the fair value of plan assets. The expected return on plan assets is determined based on the expected long-term rate of return on plan assets and the market-related value of plan assets.

Funding policy

The program regarding the amounts and timing of contributions by the employer(s), plan participants, and any other sources to provide the benefits a postretirement benefit plan specifies.

Gain or loss

A change in the value of either the accumulated postretirement benefit obligation or the plan assets resulting from experience different from that assumed or from a change in an actuarial assumption, or the consequence of a decision to temporarily deviate from the substantive plan.

Gain or loss component (of net periodic postretirement benefit cost)

The sum of (a) the difference between the actual return on plan assets and the expected return on plan assets, (b) any gain or loss immediately recognized or the amortization of the unrecognized net gain or loss from previous periods, and (c) any amount immediately recognized as a gain or loss pursuant to a decision to temporarily deviate from the substantive plan. The gain or loss component is generally the net effect of delayed recognition of gains and losses (the net change in the unrecognized net gain or loss) except that it does not include changes in the accumulated postretirement benefit obligation occurring during the period and deferred for later recognition.

Interest cost (component of net periodic postretirement benefit cost)

The accrual of interest on the accumulated postretirement benefit obligation due to the passage of time.

Market-related value of plan assets

A balance used to calculate the expected return on plan assets. Market-related value can be either fair value or a calculated value that recognizes changes in fair value in a systematic and rational manner over not more than five years. Different methods of calculating market-related value may be used for different classes of plan assets, but the manner of determining market-related value shall be applied consistently from year to year for each class of plan asset.

Measurement date

The date of the financial statements or, if used consistently from year to year, a date not more than three months prior to that date, as of which plan assets and obligations are measured.

Pay-related plan

A plan that has a benefit formula that bases benefits or benefit coverage on compensation, such as a final-pay or career-average-pay plan.

Plan amendment

A change in the existing terms of a plan. A plan amendment may increase or decrease benefits, including those attributed to years of service already rendered.

Plan assets

Assets—usually stocks, bonds, and other investments—that have been segregated and restricted (usually in a trust) to provide for postretirement benefits. The amount of plan assets includes amounts contributed by the employer (and by plan participants for a contributory plan) and amounts earned from investing the contributions, less benefits, income taxes, and other expenses incurred. Securities of the employer held by the plan are includable in plan assets provided they are transferable. If a plan has liabilities other than for benefits, those nonbenefit obligations are considered as reductions of plan assets.

Postretirement benefits

All forms of benefits, other than retirement income, provided by an employer to retirees. Those benefits may be defined in terms of specified benefits, such as health care, tuition assistance, or legal services, that are provided to retirees as the need for those benefits arises, such as certain health care benefits, or they may be defined in terms of monetary amounts that become payable on the occurrence of a specified event, such as life insurance benefits.

Plan participant

Any employee or former employee who has rendered service in the credited service period *and is expected to receive employer-provided benefits* under the postretirement benefit plan, including benefits to or for any beneficiaries and covered dependents.

Service cost (component of net periodic postretirement benefit cost)

The portion of the expected postretirement benefit obligation attributed to employee service during a period.

Settlement (of a postretirement benefit plan)

An irrevocable action that relieves the employer (or the plan) of primary responsibility for a postretirement benefit obligation and eliminates significant risks related to the obligation and the assets used to effect the settlement. Examples of transactions that constitute a settlement include (a) making lump-sum cash payments to plan participants in exchange for their rights to receive specified postretirement benefits and (b) purchasing nonparticipating insurance contracts for the accumulated postretirement benefit obligation for some or all of the plan participants.

Single-employer plan

A postretirement benefit plan that is maintained by one employer. The term also may be used to describe a plan that is maintained by related parties such as a parent and its subsidiaries.

Termination benefits

Benefits provided by an employer to employees in connection with their termination of employment. They may be either special termination benefits offered only for a short period of time or contractual benefits required by the terms of a plan only if a specified event, such as a plant closing, occurs.

Transition asset

The unrecognized amount, as of the date this Statement is initially applied, of (a) the fair value of plan assets plus any recognized accrued postretirement benefit cost or less any recognized prepaid postretirement benefit cost in excess of (b) the accumulated postretirement benefit obligation.

Transition obligation

The unrecognized amount, as of the date this Statement is initially applied, of (a) the accumulated postretirement benefit obligation in excess of (b) the fair value of plan assets plus any recognized accrued postretirement benefit cost or less any recognized prepaid postretirement benefit cost.

Unfunded accumulated postretirement benefit obligation

The accumulated postretirement benefit obligation in excess of the fair value of plan assets.

Unrecognized net gain or loss

The cumulative net gain or loss that has not been recognized as a part of net periodic postretirement benefit cost or as a part of the accounting for the effects of a settlement or a curtailment.

Unrecognized prior service cost

The portion of prior service cost that has not been recognized as a part of net periodic postretirement benefit cost, as a reduction of the effects of a negative plan amendment, or as a part of the accounting for the effects of a curtailment.

Unrecognized transition asset

The portion of the transition asset that has not been recognized either immediately as the effect of a change in accounting or on a delayed basis as a part of net periodic postretirement benefit cost, as an offset to certain losses, or as a part of accounting for the effects of a settlement or a curtailment.

Unrecognized transition obligation

The portion of the transition obligation that has not been recognized either immediately as the effect of a change in accounting or on a delayed basis as a part of net periodic postretirement benefit cost, as an offset to certain gains, or as a part of accounting for the effects of a settlement or a curtailment.

Chapter Fourteen
Accounting for Leases, Pensions and Postretirement Plans Questions

LEASES

LESSEE-CRITERIA

1. One criterion for a capital lease is that the term of the lease must equal a minimum percentage of the leased property's estimated economic life at the inception of the lease. What is this minimum percentage?

a. 51%.
b. 75%.
c. 80%.
d. 90%.

2. Lease M does not contain a bargain purchase option, but the lease term is equal to 90% of the estimated economic life of the leased property. Lease P does not transfer ownership of the property to the lessee at the end of the lease term, but the lease term is equal to 75% of the estimated economic life of the leased property. How should the lessee classify these leases?

	Lease M	*Lease P*
a.	Capital lease	Operating lease
b.	Capital lease	Capital lease
c.	Operating lease	Capital lease
d.	Operating lease	Operating lease

LESSEE-INCEPTION TO LEASE

3. On December 30, 1995, Haber Co. leased a new machine from Gregg Corp. The following data relate to the lease transaction at the inception of the lease:

Lease term	10 years
Annual rental payable at the end of each lease year	$100,000
Useful life of machine	12 years
Implicit interest rate	10%
Present value of an annuity of 1 in advance for 10 periods at 10%	6.76
Present value of annuity of 1 in arrears for 10 periods at 10%	6.15
Fair value of the machine	$700,000

The lease has no renewal option, and the possession of the machine reverts to Gregg when the lease terminates. At the inception of the lease, Haber should record a lease liability of

a. $0
b. $615,000
c. $630,000
d. $676,000

4. On January 2, 1996, Ashe Company entered into a ten-year noncancellable lease requiring year-end payments of $100,000. Ashe's incremental borrowing rate is 12%, while the lessor's implicit interest rate, known to Ashe, is 10%. Present value factors for an ordinary annuity for ten periods are 6.145 at 10%, and 5.650 at 12%. Ownership of the property remains with the lessor at expiration of the lease. There is no bargain purchase option. The leased property has an estimated economic life of 12 years. What amount should Ashe capitalize for this leased property on January 2, 1996?

a. $1,000,000
b. $614,500
c. $565,000
d. $0

LESSEE-EXECUTORY COST

5. Neal Corp. entered into a nine-year capital lease on a warehouse on December 31, 1999. Lease payments of $52,000, which includes real estate taxes of $2,000, are due annually, beginning on December 31, 2000, and every December 31 thereafter. Neal does not know the interest rate implicit in the lease; Neal's incremental borrowing rate is 9%. The rounded present value of an ordinary annuity for nine years at 9% is 5.6. What amount should Neal report as capitalized lease liability at December 31, 1999?

a. $280,000.
b. $291,200.
c. $450,000.
d. $468,000.

LESSEE-BARGAIN PURCHASE OPTION

6. Robbins, Inc., leased a machine from Ready Leasing Co. The lease qualifies as a capital lease and requires 10 annual payments of $10,000 beginning immediately. The lease specifies an interest rate of 12% and a purchase option of $10,000 at the end of the tenth year, even though the machine's estimated value on that date is $20,000. Robbins' incremental borrowing rate is 14%.

The present value of an annuity due of 1 at:
12% for 10 years is 6.328
14% for 10 years is 5.946

The present value of 1 at:
12% for 10 years is .322
14% for 10 years is .270

What amount should Robbins record as lease liability at the beginning of the lease term?
a. $62,160
b. $64,860
c. $66,500
d. $69,720

LESSEE-GUARANTEED RESIDUAL

7. On January 1, 1997, Babson, Inc., leased two automobiles for executive use. The lease requires Babson to make five annual payments of $13,000 beginning January 1, 1997. At the end of the lease term, December 31, 2001, Babson guarantees the residual value of the automobiles will total $10,000. The lease qualifies as a capital lease. The interest rate implicit in the lease is 9%. Present value factors for the 9% rate implicit in the lease are as follows:

For an annuity due with 5 payments	4.240
For an ordinary annuity with 5 payments	3.890
Present value of $1 for 5 periods	0.650

Babson's recorded capital lease liability immediately after the first required payment should be
a. $48,620
b. $44,070
c. $35,620
d. $31,070

LESSEE-INTEREST EXPENSE

8. On January 1, 1998, Harrow Co. as lessee signed a five-year noncancellable equipment lease with annual payments of $100,000 beginning December 31, 1998. Harrow treated this transaction as a capital lease. The five lease payments have a present value of $379,000 at January 1, 1998, based on interest of 10%. What amount should Harrow report as interest expense for the year ended December 31, 1998?
a. $37,900
b. $27,900
c. $24,200
d. $0

LESSEE-LEASE LIABILITY AFTER INCEPTION DATE

9. On January 1, 1997, Blaugh Co. signed a long-term lease for an office building. The terms of the lease required Blaugh to pay $10,000 annually, beginning December 30, 1997, and continuing each year for 30 years. The lease qualifies as a capital lease. On January 1, 1997, the present value of the lease payments is $112,500 at the 8% interest rate implicit in the lease. In Blaugh's December 31, 1997, balance sheet, the capital lease liability should be
a. $102,500
b. $111,500
c. $112,500
d. $290,000

10. On January 1, 1996, Day Corp. entered into a 10-year lease agreement with Ward, Inc. for industrial equipment. Annual lease payments of $10,000 are payable at the end of each year. Day knows that the lessor expects a 10% return on the lease. Day has a 12% incremental borrowing rate. The equipment is expected to have an estimated useful life of 10 years. In addition, a third party has guaranteed to pay Ward a residual value of $5,000 at the end of the lease.

The present value of an ordinary annuity of $1 at
12% for 10 years is 5.6502
10% for 10 years is 6.1446
The present value of $1 at
12% for 10 years is .3220
10% for 10 years is .3855

In Day's October 31, 1996, balance sheet, the principal amount of the lease obligation was
a. $63,374
b. $61,446
c. $58,112
d. $56,502

LESSEE-CLASSIFICATION OF LEASE LIABILITY

11. On December 30, 1998, Rafferty Corp. leased equipment under a capital lease. Annual lease payments of $20,000 are due December 31 for 10 years. The equipment's useful life is 10 years, and the interest rate implicit in the lease is 10%. The capital lease obligation was recorded on December 30, 1998, at $135,000, and the first lease payment was made on that date. What amount should Rafferty include in current liabilities for this capital lease in its December 31, 1998, balance sheet?

a. $6,500
b. $8,500
c. $11,500
d. $20,000

12. A lessee had a ten-year capital lease requiring equal annual payments. The reduction of the lease liability in year 2 should equal

a. The current liability shown for the lease at the end of year 1.
b. The current liability shown for the lease at the end of year 2.
c. The reduction of the lease obligation in year 1.
d. One-tenth of the original lease liability.

LESSEE-DEPRECIATION EXPENSE

13. On January 2, 1998, Cole Co. signed an eight-year noncancelable lease for a new machine, requiring $15,000 annual payments at the beginning of each year. The machine has a useful life of 12 years, with no salvage value. Title passes to Cole at the lease expiration date. Cole uses straight-line depreciation for all of its plant assets. Aggregate lease payments have a present value on January 2, 1998, of $108,000, based on an appropriate rate of interest. For 1998, Cole should record depreciation (amortization) expense for the leased machine at

a. $0
b. $9,000
c. $13,500
d. $15,000

14. On January 2, 1999, Nori Mining Co. (lessee) entered into a 5-year lease for drilling equipment. Nori accounted for the acquisition as a capital lease for $240,000, which includes a $10,000 bargain purchase option. At the end of the lease, Nori expects to exercise the bargain purchase option. Nori estimates that the equipment's fair value will be $20,000 at the end of its 8-year life. Nori regularly uses straight-line depreciation on similar equipment. For the year ended December 31, 1999, what amount should Nori recognize as depreciation expense on the leased asset?

a. $48,000.
b. $46,000.
c. $30,000.
d. $27,500.

LESSEE-DISCLOSURES

15. On July 1, 1999, South Co. entered into a ten-year operating lease for a warehouse facility. The annual minimum lease payments are $100,000. In addition to the base rent, South pays a monthly allocation of the building's operating expenses, which amounted to $20,000 for the year ended June 30, 2000. In the notes to South's June 30, 2000, financial statements, what amounts of subsequent years' lease payments should be disclosed?

a. $100,000 per annum for each of the next five years and $500,000 in the aggregate.
b. $120,000 per annum for each of the next five years and $600,000 in the aggregate.
c $100,000 per annum for each of the next five years and $900,000 in the aggregate.
d. $120,000 per annum for each of the next five years and $1,080,000 in the aggregate.

LESSOR-SALES TYPE LEASE

16. Winn Co. manufactures equipment that is sold or leased. On December 31, 1996, Winn leased equipment to Bart for a five-year period ending December 31, 2001, at which date ownership of the leased asset will be transferred to Bart. Equal payments under the lease are $22,000 (including $2,000 executory costs) and are due on December 31 of each year. The first payment was made on December 31, 1996. Collectibility of the remaining lease payments is reasonably assured, and Winn has no material cost uncertainties. The normal sales price of the equipment is $77,000, and the cost is $60,000. For the year ended December 31, 1996, what amount of income should Winn realize from the lease transaction?

a. $17,000
b. $22,000
c. $23,000
d. $33,000

17. Howe Co. leased equipment to Kew Corp. on January 2, 1999, for an eight-year period expiring December 31, 2006. Equal payments under the lease are $600,000 and are due on January 2 of each year. The first payment was made on January 2, 1999. The list selling price of the equipment is $3,520,000 and its carrying cost on Howe's books is $2,800,000. The lease is appropriately accounted for as a sales-type lease. The present value of the lease payments at an imputed interest rate of 12% (Howe's incremental borrowing rate) is $3,300,000.

What amount of profit on the sale should Howe report for the year ended December 31, 1999?

a. $720,000.
b. $500,000.
c. $90,000.
d. $0.

18. Peg Co. leased equipment from Howe Corp. on July 1, 1995, for an eight-year period expiring June 30, 2003. Equal payments under the lease are $600,000 and are due on July 1 of each year. The first payment was made on July 1, 1995. The rate of interest contemplated by Peg and Howe is 10%. The cash selling price of the equipment is $3,520,000, and the cost of the equipment on Howe's accounting records is $2,800,000. The lease is appropriately recorded as a sales-type lease. What is the amount of profit on the sale and interest revenue that Howe should record for the year ended December 31, 1995?

	Profit on sale	*Interest revenue*
a.	$720,000	$176,000
b.	$720,000	$146,000
c.	$45,000	$176,000
d.	$45,000	$146,000

19. In a lease that is recorded as a sales-type lease by the lessor, interest revenue

a. Should be recognized in full as revenue at the lease's inception.
b. Should be recognized over the period of the lease using the straight-line method.
c. Should be recognized over the period of the lease using the effective interest method.
d. Does **not** arise.

LESSOR-DIRECT FINANCING LEASE

20. Glade Co. leases computer equipment to customers under direct-financing leases. The equipment has no residual value at the end of the lease and the leases do not contain bargain purchase options. Glade wishes to earn 8% interest on a five-year lease of equipment with a fair value of $323,400. The present value of an annuity due of $1 at 8% for five years is 4.312. What is the total amount of interest revenue that Glade will earn over the life of the lease?

a. $51,600
b. $75,000
c. $129,360
d. $139,450

OPERATING LEASES

21. On June 1, 2000, Oren Co. entered into a five-year nonrenewable lease, commencing on that date, for office space and made the following payments to Cant Properties:

Bonus to obtain lease	$30,000
First month's rent	10,000
Last month's rent	10,000

In its income statement for the year ended June 30, 2000, what amount should Oren report as rent expense?

a. $10,000.
b. $10,500.
c. $40,000.
d. $50,000.

22. On July 1, 1996, Gee, Inc., leased a delivery truck from Marr Corp. under a 3-year operating lease. Total rent for the term of the lease will be $36,000, payable as follows:

12 months at $ 500 =	$ 6,000
12 months at $ 750 =	9,000
12 months at $1,750 =	21,000

All payments were made when due. In Marr's June 30, 1998, balance sheet, the accrued rent receivable should be reported as

a. $0
b. $9,000
c. $12,000
d. $21,000

23. Wall Co. leased office premises to Fox, Inc. for a five-year term beginning January 2, 1999. Under the terms of the operating lease, rent for the first year is $8,000 and rent for years 2 through 5 is $12,500 per annum. However, as an inducement to enter the lease, Wall granted Fox the first six months of the lease rent-free. In its December 31, 1999, income statement, what amount should Wall report as rental income?

a. $12,000.
b. $11,600.
c. $10,800.
d. $8,000.

24. Quo Co. rented a building to Hava Fast Food. Each month Quo receives a fixed rental amount plus a variable rental amount based on Hava's sales for that month. As sales increase so does the variable rental amount, but at a reduced rate. Which of the following curves reflects the monthly rentals under the agreement?

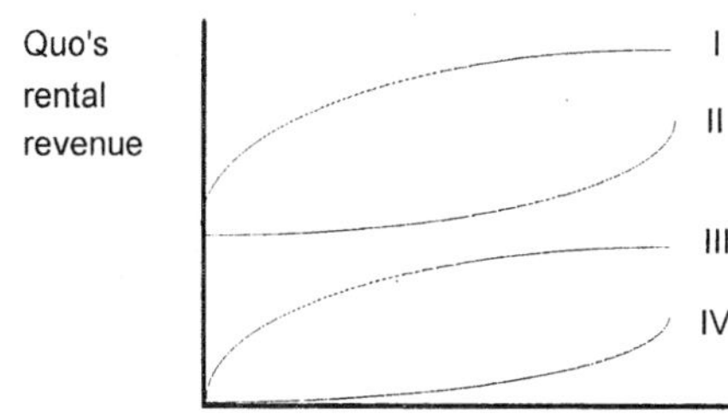

a. I
b. II
c. III
d. IV

LEASEHOLD IMPROVEMENTS

25. Star Co. leases a building for its product showroom. The ten-year non-renewable lease will expire on December 31, 2004. In January 1999, Star redecorated its showroom and made leasehold improvements of $48,000. The estimated useful life of the improvements is 8 years. What amount of leasehold improvements, net of amortization, should Star report in its June 30, 1999, balance sheet?

a. $45,600
b. $45,000
c. $44,000
d. $43,200

SALE AND LEASEBACK

MINOR PART (PV OF LEASE RENTALS ≤ 10% OF FMV OF ASSET SOLD)

26. The following information pertains to a sale and leaseback of equipment by Mega Co. on December 31, 1998:

Sales price	$400,000
Carrying amount	$300,000
Monthly lease payment	$3,250
Present value of lease payments	$36,900
Estimated remaining life	25 years
Lease term	1 year
Implicit rate	12%

What amount of deferred gain on the sale should Mega report at December 31, 1998?

a. $0
b. $36,900
c. $63,100
d. $100,000

MORE THAN A MINOR PART BUT LESS THAN SUBSTANTIALLY ALL (PV OF LEASE RENTALS > 10% BUT < 90% OF FMV OF ASSET SOLD)

27. On December 31, 1994, Parke Corp. sold Edlow Corp. an airplane with an estimated remaining useful life of ten years. At the same time, Parke leased back the airplane for three years. Additional information is as follows:

Sales price	$600,000
Carrying amount of airplane at date of sale	$100,000
Monthly rental under lease	$ 6,330
Interest rate implicit in the lease as computed by Edlow and known by Parke (this rate is lower than the lessee's incremental borrowing rate)	12%
Present value of operating lease rentals ($6,330 for 36 months @ 12%)	$190,581
The leaseback is considered an operating lease	

In Parke's December 31, 1994, balance sheet, what amount should be included as deferred revenue on this transaction?

a. $0
b. $190,581
c. $309,419
d. $500,000

SUBSTANTIALLY ALL (PV OF LEASE RENTALS ≥ 90% OF FMV OF ASSET SOLD) OR LEASED ASSET MEETS 75% OF USEFUL LIFE TEST FOR CAPITALIZATION)

28. On January 1, 1997, Hooks Oil Co. sold equipment with a carrying amount of $100,000, and a remaining useful life of 10 years, to Maco Drilling for $150,000 Hooks immediately leased the equipment back under a 10-year capital lease with a present value of $150,000 and will depreciate the equipment using the straight-line method. Hooks made the first annual lease payment of $24,412 in December 1997. In Hooks' December 31, 1997, balance sheet, the unearned gain on equipment sale should be

a. $50,000
b. $45,000
c. $25,588
d. $0

LEASES -- REVIEW QUESTIONS

29. Farm Co. leased equipment to Union Co. on July 1, 2001, and properly recorded the sales-type lease at $135,000, the present value of the lease payments discounted at 10%. The first of eight annual lease payments of $20,000 due at the beginning of each year was received and recorded on July 3, 2001. Farm had purchased the equipment for $110,000. What amount of interest revenue from the lease should Farm report in its 2001 income statement?

a. $0
b. $5,500
c. $5,750
d. $6,750

30. On January 1, 1996, Park Co. signed a 10-year operating lease for office space at $96,000 per year. The lease included a provision for additional rent of 5% of annual company sales in excess of $500,000. Park's sales for the year ended December 31, 1996, were $600,000. Upon execution of the lease, Park paid $24,000 as a bonus for the lease. Park's rent expense for the year ended December 31, 1996, is

a. $98,400
b. $101,000
c. $103,400
d. $125,000

31. On January 1, 1997, JCK Co. signed a contract for an eight-year lease of its equipment with a 10-year life. The present value of the 16 equal semiannual payments in advance equaled 85% of the equipment's fair value. The contract had no provision for JCK, the lessor, to give up legal ownership of the equipment. Should JCK recognize rent or interest revenue in 1999, and should the revenue recognized in 1999 be the same or smaller than the revenue recognized in 1998?

	1999 revenues recognized	*1999 amount recognized compared to 1998*
a.	Rent	The same
b.	Rent	Smaller
c.	Interest	The same
d.	Interest	Smaller

32. At the inception of a capital lease, the guaranteed residual value should be

a. Included as part of minimum lease payments at present value.
b. Included as part of minimum lease payments at future value.
c. Included as part of minimum lease payments only to the extent that guaranteed residual value is expected to exceed estimated residual value.
d. Excluded from minimum lease payments.

33. On December 31, 1996, Bain Corp. sold a machine to Ryan and simultaneously leased it back for one year. Pertinent information at this date follows:

Sales price	$360,000
Carrying amount	330,000
Present value of reasonable lease rentals ($3,000 for 12 months @ 12%)	34,100
Estimated remaining useful life	12 years

In Bain's December 31, 1996, balance sheet, the deferred revenue from the sale of this machine should be

a. $34,100
b. $30,000
c. $4,100
d. $0

34. An office equipment representative has a machine for sale or lease. If you buy the machine, the cost is $7,596. If you lease the machine, you will have to sign a noncancelable lease and make 5 payments of $2,000 each. At the time of the last payment you will receive title to the machine. The first payment will be made on the first day of the lease. The present value of an ordinary annuity of $1 is as follows:

Number of Periods		*Present Value*	
	10%	*12%*	*16%*
1	0.909	0.893	0.862
2	1.736	1.690	1.605
3	2.487	2.402	2.246
4	3.170	3.037	2.798
5	3.791	3.605	3.274

The interest rate implicit in this lease is approximately

a. 10%.
b. 12%.
c. Between 10% and 12%.
d. 16%.

35. As an inducement to enter a lease, Arts, Inc., a lessor, grants Hompson Corp., a lessee, nine months of free rent under a five-year operating lease. The lease is effective on July 1, 1995, and provides for monthly rental of $1,000 to begin April 1, 1996.

In Hompson's income statement for the year ended June 30, 1996, rent expense should be reported as

a. $10,200
b. $9,000
c. $3,000
d. $2,550

36. Rapp Co. leased a new machine to Lake Co. on January 1, 1996. The lease expires on January 1, 2001. The annual rental is $90,000. Additionally, on January 1, 1996, Lake paid $50,000 to Rapp as a lease bonus and $25,000 as a security deposit to be refunded upon expiration of the lease. In Rapp's 1996 income statement, the amount of rental revenue should be

a. $140,000
b. $125,000
c. $100,000
d. $90,000

37. In the long-term liabilities section of its balance sheet at December 31, 1999, Mene Co. reported a capital lease obligation of $75,000, net of current portion of $1,364. Payments of $9,000 were made on both January 2, 2000, and January 2, 2001. Mene's incremental borrowing rate on the date of the lease was 11% and the lessor's implicit rate, which was known to Mene, was 10%. In its December 31, 2000, balance sheet, what amount should Mene report as capital lease obligation, net of current portion?

a. $66,000.
b. $73,500.
c. $73,636.
d. $74,250.

38. Oak Co. leased equipment for its entire nine-year useful life, agreeing to pay $50,000 at the start of the lease term on December 31, 1998, and $50,000 annually on each December 31 for the next eight years. The present value on December 31, 1998, of the nine lease payments over the lease term, using the rate implicit in the lease which Oak knows to be 10%, was $316,500. The December 31, 1998, present value of the lease payments using Oak's incremental borrowing rate of 12% was $298,500. Oak made a timely second lease payment. What amount should Oak report as capital lease liability in its December 31, 1999, balance sheet?

a. $350,000.
b. $243,150.
c. $228,320.
d. $0.

39. Lease A does not contain a bargain purchase option, but the lease term is equal to 90 percent of the estimated economic life of the leased property. Lease B does not transfer ownership of the property to the lessee by the end of the lease term, but the lease term is equal to 75 percent of the estimated economic life of the leased property. How should the lessee classify these leases?

	Lease A	*Lease B*
a.	Operating lease	Capital lease
b.	Operating lease	Operating lease
c.	Capital lease	Capital lease
d.	Capital lease	Operating lease

RECENTLY DISCLOSED QUESTION

M96

40. On January 2, 1995, Marx Co. as lessee signed a five-year noncancelable equipment lease with annual payments of $200,000 beginning December 31, 1995. Marx treated this transaction as a capital lease. The five lease payments have a present value of $758,000 at January 2, 1995, based on interest of 10%. What amount should Marx report as interest expense for the year ended December 31, 1995?

a. $0.
b. $48,000.
c. $55,800.
d. $75,800.

PENSIONS

PENSION COST (EXPENSE)

41. The following information pertains to the 1997 activity of Ral Corp.'s defined benefit pension plan:

Service cost	$300,000
Return on plan assets	80,000
Interest cost on pension benefit obligation	164,000
Amortization of actuarial loss	30,000
Amortization of unrecognized prior service cost	70,000

Ral's 1997 pension cost was

a. $316,000
b. $484,000
c. $574,000
d. $644,000

42. The following information pertains to Lee Corp.'s defined benefit pension plan for 1998:

Service cost	$160,000
Actual and expected return on plan assets	35,000
Unexpected loss on plan assets related to a 1998 disposal of a segment	40,000
Amortization of unrecognized prior service cost	5,000
Annual interest on pension obligation	50,000

What amount should Lee report as pension expense in its 1998 income statement?

a. $250,000
b. $220,000
c. $210,000
d. $180,000

PREPAID PENSION COST OR ACCRUED PENSION COST

43. Jerry Corp., a company whose stock is publicly traded, provides a noncontributory defined benefit pension plan for its employees. The company's actuary has provided the following information for the year ended December 31, 1995:

Projected benefit obligation	$400,000
Accumulated benefit obligation	350,000
Plan assets (fair value)	410,000
Service cost	120,000
Interest on projected benefit obligation	12,000
Amortization of unrecognized prior service cost	30,000
Expected and actual return on plan assets	41,000

The market-related asset value equals the fair value of plan assets. Prior contributions to the defined benefit pension plan equaled the amount of net periodic pension cost accrued for the previous year end. No contributions have been made for 1995 pension cost. In its December 31, 1995, balance sheet, Jerry should report an accrued pension cost of

a. $203,000
b. $162,000
c. $121,000
d. $109,000

44. A company that maintains a defined benefit pension plan for its employees reports an unfunded accrued pension cost. This cost represents the amount that the

a. Cumulative net pension cost accrued exceeds contributions to the plan.
b. Cumulative net pension cost accrued exceeds the vested benefit obligation.
c. Vested benefit obligation exceeds plan assets.
d. Vested benefit obligation exceeds contributions to the plan.

45. On January 2, 1999, Loch Co. established a noncontributory defined benefit plan covering all employees and contributed $1,000,000 to the plan. At December 31, 1999, Loch determined that the 1999 service and interest costs on the plan were $620,000. The expected and the actual rate of return on plan assets for 1999 was 10%. There are no other components of Loch's pension expense. What amount should Loch report in its December 31, 1999, balance sheet as prepaid pension cost?

a. $280,000.
b. $380,000.
c. $480,000.
d. $620,000.

46. Webb Co. implemented a defined benefit pension plan for its employees on January 1, 1995. During 1995 and 1996, Webb's contributions fully funded the plan. The following data are provided for 1998 and 1997:

	1998 *Estimated*	*1997* *Actual*
Projected benefit obligation, December 31	$750,000	$700,000
Accumulated benefit obligation, December 31	520,000	500,000
Plan assets at fair value, December 31	675,000	600,000
Projected benefit obligation in excess of plan assets	75,000	100,000
Pension expense	90,000	75,000
Employer's contribution	?	50,000

What amount should Webb contribute in order to report an accrued pension liability of $15,000 in its December 31, 1998, balance sheet?

a. $50,000
b. $60,000
c. $75,000
d. $100,000

ACTUAL RETURN ON PLAN ASSETS

47. The following information pertains to Gali Co.'s defined benefit pension plan for 2001:

Fair value of plan assets, beginning of year	$350,000
Fair value of plan assets, end of year	525,000
Employer contributions	110,000
Benefits paid	85,000

In computing pension expense, what amount should Gali use as actual return on plan assets?

a. $65,000
b. $150,000
c. $175,000
d. $260,000

PROJECTED BENEFIT OBLIGATION

48. The following information pertains to Seda Co.'s pension plan:

Actuarial estimate of projected benefit obligation at 1/1/96	$72,000
Assumed discount rate	10%
Service costs for 1996	18,000
Pension benefits paid during 1996	15,000

If **no** change in actuarial estimates occurred during 1996, Seda's projected benefit obligation at December 31, 1996, was

a. $64,200
b. $75,000
c. $79,200
d. $82,200

MINIMUM PENSION LIABILITY

49. Mercer, Inc., maintains a defined benefit pension plan for its employees. As of December 31, 1996, the market value of the plan assets is less than the accumulated benefit obligation, and less than the projected benefit obligation. The projected benefit obligation exceeds the accumulated benefit obligation. In its balance sheet as of December 31, 1996, Mercer should report a minimum liability in the amount of the

a. Excess of the projected benefit obligation over the value of the plan assets.
b. Excess of the accumulated benefit obligation over the value of the plan assets.
c. Projected benefit obligation.
d. Accumulated benefit obligation.

50. Payne, Inc. implemented a defined-benefit pension plan for its employees on January 2, 2000. The following data are provided for 2000, as of December 31, 2000

Accumulated benefit obligation	$103,000
Plan assets at fair value	78,000
Net periodic pension cost	90,000
Employer's contribution	70,000

What amount should Payne record as additional minimum pension liability at December 31, 2000?

a. $0.
b. $5,000.
c. $20,000.
d. $45,000.

51. The following data relates to Nola Co.'s defined benefit pension plan as of December 31, 2000

Unfunded accumulated benefit obligation	$140,000
Unrecognized prior service cost	45,000
Accrued pension cost	80,000

Assuming that this is the first year an entry has been made in the account, what amount should Nola report as excess of additional pension liability over unrecognized prior service cost to be shown in the other comprehensive income section of the calculation of total comprehensive income for 2000.

a. $15,000
b. $35,000
c. $95,000
d. $175,000

Questions 52 and 53 are based on the following information:

The following information pertains to Hall Co.'s defined-benefit pension plan at December 31, 2001:

Unfunded accumulated benefit obligation (ABO)	$25,000
Unrecognized prior service cost	12,000
Net periodic pension cost	8,000

Hall made no contributions to the pension plan during 2001.

52. At December 31, 2001, what amount should Hall record as additional pension liability?

a $5,000
b. $13,000
c. $17,000
d. $25,000

53. Assuming that this is the first year an entry has been made in the account, what amount should Hall report as excess of additional pension liability over unrecognized prior service cost to be shown in the other comprehensive income section of the calculation of total comprehensive income for 2001.

a. $5,000
b. $13,000
c. $17,000
d. $25,000

PENSION -- DISCLOSURE

54. A company with a defined benefit pension plan must disclose in the notes to its financial statements a reconciliation of

a. The vested and nonvested benefit obligation of its pension plan with the accumulated benefit obligation.
b. The accrued or prepaid pension cost reported in its balance sheet with the pension expense reported in its income statement.
c. The accumulated benefit obligation of its pension plan with its projected benefit obligation.
d. The funded status of its pension plan with the accrued or prepaid pension cost reported in its balance sheet.

PENSION -- REVIEW QUESTIONS

55. The following information pertains to Kane Co.'s defined benefit pension plan:

Prepaid pension cost, January 1, 2001	$2,000
Service cost	19,000
Interest cost	38,000
Actual return on plan assets	22,000
Amortization of unrecognized prior service cost	52,000
Employer contributions	40,000

The fair value of plan assets exceeds the accumulated benefit obligation. In its December 31, 2001, balance sheet, what amount should Kane report as unfunded accrued pension cost?

a. $45,000
b. $49,000
c. $67,000
d. $87,000

56. On January 1, 1996, Merl Corp. adopted a defined benefit pension plan. The plan's service cost of $75,000 was fully funded at the end of 1996. Prior service cost was funded by a contribution of $30,000 in 1996. Amortization of prior service cost was $12,000 for 1996. What is the amount of Merl's prepaid pension cost at December 31, 1996?

a. $18,000
b. $30,000
c. $42,000
d. $45,000

57. Interest cost included in the net pension cost recognized by an employer sponsoring a defined benefit pension plan represents the

a. Amortization of the discount on unrecognized prior service costs.
b. Increase in the fair value of plan assets due to the passage of time.
c. Increase in the projected benefit obligation due to the passage of time.
d. Shortage between the expected and actual returns on plan assets.

58. For a defined benefit pension plan, the discount rate used to calculate the projected benefit obligation is determined by the

	Expected return on plan assets	*Actual return on plan assets*
a.	Yes	Yes
b.	No	No
c.	Yes	No
d.	No	Yes

59. On July 31, 1998, Tern Co. amended its single employee defined benefit pension plan by granting increased benefits for services provided prior to 1998. This prior service cost will be reflected in the financial statement(s) for

a. Years before 1998 only.
b. Year 1998 only.
c. Year 1998, and years before and following 1998.
d. Year 1998, and following years only.

POST-RETIREMENT BENEFITS

60. Which of the following information should be disclosed by a company providing health care benefits to its retirees?

I The assumed health care cost trend rate used to measure the expected cost of benefits covered by the plan.
II. The accumulated post-retirement benefit obligation.

a. I and II.
b. I only.
c. II only.
d. Neither I **nor** II.

61. Bounty Co. provides postretirement health care benefits to employees who have completed at least 10 years service and are aged 55 years or older when retiring. Employees retiring from Bounty have a median age of 62, and no one has worked beyond age 65. Fletcher is hired at 48 years old. The attribution period for accruing Bounty's expected postretirement health care benefit obligation to Fletcher is during the period when Fletcher is aged

a. 48 to 65.
b. 48 to 58.
c. 55 to 65.
d. 55 to 62.

62. An employer's obligation for postretirement health benefits that are expected to be provided to or for an employee must be fully accrued by the date the

a. Employee is fully eligible for benefits.
b. Employee retires.
c. Benefits are utilized.
d. Benefits are paid.

SPECIAL TERMINATION BENEFITS

63. On September 1, 1994, Howe Corp. offered special termination benefits to employees who had reached the early retirement age specified in the company's pension plan. The termination benefits consisted of lump-sum and periodic future payments. Additionally, the employees accepting the company offer receive the usual early retirement pension benefits. The offer expired on November 30, 1994. Actual or reasonably estimated amounts at December 31, 1994, relating to the employees accepting the offer are as follows:

- Lump-sum payments totaling $475,000 were made on January 1, 1995.
- Periodic payments of $60,000 annually for three years will begin January 1, 1996. The present value at December 31, 1994, of these payments was $155,000.
- Reduction of accrued pension costs at December 31, 1994, for the terminating employees was $45,000.

In its December 31, 1994, balance sheet, Howe should report a total liability for special termination benefits of

a. $475,000
b. $585,000
c. $630,000
d. $655,000

RECENTLY RELEASED QUESTIONS

1999

64. Jan Corp. amended its defined benefit pension plan, granting a total credit of $100,000 to four employees for services rendered prior to the plan's adoption. The employees, A, B, C, and D, are expected to retire from the company as follows:
"A" will retire after three years.
"B" and "C" will retire after five years.
"D" will retire after seven years.

What is the amount of prior service cost amortization in the first year?

a. $0
b. $5,000
c. $20,000
d. $25,000

65. On January 2, 1995, Loch Co. established a noncontributory defined-benefit pension plan covering all employees and contributed $400,000 to the plan. At December 31, 1995, Loch determined that the 1995 service and interest costs on the plan were $720,000. The expected and the actual rate of return on plan assets for 1995 was 10%. There are no other components of Loch's pension expense. What amount should Loch report as accrued pension cost in its December 31, 1995 balance sheet?

a. $280,000
b. $320,000
c. $360,000
d. $720,000

1999

66. Cott, Inc. prepared an interest amortization table for a five-year lease payable with a bargain purchase option of $2,000, exercisable at the end of the lease. At the end of the five years, the balance in the leases payable column of the spreadsheet was zero. Cott has asked Grant, CPA, to review the spreadsheet to determine the error. Only one error was made on the spreadsheet. Which of the following statements represents the best explanation for this error?

a. The beginning present value of the lease did **not** include the present value of the bargain purchase option.
b. Cott subtracted the annual interest amount from the lease payable balance instead of adding it.
c. The present value of the bargain purchase option was subtracted from the present value of the annual payments.
d. Cott discounted the annual payments as an ordinary annuity, when the payments actually occurred at the beginning of each period.

Chapter Fourteen
Accounting for Leases, Pension and Postretirement Plans Problems

NUMBER 1

Part a. The Jackson Company manufactured a piece of equipment at a cost of $7,000,000 which it held for resale from January 1, 1999 to June 30, 1999 at a price of $8,000,000. On July 1, 1999, Jackson leased the equipment to the Crystal Company. The lease is appropriately recorded as an operating lease for accounting purposes. The lease is for a three-year period expiring June 30, 2002. Equal monthly payments under the lease are $115,000 and are due on the first of the month. The first payment was made on July 1, 1999. The equipment is being depreciated on a straight-line basis over an eight-year period with no residual value expected.

Required:

1. What expense should Crystal appropriately record as a result of the above facts for the year ended December 31, 1999? Show supporting computations in good form.
2. What income or loss before income taxes should Jackson appropriately record as a result of the above facts for the year ended December 31, 1999? Show supporting computations in good form.

Part b. The Truman Company leased equipment from the Roosevelt Company on October 1, 1999. The lease is appropriately recorded as a capitalized lease for accounting purposes for Truman and as a sales type lease for accounting purposes for Roosevelt. The lease is for an eight-year period. Equal annual payments under the lease are $600,000 and are due on October 1 of each year. The first payment was made on October 1, 1999. The cost of the equipment on Roosevelt's accounting records was $3,000,000. The equipment has an estimated useful life of eight years with no residual value expected. Truman uses straight-line depreciation and takes a full year's depreciation in the year of purchase. The rate of interest contemplated by Truman and Roosevelt is 10%. The present value of an annuity of $1 in advance for eight periods at 10% is 5.868.

Required:

1. What expense should Truman appropriately record as a result of the above facts for the year ended December 31, 1999? Show supporting computations in good form.
2. What income or loss before income taxes should Roosevelt appropriately record as a result of the above facts for the year ended December 31, 1999? Show supporting computations in good form.

NUMBER 2

Question Number 2 consists of 10 items. Select the **best** answer for each item. **Answer all items.**

The following information pertains to Sparta Co.'s defined benefit pension plan.

Discount rate	8%
Expected rate of return	10%
Average service life	12 years

At January 1, 1999:

Projected benefit obligation	$600,000
Fair value of pension plan assets	720,000
Unrecognized prior service cost	240,000
Unamortized prior pension gain	96,000

At December 31, 1999:

Projected benefit obligation	910,000
Fair value of pension plan assets	825,000

Service cost for 1999 was $90,000. There were no contributions made or benefits paid during the year. Sparta's unfunded accrued pension liability was $8,000 at January 1, 1999. Sparta uses the straight-line method of amortization over the maximum period permitted.

Required:

1. For Items (a) through (e), calculate the amounts to be recognized as components of Sparta's unfunded accrued pension liability at December 31, 1999.

Amounts to be calculated:

(a) Interest cost.
(b) Expected return on plan assets.
(c) Actual return on plan assets.
(d) Amortization of prior service costs.
(e) Minimum amortization of unrecognized pension gain.

2. For items (f) through (j), determine whether the component increases (I) or decreases (D) Sparta's unfunded accrued pension liability.

Items to be answered:

(f) Service cost.
(g) Deferral of gain on pension plan assets.
(h) Actual return on plan assets.
(i) Amortization of prior service costs.
(j) Amortization of unrecognized pension gain.

NUMBER 3

On January 2, 1999, Elsee Co. leased equipment from Grant, Inc. Lease payments are $100,000, payable annually every December 31 for twenty years. Title to the equipment passes to Elsee at the end of the lease term. The lease is noncancelable.

Additional facts:

- The equipment has a $750,000 carrying amount on Grant's books. Its estimated economic life was 25 years on January 2, 1999.
- The rate implicit in the lease, which is known to Elsee, is 10%. Elsee's incremental borrowing rate is 12%.
- Elsee uses the straight-line method of depreciation.

The rounded present value factors of an ordinary annuity for 20 years are as follows:

12%	7.5
10%	8.5

Required:

Prepare the necessary journal entries, without explanations, to be recorded by Elsee for:

1. entering into the lease on January 2, 1999.
2. making the lease payment on December 31, 1999.
3. expenses related to the lease for the year ended December 31, 1999.

NUMBER 4

Deck Co. has just hired a new president, Palmer, and is reviewing its employee benefit plans with the new employee. For current employees, Deck offers a compensation plan for future vacations. Deck also provides postemployment benefits to former or inactive employees.

On the date of Palmer's hire, Palmer entered into a deferred compensation contract with Deck. Palmer is expected to retire in ten years. The contract calls for a payment of $150,000 upon termination of employment following a minimum three-year service period. The contract also provides that interest of 10%, compounded annually, be credited on the amount due each year after the third year.

Required:

a. Give an example of postemployment benefits. State the conditions under which Deck is required to accrue liabilities for compensated absences and postemployment benefits. State Deck's disclosure requirements if these conditions, in full or in part, are not met.

b. Describe the general accrual period for amounts to be paid under a deferred compensation contract. State the theoretical rationale for requiring accrual of these liabilities and related expenses.

c. Prepare a schedule of the expense and accrued liability related to Palmer's deferred compensation agreement to be reported in Deck's financial statements for the first four years of the contract.

NUMBER 5

At December 31, 1998, as a result of its single employer defined benefit pension plan, Bighorn Co. had an unrecognized net loss and an unfunded accrued pension cost. Bighorn's pension plan and its actuarial assumptions have not changed since it began operations in 1994. Bighorn has made annual contributions to the plan.

Required:

a. Identify the components of net pension cost that should be recognized in Bighorn's 1998 financial statements.

b. What circumstances caused Bighorn's
1. Unrecognized net loss?
2. Unfunded accrued pension cost?

c. How should Bighorn compute its minimum pension liability and any additional pension liability?

NUMBER 6

On January 2, 2001, Cody, Inc. sold equipment to Griff Co. for cash of $864,000 and immediately leased it back under a capital lease for 9 years. The carrying amount of the equipment was $540,000, and its estimated remaining economic life is 10 years. Annual year-end payments of $153,000, which include executory costs of $3,000, are based on an implicit interest rate of 10%, which is known to Cody. Cody's incremental borrowing rate is 13%. Cody uses the straight-line method of depreciation. The rounded present value factors of an ordinary annuity for 9 years are 5.76 at 10% and 5.2 at 13%.

Required:

a. What is the theoretical basis for requiring lessees to capitalize certain long-term leases? **Do not discuss the specific criteria for classifying a lease as a capital lease.**

b. Prepare the journal entries that Cody must make to record the sale and the leaseback on January 2, 2001.

c. Prepare the journal entries, including any adjusting entries, that Cody must make at December 31, 2001.

NUMBER 7

Wyatt, CPA, is meeting with Brown, the controller of Emco, a wholesaler, to discuss the following accounting issue:

Brown is aware that Statement of Financial Accounting Standards, (FAS) No. 106, *Employers' Accounting for Postretirement Benefits Other Than Pensions,* is effective for years beginning after December 15, 1999. Brown is uncertain about the benefits and beneficiaries covered by this Statement. Brown believes that, regardless of FAS 106, no estimate of postretirement obligation can be reasonable because it would be based on too many assumptions. For this reason, Brown wishes to continue to account for the postretirement benefits that Emco pays to its retirees on the pay-as-you-go (cash) basis.

Brown has asked Wyatt to write a brief memo to Brown that Brown can use to explain this issue to Emco's president.

Required:
Write a brief advisory memo from Wyatt to Brown to:

State the principal benefit covered by FAS 106 and give an example of other benefits covered by FAS 106. Explain the reasoning given in FAS 106 for requiring accruals based on estimates. Indicate the primary recipients of postretirement benefits other than pensions.

Chapter Fourteen
Solutions to Accounting for Leases, Pension and Postretirement Plans Questions

1. (b) FASB #13 states that a lease should be capitalized if at its inception the lease term is 75% or more of the economic life of the leased asset. An exception to this rule applies if the beginning of the lease term is within the last 25% of the economic life of the leased asset. In that case the lease would be considered an operating lease.

2. (b) FASB #13 states that if either of the four criteria for lease capitalization is met, the lease should be capitalized. Both Lease M and Lease P qualify as capitalized leases because their lease terms meet the criterion for 75% or more of the estimated economic life of the leased property.

3. (b) The lease is a capitalized lease since the lease term is 75% or more of the useful life of the asset. Since the rental payments are made at the end of the period, the present value of an ordinary annuity factor is used.

6.15 × $100,000 = $615,000.

4. (b)		
	Annual payments	$100,000
	Present value factor	6.145
	Capitalized lease liability	$614,500

The lower of the rate implicit in the lease (10%) or the lessee's incremental borrowing rate (12%) is used. Note that payments are made at the end of the period and the present value factor given is for an *ordinary* annuity. Therefore, the payment stream is consistent with the factor.

5. (a) The capitalized lease liability should be the annual lease payments less the executory cost (real estate taxes) times the present value factor for an ordinary annuity of 1 for nine years at 9%. The calculation would be: ($52,000 – 2,000) × 5.6 = $280,000. The real estate taxes are a period cost and should be charged to expense.

6. (c) Since the 12% interest rate implicit in the lease is less than the 14% incremental borrowing rate, the 12% rate is used. The minimum lease payments include the option payment since it is a bargain purchase option.

Present value of lease payments:	
6.328 × $10,000 =	$63,280
Present value of option payment:	
.322 × $10,000	3,220
Lease liability at the beginning of the lease term	$66,500

7. (a)		
	Present value of lease payments—$13,000 × 4.240	$55,120
	Initial payment	13,000
		$42,120
	Present value of guaranteed residual $10,000 × .65 =	6,500
	Capital lease liability at 1/1/97	$48,620

The guaranteed residual value is considered part of the minimum lease payments.

8. (a) The interest expense for 1998 is $37,900—the effective interest rate (10%) times the January 1, 1998, present value ($379,000).

9. (b)			
	Present value at 1/1/97		$112,500
	Payment made 12/30/97	$10,000	
	Interest portion for 1997 (8% × $112,500)	9,000	
	Portion applied to the liability		1,000
	Capital lease liability 12/31/97		$111,500

10. (b) The lesser of the rate implicit in the lease (10%) or the lessee's incremental borrowing rate (12%) is used. Present value of lease payments: 6.1446 × $10,000 = $61,446. The guarantee of the residual value is not related to the lessee's accounting.

11. (b) Since the first lease payment is on the first day of the lease, the total lease liability at December 31, 1998, is $115,000, the total lease minus the first payment ($135,000 – $20,000). To divide the December 31 liability into its current vs. noncurrent portions, it is helpful to look at the 1999 journal entry:

Interest expense*	$11,500	
Lease liability	8,500	
Cash		$20,000

*Effective interest rate	×	PV of lease at Jan. 1	=	Interest
10%	×	$115,000	=	$11,500

The portion of the $20,000 lease payment used to reduce the lease liability ($8,500) in 1999 would be considered a current liability at December 31, 1998.

12. (a) The portion of the lease payment which will reduce the lease obligation in year 2 is shown as a current liability at the end of year 1. The payments reduce an increased amount of the liability each year.

13. (b) The key point is that title passes to Cole at the lease expiration. This means that Cole has use of the asset for its total life and should use 12 years for the calculation of depreciation. The depreciation for 1998 would be $9,000, the total cost of $108,000 divided by the useful life of 12 years.

14. (d) In a capital lease with a bargain purchase option, the lessee will control the asset for its total useful life. Therefore, the depreciation should be allocated over the 8-year life of the asset.

$240,000 cost – 20,000 salvage value = 220,000 / 8 years = $27,500 per year

15. (c) South Co. should disclose a description of the lease agreement, annual rent obligations of $100,000 per year for each of the next five years, and the $900,000 ($100,000 × 9 years) aggregate total future payments. The $20,000 paid for annual operating cost are period expenses and would not be disclosed as a part of the future lease obligations.

16. (a)

Normal sales price (equivalent to present value of lease payments)	$77,000
Cost	60,000
Gain recognized	$17,000

Since there are no material uncertainties, the gain is recognized in full. No interest is recognized since the inception date is on the last day of the year.

17. (b)

Sales price is the present value of lease payments	$3,300,000
Less carrying value of the equipment	2,800,000
Gross profit on sale recognized in 1999	$ 500,000

Note: The list price of an asset is not always an indicator of FMV. In many cases an asset may be purchased at less than FMV.

18. (b) The profit on the sale is the difference between the cash selling price and the book value, $3,520,000 – $2,800,000 = $720,000. The interest is computed as follows:

Present value of minimum lease payments and lease obligation, 7/1/95	$3,520,000
Initial payment made 7/1/95	600,000
Liability balance	$2,920,000
Interest rate 10% =	$ 292,000
For one-half year =	$ 146,000

19. (c) In both a sales-type and a direct financing lease, interest revenue is recognized over the lease term using the interest method.

20. (a) The key point is to first calculate the annual payments required by the lease. Use the basic present value formula: Annual Payments X Present Value Factor = Present Value of Future Payments. Therefore: Annual Payments X 4.313 = $323,400; Annual payments = $323,400/4.313; Annual payments = $75,000. Then multiply the customer's $75,000 annual payment by 5 years for a total of $375,000. This figure represents Glade Co.'s gross Lease Receivable. The difference between the gross Lease Receivable and the present value of the future payments is the total amount of Interest Revenue that will be earned over the life of the lease ($375,000 - $323,400 = $51,600).

21. (b)

First month's rent		$10,000
Plus allocated portion of rent bonus for June	$30,000 / 60 months	500
Total rent expense reported on the June 30, 2000 Income Statement		$10,500

22. (b) Under an operating lease, the rent revenue is allocated equally over the term of the lease unless there are differential benefits or rents contingent upon other events. For the first 24 months, the rent revenue would be recognized at $1,000 per month or $24,000 and the collections would only have been $15,000 under the terms of the lease. Therefore, the receivable would be $9,000.

23. (c) FASB #13 states that rental revenue from an operating lease should be recognized on a straight-line basis unless an alternative basis of systematic and rational allocation is more representative of the time pattern of **physical use.** In this case the physical use pattern is the same for all five years and the total rent received of $54,000 ($4,000 for year one plus $50,000 for years two through five) should be allocated equally over the five year period. The rental income recognized for 1999 would be $10,800 ($54,000 / 5 years).

24. (a) The first point is that the rental agreement includes a fixed rental amount. The fixed rental is shown on the vertical axis at the point where lines I and II begin. Lines III and IV do not include a fixed rental and cannot be the correct answer. The second point is that as the variable rental increases, it does so at a decreasing rate. Line II is bending upwards which indicates an increasing variable rate so line II cannot be correct. Line I includes the fixed amount of rent and a variable rental that is increasing at a decreasing rate. Line I is the correct answer.

25. (c) Leasehold improvements are capitalized and amortized over the lesser of the remaining life of the lease (6 years) and the useful life of the improvements (8 years). In this case the $48,000 is amortized over 6 years resulting in an annual rate of $8,000 per year or $4,000 for six months.

The problem requires the amount of leasehold improvements net of amortization that should be reported on the balance sheet six months after the improvements were made. The amount reported should be $44,000, the original cost ($44,000) less six months amortization ($4,000).

26. (a) Since the present value of the lease payments ($36,900) is less than 10% of the value of the asset ($400,000), the entire $100,000 gain is recognized and none is deferred. The transaction represents a leaseback of a minor part of the asset.

27. (b) Since the property is leased back for more than a minor part ($190,581 > $60,000) but less than substantially all of the use of the property, the gain which is recognized is the excess of the gain ($500,000) over the present value of the lease payments or $309,419. The portion of the gain which is deferred is the present value of the lease payments ($190,581).

28. (b) The gain on the transaction must be fully deferred since the present value of the lease payments is equivalent to the sales price. The gain of $50,000 is amortized over the life of the asset (capitalized lease) and therefore has a balance of $45,000 at the end of 1997.

29. (c) The interest revenue is the present value of the Lease Receivable at July 1, 2001 less the first payment times the effective interest rate for six months.

($135,000 - $20,000) × 10% × 6/12 = $5,750

30. (c)

Regular annual rental	$ 96,000
Additional rent 5% × $100,000	5,000
Amortization of bonus	2,400
Total rent expense	$103,400

31. (d) The lease period is 80% of the useful life of the equipment which exceeds the 75% that is necessary for the lease to be a direct financing lease. The problem is silent concerning the other two criteria that must be present for the lessor to consider this a capitalized lease: collectibility of minimum lease payments is predictable and no important uncertainties exist concerning costs to be incurred in the future by the lessor. In a capitalized lease interest revenue is recognized based on the effective interest rate times the present value of the lease at the beginning of the period. Since a portion of each lease payment reduces the lease principal, the interest revenue recognized in 1999 will be smaller than that recognized in 1998.

32. (a) The guaranteed residual value is a promise made by the lessee that the lessor can sell the leased asset at the end of the lease for a guaranteed amount. Since this promise is a potential future payment, it must be included in the calculation of the present value of the lessee's future lease payments.

33. (d) Since the machine is being leased back for a minor part (present value of rentals is less than 10% of the value of the property at the date of the sale-leaseback), the sale and the lease are viewed separately and the entire $30,000 profit is recognized.

34. (d) 16%

Cost if purchased outright	$7,596
Less: Payment on first day of lease	2,000
Present value of lease payments	$5,596
% amount of each payment	2,000
Present value of $1 ordinary annuity, 4 periods	$2.798

By reference to the table in the problem $2.798 = 16%.

35. (a) The rent payments totaling $51,000 must be spread over the periods benefited—5 years. Therefore, for the year ended June 30, 1996, rent expense is computed as follows:

Total rental payments	$51,000
Number of years	÷ 5
Annual rent expense	$10,200

36. (c)

Annual rent	$90,000
Amortization of bonus ($50,000 ÷ 5)	10,000
Total rent revenue	$100,000

The security deposit is not revenue but a liability of the lessor.

37. (b) Mene Co.'s total lease obligation at December 31, 1999 was $76,364 ($75,000 + 1,364). The January 2, 2000 payment was split between the interest of $7,636 (10% × $76,364) and the lease obligation of $1,364. This payment reduced the total lease liability at December 31, 2000 to $75,000 ($76,364 – 1,364). The projected January 3, 2001 payment of $9,000 would be divided between the interest of $7,500 ($75,000 × 10%) and the principal of $1,500 ($9,000 – 1,500). Therefore, the total lease liability at December 31, 2000 of $75,000 would be allocated on the balance sheet between the $1,500 current portion payable on January 2, 2001 and the remainder of $73,500 which would be classified as a long-term liability.

38. (b) To calculate the present value of a capital lease, the lessee uses the **lower** of the lessor's implicit interest rate (if known to the lessee) or the lessee's incremental borrowing rate. In this case the lessor's implicit rate is lower and the amount capitalized is $316,500.

Present value of lease payments at 12/31/98	$316,500
Payment made on 12/31/98	(50,000)
Capital lease liability 12/31/98	266,500
Payment made on 12/31/99 (see below)	(23,350)
Capital lease liability 12/31/99	$243,150

The journal entry for the second payment is:

Interest expense	26,650	
Lease liability	23,350	
Cash		50,000

Note: The interest expense is the effective interest rate times the present value of the lease liability at the beginning of the period (10% × $266,500 = $26,650).

39. (c) Since each lease contains a lease term equal to 75% or more of the economic life of the property, each is classified as a capital lease.

40. (d)

Interest Expense	=	Effective Interest Rate	X	January 2, 1995 carrying value	X	Time Period
	=	10%	X	$758,000	X	1 year
	=	$75,800				

41. (b)

Current service cost	$300,000
Interest on P.B.O.	+ 164,000
Plan earnings	– 80,000
Amortization of unrecognized prior service cost	+ 70,000
Amortization of actuarial loss	+ 30,000
1997 pension cost	$484,000

42. (d)

Service cost	$160,000
Interest cost	50,000
Return on assets	(35,000)
Amortization of prior service cost	5,000
Pension expense	$180,000

The loss from disposal of a segment is reported as part of discontinued operations and not part of pension expense.

43. (c) Pension cost consists of the following elements:

Service cost	$120,000
Interest on P.B.O.	12,000
Amortization of prior service cost	30,000
	$162,000
Less: Return on assets	41,000
Pension cost accrued	$121,000

44. (a) The unfunded accrued pension cost is the difference between the cumulative pension cost (expense) accrued versus the cumulative contributions to the plan.

45. (c)

Pension Costs	$620,000
Less Return on Plan Assets	
(10% × $1,000,000)	(100,000)
Pension Expense	$520,000
Less contribution	(1,000,000)
Prepaid pension cost 12/31/99	$480,000

46. (d) In 1995 and 1996, there was no accrued pension liability on the books since the company fully funded the plan. In 1997, there was a $25,000 accrued pension liability on the books ($75,000 – $50,000). In order to reduce the liability to $15,000 at December 31, 1998, the company must fund the plan for $10,000 more than the 1998 expense or $100,000.

47. (b)
The best approach on this question is to set up a "T" account and plug the missing number.

PLAN ASSETS

Beginning Balance	350,000	Benefits Paid	85,000
Employer Contributions	110,000		
Actual return (Plug)	150,000		
Ending Balance	525,000		

48. (d)

Projected benefit obligation 1/1/96	$72,000
Interest in 1996 on PBO	7,200
1996 service cost	18,000
	$97,200
Pension benefits paid	–15,000
Projected Benefit Obligation at 12/31/96	$82,200

49. (b) The minimum liability is the excess of the accumulated benefit obligation over the fair value of the plan assets.

50. (b)
The journal entry to record the 2000 pension expense is:

Pension Expense	90,000	
Cash		70,000
Accrued Pension Liability		20,000

The total minimum pension liability that must be reported by Payne Inc. at December 31, 2000 is calculated as follows:

Accumulated benefit obligation 12/31/00	$103,000
Less Plan assets at fair value 12/31/00	78,000
Minimum liability to be reported	$ 25,000
Less Accrued liability recorded in the above journal entry	20,000
Additional liability to be recorded at 12/31/00	$ 5,000

51. (a)

I.	MINIMUM LIABILITY (Unfunded accumulated benefit obligation)	$140,000	
	Accrued pension cost (Liability)	(80,000)	
	Required Additional Pension Liability	60,000	
II.	JE Intangible Asset - Deferred Pension Cost	45,000	
	Excess of Additional Pension Liability over Unrecognized Prior Service Cost	15,000	
	Additional Pension Liability		60,000

Note: The amount charged to the Intangible Asset - Deferred Pension Cost can not exceed the amount of the unrecognized prior service cost.

52. (c) The key point is that the current year's pension cost has not been paid. Therefore, the year-end accrued pension liability is $8,000. The difference between the minimum pension liability of $25,000 and the accrued pension liability of $8,000 should be recorded as an additional pension liability of $17,000 ($25,000 - $8,000 = $17,000). The journal entry to record the additional pension liability is shown in the next question.

53. (a) The normal journal entry to record an additional pension liability is a debit to Intangible Asset - Deferred Pension Cost and credit Additional Pension Liability. However, if the amount of the additional pension liability exceeds the unrecognized prior service cost, this excess is debited to a stockholders' equity account. See JE.

JE Intangible Asset - Deferred Pension Cost	12,000	
Excess of Additional Pension Liability over Unrecognized Prior Service Cost	5,000	
Additional Pension Liability		17,000

54. (d) FASB #87 requires that the funded status of the pension plan be reconciled with the prepaid or accrued pension cost reported on the balance sheet. The funded status of the plan is the projected benefit obligation less the fair value of the plan assets, the unrecognized prior service cost, and the amount of any additional pension liability; plus or minus any unrecognized gains or losses or any remaining unrecognized net obligation or net asset existing at the date of the initial application of FASB #87.

55. (a)

I. Calculate Pension Expense for 2001:

A. Service Cost	$19,000
B. Interest Cost	38,000
C. Actual Return on Plan Assets	(22,000)
D. Amortization of unrecognized Prior Service Cost	52,000
Total Pension Expense	$87,000

II. Record the Journal Entry:

Pension Expense	87,000	
Cash		40,000
Prepaid/Accrued Pension Cost		47,000

III. Post to the "T" account:

PREPAID/ACCRUED PENSION COST

Beginning Balance	2,000	JE above	47,000
		Ending Balance	45,000

56. (a) The excess of the funding over the amortization of the prior service cost is the amount of the prepaid pension cost or $18,000 ($30,000 – $12,000).

57. (c) The interest cost component of net pension cost is the long-term interest rate (settlement rate) applied to the projected benefit obligation at the beginning of the year. Since the projected benefit obligation is a present value, the increase, as measured above, represents the interest cost incurred due to the passage of time.

58. (b) The discount rate applied to the projected benefit obligation is a long-term settlement rate (Pension Benefit Guarantee Corp. settlement rate, for instance).

59. (d) Prior service costs are amortized over current (1998) and future years.

60. (a) FASB #106 requires that both the assumed health care trend rate and the accumulated post-retirement benefit obligation be disclosed.

61. (b) FASB #106 states that the attribution period begins when an employee is hired and ends when the employee is eligible to receive full benefits. Fletcher began work at age 48 and after 10 years of service, age 58, will be eligible for full benefits.

62. (a) FASB #106 "requires that an employer's obligation for postretirement benefits expected to be provided to or for an employee be fully accrued by the date that employee attains full eligibility for all the benefits, even if the employee is expected to render additional service beyond that date."

63. (c) When termination benefits have been accepted and can be reasonably estimated, they should be recorded as an expense (loss) and related liability.

Amounts related to employees who accepted the offer:

Lump sum payments	$475,000
Present value of termination benefits	155,000
Total	$630,000

The reduction of pension costs does not affect the liability for special termination benefits.

64. (c) Key Point: Prior service cost is amortized over the average remaining life of the employees.
The calculation of the average remaining service life of the employees is to add the remaining service lives of A (3 years); B (5 years); C (5 years); and D (7 years) for a total of 20 years and divide by the number of employees (20 years / 4 employees = 5 years). Therefore, the amortization of the prior service cost is $100,000 divided by 5 years or $20,000.

65. (a) Pension Expense for 1995

Service and Interest Cost	$720,000
Less expected return on plan assets: 10% x 400,000	(40,000)
Pension Expense	$680,000
Less amount funded	(400,000)
Accrued Pension Liability	$280,000

66. (a) An amortization table for a lease with a bargain purchase option should have a balance equal to the bargain purchase option at the end of the lease period. The lessee then debits the lease liability and credits cash to exercise the purchase option.

Chapter Fourteen
Solutions to Accounting for Leases, Pension and Postretirement Plans Problems

NUMBER 1

a.1.

Crystal Company
COMPUTATION OF EXPENSE ON OPERATING LEASE
For the Year Ended December 31, 1999

Rental expense ($115,000 × 6 months)	$ 690,000

a.2.

Jackson Company
COMPUTATION OF INCOME BEFORE INCOME TAXES ON OPERATING LEASE
For the Year Ended December 31, 1999

Rental income ($115,000 × 6 months)	$ 690,000
Depreciation ($7,000,000 ÷ 8 years × 6 months)	437,500
	$ 252,500

b.1.

Truman Company
COMPUTATION OF EXPENSE ON LEASE RECORDED AS A PURCHASE
For the Year Ended December 31, 1999

Depreciation ($3,520,800 *[Schedule 1]* ÷ 8)	$ 440,100
Interest expense *(Schedule 2)*	73,020
	$ 513,120

Schedule 1—Computation of Purchase Price of Equipment

Equal annual payment	$ 600,000
Present value of an annuity of $1 in advance for 8 periods at 10%	× 5.868
	$3,520,800

Schedule 2—Computation of Interest Expense

Purchase price of equipment	$3,520,800
Payment made on October 1, 1999	600,000
	2,920,800
Interest rate	10%
Interest expense (October 1, 1999 to October 1, 2000)	292,080
Interest expense applicable to 1999 (3 months)	25%
	$ 73,020

b.2.

Roosevelt Company
COMPUTATION OF INCOME BEFORE INCOME TAXES
ON LEASE RECORDED AS A SALE
For the Year Ended December 31, 1999

Profit on sale:	
Sales price *(Schedule 1)*	$3,520,800
Cost of equipment	3,000,000
	$ 520,800
Interest income *(Schedule 2)*	73,020
	$ 593,820

NUMBER 2

1.

(a) $48,000. Interest cost is the discount rate times the January 1 projected benefit obligation: 8% × $600,000 = $48,000 interest cost.

(b) $72,000. The expected return on plan assets is the expected rate of return times the January 1 fair value of pension plan assets: 10% × $720,000 = $72,000 expected return on plan assets.

(c) $105,000. The problem states that there were not any contributions made or benefits paid during the year. Therefore, the actual return on plan assets is the change in the fair value of the plan assets from January 1 to December 31 of the current year: ($720,000 vs. $825,000 = $105,000 actual return on plan assets).

(d) $20,000. The amortization of the prior service cost is the January 1 unamortized prior service cost divided by the average remaining service life of the employees: $240,000 ÷ 12 years = $20,000 amortization of prior service cost.

(e) $2,000. The minimum amortization of unrecognized prior pension gain is calculated by using the "corridor" approach. The corridor approach involves four steps:

Step #1: Determine the larger of the January 1 projected benefit obligation ($600,000) and the fair value of the plan assets ($720,000). The larger is $720,000.

Step #2: Multiply the $720,000 by 10% to establish the corridor. The corridor is $72,000. If Sparta's unrecognized prior pension gain had been less than $72,000, the company would not record any amortization.

Step #3: The amount to be amortized is the excess of the unamortized prior pension gain over the corridor amount: $96,000 – $72,000 = $24,000 amount to be amortized.

Step #4: The minimum amortization is the $24,000 from Step #3 divided by the average service life of employees. In this case $24,000 ÷ 12 years = $2,000 minimum amortization of unrecognized pension gain.

2.

(f) (I) Service cost increases pension expense and accrued pension liability.

(g) (I) The deferral of a gain on pension plan assets will increase pension expense and accrued pension liability. For example, in an earlier part of this problem the actual return on plan assets was $105,000 and the expected return was $72,000. This would be included in the calculation of pension expense and the accrued pension liability as follows:

Service cost		$90,000
Interest on PBO		48,000
Actual return on plan assets	$105,000	
Less deferred gain	(33,000)	
Expected return		(72,000)
Amortization of prior service cost		20,000
Amortization of prior pension gain		(2,000)
Total pension expense—1999		$84,000

If the actual return on plan assets had been deducted, the pension expense would have decreased by $105,000, but because of the deferred gain, the deduction is only $72,000. The effect of the deferred gain is to reduce the deduction from pension expense by $33,000 and therefore increase pension expense and the accrued pension liability.

Note: The expected return on plan assets is used in calculating pension cost for the year, not the actual return. This is done to record a more consistent return rather than the more erratic return based on actual results.

(h) (D) The actual return as shown in the above calculation is adjusted by the deferred gain and deducted from pension expense and the accrued pension liability.

(i) (I) Amortization of prior service cost as shown in the above calculation increases pension expense and accrued pension liability.

(j) (D) The amortization of the unrecognized pension gain as shown above is a deduction from pension expense and the accrued pension liability.

NUMBER 3

		Debits	*Credits*
1.	January 2, 1999— to record lease:		
	Equipment	850,000	
	Capital lease liability		850,000
2.	December 31, 1999— to record payment:		
	Capital lease liability	100,000	
	Cash		100,000
3.	December 31, 1999— to record depreciation:		
	Depreciation expense	34,000	
	Accumulated depreciation		34,000
	Interest expense	85,000	
	Capital lease liability		85,000

NUMBER 4

a. An example of postemployment benefits offered by employers is continuation of health care benefits. Deck is required to accrue liabilities for compensated absences and postemployment benefits if all of the following conditions are met:

- The obligation is attributable to employees' services already rendered,
- The employees' rights accumulate or vest,
- Payment is probable, and
- The amount of the benefits can be reasonably estimated.

If an obligation cannot be accrued solely because the amount cannot be reasonably estimated, the financial statements should disclose that fact.

b. Estimated amounts to be paid under a deferred compensation contract should be accrued over the period of an employee's active employment from the time the contract is signed to the employee's full eligibility date. The theoretical rationale for accrual of these obligations to be paid in the future is that accrual matches the cost of the benefits to the period in which services are rendered, and results in recognition of a measurable liability.

c.

Deck Co.
Schedule of Deferred Compensation Amounts
For the Years 1995 through 1998

For the year ended	*Accrued liability*	*Deferred compensation expense*
12/31/95	$ 50,000	$50,000 [a]
12/31/96	$100,000	$50,000
12/31/97	$150,000	$50,000
12/31/98	$165,000	$15,000 [b]

[a] $150,000 / 3 (straight-line method)
[b] $150,000 x 10%

NUMBER 5

a. The components of Bighorn's 1998 net pension cost calculation are:

- Service cost.
- Interest cost.
- Actual return on plan assets.
- Gain or loss consisting of:
  - The difference between the actual and expected return on plan assets.
  - Any amortization of the unrecognized gain or loss from previous periods.

b. 1. Bighorn's unrecognized net loss results from differences between actuarial assumptions and experiences for both its projected benefit obligation and returns on plan assets.

2. Bighorn's unfunded accrued pension cost occurs because cumulative net pension expense exceeds cash contributed to the pension fund.

c. Bighorn's minimum pension liability equals the excess of the accumulated benefit obligation over the fair value of plan assets. Bighorn's additional pension liability would equal any excess of this minimum pension liability over the unfunded accrued pension cost.

NUMBER 6

a. The theoretical basis for capitalizing certain long-term leases is that the economic effect or substance of such leases on the lessee is that of an installment purchase. Such a lease transfers substantially all the risks and benefits incident to the ownership of property to the lessee, and obligates the lessee in a manner similar to that created when funds are borrowed.

b.

Cash	864,000	
Deferred gain		324,000
Equipment		540,000
Leased equipment	864,000	
Capital lease obligation		864,000

c.

Interest expense	86,400 [1]	
Capital lease obligation	63,600	
Executory cost	3,000	
Cash		153,000
Depreciation	96,000 [2]	
Accumulated depreciation		96,000
Deferred gain	36,000 [3]	
Depreciation		36,000

[1] 864,000 × 10% implicit interest rate
[2] 864,000 ÷ 9 year lease period
[3] 324,000 ÷ 9 year lease period

NUMBER 7

<u>Statement of Financial Accounting Standards No. 106,</u> *<u>Employers' Accounting for Postretirement Benefits Other Than Pensions.</u>*

The primary recipients of postretirement benefits other than pensions are retired employees, their beneficiaries, and covered dependents. The principle benefit covered by FAS 106 is postretirement health care benefits. Examples of other benefits include tuition assistance, legal services, life insurance benefits, day care, and housing subsidies.

The reasoning given in FAS 106 is that accrual of the obligation based on best estimates is superior to implying, by a failure to accrue, that no obligation exists prior to the payment of benefits.